06

FLORIDA

Where to Stay and Eat
for All Budgets

Must-See Sights
and Local Secrets

Ratings You Can Trust

Fodor's Travel Publications   New York, Toronto, London, Sydney, A
www.fodors.com

FODOR'S FLORIDA 2006
Editor: Paul Eisenberg

Editorial Production: David Downing
Editorial Contributors: David Downing, Richard Dworkin, Lynne Helm, Jennie Hess, Satu Hummasti, Diane P. Marshall, Gary McKechnie, Kristin Milavec, Alicia Rivas, Karen Schlesinger, Kerry Speckman, Rowland Stiteler, Cynthia Tunstall, Jim Tunstall, Chelle Koster Walton
Maps: David Lindroth *cartographer;* Bob Blake and Rebecca Baer, *map editors*
Design: Fabrizio La Rocca, *creative director;* Moon Sun Kim, *cover designer;* Guido Caroti, *art director;* Melanie Marin, *senior picture editor*
Production/Manufacturing: Robert B. Shields
Cover Photo: (St. Andrew's State Park): Visit Florida

ISBN 1-4000-1542-1

ISSN 0193-9556

SPECIAL SALES
This book is available for special discounts for bulk purchases for sales promotions or premiums. Special editions, including personalized covers, excerpts of existing books, and corporate imprints, can be created in large quantities for special needs. For more information, write to Special Markets/Premium Sales, 1745 Broadway, MD 6-2, New York, New York 10019, or e-mail specialmarkets@randomhouse.com.

AN IMPORTANT TIP & AN INVITATION
Although all prices, opening times, and other details in this book are based on information supplied to us at press time, changes occur all the time in the travel world, and Fodor's cannot accept responsibility for facts that become outdated or for inadvertent errors or omissions. So **always confirm information when it matters,** especially if you're making a detour to visit a specific place. Your experiences—positive and negative—matter to us. If we have missed or misstated something, **please write to us.** We follow up on all suggestions. Contact the Florida editor at editors@fodors.com or c/o Fodor's at 1745 Broadway, New York, NY 10019.

PRINTED IN THE UNITED STATES OF AMERICA

10 9 8 7 6 5 4 3 2 1

BE A FODOR'S CORRESPONDENT

Your opinion matters. It matters to us. It matters to your fellow Fodor's travelers, too. And we'd like to hear it. In fact, we *need* to hear it.

When you share your experiences and opinions, you become an active member of the Fodor's community. That means we'll not only use your feedback to make our books better, but we'll publish your names and comments whenever possible. Throughout our guides, look for "Word of Mouth," excerpts of your unvarnished feedback.

Here's how you can help improve Fodor's for all of us.

Tell us when we're right. We rely on local writers to give you an insider's perspective. But our writers and staff editors—who are the best in the business—depend on you. Your positive feedback is a vote to renew our recommendations for the next edition.

Tell us when we're wrong. We're proud that we update most of our guides every year. But we're not perfect. Things change. Hotels cut services. Museums change hours. Charming cafés lose charm. If our writer didn't quite capture the essence of a place, tell us how you'd do it differently. If any of our descriptions are inaccurate or inadequate, we'll incorporate your changes in the next edition and will correct factual errors at fodors.com *immediately.*

Tell us what to include. You probably have had fantastic travel experiences that aren't yet in Fodor's. Why not share them with a community of like-minded travelers? Maybe you chanced upon a beach or bistro or B&B that you don't want to keep to yourself. Tell us why we should include it. And share your discoveries and experiences with everyone directly at fodors.com. Your input may lead us to add a new listing or highlight a place we cover with a "Highly Recommended" star or with our highest rating, "Fodor's Choice."

Give us your opinion instantly at our feedback center at www.fodors.com/feedback. You may also e-mail editors@fodors.com with the subject line "Florida Editor." Or send your nominations, comments, and complaints by mail to Florida Editor, Fodor's, 1745 Broadway, New York, NY 10019.

You and travelers like you are the heart of the Fodor's community. Make our community richer by sharing your experiences. Be a Fodor's correspondent.

Happy traveling!

Tim Jarrell, Publisher

CONTENTS

Maps

CloseUps

ABOUT OUR WRITERS

Florida-raised **David Downing,** a full-time Fodor's staffer and travel columnist, is convinced that the Panhandle is the most wonderfully enigmatic region in the Sunshine State. The editor of the Compass American Guide to *Florida,* Downing has been featured on CNN and the Travel Channel, and his writing appears on fodors.com and on *New York Times* on the Web.

After being hired sight unseen by a South Florida newspaper, Fort Lauderdale–based freelance travel writer **Lynne Helm** arrived from the Midwest anticipating a couple years of palm-fringed fun. More than a quarter century later, she's still enamored of South Florida's sun-drenched charms.

Jennie Hess is a travel and feature writer based in Orlando and is the author of Fodor's *Around Orlando with Kids.* A former newspaper journalist, Hess was a publicist for Walt Disney World Resort from 1988 through 1999.

Intrepid traveler **Diane P. Marshall** has lived in Spain, France, the Philippines, California, and New York, and traveled to more than three dozen countries. She makes her home in the Keys, where she writes for numerous travel guides, newspapers, magazines, and online services.

Kristin Milavec is a former Fodor's editor who has traveled extensively but calls Sarasota home. She has also managed the production of several art-history books and a Pulitzer prize–winning war story covering Srebrenica, Bosnia.

Freelance writer **Karen Schlesinger** has been exploring various Florida cities for more than a decade and resides in the Palm Beach area. She is a regular contributor to Fodor's travel guides and provides content for various print media.

A Yankee by birth, **Kerry Speckman** moved to Jacksonville in the early 1980s and has been basking in the sun and Southern hospitality ever since. Over the years, she has been published in virtually every publication in her adopted hometown. She is a contributing writer at *Jacksonville* magazine and an entertainment writer for America Online.

Tampa Tribune staffer **Jim Tunstall** and his wife, **Cynthia,** are native Floridians who have spent much of their lives tasting the state's treasures, then escaping to their home in a radar blip called Lecanto.

From her home of more than 20 years on Sanibel Island, **Chelle Koster Walton** has written and contributed to 10 guidebooks—two of which won Lowell Thomas Awards—and written articles for *USA Today, Bridal Guide, Caribbean Travel & Life, National Geographic Traveler, Arthur Frommer's Budget Travel, Endless Vacation,* the *Boston Globe,* and other print and electronic media. Walton is cofounder of www.guidebookwriters.com.

ABOUT THIS BOOK

OUR RATINGS

Sometimes you find terrific travel experiences and sometimes they just find you. But usually the burden is on you to select the right combination of experiences. That's where our ratings come in.

As travelers we've all discovered a place so wonderful that its worthiness is obvious. And sometimes that place is so experiential that superlatives don't do it justice: you just have to be there to know. These sights, properties, and experiences get our highest rating, **Fodor's Choice**, indicated by orange stars throughout this book.

Black stars ★ highlight sights and properties we deem **Highly Recommended**, places that our writers, editors, and readers praise again and again for consistency and excellence.

By default, there's another category: any place we include in this book is by definition worth your time, unless we say otherwise. And we will.

Disagree with any of our choices? Care to nominate a place or suggest that we rate one more highly? Visit our feedback center at www.fodors.com/feedback.

BUDGET WELL

Hotel and restaurant price categories from ¢ to $$$$ are defined in the opening pages of each chapter. For attractions, we always give standard adult admission fees; reductions are usually available for children, students, and senior citizens. Want to pay with plastic? **AE, D, DC, MC, V** following restaurant and hotel listings indicate if American Express, Discover, Diner's Club, MasterCard, and Visa are accepted.

RESTAURANTS

Unless we state otherwise, restaurants are open for lunch and dinner daily. We mention dress only when there's a specific requirement and reservations only when they're essential or not accepted—it's always best to book ahead.

HOTELS

Hotels have private bath, phone, TV, and air-conditioning and operate on the European Plan (a.k.a. EP, meaning without meals), unless we specify that they use the Continental Plan (CP, with a Continental breakfast), Breakfast Plan (BP, with a full breakfast), or Modified American Plan (MAP, with breakfast and dinner) or are all-inclusive (including all meals and most activities). We always list facilities but not whether you'll be charged an extra fee to use them, so when pricing accommodations, find out what's included.

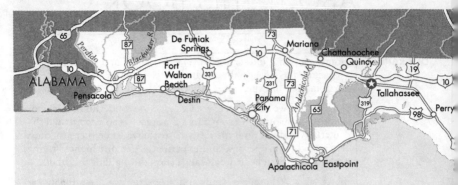

Gulf of Mexico

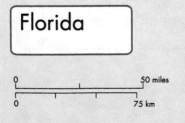

Florida

```
0                    50 miles
├────┬────┬────┼────┤
0                    75 km
```

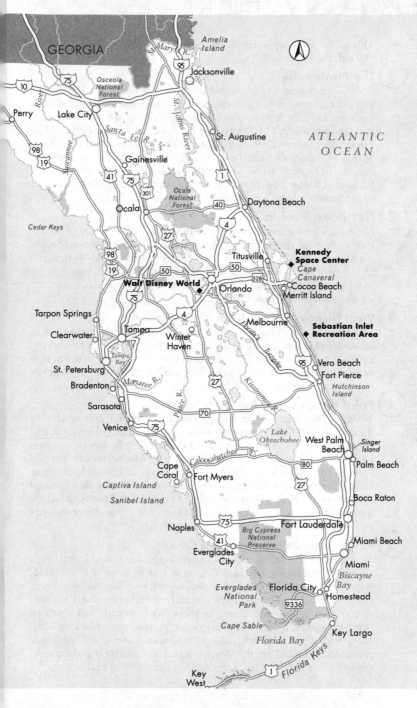

This guide begins up north in the Panhandle and takes you clockwise through the Sunshine State.

1 The Panhandle

With its magnolias, live oaks, and loblolly pines, northwest Florida has more in common with the Deep South than with the Florida of the Everglades. Even the high season is different: by May, when activities are winding down south of Tampa, the Panhandle is just gearing up. The fine beaches, however, are a constant. Perdido Key State Recreation Area, St. Joseph Peninsula State Park, and St. George Island State Park are considered by many to be some of the best beaches in the country. Tallahassee is flavored by the state government, and Pensacola has the feel of the historic old port town that it is.

2 Northeast Florida

Only a short drive separates the more than 400-year-old town of St. Augustine from the spring-break and auto-racing mecca of Daytona Beach. Along the entire northeast coast are slender barrier islands—some relatively pristine, all with fabulous beaches. Inland is the university town of Gainesville, Ocala horse country, and the backwoods scrub made famous by Marjorie Kinnan Rawlings.

3 Walt Disney World® & the Orlando Area

When Walt Disney chose 28,000 acres in Central Florida as the site of his eastern Disneyland, he forever changed the face of a cattle-and-citrus town called Orlando. Today Disney isn't the only show in town: Universal Orlando, SeaWorld, and various smaller attractions give Mickey a run for his money.

4 Palm Beach & the Treasure Coast

North of Broward, in Palm Beach County, are the northern reaches of the aptly named Gold Coast—noted for its golden sun, golden sand, and the golden bank accounts of many of the people who live or vacation here. The centerpiece of tourism is oh-so-ritzy Mediterranean-inspired Palm Beach, while the center of commerce is the larger but lower-crust West Palm Beach. Sophisticated Boca Raton and Delray Beach round out county highlights. The coast north of Palm Beach County, called the Treasure Coast, comprises Martin, St. Lucie, and Indian River counties and is also worth exploring.

5 Fort Lauderdale & Broward County

Wedged between Miami-Dade County to the south and Palm Beach County to the north, Broward County has as its hub the canal-laced, boat-friendly city of Fort Lauderdale. Downtown along the New River, Fort Lauderdale has forged a new arts and entertainment district as well as trendy shopping and dining districts. To the north and south lie ocean-side communities with varying amounts of view-blocking highrises, modest family motels, fishing piers, natural areas, and beach-side promenades. Inland are the Western-style town of Davie and the eastern fringes of the Everglades (though not the national park).

6 Miami & Miami Beach

Almost at the end of the line on Florida's east coast, Miami-Dade County throbs with energy. On the mainland is Miami itself, Florida's biggest city. This gateway to Latin America overflows with the food, language, and culture of many ethnic groups, most notably Cuban emigrés. Across Biscayne Bay, to the east, is Miami's island neighbor, Miami Beach. Its boutique art deco hotels, giant luxury resorts, and beach and café scene attract wannabes and bona fide glitterati. Other tony and chic towns around Miami, such as Coral Gables and Coconut Grove, add to the allure of this corner of the state.

7 The Florida Keys

This slender necklace of landfalls off the southern tip of Florida is strung together by a 110-mi-long highway. Though all part of Monroe County, the Keys are generally divided into Upper, Middle, and Lower. The Keys are at once a huge traffic jam, an angler's and diver's paradise, and a hideaway for those eager to "get away from it all."

8 The Everglades

Created in 1947, this national park in the southernmost extremity of the peninsula preserves a portion of the slow-moving "River of Grass"— a 50-mi-wide stream flowing through marshy grassland en route to Florida Bay. The Everglades are actually much larger than the area contained within the national park. Nevertheless, most people who visit this unique ecosystem will do so within park boundaries via only a few roads that access its western, northern, and southeastern sections. Not far away, on Florida's southeastern tip, is Biscayne National Park, a park that is 96% underwater and that contains the northern extremities of Florida's living coral reefs. Between the two parks is a corridor of "civilization" that provides motels and fast food.

9 The Lower Gulf Coast

Between the southern end of Tampa Bay and the northern reaches of the Everglades, the Lower Gulf Coast is another region that serves up what Florida is famous for: a subtropical climate; soft, sandy beaches; golf and tennis; and pockets of little-touched Florida beauty—from cypress swamps to mangrove islets. Resort communities include upscale Naples, often considered the Palm Beach of the Gulf Coast, and Fort Myers and its nearby barrier islands, Sanibel and Captiva.

10 The Tampa Bay Area

As on the Atlantic, much of the Gulf Coast is known for its barrier-island beaches, and this central section is no exception. At its heart is Tampa Bay itself, with the cities of Tampa and St. Petersburg across the water from each other. Tampa is a bustling commercial city, while St. Pete is known for its string of beach communities. Following the coast north on its way to its westward bend, you'll find fishing towns and natural areas. South of the bay, the barrier-island-flanked resorts continue, including the culturally vibrant city of Sarasota.

Florida is far more diverse than you might realize. Sure there are the world-class theme parks, with the biggest, most sparkling rides on the globe. And if you're the average visitor, that's one of the things you come for. But if you've got time to stop and smell the orange blossoms, there's a lot more here. The state is full of natural wonders and cultural experiences, from Latin-American rhythms to hip, movie-star chic. If you have at least a week, plan on flying to Orlando—an ideal gateway because of its central location (which is why Walt Disney chose it) and its abundance of direct flights.

Highlights of Florida
11 to 15 days

ORLANDO

3 or 4 days. You'll want to budget at least two days for Disney offerings. If you've got youngsters, a day at the Magic Kingdom, possibly two, is a must. If you love thrill rides, have teenagers in tow, or are a Dr. Seuss fan, Universal's Islands of Adventure is worth at least a day, as is movie-theme Universal Studios. The charming, water-based SeaWorld Orlando—with Discovery Cove—and dozens of other, smaller amusements could easily take up a week; pick the attractions most interesting to you and then hit the road. ⇨ Disney Theme Parks, and Other Theme Parks *in* Chapter 3.

TAMPA & ST. PETERSBURG

1 day. There are two must-dos when you visit these Gulf Coast cities on a 5-mi-wide bay: get a taste of Latin culture in Tampa's Ybor City (originally a Cuban cigar-manufacturing district and now a neighborhood abounding in culinary spots and hot nightclubs), and watch a classic Florida sunset at St. Pete Beach. ⇨ Tampa, and St. Petersburg *in* Chapter 10.

SANIBEL & CAPTIVA

1 day. Lee County has wonderful barrier islands, including charming Sanibel, home of the J. N. "Ding" Darling National Wildlife Refuge, where you can canoe through a rich mangrove swamp. The beaches of Sanibel and its neighbor, Captiva, have exceptional shelling, and you may see loggerhead turtles and other extraordinary wildlife. ⇨ The Coastal Islands *in* Chapter 9.

NAPLES & MARCO ISLAND

1 day. Naples, a sophisticated town 40 minutes south of Sanibel, backs up to the western Everglades. If you don't have time to access the Glades from the east, you may want to take a swamp buggy or airboat tour from Naples or Marco Island. Marco, which has great beaches and beachfront hotels, makes a good overnight stop because of a "shortcut" to Key West—a three-hour ferry as opposed to a six-hour drive. ⇨ Naples Area *in* Chapter 9.

THE FLORIDA KEYS

2 or 3 days. Key West, 100 mi by boat or bridge-laden highway from the mainland, has a classic island feel, with a laid-back culture and a quaint downtown dotted with famous watering holes. Clear waters make a snorkel or dive trip a must. It's also great fun to tour the island by moped, which you can rent at numerous spots downtown. On your way to Miami through the Middle and Upper Keys, make sure to leave time for a stop at Bahia Honda State Park, one of the loveliest spots in Florida. ⇨ The Florida Keys *in* Chapter 7.

MIAMI & MIAMI BEACH

2 or 3 days. Miami has its own spin on the urban experience, a cultural confluence of Latin vibes and subtropical hedonism mixed with an economic vibrancy based on its status as the U.S. gateway to Latin America; to envelop yourself in Latin culture, stop in the Calle Ocho district of Little Havana.

Miami is considered hot by most anyone in this hemisphere who is chic or wants to be. In Miami Beach's South Beach you're as likely to see Madonna or Elton John as you are in Hollywood. The protected natural areas of Everglades and Biscayne National Park are only 45 mi southwest. ⇨ Exploring Miami, and Miami Beach *in* Chapter 6 and Everglades National Park *in* Chapter 8.

PALM BEACH

1 or 2 days. If you feel at home at a polo match and don't shop at any place less upscale than Neiman-Marcus, Palm Beach is for you. It's the richest town, per capita, in Florida and one of the world's playgrounds for the extremely wealthy. And the rich don't choose shabby places. The sun-drenched beaches here are as impressive as the shopping and dining along Worth Avenue and the luxurious hotels, including the famous Breakers. ⇨ Palm Beach *in* Chapter 4.

Natural Wonders
5 to 8 days

Having no appreciable winter has done more for Florida than make it a good place for theme parks and golf courses. The constant spring-summer seasonal mix that has prevailed for 100 millennia or so has created beautiful forests and wetlands. If you have a map, a car, and several days you can see a side of nature here you won't see elsewhere.

BISCAYNE NATIONAL PARK & KEY LARGO

1 or 2 days. At Biscayne National Park, 30 minutes south of Miami, you can see living coral reefs by snorkeling, scuba diving, or taking a glass-bottom boat. Perhaps the best snorkeling and scuba diving, however, is another hour south at magnificent John Pennekamp Coral Reef State Park, near Key Largo, the northernmost of the Florida Keys. ⇨ Biscayne National

Jacksonville

Gainesville

250 mi

75

Wekiva
Springs
SP

FLORIDA'S TNPK.

Orlando

Walt Disney
World

80 mi

4

Tampa

15 mi

St. Petersburg

275

75

Sarasota

120 mi

75

Port Charlotte

Gulf of Mexico

Fort Myers

Captiva Island

46 mi

867

Sanibel Island

16 mi

75

Park *in* Chapter 8 and the Upper
Keys *in* Chapter 7.

THE EVERGLADES
1 or 2 days. For nature lovers,
going to Florida and not seeing
the Everglades would be like
going to Arizona and not seeing
the Grand Canyon. Miami is a
great gateway to America's
biggest protected wetland, and
you can try anything from self-
guided canoe tours (probably not
a good idea for first-timers) to
swamp buggy, airboat, and even
airplane tours, offered by several
parks and commercial operators
on U.S. 41 west of Miami. ⇨ Everglades National Park *in* Chapter 8.

Naples

15 mi

951

**Marco
Island**

80 mi

FLORIDA'S TNPK.

110 mi

Fort Pierce

*A T L A N T I C
O C E A N*

*Lake
Okeechobee*

Palm Beach

95

50 mi

95

41

Miami Beach
Miami

Everglades
NP

1

50 mi

Biscayne
NP

905

John Pennekamp
Coral Reef SP

**Key
Largo**

90 mi

1

Key West

Bahia Honda SP

ORLANDO AREA

1 or 2 days. Wekiwa Springs State Park is 45 minutes from Disney but may as well be on another planet. Here you'll find the still unspoiled, undeveloped, and un-neoned Florida, the way it was before the civilized world laid a hand on it. ⇨ Winter Park & Maitland *in* Chapter 3.

TALLAHASSEE AREA

2 days. Within an hour of Florida's capital you'll find a variety of natural treasures. Florida Caverns State Park, near Marianna, offers guided tours of a huge underground cave, where you can see Carlsbad-like formations, including stalactites and stalagmites, along with thousands of critters that live in the dark. A short drive west, near Chipley, Falling Waters State Park contains Florida's largest, and perhaps only, waterfall. The falls alone wouldn't warrant a trip to the Panhandle, but they make a nice side trip from Florida Caverns. Wild and exotic Wakulla Springs State Park, 15 mi south of Tallahassee, has glass-bottom-boat tours of impressive junglelike waterways. You can see incredible wildlife, including the ubiquitous and much-loved alligator. ⇨ Inland, and Across the Panhandle and Tallahassee *in* Chapter 1.

Great Beaches

6 to 10 days

With more than 1,200 mi of coastline, it's obvious that Florida has many beaches; and the variety of beaches—secluded beaches, people-watcher beaches, family beaches—is equaled only by the variety of reasons to visit them. You can marvel at amazing sand or fabulous sunsets, undertake countless waterborne activities, or reenergize after more tiring pursuits, since many Florida beaches are close to other popular attractions.

MIAMI AREA

1 or 2 days. Beaches in the Miami area are not unlike some Los Angeles-area beaches, with lots of male and female model would-bes rollerblading along walkways adjacent to the strand. In South Beach, a vibrant café and nightclub district faces the sand. Ten miles north at Haulover Beach you'll find Florida's only legal nude beach. (Signs mark the area.) Or try the sands at Key Biscayne's Bill Baggs Cape Florida State Park, which has a lighthouse and a great view of the Miami skyline. Along with their particular "scene, " Miami's beaches offer surprisingly clear aqua water. ⇨ South Beach-Miami Beach, Virginia Key, and Key Biscayne *in* Chapter 6.

DAYTONA BEACH & THE SPACE COAST

1 or 2 days. A sand pail's throw from one another sit one of America's most famous beaches, Daytona Beach, and one of its least spoiled, Canaveral National Seashore. Daytona is one of the few places in the nation where you can drive on the sand, which backs up right onto a hotel and nightlife strip that keeps hopping after sundown. Canaveral closes after dark, but by day you can gaze at windswept dunes and the blue Atlantic along 24 mi of beachfront and then visit the adjacent Kennedy Space Center or Merritt Island National Wildlife Refuge. ⇨ Daytona, and the Space Coast *in* Chapter 2.

ST. AUGUSTINE & AMELIA ISLAND

2 days. Heading north, you can relax on St. Augustine Beach or Vilano Beach on Anastasia Island, near historic St. Augustine. North of Jacksonville, Amelia Island has great beaches and the historic town of Fernandina Beach, which is loaded with bed-and-breakfasts. Sample the wonderful beaches, dunes, and facilities at Hannah Park in Jacksonville Beach, or explore the St. Augustine Lighthouse & Museum, near the beach and with great views of the entire St. Augustine area. ⇨ St. Augustine, and Jacksonville *in* Chapter 2.

THE PANHANDLE

1 or 2 days. The beaches of northwest Florida are justifiably renowned, routinely making the annual best-beaches list of the University of Maryland's Laboratory for Coastal Research. In fact, scenic Grayton Beach State Park, one of Florida's prettiest beaches, made the list so consistently that it has essentially been retired from contention. Halfway between Panama City and Pensacola, Grayton Beach has sugar-white sands and aqua waters as clear as you'd find in the Keys or the Bahamas. And that's just one of many fine Panhandle beaches. If you like hotels, nightclubs, and arcades near your beach blanket, visit Panama City Beach, which actively courts spring-break revelers. ⇨ Around Pensacola Bay, and the Gulf Coast *in* Chapter 1.

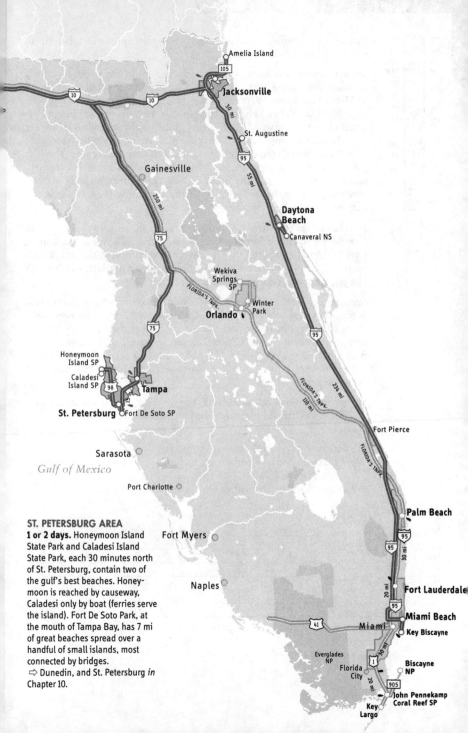

Amelia Island
105
10 Jacksonville
10
30 mi
St. Augustine
95
Gainesville
55 mi
250 mi
Daytona Beach
75
Canaveral NS
Wekiva Springs SP
FLORIDA'S TNPK.
Winter Park
Orlando
95
75
Honeymoon Island SP
Caladesi Island SP
98 **Tampa**
St. Petersburg Fort De Soto SP
FLORIDA'S TNPK.
234 mi
110 mi
Sarasota
Gulf of Mexico
Fort Pierce
Port Charlotte
FLORIDA'S TNPK.
Palm Beach
95
ST. PETERSBURG AREA
1 or 2 days. Honeymoon Island State Park and Caladesi Island State Park, each 30 minutes north of St. Petersburg, contain two of the gulf's best beaches. Honeymoon is reached by causeway, Caladesi only by boat (ferries serve the island). Fort De Soto Park, at the mouth of Tampa Bay, has 7 mi of great beaches spread over a handful of small islands, most connected by bridges.
⇨ Dunedin, and St. Petersburg *in* Chapter 10.
95
30 mi
Fort Myers
20 mi
Fort Lauderdale
95
Naples
Miami Beach
41 **Miami**
Key Biscayne
30 mi
Everglades NP
Florida City
Biscayne NP
1
20 mi
905
John Pennekamp Coral Reef SP
Key Largo

°C		°F
100		212
40		105
37		98.6
30		90
25		80
20		70
15		60
10		50
5		40
0		32
−5		20
−10		10
−15		0
−20		

Florida is a year-round state, although most visitors prefer October–April, particularly in South Florida.

Winter remains the height of the tourist season, when South Florida is crowded with "snowbirds" fleeing cold weather in the north. (It did snow in Miami once in the 1970s, but since then the average snowfall has been exactly 00.00 inches.) Hotels, bars, discos, restaurants, shops, and attractions are all crowded. Hollywood and Broadway celebrities appear in sophisticated supper clubs, and other performing artists hold the stage at ballets, operas, concerts, and theaters. From mid-December through January 2, Walt Disney World's Magic Kingdom is lavishly decorated, and there are daily parades and other extravaganzas, as well as overwhelming crowds. In the Jacksonville and Panhandle area, winter is off-season—an excellent bargain.

For the college crowd, spring vacation is still the time to congregate in Florida, especially in Panama City Beach and the Daytona Beach area; Fort Lauderdale, where city officials have refashioned the beachfront more as a family resort, no longer indulges young revelers, so it's much less popular with college students than it once was.

Summer in Florida, as smart budget-minded visitors have discovered, is often hot and very humid, but along the coast, ocean breezes make the season quite bearable and many hotels lower their prices considerably. In the Panhandle and Central Florida, summer is peak season. Theme park lines shrink only after children return to school in September. Large numbers of international visitors keep year-round visitation high at theme parks.

For senior citizens, fall is the time for discounts for many attractions and hotels in Orlando and along the Pinellas Suncoast in the Tampa Bay area.

Climate

What follows are average daily maximum and minimum temperatures for major cities in Florida.

🔲 Forecasts **Weather Channel** ⊕ www.weather.com.

KEY WEST (THE KEYS)

Jan.	76F	24C	May	85F	29C	Sept.	90F	32C
	65	18		74	23		77	25
Feb.	76F	24C	June	88F	31C	Oct.	83F	28C
	67	19		77	25		76	24
Mar.	79F	26C	July	90F	32C	Nov.	79F	26C
	68	20		79	26		70	21
Apr.	81F	27C	Aug.	90F	32C	Dec.	76F	24C
	72	22		79	26		67	19

MIAMI

Jan.	74F	23C	May	83F	28C	Sept.	86F	30C
	63	17		72	22		76	24
Feb.	76F	24C	June	85F	29C	Oct.	83F	28C
	63	17		76	24		72	22
Mar.	77F	25C	July	88F	31C	Nov.	79F	26C
	65	18		76	24		67	19
Apr.	79F	26C	Aug.	88F	31C	Dec.	76F	26C
	68	20		77	25		63	17

ORLANDO

Jan.	70F	21C	May	88F	31C	Sept.	88F	31C
	49	9		67	19		74	23
Feb.	72F	22C	June	90F	32C	Oct.	83F	28C
	54	12		72	22		67	19
Mar.	76F	24C	July	90F	32C	Nov.	76F	24C
	56	13		74	23		58	14
Apr.	81F	27C	Aug.	90F	32C	Dec.	70F	21C
	63	17		74	23		52	11

PANAMA CITY

Jan.	62F	17C	May	83F	28C	Sept.	87F	31C
	39	4		61	16		69	21
Feb.	65F	18C	June	88F	31C	Oct.	80F	27C
	41	5		68	20		55	13
Mar.	71F	22C	July	89F	32C	Nov.	71F	22C
	47	8		71	22		48	9
Apr.	77F	25C	Aug.	89F	32C	Dec.	64F	18C
	53	12		71	22		40	4

TAMPA

Jan.	70F	21C	May	86F	30C	Sept.	89F	32C
	52	11		69	21		74	23
Feb.	72F	22C	June	89F	32C	Oct.	84F	29C
	54	12		74	23		68	20
Mar.	76F	24C	July	90F	32C	Nov.	78F	26C
	59	15		75	24		61	16
Apr.	81F	27C	Aug.	90F	32C	Dec.	72F	22C
	62	17		75	24		55	13

Florida really does have seasons, and with them come festivals and events that capture special moments throughout the state. Plan well in advance if you hope to be in town for any of these celebrations.

WINTER

December	**Monthlong Victorian Seaside Christmas** (☎ 904/277–0717) takes place oceanside on Amelia Island.
	Walt Disney World's Very Merry Christmas Parade in the Magic Kingdom (☎ 407/824–4321) celebrates the season at the Magic Kingdom.
	In mid-December, the **Winterfest Boat Parade** (☎ 954/767–0686 ⊕ www.winterfestparade.com) lights up the Intracoastal Waterway in Fort Lauderdale.
Late December– early January	The **Orange Bowl and Junior Orange Bowl Festival** (☎ 305/371–4600), in the Miami area, are best known for the downtown King Orange Jamboree Parade on December 31 and the Orange Bowl Football Classic at Pro Player Stadium but also include more than 20 youth-oriented events.
	On December 31 in Tampa's Ybor City is the **Outback Bowl Blast** (☎ 813/874–2695), a street festival with live music; the next day two of the nation's best college football teams meet in the Outback Bowl. Also on New Year's Day are the **Florida Citrus Bowl** (☎ 407/423–2476) in Orlando, and the **Gator Bowl** (☎ 904/798–1700) in Jacksonville.
January	Mid-month, **Art Deco Weekend** (☎ 305/672–2014) spotlights Miami Beach's historic district with an art deco street fair along Ocean Drive, a 1930s-style Moon Over Miami Ball, and live entertainment.
	Easterlin Park in Oakland is the setting for the mid-month **South Florida Folk Festival** (☎ 800/785–8924 ⊕ www.southfloridafolkfest. com), with national touring companies, dance, and music.
	The **Florida Citrus Festival and Polk County Fair** (☎ 863/292–9810 ⊕ www.citrusfestival.com) in Winter Haven the second half of the month showcases the citrus harvest with displays and entertainment.
	The **Everglades Seafood Festival** (☎ 941/695–4100), a month-long celebration of the ocean's bounty, features free entertainment with music, crafts, and seafood each weekend.
	Early in the month, **Polo Season** (☎ 561/793–1440) opens at the Palm Beach Polo and Country Club in West Palm Beach.
	The **Winter Equestrian Festival** at **International Stadium** (☎ 561/793–5867) begins jumping in Wellington later in the month and contin-

	ues through mid-March. The festival, which includes 3,500 horses and seven major grand-prix equestrian events, then moves to the **Bob Thomas Equestrian Center** (☎ 813/740–3500) in Tampa through April.
February	During the entire month, the **Florida Renaissance Festival** (☎ 386/364–4590 or 800/373–6337 ⊕ www.ren-fest.com) in Deefield Beach draws hundreds of authentic-looking costumed festival goers each year.
	More than 300,000 visitors head to Mount Dora the first full weekend in February for the **Mount Dora Arts Festival** (☎ 352/383–0880 ⊕ www.mountdoracenterforthearts.com), the city's signature event, spotlighting more than 300 artists.
	The **Florida Strawberry Festival** (☎ 813/752–9194 ⊕ www.flstrawberryfestival.com), in Plant City, has celebrated the town's winter harvest for more than six decades with two weeks of country-music stars, rides, exhibits, and strawberry delicacies.
	The **Gasparilla Festival** (☎ 813/223–2752 or 888/224–1733 ⊕ www.gasparillapiratefest.com), on the first Saturday of the month, celebrates the legendary pirate's invasion of Tampa with street parades, an art festival, and music.
	The **Olustee Battle Festival** (☎ 396/755–1097 ⊕ www.olusteefestival.com) in Lake City is the second-largest (Gettysburg has the largest) Civil War reenactment in the nation.
	Speed Weeks (☎ 386/947–6800) is a three-week celebration of auto racing that culminates in the famous Daytona 500, at the Daytona International Speedway in Daytona Beach.
	The **Coconut Grove Art Festival** (☎ 305/447–0401), mid-month, is the state's largest.
	The **Miami International Film Festival** (☎ 305/237–3456 ⊕ www.miamifilmfestival.com) is 10 days of international, domestic, and local films.
SPRING	
Late February–early March	Early March brings the **Peace River Seafood Festival & Boat Show** (☎ 941/639–1188) in Punta Gorda, where folks gather along the town's waterfront for arts and crafts, fresh seafood, and a water-ski show.
	Bike Week (⊕ www.daytonachamber.com), one of Daytona's biggest annual events, draws 400,000 riders from across the United States for 10 days of races, plus parades and even coleslaw wrestling.

March	The **Sanibel Shell Fair** (☎ 941/472–2155), which runs for four days starting the first Thursday of the month, is the largest event of the year on Sanibel Island.
	The self-proclaimed world's largest street party, **Calle Ocho** (☎ 305/644–8888) packs 1 million people onto Miami's Southwest 8th Street for a frenetic day of live Latin music, ethnic food, and massive corporate product giveaways.
	St. Augustine's **Rhythm and Ribs Festival** (☎ 904/814–2285) spotlights the country's championship barbecuers with cook-offs, special recipes, and plenty of Southern barbecue.
	SeaFest (☎ 321/459–2200 ⊕ www.seafest.com) in Port Canaveral has loads of fun, sun, and scrumptious seafood.
	Mount Dora's **Antique Boat Festival** (☎ 352/742–8038), held the fourth weekend in March, is one of the largest in the Southeast, highlighting more than 150 antique, classic, and historic boats.
	Winter Park Sidewalk Arts Festival (☎ 407/672–6390 ⊕ www.wpsaf.org) is one of the Southeast's most prestigious outdoor fine arts festivals and spotlights internationally known artists.
	The **Sarasota Jazz Festival** (☎ 941/336–1552) is a showcase for well-known musicians from around the world.
Late March–early April	**Springtime Tallahassee** (☎850/224–5012 ⊕www.springtimetallahassee.com) is a major cultural, sporting, and culinary event in the capital.
	Nationally recognized performers and local talent entertain flocks of blues lovers during the two day **Springing the Blues Festival** (⊕ www.springingtheblues.com) at the Jacksonville Beach pavilion in early April.
	A case of the blues also hits Tampa around this time each year. The **Tampa Bay Blues Festival** (☎ 727/502–5000 ⊕ www.tampabaybluesfest.com), along the city's waterfront, donates all proceeds to three local charity organizations.
	Pensacola gyrates to the sounds of jazz during its annual **Pensacola Jazz Fest** (☎ 850/433–8382 ⊕ jazzpensacola.com).
	Fort Myers adds a touch of Latin to its jazz festival. **Latin Jazz Fest IV, Salsa on the River** (☎ 941/541–7218 ⊕ www.latinjazzfest.com), celebrates the city's growing Hispanic community with exotic foods, music, and Grammy-award-winning artists.
April	The **Delray Affair** (☎ 561/278–0424 ⊕ www.delrayaffair.com), held the weekend following Easter, is Delray Beach's biggest event and includes arts, crafts, and food.
	The **Florida Heritage Seafood Festival** (☎ 941/747–1998) takes place in Bradenton in early April.

Late April–early May	The **Conch Republic Celebration** (☎ 305/296–0213 ⊕ www.conchrepublic.com) honors the founding fathers of the Conch Republic, "the small island nation of Key West."
	The **Sun 'n' Fun Festival** (☎ 727/562–4800), held throughout Clearwater, includes an illuminated parade, a "disc golf" tournament, day and nighttime concerts, and events for kids.
	Historic downtown Fernandina Beach, chock-full of Victorian architecture, is the setting for Amelia Island's **Isle of Eight Flags Seafood Festival** (☎ 904/261–3248 ⊕ www.shrimpfestival.com). The entire historical area is filled with arts and crafts and plenty of seafood.
May	The **Air & Sea Show** (☎ 954/527–5600 Ext. 4 ⊕ www.airseashow.com) draws more than 2 million people to the Fort Lauderdale beachfront for performances by big names in aviation, such as the Navy's Blue Angels and the Air Force's Thunderbirds.
	Nationally recognized Cajun and zydeco performers, the state's largest outdoor dance floor, and 25,000 pounds of crawfish attract young and old to Fort Lauderdale's stadium for the **Cajun Zydeco Crawfish Festival** (☎ 954/828–5934) in mid-May.
	West Palm Beach celebrates everything under the sun during **Sunfest** (☎ 561/659–5980 or 800/786–3378 ⊕ www.sunfest.org).
	Top-name recording artists draw crowds to Jacksonville's Metro Park for an evening of free entertainment during the **Spring Music Fest** (☎ 904/630–3690).
	Stephen Foster State Park, near the Suwannee River in White Springs, is the gathering spot for the **Florida Folk Festival** (⊕ www.floridastateparks.org/folkfest) in late May, an event featuring nationally recognized performers.
SUMMER	
June	The **Miami-Bahamas Goombay Festival** (☎ 305/567–1399), in Miami's Coconut Grove, celebrates the city's Bahamian heritage the first weekend of the month with food, crafts, and street music all day.
	The **Billy Bowlegs Pirate Festival** (☎ 850/244–8191), in downtown Fort Walton Beach, is a week of activities in memory of a pirate who ruled the area in the late 1700s.
	Pensacola celebrates its heritage with **Fiesta of Five Flags** (☎ 904/433–6512 ⊕ www.fiestaoffiveflags.org), a weeklong event featuring treasure hunts, parades, a coronation ball, and concerts.
	The Panhandle city of Chipley celebrates its **Watermelon Festival** (☎ 850/638–6180) the last Saturday of the month; Washington County's largest event features eating and seed-spitting contests and a watermelon auction.

June–July	**Beethoven by the Beach** (☎ 954/561–2997), in Fort Lauderdale, features Beethoven's symphonies, chamber pieces, and piano concertos performed by the Florida Philharmonic.
July	Cities all over the state celebrate Independence Day with outdoor events and spectacular fireworks displays. Titusville celebrates the 4th at Sand Point Park with **Hometown USA** (☎ 321/383–8962), which includes patriotic concerts and a grand fireworks display.
	Fort Lauderdale gathers at the beach and Alexander Park for **Fourth Along the Coast** (☎ 954/761–5813), and Jacksonville's two venues include the beach and downtown's Metro Park, where the city gathers for **Freedom, Fanfare and Fireworks** (☎ 904/630–3690).
August	The **Annual Wausau Possum Funday & Parade** (☎ 850/638–7888) is held in the Possum Palace, Wausau, the first Saturday of the month in homage to the critter that once sustained the diets of the town's populace.

FALL

September	The **Anniversary of the Founding of St. Augustine** (☎ 904/825–1010), also called Days in Spain, commemorates the landing of Pedro Menendez in St. Augustine in 1565. It's held on the seaside grounds of the Mission of Nombre de Dios.
October	The **Destin Seafood Festival** (☎ 850/837–6241), held the first full weekend in the month, gives you three days to sample smoked amberjack, fried mullet, and shark kebabs.
	The **Fort Lauderdale International Boat Show** (☎ 954/764–7642), the world's largest show based on exhibit size, displays boats of every size, price, and description at the Bahia Mar marina and four other venues.
	The **Florida Manatee Festival** (☎ 352/795–3149), in Crystal River, focuses on both the river and the endangered manatee.
	Biketoberfest (☎ 800/854–1234) is highlighted by championship racing at the Daytona International Speedway, the Main Street Rally, concerts, and swap meets that last four days.
	Boggy Bayou Mullet Festival (☎ 850/729–4008 ⊕ www.mulletfestival.com) is a three-day hoedown held the third full weekend in October in celebration of the "Twin Cities," Valparaiso and Niceville, and the famed scavenger fish, the mullet.
	The **Cedar Key Seafood Festival** (☎ 352/543–5600) is held on Main Street in Cedar Key.
	The **Fall RiverFest Arts Festival** (☎ 904/328–8998) takes place downtown along the St. Johns River in Palatka.

	Fantasy Fest (☎ 305/296–1817 ⊕ www.fantasyfest.net), in Key West, is a no-holds-barred Halloween costume party, parade, and town fair.
October and November	The **Fort Lauderdale International Film Festival** (☎ 954/760–9898 ⊕ www.fliff.com) showcases three weeks of independent cinema from around the world beginning in late October.
November	The **Florida Seafood Festival** (⊕ www.floridaseafoodfestival.com) in Apalachicola's Battery Park celebrates the famous oyster harvest, with oyster-shucking-and-consumption contests and parades.
	All eyes look skyward during the **Spacecoast Birding & Wildlife Festival** (☎ 321/268–5224), formerly Flyway Fest, in Titusville.
	The **Miami Book Fair International** (☎ 305/237–3032 ⊕ www.miamibookfair.com), the largest book fair in the United States, is held on the Wolfson campus of Miami-Dade Community College.
	St. Augustine unwraps Christmas a bit early with the **Nights of Lights** (☎ 904/829–1711). More than 1 million tiny white lights illuminate the historic city beginning in mid-November for 75 days, during which time the city celebrates with historical Christmas events.

PLEASURES & PASTIMES

Beaches No point in the state is more than 60 mi from salt water. The long, lean peninsula is bordered by a 526-mi Atlantic coast from Fernandina Beach to Key West and a 792-mi coast along the Gulf of Mexico and Florida Bay from Pensacola to Key West. If you were to stretch Florida's convoluted coast in a straight line, it would extend for about 1,800 mi. What's more, if you add in the perimeter of every island surrounded by saltwater, Florida has about 8,500 mi of tidal shoreline—more than any other state except Alaska. Florida's coastline comprises more than 1,000 mi of sand beaches.

Canoeing The Everglades has areas suitable for flat-water wilderness canoeing. Other popular canoeing rivers include the Blackwater, Econlokahatchee, Juniper, Loxahatchee, Peace, Oklawaha, Suwannee, St. Marys, and Santa Fe. The Florida Department of Environmental Protection provides maps and brochures on 1,550 mi of canoe trails in various parts of the state. Also contact individual national forests, parks, monuments, reserves, and seashores for information on their canoe trails. Local chambers of commerce have information on trails in county parks. The best time to canoe in Florida is winter—the dry season—when you're less likely to get caught in a torrential downpour or become a snack for mosquitoes.

Fishing Saltwater fishing is plentiful from the Keys all the way up the Atlantic coast to Georgia and up the Gulf Coast to Alabama. Many seaside communities have fishing piers that charge admission to anglers (and usually a lower rate to spectators). These piers generally have a bait-and-tackle shop. It's easy to find a boat-charter service that will take you out into deep water. Some of the best are in the Panhandle, where Destin and Fort Walton Beach have huge fleets. The Keys, too, are dotted with charter services, and Key West has a big sportfishing fleet. You can charter anything from an old wooden craft to a luxurious waterborne palace with state-of-the-art amenities.

Inland there are more than 7,000 freshwater lakes. The largest—448,000-acre Lake Okeechobee, the third-largest natural lake in the United States—is home to bass, bluegill, speckled perch, and succulent catfish (which the locals call "sharpies"). In addition to the state's many natural freshwater rivers, South Florida also has an extensive system of flood-control canals. In 1989 scientists found high mercury levels in largemouth bass and warmouth caught in parts of the Everglades and in Palm Beach, Broward, and Dade counties and warned against eating fish from those areas. Those warnings remain in effect, and warnings have been extended to parts of northern Florida.

Golf Except in the heart of the Everglades, you'll never be far from one of Florida's more than 1,100 golf courses. Palm Beach County and Naples are the state's leading golf locales, and the PGA, LPGA, and National Golf Foundation all have headquarters in the state. And just north of St. Augustine are World Golf Village and the World Golf Hall of Fame. Many of the best golf courses in Florida allow you to play without being a member or hotel guest. Reserve tee times in advance, especially in winter. Ask about golf reservations when you make your lodging reservations.

Key Lime Time

Almost every Florida restaurant claims to make the best key lime pie. Traditional key lime pie is yellow, not green, with an old-fashioned graham cracker crust and meringue top. Some restaurants serve their key lime pie with a pastry crust; most substitute whipped cream for the more temperamental meringue. Each pie will be a little different. Try several. Even if you eat dessert first—this is, after all, your vacation—save room for a meal. Florida's cuisine changes as you move across the state, depending on who settled the area and who now operates the restaurants. You can expect seafood to be a staple on nearly every menu, however, with greater variety on the coasts, and catfish, frogs' legs, and gator tail to be popular around inland lakes and at Miccosukee restaurants along the Tamiami Trail. South Florida has a diverse assortment of Latin American restaurants and it's also easy to find island specialties born of the Bahamas, Haiti, and Jamaica. A fusion of tropical, Continental, and nouvelle cuisine—some call it Floribbean—has gained widespread popularity. It draws on exotic fruits, spices, and fresh seafood. The influence of earlier Hispanic settlements remains in Key West and Tampa's Ybor City.

Natural Areas

Although Florida is the fourth-most-populous state in the nation, more than 10 million acres of public and private recreation facilities are set aside in national forests, parks, monuments, reserves, and seashores; state forests and parks; county parks; and nature preserves owned and managed by private conservation groups. All told, Florida now has some 3,500 mi of trails, encompassing 1,550 mi of canoe and kayak trails, about 670 mi for bicycling and other uses, 900 mi exclusively for hiking, about 350 exclusively for equestrian use, plus some 30 mi of purely interpretive trails, chiefly in state parks. An active greenways development plan seeks to protect wildlife habitat as much as foster recreation.

Scuba Diving & Snorkeling

South Florida and the Keys attract most of the divers and snorkelers, but the more than 300 statewide dive shops schedule drift-, reef-, and wreck-diving trips for scuba divers all along Florida's Atlantic and Gulf coasts. The low-tech pleasures of snorkeling can be enjoyed throughout the Keys and elsewhere where shallow reefs hug the shore. Inland in northern and central Florida, you can explore more than 100 grottoes, rivers, sinkholes, and springs. In some locations you can swim near endangered manatees ("sea cows"), which migrate in from the sea to congregate around comparatively warm springs during winter.

FODOR'S CHOICE

Fodor'sChoice ★	The sights, restaurants, hotels, and other travel experiences on these pages are our editors' top picks—our Fodor's Choices. They're the best of their type in the area covered by the book—not to be missed and always worth your time. In the destination chapters that follow, you will find all the details.

LODGING

$$$$	**Amelia Island Plantation**, Northeast. The first-rate golf, tennis, and spa facilities are big draws at this sprawling, family-oriented resort, also a worthy destination for hiking, biking, and bird-watching.
$$$$	**The Breakers**, Palm Beach. The building, an opulent Italian Renaissance palace, is amazing, as is the resort's ability to balance Old World luxury with modern conveniences.
$$$$	**Casa Morada**, Islamorada. Three women hoteliers have turned this waterfront resort into an all-suites showcase befitting the French Riviera, with a Caribbean accent.
$$$$	**Delano Hotel**, South Beach. An air of surrealism surrounds this much-talked-about SoBe hotel, the hot spot for celebrities and other well-to-do visitors.
$$$$	**Don CeSar Beach Resort**, St. Pete Beach. A checkered past and stunning sands are among the treats at this cotton-candy "Pink Palace."
$$$$	**Gaylord Palms Resort**, Kissimmee. The 4-acre, glass-enclosed atrium contains environments recalling old St. Augustine, Key West, and the Everglades, all exceptionally detailed.
$$$$	**Grand Floridian Resort & Spa**, Walt Disney World. If it weren't for its modern amenities, you might think you were in one of the great hotels of the 19th century when you visit this Victorian-style charmer, Disney's flagship resort.
$$$$	**LaPlaya Beach & Golf Resort**, Naples. A Thai-style spa, rock-waterfalls pools, and a tony Miami-style beachfront restaurant are among the amenities at this resort.
$$$$	**Little Palm Island Resort & Spa**, Little Torch Key. On its own palm-fringed island 3 mi off Little Torch Key, this resort of thatch-roof villas on stilts provides a secluded, one-of-a-kind experience.
$$$$	**The Lodge & Club**, Ponte Vedra Beach. Private balconies overlooking the Atlantic are among the treats at this cozy but elegant spot.
$$$$	**Mandarin Oriental**, Miami. Attention to detail, proximity to downtown and the beaches, and a stellar restaurant, Azul, add up to a singular experience.

$$$$	**Marquesa Hotel,** Key West. In a town that prides itself on its laid-back luxe, this complex of four restored 1884 houses stands out.
$$$$	**Ponte Vedra Inn & Club,** Ponte Vedra Beach. A renowned spa is a big draw at this landmark country-club resort.
$$$$	**Renaissance Vinoy Resort,** St. Petersburg. Historic preservation yields the grandeur of St. Petersburg's early heyday and the Gatsby era.
$$$$	**Ritz-Carlton Amelia Island.** Ritz-Carltons are known for stylish elegance, superb comfort, and excellent service. This one also comes with a pristine beach, its own golf course, and the outstanding and unusual Grill restaurant.
$$$$	**Ritz-Carlton Orlando Grande Lakes,** Southwestern Orlando. With an elaborate pool area that rivals Orlando's best water parks, a huge European-style spa, and what seems like miles of marble floors, this opulent resort has something for everyone and then some.
$$$$	**Sanibel Harbour Resort & Spa,** Fort Myers. Sweeping views of San Carlos Bay as well as the sports facilities and restaurants are the draws of this high-rise resort complex.
$$$$	**WaterColor Inn,** Grayton Beach. Nature meets chic at this retreat with dune-level bungalows (with outdoor showers) as well as larger rotunda rooms, all with fabulous views of the sea.
$$$–$$$$	**Casa Monica Hotel,** St. Augustine. The turrets, towers, and wrought-iron balconies offer a hint of what's inside this late-1800s Flagler-era masterpiece.
$$$–$$$$	**Hyatt Regency Pier Sixty-Six,** Fort Lauderdale. The trademark of this high-rise resort on the Intracoastal Waterway is its rooftop Pier Top Lounge, making one 360-degree revolution every 66 minutes.
$$$–$$$$	**Marriott's Harbor Beach Resort,** Fort Lauderdale. A European spa and spacious rooms with rich tropical colors are highlights at this 16-acre property.
$$$–$$$$	**Royal Pacific Resort,** Universal Studios. The South Pacific theme extends to the beautiful, lagoon-style pool and grounds filled with tropical flora.
$$$–$$$$	**Wilderness Lodge,** Walt Disney World. This majestic hotel, incongruous in Central Florida with its surrounding fuzz of towering pines, recalls the Rocky Mountain lodges of the Teddy Roosevelt era.
$$$	**Marriott Bay Point Resort Village,** Panama City Beach. The tropical-chic guest rooms, private patios, and myriad amenities of this bayfront property are pleasant surprises.
$$$	**Sandestin Golf and Beach Resort,** Destin. Whether you've come to Sandestin for golfing, fishing, boating, dining, or just relaxing on

the beach, this classy, 2,500-acre resort situated between the Intracoastal and the Gulf of Mexico is bound to please.

RESTAURANTS	
$$$$	**The Grill**, Amelia Island. "A Seat in the Kitchen" and "blind tasting" menu are among the experiences worth paying for at the Ritz-Carlton Amelia Island's signature restaurant.
$$$$	**Victoria & Albert's**, Walt Disney World. It's expensive, but dishes like grilled prime filet over onion risotto are well worth the price.
$$$–$$$$	**Bern's Steak House**, Tampa. Tour the kitchen and wine cellar after dinner to understand just how much love and care go into the finest meal you can have in the Tampa Bay area.
$$$–$$$$	**Café Boulud**, Palm Beach. Lunch and dinner entrées on chef Daniel Boulud's signature four-muse menu reflect classic French, seasonal, vegetarian, and a rotating selection of international dishes.
$$$–$$$$	**Café Marquesa**, Key West. The hospitality machine is well oiled at this refined 50-seat contemporary restaurant adjoining the intimate Marquesa Hotel.
$$$–$$$$	**Fish Out of Water**, Grayton Beach. The Panhandle meets Manhattan at this sleek spot, where imaginative dishes with Asian and Southern accents shine as brilliantly as a Gulf sunset.
$$$–$$$$	**Matthew's**, Jacksonville. Spartan decor is the perfect foil for dazzling dishes in one of Jacksonville's trendiest neighborhoods.
$$$–$$$$	**95 Cordova**, St. Augustine. Choose from three dining rooms and consider the "tasting menu" pairing courses with outstanding wines.
$$$–$$$$	**Norman's**, Coral Gables. Chef Norman Van Aken turns out artful masterpieces of New World cuisine, combining bold tastes from Latin, American, Caribbean, and Asian traditions.
$$$–$$$$	**Sale e Pepe**, Marco Island. Pasta, sausage, and sinful pastries rule at this restaurant with patio seating overlooking the beach.
$$$–$$$$	**Shula's on the Beach**, Fort Lauderdale. Certified Angus beef is cut thick and grilled over a superhot fire at this popular steak house with sports memorabilia and large-screen TVs.
$$–$$$$	**Barracuda Grill**, Marathon. Beef, lamb, and pork shank hold their own with local fish, desserts, and a heavily Californian wine list.
$$–$$$$	**Le Coq au Vin**, Orlando. The traditional French cuisine is expertly prepared, and the setting is delightfully unstuffy.
$$–$$$$	**Les Chefs de France**, Walt Disney World. Very good French food is served daily at this Epcot charmer, which many call Disney's best.
$$–$$$$	**Mark's Las Olas**, Fort Lauderdale. Culinary star Mark Militello blends Caribbean, Southwestern, and Mediterranean flavors.

$$–$$$$ | **Pierre's,** Islamorada. The food has Asian, Indian, and Floridian accents at this spot, which marries British-colonial decadence with South Florida trendiness.

$$–$$$$ | **Wolfgang Puck Café,** Orlando. The exceptional fare is consistent visit after visit, and service is attentive, friendly, and professional.

$$$ | **Artist Point,** Walt Disney World. If you're not a guest at the Wilderness Lodge, a meal here is worth it just to see the giant totem poles and huge rock fireplace in the lobby.

$$–$$$ | **Casablanca Cafe,** Fort Lauderdale. Find an American potpourri with both tropical and Asian influences at this Moroccan-style villa.

$$–$$$ | **Spoodles,** Walt Disney World. At this stylish spot you can sample wonderful Mediterranean tapas, from Italian to Greek.

$$–$$$ | **Tamara's Cafe Floridita,** Apalachicola. This newcomer adds a uniquely South American flair to Apalachicola's up-and-coming dining scene.

$$ | **Restaurant Akershus,** Walt Disney World. The Norwegian buffet at this restaurant is as extensive as you'll find on this side of the Atlantic.

BEACHES & PARKS

Bahia Honda State Park, Bahia Honda Key. The park sprawls across both sides of the Overseas Highway, giving it 2½ mi of beautiful sandy beaches—the best in the Keys—on both the Atlantic Ocean and the Gulf of Mexico.

Bill Baggs Cape Florida State Park, Key Biscayne. Consistently voted one of South Florida's best beaches, this 414-acre park has a plethora of facilities, a historic lighthouse, and great views of the Miami skyline.

Broadwalk, Hollywood. While it's technically a walkway along the beach, this 27-foot-wide thoroughfare is ideal for strolling or biking.

Clearwater Beach. Try this happening beach, with nonstop volleyball and a nightly sunset celebration at the pier.

Delnor-Wiggins Pass State Park, Naples. Loggerhead turtles, anglers, and sun worshipers love this quiet, natural beach.

Fort Lauderdale Beachfront. Alone among Florida's major beachfront communities, Fort Lauderdale's beach remains open and uncluttered.

Grayton Beach State Park, Panhandle. The beach here is constantly ranked among the finest in the nation, but this quiet spot gets extra points for its beautifully kept campground and its brand-new cabins, which are downright stylish.

J. N. "Ding" Darling National Wildlife Refuge, Sanibel. More than half of Sanibel is occupied by this subtly beautiful refuge, 6,300 acres of wetlands and lush, jungly mangrove forests.

John Pennekamp Coral Reef State Park, Key Largo. Whenever people talk about the best diving sites in the world, this park is on the short list.

Kathryn Abbey Hanna Park, Mayport. Spectacular beaches, hiking, and biking await at this 450-acre oceanfront park just north of Atlantic Beach.

Merritt Island National Wildlife Refuge, Titusville. If you prefer wading birds over waiting in line, don't miss this 140,000-acre refuge adjacent to the Canaveral National Seashore.

Ocean Drive, Miami. A 10-block stretch from 5th to 15th Street, with a wide beach on one side and bustling art deco hotels, cafés, and boutiques on the other, is the perpetually "it" beachfront in America.

St. Andrews State Park, Panama City Beach. Families with youngsters will love the shallow, protected swimming areas and facilities galore; nature enthusiasts will be stunned by the natural beauty of Panama City Beach.

St. George Island State Park, Panhandle. Nine miles of fantastic beachfront with sand as white and fine as biscuit flour make this a must-see—and must-swim—Panhandle favorite. Florida beaches don't get any better than this.

Siesta Beach, Siesta Key. If powdery white sand as soft as down is your thing, settle in here for a while.

Wakulla Springs State Park, Wakulla Springs. A glass-bottom-boat ride deep into jungle-lined waterways might yield glimpses of alligators, snakes, waterfowl—and Old Florida.

HISTORY

Bailey-Matthews Shell Museum, Sanibel. More than a million shells from around the world are on display here.

Charles Hosmer Morse Museum, Winter Park. Stunning stained-glass windows, lamps, and watercolors designed by Louis Comfort Tiffany are the draw.

Edison & Ford Winter Estates, Fort Myers. Everything is just as Edison left it; you can imagine him tinkering with the first phonograph in the laboratory.

Ernest F. Coe Visitor Center, Everglades National Park. Engaging exhibits and films make the park's main visitor center much more than an information stop.

Henry Morrison Flagler Museum, Palm Beach. Whitehall, Flagler's mansion, is the backdrop for art and railway memorabilia.

Jacksonville Museum of Modern Art, Jacksonville. Five galleries and ArtExplorium, an interactive educational exhibit for kids, are among the draws in this 14,000-square-foot building.

Key West Museum of Art and History, Key West. This former custom house has long-term and changing exhibits on the history of Key West, including *Remember the Maine.*

Morikami Museum and Japanese Gardens, Delray Beach. The leading U.S. center for Japanese and American cultural exchange is in a model of a Japanese imperial villa.

Norton Museum of Art, West Palm Beach. The collection of 19th- and 20th-century American and European paintings includes works by Picasso, Monet, Matisse, Pollock, and O'Keeffe.

Ringling Center for the Cultural Arts, Sarasota. Two museums and a winter home for clowns is part of this complex dreamed up by circus tycoon John Ringling.

Salvador Dalí Museum, St. Petersburg. The world's most extensive collection of originals by Spanish surrealist Salvador Dalí resides here. Frequent tours by well-informed docents heighten the experience.

Ybor City, East Tampa. As in the days of yore, Ybor City's National Historic Landmark District in Tampa brings together diverse people to celebrate life like they did in the old social clubs of the cigar-making era.

SHOPS WORTH A STOP

Bal Harbour Shops, Bal Harbour. This is the swankiest shopping to be had in Florida outside of Palm Beach, with an open-air collection of 100 shops, boutiques, and department stores, from Prada to Pratesi.

Downtown Disney, Walt Disney World. After a day of beating your feet around a theme park, reserve an evening for some quiet lakeside shopping and strolling.

Jungle Drums, Captiva. Fish, sea turtles, and other wildlife are captured with utmost creativity and touches of whimsy.

Lincoln Road Mall, South Beach. The Morris Lapidus–renovated Lincoln Road, just a few blocks from the beach and convention center, is fun, lively, and friendly for people old, young, gay, and straight—and their dogs.

Ron Jon Surf Shop, Cocoa Beach. A 52,000-square-foot superstore open 24/7, Ron Jon packs appeal for sports-gear enthusiasts and the non-surfing set.

THEME PARKS

Busch Gardens, Tampa. Two of the world's largest roller coasters, good shows, and live animals are loosely brought together under a turn-of-the-last-century Africa theme on 335 acres.

Green Meadows Farm, Kissimmee. The pigs will nibble on your shoelaces and you'll get to cuddle a baby chick and milk a cow on this 40-acre family-friendly farm.

Jacksonville Zoo, Jacksonville. Rare waterfowl and the Serona Overlook, which showcases some of the world's most venomous snakes, are highlights here.

Kennedy Space Center Visitor Complex, Titusville. The home of the real *Apollo 13* illuminates the romance of the early space program. It's also one of Florida's best bargains.

SeaWorld Orlando. Weaving learning and laughter, this water-centered mega-zoo lets you get up close to all sorts of ocean life.

Sun Splash Family Waterpark, Cape Coral. Water slides and the Lilypad Walk are among the more than two dozen wet and dry attractions here.

Universal Orlando. The saucy, sassy, and hip movie-theme Universal Studios is joined by the ultracool Universal Islands of Adventure in a Universal empire.

Walt Disney World, Orlando. Don't miss a visit here: it's everything it's cracked up to be—and there's more of it every year.

VIEWS

A1A from Delray Beach. Head north through Manalapan for one of this highway's most breathtaking vistas.

Seven Mile Bridge, The Keys. Find out for yourself why this expanse—actually 6.79 mi long—is one of the most-photographed images in the Keys.

Sunshine Skyway across Tampa Bay. One of the world's great monumental sculptures carries six lanes of traffic soaring across the mouth of Florida's largest estuary.

SMART TRAVEL TIPS

Finding out about your destination before you leave home means you won't squander time organizing everyday minutiae once you've arrived. You'll be more streetwise when you hit the ground as well, better prepared to explore the aspects of Florida that drew you here in the first place. The organizations in this section can provide information to supplement this guide; contact them for up-to-the-minute details, and consult the A to Z sections that end each chapter for facts on the various topics as they relate to the state's many regions. Happy landings!

AIR TRAVEL
BOOKING

When you book, look for nonstop flights and remember that "direct" flights stop at least once. Try to avoid connecting flights, which require a change of plane. Two airlines may operate a connecting flight jointly, so ask whether your airline operates every segment of the trip; you may find that the carrier you prefer flies you only part of the way. To find more booking tips and to check prices and make online flight reservations, log on to www.fodors.com.

CARRIERS

🛪 **Major Airlines Air Canada** ☎ 888/247-2262 ⊕ www.aircanada.com. **American** ☎ 800/433-7300 ⊕ www.aa.com. **Continental** ☎ 800/525-0280 ⊕ www.continental.com. **Delta** ☎ 800/221-1212 ⊕ www.delta.com. **Northwest** ☎ 800/225-2525 ⊕ www.nwa.com. **Spirit** ☎ 800/772-7117 ⊕ www.spiritair.com. **United** ☎ 800/241-6522 ⊕ www.united.com. **US Airways** ☎ 800/428-4322 ⊕ www.usairways.com.

🛪 **Smaller Airlines AirTran** ☎ 800/247-8726 ⊕ www.airtran.com to Miami, Pensacola, Tallahassee, Fort Lauderdale, Fort Myers, Jacksonville, Orlando, Tampa, and West Palm Beach. **Jet Blue** ☎ 800/538-2583 ⊕ www.jetblue.com to Tampa, Fort Lauderdale, Fort Myers, West Palm Beach, and Orlando. **Midwest Airlines** ☎ 800/452-2022 ⊕ www.midwestairlines.com to Fort Lauderdale, Fort Myers, Orlando, and Tampa. **Southwest** ☎ 800/435-9792 ⊕ www.southwest.com to Jacksonville, Tampa, Fort Lauderdale, West Palm Beach, and Orlando.

⤴ From the U.K. American ☎ 0845/778-9789, 0207/365-0777 in London ⊕ www.aa.com. **British Airways** ☎ 0870/850-9850 ⊕ www.britishairways.com. **Continental** ☎ 0129/377-6464 or 0845/607-6760 ⊕ www.continental.com. **Delta** ☎ 0800/414-767 ⊕ www.delta.com. **Northwest** ☎ 0870/507-4074 ⊕ www.nwa.com via Detroit or Minneapolis. **United** ☎ 0845/844-4777. **Virgin Atlantic** ☎ 0870/380-2007 ⊕ www.virgin-atlantic.com.

CHECK-IN & BOARDING

Always **find out your carrier's check-in policy.** Plan to arrive at the airport about two hours before your scheduled departure time for domestic flights and 2½ to 3 hours before international flights. You may need to arrive earlier if you're flying from one of the busier airports or during peak air-traffic times. To avoid delays at airport-security checkpoints, try not to wear any metal. Jewelry, belt and other buckles, steel-toe shoes, barrettes, and underwire bras are among the items that can set off detectors.

Assuming that not everyone with a ticket will show up, airlines routinely overbook planes. When everyone does, airlines ask for volunteers to give up their seats. In return, these volunteers usually get a several-hundred-dollar flight voucher, which can be used toward the purchase of another ticket, and are rebooked on the next flight out. If there are not enough volunteers, the airline must choose who will be denied boarding. The first to get bumped are passengers who checked in late and those flying on discounted tickets, so get to the gate and check in as early as possible, especially during peak periods.

Always **bring a government-issued photo I.D.** to the airport; even when it's not required, a passport is best.

CUTTING COSTS

The least expensive airfares to Florida are priced for round-trip travel and usually must be purchased in advance. Airlines generally allow you to change your return date for a fee; most low-fare tickets, however, are nonrefundable. It's smart to call a number of airlines and check the Internet; when you are quoted a good price, book it on the spot—the same fare may not be available the next day, or even the next hour. Always check different routings and look into using alternate airports. Also, price off-peak and red-eye flights, which may be significantly less expensive than others. Travel agents, especially low-fare specialists (⇨ Discounts & Deals), are helpful.

Consolidators are another good source. They buy tickets for scheduled flights at reduced rates from the airlines, then sell them at prices that beat the best fare available directly from the airlines. (Many also offer reduced car-rental and hotel rates.) Sometimes you can even get your money back if you need to return the ticket. Carefully read the fine print detailing penalties for changes and cancellations, purchase the ticket with a credit card, and confirm your consolidator reservation with the airline.

When you fly as a courier, you trade your checked-luggage space for a ticket deeply subsidized by a courier service. There are restrictions on when you can book and how long you can stay. Some courier companies list with membership organizations, such as the Air Courier Association and the International Association of Air Travel Couriers; these require you to become a member before you can book a flight.

Many airlines, singly or in collaboration, offer discount air passes that allow foreigners to travel economically in a particular country or region. These visitor passes usually must be reserved and purchased before you leave home. Information about passes often can be found on airlines' international Web pages, which tend to be aimed at travelers from outside the carrier's home country. Also, try typing the name of the pass into a search engine, or search for "pass" within the carrier's Web site.

⤴ Consolidators AirlineConsolidator.com ☎ 888/468-5385 ⊕ www.airlineconsolidator.com; for international tickets. **Best Fares** ☎ 800/880-1234 ⊕ www.bestfares.com; $59.90 annual membership. **Cheap Tickets** ☎ 800/377-1000 or 800/652-4327 ⊕ www.cheaptickets.com. **Expedia** ☎ 800/397-3342 or 404/728-8787 ⊕ www.expedia.com. **Hotwire** ☎ 866/468-9473 or 920/330-9418 ⊕ www.hotwire.com. **Now Voyager Travel** ✉ 1717 Avenue M, Brooklyn, NY 11230 ☎ 212/459-1616 🖷 718/504-4762 ⊕ www.nowvoyagertravel.com.

Onetravel.com ⊕ www.onetravel.com. **Orbitz** ☎ 888/656-4546 ⊕ www.orbitz.com. **Priceline. com** ⊕ www.priceline.com. **Travelocity** ☎ 888/709-5983, 877/282-2925 in Canada, 0870/111-7061 in the U.K. ⊕ www.travelocity.com.

🛂 **Courier Resources Air Courier Association/ Cheaptrips.com** ☎ 800/211-5119 ⊕ www.aircourier. org or www.cheaptrips.com; $20 annual membership. **Courier Travel** ☎ 303/570-7586 🖷 313/625-6106 ⊕ www.couriertravel.org; $50 annual membership. **International Association of Air Travel Couriers** ☎ 308/632-3273 🖷 308/632-8267 ⊕ www.courier.org; $45 annual membership. **Now Voyager Travel** ✉ 1717 Avenue M, Brooklyn, NY 11230 ☎ 212/459-1616 🖷 718/504-4762 ⊕ www. nowvoyagertravel.com.

🛂 **Discount Passes All Asia Pass,** Cathay Pacific, ☎ 800/233-2742, 800/268-6868 in Canada ⊕ www.cathay-usa.com. **Boomerang Pass,** Qantas ☎ 800/227-4500, 0845/774-7767 in the U.K., 131-313 in Australia, 0800/808-767 in New Zealand (outside Auckland), 09/357-8900 in Auckland ⊕ www.qantas.com. **FlightPass,** EuropebyAir ☎ 888/387-2479 ⊕ www.europebyair.com. **Pacific Explorer Airpass,** Hideaway Holidays, ☎ 02/8799-2500 in Australia 🖷 02/9647-1267 in Australia, 530/325-4069 in the U.S. ⊕ www. hideawayholidays.com.au. **Polypass,** Polynesian Airlines, ☎ 800/264-0823 or 808/842-7659, 1300/653-737 in Australia, 0800/800-993 in New Zealand ⊕ www.polynesianairlines.com. **SAS Air Passes,** Scandinavian Airlines ☎ 800/221-2350, 0870/6072-7727 in the U.K., 1300/727-707 in Australia ⊕ www.scandinavian.net.

ENJOYING THE FLIGHT

State your seat preference when purchasing your ticket, and then repeat it when you confirm and when you check in. For more legroom, you can request one of the few emergency-aisle seats at check-in, if you're capable of moving obstacles comparable in weight to an airplane exit door (usually between 35 pounds and 60 pounds)—a Federal Aviation Administration requirement of passengers in these seats. Seats behind a bulkhead also offer more legroom, but they don't have under-seat storage. Don't sit in the row in front of the emergency aisle or in front of a bulkhead, where seats may not recline. SeatGuru.com has more information about specific seat configurations, which vary by aircraft.

Ask the airline whether a snack or meal is served on the flight. If you have dietary concerns, request special meals when booking. These can be vegetarian, low-cholesterol, or kosher, for example. It's a good idea to pack some healthful snacks and a small (plastic) bottle of water in your carry-on bag. On long flights, try to maintain a normal routine, to help fight jet lag. At night, get some sleep. By day, eat light meals, drink water (not alcohol), and **move around the cabin** to stretch your legs. For additional jet-lag tips consult *Fodor's FYI: Travel Fit & Healthy* (available at bookstores everywhere).

Smoking policies vary from carrier to carrier. Many airlines prohibit smoking on all of their flights; others allow smoking only on certain routes or certain departures. Ask your carrier about its policy.

FLYING TIMES

Flying times to Florida vary based on the city you're flying to, but typical times are 3 hours from New York, 4 hours from Chicago, 2¾ hours from Dallas, 4½-5½ hours from Los Angeles, and 8-8½ hours from London.

HOW TO COMPLAIN

If your baggage goes astray or your flight goes awry, complain right away. Most carriers require that you **file a claim immediately.** The Aviation Consumer Protection Division of the Department of Transportation publishes *Fly-Rights*, which discusses airlines and consumer issues and is available online. You can also find articles and information on mytravelrights.com, the Web site of the nonprofit Consumer Travel Rights Center.

🛂 **Airline Complaints Aviation Consumer Protection Division** ✉ U.S. Department of Transportation, Office of Aviation Enforcement and Proceedings, C-75, Room 4107, 400 7th St. SW, Washington, DC 20590 ☎ 202/366-2220 ⊕ airconsumer.ost.dot.gov. **Federal Aviation Administration Consumer Hotline** ✉ for inquiries: FAA, 800 Independence Ave. SW, Washington, DC 20591 ☎ 800/322-7873 ⊕ www.faa.gov.

RECONFIRMING

Check the status of your flight before you leave for the airport. You can do this on your carrier's Web site, by linking to a flight-status checker (many Web booking services offer these), or by calling your carrier or travel agent.

AIRPORTS

Because Florida is dotted with both major and regional airports, you can usually pick one quite close to your destination and often choose from a couple of nearby options. If you're destined for the north side of Miami-Dade County (metro Miami), or are renting a car at the airport, **consider flying into Fort Lauderdale–Hollywood International**; it's much easier to use than Miami International, and often—if not always—cheaper. The airports are only 40 minutes apart by car.

🛈 **Airport Information Daytona Beach International Airport (DAB)** ☎ 386/248-8069 ⊕ www.volusia.org/airport. **Fort Lauderdale–Hollywood International (FLL)** ☎ 954/359-6100 ⊕ www.broward.org/airport. **Jacksonville International (JAX)** ☎ 904/741-4902 ⊕ www.jaa.aero. **Miami International Airport (MIA)** ☎ 305/876-7000 ⊕ www.miami-airport.com. **Orlando International (MCO)** ☎ 407/825-2001 ⊕ www.orlandoairports.net. **Palm Beach International (PBI)** ☎ 561/471-7420 ⊕ www.pbia.org. **St. Petersburg–Clearwater International Airport (PIE)** ☎ 727/453-7800 ⊕ www.fly2pie.com. **Tampa International (TPA)** ☎ 813/870-8700 ⊕ www.tampaairport.com.

BIKE TRAVEL

Many of Florida's cities do not offer safe biking paths such as sidewalks and specially marked bike lanes. However, you will find plenty of wide open space and scenic trails twisting through the state's national and state parks.

Florida statutes require that bikers under 16 wear helmets. Bicycle passengers under four years old must be in a sling or child seat. All bikes must have lamps or reflectors—white in front and red in back, visible from 500 feet—between sunset and sunrise. *See* Sports & the Outdoors for more biking information.

BIKES IN FLIGHT

Most airlines accommodate bikes as luggage, provided they are dismantled and boxed; check with individual airlines about packing requirements. Some airlines sell bike boxes, which are often free at bike shops, for about $20 (bike bags can be considerably more expensive). International travelers often can substitute a bike for a piece of checked luggage at no charge; otherwise, the cost is about $100. Most U.S. and Canadian airlines charge $40–$80 each way.

BUSINESS HOURS

MUSEUMS & SIGHTS

Many museums in Florida are closed Monday, but offer extended hours on another weekday and are usually open on weekends. Some museums reserve a day of the week for free admission. Popular visitor attractions are usually open daily, with the exception of Thanksgiving and Christmas Day.

PHARMACIES

Most pharmacies are open seven days a week, but some close early on weekends. Many Wal-Mart stores and Walgreens pharmacies offer 24-hour pharmacy services.

BUS TRAVEL

Greyhound passes through practically every major city in Florida. For schedules and fares, **contact your local Greyhound Information Center.**

PAYING

Using a major credit card you can purchase Greyhound tickets online or by using the carrier's toll-free phone numbers. You can also purchase tickets—using cash, traveler's checks, or major credit cards—at any Greyhound terminal where tickets are sold or through one of the many independent agents representing Greyhound. A complete state-by-state list of agents is available at the Greyhound Web site.

🛈 **Bus Information Greyhound Lines** ☎ 800/231-2222 or 800/229-9424 ⊕ www.greyhound.com.

CAMERAS & PHOTOGRAPHY

The *Kodak Guide to Shooting Great Travel Pictures* (available at bookstores everywhere) is loaded with tips.

🛈 **Photo Help Kodak Information Center** ☎ 800/242-2424 ⊕ www.kodak.com.

EQUIPMENT PRECAUTIONS

Don't pack film or equipment in checked luggage, where it is much more susceptible to damage. X-ray machines used to view checked luggage are extremely powerful and therefore are likely to ruin your film. Try to ask for hand inspection of film, which becomes clouded after repeated exposure to airport X-ray machines, and keep videotapes and computer disks away from metal detectors. Always keep film, tape, and computer disks out of the sun. Carry an extra supply of batteries, and be prepared to turn on your camera, camcorder, or laptop to prove to airport security personnel that the device is real.

CAR RENTAL

In-season rates in Miami begin at $36 a day and $170 a week for an economy car with air-conditioning, an automatic transmission, and unlimited mileage. Rates in Orlando begin at $35 a day and $149 a week. Rates in Fort Lauderdale begin at $36 a day and $159 a week. Rates in Tampa begin at $34 a day and $149 a week. This does not include tax on car rentals, which varies from county to county. Bear in mind that rates fluctuate tremendously—both above and below these quoted figures—depending on demand and the season.

In the past, major rental agencies were located at the airport whereas cheaper firms weren't. Now, however, all over Florida, even the majors might be off airport property. Speedy check-in and frequent shuttle buses make off-airport rentals almost as convenient as on-site service. However, it's wise to allow a little extra time for bus travel between the rental agency and the airport.

🚗 **Major Agencies Alamo** ☎ 800/327-9633 ⊕ www.alamo.com. **Avis** ☎ 800/331-1212, 800/879-2847 or 800/272-5871 in Canada, 0870/606-0100 in the U.K., 02/9353-9000 in Australia, 09/526-2847 in New Zealand ⊕ www.avis.com. **Budget** ☎ 800/527-0700 ⊕ www.budget.com. **Dollar** ☎ 800/800-4000, 0800/085-4578 in the U.K. ⊕ www.dollar.com. **Hertz** ☎ 800/654-3131, 800/263-0600 in Canada, 0870/844-8844 in the U.K., 02/9669-2444 in Australia, 09/256-8690 in New Zealand ⊕ www.hertz.com. **National Car Rental** ☎ 800/227-7368 ⊕ www.nationalcar.com.

CUTTING COSTS

For a good deal, book through a travel agent who will shop around. Also, price local car-rental companies—whose prices may be lower still, although their service and maintenance may not be as good as those of major rental agencies—and research rates on the Internet. Consolidators that specialize in air travel can offer good rates on cars as well (⇨ Air Travel). Remember to ask about required deposits, cancellation penalties, and drop-off charges if you're planning to pick up the car in one city and leave it in another. If you're traveling during a holiday period, also make sure that a confirmed reservation guarantees you a car.

🚗 **Local Agencies Sunshine Rent-A-Car** ☎ 954/467-8100 in Fort Lauderdale. **Continental Florida Auto Rental** ☎ 800/327-3791 or 954/764-1008 in Fort Lauderdale. **U-Save Auto Rental/Specialty Van Rental** ☎ 888/440-8744 or 813/287-1872 in Clearwater, Fort Lauderdale, Miami, Orlando, Palm Harbor, Sanford, and Tampa–St. Petersburg. **Tropical Rent-A-Car** ☎ 305/294-8136 in Key West.

INSURANCE

When driving a rented car you are generally responsible for any damage to or loss of the vehicle. You also may be liable for any property damage or personal injury that you may cause while driving. Before you rent, see what coverage you already have under the terms of your personal auto-insurance policy and credit cards.

For about $9 to $25 a day, rental companies sell protection, known as a collision- or loss-damage waiver (CDW or LDW), that eliminates your liability for damage to the car; it's always optional and should never be automatically added to your bill. In most states you don't need a CDW if you have personal auto insurance or other liability insurance. However, **make sure you have enough coverage to pay for the car.** If you do not have auto insurance or an umbrella policy that covers damage to third parties, purchasing liability insurance and a CDW or LDW is highly recommended.

REQUIREMENTS & RESTRICTIONS

In Florida you must be 21 to rent a car, and rates may be higher if you're under 25.

SURCHARGES

Before you pick up a car in one city and leave it in another, ask about drop-off charges or one-way service fees, which can be substantial. Also inquire about early-return policies; some rental agencies charge extra if you return the car before the time specified in your contract while others give you a refund for the days not used. Most agencies note the tank's fuel level on your contract; to avoid a hefty refueling fee, return the car with the same tank level. If the tank was full, refill it just before you turn in the car, but be aware that gas stations near the rental outlet may overcharge. It's almost never a deal to buy a tank of gas with the car when you rent it; the understanding is that you'll return it empty, but some fuel usually remains. Surcharges may apply if you're under 25 or if you take the car outside the area approved by the rental agency. You'll pay extra for child seats (about $8 a day), which are compulsory for children under five, and usually for additional drivers (up to $25 a day, depending on location).

CAR TRAVEL

Three major interstates lead to Florida. Interstate 95 begins in Maine, runs south through the Mid-Atlantic states, and enters Florida just north of Jacksonville. It continues south past Daytona Beach, the Space Coast, Vero Beach, Palm Beach, and Fort Lauderdale, eventually ending in Miami.

Interstate 75 begins in Michigan at the Canadian border and runs south through Ohio, Kentucky, Tennessee, and Georgia, then moves south through the center of the state before veering west into Tampa. It follows the west coast south to Naples, then crosses the state through the northern section of the Everglades, and ends in Fort Lauderdale.

California and most southern states are connected to Florida by Interstate 10, which moves east from Los Angeles through Arizona, New Mexico, Texas, Louisiana, Mississippi, and Alabama; it enters Florida at Pensacola and runs straight across the northern part of the state, ending in Jacksonville.

ROAD CONDITIONS

Florida has its share of traffic problems. Downtown areas of such major cities as Miami, Orlando, and Tampa can be extremely congested during rush hours, usually 7 to 9 AM and 4 to 6 PM on weekdays. When you drive the interstate system in Florida, try to plan your trip so that you are not entering, leaving, or passing through a large city during rush hour, when traffic can slow to 10 mph for 10 mi or more. In addition, snowbirds usually rent in Florida for a month at a time, which means they all arrive on the first of the month and leave on the 31st. Believe it or not, from November to March, when the end and beginning of a month occur on a weekend, north–south routes like Interstate 75 and Interstate 95 almost come to a standstill during daylight hours. It's best to avoid traveling on these days if possible.

RULES OF THE ROAD

Speed limits are 60 mph on state highways, 30 mph within city limits and residential areas, and 70 mph on interstates and Florida's Turnpike. Be alert for signs announcing exceptions.

In Florida, you must strap a child six or younger into a child restraint device: children aged through three years must be in a separate carrier or child seat, and children four through six can be secured in a separate carrier, integrated child seat, or by a seat belt. The driver will be held responsible for passengers under the age of 16 who are not wearing a seatbelt. All front-seat passengers are required to wear seat belts.

Florida's Alcohol/Controlled Substance DUI Law is one of the toughest in the United States. A blood alcohol level of .08 or higher can have serious repercussions even for the first-time offender.

SAFETY

Before setting off on any drive, make sure you know where you're going and carry a map. At the car-rental agency or at your hotel ask if there are any areas that you should avoid. Always **keep your doors locked,** and ask questions only at toll booths, gas stations, or other obviously safe locations. Also, **don't stop if your car is bumped from behind** or if you're asked for directions. You might hesitate to foster rude behavior, but at least for now the roads are too risky to stop any place you're not familiar with (other than as traffic laws require). If you'll be renting a car and won't have a cellular phone with you, **ask the car-rental agency for a cellular phone.** Alamo, Avis, and Hertz are among the companies with in-car phones.

CHILDREN IN FLORIDA

If you are renting a car, don't forget to arrange for a car seat when you reserve. For general advice about traveling with children, consult *Fodor's FYI: Travel with Your Baby* (available in bookstores everywhere).

FLYING

If your children are two or older, ask about children's airfares. As a general rule, infants under two not occupying a seat fly at greatly reduced fares or even for free. But if you want to guarantee a seat for an infant, you have to pay full fare. Consider flying during off-peak days and times; most airlines will grant an infant a seat without a ticket if there are available seats.

Experts agree that it's a good idea to use safety seats aloft for children weighing less than 40 pounds. Airlines set their own policies: if you use a safety seat, U.S. carriers usually require that the child be ticketed, even if he or she is young enough to ride free, because the seats must be strapped into regular seats. And even if you pay the full adult fare for the seat, it may be worth it, especially on longer trips. Do **check your airline's policy about using safety seats during takeoff and landing.** Safety seats are not allowed everywhere in the plane, so get your seat assignments as early as possible.

When reserving, request children's meals or a freestanding bassinet (not available at all airlines) if you need them. But note that bulkhead seats, where you must sit to use the bassinet, may lack an overhead bin or storage space on the floor.

LODGING

Florida may have the highest concentration of hotels with organized children's programs in the United States. Activities range from simple fun and recreation to shell-hunting at Marriott's Marco Island Resort and learning about the Keys' environment from marine-science counselors at Cheeca Lodge. Sometimes kids' programs are complimentary; sometimes there's a charge. Not all accept children in diapers, and some offer programs when their central reservations services say they don't. Some programs are only offered during peak seasons or during restricted hours in less-busy times. It always pays to **confirm details with the hotel in advance.** And reserve space as soon as possible; programs are often full by the morning or evening you need them.

Most hotels in Florida allow children under a certain age to stay in their parents' room at no extra charge, but others charge for them as extra adults. Many bed-and-breakfasts and inns do not welcome young children; be sure to find out the cutoff age for any applicable discounts or age restrictions. In Orlando, in addition to the properties listed below, most properties on the Walt Disney World grounds have children's programs.

🏨 **Fort Lauderdale Marriott's Harbor Beach Resort's Beachside Buddies** ✉ 3030 Holiday Dr., Fort Lauderdale, FL 33316 ☎ 800/222-6543 or 954/525-4000, ages 5-12. **The Keys Cheeca Lodge's Camp Cheeca** ✉ MM 82, OS, Box 527, 81801 Overseas Hwy., Islamorada, FL 33036 ☎ 800/327-2888, ages 5-12. **Hawks Cay Resort's Island Adventure Club** ✉ MM 61, 61 Hawks Cay Blvd., Duck Key, FL 33050 ☎ 800/432-2242, ages 3-12.

🏨 **Miami Area Sonesta Beach Resort's Just Us Kids** ✉ 350 Ocean Dr., Key Biscayne, FL 33149 ☎ 800/766-3782 or 305/361-2021, ages 5-12.

🏨 **Northeast Florida Amelia Island Plantation's Kid's Camp Amelia** ✉ 3000 1st Coast Hwy., Amelia Island, FL 32034 ☎ 904/261-6161, ages 3-10.

🏨 **Orlando Area Holiday Inn SunSpree Resort Lake Buena Vista's Camp Holiday** ✉ 13351 State Rd. 535, Orlando, FL 32821 ☎ 800/366-6299 or 407/239-4500, ages 4-12. **Hyatt Regency Grand Cypress Resort's Camp Hyatt** ✉ 1 Grand Cypress Blvd., Orlando, FL 32836 ☎ 800/228-9000 or 407/239-1234, ages 5-12.

🏨 **Palm Beach & the Treasure Coast Club Med's Sandpiper** ✉ 3500 S.E. Morningside Blvd., Port St. Lucie, FL 34952 ☎ 800/258-2633 or 772/398-5100,

Baby Club ages 4–24 months, Petite Club ages 2–4, Mini Club ages 4–12.

🖪 Southwest Florida Marriott's Marco Island Resort's Tiki Tribes ⊠ 400 S. Collier Blvd., Marco Island, FL 34145 ☎ 800/228–9290 or 239/394–2511, ages 5–12. Radisson Suite Beach Resort's Fun Factory ⊠ 600 S. Collier Blvd., Marco Island, FL 34145 ☎ 800/333–3333 or 239/394–4100, ages 4–12. Sanibel Harbour Resort & Spa's Kids Klub ⊠ 17260 Harbour Pointe Dr., Fort Myers, FL 33908 ☎ 800/767–7777 or 239/466–4000, ages 5–12. South Seas Plantation's Explorer Fun Factory ⊠ 5400 Plantation Rd., Captiva Island, FL 33924 ☎ 800/227–8482 or 239/472–5111, ages 4–12, plus activities for teens.

CONSUMER PROTECTION

Whether you're shopping for gifts or purchasing travel services, **pay with a major credit card** whenever possible, so you can cancel payment or get reimbursed if there's a problem (and you can provide documentation). If you're doing business with a particular company for the first time, contact your local Better Business Bureau and the attorney general's offices in your state and (for U.S. businesses) the company's home state as well. Have any complaints been filed? Finally, if you're buying a package or tour, always consider travel insurance that includes default coverage (⇨ Insurance).

🖪 BBBs Council of Better Business Bureaus ⊠ 4200 Wilson Blvd., Suite 800, Arlington, VA 22203 ☎ 703/276–0100 🖷 703/525–8277 ⊕ www.bbb.org.

CRUISE TRAVEL

The port of Miami is the cruise capital of the world, with the world's largest year-round fleet. It also handles more mega-ships—vessels capable of transporting more than 2, 000 people at a time—than any other port in the world. Port Everglades, located 23 mi north of Miami, is the world's second-busiest cruise-ship terminal. Seven-day eastern and western Caribbean cruises are the most popular types of cruises leaving from Miami-area ports. To learn how to plan, choose, and book a cruise-ship voyage, consult *Fodor's FYI: Plan & Enjoy Your Cruise* (available in bookstores everywhere).

🖪 Cruise Lines Royal Caribbean ☎ 800/398–9819. Celebrity Cruises ☎ 800/437–3111. Costa Cruises Lines ☎ 800/462–6782. Crystal Cruises ☎ 800/446–6620. Cunard Cruise Line ☎ 800/728–6273. Discovery Cruises ☎ 800/866–8687. Holland America Cruises ☎ 877/724–5425. Imperial Majesty Cruise Lines ☎ 800/511–5737. Norwegian Cruises ☎ 800/327–7030. Princess Cruises ☎ 800/774–6237. Sea Escape Cruises ☎ 800/327–2005. SilverSea Cruises ☎ 800/722–9955. Windjammer Barefoot Cruises ☎ 800/327–2601.

CUSTOMS & DUTIES

IN AUSTRALIA

Australian residents who are 18 or older may bring home A$900 worth of souvenirs and gifts (including jewelry), 250 cigarettes or 250 grams of cigars or other tobacco products, and 2.25 liters of alcohol (including wine, beer, and spirits). Residents under 18 may bring back A$450 worth of goods. If any of these individual allowances are exceeded, you must pay duty for the entire amount (of the group of products in which the allowance was exceeded). Members of the same family traveling together may pool their allowances. Prohibited items include meat products. Seeds, plants, and fruits need to be declared upon arrival.

🖪 Australian Customs Service ⊘ Locked Bag 3000, Sydney International Airport , Sydney, NSW 2020 ☎ 02/6275–6666 or 1300/363263, 02/8334–7444 or 1800/020–504 quarantine-inquiry line 🖷 02/8339–6714 ⊕ www.customs.gov.au.

IN CANADA

Canadian residents who have been out of Canada for at least seven days may bring in C$750 worth of goods duty-free. If you've been away fewer than seven days but more than 48 hours, the duty-free allowance drops to C$200. If your trip lasts 24 to 48 hours, the allowance is C$50; if the goods are worth more than C$50, you must pay full duty on all of the goods. You may not pool allowances with family members. Goods claimed under the C$750 exemption may follow you by mail; those claimed under the lesser exemptions must accompany you. Alcohol and tobacco products may be included in the seven-day and 48-hour exemptions but not in the

24-hour exemption. If you meet the age requirements of the province or territory through which you reenter Canada, you may bring in, duty-free, 1.5 liters of wine *or* 1.14 liters (40 imperial ounces) of liquor *or* 24 12-ounce cans or bottles of beer or ale. Also, if you meet the local age requirement for tobacco products, you may bring in, duty-free, 200 cigarettes, 50 cigars or cigarillos, and 200 grams of tobacco. You may have to pay a minimum duty on tobacco products, regardless of whether or not you exceed your personal exemption. Check ahead of time with the Canada Border Services Agency or the Department of Agriculture for policies regarding meat products, seeds, plants, and fruits.

You may send an unlimited number of gifts (only one gift per recipient, however) worth up to C$60 each duty-free to Canada. Label the package UNSOLICITED GIFT—VALUE UNDER $60. Alcohol and tobacco are excluded.

🚩 **Canada Border Services Agency** ✉ Customs Information Services, 191 Laurier Ave. W, 15th floor, Ottawa, Ontario K1A 0L5 ☎ 800/461-9999 in Canada, 204/983-3500, 506/636-5064 ⊕ www. cbsa.gc.ca.

IN NEW ZEALAND

All homeward-bound residents may bring back NZ$700 worth of souvenirs and gifts; passengers may not pool their allowances, and children can claim only the concession on goods intended for their own use. For those 17 or older, the duty-free allowance also includes 4.5 liters of wine or beer; one 1,125-ml bottle of spirits; and either 200 cigarettes, 250 grams of tobacco, 50 cigars, *or* a combination of the three up to 250 grams. Meat products, seeds, plants, and fruits must be declared upon arrival to the Agricultural Services Department.

🚩 **New Zealand Customs** ✉ Head office: The Customhouse, 17–21 Whitmore St., Box 2218, Wellington ☎ 0800/428-786 or 09/300-5399 ⊕ www.customs. govt.nz.

IN THE U.K.

From countries outside the European Union, including the United States, you may bring home, duty-free, 200 cigarettes,

50 cigars, 100 cigarillos, or 250 grams of tobacco; 1 liter of spirits or 2 liters of fortified or sparkling wine or liqueurs; 2 liters of still table wine; 60 ml of perfume; 250 ml of toilet water; plus £145 worth of other goods, including gifts and souvenirs. Prohibited items include meat and dairy products, seeds, plants, and fruits.

🚩 **HM Customs and Excise** ✉ Portcullis House, 21 Cowbridge Rd. E, Cardiff CF11 9SS ☎ 0845/010-9000 or 0208/929-0152 advice service, 0208/929-6731 or 0208/910-3602 complaints ⊕ www.hmce. gov.uk.

DISABILITIES & ACCESSIBILITY

Although there's no single organization that offers a completely comprehensive list of motels or inns that are equipped for travelers with disabilities, you'll find helpful information and links at Florida Disabled Outdoor Association (FDOA) and Disability Travel and Recreation Resources. The Society for Accessible Travel and Hospitality is another good source.

Metro-Dade Disability Services publishes a free guidebook on the accessibility of Florida's hotels and motels, entitled *Directory of Services for the Physically Disabled in Dade County.*

🚩 **Local Resources** Florida Disabled Outdoor Association (FDOA) ☎ 850/668-7323 ⊕ www.fdoa. org. **Disability Travel and Recreation Resources** ⊕ www.makoa.org/travel.htm. **Society for Accessible Travel and Hospitality** ☎ 212/447-7284 ⊕ www.sath.org. **Miami-Dade Disability Services** ✉ 111 N.W. 1st St., Miami, FL 33128 ☎ 305/770-3131, 305/654-6530 TDD publishes a free guidebook on the accessibility of Florida's hotels and motels, entitled *Directory of Services for the Physically Disabled in Dade County.*

Deaf Services Center ✉ 1860 Boy Scout Dr., Unit B-208, Fort Myers, FL 33907 ☎ 239/461-0334, 239/461-0438 TTD. **Florida Relay Service** ☎ 800/955-8770.

LODGING

Despite the Americans with Disabilities Act, the definition of accessibility seems to differ from hotel to hotel. Some properties may be accessible by ADA standards for people with mobility problems but not for people with hearing or vision impairments, for example.

If you have mobility problems, ask for the lowest floor on which accessible services are offered. If you have a hearing impairment, check whether the hotel has devices to alert you visually to the ring of the telephone, a knock at the door, and a fire/emergency alarm. Some hotels provide these devices without charge. Discuss your needs with hotel personnel if this equipment isn't available, so that a staff member can personally alert you in the event of an emergency.

If you're bringing a guide dog, get authorization ahead of time and write down the name of the person with whom you spoke.

RESERVATIONS

When discussing accessibility with an operator or reservations agent, ask hard questions. Are there any stairs, inside *or* out? Are there grab bars next to the toilet *and* in the shower/tub? How wide is the doorway to the room? To the bathroom? For the most extensive facilities meeting the latest legal specifications, opt for newer accommodations. If you reserve through a toll-free number, consider also calling the hotel's local number to confirm the information from the central reservations office. Get confirmation in writing when you can.

TRANSPORTATION

The U.S. Department of Transportation Aviation Consumer Protection Division's online publication *New Horizons: Information for the Air Traveler with a Disability* offers advice for travellers with a disability, and outlines basic rights. Visit DisabilityInfo.gov for general information. **f7 Information and Complaints Aviation Consumer Protection Division** (⇨ Air Travel) for airline-related problems; ⊕ airconsumer.ost.dot.gov/publications/horizons.htm for airline travel advice and rights. **Departmental Office of Civil Rights** ⊠ for general inquiries, U.S. Department of Transportation, S-30, 400 7th St. SW, Room 10215, Washington, DC 20590 ☎ 202/366-4648, 202/366-8538 TTY ⊟ 202/366-9371 ⊕ www.dotcr.ost.dot.gov. **Disability Rights Section** ⊠ NYAV, U.S. Department of Justice, Civil Rights Division, 950 Pennsylvania Ave. NW, Washington, DC 20530 ☎ ADA information line 202/514-0301, 800/514-0301, 202/514-0383 TTY, 800/514-0383 TTY ⊕ www.ada.gov. **U.S. Department of**

Transportation Hotline ☎ for disability-related air-travel problems, 800/778-4838 or 800/455-9880 TTY.

TRAVEL AGENCIES

In the United States, the Americans with Disabilities Act requires that travel firms serve the needs of all travelers. Some agencies specialize in working with people with disabilities. **f7 Travelers with Mobility Problems B. Roberts Travel** ⊠ 1876 East Ave., Rochester, NY 14610 ☎ 800/444-6540 or 585/256-1680 ⊟ 585/256-1686 ⊕ www.brobertstravel.com. **Accessible Vans of America** ⊠ 37 Daniel Rd. W, Fairfield, NJ 07004 ☎ 877/282-8267, 888/282-8267, 973/808-9709 reservations ⊟ 973/808-9713 ⊕ www.accessiblevans.com. **CareVacations** ⊠ No. 5, 5110-50 Ave., Leduc, Alberta T9E 6V4, Canada ☎ 780/986-6404 or 877/478-7827 ⊟ 780/986-8332 ⊕ www.carevacations.com, for group tours and cruise vacations. **Flying Wheels Travel** ⊠ 143 W. Bridge St., Box 382, Owatonna, MN 55060 ☎ 507/451-5005 ⊟ 507/451-1685 ⊕ www.flyingwheelstravel.com.
f7 Travelers with Developmental Disabilities New Directions ⊠ 5276 Hollister Ave., Suite 207, Santa Barbara, CA 93111 ☎ 888/967-2841 or 805/967-2841 ⊟ 805/964-7344 ⊕ www.newdirectionstravel.com. **Sprout** ⊠ 893 Amsterdam Ave., New York, NY 10025 ☎ 888/222-9575 or 212/222-9575 ⊟ 212/222-9768 ⊕ www.gosprout.org.

DISCOUNTS & DEALS

Be a smart shopper and compare all your options before making decisions. A plane ticket bought with a promotional coupon from travel clubs, coupon books, and direct-mail offers or purchased on the Internet may not be cheaper than the least expensive fare from a discount ticket agency. And always keep in mind that what you get is just as important as what you save.

Theme park savvy: if visiting the Disney theme parks, consider purchasing a multi-day "Park Hopper" pass before leaving home. You'll save money by purchasing your advance tickets online at ⊕ www.disneyworld.com. You can also save by getting your tickets at a local ticket booth prior to arriving at the theme park. If you leave the park and plan to return the same day, remember to get your hand stamped for re-admission. Also, you can save as much as $10 a day by bringing your own stroller. And it's always a good idea to have lots of water on hand; refillable water bottles are quick and easy and will save you several dollars a day.

DISCOUNT RESERVATIONS

To save money, look into discount reservations services with Web sites and toll-free numbers, which use their buying power to get a better price on hotels, airline tickets (⇨ Air Travel), even car rentals. When booking a room, always **call the hotel's local toll-free number** (if one is available) rather than the central reservations number— you'll often get a better price. Always ask about special packages or corporate rates.

🔢 **Hotel Rooms Accommodations Express** ☎ 800/444-7666 or 800/277-1064. **Central Reservation Service (CRS)** ☎ 800/555-7555 or 800/548-3311 ⊕ www.crshotels.com. **Hotels.com** ☎ 800/246-8357 ⊕ www.hotels.com. **Quikbook** ☎ 800/789-9887 ⊕ www.quikbook.com. **Steigenberger Reservation Service** ☎ 800/223-5652 ⊕ www.srs-worldhotels.com. **Turbotrip.com** ☎ 800/473-7829 ⊕ w3.turbotrip.com.

PACKAGE DEALS

Don't confuse packages and guided tours. When you buy a package, you travel on your own, just as though you had planned the trip yourself. Fly/drive packages, which combine airfare and car rental, are often a good deal. In cities, ask the local visitors' bureau about hotel and local transportation packages that include tickets to major museum exhibits or other special events.

EATING & DRINKING

An antismoking amendment endorsed in 2002 by Florida voters bans smoking statewide in most enclosed indoor workplaces, including restaurants. Exemptions are permitted for stand-alone bars where food takes a back seat to the libations. If smoking matters to you one way or the other, phone the property before you go to find out how they're complying with the new regulations.

A cautionary word: raw oysters have been identified as a potential problem for people with chronic illness of the liver, stomach, or blood, or who have immune disorders. Since 1993 all Florida restaurants serving raw oysters are required to post a notice in plain view of all patrons warning of the risks associated with consuming them.

The restaurants we list are the cream of the crop in each price category. Properties indicated by ✕🏠 are lodging establishments whose restaurant warrants a special trip.

In general, when you order a regular coffee, you get coffee with milk and sugar.

CATEGORY	COST*
$$$$	over $30
$$$	$20–$30
$$	$15–$20
$	$10–$15
¢	under $10

Per person for a main course at dinner

CUTTING COSTS

Coupons are a good way to cut dining costs. You'll find coupon booklets outside supermarkets, restaurants, and shopping malls. A particularly worthy booklet is "The Best Read Guide," filled with discount coupons for dining and shopping. Many Florida restaurants have the famed "early-bird" specials and offer reduced prices if you dine early (typically before 6 PM), and many restaurants allow plate sharing for a nominal fee. You'll also find senior citizen discounts. If discount policies aren't posted, it never hurts to ask.

MEALTIMES

Unless otherwise noted, the restaurants listed in this guide are open daily for lunch and dinner.

RESERVATIONS & DRESS

Reservations are always a good idea; we mention them only when they're essential or not accepted. Book as far ahead as you can, and reconfirm as soon as you arrive. (Large parties should always call ahead to check the reservations policy.) We mention dress only when men are required to wear a jacket or a jacket and tie.

SPECIALTIES

A trip to the Tampa area or South Florida is incomplete without a taste of Cuban food. The cuisine is heavy, with pork dishes like *lechon asado*, served in garlic-based sauces. The two most typical dishes are *arroz con frijoles* (the staple side dish of rice and black beans) and *arroz con pollo* (chicken in sticky yellow rice). Key West is a mecca for lovers of key lime pie (the best is found here) and conch fritters, another local favorite. Stone crab claws, another South Florida delicacy, can be savored from November through May.

WINE, BEER & SPIRITS

Beer and wine are usually available in Florida's restaurants, whether you're dining first class or at a beachside bistro. A few chain restaurants in the major cities are also microbreweries and have a variety of premise-made beers that change with the season. Liquor is generally available at fine-dining establishments only.

ECOTOURISM

Florida's varied environment is one of its chief draws; it's also very fragile. If you're out in nature, follow the basic rules of environmental responsibility: **take nothing but pictures; leave nothing but footprints.** Most important, **be extremely careful around the dunes.** Picking the sea grasses that hold the dunes in place can result in a stiff fine, as can walking or playing or digging in the dunes. An afternoon of rough-housing can completely destroy a dune that could take years for nature to rebuild. Ecotours (⇨ Tours *in* each chapter's A to Z section) operate throughout the state and can help you see some of what makes Florida so distinct, usually in a way that makes the least impact possible.

GAY & LESBIAN TRAVEL

Destinations within Florida that have a reputation for being especially gay and lesbian friendly include South Beach and Key West and, in recent years, Fort Lauderdale and Orlando.

For details about the gay and lesbian scene, consult *Fodor's Gay Guide to the USA* (available in bookstores everywhere). ◪ Gay- & Lesbian-Friendly Travel Agencies **Different Roads Travel** ⊠ 1017 N. La Cienega Blvd., Suite 308, West Hollywood, CA 90069 ☎ 800/429-8747 or 310/289-6000 (Ext. 14 for both) 🖷 310/855-0323 ✆ lgernert@tzell.com. **Kennedy Travel**

⊠ 130 W. 42nd St., Suite 401, New York, NY 10036 ☎ 800/237-7433 or 212/840-8659 🖷 212/730-2269 ⊕ www.kennedytravel.com. **Now, Voyager** ⊠ 4406 18th St., San Francisco, CA 94114 ☎ 800/255-6951 or 415/626-1169 🖷 415/626-8626 ⊕ www.nowvoyager.com. **Skylink Travel and Tour/Flying Dutchmen Travel** ⊠ 1455 N. Dutton Ave., Suite A, Santa Rosa, CA 95401 ☎ 800/225-5759, 800/248-7471, or 707/546-9888 🖷 707/545-2112, serving lesbian travelers.

HEALTH

If you are unaccustomed to strong subtropical sun, you run a risk of sunburn and heat prostration, even in winter. So hit the beach or play tennis, golf, or another outdoor sport before 10 or after 3. If you must be out **at midday, limit strenuous exercise, drink plenty of liquids, and wear a hat.** If you begin to feel faint, get out of the sun immediately and sip water slowly. Even on overcast days, ultraviolet rays shine through the haze, so **use a sunscreen with an SPF of at least 15,** and have children wear a waterproof SPF 30 or higher.

While you're frolicking on the beach, **steer clear of what look like blue bubbles on the sand.** These are Portuguese men-of-war, and their tentacles can cause an allergic reaction. Also be careful of other large jellyfish, some of which can sting.

If you walk across a grassy area on the way to the beach, you'll probably encounter sand spurs. They are quite tiny, light brown, and remarkably prickly. You'll feel them before you see them; if you get stuck with one, just pull it out.

DIVERS' ALERT

Do not fly within 24 hours of scuba diving.

HOLIDAYS

Major national holidays are New Year's Day (Jan. 1); Martin Luther King Jr. Day (3rd Mon. in Jan.); Presidents' Day (3rd Mon. in Feb.); Memorial Day (last Mon. in May); Independence Day (July 4); Labor Day (1st Mon. in Sept.); Columbus Day (2nd Mon. in Oct.); Thanksgiving Day (4th Thurs. in Nov.); Christmas Eve and Christmas Day (Dec. 24 and 25); and New Year's Eve (Dec. 31).

INSURANCE

The most useful travel-insurance plan is a comprehensive policy that includes coverage for trip cancellation and interruption, default, trip delay, and medical expenses (with a waiver for preexisting conditions).

Without insurance you'll lose all or most of your money if you cancel your trip, regardless of the reason. Default insurance covers you if your tour operator, airline, or cruise line goes out of business—the chances of which have been increasing. Trip-delay covers expenses that arise because of bad weather or mechanical delays. Study the fine print when comparing policies.

U.K. residents can buy a travel-insurance policy valid for most vacations taken during the year in which it's purchased (but check preexisting-condition coverage).

Always **buy travel policies directly from the insurance company**; if you buy them from a cruise line, airline, or tour operator that goes out of business you probably won't be covered for the agency or operator's default, a major risk. Before making any purchase, review your existing health and home-owner's policies to find what they cover away from home.

⚂ Travel Insurers In the U.S.: **Access America** ✉ 2805 N. Parham Rd., Richmond, VA 23294 ☎ 800/284-8300 ⊠ 804/673-1469 or 800/346-9265 ⊕ www.accessamerica.com. **Travel Guard International** ✉ 1145 Clark St., Stevens Point, WI 54481 ☎ 800/826-1300 or 715/345-1041 ⊠ 800/955-8785 or 715/345-1990 ⊕ www.travelguard.com.

FOR INTERNATIONAL TRAVELERS

For information on customs restrictions, *see* Customs & Duties.

CAR RENTAL

When picking up a rental car, non-U.S. residents need a reservation voucher for any prepaid reservations that were made in the traveler's home country, a passport, a driver's license, and a travel policy that covers each driver.

CAR TRAVEL

In Florida gasoline costs $1.93–$2.20 a gallon as of this writing. Stations are plentiful. Most stay open late (24 hours along large highways and in big cities), except in rural areas, where Sunday hours are limited and where you may drive long stretches without a refueling opportunity.

Highways are well paved. Interstate highways—limited-access, multilane highways whose numbers are prefixed by "I–"—are the fastest routes. Interstates with three-digit numbers encircle urban areas, which may have other limited-access expressways, freeways, and parkways as well. Tolls may be levied on limited-access highways. So-called U.S. highways and state highways are not necessarily limited-access but may have several lanes.

Along larger highways, roadside stops with rest rooms, fast-food restaurants, and sundries stores are well spaced. State police and tow truck operators patrol major highways and lend assistance. If your car breaks down on an interstate, pull onto the shoulder and wait for help, or have your passengers wait while you walk to an emergency phone (available in most states). If you carry a cell phone, dial 911, noting your location on the small green roadside mileage markers.

Driving in the United States is on the right. Do obey speed limits posted along roads and highways. Watch for lower limits in small towns and on back roads. On weekdays between 6 and 10 AM and again between 4 and 7 PM expect heavy traffic. To encourage carpooling, some freeways have special lanes for so-called high-occupancy vehicles (HOV)—cars carrying more than one passenger.

Bookstores, gas stations, convenience stores, and rest stops sell maps (about $3) and multiregion road atlases (about $10).

CURRENCY

The dollar is the basic unit of U.S. currency. It has 100 cents. Coins are the copper penny (1¢); the silvery nickel (5¢); dime (10¢), quarter (25¢), and half-dollar (50¢); and the golden $1 coin, replacing a now-rare silver dollar. Bills are denominated $1, $5, $10, $20, $50, and $100, all mostly green and identical in size; designs and background tints vary. In addition, you may come across a $2 bill, but the chances are slim. The exchange rate at this writing is US$1.90 per British pound, $.85 per Canadian dollar, $.79 per Australian dollar, and $.71 per New Zealand dollar.

ELECTRICITY

The U.S. standard is AC, 110 volts/60 cycles. Plugs have two flat pins set parallel to each other.

EMERGENCIES

For police, fire, or ambulance, **dial 911** (0 in rural areas).

INSURANCE

Britons and Australians need extra medical coverage when traveling overseas.

🔁 **Insurance Information** In the U.K.: **Association of British Insurers** ✉ 51 Gresham St., London EC2V 7HQ ☎ 020/7600-3333 🖷 020/7696-8999 ⊕ www. abi.org.uk. In Australia: **Insurance Council of Australia** ✉ Level 3, 56 Pitt St. Sydney, NSW 2000 ☎ 02/9253-5100 🖷 02/9253-5111 ⊕ www.ica.com. au. In Canada: **RBC Insurance** ☎ 6880 Financial Dr., Mississauga, Ontario L5N 7Y5 ☎ 800/387-4357 or 905/816-2559 🖷 888/298-6458 ⊕ www. rbcinsurance.com. In New Zealand: **Insurance Council of New Zealand** ✉ Level 7, 111–115 Customhouse Quay, Box 474, Wellington ☎ 04/472-5230 🖷 04/473-3011 ⊕ www.icnz.org.nz.

MAIL & SHIPPING

You can buy stamps and aerograms and send letters and parcels in post offices. Stamp-dispensing machines can occasionally be found in airports, bus and train stations, office buildings, drugstores, and the like. You can also deposit mail in the stout, dark blue, steel bins at strategic locations everywhere and in the mail chutes of large buildings; pickup schedules are posted. You can deposit packages at public collection boxes as long as the parcels are affixed with proper postage and weigh less than one pound. Packages weighing one or more pounds must be taken to a post office or handed to a postal carrier.

For mail sent within the United States, you need a 37¢ stamp for first-class letters weighing up to 1 ounce (23¢ for each additional ounce) and 23¢ for postcards. You pay 80¢ for 1-ounce airmail letters and 70¢ for airmail postcards to most other countries; to Canada and Mexico, you need a 60¢ stamp for a 1-ounce letter and 50¢ for a postcard. An aerogram—a single sheet of lightweight blue paper that folds into its own envelope, stamped for overseas airmail—costs 70¢.

To receive mail on the road, have it sent c/o General Delivery at your destination's main post office (use the correct five-digit ZIP code). You must pick up mail in person within 30 days and show a driver's license or passport.

PASSPORTS & VISAS

When traveling internationally, carry your passport even if you don't need one (it's always the best form of I.D.) and **make two photocopies of the data page** (one for someone at home and another for you, carried separately from your passport). If you lose your passport, promptly call the nearest embassy or consulate and the local police.

Visitor visas aren't necessary for Canadian or European Union citizens, or for citizens of Australia who are staying fewer than 90 days.

🔁 **Australian Citizens** Passports Australia ☎ 131-232 ⊕ www.passports.gov.au. **United States Consulate General** ✉ MLC Centre, Level 59, 19–29 Martin Pl., Sydney, NSW 2000 ☎ 02/9373-9200, 1902/941-641 fee-based visa-inquiry line ⊕ usembassy-australia.state.gov/sydney.
🔁 **Canadian Citizens** Passport Office ✉ to mail in applications: 70 Cremazie St., Gatineau, Québec J8Y 3P2 ☎ 819/994-3500, 800/567-6868, 866/255-7655 TTY ⊕ www.ppt.gc.ca.
🔁 **New Zealand Citizens** New Zealand Passports Office ✉ For applications and information, Level 3, Boulcott House, 47 Boulcott St., Wellington ☎ 0800/22-5050 or 04/474-8100 ⊕ www. passports.govt.nz. Embassy of the United States ✉ 29 Fitzherbert Terr., Thorndon, Wellington ☎ 04/462-6000 ⊕ usembassy.org.nz. **U.S. Consulate General** ✉ Citibank Bldg., 3rd floor, 23 Customs St. E, Auckland ☎ 09/303-2724 ⊕ usembassy. org.nz.
🔁 **U.K. Citizens** U.K. Passport Service ☎ 0870/ 521-0410 ⊕ www.passport.gov.uk. **American Consulate General** ✉ Danesfort House, 223 Stranmillis Rd., Belfast, Northern Ireland BT9 5GR ☎ 028/ 9038-6100 🖷 028/9068-1301 ⊕ www.usembassy. org.uk. **American Embassy** ✉ for visa and immigration information or to submit a visa application via mail (enclose an SASE), Consular Information Unit, 24 Grosvenor Sq., London W1A 2LQ ☎ 090/ 5544-4546 or 090/6820-0290 for visa information (per-minute charges), 0207/499-9000 main switchboard ⊕ www.usembassy.org.uk.

TELEPHONES

All U.S. telephone numbers consist of a three-digit area code and a seven-digit local number. Within many local calling areas, you dial only the seven-digit number. Within some area codes, you must dial "1" first for calls outside the local area. To call between area-code regions, dial "1" then all 10 digits; the same goes for calls to numbers prefixed by "800," "888," "866," and "877"—all toll free. For calls to numbers preceded by "900" you must pay—usually dearly.

For international calls, dial "011" followed by the country code and the local number. For help, dial "0" and ask for an overseas operator. The country code is 61 for Australia, 64 for New Zealand, 44 for the United Kingdom. Calling Canada is the same as calling within the United States. Most local phone books list country codes and U.S. area codes. The country code for the United States is 1.

For operator assistance, dial "0." To obtain someone's phone number, call directory assistance at 555–1212 or occasionally 411 (free at many public phones). To have the person you're calling foot the bill, phone collect; dial "0" instead of "1" before the 10-digit number.

At pay phones, instructions often are posted. Usually you insert coins in a slot (usually 25¢–50¢ for local calls) and wait for a steady tone before dialing. When you call long-distance, the operator tells you how much to insert; prepaid phone cards, widely available in various denominations, are easier. Call the number on the back, punch in the card's personal identification number when prompted, then dial your number.

LANGUAGE

Although English is spoken everywhere in Florida, Spanish can be quite useful to know in South Florida, especially in Miami-Dade County, where Hispanics make up more than half the population. A significant percentage of Miami tourism comes from Latin America, so Spanish can be heard quite frequently in hotels, stores, and restaurants.

LODGING

Florida has every conceivable type of lodging—from tree houses to penthouses, mansions for hire to hostels. Even with occupancy rates inching above 70%, there are almost always rooms available, except maybe at Christmas and other holidays.

Children are welcome generally everywhere in Florida. Pets are another matter, so **inquire ahead of time if you're bringing an animal with you.**

In the busy seasons—over Christmas and from late January through Easter in the southern half of the state, during the summer along the Panhandle and around Jacksonville, and all over Florida during holiday weekends in summer—always **reserve ahead for the top properties.** Fall is the slowest season: rates are low and availability is high, but this is also the prime time for hurricanes. St. Augustine stays busy all summer because of its historic flavor. Key West is jam-packed for Fantasy Fest at Halloween. If you're not booking through a travel agent, call the visitors bureau or the chamber of commerce in the area you'll be visiting to check whether a special event is scheduled for the period of your trip.

The lodgings we list are the cream of the crop in each price category. We always list the facilities that are available—but we don't specify whether they cost extra: when pricing accommodations, always ask what's included.

CATEGORY	COST*
$$$$	over $220
$$$	$140–$220
$$	$100–$140
$	$80–$100
¢	under $80

All prices are for a standard double room, excluding 6% sales tax (more in some counties) and 1%–4% tourist tax.

Assume that hotels operate on the European Plan (EP, with no meals) unless we specify that they use the Continental Plan (CP, with a Continental breakfast), Breakfast Plan (BP, with a full breakfast), Modified American Plan (MAP, with breakfast and dinner), or the Full American Plan (FAP, with all meals).

Properties are assigned price categories based on the range from their least-expensive standard double room at high season (excluding holidays) to the most expensive. Properties marked ✕⬚ are lodging establishments whose restaurants warrant a special trip.

APARTMENT, HOUSE & VILLA RENTALS

If you want a home base that's roomy enough for a family and comes with cooking facilities, consider a furnished rental. These can save you money, especially if you're traveling with a group. Home-exchange directories sometimes list rentals as well as exchanges.

🔢 **International Agents Hideaways International** ✉ 767 Islington St., Portsmouth, NH 03801 ☎ 800/843-4433 or 603/430-4433 ⊟ 603/430-4444 ⊕ www.hideaways.com, annual membership $185. **Hometours International** ✉ 1108 Scottie La., Knoxville, TN 37919 ☎ 865/690-8484 or 866/367-4668 ⊕ thor.he.net/~hometour/. **Interhome** ✉ 1990 N.E. 163rd St., Suite 110, North Miami Beach, FL 33162 ☎ 800/882-6864 or 305/940-2299 ⊟ 305/940-2911 ⊕ www.interhome.us. **Vacation Home Rentals Worldwide** ✉ 235 Kensington Ave., Norwood, NJ 07648 ☎ 800/633-3284 or 201/767-9393 ⊟ 201/767-5510 ⊕ www.vhrww.com.

🔢 **Local Agents American Realty** ⬚ Box 1133, Captiva, FL 33924 ☎ 800/547-0127 ⊕ www.captiva-island.com/amrc. **Fairfield Resorts** ✉ 5259 Coconut Creek Pkwy., Margate, FL 33063 ☎ 800/251-8736 ⊕ www.fairfieldresorts.com. **Florida Keys Rental Store/Marr Properties** ⬚ Box 600, ✉ 9980 Overseas Hwy., Key Largo, FL 33037 ☎ 800/585-0584 or 305/451-3879. **Florida Sunbreak** ✉ 90 Alton Rd., Suite 16, Miami Beach, FL 33139 ☎ 800/786-2732 or 305/532-1516 ⊕ www.floridasunbreak.com. **Freewheeler Vacations** ✉ 85992 Overseas Hwy., MM 86, Islamorada, FL 33036 ☎ 866/664-2075 or 305/664-2075 ⊕ www.freewheeler-realty.com. **ResortQuest International** ✉ 35000 Emerald Coast Pkwy., Destin, FL 32541 ☎ 877/588-5800 ⊕ www.resortquest.com. **Sand Key Realty** ✉ 2701 Gulf Blvd., Indian Rocks Beach, FL 33785 ☎ 866/353-8911 or 727/595-5441 ⊕ www.sandkey.com. **Suncoast Realty** ✉ 224 Franklin Blvd., St. George Island, FL 32328 ☎ 800/341-2021.

BED & BREAKFASTS

Small inns and guest houses are increasingly numerous in Florida, but they vary tremendously, ranging from economical places that are plain but serve a good home-style breakfast to elegantly furnished Victorian houses with four-course breakfasts and rates to match. Many offer a homelike setting. In fact, many are in private homes with owners who treat you almost like family; others are more businesslike. It's a good idea to **make specific inquiries of B&Bs you're interested in.** The association listed below offers descriptions and suggestions for B&Bs throughout Florida. *Superior Small Lodging, a Guide to Fine Small Hotels,* is available through the Daytona Beach Convention and Visitors Bureau.

🔢 **Bed & Breakfast Association Florida Bed and Breakfast Inns** ⬚ Box 6187, Palm Harbor, FL 34684 ☎ 800/524-1880 or 281/499-1374 ⊕ www.florida-inns.com. *Superior Small Lodging, a Guide to Fine Small Hotels* ✉ 126 E. Orange Ave., Daytona Beach, FL 32114 ☎ 800/854-1234 or 386/255-0415.

CAMPING

Camping is popular throughout the state, especially in central Florida near the major Orlando attractions, and on the mellower west coast. Camping on nondesignated beach sites is not allowed. For information on camping facilities, contact the national and state parks and forests you plan to visit and the Florida Department of Environmental Protection.

To find a commercial campground, **pick up a copy of the free annual "Official Florida Camping Directory,"** which lists 305 campgrounds, with more than 55,000 sites. It's available at Florida welcome centers, from the Florida Tourism Industry Marketing Corporation (⇨ Visitor Information), and from the Florida Association of RV Parks & Campgrounds.

🔢 **Camping Association Florida Association of RV Parks & Campgrounds** ✉ 1340 Vickers Dr., Tallahassee, FL 32303-3041 ☎ 850/562-7151 ⊟ 850/562-7179 ⊕ www.floridacamping.com.

CONDOS

🔢 **Condo Guide** *The Condo Lux Vacationer's Guide to Condominium Rentals in the Southeast* (Vintage Books/Random House, New York; $9.95), by Jill Little.

CUTTING COSTS

Affordable lodgings can be found in even the most glittery resort towns, typically motel rooms that may cost as little as $50–$60 a night. Since beachfront properties tend to be more expensive, **look for properties a little off the beach.** Still, many beachfront properties are surprisingly affordable in places like St. Petersburg Beach, on the west coast, and Cocoa Beach, on the east coast.

If demand isn't especially high, you can often **save by showing up at a lodging in mid- to late afternoon**—desk clerks are typically willing to negotiate with travelers in order to fill those rooms late in the day. In addition, **check with chambers of commerce for discount coupons for selected properties.**

HOME EXCHANGES

If you would like to exchange your home for someone else's, join a home-exchange organization, which will send you its updated listings of available exchanges for a year and will include your own listing in at least one of them. It's up to you to make specific arrangements.

Exchange Clubs HomeLink USA ✉ 2937 NW 9th Terrace, Wilton Manors, FL 33311 ☎ 954/566-2687 or 800/638-3841 🖷 954/566-2783 ⊕ www.homelink.org; $75 yearly for a listing and online access; $45 additional to receive directories. **Intervac U.S.** ✉ 30 Corte San Fernando, Tiburon, CA 94920 ☎ 800/756-4663 🖷 415/435-7440 ⊕ www.intervacus.com; $128 yearly for a listing, online access, and a catalog; $68 without catalog.

HOSTELS

No matter what your age, you can save on lodging costs by staying at hostels. In some 4,500 locations in more than 70 countries around the world, Hostelling International (HI), the umbrella group for a number of national youth-hostel associations, offers single-sex, dorm-style beds and, at many hostels, rooms for couples and family accommodations. Membership in any HI national hostel association, open to travelers of all ages, allows you to stay in HI-affiliated hostels at member rates; one-year membership is about $28 for adults (C$35 for a two-year minimum membership in Canada, £15 in the U.K., A$52 in Australia, and NZ$40 in New Zealand); hos-

tels charge about $10–$30 per night. Members have priority if the hostel is full; they're also eligible for discounts around the world, even on rail and bus travel in some countries.

Organizations Hostelling International–USA ✉ 8401 Colesville Rd., Suite 600, Silver Spring, MD 20910 ☎ 301/495-1240 🖷 301/495-6697 ⊕ www.hiusa.org. **Hostelling International–Canada** ✉ 205 Catherine St., Suite 400, Ottawa, Ontario K2P 1C3 ☎ 800/663-5777 or 613/237-7884 🖷 613/237-7868 ⊕ www.hihostels.ca. **YHA England and Wales** ✉ Trevelyan House, Dimple Rd., Matlock, Derbyshire DE4 3YH, U.K. ☎ 0870/870-8808, 0870/770-8868, or 0162/959-2600 🖷 0870/770-6127 ⊕ www.yha.org.uk. **YHA Australia** ✉ 422 Kent St., Sydney, NSW 2001 ☎ 02/9261-1111 🖷 02/9261-1969 ⊕ www.yha.com.au. **YHA New Zealand** ✉ Level 1, Moorhouse City, 166 Moorhouse Ave., Box 436, Christchurch ☎ 0800/278-299 or 03/379-9970 🖷 03/365-4476 ⊕ www.yha.org.nz.

HOTELS

Wherever you look in Florida, it seems, you'll find lots of plain, inexpensive motels and luxurious resorts, independents alongside national chains, and an ever-growing number of modern properties as well as quite a few timeless classics. In fact, since Florida has been a favored travel destination for some time, vintage hotels are everywhere: there are grand edifices like the Breakers in Palm Beach, the Boca Raton Resort & Club in Boca Raton, the Biltmore in Coral Gables, and the Casa Marina in Key West; and smaller, historic places, like the Governors Inn in Tallahassee and the New World Inn in Pensacola.

All hotels listed have private bath unless otherwise noted.

Toll-Free Numbers Adam's Mark ☎ 800/444-2326 ⊕ www.adamsmark.com. **Baymont Inns** ☎ 800/428-3438 or 866/999-1111 ⊕ www.baymontinns.com. **Best Western** ☎ 800/528-1234 ⊕ www.bestwestern.com. **Choice** ☎ 800/424-6423 ⊕ www.choicehotels.com. **Clarion** ☎ 800/424-6423 ⊕ www.choicehotels.com. **Comfort Inn** ☎ 800/424-6423 ⊕ www.choicehotels.com. **Days Inn** ☎ 800/325-2525 ⊕ www.daysinn.com. **Doubletree Hotels** ☎ 800/222-8733 ⊕ www.doubletree.com. **Embassy Suites** ☎ 800/362-2779 ⊕ www.embassysuites.com. **Fairfield Inn** ☎ 800/228-2800 ⊕ www.marriott.com. **Four Seasons**

🕿 800/332-3442 🌐 www.fourseasons.com. **Hilton** 🕿 800/445-8667 🌐 www.hilton.com. **Holiday Inn** 🕿 800/465-4329 🌐 www.ichotelsgroup.com. **Howard Johnson** 🕿 800/446-4656 🌐 www.hojo.com. **Hyatt Hotels & Resorts** 🕿 800/233-1234 🌐 www.hyatt.com. **Inter-Continental** 🕿 800/327-0200 🌐 www.ichotelsgroup.com. **La Quinta** 🕿 800/531-5900 🌐 www.lq.com. **Marriott** 🕿 800/228-9290 🌐 www.marriott.com. **Omni** 🕿 800/843-6664 🌐 www.omnihotels.com. **Quality Inn** 🕿 800/424-6423 🌐 www.choicehotels.com. **Radisson** 🕿 800/333-3333 🌐 www.radisson.com. **Ramada** 🕿 800/228-2828, 800/854-7854 international reservations 🌐 www.ramada.com or www.ramadahotels.com. **Renaissance Hotels & Resorts** 🕿 800/468-3571 🌐 www.marriott.com. **Ritz-Carlton** 🕿 800/241-3333 🌐 www.ritzcarlton.com. **Sheraton** 🕿 800/325-3535 🌐 www.starwood.com/sheraton. **Sleep Inn** 🕿 800/424-6423 🌐 www.choicehotels.com. **Westin Hotels & Resorts** 🕿 800/228-3000 🌐 www.starwood.com/westin. **Wyndham Hotels & Resorts** 🕿 800/822-4200 🌐 www.wyndham.com.

VACATION OWNERSHIP RESORTS

Vacation ownership resorts sell hotel rooms, condominium apartments, and villas in weekly, monthly, or quarterly increments. The weekly arrangement is most popular; it's often referred to as "interval ownership" or "time sharing." Of more than 3,000 vacation ownership resorts around the world, some 500 are in Florida, with the heaviest concentration in the Walt Disney World–Orlando area. Nonowners can rent at many of these resorts by contacting the individual property or a real-estate broker in the area.

MONEY MATTERS

Prices throughout this guide are given for adults (though admission prices for children are indicated in the Walt Disney World & the Orlando Area chapter). Substantially reduced fees are almost always available for children, students, and senior citizens. For information on taxes, *see* Taxes.

ATMS

Automatic Teller Machines (ATMs) are ubiquitous in Florida. You'll find them at grocery store chains like Publix and Winn-Dixie, in shopping malls big and small, and, increasingly, at gas stations.

CREDIT CARDS

Throughout this guide, the following abbreviations are used: **AE**, American Express; **D**, Discover; **DC**, Diners Club; **MC**, MasterCard; and **V**, Visa.

🖪 Reporting Lost Cards **American Express** 🕿 800/992-3404. **Diners Club** 🕿 800/234-6377. **Discover** 🕿 800/347-2683. **MasterCard** 🕿 800/622-7747. **Visa** 🕿 800/ 847-2911.

NATIONAL PARKS

Look into discount passes to save money on park entrance fees. For $50, the National Parks Pass admits you (and any passengers in your private vehicle) to all national parks, monuments, and recreation areas, as well as other sites run by the National Park Service, for a year. (In parks that charge per person, the pass admits you, your spouse and children, and your parents, when you arrive together.) Camping and parking are extra. The $15 Golden Eagle Pass, a hologram you affix to your National Parks Pass, functions as an upgrade, granting entry to all sites run by the NPS, the U.S. Fish and Wildlife Service, the U.S. Forest Service, and the Bureau of Land Management. The upgrade, which expires with the parks pass, is sold by most national-park, Fish-and-Wildlife, and BLM fee stations. A major percentage of the proceeds from pass sales funds National Parks projects.

Both the Golden Age Passport ($10), for U.S. citizens or permanent residents who are 62 and older, and the Golden Access Passport (free), for persons with disabilities, entitle holders (and any passengers in their private vehicles) to lifetime free entry to all national parks, plus 50% off fees for the use of many park facilities and services. (The discount doesn't always apply to companions.) To obtain them, you must show proof of age and of U.S. citizenship or permanent residency—such as a U.S. passport, driver's license, or birth certificate—and, if requesting Golden Access, proof of disability. The Golden Age and Golden Access passes are available only at NPS-run sites that charge an entrance fee. The National Parks Pass is also available by mail and phone and via the Internet.

⚄ National Park Foundation ⊠ 11 Dupont Circle NW, Suite 600, Washington, DC 20036 ☏ 202/238-4200 ⊕ www.nationalparks.org. **National Park Service** ⊠ National Park Service/Department of Interior, 1849 C St. NW, Washington, DC 20240 ☏ 202/208-6843 ⊕ www.nps.gov. **National Parks Conservation Association** ⊠ 1300 19th St. NW, Suite 300, Washington, DC 20036 ☏ 202/223-6722 or 800/628-7275 ⊕ www.npca.org.

⚄ Passes by Mail & Online National Park Foundation ⊕ www.nationalparks.org. **National Parks Pass** National Park Foundation ⌓ Box 34108, Washington, DC 20043 ☏ 888/467-2757 ⊕ www.nationalparks.org; include a check or money order payable to the National Park Service, plus $3.95 for shipping and handling (allow 8 to 13 business days from date of receipt for pass delivery), or call for passes.

PRIVATE PRESERVES

⚄ Florida Sanctuary Information Audubon Florida ⊠ 444 Birckell Ave., Suite 850, Miami, FL 33131 ☏ 305/371-6399 ⊕ www.audubonofflorida.org. **Nature Conservancy** ⊠ Blowing Rocks Preserve, 575 South Beach Rd., Hobe Sound, FL 33455 ☏ 561/744-6668 ⊠ Apalachicola Bluffs and Ravines Preserve, N.W. Florida Program, 10326 N.W. Longleaf Dr., Bristol, FL 32321 ☏ 850/643-2756 ⊠ S.E. Division, 222 S. Westmonte Dr., Suite 300, Altamonte Springs, FL 32714 ☏ 407/682-3664 ⊠ Florida Keys, 55 N. Johnson Rd., Sugarloaf Shores, FL 33042 ☏ 305/745-8402 ⊠ Tiger Creek Preserve, 155 Pfundstein Rd., Babson, FL 33827 ☏ 863/635-7506 ⊠ Tallahassee Field Office, 625 N. Adams St., Tallahassee, FL 32301 ☏ 850/222-0199 ⊠ South Florida Office, 2455 E. Sunrise Blvd., Fort Lauderdale, FL 33304 ☏ 954/564-6144.

STATE PARKS

Florida's Department of Environmental Protection (DEP) is responsible for hundreds of historic buildings, landmarks, nature preserves, and parks. When requesting a free *Florida State Park Guide,* mention which parts of the state you plan to visit. For information on camping facilities at state parks, ask for the free "Florida State Parks, Fees and Facilities" and "Florida State Parks Camping Reservation Procedures" brochures. Responding to cutbacks in its budget, the DEP established Friends of Florida State Parks, a citizen support organization open to all.

⚄ State Parks Information Florida Department of Environmental Protection ⊠ Marjory Stoneman Douglas Bldg., MS 536, 3900 Commonwealth Blvd., Tallahassee, FL 32399-3000 ☏ 850/245-2118. **Friends of Florida State Parks** ☏ 850/245-3098.

PACKING

The northern part of the state is much cooler in winter than the southern part, and you'll want to take a heavy sweater if you plan on traveling north in winter months. Even in summer ocean breezes can be cool, so always **take a sweater or jacket** just in case.

The Miami area and the Naples–Fort Myers area are warm year-round and often extremely humid in summer months. Be prepared for sudden storms all over Florida in summer, but keep in mind that plastic raincoats are uncomfortable in the high humidity.

Dress is casual throughout the state, with sundresses, jeans, or walking shorts appropriate during the day; **bring comfortable walking shoes or sneakers** for theme parks. A few restaurants request that men wear jackets and ties, but most do not. Be prepared for air-conditioning working in overdrive.

You can generally swim year-round in peninsular Florida from about New Smyrna Beach south on the Atlantic coast and from Tarpon Springs south on the Gulf Coast. Be sure to **take a sun hat and sunscreen** because the sun can be fierce, even in winter and even if it's chilly or overcast.

In your carry-on luggage, pack an extra pair of eyeglasses or contact lenses and enough of any medication you take to last a few days longer than the entire trip. You may also ask your doctor to write a spare prescription using the drug's generic name, as brand names may vary from country to country. In luggage to be checked, **never pack prescription drugs, valuables, or undeveloped film.** And don't forget to carry with you the addresses of offices that handle refunds of lost traveler's checks. Check *Fodor's How to Pack* (available at online retailers and bookstores everywhere) for more tips.

To avoid customs and security delays, carry medications in their original packaging. Don't pack any sharp objects in your carry-on luggage, including knives of any size or material, scissors, nail clippers, and corkscrews, or anything else that might arouse suspicion.

To avoid having your checked luggage chosen for hand inspection, don't cram bags full. The U.S. Transportation Security Administration suggests packing shoes on top and placing personal items you don't want touched in clear plastic bags.

CHECKING LUGGAGE

You're allowed to carry aboard the aircraft one bag and one personal article, such as a purse or a laptop computer. Make sure what you carry on fits under your seat or in the overhead bin. Get to the gate early, so you can board as soon as possible, before the overhead bins fill up.

Baggage allowances vary by carrier, destination, and ticket class. On international flights, you're usually allowed to check two bags weighing up to 70 pounds (32 kilograms) each, although a few airlines allow checked bags of up to 88 pounds (40 kilograms) in first class. Some international carriers don't allow more than 66 pounds (30 kilograms) per bag in business class and 44 pounds (20 kilograms) in economy. If you're flying to or through the United Kingdom, your luggage cannot exceed 70 pounds (32 kilograms) per bag. On domestic flights, the limit is usually 50 to 70 pounds (23 to 32 kilograms) per bag. In general, carry-on bags shouldn't exceed 40 pounds (18 kilograms). Most airlines won't accept bags that weigh more than 100 pounds (45 kilograms) on domestic or international flights. Expect to pay a fee for baggage that exceeds weight limits. Check baggage restrictions with your carrier before you pack.

Airline liability for baggage is limited to $2,500 per person on flights within the United States. On international flights it amounts to $9.07 per pound or $20 per kilogram for checked baggage (roughly $640 per 70-pound bag), with a maximum of $634.90 per piece, and $400 per passenger for unchecked baggage. You can buy additional coverage at check-in for about $10 per $1,000 of coverage, but it often excludes a rather extensive list of items, shown on your airline ticket.

Before departure, itemize your bags' contents and their worth, and label the bags with your name, address, and phone number. (If you use your home address, cover it so potential thieves can't see it readily.) Include a label inside each bag and **pack a copy of your itinerary.** At check-in, make sure each bag is correctly tagged with the destination airport's three-letter code. Because some checked bags will be opened for hand inspection, the U.S. Transportation Security Administration recommends that you leave luggage unlocked or use the plastic locks offered at check-in. TSA screeners place an inspection notice inside searched bags, which are re-sealed with a special lock.

If your bag has been searched and contents are missing or damaged, file a claim with the TSA Consumer Response Center as soon as possible. If your bags arrive damaged or fail to arrive at all, file a written report with the airline before leaving the airport.

⚑ Complaints U.S. Transportation Security Administration Contact Center ☎ 866/289–9673 ⊕ www.tsa.gov.

SAFETY

Stepped-up policing of thieves who prey on tourists in rental cars has helped address what was a serious issue in the early 1990s. Still, visitors should be especially wary when driving in strange neighborhoods and leaving the airport, especially in the Miami area. Don't assume that valuables are safe in your hotel room; use in-room safes or the hotel's safety deposit boxes. Try to use ATMs only during the day or in brightly lit, well-traveled locales.

BEACH SAFETY

Before swimming, **make sure there's no undertow.** Rip currents, caused when the tide rushes out through a narrow break in the water, can overpower even the strongest swimmer. If you do get caught in one, resist the urge to swim straight back to shore— you'll tire before you make it. Instead, stay calm. Swim parallel to the shoreline until you are outside the current's pull, then work your way in to shore.

SENIOR-CITIZEN TRAVEL

Since Florida has a significant retired population, senior-citizen discounts are ubiquitous throughout the state. To qualify for age-related discounts, mention your senior-citizen status up front when booking hotel reservations (not when checking out) and before you're seated in restaurants (not when paying the bill). Be sure to have identification on hand. When renting a car, ask about promotional car-rental discounts, which can be cheaper than senior-citizen rates.

⚇ Educational Programs Elderhostel ⊠ 11 Ave. de Lafayette, Boston, MA 02111-1746 ☎ 877/426-8056, 978/323-4141 international callers, 877/426-2167 TTY ᗌ 877/426-2166 ⊕ www.elderhostel.org. Interhostel ⊠ University of New Hampshire, 6 Garrison Ave., Durham, NH 03824 ☎ 800/733-9753 or 603/862-1147 ᗌ 603/862-1113 ⊕ www.learn.unh.edu.

SPORTS & THE OUTDOORS

Recreational opportunities abound throughout Florida. The Governor's Council on Physical Fitness and Sports puts on the Sunshine State Games each July in a different part of the state.

⚇ General Information Florida Department of Environmental Protection ⊠ Office of Greenways and Trails, MS 795, 3900 Commonwealth Blvd., Tallahassee, FL 32399-3000 ☎ 877/822-5208 or 850/245-2052 ⊕ www.dep.state.fl.us for information on bicycling, canoeing, kayaking, and hiking trails.

BIKING

Biking is a popular Florida sport. Rails to Trails, a nationwide group that turns unused railroad rights-of-way into bicycle and walking paths, has made great inroads in Florida, particularly around the Tampa–St. Pete area. In addition, just about every town in Florida has its own set of bike paths and a bike rental outfit. For bike information, **check with Florida's Department of Transportation (DOT)**, which publishes free bicycle trail guides, dispenses free touring information packets, and provides names of bike coordinators around the state.

⚇ Bicycle Information Rails to Trails ☎ 850/942-2379. DOT state bicycle-pedestrian coordinator ⊠ 605 Suwannee St., MS 53, Tallahassee, FL 32399-0450 ☎ 850/245-1500.

CANOEING & KAYAKING

You can canoe or kayak along 1,550 mi of trails encompassing creeks, rivers, and springs. Both the DEP (⇨ General Information) and outfitter associations provide information on trails and their conditions, events, and contacts for trips and equipment rental.

⚇ Outfitters & Outfitting Associations Canoe Outpost System ⊠ 2816 N.W. Rte. 661, Arcadia, FL 33821 ☎ 800/268-0083 or 863/494-1215 ⊕ www.canoeoutpost.com, comprising five outfitters. Florida Professional Paddlesports Association ᗌ Box 1764, Arcadia, FL 34265 ☎ No phone ⊕ www.paddleflausa.com has a state map available online and a directory of local resources.

FISHING

In Atlantic and gulf waters, fishing seasons and other regulations vary by location and species. You will need to **buy one license for freshwater fishing and another for saltwater fishing.** Nonresident fees for a saltwater license are $31.50. Nonresidents can purchase freshwater licenses good for three days ($6.50), seven days ($16.50), or for one year ($31.50). Typically, you'll pay a $1.50 surcharge at most any marina, bait shop, Kmart, Wal-Mart, or other license vendor.

⚇ Fishing Information Florida Fish and Wildlife Conservation Commission ⊠ 620 S. Meridian St., Tallahassee, FL 32399-1600 ☎ 850/488-1960 publishes the free *Florida Fishing Handbook,* with license vendors, regional fishing guides, and educational bulletins.

JOGGING, RUNNING & WALKING

Many towns have walking and running trails, and most of Florida's beaches stretch on for miles, testing the limits of even the most stalwart runners and walkers. Local running clubs all over the state sponsor weekly public events. The Miami Runners Club has information about South Florida events. The Road Runners Club of America has chapters throughout the state.

🏃 Clubs & Events Miami Runners Club ✉ 8720 N. Kendall Dr., Suite 206, Miami, FL 33176 ☎ 305/227-1500 ⊕ www.miamirunnersclub.com. **Road Runners Club of America** ✉ Northern state info: 65 Winterbourne St. N, Orange Park, FL 32073 ☎ 904/278-2926 ✉ Southern state info: 23059 Redfish La., Cudjoe Key, FL 33042 ☎ 305/745-3027 ⊕ www.rrca.org.

PARI-MUTUEL SPORTS
Jai-alai frontons and greyhound-racing tracks are in most major Florida cities. Patrons can bet on the teams or dogs or on televised horse races.

🏃 Schedules Department of Business & Professional Regulations, Division of Pari-Mutuel Wagering ✉ 1940 N. Monroe St., Tallahassee, FL 32399 ☎ 850/488-9130 🖨 850/488-0550.

TENNIS
Tennis is extremely popular in Florida, and virtually every town has well-maintained public courts. In addition, many tennis tournaments are held in the state.

🏃 Tournament & Event Schedules USA Tennis Florida ✉ 1 Deuce Ct., Suite 100, Daytona Beach, FL 32124 ☎ 386/671-8949 🖨 386/671-8948 ⊕ www.usatennisflorida.usta.com.

WILDERNESS & RECREATION AREAS
Florida is studded with trails, rivers, and parks that are ideal for hiking, bird-watching, canoeing, bicycling, and horseback riding. *Florida Trails: A Guide to Florida's Natural Habitats,* available from Florida Tourism Industry Marketing Corporation (⇨ Visitor Information), has information on bicycling, canoeing, horseback riding, and walking trails; camping; snorkeling and scuba diving; and Florida ecosystems.

🏃 Publications Recreation Guide to District Lands 📀 Available from St. Johns River Water Management District, 4049 Reid St., Palatka, FL 32177 ☎ 386/329-4500; free for marine, wetland, and upland recreational areas.

STUDENTS IN FLORIDA
Students flock to the beaches of Florida during spring break, at its peak from early March to mid-April, but there are also special tours for students year-round. Students presenting identification qualify for discounts at most movie theaters and art museums.

🏃 I.D.s & Services STA Travel ✉ 10 Downing St., New York, NY 10014 ☎ 212/627-3111, 800/777-0112 24-hr service center ☎ 212/627-3387 ⊕ www.sta.com. **Travel Cuts** ✉ 187 College St., Toronto, Ontario M5T 1P7, Canada ☎ 800/592-2887 in the U.S., 416/979-2406 or 866/811-9020 in Canada 🖨 416/979-8167 ⊕ www.travelcuts.com.

TAXES
SALES TAX
Florida's sales tax is 6% or higher depending on the county, and local sales and tourist taxes can raise what you pay considerably, especially for certain items, such as lodging. Miami hoteliers, for example, collect roughly 12.5% for city and resort taxes. It's best to **ask about additional costs up front,** to avoid a rude awakening.

TELEPHONES
To make local calls within the 305 (Miami area) and 407 (Orlando area) calling areas, **begin calls with the local area code,** dialing a total of 10 digits.

TIME
The western portion of the Panhandle is in the Central Time Zone, but the rest of Florida is in the Eastern Time Zone.

TIPPING
Whether they carry bags, open doors, deliver food, or clean rooms, hospitality employees work to receive a portion of your travel budget. In deciding how much to give, base your tip on what the service is and how well it's performed.

In transit, tip an airport valet $1–$3 per bag, a taxi driver 15%–20% of the fare.

For hotel staff, recommended amounts are $1–$3 per bag for a bellhop, $1–$2 per night per guest for chambermaids, $5–$10 for special concierge service, $1–$3 for a doorman who hails a cab or parks a car, 15% of the green fee for a caddy, 15%–20% of the bill for a massage, and 15% of a room service bill (bear in mind that sometimes 15%–18% is automatically added to room service bills, so don't add it twice).

In a restaurant, give 15%–20% of your bill before tax to the server, 5%–10% to the maître d', 15% to a bartender, and 15% of the wine bill for a wine steward who makes a special effort in selecting and serving wine.

TOURS & PACKAGES

Because everything is prearranged on a prepackaged tour or independent vacation, you spend less time planning—and often get it all at a good price.

BOOKING WITH AN AGENT

Travel agents are excellent resources. But it's a good idea to collect brochures from several agencies, as some agents' suggestions may be influenced by relationships with tour and package firms that reward them for volume sales. If you have a special interest, find an agent with expertise in that area. The American Society of Travel Agents (ASTA) has a database of specialists worldwide; you can log on to the group's Web site to find one near you.

Make sure your travel agent knows the accommodations and other services of the place being recommended. Ask about the hotel's location, room size, beds, and whether it has a pool, room service, or programs for children, if you care about these. Has your agent been there in person or sent others whom you can contact?

Do some homework on your own, too: local tourism boards can provide information about lesser-known and small-niche operators, some of which may sell only direct.

BUYER BEWARE

Each year consumers are stranded or lose their money when tour operators—even large ones with excellent reputations—go out of business. So check out the operator. Ask several travel agents about its reputation, and try to **book with a company that has a consumer-protection program.** (Look for information in the company's brochure.) In the United States, members of the United States Tour Operators Association are required to set aside funds (up to $1 million) to help eligible customers cover payments and travel arrangements in the event that the company defaults. It's also a good idea to choose a company that participates in the American Society of Travel Agents' Tour Operator Program; ASTA will act as mediator in any disputes between you and your tour operator.

Remember that the more your package or tour includes, the better you can predict the ultimate cost of your vacation. Make sure you know exactly what is covered, and beware of hidden costs. Are taxes, tips, and transfers included? Entertainment and excursions? These can add up.

⏏ Tour-Operator Recommendations American Society of Travel Agents (⇨ Travel Agencies). **CrossSphere–The Global Association for Packaged Travel** ✉ 546 E. Main St., Lexington, KY 40508 ☎ 859/226-4444 or 800/682-8886 🖷 859/226-4414 ⊕ www.CrossSphere.com. **United States Tour Operators Association** (USTOA) ✉ 275 Madison Ave., Suite 2014, New York, NY 10016 ☎ 212/599-6599 🖷 212/599-6744 ⊕ www.ustoa.com.

TRAIN TRAVEL

Amtrak provides north–south service on two routes to the major cities of Jacksonville, Orlando, Tampa, West Palm Beach, Fort Lauderdale, and Miami, and east–west service through Jacksonville, Tallahassee, and Pensacola, with many stops in between on all routes.

⏏ Train Information Amtrak ☎ 800/872-7245 ⊕ www.amtrak.com.

TRAVEL AGENCIES

A good travel agent puts your needs first. Look for an agency that has been in business at least five years, emphasizes customer service, and has someone on staff who specializes in your destination. In addition, **make sure the agency belongs to a professional trade organization.** The American Society of Travel Agents (ASTA) has more than 10,000 members in some 140 countries, enforces a strict code of ethics, and will step in to mediate agent-client disputes involving ASTA members. ASTA also maintains a directory of agents on its Web site; ASTA's TravelSense.org, a trip planning and travel advice site, can also help to locate a travel agent who caters to your needs. (If a travel agency is also acting as your tour operator, *see* Buyer Beware *in* Tours & Packages.)

⏏ Local Agent Referrals American Society of Travel Agents (ASTA) ✉ 1101 King St., Suite 200, Alexandria, VA 22314 ☎ 703/739-2782 or 800/965-2782 24-hr hotline 🖷 703/684-8319 ⊕ www. astanet.com and www.travelsense.org. **Association**

of British Travel Agents ⊠ 68–71 Newman St., London W1T 3AH ☎ 020/7637–2444 🖷 020/ 7637–0713 ⊕ www.abta.com. **Association of Canadian Travel Agencies** ⊠ 130 Albert St., Suite 1705, Ottawa, Ontario K1P 5G4 ☎ 613/237–3657 🖷 613/ 237–7052 ⊕ www.acta.ca. **Australian Federation of Travel Agents** ⊠ Level 3, 309 Pitt St., Sydney, NSW 2000 ☎ 02/9264–3299 or 1300/363–416 🖷 02/ 9264–1085 ⊕ www.afta.com.au. **Travel Agents' Association of New Zealand** ⊠ Level 5, Tourism and Travel House, 79 Boulcott St., Box 1888, Wellington 6001 ☎ 04/499–0104 🖷 04/499–0786 ⊕ www. taanz.org.nz.

VISITOR INFORMATION

For general information about Florida's attractions, contact the office below; welcome centers are located on Interstate 10, Interstate 75, Interstate 95, and U.S. 231 (near Graceville), and in the lobby of the New Capitol in Tallahassee. For regional tourist bureaus and chambers of commerce see individual chapters.

🔢 State **Florida Tourism Industry Marketing Corporation** ⊠ 661 E. Jefferson St., Suite 300, Box 1100, Tallahassee, FL 32302 ☎ 850/488–5607 🖷 850/ 224–2938 ⊕ www.flausa.com.

🔢 In the U.K. **ABC Florida** 🗂 Box 35, Abingdon, Oxon OX14 4SF ☎ 0891/600–555, 50p per minute; send £2 for vacation pack.

🔢 Government Advisories **Consular Affairs Bureau of Canada** ☎ 800/267–6788 or 613/944–6788

⊕ www.voyage.gc.ca. **U.K. Foreign and Commonwealth Office** ⊠ Travel Advice Unit, Consular Directorate, Old Admiralty Building, London SW1A 2PA ☎ 0870/606–0290 or 020/7008–1500 ⊕ www.fco. gov.uk/travel. **Australian Department of Foreign Affairs and Trade** ☎ 300/139–281 travel advisories, 02/6261–1299 Consular Travel Advice ⊕ www. smartraveller.gov.au or www.dfat.gov.au. **New Zealand Ministry of Foreign Affairs and Trade** ☎ 04/439–8000 ⊕ www.mft.govt.nz.

WEB SITES

Do check out the World Wide Web when planning your trip. You'll find everything from weather forecasts to virtual tours of famous cities. Be sure to visit Fodors.com (⊕ www.fodors.com), a complete travel-planning site. You can research prices and book plane tickets, hotel rooms, rental cars, vacation packages, and more. In addition, you can post your pressing questions in the Travel Talk section. Other planning tools include a currency converter and weather reports, and there are loads of links to travel resources.

The state of Florida is very visitor-oriented and has a terrific Web site— ⊕ www. flausa.com—with superb links to help you find out all you want to know. It's a wonderful place to learn about everything from fancy resorts to camping trips to car routes to beach towns.

The Panhandle

WORD OF MOUTH

"I've lived in the Panhandle most of my life. The Forgotten Coast is suddenly being remembered. Come quickly. The Panhandle, as we know it, will soon be gone."

—Sunshinesue

"We just got back from St. George Island. It is near Apalachicola, which is a pretty town, well worth walking through with a lot of cute shops, more for looking than buying, unless money is not a concern. Apalachicola is very popular with fishermen. The oysters there are famous, so I ate a lot of them, and they were good. Of course this is March, but it didn't seem crowded or especially touristy. I came home feeling very relaxed."

—ebgibbs

2

By David
Downing

FLORIDA'S THIN, GREEN NORTHWEST CORNER SNUGGLES UP between
the Gulf of Mexico and the Alabama and Georgia state lines. Known
as the Panhandle, it's sometimes called "the other Florida," since in
addition to palm trees what thrives here are the magnolias, live oaks,
and loblolly pines common in the rest of the Deep South. As South
Florida's season is winding down in May, action in the northwest is
just picking up. The area is even in a different time zone: the Apalachicola
River marks the dividing line between eastern and central times. Until
World War II, when activity at the Panhandle air bases took off, this
section of the state was little known and seldom visited. But by the mid-
1950s, the 100-mi stretch along the coast between Pensacola and
Panama City was dubbed the Miracle Strip because of a dramatic rise
in property values. In the 1940s this beachfront land sold for less than
$100 an acre; today that same acre can fetch hundreds of thousands
of dollars. To convey the richness of the region, with its white sands
and sparkling green waters, swamps, bayous, and flora, public-relations
pros ditched the Redneck Riviera moniker that locals had created and
coined the phrase Emerald Coast.

It's a land of superlatives: it has the biggest military installation in the
Western Hemisphere (Eglin Air Force Base), many of Florida's most beautiful beaches, and the most productive fishing waters in the world (off
Destin). It has glitzy resorts, campgrounds where possums and deer invite themselves to lunch, and every kind of lodging in between. Students
of the past can wander the many historic districts or visit archaeological digs. For sports enthusiasts there's a different golf course or tennis
court for each day of the week, and for nature lovers there's a world of
hunting, canoeing, biking, and hiking. And most anything that happens
on water happens here, including scuba diving and plenty of fishing, both
from deep-sea charter boats or the end of a pier.

Exploring the Panhandle

There are sights in the Panhandle, but sightseeing is not the principal
activity here. The area is better known for its ample fishing and diving
spots, and for being a spot to simply relax.

Florida's westernmost city, Pensacola, with its antebellum homes and
historic landmarks, is a good place to start your trek through northwest
Florida. After exploring the museums and preservation districts, head
east to Fort Walton Beach, the Emerald Coast's largest city, and on to
neighboring Destin, where sportfishing is king. Continuing along the coast,
there are a dozen or so family-friendly communities collectively known
as the Beaches of South Walton, where sugar-white, quartz-crystal sands
and emerald-green waters make for some of the finest beaches in the
country. This is also where you'll find some of the Panhandle's newest,
most luxurious developments, such as WaterColor, where luxury meets
modern seaside-chic in the smartly designed vacation homes and intimate inns. The next resort center along the coast is Panama City Beach—
just look for the construction cranes—while to the far southeast is
historic Apalachicola, the Panhandle's oyster-fishing capital. Just south
of Apalachicola, St. George Island, a 28-mi-long barrier island bordered

Numbers in the text correspond to numbers in the margin and on the Panhandle map.

If you have 3 days

History and nature are the two biggest calling cards of this part of the Sunshine State. Visit 🏖 **Grayton Beach ❺** and **Seaside ❻** ► and take advantage of some of Florida's finest beaches. On Day 2 drive to the capital, 🏛 **Tallahassee ❸**, and soak up some of the state's past. On Day 3, make a trip to nearby **Wakulla Springs State Park ❹**, where you'll find one of the world's deepest springs—perfect for sightseeing (the glass-bottom-boat ride is a must for kids) and swimming.

1

If you have 4 days

Plant yourself in the 🏖 **Beaches of South Walton**—choose from a cabin at 🏖 **Grayton Beach State Park,** a hotel, or a beach house rental—and use the area as a base of operation. The idyllic beach here will make it hard to pull yourself away to explore the area, but here are a few ideas for your to-do list. Enjoy a picnic on the grounds of the antebellum mansion at the **Eden Gardens State Park,** set amid moss-draped live oaks—it'll give you a feel for the history of the area, a great photo-op, and a view of the intercoastal. Laze away a quiet afternoon canoeing on Western Lake at **Grayton Beach State Park,** one of the most scenic spots along the Gulf Coast. Ditch the car one day and rent a bike to explore **Seaside ❻**, a "New Urbanist" model community of shops, restaurants, and gingerbread–style, tin-roof vacation homes.

If you have 6 days

Start with the state capital, Tallahassee. Check out the local sights, including the State Capitol building, the Tallahassee Historic Trail, and Maclay Gardens State Park. Take another day to head east on 1-10, visiting **Falling Waters State Park ❿** in the morning and then exploring the cool, dark caves of the **Florida Caverns State Park ⓬** in the afternoon when things heat up: you'll be amazed that such an extensive cave system exists anywhere in the Sunshine State. On the third day head south out of town toward **Wakulla Springs State Park ❹** where you can explore the spectacular springs either with a mask and snorkel or from inside a glass bottom boat. In the afternoon, head down to **St. Marks National Wildlife Refuge and Lighthouse ⓰**, to hike, swim, or have a leisurely picnic. Eventually make your way to the coast and take Highway 98 West toward Apalachicola.

In Apalach, spend a day wandering around the historic downtown area and the waterfront, taking in the sights and shops, and be sure to sample a few of the area's number one agricultural product: oysters. Spend another day on **St. George Island ❾**—on the east end you'll find the stunningly beautiful St. George Island State Park. The next day head in the other direction to **St. Joseph Peninsula State Park,** where you can kayak on the bay side or frolic in the surf on the Gulf side—you'll also see some of the tallest sand dunes around.

by the gulf and Apalachicola Bay, has vacation homes on one end and a pristine state park on the other. Inland, a number of interesting towns and state parks lie along Interstate 10, which crosses the Suwannee River on its long eastward trek to the state capital, Tallahassee.

About the Restaurants

A staggering quantity and variety of seafood is harvested from the Panhandle's coastal waters each day, and much of it appears within hours at restaurants throughout the region. You'll find fresh oysters, crab, shrimp, scallops, and fish simply prepared at casual beachside cafés or elegantly presented at upscale resort dining rooms. Don't overlook small-town seafood shacks, where you can dine "Florida Cracker"–style on deep-fried mullet, cheese grits, cole slaw, and hush puppies. Some restaurants in resort areas and beach communities close or modify their hours during off-season, so call first if visiting during winter months.

About the Hotels

Chain hotels and motels flank the major highways in all but the smallest towns here, but because most Panhandle visitors come to stay and play for a week or more, long-term lodging is definitely the most popular and plentiful option. Beach communities all along the coast offer long-term rentals tailored to fit every lifestyle, from the simplest efficiencies to secluded bungalows to spectacular vacation homes that peek out from between powdery dunes. Do your own housekeeping and explore the area on your own, or opt to stay at one of the inclusive resorts where everything you might need or wish to do is available on-site.

WHAT IT COSTS				
$$$$	**$$$**	**$$**	**$**	**¢**
RESTAURANTS over $30	$20–$30	$15–$20	$10–$15	under $10
HOTELS over $220	$140–$220	$100–$140	$80–$100	under $80

Restaurant prices are per person for a main course at dinner. Hotel prices are for a standard double room, excluding 6% sales tax (more in some counties) and 1%–4% tourist tax.

Timing

North Florida enjoys as much sunshine as the southern part of the state, but the climate here is more temperate than tropical. Unlike in the rest of Florida, the Panhandle's high season falls roughly between Memorial Day and Labor Day, when hordes of tourists and vacationing families from neighboring states head south for the summer (up to 80% of Panhandle visitors drive in from Alabama, Georgia, and other cities in Florida). Lodging prices in the region are usually based on a four-season system: spring break and summer rates are highest, winter lowest, and fall and spring are between the two extremes. (In the Tallahassee area only, hotel room prices increase during Florida State University home-game weekends and graduation week.) If you prefer your beach less crowded or can't take the heat the Panhandle is famous for, plan to visit in the autumn—October can be the loveliest month of the year here—when warm, sunny days alternate with cool, rainy spells and there's rel-

1

Beaches

Thanks to restrictions against commercial development imposed by Eglin Air Force Base (AFB) and the Gulf Islands National Seashore, the Emerald Coast has been able to maintain several hundred miles of unspoiled beaches. Hurricane Ivan reshaped all of the coast from Navarre to Pensacola Beach, turning much of the skinny barrier island of Santa Rosa into what looks like a sand lot. But most of the reshaping of the rest of the Panhandle coastline is the work of man, not Mother Nature. The development taking place—and there is much of it—is a mixed bag: some communities, such as Grayton Beach, fearing condo-mania and overcrowding, now impose height restrictions of four stories on new construction and set quotas for population density in sensitive areas. In other areas, such as Panama City Beach, high-rises will soon form one seemingly uninterrupted wall of condos along the shore (à la Daytona Beach). Still, the Panhandle remains home to many delicate ecosystems and spectacular beaches, which are consistently rated among the finest in the United States. Maybe it's because there's no slick Panhandle PR campaign yet, or maybe it's because locals are smart enough to keep the secret to themselves, but first-time visitors are routinely stunned by the area's natural beauty—then they become repeat visitors.

Biking

Some of the nation's best bike paths run through northwest Florida's woods and dunelands, particularly on Santa Rosa Island, where you can pedal for nearly 20 mi and never lose sight of the water. Eglin AFB Reservation presents cyclists with tortuous wooded trails.

Boating

With major shipping ports at Pensacola and Panama City, and fleets of commercial and charter boats based all along the Gulf Coast, the Panhandle's waters are heavily traveled year-round. When recreational boaters add their numbers during the summer months, the region's coastal waterways can be as crowded as its coastal highways. Those arriving by boat to cruise the Intracoastal Waterway will find an abundance of full-service marinas along the way. Rentals are available for nearly every type of watercraft, but you should be familiar with state regulations and safety procedures if you want to operate a boat here; penalties are severe for those caught boating recklessly or under the influence of alcohol or drugs.

Canoeing

The Panhandle is often referred to as the Canoe Capital of Florida, and both beginners and veterans enjoy canoeing the area's abundant waterways. The shoals and rapids of the Blackwater River in the Blackwater River State Forest, 40 mi northeast of Pensacola, challenge even seasoned canoeists, while the gentler currents of sheltered marshes and inlets are less intimidating.

Fishing

The Panhandle may be known as the Emerald Coast in tourism circles, but fishermen refer to it as the Red Coast due to the abundance of red snapper that can be found in local waters. Other saltwater catches include pompano, marlin, and grouper, while in fresh water you'll find bass, catfish, and bluegill. Deep-sea fishing is immensely popular, so there are boat charters aplenty. A day costs about $575, a half day about $350.

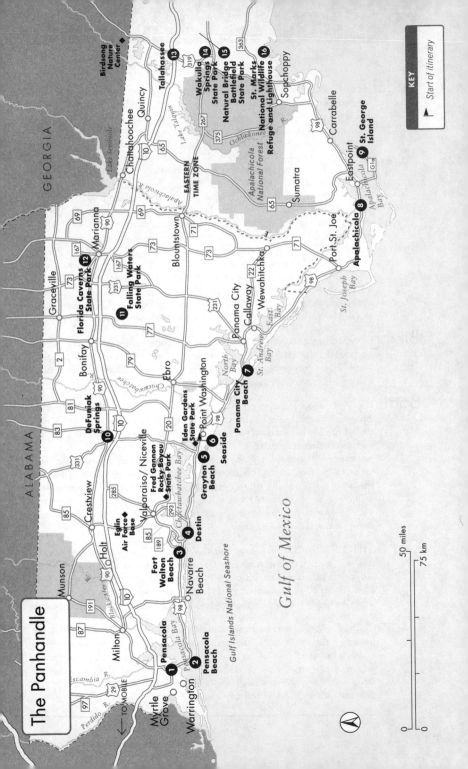

atively little humidity. Winter days can be both brilliant and bitterly cold, perfect for fishing or walking along miles of deserted beach.

AROUND PENSACOLA BAY

In the years since its founding, Pensacola has come under the control of five nations, earning this fine, old southern city its nickname, the City of Five Flags. Spanish conquistadors, under the command of Don Tristan de Luna, landed on the shores of Pensacola Bay in 1559, but discouraged by a succession of destructive tropical storms and dissension in the ranks, de Luna abandoned the settlement two years after its founding. In 1698 the Spanish once again established a fort at the site, and during the early 18th century control jockeyed back and forth among the Spanish, the French, and the British. Finally, in 1821 Pensacola passed into U.S. hands, although during the Civil War it was governed by the Confederate States of America and flew yet another flag. The city itself has many historic sights, while across the bay lies Pensacola Beach on Santa Rosa Island, an area recovering from the devastation caused by Hurricane Ivan in 2004.

Pensacola

❶ *59 mi east of Mobile, Alabama.*

Historic Pensacola consists of three distinct districts—Seville, Palafox, and North Hill—though they are easy to explore as a unit. Stroll down streets mapped out by the British and renamed by the Spanish, such as Cervantes, Palafox, Intendencia, and Tarragona. A recent influx of restaurants and bars is bringing new nightlife to the historic districts, but one-way streets can make navigating the area a bit tricky, especially at night. In late 2004, Hurricane Ivan blew through town, downing many of the town's stately oak trees, severely damaging countless homes and commercial properties, and washing out bayfront roadways and a stretch of Interstate 10. Though much progress had been made as of this writing, most of the town's historic buildings were still closed and local businesses were in a state of recovery, so call for the latest updates on openings and conditions.

The best way to orient yourself is to stop at the **Pensacola Visitor Information Center,** at the foot of the Pensacola Bay Bridge. Pick up maps here of the self-guided historic-district tours. ✉ *1401 E. Gregory St.* ☎ *850/ 434–1234 or 800/874–1234* ⊕ *www.visitpensacola.com.*

The **Seville Square Historic District** is the site of Pensacola's first permanent Spanish colonial settlement. Its center is Seville Square, a live oak–shaded park bounded by Alcaniz, Adams, Zaragoza, and Government streets. Roam these brick streets past honeymoon cottages and bayfront homes. Many of the buildings have been converted into restaurants, commercial offices, and shops.

Within the Seville district is the **Historic Pensacola Village,** a complex of several museums, whose indoor and outdoor exhibits trace the area's history back 450 years. The Museum of Industry (200 E. Zaragoza St.), in a late 19th-century warehouse, hosts permanent exhibits dedicated to the lumber, maritime, and shipping industries—once mainstays of Pensacola's economy. A reproduction of a 19th-century streetscape is displayed in the Museum of Commerce (201 E. Zaragoza St.). Also in the village are the Julee Cottage (210 E. Zaragoza St.), Dorr House (311 S. Adams St.), Lavalle House (205 E. Church St.), and Quina House (204 S. Alcaniz St.). Strolling through the area gives you a good look at many architectural styles, but to enter the museums you must purchase an all-inclusive ticket at the T. T. Wentworth Jr. Florida State Museum (included in the admission price) or the Village gift shop in the Tivoli House. *Tivoli House* ⊠ *205 E. Zaragoza St.* ☎ *850/595–5985* ⊕ *www.historicpensacola.org* ⊠ *$6, including Wentworth Museum* ⊘ *Late Aug.–early June, weekdays 10–4; early June–mid-Aug., Mon.–Sat. 10–4.*

☝ This elaborate, Renaissance Revival–style structure, Pensacola's former City Hall, now houses the **T. T. Wentworth Jr. Florida State Museum.** It has an eclectic mixture of exhibits that children find especially intriguing—particularly Discovery, a hands-on exhibit on the third floor. ⊠ *330 S. Jefferson St.* ☎ *850/595–5990* ⊠ *$6, including Historic Pensacola Village* ⊘ *Late Aug.–early June, weekdays 10–4; early June–mid-Aug., Mon–Sat. 10–4.*

Palafox Street is the main stem of the **Palafox Historic District,** which was the commercial and government hub of Old Pensacola. Note the Spanish Renaissance–style **Saenger Theater,** Pensacola's old movie palace, and the **Bear Block,** a former wholesale grocery with wrought-iron balconies that are a legacy from Pensacola's Creole past. On Palafox between Government and Zaragoza streets is a **statue of Andrew Jackson** that commemorates the formal transfer of Florida from Spain to the United States in 1821. While in the area, stop by the Veterans Memorial Park, just off Bayfront Parkway near 9th Avenue. The ¾-scale replica of the Vietnam Memorial in Washington, D.C., honors the more than 58,000 men and women who lost their lives in the Vietnam War.

Pensacola's city jail once occupied the 1906 Spanish revival–style building that is now the **Pensacola Museum of Art.** It provides a secure home (you can still see the actual cells with their huge iron doors) for the museum's permanent collections of works on paper by 20th-century artists; traveling exhibits have focused on photography, Dutch masters, regional artists, and the occasional art world icon, such as Andy Warhol. ⊠ *407 S. Jefferson St.* ☎ *850/432–6247* ⊕ *www.pensacolamuseumofart. org* ⊠ *$5, free Tues.* ⊘ *Tues.–Fri. 10–5, weekends noon–5.*

The collections of the **Civil War Soldiers Museum** hold a large number of items pertaining to Civil War medicine as well as an equally impressive collection of Civil War books. ⊠ *108 S. Palafox Pl.* ☎ *850/469–1900* ⊕ *www.cwmuseum.org* ⊠ *$5* ⊘ *Tues.–Sat. 10–4:30.*

Pensacola's affluent families, many made rich in the turn-of-the-20th-century timber boom, built their homes in the **North Hill Preservation District,** where British and Spanish fortresses once stood. Residents still occasionally unearth cannonballs in their gardens. North Hill occupies 50 blocks, with more than 500 homes in Queen Anne, neoclassical, Tudor revival, and Mediterranean styles. Take a drive through this community, but remember these are private residences. Places of general interest include the 1902 Spanish mission–style **Christ Episcopal Church; Lee Square,** where a 50-foot obelisk stands as a tribute to the Confederacy; and **Fort George,** an undeveloped parcel at the site of the largest of three forts built by the British in 1778.

The **Pensacola Naval Air Station,** established in 1914, is the nation's oldest such facility. On display in the **National Museum of Naval Aviation** (☎ 850/452–3604) are more than 200 aircraft that played an important role in aviation history. Among them are the NC-4, which in 1919 became the first plane to cross the Atlantic; the famous World War II fighter the F6 *Hellcat*; and the Skylab Command Module. Other attractions include a 14-seat motion-based simulator, as well as an IMAX theater playing *The Magic of Flight* and other educational films, such as *Dolphins* and *Everest*. ✉ *1750 Radford Blvd.* ☎ *850/452–3604, 850/453–2024 IMAX theater* ⊕ *naval.aviation.museum* 🎟 *Free, IMAX film $6.50* ⊘ *Daily 9–5.*

Dating from the Civil War, **Fort Barrancas** has picnic areas and a ½-mi woodland nature trail on its grounds. The fort, which is just northeast of the Museum of Naval Aviation, is part of the Gulf Islands National Seashore, maintained by the National Park Service. ✉ *Navy Blvd.* ☎ *850/455–5167* 🎟 *Free* ⊘ *Nov.–Feb., daily 8:30–3:45; Mar.–Oct., daily 9:30–4:45.*

off the beaten path

THE ZOO – The local zoo, near Gulf Breeze, has more than 700 animals, including many endangered species. Kids especially enjoy the petting zoo, where they can touch most every critter on Old MacDonald's farm. Other attractions yield tigers, zebras, and more unusual creatures such as African wild dogs and pygmy hippos, and there's a tall platform where you can have face-to-face meetings with giraffes. The Safari Line Limited train roams through 30 acres of free-roaming animals in their natural habitats. ✉ *5701 Gulf Breeze Pkwy., Gulf Breeze* ☎ *850/932–2229* ⊕ *www.the-zoo.com* 🎟 *$10.95 (safari train $3 extra)* ⊘ *Daily 9–4 during standard time; daily 9–5 during daylight saving time.*

Where to Stay & Eat

$$–$$$ ✕ **Dharma Blue.** Geographically speaking, this trendy spot is in downtown Pensacola, on leafy Seville Square, but culinarily speaking it's all over the map. The menu roams from Asia (sushi and spring roll appetizers) to Italy (grilled vegetables with risotto) to Mexico (lime-roasted chicken quesadilla) to the American South (fried green tomato club sandwich)—but just stick close to home and you won't be disappointed. The lunch menu includes barbecue salmon with lemon coleslaw and Texas toast, focaccia BLT, or fish-and-chips. For dinner try tomato-crusted grouper with caper cream sauce, the fish of the day (blackened, grilled, or tempura-fried), or Guinness-marinated sirloin with chipotle aioli. Dine inside under a collection of Southern folk art, or outside under café umbrellas and droopy oaks. ✉ *300 S. Alcaniz St.* ☎ *850/433–1275* 🍴 *AE, MC, V* ⊘ *No lunch Sun.*

$-$$$ ✕ **Mesquite Charlie's.** Saddle up and head on over to this Wild West saloon, with brick walls, arched doorways, mounted game, and a second-floor balcony overlooking the lobby. All that's missing are the swinging doors. The 32-ounce porterhouse is large enough to satisfy a posse of cowboys and, in a publicity schtick lifted straight from a "Simpson's" episode, the monster-sized 76-ounce sirloin is free if you finish it in less than an hour. All are charbroiled with 100% mesquite charcoal and seasoned with natural spices. ⊠ *5901 N. W St.* ☎ *850/434–0498* ▤ *AE, D, MC, V.*

¢-$$$ ✕ **McGuire's Irish Pub.** Spend anywhere from $10 to $100 for a hamburger here, depending on whether you want it topped with cheddar or served with caviar and champagne. Beer is brewed on the premises, and the wine cellar has more than 8,000 bottles. Menu items include Irish-style corned beef and cabbage and a hickory-smoked prime rib. In an old firehouse, the pub is replete with antiques, moose heads, Tiffany-style lamps, and Erin-go-bragh memorabilia. More than 275,000 dollar bills signed and dated by the pub's patrons flutter from the ceiling. ⊠ *600 E. Gregory St.* ☎ *850/433–6789* ▤ *AE, D, DC, MC, V.*

¢-$ ✕ **Ragtyme Grille.** Downtown's historic Economy Shoe Repair building now houses this intimate corner eatery that's become a favorite of local journalists (the *Pensacola News-Journal* offices are across the street). Choose from standard deli sandwiches (reubens, corned beef), po' boys, and grilled fish specials; salads—with fresh fish, fruit, or chicken—and burgers round out the menu. Grab a table inside, or relax over a beer, margarita, or glass of wine on the covered patio. Homestyle breakfast—hash browns, grits, eggs however you want them—is served on weekends. ⊠ *201 S. Jefferson St.* ☎ *850/429–9655* ▤ *AE, MC, V.*

$$ 🏨 **Residence Inn by Marriott.** In the downtown bay-front area, this immaculately kept all-suites hotel is perfect for extended stays, whether for business or pleasure. The location is ideal for exploring Pensacola's historic streets on foot—rooms in the back have views of the bay—and families will especially appreciate the fully equipped kitchens and free grocery delivery. Breakfast and evening social hour are complimentary. ⊠ *601 E. Chase St., 32502* ☎ *850/432–0202* 🖷 *850/438–7965* ⊕ *www.residenceinn.com* ⇌ *78 suites* ⌂ *Kitchens, microwaves, refrigerators, cable TV, tennis court, pool, gym, some pets allowed (fee)* ▤ *AE, D, DC, MC, V.*

★ ¢-$$ 🏨 **New World Inn.** If a small, warm, and cozy inn sounds appealing, this is the place for you. In the downtown historic area two blocks from Pensacola Bay, it contains furnishings that reflect the five periods of Pensacola's past: French and Spanish provincial, Early American, antebellum, and Queen Anne. Several rooms have four-poster mahogany beds, and the exquisite baths are handsomely appointed. The lobby's collection of signed portraits of famous former guests (and formerly famous guests!) is a hoot. ⊠ *600 S. Palafox St., 32502* ☎ *850/432–4111* 🖷 *850/432–6836* ⊕ *www.newworldlanding.com* ⇌ *14 rooms, 1 suite* ⌂ *Cable TV, meeting rooms* ▤ *AE, MC, V* ⃝ *CP.*

Nightlife & the Arts

THE ARTS The **Pensacola Little Theatre** (⊠ 400 S. Jefferson St. ☎ 850/432–2042) presents plays and musicals year-round. **Pensacola's Symphony Orches-**

tra (☎ 850/435–2533) offers 11 concerts each season at the Saenger Theatre. Productions at the restored 1926 **Saenger Theatre** (✉ 118 S. Palafox St. ☎ 850/444–7686 ⊕ www.pensacolasaenger.com) include touring Broadway shows and three locally staged operas a year.

NIGHTLIFE **Emerald City** (✉ 406 E. Wright St. ☎ 850/433–9491) is a straight-friendly gay dance bar across from the Crowne Plaza hotel downtown. Nightly drink specials, karaoke nights, and drag performances keep the party going Wednesday through Monday. After dark, **McGuire's Irish Pub** (✉ 600 E. Gregory St. ☎ 850/433–6789) welcomes those of Irish descent or anyone else who enjoys cold ale, beer, or lager. If you don't like crowds, stay away from McGuire's on Friday night and when Notre Dame games are televised. **Mesquite Charlie's** (✉ 5901 N. W St. ☎ 850/434–0498) offers country music and all the Western trappings. The **Seville Quarter** (✉ 130 E. Government St. ☎ 850/434–6211) has seven fabulous bars offering everything from disco to dueling pianos, Motown acts, blues bands, rockabilly trios—you name it. It's Pensacola's equivalent of the New Orleans French Quarter.

Sports & the Outdoors

CANOEING & **Adventures Unlimited** (✉ Rte. 87, 12 mi north of Milton ☎ 850/623–6197
KAYAKING or 800/239–6864), on Coldwater Creek, rents light watercraft as well as campsites and cabins. Canoe season lasts roughly from March through mid-November, but they rent year-round. Canoe and kayak rentals for exploring the Blackwater River—the state's only sand-bottom river, and one of only three in the world—are available from **Blackwater Canoe Rental** (✉ 6974 Deaton Bridge Rd., Milton ☎ 850/623–0235 or 800/967–6789), northeast of Pensacola off I–10 Exit 10.

DOG RACING Rain or shine, year-round there's live racing at the **Pensacola Greyhound Track.** Lounge and grandstand areas are fully enclosed and air-conditioned and have instant-replay televisions throughout. ✉ *951 Dog Track Rd., West Pensacola* ☎ *850/455–8595* ▣ *Evenings $2, matinees free* ☉ *Racing Wed.–Sat. at 7, weekends at 1.*

FISHING In a pinch you can drop a line from Old Pensacola Bay Bridge. For a full- or half-day deep-sea charter ($75–$95 per person), try the **Beach Marina** (✉ 655 Pensacola Beach Blvd. ☎ 850/932–8466), which represents several charter outfits.

GOLF There are several outstanding golf courses in and around Pensacola. **The Club at Hidden Creek** (✉ 3070 PGA Blvd., Navarre ☎ 850/939–4604) is an 18-hole course in Santa Rosa County, 20 mi from Pensacola, green fee: $29/$69 with cart. **The Moors Golf Club** (✉ 3220 Avalon Blvd., Milton ☎ 850/994–2744), is a public, 18-hole, par-70, Scottish links–style course, green fee: $33/$47. The course was designed by John LaFoy and is well known as the home of the Senior PGA Tour Emerald Coast Classic. The **Perdido Bay Golf Club** (✉ 1 Doug Ford Dr. ☎ 850/492–1223) has a well-kept 18-hole course, green fee: $35/$50 with cart. **Tiger Point Golf & Country Club** (✉ 1255 Country Club Rd., Gulf Breeze ☎ 850/932–1330) is a semiprivate 36-hole club, green fee: $35/$75 with cart.

TENNIS There are fine public tennis courts in more than 30 locations in the Pensacola area. The **Pensacola Racquet Club** (✉ 3450 Wimbledon Dr. ☎ 850/434–2434) has 10 clay and 2 hard courts, plus a pool and restaurant.

Shopping

Cordova Mall (✉ 5100 N. 9th Ave. ☎ 850/477–5563), anchored by three department stores, has specialty shops and a food court. **Harbourtown Shopping Village** (✉ 913 Gulf Breeze Pkwy., Gulf Breeze) has trendy shops and the look of a wharfside New England village.

Pensacola Beach

❷ *5 mi south of Pensacola via U.S. 98 to Rte. 399 (Bob Sikes) Bridge.*

When hurricane Opal tore across this skinny barrier island in 1995, the damaged areas were redeveloped, sand was brought in to fill the eroded beachfront, and beach facilities and parking were added to what came to be known as the "Opal Day Use Area," named in honor of the hurricane responsible for the destruction. A local bartender even invented a potent but short-lived concoction called a "Raging Opal" to commemorate the storm.

It's doubtful, however, that any public parks or cocktails will be named after Hurricane Ivan, which completely devastated the area in 2004. That's because this category IV storm, which caused a level of destruction not seen in these parts for nearly a century, wasn't an event that anyone around here cares to remember. The storm's tidal surge washed completely over the island in several places, and the obvious reminders of Ivan's visit—washed out roads, decimated homes, uprooted lives, and erased sand dunes—will be visible for years to come.

Since the national media focused its attention on Pensacola Beach for not much longer than it took the storm to do its damage, the scope of the disaster might come as a surprise to many visitors: nearly half of the island's homes were totalled and will have to be rebuilt from the ground up; all of the island's hotels were closed for months (some will never reopen); and the miles of sea oat–covered, pristine dunes, which protected the island from winter storms and gave the area its laid-back Florida look, were leveled in hours. In short, Pensacola Beach is a city changed.

But locals here know the post-Hurricane drill: dig in, dig out, and move on. As of this writing, several hotels had reopened after complete renovations, homes and condos were being demolished or rebuilt, and city and state crews had made significant progress in reconnecting roads to areas of the island rendered inaccessible by the storm. Since some of the information below is based on estimated reopening schedules, it's best to call to check on the status before venturing out to Pensacola Beach.

Dotting the 150-mi stretch between Destin and Gulfport, Mississippi is **Gulf Islands National Seashore** (☎ 850/934–2600 ⊕ www.nps.gov/guis), managed by the National Park Service. Parts of this massive seashore were damaged by Hurricane Ivan, but you'll still find great beaches and recreational spots along this beautiful stretch of island coast. It's open year-round, but there are seasonal restrictions and closings for repairs, so call ahead.

The 1,471-foot-long **Pensacola Beach Gulf Pier** bills itself as the longest pier on the Gulf of Mexico. Serious anglers will find everything they'll need—from pole rentals to bait—to land that big one, but those looking to catch only a beautiful sunset are welcome, too. Check the pier's Web site for the latest fishing reports on what's biting. ⊠ *41 Ft. Pickens Rd.* ☎ *850/934–7200* ⊕ *www.fishpensacolabeachpier.com* ⊠ *Observers $1, fishing $6.50.*

Where to Stay & Eat

¢–$$$ ✕ **Flounder's Chowder and Ale House.** Combine a gulf-front view at this casual restaurant with a fruity tropical libation, and you're all set for a night of "floundering" at its best. An eclectic collection of antiques and objets d'art contributes to the overall funkiness. The house specialty is seafood charbroiled over a hardwood fire, but the extensive menu has choices for those who don't love fish. There's live entertainment every night in season (on weekends only in off season). ⊠ *800 Quietwater Beach Blvd.* ☎ *850/932–2003* ⊟ *AE, D, DC, MC, V.*

¢–$ ✕ **The Market on the Island.** This windowless grocery/deli/wine shop/ship's store fronting a marina is one-stop shopping for all your vacation needs—and for heaps of the island's latest gossip, too. Made-to-order breakfasts (homemade biscuits, grits, and white-sausage gravy are all contenders) and lunchtime salads and sandwiches aren't fancy or adventurous, but they are fast, inexpensive, and delicious. Order from the counter, then grab a chair and wait for your number, or browse around the only store in the Panhandle that has an impressive selection of both artificial lures *and* high-end sake. The chicken-and-sausage gumbo—a must-have for visitors and a staple for locals—is so popular that it's sold by the gallon ($29.99, rice not included). ⊠ *657 Pensacola Beach Blvd.* ☎ *850/916–7192* ⊟ *AE, MC, V.*

$$$ ▥ **Hampton Inn Pensacola Beach.** The exterior's pink-and-green color scheme is reminiscent of Miami Beach's art deco buildings, and the easygoing Florida style continues inside. Directly on the gulf and centrally located, this lodging is within walking distance of several popular restaurants and shops. Most rooms have a gulf view, and all are oversized. Gulf-front rooms have private balconies. There's an evening cocktail hour, and an expansive Continental breakfast buffet is served. ⊠ *2 Via de Luna Dr., 32561* ☎ *850/932–6800 or 800/320–8108* ⊟ *850/932–6833* ⊕ *www.hamptonbeachresort.com* ⊅ *181 rooms* ⚒ *Microwaves, refrigerators, cable TV with movies, 2 pools, gym, beach, bar* ⊟ *AE, D, DC, MC, V* ☉ *CP.*

$$$ ▥ **Hilton Garden Inn.** A spacious, beige-on-white two-story atrium with ceramic tile and marble accents creates an elegant welcome to this impeccably-kept Gulf-front chain hotel. Thoughtful touches such as Neutrogena toiletries, in-room coffeemakers with complimentary coffee, and spacious desks with high-speed Internet access make this a perfect place for business or pleasure (you'll even find backup batteries in your alarm clock). Rooms, all of which were completely refitted after Hurricane Ivan came calling in 2004, have floral print bedspreads, cherry-wood fur-

nishings, and neutral-tone accents and headboards. Ask for an upper-floor room facing the Gulf for a view you won't forget. ⊠ *12 Via De Luna Dr., 32561* ☎ *850/916–2999 or 877/782–9444* 🖷 *850/934–0891* ⊕ *www.hiltongardeninn.com* ↩ *181 rooms* 🛆 *Restaurant, bar, microwaves, refrigerators, cable TV, pool, volleyball, meeting rooms* ⊟ *AE, D, DC, MC, V.*

¢–$$ 🎞 **Comfort Inn Pensacola Beach.** One of the best deals on the beach—and the first hotel to reopen after Hurricane Ivan—this spotless, four-story property sits on the bay side overlooking Little Sabine Bay, but the upper floors have views of the gulf just across the street. Breezy, floral-print fabrics and rattan furnishings lend a cheeriness to the guest rooms, and complimentary Continental breakfast and free local phone calls seal the deal. Restaurants and shops are within walking distance. ⊠ *40 Fort Pickens Rd., 32561* ☎ *850/934–5400 or 800/934–5470* 🖷 *850/932–7210* ⊕ *www.comfortinn.com* ↩ *99 rooms* 🛆 *Picnic area, microwaves, refrigerators, cable TV, pool, volleyball, meeting rooms* ⊟ *AE, D, DC, MC, V* ⑂ *CP.*

THE GULF COAST

On U.S. 98, several towns, each with its own personality, are strung along the shoreline from Pensacola southeast to St. George Island. The twin cities of Destin and Fort Walton Beach seemingly merge into one sprawling destination and continue to spread as more condominiums, resort developments, shopping centers, and restaurants crowd the skyline each year. The view changes drastically farther along the coast as you enter the quiet stretch known as the Beaches of South Walton, scattered along Route 30-A, the main coastal road. Here building restrictions prohibit high-rise developments, and the majority of dwellings are privately owned homes, most of which are available to vacationers. A total of 19 beach communities cluster along this quiet strip of Route 30-A off U.S. 98. Many are little more than a wide spot in the road, and all are among the least-known and least-developed in the Gulf Coast area, even though Grayton Beach is regularly ranked among the country's top 20 beaches. Seaside, which reached its quarter-century mark in 2006, is a thriving planned community with old-fashioned Victorian architecture, brick streets, restaurants, retail stores—and a surfeit of art galleries.

Continuing southeast on U.S. 98, you'll find Panama City Beach, whose "Miracle Strip," once crammed with carnival-like amusement parks, junk-food vendors, T-shirt shops, and go-kart tracks, is in the middle of a building frenzy that will double the number of condominiums and give the area a much needed facelift. Farther east, past the up-and-coming sleeper cities of Port St. Joe and Mexico Beach (these days, the din of construction drowns out the sounds of surf all along this coast), you'll come to the quiet blue-collar town of Apalachicola, Florida's main oyster fishery. Watch oystermen ply their trade, using long-handled tongs to bring in their catch. Cross the Apalachicola Bay via the Bryant Patton Bridge to St. George Island. This unspoiled 28-mi-long barrier island offers some of America's most scenic beaches, including St. George Island State Park, which has the longest beachfront of any state park in Florida.

Fort Walton Beach

③ *46 mi east of Pensacola.*

This coastal town dates from the Civil War but had to wait more than 75 years to come into its own. Patriots loyal to the Confederate cause organized Walton's Guard (named in honor of Colonel George Walton, onetime acting Territorial governor of West Florida) and camped at a site on Santa Rosa Sound, later known as Camp Walton. In 1940 fewer than 90 people lived in Fort Walton Beach, but within a decade the city became a boomtown, thanks to New Deal money for roads and bridges and the development of Eglin Field during World War II. The military is now Fort Walton Beach's main source of income, but tourism runs a close second.

Encompassing 724 square mi of land, **Eglin Air Force Base** includes 10 auxiliary fields and a total of 21 runways. Jimmie Doolittle's Tokyo Raiders trained here, as did the Son Tay Raiders, a group that made a daring attempt to rescue American POWs from a North Vietnamese prison camp in 1970. Off-limits to civilians, there are private tours for ROTC and military reunion groups. ⊠ *Rte. 85* ☎ *850/882–3931* ⊕ *www. eglin.af.mil.*

★ The collection at the **Air Force Armament Museum,** just outside the Eglin Air Force Base's main gate, contains more than 5,000 air force armaments from World Wars I and II and the Korean and Vietnam wars. Included are uniforms, engines, weapons, aircraft, and flight simulators; larger craft such as transport planes are exhibited on the grounds outside. A 32-minute movie about Eglin's history and its role in the development of armaments plays continuously. ⊠ *Rte. 85, Eglin Air Force Base* ☎ *850/882–4062* ⊠ *Free* ⊙ *Daily 9:30–4:30.*

John C. Beasley Wayside Park is Fort Walton Beach's seaside playground on Okaloosa Island. A boardwalk leads to the beach, where there are covered picnic tables, changing rooms, and freshwater showers. Lifeguards are on duty in summer. ⊠ *Okaloosa Island* ☎ *No phone.*

☾ Kids especially enjoy the **Indian Temple Mound and Museum,** where they can learn all about the prehistoric peoples who inhabited northwest Florida up to 10,000 years ago. It's a small museum, but the prehistoric Native American artifacts and weaponry on display are particularly fascinating, as are the few hands-on exhibits. The museum is adjacent to the 800-year-old **National Historic Landmark Temple Mound,** a large earthwork built near saltwater. ⊠ *139 Miracle Strip Pkwy. SE (U.S. 98)* ☎ *850/ 833–9595* ⊠ *$2* ⊙ *Weekdays 10–4, Sat. 9–4.*

☾ When the weather drives you off the beach, the **Gulfarium** is a great place to spend your time. Its main attraction is the Living Sea, a 60,000-gallon tank that simulates conditions on the ocean floor. See campy performances by trained porpoises, sea-lion shows, and marine-life exhibits (a new multispecies act includes dolphins and sea lions in the same show). Don't overlook the old-fashioned Dolphin Reef gift shop, where you can buy anything from conch shells to beach toys. There's also a dolphin interaction program, but you don't swim with them. Instead, you sit in a pool as spotted dolphins swim up to your lap. ⊠ *U.S. 98 E* ☏*850/ 243–9046 or 800/247–8575* ⊕ *www.gulfarium.com* ⬚ *$16.99, dolphin interaction $100* ☉ *Sept.–May, daily 9–4; June–Aug., daily 9–6.*

Where to Stay & Eat

★ **$$–$$$** ✕ **Pandora's Steakhouse and Lounge.** On the Emerald Coast the name Pandora's is synonymous with prime rib. The weather-beaten exterior gives way to a warm and cozy interior with alcoves and tables for four that lend an air of intimacy. Steaks are cooked over a wood-burning grill, and you can order your prime rib regular or extra-cut; fish aficionados should try the char-grilled yellowfin tuna or one of the daily fish specials. The mood turns a bit more gregarious in the lounge, where there's live entertainment Wednesday through Saturday. ⊠ *1120 Santa Rosa Blvd.* ☏ *850/244–8669* ⊟ *AE, D, DC, MC, V* ☉ *Closed Mon.*

$$–$$$ ✕ **Staff's.** Sip a Tropical Depression or a rum-laced Squall Line while you peruse a menu tucked into the centerfold of a tabloid-size newspaper filled with snippets of local history, early photographs, and family memorabilia. Since 1913 folks have been coming to this garage turned eatery for steaks and seafood dishes like Florida lobster and char-grilled amberjack. The grand finale is a trip to the delectable dessert bar; try a generous wedge of cherry cheesecake. ⊠ *24 Miracle Strip Pkwy. SE* ☏ *850/243–3482* ⊟ *AE, D, MC, V.*

Nightlife & the Arts

THE ARTS   Based in Fort Walton Beach, the **Northwest Florida Ballet** (☏ 850/664– 7787) has presented classical and contemporary dance performances to audiences along the Gulf Coast since 1969. Call for season schedule and ticket information as well as their current performance venue.

NIGHTLIFE   Dueling pianos (Wednesday through Sunday only) and a beachfront bar fuel the furious sing-alongs that make **Howl at the Moon** (⊠ 1450 Miracle Strip Pkwy. ☏ 850/301–0111), at the Boardwalk on Okaloosa Island, one of Fort Walton's most popular evening entertainment spots. The place rocks every night until 2 AM but can go as late as 4 AM in season.

Sports & the Outdoors

BIKING   **Eglin Air Force Base Reservation** is the size of Rhode Island—1,045 square mi, 463,448 acres—and has 810 mi of creeks and plenty of challenging, twisting wooded trails. You can bike here from 7 AM to 4:30 PM Monday through Saturday only with a $5 permit, which can be obtained from the **Jackson Guard** (⊠ 107 Rte. 85 N, Niceville ☏ 850/882– 4164).

FISHING   **Harbor Walk Marina** (⊠ 66 U.S. 98 E, Destin 32541 ☏ 850/337–8250) is a rustic-looking waterfront complex where you can get bait, gas, tackle, food, and anything else you might need for a day of fishing. Party fishing boat excursions cost as little as $40, a cheaper alternative to chartering or renting your own boat.

GOLF   The **Fort Walton Beach Golf Club** (⊠ Rte. 189 ☏ 850/833–9529) is a 36-hole municipal course whose links (Oaks and Pines) lie about 400 yards from each other. The two courses are considered by many to be one of

Florida's best public layouts, green fee: $33 with a shared cart. **Shalimar Pointe Golf & Country Club** (✉ 302 Country Club Dr., Shalimar ☎ 850/651–1416) has 18 holes with a pleasing mix of water and bunkers, green fee: $35/$45 with cart.

SCUBA DIVING Take diving lessons, arrange excursions, and rent all the necessary equipment at the **Scuba Shop** (✉ 348 Miracle Strip Pkwy. ☎ 850/243–1600). Don't expect clear Caribbean waters in the gulf: visibility is about 20–50 feet, and diving depths range between 50 feet and 90 feet—not great, but not too bad.

TENNIS Play tennis on seven Rubico and two hard courts at the **Fort Walton Racquet Club** (✉ 1819 Hurlburt Rd. ☎ 850/862–2023). There's a practice wall for solo players, too. The **Municipal Tennis Center** (✉ 45 W. Audrey Dr. ☎ 850/833–9588) has 12 lighted hard courts, four racquetball courts, and four practice walls.

Shopping

Stores in the **Manufacturer's Outlet Center** (✉ 255 Miracle Strip Pkwy.) offer well-known brands of clothing and housewares at a substantial discount. There are four department stores in the **Santa Rosa Mall** (✉ 300 Mary Esther Blvd., Mary Esther ☎ 850/244–2172), as well as 118 other shops, 15 bistro-style eateries, and a 10-screen movie theater.

Destin

❹ *8 mi east of Fort Walton Beach.*

Fort Walton Beach's neighbor lies on the other side of the strait that connects Choctawhatchee Bay with the Gulf of Mexico. Destin takes its name from its founder, Leonard A. Destin, a Connecticut sea captain who settled his family here sometime in the 1830s. For the next 100 years Destin remained a sleepy little fishing village until the strait, or East Pass, was bridged in 1935. Then recreational anglers discovered its white sands, blue-green waters, and abundance of some of the most sought-after sport fish in the world. More billfish are hauled in around Destin each year than from all other gulf fishing ports combined, giving credence to its nickname, the World's Luckiest Fishing Village. But you don't have to be the rod-and-reel type to love Destin. There's plenty to entertain the sand-pail set as well as senior citizens, and there are many nice restaurants, which you'll have an easier time finding if you remember that the main drag through town is referred to as both U.S. 98 and Emerald Coast Parkway. The name makes sense, but part of what makes the Gulf look so emerald in these parts is the contrasting whiteness of the sand on the beach. Actually, it's not sand—it's pure, powder-soft Appalachian quartz that was dropped off by a glacier a few thousand years back. Since quartz doesn't compress (and crews clean and rake the beach each evening), your tootsies get the sole-satisfying benefit of soft, sugary "sand."

☾ In addition to a seasonal water park, **Big Kahuna's Lost Paradise** has year-round family attractions, including 54 holes of miniature golf, two go-cart tracks, an arcade, thrill rides for kids of all ages, and an amphitheater. ✉ *U.S. 98 E* ☎ *850/837–4061* ⊕ *www.bigkahunas.com* ▣ *Grounds* *free, water park $29.95, miniature golf $5, go-carts $5.50* ✪ *Water park: May–Labor Day, weekends 10–5; Labor Day–mid-Sept., daily 10 AM– midnight. Water park closed mid-Sept.–Apr.*

off the beaten path

FRED GANNON ROCKY BAYOU STATE PARK – North of Destin is a quiet park offering picnic areas, nature trails, boat ramps, and 42 uncrowded campsites with electrical and water hookups. It's secluded yet easy to find. ✉ *4281 Rte. 20, Niceville* ☎ *850/833–9144* ✆ *Day use $2 per vehicle, campsites $8.48, $10.60 with electricity* ✪ *Daily 8–sunset.*

Where to Stay & Eat

$$$ ✕ **Bistro Bijoux.** Part of the Baytowne Wharf development at Sandestin Resort, this sleek spot serving Italian-tinged seafood became an instant local favorite when it opened in 2003. Starters include steamed mussels with garlic, fennel, and basil; cassoulet of shrimp and scallops; and fried-oyster salad with baby spinach and balsamic-bacon dressing. For dinner there's baked black grouper with artichokes and sun-dried tomatoes, seafood bouillabaisse, braised osso buco, steaks, and pasta and risotto dishes. The bar, with its velvet occasional chairs, minimalist fireplace, and swank decor, is one of the classiest around. In fall or spring ask for a seat on the outdoor terrace overlooking the lagoon. ✉ *9300 Emerald Coast Pkwy. W* ☎ *850/622–0760* ⊟ *AE, D, DC, MC, V* ✪ *No lunch.*

★ $$–$$$ ✕ **Marina Café.** A harbor view, impeccable service, and sophisticated fare create one of the finest dining experiences on the Emerald Coast. The ocean motif is expressed in shades of aqua, green, and sand accented with marine tapestries and sea sculptures. The chef calls his creations contemporary Continental, offering diners a choice of classic creole, Mediterranean, or Pacific Rim dishes. One regional specialty is the popular black pepper–crusted yellowfin tuna with braised spinach and spicy soy sauce. The menu changes daily, and the wine list is extensive. ✉ *404 U.S. 98 E* ☎ *850/837–7960* ⊟ *AE, D, DC, MC, V* ✪ *No lunch.*

$–$$$ ✕ **Louisiana Lagniappe.** In Louisiana when you say *lagniappe,* it means you're getting a little something extra—here it's the extra zing fresh local seafood gets when transformed into Cajun-style cuisine. You can't go wrong ordering Cajun standards like shrimp creole, crab bisque, and crawfish étouffée. Locals love the chef's innovations such as grouper coco-drie, sautéed and topped with fried crawfish, artichoke hearts, and a rich béarnaise sauce. There's outside dining overlooking Destin Harbor and delicious sunset views, whether you're dining inside or out. ✉ *775 Gulf Shore Dr., at Sandpiper Cove* ☎ *850/837–0881* ✍ *Reservations not accepted* ⊟ *AE, D, DC, MC, V* ✪ *No lunch.*

$$$–$$$$ ▥ **Henderson Park Inn.** Tucked discreetly away at the end of a quiet road bordering Henderson Beach State Park, this B&B has become Destin's premier getaway for couples seeking elegance and pampering. A green mansard roof and shingle siding are reminiscent of Queen Anne–era architecture and complement the inn's Victorian-era furnishings. Some rooms are furnished with a four-poster, canopied, or iron bed draped with fine linen. You'll find plush robes and refrigerators with ice makers in all rooms. Be sure to ask for a room with a balcony, perfect for admiring the gulf's smashing sunsets. ✉ *2700 Scenic U.S. 98 E, 32541* ☎ *850/654–0400 or 800/336–4853* 🖷 *850/654–0405* ⊕ *www.hendersonparkinn.com* 📶 *36 rooms* ⚘ *Restaurant, some microwaves, some refrigerators, cable TV, pool, beach; no kids* ▭ *AE, D, MC, V.*

$$$–$$$$ 🏨 **Holiday Inn Destin.** Lounge on sugar-white sands, get to several golf courses with ease, and walk to some of Destin's amusement parks. Common areas jazzed up with skylights and greenery are spacious and eye-pleasing. The standard rooms are uniformly bright and well kept; prices vary depending on the view. ✉ *1020 U.S. 98 E, 32541* ☎ *850/837–6181* 🖷 *850/837–1523* ⊕ *www.hidestin.com* 📶 *233 rooms* ⚘ *Restaurant, cable TV, 3 pools, beach, bar* ▭ *AE, D, DC, MC, V.*

$$$ 🏨 **Sandestin Golf and Beach Resort.** Newlyweds, conventioneers, and fam-
Fodor'sChoice   ilies all fit in at this 2,400-acre resort with villas, cottages, condominiums,
★   boat slips, and an inn. A recent addition is Baytowne Wharf, a "festival marketplace" of shops and restaurants; the Lagoons, a 7-acre family-friendly water park, is in the works. All rooms have a view, either of the gulf, Choctawhatchee Bay, a golf course, a lagoon, or a natural wildlife preserve. This resort accommodates an assortment of tastes, from the simple to the extravagant, but the gigantic suites at the Westwinds are a cut above the rest. ✉ *9300 U.S. 98 W, 32550* ☎ *850/267–8000 or 800/277–0800* 🖷 *850/267–8222* ⊕ *www.sandestin.com* 📶 *175 rooms, 250 condos, 275 villas* ⚘ *10 restaurants, some kitchens, some microwaves, some refrigerators, 4 18-hole golf courses, 15 tennis courts, pro shop, 15 pools, health club, beach, dock, 3 bars* ▭ *AE, D, DC, MC, V.*

★ $–$$ 🏨 **Bluewater Bay Golf & Tennis Resort.** Popular for its 36 holes of championship golf (on courses designed by Jerry Pate and Tom Fazio), this upscale resort is 12 mi north of Destin via the Mid-Bay Bridge on the shores of Choctawhatchee Bay. It offers vacation rentals ranging from motel rooms to villas to patio homes. Tennis courts are privately owned, but guests can use them for a special rate. ✉ *1940 Bluewater Blvd., Niceville 32578* ☎ *850/897–3613 or 800/874–2128* 🖷 *850/897–2424* ⊕ *www.bwbresort.com* 📶 *85 units* ⚘ *Restaurant, cable TV, 36-hole golf course, 19 tennis courts, 4 pools, bar, playground* ▭ *AE, D, DC, MC, V.*

Nightlife

Folks come by boat and car to **AJ's Club Bimini** (✉ 116 U.S. 98 E ☎ 850/837–1913), a supercasual bar and restaurant overlooking a marina. Nightly live music means young, lively crowds pack the dance floor. At the **Village of Baytowne Wharf** (✉ 9300 Emerald Coast Pkwy. W ☎ 850/267–8117), a nightlife and shopping development with the feel of a small village, you can amble from a piano bar to blues club to an intimate martini bar (there's about a dozen options altogether). It's inside the Sandestin Golf and Beach Resort. **Harbor Docks** (✉ 538 U.S. 98 E ☎ 850/837–2506) is another favorite with the local sea-faring set. It's famous for live music and, oddly enough, high-quality sushi. The **Hog's Breath Saloon** (✉ 541 U.S. 98 E ☎ 850/837–5991), a chain hot spot with other locations in Key West and Fort Walton Beach, presents live music Wednesday through Sunday. The food—steaks, burgers, salads—isn't bad, either. Café Grazie's **Sky Bar** (✉ 1771 U.S. 98 E ☎ 850/837–7475) draws a more mature crowd for dancing, cocktails, and live music.

Sports & the Outdoors

FISHING   Pier-fish from the 3,000-foot-long Destin Catwalk, along the East Pass Bridge. **Adventure Charters** (⊠ East Pass Marina, 288 U.S. 98 E ☎ 850/654–4070) offers deep-sea, bay-bottom, and light-tackle fishing excursions. **East Pass Bait and Tackle** (⊠ East Pass Marina, 288 U.S. 98 E ☎ 850/837–2622) sells bait, tackle, and most anything else you'd need for a day of fishing.

GOLF   **Bluewater Bay Resort** (⊠ 1950 Bluewater Blvd., Niceville ☎ 850/897–3241 or 800/874–2128), 6 mi east of Niceville via Route 20 East, has 36 holes of championship golf on courses designed by Jerry Pate and Tom Fazio, green fee: $69 with cart. The **Indian Bayou Golf & Country Club** (⊠ 1 Country Club Dr. E, off Airport Rd., off U.S. 98 ☎ 850/837–6192) has a 27-hole course, green fee: $59/$79 with cart. The 18-hole, Fred Couples-Gene Bates–designed **Kelly Plantation Golf Club** (⊠ 34851 Emerald Coast Pkwy. ☎ 850/650–7600) is a semiprivate course that runs along Choctawhatchee Bay, green fee: $60/$125 with cart. There's an 18-hole, semiprivate course, green fee: $59/$114, at **Regatta Bay Golf & Country Club** (⊠ 465 Regatta Bay Blvd. ☎ 850/337–8080). For sheer number of holes, the **Sandestin Golf and Beach Resort** (⊠ 9300 U.S. 98 W ☎ 850/267–8211) tops the list, with 72. There are four courses: Baytowne Golf Club at Sandestin, green fee: $65/$109; Burnt Pines Course, green fee: $85/$149; Links Course, green fee: $65/$109; and the Raven Golf Club, green fee: $79/$129.

SCUBA DIVING   Scuba-diving and snorkeling instruction and outings are available through **Emerald Coast Scuba** (⊠ 110 Melvin St. ☎ 850/837–0955 or 800/222–0955).

TENNIS   The **Destin Racquet & Fitness Center** (⊠ 995 Airport Rd. ☎ 850/837–7300) has six Rubico courts. **Sandestin Golf and Beach Resort** (⊠ 9300 U.S. 98 W ☎ 850/267–7110), one of the nation's five-star tennis resorts, has 15 courts with grass, hard, and Rubico surfaces.

Shopping

The **Market at Sandestin** (⊠ 9300 Emerald Coast Pkwy. W, Sandestin ☎ 850/267–8092) has about two-dozen upscale shops that peddle such goods as expensive chocolates and designer clothes in an elegant mini-mall with boardwalks. It also has the area's only Starbucks Coffee franchise. **Silver Sands Factory Stores** (⊠ 10562 Emerald Coast Pkwy. W ☎ 850/654–9771) is one of the Southeast's largest retail outlets. More than 100 shops sell top-name merchandise that ranges from gifts to kids' clothes to menswear.

Grayton Beach

❺ *18 mi east of Destin.*

The 26-mi stretch of coastline between Destin and Panama City Beach is referred to as the Beaches of South Walton. From the middle of this mostly residential stretch of the Panhandle you can see the monolithic condos of Destin and Panama City Beach in either direction, like massive bookends in the distance, flanking the area's low-slung, less imposing structures. A decidedly laid-back, refined mood prevails in these parts, where vacation homes go for millions and selecting a dinner spot is usually the day's most challenging decision. Accommodations consist primarily of private-home rentals, the majority of which are managed by local real estate firms. Also scattered along Route 30A are a growing number of boutiques selling everything from fine art to unique hand-painted furniture, to jewelry, gifts, and clothes. Inland, pine forests and hardwoods surround the area's 14 dune lakes, giving anglers ample spots to drop a line and kayakers a peaceful refuge. Grayton Beach, the oldest community in this area, has reached its 100-year mark. You can still see some of the old weathered-cypress homes scattered along sandy streets. The town has taken off with the addition of WaterColor, a high-end development of vacation homes with a stylish boutique hotel as its centerpiece. The architecture is tasteful, development is carefully regulated—no buildings taller than four stories are allowed—and bicycles and kayaks are the preferred method of transportation. Stringent building restrictions, designed to protect the pristine beaches and dunes, ensure that Grayton maintains its small-town feel and look.

Fodor'sChoice
★
The 2,133-acre **Grayton Beach State Park** is one of the most scenic spots along the Gulf Coast. Composed primarily of untouched Florida woodlands, it also has salt marshes, rolling dunes covered with sea oats, crystal-white sand, and contrasting blue-green waters. The park has facilities for swimming, fishing, snorkeling, and camping, and there's an elevated boardwalk that winds over the dunes to the beach. Even if you are just passing by, the beach here is worth the stop. Thirty fully equipped cabins are available for rent (*see* Where to Stay & Eat, *below*). ⊠ *357 Main Park Rd.* ☎ *850/231–4210* 🖼 *$3.25 per vehicle, up to 8 people* ☉ *Daily 8–sunset.*

off the beaten path

EDEN GARDENS STATE PARK – Scarlett O'Hara might be at home here on the lawn of an antebellum mansion amid an arcade of moss-draped live oaks. Furnishings in the spacious rooms date as far back as the 17th century. The surrounding grounds—the perfect setting for a picnic lunch—are beautiful year-round, but they're nothing short of spectacular in mid-March, when the azaleas and dogwoods are in full bloom. ⊠ *Rte. 395, Point Washington* ☎ *850/231–4214* 🖼 *Gardens $2, mansion tour $1.50* ☉ *Daily 8–sunset, mansion tours hourly Thurs.–Mon. 10–3.*

Where to Stay & Eat

$$$–$$$$
Fodor'sChoice
★
✕ **Fish Out of Water.** Time your appetizers to arrive at sunset here and you'll witness the best of both worlds: sea oats lumbering on gold-dusted dunes outside, and a stylish interior that sets new standards of sophistication for the entire Panhandle. Colorful, hand-blown glass accent lighting that "grows" out of the hardwood floors, plush taupe banquettes, oversize handmade lampshades, and a sleek bar area that screams New York (complete with a cloud-white curtain-wall) create an atmosphere worthy of the inventive cuisine. Influences range from Asian (Thai-style grouper with lobster-coconut broth) to Southern (Low Country shrimp and scallops with creamy grits) to classic Continental (porcini-crusted

osso buco), but all are convincingly wrought and carefully presented. The extensive wine list keeps pace with the menu offerings. ⊠ *34 Goldenrod Circle, inside WaterColor Inn* ☎ *850/534–5000* ▭ *AE, D, DC, MC, V* ⊘ *No lunch.*

$$–$$$$ ✕ **Criollas.** Inventive, contemporary, and constantly changing fare continues to win raves for this popular spot. You might choose to experience Island Hopping—a three-course dinner focusing on a particular Caribbean region or stick closer to home with Southern-inspired fare like crawfish callaloo soup, Creole pan-fried oysters, or barbecue shrimp. The menu changes seasonally, so returning diners can sample a different cuisine each visit. ⊠ *170 E. Rte. 30A* ☎ *850/267–1267* ▭ *AE, D, MC, V* ⊘ *Closed Sun. and Mon. Nov.–Jan. No lunch.*

$–$$ ✕ **Picolo Restaurant & Red Bar.** You could spend weeks here just taking in all the eclectic memorabilia—from Marilyn Monroe posters to flags to dolls—dangling from the ceiling and tacked to every available square inch of wall. The contemporary menu is small, changes daily, and is very Floridian. A baked eggplant dish stuffed with shrimp, scallops, and grilled vegetables is a popular entrée. Live blues and jazz can be heard nightly. ⊠ *70 Hotz Ave.* ☎ *850/231–1008* ▭ *No credit cards.*

¢–$ ✕ **Seagrove Village Market Café.** Grocery store in front, casual diner in back, this humble, cement-block structure on an oak-shaded lot has been a local gathering spot since 1949. It's famous in these parts for its seafood, including oyster and catfish po' boys and seafood gumbo, which you can enjoy inside in orange formica booths or on the wooden patio out back. Or, if you're feeling lucky, buy some live bait (also sold here) and try to hook your own lunch in the Gulf of Mexico, just down the street. ⊠ *2004 S. County Rd. 395, at the corner of Hwy. 30A* ☎ *850/ 231–5736* ⌕ *Reservations not accepted* ▭ *AE, MC, V* ⊘ *Closed Sun.*

$$$$ ▥ **WaterColor Inn.** Nature meets seaside chic at this boutique property,
Fodor's Choice the crown jewel of the area's latest—and largest—planned community.
★ Rooms are done in seashell tones with sea-blue comforters and accents; stylish armoires and desks look as natural and unfinished as driftwood. Dune-level bungalows have private courtyards with outdoor showers, while upper rooms have huge balconies and walk-in showers with windows overlooking the gulf. Standard rooms come with a king-size bed and a queen sleeper-sofa, but consider one of the three Rotunda rooms for something larger and more spectacular. ⊠ *34 Goldenrod Circle, 32459* ☎ *850/534–5000* 🖷 *850/534–5001* ⊕ *www.watercolorinn.com* ⇔ *60 rooms* ⌕ *Restaurant, fans, in-room safes, minibars, cable TV, in-room data ports, golf privileges, pool, hot tub, massage, beach, library, Internet, airport shuttle, no-smoking rooms.*

★ **$–$$** ▥ **Cabins at Grayton Beach State Park.** Back-to-nature enthusiasts and families like these stylish accommodations set among the sand pines and scrub oaks of this pristine state park. The two-bedroom duplexes (each named after a different species of tree found in the park), have tin roofs, white trim, and tropical wooden window louvers, and the beach is a leisurely five-minute walk away via a private boardwalk. Modern conveniences include central heat and air-conditioning and full-size kitchens complete with pots and pans. There is no daily maid service—fresh linens are provided, however—and no room phones or televisions, but gas fireplaces, barbecue grills, and screen porches add a homey touch. They're often booked solid as much as 11 months in advance, but call to check for cancellations. ⊠ *357 Main Park Rd.* ☎ *800/326–3521 for reservations* ⊕ *www.reserveamerica.com* ⤳ *30 cabins* ⚬ *Kitchens; no room phones, no room TVs* ▤ *AE, MC, V.*

Nightlife

The **Red Bar** (⊠ 70 Hotz Ave. ☎ 850/231–1008), the local watering hole, presents red-hot blues and jazz acts every night. On Friday and Saturday nights it's elbow-to-elbow at the bar.

The Outdoors

The **Santa Rosa Golf & Beach Club** (⊠ Rte. 30A, Santa Rosa Beach ☎ 850/267–2229) is a semiprivate 18-hole course that, thankfully, has little residential development beside the fairways, green fee: $69/$79 with cart.

Shopping

Gaffrey Art Gallery (⊠ 21 Blue Gulf Dr., 3 mi west of Grayton Beach, Santa Rosa Beach ☎ 850/267–0228) sells hand-painted furniture and furniture handmade by the Gaffrey family. The **Gourd Garden** (⊠ 4808 Rte. 30A ☎ 850/231–2007), housed in an old-Florida cottage, bills itself as a "curiousity shop" and sells everything from exotic plants to red Georgia clay pottery, folk art, toys, and handmade cards and stationery. It's fun just to browse. **Grayton Beach House of Art** (⊠ 133 De-Funiak St. ☎ 850/231–9997 ⊕ www.gordiehinds.com) includes works by 25 American artists, including Gordie Hinds, who gave up charter fishing and picked up a paintbrush in 2003—you have to see his work to believe it. Under the shade trees of Grayton Beach, **Magnolia House** (⊠ 2 Magnolia St. ☎ 850/231–5859) sells gift items, bath products, and accessories for the home. The **Shops of Grayton** (⊠ Rte. 283 [Grayton Rd.], 2 mi south of U.S. 98 ☎ No phone) is a colorful complex of eight Cracker-style cottages selling gifts, artwork, and antiques. At **Woodie Long Folk Art Gallery,** (⊠ 1066 B. North Bay Dr./Rte. 283 Point Washington ☎ 850/231–9961) in the living room of the artist's residence, you'll find a few of the 10,000 artworks the quirky local claims to have painted over his lifetime (a recent feature in *Smithsonian* magazine put Woodie on the art-world map).

Seaside & Rosemary Beach

▶ ❻ *2 mi east of Grayton Beach.*

This community of Victorian-style homes is so reminiscent of a storybook town that producers chose it for the set of the 1998 film *The Truman Show,* starring Jim Carrey. The brainchild of Robert Davis, **Seaside** was designed to promote a neighborly, old-fashioned lifestyle, and there's much to be said for an attractive, billboard-free village where you can park your car and walk everywhere you need to go. Pastel-color homes with white picket fences, front-porch rockers, and captain's walks are set amid redbrick streets, and all are within walking distance of the town center and its unusual cafés and shops.

The community has come into its own in the last few years, achieving a comfortable, lived-in look and feel that had escaped it since its founding more than 20 years ago: some of the once-shiny tin roofs are starting to rust around the edges, and the foliage has completely matured, creating pockets of privacy and shade. Seaside's popularity continues to soar, and the summer months can be crowded. If you're seeking a little solitude, you might prefer visiting during the off-season—between Labor Day and Memorial Day.

Farther east down Highway 30A is **Rosemary Beach,** a fledgling development that is, like many new coastal communities, a variation on the theme pioneered by Seaside's founders. A few restaurants and shops have opened, and a super-luxe boutique hotel is currently under construction, so investors are snatching up the snazzy beach houses as fast as they're built (in many cases, even before they are built). Despite the growth, the focus here is still on preserving the local environment (the landscape is comprised completely of indigenous plants) and maintaining its small town appeal. You can already see a nascent sense of community sprouting at the Town Green, a perfect patch of manicured lawn fronting the beach, where locals gather with their wine glasses to toast the sunset.

Where to Stay & Eat

★ **$$$–$$$$** ✕ **Cafe Thirty-A.** In a beautiful Florida-style home with high ceilings and a wide veranda, this restaurant has an elegant look—bolstered by white linen tablecloths—and impeccable service. The menu changes nightly and includes such entrées as chili-dusted wild king salmon, oven-roasted black grouper, and braised Arizona rabbit. Even if you're not a Southerner, you should try the appetizer of grilled Georgia quail with creamy grits and sage fritters. With nearly 20 creative varieties, the martini menu alone is worth the trip. ⊠ *3899 E. Scenic Rte. 30A, Seagrove Beach* ☎ *850/231–2166* ⊟ *AE, D, DC, MC, V* ☼ *No lunch.*

$$–$$$ ✕ **Bud & Alley's.** This down-to-earth beachside bistro has been a local favorite since 1986. Indoors are hardwood floors, ceiling fans, and 6-foot windows looking onto an herb garden; the roof-top Tarpon Club bar makes a great perch for a sunset toast (guess the exact moment the sun will disappear and win a drink). Daily salad specials are tangy introductions to such entrées as sesame-seared tuna on wild greens with a rice-wine vinaigrette and a soy dipping sauce. The Cuban steak frites, served with a flavorful tomato and avocado salsa, is a spicy local twist on a classic dish. ⊠ *Rte. 30A* ☎ *850/231–5900* ⊟ *MC, V* ☼ *Closed Tues. Oct.–Dec.*

¢–$$ ✕ **Shades Restaurant.** This is not a sports bar, so don't be fooled by the extensive (and impressive) beer list or the three televisions and the Buffalo Bills shrine in the front bar. Just grab a seat in the side room, where local artwork graces the walls, or relax on the covered patio overlooking the main square and watch the (Truman) show go by. The standout here is the seafood, from lunchtime shrimp po' boys to the always-available crab cakes, mango-and-chicken plate, and the perfectly-prepared catch of the day (the tuna and grouper are both excellent) served over equally fresh garden greens and vegetables. Breakfast, including eggs any way you want 'em, french toast sticks for kids, and beignets with fresh fruit, is served every morning from 8 to 10. ⊠ *83 Central Sq.* ☎ *850/ 231–1950* ⊟ *AE, MC, V.*

$$$–$$$$ 🏨 **Josephine's French Country Inn.** The charming rooms in this grand, Georgian-style accommodation have gulf views, four-poster beds, fireplaces, and claw-foot tubs, bringing a bit of elegance to a modern seaside spot. The daily country-style breakfast is delicious, and dinners are garnished with fresh herbs and flowers from the owners' garden. ⊠ *38 Seaside Ave., 32459* ☎ *850/231–1940 or 800/848–1840* 🖷 *850/231–2446* ⊕ *www.josephinesinn.com* ⇋ *7 rooms, 2 suites* ♿ *Dining room, microwaves, cable TV, in-room VCRs* ⊟ *AE, D, MC, V.*

★ **$$$–$$$$** 🏨 **Seaside Cottage Rental Agency.** When residents aren't using their homes, they rent out their one- to six-bedroom, porticoed, faux-Victorian cottages furnished with fully equipped kitchens, TV–VCRs, and vacuum cleaners—a perfect option for a family vacation or a large group. Gulf breezes blowing off the water remind you of the unspoiled sugar-white beaches a short stroll away. ⊠ *Rte. 30A, Box 4730, 32459* ☎ *850/231–1320 or 800/277–8696* 🖷 *850/231–2231* ⊕ *www.seasidefl. com* ⇋ *275 units* ♿ *Kitchens, 6 tennis courts, 3 pools, bicycles, badminton, croquet* ⊟ *AE, D, MC, V.*

$$–$$$ 🏨 **The Pensione at Rosemary Beach.** Penny and Mark Dragonette run this spotless, eight-room inn on the town's main square, one block from the Gulf of Mexico. In keeping with the true *pensione* concept, rooms (all with queen beds) are basic, almost dorm–style, yet comfortable—those in front have views of the gulf across the street—and thoughtful touches like chocolates, whimsical murals, and picture guides to local butterflies add a touch of homeyness. You're guaranteed peace and quiet here: children under 16, Spring Breakers, and overzealous wedding parties are not allowed. Continental breakfast is included in the room price, making this smart property one of the best bargains around. Onano, a "neighborhood café," occupies the inn's first floor. ⊠ *78 Main St., Rosemary Beach 32461* ☎ *850/231–1790* 🖷 *850/231–2995* ⊕ *www. thepensione.com* ⇋ *8 rooms* ♿ *Cable TV, in-room VCRs; no kids under 16, no smoking* ⊟ *AE, D, MC, V* ⦿ *CP.*

Nightlife

The **Medusa Rouge Wine Shoppe** (⊠ 66 Main St., Rosemary Beach ☎ 850/ 231–1219) is one of those only-in-the-Panhandle–type places: a sophisticated wine bar that hosts Monday Night Football chili bashes in a Tuscan-style courtyard. Owner Shane Hicks, a former Nashville studio musician, stocks 150 wines, fine cheeses, and artwork, too. The upstairs, open-air bar at **Bud & Alley's** (⊠Rte. 30A ☎850/231–5900) draws a friendly crowd for sunset, and the festivities usually last until the wee hours.

The Outdoors

An 8-foot-wide pathway covering 18 mi of scenic Route 30A winds past freshwater lakes, woodlands, and beaches. **Butterfly Rentals** (⊠ 3657 E. Rte. 30A ☎ 850/231–2826) rents bikes and kayaks and has free delivery and pickup. In Seaside, consult the **Cabana Man** (☎ 850/231–5046) for beach chairs, umbrellas, rafts, kayaks, and anything else you might need for a day at the beach. If there's no answer, just head to the beach and you'll find him there.

Shopping

Seaside's central square and open-air market, along Route 30A, offer a number of unique and whimsical boutiques carrying clothing, jewelry, and arts and crafts. **Perspicacity** (✉ 178 Market St. ☎ 850/231–5829), an open-air market, sells simply designed women's clothing and accessories perfect for easy, carefree beach-town casualness. At **Ruskin Place Artist Colony,** in the heart of Seaside, a collection of small shops and artists' galleries has everything from toys and pottery to fine works of art.

Panama City Beach

❼ *21 mi southeast of Seaside.*

The dizzying number of high-rises currently under construction on the Miracle Strip—about two dozen in total—has led to the formation of a new moniker for this stretch of the Panhandle: the "Construction Coast." But the vast majority of the new buildings are condominiums, not hotels, and many of the older mom-and-pop motels that once gave this town its beach-resort flavor have fallen victim to the wrecking ball. But this is not all bad news. Land values have risen so dramatically in the last few years that many of the attractions that gave parts of this area a seedy reputation (i.e.: strip joints, dive bars) have been driven out, replaced by new retailers and the occasional franchise "family" restaurant or chain store. Of course, with the 2004 closing of the Miracle Strip amusement park—once the defining icon of Panama City Beach—things will be different but, truth be told, in the last decade or so Panama City had become a shabby impostor of its former self, and many here welcome the change.

The one constant in this sea of change, however, is the area's natural beauty that, in some areas at least, manages to excuse its gross overcommercialization. The beaches along the Miracle Strip, with their powder-soft sand and translucent emerald waters, are some of the finest in the state; in one sense, anyway, it's easy to understand why so many condos are being built here. And St. Andrew's State Park, on the southern end of the beaches, is treasured by locals and visitors alike.

The area's incredible white sands, navigable waterways, and plentiful marine life that attracted Spanish conquistadors today draw invaders of the vacationing kind—namely families, the vast majority of whom hail from nearby Georgia and Alabama.

Once part of the now-defunct Miracle Strip Amusement Park operation, **Shipwreck Island,** a 6-acre water park, offers everything from speedy slides and tubes to the slow-moving Lazy River. ✉ *12000 Front Beach Rd.* ☎ *850/234–0368* ⊕ *www.shipwreckisland.com* ✂ *$27* ☉ *Mid-Apr.–May, weekends 10:30–5; June–early Sept., daily 10:30–5.*

At the unique **Museum of Man in the Sea** see rare examples of breathing apparatus and diving equipment, some dating as far back as the 1600s, in addition to exhibits on Florida's historic shipwrecks. There are also treasures recovered from famous wrecks, including artifacts from the Spanish galleon *Atocha,* and live creatures found in the area's coastal waters. ⊠ *17314 Panama City Beach Pkwy.* ☎ *850/235–4101* 🖃 *$5* ⊙ *Daily 1–4.*

☺ **Gulf World** is the resident marine park, with a tropical garden, tropical bird theater, and alligator and otter exhibits. The stingray petting pool and the shark-feeding and scuba demonstrations are popular with the kids, but the old favorites—performing sea lions, otters, and bottle-nosed dolphins—still hold their own. There's a nighttime laser light show six days a week in season. ⊠ *15412 Front Beach Rd.* ☎ *850/234–5271* ⊕ *www.gulfworldmarinepark.com* 🖃 *$21* ⊙ *Late May–early Sept., daily 9 AM–4 PM; call for hrs at other times of yr.*

☺ At the eastern tip of Panama City Beach, the **St. Andrews State Park** in-

Fodor'sChoice cludes 1,260 acres of beaches, pinewoods, and marshes. There are com-

★ plete camping facilities here and a snack bar, too, as well as places to swim, pier-fish, or hike the dunes along clearly marked nature trails. Board a ferry to **Shell Island**—a barrier island in the Gulf of Mexico with some of the best shelling north of Sanibel Island. A rock jetty creates a calm, shallow play area that is perfect for young children. Come to this spectacular park for a peek at what the entire beach area looked like before developers got ahold of it. ⊠ *4607 State Park La.* ☎ *850/233–5140* 🖃 *$5 per vehicle, up to 8 people* ⊙ *Daily 8–5.*

Where to Stay & Eat

$–$$$$ ✗ **Capt. Anderson's.** Come early to watch the boats unload the catch of the day on the docks, and be among the first to line up to eat in this noted restaurant. A nautical theme is reinforced by tables made of hatch covers in the attached bar, which attracts long-time locals. The Greek specialties aren't limited to feta cheese and shriveled olives; charcoal-broiled fish and steaks have a prominent place on the menu as well. If you're visiting in the off-season, call to make sure they are adhering to the posted hours before venturing out. ⊠ *5551 N. Lagoon Dr.* ☎ *850/234–2225* 🖎 *Reservations not accepted* ⊟ *AE, D, DC, MC, V* ⊙ *Closed Nov.–Jan. and Sun. No lunch.*

$$–$$$ ✗ **Boar's Head.** An exterior that looks like an oversize thatch-roof cottage sets the mood for dining in this ersatz-rustic restaurant and tavern. Prime rib has been the number one people-pleaser since the house opened in 1978, but blackened seafood and broiled shrimp with crab-meat stuffing are popular, too. ⊠ *17290 Front Beach Rd.* ☎ *850/234–6628* ⊟ *AE, D, DC, MC, V* ⊙ *No lunch.*

¢–$$$ ✗ **The Boatyard.** The same folks who operate Schooners on the beach side opened this larger, more stylish establishment overlooking a marina on the Grand Lagoon. For starters, try the fried peanut-crusted crab claws, or the conch fritters with hot pepper jelly and wasabi mayonnaise. For dinner, choose from the Ceasar salad with Apalachicola oyster fritters, the lobster sandwich, or the aptly named Fried Shrimp You Can't Live Without. The coconut- and plantain-crusted grouper is a knock-out, as is the pan-roasted catch with bacon, mushrooms, and grits (this is definitely the South). There's a kids menu, an extensive wine list and full bar, and the upstairs deck area is a great place to get away from the beach for a long, lazy lunch or romantic sunset dinner. Be aware that the Boatyard kicks into high gear at sundown, transforming into one of the hottest nightspots in town. ✉ *5325 N. Lagoon Dr.* ☎ *850/249–9273* 🖃 *AE, D, DC, MC, V.*

¢–$$$ ✕ **Schooner's.** Billing itself as the "last local beach club," this beachfront spot is the perfect place for a casual family lunch or early dinner: kids can have burgers and play on the beach while Mom and Dad enjoy grown-up drinks and more substantial fare such as homemade gumbo, steak, or simply prepared seafood. Late-night crowds pile in for live music and dancing. ✉ *5121 Gulf Dr.* ☎ *850/235–3555* 🖃 *AE, D, MC, V.*

¢–$$ ✕ **Billy's Steamed Seafood Restaurant, Oyster Bar, and Crab House.** Roll up your sleeves and dig into some of the gulf's finest blue crabs and shrimp seasoned to perfection with Billy's special recipe. Homemade gumbo, crawfish, and the day's catch as well as sandwiches and burgers round out the menu. The taste here is in the food, not the surroundings, but you can eat on an outdoor patio in the cooler months. ✉ *3000 Thomas Dr.* ☎ *850/235–2349* 🖃 *AE, D, MC, V.*

¢–$$ ✕ **Montego Bay.** A tiki-style bar is the focal point at this former beach cottage where you're guaranteed friendly service and reasonably priced seafood, chicken, and steak dishes. Appetizers include deep-fried Cajun crawfish and "gator bites" (if you've never eaten fried alligator tail, try it here: it's nowhere near as exotic as you might think), calamari, chicken wings, and coconut shrimp. Main courses range from fresh fish (fried, sautéed, or grilled) to caramelized ribs, grilled sirloin, and Jamaican jerk chicken. There's a special menu just for kids, and beer, wine, and frozen specialty drinks for adults. ✉ *4920 Thomas Dr.* ☎ *850/233–6033* 🖃 *AE, D, DC, MC.*

¢ ✕ **Coram's.** Don't feel slighted if you're the only one in the place the waitress doesn't know by name—she'll know it by the time you leave (and "Hun" will do in the meantime). More than a local institution, this plain-Jane, diner-style restaurant with parking-lot views makes up for in taste and price what it lacks in atmosphere. Locals flock here for hearty breakfasts—the fluffy omelets are ample enough for two—lunchtime salads and sandwiches, and a dinner menu that includes barbecue pork, fish specials, and steaks and roast beef preparations served with mashed potatoes. For solid food at criminally low prices 24/7, you just can't beat this place. ✉ *2016 Thomas Dr.* ☎ *850/234–8373* ⌔ *Reservations not accepted* 🖃 *No credit cards.*

★ $$$–$$$$ 🏨 **Edgewater Beach Resort.** Luxurious one-, two-, and three-bedroom apartments in beachside towers and golf-course villas are elegantly furnished with wicker and rattan. The resort centerpiece is a Polynesian-style lagoon pool with waterfalls, reflecting ponds, footbridges, and more than 20,000 species of tropical plants. This resort is a good option for longer stays or family vacations. ✉*11212 Front Beach Rd., 32407* ☎*850/235–4044 or 800/874–8686* 🖷 *850/233–7529* ⊕ *www.edgewaterbeachresort.com* ⤴ *520 apartments* ⌂ *2 restaurants, cable TV, 9-hole golf course, 11 tennis courts, hair salon, spa, beach, 2 bars* 🖃 *D, DC, MC, V.*

$$$ 🏨 **Legacy by the Sea.** Every room at this all-suite, 14-story, pastel-peach hotel has a private balcony with commanding Gulf views. Rooms are designed with families in mind, from the fully-equipped kitchens, to the two televisions and waterproof sofa cushions, to the door that conve-

niently separates the bedroom area from the rest of the unit. There's a gulf-front pool and hot tub area (with a kiddie pool), and freebies include Continental breakfast, daily newspaper, local calls, and an airport shuttle. Shopping, dining, and attractions are within walking distance, and a variety of watersport options, including parasailing and jet skiing, are offered by on-site concessionaires. The hotel's closed-circuit cable channel airing nothing but live security camera feeds (inside the elevator, around the pool, in the common areas) makes keeping an eye on the kids a breeze—and keeping an eye on unsuspecting adults a hoot. ✉ *15325 Front Beach Rd., 32413* ☎ *850/249–8601 or 888/886–8917* 🖷 *850/249–8601* ⊕ *www.legacybythesea.com* ⇆ *278 rooms, 78 suites* ⚫ *Full kitchens, cable TV, pool, hot tub, kiddie pool, airport shuttle* ⊟ *AE, D, DC, MC, V.*

$$$ 🏨 **Marriott Bay Point Resort Village.** Across the Grand Lagoon from St.
Fodor'sChoice Andrews State Park, this expansive property exudes sheer elegance.
★ The tropical-chic feel starts in the light-filled lobby, with its polished marble floors, glowing chandeliers, potted palms, and colorful floral paintings. Quiet guest rooms continue the theme with light wood furnishings and armoires, floral-print fabrics, and private balconies or patios overlooking the lush grounds and peaceful bay. Rooms on the upper floors of the main building have expansive views of the bay and the gulf beyond, and villas are a mere tee-shot away from the hotel. A meandering boardwalk (which doubles as a jogging trail) leads to a private bayside beach where an open-air bar and water sports await. ✉ *4200 Marriott Dr., 32408* ☎ *850/236–6000 or 800/874–7105* 🖷 *850/236–6158* ⊕ *www.marriottbaypoint.com* ⇆ *278 rooms, 78 suites* ⚫ *5 restaurants, some microwaves, some refrigerators, cable TV, 2 golf courses, 6 pools, gym, marina, 2 bars, airport shuttle* ⊟ *AE, D, DC, MC, V.*

$–$$$ 🏨 **Holiday Inn Sunspree Resort.** The pool area at this expansive, kidney-shape beachfront resort yields waterfalls, faux-rock formations, lush foliage, thatch-roofed huts, and Jamon, billed as the resort's own "Polynesian Islander," who lights the poolside torches every night. You might see why this tiki-schtick appeals to Spring Breakers, who flock to the place in huge numbers, but if peace and quiet are your thing in spring, this is the wrong place—and the wrong town. The rest of the year, though, it's a pleasant enough retreat for families: kids enjoy the myriad planned activities of the Splash Around Kids Club and the beach-front game room, and parents can simply relax at the in-pool grotto bar. All rooms have terra-cotta tile floors, tropical-print bedspreads, wicker furnishings, and private balconies with views of the Gulf. If you want a decent place to plant the whole family without having to leave the grounds for food or entertainment, this is it. ✉ *11127 Front Beach Rd., 32407* ☎ *850/234–1111* 🖷 *850/235–1907* ⊕ *www.holidayinnsunspree.com* ⇆ *337 rooms, 4 suites* ⚫ *1 restaurant, in-room safes, some in-room hot tubs, microwaves, refrigerators, cable TV, in-room data ports, driving range, putting green, pool, gym, hot tub, sauna, steam room, beach, 2 bars, children's programs (ages 3–18), laundry facilities, business services* ⊟ *AE, D, DC, MC, V.*

Nightlife & the Arts

THE ARTS Broadway touring shows, top-name entertainers, and concert artists are booked into the **Marina Civic Center** (⊠ 8 Harrison Ave., Panama City ☎ 850/769–1217 or 850/763–4696 ⊕ www.marinaciviccenter.com).

NIGHTLIFE **The Boatyard** (⊠ 5325 North Lagoon Dr. ☎ 850/249–9273) is a multi-level, indoor–outdoor waterfront nightclub and restaurant that presents a regular lineup of bands, ranging from blues to steel drums, to classic rock and beyond (DJs round out the entertainment roster). There's never a cover for locals, so act like a local, if you dare. **Pineapple Willy's** (⊠ 9875 S. Thomas Dr. ☎ 850/235–0928) is an eatery and bar geared to families and tourists—as well as sports fans. **Schooner's** (⊠ 5121 Gulf Dr. ☎ 850/235–3555), a beachfront bar and restaurant, draws huge crowds of mostly locals for live music and late-night dancing on weekends.

Sports & the Outdoors

CANOEING Rentals for a trip down Econofina Creek, "Florida's most beautiful canoe trail," are supplied by **Econofina Creek Canoe Livery** (⊠ Strickland Rd., north of Rte. 20, Youngstown ☎ 850/722–9032).

DOG RACING Find pari-mutuel betting year-round and live greyhound racing five nights and two afternoons a week at the **Ebro Greyhound Park.** Simulcasts of thoroughbred racing from the Miami area are also shown throughout the year. Schedules change periodically, so call for details. ⊠ *Rte. 79 and Hwy. 20, Ebro* ☎ *850/234–3943* ⌑ *General $2, clubhouse $1 extra.*

GOLF The **Hombre Golf Club** (⊠ 120 Coyote Pass ☎ 850/234–3673) has a 27-hole course that occasionally hosts professional tours, green fee: $45/$75 with cart. **Marriott Bay Point Resort** (⊠ 4200 Marriott Dr. ☎ 850/235–6950 or 850/235–6949) has a country club with two courses open to the public: the Lagoon Legends and the Club Meadow, green fee: $60/$90 each.

TENNIS The tennis center at **Marriott Bay Point Resort** (⊠ 4200 Marriott Dr. ☎ 850/235–6910) has 10 Har-Tru tennis courts.

Shopping

Stores in the **Manufacturer's Outlet Center** (⊠ 105 W. 23rd St., Panama City) offer well-known brands at a substantial discount. The **Panama City Mall** (⊠ 2150 Martin Luther King Jr. Blvd., Panama City ☎ 850/785–9587) has a mix of some 100 franchise shops and national chain stores.

en route Off of U.S. Highway 98 on the way to Apalachicola, you'll see signs for **St. Joseph Peninsula State Park,** a 2,526-acre gem situated on Cape San Blas, a crescent-shape peninsula separating St. Joseph's Bay from the Gulf of Mexico. The park offers swimming, picnicking, fishing, sunbathing, and you can hike for miles without seeing another human being in the 1,750-acre wilderness preserve that covers the peninsula's far end. Thirty furnished, loft-style cabins are on the bay side (Hurricane Ivan damaged some of them and they're often booked up to a year in advance, so plan ahead), and the 119 campsites have full hookups, picnic tables, barbecue grills—as well as a group of skittish white-tailed deer who call the place home. The gulf side of the peninsula is great for boating and sailing, while the shallow, protected bayside is perfect for kayaking and fishing. Since there are no restaurants, grocery stores, or commercial operations of any kind allowed in the park, be sure to bring everything you'll need for a day—or a week—at the beach with you. ⊠ *8899 Cape San Blas Rd.* ☎ *850/227–1327, 800/326–3521 for camping and cabin reservations* ⊕ *www.floridastateparks.org* ☉ *Daily 8* AM*–sunset.*

Apalachicola

8 *65 mi southeast of Panama City Beach.*

Meaning "land of the friendly people" in the language of its original Native American inhabitants, Apalachicola—known in these parts as simply Apalach—lies on the Panhandle's southernmost bulge. European settlers began arriving in 1821, and by 1847 the southern terminus of the Apalachicola River steamboat route was a bustling port town. Although the town is now known as the Oyster Capital of the World, oystering became king only after the local cotton industry flagged—the city's extrawide streets, built to accommodate bales of cotton awaiting transport, are a remnant of that trade—and the sponge industry moved down the coast after depleting local sponge colonies. But the newest industry here is tourism, and visitors have begun discovering the Forgotten Coast, as the area is known, flocking to its intimate hotels and B&Bs, dining at excellent restaurants, and browsing through unique shops selling everything from handmade furniture to brass fixtures recovered from nearby shipwrecks. If you like oysters or you want to go back in time to the Old South of Gothic churches and spooky graveyards, Apalachicola is a good place to start.

Drive by the **Raney House**, circa 1850, and **Trinity Episcopal Church**, built from prefabricated parts in 1838. The town is at a developmental turning point, pulled in one direction by well-intentioned locals who want to preserve Apalachicola's port-town roots and in the other by long-time business owners who fear preservation will inhibit commercial growth. For now, however, the city exudes a refreshing authenticity—think Key West in the early 1960s—that many others in the Sunshine State lost long ago, one that might be lost to Panama City Beach–style overdevelopment unless local government institutes an official historic preservation committee.

Stop in at the **John Gorrie Museum State Park,** which honors the physician credited with inventing ice-making and, almost, air-conditioning. Although he was hampered by technology, later air-conditioning patents utilized Gorrie's discoveries. Exhibits of Apalachicola history are displayed here as well. ⊠ *Ave. D and 6th St.* ☎ *850/653–9347* ☜ *$1* ☉ *Thurs.–Mon. 9–5.*

Where to Stay & Eat

$$-$$$ ✕ **Nola's Grill.** Hobnob with Apalachicola aristocracy as you eat in a serene, Edwardian-style dining room at the town's traditional hotel. The place is a bit formal—crisp, creased linen tablecloths and atmospheric lighting—and the food's impeccable. The menu changes seasonally, but count on fresh seafood, namely oyster, shrimp, and grouper preparations. Even if you've eaten dinner elsewhere, make sure to stop by the cozy wooden bar for an after-dinner drink and a taste of Apalachicola of yesteryear. ⊠ *51 Ave. C* ☎ *850/653–2191* ⊟ *AE, MC, V.*

$$-$$$ ✕ **Tamara's Cafe Floridita.** Tamara, a native Venezuelan, brings the food
Fodor'sChoice and warmth of her homeland to this colorful bistro, which mixes Florida
★ flavors with South American flair. For starters, try the creamy black bean soup or the pleasantly spicy oyster stew; for dinner choose from seafood paella, prosciutto-wrapped salmon with mango-cilantro sauce, or margarita chicken and scallops with a tequila-lime glaze. All entrées come with black beans and rice, fresh vegetables, and focaccia bread, but if you still have room for dessert try the fried banana split or the *tres leches,* a South American favorite. The chef, who keeps watch over the dining room from an open kitchen, is happy to accommodate most any whim. ⊠ *17 Ave. E* ☎ *850/653–4111* ⊟ *AE, MC, V.*

$-$$$ ✕ **Boss Oyster.** Eat your oysters fried, Rockefeller-style, or on the half shell at this laid-back eatery overlooking the Apalachicola River. Eat 'em alfresco at picnic tables or inside in the busy, rustic dining room, but don't let the modest surroundings fool you—oysters aren't cheap here or anywhere in Apalach. If you're allergic to seafood, don't worry. The menu also includes such staples as steak and pizza. ⊠ *125 Water St.* ☎ *850/653–9364* ⊟ *AE, D, DC, MC, V.*

★ **$-$$$** ✕ **Magnolia Grill.** Chef-owner Eddie Cass has earned local and regional acclaim from major food critics who have discovered the culinary pearl in this small oyster town. Such dishes as Magnolia Grill Surf and Turf, which weds oak-grilled pork tenderloin with béarnaise sauce to jumbo shrimp with New England crabmeat stuffing and lobster sauce, pleasingly unite the flavors of Eddie's native New England and the coastal South. Dinners here tend to be leisurely events (this is the South, after all)—and the stellar desserts—anything chocolate will wow you—deserve an hour of their own. Because the restaurant is small, reservations are recommended. ⊠ *99 11th St.* ☎ *850/653–8000* ⊟ *MC, V* ۞ *Closed Sun. No lunch.*

$-$$$ ✕ **Owl Café.** This old-fashioned, charming lunch and dinner spot pleases modern palates, both in the white-linen elegance of the dining room and in the colorful garden terrace. The food is an artful blend of old and new as well: Grandma's chicken sandwich seems as much at home on the lunch menu as the crab quesadillas. Dinner seafood specials are carefully prepared, but special requests are sometimes met with resistance from the kitchen. Fine wines for adults and special menu selections for children make this a family-friendly place. ⊠ *15 Ave. D* ☎ *850/653–9888* ⊟ *AE, MC, V* ۞ *Closed Sun.*

$$$-$$$$ ▦ **The Consulate.** These four elegant suites, on the second story of the former offices of the local French Consul, range in size from 650 to 1,650 square feet and combine a 19th-century feel with 21st-century luxury.

Exposed wooden beams and brick walls, 13-foot ceilings, hardwood floors, and antique architectural details add more than a hint of charm, while custom-built kitchens, full-size washers and dryers, and cordless room phones make living easy. The two front units share an expansive balcony, where you can take in the constant parade of fishing vessels headed out the Intracoastal. The homelike amenities make this a popular spot for families, larger groups, and even wedding parties, and discounts are given for stays longer than two nights. The Grady Market, a locally owned art and clothing boutique, occupies the building's first floor. ⊠ 76 Water St., 32320 ☎ 850/653–1515 or 877/239–1159 ⊞ 850/653–1516 ⊕ www.consulatesuites.com ⇋ 4 suites ⌂ Kitchens, cable TV, in-room VCRs ⊟ AE, MC, V.

$–$$$$ ⊡ **Coombs House Inn.** Nine fireplaces and an ornate oak staircase with lead-glass windows on the landing lend authenticity to this restored 1905 mansion. No two guest rooms are alike, but all are appointed with Victorian-era settees, four-poster or sleigh beds, English chintz curtains, and Asian rugs on polished hardwood floors. A full breakfast is served in the dining room. Eighty steps away is Coombs House East, and, beyond that, a renovated carriage house. Popular for weddings and receptions, these may be the most elegant homes in Apalachicola. Free tours are offered in the afternoon if the accommodations are not in use. ⊠ 80 6th St., 32320 ☎ 850/653–9199 ⊞ 850/653–2785 ⊕ www.coombshouseinn. com ⇋ 18 rooms ⌂ Dining room, cable TV, bicycles; no smoking ⊟ D, MC, V.

$–$$ ⊡ **Gibson Inn.** One of a few inns on the National Register of Historic Places still operating as a full-service facility, this turn-of-the-20th-century hostelry in the heart of downtown is easily identified by its wraparound porches, fretwork, and captain's watch. Rooms are furnished with period pieces, such as four-poster beds, antique armoires, and pedestal lavatories, which have wide basins and porcelain fixtures. ⊠ 51 Ave. C, 32320 ☎ 850/653–2191 ⊞ 850/653–3521 ⊕ www. gibsoninn.com ⇋ 30 rooms, 2 suites ⌂ Restaurant, cable TV, bar, some pets allowed ⊟ AE, MC, V.

¢–$$ ⊡ **Best Western Apalach Inn.** Basic but impeccably kept, this modern property 1 mi from the downtown waterfront area has everything you need for a convenient, inexpensive overnight. Standard guest rooms are done in earth tones with wicker headboards and burgundy-print curtains and bedspreads. A large swimming pool, free local calls, and a complimentary Continental breakfast are unexpected bonuses. ⊠ 249 U.S. 98 W, 32320 ☎ 850/653–9131 ⊞ 850/653–9136 ⊕ www.bwapalachinn. com ⇋ 42 rooms ⌂ Cable TV, in-room data ports, pool ⊟ AE, D, MC, V ⏹ CP.

¢–$ ⊡ **Rancho Inn.** This mom-and-pop operation—the owners live on-site—prides itself on its homeyness and personalized service. Rooms are spotless, if a little dated in their beige-and-brown color schemes (a few have undergone recent renovations), but 27-inch color TVs (complete with HBO and other premium channels) and in-room coffeemakers, refrigerators, and microwaves make it a hard-to-beat option for those on a budget. The owners advertise "never smoked-in rooms"—and impose fines of $100 for guests who light up in them. ⊠ 240 U.S. 98 W, 32320

☎ *850/653–9435* 🖨 *850/653–9180* ⊕ *www.ranchoinn.com* 🛏 *31 rooms, 1 suite* ♿ *Microwaves, refrigerators, cable TV with movies, pool* 🖃 *AE, D, MC, V.*

Shopping

The **Tin Shed** (✉ 170 Water St., Apalachicola ☎ 850/653–3635) has an impressive collection of antiques and knickknacks, from antique brass luggage tags to 1940s-era nautical charts to sponge-diver wetsuits to hand-glazed tiles and architectural elements salvaged from demolished buildings. The **Grady Market** (✉ 76 Water St., Apalachicola ☎ 850/653–4099) is a collection of more than a dozen boutiques, including several antiques dealers and the gallery of Richard Bickel, known for his stunning black-and-white photographs of local residents. **Avenue E** (✉ 15 Ave. E, Apalachicola ☎ 850/653–1411) is a stylish store specializing in reasonably priced antique and reproduction pieces, including furniture, lamps, artwork, and interior accessories.

St. George Island

9 *8 mi southeast of Apalachicola.*

Pristine St. George Island sits 5 mi out into the Gulf of Mexico just south of Apalachicola. Accessed via the Bryant Patton Bridge off U.S. 98, the island is bordered by both Apalachicola Bay and the gulf, offering vacationers the best of both. The rich bay is an angler's dream, while the snowy-white beaches and clear gulf waters satisfy even the most finicky beachgoer. Indulge in bicycling, hiking, canoeing, and snorkeling or find a secluded spot for reading, gathering shells, or bird-watching. Accommodations mostly take the form of privately owned, fully furnished condos and single-family homes, which allow for plenty of privacy.

Fodor'sChoice ★ **St. George Island State Park** gives you Old Florida at its undisturbed best. On the east end of the island are 9 mi of undeveloped beaches and dunes—the longest beachfront of any state park in Florida. Sandy coves, salt marshes, oak forests, and pines provide shelter for many species, including such birds as bald eagles and ospreys. Spotless rest rooms and plentiful parking make a day at this park a joy. ☎ *850/927–2111* 🅿 *$4 per vehicle, up to 8 people* ☉ *Daily 8–sunset.*

off the beaten path

CARRABELLE – Where, exactly, is Carrabelle? Why, it's between Sopchoppy and Wewahitchka, of course. Known locally as "a quaint drinking village with a fishing problem," one of the last true fishing ports on the Gulf Coast is most famous for having the World's Smallest Police Station, a former phone booth off U.S. 98 (you can buy the postcard at the nearby general store). Talk a walk around the docks and watch the gulls compete for handouts above the rusted shrimp boats. But do it soon: a major condo development in the works on nearby Timber Island will soon put this sleepy port on the snowbird map. ✉ *15 mi east of St. George Island on U.S. 98.*

Where to Stay & Eat

$–$$$ ✗ **Blue Parrot.** You'll feel like you're sneaking in the back door as you climb the side stairs leading to an outdoor deck overlooking the gulf.

Or if you can, grab a table indoors. During special-event weekends, the place is packed, and service may be a little slow. The food is hard to beat if you're not looking for anything fancy. Baskets of shrimp, oysters, and crab cakes—fried or char-grilled and served with fries—are more than one person can handle. Daily specials are listed on the blackboard. ⊠ *68 W. Gorrie Dr.* ☎ *850/927–2987* ⊟ *AE, D, MC, V.*

$–$$$ ✕ **Lorenzo's Italian Restaurante.** Like a stereotypically cheesy Italian restaurant straight out of central casting—red-and-white-checkered tablecloths, waiters in crumpled bowties, a grand piano—this place has no reason to be good, but it is. Locals put up with erratic hours and occasional long waits to enjoy such classics as lasagna, fettuccine with clams, and fried eggplant. The pizzas, on the large side and made with whatever fresh ingredients the owner is able to procure (this is the Panhandle, after all), are particularly satisfying. ⊠ *U.S. 98* ☎ *850/697–4084* ⊟ *AE, D, MC, V* ۞ *Closed Sun.*

¢–$$ ✕ **That Place on 98.** This place used to be as folksy and unassuming as its name suggests—that is, until the owner decided on an eye-popping turquoise and pink color scheme. Lucky for you, though, because now you *can't* miss it, washed up on the shores of Apalachicola Bay like a Benjamin Moore shipwreck. Nonetheless, it's one of the most authentic seafood shacks on the entire Gulf coast, and it's *the* place to go if you're looking for fresh oysters. Get them any way you like them: on the half-shell, steamed, fried, Rockefellered, or 98'ed (baked with bacon, onions, garlic, and mozzarella). Fresh fish dishes, chicken, beef, and Greek salads round out the menu. ⊠ *500 Hwy. 98* ☎ *850/670–9898* ۞ *Closed Wed.*

¢ ✕ **BJs.** In any other locale you might think twice before dining at a restaurant that advertises "kegs-to-go" on the menu, but this is an island, so establishments tend to wear several hats (some even sell live bait). Fear not. This simple beach shack serves solid, if predictable, sandwiches (grilled chicken, turkey club, BLT), salads (Caesar, tuna, fried chicken), and appetizers (Buffalo wings, cheese sticks, onion rings), but the pizza is definitely worth stopping for. Pies range from white pizza with chicken and bacon, to shrimp-and-mozzarella, to build-your-own personal pie (choose from 15 toppings). There's beer and wine, and pool tables to pass the time while you wait for your order. ⊠ *105 W. Gulf Beach Dr.* ☎ *850/927–2805* ⌂ *Reservations not accepted* ⊟ *MC, V.*

¢ ✕ **Carrabelle Junction.** Stop by this eclectic spot for a cup of gourmet coffee—no small feat in these parts—and freshly made classic sandwiches ranging from tuna salad to BLTs. Or grab a seat outside and have a cold beer, a glass of wine, or a scoop of ice cream while enjoying the music that Ron, the proprietor (who ran a similar place in San Francisco for 20-odd years), spins on a real record player. There's local artwork for sale, and at the Wednesday open-mike night area musicians treat the crowd to bluegrass, rock, and country tunes. ⊠ *88 Tallahassee St., Carrabelle* ☎ *850/697–9550* ⊟ *No credit cards* ۞ *No dinner.*

$$–$$$ ▣ **St. George Inn.** A little piece of Key West smack in the middle of the Panhandle, this cozy inn has tin roofs, hardwood floors, wraparound porches—even a widow's walk. Personal touches like private porches and in-room coffeemakers keep things homey. Both beach and bay are within view, and several restaurants and a convenience store are within walking distance. Two larger suites have full kitchens, and the pool is heated for year-round swimming. Specials are posted on the inn's Web site during off-season, when prices can drop by more than half. ⊠ *135 Franklin Blvd., 32320* ☎ *850/927–2903, 850/927–2666, 800/332–5196 reservations* ⊕ *www.stgeorgeinn.com* �’ *15 rooms, 2 suites* ⚭ *Some kitchens, refrigerators, cable TV, pool* ⊟ *MC, V.*

The Outdoors
BOATING For a **boat tour** (⬚ Box 696, Carrabelle 32322 ☎ 850/697–3989) of St. George Sound and Apalachicola Bay, call charter captain A. P. Whaley. He's famous in these parts for his uncanny ability to attract dolphin to the stern of his boat, the *Gat V.*

INLAND ACROSS THE PANHANDLE

Farther inland, where the northern reaches of the Panhandle butt up against the back porches of Alabama and Georgia, you'll find a part of Florida that goes a long way toward explaining why the state song is "Suwannee River" (and why its parenthetical title is "Old Folks at Home"). Stephen Foster's musical genius notwithstanding, the inland Panhandle area is definitely more Dixie than Sunshine State, with few lodging options other than the chain motels that flank the Interstate 10 exits and a decidedly slower pace of life than on the tourist-heavy Gulf Coast. But the area's natural attractions—hills and farmlands, untouched small towns, pristine state parks—make for great day trips from the coast should the sky turn gray or the skin red. Explore underground caverns where eons-old rock formations create bizarre scenes, visit one of Florida's up-and-coming wineries, or poke around small-town America in DeFuniak Springs.

DeFuniak Springs
🔟 *28 mi east of Crestview.*

This scenic spot has a rather unusual claim to fame: at its center lies a nearly perfectly symmetrical spring-fed lake, one of only two such naturally circular bodies of water in the world (the other is in Switzerland). In 1848 the Knox Hill Academy was founded here, and for more than half a century it was the only institution of higher learning in northwestern Florida. In 1885 the town was chosen as the location for the New York Chautauqua educational society's winter assembly. The Chautauqua programs were discontinued in 1922, but DeFuniak Springs attempts to revive them, in spirit at least, by sponsoring a county-wide Chautauqua Festival in April. Christmas is a particularly festive time here, when the sprawling, Victorian houses surrounding the lake are decorated to the nines.

By all accounts, the 16-foot by 24-foot **Walton-DeFuniak Public Library** is Florida's oldest library continuously operating in its original building. Opened in 1887, the original space has been added to over the years and it now contains nearly 30,000 volumes, including some rare books, many older than the structure itself. The collection also includes antique musical instruments and impressive European armor. ✉ *3 Circle Dr.* ☎ *850/892–3624* ⊙ *Mon. and Wed.–Sat. 9–5, Tues. 9–8.*

The **Chautauqua Winery** (✉ I–10 and U.S. 331 ⊕ www.chautauquawinery. com ☎ 850/892–5887) opened in 1989, and its vintages have slowly won respect from oenophiles wary of what was once considered to be an oxymoron at best: "Florida wine." But the state has history on its side: according to historical records, the first wine produced by Europeans in the New World was made in Florida in 1562 by French Huguenots (obviously, this pre-dated their little-known Siege of Napa Valley). Take a free tour to see how ancient art blends with modern technology; then retreat to the tasting room and gift shop.

Some of the finest examples of Victorian architecture in the state can be seen on a walking tour of **Circle Drive.** In addition to the Walton-De-Funiak Public Library, the Dream Cottage and the Pansy Cottage are beautiful Victorian specimens. Most of the other notable structures are private residences, but you can still admire them from the street.

Where to Stay & Eat

¢–$$ ✕🏨 **Hotel De Funiak.** You can't miss this Depression-era two-story red-brick structure on a quiet corner a few blocks from peaceful Lake De-Funiak—just look for the two-tone 1937 Buick permanently moored out front. Each room has a different theme decor, from Oriental to art deco to French Country, and contains a combination of period antiques and reproductions, many of which can be purchased on the spot. It's one of the nicer places to stay in this part of the Panhandle. The hotel's Lake Room serves Gulf Coast Regional cuisine—the fresh seafood comes from the Gulf, only 30 minutes away—in a period setting reminiscent of a bordello; the more casual Lake Café serves breakfast and lunch. ✉ *400 E. Nelson Ave., 32433* ☎ *850/892–4383 or 877/333–8642* 🖷 *850/ 892–5346* ⊕ *www.hoteldefuniak.com* 🛏 *8 rooms, 4 suites* ⚐ *Restaurant, cable TV, library; no smoking* ▭ *AE, D, MC, V* ⊙l *CP.*

Falling Waters State Park

⑪ *35 mi east of DeFuniak Springs.*

This site of a Civil War–era whiskey distillery and, later, an exotic plant nursery—some imported species still thrive in the wild—is best known for also being the site of one of Florida's most notable geological features—the Falling Waters Sink. The 100-foot-deep cylindrical pit provides the background for a waterfall, and there's an observation deck for viewing this natural phenomenon. The water free-falls 67 feet to the bottom of the sink, but where it goes after that is a mystery. ✉ *Rte. 77A, Chipley* ☎ *850/638–6130* ⊕ *www.dep.state.fl.us/parks* 🎫 *$4 per vehicle, up to 8 people* ⊙ *Daily 8–sunset.*

Florida Caverns State Park

★ ⑫ *13 mi northeast of Falling Waters off I–10 on U.S. 231.*

Take a ranger-led cave tour to see stalactites, stalagmites, and "waterfalls" of solid rock at these underground caverns where the temperature hovers at an oh-so-pleasant 68°F year-round. Some of the caverns are off-limits to the public or open for scientific study only with a permit, but you'll still see enough to fill a half day or more—and you'll be amazed that caverns of this magnitude exist anywhere in the Sunshine State. Between Memorial Day and Labor Day, rangers offer guided lantern tours on Friday and Saturday nights. There are also hiking trails, campsites, and areas for swimming, horseback riding, and canoeing on the Chipola River. ⊠ *Rte. 166, Marianna* ☎ *850/482–9598, 800/ 326–3521 for camping reservations* ⊠ *Park $4 per vehicle, up to 8 people; caverns $5* ⊙ *Daily 8–sunset; cavern tours daily 9–4.*

TALLAHASSEE

⑬ *61 mi southeast of Florida Caverns.*

Interstate 10 rolls east over the timid beginnings of the Appalachian foothills and through thick pines into the state capital, with its canopies of ancient oaks and spring bowers of azaleas. Along with Florida State University, the perennial Seminoles football champions, and FAMU's fabled "Marching 100" band, the city also has more than a touch of the Old South. Tallahassee maintains a tranquillity quite different from the sun-and-surf hedonism of the major coastal towns. Acknowledging the cosmopolitan pace of other Florida cities, residents claim their hometown is "Florida with a southern accent." Vestiges of the city's colorful past are found throughout; for example, in the capitol complex, the turn-of-the-20th-century Old Capitol building is strikingly paired with the New Capitol skyscraper. Tallahassee's tree-lined streets are particularly memorable—among the best "canopy roads" (as they are called) are St. Augustine, Miccosukee, Meridian, Old Bainbridge, and Centerville, all dotted with country stores and antebellum plantation houses.

Downtown

a good walk

The downtown area is compact enough so that most sights can be seen on foot, although it's also served by a free, continuous shuttle trolley. Start at the capitol complex, which contains the **Old Capitol** ▶ and its counterpoint, the **New Capitol.** Across the street from the older structure is the restored **Union Bank Building,** and two blocks west of the new statehouse you'll find the **Museum of Florida History,** with exhibits on many eras of the state's history and prehistory. If you really want to get a feel for Old Tallahassee, walk the **Downtown Tallahassee Historic Trail** as it wends its way from the capitol complex through several of the city's historic districts.

TIMING   You can't do justice to the capitol complex and downtown area in less than two hours. Allow four hours to walk the 8-mi stretch of the historic trail. If you visit between March and April, you'll find flowers in bloom and the Springtime Tallahassee festival in full swing.

What to See

Downtown Tallahassee Historic Trail. A route originally mapped and documented by an eager Eagle Scout as part of a merit-badge project, this trail has become a Tallahassee sightseeing staple. The starting point is the New Capitol, where you can pick up maps and descriptive brochures at the visitor center. You'll walk through the **Park Avenue and Calhoun Street historic districts,** which will take you back to Territorial days and the era of postwar reconstruction. The trail is dotted with landmark churches and cemeteries, along with outstanding examples of Greek revival, Italianate, and Prairie-style architecture. Some houses are open to the public. The **Brokaw-McDougall House** (⊠ 329 N. Meridian St. ⊙ Weekdays 9–3 ⊡ Free) is a superb example of the Greek revival and Italianate styles. The **Meginnis-Monroe House** (⊠ 125 N. Gadsden St. ⊡ Free ⊙ Tues.–Sat. 10–5, Sun. 2–5) served as a field hospital during the Civil War and is now an art gallery.

Museum of Florida History. If you thought Florida was founded by Walt Disney, stop here. Covering 12,000 years, the displays explain Florida's past by highlighting the unique geological and historical events that have shaped the state. Exhibits include a mammoth armadillo grazing in a savannah, the remains of a giant mastodon found in nearby Wakulla Springs, and a dugout canoe that once carried Indians into Florida's backwaters. ⊠ *500 S. Bronough St.* ☎ *850/245–6400* ⊕ *dhr.dos.state.fl.us/ museum* ⊡ *Free* ⊙ *Weekdays 9–4:30, Sat. 10–4:30, Sun. noon–4:30.*

★ **New Capitol.** This modern skyscraper looms up 22 stories directly behind the low-rise Old Capitol. From the fabulous 22nd-floor observation deck, on a clear day, catch a panoramic view of Tallahassee and the surrounding countryside—all the way into Georgia. Also on this floor is the Florida Artists Hall of Fame, a tribute to Floridians such as Ray Charles, Burt Reynolds, Tennessee Williams, Ernest Hemingway, and Marjorie Kinnan Rawlings. To pick up information about the area, stop at the Florida Visitors Center, on the plaza level. There are guided tours from 9 to 3 on the hour (none at noon), booked in advance. ⊠ *400 S. Monroe St.* ☎ *850/488–6167* ⊡ *Free* ⊙ *Visitor center weekdays 8–5, self-guided or guided tours weekdays 8–5.*

★ ⮞ **Old Capitol.** The centerpiece of the capitol complex, this pre–Civil War structure has been added to and subtracted from several times. Having been restored, the jaunty red-and-white stripe awnings and combination gas-electric lights make it look much as it did in 1902. Inside, historically accurate legislative chambers and exhibits offer a very interesting peek into the past. ⊠ *S. Monroe St. at Apalachee Pkwy.* ☎ *850/487–1902* ⊡ *Free* ⊙ *Self-guided or guided tours weekdays 9–4:30, Sat. 10–4:30, Sun. noon–4:30.*

Union Bank Building. Chartered in 1833, this is Florida's oldest bank building. Since it closed in 1843, it has played many roles, from ballet school to bakery. It has been restored to what is thought to be its original appearance and currently houses Florida A&M's Black Archives Extension, which depicts black history in Florida. Call ahead for hours, which are subject to change, and directions. ⊠ *Calhoun St. at Apalachee Pkwy.* ☎ *850/487–3803* ⊡ *Free* ⊙ *Weekdays 9–4.*

Away from Downtown

What to See

Alfred Maclay Gardens State Park. Starting in December the grounds are afire with azaleas, dogwood, and other showy or rare plants. Allow half a day to wander past the reflecting pool into the tiny walled garden, and around the lakes and woodlands. The Maclay residence (open January through April only), furnished as it was in the 1920s; picnic areas; and swimming and boating facilities are open to the public. The gardens are both peaceful and perfect. ⊠ *3540 Thomasville Rd.* ☎ *850/487–4556* 🏷 *$4 per vehicle, up to 8 people; extra $4 per person for garden admission, Jan.–Apr.; free rest of yr* ☉ *Daily 8–sunset.*

Lake Jackson Mounds Archaeological State Park. Here are waters to make bass anglers weep. For sightseers, Indian mounds and the ruins of an early 19th-century plantation built by Colonel Robert Butler, adjutant to General Andrew Jackson during the siege of New Orleans, are found along the shores of the lake. ⊠ *3600 Indian Mounds Rd.* ☎ *850/562–0042* 🏷 *$2* ☉ *Daily 8–sunset.*

San Luis Archaeological and Historic Site. This museum focuses on the archaeology of 17th-century Spanish mission and Apalachee Indian town sites. In its heyday, in 1675, the Apalachee village here had a population of at least 1,400. Threatened by Creek Indians and British forces in 1704, the locals burned the village and fled. Take self-guided tours and watch scientists conducting digs daily (usually). The museum's popular "Living History" program is held on the third Saturday of the month (10 AM–2 PM). ⊠ *2020 W. Mission Rd.* ☎ *850/487-3711* 🏷 *Free* ☉ *Tues.–Sun. 10–4.*

☾ **Tallahassee Museum of History and Natural Science.** It could have been dull, but this bucolic park showcases a peaceful and intriguing look at Old Florida. A working 1880s pioneer farm offers daily hands-on activities for children, such as soap making and blacksmithing. A boardwalk meanders through the 52 acres of natural habitat that make up the zoo, which has such varied animals as panthers, bobcats, white-tailed deer, and black bears. Also on-site are nature trails, a one-room schoolhouse dating from 1897, and an 1840s Southern plantation manor, where you can usually find someone cooking on the weekends. ⊠ *3945 Museum Dr.* ☎ *850/576-1636* 🏷 *$6.50* ☉ *Mon.–Sat. 9–5, Sun. 12:30–5.*

> **off the beaten path**

BIRDSONG NATURE CENTER – This 500-acre preserve's 12 mi of nature trails, with lakes, woodlands, deer—and a skittish Florida bobcat or two—provide a taste of what all of North Florida and southern Georgia used to look like. Visitors come here for the exact opposite reason they go to Disney—to bask in the natural environment, learn about natural history and preservation, and get away from it all. The Evening Sky program, a nighttime study of stars and constellations, is especially popular, and the 20-minute drive north on Meridian Road out of Tallahassee, beneath canopies of oaks whose beards of Spanish moss hang from above like soft, green stalactites, is an adventure in itself. ⊠ *2106 Meridian Rd.,*

Thomasville, GA 31792 ☎ *229/377–4408* ⊕ *tfn.net/birdsong* 🖃 *$5*
⊙ *Wed., Fri., and Sat. 9–5, Sun. 1–5.*

Where to Stay & Eat

$–$$$$ ✕ **Nicholson's Farmhouse.** The name says a lot about this friendly, informal country place with an outside kitchen and grill. A few miles out in the Tallahassee countryside, the steak house is a retreat from the already calming capital city. A farm, gift shop, and mule-drawn-wagon rides (Fridays only; weather permitting) create a rural retreat where you can enjoy hand-cut steaks, chops, and seafood. ✉ *From U.S. 27 follow Rte. 12 toward Quincy and look for signs* ☎ *850/539–5931* 🖃 *AE, D, MC, V* 🍴 *BYOB* ⊙ *Closed Sun. and Mon. No lunch.*

$–$$$ ✕ **Chez Pierre.** You'll feel as if you've entered a great-aunt's old plantation home in this restored 1920s house set back from the road in historic Lafayette Park. Since 1976, its warm, cozy rooms, gleaming hardwood floors, and large French doors separating dining areas have created an intimate place to go for authentic French cuisine. Try the tournedos of beef or one of the special lamb dishes. Sunday brunch is one of the most popular around. ✉ *1215 Thomasville Rd.* ☎ *850/222–0936* 🖃 *AE, D, DC, MC, V.*

¢–$$$ ✕ **Andrew's 228.** Part of a smart complex in the heart of the political district, this two-story "urban Tuscan villa" (contradiction noted) is the latest of owner Andy Reiss's restaurant incarnations to occupy the same space (the last was Andrew's Second Act). The high-price entrées were thrown out with the old decor; instead choose from daily pastas ($9–$14), grilled steak or chicken dinner sandwiches ($10), or more substantive classics like (urban?) Tuscan chicken ($13.50) and filet mignon. It's a noisy, vivacious spot—think exposed brick with arched ceilings, dim lighting, banquettes—on one of downtown's most high-profile corners. As you might expect, the all-you-can eat soup and salad lunch special ($5.95) is wildly popular in this college town—as is the bar menu of some 600 martinis. ✉ *228 S. Adams St.* ☎ *850/222–3444* 🖃 *AE, D, MC, V.*

¢–$ ✕ **Hopkins' Eatery.** Locals in the know flock here for superb salads, homemade soups, and sandwiches—expect a short wait at lunchtime—via simple counter service. Kids will like the traditional PBJ sandwich (offered with bananas and sprouts, if they dare); adults might opt for a chunky chicken melt, smothered beef, or garden vegetarian sub. The spearmint iced tea is a must-have, as is a slice of freshly baked chocolate cake. A second location on North Monroe Street offers the same menu. ✉ *1415 Market St.* ☎ *850/668–0311* ✉ *1840 N. Monroe St.* ☎ *850/386–1809* 🖃 *AE, D, DC, MC, V* ⊙ *Closed Sun. No dinner Sat.*

¢–$ ✕ **Rice-Bowl Oriental.** Bamboo woodwork and thatched-roof booths lend an air of authenticity to this Asian-hybrid spot tucked away in a Tallahassee strip mall. Chinese, Japanese, Thai, and Vietnamese favorites are all represented here, from General Tso's Chicken to fresh sushi to green curry and rice noodle dishes. The all-you-can-eat lunch buffet (offered Sunday–Friday; $6.95), complete with entrées, salads, soups, and fresh sushi, just might be one of the best deals in town. ✉ *3813 N. Monroe St.* ☎ *850/514–3632* 🖃 *AE, D, DC, MC, V.*

¢ ✕ **Decent Pizza.** The name is terribly modest—the pizza here is much more than decent, and the prices are more than reasonable. A couple of FSU grads opened this simple pizzeria, which became an instant hit with those on an undergraduate budget: slices and salads start at $2.50 each, and at a buck each, draft beers are cheaper than sodas (how's *that* for a bad excuse to save the 'rents some money?). Choose from more than 30 toppings for regular red-sauce, pesto, or white pies. ⊠ *1026 N. Monroe St.* ☎ *850/222–6400* ⌕ *Reservations not accepted* ▤ *MC, V.*

★ **$$–$$$$** ▥ **Governors Inn.** Only a block from the capitol, this plushly restored historic warehouse is abuzz during the week with politicians, press, and lobbyists. It's a perfect location for business travelers and on weekends for tourists who want to visit downtown sites. Rooms are a rich blend of mahogany, brass, and classic prints. The VIP treatment includes cocktails, robes, shoe shine, and a daily paper. ⊠ *209 S. Adams St., 32301* ☎ *850/681–6855 or 800/342–7717* 🖷 *850/222–3105* ⊕ *www.thegovinn. com* ⇋ *28 rooms, 12 suites* ⌕ *Cable TV, laundry service, parking (fee)* ▤ *AE, D, DC, MC, V* ⦿ *CP.*

$–$$$ ▥ **DoubleTree Hotel Tallahassee.** This hotel a mere two blocks from the capitol hosts heavy hitters from the worlds of politics and media. Since it's also an easy walk from the Florida State University campus, it welcomes plenty of FSU fans during football season. Rooms, which overlook either a city park or the Capitol, are basic, but clean, with beige-tone wallpaper and occasional chairs and green-and-yellow stripe bedspreads. Most have two full-size beds, which can be pushed together to create an ersatz "king" bed. ⊠ *101 S. Adams St., 32301* ☎ *850/224–5000* 🖷 *850/513–9516* ⇋ *243 rooms* ⌕ *Restaurant, cable TV, in-room data ports, pool, gym, bar* ▤ *AE, D, DC, MC, V.*

¢ ▥ **Shoney's Inn.** The quiet courtyard with its own pool and the darkly welcoming cantina (where a complimentary Continental breakfast is served) convey the look of Old Spain. Rooms are furnished in heavy Mediterranean style—and come with two double beds or one king. Rates jump $30 on FSU football home-game weekends. ⊠ *2801 N. Monroe St., 32303* ☎ *850/386–8286* 🖷 *850/422–1074* ⊕ *www.shoneysinn. com* ⇋ *113 rooms, 27 suites* ⌕ *Cable TV, pool* ▤ *AE, D, MC, V* ⦿ *CP.*

Nightlife & the Arts

The Arts
Florida State University (☎ 850/644–4774 School of Music, 850/644–6500 School of Theatre ⊕ www.music.fsu.edu) annually hosts more than 400 concerts and recitals given year-round by its School of Music, and many productions by its School of Theatre. The **Monticello Opera House** (⊠ 185 W. Washington [U.S. 90 E], Monticello ☎ 850/997–4242) presents concerts and plays in a restored 1890s gaslight-era opera house. The **Tallahassee Little Theatre** (⊠ 1861 Thomasville Rd. ☎ 850/224–8474 ⊕ www.tallahasseelittletheatre.org) has a five-production season that runs from September through May. The season of the **Tallahassee Symphony Orchestra** (☎ 850/224–0461 ⊕ www.tsolive.org) usually runs from October through April; performances are usually held at Florida State University's Ruby Diamond Auditorium.

Nightlife

Waterworks (✉ 1133 Thomasville Rd. ☎ 850/224–1887), with its retro-chic tiki-bar fittings, attracts jazz fans and hipsters of all ages for cocktails and DJ-spun dance music. On Friday night there's a banjo player, a retro-cool treat. **Floyd's Music Store** (✉ 666-1 W. Tennessee St. ☎ 850/222–3506) hosts some of the hottest local and touring acts around. Other performers, from dueling pianos to Dave Matthews cover bands to assorted DJs, round out the schedule. Don't let the name fool you: the **Late Night Library** (✉ 809 Gay St. ☎ 850/224–2429) is the quintessential college-town party bar with dancing, drinking, cavorting—you get the picture.

Side Trips

South to the Gulf

South of the capital and east of the Ochlockanee River are several fascinating natural and historic sites. These sites are near one another, so string several together on an excursion from Tallahassee.

⓮ Known for having one of the deepest springs in the world, **Wakulla Springs**
Fodor'sChoice **State Park** remains relatively untouched, retaining the wild and exotic
★ look it had in the 1930s, when Tarzan movies were made here. Take a glass-bottom boat deep into the lush, jungle-lined waterways to catch glimpses of alligators, snakes, nesting limpkins, and other waterfowl. An underground river flows into a pool so clear that you can see the bottom more than 100 feet below. The park is 15 mi south of Tallahassee on Route 61. If you can't pull yourself away from this idyllic spot, spend the night in the 1930s lodge. ✉ *550 Wakulla Park Dr., Wakulla Springs* ☎ *850/922–3632* 💲 *$4 per vehicle, up to 8 people; boat tour $4.50* ☉ *Daily 8–sunset, boat tours hourly 9:30–4:30.*

⓯ **Natural Bridge Battlefield State Park** marks the spot where in 1865 Confederate soldiers stood firm against a Yankee advance on St. Marks. The Rebs held, saving Tallahassee—the only southern capital east of the Mississippi that never fell to the Union. Ten miles southeast of Tallahassee, the site is a good place for a hike and a picnic. Visit the first week in March (call for schedule) to see a reenactment of the battle. ✉ *Natural Bridge Rd., off Rte. 363, Woodville* ☎ *850/922–6007* 💲 *Free* ☉ *Daily 8–sunset.*

⓰ As its name suggests, **St. Marks National Wildlife Refuge and Lighthouse** is of both natural and historical interest. The once-powerful Fort San Marcos de Apalache was built nearby in 1639, and stones salvaged from the fort were used in the lighthouse, which is still in operation. In winter the refuge is the resting place for thousands of migratory birds, but the alligators seem to like it year-round (keep your camera ready and you're bound to get a photo op). The visitor center has information on more than 75 mi of marked trails, some of which wend through landscapes with foliage more reminiscent of North Carolina than Florida. Twenty-five miles south of Tallahassee, the refuge can be reached via Route 363. ✉ *1255 Lighthouse Rd., St. Marks* ☎ *850/925–6424* ⊕ *saintmarks.fws.gov* 💲 *$4 per vehicle* ☉ *Refuge daily sunrise–sunset; visitor center weekdays 8–4, weekends 10–5.*

Spreading north of Apalachicola and west of Tallahassee and U.S. 319 is the **Apalachicola National Forest,** with campsites, hiking trails, picnic areas, and plentiful lakes for old-fashioned swimmin'. Honor-system fees range from $3 admission to $8 camping. ☎ *850/643–2282.*

CANOEING **TNT Hideaway** (✉ U.S. 98 at the Wakulla River, St. Marks ☎ 850/925–6412), 18 mi south of Tallahassee, arranges canoe trips on the spring-fed Wakulla River. An average trek takes about three hours, and a four-hour canoe rental for two costs $20.

WHERE TO STAY & EAT ¢–$ ✕☆ **Wakulla Springs State Park and Lodge.** Built in 1937, this is a pre-served piece of Florida history on the grounds of Wakulla Springs State Park. There's a huge fireplace in the lobby; broad, painted Moorish-style beams across the ceiling; and cozy, if spartan, rooms. Activities are at a minimum, so if you put relaxation at a premium, this might be your place. The facility serves three meals a day in a sunny, simple room that seems little changed from the 1930s. Schedule lunch here to sample the famous bean soup, home-baked muffins, and a slab of pie. In the soda shop, order a "ginger yip" (ice cream, whipped cream, and ginger ale) or buy a wind-up toy alligator as a memento of your stay. ✉ *550 Wakulla Park Dr., Wakulla Springs 32327* ☎ *850/224–5950* 🖶 *850/ 561–7251* ➽ *27 rooms* ♿ *Restaurant, beach* ▤ *AE, D, MC, V.*

THE PANHANDLE A TO Z

To research prices, get advice from other travelers, and book travel arrangements, visit www.fodors.com.

AIR TRAVEL

CARRIERS Pensacola Regional Airport is served by Air Tran, American Eagle, Continental, Delta, Northwest, and US Airways. Okaloosa County Regional Airport is served by Atlantic Southeast, Delta, Northwest, and US Airways Express. Panama City–Bay County International Airport is served by Delta Connection, Northwest Airlink, and Chautauqua Airlines. Tallahassee Regional Airport is served by Atlantic Southeast/ Delta, Delta, Delta Connection/Chautauqua, Northwest, and US Airways Express.

🔢 **Airlines & Contacts AirTran** ☎ 800/247-8726. **Continental** ☎ 800/523-3273. **Delta** ☎ 800/221-1212. **Northwest** ☎ 800/225-2525. **Northwest Airlink** ☎ 800/225-2525. **US Airways/US Airways Express** ☎ 800/428-4322.

AIRPORTS

AIRPORT TRANSFERS A trip from Pensacola Regional Airport via Yellow Cab costs about $14 to downtown and $24 to Pensacola Beach. A ride from the Okaloosa County Regional Airport via Checker Cab costs $18 to Fort Walton Beach and $24 to Destin. Bluewater Car Service charges $15–$17 to Fort Walton Beach and $28 to Destin. Yellow Cab charges about $15–$27 from Panama City–Bay County International Airport to the beach area, depending on the location of your hotel. DeLuxe Coach Limo Service provides van service to downtown Panama City and to Panama City Beach for $1.25 per mile. Yellow Cab travels from Tallahassee Regional Airport to downtown for $13–$16. Some Tallahassee hotels provide free shuttle service.

🔢 **Airport Information Okaloosa County Regional Airport** ☎ 850/651-7160 ⊕ www. okaloosacountyairports.com. **Panama City–Bay County International Airport** ☎ 850/

763–6751 ⊕ www.pcairport.com. **Pensacola Regional Airport** ☎ 850/436–5005
⊕ www.flypensacola.com. **Tallahassee Regional Airport** ☎ 850/891–7800 ⊕ talgov.
com/citytlh/aviation.

🛂 Airport Transportation Contacts **Okaloose County Airport: Gulf Coast Shuttle Service** ☎ 850/642–1042. **Panama City Beach: A Airport Limo** ☎ 850/233–0029. **Pensacola: All Airports Taxi and Shuttle** ☎ 850/622–1979 or 800/643–4711. **Tallahassee: Capital Transportation** ☎ 850/580–8080.

BUS TRAVEL
Greyhound has stations in Crestview, DeFuniak Springs, Fort Walton Beach, Panama City, Pensacola, and Tallahassee. The Baytown Trolley serves Bay County including downtown Panama City and the beaches ($1). In Pensacola, Escambia County Area Transit (ECAT) provides regular citywide bus service ($1), downtown trolley routes, tours through the historic district (25¢), and from Memorial Day to Labor Day free trolley service on Friday, Saturday, and Sunday.

🛂 Bus Information **Baytown Trolley** ☎ 850/769–0557. **Escambia County Area Transit** ☎ 850/595–3228. **Greyhound Lines** ☎ 800/231–2222, 850/682–6922 in Crestview, 850/892–5566 in DeFuniak Springs, 850/243–1940 in Fort Walton Beach, 850/785–6111 in Panama City, 850/476–4800 in Pensacola, 850/222–4240 in Tallahassee.

CAR RENTAL
🛂 **Alamo** ☎ 800/462–5266. **Avis** ☎ 800/331–1212. **Budget** ☎ 800/527–7000. **Hertz** ☎ 800/654–3131. **National** ☎ 800/227–7368.

CAR TRAVEL
The main east–west arteries across the top of the state are I–10 and U.S. 90. Pensacola is about an hour's drive east of Mobile. Tallahassee is 3½ hours west of Jacksonville. It takes about four hours from Pensacola to Tallahassee. Driving along I–10 can be monotonous, but U.S. 90 piques your interest by routing you along the main streets of several county seats. U.S. 98 snakes eastward along the coast, splitting into 98 and 98A at Inlet Beach before rejoining at Panama City and continuing on to Port St. Joe and Apalachicola. The view of the gulf from U.S. 98 can be breathtaking, especially at sunset, but ongoing construction projects, frequent 35 mph speed limits, and growing congestion make it slow going most of the time. If you need to get from one end of the Panhandle to the other in a timely manner, you're better off driving inland to I–10, where the speed limit runs as high as 70 mph in places. Even with the extra time it takes to drive inland, you'll wind up getting where you need to go much more quickly. Route 399 between Pensacola Beach and Navarre Beach was completely destroyed by Hurricane Ivan and, as of this writing, was not open. Major north–south highways that weave through the Panhandle are (from east to west) U.S. 231, U.S. 331, Route 85, and U.S. 29. From U.S. 331, which runs over a causeway at the east end of Choctawhatchee Bay between Route 20 and U.S. 98, the panorama of barge traffic and cabin cruisers on the twinkling waters of the Intracoastal Waterway will get your attention.

EMERGENCIES

Ambulance or Police Emergencies ☎ 911.

24-Hour Medical Care Destin Urgent Care and Diagnostic Center ✉ 996 Airport Rd., Destin ☎ 850/837-9194. **Fort Walton Beach Medical Center** ✉ 1000 Mar-Walt Dr., Fort Walton Beach ☎ 850/862-1111. **Gulf Coast Medical Center** ✉ 449 W. 23rd St., Panama City ☎ 850/769-8341. **Tallahassee Memorial Hospital** ✉ Magnolia Dr. and Miccosukee Rd., Tallahassee ☎ 850/431-1155. **West Florida Hospital** ✉ 8383 N. Davis Hwy., Pensacola ☎ 850/494-4000.

LODGING

In the Beaches of South Walton, two of the larger vacation-rental management companies that handle furnished rentals and offer free vacation guides are Abbott Resorts and Rivard of South Walton. On St. George Island, fully furnished homes can be rented through Suncoast Realty and Prudential Resort Realty.

HOME & CONDO RENTALS

Local Agents Abbott Resorts ☎ 800/336–4853 🌐 www.abbott-resorts.com. **Suncoast Realty** ☎ 800/341–2021 🌐 www.uncommonflorida.com. **Prudential Resort Realty** ☎ 800/332–5196 🌐 www.forgottencoastrealtor.com. **Rivard of South Walton** ☎ 800/423–3215 🌐 www.rivardnet.com.

MEDIA

NEWSPAPERS & MAGAZINES

Check the *Weekender,* the weekly entertainment magazine of the *Pensacola News Journal,* or the *Pensacola Downtown Crowd* to find out what's happening around the region and in the historic district. For the latest information in the Destin and Fort Walton areas, look for the *Emerald Coast's Insider Magazine. Chuck Spicer's Coast Line* (🌐 www.forgottencoastline.com) offers an informative and offbeat perspective on Florida's "Forgotten Coast" between Mexico Beach in Bay County and St. Marks in Wakulla County. In Tallahassee, the entertainment section of the *Tallahassee Democrat* is the most comprehensive local arts and entertainment guide.

TRAIN TRAVEL

Amtrak connects the Panhandle to the east and west coasts via the transcontinental *Sunset Limited* route, with station stops in Pensacola, Crestview, and Tallahassee.

Train Information Amtrak ☎ 800/872-7245.

VISITOR INFORMATION

All local visitor information centers are open weekdays, and many are open on Saturday—or all weekend—as well. In winter these hours might be curtailed, so call ahead or check the Web sites listed below for schedules. The Panhandle is blessed with many beautiful areas that are being preserved as parks by the state of Florida. Check out the Florida Department of Environmental Protection's excellent parks Web site for hours and admission fees, as well as photos and brief histories of the parks.

Tourist Information Apalachicola Bay Chamber of Commerce ✉ 122 Commerce St., Apalachicola 32320 ☎ 850/653-9419 🌐 www.apalachicolabay.org. **Beaches of South Walton Visitor Information Center** ✉ U.S. 331 and U.S. 98, Santa Rosa Beach 32459 ☎ 850/267-1216 or 800/822-6877 🌐 www.beachesofsouthwalton.com. **Destin**

Chamber of Commerce ✉ 4484 Legendary Dr., Destin 32541 ☎ 850/837-6241 ⊕ www. destinchamber.com. **Emerald Coast Convention & Visitors Bureau** ✉ 1540 Miracle Strip Pkwy. SE, Fort Walton Beach 32548 ☎ 850/651-7131 or 800/322-3319 ⊕ www.destin-fwb.com. **Florida Department of Environmental Protection-Parks Division** ☎ 850/245-2157 Information Line ⊕ www.dep.state.fl.us/parks. **Panama City Beach Convention & Visitors Bureau** ✉ 17001 Panama City Beach Pkwy., Panama City Beach 32413 ☎ 850/233-5070 or 800/722-3224 ⊕ www.800pcbeach.com. **Pensacola Visitor Information Center** ✉ 1401 E. Gregory St., Pensacola 32502 ☎ 850/434-1234 or 800/874-1234 ⊕ www.visitpensacola.com. **Tallahassee Area Convention and Visitors Bureau** ✉ 106 E. Jefferson St., Tallahassee 32301 ☎ 850/413-9200 or 800/628-2866 ⊕ www. seetallahassee.com. **Walton County Chamber of Commerce** ✉ 95 Circle Dr., DeFuniak Springs 32433 ☎ 850/892-3191 ⊕ www.waltoncountychamber.com.

Northeast Florida

WORD OF MOUTH

"[In the St. Augustine historic district] there are several things you can do within easy walking distance. Shopping on George Street and the side streets is a must. There is a trolley tour of town that allows on/off privileges. You can also take a carriage ride tour. Flagler College, in the old Ponce de Leon Hotel, offers hour-long tours of its impressive building.

For something really cool that not many people see, head through the breezeways of the Lightner Museum (the Alcazar Hotel, back in the day) and toward the right out back to the antique mall. It's actually housed in the hotel's former indoor swimming pool! Very impressive."

—xrae

Updated by
Kerry
Speckman

SOME OF THE OLDEST SETTLEMENTS IN THE STATE—indeed in all of the United States—are in northeastern Florida, although the region didn't get much attention until the Union army came through during the Civil War. The soldiers' rapturous accounts of the mild climate, pristine beaches, and lush vegetation captured the imagination of folks up north. First came the speculators and the curiosity seekers. Then the advent of the railroads brought more permanent settlers and the first wave of winter vacationers. Finally, the automobile transported the full rush of snowbirds, seasonal residents escaping from harsh northern winters. They still come, to sop up sun on the beach, to tee up year-round, to bass-fish and bird-watch in forests and parks, and to party in the clubs and bars of Daytona, a popular spring-break destination. The region is remarkably diverse. Tortured, towering live oaks; plantations; and antebellum-style architecture recollect the Old South. The mossy marshes of Silver Springs and the St. Johns River look as untouched and junglelike today as they did generations ago. Horse farms around Ocala resemble Kentucky's bluegrass country or the hunt clubs of Virginia. St. Augustine is a showcase of early U.S. history, and Jacksonville is a young but sophisticated metropolis. Yet these are all but light diversions from northeastern Florida's primary draw—absolutely sensational beaches. Hugging the coast are long, slender barrier islands whose entire eastern sides make up a broad band of spectacular sand. Except in the most populated areas, development has been modest, and beaches are lined with funky, appealing little towns.

Exploring Northeast Florida

The region defies any single description. Much of its tourist territory lies along the Atlantic coast, both on the mainland and on the barrier islands just offshore. A1A (mostly called Atlantic Avenue) is the main road on all the barrier islands, and it's here that you find the best beaches. Both Jacksonville, the region's only real high-rise city, and the relatively remote Amelia Island, just south of the Georgia border, are in the far northeast. St. Augustine, about a 45-minute drive south of Jacksonville on I–95, is the historic capital of this part of Florida. Farther south along the coast, the diversity continues among neighbors like Daytona Beach, where annual events are geared toward spring-breakers, auto racers, and bikers; New Smyrna Beach, which offers quiet appeal; and Cocoa Beach, the ultimate boogie-board beach town. Inland are charming small towns, the sprawling Ocala National Forest, and bustling Gainesville, home of the University of Florida.

About the Restaurants

The ocean, St. Johns River, and numerous lakes and smaller rivers are teeming with fish, and so, naturally, seafood dominates local menus. In coastal towns, catches are often from the restaurant's own fleet. Shrimp, snapper, swordfish, and grouper are especially prevalent.

About the Hotels

For the busy seasons—during summer in and around Jacksonville, and during summer holiday weekends all over Florida—always reserve well ahead for the top properties. Jacksonville beaches' hotels fill up quickly for the PGA Players Championship in late March. Daytona Beach presents similar lodging dilemmas during the Daytona 500 (mid-February), Bike Week (late February–early March), Spring Break (March), and the Pepsi 400 (early July). St. Augustine stays busy all year because of its historic character. Fall is the slowest season: rates are low and availability is high, but it is also the prime time for hurricanes.

	WHAT IT COSTS				
	$$$$	$$$	$$	$	¢
RESTAURANTS	over $30	$20–$30	$15–$20	$10–$15	under $10
HOTELS	over $220	$140–$220	$100–$140	$80–$100	under $80

Restaurant prices are per person for a main course at dinner. Hotel prices are for a standard double room, excluding 6% sales tax (more in some counties) and 1%–4% tourist tax.

Timing

Fair weather is one of the many factors drawing residents to the area. The temperature dips to the low 50s in Jacksonville and low 60s in Cocoa Beach in winter and hovers around 80 in summer throughout the area. The ocean warms up by March, when college kids on spring break often pack the beaches—but this is also the best month to see the azalea gardens in bloom. Midsummer is hot, yet breezy, as long as you stick to the beaches; inland, the heat and humidity can be stifling.

JACKSONVILLE

①–⑩ *399 mi north of Miami.*

One of Florida's oldest cities and at 730 square mi the largest city in the continental United States, Jacksonville makes for an underrated vacation spot. It offers appealing downtown riverside areas, handsome residential neighborhoods, the region's only skyscrapers, a thriving arts scene, and, for football fans, the NFL Jaguars and the NCAA Gator Bowl. Remnants of the Old South flavor the city, especially in the Riverside/Avondale historic district where moss-draped oak trees frame Prairie-style bungalows and Tudor Revival mansions, and palm trees, Spanish bayonet, and azaleas populate Jacksonville's landscape.

Exploring Jacksonville

Because Jacksonville was settled along both sides of the twisting St. Johns River, a number of attractions are on or near a riverbank. Both sides of the river, which is spanned by myriad bridges, have downtown areas and waterfront complexes of shops, restaurants, parks, and museums; some attractions can be reached by water taxi or Skyway Express monorail system—scenic alteratives to driving back and forth across the bridges—but a car is generally necessary.

Numbers in the text correspond to numbers in the margin and on the Jacksonville map.

Numbers in the text correspond to numbers in the margin and on the Northeast Florida and St. Augustine maps.

If you have 3 days

Spend your first night in ▦ **Jacksonville** ❶ ▶ –⑩, using it as a base to explore the **Jacksonville Museum of Modern Art** ❼ or the **Cummer Museum of Art and Gardens** ❹, as well as Fort Clinch State Park on **Amelia Island** ⑬, which has one of the best-preserved brick forts in the United States. Take Interstate 95 south to **St. Augustine** ⑭–㉜ and see the restored **Colonial Spanish Quarter** ⑰ and the **Castillo de San Marcos National Monument** ⑱ before continuing down the coast. Enjoy Canaveral National Seashore—accessible from either ▦ **New Smyrna Beach** ㉟ or ▦ **Cocoa Beach** ㊴—and don't miss the Kennedy Space Center Visitor Complex in **Titusville** ㊱.

If you have 5 days

Before leaving **Jacksonville** ❶ ▶ –⑩ try to visit the three largest museums, the **Jacksonville Museum of Modern Art** ❼, the **Cummer Museum of Art and Gardens** ❹, and the **Museum of Science and History** ❺. Then focus your sightseeing on **Amelia Island** ⑬, including its historic district and Fort Clinch State Park. Going south on Interstate 95, stop in **St. Augustine** ⑭–㉜. Follow the Old City Walking Tour suggested by the **Visitor Information and Preview Center** ⑭ and stroll through the restored **Colonial Spanish Quarter** ⑰. Consider taking the slightly longer but more scenic Route A1A to **Daytona Beach** ㉞; visit the Museum of Arts and Sciences and the famous beaches. For your last night, stay in ▦ **New Smyrna Beach** ㉟ or ▦ **Cocoa Beach** ㊴, both within reach of Canaveral National Seashore and Kennedy Space Center.

If you have 10 days

As in the previous two itineraries, start in ▦ **Jacksonville** ❶ ▶ –⑩ and visit the attractions mentioned above; by staying three nights, however, you'll have time to make the drive north to Kingsley Plantation, Florida's oldest remaining plantation, on Fort George Island, and hike or picnic in Fort Clinch State Park on **Amelia Island** ⑬. Next, head to ▦ **St. Augustine** ⑭–㉜. Three days here enable you to conduct a more leisurely exploration of the extensive historic district and to take in the **Lightner Museum** ㉑, in what was originally one of Henry Flagler's fancy hotels. Another three-day stay, this time based at ▦ **Daytona Beach** ㉞, ▦ **New Smyrna Beach** ㉟, or ▦ **Cocoa Beach** ㊴, allows you to cover Daytona's Museum of Arts and Sciences, drive along the shoreline, spend some time at the beach, and see Canaveral National Seashore, as well as the Kennedy Space Center Visitor Complex near **Titusville** ㊱. Then head inland for a day in **Ocala National Forest** ㊸, a beautiful wilderness area.

a good tour

Start your morning at the riverfront campus of Jacksonville University, site of the **Alexander Brest Museum** ❶ ▶. After browsing the collections, head south on University Boulevard and east on Arlington Expressway to **Kona Skatepark** ❷, where you can practice your sausage grinds or watch X-treme athletes riding the concrete wave. Even if you've just worked up a virtual sweat, you'll want to cool off, so go east on Atlantic Boulevard, over the Hart Bridge, to **Kids Kampus** ❸, a 10-acre recreational facility with a splash park. Next, head west on Gator Bowl Boulevard–Bay Street and follow the signs for Riverside to get to another riverfront landmark, the **Cummer Museum of Art and Gardens** ❹. After touring the museum and its grounds, head back on Riverside Avenue toward the Acosta Bridge and take the first exit, San Marco Boulevard. Two blocks north is the **Museum of Science and History** ❺. Walk a block south to the Automated Skyway Express station and take a monorail across the river to the **Jacksonville Landing** ❻, where you can shop and grab some lunch. Afterward, walk four blocks north to the **Jacksonville Museum of Modern Art** ❼. Head back to the Landing to recross the river, but for the return trip, catch a water taxi. On the road again, go back over the Acosta Bridge and stay on Broad Street to 1st Street, where you'll find the **Karpeles Manuscript Library Museum** ❽. Next, proceed west on State Street to Interstate 95 North, then take the Heckscher Drive exit east to Zoo Road for the **Jacksonville Zoo** ❾. Finally, head back to Interstate 95 North and exit east at Dunn Avenue, which becomes Busch Road, and visit the **Anheuser-Busch Jacksonville Brewery** ❿.

TIMING   Jacksonville's sprawl dictates a generous amount of time for reaching and touring these sights. Allow at least two days, six hours a day (including driving time), budgeting at least an hour for each attraction, more for the zoo and the modern art museum.

What to See

▶ ❶ **Alexander Brest Museum.** Boehm and Royal Copenhagen porcelain and Steuben glass are among the collections at this Jacksonville University museum. Also on display are cloisonné pieces, pre-Columbian artifacts, and one of the finest collections of ivory from the early 17th to the late 19th century. ✉ *Jacksonville University, Phillips Fine Arts Bldg., 2800 University Blvd. N* ☎ *904/744–3950 Ext. 3371* ⌧ *Free* ☉ *Weekdays 9–4:30, Sat. noon–5.*

❿ **Anheuser-Busch Jacksonville Brewery.** If you're a beer connoisseur, don't miss a guided or self-guided tour here, which takes you through the entire brewing and bottling process. There are free beer tastings and logo-filled gift shops. You must be at least 18 to visit the brewery or shops. ✉ *111 Busch Dr.* ☎ *904/696–8373* ⊕ *www.budweisertours.com* ⌧ *Free* ☉ *Mon.–Sat. 10–4; guided tours Mon.–Sat. 10–3 on the half hr.*

❹ **Cummer Museum of Art and Gardens.** The world-famous Wark Collection of early-18th-century Meissen porcelain is just one reason to visit this former riverfront estate, which includes 12 permanent galleries with more than 5,000 items spanning more than 8,000 years and 3 acres of gardens reflecting Northeast Florida's blooming seasons and indigenous varieties. For the kids, Art Connections allows them to "experience" art through hands-on, interactive exhibits. ✉ *829 Riverside Ave.* ☎ *904/356–6857* ⊕ *www.cummer.org* ⌧ *$6, free Tues. 4–9* ☉ *Tues. and Thurs. 10–9, Wed., Fri., and Sat. 10–5, Sun. noon–5. Closed Mon.*

❻ **Jacksonville Landing.** During the week, the riverfront festival marketplace here caters to locals and tourists alike, with more than 40 specialty shops with home furnishings, apparel, and toys, nine full-service restaurants—

2

Beaches

The northeast has luxuriously long beaches. Some are hard-packed white sand, while others have slightly reddish sand with a coarse, grainy texture. Waves are normally gentle, and many areas are safe for swimming. However, take care when the surf is up and obey lifeguard instructions. The very fragile dunes, held in place by sea grasses, are responsible for protecting the shore from the sea; Florida law mandates that you neither pick the sea oats nor walk on or play in the dunes. A single afternoon of careless roughhousing can destroy a dune forever. The area's most densely developed beaches, with rows of high-rise condominiums and hotels, are in Daytona and Cocoa Beach. Elsewhere, coastal towns are still mostly small and laid-back, and beaches are crowded only on summer weekends.

Bird-Watching

Florida's diverse habitat is a bird-watcher's heaven. The wetlands, marshes, and warm weather attract hundreds of migratory birds, many of which are rare and seldom seen. The Great Florida Birding Trail (www.floridabirdingtrail.com), a program of the Florida Fish and Wildlife Conservation Commission, maps out Northeast Florida's best birding locations. What you can see through your binoculars depends on the season, location, and time of day.

Canoeing

Inland, especially in Ocala National Forest, sparkling-clear spring "runs" may be mere tunnels through tangled jungle growth. You can also canoe the grassy marshes near the coast and the maze of shallow inlets along the inland waterway side of Canaveral National Seashore.

Fishing

From cane-pole fishing in a roadside canal to throwing a line off a pier to deep-sea fishing from a luxury charter boat, options abound. There's no charge (or a nominal one) to fish from many causeways, beaches, and piers. Deep-sea fishing charters are available up and down the coast.

Skydiving

DeLand is the skydiving capital of the world. Spectators can watch high-flying competitions, while those interested in swooping down from an airplane from thousands of feet up can try solo or tandem jumping.

---

including a brew pub, Italian bistro, and steak house—and an internationally-flavored food court. On weekends the Landing hosts special events, including the American Cancer Society Duck Race, and the Florida–Georgia game after-party in the courtyard, directly on the St. Johns River. ⊠ *2 Independent Dr.* ☎ *904/353–1188* ⊕ *www. jacksonvillelanding.com* ⊡ *Free* ⊙ *Mon.–Thurs. 10–8, Fri. and Sat. 10–9, Sun. noon–5:30; some restaurants open earlier and close later.*

❼ **Jacksonville Museum of Modern Art.** In this loftlike, 14,000-square-foot
Fodor'sChoice building, the former headquarters of the Western Union Telegraph Com-
★ pany, a permanent collection of 20th-century art shares space with traveling exhibitions. The museum encompasses five galleries and

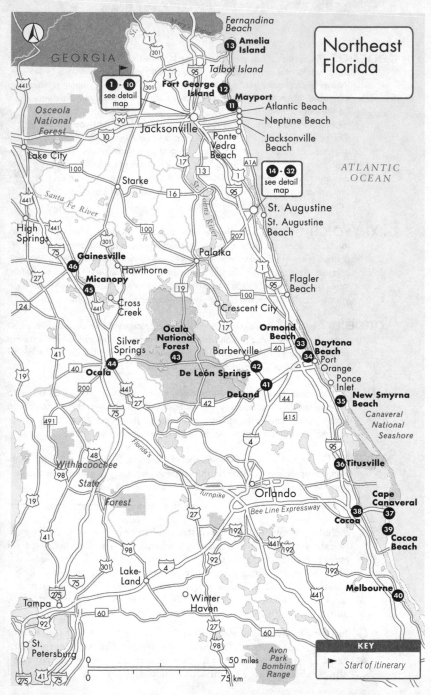

GEORGIA

Northeast Florida

Fernandina Beach

13 Amelia Island

Talbot Island

Fort George Island

1 - 10 see detail map

12

11 Mayport

Atlantic Beach

Neptune Beach

Jacksonville Beach

Jacksonville

Ponte Vedra Beach

Osceola National Forest

Lake City

Starke

High Springs

Santa Fe River

14 - 32 see detail map

St. Augustine

St. Augustine Beach

ATLANTIC OCEAN

Palatka

Gainesville

46

Hawthorne

Micanopy

45

Cross Creek

Flagler Beach

Crescent City

Silver Springs

Ocala National Forest

43

Barberville

Ormond Beach

33

Daytona Beach

34

Port Orange

Ocala

44

De León Springs 42

DeLand

41

Ponce Inlet

35 New Smyrna Beach

Canaveral National Seashore

Withlacoochee State Forest

Florida's Turnpike

Orlando

Bee Line Expressway

36 Titusville

Cape Canaveral

38

37

Cocoa

39 Cocoa Beach

Lake-Land

Winter Haven

Tampa

Melbourne 40

St. Petersburg

Avon Park Bombing Range

50 miles

0

0   75 km

KEY

▶ *Start of itinerary*

ArtExplorium, a highly interactive educational exhibit for kids, as well as a funky gift shop and Cafe Nola, open for breakfast, lunch, and weekly wine-tasting events. JMOMA also hosts film series, lectures, and workshops. ⊠ *Hemming Plaza, 333 N. Laura St.* ☎ *904/366–6911* ⊕ *www. jmoma.org* ≊ *$6, free Wed. 5–9 and Sun.* ☉ *Tues. and Fri. 11–5, Wed. and Thurs. 11–9, Sat. 11–4, Sun. noon–4; hours subject to change.*

ⓒ ❾ **Jacksonville Zoo.** Among the zoo's outstanding exhibits is its collection
Fodor's Choice of rare waterfowl and the Serona Overlook, which showcases some of
★ the world's most venomous snakes. The Florida Wetlands is a 2½-acre area with black bears, bald eagles, white-tailed deer, and other animals native to Florida. The African Veldt has alligators, elephants, and white rhinos, among other species of African birds and mammals. Kids get a kick out of the petting zoo, and everyone goes bananas over Great Apes of the World. The zoo's newest exhibit, the Range of the Jaguar, includes 4 acres of exotic big cats as well as 20 other species of animals. ⊠ *8605 Zoo Pkwy., off Heckscher Dr. E* ☎ *904/757–4463* ⊕ *www.jaxzoo. org.* ≊ *$9.50* ☉ *Daily 9–5.*

❽ **Karpeles Manuscript Library Museum.** Preserving and presenting original works of authors, scientists, composers, philosophers, and world leaders is the mission of this museum, in a 1921 neoclassical building on the outskirts of downtown. On display are a changing selection of priceless manuscripts, which have included the original draft of the Bill of Rights, the Emancipation Proclamation signed by Abraham Lincoln, handwritten manuscripts of Edgar Allan Poe and Charles Dickens, and musical scores by Beethoven and Mozart. Also on the premises are an antique-book library, with volumes dating from the late 1800s, and a children's museum. ⊠ *101 W. 1st St.* ☎ *904/356–2992* ⊕ *www.rain. org/~karpeles/jaxfrm.html* ≊ *Free* ☉ *Tues.–Sat. 10–3.*

ⓒ ❸ **Kids Kampus.** Directly on the St. Johns River adjacent to Metropolitan Park, this 10-acre recreational facility, developed by local educators, encourages children's natural curiosity with climbing and sliding apparati, engaging playscapes, mini-representations of Jacksonville landmarks, like Bay Street, Kings Road, and the main post office, and a splash park. The "kampus" also has a picnic pavilion and jogging trail. ⊠ *1410 Gator Bowl Blvd.* ☎ *904/630–5437* ≊ *Free* ☉ *Mar.–Oct., Mon.–Sat. 8–8, Sun. 10–8; Nov.–Feb., Mon.–Sat. 8–6, Sun. 10–6.*

ⓒ ❷ **Kona Skatepark.** Built back in the '70s—before most of its patrons were even born—this X-treme sport outpost still has its original bowls, plus updates like an 80-foot-wide vertical ramp, two street courses, and one of the area's few snake runs (a high-speed, downhill run with banked turns). Skateboard legend Tony Hawk digs the park's retro feel so much that he named it one of his five favorite U.S. skate parks. For those less experienced, the park, which also caters to in-line skaters, rents boards, skates, and safety equipment (required of all skaters) and offers lessons. ⊠ *8739 Kona Ave.* ☎ *904/725–8770, 866/758–5662* ⊕ *www. konaskatepark.com* ≊ *$10* ☉ *Weekdays noon–10, Sat. 10–10, Sun. 1–9.*

ⓒ ❺ **Museum of Science and History.** Permanent exhibits here include Atlantic Tails, a hands-on exploration of whales, dolphins, and manatees; Cur-

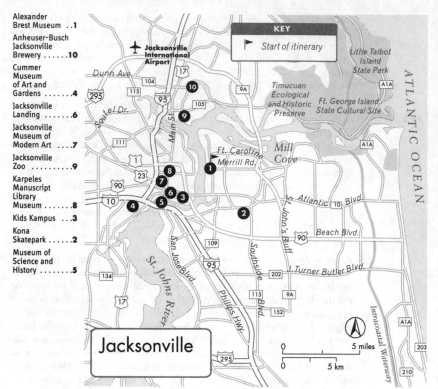

rents of Time, chronicling 12,000 years of northeast Florida history; the
HoloZone, a virtual-reality exhibit that puts guests right in the action;
and the Universe of Science, a state-of-the-art center that investigates
the world of science. The Alexander Brest Planetarium hosts daily shows
on astronomy and, on weekends, Cosmic Concerts, 3-D laser shows set
to pop music. ⊠ *1025 Museum Circle* ☎ *904/396–6674* ⊕ *www.
themosh.org.* ☜ *$7, Cosmic Concerts $3–$6* ☉ *Weekdays 10–5, Sat.
10–6, Sun. 1–6.*

**off the
beaten
path**

FORT CAROLINE NATIONAL MEMORIAL – Spread over 130 acres
along the St. Johns River 13 mi northeast of downtown Jacksonville
(via Route 113), this site holds both historical and recreational
interest. The original fort was built in the 1560s by French
Huguenots, who were later slaughtered by the Spanish in the first
major clash between European powers for control of what would
become the United States. An oak-wood pathway leads to a replica of
the original fort—a great, sunny place to picnic (bring your own food
and drink), stretch your legs, and explore a small museum. There's
also a 1-mi self-guided trail with signs describing natural and cultural
history. ⊠ *12713 Fort Caroline Rd.* ☎ *904/641–7155* ⊕ *www.nps.
gov/foca* ☜ *Free* ☉ *Museum daily 9–5.*

Where to Stay & Eat

$$$-$$$$
Fodor'sChoice
★ ✕ **Matthew's.** Chef-owner Matthew Medure creates masterpieces in one of Jacksonville's trendiest neighborhoods. The dramatically spare decor—stainless steel, polished bronze, and terrazzo flooring—is a perfect foil for his dazzling food. The menu changes nightly but might include lemon-roasted Amish chicken with honey-truffle spaghetti squash or herb-roasted rack of lamb with mustard pistachio crust. Complement your meal with one of 450 wines (topping out at $1,100 per bottle), then dive into one of the baked warm soufflés for dessert. ⊠ *2107 Hendricks Ave., San Marco* ☎ *904/396–9922* ⊟ *AE, D, DC, MC, V* ☾ *Closed Sun. No lunch.*

$$$-$$$$ ✕ **Wine Cellar.** Tables are well spaced in cozy dining areas on several levels and on an outdoor patio in this elegant candlelit spot with exposed brick walls. Try the filet mignon served over a potato, leek and Asiago tart, topped with wild mushroom demi-glace. Chocolate truffle torte, key lime pie, and cheesecake du jour are dessert highlights. The wine list includes more than 250 choices. ⊠ *1314 Prudential Dr., San Marco* ☎ *904/398–8989* ⊟ *AE, D, DC, MC, V* ☾ *Closed Sun. No lunch Sat.*

$$-$$$$ ✕ **River City Brewing Company.** Take one of the free daily brewery tours (by appointment only) at this brewpub overlooking the river and then sample the day's brew. Lunch leans toward sandwiches and salads; dinner includes shrimp, fresh fish, grilled steaks, and seafood jambalaya. During the warmer months, young professionals flock to the deck for Friday happy hour. On weekend nights, local bands and DJs entertain both inside and out. Sunday brunch is a scrumptious event. If you miss brunch, catch the Sunday-night seafood buffet. ⊠ *835 Museum Circle, Southbank Riverwalk* ☎ *904/398–2299* ⊟ *AE, D, DC, MC, V.*

★ $-$$$$ ✕ **Bistro Aix.** Locals head for the patio for a delightful candlelight dinner when the weather is nice; indoors, there are romantic velvet drapes, banquettes, and exposed brick walls. Grilled salmon or filet mignon are good choices. Crispy, thin-crust pizzas, baked in the wood-burning oven, pastas, and salads are among the lighter choices. Belgian chocolate cake, served warm and topped with vanilla whipped cream, caps a perfect evening. Call ahead for preferred seating. ⊠ *1440 San Marco Blvd., San Marco* ☎ *904/398–1949* ⚠ *Reservations not accepted* ⊟ *AE, D, DC, MC, V* ☾ *No lunch weekends.*

$-$$$ ✕ **Biscottis.** The local artwork on the redbrick walls is a mild distraction from the jovial crowds jockeying for tables in this midsize restaurant. Elbows almost touch, but no one seems to mind. The menu offers the unexpected: wild-mushroom ravioli with a broth of corn, leek, and dried apricot; or curry grilled swordfish with cucumber fig bordelaise. Don't be too quick to pass up either the daily specials or the mouthwatering desserts. ⊠ *3556 St. Johns Ave., Avondale* ☎ *904/387–2060* ⚠ *Reservations not accepted* ⊟ *AE, MC, V.*

★ ¢-$$$ ✕ **bb's.** Sleek yet cozy, this hip bistro is as popular with corporate muckety-mucks looking to close a deal as it is with thirtysomething lovebirds seemingly on the verge of popping the question. The modern decor, which includes concrete floors and a stainless-steel wine bar, provides an interesting backdrop for comfort food–inspired entrées and daily specials that might include char-grilled beef tenderloin, prosciutto-wrapped pork chops, or mushroom triangoli ravioli. On the lighter side, grilled pizzas, sandwiches, and salads, especially warm goat cheese salad, are favorites. Although a wait is practically guaranteed, you can pass the time sizing up the display of decadent desserts. ⊠ *1019 Hendricks Ave., San Marco* 🕾 *904/306–0100* ⌖ *Reservations not accepted* ▤ *AE, D, DC, MC, V* ☺ *Closed Sun.*

¢–$$ ✕ **Clark's Fish Camp.** It's out of the way and hard to find, but every mile
Fodor'sChoice and missed turn will be forgiven once you step inside this former bait
★ shop overlooking Julington Creek. Clark's has one of the largest menus in town, with more than 160 appetizers and entrées, including the usual—shrimp, catfish, and oysters—and the unusual—ostrich, rattlesnake, and kangaroo. In keeping with the more bizarre entrées is the decor, best described as Early American Taxidermy: hundreds of stuffed birds and critters gaze upon you in the main dining room, while preserved lions, gazelles, baboons, even a rhino, keep a watchful eye in the bar. Creepy sounding, yes, but the kitsch is strangely comforting. Reservations are accepted for parties of eight or more; call-ahead service is available for everyone else. ⊠ *12903 Hood Landing Rd., Mandarin* 🕾 *904/268–3474* ▤ *D, MC, V* ☺ *No lunch weekdays.*

¢–$$ ✕ **Mossfire.** The tongue-in-cheek name of this Southwest-inspired restaurant speaks to the sassy waitstaff and patrons who frequent it (the city's Great Fire of 1901 was started when a mattress factory, which processed moss, caught fire). Dinner entrées range from fish tacos and crab cake salad to New York strip loin and pecan chicken. The dimly lit upstairs lounge has a coffeehouse vibe—with a handful of cozy booths, two-tops, and leather couches, also with a Southwestern flair—and showcases local bands Friday and Saturday evenings. ⊠ *1537 Margaret St., Riverside* 🕾 *904/355–4434* ⌖ *Reservations not accepted* ▤ *AE, MC, V.*

¢–$ ✕ **Al's Pizza.** While it fits the criteria of a neighborhood pizza joint—cheap, casual, and frequented by locals—this funky-chic pizzeria looks more like a hangout for L.A. hipsters than Jacksonvillians low on dough. Both in-town locations are slick, art deco–inspired spaces with colorful palettes, wood-and-steel accents, and original artwork throughout. As to be expected, the main draw is the pizza, particularly Al's gourmet white pizza, but eggplant parmigiana, stuffed shells, and lasagna are also good. The location in Riverside caters to its more upscale clientele with table service and a separate bar area. ⊠ *1620 Margaret St. #201, Riverside* 🕾 *904/388–8384* ⊠ *14286 Beach Blvd., Intracoastal West* 🕾 *904/223–0991* ⌖ *Reservations not accepted* ▤ *AE, D, MC, V.*

¢–$ ✕ **La Nopalera.** For diners seeking authentic Mexican food in Jacksonville, this family-owned restaurant is numero uno. The menu is as standard—tacos, burritos, enchiladas, and fajitas with rice and beans as sides—as the decor, limited to serapes and neon beer signs on the walls and faded piñatas hanging from the ceiling. But huge and inexpensive portions keep customers loyal. ⊠ *1621 Hendricks Ave., San Marco* 🕾 *904/399–1768* ⊠ *8818 Atlantic Blvd., Regency* 🕾 *904/720–0106* ⌖ *Reservations not accepted* ▤ *AE, D, MC, V* ☺ *Closed Sun.*

★ ¢ ✕ **European Street.** Wicker baskets and lofty shelves brimming with European confections and groceries like Toblerone and Nutella fill practically every inch of space not occupied by café tables. The menu can be similarly overwhelming, with nearly 100 deli sandwiches and salads. Notable are raspberry almond chicken salad, stuffed turkey wrap with cranberry sauce and stuffing, and the "Blue Max," with pastrami, corned beef, Swiss cheese, sauerkraut, hot mustard, and blue-cheese dressing. This spot is favored by area professionals looking for a quick lunch, as well as the under-forty set doing 23-ounce curls with one of the restaurant's 20-plus beers on tap (plus more than 100 in bottles). ⊠ *2753 Park St., Riverside* ☎ *904/384–9999* ⊠ *1704 San Marco Blvd., San Marco* ☎ *904/398–9500* ⊠ *5500 Beach Blvd., Southside* ☎ *904/398–1717* ⚑ *Reservations not accepted* ▭ *AE, MC, V.*

¢ ✕ **The Loop Pizza Grill.** Standing in line to place their orders, first-time diners may think this Jacksonville-based chain is just another fast-food joint. But one look at the menu, chock-full of designer salads, specialty pizzas, and upscale sandwiches, not to mention the stylish dining room complete with upholstered booths, funky light fixtures, and tiled floors, and they'll think they're in McDreamland. The big sellers here are the burgers (the Loop 'N Cheddar and Loop 'N Blue, in particular) and pizzas (both California-thin and Chicago-thick), but sandwiches like the portobello mushroom and cajun chicken merit special mention. The onion rings and milk shakes are among the best in town. ⊠ *2014 San Marco Blvd., San Marco* ☎ *904/399–5667 or 904/725–0850* ⊠ *14444 Beach Blvd., San Pablo* ☎ *904/223–6611 or 904/448–0322* ⊠ *9965 San Jose Blvd., Mandarin* ☎ *904/262–2210* ⊠ *4000 St. Johns Ave., Avondale* ☎ *904/384–7301* ⊠ *8221 Southside Blvd., Baymeadows* ☎ *904/645– 7788* ⚑ *Reservations not accepted* ▭ *AE, D, MC, V.*

¢ ✕ **Tidbits.** Don't be put off by the herd of customers waiting to order: the line moves fast and any wait is well worth it. Catering to downtown and San Marco worker bees, this lunch-only restaurant serves sandwiches and salads that are as fresh as they are delicious. Sandwiches include the chicken supreme pita, french dip, and veggie surprise; salads include a chicken and fruit plate and the top-selling Tidbit Special, with seasoned chicken chunks and pasta on a bed of lettuce topped with avocado and cheddar. Try Clara's potato salad, which has become legendary in these parts. ⊠ *1076 Hendricks Ave., San Marco* ☎ *904/396–0528* ⚑ *Reservations not accepted* ⊘ *Closed weekends. No dinner.*

★ $$$–$$$$ ▣ **Omni Jacksonville Hotel.** The 16-story ultramodern facility is in the heart of downtown. The splashy marble-floor lobby leads to the reception area, an upscale bar and lounge, and a restaurant with cozy banquettes and tables that look up to a soaring atrium. Further cementing its reputation as the city's most glamorous, the hotel has undergone a $4.5-million makeover including "downtown urban style" guest rooms (think dark wood, stainless steel and flat-screen TVs) and an expanded fitness center. It also scores high marks for its family-oriented atmosphere, including Nintendo in every room, no adult films, and the Omni Kids Rule program. Bell service is also exemplary: with most porters having 10-plus years on the job, they can, and will, help you find just about anything. ⊠ *245 Water St., 32202* ☎ *904/355–6664 or 800/843–6664* 🖷 *904/791–4812* ⊕ *www.omnijacksonville.com* ⇋ *354 rooms, 4 suites* ⚘ *Restaurant, coffee shop, room service, minibars, cable TV with* *movies and video games, in-room data ports, pool, gym, bar, shop, children's programs (ages 3–10), dry cleaning, concierge, Internet, business services, meeting rooms, parking (fee), some pets allowed (fee), no-smoking floors* ⊟ *AE, D, DC, MC, V.*

$$$ 🏨 **Embassy Suites Hotel.** The Baymeadows location makes Jacksonville's only full-service, all-suites hotel convenient to a number of restaurants, clubs, and shops. All units feature a balcony and overlook the six-story atrium. Each has a separate living room with sleep sofa, a refrigerator, and a microwave. A cooked-to-order breakfast and a two-hour cocktail reception on weekdays are also included in the rate. ✉ *9300 Baymeadows Rd., 32256* ☎ *904/731–3555 or 800/362–2779* 📠 *904/731–4972* ⊕ *www.embassysuitesjax.com* 🛏 *277 suites* ⚓ *Restaurant, room service, kitchenettes, microwaves, refrigerators, cable TV with movies and video games, in-room data ports, indoor pool, gym, hot tub, sauna, steam room, bar, dry cleaning, laundry facilities, laundry service, business services, Internet, meeting rooms, free parking, no-smoking floors* ⊟ *AE, DC, MC, V* ⏲ *BP.*

★ $$$ 🏨 **Plantation Manor Inn.** Stately, yet cozy, this three-story Greek Revival plantation home has been divvied up into nine unique guest rooms, each with elegant antique furniture, Oriental rugs, and artwork. Authenticity aside, innkeepers Kathy and Jerry Ray understand the need for modern conveniences and equip each room with a private bath, hair dryer, iron and ironing board, and high-speed Internet access. The tranquil garden has a lap pool and hot tub. ✉ *1630 Copeland St., 32204* ☎ *904/384–4630* 📠 *904/387–0960* ⊕ *www.plantationmanorinn.com* 🛏 *9 rooms* ⚓ *Dining room, cable TV, some in-room VCRs, in-room data ports, pool, outdoor hot tub, Internet, business services, meeting rooms, free parking; no kids under 12, no smoking* ⊟ *AE, DC, MC, V* ⏲ *BP.*

★ $$–$$$ 🏨 **Adam's Mark.** In Jacksonville, it doesn't get much more convenient than this downtown, waterfront hotel. Perched on the north bank of the St. Johns River, the nine-story property is within walking distance of the Jacksonville Landing, Florida Theatre, and T-U Center, as well as corporate office towers and the county courthouse. Fortunately, luxury is not forsaken for convenience. A glitzy, grand lobby greets guests, who have access to a full range of amenities, including an exceptional Italian restaurant with opera-singing servers and a rooftop swimming pool. Rooms were designed with the business traveler in mind and include a large work desk, two-line speaker phone with voice mail, and a data port. Upgrade to a VIP Club Level room and you'll enjoy a private lounge where a complimentary breakfast is served every morning, hors d'oeuvres every night. ✉ *225 Coastline Dr. E, 32202* ☎ *904/633–9095 or 800/444–2326* 📠 *904/633–9988* ⊕ *www.adamsmark.com/ jacksonville* 🛏 *966 rooms, 21 suites* ⚓ *2 restaurants, room service, some refrigerators, cable TV with movies and video games, in-room data ports, pool, gym, sauna, lobby lounge, sports bar, shop, dry cleaning, laundry facilities, laundry service, concierge, concierge floor, Internet, business services, convention center, parking (fee), no-smoking floors* ⊟ *AE, D, DC, MC, V.*

★ $$–$$$ 🏨 **Hilton Jacksonville Riverfront.** Sitting on the water, this handsome eight-story hotel has a commanding presence. Its location on the south side of the St. Johns River puts it within easy walking distance of museums, restaurants, and the water taxi; Ruth's Chris Steak House is one of the on-site restaurants. Spacious rooms have walk-out balconies and city or river views. Guests truly wanting to live like a king can book the San Marco (aka the Elvis Room), a premier suite with Jacuzzi tub and two balconies that Presley called home during numerous trips to Jacksonville. Or celebrate a special occasion aboard the hotel's private yacht, the *Jacksonville Princess.* ⊠ *1201 Riverplace Blvd., 32207* ☎ *904/ 398–8800* 🖷 *904/398–9170* ⊕ *www.jacksonvillehilton.com* 🛏 *292 rooms, 30 suites* ♿ *2 restaurants, room service, some kitchenettes, cable TV with movies and video games, in-room data ports, pool, gym, outdoor hot tub, massage, marina, 2 bars, shop, dry cleaning, laundry service, Internet, business services, meeting rooms, parking (fee), no-smoking floors* ▤ *AE, D, DC, MC, V.*

★ **$$–$$$** 🖭 **The Inn at Oak Street.** Built in 1902 as a private residence, the three-story, 6,000-square-foot Frame Vernacular–style building was restored and reopened as a charming bed-and-breakfast in 2003. Rooms include the cozy and romantic Boudoir room, with four-poster bed and inlaid-tile fireplace, and the more modern St. John's Room, with cobalt-hue walls and geometric bedspread. Each room has a private bath—some with whirlpool tubs and others with double-head showers—and second-story rooms offer balconies. Mornings start with a tasty breakfast in the dining room or on the enclosed porch; evenings wind down with wine and refreshments in the parlor. ⊠ *2114 Oak St., 32204* ☎ *904/ 379–5525* ⊕ *www.innatoakstreet.com* 🛏 *6 rooms* ♿ *Fans, cable TV, in-room VCRs, in-room data ports, massage, library, Internet, business services, free parking; no kids under 12, no smoking* ▤ *AE, D, MC, V* ⦿*I BP.*

$$–$$$ 🖭 **Radisson Riverwalk Hotel.** The Riverwalk complex connects to this bustling five-story hotel. Rooms are done in blond wood with pastel striped fabrics and have either a king-size or two double beds. Four restaurants, a museum, and the water taxi to the Jacksonville Landing are within walking distance. Units overlooking the St. Johns River command the highest prices. ⊠ *1515 Prudential Dr., 32207* ☎ *904/396–5100* 🖷 *904/ 396–7154* ⊕ *www.radisson.com/jacksonvillefl* 🛏 *322 rooms, 19 suites* ♿ *Restaurant, room service, some refrigerators, cable TV with movies and video games, in-room data ports, 2 tennis courts, pool, gym, bar, shop, dry cleaning, laundry facilities, Internet, business services, convention center, some free parking, no-smoking rooms* ▤ *AE, DC, MC, V.*

$ 🖭 **House on Cherry Street.** Pewter, Oriental rugs, antique canopy beds, and other remnants of a rich past furnish this early-20th-century treasure. Afternoon tea doesn't come any fresher: select your favorite blend from owner Victoria Freeman's own tea garden and have it brewed right on the spot. Fresh flowers in rooms are a nice touch. The parks and gardens of the chic Avondale district are a walk away. ⊠ *1844 Cherry St., 32205* ☎ *904/384–1999* 🖷 *904/387–4007* ⊕ *www.houseoncherrystreet. com* 🛏 *4 rooms, 3 suites* ♿ *Dining room, fans, some refrigerators, bicycles, croquet, horseshoes, laundry facilities, Internet, business services, meeting rooms, free parking; no room phones, no kids under 12, no smoking* ▤ *AE, MC, V* ⦿*I CP.*

Nightlife & the Arts

THE ARTS   The **Alhambra Dinner Theater** (✉ 12000 Beach Blvd. ☎ 904/641–1212) serves up professional theater along with a menu that's often altered with each new play. Northeast Florida's major presenter of professional national and international touring attractions is the **FCCJ Artist Series** (✉ 501 W. State St. ☎ 904/632–3373). **The Florida Theatre** (✉ 128 E. Forsyth St. ☎ 904/355–5661) presents concerts, dance productions, and special events, as well as a classic-movie series. The **Jacksonville Symphony Orchestra** (☎ 904/354–5547) performs at the Jacoby Music Hall in the Times-Union Center for the Performing Arts and gives outdoor concerts at downtown's Metro Park. Opened in late 2003, the 16,000-seat **Jacksonville Veterans Memorial Arena** (✉ 300 A. Philip Randolph Blvd. ☎ 904/630–3900) is the latest addition to the city's entertainment complex. It hosts concerts, special events, and sporting events, and is home to the Jacksonville Barracudas hockey team. **Metropolitan Park** (✉ 1410 Gator Bowl Blvd. ☎ 904/630–0837) is a 27-acre riverfront venue that hosts the city's major musical and cultural events, such as the Jacksonville Jazz Festival in April, and Freedom, Fanfare and Fireworks on July 4. Florida Community College at Jacksonville's South Campus is the site of the **Nathan H. Wilson Center for the Arts** (✉ 11901 Beach Blvd. ☎ 904/646–2222), a performing- and visual-arts facility showcasing multidisciplinary productions by students and professional artists. Dubbed "the Harlem of the South" in the 1920s, historic La Villa is the site of the **Ritz Theatre** (✉ 829 N. Davis St. ☎ 904/632–5555), which hosts musical and theatrical events of particular interest to the African-American community. The oldest continuously operating community theater in the United States, **Theatre Jacksonville** (✉ 2032 San Marco Blvd. ☎ 904/396–4425) presents outstanding productions ranging from Shakespeare to programs for children. The **Times-Union Center for the Performing Arts** (✉ 300 W. Water St. ☎ 904/633–6110) draws rock bands, musicals, and children's shows. The **University of North Florida Fine Arts Center** (✉ 4567 St. Johns Bluff Rd. S, Bldg. 45 ☎ 904/620–2878) presents dance and comedy troupes and other shows.

NIGHTLIFE   **Buffalo Wild Wings** (✉ 9550 Baymeadows Rd. #26 ☎ 904/448–1293), or "BW3" to the locals, is *the* place to watch college and pro football. Inside the Ramada Inn Mandarin, the **Comedy Zone** (✉ 3130 Hartley Rd. ☎ 904/292–4242) is the area's premier comedy nightclub. Stylish dress is required at **Endo Exo** (✉ 1224 Kings Ave. ☎ 904/396–7733), a cozy lounge with live music on the outdoor deck. Crowds head to **Dave & Buster's** (✉ 7025 Salisbury Rd. ☎ 904/296–1525) for its huge video-game room and for a part in the whodunit at the mystery theater Saturday night. **57 Heaven** (✉ 8136 Atlantic Blvd. ☎ 904/721–5757) draws a crowd in their forties and fifties with its selection of oldies but goodies and shag contests. **Fuel Coffeehouse** (✉ 1037 Park St. ☎ 904/425–3835) in Five Points is the hippest place to get your java on, as well as enjoy a pick-up chess game, live music, underground films, and spoken-word performances. **Harmonious Monks** (✉ 10550 Old St. Augustine Rd. ☎ 904/880–3040) has the "world's most talented wait staff" who perform throughout the night and encourage customers to dance on the bar. **Jack Rabbits** (✉ 1528 Hendricks Ave. ☎ 904/398–7496) welcomes the latest and greatest indie bands and rock stars in-the-making. Fans of Christian music flock to the **Murray Hill Theatre** (✉ 932 Edgewood Ave. S ☎ 904/388–7807), a no-smoking, no-alcohol club. **River City Brewing Company** (✉ 835 Museum Circle ☎ 904/398–2299) showcases local bands or DJs Thursday through Saturday nights. Fronting on San Marco Boulevard, **Square One** (✉ 1974 San Marco Blvd. ☎ 904/306–9004) is an upscale singles scene with live music on weekends.

Sports & the Outdoors

Baseball
The **Jacksonville Suns** (✉ 301 A. Phillip Randolph Blvd. ☎ 904/358–2846), the AA minor-league affiliate of the Los Angeles Dodgers, play at the Baseball Grounds of Jacksonville, their new $25-million ballpark.

Dog Racing
Jacksonville Greyhound Racing splits its live racing season between two tracks. In town, the **Jacksonville Kennel Club** (✉ 1440 N. McDuff Ave. ☎ 904/646–0001) runs greyhound races from late May through early September. At the **Orange Park Kennel Club** (✉ 455 Park Ave., Orange Park, ½ mi south of I–295 ☎ 904/646–0001), the dogs hit the track from early September through late May. **The "Best Bet" at St. Johns** (✉ 6322 Race Track Rd. ☎ 904/646–0001) is a simulcast-only facility that includes a 14,000-square-foot poker room.

Football
ALLTELL Stadium (✉ 1 ALLTEL Stadium Pl.) is home to the NFL **Jacksonville Jaguars** (☎ 904/633–6000, 904/633–2000 tickets). Jacksonville kicks off each year with its own New Year's bowl game, the **Toyota Gator Bowl** (☎ 904/798–1700), which usually hosts NCAA top-10 teams from the SEC, ACC, or Big East conference. Billed as the "World's Largest Outdoor Cocktail Party," the **Florida/Georgia Game** (☎ 904/630–3690) celebrates one of college football's most heated rivalries.

Golf
The **Eagle Harbor Golf Club** (✉ 2217 Eagle Harbor Pkwy., Orange Park ☎ 904/269–9300) has an 18-hole, par-72 course designed by Clyde Johnston and has a driving range, club rentals, and discount packages; green fee: $46/$56. The 18-hole, 71-par **Golf Club of Jacksonville** (✉ 10440 Tournament La. ☎ 904/779–0800), 15 mi west of downtown, has a driving range and rents clubs; green fee: $26/$48. **Windsor Parke Golf Club** (✉ 13823 Sutton Park Rd. ☎ 904/223–4972) has 18 holes (par 72) on tree-lined fairways and amid natural marshlands, green fee: $39/$49.

Hockey
The **Jacksonville Barracudas,** affiliated with the Southern Professional Hockey League, play at the **Jacksonville Veterans Memorial Arena** (✉ 300 A. Philip Randolph Blvd. ☎ 904/367–1423).

Tennis
Boone Park (✉ 3730 Park St. ☎ 904/384–8687) is a public tennis facility with hard and clay courts as well as picnic and rest-room facili-

ties. **Southside Tennis Complex** (⊠ 1539 Hendricks Ave. ☎ 904/399–1761) has hard and clay courts, picnic areas, and rest rooms.

Skydiving

The city's only drop zone, **Skydive Jacksonville** (⊠ Herlong Airport, Normandy Blvd., 3 mi west of I–295 ☎ 904/387–5867) offers tandem jumps, static line jumps, and accelerated freefall. Prices range from $160 to $275 per person, including equipment rental and instruction. Videography and still photography services cost extra.

Shopping

At **Five Points** (⊠ Intersection of Park, Margaret, and Lomax Sts., Riverside) you'll find a small but funky shopping district of new and vintage clothing boutiques, shoe stores, and antiques shops, as well as a handful of eateries and bars. **The Shoppes of Avondale** (⊠ St. Johns Ave.) highlight upscale clothing and accessories boutiques, art galleries, home-furnishing shops, a chocolatier, and trendy restaurants. **San Marco Square** (⊠ intersection of San Marco and Atlantic Blvds.) has dozens of interesting apparel, home, and jewelry stores and restaurants in 1920s Mediterranean revival-style buildings.

Jacksonville Beaches

20 mi east of Jacksonville on U.S. 90 (Beach Blvd.).

Separated from the mainland by the Intracoastal Waterway, Jacksonville's main beaches run along the barrier island that includes the laid-back towns of Jacksonville Beach, Neptune Beach, Atlantic Beach, and Ponte Vedra Beach. The northernmost of Jacksonville's beaches, Atlantic Beach is more subdued but a favorite with local surfers. Adjacent Neptune Beach is largely residential and draws bicyclists and in-line skaters who cruise up and down 1st Street. Just south is Jacksonville Beach, which has a decidedly more active shoreline, with volleyballs and Frisbees buzzing through the air and portable radios blaring everything from Nelly to Van Halen. With multimillion-dollar homes stretching for miles, Ponte Vedra is the most difficult beach to access, but makes for a lovely drive down A1A. Lifeguards are on duty on the more populated stretches of the beaches from 10 to 6 in summer.

Where to Stay & Eat

$$–$$$
Fodor'sChoice
★

✕ **Restaurant Medure.** At more than 4,500 square feet, this chic Ponte Vedra restaurant is more spacious than its sister restaurant, Matthew's, in Jacksonville. And with its uplit floor-to-ceiling wine cellars, patina-stained concrete floors, overstuffed leather chairs, and room dividers constructed of oak branches and brushed aluminum, it's decidedly more urban. What is a constant, however, is Chef Matthew Medure's deliciously eclectic menu including popular carry-overs from Matthew's such as pan-seared foie gras and sea scallops with sweet corn grits, and Medure originals like meatloaf with horseradish potato puree and mushrooms and pork tenderloin with bacon-onion compote. ⊠ *818 N. A1A Ponte Vedra Beach* ☎ *904/543-3797* ▤ *AE, D, DC, MC, V* ⊗ *No lunch.*

$–$$$ ✕ **Lighthouse Grille.** Char-grilled New York strip, filet mignon, giant porterhouse steak, tender prime rib—it's the high-quality beef that draws the dinner crowds to this snappy-looking spot. The dining room has a marble-topped bar and polished hardwood floors; an open-air deck looks out to the Intracoastal Waterway. Local fish and shrimp are on the menu, too, and the sensational house salad, with crumbled bacon, chopped eggs, and almonds, is large enough to be a meal. ⊠ *2600 Beach Blvd., Jacksonville Beach* ☎ *904/242–8899* ▤ *AE, D, DC, MC, V.*

★ **$–$$$** ✕ **Ragtime Tavern.** A New Orleans theme prevails at this loud place that attracts a sophisticated young bunch in their twenties and thirties. Bayou bouillabaisse (lobster, shrimp, scallops, fish, crab, clams, and crawfish in a creole court bouillon) and ragtime shrimp (deep-fried fresh shrimp rolled in coconut) are the true specialties here, along with microbrews made on premises. If you aren't into creole and Cajun, try a po' boy sandwich or fish sizzled on the grill. ⊠ *207 Atlantic Blvd., Atlantic Beach* ☎ *904/241–7877* ⌣ *Reservations not accepted* ▤ *AE, D, DC, MC, V.*

$–$$ ✕ **Homestead.** A two-story log cabin built in 1934 and recently renovated, this down-home place serving classic Southern cooking is always busy. The specialty is skillet-fried chicken with rice and gravy, but newer, regional fare includes crispy Parmesan-crusted rainbow trout, pan-fried Georgia quail, Memphis-style barbecued duck, and low-country braised lamb shank. Sunday gospel brunch is also popular, as are pre-dinner drinks in the Coppertop Pub. ⊠ *1712 Beach Blvd., Jacksonville Beach* ☎ *904/249–9660* ▤ *AE, D, MC, V* ⊘ *No lunch.*

¢–$$ ✕ **Sticky Fingers.** In the South, barbecue joints are a dime a dozen, yet this Atlantic Beach smokehouse manages to stand out year after year. Perhaps it's the atypical environment—meals are served on real dishes rather than paper plates, soft lighting replaces harsh fluorescents, and B. B. King plays in the background instead of Billy Ray Cyrus. Maybe it's the proprietor, Don Nicol, who will bend over backwards to make sure you're satisfied. Probably, it's the classic, Memphis-style smoked ribs slow cooked over aged hickory and available in five versions, including Memphis-style dry, Tennessee whiskey, and Carolina sweet. A full bar sweetens the deal. ⊠ *363 Atlantic Blvd. #1, Atlantic Beach* ☎ *904/241–7427* ▤ *AE, D, MC, V.*

¢–$ ✕ **Al's Pizza.** Like its city counterparts, the beach locations of this popular restaurant defy all expectations of a neighborhood pizza joint. Bright colors and geometric patterns accent the dining room, which also takes on an industrial feel. The menu is fairly predictable; there's pizza by the slice and by the pie, plus standbys like lasagna and ravioli. ⊠ *303 Atlantic Blvd., Atlantic Beach* ☎ *904/249–0002* ⊠ *635 A1A N, Ponte Vedra Beach* ☎ *904/543–1494* ⌣ *Reservations not accepted* ▤ *AE, D, MC, V.*

$$$$ ▥ **The Lodge & Club.** The Spanish roof tiles and white-stucco exterior
Fodor'sChoice yield a look that's Mediterranean-villa grand luxe. Rooms have cozy
★ window seats, appealing artwork, and private balconies overlooking the Atlantic; some units include a whirlpool tub and gas fireplace. The restaurant, the bar, and the heated pools offer more ocean views. Guests have full access to sports, recreation, and spa facilities at its sister property, Ponte Vedra Inn & Club, less than 2 mi away. ⊠ *607 Ponte Vedra*

Blvd., Ponte Vedra Beach 32082 ☎ *904/273–9500 or 800/243–4304* 🖷 *904/273–0210* ⊕ *www.pvresorts.com* 🛏 *42 rooms, 24 suites* ♨ *Restaurant, picnic area, snack bar, room service, BBQs, fans, in-room safes, some in-room hot tubs, some kitchenettes, minibars, some refrigerators, cable TV with movies and video games, in-room data ports, golf privileges, 3 pools, gym, health club, hair salon, hot tub, spa, beach, windsurfing, fishing, bicycles, volleyball, bar, lounge, piano bar, shops, babysitting, children's programs (ages 4–12), playground, dry cleaning, laundry service, concierge, Internet, business services, meeting rooms, parking (fee), no-smoking rooms* ☰ *AE, D, DC, MC, V.*

$$$$
Fodor's Choice
★
🏨 **Ponte Vedra Inn & Club.** Accommodations at this 1928 landmark country-club resort are in a series of white-stucco Spanish-style buildings lining the beach; rooms are extra-large, and most have ocean views. The main house holds the registration area and some common spaces, including a big living room with fireplace. The Inn's renowned full-service spa attracts the rich and famous, including actors, supermodels, and former First Ladies. ⊠ *200 Ponte Vedra Blvd., Ponte Vedra Beach 32082* ☎ *904/285–1111 or 800/234–7842* 🖷 *904/285–2111* ⊕ *www. pvresorts.com* 🛏 *250 rooms, 45 suites* ♨ *3 restaurants, café, coffee shop, dining room, picnic area, 3 snack bars, room service, BBQs, fans, in-room safes, some in-room hot tubs, some kitchenettes, minibars, some microwaves, some refrigerators, cable TV with movies, some in-room VCRs, in-room data ports, 2 18-hole golf courses, putting green, 15 tennis courts, pro shop, 3 pools, fitness classes, health club, outdoor hot tub, spa, beach, boating, fishing, bicycles, billiards, volleyball, 4 bars, lounge, piano bar, library, shops, babysitting, children's programs (ages 4–12), playground, laundry service, concierge, Internet, business services, convention center, meeting rooms, travel services, free parking, no-smoking floors* ☰ *AE, D, DC, MC, V.*

$$$–$$$$ 🏨 **Sawgrass Marriott Resort and Beach Club.** The main building and lobby areas feel more like a business hotel than a plush resort—the property does include a 46,000-square-foot high-tech business center—but the grounds are beautiful and the rooms are spacious, with deep-color carpets and drapes, wood furniture, and roomy bathrooms. This is truly a full-service resort, whether you've come to laze about (guests also have access to the Cabana Club, a private beach club nearby) or spend some time on the courts. ⊠ *1000 PGA Tour Blvd., Ponte Vedra Beach 32082* ☎ *904/285–7777 or 800/457–4653* 🖷 *904/285–0259* ⊕ *www. sawgrassmarriott.com* 🛏 *508 rooms, 24 suites* ♨ *6 restaurants, room service, some kitchens, minibars, some microwaves, some refrigerators, cable TV with movies and video games, in-room data ports, golf privileges, 9 tennis courts, pro shop, 2 pools, wading pool, health club, hot tub, sauna, steam room, bicycles, 4 bars, lounge, shop, babysitting, children's programs (ages 3–12), playground, dry cleaning, laundry facilities, laundry service, concierge, Internet, business services, meeting rooms, some free parking, some pets allowed (fee), no-smoking floors* ☰ *AE, D, DC, MC, V.*

$$–$$$$ 🏨 **Sea Turtle Inn.** Some of the rooms at this eight-story hotel overlooking the Atlantic have full oceanfront views and private balconies; all rooms are spacious and have "turtle windows," made of light-deflective glass

designed to prevent sea turtles and their hatchlings from mistaking indoor lighting for natural light (which would disorient them in their journey from beach to sea). This is a great spot for families because of its homelike amenities and convenient location. ⊠ *1 Ocean Blvd., Jacksonville Beach 32233* ☎ *904/249–7402 or 800/874–6000* 🖷 *904/249–1119* ⊕ *www.seaturtle.com* ⇆ *193 rooms, 3 suites* ⚲ *Restaurant, some microwaves, refrigerators, cable TV with movies, in-room VCRs, in-room data ports, pool, beach, bicycles, volleyball, 2 bars, shop, dry cleaning, laundry service, Internet, convention center, some free parking, no-smoking rooms* ☰ *AE, D, MC, V.*

$–$$$ 🏨 **Comfort Inn Oceanfront.** The Atlantic Ocean is the front yard of this seven-story hotel, which offers water views from the private balconies of each of its pastel-color rooms. Families enjoy the four waterfalls that cascade into a giant, heated, free-form pool. ⊠ *1515 N. 1st St., Jacksonville Beach 32250* ☎ *904/241–2311 or 800/654–8776* 🖷 *904/249–3830* ⊕ *www.comfortinnjaxbeach.com* ⇆ *177 rooms, 15 suites* ⚲ *Restaurant, in-room safes, microwaves, refrigerators, cable TV with movies and video games, in-room data ports, pool, exercise equipment, outdoor hot tub, beach, volleyball, bar, video game room, shop, dry cleaning, Internet, business services, meeting rooms, free parking, no-smoking rooms* ☰ *AE, D, DC, MC, V* ⎮◎⎮ *CP.*

$$ 🏨 **Sea Horse Oceanfront Inn.** Lacking the hoity-toity decor and amenities of other beachfront properties, this modest motel caters to guests seeking an ultracasual, laid-back vibe. Every room has an ocean view, and beachcombers will appreciate the private beach walk-over. Visit the enticing poolside Lemon Bar. ⊠ *120 Atlantic Blvd., Neptune Beach 32266* ☎ *904/246–2175 or 800/881–2330* 🖷 *904/246–4256* ⊕ *www.seahorseresort.com* ⇆ *39 rooms, 1 suite* ⚲ *Picnic area, some kitchenettes, some microwaves, refrigerators, cable TV, golf privileges, pool, beach, bar, some free parking, no-smoking rooms* ☰ *AE, D, MC, V.*

Nightlife

A groovy, low-key lounge during the week, **The Atlantic** (⊠ 333 N. 1st St., Jacksonville Beach ☎ 904/249–3338) turns into a jam-packed, sweat-soaked dance club on weekends. **Freebird Live** (⊠ 200 N. 1st St., Jacksonville Beach ☎ 904/246–2473) pays tribute to Jacksonville's own Lynyrd Skynyrd and hosts live music five nights a week, with acts ranging from the Fabulous Thunderbirds to Ziggy Marley. Hoist a pint o' Guinness and sing along with Emerald Isle troubadours at **Lynch's Irish Pub** (⊠ 514 N. 1st St., Jacksonville Beach ☎ 904/249–5181). The beautiful people gather at the **Ocean Club** (⊠ 401 N. 1st St., Jacksonville Beach ☎ 904/242–8884) for dancing, flirting, and drinking, not necessarily in that order. The oldest bar in Jacksonville and the beaches, **Pete's Bar** (⊠ 117 1st St., Neptune Beach ☎ 904/249–9158) is notable for the cheapest drinks, cheapest pool tables, and most colorful clientele in town. On Friday and Saturday nights the **Ragtime Tavern** (⊠ 207 Atlantic Blvd., Atlantic Beach ☎ 904/241–7877) resonates with live music, from jazz to blues to progressive to good old rock and roll. Entertainment at the **Sun Dog** (⊠ 207 Atlantic Blvd., Neptune Beach ☎ 904/241–8221) often includes acoustic guitarists. With nearly 80 TVs and an impressive menu, **Sneakers Sports Grille** (⊠ 111 Beach

Blvd., Jacksonville Beach ☎ 904/482–1000) is the go-to sports bar at the beach.

Sports & the Outdoors

BIKING **American Bicycle Company** (✉ 240 S. 3rd St., Jacksonville Beach ☎ 904/ 246–4433) rents beach cruisers by the hour and by the day. **Ponte Vedra Bicycles** (✉ 250 Solana Rd., Ponte Vedra Beach ☎ 904/273–0199) includes free bike maps with your rental.

FISHING **North Florida Fishing Charters** (✉ 2221 Larchmont Rd., Jacksonville ☎ 904/346–3868) specializes in in-shore light tackle fishing from St. Augustine to Amelia Island.

Mayport

⓫ *20 mi northeast of Jacksonville.*

Dating back more than 300 years, this is one of the oldest fishing communities in the United States. It has several excellent and very casual seafood restaurants and a large commercial shrimp-boat fleet. It's also the home to the third-largest naval facility in the country, Naval Station Mayport.

Fodor'sChoice **Kathryn Abbey Hanna Park** is a 450-acre oceanfront property just north ★ of Atlantic Beach. It's filled with spectacular beaches, biking and hiking trails, wooded campsites, and a 60-acre freshwater lake, perfect for swimming, kayaking, and canoeing. The lake area also includes picnic tables, grills, and a quarter-acre water park with fountains and squirting hoses. Throughout the park there are rest rooms, showers, and snack bars, open April through Labor Day, as well as lifeguards supervising all water activities during summer. Surfers in the know head to "the poles" for the best wave action in town. Camping fees range from $14 to $30 per day. ✉ 500 Wonderwood Dr. ☎ 904/249–4700 ⊕ www. cr.nps.gov/goldcres/sites/kingsley.htm ≈ $1 ☉ Daily 8–sunset.

en route The arrival of the **St. Johns River Ferry** in 1948 was a huge convenience to local residents, plus a fun activity to share with kids. The ferry (the *Jean Ribault*) continues to delight passengers young and old, as they drive aboard the 153-foot vessel and embark on the 10-minute cruise across the river. ☎ 904/241–9969 ⊕ www. stjohnsriverferry.com ≈ $2.50 per motorcycle, $2.75 per car, $4.50 per RV, pedestrians and bicyclists 50¢ ☉ Daily 6:20 AM–10 PM, departing every ½ hr.

Fort George Island

⓬ *25 mi northeast of Jacksonville.*

One of the oldest inhabited areas of Florida, Fort George Island is lush with foliage, natural vegetation, and wildlife. A 4-mi nature and bike trail meanders through the island, revealing shell mounds dating as far back as 6,000 years.

Built in 1792 by Zephaniah Kingsley, an eccentric slave trader, the **Kingsley Plantation** is the oldest remaining cotton plantation in the state. The ruins of 23 tabby (a cementlike mixture of sand and crushed shells) slave houses, a barn, and the modest Kingsley home are open to the public and reachable by ferry or bridge. ⊠ *A1A–Hecksher Dr., just north of St. Johns River Ferry, Fort George Island* ☎ *904/251–3537* ▣ *Free* ⊙ *Daily 9–5; ranger talks weekdays at 1, weekends at 1 and 3.*

| off the beaten path | **TALBOT ISLAND STATE PARKS** – The Talbot Island State Parks, including Big and Little Talbot islands, have 17 mi of gorgeous beaches, sand dunes, and golden marshes that hum with birds and native waterfowl. Come to picnic, fish, swim, snorkel, or camp. Little |

★ Talbot Island, one of the few undeveloped barrier islands in Florida, has river otters, marsh rabbits, raccoons, bobcats, possums, and gopher tortoises. A 4-mi nature trail winds across Little Talbot, and there are several smaller trails on Big Talbot. ⊠ *12157 Heckscher Dr., Talbot Island* ☎ *904/251–2320* ⊕ *www.floridastateparks.org/littletalbotisland* ▣ *$4 per vehicle, up to 8 people* ⊙ *Daily 8–sunset.*

Amelia Island (Fernandina Beach)

⑬ *35 mi northeast of Jacksonville.*

At the northeasternmost reach of Florida, Amelia Island has beautiful beaches with enormous sand dunes along its eastern flank, a state park with a Civil War fort, sophisticated restaurants, interesting shops, and accommodations that range from B&Bs to luxury resorts. The town of Fernandina Beach is on the island's northern end; a century ago casinos and brothels thrived here, but those are gone. Today there's little reminder of the town's wild days, though one event comes close: the Isle of Eight Flags Shrimp Festival, held during the first weekend of May in Fernandina, attracts more than 150,000 people a year.

★ The **Amelia Island Historic District,** in Fernandina Beach, has more than 50 blocks of buildings listed on the National Register of Historic Places; 450 ornate structures built prior to 1927 offer some of the nation's finest examples of Queen Anne, Victorian, and Italianate homes. Many date to the haven's mid-19th-century glory days. Pick up a self-guided-tour map at the chamber of commerce, in the old train depot—once a stopping point on the first cross-state railroad.

Founded in 1859, **St. Peter's Episcopal Church** (⊠ 801 Atlantic Ave., Fernandina Beach ☎904/261–4293) is a Gothic revival structure with Tiffany glass–style memorials and a turn-of-the-20th-century L. C. Harrison organ with magnificent hand-painted pipes.

One of the country's best-preserved and most complete brick forts is at
★ **Fort Clinch State Park.** Fort Clinch was built to discourage further British intrusion after the War of 1812 and was occupied in 1863 by the Confederacy; a year later it was retaken by the North. During the Spanish-American War it was reactivated for a brief time but for the most part

wasn't used. The 1,086-acre park has camping, nature trails, carriage rides, a swimming beach, and surf and pier fishing. Wander through restored buildings, including furnished barracks, a kitchen, and a repair shop. Scheduled periodically are living-history reenactments of Civil War garrison life. ⊠ *2601 Atlantic Ave., Fernandina Beach* ☎ *904/277–7274* ⊕ *www.floridastateparks.org/fortclinch* 🔁 *$5 per vehicle, up to 8 people* ☺ *Daily 8–sunset.*

Amelia Island's eastern shore includes **Main Beach,** a 13-mi stretch of white-sand beach edged with dunes, some 40 feet high. It's one of the few beaches in Florida where horseback riding is allowed.

Where to Stay & Eat

$$$$
Fodor'sChoice
★ ✕ **The Grill.** Like the resort in which it resides, the Ritz-Carlton's signature restaurant is quietly elegant. Rich wood wall panels and an elaborate gold chandelier hanging from the vaulted ceiling create a traditional feel, while multi-color upholstered chairs and a vivid patterned carpet add a contemporary splash. The key design element, however, is the view of the Atlantic Ocean. Equally outstanding is the menu, which includes pan-roasted jumbo sea scallops and a surf and turf with a petite veal filet and Maine lobster. The impressive wine list tops 500 bottles. Choose the chef's tasting menu to have the chef personalize a multicourse dinner. Or, reserve A Seat in the Kitchen, a private dining room within the kitchen where you'll watch the chefs at work and enjoy a customized five-course meal. Sunday brunch is a feast in itself. Collared shirts are required. ⊠ *Ritz-Carlton, Amelia Island, 4750 Amelia Island Pkwy.* ☎ *904/277–1100* ⚑ *Reservations essential* ☐ *AE, DC, MC, V* ☺ *No lunch.*

★ **$$$–$$$$**
✕ **Beech Street Grill.** Hardwood floors, high ceilings, and marble fireplaces adorn many rooms on two floors to create a pleasant environment in this 1889 sea captain's house. An extensive menu includes such house favorites as roasted lamb with mint and apple salsa, Parmesan-crusted red snapper with mustard-basil cream sauce, and crab-stuffed local shrimp with *tasso* (a smoked cajun ham) gravy. A blackboard lists four or five fresh fish specials nightly. The outstanding wine list includes some coveted Californians. ⊠ *801 Beech St., Fernandina Beach* ☎ *904/277–3662* ⚑ *Reservations essential* ☐ *AE, D, DC, MC, V* ☺ *No lunch.*

$$–$$$
✕ **Down Under.** Fresh local fish is the specialty of this casual place beneath the overpass of the A1A bridge. Enjoy the glorious views of the tranquil Intracoastal Waterway and order baskets of fried shrimp or fried oysters; dine on stuffed tuna, shrimp scampi, or grilled tuna; or go for the seafood platter. For landlubbers, chicken and steak are available. ⊠ *Intracoastal Waterway, under the Rte. A1A bridge, Fernandina Beach* ☎ *904/261–1001* ☐ *AE, D, MC, V* ☺ *No lunch.*

$–$$$
✕ **Verandah Restaurant.** Despite being located on Amelia Island Plantation, this family-friendly restaurant is open to non-resort guests, many of whom drive from Jacksonville to dine here. The dining room has a casual hotel restaurant vibe to it, with floral prints and roomy booths, but the menu is all business. Fresh seafood dishes are a highlight, including red snapper with pecan and crab meunière, pasta paella, and surf and turf, served with filet mignon and pan-roasted lobster tail. Don't miss the ultra-rich she-crab Amelia, served with a dash of sherry, which

just might be the best crab soup in northeast Florida. ⊠ *6800 1st Coast Hwy.* ☎ *904/321–5050* ⊟ *AE, D, MC, V* ⊘ *No lunch.*

$–$$ ✕ **O'Kane's Irish Pub.** The authentic Irish fare here includes shepherd's pie, steak and Guinness pie, and fish-and-chips. Also on the menu are sandwiches, ribs, pasta, and soup served in a bowl of sourdough bread (you eat the whole thing). The quiet dining room in back has an old-fashioned tin ceiling and upholstered chairs. This is one of the few bars where the Irish coffee is prepared as it is in Ireland—with very cold, barely whipped, heavy cream floating on top. ⊠ *318 Centre St., Fernandina Beach* ☎ *904/ 261–1000* ⌕ *Reservations not accepted* ⊟ *AE, D, MC, V.*

$$$$ ▦ **Amelia Island Plantation.** The first-rate golf, tennis, and spa facilities
Fodor'sChoice   are big draws at this sprawling, family-oriented resort where accom-
★   modations include full-service hotel rooms as well as home and condo (or "villa") rentals. The hotel rooms tend to be large, with comfortable seating areas, balconies, and ocean views. Much of the hotel lobby is devoted to a piano bar, which stays busy late into the evening. With its ancient oaks, marshes, and lagoons, the resort is also a worthy destination for hiking, biking, and bird-watching, and one of the few places in northeast Florida to rent Segways (guided nature tours aboard the "human transporters" are $80). Good dining and shopping options mean you don't have to leave the property. ⊠ *6800 1st Coast Hwy., 32034* ☎ *904/261–6161 or 800/874–6878* ⊟ *904/277–5945* ⊕ *www.aipfl.com* ⌔ *249 rooms, 418 1-, 2-, and 3-bedroom villas* ⌕ *9 restaurants, grocery, room service, in-room safes, some kitchenettes, some microwaves, some refrigerators, cable TV with movies and video games, some in-room VCRs, in-room data ports, 3 18-hole golf courses, 23 tennis courts, pro shop, 23 pools (1 indoor), health club, spa, beach, fishing, bicycles, hiking, horseback riding, racquetball, volleyball, 3 bars, shops, babysitting, children's programs (ages 3–10), playground, dry cleaning, laundry service, Internet, business services, meeting rooms, airport shuttle, nosmoking rooms* ⊟ *AE, D, MC, V.*

$$$–$$$$ ▦ **The Ritz-Carlton, Amelia Island.** The elegance, superb comfort, excel-
Fodor'sChoice   lent service, and exquisite beach are enough to make you swoon. All
★   accommodations in the eight-story building have balconies and ocean views; suites and rooms are spacious and luxurious and are furnished with heavy print draperies, plush carpet, framed prints, and comfortable upholstered chairs. Public areas are exquisitely maintained, and fine cuisine can be had at a choice of restaurants, including the acclaimed Grill. ⊠ *4750 Amelia Island Pkwy., 32034* ☎ *904/277–1100* ⊟ *904/ 261–9064* ⊕ *www.ritzcarlton.com/resorts/amelia_island* ⌔ *444 rooms, 45 suites* ⌕ *3 restaurants, room service, in-room safes, minibars, cable TV with movies and video games, in-room data ports, 18-hole golf course, putting green, 9 tennis courts, 2 pools (1 indoor), wading pool, health club, hair salon, spa, beach, boating, jet skiing, parasailing, fishing, bicycles, billiards, horseback riding, 3 bars, shop, babysitting, children's programs (ages 5–12), playground, dry cleaning, laundry service, concierge, concierge floor, Internet, business services, convention center, nosmoking floors* ⊟ *AE, D, DC, MC, V.*

★ $$$–$$$$ ▦ **Elizabeth Pointe Lodge.** The inn, built to resemble a (supersize) Nantucket shingle-style house, is just behind the dunes. Oceanside units have great water views, albeit through disappointingly small windows. A chair-lined porch offers everyone a chance to rock in ocean breezes, and on cold nights guests can cluster around the living-room fireplace. An adjacent cottage has additional rooms and a suite. The restaurant is open for lunch only. ☒ *98 S. Fletcher Ave., 32034* ☎ *904/277–4851 or 800/772–3359* ☒ *904/277–6500* ⊕ *www.elizabethpointelodge.com* ⤶ *24 rooms, 2 suites, 1 2-bedroom cottage* ᗌ *Some in-room hot tubs, cable TV, beach, library, laundry service, concierge, Internet, business services, meeting rooms, free parking; no smoking* ⊟ *AE, D, MC, V* ⭘ *BP.*

$$–$$$$ ▦ **Amelia Hotel & Suites.** A block from the beach, this mid-size inn is not only convenient but an economical and family-friendly alternative to the luxury resorts and romantic B&Bs that populate the area. The beach and several restaurants are within walking distance, particularly convenient for families with children. Parents will also appreciate the hotel-wide no-smoking policy and Continental breakfast served each morning in the lobby. Rooms are modestly furnished and have ocean or pool views. ☒ *1997 S. Fletcher Ave., Fernandina Beach 32034* ☎ *904/261–5735* ⊕ *www.ameliahotelandsuites.com* ⤶ *90 rooms, 18 suites* ᗌ *Some in-room hot tubs, some kitchenettes, some microwaves, some refrigerators, cable TV, in-room data ports, pool, business services, meeting rooms; no smoking* ⊟ *AE, D, MC, V* ⭘ *CP.*

$$–$$$$ ▦ **Ash Street Inn.** A white picket fence frames the yard of this appealing inn a block from the heart of downtown Fernandina Beach. Rooms are spacious and individually done with bedspreads and fabrics and, in some cases, window treatments and antiques. Some rooms have claw-foot tubs, others have whirlpools, and one has a working fireplace. The rate includes a three-course breakfast that can be enjoyed either in the bright dining room or out on the porch. ☒ *102 S. 7th St., Fernandina Beach 32034* ☎ *904/277–6660 or 800/277–6660* ☒ *904/277–4646* ⊕ *www.ashstreeinn.net* ⤶ *10 rooms* ᗌ *Some in-room hot tubs, some kitchenettes, cable TV, in-room VCRs, in-room data ports, golf privileges, pool, massage, bicycles, library, Internet, meeting rooms, free parking, some pets allowed (fee); no smoking* ⊟ *AE, D, MC, V* ⭘ *BP.*

$$–$$$ ▦ **Hoyt House Bed & Breakfast.** A redbrick walkway leads to this fine example of Queen Anne Victorian architecture (built in 1905). Relax in one of the rockers on the wide veranda. Shade trees keep the B&B's yard cool. Inside, inviting rooms show off antique and reproduction furniture, down quilts, and walls painted in rich hues. All rooms have private baths, and one has a whirlpool. In the late afternoon guests congregate in the parlor for complimentary wine and cheese. The house is in the historic district, at the edge of Fernandina Beach. ☒ *804 Atlantic Ave., 32034* ☎ *904/277–4300 or 800/432–2085* ☒ *904/277–9626* ⊕ *www.hoythouse.com* ⤶ *10 rooms* ᗌ *Some in-room hot tubs, cable TV, in-room VCRs, pool, hot tub, bicycles, Internet, business services, meeting rooms, free parking, some pets allowed (fee); no kids under 12, no smoking* ⊟ *AE, D, MC, V* ⭘ *BP.*

$–$$$ ▦ **Florida House Inn.** The rambling two-story clapboard main building, more than 100 years old, is definitely of another era, with creaking floors and small doors. Rooms have handmade quilts and hooked rugs but also include such modern amenities as king-size beds and whirlpool tubs. Some even have fireplaces. Two carriage houses across the street offer additional rooms. Guests often relax in the cozy parlor and dine in the restaurant, which serves heaping quantities at family-style breakfasts, lunches, and dinners. ⊠ *22 S. 3rd St., 32034* ☎ *904/261–3300 or 800/ 258–3301* 🖷 *904/277–3831* ⊕ *www.floridahouseinn.com* ⤳ *17 rooms, 1 suite* ⌂ *Restaurant, fans, some in-room hot tubs, cable TV, bicycles, pub, business services, free parking, some pets allowed (fee); no smoking* ☱ *AE, D, MC, V.*

HORSEBACK **Country Day Stables** in Callahan (☎ 904/879–9383) offers individual and
RIDING group rides, including private picnic outings, on its 40-acre ranch. Reservations are required. **Kelly Seahorse Ranch** (⊠ 7500 1st Coast Hwy., Amelia Island ☎ 904/491–5166) takes guests on horseback rides on the beach.

Shopping

Within the Amelia Island Historic District are numerous shops, art galleries, and boutiques, many clustered along cobblestone Centre Street. The **Island Art Association Co-op Gallery** (⊠ 18 N. 2nd St., Fernandina Beach ☎ 904/261–7020) displays and sells paintings, prints, and other artwork by locals.

ST. AUGUSTINE

⓮–㉜ *35 mi south of Jacksonville.*

Founded in 1565 by Spanish explorers, St. Augustine is the nation's oldest city and has a wealth of historic buildings and attractions. In addition to the historic sites on the mainland, the city has 43 mi of beaches on two barrier islands to the east, both reachable by causeways. Several times a year St. Augustine holds historic reenactments, such as December's Grand Christmas Illumination, which commemorates the town's British occupation.

Exploring St. Augustine

The core of any visit is a tour of the historic district, a showcase for more than 60 historic sites and attractions, plus 144 blocks of houses listed on the National Register of Historic Places. You could probably spend several weeks exploring these treasures, but don't neglect other, generally newer, attractions found elsewhere in town.

Numbers in the text correspond to numbers in the margin and on the St. Augustine map.

a good walk

A good place to start is the **Visitor Information and Preview Center ⓮** ▶ : pick up maps, brochures, and information. It's on San Marco Avenue between Castillo Drive and Orange Street. From there cross Orange Street to reach the **City Gate ⓯**, the entrance to the city's restored area. Walk south on St. George Street to the **Oldest Wooden Schoolhouse ⓰**. Directly across from it is the **Colonial Spanish Quarter ⓱**. Go out Fort Alley and cross San Marco Avenue to the impressive **Castillo de San Marcos National Monument ⓲**. Now head west on Cuna Street and turn left on Cordova Street. Walk south three blocks to Valencia Street and turn right. At the end of the block is the splendid **Flagler Memorial Presbyterian Church ⑲**. Head one block south on Sevilla Street and turn left on King Street to find the **Museum of Historic St. Augustine Government House ⑳** and three more of Henry Flagler's legacies: the **Lightner Museum ㉑**, **Flagler College ㉒**, and the Casa Monica Hotel. Continue two blocks east on King Street and turn right onto St. George Street to reach the **Ximenez-Fatio House ㉓**. Afterward, head a few blocks south down Aviles Street to St. Francis Street for a look at a microcosm of the city's history, the **Oldest House ㉔** (not to be confused with the Oldest Wooden Schoolhouse). Head back north to the Bridge of Lions, the **Plaza de la Constitución ㉕**, and the **Basilica Cathedral of St. Augustine ㉖**. You have to cross the Bridge of Lions to get to Anastasia Island and the historic **St. Augustine Lighthouse & Museum ㉗**, but it's worth the effort.

Several attractions are beyond this walk, including two of particular historic note: the **Mission of Nombre de Dios ㉘**, north of the visitor center, is the site of America's first Christian mass; and well north of the city's cluster of sights is the **Fountain of Youth National Archeological Park ㉙**, marking the location of the famed spring. For recreation, also consider **Vilano Beach ㉚**, north of the city, as well as **St. Augustine Beach ㉛** and **Anastasia State Park ㉜**, both on Anastasia Island.

TIMING Allot eight hours for the tour, covering it in two days if possible. Though most sights keep the same hours (daytime only), a few are not open on Sunday. Weekday mornings generally have the smallest crowds.

What to See

㉜ **Anastasia State Park.** With 1,700 protected acres of bird sanctuary, this Anastasia Island park draws families that like to hike, bike, camp, swim, and play on the beach. ✉ *1340 Rte. A1A S, Anastasia Island* ☎ *904/461–2033* ⊕ *www.floridastateparks.org/anastasia* ✇ *$5 per vehicle, up to 8 people* ⊘ *Daily 8–sunset.*

㉖ **Basilica Cathedral of St. Augustine.** The cathedral has the country's oldest written parish records, dating from 1594. Restored in the mid-1960s, the current structure (1797) had extensive changes after an 1887 fire. ✉ *40 Cathedral Pl.* ☎ *904/824–2806* ✇ *Donation welcome* ⊘ *Weekdays 7–5.*

★ ⑱ **Castillo de San Marcos National Monument.** This massive structure is three centuries old, and it looks every second of it. The fort was constructed of coquina, a soft limestone made of broken shells and coral. Built by the Spanish to protect St. Augustine from British raids (English pirates were handy with a torch), the fort was used as a prison during the Revolutionary and Civil wars. Park rangers provide an introductory narration, after which you're on your own to explore the moat, turrets, and 16-foot-thick walls. Garrison rooms depict the life of the era, and special cannon-firing demonstrations are held on weekends from Memorial Day to Labor Day. Children under 17 must be accompanied by an adult. ✉ *1 Castillo Dr.* ☎ *904/829–6506* ⊕ *www.nps.gov/casa* ✇ *$5* ⊘ *Daily 8:45–4:45.*

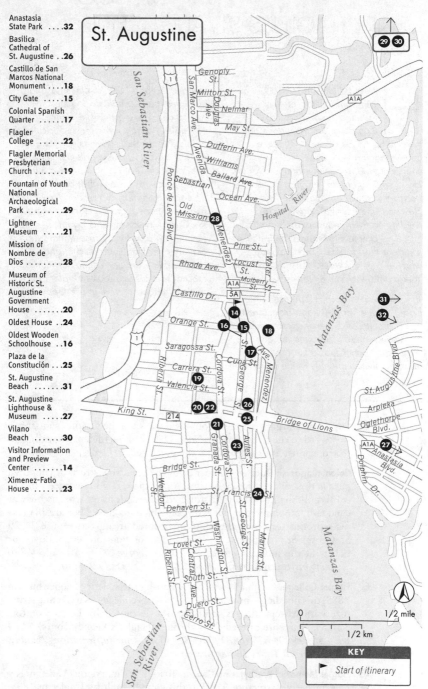

St. Augustine

KEY

▶ *Start of itinerary*

CloseUp
HENRY FLAGLER'S ST. AUGUSTINE LEGACY

HENRY MORRISON FLAGLER, *who, with John D. Rockefeller, founded the Standard Oil Company, first visited the tiny town of St. Augustine in 1885 while honeymooning with his second wife. His choice proved to be very fortunate for the city. It was during this trip that Flagler decided to make St. Augustine "the Newport of the South": a winter resort for wealthy northern industrialists. And to get his select clientele to Florida, he built the luxurious Florida East Coast Railway, which eventually would stretch from New York all the way to the Florida Keys.*

To incorporate the city's Spanish heritage, Flagler chose Spanish Renaissance revival as his architectural theme. He created the St. Augustine Golf Club and the St. Augustine Yacht Club so there would be leisure activities to enjoy in the warm climate. He also built the city's hospital, churches, the city hall, and winter residences. The most visible manifestations of Flagler's dream were the spectacular hotels with castlelike towers, turrets, and red-tile roofs. His most opulent hotel resort, the Ponce de León, is now a private four-year liberal-arts college that bears his name; another flagship resort, the Alcazar, has been turned into the Lightner Museum; the Casa Monica Hotel is again functioning as a luxury resort, more than a century after Flagler created it; and despite the wrath of multiple hurricanes, most of the railroad routes Flagler built and developed are still in use today.

---

⑮ City Gate. The gate is a relic from the days when the Castillo's moat ran westward to the river, and the Cubo Defense Line (defensive wall) protected against approaches from the north. ⊠ *St. George St.*

⑰ Colonial Spanish Quarter. Wander through the narrow streets at your own pace in this village with eight sites. Along the way you may see a blacksmith building his shop (a historic reconstruction) or artisans busy at candle-dipping, spinning, weaving, or cabinetmaking. They are all making reproductions for use within the restored area. **Triay House** (⊠ 29 St. George St.) has period artifacts and an orientation center. Buy your tickets at the museum store. ⊠ *33 St. George St.* ☎ *904/825–6830* ⊕ *www.historicstaugustine.com* ⊠ *$6.50* ⊘ *Daily 9–5:30.*

㉒ Flagler College. Originally one of two posh hotels Henry Flagler built in 1888, this building—now a small liberal arts college—is a riveting structure with towers, turrets, and arcades decorated by Louis Comfort Tiffany. Tours are offered daily through Flagler's Legacy Tours. ⊠ *74 King St.* ☎ *904/829–6481, 904/823–3378 tour information* ⊕ *www.flagler.edu* ⊠ *Tours $6 per person.*

⑲ Flagler Memorial Presbyterian Church. To look at a marvelous Venetian Renaissance–style structure, head to this church, built by Flagler in 1889.

The dome towers more than 100 feet and is topped by a 20-foot Greek cross. ☒ *Valencia and Sevilla Sts.* ☎ *904/829–6451* ⊘ *Weekdays 8:30–4:30.*

㉙ Fountain of Youth National Archaeological Park. Well north of St. Augustine's main sights is this tribute to explorer Ponce de León, marking the location of the legendary spring that flowed through folklore as the Fountain of Youth. In the complex is a springhouse, an explorer's globe, a planetarium, a Native American village, and exhibits about early Timucuan Indian inhabitants. The spring has been here for more than 4,000 years and is rich in iron and sulfur. Since León's discovery, people have made pilgrimages here to sip from the waters. Taste it if you must, but be prepared—there's a reason sulfur-flavor beverages have never been marketed. ☒ *11 Magnolia Ave.* ☎ *904/829–3168 or 800/356–8222* ⊕ *www.fountainofyouthflorida.com* ☒ *$6* ⊘ *Daily 9–5.*

★ ㉑ Lightner Museum. In his quest to turn Florida into an American Riviera, Henry Flagler built two fancy hotels in 1888—the Ponce de León, which became Flagler College, and the Alcazar, which now houses this museum. The building showcases three floors of furnishings, costumes, and Victorian art glass, plus ornate antique music boxes (demonstrations daily at 11 and 2). The Lightner Antiques Mall perches on three levels of what was the hotel's indoor pool. ☒ *75 King St.* ☎ *904/824–2874* ⊕ *www. lightnermuseum.org* ☒ *$8* ⊘ *Museum daily 9–5.*

㉘ Mission of Nombre de Dios. The site, north of the historic district, commemorates where America's first Christian mass was celebrated. A 208-foot stainless-steel cross marks the spot where the mission's first cross was planted. ☒ *San Marco Ave. and Old Mission Rd.* ☎ *904/824–2809* ⊕ *www.missionandshrine.org* ☒ *Donation requested* ⊘ *Weekdays 8–5, Sat. 9–5, Sun. 9:30–5.*

㉒ Museum of Historic St. Augustine Government House. With a collection of more than 300 artifacts from archaeological digs and Spanish shipwrecks off the Florida coast, this museum reflects five centuries of history. ☒ *48 King St.* ☎ *904/825–5033* ☒ *$2.50* ⊘ *Daily 9–4:30.*

㉔ Oldest House. Known as the Gonzalez-Alvarez House, the Oldest House is a National Historic Landmark. The current site dates from the early 1700s, but a structure has been on this site since the early 1600s. Much of the city's history is seen in the building's changes and additions, from the coquina blocks—which came into use to replace wood soon after the town burned in 1702—to the house's enlargement during the British occupation. ☒ *14 St. Francis St.* ☎ *904/824–2872* ⊕ *www. staugustinehistoricalsociety.org* ☒ *$7* ⊘ *Daily 9–5.*

⑯ Oldest Wooden Schoolhouse. Automated mannequins of a teacher and students relate the school's history. The tiny 18th-century building of cypress and cedar is thought to be one of the nation's oldest schoolhouses. Because it was the closest structure to the city gate, it served as a guardhouse and sentry shelter during the Seminole Wars. ☒ *14 St. George St.* ☎ *904/824–0192* ⊕ *www.oldestschoolhouse.com* ☒ *$3* ⊘ *Daily 9–5.*

㉕ Plaza de la Constitución. The central area of the original settlement was laid out in 1598 by decree of King Philip II, and little has changed since.

At its center is a monument to the Spanish constitution of 1812, while at the east end is a public market dating from early American days. Just beyond is a statue of Juan Ponce de León, who "discovered" Florida in 1513. ⊠ *St. George St. and Cathedral Pl.*

③① **St. Augustine Beach.** This very popular strand is the closest beach to downtown. It's on the northern end of Anastasia Island, directly east of town. ⊠ *1200 Rte. A1A S* ☎ *No phone* ☞ *Free.*

②⑦ **St. Augustine Lighthouse & Museum.** Its beacon no longer guides ships to St. Augustine's shores, but the historic lighthouse continues to draw thousands of visitors each year. The 1874 structure replaced an earlier lighthouse built by the Spanish when the city was founded in 1565. The visitor center has an exhibit gallery and a store. ⊠ *81 Lighthouse Ave.* ☎ *904/829–0745* ⊕ *www.staugustinelighthouse.com* ☞ *$7.50* ⊘ *Daily 9–6.*

③⓪ **Vilano Beach.** Once-quiet Vilano Beach, just north of St. Augustine, is slowly blossoming into a bustling community with a town center, cozy restaurants and outdoor cafés, condos, and hotels. ⊠ *3400 Coastal Hwy., across the St. Augustine Inlet* ☎ *No phone* ☞ *Free.*

▶ ①④ **Visitor Information and Preview Center.** An entertaining film on the founding of St. Augustine, *Struggle to Survive,* is shown hourly 9–4. ⊠ *10 Castillo Dr.* ☎ *904/825–1000* ☞ *Free, movie $1* ⊘ *Daily 8:30–5:30.*

②③ **Ximenez-Fatio House.** Built as a merchant's house and store in 1797, the place became a tourist boardinghouse in the 1800s. It's been restored to look like it did during its inn days. ⊠ *20 Aviles St.* ☎ *904/829–3575* ⊕ *www.oldcity.com/sites/ximenez* ☞ *$5* ⊘ *Mon.–Sat. 11–4.*

off the beaten path

★

WORLD GOLF HALL OF FAME – This stunning tribute to the game of golf is the centerpiece of **World Golf Village,** an extraordinary complex that includes 36 holes of golf, a golf academy, two resorts, and a convention center. The Hall of Fame has an IMAX theater as well as more than 70 exhibits combining historical artifacts with the latest in interactive technology. Stand up to the pressures of the TV camera and crowd noise as you try to sink a final putt, or have your swing computer-analyzed. ⊠ *1 World Golf Pl.* ☎ *904/940–4123* ⊕ *www.worldgolfhalloffame.org* ☞ *$15, IMAX film $7.50, combined ticket $17* ⊘ *Mon.–Sat. 10–6, Sun. noon–6.*

Where to Stay & Eat

$$$–$$$$
Fodor'sChoice
★

✕ **95 Cordova.** Tucked away on the 1st floor of the Casa Monica Hotel, this restaurant serves classic cuisine with an international flair. Sup in one of three dining rooms, including the main room with intricate Moroccan-themed chandeliers, wrought-iron chairs, and heavy wood columns, or the Sultan's Room, a gold-dipped space accented with potted palms and a silk-draped ceiling. The exotic furnishings are inherently romantic, but still lend an appropriate feel to dinner with friends or business associates. Innovative dishes change seasonally and highlight local seafood and produce. The "Tasting Menu" offers diners six international courses paired with the restaurant's outstanding wines. ⊠ *115 Cordova St.* ☎ *904/810–6810* ▤ *AE, D, MC, V.*

★ **$$–$$$** ✕ **Columbia.** Arroz con pollo, fillet *salteado* (with a spicy sauce), and a fragrant seafood paella: this heir to the original Columbia, founded in Tampa in 1905 and still going strong, serves the same time-honored Cuban and Spanish dishes. Befitting its cuisine, the restaurant has a white stucco exterior and an atrium dining room full of palm trees, hand-painted tiles, and decorative arches. Sunday's Fiesta Brunch has everything from cheeses and cold meats to Belgian waffles. ⊠ *98 St. George St.* ☎ *904/ 824–3341, 800/227–1905 in Florida* ⊟ *AE, D, DC, MC, V.*

★ **$$–$$$** ✕ **La Parisienne.** Attentive and enthusiastic in its approach to honest bistro cuisine, this tiny place in a white stucco building with a little flower-filled courtyard is a true find (which, unfortunately, everyone seems to have found). Try grilled rack of lamb, roasted duck, or seafood chowder with pompano, clams, mussels, and oysters, and be sure to save room for the pastries. There's brunch on weekends. ⊠ *60 Hypolita St.* ☎ *904/ 829–0055* ⊟ *AE, D, DC, MC, V.*

$–$$$ ✕ **Fiddler's Green.** Spectacular views of the Atlantic and St. Augustine Inlet complement the open-flame-grilled seafood and steaks. Coconut shrimp comes with citrus-mustard salsa; Italian-seasoned crab cakes are made with fresh blue crabs and served with a mustard sauce. Also worthy are the New York strip and filet mignon. ⊠ *2750 Anahma Dr., Vilano Beach* ☎ *904/824–8897* ⊟ *AE, D, DC, MC, V* ⊗ *Closed Mon. No lunch.*

$–$$$ ✕ **O.C. White's Seafood & Spirits.** Waterfront views add to the charm of dining at this bayfront eatery, which makes its home in the General Worth house, circa 1791. Local favorites include coconut shrimp, blue crab cakes, Caribbean jerk chicken, and Alaskan snow-crab clusters. Beef lovers may want to try the 20-ounce porterhouse or the 12-ounce New York strip. Ask for an upstairs table to admire the marina. ⊠ *118 Avenida Menendez* ☎ *904/824–0808* ⊟ *AE, D, MC, V.*

★ **$–$$$** ✕ **Salt Water Cowboys.** Rustic handmade twig furniture and 100-year-old hardwood floors are reminders that this spot, hidden in the salt marshes flanking the Intracoastal Waterway, began as a secluded fish camp. Clam chowder, oyster stew, barbecue ribs, and crispy fried chicken are standard fare, along with blackened and broiled seafood, steamed oysters, and steak. For more adventuresome palates, the menu includes frogs' legs, alligator, and cooter (fried soft-shell turtle rolled in seasoned bread crumbs). ⊠ *299 Dondanville Rd.* ☎ *904/471–2332* ⊟ *AE, D, DC, MC, V* ⊗ *Closed Mon. No lunch.*

¢–$$ ✕ **Harry's Seafood Bar and Grill.** Although this casual eatery calls itself a seafood bar and grill, you might think you're on Bourbon Street when you step inside and get a whiff of the spicy cooking. Red beans with rice and sausage, shrimp and crab étouffée, and jambalaya are house specialties, but the menu also includes lobster and seafood pasta, catfish Pontchartrain, and tasty desserts such as bayou brownies and bananas Foster. Tables are in several small rooms and are almost always full. ⊠ *46 Avenida Menendez* ☎ *904/824–7765* ⊟ *AE, D, MC, V.*

$$$–$$$$ ⊞ **Casa Monica Hotel.** Hand-stenciled Moorish columns and arches,
Fodoŕ**sChoice** hand-crafted chandeliers, and gilded iron tables decorate the lobby of
★ this late-1800s Flagler-era masterpiece. A retreat for the nation's wealthiest until the Great Depression put it out of business, it has returned to

its perch as St. Augustine's grande dame. The turrets, towers, and wrought-iron balconies offer a hint of what's inside. Rooms—dressed in blues, greens, and whites—include wrought-iron two- and four-poster beds and mahogany writing desks and nightstands. The downtown location is within walking distance of many attractions. Guests also have access to the Serenata Beach Club, including three pools, private beach access, and beach equipment rentals. ✉ *95 Cordova St., 32084* ☎ *904/ 819–6087 or 800/648–1888* 🖷 *904/827–0426* ⊕ *www.casamonica. com* 🛏 *138 rooms, 14 suites* ⏚ *Restaurant, coffee shop, picnic area, snack bar, room service, in-room safes, some in-room hot tubs, some kitchenettes, some microwaves, some refrigerators, cable TV with movies and video games, in-room data ports, golf privileges, pool, exercise equipment, outdoor hot tub, massage, bicycles, billiards, bar, shops, dry cleaning, laundry service, concierge, Internet, business services, meeting rooms, parking (fee), no-smoking floors* ⊟ *AE, DC, MC, V.*

★ **$$$–$$$$** 🏨 **Casablanca Inn Bed & Breakfast on the Bay.** Breakfast comes with scenic views of the Matanzas Bay at this restored 1914 Mediterranean revival stucco-and-stone house, just north of the historic Bridge of Lions. Rooms vary in size and shape; some have separate sitting rooms, some have views of the bay, and some have whirlpool tubs, but all are decorated with period and reproduction furniture. You can enjoy breakfast on the patio or in the sunny dining room. In the evening, you can sip complimentary sherry in the cozy parlor. ✉ *24 Avenida Menendez, 32084* ☎ *904/829–0928 or 800/826–2626* 🖷 *904/826–1892* ⊕ *www. casablancainn.com* 🛏 *23 rooms, 13 suites* ⏚ *Dining room, fans, some in-room hot tubs, free parking; no phones in some rooms, no kids under 12, no smoking* ⊟ *AE, D, MC, V* ⎚⎓ *BP.*

$$–$$$$ 🏨 **Centennial House Bed & Breakfast.** Wide steps lead up to the entrance of this charming B&B in a fully restored 19th-century frame house in the heart of downtown St. Augustine. Each room is different, but all are painted in deep hues and have 10-foot-high ceilings and a mix of antiques and reproduction furniture. Some rooms have gas fireplaces and some have whirlpools. The brick courtyard is a peaceful outdoor space for taking a break. ✉ *26 Cordova St., 32084* ☎ *904/810–2218 or 800/611–2880* 🖷 *904/810–1930* ⊕ *www.centennialhouse.com* 🛏 *8 rooms* ⏚ *Dining room, some in-room hot tubs, cable TV, in-room VCRs, massage, Internet, business services, free parking; no kids under 10, no smoking* ⊟ *MC, V* ⎚⎓ *BP.*

★ **$$–$$$$** 🏨 **Grande Villas at World Golf Village.** Watch the action at the 17th and 18th holes from many rooms at this golfer's haven. One- and two-bedroom units are in three six-story pink-and-green buildings that overlook a golf course and lakes in World Golf Village. Rooms are richly appointed, painted deep shades of green or ocher, and decorated with framed prints and earth-tone fabrics. All units have a separate living room, a full kitchen, a washer and dryer, and a balcony. Nongolfers can spend their time relaxing by the pool or on the tennis courts. ✉ *100 Front Nine Dr., 32092* ☎ *904/940–2000 or 800/456–0009* 🖷 *904/940–2076* ⊕ *www. bluegreenonline.com* 🛏 *134 villas* ⏚ *In-room safes, some in-room hot tubs, kitchens, kitchenettes, microwaves, refrigerators, cable TV with movies, in-room VCRs, golf privileges, 2 tennis courts, pool, wading* *pool, gym, outdoor hot tub, basketball, volleyball, babysitting, play-ground, dry cleaning, laundry facilities, concierge, Internet, business ser-vices, convention center, meeting rooms, free parking* ⊟ *AE, D, DC, MC, V.*

★ **$$-$$$$** ⊞ **Renaissance Resort at World Golf Village.** If you want to be within walk-ing distance of all World Golf Village has to offer, this full-service re-sort is an excellent choice. The 10-story building dwarfs the surrounding palm trees and overlooks a peaceful lake. Rooms and suites surround a soaring atrium, at the bottom of which is a restaurant set amid trop-ical foliage and cool streams. Units are oversize and are furnished in muted pastels. The hotel has an IMAX movie theater, adjoins a convention cen-ter, is adjacent to the World Golf Hall of Fame, and borders the cham-pionship golf course. ⊠ *500 S. Legacy Trail, 32092* ☎ *904/940–8000 or 888/740–7020* ⊟ *904/940–8008* ⊕ *www.worldgolfrenaissance.com* ⇗ *300 rooms, 28 suites* ⌂ *Restaurant, some in-room hot tubs, some kitchenettes, some microwaves, some refrigerators, cable TV with movies and video games, in-room data ports, golf privileges, putting green, pool, gym, outdoor hot tub, billiards, bar, video game room, shops, babysit-ting, playground, dry cleaning, laundry facilities, concierge, Internet, busi-ness services, convention center, meeting rooms, free parking, no-smoking floors* ⊟ *AE, D, DC, MC, V.*

$$-$$$$ ⊞ **St. Francis Inn Bed & Breakfast.** If the walls could whisper, this late-18th-century house in the historic district would tell tales of slave up-risings, buried doubloons, and Confederate spies. The inn, a guest house since 1845, offers rooms, suites, a room in the former carriage house, and a five-room cottage. Furnishings are a mix of antiques and just plain old. ⊠ *279 St. George St., 32084* ☎ *904/824–6068 or 800/824–6062* ⊟ *904/810–5525* ⊕ *www.stfrancisinn.com* ⇗ *13 rooms, 4 suites, 1 2-bedroom cottage* ⌂ *Dining room, some in-room hot tubs, some kitch-enettes, some microwaves, some refrigerators, cable TV, some in-room VCRs, in-room data ports, pool, bicycles, free parking; no kids under 10 in main house, no smoking* ⊟ *MC, V* ⊙*I BP.*

$-$$$ ⊞ **Carriage Way Bed and Breakfast.** The grandly restored Victorian man-sion is within walking distance of the old town. Innkeepers Bill John-son and his family see to such welcoming touches as fresh flowers, home-baked breads, and evening cordials. Special-occasion breakfasts, flowers, picnic lunches, romantic dinners, or a simple family supper can be arranged with advance notice. ⊠ *70 Cuna St., 32084* ☎ *904/829–2467 or 800/908–9832* ⊟ *904/826–1461* ⊕ *www.carriageway.com* ⇗ *11 rooms* ⌂ *Some in-room hot tubs, some kitchenettes, bicycles, In-ternet, business services, meeting rooms, free parking; no room TVs, no smoking* ⊟ *D, MC, V* ⊙*I BP.*

$-$$$ ⊞ **Old City House Inn and Restaurant.** It's hardly noticeable amid the pala-tial Flagler-era architecture of the historic district, but this small two-story inn is certainly worth a visit. Touches of Paris, Venice, and India are just a few of the surprises within its coquina walls, where innkeep-ers Ilse and James Philcox, both avid travelers, have decorated the rooms to reflect different international cities or themes. Although it's downtown and near busy attractions, the property's tall brick walls and lush foliage offer ample privacy. Each room has its own entrance, and a 2nd-floor deck is perfect for taking in sunsets. ⊠ *115 Cordova St., 32084* ☎ *904/826–0113* ⊕ *www.oldcityhouse.com* ⤴ *7 rooms* ⚴ *Restaurant, some in-room hot tubs, cable TV, some in-room VCRs, free parking; no kids under 10, no smoking* ⊟ *AE, MC, V* ⊚| *BP.*

¢–$$$ 🏨 **Monterey Inn.** Location—right across from the Castillo de San Marcos National Monument and across the street from Matanzas Bay—is the draw of this modest two-story motel. Rooms are on the plain side. It's within walking distance of many restaurants and sights. ⊠ *16 Avenida Menendez, 32084* ☎ *904/824–4482* 🖶 *904/829–8854* ⊕ *www. themontereyinn.com* ⤴ *59 rooms* ⚴ *Café, some kitchenettes, some microwaves, some refrigerators, cable TV, in-room data ports, pool, business services, free parking; no smoking* ⊟ *AE, D, DC, MC, V.*

$–$$ 🏨 **Kenwood Inn.** For more than a century, this stately Victorian inn has welcomed wayfarers, and the Constant family continues the tradition. In the heart of the historic district, the inn is near restaurants and sightseeing. A Continental buffet breakfast of home-baked cakes and breads is included. ⊠ *38 Marine St., 32084* ☎ *904/824–2116 or 800/824–8151* 🖶 *904/824–1689* ⊕ *www.thekenwoodinn.com* ⤴ *14 rooms, 3 suites* ⚴ *Cable TV, pool, bicycles, Internet, free parking; no room phones, no kids under 8, no smoking* ⊟ *D, MC, V* ⊚| *CP.*

Nightlife

The **Mill Top Tavern** (⊠ 19½ St. George St. ☎ 904/829–2329) is one of the city's hottest night spots. If you're staying on Anastasia Island, the **Oasis Deck and Restaurant** (⊠ 4000 Rte. A1A S, at Ocean Trace Rd., St. Augustine Beach ☎ 904/471–3424) is your best bet for nightly entertainment, offering 24 draft beers and beach access. Something is always happening at **Scarlett O'Hara's** (⊠ 70 Hypolita St. ☎ 904/824–6535). Some nights it's blues or jazz bands; on others it might be disco, Top 40, or karaoke; and many nights the early and late-night entertainment are completely different. **Trade Winds** (⊠ 124 Charlotte St. ☎ 904/829–9336) showcases bands every night, from country and western to rock.

Sports & the Outdoors

Biking

Rent bikes to ride on the beach or in the bike lanes along A1A at **Bike America** (⊠ 3936 Rte. A1A S, St. Augustine Beach ☎ 904/461–5557).

Fishing

K-2 Sport Fishing (⊠ U.S. 1 and Rte. 207 ☎ 904/824–9499) offers 10- and 12-hour charters in addition to overnight and extended-stay trips. Charter the *Sea Love II* (⊠ 250 Vilano Rd. ☎ 904/824–3328), or sign up to join a half- or full-day fishing trip.

Golf

Ocean Hammock (⊠ 105 16th Rd., Palm Coast ☎ 386/447–4611) at the Palm Coast Golf Resort is considered among the best open-to-the-public courses in the state. Green fee: $205. Golfers looking for a more reasonably-priced round at Palm Coast can check out **Hampton Golf at Matanzas Woods** (⊠ 398 Lakeview Blvd., Palm Coast ☎ 386/446–

6330), green fee: $30/$80. Like Matanzas Woods, **Pine Lakes at Hampton Golf** (✉ 400 Pine Lakes Pl., Palm Coast ☎ 386/445–0852) was designed by Arnold Palmer and Ed Seay and is also reasonably priced, green fee: $30/$80. Find 72 holes at the **Sheraton Palm Coast** (✉ 300 Clubhouse Dr., Palm Coast ☎ 800/654–6538). Green fee: $45/$65. As part of its complex, **World Golf Village** (✉ 21 World Golf Pl. ☎ 904/940–4000) has two 18-hole layouts named for and partially designed by golf legends Sam Snead, Gene Sarazen, Arnold Palmer, and Jack Nicklaus. The courses are the Slammer & Squire (☎ 904/940–6088), green fee: $99/$150, and the King & Bear (☎ 904/940–6200), green fee: $150/$175.

Tennis

Ron Parker Memorial Field (✉ 901 Pope Rd.) has two lighted tennis courts and four paddleball courts. Public courts are available at **Treaty Park** (✉ 1595 Wildwood Dr.). It has six lighted tennis courts, eight paddleball and eight racquetball courts, and a skate park with ramps and jumps.

Water Sports

Rent surfboards, skim boards, and body boards at the **Surf Station** (✉ 1020 Anastasia Blvd. ☎ 904/471–9463). Or head off into the wild blue yonder, 1,400 feet over the ocean, with **Smile High Parasail** (✉ 111 Avenida Menendez ☎ 904/819–0980).

Shopping

Just north of St. Augustine, at Exit 95 on Interstate 95, is the **St. Augustine Premium Outlets Center** (✉ 2700 State Rd. 16 ☎ 904/825–1555 ⊕ www.staugustineoutlets.com), with 95 designer and brand-name outlets. **Belz Factory Outlet World** (✉ 500 Belz Outlet Rd. ☎ 904/826–1311) has 75 name-brand stores. In town, be sure to walk along car-free **St. George Street** (✉ Between Cathedral Pl. and Orange St.) to check out the art galleries and one-of-a-kind shops with candles, home accents, handmade jewelry, aromatherapy products, pottery, books, and clothing.

Side Trips from St. Augustine

Marineland of Florida

🕙 *18 mi south of St. Augustine.*

Constructed in 1938, the world's first oceanarium has earned a spot on the National Register of Historic Places, and though it may be showing its age, it's still worth a visit. Watch divers put dolphins through daily training routines, view underwater feedings, and participate in several interactive programs, including diving, snorkeling, and a touch-and-feel dolphin encounter (extra cost). You can meet an African penguin, too, also extra. ✉ *9600 Ocean Shore Blvd., Marineland* ☎ *904/460–1275 or 888/279–9194* ⊕ *www.marineland.net* 🎟 *$14* 🕙 *Fri.–Mon. 9:30–4:30.*

Ravine State Gardens

35 mi southwest of St. Augustine.

For a great picnic spot, make your way to one of the state's wonderful azalea gardens, which took root during the Depression as a WPA project. The ravines are atypical of flat Florida. They're steep and deep, threaded with brooks and rocky outcroppings, and floored with flatlands. Although any month is a good time to hike the shaded glens, for a truly stunning scene, head here in February and March when the azaleas are in full bloom. ⊠ *1600 Twig St., Palatka* ☎ *386/329–3721* 🔄 *$4 per vehicle, up to 8 people* ⊘ *Daily 8–sunset.*

DAYTONA & THE SPACE COAST

This section of coast covers only 75 mi, but it offers considerable variety, from the unassuming bedroom community of Ormond Beach to the Spring Break Capital of Daytona Beach, to the world's only launch site for the Space Shuttle in Cape Canaveral. On the northernmost tip of the coast sits Ormond Beach, established at the turn of the 20th century as a tourist haven for the rich and famous, now catering to families and seniors seeking a quiet escape. To the south is Daytona Beach. Primarily associated with auto racing and spring break, the World's Most Famous Beach is fronted with a mixture of tall condos and apartments, hotels, low-rise motels and flashy nightclubs. Farther south is the small town of New Smyrna Beach, its beach lined with private houses, some empty land, and an occasional taller condominium. Just below it lies the Canaveral National Seashore and the John F. Kennedy Space Center. Still farther south, the laid-back town of Cocoa Beach attracts visitors on weekends all year, as it's the closest beach to Orlando. While the hurricanes of 2004 caused hundreds of millions of dollars in damage to the area, including 40% of all hotel/motel rooms in Daytona Beach, most commercial properties have since reopened, many having undergone considerable renovations. Some smaller, family-owned entities, however, continue to rebuild.

Ormond Beach

33 *60 mi south of St. Augustine.*

The town got its reputation as the birthplace of speed because early car enthusiasts such as Alexander Winton, R. E. Olds, and Barney Oldfield raced their autos on the sands here. The Birthplace of Speed Antique Car Show and Swap Meet is held every Thanksgiving, attracting enthusiasts from across the nation. Ormond Beach borders the north side of Daytona Beach on both the mainland and the barrier island; nowadays you can't tell you've crossed from one to the other unless you notice the sign.

The scenic **Tomoka State Park,** 3 mi north of Ormond Beach, is perfect for fishing, camping, hiking, and boating. It is the site of a Timucuan Indian settlement discovered in 1605 by Spanish explorer Alvaro Mexia. Wooded campsites, bicycle and walking paths, and guided canoe tours on the Tomoka and Halifax rivers are the main attractions. ⊠ *2099 N. Beach St.* ☎ *386/676–4050, 800/326–3521 (Reserve America) for camping reservations* 🗏 *386/676–4060* ⊕ *www.floridastateparks.org/ tomoka* 🔄 *$4 per vehicle, up to 8 people* ⊘ *Daily 8–sunset.*

★ Listed on the National Register of Historic Places, the **Casements,** the restored winter retreat of John D. Rockefeller, is now a cultural center and museum. Take a tour through the period Rockefeller Room, which contains some of the family's memorabilia. The estate and its formal gardens host an annual lineup of events and exhibits; there's also a permanent exhibit of Hungarian folk art and musical instruments. ⌧ *25 Riverside Dr.* ☎ *386/676–3216* ⊕ *www.ormondbeach.org* ✉ *Donations accepted* ☉ *Weekdays 8:30–5, Sat. 9–noon, tours 10–2:30.*

Take a walk through 4 acres of lush tropical gardens, past fish ponds and fountains, at the **Ormond Memorial Art Museum and Gardens.** The museum has historical displays, symbolic religious paintings by Malcolm Fraser, and special exhibits by Florida artists. ⌧ *78 E. Granada Blvd.* ☎ *386/676–3347* ⊕ *www.ormondartmuseum.org* ✉ *Donations accepted* ☉ *Weekdays 10–4, weekends noon–4.*

Where to Stay & Eat

★ **$$$$** ✕ **La Crepe en Haut.** Outside stairs lead up to this quiet and elegant French restaurant with several dining rooms and many window tables. Consider starting with onion soup, and then try fillet of beef with burgundy sauce or roasted duck with berries. Leave room for a sweet fruit tart or a slice of creamy cheesecake. The wine list includes excellent French labels. If you're in search of lighter fare, stop by the Bistro, next door but with the same kitchen. ⌧ *142 E. Granada Blvd.* ☎ *386/673–1999* ▭ *AE, MC, V* ☉ *Closed Mon. No lunch Sat.*

$–$$$$ ▦ **Best Western Mainsail Inn & Suites.** The rooms and suites (they have two bedrooms) are basic but comfortably furnished; rates are very reasonable; and management is caring. Plus, the three-story, U-shape building is right on the beach. ⌧ *281 S. Atlantic Ave., 32176* ☎ *386/677–2131 or 800/843–5142* 🖷 *386/676–0323* ⊕ *www.bestwesternmainsail.com* ⇆ *44 rooms, 9 suites* ⚐ *In-room safes, some in-room hot tubs, some kitchenettes, cable TV, pool, wading pool, beach, dry cleaning, laundry service, business services, free parking, no-smoking rooms* ▭ *AE, D, MC, V* ⦿l *CP.*

Daytona Beach

③④ *65 mi south of St. Augustine.*

Best known for the Daytona 500, Daytona has been the center of automobile racing since cars were first raced along the beach here in 1902. February is the biggest month for race enthusiasts, and there are weekly events at the International Speedway. During race weeks, bike weeks, spring-break periods, and summer holidays, expect extremely heavy traffic along the strip as well as on the beach itself, since driving on the sand is allowed; areas marked "no car zones" are less frenetic and more family friendly. On the mainland, near the Inland Waterway, several blocks of Beach Street have been "street-scaped," and shops and restaurants open onto an inviting, broad brick sidewalk.

Memorabilia from the early days of beach automobile racing are on display at the **Halifax Historical Museum,** as are historic photographs, Native American artifacts, a postcard exhibit, and a video that details city history. There's a shop for gifts and antiques, too. ⊠ *252 S. Beach St.* ☎ *386/255–6976* ⊕ *www.halifaxhistorical.org* ☑ *$3, free Sat.* ☉ *Tues.–Fri. 10–4, Sat. 10-noon.*

★ ⓒ   The interactive motor-sports attraction at **Daytona USA** lets you experience the thrill of a race from the driver's seat with its Dreamlaps motion simulator. For the truly brave, Accelerator Alley puts the pedal to the metal with speeds reaching 200 mph. Participate in a pit stop on a NASCAR Winston Cup stock car or computer-design your own race car. There's also an exhibit of the history of auto racing. Several cars are on display, including the late Dale Earnhardt's Number 3 Chevrolet Monte Carlo, which he drove to victory in the 1998 Daytona 500, and Sir Malcolm Campbell's fully restored Bluebird V, which reached 276 mph in the 1935 Daytona race, when races were still held on the beach. ⊠ *1801 W. International Speedway Dr.* ☎ *386/947–6800* ⊕ *www.daytonausa. com* ☑ *$21.50* ☉ *Daily 9–7.*

One of only a dozen photography museums in the country, the **Southeast Museum of Photography,** at Daytona Beach Community College, has changing historical and contemporary exhibits. ⊠ *1200 W. International Speedway Blvd., Bldg. 100* ☎ *386/254–4475* ⊕ *www.smponline.org* ☑ *Donation welcome* ☉ *Mon. and Wed.–Fri. 10–4, Tues. 11–7, weekends 1–5.*

The humanities section of the **Museum of Arts and Sciences,** one of the largest museums in Florida, includes displays of Chinese art, and glass, silver, gold, and porcelain examples of decorative arts. The museum also has pre-Castro Cuban art, Florida Native American items, pre-Columbian art, Indian and Persian miniature paintings, and an eye-popping complete skeleton of a giant sloth that is 13 feet long and 130,000 years old. ⊠ *1040 Museum Blvd.* ☎ *386/255–0285* ⊕ *www.moas.org* ☑ *$8* ☉ *Tues.–Fri. 9–4, weekends noon–5.*

★   **Daytona Beach,** which bills itself as the World's Most Famous Beach, permits you to drive your car right up to your beach site, spread out a blanket, and have all your belongings at hand; this is especially convenient for beachgoers who are elderly or have disabilities. However, heavy traffic during summer and holidays makes it dangerous for children, and families should be extra careful or stay in the designated car-free zones. The speed limit is 10 mph. To get your car on the beach, look for signs on Route A1A indicating beach access via beach ramps. Sand traps are not limited to the golf course, though—cars can get stuck.

off the beaten path   **PONCE INLET –** At the southern tip of the barrier island that includes Daytona Beach is this sleepy town with a small marina, a few bars, and informal fish restaurants. Boardwalks traverse delicate dunes and provide easy access to the beach, although storms have caused serious erosion. Marking this prime spot is the bright-red, century-old **Ponce de León Lighthouse,** a historic monument and museum, the tallest lighthouse in the state and the second tallest in the country. Climb to the top of the lighthouse tower for a bird's-eye view of Ponce Inlet. ⊠ *4931 S. Peninsula Dr.* ☎ *386/761–1821* ⊕ *www.ponceinlet.org* ☑ *$5* ☉ *Early Sept.–mid-May, daily 10–5; mid-May–early Sept., daily 10–9.*

Where to Stay & Eat

★ **$$-$$$** ✕ **Gene's Steak House.** Quiet and intimate, this family-operated restaurant, a bit west of town, has long upheld its reputation as *the* place for steaks in the area. Signature entrées include filet mignons, sirloins, and porterhouses. Seafood is also available. The wine list is one of the state's largest. ✉ *3674 W. International Speedway Blvd. (U.S. 92)* ☎ *386/255–2059* ☰ *AE, DC, MC, V* ☉ *Closed Sun. and Mon. No lunch.*

$-$$$ ✕ **Aunt Catfish's on the River.** Hot cinnamon rolls and hush puppies come with any entrée, one of the lures attracting locals and visitors alike. Other draws are a terrific salad bar, Southern-style fried chicken, and seafood (fried shrimp, fried catfish, and crab cakes are specialties). It's on the west bank of the Intracoastal Waterway (off U.S. 1, before crossing the Port Orange Causeway), just south of Daytona. ✉ *4009 Halifax Dr., Port Orange* ☎ *386/767–4768* ⌖ *Reservations not accepted* ☰ *AE, MC, V.*

★ **$-$$$** ✕ **Rosario Ristorante.** Excellent northern-Italian fare drives this busy place. Tender veal marsala and fresh local grouper poached in white wine are among the high points, but the menu also has a full page of pastas, including tortellini *alla Rosario* (stuffed with ricotta cheese, prosciutto, and mushrooms in a creamy cheese sauce) and spaghetti *puttanesca* (with sun-dried tomatoes, olives, capers, and anchovies). Save room for the sweet cannoli. ✉ *448 S. Beach St.* ☎ *386/258–6066* ☰ *MC, V* ☉ *Closed Sun. and Mon. No lunch.*

$-$$ ✕ **Anna's Italian Trattoria.** White table linens and flowers complement delightful Italian fare at this cozy spot. Choose from a long list of delicious pastas, such as the spaghetti with Italian sausage and onions, angel-hair pasta with fresh chopped tomatoes and garlic, or spinach-stuffed ravioli. Try one of the many classic Italian desserts here. ✉ *304 Seabreeze Blvd.* ☎ *386/239–9624* ☰ *MC, V* ☉ *No lunch.*

¢-$$ ✕ **McK's Dublin Station.** Crowds fill up the bar, the tables, and the cozy booths in this lively tavern. The fare is simple, hearty, and generous; cheeseburgers are thick and juicy, the chili is extra-spicy, and a big slice of homemade meat loaf comes with mashed potatoes. There's a long list of stuffed sandwiches. Onion rings are a specialty. ✉ *218 S. Beach St.* ☎ *386/238–3321* ☰ *AE, MC, V* ☉ *Closed Sun.*

$$$-$$$$ ▦ **The Shores Resort & Spa.** Formerly the Hilton Daytona Oceanfront, this 11-story beachfront resort underwent a $10 million facelift in 2004. Rooms are spacious and have views of either the ocean or intracoastal waterway. Rustic furniture and beds swathed in mosquito netting lend themselves to the Old Florida decor, but there's nothing primitive about the hotel's amenities, including a luxury bed and a 42-inch plasma, flat-screen TV in every room; the Indonesian-inspired SpaTerre; and Baleen restaurant and lounge overlooking the Atlantic Ocean. ✉ *2637 S. Atlantic Ave., 32219* ☎ *386/767–7350 or 800/525–7350* ☎ *386/760–3651* ⊕ *www.daytonabeach.hilton.com* ➳ *212 rooms, 2 suites* ⌖ *Restaurant, room service, in-room safes, minibars, cable TV with movies, in-room DVD players, in-room data ports, pool, wading pool, gym, hair salon, outdoor hot tub, spa, beach, 2 bars, video game room, dry cleaning, laundry service, Internet, business services, meeting rooms, free parking, no-smoking floors* ☰ *AE, D, DC, MC, V.*

★ **$$–$$$$** ⬛ **Adam's Mark Daytona Beach Resort.** Daytona's most luxurious high-rise hotel has two towers that sit on a traffic-free beach. Every room has a great ocean view and is comfortably furnished in pleasing pastels and blond oak. Spacious sun decks and pools are perfect for those not into the beach. Dine in the resort's food court or live it up in an elegant restaurant. ✉ *100 N. Atlantic Ave., 32118* ☎ *386/254–8200 or 800/444–2326* 🖷 *386/253–8841* ⊕ *www.adamsmark.com/ daytonabeach* ➩ *742 rooms, 52 suites* ⚘ *3 restaurants, food court, room service, some minibars, cable TV with movies and video games, in-room data ports, indoor-outdoor pool, outdoor pool, wading pool, 2 health clubs, massage, beach, volleyball, 3 bars, video game room, shops, playground, laundry facilities, laundry service, concierge, Internet, business services, convention center, free parking, no-smoking floors* ▭ *AE, D, DC, MC, V.*

$$–$$$ ⬛ **Perry's Ocean-Edge Resort.** Long regarded as a family resort, Perry's is known for its free homemade doughnuts and coffee—a breakfast ritual served in the lush solarium. Units are in one of four buildings, ranging from two to six stories that face the beach. Most of the rooms have kitchens and great ocean views. There are several pools, a wide beach, and a putting green. ✉ *2209 S. Atlantic Ave., 32118* ☎ *386/255–0581 or 800/447–0002* 🖷 *386/258–7315* ⊕ *www.perrysoceanedge.com* ➩ *200 rooms* ⚘ *Café, kitchens, cable TV, in-room data ports, putting green, 3 pools (1 indoor), fitness classes, gym, spa, beach, horseshoes, shuffleboard, volleyball, children's programs (ages 4–12), playground, laundry facilities, laundry service, Internet, free parking, no-smoking rooms* ▭ *AE, D, DC, MC, V.*

$–$$ ⬛ **Beach Quarters Resort.** Freshly-baked free goodies and coffee, served in the home-style Galley overlooking the ocean, are one of the special touches at this all-suites inn. The one- and two-bedroom units are done in bright yellows with teal or red-and-blue accents and have coordinating window treatments and oak furnishings. Each unit has a private balcony and full kitchen. Penthouse suites have electric fireplaces. ✉ *3711 S. Atlantic Ave., Daytona Beach Shores 32127* ☎ *386/767–3119 or 800/332–3119* 🖷 *386/767–0883* ⊕ *www.thebeachquarters. com* ➩ *26 suites* ⚘ *Restaurant, kitchens, cable TV, in-room VCRs, pool, beach, laundry facilities, business services, free parking* ▭ *AE, D, MC, V.*

★ **$–$$** ⬛ **Live Oak Inn.** Two restored homes next door to each other, both listed on the National Register of Historic Places, make up this lovely B&B. Each room is beautifully furnished with antiques. Some have long enclosed porches and look out over the marina or onto gardens. Three have whirlpools. The first floor contains a small lounge and reception area. ✉ *444 S. Beach St., 32114* ☎ *386/252–4667* 🖷 *386/ 239–0068* ➩ *10 rooms* ⚘ *Dining room, some in-room hot tubs, free parking; no smoking* ▭ *AE, D, MC, V* ⦿ *CP.*

Nightlife & the Arts

THE ARTS Jazz, big band, blues, and folk acts perform at the outdoor, oceanfront **Daytona Beach Bandshell** (✉ 250 N. Atlantic Ave. ☎ 386/671–3420). Internationally acclaimed orchestras and soloists appear as part of the **Daytona Beach Symphony Society** (✉ 140 S. Beach St., Ste. 107 ☎ 386/

253–2901). Touring Broadway shows, symphony orchestras, international ballet companies, and popular entertainers appear at the **Volusia County Ocean Center** (⊠ 101 N. Atlantic Ave. ☎ 386/254–4545, 800/858–6444 in Florida). Affiliated with Bethune Cookman College, the 2,500-seat **Mary McLeod Bethune Performing Arts Center** (⊠ 698 W. International Speedway Blvd. ☎ 386/481–2778) showcases performing and visual arts productions by students and professional touring companies. **Peabody Auditorium** (⊠ 600 Auditorium Blvd. ☎ 386/671–3461) is used for concerts and programs year-round. **Seaside Music Theater** (⊠ 176 N. Beach St. ☎ 386/252–6200 or 800/854–5592) presents musicals in two venues January through February and June through August.

NIGHTLIFE **Ocean Walk** (⊠ 250 N. Atlantic Ave. ☎ 386/566–6876) is a lively, always hopping cluster of shops, restaurants, and bars right on the ocean. At **Razzles Nightclub** (⊠ 611 Seabreeze Blvd. ☎ 386/257–6236), DJs play high-energy dance music from 8 PM to 3 AM.

Sports & the Outdoors

AUTO RACING The massive **Daytona International Speedway** (⊠ 1801 W. International Speedway Blvd. ☎ 386/254–2700), on Daytona's major east–west artery, has year-round auto and motorcycle racing, including the Daytona 500 in February and the Pepsi 400 in July. When races aren't on, you can take a 20-minute tour (daily 9:30–4, on the half hour).

DOG RACING Bet on the dogs every day but Sunday year-round at the **Daytona Beach Kennel Club and Poker Room** (⊠ 2201 W. International Speedway ☎ 386/252–6484).

FISHING Contact **Critter Fleet Marina** (⊠ 4950 S. Peninsula Dr., Ponce Inlet ☎ 386/767–7676) for full- or half-day deep-sea party trips. **Half-n-Half Charters** (⊠ 79 E. Dunlawton Ave. ☎ 386/767–0583) offers 5-, 8-, 10-, and 12-hour fishing excursions.

GOLF **Indigo Lakes Golf Club** (⊠ 312 Indigo Dr. ☎ 386/254–3607) has 18 holes of golf, green fee: $42/$70. The public courses at **LPGA International** (⊠ 1000 Champions Dr., Daytona Beach ☎ 386/523–2001) yield 36 holes, green fee: $75/$95. **Pelican Bay South Country Club** (⊠ 550 Sea Duck Dr. ☎ 386/788–6496) rents clubs and has a pro shop and a restaurant, in addition to 18 holes, green fee: $35/$55. There's an 18-hole course at **Spruce Creek Golf & Country Club** (⊠ 1900 Country Club Dr., Port Orange ☎ 386/756–6114), along with practice and driving ranges, rental clubs, a pro shop, and a restaurant, green fee: $45/$55.

WATER SPORTS Catch air at **Blue Sky Parasail** (⊠ 2025 S. Atlantic Ave. ☎ 386/334–2191). Rent surfboards or boogie boards at any **Salty Dog** (⊠ 700 E. International Speedway Blvd. ☎ 386/258–0457 ⊠ 100 S. Atlantic Ave. ☎ 386/253–2755 ⊠ Bellair Plaza, 2429 N. Atlantic Ave. ☎ 386/673–5277).

Shopping

Daytona Flea & Farmer's Market (⊠ 2987 Belleview Ave. ☎ 386/253–3330 ⊕ www.daytonafleamarket.net) is one of the largest in the South. The **Volusia Mall** (⊠ 1700 W. International Speedway Blvd. ☎ 386/253–6783) has more than 100 stores, including Burdines and Dillards.

New Smyrna Beach

㉟ *19 mi south of Daytona Beach.*

The long, dune-lined beach of this small town abuts the Canaveral National Seashore. Behind the dunes sit beach houses, small motels, and an occasional high-rise (except at the extreme northern tip, where none are higher than seven stories). Canal Street, on the mainland, and Flagler Avenue, with many beachside shops and restaurants, have both been "street-scaped" with wide brick sidewalks and stately palm trees. The town is also known for its internationally recognized artists' workshop.

Changing exhibits every two months, the **Atlantic Center for the Arts** has works of internationally known artists. Media include sculpture, mixed materials, video, drawings, prints, and paintings. Intensive three-week workshops are periodically run by visual, literary, and performing master artists such as Edward Albee, James Dickey, and Beverly Pepper. ✉ *1414 Art Center Ave.* ☎ *386/427–6975* ⊕ *www.atlanticcenterforthearts. org* 🔲 *Free* ☉ *Weekdays 9–5, Sat. 10–2.*

In a warehouse that has been converted into a stunning high-ceiling art gallery, **Arts on Douglas** has a new exhibit of works by a Florida artist every month. Representing more than 60 artists, the gallery has previously hosted exhibits on the handmade jewelry of Mary Schimpff Webb and landscape and still-life oils by Barbara Tiffany. The gallery also hosts an open reception every first Saturday of the month from 4 to 7 PM. ✉ *123 Douglas St.* ☎ *386/428–1133* 🔲 *Free* ☉ *Tues.–Fri. 11–6, Sat. 10–2, and by appointment.*

Smyrna Dunes Park is on the northern tip of its barrier island. Here 1½ mi of boardwalks crisscross sand dunes and delicate dune vegetation to lead to beaches and a fishing jetty. Botanical signs identify the flora, and there are picnic tables and an information center. ✉ *N. Peninsula Ave.* ☎ *386/424–2935* 🔲 *$3.50 per vehicle, up to 8 people* ☉ *Daily 6 AM–sunset.*

New Smyrna Beach's public beach extends 7 mi from the northernmost part of the barrier island south to the Canaveral National Seashore. It's mostly hard-packed white sand and at low tide can be stunningly wide. The beach is lined with heaps of sandy dunes, but because they're endangered, it's against the law to walk on or play in them or to pick the sea grass, which helps to stabilize the dunes. Note that from sunrise to sunset cars are allowed on certain sections of the beach (speed limit: 10 mph). In season there's a nominal beach access fee for cars.

★ Miles of grassy, windswept dunes and a virtually empty beach await you at **Canaveral National Seashore**, a remarkable 57,000-acre park with 24 mi of undeveloped coastline. Stop at any of the six parking areas and follow the wooden walkways to the beach. Ranger-led weekly programs include canoe trips and sea-turtle talks. ✉ *7611 S. Atlantic Ave.* ☎ *386/428–3384* ⊕ *www.nps.gov/cana* 🔲 *$5 per vehicle* ☉ *Nov.–Mar., daily 6–6, Apr.–Oct., daily 6 AM–8 PM; call for Playalinda Beach hrs.*

Where to Stay & Eat

$$–$$$ ✕ **New Smyrna Steakhouse.** Superb steaks and ribs bring locals and visitors to this dark, busy spot. Booths are lit by individual, low-hanging lamps that provide intimacy but enough light to read the menu. Try the 12-ounce New York strip or sirloin, the 22-ounce porterhouse, the 8-ounce filet mignon, or a rack of tender ribs. Other good choices are the cajun pizza, shrimp Caesar salad, and mesquite chicken. ⊠ *723 3rd Ave.* ☎ *386/424–9696* ⊟ *AE, D, MC, V.*

$$–$$$ ✕ **Norwood's Seafood Restaurant.** Fresh local fish and shrimp are the specialties at this casual New Smyrna Beach landmark, open since 1945. Built as a gas station, the building later served as a general store and piggy bank factory, but the remodeled interior belies this back story; the place is replete with wood, from the chairs and booths to the walls and rafters. Order steak, blackened chicken breast, or pasta. Prices are reasonable, and more than 3,000 bottles of wine are on hand. ⊠ *400 E. 2nd Ave.* ☎ *386/428–4621* ⊟ *AE, D, MC, V.*

★ $–$$$ ✕**Spanish River Grill.** Michelle and Henry Salgado own this first-rate restaurant, which many consider the best in New Smyrna Beach. Henry combines his Cuban grandmother's recipes with local ingredients for knockout results. Start with fried green plantains or clams tossed with garlic and avocado. For the main course, try some seafood, the incredible paella, or a tender rib-eye steak stuffed with chorizo. Be sure to save room for one of Michelle's desserts. ⊠ *737 E. 3rd Ave.* ☎ *386/424–6991* ⊟ *AE, MC, V* ⊘ *Closed Mon. No lunch.*

★ $–$$$ ✕ **Victor's Backstreet Cuisine.** A blue neon sign lights the way to this tiny restaurant. Although the interior is humble—specials scrawled on a blackboard, tightly arranged wooden tables, and a small, open kitchen—the fare here is definitely bold. Spicy barbecue ribs, herb-seasoned tuna or chicken on a dense berry sauce, and sirloin with datil-pepper salsa are just some of the many choices. Specials could be filet mignon or ostrich prepared with a twist. You'll see Victor in the kitchen, working his culinary magic, and in the photos on the walls, accepting accolades. On weekends reservations are a must. ⊠ *103 Pine St.* ☎ *386/426–5000* ⊟ *No credit cards* ⊘ *Closed Mon. and Tues. No lunch.*

$–$$ ✕**Captain J. B.'s Famous Fishing Camp and Seafood Restaurant.** Better known simply as J. B.'s, this local landmark is on the eastern shore of the Indian River. Crowds gather around the picnic-style tables inside and out or belly up to the bar to dine on mounds of spicy seafood, fresh crabs, cajun alligator, or crab cakes. It's a great place to catch the sunset, and there's live music Saturday and Sunday afternoons. ⊠ *859 Pompano Ave.* ☎ *386/427–5747* ⊟ *AE, D, MC, V.*

$–$$ ✕ **Chase's on the Beach.** Eat on the deck beneath the stars—gazing at either the ocean or the pool—or dine indoors. Barefooted beachgoers wander up for beverages, hamburgers, and salads during the day (shoes required inside), whereas the evening crowd comes for fried shrimp, grouper sandwiches, and weekend entertainment. ⊠ *3401 S. Atlantic Ave.* ☎ *386/423–8787* ⊟ *AE, D, MC, V.*

★ $$–$$$ ▥ **Riverview Hotel, Restaurant and Spa.** A landmark since 1886, this former bridge tender's home is set back from the Intracoastal Waterway at the edge of the North Causeway, which still has an operating drawbridge. Rooms open out to plant-filled verandas and balconies, and views look either through trees to the Intracoastal or onto the private courtyard and pretty pool. Each room is furnished differently with charming antique touches, such as an old washbasin, a quilt, or a rocking chair. Continental breakfast is served in your room. The inn has a full-service spa, an excellent gift shop, and is near art galleries and stores. ⊠ *103 Flagler Ave., 32169* ☎ *386/428–5858 or 800/945–7416* 🖷 *386/423–8927* ⊕ *www.riverviewhotel.com* 🖎 *18 rooms, 1 suite* ⚲ *Restaurant, fans, in-room safes, cable TV, in-room data ports, pool, bicycles, bar, laundry service, Internet, business services, meeting rooms, free parking* 🚭 *AE, D, DC, MC, V* ⦿*CP.*

¢–$$ 🖾 **Coastal Waters Inn.** Popular with families, this three-story blue-and-white beachfront hotel has one- and two-bedroom suites with kitchens as well as standard rooms. Some units have excellent ocean views, and many have balconies or patios. Furnishings are spare but comfortable. The beach is nearby. ⊠ *3509 S. Atlantic Ave., 32169* ☎ *386/428–3800 or 800/321–7882* 🖷 *396/423–5002* ⊕ *www.coastalwatersinn.com* 🖎 *8 rooms, 32 suites* ⚲ *Some kitchenettes, some microwaves, some refrigerators, cable TV, pool, wading pool, beach, laundry facilities, Internet, business services, free parking, no-smoking rooms* 🚭 *AE, D, MC, V.*

The Arts

The **Little Theater of New Smyrna Beach** (⊠ 726 3rd Ave. ☎ 386/423–1246) has been offering productions for more than half a century. The six productions a season vary from comedy to mystery to drama.

The Outdoors

BOATING **Florida Coastal Cruises, Inc.** (⊠ Seaharvest Marina ☎ 386/428–0201 or 800/881–2628) is a relaxed and wonderful way to experience some of the natural beauty of the New Smyrna Beach area. The good ship *Manatee* and its skipper offer lunch, sunset, and dinner cruises.

Shopping

Flagler Avenue (⊠North Causeway) is the major entranceway to the beach, and art galleries, gift shops, and surf shops line the street. **Arts on Douglas** (⊠ 123 Douglas St. ☎ 386/428–1133) displays works by 60 artists plus a solo exhibit, which changes monthly.

Titusville

36 *17 mi north of Cocoa.*

It's unusual that such a small, easily overlooked community could accommodate what it does, namely the Kennedy Space Center, the nerve center of the U.S. space program, and the magnificent Merritt Island National Wildlife Refuge.

⟳ The must-see **Kennedy Space Center Visitor Complex,** just southeast of Titusville, is one of Central Florida's most popular sights. Following the lead of the theme parks, they've switched to a one-price-covers-all admission. To get the most out of your visit to the space center, take the bus tour (included with admission), which makes stops at several facilities. Buses depart every 15 minutes, and you can get on and off any

FodorsChoice
★

bus whenever you like. As you approach the Kennedy Space Center grounds, tune your car radio to AM1320 for attraction information.

The first stop on the tour is the **Launch Complex 39 Observation Gantry,** which has an unparalleled view of the twin space-shuttle launch-pads. At the **Apollo Saturn V Center,** don't miss the presentation at the Firing Room Theatre, where the launch of America's first lunar mission, 1968's *Apollo VIII,* is re-created with a ground-shaking, window-rattling lift-off. At the **Lunar Surface Theatre,** recordings from *Apollo XI* offer an eerie and awe-inspiring reminder that when Armstrong and Aldrin landed, they had less than 30 seconds of fuel to spare. In the hall it's impossible to miss the 363-foot-long *Saturn V* rocket. A spare built for a moon mission that never took place, this 6.2-million-pound spacecraft has enough power to throw a fully loaded DC-3 all the way to the sun and back!

Exhibits near the center's entrance include the **Early Space Exploration** display, which highlights the rudimentary yet influential Mercury and Gemini space programs; **Robot Scouts,** a walk-through exhibit of unmanned planetary probes; and the **Exploration in the New Millennium** display, which offers you the opportunity to touch a piece of Mars (it fell to the Earth in the form of meteorite). Don't miss the outdoor **Rocket Garden,** with walkways winding beside spare rockets from early Atlas spacecraft to a Saturn 1. Children love the space playground, with a one-fifth-scale space shuttle and a crawl-through, multi-level tower, about right for kids 3 and older. Also fun for kids is a full-scale reproduction of a space shuttle, *Explorer* : you can walk through the payload bay, cockpit, and crew quarters. Within the garden there's also a museum filled with exhibits on spacecraft that have explored the last frontier, and a theater showing several short films.

The most moving exhibit is the **Astronauts Memorial,** a tribute to those who have died while in pursuit of space exploration. A 42½-foot-high by 50-foot-wide "Space Mirror" tracks the movement of the sun throughout the day, using reflected sunlight to brilliantly illuminate the names of the 24 fallen astronauts that are carved into the monument's 70,400-pound polished granite surface.

During the **Astronaut Encounter,** in a pavilion near the center's entrance, an astronaut who's actually flown in space hosts a daily Q&A session to tell visitors about life in zero gravity, providing insights to an experience only a few hundred people have ever shared. If you'd like to have a closer encounter with an astronaut, you can purchase a special ticket option to **Lunch with an Astronaut** for $20 for adults and $13 for kids—which includes your regular KSC admission. For an added fee and a more in-depth experience ($22 adults, $16 children 3-11), take the **NASA Up Close** tour, which brings visitors to sights seldom accessible to the public, such as the NASA Press Site Launch Countdown Clock, the Vehicle Assembly Building, the shuttle landing strip, and the 6-million-pound crawler that transports the shuttle to its launchpad.

The only back-to-back twin **IMAX theater complex** in the world is in the complex, too. *The Dream Is Alive,* an awesome 40-minute film narrated by Walter Cronkite and shot mostly by the astronauts, takes you from astronaut training and a thundering shuttle launch to an astronaut's-eye view of life aboard the shuttle while in space. **Space Station IMAX 3-D** follows astronauts and cosmonauts on their missions, with the 3-D effects putting you in space with them. ⊠ *Rte. 405, Kennedy Space Center* ☎ *321/449–4400 or 800/572–4636 (launch hotline)* ⊕ *www. kennedyspacecenter.com* ⊠ *General 1-day admission includes bus tour and IMAX movies, $30 adults, $20 children 3–11; Maximum Access Badge, valid for 2 days, includes bus tour, IMAX movies, and the Astronaut Hall of Fame, $37 adults, $27 children 3–11; NASA Up Close Tour: $22 plus admission* ☉ *Space Center daily 9 AM–5:30, last regular tour 3 hrs before closing; closed certain launch dates; IMAX I and II Theaters daily 10–5:40.*

The original Mercury 7 team and the later Gemini, Apollo, Skylab, and shuttle astronauts contributed to make the **United States Astronaut Hall of Fame** the world's premium archive of astronauts' personal stories. Authentic memorabilia and equipment from their collections tell the story of human space exploration. You'll watch videotapes of historic moments in the space program and see one-of-a-kind items like Wally Schirra's relatively archaic Sigma 7 Mercury space capsule, Gus Grissom's spacesuit (colored silver only because NASA thought silver looked more "spacey"), and a flag that made it to the moon. The exhibit **First on the Moon** focuses on crew selection for *Apollo 11* and the Soviet Union's role in the space race. Definitely don't miss the **Astronaut Adventure**, a hands-on discovery center with interactive exhibits that help you learn about space travel. One of the more challenging activities is a space-shuttle simulator that lets you try your hand at landing the craft—and afterward replays a side view of your rolling and pitching descent.

If that gets your motor going, consider enrolling in **ATX (Astronaut Training Experience.** Held at the Hall of Fame, this is an intense full-day experience where you can dangle from a springy harness for a simulated moonwalk, spin in ways you never thought possible in a multi-axis trainer, and either work Mission Control or helm a space shuttle (in a full-scale mock-up) during a simulated landing. Veteran NASA astronauts helped design the program, and you'll hear first-hand from them as you progress through your training. Space is limited (no pun intended), so call ☎ 321/449–4400 well in advance. Included in the $225 program is your astronaut gear, lunch, and a VIP tour of the Kennedy Space Center. ⊠ *6225 Vectorspace Blvd., off Rte. 405* ☎ *321/452–2121 or 800/572–4636* ⊕ *www.kennedyspacecenter.com* ⊠ *AHOF only: $17 adults, $13 children 6–12; Maximum Access Pass, valid for 2 days, combines the Kennedy Space Center Visitor Complex and the Astronaut Hall of Fame, $37 adults, $27 children 3–11* ☉ *Daily 9–6.*

If you've ever wondered why cops deserve your respect, pay a visit to the **American Police Hall of Fame and Museum.** Opened in late 2003, it is adjacent to the Astronaut Hall of Fame and, in its own way, is just as impressive. In addition to memorabilia like the Robocop costume and Bladerunner car from the films, there are informative displays on what cops face every day: drugs, homicides, and criminals who can create knives from dental putty and guns from a bicycle spoke (really). At times, it can be a gruesome chamber of horrors with autopsy photos of criminals and chilling mock-ups of prison cells, gas chambers and an electric chair. An eerie example of law enforcement memorabilia is a piece of a WTC tower fused with the plane that hit it. Other historical exhibits include invitations to hangings, police patches, how you collect evidence at a crime scene and, most importantly, a rotunda where more than 7,000 names are etched in marble to honor police officers who have died in the line of duty. Cops, gun nuts, and curious tourists are taken by the 24-lane shooting range that provides rental guns (weekdays noon–7 PM, weekends noon–5 PM). ⊠ *6350 Horizon Dr.* ☎ *321/264-0911* ⊕ *www. aphf.org* ⊠ *$12 adults, $8 children 4–12* ⊙ *Daily 10–6.*

Although its exterior looks sort of squirrelly, what's inside the **Valiant Air Command Warbird Air Museum** is certainly impressive. Aviation buffs won't want to miss memorabilia from both world wars, Korea, and Vietnam, as well as extensive displays of vintage military flying gear and uniforms. There are posters used to identify Japanese planes, plus there's a Huey helicopter and the cockpit of an F-106 that you can sit in (but can't start). In the north hangar it looks like activity day at the senior center as a volunteer team of retirees busily restores old planes. It's an inspiring sight, and a good place to hear some war stories. In the lobby gift shop they sell real flight suits ($40), old flight magazines, bomber jackets, books, and T-shirts. ⊠ *6600 Tico Rd.* ☎ *321/268–1941* ⊕ *www. vacwarbirds.org* ⊠ *$9 adults, $5 children 4–12* ⊙ *Daily 10–6.*

★ The 57,000-acre **Canaveral National Seashore** is on a barrier island that's home to more than 1,000 species of plants and 300 species of birds and other animals. The unspoiled area of hilly sand dunes, grassy marshes, and seashell-sprinkled beaches is a large part of NASA's buffer zone. Surf and lagoon fishing are available, and a hiking trail leads to the top of a Native American shell midden at Turtle Mound. A visitor center is on Route A1A. Weekends are busy, and parts of the park are closed before launches, sometimes as much as two weeks in advance, so call ahead.

Part of the national seashore, remote **Playalinda Beach** has pristine sands and is the longest stretch of undeveloped coast on Florida's Atlantic seaboard. Its isolation explains why a remote strand of the beach is popular with nude sunbathers. Aside from them, hundreds of giant sea turtles come ashore here May through August to lay their eggs. There are no lifeguards, but park rangers patrol. Eight parking lots anchor the beach at 1-mi intervals. Take bug repellent in case of horseflies. To get here, follow U.S. 1 north into Titusville to Route 406 (I–95 Exit 80), follow Route 406 east across the Indian River, and then take Route 402 east for 12 mi. ⊠ *Southern end: Rte. 402* ☎ *321/267–1110* ⊠ *Northern end: 7611 S. Atlantic Ave., New Smyrna Beach* ☎ *386/428–3384* ⊕ *www.nps.gov/cana* ⊠ *$5 per car* ⊙ *Apr.–Oct., daily 6 AM–8 PM; Nov.–Mar., daily 8 AM–6 PM.*

Fodor's Choice ★ If you prefer wading birds over waiting in line, don't miss the 140,000-acre **Merritt Island National Wildlife Refuge**, which adjoins the Canaveral National Seashore. It's an immense area dotted by brackish estuaries and marshes and patches of land consisting of coastal dunes, scrub oaks, pine forests and flatwoods, and palm and oak hammocks. You can borrow field guides and binoculars at the visitor center to track down various types of falcons, osprey, eagles, turkeys, doves, cuckoos, loons, geese, skimmers, terns, warblers, wrens, thrushes, sparrows, owls, and woodpeckers. A 20-minute video about refuge wildlife and accessibility—only 10,000 acres are developed—can help orient you. You might take a self-guided tour along the 7-mi **Black Point Wildlife Drive.** The dirt road takes you back in time, where there are no traces of encroaching malls or mankind and it's easy to visualize the Indian tribes who made this their home 7,000 years ago. On the **Oak Hammock Foot Trail,** you can see wintering migratory waterfowl and learn about the plants of a hammock community. If you exit the north end of the refuge, look for the **Manatee Observation Area** just north of the Haulover Canal (maps are at the visitor center). They usually show up in spring and fall. There are also fishing camps scattered throughout the area. The refuge is closed four days prior to a shuttle launch. ⊠ *Rte. 402, across Titusville causeway* ☎ *321/861–0667* ⊕ *merrittisland.fws.gov* ☜ *Free* ☉ *Daily sunrise–sunset, visitor center open weekdays 8–4:30, Sat. 9–5.*

Bringing people closer to nature since the early 1980s, **Space Coast Nature Tours** sets sail on the Indian River, using stable pontoon boats, quiet electric motors, and knowledgeable guides to enhance the experience. The true nature of the coast is revealed when you skim in close to bird rookeries, past manatees, and alongside dolphins on the 90-minute cruise. On the journey, you'll also spy wading birds, shore birds, birds of prey, migratory birds, alligators, and the massive space shuttle launch pads just seven miles away. ⊠ *451 Marina Road (Titusville Municipal Marina, slip A-23)* ☎ *321/267–4551* ⊕ *www.spacecoastnaturetours.com* ☜ *$17 adults, $15 children* ☉ *Regularly scheduled tours daily except Sun. at 10:30 and 1:30.*

Where to Stay & Eat

★ ¢–$$$ ✕ **Dixie Crossroads.** This sprawling restaurant is always crowded and festive, but it's not just the setting that draws the throngs; it's the seafood. The specialty is the difficult-to-cook rock shrimp, which is served fried or broiled. Other standouts include clam strips and the all-you-can-eat catfish. Often the wait for a table can last 90 minutes, but if you don't have time to wait, you can order takeout or eat in the bar area. ⊠ *1475 Garden St., 2 mi east of I–95 Exit 80* ☎ *321/268–5000* ⚑ *Reservations not accepted* ▤ *AE, D, DC, MC, V.*

$$ ▥ **Holiday Inn Riverfront Kennedy Space Center.** Because it offers great views of lift-offs, this hotel, on the shores of the Indian River, books up fast when a launch is scheduled. Rooms are comfortable but modestly furnished. The beach is a car ride away, but there's a big pool. ⊠ *4951 S. Washington Ave., 32780* ☎ *321/269–2121* ⚏ *321/267–4739* ⊕ *www. holidayinnksc.com* ⇄ *117 rooms, 2 suites* ⚭ *Restaurant, some microwaves, some refrigerators, cable TV, in-room data ports, pool, wading pool, exercise equipment, volleyball, lounge, playground, laundry service, business services, meeting rooms, some pets allowed (fee), no-smoking rooms* ▤ *AE, D, DC, MC, V.*

Cape Canaveral

③⑦ *5 mi north of Cocoa.*

This once-bustling commercial fishing area is still home to a small shrimping fleet, charter boats, and party fishing boats, but its main business these days is as a cruise-ship port. Cocoa Beach itself isn't the spiffiest place around, but what *is* becoming quite clean and neat is the north end of the port where the Carnival, Disney, and Royal Caribbean cruise lines set sail. Port Canaveral is now Florida's second-busiest cruise port, which makes this a great place to catch a glimpse of these giant ships even if you're not headed out to sea.

Jetty Maritime Park serves a wonderful taste of the real Florida. At Port Canaveral's south side, there are assorted restaurants and marine shops, a 4½-acre beach, more than 150 campsites for tents and RVs, picnic pavilions, and a 1,200-foot-long fishing pier that doubles as a perfect vantage point from which to watch a lift-off of the space shuttle. A jetty constructed of giant boulders adds to the landscape, and a walkway that crosses it provides access to a less-populated stretch of beach. Real and rustic, this is Florida without the theme-park varnish. ⊠ *400 E. Jetty Rd., Cape Canaveral* ☎ *321/783–7111* ☞ *$5 per car, $7 for RVs, for fishing or beach; camping $18–$24 for basic, $22–$28 with water–electric, $25–$31 full hook-up* ⊙ *Daily 7 AM–9 PM.*

Where to Stay

$$–$$$ 🏨 **Radisson Resort at the Port.** This resort directly across the bay from Port Canaveral is not on the ocean, but it does provide complimentary transportation to the beach, Ron Jon Surf Shop, and the cruise ship terminals at Port Canaveral. Rooms have wicker furniture, hand-painted wallpaper, coffeemakers, and ceiling fans. The pool is tropically landscaped and replete with a cascading 95-foot mountain waterfall. ⊠ *8701 Astronaut Blvd., Cape Canaveral* ☎ *321/784–0000* 🖷 *321/784–3737* ⊕ *www.radisson.com/capecanaveralfl* ⇄ *284 rooms, 72 suites* ⚑ *Restaurant, some in-room safes, some in-room hot tubs, some kitchenettes, some microwaves, some refrigerators, cable TV with movies and video games, in-room data ports, tennis court, 2 pools, gym, hot tub, bar, playground, laundry facilities, laundry service, business services, convention center, airport shuttle* ⊟ *AE, DC, MC, V.*

Sports & the Outdoors

Cape Marina (⊠ 800 Scallop Dr. ☎ 321/783–8410) books 8-, 10-, and 16-hour fishing charters in search of the elusive wahoo, tuna, dolphin, mackerel, snapper, grouper, amberjack, marlin, and sailfish.

Cocoa

③⑧ *50 mi east of downtown Orlando, 60 mi east of Walt Disney World.*

Not to be confused with the seaside community of Cocoa Beach, the small town of Cocoa sits smack dab on mainland Florida and faces the Intracoastal Waterway, known locally as the Indian River. There's a planetarium and a museum, as well as a rustic fish camp along the St. Johns

River, a few miles inland. Perhaps Cocoa's most interesting feature is restored **Cocoa Village**. Folks in a rush to get to the beach tend to overlook this Victorian-style village, but it's worth a stop. Within the cluster of restored turn-of-the-20th-century buildings and cobblestone walkways, you can enjoy several restaurants, indoor and outdoor cafés, snack and ice cream shops, and almost 50 specialty shops and art galleries. To get to Cocoa Village, head east on Route 520—named King Street in Cocoa—and when the streets get narrow and the road curves, make a right onto Brevard Avenue; follow the signs for the free municipal parking lot.

As its name suggests, **Porcher House** was the home of E. P. Porcher, one of Cocoa's pioneers and the founder of the Deerfield Citrus groves. The Porcher home, built in 1916 and now a national historic landmark, is an example of 20th-century classical revival–style architecture incorporating local coquina rock. The house is open to the public for self-guided tours. ⊠ *434 Delannoy Ave., Cocoa Village* ☎ *321/639–3500* 🖃 *Donation welcome* ⊙ *Weekdays 9–5.*

Ⓒ The **Brevard Community College Planetarium and Observatory,** one of the largest public-access observatories in Florida, has a 24-inch telescope through which visitors can view objects in the solar system and deep space. On the campus of Brevard Community College, the planetarium has two theaters, one showing a changing roster of nature documentaries, the other hosting laser light as well as changing planetarium shows. Science Quest Exhibit Hall has hands-on exhibits, including scales calibrated to other planets (on the moon, Vegas-era Elvis would have weighed just 62 pounds). The International Hall of Space Explorers displays exhibits on space travel. Show schedules and opening hours may vary, so it's best to call ahead. Travel 2½ mi east of I–95 Exit 75 on Route 520, and take Route 501 north for 1¾ mi. ⊠ *1519 Clearlake Rd.* ☎ *321/433–7373* ⊕ *www.brevardcc.edu/planet* 🖃 *Observatory and exhibit hall free; film or planetarium show $6, both shows $10; laser show $6, triple combination $14* ⊙ *Call for current schedule.*

To see what the local lay of the land looked like in other eras, check out
Ⓒ the **Brevard Museum of History & Science.** Hands-on activities for children are the draw here. Not to be missed is the Windover Archaeological Exhibit of 7,000-year-old artifacts indigenous to the region. In 1984, a shallow pond revealed the burial ground for more than 200 Native Americans who lived in the area about 7,000 years ago. Preserved in the muck were bones and, to the archaeologists' surprise, the brains of these ancient people. Don't overlook the hands-on discovery rooms and the collection of Victoriana. The museum's nature center has 22 acres of trails encompassing three distinct ecosystems—sand pine hills, lake lands, and marshlands. ⊠ *2201 Michigan Ave.* ☎ *321/632–1830* ⊕ *www.brevardmuseum.com* 🖃 *$5.50, trails free* ⊙ *Mon.–Sat. 10–4, Sun. noon–4.*

The **Lone Cabbage Fish Camp** is a strange Old Florida riverfront restaurant and attraction. In reality just a clapboard shack, it's offbeat and extremely casual. There's a dock where you can buy bait and fish, a Florida Cracker restaurant inside, and if you want to see the river's wildlife up close, there are airboat rides—including specially arranged nighttime tours as well as longer and more thrilling rides aboard shorter and more nimble watercraft. The camp is about 9 mi west of Cocoa's city limits, 4 mi west of I–95. ⊠ *8199 Rte. 520* ☎ *321/632–4199* ⊕ *www.twisterairboatrides.com* ⊠ *Airboat ride $17* ☉ *Airboat rides daily 10–6.*

Where to Stay & Eat

★ **$$–$$$** ✕ **Black Tulip Restaurant.** Two intimate dining rooms invite romance at this Cocoa Village bistro, which takes pride in its 50-plus label wine menu. Appetizers include tortellini with meat sauce and crab-stuffed mushrooms. Select such entrées as fettuccine primavera Alfredo; sautéed pork loin simmered with apples, brandy, and cream; roast duckling with peaches and cashews; or fillet medallions with artichoke sauce. Lighter lunch selections include sandwiches, salads, and quiches. Don't miss the chocolate mousse pie and the warm apple strudel. ⊠ *207 Brevard Ave.* ☎ *321/ 631–1133* ⊟ *AE, D, DC, MC, V* ☉ *Closed Sun. June–Oct.*

$$–$$$ ✕ **Café Margaux.** Dine inside or out at this charming, cozy Cocoa Village spot with its eclectic, creative mix of French and Italian cuisine. The lunch menu includes black sesame–coated chicken over mesclun greens, as well as lump crab cakes over pancetta and roasted corn relish. Dinners are equally exotic, with oak-smoked Norwegian salmon rosettes, and samplers like a baked Brie coated in pecans. ⊠ *220 Brevard Ave.* ☎ *321/639–8343* ⊟ *AE, DC, MC, V* ☉ *Closed Sun. and Tues.*

¢–$ ✕ **Lone Cabbage Fish Camp.** This is down-home, no-nonsense dining in a rustic setting. Set your calorie counter for plates of catfish, frogs' legs, turtle, and alligator (as well as burgers and hot dogs). There's a fish fry and country-and-western hoedown every Sunday. ⊠ *8199 Rte. 520* ☎ *321/632–4199* ⊟ *AE, MC, V.*

$$ 🏨 **Indian River House Bed & Breakfast.** Three miles north of Cocoa Village, this charming 1903 home overlooks the Intracoastal Waterway. Three rooms have water views and all are individually and comfortably decorated. You can spot the space shuttle as well as dolphins and egrets from the dock, where canoes and kayaks await guests. A full breakfast is included. ⊠ *3113 Indian River Dr., 32922* ☎ *321/631–5660* ⊕ *www. indianriverhouse.com* ⊠ *4 rooms* ⚲ *Some in-room data ports, dock, boating, bicycles; no TV in some rooms, no kids under 12* ⊟ *AE, MC, V* ❌ *BP.*

Nightlife & the Arts

In 1918 this building was a Ford dealership that sold Model Ts. After that, it evolved into the Aladdin Theater, a vaudeville house, and then did a turn as a movie theater before being purchased by Brevard Community College. Today, the **Cocoa Village Playhouse** (⊠ 300 Brevard Ave. ☎ 321/636–5050) is the area's community theater. The September through June performance schedule has musicals starring local talent. The rest of the year the stage hosts touring professional productions, concerts, and, in summer, shows geared to children on vacation.

Shopping

You could spend hours browsing in the many boutiques and shops of **Cocoa Village,** along Brevard Avenue and Harrison Street, which has the densest concentration of shops. Kids come to a screeching halt when they catch sight of the dizzying selection of toys displayed in the storefront windows of **Annie's Toy Chest** (✉ 405 Brevard Ave. ☎ 321/632–5890). The **Bath Cottage** (✉ 425 Brevard Ave. ☎ 321/690–2284) has fine soaps, aromatherapy candles, plush towels, and elegant shower curtains, as well as colorful blown-glass balls, drawer pulls, and table lamps.

For some terrific sculptures of fish, follow the brick path back to the **Harry Phillips Gallery** (✉ 116-B Harrison St. ☎ 321/636–4160). If you like to cook, or even just like to eat, spend some time wandering through the many kitchen and cooking items—handsome ceramic bowls, colorful glassware, regional cookbooks, exotic soup mixes—and gourmet ingredients at **The Village Gourmet** (✉ 9 Stone St. ☎ 321/636–5480). Take a break from the heat with a hand-packed ice cream cone from the **Village Ice Cream & Sandwich Shop** (✉ 120-B Harrison St. ☎ 321/632–2311).

The Outdoors

BIKING Rent a beach-cruiser bike from **Matt's Bicycle Center** (✉ 166 N. Atlantic Ave. ☎ 321/783–1196) and ride like the wind up and down the strand.

FISHING **Cape Marina** (✉ 800 Scallop Dr., Port Canaveral ☎ 321/783–8410) has 8- and 10-hour charter-fishing trips.

Cocoa Beach

39 *65 mi east of Orlando, 70 mi east of Walt Disney World.*

After crossing a long and high bridge just east of Cocoa Village, you'll be dropped down upon a barrier island. A few miles further and you'll reach the Atlantic Ocean and picture-perfect **Cocoa Beach** at Route A1A. This is one of the Space Coast's nicest beaches, with many wide stretches that are excellent for biking, jogging, power walking, or strolling. In some places there are dressing rooms, showers, playgrounds, picnic areas with grills, snack shops, and surf-side parking lots. Beach vendors offer necessities, and guards are on duty in summer. Cocoa Beach is considered the capital of Florida's surfing community.

Stretching far over the Atlantic, the **Cocoa Beach Pier** (✉ 401 Meade Ave. ☎ 321/783–7549 ⊕ www.cocoabeachpier.com) is an everyday gathering spot as well as a beachside grandstand for space-shuttle launches. There are several souvenir shops, bars, and restaurants, as well as a bait-and-tackle shop. It costs $3 to park here, and another $1 for access to the fishing part of the pier that dangles 800 feet out into the Atlantic. Don't expect pristine Disney cleanliness here; this is a weather-beaten, sandy hangout for people who love the beach.

When the children have had enough of the beach, take them to **Extreme Fun Center** to tire them out. There are mazes to climb around and get lost in, three tracks of go-carts for children and adults, 70 video games, a "soft play" playground, batting cages for both softball and hardball, laser tag, and 36 holes of miniature golf with a jungle theme featuring Pinky, a life-size elephant who sports pachyderm-size sunglasses. Hey, it's Florida. Don't go in the middle of the day in summer; you could wilt from the drop-dead heat. ✉ *8801 Astronaut Blvd., Cape Canaveral*

☎ *321/783–0595* 🅿 *Parking free; go-carts $4.50–$8.50; miniature golf and laser tag $5; call for off-season price specials* ☉ *Sun.–Thurs. 10–10, Fri.–Sat. 10–midnight.*

Sydney Fisher Park at Cocoa Beach (✉ 2100 block of Rte. A1A) has showers, playgrounds, changing areas, picnic areas with grills, snack shops, and plenty of well-maintained, inexpensive surfside parking lots. Beach vendors carry necessities for sunning and swimming. The parking fee is $3 for cars and $5 for RVs.

Where to Stay & Eat

★ **$$–$$$$** ✕ **Bernard's Surf.** Since 1948 this family operation has served numerous fresh seafood entrées, from swordfish, cobia, and pompano to lobster and shrimp. The house specialty is snapper under a creamy seafood sauce. Landlubbers can choose pork chops or steak. Try the tableside Caesar salad, and save room for the cheesecake. ✉ *2 S. Atlantic Ave.* ☎ *321/783–2401* ▤ *AE, D, MC, V* ☉ *No lunch.*

★ **$$–$$$$** ✕ **Mango Tree Restaurant.** Candles, fresh flowers, and rattan basket chairs set a romantic mood in the intimate dining room, designed to evoke the feel of a South Pacific plantation. *Lobsterocki* (Maine lobster wrapped in bacon with teriyaki cream sauce), baked Brie, or rare seared tuna are good appetizer choices. For a main course, try Indian River crab cakes, coq au vin, or veal Française (scaloppine with mushroom sauce). ✉ *118 N. Atlantic Ave.* ☎ *321/799–0513* ▤ *AE, MC, V* ☉ *Closed Mon. No lunch.*

$$–$$$ ✕ **Heidelberg.** As the name suggests, the cuisine here is definitely German, from the sauerbraten served with potato dumplings and red cabbage to the beef Stroganoff and spaetzle to the classically prepared Wiener schnitzel. All the soups and desserts are homemade; try the apple strudel and the rum-zapped almond-cream tortes. Elegant interior touches include crisp linens and fresh flowers. You can also dine inside the jazz club, Heidi's, where there's live music every day but Monday. It's not just local talent, either; jazz greats like Boots Randolph and Mose Allison have played here. ✉ *7 N. Orlando Ave., opposite City Hall* ☎ *321/783–6806* ▤ *AE, MC, V* ☉ *Closed Mon. No lunch Sun.*

$–$$ ✕ **Atlantic Ocean Grille.** Jutting five hundred feet out over the ocean on Cocoa Beach Pier, this casual seafood restaurant has floor-to-ceiling windows that overlook the water. Among the excellent fresh-fish options are mahimahi and grouper, which you can order broiled, blackened, grilled, or fried. ✉ *401 Meade Ave., Cocoa Beach Pier* ☎ *321/783–7549* ▤ *AE, D, DC, MC, V* ☉ *No lunch.*

¢–$$ ✕ **Rusty's Seafood & Oyster Bar.** Oysters, prepared raw, steamed, or casino style, are just one of the draws at this casual eatery with a Hooters motif—waitresses are dressed in very short shorts. Other menu items include seafood gumbo, spicy wings, steamed crab legs, burgers, and baskets of fish-and-chips, clam strips, or fried calamari. ✉ *2 S. Atlantic Ave.* ☎ *321/783–2401* ✉ *628 Glen Cheek Dr., Port Canaveral* ☎ *321/ 783–2033* ▤ *AE, D, MC, V.*

¢–$ ✕ **The Boardwalk.** Finger food reigns at this open-air bar on Cocoa Beach Pier, and you can count on live entertainment every night but Tuesday and Thursday. At the Friday-night Boardwalk Bash there are $7 lobsters and $2 ribs. ⊠ *401 Meade Ave., Cocoa Beach Pier* ☎ *321/783–7549* ⊟ *AE, D, DC, MC, V.*

¢–$ ✕ **Fischer's Bar and Grill.** This casual eatery, owned by the same family that runs the more upscale Bernard's Surf, is a perfect spot for winding down after a tough day at the beach. Although complete dinners are available, people tend to come for the salads, pasta, burgers, and platters of tasty fried shrimp. The family's fleet of fishing boats brings in fresh seafood daily. Happy hour is from 4 to 7. ⊠ *2 S. Atlantic Ave.* ☎ *321/783–2401* ⊟ *AE, D, MC, V.*

¢–$ ✕ **Oh Shucks Seafood Bar.** At the only open-air seafood bar on the beach, the main item is oysters, served on the half shell. It also serves burgers, and there's live entertainment on Friday and Saturday. ⊠ *401 Meade Ave., Cocoa Beach Pier* ☎ *321/783–7549* ⊟ *AE, D, DC, MC, V.*

★ $$$–$$$$ ▦ **Inn at Cocoa Beach.** One of the area's best, this charming oceanfront inn has spacious, individually decorated rooms with four-poster beds, upholstered chairs, and balconies or patios; most have ocean views. Deluxe rooms are much larger, with a king-size bed, sofa, and sitting area; most also have a dining table. Jacuzzi rooms are different sizes; several have fireplaces, and all have beautiful ocean views. Included in the rate are evening wine and cheese and a sumptuous Continental breakfast. ⊠ *4300 Ocean Beach Blvd., 32931* ☎ *321/799–3460, 800/343–5307 outside Florida* 🖷 *321/784–8632* ⊕ *www.theinnatcocoabeach.com* ⇗ *50 rooms* ↺ *Dining room, in-room safes, some in-room hot tubs, cable TV, in-room VCRs, pool, exercise equipment, gym, massage, beach, bicycles, shuffleboard, dry cleaning, meeting rooms, free parking* ⊟ *AE, D, MC, V* ❧❍❙ *BP.*

$$$ ▦ **Doubletree Oceanfront Hotel.** Following significant hurricane damage in 2004, this oceanfront hotel underwent an $8 million top-to-bottom renovation. Guest rooms are comfortably furnished with dark oak furniture, colorful tropical prints, and cheerful yellow walls. Most rooms are oceanfront with superb water views and private balconies. The five-story hotel is a favorite of families as well as Orlandoans on weekend getaways. ⊠ *2080 N. Atlantic Ave., 32931* ☎ *321/783–9222* 🖷 *321/799–3234* ⊕ *www.cocoabeachdoubletree.com* ⇗ *148 rooms, 12 suites* ↺ *Restaurant, picnic area, microwaves, refrigerators, cable TV with movies and video games, in-room data ports, pool, gym, shuffleboard, bar, Internet, business services, meeting rooms, no-smoking floors* ⊟ *AE, D, DC, MC, V.*

★ $$–$$$ ▦ **Cocoa Beach Hilton Oceanfront.** At seven stories, this is one of the tallest buildings in Cocoa Beach as well as one of the best hotels. Dense natural foliage separates the property from the roadway. Rooms are comfortably but not lavishly furnished. Most have ocean views, but for true drama get a room on the east end, facing the water. The hotel's best feature is its location, right on the beach. In season, a band plays reggae music poolside on weekends. ⊠ *1550 N. Atlantic Ave., 32931* ☎ *321/799–0003* 🖷 *321/799–0344* ⊕ *www.cocoabeachhilton.com* ⇗ *296 rooms, 11 suites* ↺ *2 restaurants, room service, cable TV with movies and video games, in-room data ports, pool, exercise equipment, beach, volleyball, bar, video game room, dry cleaning, laundry facilities, Internet, meeting rooms, free parking, no-smoking rooms* ⊟ *AE, D, DC, MC, V.*

$$–$$$ 🏨 **Ocean Suite Hotel.** A boxy five-story building with a great location, this modest property is just a half block south of Cocoa Beach Pier. Ideal for families or business travelers, each suite has two TVs, a separate living room, wet bar area with sink, refrigerator, microwave, dinette set, hideaway sofa bed, two telephone lines with data ports, and desks. All suites have a private balcony. Breakfast is the only meal served at the on-site restaurant. ⊠ *5500 Ocean Beach Blvd., 32931* ☎ *321/784–4343 or 800/367–1223* 🖷 *321/783–6514* ⊕ *www.oceansuiteshotel.com* ⇨ *50 suites* ⚬ *Restaurant, microwaves, refrigerators, cable TV, in-room data ports, pool, laundry facilities, business services, Internet, no-smoking rooms* ⊟ *AE, D, DC, MC, V.*

★ **$$–$$$** 🏨 **Wakulla Suites Resort.** This two-story motel is clean and comfortable and just off the beach. Some rooms are a block away from the water, and a few are just a walk down the boardwalk. The bright rooms are fairly ordinary, decorated in tropical prints. Completely furnished five-room suites, designed to sleep six, are great for families; each includes two bedrooms and a living room, dining room, and fully equipped kitchen. ⊠ *3550 N. Atlantic Ave., 32931* ☎ *321/783–2230 or 800/992–5852* 🖷 *321/783–0980* ⊕ *www.wakulla-suites.com* ⇨ *116 suites* ⚬ *Restaurant, kitchens, cable TV with movies, pool, shuffleboard, dry cleaning, laundry facilities, business services, free parking, no-smoking rooms* ⊟ *AE, D, DC, MC, V.*

$–$$$ 🏨 **Holiday Inn Cocoa Beach Oceanfront Resort.** When two adjacent beach hotels were redesigned and a promenade park landscaped between them, the Holiday Inn Cocoa Beach Resort was born. Standard rooms are plush, modern, and designed in bright tropical colors; suites and villas have a Key West feel with louvered doors and rattan ceiling fans. Lodging options include standard and king rooms; oceanfront suites, which have a living room with sleeper sofa; villas; or bi-level lofts. Kids are given the royal treatment with specially-designed KidsSuites that feature playrooms and a pirate ship pool with water-blasting cannons. ⊠ *1300 N. Atlantic Ave., 32931* ☎ *321/783–2271 or 800/206–2747* 🖷 *321/784–8878* ⊕ *www.hicentralflorida.com/cocoa.html* ⇨ *500 rooms, 119 suites* ⚬ *Restaurant, snack bar, BBQs, some kitchenettes, some microwaves, some refrigerators, cable TV with movies and video games, in-room data ports, 2 tennis courts, pool, gym, hot tub, shuffleboard, volleyball, 3 bars, video game room, shop, dry cleaning, laundry facilities, laundry service, Internet, business services, meeting rooms, free parking* ⊟ *AE, DC, MC, V.*

¢–$$$ 🏨 **Cocoa Beach Oceanside Inn.** This five-story property is right on the beach, adjacent to the Cocoa Beach Pier and on the beach closest to Kennedy Space Center. All rooms are done in the typical tropical Florida pastel style that seems to cool you off after a day in the sun, and each has an oceanfront balcony. After the salty sea, the freshwater pool is a welcome change. ⊠ *1 Hendry Ave., 32931* ☎ *321/784–3126 or 800/874–7958* 🖷 *321/799–0883* ⊕ *www.cocoabeachoceansideinn.com* ⇨ *76 rooms, 2 suites* ⚬ *2 restaurants, some in-room hot tubs, some refrigerators, cable TV with movies, some in-room data ports, pool, beach, bar, laundry service, business services, no-smoking rooms* ⊟ *AE, D, MC, V* ⏏⚬⏐ *CP.*

Nightlife

The **Cocoa Beach Pier** (✉ 401 Meade Ave. ☎ 321/783–7549) is for locals, beach bums, surfers, and people who don't mind the weatherworn wood and sandy, watery paths. At the Mai Tiki they claim that "No Bar Goes This Far," which is true, considering it's at the end of the 800-foot pier. Come to the Boardwalk Friday night for the Boardwalk Bash, with live acoustic and rock-and-roll music; drop in Saturday for more live music; and come back Wednesday evening to catch the reggae band.

Coconuts on the Beach (✉ 2 Minuteman Causeway ☎ 321/784–1422), a beachfront hangout that's long been the local party place, attracts a younger crowd. There are karaoke nights, ladies' nights, 25¢-beer nights, and volleyball tournaments, plus live music on Thursday, Friday, and Saturday. Burgers, salads, and sandwiches are on the menu. For great live jazz, head to **Heidi's Jazz Club** (✉ 7 Orlando Ave. ☎ 321/783–4559 ⊕ www.heidisjazzclub.com). Local and nationally known musicians play Tuesday through Sunday, with showcase acts usually appearing on weekends.

Sports & the Outdoors

The **Space Coast Office of Tourism** (✉ 2725 Judge Fran Jamieson Way, B-105, Viera ☎ 800/936–2326) publishes a lengthy, detailed list of outdoor adventures, from horseback rides to airboat rides to sea turtle walks. It also lists surfing and sailing schools and fishing charters.

The **Cocoa Beach Country Club** (✉ 5000 Tom Warriner Blvd. ☎ 321/868–3351) is actually an extensive public sports complex that's owned by the city and open to anyone. Its facilities include a 27-hole championship golf course (green fee: $25/$30); an Olympic-size swimming pool; 10 lighted tennis courts; a restaurant and snack bar; and a riverside pavilion with picnic tables. Seventeen lakes on the golf course provide a habitat that attracts an abundance of waterfowl and other birds, with species listed and information offered at each hole.

BIKING Although there are no bike trails as such in the area, cycling is allowed on the beaches and the Cocoa Beach Causeway. Bikes can be rented hourly, daily, or weekly at **Ron Jon Surf Shop** (✉ 4151 N. Atlantic Ave., Rte. A1A ☎ 321/799–8888). Locks are available.

FISHING The **Cocoa Beach Pier** (✉ 401 Meade Ave. ☎ 321/783–7549) has a bait-and-tackle shop and a fishing area. Although most of the pier is free to walk on, there's a $1 charge to enter the fishing area at the end of the 800-foot-long boardwalk, and a $3.50 fishing fee. You can rent rods and reels here.

SURFING If you can't tell a tri-skeg stick from a hodaddy shredding the lip on a gnarly tube, then you may want to avail yourself of the **Cocoa Beach Surfing School** (✉ 150 E. Columbia La. ☎ 321/868–1980). They teach grommets (dudes) and gidgets (chicks) from kids to seniors. Private lessons range from $50 for a one-hour lesson to $120 for three hours. Group lessons are $60 per person for three hours. No credit cards; cash and traveler's checks only.

Shopping

Merritt Square Mall (✉ 777 E. Merritt Island Causeway, Merritt Island ☎ 321/452–3272), the area's only major shopping mall, is about a 20-minute ride from the beach. Stores include Burdines, Dillard's, JCPenney, Sears Roebuck, Bath & Body Works, Foot Locker, Waldenbooks, and roughly 100 others. There's a six-screen multiplex, along with a food court and several restaurant chains.

Fodor's Choice ★ It's impossible to miss the **Ron Jon Surf Shop** (✉ 4151 N. Atlantic Ave., Rte. A1A ☎ 321/799–8888 ⊕ www.ronjons.com). With a giant surfboard and an aqua, teal, and pink art-deco facade, Ron Jon takes up nearly two blocks along A1A. What started in 1963 as a small T-shirt and bathing-suit shop has evolved into a 52,000-square-foot superstore that's open every day 'round the clock. The shop has water-sports gear as well as chairs and umbrellas for rent, and sells every kind of beachwear, surf wax, plus the requisite T-shirts and flip-flops. For up-to-the-minute surfing conditions, call the store and press 3 and then 7 for the **Ron Jon Surf and Weather Report.**

Melbourne

40 *20 mi south of Cocoa.*

Despite its dependence on the high-tech space industry, this town is decidedly laid-back. While the majority of the city is located on mainland Florida, a small portion trickles onto a barrier island, separated by the Indian River Lagoon, and accessible by several inlets, including the Sebastian Inlet.

★ ☺ It took 20,000 volunteers two weeks to turn 56 acres of forest and wetlands into the **Brevard Zoo,** the only American Zoo and Aquarium Association–accredited zoo built by a community. Stroll along the shaded boardwalks and get a close-up look at alligators, crocodiles, giant anteaters, marmosets, jaguars, eagles, river otters, kangaroos, exotic birds, and kookaburras. Alligator, crocodile, and river otter feedings are held on alternate afternoons—although the alligators do not dine on the otters. Stop by Paws-On, an interactive learning playground where kids and adults can crawl into human-size gopher burrows, beehives, and spider webs; get cozy with several domestic animals in Animal Encounters; have a bird hop on your shoulder in the Australian Free Flight Aviary; and step up to the Wetlands Outpost, an elevated pavilion that's a gateway to 22 acres of wetlands through which you can paddle kayaks and keep an eye open for the 4,000 species of wildlife that live in these waters and woods. Overnight Zoo Safaris for kids ages 7–14 include a nighttime zoo safari by flashlight and marshmallows cooked over a campfire. Picnic tables, a snack bar, and a gift shop complete the daytime picture. ✉ *8225 N. Wickham Rd.* ☎ *321/254–9453* ⊕ *www.brevardzoo. org* ✑ *$9; kayak trips $3 per person; train ride $3* ☉ *Daily 10–5.*

The **King Center for the Performing Arts** is one of the premier performance centers in Central Florida. Oddly enough, top-name performers often bypass Orlando to appear in this comfortable 2,000-seat hall. Call for a performance schedule. ✉ *3865 N. Wickham Rd.* ☎ *321/242–2219 box office.*

SATELLITE BEACH – The beaches of this sleepy little community just south of Patrick Air Force Base, about 15 mi south of Cocoa Beach on A1A, are cradled between the balmy Atlantic Ocean and biologically diverse Indian River Lagoon. It's a popular spot for family vacations because of its slow pace and lack of crowds.

PARADISE BEACH – Small and scenic, this 1,600-foot stretch of sand is part of a 10-acre park north of Indialantic, about 20 mi south of Cocoa Beach on A1A. It has showers, rest rooms, picnic tables, a refreshment stand, and lifeguards in summer.

Sports & the Outdoors

BASEBALL Even though they play in our nation's capital during the regular season, the **Washington Nationals** (✉ 5800 Stadium Pkwy. ☎ 321/633–9200 ⊕ www.washingtonnationals.com), formerly the Montreal Expos, use Melbourne's Space Coast Stadium for their spring-training site. Seats are still pretty cheap: $7–$18. For the rest of the season, the facility is home to the Brevard County Manatees, one of the Nationals' minor-league teams.

GOLF **Baytree National Golf Links** (✉ 8207 National Dr. ☎ 321/259–9060 or 888/955–1234) is an 18-hole course, green fee: $26/$79. **Viera East Golf Club** (✉ 2300 Clubhouse Dr., Viera, 5 mi from Melbourne ☎ 321/639–6500 or 888/843–7232) has a public 18-hole course, green fee: $25/$59.

INLAND TOWNS

Inland, peaceful little towns are separated by miles of two-lane roads running through acres of dense forest and flat pastureland and skirting one lake after another. There's not much else to see but cattle, though you may catch a glimpse of the few hills found in the state. Gentle and rolling, they're hardly worth noting to folks from true hill country, but they're significant enough in Florida for much of this area to be called the "hill and lake region."

DeLand

41 *21 mi southwest of Daytona Beach.*

The quiet town is home to Stetson University, established in 1886 by hat magnate John Stetson. Several inviting state parks are nearby; as for activities, there's great manatee-watching during the winter as well as skydiving for both spectators and participants.

Soaring ceilings and neoclassical furnishings provide the backdrop at the **Duncan Gallery of Art,** on the Stetson University campus. The gallery hosts exhibits by southwestern and national artists and Stetson students. ✉ *Stetson University, Sampson Hall, Michigan and Amelia Aves.* ☎ *386/822–7266* 🖼 *Donation welcome* ⊙ *Tues.–Sat. 10–4, Sun. 1–4.*

The **DeLand Museum of Art,** in the Cultural Arts Center across from Stetson University, has nationally recognized exhibits of painting, photography, sculpture, and fine crafts. ⊠ *600 N. Woodland Blvd.* ☎ *386/734–4371* 🖃 *Donation welcome* ⊘ *Tues.–Sat. 10–4, Sun. 1–4.*

One of the largest private collections of gems and minerals in the world can be found in the **Gillespie Museum of Minerals,** on the Stetson University campus. ⊠ *Stetson University, Michigan and Amelia Aves.* ☎ *386/822–7330* 🖃 *$2* ⊘ *Tues.–Fri. 10–4.*

February is the top month for sighting manatees, but they begin to head here in November, as soon as the water gets cold enough (below 68°F). **Blue Spring State Park,** once a river port where paddle wheelers stopped to take on cargoes of oranges, also contains a historic homestead that is open to the public. You can hike, camp, or picnic here. Your best bet for spotting a manatee is to walk along the boardwalk. ⊠ *2100 W. French Ave., Orange City* ☎ *386/775–3663* ⊕ *www.dep.state.fl.us/parks/district3/bluespring* 🖃 *$5 per vehicle, up to 8 people* ⊘ *Daily 8–sunset.*

Where to Stay & Eat

¢ ✕ **Dublin Station.** The large, dimly lighted bar and restaurant has dark wood walls, a wooden floor, and a thoroughly Irish streak. In addition to lagers and ales, meat pies, and fish-and-chips, there are chops, steaks, burgers, and salads. Seating is at a long bar, at tables in a lounge and dining room, in comfortable booths, or outside along the sidewalk. But whether it's day or night, the place is always busy. ⊠ *105 W. Indiana Ave.* ☎ *386/740–7720* ▤ *AE, MC, V* ⊘ *Closed Sun. and Mon.*

¢ ✕ **Original Holiday House.** The original location of what has become a small chain of buffet restaurants is enormously popular with senior citizens, families, and college students (it's across from the Stetson University campus). Choose from three categories: salads only, salads and vegetables only, or the full buffet. The lunch and dinner buffets are $8.45. ⊠ *704 N. Woodland Blvd.* ☎ *386/734–6319* 🖄 *Reservations not accepted* ▤ *D, MC, V.*

¢–$ 🏨 **Holiday Inn DeLand.** Picture a snazzy big-city hotel run by friendly, small-town folks with city savvy. An enormous painting by nationally known local artist Fred Messersmith dominates the plush lobby. Rooms are done in subdued colors and styles; prestige suites have housed the likes of Tom Cruise. Tennis and golf privileges at the DeLand Country Club are offered. ⊠ *350 E. International Speedway Blvd. (U.S. 92), 32724* ☎ *386/738–5200* 🖷 *386/943–9091* ⊕ *www.ichotelsgroup.com* 🛏 *148 rooms, 12 suites* 🏷 *Restaurant, cable TV, in-room data ports, pool, gym, hot tub, billiards, bar, dry cleaning, laundry facilities, laundry service, Internet, business services, some pets allowed (fee), no-smoking rooms* ▤ *AE, D, DC, MC, V.*

¢ 🏨 **University Inn.** For years this has been the choice of business travelers and visitors to Stetson University. The inn is adjacent to campus and next door to the Original Holiday House restaurant. ⊠ *644 N. Woodland Blvd., 32720* ☎ *386/734–5711 or 800/345–8991* 🖷 *386/734–5716* ⊕ *www.universitydeland.com* 🛏 *60 rooms, 1 suite* 🏷 *Microwaves, refrigerators, cable TV, in-room data ports, pool, gym, business services,* *meeting rooms, free parking, some pets allowed (fee), no-smoking rooms* ⊟ *AE, D, DC, MC, V* ◎ *CP.*

The Outdoors

BOATING AND
FISHING

BOATING AND FISHING   Pontoon boats, houseboats, and bass boats for the St. Johns River are available from **Hontoon Landing Marina** (⊠ 2317 River Ridge Rd. ☎ 386/734–2474 or 800/248–2474). The marina also rents bass boats and offers fishing-guide service. One of the savviest guides to St. Johns River bass fishing is Bob Stonewater of **Bob Stonewater's Big Bass Fishing** (☎ 386/736–7120). He'll tow his boat to the launch to meet clients for the day's fishing.

SKYDIVING   In addition to hosting competitions, DeLand has tandem jumping; you are literally attached to an experienced instructor-diver, which means that even novices are able to take their maiden voyage after one day. **Skydive DeLand** (⊠ 1600 Flightline Blvd. ☎ 386/738–3539), open daily 8 AM–sunset, offers lessons.

De León Springs

42   *7 mi northwest of DeLand, 26 mi southwest of Daytona Beach.*

The town (population 1,500) is a small spot on the map just outside the eastern edge of the Ocala National Forest.

Near the end of the 19th century, **De León Springs State Recreation Area** was promoted as a fountain of youth to winter guests. Today visitors are attracted to the year-round 72°F springs for swimming, fishing, canoeing, and kayaking. Nature trails draw hikers and outdoor enthusiasts. Explore an abandoned sugar mill at **Lake Woodruff National Wildlife Refuge**—accessible through DeLeón Springs—which also has plenty of lakes, creeks, and marshes for scuba diving, canoeing, and hiking. ⊠ *Ponce de León Blvd. at Burt Parks Rd., east off U.S. 17* ☎ *386/985–4212* ⊕ *www.floridastateparks.org/deleonsprings* ⊡ *$5 per vehicle, up to 8 people* ⊙ *Daily 8–sunset.*

Where to Eat

$–$$$ ✕ **Karlings Inn.** A sort of Bavarian Brigadoon set beside a forgotten highway, this restaurant is decorated like a Black Forest inn inside and out. Karl Caeners oversees the preparation of the sauerbraten, red cabbage, and succulent roast duckling, as well as charcoal-grilled steaks, seafood, and fresh veal. The menu has Swiss, German, French, and Italian selections, and house specialties include blue-crab cakes with spicy apricot sauce, seafood sausages (a blend of scallops, shrimp, and fish) served with a smoked chorizo and toasted garlic sauce, and roasted duck with Montmorency sauce. Ask to see the dessert tray. ⊠ *4640 N. U.S. Hwy. 17* ☎ *386/985–5535* ⊟ *MC, V* ⊙ *Closed Sun. and Mon. No lunch.*

¢   ✕ **The Old Spanish Sugar Mill Grill and Griddle House.** You may enjoy poking around the old sugar mill, but there's a lot more fun inside: pitchers of homemade batter arrive at your table, where you do the pouring and flipping. Top the pancakes off with blueberries, bananas, pecans, or whatever else is available. Side items include sausage, ham, bacon, eggs, and homemade breads. Although breakfast fare is available until

4 PM (the place closes at 5), salads and sandwiches are also on the menu during lunch hours. You have to pay the $5 admission to the park to eat at the restaurant. ⊠ *De León Springs State Recreation Area, Ponce de León Blvd. at Burt Parks Rd., east off U.S. 17* ☎*386/985–5644* ☐*MC, V* ⌲ *Reservations not accepted* ⊘ *No dinner.*

Ocala National Forest

㊸ *Eastern entrance 40 mi west of Daytona Beach, northern entrance 52 mi south of Jacksonville.*

This delightful 389,000-acre wilderness with lakes, springs, rivers, hiking trails, campgrounds, and historic sites has three major recreational areas (listed here from east to west): **Alexander Springs** (⊠ Off Rte. 40 via Rte. 445 S) has a swimming lake and a campground; **Salt Springs** (⊠ Off Rte. 40 via Rte. 19 N) has a natural saltwater spring where Atlantic blue crabs come to spawn each summer; **Juniper Springs** (⊠ Off Rte. 40) includes a stone waterwheel house, a campground, a natural-spring swimming pool, and hiking and canoe trails. About 30 campsites are sprinkled throughout the park and range from bare sites to those with electric hook-ups, showers, and bathrooms. Note that credit cards aren't accepted. ⊠ *Visitor center, 17147 E. Hwy. 40, Silver Springs* ☎*352/ 625–2520* ⊕ *www.southernregion.fs.fed.us/florida/recreation/index oca.shtml* ☞ *Free.*

The Outdoors

CANOEING The 7-mi **Juniper Springs run** is a narrow, twisting, and winding canoe ride, which, although exhilarating, is not for the novice. You must arrange with the canoe-rental concession at **Juniper Wayside Park** (⊠ Rte. 40 ☎ 352/625–2808) for rehaul—getting picked up and brought back to where you started—but it's included in the rental price.

FISHING **Captain Tom's Custom Charters** (⊠ Rte. 40, Silver Springs ☎ 352/546– 4823) allows you to charter fishing trips ranging from three hours to a full day, and offers sightseeing cruises as well.

HORSEBACK The stable closest to Ocala that's open to the public, **Fiddler's Green Ranch**
RIDING (⊠ Demko Rd., Altoona ☎ 352/669–7111) organizes trail rides into the national forest.

Ocala

㊹ *78 mi west of Daytona Beach, 123 mi southwest of Jacksonville.*

This is horse country. Here at the forest's western edge are dozens of horse farms with grassy paddocks and white wooden fences. Hills and sweeping fields of bluegrass make the area feel more like Kentucky than Florida, which is entirely appropriate. The peaceful town is considered a center for thoroughbred breeding and training, and Kentucky Derby winners have been raised in the region's training centers. Sometimes the farms are open to the public.

The **Appleton Museum of Art,** a three-building cultural complex, is a marble-and-granite tour de force with a serene esplanade and reflecting pool. The collection lives up to its surroundings, thanks to more than 6,000 pre-Columbian, Asian, and African artifacts and 19th-century objets d'art. ✉ *4333 N.E. Silver Springs Blvd.* ☎ *352/236–7100* ⊕ *www. appletonmuseum.org* ☜ *$6* ⊗ *Tues.–Sun. 10–6.*

Retired drag racer Don Garlit pays tribute to the cars and the drivers of that sport at **Garlit's Museum of Drag Racing.** Among his extensive collection is the only car in history to run more than 290 mph in the quarter-mile, the 1963 Pontiac Firebird Jet. ✉ *13700 S.W. 16th Ave.* ☎ *877/ 271–3278* ⊕ *www.garlits.com* ☜ *$12* ⊗ *Daily 9–5.*

off the beaten path

SILVER SPRINGS – The 350-acre natural theme park outside Ocala at the western edge of the Ocala National Forest has the world's largest collection of artesian springs. The state's first tourist attraction, it was established in 1890 and is listed on the National Register of Historic Landmarks. Today the park presents wild-animal displays, glass-bottom boat tours in the Silver River, a Jeep safari through 35 acres of wilderness, and walks through natural habitats. Exhibits include the Panther Prowl, which enables visitors to watch and photograph the endangered Florida panther, and the Big Gator Lagoon, a ½-acre swamp featuring alligators. New attractions include the Fort King River Cruise and the Lighthouse Ride, a combination carousel/gondola ride giving guests a bird's eye view of the park. A great place to cool off, **Silver Springs Wild Waters** (☎ 352/236– 2121 ⊕ www.wildwaterspark.com) has a 450,000-gallon wave pool and eight water slides and high-speed flumes. The water park is open March through September 10–5 (call for operating schedule); admission is $23.99. ✉ *Rte. 40, Exit 352 east off I–75 or Exit 268 west off I–95* ☎ *352/236–2121* ⊕ *www.silversprings.com* ☜ *$32.99, $35.99 including Wild Waters* ⊗ *Daily 10–5.*

Where to Stay & Eat

$$–$$$ ✕ **Arthur's.** Don't pass up this elegant restaurant, in an open area at the back of the lobby in the Ocala Silver Springs Hilton. Filet mignon with port sauce and chicken breast stuffed with spinach and sun-dried tomatoes are favorites. The Sunday brunch is a must. ✉ *3600 S.W. 36th Ave.* ☎ *352/854–1400* ▤ *AE, D, DC, MC, V* ⊗ *No lunch Sat.*

★ $–$$$$ ▥ **Seven Sisters Inn.** A pair of showplace Queen Anne mansions functions as a B&B. Each room has period antiques and its own bath; some rooms have a fireplace, some a canopy bed. A loft furnished with wicker sleeps four. Rates include a delicious breakfast and afternoon tea. ✉ *820 S.E. Fort King St., 32671* ☎ *352/867–1170 or 800/250–3496* 🖷 *352/ 867–5266* ⊕ *www.7sistersinn.com* ↝ *13 rooms* ⚘ *Dining room, some in-room hot tubs, in-room data ports, some in-room VCRs, bicycles, library, Internet, free parking; no kids under 12, no smoking* ▤ *AE, D, MC, V* ⼝ *BP.*

$$–$$$ ▥ **Ocala Silver Springs Hilton.** A winding, tree-lined boulevard leads to this nine-story pink tower nestled in a wooded patch of countryside just off Interstate 75 and a bit removed from downtown. The marble-floor lobby has a piano bar. The spacious guest rooms are decorated in stripes and floral prints in autumn shades of forest green, sand, and burnt orange.

✉ 3600 S.W. 36th Ave., 34474 ☎ 352/854–1400 or 877/602–4023 📠 352/854–6073 ⊕ www.hiltonocala.com ⌨ 197 rooms, 8 suites ⚭ Restaurant, room service, some microwaves, some refrigerators, cable TV with movies and video games, in-room data ports, 1 tennis court, pool, wading pool, gym, hot tub, volleyball, bar, piano bar, comedy club, shop, dry cleaning, laundry service, Internet, business services, meeting rooms, no-smoking floors ☰ AE, D, DC, MC, V.

Sports & the Outdoors

GOLF Twenty miles south of Ocala, **El Diablo Golf & Country Club** (✉ 10405 N. Sherman Dr., Citrus Springs ☎ 352/465–0986 or 877/353–4225) has a public 18-hole course, green fee: $25/$55.

JAI ALAI One of the speediest of sports, jai alai is played year-round at **Ocala Jai–Alai** (✉ 4601 N.W. Hwy. 318, Orange Lake ☎ 352/591–2345).

Micanopy

⑮ *36 mi north of Ocala.*

Though this was the state's oldest inland town, site of both a Timucuan Indian settlement and a Spanish mission, there are few traces left from before white settlement, which began in 1821. Micanopy (pronounced micka-*no*-pea) does still draw those interested in the past, however. The main street of this beautiful little town has quite a few antiques shops, and in fall roughly 200 antiques dealers descend on the town for the annual Harvest Fall Festival.

★ A 20,000-acre wildlife preserve with ponds, lakes, trails, and a visitor center with a museum, **Paynes Prairie State Preserve** is a wintering area for many migratory birds where alligators and a wild herd of American bison also roam. There was once a vast lake here, but a century ago it drained so abruptly that thousands of beached fish died in the mud. The remains of a ferry stranded in the 1880s can still be seen. Swimming, boating, picnicking, and camping are permitted. ✉ *Off U.S. 441, 1 mi north of Micanopy* ☎ *352/466–3397* 💲 *$4 per vehicle, up to 8 people* ☉ *Daily 8–sunset.*

off the beaten path

MARJORIE KINNAN RAWLINGS STATE HISTORIC SITE – The presence of Rawlings, whose works include *The Yearling* and *Cross Creek*, permeates this home where the typewriter rusts on the ramshackle porch, the closet where she hid her booze during Prohibition yawns open, and clippings from her scrapbook reveal her legal battles and marital problems. Bring lunch, and picnic in the shade of one of Rawlings' trees. Then visit her grave a few miles away at peaceful Island Grove. ✉ *Rte. 325, Hawthorne* ☎ *352/466–3672* ⊕ *www.dep.state.fl.us* 💲 *$2 per vehicle, up to 8 people; tours $3* ☉ *Thurs.–Sun. 10–4; tours at 10, 11, and hourly 1–4 Oct.–July.*

Where to Stay

$–$$ 🏨 **Herlong Mansion.** Spanish moss clings to the stately oak trees surrounding this restored mansion built in the early 1900s. The imposing Greek revival–style B&B has Corinthian columns and wide verandas perfect for relaxing in a rocker. Rooms and suites have period furniture, Oriental rugs, lead-glass windows, and claw-foot tubs; some rooms have whirlpools. A multicourse breakfast, which is included in the rate, is an event here. ⊠ *402 N.E. Cholokka Blvd., 32667* ☎ *352/466–3322 or 800/437–5664* ⊕ *www.herlong.com* ➪ *5 rooms, 4 suites, 2 cottages* ⚘ *Dining room, some in-room hot tubs, some refrigerators, piano, free parking; no room phones, no TV in some rooms, no kids under 12, no smoking* ⊟ *AE, D, MC, V* ¶◉¶ *BP.*

Gainesville

46 *11 mi north of Micanopy on U.S. 441.*

The University of Florida anchors this sprawling town. Visitors are mostly Gator football fans and parents of university students, so the styles and costs of accommodations are primarily aimed at budget-minded travelers rather than luxury-seeking vacationers. The surrounding area encompasses several state parks and interesting gardens and geological sites.

☙ On the campus of the University of Florida, the **Florida Museum of Natural History** has several interesting replicas, including a Maya palace, a typical Timucuan household, and a full-size replica of a Florida cave. The collections from throughout Florida's history warrant at least half a day. ⊠ *University of Florida, S.W. 34th St. at Hull Rd.* ☎ *352/846–2000* ⊕ *www.flmnh.ufl.edu* ➩ *Free* ☉ *Mon.–Sat. 10–5, Sun. 1–5.*

About 10,000 years ago an underground cavern collapsed and created a geological treat. At **Devil's Millhopper State Geological Site,** see the botanical wonderland of exotic subtropical ferns and trees growing in the 500-foot-wide, 120-foot-deep sinkhole. You pass a dozen small waterfalls as you head down 232 steps to the bottom. ⊠ *4732 Millhopper Rd., off U.S. 441* ☎ *386/462–7905* ➩ *$2 per vehicle, up to 8 people* ☉ *Daily 9–5.*

Where to Stay & Eat

$–$$$$ ✕ **Paramount Grill.** You may be rubbing elbows with your neighbor, but the meal is definitely worth the inconvenience. Try one of the five house salads and such entrées as pan-roasted pork tenderloin with creamy blue-cheese polenta and apple-cider lemon-thyme reduction sauce, or Asian spiced tuna over wasabi pancakes with grilled green tomatoes, served with sweet sesame vinaigrette and a gingered spinach salad. If you miss dinner here, try the Sunday brunch. ⊠ *12 S.W. 1st Ave.* ☎ *352/378–3398* ⊟ *AE, MC, V* ☉ *No lunch Sat. and Sun.*

$$$ ✕ **Melting Pot.** Eating is a group activity at this fondue spot; sit downstairs or upstairs in the cozy loft. Dip slivers of fish or steak in sizzling hot oil, or cubes of crusty French bread in pots of melted cheese. Save room for dessert—more fondue, naturally—bits of fruit you dip into rich melted chocolate. ⊠ *418 E. University Ave.* ☎ *352/372–5623* ⊟ *AE, D, DC, MC, V* ☉ *No lunch.*

★ **$$–$$$** ✕ **Sovereign.** Crystal and candlelight set a tone of restrained elegance in this 1878 carriage house. An iron gate and a narrow walkway lead back to the elegant dining room. Veal specialties are notable, particularly the saltimbocca, braised in white wine, flavored with sage, and topped with ham. Beef Wellington and rack of baby lamb are dependable choices, too. ⊠ *12 S.E. 2nd Ave.* ☎ *352/378–6307* ⚲ *Reservations essential* ▭ *AE, D, DC, MC, V* ⊘ *Closed Sun. No lunch.*

$–$$$ ✕ **Emiliano's Cafe.** Linen tablecloths and art deco-ish artwork create a casual, elegant feel here. Dine indoors or beneath the stars on the sidewalk café. Start with the Gallician stew (a family recipe) or the black bean soup, and then move on to one of the chef's signature dishes—Spanish saffron rice with shrimp, clams, mussels, fresh fish, chicken, artichoke hearts, peas, asparagus, and pimientos. Also worthy is the beef tenderloin encrusted with crushed coriander seed and black peppercorns and served over julienned yucca fries topped with a mango cabernet sauce. ⊠ *7 S.E. 1st Ave.* ☎ *352/375–7381* ▭ *AE, D, MC, V* ⊘ *Closed Mon.*

$–$$ ✕ **Bistro 1245.** Get high-quality meals at bargain-basement prices. The butternut-squash bisque and the seared-tuna club sandwich served with bacon, lettuce, and tomato are favorite menu items. For a lighter meal, and a lighter price, order off the lunch menu in the evening. ⊠ *1245 W. University Ave.* ☎ *352/376–0000* ▭ *AE, D, DC, MC, V.*

¢ ✕ **Market Street Pub.** The large, British-style pub brews its own beer and serves homemade sausage, fish-and-chips, salads, and hearty sandwiches. Dine indoors, or outdoors at the sidewalk café. The pub has live music on weekends and a DJ some weeknights. ⊠ *120 S.W. 1st Ave.* ☎ *352/377–2927* ⚲ *Reservations not accepted* ▭ *AE, D, MC, V* ⊘ *Closed Sun. and Mon. No lunch.*

$–$$$ ▥ **Sweetwater Branch Inn Bed & Breakfast.** You'll find such modern conveniences as data ports, hair dryers, and business services mixed with Southern charm and hospitality all wrapped up in two grand Victorian homes surrounded by lush tropical gardens. Gleaming hardwood floors and antique furnishings lend a European flair to nicely appointed rooms. The Sweetwater is in historic downtown, adjacent to the University of Florida, and within walking distance of many of the area's better restaurants and entertainment venues. ⊠ *625 E. University Ave., 32601* ☎ *352/373–6760 or 800/595–7760* ⊜ *352/371–3771* ⊕ *www.sweetwaterinn.com* ⇴ *13 rooms, 3 suites* ⚲ *Some in-room hot tubs, some kitchenettes, some microwaves, some refrigerators, in-room data ports, Internet, business services, meeting rooms, free parking; no smoking* ▭ *AE, MC, V.*

$–$$ ▥ **The Magnolia Plantation Bed and Breakfast Inn.** You'll be within minutes of historic downtown and the University of Florida, and owners Joe and Cindy Montalto will welcome you like old friends, whether you stay in the main house or in one of the adorable cottages. The inn's unique French Second Empire architecture is one of only a handful of such examples found in the southeastern United States. The lush gardens and gazebos offer quiet, shady spots to relax. All rooms have a private bath with claw-foot tub (except for one room, which features a whirlpool tub). A full breakfast is standard fare and is served in the formal dining room or in the privacy of your cottage. ⊠ *309 S.E. 7th St., 32601* ☎ *352/375–6653 or 800/201–2379* ⊜ *352/338–0303* ⊕ *www. magnoliabnb.com* ⇴ *5 rooms, 6 cottages* ⚲ *Some in-room hot tubs, some kitchenettes, some microwaves, some refrigerators, some in-room data ports, laundry facilities, Internet, business services, free parking; no TV in some rooms, no smoking* ▭ *AE, D, MC, V.*

¢–$$ 🏨 **Residence Inn by Marriott.** One- and two-bedroom suites with a kitchen and fireplace make a cozy pied-à-terre. Happy hour with complimentary beer and wine is part of the hospitality. The central location is convenient for the university or business traveler. ✉ *4001 S.W. 13th St., at U.S. 441 and Rte. 331, 32608* ☎ *352/371–2101* 🖷 *352/377–2247* ⊕ *www.marriott.com* 🛏 *80 suites* ⚐ *Kitchens, cable TV, in-room data ports, pool, gym, hot tub, basketball, volleyball, dry cleaning, laundry service, Internet, meeting rooms, free parking, some pets allowed (fee), no-smoking floors* 🖃 *AE, D, DC, MC, V* ❢❶ *CP.*

¢–$ 🏨 **LaQuinta Inn.** If you're visiting someone at the university, you might appreciate that this property is both an economical choice and a mere five minutes from campus. It's also within walking distance of many downtown restaurants and nightspots. ✉ *920 N.W. 69th Terr., 32605* ☎ *352/332–6466* 🖷 *352/332–7074* 🛏 *134 rooms, 5 suites* ⚐ *Some kitchenettes, some microwaves, some refrigerators, cable TV with movies, in-room data ports, pool, Internet, business services, meeting rooms, free parking, some pets allowed* 🖃 *AE, D, MC, V* ❢❶ *CP.*

Nightlife

Locals head to **Calico Jack's Oyster Bar** (✉ 3501 S.W. 2nd Ave.) for seafood, beer and live music. Get your caffeine and live-music fix at **Common Grounds** (✉ 919 W. University Ave. ☎ 352/372–7320), which spotlights an eclectic mix of bands. Gainesville's oldest bar, **Lillian's Music Store** (✉ 112 S.E. 1st St. ☎ 352/372–1010), has rock and Top 40 music, bands, and karaoke.

Sports & the Outdoors

AUTO RACING The **Gainesville Raceway** (✉ 11211 N. County Rd. 225 ☎ 352/377–0046, 626/914–4761 for National Hot Rod Association) is the site of professional and amateur auto and motorcycle races, including Gatornationals in March, as well as a drag-racing school.

FOOTBALL The games of the **University of Florida Gators** (✉ Ben Hill Griffin Stadium, 111 North-South Dr. ☎ 352/375–4683) are extremely well attended and tickets are difficult to get.

NORTHEAST FLORIDA A TO Z

To research prices, get advice from other travelers, and book arrangements, visit www.fodors.com.

AIR TRAVEL

The main airport for the region is Jacksonville International (JAX). It's served by Airtran, American, Comair, Continental and Continental Connection/Express, Delta, Executive, Midway, Northwest, Southeast, United Express, US Airways and US Airways Express. Continental, Delta and Vintage Props & Jets serve Daytona Beach International Airport (DAB). Gainesville Regional Airport (GNV) is served by Delta Connection and US Airways Express. Although Orlando isn't part of the area, visitors to northeastern Florida often choose to arrive at Orlando International Airport (MCO) because of the huge number of convenient flights. Driving east from Orlando on the Beeline Expressway brings you

to Cocoa Beach in about an hour. Reach Daytona, about a two-hour drive, by taking the Beeline Expressway to Interstate 95 and driving north.
Airlines & Contacts Airtran ☎ 800/247-8726. **American** ☎ 800/433-7300. **Comair** ☎ 800/354-9822. **Continental and Continental Connection/Express** ☎ 800/523-3273. **Delta** ☎ 800/221-1212. **Delta Connection** ☎ 800/282-3424. **Executive** ☎ 800/423-7300. **Midway** ☎ 800/466-4392. **Northwest** ☎ 800/225-2525. **Southwest** ☎ 800/435-9792. **United Express** ☎ 800/241-6522. **US Airways and US Airways Express** ☎ 800/428-4322. **Vintage Props & Jets** ☎ 800/852-0275.

AIRPORTS

Airport Information Daytona Beach International Airport (DAB) ☎ 386/248-8069 ⊕ www.flydaytonafirst.com. **Gainesville Regional Airport** (GNV) ☎ 352/373-0249 ⊕ www.gra-gnv.com. **Jacksonville International Airport** (JAX) ☎ 904/741-4902 ⊕ www.jaxairports.org. **Orlando International Airport** (MCO) ☎ 407/825-2001 ⊕ www.orlandoairports.net.

TRANSFERS   At Jacksonville International, free shuttles run from the terminal to all parking lots (except the garage) around the clock. Taxi service is available from a number of companies, including Gator City Taxi and Yellow Cab, with fares to downtown approximately $28 and $45 to the beaches and Amelia Island. Shuttle service is available from Gator City Shuttle for approximately $24 for one to four people going downtown, $40 for one to four people going to the beaches and Amelia Island. Limousine service is available from Carey Jacksonville for approximately $65 to downtown and $74 to the beaches and Amelia Island (one to four people), and reservations are required. From Daytona Beach International Airport, taxi fare to beach hotels runs about $17–$22. Taxi companies include Yellow Cab and Checker Cab. DOTS Transit Service has scheduled service connecting the Daytona Beach and Orlando International airports, the Sheraton Palm Coast area, DeLand (including its train station), New Smyrna Beach, Sanford, and Deltona; fares are $27 one-way and $49 round-trip between the Daytona and Orlando airports, $24 one-way and $43 round-trip from the Orlando airport to DeLand or Deltona. From the Gainesville Regional Airport, taxi fare to the center of Gainesville is about $15; some hotels provide free airport pickup.
Carey Jacksonville ☎ 904/246-3741. **Checker Cab** ☎ 800/566-4222. **DOTS Transit Service** ☎ 386/257-5411 or 800/231-1965. **Gator City Shuttle** ☎ 904/741-6650. **Gator City Taxi** ☎ 904/741-0008. **Yellow Cab** ☎ 888/442-8294.

BOAT & FERRY TRAVEL

Connecting the north and south banks of the St. Johns River, in Jacksonville, the S.S. Marine Taxi runs between several locations, including the Hilton Jacksonville Riverfront and the Jacksonville Landing. During football season, the water taxi also makes trips to ALLTEL Stadium on game days and for special events like the Florida–Georgia game. The one-way trip takes about five minutes. The ferry runs 11–10 daily (except during rain or other bad weather). Round-trip fare is $5; one-way fare is $3.
Boat & Ferry Information S.S. Marine Taxi ☎ 904/733-7782.

BUS TRAVEL

Greyhound Lines serves the region, with full-service terminals in Jacksonville, Daytona Beach, Cocoa Beach, Ocala, and Gainesville, and additional stops in St. Augustine, New Smyrna Beach, and DeLand. The Jacksonville Transportation Authority (JTA) serves Jacksonville and the beaches with weekday service to Orange Park, Palatka, and Green Cove Springs. Daytona Beach has an excellent bus network, Votran, which serves the beach area, airport, shopping malls, and major arteries, including service to DeLand and New Smyrna Beach and the Express Link to Orlando. Exact fare is required for Votran ($1–$2) and JTA (75¢–$1.50).

🚌 **Bus Information Greyhound Lines** ☎ 800/231-2222, 321/636-6531 in Cocoa Beach, 904/255-7076 in Daytona Beach, 352/376-5252 in Gainesville, 904/356-9976 in Jacksonville, 352/732-2677 in Ocala ⊕ www.greyhound.com. **Jacksonville Transportation Authority** ☎ 904/743-3582 ⊕ www.jtaonthemove.com. **Votran** ☎ 386/756-7496 ⊕ www.votran.com.

CAR TRAVEL

East-west traffic travels the northern part of the state on Interstate 10, a cross-country highway stretching from Los Angeles to Jacksonville. Farther south, Interstate 4 connects Florida's west and east coasts. Signs on Interstate 4 designate it an east–west route, but actually the road rambles northeast from Tampa to Orlando, then heads north–northeast to Daytona. Two interstates head north–south on Florida's peninsula: Interstate 95 on the east coast (from Miami to Houlton, Maine) and Interstate 75 on the west. If you want to drive as close to the Atlantic as possible and are not in a hurry, stick with A1A. It runs along the barrier islands, changing its name several times along the way. Where there are no bridges between islands, cars must return to the mainland via causeways; some are low, with drawbridges that open for boat traffic on the inland waterway, and there can be unexpected delays. The Buccaneer Trail, which overlaps part of Route A1A, goes from St. Augustine north to Mayport (where a ferry is part of the state highway system), through marshlands and beaches, to the 300-year-old seaport town of Fernandina Beach, and then finally into Fort Clinch State Park. Route 13, also known as the William Bartram Trail, runs from Jacksonville to East Palatka along the east side of the St. Johns River through tiny hamlets. It's one of the most scenic drives in North Florida—a two-laner lined with huge oaks that hug the riverbanks—very Old Florida. U.S. 17 travels the west side of the river, passing through Green Cove Springs and Palatka. Route 40 runs east–west through the Ocala National Forest, giving a nonstop view of stately pines and bold wildlife; short side roads lead to parks, springs, picnic areas, and campgrounds.

EMERGENCIES

All of the following hospitals have 24-hour emergency rooms.

🚨 **Emergency Services** ☎ 911.

🚨 **Hospitals Baptist Medical Center** ✉ 800 Prudential Dr., Jacksonville ☎ 904/202-2000. **Baptist Medical Center Beaches** ✉ 1350 13th Ave. S, Jacksonville Beach ☎ 904/247-2900. **Bert Fish Medical Center** ✉ 401 Palmetto St., New Smyrna Beach ☎ 386/424-5000. **Florida Hospital Ormond** ✉ 875 Sterthouse Ave., Ormond Beach ☎ 386/672-4161. **Halifax Medical Center** ✉ 303 N. Clyde Morris Blvd., Daytona ☎ 386/254-

4100. **Munroe Regional Medical Center** ⊠ 1500 S.W. 1st Ave., Ocala ☎ 352/351-7200. **Orange Park Medical Center** ⊠ 2001 Kingsley Ave., Orange Park ☎ 904/276-8500. **Shands at Alachua General** ⊠ 801 S.W. 2nd Ave., Gainesville ☎ 352/372-4321. **Shands Jacksonville** ⊠ 655 W. 8th St., Jacksonville ☎ 904/549-4217. **St. Luke's Hospital** ⊠ 4201 Belfort Rd., Jacksonville ☎ 904/296-3700. **St. Vincent's Medical Center** ⊠ 1800 Barrs St., Jacksonville ☎ 904/308-7300.

MEDIA

NEWSPAPERS & MAGAZINES
Local daily papers include the *Daytona Beach News-Journal,* Jacksonville's *Florida Times-Union, St. Augustine Record, Ocala Star-Banner,* and *Gainesville Sun.* Weekly and biweekly papers include Jacksonville's *Folio Weekly, Beaches Leader, Jacksonville Business Journal, Fernandina Beach News-Leader,* and *DeLand-Deltona Beacon.* Monthly publications include Jacksonville's *Water's Edge, Jacksonville Magazine, Ocala Magazine,* and *Gainesville Today.*

RADIO
The Jacksonville dial has a serviceable smattering of stations: WFSJ 97.9 FM plays Top 40; WKQL 96.9 FM, oldies; WQIK 99.9, country; WAPE 95.1, contemporary rock; and WOKV 690 AM, talk radio.

TOURS

In Jacksonville, River Cruises has relaxing lunch and dinner–dancing cruises and private sightseeing charters aboard the *Annabelle Lee* and *Lady St. Johns* paddleboats; schedules vary with the season. Departing from the Jacksonville Landing every Friday and Saturday evening, Jacksonville Haunted History Tours takes guests on a 90-minute, lantern-guided tour of the city's favorite haunts. The Jacksonville Historical Society arranges tours only for groups of 20 or more. In St. Augustine, Old Town Trolley Tours conducts fully narrated tours covering more than 100 points of interest. As the nation's oldest continually operated carriage company, the St. Augustine Transfer Company offers historic and ghost tours via horse-drawn carriage, as well as the Spirits of St. Augustine Ghost Walk. In Daytona Beach, A Tiny Cruise Line leaves from the public marina and explores the Intracoastal Waterway. Tour Time, Inc. offers custom group and individual motorcoach tours of Jacksonville, Amelia Island, and St. Augustine, as well as overnight trips to Silver Springs, Kennedy Space Center, Orlando, Okefenokee Swamp, and Savannah. Prior arrangements are required.

🚢 **River Cruises** ☎ 904/396-2333 ⊕ www.rivercruise.com. **Jacksonville Haunted History Tours** ☎ 904/276-2098 ⊕ jhht.cjb.net. **Jacksonville Historical Society** ☎ 904/665-0064 ⊕ www.jaxhistory.com. **Old Town Trolley Tours** ☎ 904/829-3800 ⊕ www.historictours.com/staugustine. **St. Augustine Transfer Company** ☎ 904/829-2391 ⊕ www.staugustinetransfer.com. **A Tiny Cruise Line** ☎ 386/226-2343 ⊕ www.visitdaytona.com/tinycruise. **Tour Time, Inc.** ☎ 904/282-8500 or 800/822-4278 ⊕ www.tourtimeinc.com.

TRAIN TRAVEL

Amtrak schedules stops in Jacksonville, Daytona Beach, DeLand, Waldo (near Gainesville), Ocala, and Palatka. The Auto Train carries cars between Orlando and Lorton, Virginia (just south of Washington, D.C.). Schedules vary depending on the season.

🚆 **Train Line Amtrak** ☎ 800/872-7245 ⊕ www.amtrak.com.

VISITOR INFORMATION
Most visitor information offices are open weekdays from 8 or 9 to 5.
The St. Augustine Visitor Information Center is open daily 8:30–5:30.
🚹 Tourist Information **Amelia Island–Fernandina Beach Chamber of Commerce**
✉ 961687 Gateway Blvd., Suite 101G, Amelia Island 32034 ☎ 904/261-3248 or 800/226-
3542 ⊕ www.islandchamber.com. **Cocoa Beach Area Chamber of Commerce** ✉ 400
Fortenberry Rd., Merritt Island 32952 ☎ 321/459-2200 ⊕ www.cocoabeachchamber.
com. **Daytona Convention and Visitors Bureau** ✉ 126 E. Orange Ave., Daytona 32114
☎ 800/544-0415 ⊕ www.daytonabeach.com. **Gainesville Visitors and Convention Bureau** ✉ 30 E. University Ave., Gainesville 32601 ☎ 352/374-5231 ⊕ www.visitgainesville.
net. **Jacksonville and The Beaches Convention & Visitors Bureau** ✉ 550 Water St.,
Suite 1000, Jacksonville 32202 ☎ 904/798-9100 or 800/733-2668 ⊕ www.jaxcvb.com.
Ocala/Marion County Chamber of Commerce ✉ 110 E. Silver Springs Blvd., Ocala 34470
☎ 352/629-8051 ⊕ www.ocalacc.com. **St. Augustine, Ponte Vedra & The Beaches
Visitor & Convention Bureau** ✉ 88 Riberia St., #400, St. Augustine 32084 ☎ 904/
829-1711 or 800/653-2489 ⊕ www.visitoldcity.com.

Walt Disney World®
& the Orlando Area

WORD OF MOUTH

"The best times to go to WDW [are] after Spring Break up till mid May. We sometimes go the week before Mother's Day and it is wonderful. Also the weeks before Thanksgiving—and after Thanksgiving up till mid-December."

—Annabel

"If you are going to watch a parade at the Magic Kingdom, watch from Frontierland and not Main Street. The crowds are thinner."

—ilisa

"Mount Dora is a great place to spend a day. It is quaint, has some interesting shops and places to eat. The town is situated on a beautiful lake. Wekiva Springs is just north of Orlando. The canoe trip is really fun and it too is 'real Florida.' "

—LindyE

Updated by
Jennie Hess

LONG BEFORE "IT'S A SMALL WORLD" ECHOED THROUGH THE PAL-METTO SCRUB, other theme parks tempted visitors away from the beaches into the heart of Central Florida. Interstate 4 hadn't even been built when Dick and Julie Pope created Cypress Gardens, one of the region's oldest attractions. But when Walt Disney World (WDW) opened on October 1, 1971, and was immediately successful, the Central Florida theme-park scene became big business. Since then, Disney has bolstered its flagship theme park, the Magic Kingdom, with three others—Epcot, Disney–MGM Studios, and Disney's Animal Kingdom—which, together with the company's two water parks, myriad hotels, retail establishments, sports facility, nighttime entertainment centers, and restaurants, form what is today known collectively as the Walt Disney World Resort. And through 2006, this vacation kingdom will host the Happiest Celebration on Earth to honor the 50th anniversary of Walt's original theme park, Disneyland in Anaheim, California. Festival decorations, new attractions, and shows add extra pixie dust to all four theme parks. Disney's success has spurred major competition to town, namely SeaWorld and Discovery Cove, and Universal Studios and Islands of Adventure. Smaller attractions such as the Orlando Science Center and WonderWorks, among others, also bid for your business.

The problem if you have tight schedules or slim wallets is that each park is worth a visit. The Magic Kingdom, Epcot, Disney's Animal Kingdom, and SeaWorld are not to be missed. Of the two movie parks, Universal Studios and Disney–MGM Studios, the former is larger and rooted more in contemporary film; the latter projects the ambience of Hollywood in its heyday while incorporating modern movie and television themes. Islands of Adventure has more thrills for big kids and adults, and will bring out the child in everyone. Two dining, shopping, and entertainment centers stand out: CityWalk at Universal and Downtown Disney at Walt Disney World Resort. If there's time, you shouldn't miss Cirque du Soleil's acrobats, theatrics, and stunning choreography of "La Nouba," a show created for Cirque's Downtown Disney theater. DisneyQuest at Downtown Disney is an indoor theme park with several hours' worth of virtual-reality attractions. At CityWalk, sports bars and establishments with musical themes—such as Jimmy Buffet and Motown—lend lots of dining fun to its eateries. Your best bet is to poll family or group members on their theme-park wishes, then develop a strategy to enjoy the top picks.

It's easy to forget that this ever-expanding fantasy world grew up around a sleepy farming town founded as a military outpost, Fort Gatlin, in 1838. Although not on any major waterway, Orlando was surrounded by small spring-fed lakes, and transplanted northerners planted sprawling oak trees to vary the landscape of palmetto scrub and citrus groves. Most development is in southwest Orlando, along the Interstate 4 corridor south of Florida's Turnpike. Orlando itself has become a center of international business, and north of downtown are several handsome, prosperous suburbs, most notably Winter Park, which retains its Old Florida charm.

Numbers in the text correspond to numbers in the margin and on the Orlando Area map.

If you have 4 days

No stay in the area would be complete without a visit to the **Magic Kingdom ❶ ▶**. The next day, take your pick between the more sophisticated **Epcot ❷** and state-of-the-art **Universal Islands of Adventure ❿**. On Day 3, see **Universal Studios ❾** or the smaller and more manageable **Disney–MGM Studios ❸**. On your fourth day go for **Disney's Animal Kingdom ❹** or **SeaWorld Orlando ❼**. Be sure to catch fireworks one night and one of the local dinner-show extravaganzas on another.

If you have 6 days

Spend the first four days exploring in this order: **Magic Kingdom ❶ ▶**, **Universal Islands of Adventure ❿**, **Epcot ❷**, and **Disney's Animal Kingdom ❹** or **Universal Studios ❾**. At night make sure you get to some fireworks, sample at least one of the now-ubiquitous themed dining experiences, and visit Pleasure Island, Downtown Disney, or CityWalk at Universal. After all that theme park-ing, you'll need a rest. Depending on your interests and the ages of your children, use Day 5 to relax and play at a Disney water park like Typhoon Lagoon, or venture into Orlando and Winter Park. Take a leisurely boat tour and visit the **Charles Hosmer Morse Museum of American Art ⓭** or the **Orlando Science Center ⓱** for its great interactive activities before relaxing at your hotel. The sixth day should be for **SeaWorld Orlando ❼** or the more intimate **Discovery Cove ❽**. On your last evening take in Cirque du Soleil's "La Nouba" or a dinner show, perhaps SeaWorld's luau, Disney's Hoop-Dee-Doo Revue, or Kissimmee's Arabian Nights show.

If you have 8 days

You'll have time to see *all* the theme parks, but pacing is key. To ensure that the go-go Orlando tourism scene doesn't wear you down, intersperse theme-park outings with low-key sightseeing or shopping. Start with the **Magic Kingdom ❶ ▶**, staying late the first night for the fireworks. The second day, tackle **Epcot ❷** and hit Downtown Disney Pleasure Island that evening. Set aside the third day for a visit to slower-paced **SeaWorld Orlando ❼**, making luau reservations when you enter the park; or, make reservations before your trip to visit **Discovery Cove ❽** to swim with dolphins and other sea creatures. On your fourth day it's back to the theme parks—either **Disney–MGM Studios ❸** or **Universal Studios ❾**, or **Blizzard Beach ❺** or **Typhoon Lagoon ❻** for slower-paced fun. On your fifth and sixth days take in **Disney's Animal Kingdom ❹** and **Universal Islands of Adventure ❿**. Have dinner at a restaurant that suits your fancy. If it rains on one of these days, substitute the indoor adventures of DisneyQuest. On Day 7, a day of (relative) rest, enjoy a boat tour through Winter Park and visit the **Charles Hosmer Morse Museum of American Art ⓭** or the **Orlando Science Center ⓱**. In late afternoon, stroll along downtown's Lake Eola, paddle a swan boat, and grab dinner on the porch of the Lake Eola Yacht Club or at Panera Bread. On your eighth day drive out to **Historic Bok Sanctuary,** and explore Downtown Disney in the evening.

EXPLORING WALT DISNEY WORLD® & THE ORLANDO AREA

No doubt about it, the Disney parks have a special magic. You probably know lots about the Magic Kingdom, Epcot, Disney–MGM Studios, and Disney's Animal Kingdom. But there are also two wonderful water parks, Typhoon Lagoon and Blizzard Beach, as well as the indoor excitement at DisneyQuest. Before venturing into one of the big four, study the park's guidemap to note FASTPASS attractions. With your park ticket, make a free appointment to return to these locations later to gain quick admission and avoid long lines. One hitch: you usually can't make appointments for more than one FASTPASS attraction at a time. If you ask the attraction host, however, he or she can help you navigate the system. Everyone leaves the theme parks with a different opinion about what was "the best." Some attractions get raves from all visitors, while others are enjoyed most by young children or older travelers. To take this into account, our descriptions rate each attraction with ★, ★★, or ★★★, depending on the strength of its appeal to the visitor group noted by the italics preceding the stars. "Young children" refers to kids ages five to seven; "very young children" are those (ages four and under) who probably won't meet the height requirements of most thrill rides anyway (for safety reasons). However, since youngsters come in different heights and confidence levels, exercise your parental judgment when it comes to the scarier rides.

Timing

If you're traveling without youngsters, avoid school-holiday periods. If you have preschoolers, follow the same course; crowds can overwhelm small fry. With school children, it's nice to avoid prime break times, but it's not always possible. Since the parks staff up in peak season, bigger crowds don't always mean longer lines, and busy periods bring longer hours and added entertainment and parades. Nevertheless, to steer clear of crowds, avoid Christmas, late March, the Easter weeks, and mid-June–mid-August, especially July 4 (it's too hot, anyway). Try to vacation in late May or early June, as soon as the school year ends; in late August; or at Thanksgiving; or the first two weeks of December, which are not as busy as other holidays.

Magic Kingdom

▶ ❶ *Take the Magic Kingdom–U.S. 192 exit (Exit 64) off I–4; from there it's 4 mi along Disney's main entrance road and another mile to the parking lot; be prepared for serious traffic.*

The Magic Kingdom is the heart and soul of the Disney empire. Comparable to California's Disneyland, it was the first Disney outpost in Florida when it opened in 1971, and it's the park that traveled, with modifications, to France and Japan. For a park that wields such worldwide influence, the Magic Kingdom is surprisingly small: at barely 98 acres, it's the tiniest of Walt Disney World Resort's big four. However, the unofficial theme song—"It's a Small World After All"—doesn't

3

Boating

The Orlando area has one of the highest concentrations of lakes—both large and small—of anywhere in the continental United States, many of them right on WDW property. The lakes and the St. Johns River east of town provide popular vacation spots for recreational houseboaters.

Orlando Dining: A Ride in Itself

If they batter it, fry it, microwave it, torture it under a heat lamp until it's ready to sign a confession, and serve it with a side of fries, it's in Central Florida. On the other hand, renowned chefs such as Emeril Lagasse and Wolfgang Puck have places here, several Disney fine-dining restaurants have earned critical raves, and even the less lofty restaurant names try to put their best food forward in Orlando, where meals are consumed by millions of globally diverse visitors. The McDonald's on International Drive, for example, is the largest in the nation. This fiercely competitive dining market even brings out the best from the hometown eateries that predate Disney. The result is that dining choices in Orlando are like entertainment choices: there are simply more than you can sample on any one trip.

Golf

Professional golfers have been coming to Orlando for decades. Some of the greats, like Arnold Palmer, have established winter homes in the city. Not surprisingly, the city offers some of the best golfing anywhere, including courses designed by PGA pros and by the elite of professional golf-course designers, such as Pete Dye, Tom Fazio, and Robert Trent Jones.

Shopping

It's only fitting that the world's number one tourist destination should offer excellent shopping. Every year, it seems, a new mall opens and the current hot ticket is the chichi Mall at Millenia east of Universal Studios. Disney and Universal have their own shopping "theme parks"—Downtown Disney and CityWalk, respectively. If you prefer shopping with a more eclectic feel, the tony shops and bistros of Winter Park's Park Avenue are a must.

---

hold true when it comes to the Magic Kingdom attractions. Packed into seven different "lands" are nearly 50 major crowd-pleasers, and that's not counting all the ancillary shops, eateries, live entertainment, roaming cartoon characters, fireworks, parades, and, of course, the sheer pleasure of strolling through the beautifully landscaped and manicured grounds. The park is laid out on a north–south axis, with Cinderella Castle at the epicenter and the various lands surrounding it in a broad circle. Upon passing through the entrance gates, you immediately enter **Town Square,** a central connection point that directly segues into **Main Street, U.S.A.,** a boulevard filled with Victorian-style stores and dining spots. Main Street runs due north and ends at the Hub, a large tree-lined circle, known as Central Plaza, in front of Cinderella Castle. Rope Drop, the ceremonial stampede that kicks off each day, occurs at points along Main Street and the Hub.

Orlando Area

Central Florida Zoological Park

ALTAMONTE SPRINGS

Flea World

Wekiwa Springs State Park

Altamonte Mall

APOPKA
TO MOUNT DORA

MAITLAND

Bear Lake

North Orange Blossom Tr.

LOCKHART

Park Ave.

WINTER PARK

Lake Apopka

Fairbanks Ave.

Forrest

Lake Fairview

Virginia Dr.

Colonial

PINE HILLS

ORLANDO

East–West Expwy.

Florida's Tnpk.

Lake Down

Lake Butler

WINDERMERE

Lake Tibet

Lake Sheen

Big Sand Lake

TO ORLANDO INTERNATIONAL AIRPORT

Turkey Lake Rd.

Sand Lake Rd.

Bee Line Expwy.

International Dr.

Florida Mall

Central Florida Pkwy.

South Orange Blossom Tr.

WALT DISNEY WORLD RESORT

KISSIMMEE

CELEBRATION

Irlo Bronson Memorial Hwy.

Historic Bok Sanctuary

Cypress Gardens

0   5 miles

0   5 km

KEY

Start of itinerary

As you move clockwise from the Hub, the Magic Kingdom's lands begin with **Adventureland, Frontierland,** and **Liberty Square.** Next, **Fantasyland** is directly behind Cinderella Castle—in the castle's courtyard, as it were. **Mickey's Toontown Fair** is set off the upper right-hand corner—that's northeast, for geography buffs—of Fantasyland. And **Tomorrowland,** directly to the right of the Hub, rounds out the circle.

Main Street, U.S.A.

With its pastel Victorian-style buildings filled with charming shops, Main Street is more than a mere conduit to the other enchantments of the Magic Kingdom. It's where the spell is first cast.

Walt Disney World Railroad. Step right up to the elevated platform above the Magic Kingdom's entrance for a ride into living history. The 1½-mi track runs along the perimeter of the Magic Kingdom, with much of the trip through the woods. You'll pass Tom Sawyer Island and other attractions; stops are in Frontierland and Mickey's Toontown Fair. Although the ride provides a good introduction to the layout of the park, it's best for parents with small children or as relief for tired feet and dragging legs later in the day. ☞ *Audience: All ages. Rating:* ★★.

Adventureland

From the scrubbed brick, manicured lawns, and meticulously pruned trees of the Central Plaza, an artfully dilapidated wooden bridge leads to Adventureland, Disney's jungle homage.

Enchanted Tiki Room Under New Management. In its original incarnation as the Enchanted Tiki Birds, this was Disney's first audio-animatronics attraction. The updated version includes avian stars of two popular Disney animated films: Zazu from *The Lion King* and *Aladdin*'s Iago. ☞ *Audience: All ages. Rating:* ★.

Jungle Cruise. Cruise through three continents and along four rivers—the Congo, the Nile, the Mekong, and the Amazon—past all manner of animals from bathing elephants to slinky pythons. The guide's spiel is surprisingly funny, with just the right blend of cornball humor and gentle snideness. ☞ *Audience: All ages. Rating:* ★★★.

The Magic Carpets of Aladdin. In this jewel-tone "carpet" ride around a giant genie's bottle, you control your own four-passenger, state-of-the-art carpet with a front-seat lever that moves it up and down and a rear-seat button that pitches it forward or backward. Part of the fun is trying to dodge the right-on aim of a water-spewing "camel." Though short, the ride is a big hit with kids, who are also dazzled by the colorful gems implanted in the pavement around the attraction. ☞ *Audience: All ages; parents must ride with toddlers. Rating:* ★★★.

Pirates of the Caribbean. Classic Disney, this boat ride has memorable vignettes, incredible detail, a gripping story, and catchy music whose relentless yo-ho-ing can only be eradicated by "It's a Small World." It also enjoys new star status in the wake of the wildly successful hit film starring Johnny Depp—watch for scenes along the ride that producers pirated for the film. Emerging from a pitch-black time tunnel, you're in the middle of a furious battle. A pirate ship, cannons blazing, is attacking a stone fortress. Cannonballs splash into the water just off your bows,

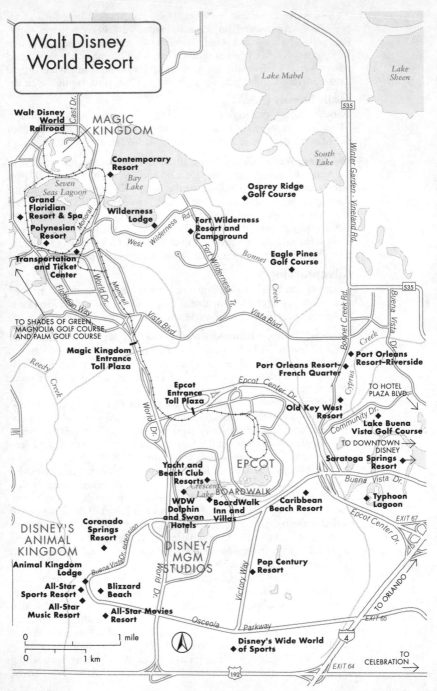

Walt Disney World Resort

Walt Disney World Railroad

MAGIC KINGDOM

Cast Dr.

Lake Mabel

Lake Sheen

535

Contemporary Resort

Bay Lake

South Lake

Osprey Ridge Golf Course

Seven Seas Lagoon

Winter Garden - Vineland Rd.

Grand Floridian Resort & Spa

Polynesian Resort

Wilderness Lodge

West Wilderness Rd.

Fort Wilderness Resort and Campground

Eagle Pines Golf Course

Bonnet Creek

Transportation and Ticket Center

Monorail

Fort Wilderness Tr.

Floridian Way

World Dr.

Monorail

Vista Blvd

Vista Blvd

535

Bonnet Creek Rd.

Buena Vista Dr.

TO SHADES OF GREEN, MAGNOLIA GOLF COURSE, AND PALM GOLF COURSE

Reedy Creek

Magic Kingdom Entrance Toll Plaza

Cyprus Creek

Port Orleans Resort–Riverside

Port Orleans Resort– French Quarter

Epcot Center Dr.

World Dr.

Epcot Entrance Toll Plaza

TO HOTEL PLAZA BLVD

Old Key West Resort

Community Dr.

Lake Buena Vista Golf Course

EPCOT

TO DOWNTOWN DISNEY

Saratoga Springs Resort

Yacht and Beach Club Resorts

Crescent Lake

BOARDWALK

Buena Vista Dr.

DISNEY'S ANIMAL KINGDOM

WDW Dolphin and Swan Hotels

BoardWalk Inn and Villas

Caribbean Beach Resort

Typhoon Lagoon

Epcot Center Dr.

EXIT 67

Coronado Springs Resort

Buena Vista Dr. extension

DISNEY- MGM STUDIOS

Animal Kingdom Lodge

World Dr.

Victory Way

Pop Century Resort

TO ORLANDO

All-Star Sports Resort

Blizzard Beach

All-Star Music Resort

All-Star Movies Resort

EXIT 65

Osceola Parkway

0   1 mile

0   1 km

Disney's Wide World of Sports

192

EXIT 64

TO CELEBRATION

and audio-animatronics pirates hoist the Jolly Roger. ☞ *Audience: All but young children. Rating:* ★★★.

Swiss Family Treehouse. Based on the classic novel by Johann Wyss about the adventures of the Robinson family, who were shipwrecked on the way to America, the tree house shows what you can do with a big banyan and a lot of imagination. The rooms are furnished with patchwork quilts and mahogany furniture, and great Disney detail abounds. ☞ *Audience: All ages; toddlers unsteady on their feet may have trouble with the stairs. Rating:* ★★.

Frontierland

Frontierland, in the northwest quadrant of the Magic Kingdom, invokes the American frontier. Banjo and fiddle music twang from tree to tree, and you can walk around munching on the biggest turkey drumsticks you've ever seen.

Big Thunder Mountain Railroad. As any true roller-coaster lover can tell you, this three-minute ride is relatively tame. The thrills are there, however, thanks to the intricate details and stunning scenery along every inch of the 2,780-foot-long wooden track. Set in gold-rush days, the runaway train rushes and rattles past animatronic donkeys, chickens, a goat, and a grizzled old miner surprised in his bathtub. ☞ *Audience: All but young children. No pregnant women or guests with back, neck, or leg braces; minimum height: 40″. Rating:* ★★★.

Country Bear Jamboree. Wisecracking, corn-pone audio-animatronics bears joke, sing, and play country music and 1950s rock and roll in this stage show. ☞ *Audience: All ages. Rating:* ★★★.

Fodor'sChoice ★ **Splash Mountain.** Based on the animated sequences in Disney's 1946 film *Song of the South,* this incredibly popular log-flume ride highlights a menagerie of Brer beasts (including Brer Rabbit, Brer Bear, and Brer Fox). You get one heart-stopping pause at the top, and then plummet. ☞ *Audience: All but very young children. No pregnant women or guests with back, neck, or leg braces; minimum height: 40″. Rating:* ★★★.

Tom Sawyer Island. The island—actually two islands connected by an old-fashioned swing bridge—is a natural playground, all hills and trees and rocks and shrubs. Check out the caves, Harper's Mill, and the rustic playground. ☞ *Audience: All ages. Rating:* ★★.

Liberty Square

The weathered siding gives way to neat clapboard and solid brick; the mesquite and cactus are replaced by stately oaks, and the rough-and-tumble western frontier gently slides into Colonial America in Liberty Square.

Hall of Presidents. This multimedia tribute to the Constitution starts with a film, narrated by writer Maya Angelou, that discusses the Constitution as the codification of the spirit that founded America, then goes on to a roll call of all U.S. presidents (animatronic robots, the first to be introduced at the park). The detail is lifelike—right down to the brace on Franklin Delano Roosevelt's leg, or the way the presidents shift their bodies or gaze toward whichever chief is pontificating, a subtle effect quite capable of imparting a pleasant chill. It's worth lingering in the lobby for a few minutes before or after the show to survey the reproductions of presidential portraits as well as odd bits of memorabilia. ☞ *Audience: Older children and adults. Rating:* ★★.

Haunted Mansion. Part walk-through, part ride on a "doom buggy," this eight-minute ride is scary but not terrifying, and the special effects are a howl. Catch the glowing bats' eyes on the wallpaper, the wacky inscriptions on the tombstones, and the dancing ghosts. ☞ *Audience: All but young children. Rating:* ★★★.

Liberty Square Riverboat. A real old-fashioned steamboat takes you on a trip that is slow and not exactly thrilling, but it's a relaxing break for all concerned. ☞ *Audience: All ages. Rating:* ★.

Fantasyland

Many of the rides here are for children, and the lines move slowly. If you're traveling without young kids, skip this area, with the possible exception of Cinderella's Golden Carrousel, it's a small world, and one classic FASTPASS attraction: Peter Pan's Flight. If small children are along, look for Pooh's new Hundred Acre Wood playground (unavailable for viewing as of this writing).

Cinderella Castle. At 180 feet, this castle is more than 100 feet taller than Disneyland's Sleeping Beauty Castle and, with its elongated towers and lacy fretwork, immeasurably more graceful.

Cinderella's Golden Carrousel. The whirling, musical heart of Fantasyland, this antique merry-go-round has 90 prancing horses, each completely different. The band organ plays favorite Disney tunes. ☞ *Audience: All ages. Rating:* ★★.

Dumbo the Flying Elephant. Jolly Dumbos fly around a central column, each pachyderm packing a couple of kids and a parent. It's one of Fantasyland's most popular rides. Alas, the ears do not flap. Ride very early to avoid tedious lines. ☞ *Audience: Young children and the young at heart. Rating:* ★★.

it's a small world. Visiting the Magic Kingdom and not stopping here—why, the idea is practically un-American. Freshly renovated with features that include the whimsical entrance and clock tower modeled after Disneyland's "small world" attraction, this new-and-improved ride adds stereo sound for the first time. Barges inch through several brightly colored rooms, each representing a continent and each crammed with musical moppets dressed in national costumes and singing "It's a Small World After All." But somehow by the time you reach the end of the 11-minute trip, you're grinning and humming, too—as has almost everyone who's gone on the ride since it debuted at the 1964–65 New York World's Fair. ☞ *Audience: All ages. Rating:* ★★.

Mad Tea Party. In this ride based on the 1951 Disney film about a girl named Alice who tumbles into Wonderland, you hop into oversize pastel teacups and whirl for two minutes around a giant platter. Check out the soused mouse that pops out of the teapot centerpiece. ☞ *Audience: All ages. Rating:* ★.

The Many Adventures of Winnie the Pooh. The famous honey lover and his exploits in the Hundred Acre Wood are the theme for this charmer. ☞ *Audience: All ages.* ★★★.

Mickey's PhilharMagic. Mickey Mouse may be the headliner here, but it's Donald Duck's misadventures—reminiscent of Mickey's in The Sorcerer's

Apprentice from *Fantasia*—that set the comic pace in this gorgeous 3-D animated film. Beautifully scored and studded with sensory effects, the movie takes you on a whimsical romp that includes a whirlwind magic carpet ride with Aladdin and Jasmine and an "electrifying" dip under the sea with Ariel from *The Little Mermaid*. The film startles with its special-effects technology—you'll smell a fresh-baked apple pie and feel the rush of air as champagne corks pop. The 3-D effects pop more sharply if you sit toward the center of the theater, so avoid the edges as you file inside. ☞ *Audience: All ages. Rating:* ★★★.

Peter Pan's Flight. Aboard two-person magic sailing ships with brightly striped sails, you soar into the moonlit skies above London en route to Never Land. ☞ *Audience: All ages. Rating:* ★★★.

Snow White's Scary Adventures. This three-minute trip is complete with the evil queen, but there are also the Prince and Snow White and an honest-to-goodness kiss followed by a happily-ever-after ending. ☞ *Audience: All ages; toddlers may be scared. Rating:* ★.

Mickey's Toontown Fair

For a company that owes its fame to a certain endearing, big-eared little fellow, Walt Disney World Resort is astonishingly mouse-free. Until, that is, you arrive here: everything is child size. Pastel houses are positively lilliputian, with miniature driveways, toy-size picket fences, and signs scribbled with finger paint.

Barnstormer at Goofy's Wiseacres Farm. Traditional red barns and farm buildings form the backdrop here. The real attraction is the Barnstormer, a kid-size roller coaster with cars resembling 1920s crop-dusting biplanes. ☞ *Audience: Young children. Rating:* ★★★.

Donald's Boat. A cross between a tugboat and a leaky ocean liner, the *Miss Daisy* is actually a water-play area. ☞ *Audience: Young children and their families. Rating:* ★★.

Judge's Tent. If you want to spend a few moments with the Big Cheese himself, load your camera, dig out a pen, and get in line here. You'll catch Mickey in his personal dressing room for the ideal photo op and autograph-session memories. ☞ *Audience: Young children and families. Rating:* ★★★.

Mickey's Country House. This slightly goofy architectural creation is right in the heart of Toontown Fairgrounds. Inside, a radio in the living room is "tooned" to scores from Mickey's favorite football team, from Duckburg University, while his clothes are neatly arranged in his bedroom beside Mickey's baby pictures and a photo of Minnie. ☞ *Audience: All ages, although teens may be put off by the terminal cuteness. Rating:* ★★.

Minnie's Country House. A peek inside this baby-blue-and-pink house reveals Minnie's lively lifestyle. In addition to her duties as editor of *Minnie's Cartoon Country Living* magazine, the Martha Stewart of the mouse set also quilts, paints, and gardens. ☞ *Audience: All ages, although teens may be put off. Rating:* ★★.

Toon Park. Another play area, this spongy green meadow is filled with foam topiary in the shapes of goats, cows, pigs, and horses. Kids can jump and hop on interactive lily pads to hear animal topiaries moo, bleat, and whinny. ☞ *Audience: Young children, mainly. Rating:* ★.

Toontown Hall of Fame. Stop here to collect an autograph and a hug from Disney characters such as Pluto and Goofy, and check out the blue-ribbon-winning entries from the Toontown Fair. **County Bounty** sells stuffed animals and all kinds of Toontown souvenirs, including autograph books. ☞ *Audience: Young children. Rating:* ★★.

Tomorrowland

Rather than predict a tomorrow destined for obsolescence, the focus here is on "the future that never was"—the future envisioned by sci-fi writers and moviemakers in the 1920s and '30s, when space flight, laser beams, and home computers belonged in the world of fiction, not fact.

Astro-Orbiter. The superstructure of revolving planets has come to symbolize the new Tomorrowland as much as Dumbo represents Fantasyland. The ride is a sort of Dumbo for grown-ups, but with Buck Rogers–style vehicles rather than elephants. You can control the altitude if not the velocity. ☞ *Audience: All ages. Rating:* ★★.

Fodor's Choice ★ **Buzz Lightyear's Space Ranger Spin.** Based on the wildly popular *Toy Story,* this ride gives you a toy's perspective as it pits you and Buzz against the world. You're seated in a steadily-moving vehicle equipped with a laser gun with which you shoot at targets to help Disney's macho spaceman save the universe. As Buzz likes to say, "To infinity—and beyond!" ☞ *Audience: Kids 3–100. Rating:* ★★★.

Carousel of Progress. This 20-minute show in a revolving theater, first seen at the 1964–65 World's Fair, traces the impact of technological progress from the turn of the 20th century into the near future. In each decade an audio-animatronics family sings the praises of the new gadgets that technology has wrought. The Carousel is only open during peak season. ☞ *Audience: All ages. Rating:* ★.

Stitch's Great Escape. Once again, Disney seizes upon a hit film to create a crowd-pleasing attraction. This time the film is *Lilo & Stitch,* and the attraction is built around a back-story to the film, about the mischievous alien, Stitch, before he meets Lilo in Hawaii. You are invited, as a new security recruit to the Galactic Federation Prisoner Teleport Center, to enter the high-security teleportation chamber, where the ill-mannered Stitch is being processed for prison. In the form of a 3½-foot-tall audio-animatronics figure, Stitch escapes his captors and wreaks havoc on the room during close encounters with the audience that involve sensory effects, tactile surprises, and a bit too much darkness. ☞ *Audience: All but young children—darkness and startling noises may frighten them. Rating:* ★★.

Space Mountain. The 180-foot-high, gleaming white-concrete cone is a Magic Kingdom icon. Inside is a roller coaster that may well be the world's most imaginative. The ride only lasts two minutes and 38 seconds and attains a top speed of a mere 28 mph, but the devious twists and drops and the fact that it's all in the dark make it seem twice as long and four times as thrilling. ☞ *Audience: All but young children. No pregnant women or guests with back, neck, or leg braces; minimum height: 44". Rating:* ★★★.

Timekeeper. This time-traveling adventure uses the voice of Robin Williams, who introduces you to famous inventors and visionaries of the machine age, such as Jules Verne and H. G. Wells. It's only open during peak season. ☞ *Audience: All ages. Rating:* ★★.

Tomorrowland Speedway. Be prepared for instant addiction among kids: brightly colored Mark VII model gasoline-powered cars swerve around the four 2,260-foot tracks with much vroom-vroom-vroom-ing. ☞ *Audience: Older children. Minimum height: 52" to drive; be sure to check your youngster's height before lining up. Rating:* ★.

Tomorrowland Transit Authority—TTA. All aboard for a nice, leisurely ride around the perimeter of Tomorrowland, circling the Astro-Orbiter and eventually gliding through the middle of Space Mountain. ☞ *Audience: All ages. Rating:* ★.

Entertainment

Beginning at 3 every day, the 15-minute-long **Share a Dream Come True** parade proceeds through Frontierland and down Main Street; there are floats, cartoon characters, dancers, singers, and much waving and cheering. The processions pack particular appeal for the 3-and-under set, and the break doubles as a nice opportunity to dig into a midday snack. The magic truly comes out at night (during busier times of the year) when **SpectroMagic** rolls down Main Street, U.S.A. in a splendidly choreographed surge of electro-luminescent, fiber-optic, and prismatic lighting effects. **Wishes,** the charming fireworks show in the Magic Kingdom, is well worth waiting around for (starting times for evening shows vary according to what time the sun sets).

Epcot

❷ *Take the Epcot–Downtown Disney exit (Exit 67) off I-4.*

Walt Disney World was created because of Walt Disney's dream of EPCOT, the Experimental Prototype Community of Tomorrow, which would reap the miraculous harvest of technological achievement. The permanent community that he envisioned has not yet come to be. Instead, there's Epcot—which opened in 1982, 16 years after Disney's death—a showcase, ostensibly, for the concepts that would be incorporated into the real-life Epcots of the future. Epcot is that rare paradox—an educational theme park—and a very successful one, too. In recent years, thrill rides have been added to provide a much-needed adrenaline rush. Bottom line: Epcot is best for school-age children and adults, and prime times to visit are during the spring International Flower & Garden Festival or the fall International Food and Wine Festival. The two parts of Epcot are separated by the 40-acre World Showcase Lagoon. The northern half, **Future World,** is where the monorail drops you off and is the official entrance. The southern half, **World Showcase,** is accessible from Future World and the park's International Gateway entrance between the France and U.K. pavilions. Walk or take a launch from the Dolphin and Swan hotels and Disney's Yacht and Beach Club and BoardWalk resorts.

Future World

Future World is made up of two concentric circles of pavilions. The inner core is composed of the Spaceship Earth geosphere and, just beyond it, the large, computer-animated Fountain of Nations, bracketed by the crescent-shape Innoventions East and West. The outer ring comprises seven pavilions. On the east side they are, in order, the Universe of Energy, Wonders of Life, Test Track, and the new Mission: SPACE. With the exception of the Wonders of Life, the pavilions present a single, self-contained ride and an occasional post-ride showcase; a visit rarely takes more than 30 minutes, but it depends on how long you spend in the post-ride area. On the west side there are the Living Seas, the Land, and Imagination! Like the Wonders of Life, these blockbuster exhibits contain both rides and interactive displays; count on spending at least 1½ hours per pavilion—and wanting to stay longer.

Imagination! Have a sensory adventure through sound, illusion, gravity, dimensions, and color, along with a behind-the-scenes tour of what you see in the *Honey, I Shrunk the Audience* film.

FodorsChoice
★
Honey, I Shrunk the Audience is one of the more popular attractions in Epcot. This 3-D adventure utilizes the futuristic "shrinking" techniques demonstrated in the films that starred Rick Moranis. Be prepared to laugh and scream your head off, courtesy of the special in-theater effects, moving seats, and 3-D film technology. Don't miss this one. ☞ *Audience: All but very young children. Rating:* ★★★ .

The pavilion's **Image Works** is an electronic fun house with interactive games and wizardry. ☞ *Audience: All ages. Rating:* ★★★ .

Innoventions. In this two-building, 100,000-square-foot attraction, continually updated to reflect the latest technology, are live stage demonstrations, hands-on displays, and exhibits that highlight gadgets that affect daily living. Each major exhibition area is presented by a leading manufacturer. ☞ *Audience: All ages. Rating:* ★★★ .

The Land. Shaped like an intergalactic greenhouse, the enormous skylighted The Land pavilion dedicates 6 acres and a host of attractions to a popular and important topic: food and the environment in which it grows. *Circle of Life* is a film with three stars of *The Lion King*—Simba the lion, Timon the meerkat, and Pumbaa the waddling warthog—in an enlightening and powerful message about protecting the world's environment for all living things. ☞ *Audience: All ages, although some toddlers may nap. Rating:* ★★ .

Soarin'. If you've ever wondered what it's like to fly, or at least hang glide, this is your chance to enjoy the sensation without actually taking the plunge. Opened in 2005, Soarin' is based on the popular attraction "Soarin' Over California" at Disney's California Adventure in Anaheim. This latest Epcot adventure uses motion-based technology to literally lift you in your seat 40 feet into the air within a giant projection-screen dome. As you soar above the Golden Gate Bridge, Napa Valley, and other wonders of California, you feel the wind and smell fragrant orange blossoms that surround you. The accompanying orchestral musical score created by Jerry Goldsmith ("Mulan," "Star Trek") builds on the thrill, and the crispness and definition of the film projection at twice the rate of a typical motion picture adds realism. ☞ *Audience: Adults and children 40" or taller. Rating:* ★★ .

The main event is a boat ride called **Living with the Land,** piloted by an informative, overalls-clad guide. You cruise through three biomes—rain forest, desert, and prairie ecological communities—and into an experimental greenhouse that demonstrates how food sources may be grown in the future, on this planet and in outer space. ☞ *Audience: All but very young children. Rating:* ★★★.

Living Seas. On Epcot's western outer ring is the first satellite pavilion, Living Seas, a favorite among children. Time and technology have caught up with the 5.7-million-gallon aquarium at the pavilion's core, so what was once revolutionary has now been equaled by top aquariums around the country.

The two-level **Sea Base Alpha,** a typical Epcot playground in the guise of an underwater research facility is dedicated to specific subjects, such as ocean ecosystems, porpoises, and the endangered Florida manatee. Fully interactive, the attraction offers films, touchy-feely sections, mini-aquariums, and video quizzes. ☞ *Audience: All but very young children. Rating:* ★★.

The three-minute **Caribbean Coral Reef Ride,** an underwater shuttle to Sea Base Alpha, is simply too short. In addition to watching the aquarium's full-time denizens, you may catch sight of a diver testing out the latest scuba equipment, surrounded by a cloud of parrot fish. Afterward you may want to circumnavigate the tank at your own speed on an upper level, pointing out barracudas, stingrays, sea turtles, and even sharks. ☞ *Audience: All. Rating:* ★★.

Spaceship Earth. Balanced like a giant golf ball waiting for some celestial being to tee off, the multifaceted silver geosphere of Spaceship Earth is to Epcot what the Cinderella Castle is to the Magic Kingdom.

The **Spaceship Earth ride** explores human progress and the continuing search for better forms of communication. Scripted by Ray Bradbury and narrated by Jeremy Irons, the journey begins in the darkest tunnels of time. It proceeds through history and ends poised on the edge of the future. ☞ *Audience: All ages, but persons who experience anxiety in dark, narrow, or enclosed spaces should not ride. Rating:* ★★.

Fodor'sChoice **Test Track.** This small-scale version of a General Motors test track is billed
★ as "the longest and fastest ride in Walt Disney World history." The heart-pounding trip takes you through seven tests and reaches speeds near 65 mph at the end, when your vehicle bursts from the building to an outdoor finale. ☞ *Audience: All but young children. No pregnant women or guests with back, neck, or leg braces; minimum height: 40". Rating:* ★★★.

Fodor'sChoice **Mission: SPACE.** It's the year 2036, and you're one of four astronauts-
★ in-training to board one of the attraction's 40 X-2 rocket capsules. You receive instructions before "liftoff," and soon you see and feel the capsule tilt skyward as the launch gantry appears on the individual screen before you. You're flattened against the back of your seat during "launch" (which is accomplished through rapid spinning of your vehicle via state-of-the-art centrifuge technology—though you won't actually sense that), and you experience the rumble of turbulence and even the sensation of weightlessness in outer space. Created with the help of former NASA scientists and astronauts, the ride lets riders "partic-

ipate" in carrying out the mission by pressing buttons and manipulating a joystick. In the capsule, you're instructed to keep your head back against the seat and look straight ahead for the duration of the ride to avoid motion sickness. If you think your children won't follow these instructions, keep them off the ride. In the summer of 2005, a 4-year-old boy died while on Mission: SPACE; as of this writing, there's no evidence to indicate whether he had a pre-existing condition. Engineers have ascertained that the ride did not malfunction. ☞ *Audience: Anyone 44″ or taller who doesn't suffer from balance problems, motion sickness, or have health problems related to the heart, back, and neck. Rating:* ★★★.

Universe of Energy. The first of the pavilions on the left, or east, side of Future World is in a large, lopsided pyramid sheathed in thousands of mirrors—solar collectors that power the attraction within.

One of the most technologically complex shows at Epcot, **Ellen's Energy Adventure** stars comedian Ellen DeGeneres as a woman who dreams she's a contestant on *Jeopardy!*, only to discover that all the categories are about a subject she knows nothing about—energy. With help from Bill Nye the Science Guy, you get a crash course in Energy 101. The exhibit combines a ride, three films that could use some updating, some of the largest audio-animatronics creatures ever built, 250 prehistoric trees, and enough cold, damp fog to make you think you've been transported into a defrosting refrigerator. ☞ *Audience: All ages. Rating:* ★★.

Wonders of Life. A towering statue of a DNA double helix stands outside the gold-crowned dome of one of the most popular wonders of Epcot. The attraction takes an amusing but serious and educational look at health, fitness, and modern lifestyles. Check the park schedule, as this pavilion is now open only during peak travel season.

The flight simulator—**Body Wars**—takes you on a bumpy platelet-to-platelet ride through the human circulatory system. ☞ *Audience: All but young children. No pregnant women or guests with heart, back, or neck problems or motion sickness; minimum height: 40″. Rating:* ★★★.

The engaging **Cranium Command** shows how the cranium manages to make the heart, the uptight left brain, the laid-back right brain, the stomach, and an ever-alert adrenal gland all work together as their host, a 12-year-old boy, suffers the slings and arrows of a typical day. ☞ *Audience: All ages. Rating:* ★★★.

The **Fitness Fairground,** an educational playground that teaches adults and children about good health, takes up much of Wonders of Life. There are games in which you can pedal around the world on a stationary bicycle and guess your stress level. ☞ *Audience: All ages. Rating:* ★★.

Starring Martin Short, *The Making of Me* is a valuable film on human conception and childbearing, using animation and actual footage from a live birth to explain where babies come from. Some scenes are explicit, but all the topics are handled with gentle humor and great delicacy. ☞ *Audience: All but very young children. Rating:* ★★★.

World Showcase

The 40-acre World Showcase Lagoon is 1⅓ mi around, but in that space you circumnavigate the globe, or at least explore it, in pavilions representing 11 countries in Europe, Asia, North Africa, and the Americas. In each pavilion native food, entertainment, art and handicrafts, and usually a multimedia presentation showcase the particular culture and people; architecture and landscaping re-create well-known landmarks.

Mexico. In a spectacular Maya pyramid surrounded by a tangle of tropical vegetation, Mexico has an exhibit of pre-Columbian art, a restaurant, and, of course, a shopping plaza. The cool, dark insides of the pyramid provide a welcome respite from a hot Orlando day. True to its name, the **El Río del Tiempo** boat ride takes you on a ho-hum trip down the river of time. ☞ *Audience: All ages.*

Norway. Here rough-hewn timbers and sharply pitched roofs are brightened by bloom-stuffed window boxes. The pavilion complex contains a 14th-century stone fortress that mimics Oslo's Akershus, cobbled streets, rocky waterfalls, and a wood-stave church, modeled after one built in 1250, with wooden dragons glaring from the eaves. The church has an exhibit that tells the story of two early-20th-century polar expeditions by using vintage artifacts, and the pavilion's shops sell spears, shields, and other Viking necessities. Norway also has a dandy boat ride: **Maelstrom,** in which dragon-headed longboats take a voyage through time that, despite its scary name and encounters with evil trolls, is actually more interesting than frightening. Let the kids frolic on the Age of the Vikings playground area, which replicates an old ship. ☞ *Audience: All ages.*

China. A shimmering red-and-gold three-tier replica of Beijing's Temple of Heaven towers over a serene Chinese garden, an art gallery displaying treasures from the People's Republic, a spacious emporium devoted to Chinese goods, and two restaurants. *Reflections of China,* a sensational panorama of the land and people, is dramatically portrayed on a 360-degree CircleVision screen that includes new scenes of Hong Kong, Shanghai, and Macao. ☞ *Audience: All ages, although no strollers permitted and small children have to be held aloft to see.*

Germany. In this jovial make-believe village you'll hear the hourly chimes from the glockenspiel on the clock tower, musical toots and tweets from multitudinous cuckoo clocks, and the satisfied grunts of hungry visitors chowing down on hearty German cooking. The oompah-band show in the Biergarten restaurant is also scheduled at times in the courtyard. Germany has the most shops of any pavilion. ☞ *Audience: Adults and older children.*

Italy. The star here is the Piazza San Marco, complete with a re-creation of Venice's Doge's Palace that's accurate right down to the gold leaf on the ringlets of the angel perched 100 feet atop the campanile, gondolas tethered to a seawall stained with age, and Romanesque columns, Byzantine mosaics, Gothic arches, and stone walls that have been carefully antiqued to look historic. ☞ *Audience: Adults and older children.*

American Adventure. The pavilion's superlative attraction is a 100-yard dash through history called the **American Adventure.** To the music of a piece called "The Golden Dream," it combines evocative sets, one of the world's largest rear-projection screens (72 feet wide), enormous movable stages, and 35 lifelike audio-animatronics players. ☞ *Audience: All ages.*

Japan. A brilliant vermilion torii gate, derived from the design of Hiroshima Bay's much-photographed Itsukushima Shrine, epitomizes the striking yet serene mood here. Disney horticulturists deserve a hand for their achievement in constructing out of all-American plants and boulders a very Japanese landscape, complete with rocks, pebbled streams, pools, and hills. The peace is occasionally disturbed by performances of traditional Japanese drumming. ☞ *Audience: Adults and older children.*

Morocco. You don't need a magic carpet to be instantaneously transported into an exotic culture—just walk through the pointed arches of the Bab Boujouloud gate. Koutoubia Minaret, a replica of the prayer tower in Marrakesh, acts as Morocco's landmark. Traditional winding alleyways, each corner bursting with carpets, brasses, leather work, and other North African craftsmanship, lead to a beautifully tiled fountain and lush gardens. ☞ *Audience: Adults and older children.*

France. The scaled-down model of the Eiffel Tower ought to clue you in to the fact that you've arrived in France, specifically Paris; but if that doesn't set the scene for you, poignant accordion music wafts out of concealed speakers and delicious aromas waft from the Boulangerie Pâtisserie bakeshop. The intimate Palais du Cinéma screens the film *Impressions de France,* homage to the glories of the country: the vineyards at harvesttime, Paris on Bastille Day, the Alps, Versailles, Normandy's Mont-St-Michel, and the stunning châteaux of the Loire Valley. ☞ *Audience: Adults and older children.*

United Kingdom. A pastiche of "There will always be an England" architecture, the United Kingdom rambles between the elegant mansions lining a London square to the bustling, half-timbered shops of a village High Street to the thatched-roof cottages of the countryside. The pavilion has no single major attraction. Instead, wander through shops selling tea and tea accessories, Welsh handicrafts, Royal Doulton figurines, and woolens and tartans. Check the entertainment schedule for performances of the British Invasion, a four-man band with a sound so like the Beatles that you'll feel the '60s all over again. ☞ *Audience: Adults and older children.*

Canada. "Oh, it's just our Canadian," said a typically modest native guide upon being asked the model for the striking rocky chasm and tumbling waterfall that represent just one of the high points of Canada. The top attraction is the CircleVision film *O Canada!* And that's just what you'll say after the stunning opening shot of the Royal Canadian Mounted Police literally surrounding you as they circle the screen. ☞ *Audience: All ages, although no strollers permitted and toddlers have to be held aloft to see.*

Entertainment

Most pavilions have entertainment; schedules are in the Times Guide that accompanies your park map. Above the lagoon every night, about a half hour before closing, don't miss the spectacular **IllumiNations** sound-and-light show, with fireworks, lasers, fountains, and lots of special effects to the accompaniment of a terrific score.

Disney–MGM Studios

❸ *Take the Disney–MGM Studios exit (Exit 64) off I–4.*

Inspired by Walt Disney's roots in show business and animated film, Disney–MGM Studios blends theme park with fully functioning movie and television production center, breathtaking rides with instructional tours, nostalgia with high-tech wonders. The park is suited for young and old, with more mature visitors appreciating cinematic references that hark back to the 1920s and '30s, while the youngsters hone in on popular film and TV of today. Surprisingly, the entire park is rather small—only 110 acres, a quarter the size of Universal Studios—with about 20 major attractions. When the lines are minimal, or by using FASTPASS, the park can be easily covered in a day with time for repeat rides.

Unpredictable Florida showers will send you scurrying for your disposable ponchos regardless of where you are, but if rain's in the forecast, Disney–MGM's preponderance of indoor, show-based attractions may leave you less soggy at day's end than the more ride-oriented parks.

Hollywood Boulevard

With its palm trees, pastel buildings, and flashy neon, Hollywood Boulevard paints a rosy picture of Tinseltown in the 1930s. The sense of having walked right onto a movie set is enhanced by the art deco–style storefronts, strolling brass bands, and roving actors dressed in costume and playing everything from would-be starlets to nefarious agents. The set is marred only by the Sorcerer Mickey hat icon that blocks a once-nostalgic view of the park's magnificent Chinese Theater reproduction. Hollywood and Sunset boulevards have souvenir shops and memorabilia collections galore.

Great Movie Ride. In a fire-engine-red pagoda replica of Grauman's Chinese Theater, this 22-minute tour full of Disney magic captures great moments in film—from Gene Kelly clutching that familiar lamppost as he sings the title song from *Singin' in the Rain* to the Munchkins of Oz and some of the slimier characters from *Alien*. A generic live "gangster" temporarily abducts your tram and engages in a shootout with other ne'er-do-wells, a scenario that might jar young ones more for the gunfire than the drama. A compilation of great movie clips is a fun and promising warm-up to boarding the ride—unless you're still in line when the reel repeats. ☞ *Audience: All but young children, for whom it may be too intense. Rating:* ★★.

Sunset Boulevard

This avenue pays tribute to famous Hollywood monuments.

Beauty and the Beast—Live on Stage. This very popular stage show takes place in the Theater of the Stars, a re-creation of the famed Hollywood Bowl. The long-running production is a lively, colorful, and well-done condensation of the animated film. As you arrive or depart, it's fun to check out set-in-cement handprints and footprints of the television celebrities who've visited Disney–MGM Studios. ☞ *Audience: All ages. Rating:* ★★★.

Fodor'sChoice **Rock 'n' Roller Coaster Starring Aerosmith.** On WDW's wildest roller
★ coaster, the twists and turns are accentuated by a synchronized rock sound-
track that resonates from speakers mounted in each vehicle. ☞ *Audi-*
ence: Older children and adults. No pregnant women or guests with heart,
back, or neck problems or motion sickness; minimum height: 44″. Rat-
ing: ★★★.

Fodor'sChoice **Twilight Zone Tower of Terror.** Ominously overlooking Sunset Boulevard
★ is a 13-story structure that's reputedly the now-deserted Hollywood Tower
Hotel. You take an eerie stroll through the dimly lighted lobby and de-
caying library to the boiler room before boarding the hotel's giant elevator. As you head upward past seemingly deserted hallways, ghostly
former residents appear around you, until suddenly—faster than you
can say "Where's Rod Serling?"—the creaking vehicle abruptly plunges
downward in a terrifying 130-foot free-fall drop, only to repeat with
several stomach-churning ups and downs. ☞ *Audience: Older chil-*
dren and adults. No pregnant women or guests with heart, back, or neck
problems; minimum height: 40″. Rating: ★★★.

Animation Courtyard

Fodor'sChoice **The Magic of Disney Animation.** This tour through the Disney animation
★ process takes you inside the magic of filmmaking as you follow the many
steps of 2-D animation. You begin the tour in a small theater with a performance of *Drawn to Animation,* where a live-and-in-person Disney
actor plays the role of animator interacting comically with the wise-crack-
ing animated character, Mushu, from *Mulan,* who prances between
two screens above the stage. Next is the creative zone, where kiosks of
computer touch screens invite you to add color to your favorite characters and even find out which Disney character is most like you. Watch
for popular Disney film characters, including The Incredibles, to appear
in this area for autographs and photos. The final stop is the Animation
Academy, a delightful crash course in how to draw an animated character. Children and adults can sit side-by-side at one of 38 backlit draft-
ing tables as an artist gives easy-to-follow instructions on drawing a Disney
character. Your sketch of Donald Duck (or the character du jour) is your
souvenir. ☞ *Audience: All but toddlers, who may be unwilling to sit*
still for the Animation Academy. Rating: ★★★.

Playhouse Disney—Live on Stage! The former Soundstage Restaurant now
has one of the best shows for young children anywhere at Walt Disney
World. There's a perky host on a larger-than-life "storybook stage" that
presents stars of several popular Disney Channel shows. Curiously, the
theater is devoid of seating, so you'll be corralled to sit on the carpet, but
preschoolers and even toddlers can sing and, towards the end of the show,
dance, as the Bear in the Big Blue House, Rolie Polie Olie, Stanley, Pooh
and friends cha-cha-cha their way through positive life lessons. Seeing the
Bear characters "in person" is a particular thrill because these Henson
creations appear in size and scale exactly as they do on the live-action TV
series. ☞ *Audience: Toddlers and preschoolers. Rating:* ★★★.

Voyage of the Little Mermaid. A boxy building on Mickey Avenue invites
you to join Ariel, Sebastian, and the rest of the underwater gang in this
stage show, which condenses the movie into a marathon presentation
of greatest hits. ☞ *Audience: All ages. Rating:* ★★.

Walt Disney: One Man's Dream. This photo, film, and audio tour leads you through Walt's life in the old Walt Disney Theater. If you're a baby boomer, it's a real nostalgia trip to see Walt resurrected on film as his "Wonderful World of Color" intro splashes across the screen. And if you're into artifacts, there's plenty of Walt memorabilia to view as you absorb the remarkable history of this entertainment legend. ☞ *Audience: Ages 10 and up. Rating:* ★★.

Mickey Avenue

Disney–MGM Studios Backlot Tour. This combination tram ride and walking tour is a 60-minute exploration of the back-lot building blocks of movies: set design, costumes, props, lighting, and special effects. During a demonstration of the latter, you have the option of volunteering as an "extra," a humbling experience that will certainly delight any companions you've brought along. At Catastrophe Canyon, the tram bounces up and down in a simulated earthquake, an oil tanker explodes in gobs of smoke and flame, and a water tower crashes to the ground, touching off a flash flood. ☞ *Audience: All but young children. Rating:* ★★.

Who Wants to Be a Millionaire—Play It! The syndicated TV show is now also a live stage show on Soundstages 2 and 3, where you'll have your own fastest-finger buttons and a chance at the hot seat next to the show's celebrity "Regis." You don't vie for $1 million, but you do build points to get a shot at some parting prizes. ☞ *Audience: Ages 5 and up. Rating:* ★★★.

New York Street

The **Lights, Motors, Action! Extreme Stunt Show** is modeled after the high-octane Walt Disney Studios Stunt Show Spectacular at Disneyland Paris. Here, Disney designers made it their mission to reveal the secrets behind Hollywood's greatest stunts, including those heart-pounding car chases common to the big screen. The scene: a 177,000-square-foot Mediterranean village "set" inside a 5,000-seat stadium. The premise: filmmakers are producing a spy thriller on the set, and the director is setting up different out-of-sequence stunts between heroes and villains that include high-speed spinouts, two-wheeled driving, jumps, pyrotechnic explosions, high falls, and even watercraft stunts on the set's canal. The payoff: besides experiencing the thrill of seeing choreographed stunts live, you will see how the "director" combines the stunt shots to create a completed scene, which plays on the stadium's mammoth video wall. ☞ *Audience: All, though young children may be frightened by loud noises.*

Honey, I Shrunk the Kids Movie Set Adventure. Let the kids run free in this state-of-the-art playground based on the movie about lilliputian kids in a larger-than-life world. They can slide down a gigantic blade of grass, crawl through caves, and climb a mushroom mountain. ☞ *Audience: Children and those who love them. Rating:* ★★★.

Jim Henson's MuppetVision 3-D. You don't have to be a Miss Piggy–phile to get a kick out of this combination 3-D movie and musical revue. The theater was constructed especially for this show, with special effects built into the walls and ceilings. ☞ *Audience: All ages. Rating:* ★★★.

Echo Lake

In the center of this idealized California is cool, calm Echo Lake, fringed with trees and benches and ringed with landmarks: pink-and-aqua restaurants trimmed in chrome; Min and Bill's Dockside Diner with fast snacks; and Gertie, a Sinclair gas station dinosaur that dispenses ice cream, Disney souvenirs, and the occasional puff of smoke in true magic-dragon fashion.

Indiana Jones Epic Stunt Spectacular! Don't leave Disney–MGM Studios without seeing this 30-minute show with the stunt choreography of veteran coordinator Glenn Randall (*Raiders of the Lost Ark, Indiana Jones and the Temple of Doom, E. T.,* and *Jewel of the Nile* are among his credits). ☞ *Audience: All but young children. Rating:* ★★★.

Sounds Dangerous Starring Drew Carey. This show is a delightful, multi-faceted demonstration of the use of movie sound effects. It stars Drew Carey in a hilarious movie that lets you play detective. Once the theater turns pitch black, you'll hear sounds that create the effects that are used on the screen. Don't see the show if you're afraid of the dark. ☞ *Audience: All but very young children. Rating:* ★★.

Star Tours. Although the flight-simulator technology used for this ride was long ago surpassed by other thrill rides, most notably Universal Studios' *Back to the Future . . . The Ride,* this *Star Wars* experience is still a pretty good trip. While much of the action happens onscreen, you'll feel like you're lurching through space as your seat shakes and vibrates. The surrounding "set" is also quite thoughtful: beloved droids from the movies tune up equipment on the fringes as you queue up in the boarding area, and you'll exit through present-day airport corridors with futuristic signs, a convincing little touch. ☞ *Audience: Older children and adults. No pregnant women or guests with heart, back, or neck problems or motion sickness. Children must be 40", and those under 7 must be accompanied by an adult. Rating:* ★★★.

Entertainment

The live *Beauty and the Beast* stage show is a winner. And don't miss the **Disney Stars and Motor Cars** parade, which wends its way up Hollywood Boulevard. The after-dark fireworks show **Fantasmic!** is the perfect finale to the day, with its cast of Disney characters, fountains, lasers, and dramatic musical score. You can reserve seating for the show by booking a Fantasmic! dinner package.

Disney's Animal Kingdom

❹ *Take the Disney's Animal Kingdom exit (Exit 65) off I–4.*

Humankind's enduring love for animals is the inspiration for Disney's fourth theme park in Orlando, which explores the story of all animals—real, imaginary, and extinct—in true Disney fashion, via carefully re-created and dramatic landscapes, rides, peppy musical shows, shops, and eateries.

The park is laid out very much like the Magic Kingdom; its focal point is the spectacular **Tree of Life,** in **Discovery Island.** From there, all the other "lands" are laid out like the spokes of a wheel. At the entrance is the **Oasis,** with guest relations, and to its right is **DinoLand U.S.A.** In the northeast corner is **Asia,** and **Africa** is on the northwest side. South of Discovery Island, immediately west of the Oasis, is **Camp Minnie-Mickey,** a character-greeting and show area. Make sure you arrive early, when the animals are at their liveliest, or you may miss out on some of the best reasons to go.

While Animal Kingdom has its share of rides and run-around activities, it's decidedly more laid-back than its sister parks, so consider sliding in a visit here between intense Magic Kingdom outings or other highly caffeinated stops.

Discovery Island
Primarily the site of the Tree of Life and "It's Tough to Be a Bug!" inside the Tree of Life Theater, this land also has live animal habitats, two eateries, several gift shops, and some visitor services, such as the baby-care center and lost and found.

Fodor'sChoice
★

Tree of Life. The imposing park centerpiece is 14 stories high and 50 feet wide, and its roots, trunk, and branches are covered with 325 intricate carvings of animal forms. More than 100,000 fabric leaves in several shades of green form its realistic canopy. Once inside the Tree of Life Theater's mammoth trunk, you'll be serenaded by crickets and get a bug's-eye view of life in the whimsical *It's Tough to Be a Bug!,* complete with in-theater special effects. ☞ *Audience: All but very young children, who might be frightened of the dark and some bug effects. Rating:* ★★★.

DinoLand U.S.A.
Just as it sounds, this is the place to come in contact with creatures prehistoric.

Boneyard. Youngsters can slide, bounce, and slither around this archaeological dig site–cum–playground and even unearth a woolly mammoth in the area's huge sandbox. A climbing area that allows you to ascend a mountain of woven rope is a big draw, surprisingly manageable—and, inevitably, climbable again and again—for kids as young as 4. ☞ *Audience: Young children and their families. Rating:* ★★★.

DINOSAUR. When your car rouses a cantankerous Carnotaurus from his Cretaceous slumber, it's show time on this thrill ride. Travel back 65 million years on a twisting start-stop adventure and try to save the last living iguanodon as a massive asteroid hurtles toward Earth. ☞ *Audience: All ages who don't mind scary creatures in the dark and are tall enough to meet the minimum height requirement of 40". No pregnant women or guests with heart, back, or neck problems. Rating:* ★★★.

Fossil Fun Games. This carnival-style midway includes games like Whack a Packycephalosaur and the mallet-strength challenge Dino-Whamma. The prehistoric fun comes at a price, however, and stone currency is not accepted.

Primeval Whirl. In this free-spinning, four-passenger outdoor "time machine" your vehicle heads on a brief journey back in time, twisting and turning along a compact track, and even venturing into the jaws of a dinosaur "skeleton." The more weight there is in the vehicle, the more you spin. ☞ *Audience: All but very young children. Minimum height: 48". Rating:* ★★★.

Tarzan Rocks! This live musical stage show, based on the animated film, includes live acrobatics, extreme stunts, and a rock performance that showcases the buff jungle dude and his toned jungle honey. ☞ *Audience: All ages. Rating:* ★★.

TriceraTop Spin. Until this opened, there wasn't a true "kiddie ride" anywhere at Disney's Animal Kingdom. TriceraTop Spin is designed for playful little dinophiles who'll get a kick out of whirling around a giant spinning toy top in their dino-mobiles. ☞ *Audience: Toddlers and young children and their families. Rating:* ★★.

Asia

This is a typical rural village and an exotic rain forest where trees grow from a crumbling tiger shrine and two massive towers, one representing Thailand, the other Nepal.

Flights of Wonder. An outdoor show on the *Caravan Stage,* it highlights spectacular demonstrations of skill by falcons, hawks, and other rare and fascinating birds that swoop down over the audience. ☞ *Audience: All but those who might be frightened by the low-flying birds. Rating:* ★★.

Kali River Rapids. Run the Chakranadi River through a huge bamboo tunnel and a series of sharp twists, turns, and one steep, very wet drop while passing rain forests, burning woodlands, and temple ruins. ☞ *Audience: Older children and adults. No guests with heart, back, or neck problems or motion sickness; minimum height: 42". Rating:* ★★★.

Maharajah Jungle Trek. Get a wonderful up-close view of jungle animals— including magnificent tigers, a Komodo dragon, and fascinating fruit bats—along this trail. At the end, you walk through an aviary set with a lotus pool. ☞ *Audience: Older children and adults. Rating:* ★★★.

Africa

Predominantly an enclave for wildlife from the continent, this is all forests and grasslands; the focus is on live animals. **Harambe,** on the northern banks of Discovery River, is Africa's starting point. Inspired by the small town of Lamu, Kenya, this coastal "village" spotlights Swahili architecture, food, and shopping with African themes.

Fodor'sChoice ★ **Kilimanjaro Safaris.** A re-created African safari may not be a new idea, but this one goes a step beyond merely observing zebras and lions. Open-sided safari vehicles take you over some 100 acres of savanna, forest, rivers, and rocky hills to see herds of African animals including elephants, rhinos, giraffes, hippos, and even cheetahs in extremely authentic settings. There's even a wee bit of Disney's famous audio-animatronics animal action near the end that links the ride to its "let's-get-the-poachers" story line. Do this early in the day when animals are friskiest, and use FASTPASS if the wait is more than 30 minutes. ☞ *Audience: All ages. Parents can hold small tykes and explain the ride's poacher theme. Rating:* ★★★.

Pangani Forest Exploration Trail. Take a nature walk among streams and waterfalls to see a family and a bachelor group of lowland gorillas, hippos (viewed from under the water), meerkats, exotic birds, and even naked mole rats. This is one of the best experiences in the park if the weather is cool enough for the animals to be active. ☞ *Audience: All ages. Rating:* ★★★.

Rafiki's Planet Watch. Take the Wildlife Express steam train to this unique center of eco-awareness. At Habitat Habit!, cotton-top tamarins play while you learn how to live with all Earth's animals. At Conservation Station, there are animal experts, interactive exhibits, and information on worldwide efforts to protect endangered species and their habitats and about the park's behind-the-scenes operations. At Affection Section, children can get face-to-face with goats and other small critters. ☞ *Audience: All ages. Rating:* ★★.

Camp Minnie-Mickey

This Adirondack-style land is a meet-and-greet area where Disney characters gather for picture-taking and autographs. Very small children may be wary around the larger-than-life renditions of Mickey Mouse, Goofy, and other characters, but everyone else will have a blast. Live performances are also staged here.

★ **Festival of the Lion King.** If you think you've seen enough Lion King to last a lifetime, you're wrong, unless you've seen this show. In an open-air theater-in-the-round, it's a delightful tribal celebration of song, dance, acrobatics, and other surprising performances on huge moving stages and with giant moving floats. ☞ *Audience: All ages. Rating:* ★★★.

Pocahontas and Her Forest Friends. This show based on the Disney film stars live animals in a lesson on nature and how to preserve endangered species. Pocahontas is your official hostess, talking on the subject and breaking out in song, including "Colors of the Wind." ☞ *Note: May not be scheduled daily during slower season—check entertainment guidemap. Audience: All ages. Rating:* ★★.

The Disney Water Parks

Visit the water parks first thing in the morning or late in the afternoon to avoid crowds, or when the weather clears up after a thundershower. (Typically, rainstorms drive away the crowds, and lots of people simply don't come back.) If you plan to make a whole day of it, avoid weekends—Typhoon Lagoon and Blizzard Beach are big among locals as well as visitors.

Blizzard Beach

❺ Blizzard Beach promises the seemingly impossible—a seaside playground with an alpine theme. The Disney Imagineers have gone all out to create a ski resort in the midst of a tropical lagoon. The snow-in-Florida motif provides lots of puns and sight gags. The park centers on **Mt. Gushmore,** a faux "snowcapped" mountain that looks real from a distance until you discover it's a set-designer's trick, with all sorts of ways, such as toboggan and sled runs, to get down. At the base of the mountain there's a sandy beach featuring the obligatory wave pool, a lazy river, and play areas for young children and preteens. Mt. Gushmore's big gun is **Summit Plummet,** which Disney bills as "the world's tallest, fastest free-fall speed slide." From the top it's a wild 55-mph plunge straight down to a splash landing at the base of the mountain. **Teamboat Springs** is a "white-water raft ride" in which six-passenger rafts zip along a twisting series of rushing waterfalls. Of course, no water park would be complete without a flume ride—here there are three.

Typhoon Lagoon

❻ Typhoon Lagoon will whirl and wow you for the better part of a day: bobbing in 4-foot waves in a surf lagoon the size of two football fields, speeding down arrow-straight water slides and around twisty storm slides, and bumping through white-water rapids. Your inner thrill-seeker will go crazy over the park's new **Crush 'N' Gusher,** Central Florida's first "water coaster." Designed to propel you uphill and down along a series of flumes, caverns, and spillways, this ride should satisfy the most enthusiastic daredevil. Try snorkeling in **Shark Reef,** a 360,000-gallon tank with an artificial coral reef and 4,000 real tropical fish. Or grab an inner tube and float along 2,100-foot **Castaway Creek,** which circles the entire park. It takes about 30 minutes to do the circuit; stop as you please along the way. If you want to get scared out of your wits in three seconds flat, slide down **Humunga Kowabunga,** with a drop of more than 50 feet. A children's area, **Ketchakiddie Creek,** replicates adult rides on a smaller scale. The park is popular; in fact, in summer and on weekends it often reaches capacity (7,200) by mid-morning.

Tips for Making the Most of Your Visit

- Arrive at the theme parks early—30–45 minutes before opening—so you can check belongings into lockers and rent strollers and wheelchairs.

- See the three-star attractions first thing in the morning, at the end of the day, or during a parade, using FASTPASS whenever possible.

- Eat in a restaurant that takes priority-seating reservations, bring your own food discreetly (a big time *and* money saver), or have meals before or after mealtime rush hours (from 11 to 2 and again from 6 to 8).

- If a meal with the characters is in your plans, save it for the end of your trip, when your youngsters will have become accustomed to these large, looming figures.

- Familiarize yourself with all age and height restrictions to avoid having children get excited about rides they're too short or too young to experience.

- Call ahead to check on operating hours and parade times, which vary greatly throughout the year.

Walt Disney World Resort A to Z

ADMISSION FEES

Visiting Walt Disney World Resort is not cheap, especially if you have a child or two along. Everyone 10 and older pays adult prices; reductions are available for children ages 3 through 9. Children under three get in free. You won't find discounted tickets at the park, so buy ahead

20 ROMANTIC THINGS TO DO AT WALT DISNEY WORLD®

NOT EVERYTHING AT DISNEY WORLD *involves children. Get a babysitter (available for a fee through WDW) and enjoy some private time, just the two of you.*

1. Dine on gourmet fare at the very grand Victoria & Albert's restaurant in the Grand Floridian.

2. Have dinner at the California Grill and watch the Magic Kingdom fireworks.

3. Rent a boat to take a cruise on the Seven Seas Lagoon or the waterways leading to it. Bring champagne and glasses.

4. Take a nighttime whirl on Cinderella's Golden Carrousel in Fantasyland. Sparkling lights make it magical.

5. Have your picture taken and grab a kiss in the heart-shape gazebo in the back of Minnie's Country House.

6. Sit on the beach at the Grand Floridian at sunrise or at dusk—a special time.

7. Plan a day of pampering at the Grand Floridian Spa.

8. Buy a faux diamond ring at the Emporium on Main Street in the Magic Kingdom. Propose to your sweetheart at your favorite spot in the World.

9. Have a caricature drawn of the two of you at the Marketplace.

10. Sit by the fountain in front of Epcot's France pavilion and have some wine or a pastry and coffee.

11. Have a drink at the cozy Yachtsman's Crew bar in the Yacht Club hotel.

12. After dinner at Narcoosee's in the Grand Floridian, watch the Electrical Water Pageant outside.

13. Take a walk on the BoardWalk. Watch IllumiNations from the bridge to the Yacht and Beach Club. Then boogie at Atlantic Dance.

14. Tie the knot all over again at the Wedding Pavilion. Invite Mickey and Minnie to the reception.

15. Rent a hot-air balloon for a magical tour of Walt Disney World.

16. Every night is New Year's Eve at Pleasure Island. Declare your love amid confetti and fireworks.

17. Enjoy a British lager outside at Epcot's Rose & Crown Pub—a perfect IllumiNations viewing spot. Book ahead and ask for a table with a view.

18. Have your picture taken with Mickey at Toontown Fair.

19. Have dinner at Alfredo's in Epcot, right after IllumiNations—request an 8:55 reservation. After dinner, since the park is officially closed, it's incredibly lovely.

20. Book the Fantasmic! dinner package at the Hollywood Brown Derby in Disney–MGM Studios to dine in leisure and get reserved seating at the show.

if you're looking for a deal. Prices change often and, in early 2005, Disney introduced an entirely new ticketing system called **Magic Your Way,** so be sure to call for the most up-to-date information.

Until **Magic Your Way** ticketing was introduced, you were stuck with purchasing either one-day, one-park tickets, or passes that included park-hopping perks to the Magic Kingdom, Epcot, Disney–MGM Studios, and the Animal Kingdom for four or more days. If you were hoping for a two- or three-day ticket with park-hopping privileges, your only option was to stay at a Disney-owned resort and opt for tailoring your pass to your length of stay.

The new system is somewhat complicated, but it does provide plenty of ways to save, depending on your vacation plans. One thing is clear: the more days you spend in the Disney parks, the greater your savings on ticket prices. The system begins with a base ticket good for one park, one day; two parks, two days; continuing up to seven days. For true Disneyphiles, there's even a 10-day ticket. The more days you visit, the greater the discounts per day. (A one-day ticket costs $59.75 for anyone ages 10 and up; a two-day base ticket costs $119, offering a per-day savings of only 25 cents; a five-day base pass costs $193, with a per-day savings of $21.15.)

Next, you can tailor your ticket packages to your itinerary. One option allows you to add the **Park Hopper** perk to your passes, so that you can visit several parks each day. If you remember the old Disney Park Hopper pass, banish it from your memory bank—this one simply augments your base ticket. It costs $35, no matter how many days your park ticket covers. So it's an expensive option for a one-, two-, or even three-day ticket. If you add the Park Hopper option to a four-day ticket, the cost breaks down to $8.75 a day; it's just $5 per day for a seven-day ticket.

Another option is called the **Magic Plus Pack,** which adds to your ticket a choice of visits to Disney entertainment and recreation facilities beyond the four major theme parks. Included are Typhoon Lagoon and Blizzard Beach water parks, Pleasure Island, DisneyQuest, and Disney's Wide World of Sports complex. The shorter your stay, the more you'll pay; for instance, if you add the $45 Plus Pack cost to a one-, two-, or three-day ticket, you're only entitled to two non-theme-park visits. If you add the same $45 perk to a four- or five-day ticket, you get three visits; a seven-day ticket with the Magic Plus Pack option gives you a chance to experience all five extra attractions.

If you plan to buy tickets for at least four days, but you'd like to keep to a budget, your best bet is to pass on the Park Hopper option and go straight to the Magic Plus Pack choice—even though you won't be able to park hop, you can experience four theme parks in four days and enjoy some of the other attractions.

Be warned that it's not easy to "do" more than one park in a day, but if you want to take in the attractions of, say, the Magic Kingdom and then nip over for dinner at Epcot's World Showcase, park hopability may be attractive. Another way to save time is with **FASTPASS,** a free system that allows you to get a timed ticket to popular attractions and then return at an appointed time instead of waiting in line.

Tickets and passes to all Walt Disney World Resort parks can be purchased at park entrances, at admission booths at the Transportation and Ticket Center (TTC), in all on-site resorts (if you're a registered guest), and at the Walt Disney World kiosk at Orlando International Airport (second floor, main terminal). American Express, Visa, and MasterCard are accepted, as are cash, personal checks (with ID), and traveler's checks. Many offices of the American Automobile Association (AAA) sell discounted tickets. Check with your local office. Tickets are also available at Disney stores nationwide, so you may want to purchase them at home before you leave. Some tickets may be available at hotels and stores off WDW property. Although these outlets may not save you much—or any—money, they could save time waiting in line at the park. You can also purchase tickets at ⊕ www.disneyworld.com. Save 5%–7% on each ticket, which can add up to $50 or more depending on the number of people in your family and the package you buy.

GETTING AROUND

Walt Disney World Resort has its own transportation system, with boats, buses, and monorails to get you wherever you want to go. It's a fairly simple system—if in doubt, ask the nearest Disney staffer the best way to get where you're going. In general, allow 45–60 minutes to get to your destination. Monorails, launches, buses, and trams operate from early in the morning until at least midnight. (Hours are shorter when the park closes earlier.) Even if you've rented a vehicle in Orlando, it's worthwhile to avail yourself of the public transportation provided within the resort. Some connections can be a little convoluted, but are still convenient: for instance, if you want to reach Downtown Disney from MGM Studios, your best bet is to catch a bus to one of the on-property hotels and then take another bus to get downtown.

OPENING & CLOSING TIMES

Operating hours for the Magic Kingdom, Epcot, Disney–MGM Studios, and Disney's Animal Kingdom vary widely throughout the year. In general, the longest days are in summer and over the year-end holidays, when the Magic Kingdom is open until 10 or 11 (later on New Year's Eve), Epcot is open until 9 or 9:30, and Disney–MGM Studios is open until at least 7, sometimes 8:30. There are so many variations, it pays to call ahead or check the parks' Web site calendar. The Magic Kingdom, Epcot's Future World, and Disney–MGM officially open at 9. Disney's Animal Kingdom opens at 9 and closes at 5, though hours expand from 8 AM to 7 or 8 PM during peak times. The World Showcase at Epcot opens at 11. Parking lots open at least an hour earlier. Arrive at the Magic Kingdom turnstiles before the official opening time; breakfast in a restaurant on Main Street, which opens before the rest of the park; and be ready to dash to one of the popular attractions in other areas as soon as officially possible. Arriving in Epcot, Disney–MGM Studios, or Disney's Animal Kingdom, make dinner reservations before the crowds arrive—in fact, try to reserve tables even before you arrive, utilizing Disney's central reservations number (⇨ Visitor Information). Try to

MAGIC YOUR WAY PRICE CHART

TICKET OPTIONS								
TICKET	**10-DAY**	**7-DAY**	**6-DAY**	**5-DAY**	**4-DAY**	**3-DAY**	**2-DAY**	**1-DAY**
BASE TICKET								
Ages 10-up	$208	$199	$196	$193	$185	$171	$119	$59.75
Ages 3-9	$167	$160	$157	$155	$148	$137	$96	$48

Base Ticket admits guest to one of the four major theme parks per day's use.
Park choices are: Magic Kingdom, Epcot, Disney-MGM Studios, Disney's Animal Kingdom.

ADD: Park Hopper	$35	$35	$35	$35	$35	$35	$35	$35

Park Hopper option entitles guest to visit more than one theme park per day's use. Park choices are any combination of Magic Kingdom, Epcot, Disney-MGM Studios, Disney's Animal Kingdom.

ADD: Water Parks & More	$45 5 visits	$45 5 visits	$45 4 visits	$45 3 visits	$45 3 visits	$45 2 visits	$45 2 visits	$45 2 visits

Water Parks & More option entitles guest to a specified number of visits (between 2 and 5) to a choice of entertainment and recreation venues. Choices are Blizzard Beach, Typhoon Lagoon, Disney-Quest, Pleasure Island, and Wide World of Sports.

ADD: No Expiration	$100	$55	$45	$35	$15	$10	$10	n/a

No expiration means that unused admissions on a ticket may be used any time in the future. Without this option, tickets expire 14 days after first use.

MINOR PARKS AND ATTRACTIONS		
TICKET	**AGES 10-UP**	**AGES 3-9**
TYPHOON LAGOON OR BLIZZARD BEACH 1-Day 1-Park	$34	$28
DISNEYQUEST 1-Day	$34	$28
DISNEY'S WIDE WORLD OF SPORTS COMPLEX	$10.05	$7.48
CIRQUE DU SOLEIL'S *LA NOUBA*	$59-$87	$44-$65
PLEASURE ISLAND 1-Night Multi-Club Ticket	$20.95	$20.95

*Admission to *Pleasure Island* clubs is restricted to guests 18 or older unless accompanied by an adult 21 or older. For some clubs all guests must be 21 or older.

*All prices are subject to Florida sales tax

take in some of the attractions and pavilions well before the major crowds descend later in the morning.

PARKING

Every theme park has a parking lot—and all are huge. Always write down exactly where you parked your car and take the note with you. Parking-area trams deliver you to the park entrance. For each lot the cost is $8 for cars (free to WDW resort guests with ID). At Typhoon Lagoon and Blizzard Beach, parking is free.

VISITOR INFORMATION

For general information for Walt Disney World call either the information number or the switchboard. For all accommodations and shows call the central reservations number. There's a single number for all dining reservations. To inquire about resort facilities, call the individual property. For child-care information call KinderCare. One of the easiest ways to get information is via the Web site ⊕ www.disneyworld.com.
🔏 **Walt Disney World Information** ☎ 407/824-4321. **WDW switchboard** ☎ 407/824-2222. **WDW Central Reservations** ☎ 407/934-7639. **WDW Dining Reservations** ☎ 407/939-3463.

Disney–MGM Studios TV-show tapings ☎ 407/560-4651. **Kid's Nite Out** ☎ 407/828-0920 for in-room, 407/827-5437 for drop-off at Kindercare. **Pleasure Island** ☎ 407/934-7781. **Water Parks** ☎ 407/824-4321.

UNIVERSAL ORLANDO

The "umbrella" that is Universal Orlando contains Universal Studios (the original movie theme park), Islands of Adventure (the second theme park), and CityWalk (the dining-shopping-nightclub complex). Although it's bordered by residential neighborhoods and thickly trafficked International Drive, Universal Orlando is surprisingly expansive, intimate, and accessible, with two massive parking complexes, easy walks to all attractions, and a motor launch that cruises to the hotels. While Universal Orlando emphasizes "two parks, two days, one great adventure," you may find the presentation, creativity, and cutting-edge technology bringing you back for more.

Universal Studios

❾ *Near the intersection of I–4 and Florida's Tpke. Heading eastbound on I–4, take Exit 75A. Heading west on I–4, take Exit 74B and follow the signs.*

Universal Studios is a theme park with attitude. It's saucy, sassy, and hip, geared to those who like their rides loud and scary. If you want to calm down, there are quiet, shaded parks and a children's area where adults can enjoy a respite while the kids are ripping through assorted playlands at 100 mph. There are some, however, who miss the sort of connection that Disney forges with the public through its carefully developed history of singable songs and cuddly characters. The park's 444 acres are a bewildering conglomeration of stage sets, shops, reproductions of New York and San Francisco, and anonymous soundstages with theme attractions, as well as genuine moviemaking paraphernalia. On a map it looks easy. On foot, a quick run through the park to hit the top rides first is difficult, since it involves a few long detours and some backtracking. Attractions here are geared more to teenagers and adults than to the stroller set.

PRODUCTION CENTRAL Composed of six huge warehouses with working soundstages, this area also has new attractions that should prove popular with kids. Follow Nickelodeon Way left from the Plaza of the Stars.

Jimmy Neutron's Nicktoon Blast. Stepping into the void left by the departed Hanna-Barbera attraction, Jimmy has arrived with a similar virtual reality ride. The boy genius is joined by a large collection of Nickelodeon characters, including SpongeBob SquarePants and the Rugrats, as he demonstrates his latest invention (the powerful Mark IV rocket). Your "rocket car" dives and bounces as things go awry when evil egg-shape aliens make off with the rocket and threaten to dominate the world. ☞ *Audience: All ages except children under 40"; smaller children can experience the attraction from stationary seats. Rating:* ★★★.

Nickelodeon Studios. When Orlando was expected to become "Hollywood East," this was the centerpiece of a busy production center. Now, however, all of the cable network's productions have picked up and moved out west. So what's the big attraction? Several times a day, parents and kids get to sit in a mock studio where the audience is divided into teams and an emcee conducts various games familiar to Nick viewers. The winning kid has the option of getting creamed with a pie or getting slimed—and slime usually wins. It's nothing special, but kids may enjoy an attraction especially designed for them. ☞ *Audience: All ages, but especially grade-schoolers. Rating:* ★.

Fodor'sChoice
★ **Shrek 4-D.** Mike Myers, Eddie Murphy, Cameron Diaz, and John Lithgow reprise their respective vocal roles as the ogre, Shrek; his chatterbox companion, Donkey; his bride, Princess Fiona; and the vengeful Lord Farquaad in this animated 3-D saga. "OgreVision" glasses provide the 3-D film effects, while specially built seats and sensory sensations add "4-D" surprises to the show. The movie picks up with Shrek, Princess Fiona, and Donkey leaving for a honeymoon at Fairytale Falls, but things are interrupted by the ghost of Lord Farquaad. The showdown puts you at the center of an adventure that includes a battle between fire-breathing dragons and a plunge down a deadly waterfall. ☞ *Audience: All ages. Rating:* ★★★.

NEW YORK Here the Big Apple is rendered with surprising detail, right down to the cracked concrete and slightly stained cobblestones.

Revenge of the Mummy. The Brendan Fraser film was seat-of-the-pants fun, and a $40 million ride promises an unusual fusion of special effects that combine roller coaster technology, pyrotechnics, and some super-scary skeletal warriors into a spine-tingling journey through Egyptian burial chambers and underground passageways. The "psychological thrill ride" was designed in collaboration with *The Mummy* director Stephen Sommers and replaced the old Kongfrontation in spring 2004. ☞ *Audience: All but young children, who may be frightened. Minimum height: 48" Rating:* ★★★.

TWISTER . . . Ride It Out. Here's your chance to see a tornado up close and personal, in the form of an ominous five-story-high funnel cloud that circulates some 2 million cubic feet of air around the theater and creates a terrifying freight-train sound. ☞ *Audience: All but young children. Rating:* ★★★.

SAN FRANCISCO– AMITY

This area combines two sets. One part is the wharves and warehouses of San Francisco's Embarcadero and Fisherman's Wharf districts, with cable-car tracks and the distinctive redbrick Ghirardelli chocolate factory; the other is the New England fishing village terrorized by the shark in *Jaws.*

Beetlejuice's Graveyard Revue. A Transylvanian castle is the backdrop for Beetlejuice, who takes the stage and warms up the audience with his snappy lines and sarcastic attitude. Frankenstein's monster and his bride, the Werewolf, and Dracula soon appear, doffing their traditional costumes in favor of glitzy threads and singing the greatest hits of such diverse artists as Ricky Martin, Santana, Gloria Gaynor, and the Village People. Be prepared for some serious weirdness. ☞ *Audience: Older children and adults. Rating:* ★★.

Earthquake—The Big One. This is another headliner in Universal's "adrenaline alley." The preshow reproduces choice scenes from the movie *Earthquake,* then takes you onto San Francisco Bay Area Rapid Transit subway cars to ride out an 8.3 Richter-scale tremor and its consequences: fire, flood, blackouts. Stay away from this one if you are claustrophobic or have a fear of loud noises. ☞ *Audience: All but young children. No pregnant women or guests with heart, back, or neck problems or motion sickness; minimum height: 40″ to ride alone. Rating:* ★★★.

Jaws. Stagger out of San Francisco into the town of Amity, and stand in line for this terror-filled boat trip with explosions, noise, shaking, and gnashing of sharp shark teeth. The special effects shine, especially the heat and fire from electrical explosions. Try it after dark for an extra thrill, then cancel the following day's trip to the beach. ☞ *Audience: All but young children. No pregnant women or guests with heart, back, or neck problems or motion sickness. Rating:* ★★★.

WORLD EXPO

The southeastern corner of the park has some very exciting attractions.

Back to the Future . . . The Ride. Universal's flight-simulator ride involves a one-of-a-kind seven-story Omnimax screen surrounding your DeLorean-shape simulator. Having no sense of perspective (or seat belts) makes this the rocking, rolling, pitching equivalent of a hyperactive paint mixer. It's perpetually scary, jarring, and jolting. If you like your rides shaken, not stirred, this one'll be worth the wait—and the queasy feeling that'll follow you around afterward. ☞ *Audience: Older children and adults. No pregnant women or guests with heart, back, or neck problems or motion sickness; minimum height: 40″. Rating:* ★★★.

Men in Black—Alien Attack. This star attraction is billed as the world's first "ride-through video game." With your on-board laser gun, you set off on a trip through New York streets, firing at aliens to rack up points. Keep in mind they can fire back at you and send your car spinning out of control. Depending on your score, the ride concludes with one of 35 endings, ranging from a hero's welcome to a loser's farewell. *Audience: Older children and adults. Minimum height: 42"; children 42–48" must ride with an adult. Rating:* ★★★.

WOODY WOODPECKER'S KIDZONE This area was opened so that toddler and elementary-school kids could have something to shout about.

A Day in the Park with Barney. After a cute stand-in-line pre-show you'll enter a theater where the beloved TV playmate and Baby Bop dance and sing though the clap-along, sing-along monster classics, including "If You're Happy and You Know It" and (of course) "I Love You." A fairly elaborate play area, accessible before or after the show, has hands-on activities—a water harp, wood-pipe xylophone, and musical rocks—and propels already excited preschoolers to even greater heights. Immediately after the show, Barney plants himself in this area to allow you and your youngsters the chance to line up for a photo op. ☞ *Audience: Young children. Rating:* ★★.

Fodor'sChoice ★ **Animal Planet Live!** An ark of animals is the star here: a raccoon opens the show, Lassie makes a brief appearance, there's a dog decathlon, and you'll also see Gizmo, the parrot from *Ace Ventura: Pet Detective.* Grand-finale highlights include impressions by Bailey the orangutan of, among others, Ricky Martin, then an overpoweringly adorable chimpanzee, and finally a sneak peek at a boa constrictor. It's a fun show that shouldn't be missed. ☞ *Audience: All ages. Rating:* ★★★.

Curious George Goes to Town. The celebrated simian visits the Man with the Yellow Hat in a no-line, no-waiting interactive aqua play area that attracts kids like fish to water. Yes, there's water, water everywhere, especially atop the clock tower, which periodically dumps 500 gallons down a roof and straight onto a screaming passel of preschoolers. Kids love the levers, valves, pumps, and hoses that gush at the rate of 200 gallons per minute. At the head of the square, footprints lead to a popular dry-play area, where youngsters can frolic among thousands of foam balls raining down from a cage or projected from kid-fired guns and cannons positioned around the large room. Getting pelted with the balls is not uncommon and, after you take a few to the head, not that bothersome. ☞ *Audience: Water-babies of all ages. Rating:* ★★★.

E. T. Adventure. This trip aboard bicycles mounted on a movable platform takes you through fantastic forests and across the moon in an attempt to help the endearing extraterrestrial find his way back to his home planet. ☞ *Audience: All ages. No guests with heart, back, or neck problems or motion sickness. Rating:* ★★★.

Fievel's Playland. Based on the adventures of Steven Spielberg's mighty mini-mouse, this gigantic playground incorporates a four-story net climb, tunnel slides, water-play areas, ball crawls, a 200-foot water slide, and a harmonica slide that plays music when you slide along the openings. ☞ *Audience: Young children and their families. Rating:* ★★.

Woody Woodpecker's Nuthouse Coaster. This low-speed, mild-thrill roller coaster (top speed 22 mph) makes it a safe bet for younger kids and action-phobic adults. ☞ *Audience: Young children and their parents. Minimum height 36"; children 36–48" must ride with an adult. Rating:* ★★★.

HOLLYWOOD   Angling off to the right of Plaza of the Stars, Rodeo Drive forms the backbone of Hollywood.

Lucy: A Tribute. This walk-through collection of Lucille Ball's costumes and other memorabilia plus trivia quizzes and short spots from the series is best for real fans of the ditsy redhead. ☞ *Audience: Adults. Rating:* ★.

Terminator 2 3-D. In his pre-Sacramento days, Arnold said he'd be back, and he is, in this exciting, technologically advanced 3-D adventure that mixes live action and film. Icy fog, live actors, gunfights, and a fantastically chilling grand finale keep tension high and the pace moving at 100 mph. Kids may be scared silly. ☞ *Audience: All but young children. Rating:* ★★★.

Fodor'sChoice   **Universal Horror Make-up Show.** On display in the entertaining preshow
★   area are masks and props and rubber skeletons from the film *Scorpion King*—all great backdrops for a family photo. The real fun kicks off in the theater when a host brings out a "special-effects expert" to describe what goes into (and what oozes out of) some of the creepiest movie effects (corn syrup and food coloring makes for a dandy blood substitute, for example). Add knives, guns, loose limbs, one-liners, and a surprise ending for edge-of-your-seat fun. Actors create a completely entertaining mix of movie secrets and comedy club timing. ☞ *Audience: Preteens to adults. Rating:* ★★★.

Entertainment

Don't miss Universal's seasonal evening parties—most notably Mardi Gras (early February through early April), Fiesta Caliente (May), Rock the Universe (Christian music, September), the popular Halloween Horror Nights (October), and Grinchmas (November and December). Except for Halloween and Rock the Universe, these festivals are included with park admission.

Universal Islands of Adventure

🔟 *Near the intersection of I–4 and Florida's Tpke. Heading east on I–4, take Exit 75A; heading west, take Exit 74B.*

The creators of Islands of Adventure elevated theme-park attractions to a new level. From Marvel Super Hero Island and Toon Lagoon to Seuss Landing, Jurassic Park, and the Lost Continent, every section of the park—from the architecture to the landscaping to the technology of the rides—is truly impressive; they may have out-Disneyed Disney. A few drawbacks are a layout that's not easy to grasp and some rides and venues that are still shuttered or empty or lack a rousing ending.

SEUSS LANDING   This whimsical 10-acre island is the only place in the world where the books of Dr. Seuss come to life. Make it a mandatory stop, since this is the most visually stunning piece of real estate in America.

Caro-Seuss-el. The centerpiece of Seuss Landing looks like it came straight from the pages of a Dr. Seuss book. Merry-go-round mounts are strange, bespotted, bewhiskered, and wonderfully colorful. Take a dog-alope or a cowfish for a spin. ☞ *Audience: All ages. Children under 48″ must be accompanied by an adult. Rating:* ★★★.

The Cat in the Hat. Take a cleverly chaotic journey aboard a whirling, spinning "couch" through the pages of Dr. Seuss's most famous book, about the topsy-turvy day that the Cat came to play. ☞ *Audience: All ages. Children under 48″ must be accompanied by an adult. Rating:* ★★.

If I Ran the Zoo. In this maze of a playground, children can climb, jump, push buttons, get splashed in interactive fountains, and work with each other to animate strange and wonderful Seussian animals. ☞ *Audience: Young children. Rating:* ★★★.

One Fish, Two Fish, Red Fish, Blue Fish. It's a long wait for this ride, where you steer a rising and falling Seussian-style fish to the accompaniment of a Jamaican-style song. Ignore the song's hints and you'll be splashed by a squirting post. ☞ *Audience: Young children. Children under 48″ must be accompanied by an adult. Rating:* ★★.

LOST CONTINENT Ancient myths from around the world inspired this land. A visit transports you through time, past a crumbling statue of Poseidon, the Greek god of the sea, toward a revered city buzzing with humanity.

Fodor'sChoice **Dueling Dragons.** After enduring a ½-mi-long line, you board "Ice ★ Coaster" or "Fire Coaster" to whiz past the trees of a medieval forest, over Dragon Lake, and past oncoming cars during five inversions, three near misses, and top speeds of 55–60 mph. Cars are suspended from the track, your feet dangle freely, and your legs swing off toward the wild blue yonder. ☞ *Audience: Older children, teens, and adults. Minimum height: 54″. No pregnant women or guests with heart, back, or neck problems. Rating:* ★★★.

Fodor'sChoice **Eighth Voyage of Sindbad.** Seven voyages were not enough for Sindbad. ★ So he strikes out again on his continuing search for enormous riches, encountering life-threatening perils along the way. Staged in a 1,700-seat theater, this edge-of-your-seat stunt show has water explosions, flames, and pyrotechnic effects. ☞ *Audience: Older children and adults. Rating:* ★★★.

Flying Unicorn. This low-key children's coaster places kids on the back of a unicorn for a very, very brief ride through a mythical forest. ☞ *Audience: Younger children. Minimum height: 36″. Rating:* ★★★.

Poseidon's Fury: Escape from the Lost City. The multimedia presentation here is an exciting battle between Poseidon (water) and his archenemy, Zeus (fire). Their "weapons" consist of more than 350,000 gallons of water and 200 flame effects, including scorching fireballs that erupt all around you. Although the first 15 minutes don't offer much, the finale is loud, powerful, and hyperactive. The show is part theater, part walk-through. ☞ *Audience: Older children and adults. Rating:* ★★.

JURASSIC PARK As you venture through the junglelike vegetation here and find yourself surrounded by the high-tension wires and warning signs, you'll get the feeling you've stepped into the Jurassic Park of Steven Spielberg's blockbuster movie.

Camp Jurassic. This clever park-within-a-park is loads of fun. You—or your kids—race along footpaths through the forests, slither down slides, clamber over swinging bridges and across boiling streams, scramble up net climbs and rock formations, and explore mysterious caves full of faux lava. ☞ *Audience: All. Rating:* ★★.

Jurassic Park Discovery Center. Get close to skeletal remains of a massive Tyrannosaurus rex and laboratories where biochemists develop the technology to bring these prehistoric creatures to life. One of the many demonstration areas shows a realistic-looking raptor being hatched. ☞ *Audience: All. Rating:* ★★.

Jurassic Park River Adventure. The climax of this ride is an 85-foot plunge straight down the longest, fastest, steepest water descent ever built. Before that, however, you'll meander through a three-dimensional Jurassic Park that's scarily similar to the cinematic version—where you discover that you've become the prey of a terrifying T. rex. ☞ *Audience: All but young children. Minimum height: 42". No pregnant women or guests with heart, back, or neck problems. Rating:* ★★★.

Pteranodon Flyers. The intent was good, but the prehistoric bird's-eye view of the Jurassic Park compound is a slow and time-consuming distraction. Go for it only if there's no one in line. ☞ *Audience: All ages. Adults must be accompanied by a child 36" to 56" tall. Rating:* ★.

TOON LAGOON Here's your chance to leap into the Sunday funnies and romp around the animated universe with some pretty famous characters—more than 150 in all—in an environment that melts the boundaries between imagination and reality.

Dudley Do-Right's Ripsaw Falls. Based on the popular 1960s cartoon, this flume ride will take you on a wet and wild ride as you try to help Dudley rescue Nell from Snidely Whiplash. ☞ *Audience: All but young children. Minimum height: 44"; children under 48" must be accompanied by an adult. No pregnant women or guests with heart, back, or neck problems. Rating:* ★★★.

Me Ship, the Olive. This is a huge, interactive playground-boat where you and your kids can wander about, stopping occasionally to fire water cannons at passengers in the Bilge-Rat Barges. Here's your chance to get even. ☞ *Audience: Young children. Rating:* ★★.

Popeye & Bluto's Bilge-Rat Barges. A churning, turning white-water raft ride spins and drops you into whirlpools and eddies and then a fully operational boat wash. You will get wet—and so will your possessions. There are lockers at the boarding area for anything you'd prefer to keep dry. ☞ *Audience: All but young children. Minimum height: 48"; children under 48" must be accompanied by an adult. No pregnant women or guests with heart, back, or neck problems or motion sickness. Rating:* ★★★.

MARVEL SUPER This island puts you smack in the middle of scenes straight from the pages
HERO ISLAND of Marvel comics' greatest adventures.

Fodor'sChoice **Amazing Adventures of Spider-Man.** The thrill of this ride will validate
★ any time you've spent standing on line. Unlike any other ride at any theme park anywhere, it combines moving vehicles, 3-D film, simulator technology, and special effects. No matter how many times you visit this attraction, you'll cringe when Doc Oc breaks through a brick wall, raises your car to the top of a skyscraper, and then releases you for a 400-foot sensory free fall to the pavement below. ☞ *Audience: All but young children. Minimum height: 40"; children under 48" must be accompanied*

by an adult. No pregnant women or guests with heart, back, or neck problems. Rating: ★★★.

Dr. Doom's Fearfall. It looks scary, but it's a letdown when you're elevated and dropped a few hundred feet and . . . well, that's it. Skip it if the line is too long. ☞ Audience: Older children and adults. Minimum height: 52". No pregnant women or guests with heart, back, or neck problems or motion sickness. Rating: ★.

Incredible Hulk Coaster. One of Islands' two blockbuster coasters dominates the lagoonside scenery with its spaghetti of tracks in a neon shade of green that recalls the skin of mild-mannered Bruce Banner turned Hulk. Racing along the track, you spin through seven rollovers and plunge into two deep, foggy, subterranean enclosures. Afterward, the Hulk's not the only one who's green. ☞ Audience: Older children and adults. Minimum height: 54". No pregnant women or guests with heart, back, or neck problems. Rating: ★★★.

Storm Force Accelatron. This whirling indoor ride is supposed to demonstrate the power of nature. Strip away the veneer, however, and what you've got is a mirror image of Disney World's popular twirling teacups. ☞ Audience: Older children and adults. No pregnant women or guests with heart, back, or neck problems. Minimum height: 54". Rating: ★★.

Tips for Making the Most of Your Visit

- Universal Express is available to all park guests at all attractions. You check in at the ride entrance, are assigned a time, and then return later to bypass the line and ride within minutes. Universal Express PLUS is a perk priced from $15 to $25 (depending on the season) that allows you to cut to the front of the line all day long without waiting for a previous Universal Express pass to expire.

- If you're staying at a Universal resort, use your room key as your Express ticket to bypass the line at almost all Universal attractions.

- In peak seasons, resort hotel guests are admitted to Universal parks an hour before regular park goers.

- Call a day or two before your visit to get official park hours, and arrive in the parking lot 45 minutes early. See the biggest attractions first.

- Be sure to write down your parking location.

- Have a filling snack around 10:30, lunch after 2, and dinner at 8 or later. Or lunch on the early side at a place that takes reservations; then have dinner at 5. Be sure to make your reservations ahead of time or, at the very least, when you enter the park.

Universal Orlando A to Z

ADMISSION FEES

One-day, one-park tickets for Universal Studios or Islands of Adventure cost $63.64 for adults and $51.12 for children. For a one-day, two-park visit, the cost is $84.09 for adults, $72.37 for children (tax included).

A two-day, two-park ticket, which is a good option since it includes a bonus pass for a free third day and admission to CityWalk clubs, is $111.78 for an adult and $101.13 for children aged three to nine. **Universal Express passes** are included in the price of admission. Guests of on-site resorts can use their hotel key cards to access express lines, while guests staying off-site must use their paper tickets to make reservations for express-line access. If you're staying off-site, consider purchasing the **Universal Express PLUS pass** for an extra $15 to $25. The PLUS pass gives you express-line access without having to make reservations. Hint: there are discount coupons for most theme parks in tourist-friendly fliers distributed around the parks, and the money you save through them may offset the cost of the PLUS pass. Tickets do not have to be used on consecutive days, but must be used within seven days of your first visit. You can get tickets in advance by mail through **Ticketmaster** (☎ 800/745–5000) or by contacting **Universal Studios Vacations** (☎ 888/322–5537).

The **Orlando FlexTicket** is similar to Walt Disney World's pass system. The four-park version gets you into Universal Studios, Islands of Adventure, Wet 'n Wild, and SeaWorld for $191.64 adults, $155.43 children three to nine, including tax, and five-park versions allow you 14 consecutive days of unlimited admission to all of the above as well as Busch Gardens Tampa ($228.92 and $191.64 adults/kids, including tax). SeaWorld–Busch Gardens combination Value Tickets, which include one day at each park, cost $85.95 for adults and $72.95 for children three to nine, with tax included.

PARKING

Universal's single parking-garage complex, which serves both theme parks and CityWalk, is one of the world's largest car parks. Because your vehicle is covered, it's not so sweltering at the end of the day even when it's hot. The cost is $8 for cars, $10 for campers. Valet parking is available for $16.

VISITOR INFORMATION

Universal Orlando (✉ 1000 Universal Studios Plaza, Orlando 32819-7610 ☎407/363–8000 or 888/331–9108 ⊕ www.universalorlando.com).

SEAWORLD & DISCOVERY COVE

Theme parks grow so well in the sandy Central Florida soil that you might almost imagine a handful of seeds scattered across the fertile Interstate 4 belt, waiting for the right combination of money and vision to nurture them into the next Walt Disney World.

SeaWorld Orlando

❼ *Near the intersection of I–4 and the Beeline Expressway; take I–4 to Exit 71 or 72 and follow signs.*

There's a whole lot more to SeaWorld than Shamu, its mammoth killer-whale mascot. Sure, you can be splashed by Shamu, stroke a dolphin or stingray, see manatees face-to-snout, learn to love an eel, and be spat upon by a walrus, but far from incidental is that this is also the world's largest marine adventure park—yet it can be tackled comfortably in a day, if necessary. Every attraction at SeaWorld is devoted to demonstrating the ways that humans can protect the mammals, birds, fish, and reptiles that live in the ocean and its tributaries. The presentations are gentle reminders of our responsibility to safeguard the environment, and you'll find that SeaWorld's use of humor plays a major role in this education. First-timers may be slightly confused by the lack of distinct "lands" here—SeaWorld's performance venues, attractions, and activities surround a 17-acre lake, and the artful landscaping and curving paths sometimes lead to wrong turns. But armed with a map that lists show times, you can plan a chronological approach that flows easily from one attraction to the next.

Dolphin Nursery. In a large pool, dolphin moms and babies (with birth dates posted on signs) play and leap and splash. You can't get close enough to pet or feed them (you can do this at the park's Key West attraction), so you'll have to be content peering from several feet away and asking the host questions during a regular Q and A session. Here's a popular answer: No, you can't take one home. ☞ *Audience: All ages. Rating:* ★★.

★ **SeaWorld Theater—*Pets Ahoy*.** SeaWorld Theater is the venue for the lively and highly entertaining *Pets Ahoy*. A dozen dogs, 18 cats, and an assortment of ducks, doves, parrots, and a pig (nearly all rescued from the local animal shelter) perform a series of incredible and complex stunts. The show builds to a fun—and funny—finale. Stick around after the show for a chance to shake paws with the stars. ☞ *Audience: All ages. Rating:* ★★★.

Tropical Reef. In this soothing indoor attraction, more than 30 separate aquariums are aswim with tropical fish from around the world. ☞ *Audience: All ages. Rating:* ★★.

Turtle Point. At this re-creation of a small beach and lagoon, many of the sea turtles basking in the sun or drifting in the water were rescued from predators or fishing nets. Injuries make it impossible for these lumbering beauties to return to the wild. An educator is usually on hand to answer questions. ☞ *Crowds: Sporadically crowded, but generally enough space for all to get a good view. Strategy: Go anytime. Audience: All ages. Rating:* ★★.

Key West at SeaWorld. In this laid-back area, you'll be able to purchase fish at designated times and feed some of the nearly two-dozen Atlantic bottle-nose dolphins. The creatures are relatively easy to pet once they begin surfacing for food but almost impossible to touch otherwise, so stick around until feeding time. At the nightly sunset celebration, kids can get their faces painted and have their pictures taken with a larger-than-human-size Shamu or Dolly Dolphin. ☞ *Audience: All ages. Rating:* ★★★.

Stingray Lagoon. Buy a batch of smelts to feed the rays and stroke their velvety skin. Don't worry about getting stung—these slippery swimmers just want food. ☞ *Audience: All ages. Rating:* ★★★.

Manatees: The Last Generation? The lumbering, whiskered manatees look like a cross between walruses and air bags, and this display devoted to them is striking. After a short film, watch the gentle giants swim placidly alongside native fish in their 300,000-gallon tank. Keep an eye out for mamas and their calves. ☞ *Audience: All ages. Rating:* ★★★.

Journey to Atlantis. Combining elements of a high-speed water ride and roller coaster with LCD technology, lasers, and holographic illusions, this thriller plunges you into the world of Greek mythology and down two of the fastest, steepest drops anywhere. You will get soaked, so bring a change of clothes (including underwear). ☞ *Audience: Older children and adults. Not recommended for pregnant women or guests with heart problems or a fear of dark, enclosed spaces; minimum height: 42". Rating:* ★★★.

Fodor'sChoice **Kraken.** Big draws for coaster enthusiasts on this high-intensity ride are
★ the seven inversions and moments of weightlessness, courtesy of zero-G rolls. Folks around these parts claim this is the tallest (149 feet) and fastest (up to 65 mph), and—backless sandal and flip-flop wearers beware—only floorless coaster in Florida. If you're a thrill ride–deprived parent and you're permitted to break away for just one ride, this is the one. A separate line develops toward the front of the attraction for those who want to ride the first car, but the second or third rows are just as worthy, and the wait is shorter. ☞ *Audience: Older children and adults. Not recommended for pregnant women or guests with heart problems. Minimum height: 54". Rating:* ★★★.

Penguin Encounter. A refrigerated re-creation of Antarctica, the exhibit has 17 species of penguins; a Plexiglas wall on your side of the tank lets you see that the penguins are cute as can be, waddling across icy promontories and plopping into frigid waters to display their aquatic skills. A similar viewing area for puffins and murres (a kind of seabird) is just as entertaining. ☞ *Audience: All ages. Rating:* ★★.

Pacific Point Preserve. A nonstop chorus of "aarrrps" and "yawps" leads, no, not to a frat-house keg party but to fun-loving California sea lions and harbor and fur seals on a 2½-acre rocky promontory. Just call it Bark Avenue. ☞ *Audience: All ages. Rating:* ★★★.

Fodor'sChoice **Sea Lion & Otter Stadium.** A wildly inventive, multilevel pirate ship
★ forms the set for *Clyde and Seamore Take Pirate Island*. SeaWorld's celebrated sea lions, otters, and walruses prevail over pirate treachery in this swashbuckler of a saga. Arrive early to catch the preshow—the mime is definitely one of the best you'll ever see. ☞ *Audience: All ages. Rating:* ★★★.

Shark Encounter. Within this large, innocuous white structure are some thoroughly creepy critters: eels, barracuda, sharks, and poisonous fish. You walk through a series of four Plexiglas tubes, surrounded by tanks containing the world's largest collection of such animals—a half dozen species of shark, for example—in some 300,000 gallons of water. The entrance to the attraction has changed to make room for a tony sit-down venue, **Sharks Underwater Grill,** where diners, somewhat perversely, can order fresh fish as well as Floribbean cuisine while watching their entrées' cousins. ☞ *Audience: All ages. Rating:* ★★★.

Odyssea. Odyssea is the follow-up to the long-running and successful show *Cirque de la Mer,* although the new show is not quite as funny or entertaining. Peruvian silent comic Cesar Aedo appears as an innocent spectator who's whisked into an underwater world where he witnesses the performances of sea creatures. You'll see a contortionist in a clam shell, gymnasts twirling on ropes in a "kelp bed," and trampoline artists as penguins—even a giant, accordionlike "tube worm" who, well, you just have to see it. All in all, it's fun entertainment. ☞ *Audience: All ages. Rating:* ★★★.

Shamu: Close Up! For unprecedented underwater viewing of a whale breeding and nursery area, this is the place to be. Follow the signs to the underground viewing stations for a unique glimpse of favorite whale pastimes: tummy-rubbing and back-scratching. ☞ *Audience: All ages. Rating:* ★★★.

Clydesdale Hamlet. At its core, this is a walk around the stable where the hulking Clydesdale horses live and a look at the corral where they romp and play. A statue of a mighty stallion—which kids are encouraged to climb upon—is a good photo opportunity. ☞ *Audience: All ages. Rating:* ★.

FodorśChoice
★
Shamu Stadium. The home of SeaWorld's orca mascot, the stadium is hands down the most popular attraction in the park. Several of *The Shamu Adventure* shows daily showcase the whales' acrobatic, spectator-drenching antics. The show is interspersed with filmed segments of animal expert Jack Hanna talking about whales and their habitats, and a trivia game that puts audience members on the spot—as well as on the tremendous view screen. In the slightly funkier nighttime *Shamu Rocks America,* the famous orca jumps to the beat of "God Bless the USA." Take the splash zone—the first several stadium rows near the tank—seriously, and bring a change of clothes, just in case. ☞ *Audience: All ages. Rating:* ★★★.

Shamu's Happy Harbor. If you want to take a break while your kids exhaust the last ounce of energy that their little bodies possess, bring them here. This 3-acre outdoor play area has crawlable, climbable, explorable, bounceable, and get-wet activities. ☞ *Audience: Toddlers through grade-schoolers. Rating:* ★★★.

Wild Arctic. Inside this pseudo–ice station you embark on a flight-simulator helicopter ride leading to rooms with interactive, educational displays. If your stomach can handle the rolls and pitches of a virtual helicopter, it makes for scary, enjoyable, (and maybe queasy) fun. Afterward, there are above- and below-water viewing stations where you can watch beluga whales blowing bubble rings, polar bears padding around with their toys, and groaning walruses trying to hoist themselves onto a thick shelf of ice. There's a nonmoving option for those too small for or not interested in the jostling ride. ☞ *Audience: All ages. Minimum height: 42″ for motion option. Rating:* ★★★.

The Waterfront. A boardwalk leads from Shamu Stadium across the lagoon to this stretch of a nautical neighborhood lined with shops, eateries, kiosks, and street performers. Although there are scheduled performances, chances are you'll just wander through the area en route to another attraction and catch some strolling musicians on the street or perhaps in one of the restaurants like **Voyagers Wood Fired Pizzas,** where chefs Dominick and Luigi flip jokes along with pies. Shops offer an impressive amount of exotic goods and include the **Tropica Trading Company,** with gifts from Bali, Indonesia, Italy, and South America; and **Allura's Treasure Trove,** a toy shop where you can design your own porcelain dolls. In summer and on holidays, the Waterfront is the base for a fireworks show. ☞ *Audience: Everyone. Rating:* ★★★.

Sky Tower. The focal point of the park is this 400-foot-tall tower, which is the main mast for a revolving double-decker platform. During the six-minute rotating round-trip, you'll get a bird's-eye-view of the park. There's a separate $3 admission. ☞ *Audience: All ages. Rating:* ★★.

SeaWorld Orlando Information

✉ *7007 Sea Harbor Dr., International Drive Area, Orlando 32821* ☎ *407/351–3600, 800/327–2424, or 800/432–1178 Ext. 5* ⊕ *www. seaworld.com* 🖃 *$57.46 adults, $47.78 children 3–9; 10% discount for online purchase; SeaWorld sometimes offers its "2nd Day Free" promotion, a complimentary pass you can use to return within 7 days— the passes are handed out near the exit to customers leaving the park. Make sure your entire party is together when arranging the following day's admission. The Orlando FlexTicket, which covers SeaWorld, other Busch parks, and the Universal parks, is similar to Walt Disney World's pass system. The base price of four-park versions that allow you up to 14 consecutive days of unlimited admission to Universal Orlando parks, Wet 'n Wild, and SeaWorld is $191.65 adults, $155.44 children 3–9, and the five-park versions that allow 14 consecutive days of unlimited admission to all of the above as well as Busch Gardens are $229.10 and $191.82. SeaWorld–Busch Gardens combination Value Tickets, which include one day at each park, cost $95.98 for adults and $86.39 for children 3–9, including tax. For more information, call* ☎ *800/ 224–3838 or visit www.orlandoflexticket.com* ☉ *Daily 9–6 or 7, until as late as 11 summer and holidays; educational programs daily, some beginning as early as 6:30* AM.

Discovery Cove

❽ *Near the intersection of I–4 and the Beeline Expressway; take I–4 to Exit 71 or 72 and follow signs.*

Making a quantum leap from the traditional theme park, SeaWorld took a chance when it opened Discovery Cove, a 32-acre limited-admission park that's a re-creation of the Caribbean complete with coral reefs, sandy beach, margaritas, and dolphins. Here's how it works: after entering a huge thatch-roof tiki building, you register and are given a time to swim with the dolphins, the highlight of your Discovery Cove day. You're issued a photo ID that allows you to charge drinks during the day, and that's all you need to worry about. With your admission, everything else is included—lockers, food, mask, fins, snorkel, wetsuit, swim vest, towels, and admission to SeaWorld Orlando or Busch Gardens.

Once inside, you are awash in rocky lagoons surrounded by lush landscaping, intricate coral reefs, and underwater ruins. The pool where snorkeling lessons are taught has cascading waterfalls, and white beaches are fringed with thatch huts, cabanas, and hammocks. Exciting encounters with animal species from the Bahamas, Tahiti, and Micronesia are part of the experience. A free-flight aviary is aflutter with exotic birds, which you reach via a quiet walkway or by swimming in a river and then beneath a waterfall.

Although $249 per person may seem steep, if you skip the dolphin swim it's only $149 in summer and as low as $129 in fall. Then when you consider that a dolphin swim in the Florida Keys runs approximately $150, and SeaWorld throws in a complimentary seven-day admission to SeaWorld *or* Busch Gardens, it begins to feel like a bargain.

Discovery Cove Information

☎ 877/434–7268 *reservations line daily 9–8* ⊕ *www.discoverycove.com* ☉ *Daily 9–5:30, with extended hrs summer and holidays. Allow a full day to see all shows and attractions.*

ELSEWHERE IN THE AREA

Once you've exhausted the theme parks, or have been exhausted by them, turn your attention to a wealth of other area offerings. Although you'll find plenty of other recreational activities of interest to kids, there are also museums and parks and gardens galore, highlighting the cultural and natural heritage of this part of the South.

Kissimmee

10 mi east of Walt Disney World Resort; take I–4 Exit 64A.

Although Kissimmee is primarily known as the gateway to Walt Disney World, its non-WDW attractions just might tickle your fancy.

☺ ⑫ Long before Walt Disney World, there was campy **Gatorland,** which has endured since 1949 without much change, despite major competition. Through the monstrous aqua gator-jaw doorway—a definite photo op—lie thrills and chills in the form of thousands of alligators and crocodiles swimming and basking in the Florida sun. There's a Gator Wrestling Cracker-style show, and although there's no doubt who's going to win the match, it's still fun to see the handlers take on those tough guys with the beady eyes. In the educational Up Close Encounters Snake Show, high drama is provided by the 30–40 rattlesnakes that fill the pit around the speaker. ✉ *14501 S. Orange Blossom Trail, between Orlando and Kissimmee* ☎ *407/855–5496 or 800/393–5297* ⊕ *www.gatorland.com* ☜ *$21.25 adults, $10.60 children 3–12; discount coupons online* ☉ *Daily 9–5.*

Friendly farmhands keep things moving on the two-hour guided tour
☺ of **Green Meadows Farm**—a 40-acre property with almost 300 animals.
Fodor'sChoice There's no waiting in line because tours are always starting. Everyone
★ can milk the mama cow, and chickens and geese are turned loose in their yard to run and squawk while city slickers try to catch them. Children

take a quick pony ride, and everyone gets jostled about on the old-fashioned hayride. Youngsters come away saying, "I milked a cow, caught a chicken, petted a pig, and fed a goat." Take U.S. 192 for 3 mi east of I–4 to South Poinciana Boulevard; turn right and drive 5 mi. ☒ *1368 S. Poinciana Blvd.* ☏ *407/846–0770* ⊕ *www.greenmeadowsfarm.com* ☜ *$18 age 3 and up; discount coupons online* ☉ *Daily 9:30–5:30; last tour begins at 4.*

⊙ ⑪ **Water Mania** has all the requisite rides and slides without Walt Disney World's aesthetics. However, it's the only water park around to have **Wipe Out**, a surfing simulator, where you grab a body board and ride a continuous wave form. The giant Pirate Ship in the **Pirate's Lagoon**, one of two children's play areas, is equipped with water slides and water cannons. The **Abyss** is an enclosed tube slide through which you twist and turn on a one- or two-person raft through 380 feet of deep-blue darkness. This 36-acre park also has a sandy beach, go-carts, a picnic area, snack bars, gift shops, a miniature golf course, and periodic concerts. It's 1½ mi from Walt Disney World, about ¼ mi east of I–4. Be sure to call for opening and closing times, which can vary due to weather. Also call for unadvertised special rates during certain off-season times. ☒ *6073 W. Irlo Bronson Memorial Hwy.* ☏ *407/396–2626 or 800/527–3092* ⊕ *www.watermania-florida.com* ☜ *$28.84 adults, $22.42 ages 3–9, discount coupons online; parking $6* ☉ *Mid-Mar.–early Sept., daily 10–5; rest of Sept., weekdays 11–5, weekends 10–5; Oct., Thurs.–Sun. 11–5.*

> [!NOTE] off the beaten path
HISTORIC BOK SANCTUARY – Perfect for a quick back-to-nature fix is this appealing but often overlooked sanctuary of plants, flowers, trees, and wildlife. Shady paths meander through a peaceful world of pine forests, silvery moats, mockingbirds and swans, blooming thickets, and hidden sundials. The majestic 200-foot Bok Tower is constructed of coquina (from seashells) and pink, white, and gray marble and has a carillon with 57 bronze bells that ring out each day at 3 during a 45-minute recital, which may include early American folk songs, Appalachian tunes, Irish ballads, or Latin hymns. The bells also are featured in recordings played every half hour after 10 AM, and moonlight recitals are sometimes held. To reach the gardens, take Interstate 4 Exit 55 and head south along U.S. 27, away from the congestion of Orlando and past quite a few of Central Florida's citrus groves. ☒ *1151 Tower Blvd., Lake Wales* ☏ *863/676–1408* ☜ *$8 adults, $3 children 5–12, free Sat. 8–9; Pinewood Estate general tour $5 adults, $3 children 5–12; holiday tour $15 adults, $8 children 5–12* ☉ *Daily 8–6; Pinewood House tours mid-Sept.–mid-May, Tues. and Thurs. at 12:30 and 2, Sun. at 2.*

International Drive Area, Orlando

7 mi northeast of Walt Disney World Resort; take I–4 Exit 74 or 75.

Between WDW and downtown Orlando are several attractions that kids adore. Unfortunately they may put some wear and tear on parents.

A 10-foot-square section of the Berlin Wall, a pain and torture chamber, a Rolls-Royce constructed entirely of matchsticks—these and almost
⊙ ⑬ 200 other oddities speak for themselves at **Ripley's Believe It or Not! Mu-**

seum, in the heart of tourist territory. It's said that the fruits of Robert Ripley's explorations are to reality what Walt Disney World is to fantasy. ⊠ *8201 International Dr., International Drive Area* ☎ *407/363–4418 or 800/998–4418* ⊠ *$16.95 adults, $11.95 children 4–12* ⊙ *Daily 9 AM–1 AM; last tickets sold at midnight.*

★ ☉ ⑭ A playground of 75 entertaining and educational interactive experiences awaits at **WonderWorks.** Find yourself in the middle of an earthquake or a hurricane, swim with sharks, play in the largest laser-tag arena in the world, design and ride your own awesome roller coaster, or even play basketball with a 7-foot opponent. ⊠ *9067 International Dr., International Drive Area* ☎ *407/352–8655* ⊠ *$17.95 adults, $12.95 children 4–12. Packages include laser tag and Magical Dinner Show* ⊙ *Daily 9 AM–midnight.*

Downtown Orlando & Environs

15 mi northeast of Walt Disney World Resort; take I–4 Exit 83B if you're heading westbound, Exit 83A if eastbound, or Exit 85 for Loch Haven Park sights.

Downtown Orlando is a dynamic community that's constantly growing and changing. Numerous parks, many of which surround lakes, provide pleasant relief from the tall office buildings. One such is Lake Eola, which has a delightful playground at one end and a walkway around its circumference that invites strolling. Just a few steps from downtown are delightful residential neighborhoods with brick-paved streets and live oaks dripping with Spanish moss.

☉ In the heart of downtown is **Lake Eola Park,** with its signature fountain in the center. The security here is such that families with young children use the well-lighted playground in the evening and downtown residents toss bread to the ducks, swans, and birds and walk their dogs late at night. Festivals and concerts are scheduled throughout the year. The most fun to be had in the park is a ride in a swan-shape pedal boat. You can even book a ride in an authentic 32-foot Venetian gondola, where dinner or snacks and beverages are served while a gondolier plays favorite tunes. Lake-view and patio dining include: **Lee's Lakeside** (which prepares the steak and lobster for GondEola dinner cruises); **Eola Yacht Club,** and **The Terrace on Lake Eola.** The view at dusk, as the fountain lights up in all its colors and the sun sets behind Orlando's ever-growing skyline, is spectacular. ⊠ *Robinson St. and Rosalind Ave.* ☎ *407/246–2827 park, 407/658–4226 gondola and swan boats* ⊠ *Boat rental $10 per half hr, maximum 3 adults or 2 adults and 2 children per boat; children under 10 must be with an adult. GondEola packages $45–$150 per couple, not including tax and gratuity* ⊙ *Park daily 6 AM–midnight; swan boats daily 10–8; gondola rides 5 PM–midnight.*

⑯ Journey back in time at the **Orange County Regional History Center** to discover how Florida's Paleo-Indians hunted and fished the land; what the Sunshine State was like when Spaniards first arrived in the New World; and how life in Florida was different when citrus was king.

✉ *65 E. Central Blvd.* ☎ *407/836–8500 or 800/965–2030* ⊕ *www. thehistorycenter.org* 💲 *$7 adults; $3.50 children 3–12* ⊙ *Mon.–Sat. 10–5, Sun. noon–5.*

⑮ The former estate of citrus entrepreneur Harry P. Leu, **Harry P. Leu Gardens** provides a quiet respite. On the grounds' 50 acres is a collection of historical blooms, many varieties of which were established before 1900. ✉ *1920 N. Forest Ave., Downtown Orlando* ☎ *407/246–2620* ⊕ *www.leugardens.org* 💲 *$5; $1 children in kindergarten through 12th grade* ⊙ *Garden daily 9–5, guided house tours daily 10–3:30.*

★ ☺ ⑰ With all the high-tech glitz and imagined worlds of the theme parks, which are closer to where most stay, is it worth visiting the **Orlando Science Center,** a reality-based science museum in Orlando proper? Absolutely. Multiple themed display halls have exciting hands-on exhibits covering mechanics, electricity and magnetism, math, health and fitness, nature, the solar system, and light, lasers, and optics. Walk through an enormous open mouth (literally) and take a journey through the human body (figuratively). New exhibits are added periodically; one of the most recent, **Touch the Sky,** reveals the wonders of aviation aboard a flight simulator, in a wind tunnel, and on a control-tower tour. The **CineDome,** a movie theater with an eight-story screen, offers large-format Iwerks films, planetarium programs, and, on weekends, laser-light shows. Friday and Saturday nights, visitors can peer through Florida's largest publicly accessible refractor telescope to view planets and many of their moons, plus other galaxies and nebulas. The center also has its own performance troupe, the Einstein Players. ✉ *777 E. Princeton St.* ☎ *407/514–2000* 💲 *Unlimited ticket includes exhibits, films, and planetarium shows, $14.95 adults, $9.95 children 3–11; after 6 Fri. and Sat. $9.95; parking $3.50* ⊙ *Tues.–Thurs. 9–5, Fri. and Sat. 9–9, Sun. noon–5. Open Mon. 9–5 school holidays and Memorial Day–mid-Aug.*

Winter Park & Maitland

20 mi northeast of WDW; take I–4 Exit 87 to Winter Park and head east 3 mi on Fairbanks Ave., or take I–4 Exit 90A, then Maitland Blvd. east, and turn right (south) on Maitland Ave.

Spend a pleasant day in upscale Winter Park shopping at chic boutiques, eating at a cozy café, visiting museums, and taking in the scenery along Park Avenue, with its hidden alleyways that lead to peaceful nooks and crannies. Away from the avenue, moss-covered trees form a canopy over brick streets, and old estates surround canal-linked lakes. Just north are two important Maitland stops, the Holocaust Memorial Resource and Education Center and the Audubon Center for Birds of Prey.

⑱ Lovely, shady, and green, **Central Park,** with a stage and gazebo, is Winter Park's gathering place, often the scene of concerts and monthly movies in the park. ✉ *Park Ave.*

⑲ Many works of Louis Comfort Tiffany, including immense stained-glass windows, lamps, watercolors, and desk sets, are at the **Charles Hosmer Morse Museum of American Art.** The 1,082-square-foot Tiffany

Fodor$Choice ★

Chapel was built for the 1893 World's Fair. ✉ *445 N. Park Ave.* ☎ *407/ 645–5311* ✆ *$3; $1 students, children under 12 free* ⊙ *Tues.–Sat. 9:30–4, Sun. 1–4; Fri. 9:30–8 Sept.–May.*

★ ㉑ From the dock at the end of Morse Avenue, depart for the **Scenic Boat Tour,** a Winter Park tradition that's been in continuous operation for more than 60 years. The one-hour pontoon boat tour, narrated by your captain, leaves hourly and cruises along 12 mi of Winter Park's opulent lakeside estates, through narrow canals, and across three lakes. ✉ *312 E. Morse Blvd.* ☎ *407/644–4056* ⊕ *www.scenicboattours.com* ✆ *$8; $4 children 2–11* ⊙ *Daily 10–4.*

㉒ A private liberal arts school, **Rollins College** was once the late Mister (Fred) Rogers's neighborhood—yes, he was an alumnus. You'll see the **Knowles Memorial Chapel,** built in 1932, and the **Annie Russell Theatre,** a 1931 building often used for local theatrical productions. The **Cornell Fine Arts Museum** has interesting 19th- and 20th-century American and European paintings, decorative arts, and sculpture. ✉ *End of Holt Ave.* ☎ *407/646–2526* ✆ *Museum free* ⊙ *Museum Tues.–Fri. 10–5, weekends 1–5.*

⓴ Exhibits at the **Holocaust Memorial Resource and Education Center of Central Florida** are arranged in chronological order and include a large number of photographs and audiovisual presentations. ✉ *851 N. Maitland Ave., Maitland* ☎ *407/628–0555* ✆ *Free* ⊙ *Mon.–Thurs. 9–4, Fri. 9–1, Sun. 1–4.*

More than 20 bird species, including hawks, eagles, owls, falcons, and ♻ vultures, make their home at **Audubon's Center for Birds of Prey.** This small wildlife rehabilitation center takes in more than 600 injured wild birds of prey each year. Fewer than half the birds are able to return to the wild; permanently injured birds live at the center on outdoor perches or in the center's aviaries. From Maitland Avenue, turn right on U.S. 17–92, right on Lake Avenue, and right on Audubon Way. ✉ *1101 Audubon Way* ☎ *407/644–0190* ⊕ *www.audubonofflorida.org/ conservation/cbop.htm* ✆ *$5* ⊙ *Tues.–Sun. 10–4.*

off the beaten path

WEKIWA SPRINGS STATE PARK – Where the tannin-stained Wekiva River meets the crystal-clear Wekiva headspring, you'll find this 6,400-acre park good for camping, hiking, picnicking, swimming, canoeing, fishing, and watching for alligators, egrets, and deer.

Fodor's Choice Although it can be crowded on weekends, on weekdays it's Walden Pond, ★ Florida style. Take Interstate 4 Exit 94 and turn left on Route 434 and right on Wekiwa Springs Road. ✉ *1800 Wekiva Circle, Apopka* ☎ *407/ 884–2008* ✆ *$5 per vehicle* ⊙ *Daily 8–sunset.*

Sports & the Outdoors

GOLF **DeBary Golf & Country Club** (✉ 300 Plantation Dr., DeBary ☎ 386/668– 1709) is an 18-hole course 10 mi north of Winter Park, green fee: $24/$40.

Celebration

10 mi southeast of WDW; take I–4 to Exit 64A and follow the Celebration signs.

This Disney-created community reminds some locals of something out of the 1970s film *The Stepford Wives*. But Celebration, which draws on vernacular architecture from all over the United States and was based on ideas from some of America's top architects and planners, can be a great retreat from the theme parks and from the garish reality of the U.S. 192 tourist strip 1 mi to the east. The town is so perfect it could be a movie set, and it's a delightful place to spend a morning or afternoon. Sidewalks are built for strolling, restaurants have outdoor seating with lake views, and inviting shops beckon. After a walk around the lake, take your youngsters over to the huge interactive fountain, and have fun getting wet. Starting after Thanksgiving and continuing on through the new year, honest-to-goodness snow sprinkles softly over Main Street each evening, to the delight of children of all ages.

Sports & the Outdoors

GOLF **Celebration Golf Club Service** (⊠ 701 Golf Park Dr. ☎ 407/566–4653 or 888/275–2918) is an 18-hole course designed by Robert Trent Jones and Robert Trent Jones Jr., green fee: $45/$130.

Mount Dora

35 mi northwest of Orlando and 50 mi north of WDW; take U.S. 441 (Orange Blossom Trail in Orlando) north or take I–4 to Exit 92, then take Rte. 436 west to U.S. 441, and follow the signs.

Built around the unspoiled Lake Harris chain of lakes, the valley community of Mount Dora has a slow and easy pace, a rich history, New England–style charm, and excellent antiquing. Although the population is less than 8,000, there's plenty of excitement here. The first weekend in February is the annual Mount Dora Art Festival. Attracting more than 200,000 people over a three-day period, it's one of Central Florida's major outdoor events. During the year there's a sailing regatta, a bicycle festival, and a crafts fair, or take in the historic buildings along Donnelly Street or 5th Avenue any time of year.

Sports & the Outdoors

GOLF About 5 mi northwest of Mt. Dora, **Deer Island Golf & Lake Club** (⊠ 18000 Eagles Way, Tavares ☎ 352/343–7550 or 800/269–0006) is a year-round, 18-hole course, green fee: $25/$65. **Harbor Hills Country Club** (⊠ 6538 Lake Griffin Rd., Lady Lake ☎ 352/753–7711 or 352/753–7000), about 15 mi northwest of Mt. Dora, has 18 holes, green fee: $28/$55.

WHERE TO EAT

Because tourism is king here, casual dress is the rule, and few restaurants require fancy attire. Reservations are always a good idea; otherwise the entire Ecuadoran soccer team or the Platt City High School senior class may arrive moments before you and keep you waiting a long, long time. Save that experience for the theme parks. For restaurants within Walt Disney World Resort, priority-seating reservations are easy to make, thanks to its **central reservations line** (☎ 407/939–3463 or 407/560–7277). Universal Orlando, which has become a major player in the culinary wars, also has its own reservations line (☎ 407/224–9255). Orlando is not big, but getting to places is frequently complicated, so always call for directions.

WHAT IT COSTS				
	$$$$	$$$	$$	$	¢
AT DINNER	over $30	$20–$30	$15–$20	$10–$15	under $10

Restaurant prices are per person for a main course at dinner.

Epcot

Canadian
$$–$$$ ✕ **Le Cellier Steakhouse.** A good selection of Canadian beer joins the best Canadian wine cellar in the state at this charming eatery. Aged beef is king, although many steaks appear only on the dinner menu. Carnivores should hone in on the herb-crusted prime rib, while seafood lovers might sample the popular maple-ginger glazed Canadian salmon. Desserts include a crème brûlée made with maple sugar and a Canadian Club chocolate cake. ⊠ *Canada* ▤ *AE, MC, V.*

English
$–$$ ✕ **Rose & Crown.** If you're an Anglophile and you love a good, thick beer, this is the place to soak up both the suds and the British street culture. "Wenches" serve up traditional English fare—fish-and-chips, meat pies, Yorkshire pudding, and the ever-popular bangers and mash, English sausage over mashed potatoes. A good and somewhat eclectic choice is the English pie sampler, with both chicken-and-leek and pork-and-cottage pies (pork with carrots topped with mashed potatoes and cheddar cheese), plus a side of green beans. For vegetarians, there's even an offering of curried veggies and tofu on the menu. For dessert, try the sticky toffee pudding with butter rum sauce. If you are not driving soon after the meal, try the Imperial Ale sampler—five 6-ounce glasses for $9.35. The terrace has a splendid view of IllumiNations. ⊠ *United Kingdom* ▤ *AE, MC, V.*

French
★ $$$–$$$$ ✕ **Bistro de Paris.** The great secret in the France pavilion—and, indeed, in all of Epcot—is the Bistro de Paris, upstairs from Les Chefs de France. The sophisticated menu reflects the cutting edge of French cooking; representative dishes include roasted rack of venison with black-pepper sauce, pan-seared lobster served in its own bisque, and seared scallops with black truffle potato puree. Escargot, as an appetizer, is a relative bargain at $10. Save room for the Grand Marnier–flambéed crepes. Come late, ask for a window seat, and plan to linger to watch the nightly Epcot light show. Moderately priced French wines are available by the glass. ⊠ *France* ▤ *AE, MC, V.*

$$–$$$$ ✕ **Les Chefs de France.** What some consider the best restaurant at Dis-
Fodor'sChoice ney was created by three of France's most famous chefs: Paul Bocuse,
★ Gaston Lenôtre, and Roger Vergé. Classic escargots, a good starter, are
prepared in a casserole with garlic butter; you might follow up with duck
à l'orange or chicken Cordon Bleu and end with crepes *au chocolat.*
⊠ *France* ⊟ *AE, MC, V.*

German

☾ **$$** ✕ **Biergarten.** Oktoberfest runs 365 days a year here. The cheerful,
sometimes raucous crowds are what you would expect in a place with
an oompah band. Waitresses in Bavarian garb serve *breseln,* fresh, hot
German pretzels. Both the menu and the level of frivolity are the same
at lunch and dinner, with a huge assortment of classic German fare in
the one-price all-you-can-eat buffet ($19.99 for adults, $7.99 for kids
ages 3–11 at dinner). For that price, there are mountains of sauerbraten,
bratwurst, chicken schnitzel, as well as a good apple strudel and Black
Forest cake. And if you aren't feeling too Teutonic, there's a great rotisserie chicken and roast pork in unlimited amounts. Patrons pound
pitchers of all kinds of beer and wine on the long communal tables—
even when the yodelers, singers, and dancers aren't egging them on.
⊠ *Germany* ⊟ *AE, MC, V.*

Italian

★ ✕ **L'Originale Alfredo di Roma Ristorante.** Waiters skip around singing arias,
☾ **$$–$$$$** a show in itself. Their voices and the restaurant's namesake dish, made
with mountains of imported Italian butter, account for its popularity.
The classic dish—fettuccine with cream, butter, and loads of freshly grated
Parmesan cheese—was invented by Alfredo de Lelio. (Disney and de Lelio's
descendants both had a hand in creating this restaurant.) Besides the
excellent pasta, try the chef's tip of the hat to Florida—roasted grouper
with a lemon, butter, and white wine sauce, or the slow-roasted chicken
with a white grape sauce, served with polenta. Dessert offerings include
a good tiramisu and an even better cannoli. ⊠ *Italy* ⊟ *AE, MC, V.*

Japanese

$$–$$$$ ✕ **Mitsukoshi.** Three restaurants are enclosed in this complex, which overlooks tranquil gardens. Yakitori House, a gussied-up fast-food stand in
a small pavilion, is modeled after a teahouse in Kyoto's Katsura Summer Palace. At the Tempura Kiku, diners watch the chefs prepare sushi,
sashimi, and tempura. In the five Teppanyaki dining rooms, chefs fre-
netically chop vegetables, meat, and fish and stir-fry them at the grills
set into the communal tables. The lounge offers one of Epcot's great bargains, the 12-piece, deluxe sushi platter for $21.25—a great price for
that much sushi anywhere these days. Grown-ups might also go for the
sake martini. ⊠ *Japan* ⊟ *AE, MC, V.*

Mexican

$$–$$$ ✕ **San Angel Inn.** In the dark, grottolike main dining room, a deep pur-
ple, dimly lit mural of a night scene in Central Mexico seems to envelop
the diners. San Angel is a popular respite for the weary, especially when
the humidity outside makes Central Florida feel like equatorial Africa.
At dinner, guitar and marimba music fills the air. Start with the *queso*

fundido (melted cheese and Mexican chorizo sausage served with soft tortillas) and then try the authentic *mole poblano* (chicken simmered in a rich sauce of chiles, green tomatoes, ground tortillas, cocoa, cumin, and 11 other spices). Another standout is the *puntas de filete* (tender beef tips sautéed with onions and chile poblano strips), served with rice and refried beans. The traditional flan dessert has a special spin—a piña colada sauce and a fresh strawberry on top. ⊠ *Mexico* ⊟ *AE, MC, V.*

Moroccan

$$–$$$ ✕ **Marrakesh.** Chef Abrache Lahcen of Morocco presents the best cooking of his homeland in this ornate eatery. Start with harira soup, flavored with tomatoes, lentils, and lamb. Also try the couscous, the national dish of Morocco, which is rolled semolina steamed and served with seasonal vegetables. Another good choice is the Mediterranean seafood platter with shrimp ragout, broiled salmon, and seafood bastilla. A good way to try a bit of everything is the Marrakesh Feast ($27.75 per person), which includes chicken bastilla and beef *brewat* (minced beef in a layered pastry dusted with cinnamon and powered sugar), plus vegetable couscous and assorted Moroccan pastries. ⊠ *Morocco* ⊟ *AE, MC, V.*

Scandinavian

$$
Fodor'sChoice
★ ✕ **Restaurant Akershus.** The Norwegian buffet at this restaurant is as extensive as you'll find on this side of the Atlantic. Appetizers usually include herring and cold seafood, including gravlax (cured salmon served with mustard sauce) or *fiskepudding* (a seafood mousse with herb dressing). Next, pick up cold salads and meats, and on your last foray, fill up on hot lamb, veal, or venison. Try some grilled salmon, venison stew, or a trio of grilled sausages. The à la carte desserts include raspberry tarts, bread pudding, and chocolate mousse with strawberry sauce. ⊠ *Norway* ⊟ *AE, MC, V.*

Seafood

⟳ $$–$$$$ ✕ **Coral Reef Restaurant.** Part of the attraction here is the view of the giant Living Seas aquarium: the three-tiered seating area gives every diner a good view. Edible attractions include grilled basil-stuffed salmon, grilled Ahi tuna, and Dublin mussels, cockles, and clams steamed in Harp beer broth. A great appetizer: crab fritters with spicy marinara. Finish with tiramisu in Kahlua and espresso with raspberry sauce. ⊠ *The Living Seas* ⊟ *AE, MC, V.*

Elsewhere in Walt Disney World Resort

African

$$–$$$ ✕ **Jiko.** The specialty here is African-style cooking, such as steamed golden bass with spicy Chaka-Laka sauce. The menu changes periodically but typically includes such entrées as chermoula roasted chicken with mashed potatoes, and pomegranate-glazed quails stuffed with saffron basmati rice. Try one of the flatbreads ($7–$9.50), with an optional ($7.75) trio of African dips that will take your palate to the wild continent. For dessert try a non-African treat, baklava. Jiko also reportedly has one of the most extensive collections of South African wines in the country. ⊠ *Disney's Animal Kingdom Lodge* ☎ *407/939–3463* ⚠ *Reservations essential* ▭ *AE, D, MC, V.*

☕ **$–$$$** ✕ **Boma.** Boma takes Western-style ingredients and prepares them with an African twist. The dozen or so walk-up cooking stations have such entrées as spit-fired roast pork, durban-spiced roasted chicken, malabu pepper steak and banana leaf–wrapped seafood (sea bass or salmon). Zebra bones dessert is chocolate mousse covered with white chocolate and striped with dark chocolate. Picky kids have their own chicken-tender, macaroni and cheese, and spaghetti station. All meals are prix fixe ($24 for adults, $10 for children 3–11). The South African wine list is outstanding. Priority seating reservations are essential if you are not a guest at the hotel. ⊠ *Disney's Animal Kingdom Lodge* ☎ *407/939–3463* ⚠ *Reservations essential* ▭ *AE, D, DC, MC, V* ☾ *No lunch.*

American/Casual

¢–$$ ✕ **ESPN Sports Club.** Not only can you watch sports on big-screen TV here, but you can periodically see ESPN programs being taped in the club itself and be part of the audience of sports radio talk shows. Food ranges from an outstanding half-pound burger to grilled chicken and shrimp in penne pasta. For starters, try the macho nachos—tortilla chips piled high with spicy ground beef, shredded cheddar cheese, pico de gallo, sour cream, and sliced jalapeños. Finish with apple brown Betty, made with fresh apples and cinnamon baked with granola streusel topping. This place is open until 2 AM on Friday and Saturday. ⊠ *Disney's BoardWalk* ☎ *407/939–5100* ▭ *AE, MC, V.*

★ ☕ ¢–$$ ✕ **Rainforest Café.** People start queuing up half an hour before the 10:30 AM opening of this 30,000-square-foot jungle fantasy in Downtown Disney Marketplace, drawn as much by the gimmicks (man-made rainstorms, volcano eruptions) as the menu. But the food is nevertheless worthwhile. Top choices include Eyes of the Ocelot, a nice meat loaf topped with sautéed mushrooms; and Mojo Bones, tender ribs with barbecue sauce. Best dessert: Tortoise pie—actually chocolate espresso ice cream and Oreo cookies. Breakfast is served only at the Animal Kingdom location, beginning at 7:30. ⊠ *Downtown Disney Marketplace or Disney's Animal Kingdom* ☎ *407/827–8500 D.D.M., 407/938–9100 D.A.K., 407/939–3463 D.A.K.* ▭ *AE, D, DC, MC, V.*

Cajun/Creole

¢–$$$ ✕ **House of Blues.** From the outside, House of Blues resembles an old factory; the inside looks like an old church, complete with angelic frescoes. In any case, the Southern cooking is truly righteous. Best bets are smoked baby back ribs (worth the $20 price tag), cajun meat loaf, and Louisiana crawfish and shrimp étouffée, as well as the Elwood sandwich—blackened chicken with chili-garlic mayonnaise and sour cream. For dessert, try the white-chocolate banana-bread pudding with crème anglaise. The place gets noisy when the live music plays (11 PM–2 AM); lunches can be almost serene. Sunday gospel brunch ($30 adults, $15 children 4–12) is a feast worth its price tag. ⊠ *Downtown Disney West Side* ☎ *407/934–2583* ▭ *AE, D, MC, V.*

Contemporary

$$$$ ✗ **Victoria and Albert's.** At this Disney fantasy, the servers work in man-
Fodor'sChoice woman pairs, reciting specials in tandem. It's one of the plushest fine-
★ dining experiences in Florida: a regal meal in a lavish, Victorian-style
room. The seven-course, prix-fixe menu ($95; wine is an additional $50)
changes daily. Appetizer choices might include veal sweetbreads or ar-
tichokes in a mushroom-based sauce; entrées may be grilled prime filet
over cipollini onion risotto or veal tenderloin with cauliflower potato
puree. There are two seatings, at 5:45 and 9. In July and August, there's
usually just one seating—at 6:30. The chef's table dinner event is
$115–$162 (with wine pairing) per person. ⊠ *Grand Floridian* ☎ 407/
939–3463 ⚱ *Reservations essential* 🏛 *Jacket required* ⊟ *AE, MC, V*
⊘ *No lunch.*

$$$–$$$$ ✗ **Cítricos.** Although the name implies that you might be eating lots of
local citrus-flavored specialties, you won't find them here, aside from
drinks like a Citropolitan martini, infused with lemon and lime liqueur,
and an orange chocolate mousse for dessert. Standout entrées include
grilled pork tenderloin with celery root mash, baby carrots, and red wine
sauce; and roasted free range chicken with vegetable quinoa and tomato-
cilantro sauce. The wine list, one of Disney's most extensive, includes
vintages from around the world. Many are available by the glass.
⊠ *Grand Floridian* ☎ *407/939–3463* ⊟ *AE, MC, V.*

★ **$$–$$$$** ✗ **California Grill.** The view of the surrounding Disney parks from this
rooftop restaurant is as stunning as the food, and you can watch the
nightly Magic Kingdom fireworks from the patio. Start with the brick-
oven flatbread with grilled duck sausage or the *unagi* (eel) sushi. Try
the oak-fired beef filet with three-cheese potato gratin and tamarind barbecue sauce. Good dessert choices include orange crepes with Grand
Marnier custard, raspberries, and blackberry coulis, and the trio of
butterscotch, orange, and vanilla crème brûlée. ⊠ *Contemporary Resort* ☎ *407/939–3463* ⊟ *AE, MC, V.*

☾ **$$–$$$$** ✗ **Wolfgang Puck Café.** Within this single restaurant are the informal Puck
Fodor'sChoice Express, a café (with sushi bar), and a formal upstairs dining room. Must-
★ tries at Express include the pizzas, with toppings such as Thai chicken
with mozzarella and Granny Smith apples. The café has pastas with sauces
sublimely laced with chunks of lobster, salmon, or chicken. The café and
dining room usually offer a fresh ravioli (try the roasted pumpkin ravi-
oli with port wine glaze). If available, the hoisin barbecue ribs are wor-
thy either as a starter or main course. There's a good kids' menu, too.
Service is attentive, friendly, and professional. Special five-course prix-
fixe dinners upstairs ($100 with wine, $65 without) require 24-hours no-
tice. ⊠ *Downtown Disney West Side* ☎ *407/938–9653* ⊟ *AE, MC, V.*

$$$ ✗ **Artist Point.** If you're not a guest at the Wilderness Lodge, a meal here
Fodor'sChoice is worth it just to see the giant totem poles and huge rock fireplace in
★ the lobby. The specialty is cedar-plank salmon served with potato puree
and roasted fennel and truffle butter (worth its $28 price tag), and there
are always some unusual offerings on the menu, like grilled buffalo sir-
loin with sweet potato–hazelnut gratin and sweet onion jam. For dessert,
try the wild berry cobbler or flourless chocolate whiskey cake with
pecans and raspberry sorbet. There's a good northwestern U.S. wine list,

and wine pairings for the meal cost $18 to $23 per person. ✉ *Wilderness Lodge* ☎ *407/939–3463* ♨ *Reservations essential* 🖃 *AE, MC, V.*

Continental

$$$$ ✕ **Arthur's 27.** The haute cuisine here comes with a magnificent view from the 27th floor of the Wyndham Palace Resort, overlooking all of Disney World. The menu changes often, but typical dishes include appetizers such as sugar-cane–seared pork tenderloin, and entrées such as the consistently well-prepared truffle-stuffed veal chop. There are also more exotic choices, such as buffalo medallions or roasted capon. The best dessert is the stellar Grand Marnier soufflé. There are also prix-fixe options: $68 for five courses, $62 for four. ✉ *Wyndham Palace Resort & Spa, 1900 Buena Vista Dr., I–4 Exit 68, Lake Buena Vista* ☎ *407/827–3450* ♨ *Reservations essential* 🖃 *AE, D, DC, MC, V.*

Cuban

$$–$$$ ✕ **Bongos Cuban Café.** Singer Gloria Estefan's Cuban eatery is inside a two-story building shaped like a pineapple. Hot-pressed Cuban sandwiches, black bean soup, deep-fried plantain chips, and beans and rice are luncheon mainstays. One of the best entrées is *La Habana*: lobster, shrimp, scallops, calamari, clams, and mussels in a piquant creole sauce. Other worthwhile offerings include *masitas de puerco* (pork chunks served with grilled onions) and *enchilada de camarones* (shrimp in a creole sauce). There's live Latin music on Friday and Saturday. ✉ *Downtown Disney West Side* ☎ *407/828–0999* ♨ *Reservations not accepted* 🖃 *AE, D, DC, MC, V.*

Italian

$$$–$$$$ ✕ **Portobello Yacht Club.** The northern-Italian cuisine here is uniformly good. *Spaghettini alla portobello* (with scallops, clams, and Alaskan king crab) is outstanding; other fine dishes include charcoal-grilled rack of lamb served with creamy risotto cake and rigatoni *alla Calabrese,* with sausage, mushrooms, tomatoes, and black olives. There's always a fresh-catch special, as well as tasty wood-oven pizza. ✉ *Pleasure Island* ☎ *407/934–8888* 🖃 *AE, MC, V.*

Mediterranean

☼ **$$–$$$** ✕ **Spoodles.** The international tapas-style menu here draws on the best
Fodor'sChoice foods of the Mediterranean, from tuna with sun-dried tomato couscous
★ to Italian fettuccine with rich Parmesan cream sauce. Oak-fired flatbreads with such toppings as roasted peppers make stellar appetizers. For an unusual entrée, try Spanish peppers stuffed with roasted vegetables and chick peas, or pilaf with almonds, topped with manchego cheese. For dessert try the cheesecake with banana slices and hazelnut filo, or go straight for the dessert tower that lets you taste everything on the dessert cart. The children's dinner menu includes fried chicken fingers, burgers, and hot dogs. There's also a walk-up pizza window, in case you prefer to stroll the boardwalk and snack. ✉ *Disney's BoardWalk* ☎ *407/ 939–3463* 🖃 *AE, MC, V.*

Seafood

$$$–$$$$ ✕ **Fulton's Crab House.** Set in a faux riverboat docked in a lagoon between Pleasure Island and the Marketplace, this fish house offers fancy, if expensive, dining. The signature seafood is flown in daily. Dungeness crab from the Atlantic banks, Alaskan king crab, Florida stone crab: it's all fresh. Start with crab and lobster bisque, then try one of the many combination entrées, like the gulf shrimp and dungeness crab cake platter. Sublime cappuccino ice cream cake is $13, but one order is easily enough for two. ⊠ *Downtown Disney MarketPl.* ☎ *407/934–2628* ▤ *AE, MC, V.*

$$–$$$ ✕**Flying Fish.** One of Disney's better restaurants, this fish house's best dishes include potato-wrapped red snapper, and pork chop with blue-cheese potato gratin. "Peeky toe" crab cakes with ancho-chili rémoulade is an appetizer that never leaves the frequently changing menu—try it and you will see why. Save room for the banana napoleon with crispy phyllo dough, vanilla crème brûlée, and warm caramel sauce. ⊠ *Disney's BoardWalk* ☎ *407/939–2359* ▤ *AE, MC, V.*

$–$$$ ✕**Landry's Seafood House.** In a fake warehouse building—popular architecture in Central Florida—this branch of a nationwide chain delivers good seafood at reasonable prices. The food is first-rate, especially cajun dishes like fresh-caught fish Pontchartrain, broiled fish with slightly spicy seasoning and a creamy white-wine sauce that's topped with a lump of crabmeat. For starters try seafood gumbo or fried calamari. Combination platters abound, including the $15 seafood platter, which lets you sample crab fingers, fried oysters, shrimp and catfish fillet. ⊠ *8800 Vineland Ave., Rte. 535, Lake Buena Vista* ☎ *407/827–6466* ▤ *AE, D, DC, MC, V.*

Steak

$$$–$$$$ ✕**Shula's Steak House.** The hardwood floors, dark-wood paneling, and pictures of former Miami Dolphins coach Don Shula make this restaurant resemble an annex of the NFL Hall of Fame. Among the best selections are the porterhouse and prime rib. Finish the 48-ounce porterhouse and you get a football with your picture on it, but it's not an easy task to eat three pounds of red meat at one sitting, unless you're a polar bear. The least expensive steak, the 20-ounce Kansas City strip, is $31, but worth it if you like aged beef. If you're not a carnivore, go for Norwegian salmon, Florida snapper, or a huge (up to 4 pounds) Maine lobster. Save room for chocolate soufflé, a relative bargain at $13 for a serving for two. Note that there's a no-kids policy here. ⊠ *Walt Disney World Dolphin* ☎ *407/934–1362* ▤ *AE, D, DC, MC, V* ⊗ *No lunch.*

$$–$$$$ ✕**Yachtsman Steakhouse.** Aged beef, the attraction at this steak house in the ultrapolished Yacht and Beach Club, can be seen mellowing in the glassed-in butcher shop near the entryway. Slow-roasted prime rib is superb, as is roasted Chilean sea bass. The tasty surf and turf is an 8-ounce filet mignon and a 6-ounce lobster tail. For dessert, try the tower of chocolate, a chocolate layer cake with wine-marinated cherries. ⊠ *Yacht and Beach Club* ☎ *407/939–3463* ▤ *AE, MC, V* ⊗ *No lunch.*

☼ $–$$$ ✕**Concourse Steak House.** If you've always liked that trademark monorail that runs from the Magic Kingdom into the Contemporary Resort, you might want to have a meal here, set as it is one story below the train (the tracks run above). The place isn't as noisy as you'd expect it to be. Beef selections include a well-prepared Kansas City strip and a succulent prime rib. Among other entrées are herb-crusted salmon and a vegetarian selection, penne pasta with basil pesto, to which you can add shrimp, chicken, or sirloin steak. For dessert, try the New York cheesecake and Grand Marnier mousse combo, a relative bargain at $6. ⊠ *Contemporary Resort* ☎ 407/939–3463 ☐ *AE, MC, V.*

Universal's CityWalk

Take I–4 Exit 74B if you're heading westbound, 75A if eastbound.

American/Casual

★ $$$–$$$$ ✕ **Emeril's.** The popular eatery is a culinary shrine to celebrity chef Emeril Lagasse, who occasionally appears here. The menu changes frequently, but you can always count on New Orleans treats like andouille sausage, shrimp, and red beans appearing in some form or fashion. Entrées may include chili-glazed chicken with black bean avocado tart and roasted quail with andouille-cornbread stuffing. Wood-baked pizza, topped with exotic mushrooms, is stellar. Save room for Emeril's ice cream parfait, which has banana daiquiri ice cream topped with hot fudge and caramel sauce, walnuts, and a double-chocolate fudge cookie. ⊠ *6000 Universal Blvd., at Universal Orlando's CityWalk* ☎ 407/224–2424 ⌕ *Reservations essential* ☐ *AE, D, MC, V.*

¢–$$ ✕ **Hard Rock Cafe Orlando.** Built to resemble Rome's Colosseum, this 800-seat restaurant is the largest of the 100-odd Hard Rocks in the world, but getting a seat at lunch can still require a long wait. The music is always loud and the walls are filled with rock memorabilia. The most popular menu item is still the burger, with baby-back ribs and the homemade-style meat loaf both strong contenders. If you don't eat red meat, then try the roasted vegetable pasta with pesto. The best dessert is the $5 chocolate chip cookie (it's big), which is covered with ice cream. ⊠ *6000 Universal Blvd., at Universal Orlando's CityWalk* ☎ 407/224–3663 or 407/351–7625 ⌕ *Reservations not accepted* ☐ *AE, D, DC, MC, V.*

¢–$$ ✕ **Jimmy Buffett's Margaritaville.** Parrot-heads can probably name the top two menu items before they even walk in the door. You've got your cheeseburger, featured in the song "Cheeseburger in Paradise," and, of course, your Ultimate Margarita. The rest of the menu is an eclectic mix of quesadillas, chowder, crab cakes, jambalaya, jerk salmon, and a pretty decent steak. Worthy dessert choices include Last Mango in Paradise cheesecake, key lime pie, and a tasty chocolate banana bread pudding. ⊠ *6000 Universal Blvd., at Universal Orlando's CityWalk* ☎ 407/224–2155 ☐ *AE, D, MC, V.*

¢–$$ ✕ **NASCAR Café Orlando.** If you're a racing fanatic, this is your place. If the memorabilia on the walls is not enough for you, a couple of actual race cars hang from the ceiling. The food is decent: highlights include a good chicken mushroom soup (with grilled chicken and shiitake mushrooms), fried chicken over smashed potatoes, smoky mountain barbecue ribs, and the Thunder Road burger, with melted pimento cheese and sautéed onions. Aside from white-chocolate cheesecake, desserts are largely forgettable. ⊠ *6000 Universal Blvd., at Universal Orlando's CityWalk* ☎ 407/224–3663 ☐ *AE, D, MC, V.*

¢–$$ ✕**NBA City.** The NBA memorabilia and video games are great, but the food is actually the real draw here. Best choices include appetizers of sweet and spicy smoked wings and pecan chicken tenders with orange marmalade sauce. For an entrée, try grilled lemon chicken served with garlic risotto and roasted poblano peppers and artichokes. The brick-oven pizzas include an unusual BLT variety. Finish with Vermont maple syrup pecan tart with fresh cream. The big-screen TVs, which naturally broadcast nonstop basketball action, probably won't surprise you, but the relatively quiet bar upstairs, with elegant blond-wood furniture, probably will. ⊠ *6000 Universal Blvd., at Universal Orlando's CityWalk* ☎ *407/363–5919* ⊟ *AE, D, MC, V.*

¢–$ ✕**Pat O'Brien's Orlando.** Head to this clone of the famous New Orleans bar to sip its famous (and super-sweet, and fairly strong) drink, the hurricane, and munch on bayou-inspired snacks like crawfish nachos, Cajun shrimp, and alligator bites. Try the po' boys, French-bread sandwiches filled with tangy shrimp and sausage, or the *muffuletta* sandwiches, made with salami, ham, provolone, and olives. Pat's also has a good jambalaya, the spicy stew of sausage and chicken. There's live music nightly ($2 cover charge). ⊠ *6000 Universal Blvd., at Universal Orlando's CityWalk* ☎ *407/224–9255* ⊟ *AE, D, MC, V.*

Universal Islands of Adventure

Take I–4 Exit 74B if you're heading westbound, 75A if eastbound.

American/Casual

☾ ¢ ✕**Green Eggs and Ham Cafe.** This Dr. Seuss–inspired spot is the only place in Orlando where the eggs are intentionally green. They're served (tinted with food coloring) in an egg-and-ham sandwich, the most popular item at this walk-up, outdoor eatery, which looks like a hallucinatory McDonald's. There's also a fairly tasty "green" garden salad, as well as some other conventional fare, including a normal cheeseburger, fries, and "frings," a type of onion ring. ⊠ *6000 Universal Blvd., Seuss Landing section at Universal Studios Islands of Adventure* ☎ *407/224–9255* ⊟ *AE, D, MC, V.*

American/Contemporary

☾ $–$$ ✕**Confisco Grille.** You could walk right past this Mediterranean eatery, but if you want a good meal and sit-down service, don't pass by too quickly. The menu changes often, but typical entrées include pan-seared pork medallions with roasted garlic and red peppers, baked cod with spinach and mashed potatoes, and Thai noodles with chicken, shrimp, tofu, and bean sprouts. Save room for the chocolate banana-bread pudding or crème brûlée. You can catch the Dr. Seuss characters at breakfast. ⊠ *6000 Universal Blvd., Port of Entry section at Universal Studios Islands of Adventure* ☎ *407/224–9255* ⊟ *AE, D, MC, V* ☉ *No lunch.*

$–$$ ✕**Mythos.** The name sounds Greek, but the dishes are eclectic. The menu, which changes frequently, usually includes standouts like meat loaf, roast pork tenderloin, and assorted wood-fired pizzas. Among the creative desserts is a fine pumpkin cheesecake. But the building itself is enough to grab your attention. It looks like a giant rock formation from the outside and a huge cave (albeit one with plush upholstered seating) from the inside. Mythos also has a waterfront view of the big lagoon in the center of the theme park. ⊠ *6000 Universal Blvd., Lost Continent at Universal Studios Islands of Adventure* ☎ *407/224–9255* ⊟ *AE, D, MC, V.*

Portofino Bay Hotel

Italian

$$$–$$$$ ✕ **Bice.** Gone is Delfino Riviera, the hotel's former top-billed restaurant, replaced with the somewhat trendier and pricier Bice (pronounced *beach-ay,* which is an Italian nickname for Beatrice, as in Beatrice Ruggeri, who founded the original, Milan location of this family restaurant in 1926). But the word "family" does not carry the connotation "mom and pop" at Bice, with white-starched tablecloths and locations in top-dollar hotels and malls around the United States. The restaurant retains its frescoed ceilings and marble floors, and of course, the great views of the resort's man-made bay just outside the picture windows. This restaurant is expensive, but worthy are the one-pound veal chop with polenta and Parmesan and the veal Milanese. Desserts, ranging from the basic tiramisu to the chocolate soufflé cake with vanilla ice cream and honey, are standouts. ⊠ *5601 Universal Blvd., Universal Orlando* ☎ *407/503–1415* ⊕ *www.portofinobay.com* ⊟ *AE, D, DC, MC, V* ☉ *No lunch.*

$$–$$$ ✕ **Mama Della's.** The premise here is that Mama Della is a middle-aged Italian housewife who has opened up her home as a restaurant. "Mama" is always on hand (there are several of them, working in shifts), strolling among the tables and making small talk. The food, served family style, is excellent. The menu has Italian traditions like chicken cacciatore and spaghetti with sirloin meatballs or Bolognese sauce, and all the pastas are made in-house. The quality of the food experience starts with hot garlic bread and continues through the dessert course; tiramisu and Italian chocolate torte both make sure bets. ⊠ *5601 Universal Blvd.* ☎ *407/503–1000* ⊟ *AE, D, DC, MC, V* ☉ *Closed Mon. No lunch.*

Hard Rock Hotel

Steak

$$–$$$$ ✕ **The Palm.** With its dark-wood interior and hundreds of framed celebrity caricatures, this restaurant resembles its famed New York City namesake. Steaks are the reason to dine here, but most are available only at dinner. The steak filet cooked on a hot stone is a specialty, as is Double Steak, a 36-ounce New York strip for two (or one ambitious carnivore). There are several veal dishes on the menu, along with a 3-pound Maine lobster, and linguine with red clam sauce. ⊠ *1000 Universal Studios Plaza* ☎ *407/503–7256* ⊟ *AE, D, DC, MC, V* ☉ *No lunch weekends.*

International Drive, Orlando

Take I–4 Exit 72 or 74A.

American/Casual

$–$$$ ✕ **B-Line Diner.** As you might expect from its hotel location, this slick, 1950s-style diner with red vinyl counter seats is not exactly cheap, but the salads, sandwiches, and griddle foods are tops. The greatest combo ever, a thick, juicy burger served with fries and a wonderful milk shake, is done beautifully. You can get pork chops and fried snapper as well. Desserts include hazelnut orange cake and banana splits. It's open 24 hours. ⊠ *Peabody Orlando, 9801 International Dr., International Drive Area* ☎ *407/352–4000* ☐ *AE, D, DC, MC, V.*

$–$$$ ✗ **Dan Marino's Town Tavern.** Part of a Florida sports bar chain begun by the former Miami Dolphins quarterback, the Tavern mixes burgers and steaks with some sophisticated surprises, including seared tuna and tips of filet mignon in a mushroom merlot sauce served over mashed potatoes. ⊠ *Pointe*Orlando, 9101 International Dr., International Drive Area* ☎ *407/363–1013* ☐ *AE, MC.*

Caribbean

🍴 $–$$$ ✗ **Bahama Breeze.** Even though the lineage is corporate, the menu here is creative and tasty. The casual fun and the Caribbean cooking draw a crowd, so be prepared for a wait. Meanwhile, you can sip piña coladas and other West Indian delights on a big wooden porch. The food is worth the wait. Start with fried coconut prawns marinated in coco lopez. For an entrée, try West Indies ribs with guava glaze, and finish with home-made key lime pie. A large outdoor dining area opens at 4 PM for drinks, appetizers, and desserts only. ⊠ *8849 International Dr., International Drive Area* ☎ *407/248–2499* ⊠ *8735 Vineland Ave., I–4 Exit 68, International Drive Area* ☎ *407/938–9010* ⌾ *Reservations not accepted* ☐ *AE, D, DC, MC.*

Chinese

$–$$$$ ✗ **Ming Court.** A walled courtyard and serene pond make you forget you're on International Drive. The extensive menu includes simple chicken Szechuan, jumbo shrimp with honey-glazed walnuts, and aged filet mignon grilled in spicy Szechuan sauce. Flourless chocolate cake, certainly not Asian, has been a popular standard for years. ⊠ *9188 International Dr., International Drive Area* ☎ *407/351–9988* ☐ *AE, D, DC, MC, V.*

Contemporary

$$–$$$ ✗ **Café Tu Tu Tango.** The food here is served tapas-style—everything is appetizer-size. The eclectic menu is fitting for a restaurant on International Drive. If you want a compendium of cuisines at one go, try black bean soup with cilantro sour cream, grilled baby lamb chops with curried apple chutney, coconut curry mussels, and Barcelona stir fry. The restaurant is supposedly a crazy artist's loft; artists paint at easels while diners sip drinks like Matisse Margaritas. Although nothing costs more than $8, it's not hard to spend $50 for lunch for two. ⊠ *8625 International Dr., International Drive Area* ☎ *407/248–2222* ⌾ *Reservations not accepted* ☐ *AE, D, DC, MC, V.*

Italian

$$–$$$ ✗ **Bergamo's.** If you're wondering what became of your waiter, don't fret; he or she might be the one belting out that Broadway or opera standard. In this twist on dinner theater, you'll get song, food, and wine at

once. The large and elegant dining space, with plush red carpeting, patterned wallpaper, and wood trim, has a drawing-room feel underscored by the piano player in the center of the room. Management does not rely on the entertainment alone to fill seats: the food is very worthwhile. Try the linguine *pescatore* (fisherman's linguine), with lobster, shrimp, crab meat and mussels; or the classic osso buco with risotto Milanese. And while mango-basil cheesecake sounds a tad strange, most who try it like it. Bergamo's is in the Mercado Shopping Village; keep an eye out for the restaurant's name lit in red, especially if you're arriving after dark. ⊠ *8445 International Dr., I–4 Exit 74A, International Drive Area* ☏ *407/352–3805* ▤ *AE, D, DC, MC, V* ✆ *No lunch.*

Seafood

$$$–$$$$ ✕ **Atlantis.** Given the expansive modern lobby with glass elevators that houses this spot, you'll feel like you've taken a strange (though fortuitous) turn into another era: a harpist plays in the dining room, which is outfitted with frescoes, dark-wood paneling, and plush green carpet. Waiters bring forth entrées on silver-domed trays. Go for a lobster dish or a grilled fish, such as yellowfin tuna or salmon. There are also worthy red-meat dishes, including roast loin of lamb, and the obligatory surf-and-turf combo—in this case sirloin served with lobster and pesto sauce. Desserts include some fine soufflés, which must be ordered 30 minutes in advance. ⊠ *Renaissance Orlando Resort, 6677 Sea Harbor Dr., International Drive Area* ☏ *407/351–5555* ▤ *AE, MC, V* ✆ *No lunch.*

Steak

★ $$–$$$$ ✕ **Vito's Chop House.** There's a reason they keep the blinds closed most of the time: it's for the wines' sake. The dining room doubles as the cellar, with hundreds of bottles stacked in every nook and cranny. The steaks and the wood-grilled pork chops are superb. A "get it while they last" entrée is the popular wood-roasted chicken cacciatore, and a second house favorite is fried lobster tails on linguine with marinara sauce. Worthwhile desserts include grilled peach di Vito, an excellent key lime pie, and Italian wedding cake. ⊠ *8633 International Dr., International Drive Area* ☏ *407/354–2467* ⚖ *Reservations essential* ▤ *AE, D, DC, MC, V* ✆ *No lunch.*

Thai

$–$$ ✕ **Siam Orchid.** One of Orlando's more elegant Asian restaurants is in a gorgeous structure a bit off International Drive. Waitresses, who wear costumes from Thailand, serve authentic fare such as Siam wings—chicken wings stuffed to look like drumsticks—and *pla rad prikm,* a whole, deep-fried fish served with a sauce flavored with red chilies, bell peppers, and garlic. Pad thai can be ordered with beef, pork, seafood, or just vegetables. If you like your food spicy, remember to say "Thai hot"—but be sure you mean it. ⊠ *7575 Universal Blvd., International Drive Area* ☏ *407/ 351–0821* ▤ *AE, DC, MC, V.*

Downtown Orlando

Take I–4 Exit 83B if you're heading westbound, Exit 83A if eastbound, unless otherwise noted.

Contemporary

★ $$$–$$$$ ✕ **Manuel's on the 28th.** Restaurants with great views don't always have much more than that to offer, but this lofty spot on the 28th floor is also a culinary landmark. The menu changes regularly, but there's always a representative sampling of fish, Angus beef, pork, and duck. Dinner offerings may include sea scallops covered in macadamia nuts, Black Angus filet mignon, and even wild boar loin marinated in coconut milk. Try the smoked confit of duck with Boursin cheese appetizer. For dessert, try baked apples wrapped in pastry and topped with caramel sauce. ⊠ *Bank of America Bldg., 390 N. Orange Ave., Suite 2800, Downtown Orlando* ☎ *407/246–6580* ⊟ *AE, D, DC, MC, V* ☉ *Closed Sun. and Mon. No lunch.*

$$–$$$$ ✕ **The Boheme Restaurant.** The company that operates Manuel's on the 28th also runs the Boheme. No panorama here, but the food is every bit as adventurous. The menu changes frequently. As a prelude, try escargot nouvelle with mushrooms stuffed into a puffed pastry. Entrées include such dishes as roasted Chilean sea bass with pecorino crust and lobster sauce, and corn-fed Angus beef, which is always on the menu. At breakfast, French toast with triple sec–strawberry glaze is an excellent way to awaken your palate. Sunday brunch is worthwhile: you can get prime rib and sushi as well as omelets. ⊠ *Westin Grand Bohemian, 325 S. Orange Ave., Downtown Orlando* ☎ *407/313–9000* ⌖ *Reservations essential* ⊟ *AE, D, DC, MC, V.*

$–$$$ ✕ **Harvey's Bistro.** A loyal business crowd peoples this clubby café at lunch. It also attracts a nighttime following by staying open until 11 on weekends. Smoked duck and spinach pizza is a top starter. Pasta favorites include chicken Stroganoff, duck and shrimp in Asian peanut sauce on linguine, and salmon with lobster Alfredo sauce. Harvey's has tasty pot roast, a pan-seared tenderloin, and meat loaf baked in parchment. ⊠ *Bank of America Bldg., 390 N. Orange Ave., Downtown Orlando* ☎ *407/246–6560* ⊟ *AE, D, DC, MC, V* ☉ *Closed Sun. No lunch Sat.*

¢–$ ✕ **The Globe.** A block from busy Orange Avenue, on a brick street with almost no traffic, The Globe offers tables with big umbrellas. Standouts on the eclectic menu include the crab cake sandwich, tempura Monte Cristo, and Gung Ho noodle bowl, with roast pork, chicken and shrimp sautéed with Oriental veggies. Good desserts include triple chocolate cake and the bread pudding with rum butter sauce. ⊠ *27 Wall Street Plaza, Downtown Orlando* ☎ *407/849–9904* ⊟ *AE, D, DC, MC, V.*

¢ ✕ **JW's Southern Fixins.** The red-and-white plastic tablecloths here appear to have belonged to the last three restaurants that occupied this little building, but if you believe in the nobility of simple cuisine well prepared, this place will look like a palace to you. The best bet is slow-roasted pork ribs, although the meat loaf is also a competitor for the top spot. There is no set menu—it's written daily on a blackboard—but you can count on the availability of collard greens and black-eyed peas. The best dessert is the homemade-tasting pumpkin pie. No alcoholic beverages are permitted here. ✉ *900 W. Colonial Dr., Central Orlando* ☎ *407/236–9411* ☰ *AE, D, DC, MC, V* ✹ *Closed Sun.*

Elsewhere in Orlando

American/Casual

★ ¢–$$ ✕ **White Wolf Café.** A perfect fit for Orlando's small but vibrant antiques-and-art-gallery district, this urbane bistro offers a fine menu and a good sidewalk café area. A great appetizer is the *lavosh* (Mediterranean-style cracker bread), topped with artichoke hearts, sun-dried tomatoes, and mozzarella. Entrées usually include a mahimahi fillet served with mango Thai chili sauce and chicken breast with mozzarella baked in French bread and topped with marinara. For dessert, try chocolate hazelnut torte or a chocolate-chip truffle cookie. There's live music on Friday and Saturday nights. ✉ *1829 N. Orange Ave., Central Orlando* ☎ *407/895–5590* ☰ *AE, MC, V.*

¢–$ ✕ **Seasons 52.** Every week of the year is its own season with its own special cuisine. At least that's the concept behind the restaurant name, and the company behind this restaurant knows a bit about restaurant concepts: it's Darden Restaurants, purveyors of Olive Garden, Red Lobster, Bahama Breeze, and Smokey Bones Barbecue. The idea at Seasons 52 is to serve fresh ingredients at their peak, so the menu changes often. But typical offerings (all with low calorie counts) include sesame pork chops with chilled asparagus or grilled sea scallops. "Mini indulgence" desserts, like butterscotch pudding and rocky road ice cream, are designed to keep calories in check. Although the cuisine is haute, prices are low. ✉ *7700 Sand Lake Rd.* ☎ *407/354–5212* ☰ *AE, D, DC, MC, V* ✹ *No lunch.*

Contemporary

$$–$$$$ ✕ **Chatham's Place.** In Florida, grouper is about as ubiquitous as Coca-Cola, but to discover its full potential, try the rendition here: sautéed in pecan butter and flavored with cayenne, it's one of the best dishes in Orlando. Other good entries include chicken piccata and filet mignon served with peppercorn-cognac sauce. The most popular appetizer is Maryland-style crab cakes, but the New Orleans–style shrimp brochette is also noteworthy. The chef does wonders with desserts like pecan–macadamia nut pie. Take I–4 Exit 74A. ✉ *7575 Dr. Phillips Blvd., Southwestern Orlando* ☎ *407/345–2992* ☰ *AE, D, DC, MC, V.*

$–$$$$ ✕ **HUE.** On the ground floor of a condo high-rise on the edge of Lake Eola, this place takes its name from a self-created acronym: Hip Urban Environment. The food is both good and eclectic, with offerings ranging from succulent duck tostados with black beans, jack cheese, and salsa, to crispy oysters with garlic mayo, to wood-grilled New York strip steak with red wine demi-glace. There's a large sidewalk dining area. ✉ *629 E. Central Blvd., Thornton Park* ☎ *407/849–1800* 🖷 *407/872–3348* ◇ *Reservations not accepted* ☰ *AE, D, DC, MC, V.*

Cuban

★ $–$$$ ✕ **Numero Uno.** To the followers of this long-popular Latin restaurant, the name is accurate. Downtowners have been filling the place for years. It bills itself as "the home of paella," and that's probably the best choice. If you have a good appetite and you either called to order ahead or can spare the 75-minute wait, then try the *boliche,* a tender eye round roast stuffed with spicy chorizo in a tomato-based sauce with a side order of plantains. Otherwise, you can go for traditional Cuban fare like shredded flank steak or arroz con pollo. Finish with *tres leches,* made with regular, evaporated, and sweetened condensed milk. Take I–4 Exit 81A or 81B. ⊠ *2499 S. Orange Ave., Central Orlando* ☎ *407/841– 3840* ▤ *AE, D, DC, MC, V.*

French

$$–$$$$
Fodor'sChoice
★

✕ **Le Coq au Vin.** Chef-owner Louis Perrotte is something of a culinary god in Orlando, but he doesn't let it go to his head. He operates a modest little kitchen in a small house in south Orlando. Perrotte's homey eatery is usually filled with locals who appreciate the lovely traditional French fare: braised chicken with red wine, mushrooms, and bacon; bronzed grouper with toasted pecans; and Long Island duck with green peppercorns. The menu changes seasonally, but the house-namesake dish is always available and excellent. For dessert, try Grand Marnier soufflé or the exquisite crème brûlée. ⊠ *4800 S. Orange Ave., Central Orlando* ☎ *407/851–6980* ▤ *AE, DC, MC, V* ☻ *Closed Mon.*

Hawaiian

$$–$$$

✕ **Roy's.** Chef Roy Yamaguchi has more or less perfected his own cuisine type—Hawaiian fusion, replete with tropical fruit–based sauces and imagination. The menu changes daily, but typical dishes include treats like hickory-smoked and grilled ostrich loin, and macadamia nut–crusted bass with Thai curry-peanut sauce. Frequently served desserts include macadamia-nut tart and coconut-crusted, fried cheesecake. If your tastes prefer to remain on the mainland, go for classics like wood-fired, homemade-style meat loaf and warm apple crumb pie with vanilla-bean ice cream. ⊠ *7760 W. Sand Lake Rd., I–4 Exit 74A, Sand Lake Rd. Area* ☎ *407/352–4844* ▤ *AE, D, DC, MC, V.*

Italian

$$–$$$$

✕ **Christini's.** Locals, visitors, and Disney execs gladly pay the price at Christini's, one of the city's best places for northern Italian. Owner Chris Christini is on hand nightly to make sure that everything is perfect. Try fettuccine *alla Christini* (the house-specialty fettuccine Alfredo) or veal piccata. The multicourse dinner often takes a couple of hours or more, but if you like Italian minstrels at your table, this place should please you. Take I–4 Exit 74A. ⊠ *7600 Dr. Phillips Blvd., Dr. Phillips Marketplace, Sand Lake Rd. area* ☎ *407/345–8770* ▤ *AE, D, DC, MC, V.*

★ ☪ ¢–$

✕ **Alfonso's Pizza & More.** This is a strong contender for the best pizza in Orlando (in the non–wood-fired-oven division). Since it's just across the street from a high school, things get frenzied at lunch. The hand-tossed pizza's toppings include pepperoni and pineapple. The calzones and some of the pastas, like fettuccine Alfredo, are worthy as well. There are also subs and salads for lighter fare. The secret to the superior pizza is simple: the dough and all the sauces are made from scratch daily. Take I–4 Exit 84 to the College Park neighborhood. ⊠ *3231 Edgewater Dr., College Park* ☎ *407/872–7324* ▤ *MC, V.*

Steak

$$–$$$$ ✕ **Del Frisco.** Locals like this quiet, uncomplicated steak house. Del Frisco delivers carefully prepared, corn-fed beef and attentive service. When your steak arrives, the waiter asks you to cut into it and check that it was cooked as you ordered it. The simple menu includes T-bones, porterhouses, filets mignons, Maine lobster, Alaskan crab, and lobster bisque. Bread is baked daily at the restaurant, and the bread pudding, with a Jack Daniels sauce, is worth a try. There's a piano bar next to the dining room. ✉ *729 Lee Rd., Central Orlando* ☎ *407/645–4443* ▤ *AE, D, DC, MC, V* ☉ *Closed Sun. No lunch.*

$$–$$$ ✕ **Linda's La Cantina.** As the menu says, management "cannot be responsible for steaks cooked medium-well and well done," and despite that stuffy-sounding caveat, this down-home steak house has been a favorite among locals since the Eisenhower administration. The menu is short and to the point, including about a dozen steaks and just enough ancillary items to fill up a page. Among the best cuts is La Cantina large T-bone—more beef than most can handle—for $22. With every entrée you get a heaping order of spaghetti (which isn't particularly noteworthy) or a baked potato. ✉ *4721 E. Colonial Dr., Central Orlando* ☎ *407/894–4491* ▤ *AE, D, MC, V.*

Vietnamese

★ ¢ ✕ **Little Saigon.** This local favorite represents one of the best of Orlando's ethnic restaurants. Sample the summer rolls (spring-roll filling in a soft wrapper) with peanut sauce, or excellent Vietnamese crepes, filled with shredded pork and noodles. Move on to grilled pork and egg, served atop rice noodles, or the traditional soup, filled with noodles, rice, vegetables, and your choice of chicken or seafood; ask to have extra meat in the soup if you're hungry, and be sure they bring you mint and bean sprouts to sprinkle in. Beer and wine are available. ✉ *1106 E. Colonial Dr., Central Orlando* ☎ *407/423–8539* ▤ *MC, V.*

Outlying Towns

Contemporary

¢–$$ ✕ **Dexter's.** The good wine list and imaginative menu tend to attract quite a crowd of locals. A "don't miss" entrée is chicken tortilla pie, a stack of cheese-laden puffy fried tortillas that looks like a spaceship, or try the garlic bucatini with fresh pesto (with or without chicken), or the mesquite-grilled chicken quesadilla with fire-roasted poblano peppers. The East Washington location is in gentrified Thornton Park, just east of downtown Orlando; you may be the only out-of-towner there. ✉ *558 W. New England Ave., Winter Park* ☎ *407/629–1150* ✉ *808 E. Washington St., Orlando* ☎ *407/648–2777* ⌖ *Reservations not accepted* ▤ *AE, D, DC, MC, V.*

Continental

$$$$ ✕ **Chalet Suzanne.** If you are on your way south, or are visiting Historic Bok Sanctuary, consider making time for a good meal at this family-owned country inn. Many devotees come for the traditional dinner—all lunch and dinner meals are prix-fixe affairs—or for a sophisticated breakfast of eggs Benedict or Swedish pancakes with lingonberries. The best meal,

if you are on a budget, is lunch. The house-signature chicken Suzanne (baked and carefully basted) is tender and worth the dinner price of $59, but it's just as tasty at lunch for $32. ☒ *3800 Chalet Suzanne Dr., I–4 Exit 55, Lake Wales* ☎ *863/676–6011* ▤ *AE, DC, MC, V* ✆ *Closed Mon. June–Aug.*

$$–$$$ ✕ **Chef Justin's Park Plaza Gardens.** Sitting at the sidewalk café and bar is like sitting on the main street of the quintessential American small town. But the locals know the real gem is hidden inside—an atrium with live ficus trees, a brick floor, and brick walls that give the place a Vieux Carré feel. Chef Justin Plank's menu combines the best of French and Italian cuisine with an American twist. You might have onion soup or a turkey and Brie croissant sandwich for lunch, and baked grouper or herbed pork tenderloin for dinner. Sunday brunch frequently includes live jazz. ☒ *319 Park Ave. S, Winter Park* ☎ *407/645–2475* ▤ *AE, D, DC, MC, V.*

Italian

$$–$$$$ ✕ **Antonio's La Fiamma.** The wood-burning grill and oven do more than give the place a delightful smell. They're used to turn out great grilled fish dishes, delicious pizzas, and homemade bread. Try the *capesante alla vesuviana* (scallops with a puree of cannellini beans and tomato) or the equally compelling *lombata alla verdi* (veal chop and mushrooms topped with baked goat cheese). For a quick bite, the deli-style venue downstairs has many of the same menu items. ☒ *611 S. Orlando Ave., U.S. 17–92, Maitland* ☎ *407/645–5523* ▤ *AE, MC, V* ✆ *Closed Sun.*

★ $$–$$$$ ✕ **Enzo's on the Lake.** This is one of Orlando's foodies' favorite restaurants, even though it's on a tacky stretch of highway filled with used-car lots. Enzo Perlini, the Roman charmer who owns the place, has turned a rather ordinary lakefront house into an Italian villa. It's worth the trip, about 45 minutes from WDW, to sample the antipasti. Mussels in the shell, with a broth of tomatoes, olive oil, and garlic, make a great appetizer. Fettuccine *all'aragosta e gamberi* (homemade fettuccine with lobster and shrimp in a saffron salsa) is very popular. Also try the grilled veal chop served in a shiitake-and-champignon-mushroom white wine sauce. ☒ *1130 S. U.S. 17–92, Longwood* ☎ *407/834–9872* ▤ *AE, DC, MC, V* ✆ *Closed Sun.*

Seafood

$$–$$$$ ✕ **Black Fin.** The interior feels like an old mansion, even though Black Fin is inside a modern shopping complex. Representative offerings at this fish-focused restaurant include shrimp scampi linguine, grilled striped bass with peach-mango chutney, and Parmesan-crusted Chilean sea bass with lemon butter. There are also such standards as broiled Caribbean lobster, Alaskan king crab, and a lobster and filet mignon combo. There's a large selection of fresh oyster appetizers prepared on the half shell, including Florentine, broussard, or spicy hot. Save room for the chocolate Kahlua mousse cake. ☒ *460 N. Orlando Ave., Winter Park* ☎ *407/691–4653* ▤ *AE, D, DC, MC, V.*

WHERE TO STAY

Your basic options come down to properties that are (1) owned and operated by Disney on WDW grounds, (2) not owned or operated by Disney but on Disney property, and (3) not on WDW property. There are advantages to each. If you're coming to Orlando for only a few days and are interested solely in the Magic Kingdom, Epcot, and the other Disney attractions, the resorts on Disney property—whether or not they're owned by Disney—are the most convenient. But if you plan to spend time sightseeing in and around Orlando, it makes sense to look into the alternatives. On-site hotels are generally more expensive, although there are some moderately priced establishments on Disney property. But Orlando is not huge, and even apparently distant properties are only a half hour's drive from Disney entrance gates. Some good but inexpensive hotels can also be found in Kissimmee, 10 minutes from Disney World. As a rule, the greater the distance from Walt Disney World Resort, the lower the room rates. Reservations should be made several months in advance—as much as a year in advance for the best rooms during high season. Many hotels and attractions offer discounts up to 40% from September to mid-December. Orlando lodging prices tend to be a little higher than elsewhere in Florida, but in all but the smallest motels there is little or no charge for children under 18 who share a room with an adult.

WHAT IT COSTS					
	$$$$	$$$	$$	$	¢
FOR 2 PEOPLE	over $220	$140–$220	$100–$140	$80–$100	under $80

Hotel prices are for a standard double room, excluding 6% sales tax (more in some counties) and 1%–4% tourist tax.

In WDW: Disney-Owned Properties

All on-site accommodations that are owned by Disney may be booked through the **Walt Disney World Central Reservations Office** (⌷ Box 10100, Suite 300, Lake Buena Vista 32830 ☎ 407/934–7639 ⊕ www.disneyworld.com). People with disabilities can call **WDW Special Request Reservations** (☎ 407/939–7807) to get information or book rooms at any of the on-site Disney properties.

Disney-owned accommodations are noted on the Walt Disney World Resort map.

Magic Kingdom Resort Area
Take I–4 Exit 62, 64B, or 65.

$$$$ ▣ **Contemporary Resort.** Looking like an intergalactic docking bay, this 15-story, flat-top pyramid bustles from dawn to after midnight. Upper floors of the main tower (where rooms are more expensive) offer a great view of all the day and night activities in and around the Magic Kingdom. Rooms are bright and colorful with incredible views of the evening fireworks show. Best reason to stay: location, location, location. The monorail runs through the Tower lobby so it only takes minutes to get to the Magic Kingdom and Epcot. Restaurants include the character-meal palace Chef Mickey's, the laid-back Concourse Steak House, and the top-floor and top-rated California Grill. ☎ 407/824–1000 ⤿ 407/824–3539 ⤳ *1,013 rooms, 25 suites* ⚬ *3 restaurants, snack bar, room*

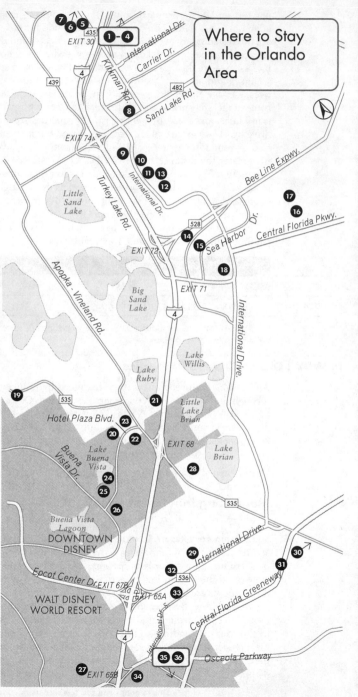

Where to Stay in the Orlando Area

service, in-room safes, some refrigerators, cable TV, in-room data ports, golf privileges, 6 tennis courts, 3 pools, wading pool, health club, hair salon, 2 hot tubs, massage, beach, boating, marina, waterskiing, basketball, volleyball, 2 lobby lounges, video game room, shops, babysitting, children's programs (ages 4–12), playground, laundry facilities, laundry service, concierge, concierge floor, high speed Internet, business services, convention center, meeting rooms, no-smoking rooms ▤ *AE, D, DC, MC, V.*

$$$$
Fodor'sChoice
★
🏨 **Grand Floridian Resort & Spa.** This Victorian-style property on the shores of the Seven Seas Lagoon has a red gabled roof, delicate gingerbread, rambling verandas, and brick chimneys. Rooms have ornate hardwood furniture and fancy-print carpeting. Add a dinner or two at Victoria and Albert's, or Cítricos, and you'll probably spend more in a weekend here than on an average mortgage payment, but you'll have the memory of the best Disney offers. The Grand Floridian is what Disney considers its flagship resort—no other has better amenities or higher rates, but you won't look out of place walking through the lobby in flip-flops and shorts. ☎ *407/824–3000* 🖷 *407/824–3186* ♨ *900 rooms, 90 suites* ♿ *5 restaurants, snack bar, room service, in-room safes, cable TV, in-room data ports, golf privileges, 2 tennis courts, 3 pools, wading pool, health club, hair salon, massage, spa, beach, boating, marina, waterskiing, croquet, shuffleboard, volleyball, 4 lounges, video game room, babysitting, children's programs (ages 4–12), playground, laundry facilities, laundry service, concierge, concierge floor, high speed internet, business services, convention center, meeting rooms, no-smoking rooms* ▤ *AE, D, DC, MC, V.*

$$$$
🏨 **Polynesian Resort.** If it weren't for the kids in Mickey Mouse caps, you might think you were in Fiji. A three-story tropical atrium fills the lobby. Orchids bloom alongside coconut palms and banana trees, and water cascades from volcanic rock fountains. A mainstay here is the evening luau (Wednesday through Sunday), in which Polynesian dancers perform before a feast that includes Hawaiian-style roast pork. Rooms sleep five, since they all have two queen-size beds and a daybed. Lagoon-view rooms—which overlook the Electrical Water Pageant—are the most peaceful and the priciest. Most rooms have a balcony or patio. ☎ *407/824–2000* 🖷 *407/824–3174* ♨ *853 rooms, 5 suites* ♿ *4 restaurants, snack bar, room service, in-room safes, cable TV, in-room data ports, golf privileges, 2 pools, wading pool, health club, hair salon, massage, beach, boating, volleyball, bar, lobby lounge, video game room, babysitting, children's programs (ages 4–12), playground, laundry facilities, laundry service, concierge, concierge floors, high speed Internet, business services, no-smoking rooms* ▤ *AE, D, DC, MC, V.*

$$$–$$$$
Fodor'sChoice
★
🏨 **Wilderness Lodge.** The architects outdid themselves with this seven-story hotel, modeled after the majestic National Park lodges of America's Great Northwest. The five-story lobby, supported by towering tree trunks, has an 82-foot-high, three-sided fireplace made of rocks from the Grand Canyon and lit by enormous tepee-shape chandeliers. Two 55-foot-tall hand-carved totem poles complete the illusion. Rooms have leather chairs, patchwork quilts, and cowboy art. Each has a balcony or a patio. The hotel's showstopper is its Fire Rock Geyser, a faux Old

Faithful, near the large pool, which begins as a hot spring in the lobby. ☎ 407/824–3200 ⌨ 407/824–3232 ☞ *728 rooms, 31 suites ♿ 3 restaurants, some room service, cable TV with movies, in-room data ports, pool, wading pool, 2 hot tubs, beach, boating, bicycles, 2 lobby lounges, video game room, babysitting, children's programs (ages 4–12), laundry facilities, laundry service, concierge, concierge floor, high speed Internet, no-smoking rooms* ▤ *AE, D, DC, MC, V.*

★ ☕ **Fort Wilderness Resort and Campground.** For a calm spot amid the theme-
¢–$$$$ park storm, go no farther than the 700 acres of scrubby pine and tiny streams known as Fort Wilderness, on Bay Lake and about a mile from the Wilderness Lodge. Bringing a tent or RV is one of the cheapest ways to stay on WDW property, especially since sites, with outdoor grills and picnic tables, accommodate up to 10. Comfortable Wilderness Cabins put the relaxed friendliness of Fort Wilderness within reach of families who haven't brought their own RV and don't want to camp out. Cabins can accommodate four grown-ups and two children. ☞ *784 campsites (695 full hook-ups, 90 partial hook-ups), 408 cabins ♿ Cafeteria, grocery, snack bar, 2 tennis courts, 2 pools, beach, boating, bicycles, basketball, horseback riding, shuffleboard, volleyball, playground, laundry facilities* ☎ *407/824–2900* ⌨ *$58–$329* ▤ *AE, MC, V.*

Epcot Resort Area
Take I–4 Exit 64B, 65 or 67.

★ $$$$ ▦ **BoardWalk Inn and Villas.** A beautiful re-creation of Victorian-era Atlantic City, WDW's smallest deluxe hotel, off the Boardwalk entertainment area, is the crowning jewel of the BoardWalk complex. WDW's architectural master, Robert A. M. Stern, designed this inn to mimic 19th-century New England building styles. Rooms have floral-print bedspreads and blue-and-white painted furniture. A 200-foot water slide in the form of a classic wooden roller coaster cascades into the pool area. You can ride surrey bikes, watch the game at the ESPN Sports Club or dine at some of Disney's better restaurants. ☎ *407/939–5100 inn, 407/939–6200 villas* ⌨ *407/939–5150* ☞ *370 rooms, 19 suites, 526 villas ♿ 4 restaurants, room service, in-room safes, in-room data ports, golf privileges, miniature golf, tennis court, pool, gym, health club, fishing, croquet, lobby lounge, nightclub, video game room, babysitting, children's programs (ages 4–12), laundry facilities, laundry service, concierge, high speed Internet, business services, convention center, no-smoking rooms* ▤ *AE, D, DC, MC, V.*

★ $$$$ ▦ **Yacht and Beach Club Resorts.** Straight out of a Cape Cod summer, these properties on Seven Seas Lagoon are coastal-style inns on a grand Disney scale. The five-story Yacht Club has hardwood floors, a lobby full of gleaming brass and polished leather, an oyster-gray clapboard facade, and evergreen landscaping; there's even a lighthouse on its pier. Rooms have white-and-blue naval flags on the bedspreads and a small ship's wheel on the headboard. At the Beach Club, a croquet lawn and cabana-dotted, white-sand beach set the scene. Stormalong Bay, a 3-acre water park with water slides and whirlpools, is part of this Club. ☎ *407/934–8000 Beach Club, 407/934–7000 Yacht Club* ⌨ *407/934–3850 Beach Club, 407/934–3450 Yacht Club* ☞ *1,213 rooms, 112 suites ♿ 4* *restaurants, snack bar, room service, in-room safes, cable TV with movies, in-room data ports, golf privileges, 2 tennis courts, 3 pools, gym, health club, hair salon, massage, sauna, beach, boating, bicycles, croquet, volleyball, 3 lobby lounges, video game room, babysitting, children's programs (ages 4–12), laundry service, concierge, high speed Internet, business services, convention center, no-smoking rooms* ▭ AE, D, DC, MC, V.

★ **$$–$$$** ▦**Caribbean Beach Resort.** Awash in dizzying Caribbean colors, this hotel complex was the first of Disney's moderately priced accommodations. Six palm-studded "villages" share 45-acre Barefoot Bay and its white-sand beach. A promenade circles the lake, and bridges over it connect to a 1-acre path-crossed play and picnic area called Parrot Cay. The Old Port Royale complex, decorated with pirates' cannons, tropical birds, and statues, has a food court, full-service restaurant, and pool with waterfalls and a big water slide. The lake area is filled with recreation options, and bikes and small boats are for rent by the day or the hour. Rooms are done in soft pastel colors like turquoise and peach, with white wood furniture. ☎407/934–3400 ᕫ407/934–3288 ➳2,112 rooms ♿ *Restaurant, food court, some room service, in-room safes, cable TV with movies, in-room data ports, golf privileges, 7 pools, wading pool, hot tub, beach, boating, bicycles, lobby lounge, video game room, babysitting, playground, laundry facilities, laundry service, no-smoking rooms* ▭ AE, D, DC, MC, V.

★ **$$–$$$** ▦**Coronado Springs Resort.** This moderately priced hotel on yet another Disney-made lake serves two constituencies. Because of its on-property convention center, it's popular with business groups. But family vacationers come for its casual Southwestern architecture; its wonderful, lively, Mexican-style Pepper Market food court; and its elaborate swimming pool complex, which has a Maya pyramid with a big water slide. There's a full-service health club, but if you like jogging, walking, or biking you're in the right place—a sidewalk circles the property's 15-acre lake. ☎407/939–1000 ᕫ407/939–1001 ➳1,967 rooms ♿ *2 restaurants, food court, room service, cable TV with movies, golf privileges, 4 pools, health club, hair salon, boating, bicycles, bar, video game room, babysitting, laundry service, high-speed Internet, convention center* ▭ AE, D, DC, MC, V.

Disney's Animal Kingdom Area
Take I–4 Exit 64B or 65.

★ **$$$$** ▦**Animal Kingdom Lodge.** Giraffes, zebras, and other African wildlife roam three 11-acre savannas separated by wings of this grand hotel. The atrium lobby exudes African style, from the inlaid carvings on the hardwood floors to the massive faux-thatched roof almost 100 feet above. Cultural ambassadors, natives of Africa, give talks about their homelands, the animals, and the artwork on display; in the evening, they tell folk stories around the fire circle on the Arusha Rock terrace. All of the somewhat tentlike rooms (with drapes descending from the ceiling) have a bit of African art, including carved headboards and watercolors, pen-and-ink, or other kinds of original African prints. The resort's two restaurants offer authentic African cooking and impressive South African wine and beer lists. Most of the guest rooms have balconies with a spectacular view of the private wildlife reserve. ☎ 407/934–7639 📠 407/934–7629 ✒ *1,293 rooms ◊ 3 restaurants, cable TV with movies, golf privileges, 2 pools, health club, spa, bar, lobby lounge, babysitting, children's programs (ages 4–12), playground, laundry facilities, laundry service, high-speed Internet, business services* 🗎 *AE, D, DC, MC, V.*

Downtown Disney/Lake Buena Vista/ WDW Resort Area
Take I–4 Exit 67 or 68.

$$$$ 🏨 **Old Key West Resort.** A red-and-white lighthouse helps you find your way through this marina-style resort, which is part of the Disney Vacation Club network but is available to non-members of the time-share club. Freestanding villas resemble turn-of-the-20th-century Key West houses, with white clapboard siding and private balconies that overlook the waterways winding through the grounds. The one-, two-, or three-bedroom houses have whirlpools in the master bedrooms, full-size kitchens, full-size washers and dryers, and outdoor patios. The 2,265-square-foot three-bedroom grand villas accommodate up to 12 adults. ☎ 407/827–7700 📠 407/827–7710 ✒ *761 units ◊ Restaurant, snack bar, microwaves, cable TV with movies, golf privileges, 3 tennis courts, 4 pools, health club, 4 hot tubs, spa, boating, bicycles, basketball, shuffleboard, lobby lounge, video game room, babysitting, playground, laundry facilities, laundry service, high-speed Internet* 🗎 *AE, D, DC, MC, V.*

$$$$ 🏨 **Saratoga Springs Resort.** The newest Disney resort, which opened in May 2004, is also the largest Disney Vacation Club property ever, with 552 units on 16 acres. Non–club members can book rooms, too. A cluster of three- and four-story residential-style buildings, decorated in and out to look like the 19th-century resorts of upstate New York, overlook a giant pool with man-made hot springs surrounded by faux boulders. Standard rooms include microwaves and refrigerators, while suites have full kitchens. Three-bedroom family suites, occupying two levels, have dining rooms, living rooms, and four bathrooms. Dark wood, early American–style furniture, and overstuffed couches give the rooms a homey, rural–New England look. A ferry boat and a walkway connect the resort with Downtown Disney. ☎ 407/934–7639 ✒ *552 units ◊ Restaurant, snack bar, in-room safes, microwaves, cable TV with movies, in-room data ports, golf privileges, 2 tennis courts, 2 pools, health club, 4 hot tubs, spa, boating, bicycles, basketball, shuffleboard, lobby lounge, theater, video game room, high-speed Internet, business services, no smoking rooms* 🗎 *AE, D, DC, MC, V.*

$$–$$$ 🏨 **Port Orleans Resort–French Quarter.** This vision of New Orleans has ornate row houses with vine-covered balconies, clustered around squares planted with magnolias. Lamp-lighted sidewalks are named for French Quarter thoroughfares. The resort began a two-year renovation of all guest rooms in summer 2004. The French Quarter rooms are the first step of the renovation, with new furniture, bed and wall coverings, and carpeting. The food court serves such Crescent City specialties as jambalaya and beignets. Doubloon Lagoon, one of Disney's most exotic pools, includes a sea serpent water slide that "swallows" swimmers and then spits them into the water. ☎ *407/934–5000* ≞ *407/934–5353* ➪ *1,008 rooms △ Restaurant, in-room safes, cable TV with video games, in-room data ports, golf privileges, pool, wading pool, hot tub, boating, bicycles, croquet, lobby lounge, babysitting, laundry facilities, laundry service, no-smoking rooms* ▤ *AE, D, DC, MC, V.*

$$–$$$ 🏨 **Port Orleans Resort–Riverside.** Disney's Imagineers drew inspiration from the Old South for this sprawling resort. Buildings look like plantation-style mansions and rustic bayou dwellings. Rooms accommodate up to four in two double beds. Elegantly decorated, they have wooden armoires, quilted bedspreads, and gleaming brass faucets; a few rooms have king-size beds. The registration area looks like a steamboat interior, and the 3½-acre, old-fashioned swimming-hole complex called Ol' Man Island has a pool with slides, rope swings, and a nearby play area. ☎ *407/934–6000* ≞ *407/934–5777* ➪ *2,048 rooms △ Restaurant, snack bar, in-room safes, cable TV with movies, in-room data ports, golf privileges, 6 pools, boating, bicycles, lobby lounge, video game room, babysitting, playground, laundry facilities, laundry service, no-smoking rooms* ▤ *AE, D, DC, MC, V.*

All-Star Village & Pop Century Resort
Take I–4 Exit 64B.

¢–$$ 🏨 **All-Star Sports, All-Star Music, and All-Star Movies Resorts.** These Disney economy resorts depict five sports themes, five music themes, and movie themes from *Fantasia, 101 Dalmatians,* and *The Mighty Ducks* to *The Love Bug.* Stairwells shaped like giant bongos frame Calypso, whereas in the Sports resort, 30-foot tennis rackets strike balls the size of small cars, and in the Movies resort, giant icons like *Toy Story*'s Buzz Lightyear frame each building. Each room has two double beds, a closet rod, an armoire, and a desk. The All-Star resorts are as economically priced as most any hotel in Orlando and you are just next door to Disney's Blizzard Beach water park. The food courts sell standard fast food, or you can have pizza delivered to your room. Don't take a room near the food courts or pools if a little noise bothers you. ☎ *407/939– 5000 Sports, 407/939–6000 Music, 407/939–7000 Movies* ≞ *407/939– 7333 Sports, 407/939–7222 Music, 407/939–7111 Movies* ➪ *1,920 rooms at each △ 3 food courts, some room service, in-room safes, cable TV with movies, in-room data ports, golf privileges, 6 pools, 3 bars, video game rooms, babysitting, playground, laundry facilities, laundry service, Internet, no-smoking rooms* ▤ *AE, D, DC, MC, V.*

¢–$$ 🏨 **Pop Century Resort.** This budget-hotel megaplex follows the success of the moderately priced, gargantuan All-Star Resorts. Three-story-tall jukeboxes and bowling pins herald its arrival, and the pop-culture theme continues with huge sculptures of Big Wheel tricycles, Rubik's Cubes, and Play-Doh cans scattered about the grounds. Brightly colored rooms are functional for families, with two double beds or one king. A big food court, cafeteria-style eatery, and room-delivery pizza service offer reasonably priced food. During a second construction phase, the resort aims to double its number of rooms. ☎ *407/934–7639* ➪ *2,880 rooms △ Food court, some room service, in-room safes, cable TV with* *movies, in-room data ports, golf privileges, 2 pools, health club, hair salon, bar, video game room, babysitting, playground, laundry service, no-smoking rooms* ▭ *AE, D, DC, MC, V.*

In WDW: Other Hotels

Epcot Resort Area hotels are also noted on the Walt Disney World Resort map.

Epcot Resort Area
Take I–4 Exit 67.

★ **$$$$** ▣ **Walt Disney World Dolphin.** The Dolphin and Swan have been redesigned with a fresh, contemporary look by Michael Graves, the hotels' original, world-renowned architect. Outside, a pair of 56-foot-tall sea creatures bookend the 25-story glass pyramid of a building. The fabric-draped lobby inside resembles a giant sultan's tent. All rooms have either two queen beds or one king and bright, beach-inspired bedspreads and drapes. Pillow-top mattresses, white goose-down comforters, and overstuffed pillows makes this one of the most comfortable resting places in the Kingdom. Extensive children's programs include Camp Dolphin summer camp and the five-hour Dolphin Dinner Club. Grotto Pool has a big water slide. Todd English's BlueZoo is the trendiest eatery in the place, but the kids may prefer Tubbi's Buffeteria, where you can get macaroni and cheese 24 hours a day; connected to Tubbi's is a sundry shop, also open 24 hours. ✉ *1500 Epcot Resorts Blvd., Lake Buena Vista 32830* ☎ *407/934–4000 or 800/227–1500* ▤ *407/934–4884* ⊕ *www.swandolphin.com* ↪ *1,509 rooms, 136 suites* ♨ *9 restaurants, room service, in-room safes, cable TV with movies and video games, in-room data ports, golf privileges, 4 tennis courts, 5 pools, wading pool, gym, massage, spa, beach, boating, volleyball, 3 lobby lounges, video game room, babysitting, children's programs (ages 4–12), concierge, concierge floor, high-speed Internet, business services, convention center, no-smoking rooms* ▭ *AE, D, DC, MC, V.*

$$$$ ▣ **Walt Disney World Swan.** Facing the Dolphin across Crescent Lake, the Swan is another example of the postmodern entertainment architecture characteristic of Michael Graves. Two 46-foot swans grace the rooftop of this coral-and-aquamarine hotel, and the massive main lobby, with a fountain as its hub, provides a playful mix of tropical imagery, popping with shades of green, gold, and peach. Guest rooms are quirkily decorated with floral and geometric patterns, pineapples painted on furniture, and exotic bird-shape lamps. Every room has two ultra comfortable queen beds or one king, and two phone lines (one data port); some have balconies. The property sprawls, but in a functional, accessible way; you can reach the lobby's grab-and-go eatery or get to the pool without trekking a mile. ✉ *1200 Epcot Resorts Blvd., Lake Buena Vista 32830* ☎ *407/934–3000 or 800/248–7926* ▤ *407/934–4499* ⊕ *www.swandolphin.com* ↪ *756 rooms, 55 suites* ♨ *6 restaurants, room service, cable TV with movies and video games, golf privileges, 4 tennis courts, 5 pools, gym, massage, spa, beach, boating, 2 lobby lounges, video game room, babysitting, children's programs (ages 4–12), play-*

ground, concierge, high-speed Internet, convention center ▤ *AE, DC, MC, V.*

Downtown Disney Resort Area
Take I–4 Exit 68.

A number of non-Disney-owned resorts are clustered on Disney property not far from Downtown Disney, and several more sprawling, high-quality resorts are just outside the park's northernmost entrance. Several of these hotels market themselves as "official" Disney hotels, meaning that they have special agreements with Disney that allow them to offer their guests such perks as early or extended park admission on specified days. The Hotel Plaza Boulevard resorts are within walking distance of Downtown Disney Marketplace and offer shuttle service.

$$$–$$$$ 🏨 **Hilton at WDW Resort.** It's not palatial, but this Hilton is still a fine, upscale hotel that's only a five-minute walk from Downtown Disney Marketplace. An ingeniously designed waterfall tumbles off the covered entrance and into a stone fountain surrounded by palm trees. Rooms are upbeat and cozy. The evening seafood-tasting buffet in the lobby will tempt you to step into the on-site restaurant, Finn's. ✉ *1751 Hotel Plaza Blvd., Downtown Disney, 32830* ☎ *407/827–4000, 800/782–4414 reservations* 🖷 *407/827–6369* ⊕ *www.hilton.com* ⇆ *814 rooms, 27 suites* ⌂ *7 restaurants, room service, cable TV with movies, 3 pools, health club, outdoor hot tub, lobby lounge, babysitting, children's programs (ages 3–12), laundry facilities, laundry service, business services, high-speed Internet* ▤ *AE, DC, MC, V.*

$$–$$$ 🏨 **DoubleTree Guest Suites in the WDW Resort.** Comfortable one- and two-bedroom suites are decorated in tasteful hues, with blue carpeting and orange drapes and bedspreads. Each bedroom has either a king bed or two doubles. Units come with three TVs, including one in the bathroom, and a wet bar, microwave, refrigerator, and coffeemaker. The smallish lobby has a charming feature—a small aviary with birds from South America and Africa. There's a special "registration desk" for kids, where they can get coloring books and balloons. ✉ *2305 Hotel Plaza Blvd., Downtown Disney, 32830* ☎ *407/934–1000 or 800/222–8733* 🖷 *407/934–1015* ⊕ *www.doubletreeguestsuites.com* ⇆ *229 units* ⌂ *Restaurant, room service, microwaves, refrigerators, cable TV with movies, golf privileges, 2 tennis courts, pool, wading pool, gym, hot tub, 2 bars, laundry facilities, laundry service, high-speed Internet, business services* ▤ *AE, DC, MC, V.*

★ $$$$ 🏨 **Wyndham Palace Resort & Spa in the WDW Resort.** This luxury hotel gets kudos as much for its on-site charms (such as a huge health spa) as for its location—100 yards from the nearest Wolfgang Puck's, in Downtown Disney. All rooms have balconies or patios, as well as high-speed Internet access. At the Top of the Palace, the club-bar on the 27th floor, guests receive a free glass of champagne to accompany the wonderful view of the sun sinking into the Disney complex. Book early if you want a meal at the rooftop restaurant, Arthur's 27. ✉ *1900 Buena Vista Dr., Downtown Disney, 32830* ☎ *407/827–2727 or 800/327–2990* 🖷 *407/827–6034* ⊕ *www.wyndhampalaceresort.com* ⇆ *1,014 rooms, 209* suites ♿ *4 restaurants, patisserie, snack bar, some room service, cable TV with movies, tennis courts, 3 pools, health club, hot tub, spa, volleyball, 4 lounges, video game room, babysitting, children's programs (ages 4–12), playground, laundry facilities, laundry service, high-speed Internet, convention center* ▤ *AE, D, DC, MC, V.*

¢–$$ 🏨 **Best Western Lake Buena Vista Resort Hotel.** This 18-story property has an attractive mural of Florida wildlife and landscapes gracing the lobby, though the view of a junglelike wetland out the windows of the atrium restaurant is more compelling. Most rooms have private balconies with spectacular views of nightly Disney firework shows. Disney shuttles are available, but the walk to Downtown Disney is easy. With standard rooms as cheap as $99 a night in high season (April), the hotel offers one of the best bargains on Hotel Row. ✉ *2000 Hotel Plaza Blvd., Downtown Disney, 32830* ☎ *407/828–2424 or 800/348–3765* 🖷 *407/828–8933* ∰ *www.orlandoresorthotel.com* ⮐ *325 rooms* ♿ *Restaurant, snack bar, room service, cable TV with movies, pool, wading pool, lobby lounge, playground, laundry facilities, laundry service, high-speed Internet, business services* ▤ *AE, D, DC, MC, V.*

$–$$ 🏨 **Grosvenor Resort.** This pink high-rise (the name is pronounced *Grovener*) is nondescript on the outside but quite pleasant on the inside. Blond-wood furniture and rose carpeting make the rooms homey, and those in the tower have a great view of Downtown Disney. Public areas are decorated in an easygoing Caribbean style. One of the restaurants, Baskervilles, hosts a Disney character breakfast three days a week and a Saturday murder-mystery dinner show. A free shuttle takes you to all Disney theme parks. ✉ *1850 Hotel Plaza Blvd., Downtown Disney 32830* ☎ *407/828–4444 or 800/624–4109* 🖷 *407/828–8192* ∰ *www. grosvenorresort.com* ⮐ *626 rooms, 5 suites* ♿ *3 restaurants, room service, in-room safes, refrigerators, cable TV with movies, in-room VCRs, in-room data ports, 2 tennis courts, 2 pools, wading pool, hot tub, basketball, volleyball, lobby lounge, video game room, babysitting, playground, laundry service, high-speed Internet, business services, meeting rooms, no-smoking rooms* ▤ *AE, DC, MC, V.*

Universal Orlando
Take I–4 Exit 74B if you're heading westbound, 75A if eastbound.

$$$$ 🏨 **Hard Rock Hotel.** It's not quite as plush as Portofino Bay, but then, the price tag isn't quite as high. Inside the California mission–style building, you'll find lots of rock-music memorabilia, including the slip Madonna wore in her "Like a Prayer" video. Rooms have white walls and black-and-white photos of pop icons. The pool is surrounded by a sand beach and has an underwater sound system pumping music into the water. The hotel offers the option of bringing your family pet, with no weight limitation. ✉ *5800 Universal Blvd., Universal Studios, 32819* ☎ *407/503–7625 or 800/232–7827* 🖷 *407/503–7655* ∰ *www. universalorlando.com* ⮐ *621 rooms, 29 suites* ♿ *3 restaurants, room service, refrigerators, cable TV with movies, in-room VCRs, 2 pools, health club, 3 bars, video game room, babysitting, children's programs (ages 4–14), laundry service, high-speed Internet, business services, pets allowed* ▤ *AE, D, DC, MC, V.*

$$$$ ⊡ **Portofino Bay Hotel.** Built to resemble the Italian Riviera town of Portofino, this hotel complex holds monthly Italian wine tastings and even has a boccie ball court. Other touches include gelato machines around the pool, a wood-fire pizzeria, and two great Italian restaurants. The massive pool has a Roman aqueduct–style water slide. The hotel offers an unusual feature for such an upscale resort: for a fee, you can bring your pets with you; room service for pets is also available. ⊠ *5601 Universal Blvd., Universal Studios, 32819* ☎ *407/503–1000 or 800/232–7827* ⊟ *407/224–5311* ⊕ *www.universalorlando.com* ⤙ *699 rooms, 51 suites* ♨ *3 restaurants, pizzeria, room service, cable TV with movies, in-room VCRs, 3 pools, health club, massage, spa, boccie, bar, babysitting, children's programs (ages 4–14), playground, laundry service, high-speed Internet, convention center, pets allowed* ⊟ *AE, D, DC, MC, V.*

$$$–$$$$ ⊡ **Royal Pacific Resort.** The hotel entrance—a footbridge across a tropical stream—sets the tone for the South Pacific theme of this hotel. The resort's focal point is a 12,000-square-foot lagoon–style swimming pool (Orlando's largest) with its own sand beach. Emeril Lagasse's newest Orlando restaurant, Tchoup Chop, brings in crowds. Pet-friendly guest rooms are available with advance notice. ⊠ *6300 Hollywood Way, Universal Studios, 32819* ☎ *407/503–3000 or 800/232–7827* ⊟ *407/503–3010* ⊕ *www.universalorlando.com* ⤙ *1,000 rooms, 113 suites* ♨ *3 restaurants, room service, in-room VCRs, putting green, pool, wading pool, exercise equipment, health club, hot tub, massage, sauna, steam room, 2 bars, lobby lounge, children's programs (ages 4–14), laundry facilities, laundry service, high-speed Internet, convention center* ⊟ *AE, DC, MC, V.*

FodorsChoice
★

Orlando

International Drive
Take I–4 Exit 28 or 29.

If you plan to visit other attractions besides Walt Disney World, the sprawl of newish hotels, restaurants, and shopping malls known as International Drive—"I–Drive" to locals—makes a convenient base. Parallel to Interstate 4, it's just a few minutes south of downtown Orlando. It's also near SeaWorld and Universal Orlando as well as several popular dinner theaters.

$$$$ ⊡ **JW Marriott Orlando Grande Lakes.** Though it caters to a convention clientele, this is an appealing place for tourists with a flexible budget. Rooms, at 420 square feet, are on the large side, and most have balconies that overlook the resort's huge pool complex, the spa building, and beyond those, the golf course. Wander down a long connector hallway to the adjoining Ritz-Carlton, where you can use your room charge card in the restaurants and shops. ⊠ *4040 Central Florida Pkwy., International Drive Area, 32837* ☎ *407/206–2300 or 800/228–9290* ⊟ *407/393–4001* ⊕ *www.grandelakes.com* ⤙ *1,000 rooms, 57 suites* ♨ *4 restaurants, room service, cable TV with movies, in-room data ports, 18-hole golf course, 2 pools, health club, hot tubs (indoor and outdoor), spa, 2 bars, lobby lounge, laundry service, concierge, concierge floor,* high-speed Internet, business services, meeting rooms, no-smoking rooms ⊟ AE, D, DC, MC, V.

★ $$$$ 🏨 **Peabody Orlando.** At 11 AM the celebrated Peabody ducks exit a private elevator and waddle across the lobby to the marble fountain where they pass the day, basking in their fame. At 5 they repeat the ritual in reverse. Built by the owners of the landmark Peabody Hotel in Memphis, this 27-story structure has an impressive interior, with gilt and marble halls. Some of the oversize upper-floor rooms have panoramic views of WDW. ⊠ 9801 International Dr., International Drive Area, 32819 ☎ 407/352–4000 or 800/732–2639 🖷 407/354–1424 ⊕ www. peabodyorlando.com ⇆ 891 rooms ₺ 3 restaurants, room service, cable TV with movies, golf privileges, 4 tennis courts, pool, wading pool, health club, hot tub, massage, spa, 2 lobby lounges, babysitting, concierge, high-speed Internet, convention center ⊟ AE, D, DC, MC, V.

$$$$ 🏨 **Ritz-Carlton Orlando Grande Lakes.** Orlando had more than 110,000
FodorśChoice hotel rooms before it had a single Ritz-Carlton, but Marriott Interna-
★ tional, Inc., the parent company of Ritz-Carlton, decided to make up for its absence. In addition to having the trendy Norman's restaurant, the hotel also has a waterpark complex. The hotel caters to the convention crowd, but also to families, with extensive children's programs. An enclosed hallway connects the Ritz-Carlton to a JW Marriott Hotel, and the two share some amenities, including a huge spa. ⊠ 4012 Central Florida Pkwy., International Drive Area, 32837 ☎ 407/206–2400 or 800/576–5760 🖷 407/529–2240 ⊕ www.grandelakes.com ⇆ 584 rooms, 156 suites ₺ 4 restaurants, room service, cable TV with movies, in-room data ports, 18-hole golf course, pool, wading pool, health club, hot tubs (indoor and outdoor), spa, 2 bars, lobby lounge, children's programs (ages 4–12), laundry service, concierge, concierge floor, high-speed Internet, business services, meeting rooms, no-smoking rooms ⊟ AE, D, DC, MC, V.

$$$ 🏨 **Renaissance Orlando Resort at SeaWorld.** The hotel's 10-story atrium is full of waterfalls, goldfish ponds, and palm trees; as you shoot skyward in sleek, glass elevators, look for exotic birds—on loan from Sea-World across the street—twittering in the hand-carved, gilded Venetian aviary. Rooms have more floor space than the average Central Florida hotel, plus nice touches like high-speed Internet connections, speakers, and two-line phones. Atlantis, the formal restaurant, is something of an undiscovered gem, with Mediterranean cuisine. The hotel completed a $4-million renovation in 2004. ⊠ 6677 Sea Harbor Dr., International Drive Area, 32821 ☎ 407/351–5555 or 800/468–3571 🖷 407/351–4618 ⊕ www.renaissancehotels.com ⇆ 778 rooms ₺ 4 restaurants, room service, cable TV with movies, golf privileges, 4 tennis courts, pool, wading pool, health club, hair salon, hot tub, massage, sauna, volleyball, 3 lounges, babysitting, laundry service, high-speed Internet, convention center ⊟ AE, D, DC, MC, V.

$$–$$$ 🏨 **Staybridge Suites–International Drive.** Parents can use that trump-card disciplinary option "Go to your room!" at this hotel. Sleeping from four to eight people, the one- and two-bedroom units at the all-suites Staybridge are a great option for families. Two-bedroom units, the most popular, have fully equipped kitchens, plus a living room with TV and VCR,

and another TV in one bedroom. Plush landscaping makes the place seem secluded. ⊠ *8480 International Dr., I–4 Exit 74A, International Drive Area, 32819* ☎ *407/352–2400 or 800/238–8000* 🖷 *407/352–4631* ⊕ *www.lbvorlando.staybridge.com* ⇲ *146 suites* ♿ *Grocery, kitchens, microwaves, refrigerators, cable TV with movies, pool, wading pool, gym, hot tub, lobby lounge, video game room, laundry facilities, laundry service, high-speed Internet, meeting rooms* ▤ *AE, D, DC, MC, V.*

$–$$ 📺 **DoubleTree Castle Hotel.** You won't really think you're in a castle at this mid-price hotel, although the tall gold-and-silver-color spires, medieval-style mosaics, and arched doorways may make you feel like reading Harry Potter. Take your book to either the rooftop terrace or the inviting courtyard, which has a big, round swimming pool. Café Tu Tu Tango, one of the better restaurants in this part of Orlando, has a zesty multicultural menu. ⊠ *8629 International Dr., International Drive Area, 32819* ☎ *407/345–1511 or 800/952–2785* 🖷 *407/248–8181* ⊕ *www.doubletreecastle.com* ⇲ *216 rooms* ♿ *2 restaurants, room service, minibars, refrigerators, cable TV with movies, pool, gym, hot tub, lobby lounge, video game room, laundry service, high-speed Internet, business services* ▤ *AE, D, DC, MC, V.*

$–$$ 📺 **Enclave Suites at Orlando.** With three 10-story buildings surrounding an office, restaurant, and recreation area, this all-suites lodging is less a hotel than a condominium complex. Here, what you would spend for a normal room in a fancy hotel gets you a complete apartment, with more space than you find in many all-suites hotels. KidsQuarter suites, which sleep up to six people and offer blond-wood bunk beds in the kids' room, are designed to provide a homelike environment, although your home may not have the great Shamu murals found in the kids' rooms here. All units have full kitchens, living rooms, two bedrooms, and small terraces with a view of a nearby lake. There's free transportation to SeaWorld, Wet 'n Wild, and Universal Orlando, but Wet 'n Wild is an easy walk. A free hot breakfast buffet is served daily. ⊠ *6165 Carrier Dr., International Drive Area, 32819* ☎ *407/351–1155 or 800/457–0077* 🖷 *407/351–2001* ⊕ *www.enclavesuites.com* ⇲ *352 suites* ♿ *Food court, grocery, pizzeria, snack bar, tennis court, 3 pools (1 indoor), 2 wading pools, gym, hot tub, playground, laundry facilities, laundry service, business services* ▤ *AE, D, DC, MC, V.*

$–$$ 📺 **Parc Corniche Condominium Suite Hotel.** A good bet for golf enthusiasts, the suites-only resort is framed by a Joe Lee–designed course. Each of the one- and two-bedroom suites has a kitchen complete with dishes and a dishwasher, plus a patio or balcony with golf-course views. The largest accommodations, with two bedrooms and two baths, can sleep up to six. A complimentary Continental breakfast is served daily, and SeaWorld is only a few blocks away. Wireless high-speed Internet is available, but only in the lobby. ⊠ *6300 Parc Corniche Dr., International Drive Area, 32821* ☎ *407/239–7100 or 800/446–2721* 🖷 *407/239–8501* ⊕ *www.parccorniche.com* ⇲ *210 suites* ♿ *Restaurant, room service, babysitting, playground, laundry facilities, laundry service, high-speed Internet, business services* ▤ *AE, D, DC, MC, V* ⑩ *BP.*

$–$$ 📺 **Rosen Plaza Hotel.** Harris Rosen, the largest independent hotel owner in the Orlando market, loves to offer bargains, and you'll find one here.

This is essentially a convention hotel, although leisure travelers like the prime location and the long list of amenities. Newly decorated rooms are larger than the usual standard rooms, with two queen-size beds. Two upscale restaurants, Jack's Place and Café Matisse, offer great steaks and a fine buffet, respectively, but the best food option is the pizza at Rossini's. You can also grab quick eats at the reasonably priced 24-hour deli. All Rosen conference hotels now offer a service called "BAGS," by which you can get your airline boarding passes and check your bags through to your next destination in the hotel lobby, allowing you to go right to your gate at Orlando International when you leave. ⊠ 9700 *International Dr., International Drive Area, 32819* ☎ *407/996–9700 or 800/627–8258* 📠 *407/996–9119* 🌐 *www.rosenplaza.com* 🛏 *810 rooms* ♿ *2 restaurants, coffee shop, ice-cream parlor, pizzeria, room service, cable TV, pool, hot tub, bar, lobby lounge, nightclub, video game room, babysitting, laundry facilities, laundry service, high-speed Internet, meeting rooms* 🍴 *AE, D, DC, MC, V.*

$–$$ 🏨 **Sheraton Studio City.** Atop this Sheraton is a giant silver globe suitable for Times Square on New Year's Eve. But the interior has a Hollywood theme, with movie posters and black-and-white art deco touches. Most rooms have two queen beds. The top three floors offer star-studded concierge accommodations, and the Concierge Lounge offers complimentary Continental breakfast each morning and beverages, snacks, and hors d'oeuvres in the evening with luxury suites. The 21st floor houses 15 spacious deluxe rooms with full window walls to view the surrounding area. Free shuttles go to the major theme parks and shopping malls. ⊠ *5905 International Dr., International Drive Area, 32819* ☎ *407/351–2100 or 800/327–1366* 📠 *407/345–5249* 🌐 *www. sheratonstudiocity.com* 🛏 *302 rooms* ♿ *Restaurant, room service, cable TV with movies and video games, pool, wading pool, hair salon, hot tub, bar, lobby lounge, video game room, laundry service, high-speed Internet, business services* 🍴 *AE, D, DC, MC, V.*

$ 🏨 **Inn of America** This former Fairfield Inn by Marriott became an Inn of America in January 2005, remaining the same understated, few-frills, three-story hotel that becomes a natural for single travelers or small families on a tight budget. It's squeezed between International Drive and I–4, and although it doesn't have many amenities, there are nice perks such as complimentary coffee and tea, free local phone calls, and in-room, wireless, high-speed Internet access. ⊠ *8342 Jamaican Ct., International Drive Area, 32819* ☎ *407/363–1944* 📠 *407/363–4844* 🌐 *www. innofamerica.com* 🛏 *134 rooms* ♿ *Room TVs with movies, pool, high-speed Internet, business services* 🍴 *AE, D, DC, MC, V.*

★ ¢–$ 🏨 **Travelodge Orlando Convention Center.** If you don't want a room with just the bare essentials yet don't have the budget for luxury, this three-story motel is a find. The rooms are comfy if not spectacular; all have two double beds. Children 17 and under stay free in their parents' room (maximum of four people per room). The hotel is ¼ mi from SeaWorld. Free transportation is provided to theme parks. ⊠ *6263 Westwood Blvd., International Drive Area, 32821* ☎ *407/345–8000 or 800/346–1551* 📠 *407/345–1508* 🌐 *www.travelodge.com* 🛏 *144 rooms* ♿ *Restaurant, room TVs with movies, 2 pools, exercise equipment, bar, video* *game room, laundry facilities, laundry service, business services* ▭ *AE, DC, MC, V.*

Downtown Disney/Lake Buena Vista Area
Take I–4 Exit 68.

Many people choose to stay in one of the resorts a bit farther east of Downtown Disney because, though equally grand, they tend to be less expensive than those right on Hotel Plaza Boulevard. Perennially popular with families are the all-suites properties, many with in-room kitchens, just east of Lake Buena Vista Drive. The 1,100-room Marriott Village at Lake Buena Vista, across I–4 from Downtown Disney, is popular for its gated, secure cluster of three hotels, a multi-restaurant complex, a video-rental store, a 24-hour convenience store, and a Hertz rental-car station.

★ $$$$ ▦ **Hyatt Regency Grand Cypress Resort.** This spectacular resort offers every amenity imaginable, including a 45-acre nature preserve. Golf facilities, among them a high-tech golf school, are first-class. The 800,000-gallon pool resembles an enormous grotto fed by 12 waterfalls. There's even a small lake, with a white-sand beach. A striking 18-story atrium is filled with tropical plants, ancient Chinese sculptures, and tropical birds. Accommodations are divided between the Hyatt Regency Grand Cypress and the Villas of Grand Cypress. The hotel's fine dining room, La Coquina, offers one of the best Sunday brunches in the Orlando area. ⊠ *1 Grand Cypress Blvd., Lake Buena Vista Area, 32836* ☎ *407/239–1234 or 800/233–1234* ☐ *407/239–3800* ⊕ *www.hyattgrandcypress.com* ⇌ *750 rooms* ⌂ *5 restaurants, room service, cable TV with movies, 18-hole golf course, 9-hole golf course, 12 tennis courts, 2 pools, health club, 3 hot tubs, massage, spa, boating, bicycles, horseback riding, 4 lobby lounges, babysitting, children's programs (ages 5–12), laundry service, high-speed Internet, convention center* ▭ *AE, D, DC, MC, V.*

$$$$ ▦ **Orlando World Center Marriott.** At 2,000 rooms, this is one of the largest hotels in Orlando, and one very popular with conventions. Rooms have patios or balconies. One of the pools here is the largest in Florida. Upscale villas are available for daily and weekly rentals. The hotel's Hawk's Landing Steakhouse and Grille is among the better beef-centric restaurants in the Disney area. ⊠ *8701 World Center Dr., I–4 Exit 67, Buena Vista 32821* ☎ *407/239–4200 or 800/228–9290* ☐ *407/238–8777* ⊕ *www.marriottworldcenter.com* ⇌ *2,000 rooms, 98 suites, 259 villas* ⌂ *7 restaurants, ice-cream parlor, room service, cable TV with movies, golf, 4 pools (1 indoor), wading pool, health club, hair salon, 4 hot tubs, 2 lobby lounges, babysitting, children's programs (ages 4–12), laundry facilities, laundry service, high-speed Internet, convention center* ▭ *AE, D, DC, MC, V.*

$$$–$$$$ ▦ **Nickelodeon Family Suites by Holiday Inn.** This is a former Holiday Inn Family Suites transformed, by a $20-million renovation, into a Nick-theme environment, complete with the company's signature entertainment and style. The hotel includes Nick-decorated bedrooms for kids, two pools with waterslides and flumes, poolside game areas, wake-up calls from Nick stars, daily character breakfasts, and live entertainment with Nick characters. The hotel also offers three-bedroom suites, with

two baths and fully functional kitchen. Say the word "location" three times to remind yourself that this property is just a few short minutes and turns away from the Disney park exits; it's ultraconvenient to Sea-World as well. ✉ *14500 Continental Gateway, I–4 Exit 67, Lake Buena Vista Area, 32821* ☏ *407/387–5437 or 877/387–5437* 🖷 *407/387–1490* 🌐 *www.nickhotels.com* 🛏 *800 suites* ♿ *3 restaurants, ice-cream parlor, room service, in-room safes, microwaves, refrigerators, cable TV with movies, in-room data ports, 2 pools, health club, hair salon, 2 hot tubs, 2 lobby lounges, babysitting, children's programs (ages 4–12), laundry facilities, laundry service, business services, no-smoking rooms* ▭ *AE, D, DC, MC, V.*

$$$ 🏨 **Embassy Suites Hotel Lake Buena Vista.** Some locals are shocked by the wild turquoise, pink, and peach facade, but the Embassy Suites resort is an attractive option for other reasons. It's 1 mi from Walt Disney World, 3 mi from SeaWorld, and 7 mi from Universal Orlando. Each suite has a living room and two TVs. The central atrium lobby, soothed by the sounds of a rushing fountain, is a great place to enjoy the complimentary full breakfast and evening cocktails. The hotel offers "pet-friendly" suites for guests with pets weighing 25 pounds or less. ✉ *8100 Lake Ave., Lake Buena Vista 32836* ☏ *407/239–1144, 800/257–8483, or 800/ 362–2779* 🖷 *407/239–1718* 🌐 *www.embassysuitesorlando.com* 🛏 *333 suites* ♿ *2 restaurants, room service, cable TV with movies, tennis court, indoor-outdoor pool, wading pool, gym, hot tub, basketball, shuffleboard, volleyball, lobby lounge, babysitting, children's programs (ages 4–12), playground, high-speed Internet, meeting room* ▭ *AE, D, DC, MC, V* ⅋ *BP.*

$$$ 🏨 **Sheraton's Vistana Resort.** Consider this peaceful resort if you're interested in tennis. Enjoy free use of clay and all-weather courts; lessons are available for a fee. Spread over 135 landscaped acres, the spacious, tastefully decorated villas and town houses come in one- and two-bedroom versions with living room, a full kitchen, and washer and dryer. ✉ *8800 Vistana Center Dr., Lake Buena Vista 32821* ☏ *407/239– 3100 or 800/208–0003* 🖷 *407/239–3111* 🌐 *www.vistana.com/resorts/ vistana* 🛏 *1,700 units* ♿ *2 restaurants, grocery, microwaves, cable TV with movies, miniature golf, 13 tennis courts, 7 pools, 5 wading pools, health club, 8 hot tubs, massage, basketball, shuffleboard, lobby lounge, babysitting, children's programs (ages 4–12), meeting rooms* ▭ *AE, D, DC, MC, V.*

$$–$$$ 🏨 **Buena Vista Suites.** In this suites-only property, you get two rooms (a bedroom and a living room with a fold-out sofa bed), a small kitchen area with a coffeemaker, sink, microwave, and refrigerator, two TVs, and two phones. King suites have a king bed and a whirlpool bath. The hotel serves a complimentary breakfast buffet and provides shuttle transportation to the Walt Disney World theme parks. ✉ *8203 World Center Dr., Southwestern Orlando, 32821* ☏ *407/239–8588 or 800/ 537–7737* 🖷 *407/239–1401* 🌐 *www.buenavistasuites.com* 🛏 *280 suites* ♿ *Restaurant, room service, microwaves, refrigerators, cable TV with movies, 2 tennis courts, outdoor pool, wading pool, gym, hot tub, laundry facilities* ▭ *AE, D, DC, MC, V* ⅋ *BP.*

★ **$$–$$$** ⊞ **PerriHouse Bed & Breakfast Inn.** An eight-room bed-and-breakfast inside a serene bird sanctuary offers you a chance to split your time between sightseeing and spending quiet moments bird-watching. The 13-acre sanctuary has observation paths, a pond, a feeding station, and a small birdhouse museum. Lush plantings make it attractive to bobwhites, downy woodpeckers, red-tail hawks, and the occasional bald eagle. Some rooms have four-poster beds and fireplaces. ✉ *10417 Vista Oak Ct., Lake Buena Vista 32836* ☎ *407/876–4830 or 800/780–4830* ⊟ *407/876–0241* ⊕ *www.perrihouse.com* ⇆ *8 rooms* ♻ *Cable TV, golf privileges, pool, hot tub* ⊟ *AE, D, DC, MC, V* ❏ *CP.*

¢–$$ ⊞ **Holiday Inn SunSpree Resort Lake Buena Vista.** This place is as kid-oriented as it gets. The little ones have their own registration desk, and there's usually a costumed clown to hand out balloons and other treats. Off the lobby you'll find the CyberArcade; Camp Holiday, a free, supervised activity program; a small theater where clowns perform weekends at 7 PM; and a buffet restaurant where kids accompanied by adults eat free at their own little picnic tables. Families love the Kidsuites, playhouse-style rooms within a larger room. ✉ *13351 Rte. 535, Lake Buena Vista 32821* ☎ *407/239–4500 or 800/366–6299* ⊟ *407/239–7713* ⊕ *www. kidsuites.com* ⇆ *507 rooms* ♻ *Restaurant, grocery, microwaves, refrigerators, cable TV with movies and video games, pool, wading pool, gym, 2 hot tubs, basketball, Ping-Pong, bar, lobby lounge, theater, video game room, children's programs (ages 4–12), playground, laundry facilities, laundry service, high-speed Internet, business services* ⊟ *AE, D, DC, MC, V.*

Downtown Orlando

Downtown Orlando, north of Walt Disney World and slightly north of the International Drive area, is a thriving business district with a tourist fringe in the form of Church Street Station. To get there take Exit 83 off Interstate 4 if you're heading west, Exit 82C if eastbound.

$$$–$$$$ ⊞ **Westin Grand Bohemian.** This European–style property is downtown Orlando's only luxury hotel. Opposite City Hall, the Grand Bohemian showcases more than 100 pieces of art—including a Bösendorfer piano, one of only two in the world, which sits in a posh ground-floor lounge. Rooms are more sedate (despite the red-and-purple curtains), and all have three phones and interactive television. Off the main lobby are a Starbucks and an art gallery. The business center is open 24 hours. ✉ *325 S. Orange Ave., Downtown Orlando, 32801* ☎ *407/313–9000 or 866/663–0024* ⊟ *407/313–9001* ⊕ *www.grandbohemianhotel.com* ⇆ *250 rooms, 36 suites* ♻ *Restaurant, room service, cable TV with movies, pool, gym, massage, bar, concierge, high-speed Internet, business services, parking (fee)* ⊟ *AE, D, MC, V.*

★ **$$–$$$** ⊞ **Eō Inn & Urban Spa.** The entrance to this boutique hotel is at the rear of the building, behind Panera Bread, the bakery and restaurant on the ground floor. Consequently, this charming three-story hotel in a 1923 building is somewhat of an undiscovered gem. The spa offers many services, from Swedish massage to beauty treatments. Rooms have black-and-white photographs on the walls and thick down comforters on the beds, as well as high-speed Internet connections. Best of all, Lake Eola, with its 1-mi walking path, is across the street—treat yourself to a king suite overlooking the lake. ✉ *227 N. Eola Dr., off E. Robinson St., Thornton Park 32801* ☎ *407/481–8485 or 888/481–8488* 🖷 *407/481–8495* 🌐 *www.eoinn.com* 🛏 *17 rooms* ᗜ *In-room safes, cable TV with movies, in-room data ports, hot tubs (indoor and outdoor), massage, sauna, spa, laundry service, high-speed Internet, business services, no-smoking rooms* ☰ *AE, D, DC, MC, V.*

Kissimmee

Take I–4 Exit 64A, unless otherwise noted.

$$$$ 🏨 **Gaylord Palms Resort.** With a huge atrium that re-creates such Florida
Fodor's Choice locales as the Everglades, Key West, and old St. Augustine under a 4-
★ acre glass roof, this massive property, 5 mi from WDW, is arguably Orlando's most elaborate hotel. The five dramatic atrium restaurants include the Old Hickory Steak House, in an old warehouse overlooking the alligator-ridden Everglades, and Sunset Sam's Fish Camp, set on a 60-foot fishing boat docked on the hotel's indoor ocean. Sam's entertainment makes it a particularly worthwhile destination for families. Face painters, fire swallowers, and staffers on stilts are among those that help keep the kids engaged and in their seats. The hotel aims to keep you on site with extensive children's programs, two pool areas, and a huge Canyon Ranch spa. The newest guest room amenity is Gaylord iConnect, a computer system, complete with a 15-inch flat screen monitor that allows you to connect not only to the Internet, but to an in-hotel network with which you can do everything from book dinner reservations to keep up with on-property activities. ✉ *6000 Osceola Pkwy., I–4 Exit 65, Kissimmee 34746* ☎ *407/586–0000* 🖷 *407/586– 1999* 🌐 *www.gaylordpalms.com* 🛏 *1,406 rooms, 86 suites* ᗜ *4 restaurants, cable TV with movies, golf privileges, 2 pools, gym, hot tub, massage, spa, 2 bars, lobby lounge, children's programs (ages 4–12), laundry service, convention center, high-speed Internet, meeting rooms* ☰ *AE, D, DC, MC, V.*

★ **$$$** 🏨 **Celebration Hotel.** Like everything in the fantasy-driven, Disney-created town of Celebration, this 115-room hotel borrows from the best of several centuries. The lobby resembles that of the grand Victorian-era hotels, with hardwood floors and decorative millwork on the walls and ceilings. Rooms may look as if they date from the early 1900s, but each has a 25-inch TV, two phone lines, high-speed Internet access port, and a six-channel stereo sound system. The entire hotel, including all guest rooms, is non-smoking. Though it's less than 1 mi south of the U.S. 192 tourist strip in Kissimmee, the hotel's surroundings are serene. ✉ *700 Bloom St., Celebration 34747* ☎ *407/566–6000 or 888/499– 3800* 🖷 *407/566–1844* 🌐 *www.celebrationhotel.com* 🛏 *115 rooms* ᗜ *2 restaurants, cable TV with movies, in-room data ports, golf privileges, pool, health club, hot tub, lobby lounge, laundry service; no smoking* ☰ *AE, D, DC, MC, V.*

$–$$ 🏨 **Magical Memories Villas.** Despite the name, this resort is not affiliated with Disney, but the real magical moment here is when you pay your bill—two-bedroom villas start at $89 a night. Lodging choices include two-, three-, and four-bedroom villas, plus three-, four-, and five-bedroom private pool homes. Furnishings are pretty standard, and the villas or homes includes a fully equipped kitchen, spacious living and dining areas, master bedroom with en-suite bath, two cable TVs, and VCR. All accommodations include an in-unit washer and dryer, and a set of linens and towels. Pets are accepted at some units with a pet fee. ⊠ *5075 West Irlo Bronson Memorial Hwy., 34746* ☎ *407/390–8200 or 800/736–0402* 🖶 *407/390–0718* ⊕ *www.magicalmemories.com* ⇨ *140* ♿ *Tennis court, pool, gym, spa, billiards, volleyball, video game room, laundry facilities, some pets allowed (fee), no-smoking rooms* ⊟ *D, MC, V.*

★ **$–$$** 🏨 **Radisson Resort Parkway.** Bright and spacious, this Radisson may offer the best deal in the neighborhood: an attractive location amid 1½ acres of lush tropical foliage, good facilities, and competitive prices. The focal point of the resort is the giant free-form pool with waterfalls and waterslide plus two outdoor whirlpools and a kiddies' wading pool. Its delicatessen comes in handy when you want to assemble a picnic, and there's an on-site Pizza Hut. Rooms with the best view and light face the pool, which has a 40-foot water slide. Off the lobby is a lively sports bar. A full breakfast buffet for two adults is available at $10 above the standard room rate. Children 10 and under eat free when accompanied by their parents. ⊠ *2900 Parkway Blvd., Kissimmee 34746* ☎ *407/396–7000 or 800/634–4774* 🖶 *407/396–6792* ⊕ *www.radissonparkway.com* ⇨ *712 rooms, 8 suites* ♿ *2 restaurants, snack bar, cable TV with movies, 2 tennis courts, 2 pools, wading pool, gym, 2 hot tubs, sauna, volleyball, lobby lounge, sports bar, laundry facilities, laundry service, high-speed Internet, meeting rooms* ⊟ *AE, D, DC, MC, V.*

Orlando Suburbs

Travel farther afield and find more comforts and facilities for the money, and maybe even some genuine Orlando charm—of the warm, cozy, one-of-a-kind country inn variety.

$$$–$$$$ 🏨 **Chalet Suzanne.** A world away from the world of Disney, this quiet, family-owned country inn was constructed in the 1930s, and subsequent updates have not taken away its original architectural charm. Although painted tropical pink and aqua, the buildings otherwise resemble a Swiss village. Some of the lovely antiques-dotted guest rooms have original tile baths, whereas others have whirlpools. The best overlook a lake or garden. Perhaps the biggest treat is a meal in the inn's elegant restaurant, where a six-course dinner is the house specialty. Wireless high-speed Internet access is available near the office and in the pool area. Take I–4 Exit 55 and U.S. 27 south. ⊠ *3800 Chalet Suzanne La., 33859* ☎ *863/676–6011 or 800/433–6011* 🖶 *863/676–1814* ⊕ *www.chaletsuzanne.com* ⇨ *30 rooms* ♿ *Restaurant, cable TV, high-speed Internet, pool, lake, badminton, croquet, volleyball, bar* ⊟ *AE, D, DC, MC, V* ¶◯¶ *BP.*

$$–$$$$ 🏨 **Park Plaza Hotel.** Small and intimate, this 1922 establishment in the upscale shopping district along Park Avenue feels almost like a private home. Best accommodations are front garden suites with a living room, which opens onto a long balcony usually abloom with impatiens and bougainvillea. There's not much for kids here, but for adults, a half-dozen sidewalk cafés are within a block, and the Charles Hosmer Morse Museum of Art and the wonderful Scenic Boat Tour are within a few blocks. Take I–4 Exit 87. ✉ *307 Park Ave. S, 32789* ☎ *407/647–1072 or 800/228–7220* 🖨 *407/647–4081* ⊕ *www.parkplazahotel.com* ⟿ *27 rooms* ⚭ *Restaurant, room service, cable TV, lobby lounge, laundry service; no kids under 5* ▭ *AE, DC, MC, V.*

NIGHTLIFE & THE ARTS

A fair number of the millions who pour through Orlando each year are adults traveling without children. After years of denial, Disney heeded the command of the profits and built Pleasure Island and later West Side to complete the Downtown Disney entertainment complex, which also includes the Marketplace. In response, Universal Orlando opened CityWalk to siphon off from Disney what Disney had siphoned off from downtown Orlando, which is now struggling to find its footing amid the increased competition. If you're here for at least two nights and don't mind losing some sleep, reserve one evening for Downtown Disney and the next for CityWalk.

The Arts

When the fantasy starts wearing thin, check out the Orlando arts scene in the *Orlando Weekly* (⊕ www.orlandoweekly.com), a free local entertainment and opinion newspaper that accurately tracks Orlando culture, lifestyles, and nightlife. Perhaps your best source of up-to-the-week information is in Friday's *Orlando Sentinel* (⊕ www.orlandosentinel. com). The handy Calendar section carries reviews of plays, nightclubs, live music venues, restaurants, and attractions, and also contains a few tourist-oriented coupons.

The area has a fairly active agenda of dance, classical music, opera, and theater, much of which takes place at the **Carr Performing Arts Centre** (✉401 W. Livingston St., Orlando ☎407/849–2577 ⊕ www.orlandocentroplex. com). The **Broadway Series** (☎ 407/839–3900 Ticketmaster) has top-notch touring shows such as *Beauty and the Beast, Fame,* and *Phantom of the Opera.*

The downtown Orlando Arena was given a name change thanks to a large check from a major corporation; the clunkily named **TD Waterhouse Centre** (✉ 600 W. Amelia St., Orlando ☎ 407/849–2020 ⊕ www. orlandocentroplex.com) plays host to many big-name performers and sports events.

During the school year, the Bach Festival organization at **Rollins College** (✉ Winter Park ☎ 407/646–2233) has a three-part concert series that's open to the public and is usually free. The choral series is held at Rollins's Knowles Memorial Chapel. The second part, the visiting-artists series at the Annie Russell Theater, showcases internationally celebrated artists who have performed at venues such as Carnegie Hall. In late February and early March, internationally recognized artists appear at the **Bach Music Festival** (☎ 407/646–2182 ⊕ www.bachfestivalflorida. org), a Winter Park tradition since 1936 and the last in the trilogy. Call or check the Web site for festival locations, which may include the Annie Russell Theater, Knowles Memorial Chapel, and the First Congregational Church of Winter Park.

Nightlife

Bars, Lounges & Nightclubs

WALT DISNEY WORLD RESORT — When you enter the fiefdom known as Walt Disney World, you're likely to see as many watering holes as cartoon characters. Nightlife awaits at several Disney shopping and entertainment complexes—everywhere you look, rockers, bluesmen, and DJs are tuning up and turning on their amps after dinner's done. Plus, two long-running dinner shows provide an evening of song, dance, and dining, all for a single price. Get information on WDW nightlife from the Walt Disney World information hot line (☎ 407/824–4321 or 407/824–4500) or check online at ⊕ www. disneyworld.com. Disney nightspots accept American Express, MasterCard, and Visa, and you can charge your bill to your room if you're staying at a Disney-owned property. The **Laughing Kookaburra** (⊠ Wyndham Palace, Lake Buena Vista ☎ 407/827–3722) has been a longtime favorite of locals, with standard-issue happy hours, Ladies' Nights, and live music.

Disney's BoardWalk (☎ 407/939–3492 entertainment hotline), across Crescent Lake from the Yacht and Beach Club Resorts, recalls an Atlantic City–style, turn-of-the-last-century amusement complex by the shore, complete with restaurants, clubs, souvenir sellers, surreys, saltwater taffy vendors, and shops. When the lights go on after sunset, take a nostalgic, romantic stroll. In true Disney fashion, the sports motif at the **ESPN Club** (☎ 407/939–1177) is carried into every nook and many of the crannies. The vibe is rugged and boisterous at **Jellyrolls** (☎ 407/ 560–8770), which has comedians at dueling grand pianos and a singalong piano bar. Wander the promenade and you'll also come across **Atlantic Dance** (☎ 407/939–2444) for Top 40 dance tunes, and **Big River Grille & Brewing Works** (☎ 407/560–0253). Cover charges vary depending on the day of the week. For information on all BoardWalk events, call the entertainment hotline.

Many Disney clubs are at **Pleasure Island,** a 6-acre after-dark entertainment complex connected to the rest of Downtown Disney by footbridges. Despite its location on Disney property, the entertainment has real grit and life, even against the backdrop of the facility's gimmicky underlying concept: every night is New Year's Eve, complete with a nightly countdown to midnight and fireworks. In addition to seven clubs and an Irish pub, you'll find a few restaurants and shops. A pay-one-price admission gets you into all the clubs and shows. Children accompanied by an adult are admitted to all clubs except BET SoundStage and Mannequins.

Fodor'sChoice
★

Adventurer's Club re-creates a private club of the 1930s. Much of the entertainment is found in looking at exotic accent pieces that clutter the walls; the rest is in watching actors lead sing-alongs and share tall tales from their adventures. **BET SoundStage Club** is backed by Black Entertainment Television and pays tribute to all genres of African-American music through videos and live performances. The blend has attracted legions of locals who proclaim this the funkiest nightspot in Central Florida (and perhaps also the loudest). The comedians at the **Comedy Warehouse** perform improv games, sing improvised songs, and create off-the-cuff sketches based largely on suggestions from the audience. At **8TRAX,** groove to the recorded music of Donna Summer or the Village People while the disco balls spin. You'll either love or tolerate **Mannequins'** high-tech style, complete with Top 40 hits; a revolving dance floor; elaborate lighting; suggestive, over-the-top Disney dancers; and such special effects as bubbles and snow. **Motion** plays dance music from Zoot Suit Riot to the latest techno junk. The two-story warehouse look is stark, with the emphasis put on the dance floor and the club's twirling lights and thumping sound system. A traditional Irish pub with music, a menu of treats, and a bit o' Blarney just opened at the site of the old Pleasure Island Jazz Company. The **Rock & Roll Beach Club** throbs with live rock music from the '60s to the '90s. ⊠ *Off Buena Vista Dr., Downtown Disney* ☎ *407/934–7781 or 407/824–4500* ▦ *Pay-one-price admission to clubs $20.95 plus tax, shops and restaurants open to all 10:30–7* ◷ *Clubs daily 7 PM–2 AM; shops and restaurants daily 10:30 AM–2 AM.*

Fodor'sChoice
★

Fodor'sChoice
★

Downtown Disney West Side is a pleasingly hip outdoor complex of shopping, dining, and entertainment. A 24-screen AMC cinema shows first-run movies. For something a little different, drop by for a beer and a *baba-lu* at Gloria Estefan's **Bongos Cuban Café** (☎ 407/828–0999). **Cirque du Soleil** (☎ 407/939–7600) starts at 100 mph and accelerates from there. It's 90 minutes of extraordinary acrobatics, avant-garde stagings, costumes, choreography, and a grand finale that'll make you double-check Newton's laws of motion. Shows featuring 72 performers are scheduled twice daily, five days a week (call for current performance schedule). Adjacent to the **House of Blues** (☎ 407/934–2583) restaurant, which itself showcases cool blues starting at 11, HOB's up-close-and-personal concert venue presents local and nationally known artists playing everything from reggae to rock to R&B. **DisneyQuest** is a five-story video–virtual-reality mini-theme park, and there's a **Wolfgang Puck Cafe,** a **Virgin Megastore,** plus an avenue of eclectic shops. ⊠ *Off Buena Vista Dr., Downtown Disney* ☎ *407/824–4321 or 407/824–2222.*

Universal's CityWalk meets the Downtown Disney challenge with its open and airy gathering place, which includes clubs ranging from quiet jazz retreats to over-the-top discotheques. **Bob Marley—A Tribute to Freedom** is a loud reggae club–restaurant with more than a touch of Jamaica. **City Jazz** has taken on a split personality, with cool jazz and high-energy funk sharing the venue several days a week with a Bonkerz Comedy Club routine. **the groove** has wild lighting, visual effects, disco chrome, and funk music that will have you shakin' your groove thang all night long. The world's largest **Hard Rock Cafe** adjoins the chain's first dedicated live concert venue, **Hard Rock Live.** **The Latin Quarter** is crowded and pulsing and feels like a 21st-century version of Ricky Ricardo's Tropicana, with food and entertainment from 21 Latin American countries. The 20-screen **Loew's Universal Cineplex** (☎ 407/354–5998 tickets, 407/354–3374 box office) can offer an escape from the crowds. **Jimmy Buffett's Margaritaville** has proven itself popular with Parrotheads and margarita drinkers. The former Motown Cafe is evolving as a new club called **Decades.** The **NASCAR Café** is the only NASCAR-sanctioned specialty restaurant with full-size stock cars and racing memorabilia. Having teamed up with the Hard Rock Cafe, the NBA and WNBA see a demand for the basketball-theme **NBA restaurant.** An exact duplicate of the New Orleans favorite, **Pat O'Brien's** blows into Orlando with its signature drink, the hurricane, as well as dueling pianos and a "flaming fountain" patio. Clubs charge individual covers; you can buy a Party Pass (a one price–all clubs admission) for $9.95; or a Party Pass-and-a-Movie for $13. Making these deals even better is the fact that after 6 PM the $8 parking fee drops to nothing. ☎ *407/363–8000 Universal main line, 888/331–9108, 407/224–2692 CityWalk guest services* ⊕ *www.citywalkorlando.com.*

ORLANDO For several years, downtown Orlando clubs had a monopoly on nighttime entertainment—which came to a close when Disney and Universal muscled their way in. Nightspots still attract office workers after hours, but the once-popular Church Street Station entertainment complex has closed. Down Orange Avenue, cool clubs are now sitting beside grungy tattoo and piercing parlors that are making the downtown area look tired, though a revitalization project is currently underway. There are some gems in the surrounding neighborhoods and clubs that are worth a visit—if you're willing to seek them out.

Devoid of stand-up comedians, lively **Sak Comedy Lab** (✉ 380 W. Amelia Ave., Downtown Orlando ☎ 407/648–0001) is where you'll find Orlando's premier comedy troupe. Duel of Fools is the regular cast; the Sak Comedy Lab Rats are apprentices with potential, and the Generation S show spotlights Lab Rats with promise. Wayne Brady, star of *Whose Line Is It Anyway?,* got his start here. The troupe plays to sold-out audiences Tuesday–Saturday.

Perhaps the favorite live-music venue of locals, **Social** (✉ 54 N. Orange Ave. ☎ 407/246–1419 ⊕ orlandosocial.com) is a great place to see touring and local musicians. You can sip trademark martinis while listening to anything from alternative rock to rockabilly to undiluted jazz. Matchbox Twenty and Seven Mary Three both got their starts here.

Socialite Paris Hilton lent her name and business acumen to **Club Paris** (✉ 122 W. Church St. ☎ 407/832-7409), a new nightclub that premiered in late 2004. Three million dollars helped refurbish part of the defunct Church Street Station, and now a South Beach–style courtyard sets the tone for entry. The floor is monitored by "fashion police" who award the trendiest patrons a free bar tab for the evening. There's plenty of room to dance (20,000 square feet) to New York–style DJ noise, as well as varied music on themed nights: Latin, Ladies, Fashion, and '80s. If you're considered worthy or are willing to pay an added admission, you can go upstairs to the VIP club. This might well be the hottest club in Orlando.

Dinner Shows

For a single price, these hybrid eatery-entertainment complexes deliver a theatrical production and a multicourse dinner. Performances might include jousting or jamboree tunes, and some meals tend to be better than average. Unlimited beer, wine, and soda are usually included, but mixed drinks (often *any* drinks before dinner) will cost you extra. What the shows lack in substance and depth they make up for in grandeur and enthusiasm; children often love them. Seatings are usually sometime between 7 and 9:30, but an extra show may be added during peak tourist periods. Always make reservations in advance, especially for weekends and shows at Walt Disney World Resort.

WALT DISNEY WORLD RESORT   Staged at rustic Pioneer Hall, the **Hoop-Dee-Doo Revue** may be corny, but it's also the liveliest show in Walt Disney World. A troupe of jokers called the Pioneer Hall Players stomp their feet, wisecrack, sing, and dance while the audience chows down on barbecued ribs, fried chicken, corn on the cob, strawberry shortcake, and all the fixins. Shows during busy seasons sell out months in advance. ⊠ *Fort Wilderness Resort, Walt Disney World* ☎ *407/939–3463 in advance, 407/824–2803 day of show* 🍽 *$50.22 adults, $25.43 children 3–11* ☾ *Daily at 5, 7:15, and 9:30* ☞ *No smoking.*

Spirit of Aloha is the new name for the long-running Polynesian Luau. The show is still an outdoor barbecue with entertainment in line with its colorful South Pacific style. Its fire jugglers and hula-drum dancers are entertaining for the whole family, if never quite as endearing as the napkin twirlers at the Hoop-Dee-Doo Revue. The hula dancers' navel maneuvers, however, are something to see. You should try to make reservations at least a month in advance. ⊠ *Polynesian Resort, Walt Disney World* ☎ *407/939–3463 in advance, 407/824–1593 day of show* 🍽 *$50.22 adults, $25.43 children 3–11* ☾ *Tues.–Sat. at 5:15 and 8* ☞ *No smoking.*

AROUND ORLANDO   An elaborate palace outside, **Arabian Nights** is more like an arena within, with seating for more than 1,200. The show includes eerie fog, an Arabian princess, and a buffoonish genie, but the real stars are the 60 fabulous horses that perform in acts representing horse-loving cultures from around the world. The three-course dinners of prime rib or vegetarian lasagna are functional but not very flavorful. Ask about discount offers. ⊠ *6225 W. Irlo Bronson Memorial Hwy., Kissimmee* ☎ *407/239–9223, 800/553–6116, 800/533–3615 in Canada* 🍽 *$47 adults, $29 children 3–11* ☾ *Shows nightly; times vary* ▭ *AE, D, MC, V.*

Capone's Dinner and Show returns to the gangland Chicago of 1931, when mobsters and their dames represented the height of underworld society. The evening begins in an old-fashioned ice-cream parlor, but say the secret password and you are ushered inside Al Capone's private Underworld Cabaret and Speakeasy. Dinner is an unlimited Italian buffet that's heavy on pasta. ⊠ *4740 W. Irlo Bronson Memorial Hwy.* ☎ *407/397–2378* 🕮 *$39.95 adults, $23.95 children 4–12* ⊘ *Daily at 7:30* ⊟ *AE, D, MC, V.*

For real old-fashioned family-fun entertainment, **Dolly Parton's Dixie Stampede Dinner & Show** can't be beat. Opened in June 2003, the show gets the audience involved in a competition between the North and South as you cheer during events that include ostrich and pig races. The country-style show has singing, dancing, comedy, eight buffalo, and fast-paced acrobatic horsemanship with 32 magnificent horses. The finale includes a patriotic tribute written by Dolly Parton. After the show you can meet the horses and performers. ⊠ *8251 Vineland Ave.* ☎ *407/238–4455 or 866/443–4943* ⊕ *www.dixiestampede.com* 🕮 *$46.99 adults, $19.99 children 3–11* ⊘ *Shows usually 7 PM with more shows or special holiday shows added in season; call ahead* ⊟ *AE, D, MC, V.*

In **Medieval Times,** no fewer than 30 charging horses and a cast of 75 knights, nobles, and maidens perform in a huge, ersatz-medieval manor house. The two-hour tournament includes sword fights, jousting matches, and other games, and the bill of fare is heavy on meat and potatoes. ⊠ *4510 W. Irlo Bronson Memorial Hwy., Kissimmee* ☎ *407/239–0214 or 800/229–8300* 🕮 *$45.95 adults, $29.95 children 3–11* ⊘ *Performances usually daily at 8; call ahead* ⊟ *AE, D, MC, V.*

At **Sleuths Mystery Dinner Show,** your four-course meal is served up with a healthy dose of conspiracy. If you haven't got a clue, then stop here and question the characters in an attempt to solve the mystery. ⊠ *7508 Universal Blvd.* ☎ *407/363–1985 or 800/393–1985* 🕮 *$46.95 adults, $23.95 children 3–11* ⊘ *Weekdays 7:30, sometimes 8:30; Sat. 6, 7:30, and 9; Sun. 7:30* ⊟ *AE, D, MC, V.*

Movies
In addition to the theaters at Downtown Disney and CityWalk, check out the impressive **Muvico Pointe 21.** It has 21 screens and stadium seating. ⊠ *Pointe*Orlando, 9101 International Dr., International Drive Area* ☎ *407/903–0555* 🕮 *After 6 PM, $8 adults, $5 children; matinees $6.*

SPORTS & THE OUTDOORS

Orlando is the place to visit if you want to be outside. You'll find just about every outdoor sport here—unless it involves a ski lift—that you'll find anywhere else in the country. The city also holds a hot ticket as a professional-sports town. In addition to hosting the NBA Magic, Orlando lays claim to the Walt Disney Speedway. **Disney's Wide World of Sports** (☎ 407/828–3267) has tournament-type events in more than 30 individual and team sports; serves as the spring-training home of the Atlanta Braves; and offers participatory sports for guests, including basketball, football, baseball, and soccer, as part of its Multi Sport Experience.

Fodor'sChoice
★

Auto Racing
The **Richard Petty Driving Experience** allows you to ride in or even drive a NASCAR-style stock car on a real racetrack. Depending on what you're

CloseUp

FLORIDA SPRING TRAINING: PLAY BALL!

ALTHOUGH THE MAJORITY of Americans are addicted to baseball for only a few days each October, there are some whose passion for this pastime burns year-round. The scant months when the "Boys of Summer" aren't actually on the field is far too long for those who head south to watch the "Boys of Spring" get back to business at Florida's many spring training camps.

If you're cruising the state in March, you can join them at any of the 20 major-league spring-training camps spread across Central and South Florida. While the action on the field won't have any bearing on the outcome of the World Series, the atmosphere brings baseball back to its roots. When you're watching from wooden stands or stretched out on the lawn, the simplicity of the sport is in sharp focus. Here, there are no massive stadiums backed by software companies or financial institutions. The millionaires on the field are back on the sandlots where they learned to play. And since managers want to give every player a shot, chances are you'll see the entire roster playing a few innings at least—and you'll usually have a shot at getting a player's autograph before the game begins.

So while you're roaming around Central Florida and find yourself near a spring-training stadium, drop into one of these fields of dreams. Armed with a carton of popcorn, a soft drink, and a hot dog, you'll be able to savor the American pastime without the pretense.

Atlanta Braves. At Disney's Wide World of Sports Complex, the Atlanta Braves play in a sparkling stadium complete with towering archways and ballroom-style common areas. These luxuries aside, the sloping lawns that run along side the first- and third-base lines are perfect for stretching out a blanket and watching the game. ⊠ Disney Baseball Stadium, 710 S. Victory Way, Kissimmee ☎ 407/828–3267 or 407/939–4263 🎫 $12.50–$20.50.

Cleveland Indians. Upgraded seats aside, the feel in this stadium still has traces of the past (poles erected in the middle of the seating sections). The Indians were ready to leave Arizona and head to Homestead, but Hurricane Andrew forced them to go north. This is a good bet for fans who want to watch the game in a bucolic Florida town. ⊠ Chain of Lakes Park, Cypress Gardens Blvd., Winter Haven ☎ 866/488–7423 for phone sales 🎫 $5–$21.

Detroit Tigers. If you thought Florida was discovered by Walt Disney, consider this: the Detroit Tigers have been training in the Sunshine State each spring since 1934 (the mouse didn't come to stay until 1971). Named after the city's parks director, this slow-paced stadium is in a laid-back southern city where you can settle in and watch the game minus the taint of corporate money. ⊠ Joker Marchant Stadium, 2301 Lakeland Hills Blvd., Lakeland ☎ 863/686–8075 🎫 $7–$16.

Houston Astros. Just a hop, skip, and jump from the theme parks is a chance to see the Houston Astros in spring-training action. ⊠ Osceola County Stadium, 1000 Bill Beck Blvd., Kissimmee ☎ 407/933–2520 or 407/839–3900 🎫 $9–$14.

willing to spend—prices range from $95 to $1,249—you can do everything from riding shotgun for three laps on the 1-mi track to taking driving lessons, culminating in your very own solo behind the wheel. The Richard Petty organization has a second Central Florida location at the Daytona International Speedway, but it offers rides with experienced drivers rather than allowing you to drive a race car. ⊠ *Walt Disney Speedway* ☎ *800/237–3889* ⊕ *www.1800bepetty.com.*

Basketball

Fodor'sChoice The **Orlando Magic** has driven the city to new heights of hoop fanati-
★ cism, though tickets aren't unattainable. Nosebleed seats run as low as $10; front-and-center viewing goes for up to $150. ⊠ *TD Waterhouse Centre, 600 W. Amelia St., Orlando, 2 blocks west of I–4 Exit 41* ☎ *407/839–3900 Ticketmaster* ⊕ *www.nba.com/magic.*

Biking

The most scenic bike riding in Orlando is on Walt Disney World Resort property, along roads that take you past forests, lakes, golf courses, and Disney's wooded resort villas and campgrounds. You can rent bikes for $4 per hour and surrey bikes for $18 (two-seater) and $22 (four-seater) per half hour at the **Barefoot Bay Marina** (☎ 407/934–2850), open daily 10–5. Bike rentals at **Coronado Springs Resort** (☎ 407/939–1000) near Disney–MGM Studios are $8 per hour or $22 per day and surrey bikes are $17 (2 seater) and $21 (4 seater) per half hour. The resort's odd surrey bikes, which look like old-fashioned carriages, are a great way to take your family on a sightseeing tour, and with their covered tops, provide a rare commodity at Disney—shade. At **Fort Wilderness Bike Barn** (☎ 407/824–2742), bicycles rent for $8 per hour and $21 per day. At the **BoardWalk Resort** (☎ 407/939–6486, 407/560–8754 surrey bikes), near Disney–MGM Studios, two types of bikes are available at two separate kiosks. Surrey bikes cost $18, $20, and $23 per half hour, depending on the size of the bike. Regular bicycles are $7 per hour.

Orlando has three good bike trails. The **West Orange Trail** (⊠ 3535 Damon Rd., Apopka ☎ 407/654–5144) runs some 22 mi through western Orlando and the neighboring towns of Winter Garden and Apopka. The **Cady Way Trail** is a local favorite that connects eastern Orlando with the well-manicured enclave suburb of Winter Park. The pleasant trail is only 3½ mi long, with water fountains and shaded seating along the route. The best access point is the parking lot at the southern trailhead, immediately adjacent to the east side of the Orlando Fashion Square Mall (3201 E. Colonial Dr., about 3 mi east of I–4 Exit 83B). You can also enter the trail on its east end, at Cady Way Park (1300 S. Denning Ave.). **Cross Seminole Trail** has been designated as part of the Florida National Scenic Trail and is scheduled to become part of a 30-mi link of trails that run through the cities north of downtown to eventually connect with Cady Way Trail. At this writing, 3.7 mi of the trail is open; it runs through heavily vegetated landscape, which is both peaceful and picturesque.

Fishing

Central Florida is covered with freshwater lakes and rivers teeming with all kinds of fish, especially largemouth black bass, but also perch, catfish, sunfish, and pike. To fish in most Florida waters—but not at Walt Disney World Resort—anglers over 16 need a fishing license, available at bait-and-tackle shops, fishing camps, and sporting-goods stores.

WALT DISNEY WORLD RESORT Fishing without a guide is permitted in the canals around the Dixie Landings and Port Orleans resorts and at Fort Wilderness Resort and Campground. **Bay Lake Fishing Trips** (☎ 407/939–7529) takes two-hour fishing excursions on regularly stocked Bay Lake and Seven Seas Lagoon.

AROUND ORLANDO Top fishing waters include Lake Kissimmee, the Butler and Conway chains of lakes, and Lake Tohopekaliga (also known as Lake Toho). Arrange for a guide through one of the excellent area fishing camps. **East Lake Fish Camp** (✉ 3705 Big Bass Rd., Kissimmee ☎ 407/348–2040) is on East Lake Tohopekaliga. **Lake Toho Resort** (✉ 4715 Kissimmee Park Rd., St. Cloud ☎ 407/892–8795 ⊕ www.laketohoresort.com) is on West Lake Tohopekaliga. **Richardson's Fish Camp** (✉ 1550 Scotty's Rd., Kissimmee ☎ 407/846–6540) is also on West Lake Tohopekaliga.

Golf

Golf is extremely popular in Central Florida. Be sure to reserve tee times well in advance.

Golfpac (✉ 483 Montgomery Pl., Altamonte Springs 32714 ☎ 407/260–2288 or 800/327–0878 ⊕ www.golfpactravel.com) packages golf vacations and prearranges tee times at more than 78 courses around Orlando. Rates vary based on hotel and course.

WALT DISNEY WORLD RESORT

Fodor's Choice
★

Walt Disney World (☎ 407/939–4653) has five championship 18-hole courses—all on the PGA Tour route: **Eagle Pines** (✉ Bonnet Creek Golf Club, Walt Disney World), green fee: $89/$154; **Lake Buena Vista** (✉ Lake Buena Vista Dr., Walt Disney World), green fee: $69/$119; **Magnolia** (✉ Shades of Green, Walt Disney World), green fee: $79/$144; **Osprey Ridge** (✉ Bonnet Creek Golf Club, Walt Disney World), green fee: $99/$169; and the **Palm** (✉ Shades of Green, Walt Disney World), green fee: $74/$139. Except for **Oak Trail** (✉ Shades of Green, Walt Disney World), a 9-hole layout for novice and preteen golfers, these courses are among the busiest and most expensive in the region.

The three original Disney courses—Lake Buena Vista, Magnolia, and the Palm—have the same fees and discount policies regardless of season and are slightly less expensive than Eagle Pines and Osprey Ridge, whose fees change during the year. All offer a twilight discount rate, $20/$80, which goes into effect between 2 and 3, depending on the season.

AROUND ORLANDO Green fees at most non-Disney courses fluctuate with the season. A twilight discount applies after 2 in busy seasons and after 3 during the rest of the year; the discount is usually half off the normal rate.

★ You can only play at **Arnold Palmer's Bay Hill Club** (✉ 9000 Bay Hill Rd. ☎ 407/876–2429 or 888/422–9445) if you're invited by a member or stay at the club's on-property hotel, but room rates that include a round of golf run as low as $189 per person in summer. The course at the **Celebration Golf Club** (✉ 701 Golf Park Dr., Celebration ☎ 407/566–4653) was designed by Robert Trent Jones Jr. and Sr. and is 1 mi off the U.S.192 strip; green fee: $45/$130. **Champions Gate Golf Club** (✉ 1400

Masters Blvd., Champions Gate ☎ 407/787–4653 or 888/558–9301), near Walt Disney World, has the feel of the best British Isles courses; green fee: $59/$140. **Cypress Creek Country Club** (⊠ 5353 Vineland Rd. ☎ 407/351–2187) is a demanding course with 16 water holes and lots of trees; green fee: $40/$55. The **Falcon's Fire Golf Club** (⊠ 3200 Seralago Blvd., Kissimmee ☎ 407/239–5445) course was designed by Rees Jones, green fee: $85/$130. **The Villas of Grand Cypress Golf Club** (⊠ 1 N. Jacaranda Dr. ☎ 407/239–1909 or 800/835–7377) has 45 holes of golf, green fee: $115/$180. **Hawk's Landing Golf Course** (⊠ Marriott's Orlando World Center, 8701 World Center Dr. ☎ 407/238–8660) includes 16 water holes, lots of sand, and exotic landscaping; green fee: $65/$165. The Tom Fazio–designed, semi-private **Legacy Club at Alaqua Lakes** (⊠ 1700 Alaqua Lakes Blvd., Longwood ☎ 407/444–9995) has 18 holes, green fee: $99/$109. The 18-hole, semi-private course at **MetroWest Country Club** (⊠ 2100 S. Hiawassee Rd., Orlando ☎ 407/299–1099) was designed by Robert Trent Jones, green fee: $59/$94. **Mission Inn Golf & Tennis Resort** (⊠ 10400 Rte. 48, Howey-in-the-Hills ☎ 352/324–3885 or 800/874–9053) has two courses, green fee: $60/$125. **Orange County National Golf Center & Lodge** (⊠ 16301 Phil Ritson Way, Winter Garden ☎ 407/656–2626 or 888/727–3672) has two public, par-72, 18-hole courses: the Crooked Cat Course, green fee: $19/$65, and the Panther Lake course, green fee: $19/$75. There are 54 holes to play at the **Orange Lake Resort & Country Club** (⊠ 8505 W. Irlo Bronson Memorial Hwy., Kissimmee ☎ 407/239–0000 or 800/877–6522); among them are the 18 holes at the Legends at Orange Lake course, green fee: $31/$135. Overlooking Lake Minneola, **Palisades Country Club** (⊠ 16510 Palisades Blvd., Clermont ☎ 352/394–0085) has a Joe Lee–designed course, green fee: $30/$55. The exceptionally long public course at **Southern Dunes Golf & Country Club** (⊠ 2888 Southern Dunes Blvd., Haines City ☎ 941/421–4653 or 800/632–6400), great for low handicappers, has 18 holes, green fee: $35/$110. The low-key 9-hole **Winter Park Municipal Golf Club** (⊠ 761 Old England Ave., Winter Park ☎ 407/623–3339) is incredibly inexpensive; green fee: $10.

Horseback Riding

Fort Wilderness Resort and Campground (⊠ Fort Wilderness Resort ☎ 407/824–2832) offers tame trail rides through backwoods. Children must be at least nine to ride, and adults must weigh less than 250 pounds. Trail rides are $32 for 45 minutes, and hours of operation vary by season. You must check in 30 minutes prior to your ride, and reservations are essential. Both horseback riding and camping are open to nonguests.

FodorsChoice ★ **Grand Cypress Equestrian Center** (⊠ Hyatt Regency Grand Cypress Resort, 1 Equestrian Dr., Orlando ☎ 407/239–4608) gives private lessons in hunt seat, jumping, combined training, dressage, and western. Supervised novice and advanced group trail rides are available daily between 8:30 and 5. Trail rides are $45 per hour for novice, $100 per hour for advanced. Private lessons are $55 per ½ hour and $100 per hour. Call at least a week ahead for reservations in winter and spring.

Basic and longer, more advanced nature-trail tours along beautifully wooded trails near Kissimmee are available at **Horse World Riding Sta-**

bles (✉ 3705 S. Poinciana Blvd., Kissimmee ☎ 407/847–4343), open daily between 9 and 5. Pony rides are also available, and the stables area has picnic tables, farm animals you can pet, and a pond to fish in. Trail rides are $39 for basic, $47 for intermediate, and $69 for advanced. The basic trail ride for children 5 and under is $15, and the stables offers birthday party packages for kids, as well as hay rides for groups. Reservations a day in advance are recommended for the advanced trails.

Miniature Golf

The **Fantasia Gardens Miniature Golf Course** (☎ 407/560–4870) is heavily themed in imagery from Disney's *Fantasia*. It's adjacent to the Swan and Dolphin resort complex and is near the Disney–MGM Studios. Games are $10.70 for adults, $8.56 for children ages three through nine, and there's a 50% discount for the second consecutive round played, which is also valid at the Winter Summerland course. With everything from Fodor'sChoice sand castles to snow banks, the **Winter Summerland Miniature Golf** ★ **Course** (☎ 407/560–7161) is allegedly where Santa and his elves spend their summer vacation. The course is adjacent to Blizzard Beach and is close to the Coronado Springs and All-Star Resorts. Adults play for $10.70, and children ages three to nine play for $8.56. A 50% discount on the second consecutive round played can be used here or at Fantasia Gardens.

Rock Climbing

The **Aiguille Rock Climbing Center,** in the Orlando suburb of Longwood, has all the cliffs you can handle. Climbers reach a height of 45 feet on 6,500 square feet of rock-studded walls. ✉ *999 Charles St., Longwood* ☎ *407/332–1430 ⊕ www.climborlando.com ⊠ Day passes $15 adults; equipment rental $6.50, including proper shoes and harness; private rock-climbing instruction $40 per hr for one person; reservation required ⊙ Weekdays 10–10, Sat. 10–11, Sun. noon–7.*

Water Sports

Marinas at the Caribbean Beach Resort, Contemporary Resort, Dixie Landings Resort, Downtown Disney Marketplace, Fort Wilderness Resort and Campground, Grand Floridian, Polynesian Resort, Port Orleans Resort, Wilderness Lodge, and Yacht and Beach clubs rent Sunfish, catamarans, motor-powered pontoon boats, pedal boats, and tiny two-passenger Water Sprites—a hit with kids—for use on their nearby waters: Bay Lake, Seven Seas Lagoon, Lake Buena Vista, Club Lake, or Buena Vista Lagoon. The Polynesian Resort marina also rents outrigger canoes, and Fort Wilderness rents canoes for paddling along the placid canals in the area. To sail or water-ski on Bay Lake or the Seven Seas Lagoon, stop at the Fort Wilderness, Contemporary, Polynesian, or Grand Floridian marina.

SHOPPING

Factory Outlets

The International Drive area is filled with outlet stores. At the northern tip of I–Drive, **Belz Factory Outlet World** (✉ 5401 W. Oak Ridge Rd.,

Orlando ☎ 407/354–0126 or 407/352–9611 ☉ Mon.–Sat. 10–9, Sun. 10–6) is the area's largest collection of outlets—more than 170—in two malls and four nearby annexes. **Orlando Premium Outlet** (✉ 8200 Vineland Rd. ☎ 407/238–7787 ⊕ www.premiumoutlets.com ☉ Mon.–Sat. 10–10, Sun. 10–9), with its collection of 127 upscale shops in an open-air layout, is capitalizing on its proximity to Disney (it's at the confluence of I–4, Highway 535, and International Drive). It can be tricky to reach—you have to turn off Highway 535 and find the very subtle entrance to Little Lake Bryan Road (*hint*: it parallels I–4).

Flea Markets
Flea World (✉ 3 mi east of I–4 Exit 98 on Lake Mary Blvd., then 1 mi south on U.S. 17–92, Sanford ☎ 407/321–1792) claims to be America's largest flea market under one roof. It sells predominantly merchandise—everything from car tires and pet tarantulas to coffee, leather lingerie, and beaded evening gowns. It's open Friday–Sunday 9–6. Kids love **Fun World,** next door, which offers miniature golf, arcade games, go-carts, bumper cars, bumper boats, kiddie rides, and batting cages.

★ On weekends, **Renninger's Twin Markets** (✉ U.S. 441, Mount Dora ☎ 352/383–8393) hosts hundreds of dealers. At the top of the hill, 400 flea-market dealers sell household items, garage-sale surplus, produce, baked goods, and pets. At the bottom of the hill, 200 antiques dealers sell ephemera, old phonographs, deco fixtures, and antique furniture. Both markets are open every weekend, but on certain weekends, the antiques market has Antique Fairs, attracting about 500 dealers. The really big shows, however, are the three-day Extravaganzas, which draw up to 1,500 dealers. Depending on the day of the week, entrance to Extravaganzas costs $3–$10, but the other markets are free. Hours are weekends 9 to 5.

Shopping Areas, Malls & Department Stores
WALT DISNEY WORLD RESORT Shopping is an integral part of the Disney experience, going far beyond the surfeit of Disney trinkets found in every park. The area known as Downtown Disney contains three shopping-entertainment areas with plenty of just about everything. If you're staying at a Disney property, a nice perk awaits: if you buy anything from a store inside any Disney park, you can ask the salesperson to have it delivered to your room so you don't have to lug it around all day long. The service is free, and your purchase will be waiting for you on your bed when you return to your room. **Downtown Disney Marketplace,** a pleasant complex of shops,

Fodor'sChoice ★ includes the **World of Disney** (☎ 407/828–1451), the Disney superstore to end all Disney superstores, and the refurbished **LEGO Imagination Center** (☎ 407/828–0065), with an impressive backdrop of elaborate Lego sculptures and an excellent outdoor play area for kids. Among the standouts over at **Downtown Disney West Side** are **Guitar Gallery** (☎ 407/827–0118), which sells videos, music books, accessories, and guitars, guitars, and more guitars; and the enormous **Virgin Megastore** (☎ 407/828–0222), with a music, video, and book selection as large as its prices. Don't miss **Hoypolloi,** with its gallery full of museum-quality art and jewelry. Sandwiched between those two key shopping spots is **Downtown Disney Pleasure Island,** with several trendy boutiques and gift shops.

UNIVERSAL ORLANDO **Universal's CityWalk** (☎ 407/363–8000) brings themed shopping experiences along with its cornucopia of restaurants, clubs, bars, and cafés. Retailers include **Endangered Species** (☎ 407/224–2310), with products representing endangered animals, ecosystems, and cultures worldwide; **Cigarz** (☎ 407/370–2999), for hand-rolled cigars; **All Star Collectibles** (☎ 407/224–2380), for sports junkies, with one-of-a-kind items and paraphernalia; and **Universal Studios Store** (☎ 407/224–2207), for a slew of official merchandise.

ORLANDO The necessities, such as a 24-hour grocery and pharmacy, post office, bank, and cleaners, are all at **Crossroads of Lake Buena Vista** (⊠ Rte. 535 and I–4, Lake Buena Vista), across from Downtown Disney Marketplace. **Florida Mall** (⊠ 8001 S. Orange Blossom Trail), 4½ mi east of Interstate 4 and International Drive, is the largest mall in Central Florida, with 2 million square feet of shopping action with big-name chain stores, 260 specialty shops, and one of the better food courts around. **Mall at Millenia** (⊠ 4200 S. Conroy Rd. ☎ 407/363–3555 ⊙ Mon.–Sat. 10–9:30, Sun. 11–7), at 1.2 million square feet, is the latest arrival in Orlando's retail wars. A few minutes northwest of Universal Orlando, it has several stores exclusive to the area, including Neiman-Marcus and Bloomingdale's, and several good restaurants. The retro-nouveau design of the mall's furnishings incorporates tiles made with 250-million-year-old fossils as well as a dozen LED screens suspended in the mall rotunda broadcasting entertainment and fashion shows. A currency exchange counter is handy for international guests (who make up a third of the mall's shoppers). It's easy to reach: take Exit 78 off I–4. At **Mercado** (⊠ 8445 International Dr., International Drive Area), there are some specialty shops and a food court.

Orlando Fashion Square (⊠ 3201 E. Colonial Dr.), 3 mi east of Interstate 4 Exit 83B, has 165 shops, including Macy's, JCPenney, Sears Roebuck, Ann Taylor Loft, and Lerner. **Pointe*Orlando** (⊠ 9101 International Dr., International Drive Area) is across from the Orange County Convention Center and has more than 60 specialty shops, including A/X Armani Exchange, Abercrombie & Fitch, Gap, and Tommy Hilfiger.

In a sparkling 150,000-square-foot Western-style lodge, **Outdoor World** (⊠ 5156 International Dr. ☎ 407/563–5200) packs in countless fishing boats, RVs, tents, rifles, deep-sea fishing gear, freshwater fishing tackle, scuba equipment, fly-tying materials (classes are offered, too), a pro shop, outdoor clothing, Uncle Buck's Cabin (a restaurant and snack bar), and a shooting gallery. If you're an outdoor enthusiast, this is a must-see. The huge, multilevel **Sports Dominator** (⊠ 6464 International Dr. ☎ 407/354–2100) could probably equip all the players of Major League Baseball and the NFL, NBA, and NHL combined. Each sport receives its own section, crowding the floor with soccer balls, golf clubs, catcher's mitts, jerseys, bows, and a few thousand more sports items.

ORLANDO SUBURBS The New England–style village of **Mount Dora** is recognized as the antiques capital of Florida. Trendy and swank **Park Avenue** (⊠ Winter Park) has a collection of chic boutiques and bistros and is the perfect place for a romantic evening stroll.

WALT DISNEY WORLD® & THE ORLANDO AREA A TO Z

To research prices, get advice from other travelers, and book travel arrangements, visit www.fodors.com.

AIR TRAVEL

CARRIERS More than 20 scheduled airlines and more than 30 charter firms operate into and out of Orlando International Airport, providing direct service to more than 100 cities in the United States and overseas.

🛪 Major Airlines Air Tran ☎ 800/247-8726. Alaska Airlines ☎ 800/252-7522. America West ☎ 800/235-9292. American ☎ 800/433-7300. Continental ☎ 800/523-3273. Delta ☎ 800/221-1212. Northwest/KLM ☎ 800/225-2525. United Airlines ☎ 800/241-6522. US Airways ☎ 800/428-4322.

🛪 Smaller Airlines ATA ☎ 800/225-2995. Frontier ☎ 800/432-1359. JetBlue ☎ 800/538-2583. Midwest Express ☎ 800/452-2022. Song ☎ 800/359-7664. Southwest ☎ 800/435-9792. Spirit ☎ 800/772-7117.

AIRPORTS

The Orlando airport (MCO on your baggage tag) is ultramodern, huge, and growing all the time. However, it's relatively easy to navigate. Just follow the excellent signs. Monorails shuttle you from gate areas to the core area, where you'll find baggage claim. The complex is south of Orlando and northeast of Walt Disney World.

🛪 Airport Information Orlando International Airport (MCO) ☎ 407/825-2001.

AIRPORT TRANSFERS Find out in advance whether your hotel offers a free airport shuttle; if not, ask for a recommendation. Lynx operates public buses between the airport and the main terminal downtown. Although the cost is very low, other options are preferable, since the terminal is far from most hotels used by theme-park vacationers. Mears Transportation Group meets you at the gate, helps you with your luggage, and whisks you away, either in an 11-passenger van, a town car, or a limo. Vans run to and along U.S. 192 every 30 minutes; prices range from $17 one-way for adults ($13 for children 4–11) to $29 round-trip for adults ($21 children 4–11). Limo rates run around $44–$70 for a town car that accommodates three or four and $125 for a stretch limo that seats six. Town & Country charges $35–$55 one-way for up to seven people. Taxis take only a half hour to get from the airport to most hotels used by WDW visitors. They charge about $30 to the International Drive area, about $10 more to the U.S. 192 area. If you're staying at a Disney hotel, then make arrangements to use Disney's Magical Express. It provides airport shuttle, luggage delivery, and airline check-in for Disney hotel guests. The round-trip service is complimentary for the 18-month duration of the Happiest Celebration on Earth event beginning May 2005.

🛪 Buses & Limos Lynx ✉ 1200 W. South St., Orlando ☎ 407/841-8240 or 800/344-5969 ⊕ www.golynx.com. Mears Transportation Group ☎ 407/423-5566 ⊕ www.mearstransportation.com. Town & Country Transportation ☎ 407/828-3035.

BUS TRAVEL

Greyhound Lines buses stop in Orlando. If you're staying along International Drive, in Kissimmee, or in Orlando proper, ride public buses to get around the immediate area. To find out which bus to take, ask your hotel clerk or call Lynx. Scheduled service and charters linking just about every hotel and major attraction in the area are available from Mears Transportation Group. In addition, many hotels run their own shuttles especially for guests; to arrange a ride, ask your hotel concierge, inquire at the front desk, or phone the company directly. One-way fares are usually $8–$10 per adult, a couple of dollars less for children ages 4–11, between major hotel areas and the WDW parks. I-Ride trolleys run daily 8 AM–10:30 PM. Exact change is necessary—adult fare (75¢); children under 12 ride free. Passes for unlimited rides are $2 for one day, $3 for three days, $5 for five days, and $7 for one week.

🚌 **Bus Information Greyhound Lines** ☎ 800/231-2222 ✉ 555 N. John Young Pkwy., Orlando ☎ 407/292-3422. **Lynx** ☎ 407/841-8240. **Mears Transportation Group** ☎ 407/423-5566. **I-Ride Trolley** ☎ 407/248-9590 or 866/243-7483 ⊕ www.iridetrolley.com.

CAR TRAVEL

The Beeline Expressway (State Road 528) is the best way to get from Orlando International Airport to area attractions; however, it's a toll road, so expect to pay about $1.25 in tolls to get from the airport to I–4. Depending on the location of your hotel, follow the expressway west to International Drive, and either exit at SeaWorld for the International Drive area or stay on the Beeline to I–4, and head either west for Walt Disney World and U.S. 192–Kissimmee or east for Universal Studios and downtown Orlando. Call your hotel for the best route. Interstate 4 is the main artery in Central Florida, linking the Gulf Coast in Tampa to the Atlantic coast in Daytona Beach. While I–4 is an east–west highway, it actually follows a north–south track through the Orlando area, so traveling north on I–4 through Orlando would actually be heading east toward Daytona, and traveling south would actually be traveling west toward Tampa. So **think north when I–4 signs say east and think south when the signs say west.** In 2002 the Florida Department of Transportation changed the exit numbers of several major interstates, including I–4, which intersects Orlando and Walt Disney World. The WDW exits are 64B, 65, 67, and 68, but locals and older maps may still cite the old exits, 25, 24D, 26D, and 27, respectively. The new highway signs display both the old and new exit numbers. Two other main roads you're likely to use are International Drive, also known as I–Drive, and U.S. 192, sometimes called the Spacecoast Parkway or Irlo Bronson Memorial Highway. Get onto International Drive from I–4 Exits 72 (formerly Exit 28), 74A (formerly Exit 29), and 75B (formerly Exit 30B). U.S. 192 cuts across I–4 at Exits 64A (formerly 25A) and 64B (formerly 25B).

DISCOUNTS & DEALS

There are plenty of ways to save money while you're in the Orlando area. Coupon books, such as those available from Entertainment Travel Editions for around $30, can be good sources for discounts on rental cars, admission to attractions, meals, and other typical purchases.

1. Shop around carefully for theme-park tickets. Discounted theme-park tickets are widely available. Be sure to **look into combination tickets** and second-day-free tickets that get you admission to multiple theme parks or two days' admission for the price of one to a single park. The Orlando FlexTicket is just one example of the combination tickets available. Also visit the Orlando–Orange County Convention and Visitors Bureau on International Drive (⇨ Visitor Information) or stop in one of the many ticket booths around town, including the Tourism Bureau of Orlando, Know Before You Go, and the Tourist Information Center of Orlando. Do watch out for extra-cheap tickets (they may be expired) and discounts that require you to take time-share tours—unless you're interested in a time-share, that is.

If you're a member of the American Automobile Association, be sure to ask at your local club about getting discounted tickets. Find out if your employer belongs to the Universal Fan Club or the Magic Kingdom Club, which offer discount schemes to members' employees. Take advantage of next-day-free offers on tickets, which are often available. You'll get into a theme park a second day for the price of a one-day ticket. At Busch Gardens, go for the Twilight Tickets, available after 3 PM.

2. Buy your tickets as soon as you know you're going. Prices typically go up at least once a year, so you might beat a price hike—and save a little money.

3. Stay at hotels on U.S. 192 around Kissimmee and on International Drive that offer free transportation to and from the park. Getting to and from the parks may take a little extra time, but you won't have to pay to rent a car—or to park it.

4. In deciding whether to rent a car, do the math. Weigh the cost of renting against what it will cost to get your entire party to and from the airport and the theme parks and any other places you want to go. If you are traveling with a group of more than four, renting a car may be cheaper than other options.

5. Choose accommodations with a kitchen and where kids eat free. Stock up on breakfast items in a nearby supermarket, and save time—and money—by eating your morning meal in your hotel room.

6. Watch your shopping carefully. Theme-park merchandisers are excellent at displaying the goods so that you (or your children) can't resist them. You may find that some of the items for sale are also available at home—for quite a bit less. One way to cope is to give every member of your family a souvenir budget—adults and children alike.

7. Shop around for vacation packages. But when you do, buy a package that gives you exactly the features you want. Don't go for one that includes admission to parks or other sites you don't care about.

8. Avoid holidays and school vacation times or go off-season. You'll see more in less time, and lodging rates are lower.

9. If you fly to Orlando, check around for the lowest airline prices and buy cheaper, nonrefundable tickets if you are sure of the dates you want.

10. If you plan to eat in a full-service restaurant, have a large, late breakfast, and then eat lunch late in the day in lieu of dinner.

EMERGENCIES

Dial 911 for police or ambulance. All the area's major theme parks (and some of the minor ones) have first-aid centers. The most accessible hospital in the International Drive area is the Orlando Regional Medical Center–Sand Lake Hospital.

🚹 **Police or ambulance** ☎ 911.

🚹 Doctors & Dentists **Dental Emergency Service** ☎ 407/331-2526.

🚹 Hospitals & Clinics **Centra Care** ✉ 4320 W. Vine St., Kissimmee ☎ 407/390-1888 ✉ 12500 S. Apopka Vineland Rd., Lake Buena Vista ☎ 407/934-2273. **Florida Hospital Celebration Health** ☎ 407/764-4000 is near downtown Celebration. **Main Street Physicians** ✉ 8324 International Dr., Orlando ☎ 407/370-4881. **Orlando Regional Medical Center/Sand Lake Hospital** ☎ 407/351-8500, near International Drive.

🚹 24-Hour Pharmacies **Walgreens** ✉ 5501 S. Kirkman Rd. ☎ 407/248-0315 ✉ 7650 W. Sand Lake Rd. ☎ 407/238-0400. **CVS** ✉ 5308 W. Irlo Bronson Memorial Hwy. ☎ 407/390-9185.

MEDIA

NEWSPAPERS & MAGAZINES
The *Orlando Sentinel* is the area outlet for news; *Orlando Magazine* is a monthly publication. Both are mainstream. The *Orlando Weekly* is the alternative newspaper for the city, covering and criticizing local politics and recommending bars and clubs favored by college students, beatniks, and bohemians. The free weekly is found in distinctive red racks throughout the city.

RADIO
WRUM (100.3 FM) features Latin rhythms. You'll find country music at WPCV (97.5 FM) and WWKA (92 FM). WMFE (90.7 FM) is the local National Public Radio affiliate. WDBO (580 AM) is an excellent source of news and traffic; WFLA (540 AM) has a limited news offering and several popular talk shows.

TAXIS

Taxi fares start at $3.25 for the first mile and cost $1.75 for each mile thereafter. Sample fares: to WDW's Magic Kingdom, about $25 from International Drive, $14–$18 from U.S. 192. To Universal Studios, $10–$14 from International Drive, $27–$34 from U.S. 192. To Church Street or downtown, $22–$28 from International Drive, $32–$44 from U.S. 192. For information on getting to or from the airport by taxi, *see* Airport Transfers.

🚹 Taxi Companies **A-1 Taxi** ☎ 407/328-4555. **Checker Cab Company** ☎ 407/699-9999. **Star Taxi** ☎ 407/857-9999.

TRAIN TRAVEL

If you want to have your car in Florida without driving it there, consider a 900-mi shortcut with Amtrak's **Auto Train,** which departs for Florida from Lorton, Virginia, near Washington, D.C. Its southern terminus—Sanford, Florida—is 23 mi north of Orlando.

FARES & SCHEDULES The Auto Train runs daily, with one departure at 4 PM (car boarding ends one hour earlier). You'll arrive in Sanford around 8:30 the next morning. Fares vary depending on class of service and time of year, but expect to pay between $229 and $445 for a basic sleeper seat and car passage each way. For a group of four and one car, the cost is about $800 total. You must be traveling with an automobile to ride on the Auto Train.

🔊 **Auto Train** ☎ 407/321-3873 or 877/754-7495.

VISITOR INFORMATION

🔊 Tourist Information **Kissimmee/St. Cloud Convention and Visitors Bureau** ✉ 1925 Irlo Bronson Memorial Hwy., Kissimmee, FL 34744 ☎ 407/847-5000 or 800/327-9159. **Orlando/Orange County Convention & Visitors Bureau** ✉ 8723 International Dr., Orlando, FL 32819 ☎ 407/363-5871. **Winter Park Chamber of Commerce** ✉ Box 280, Winter Park, FL 32790 ☎ 407/644-8281.

Palm Beach & the Treasure Coast

4

Updated by
Karen
Schlesinger

MUCH LIKE A KALEIDOSCOPE, this multifaceted section of Atlantic coast resists categorization for good reason. The territory from Palm Beach south to Boca Raton defines the northern portion of the Gold Coast. North of Palm Beach you'll uncover the comparatively undeveloped Treasure Coast—liberally sprinkled with coastal gems—where towns and wide open spaces along the road await your discovery. Altogether, there's a delightful disparity, from Palm Beach, pulsing fast with plenty of old-money wealth, to low-key Hutchinson Island, Manalapan, and Briny Breezes. Seductive as the beach scene interspersed with eclectic dining options can be, you should also take advantage of flourishing commitments to historic preservation and the arts as town after town yields intriguing museums, galleries, theaters, and gardens.

Long reigning as the epicenter of where the crème de la crème go to shake off winter's chill, Palm Beach continues to be a seasonal hotbed of platinum-grade consumption. Rare is the visitor to this region who can resist popping over to the island for a peek. Yes, other Florida favorites such as Jupiter Island actually rank higher on the per capita wealth meters of financial intelligence sources such as *Worth* magazine. But there's no competing with the historic social supremacy of Palm Beach, long a winter address for heirs of icons named Rockefeller, Vanderbilt, Colgate, Post, Kellogg, and Kennedy. Yet even newer power brokers with names like Kravis, Peltz, and Trump are made to understand that strict laws govern everything from building to landscaping, and not so much as a pool awning gets added without a town council nod. If Palm Beach were to fly a flag, it's been observed, there might be three interlocking Cs, standing not only for Cartier, Chanel, and Christian Dior but also for clean, civil, and capricious. Only three bridges allow access to the island, and huge tour buses are a no-no. Yet when a freighter once ran aground near a Palm Beach socialite's pool, she was quick to lament not having "enough Bloody Mary mix for all these sailors."

To learn who's who in Palm Beach, it helps to pick up a copy of the *Palm Beach Daily News*—locals call it the Shiny Sheet because its high-quality paper avoids smudging society hands or the Pratesi linens—for, as it is said, to be mentioned in the Shiny Sheet is to be Palm Beach. All this fabled ambience started with Henry Morrison Flagler, Florida's premier developer, and cofounder, along with John D. Rockefeller, of Standard Oil. No sooner did Flagler bring the railroad to Florida in the 1890s, than he erected the famed Royal Poinciana and Breakers hotels. Rail access sent real estate prices soaring, and ever since, princely sums have been forked over for personal stationery engraved with the 33480 zip code of Palm Beach. To service Palm Beach with servants and other workers, Flagler also developed an off-island community a mile or so west. West Palm Beach now bustles with its own affluent identity, even if there's still no competing with one of the world's toniest island resorts.

With Palm Beach proper representing only 1% of Palm Beach County's land, remaining territory is given over to West Palm and other classic Florida coastal towns, along with—to the west—citrus farms, the Arthur

R. Marshall–Loxahatchee National Wildlife Refuge, and Lake Okeechobee, a bass-fishing hot spot and Florida's largest lake. Well worth exploring is the Treasure Coast territory, covering northernmost Palm Beach County, plus Martin, St. Lucie, and Indian River counties. Despite a growing number of malls and beachfront condominiums, much of the Treasure Coast's shoreline remains blissfully undeveloped. Along the coast, the broad tidal lagoon called the Indian River separates barrier islands from the mainland. Inland there's cattle ranching in tracts of pine and palmetto scrub, along with sugar and citrus production. Shrimp farming utilizes techniques for acclimatizing shrimp from saltwater—land near seawater is costly—to fresh water, all the better to serve demand from restaurants popping up all over the region.

Exploring Palm Beach & the Treasure Coast

Palm Beach, with Gatsby-era architecture, stone and stucco estates, extravagant landscaping, and highbrow shops, can reign as the focal point for your sojourn any time of year. From Palm Beach, head off in any of three directions: south via the Gold Coast toward Boca Raton along an especially scenic route known as A1A, back to the mainland and north to the barrier-island treasures of the Treasure Coast, or west for more rustic inland delights.

About the Restaurants

Not surprisingly, numerous elegant establishments offer upscale Continental and contemporary fare, but the area also teems with casual waterfront spots serving up affordable burgers and fresh seafood feasts. Grouper, fried or blackened, is especially popular here, along with the ubiquitous shrimp. An hour west from the coast, around Lake Okeechobee, dine on catfish, panfried to perfection and so fresh it seems barely out of the water. Early-bird menus, a Florida hallmark, typically entice the budget-minded with several dinner entrées at reduced prices when ordered during certain hours, usually before 5 or 6 PM.

About the Hotels

Palm Beach has a number of smaller hotels in addition to the famous Breakers. Lower-priced hotels and motels can be found in West Palm Beach and Lake Worth. To the south, the coastal town of Manalapan has the Ritz-Carlton, Palm Beach; and the posh Boca Raton Resort & Club is near the beach in Boca Raton. To the north in suburban Palm Beach Gardens is the PGA National Resort & Spa. To the west, small towns near Lake Okeechobee offer country-inn accommodations.

WHAT IT COSTS				
$$$$	**$$$**	**$$**	**$**	**¢**
RESTAURANTS over $30	$20–$30	$15–$20	$10–$15	under $10
HOTELS over $220	$140–$220	$100–$140	$80–$100	under $80

Restaurant prices are per person for a main course at dinner. Hotel prices are for a standard double room, excluding 6% sales tax (more in some counties) and 1%–4% tourist tax.

4

Numbers in the text correspond to numbers in the margin and on the Gold Coast and Treasure Coast and the Palm Beach and West Palm Beach maps.

If you have 3 days

When time is tight, make ⊠ **Palm Beach** ❶ ⌐ – ⓫ your base. On the first day, start downtown on **Worth Avenue** ❼ to window-shop and gallery-browse. After a *très* chic bistro lunch, head for that other must-see on even the shortest itinerary, the **Henry Morrison Flagler Museum** ❷. Your second day is for the beach. Consider either Lantana Public Beach or Oceanfront Park in **Boynton Beach** ㉕. Budget your last day for exploring other attractions, such as the Morikami Museum and Japanese Gardens in nearby **Delray Beach** ㉗, or Lion Country Safari in ⊠ **West Palm Beach** ⓬ – ㉒, yielding tastes of Africa.

If you have 5 days

Stay in ⊠ **Palm Beach** ❶ ⌐ – ⓫ for two nights. The first day visit the **Henry Morrison Flagler Museum** ❷ and the luxury hotel known as the **Breakers** ❹, another Flagler legacy. Then head to **Worth Avenue** ❼ for lunch and afternoon shopping, even if it's only the window variety. On the second day, drive over to ⊠ **West Palm Beach** ⓬ – ㉒ and the **Norton Museum of Art** ⓭, with many 19th- and 20th-century paintings and sculptures. On Day 3, choose between an overnight visit to ⊠ **Lake Okeechobee,** the world's bass-fishing capital, or Palm Beach for another night and a drive of a half hour or so to explore the Arthur R. Marshall–Loxahatchee National Wildlife Refuge. Or head for the **National Croquet Center** ⓲. Go to ⊠ **Boca Raton** ㉘ on the fourth day, and check into a hotel near the beach before spending the afternoon wandering through Mizner Park's shops. On your fifth day, meander through Mizner Park's Boca Raton Museum of Art in the morning and get some sun at South Beach Park after lunch.

If you have 7 days

Stay two nights in ⊠ **Palm Beach** ❶ ⌐ – ⓫, spending your first day enjoying the stellar sights mentioned in the 5 day itinerary. On Day 2, rent a bicycle and follow the bike path along Lake Worth, which provides great glimpses at backyards of many Palm Beach mansions. Drive north on Day 3, going first to the mainland and then across Jerry Thomas Bridge to Singer Island and John D. MacArthur Beach State Park. Spend the third night farther north, on ⊠ **Hutchinson Island** ㉞, and relax the next morning on the beach at your hotel. On your way back south, explore **Stuart** ㉝ and its intriguing historic downtown area, and pause at the Arthur R. Marshall–Loxahatchee National Wildlife Refuge before ending up in ⊠ **Boca Raton** ㉘, for three nights at a hotel near the beach. Split Day 5 between shopping at Mizner Park and sunning at South Beach Park. Day 6 is for cultural attractions: the Boca Raton Museum of Art followed by the Atlantic Avenue galleries and the Morikami in **Delray Beach** ㉗. On your last day, check out one of Boca's other two beaches, Spanish River and Red Reef parks.

Timing

The weather is optimum November through May, but the trade-off is that roadways and facilities are more crowded and prices higher. In summer, to spend much time outside, it helps to have a tolerance for heat, humidity, and afternoon downpours. No matter when you visit, bring insect repellent for outdoor activities.

PALM BEACH

78 mi north of Miami.

Setting the tone in this town of unparalleled Florida opulence is the ornate architectural work of Addison Mizner, who began designing homes and public buildings here in the 1920s and whose Moorish-Gothic style has influenced virtually all community landmarks. Thanks to Mizner and his lasting influence, Palm Beach remains a playground of the rich, famous, and discerning.

Exploring Palm Beach

For a taste of what it's like to jockey for position in this status-conscious town, stake out a parking place on Worth Avenue, and squeeze in among the Mercedeses and Bentleys. Actually, the easiest, most affordable way to reach Worth Avenue is by foot, since there's little on-street parking and space is at a premium at nearby lots. Away from downtown, along County Road and Ocean Boulevard (the shore road, also designated as Route A1A), are Palm Beach's other defining landmarks: residences that are nothing short of palatial, topped by the seemingly de rigueur barrel-tile roofs and often fronted by 20-foot-thick hedgerows. The low wall that separates the dune-top shore road from the sea hides shoreline that varies in many places from expansive to eroded. Here and there, where the strand deepens, homes are built directly on the beach.

a good tour

Start on the island's north end with a quick drive through the bit of sandstone and limestone intrigue called the **Canyon of Palm Beach** ❶ ▶ on Lake Way Road. Drive south, across Royal Poinciana Way, to the **Henry Morrison Flagler Museum** ❷, a 73-room palace Flagler built for his third wife. From here, backtrack to Royal Poinciana Way, turn right, and follow the road until it ends at North County Road and the Spanish-style **Palm Beach Post Office** ❸. Here County Road changes from north to south designations. Head southbound and look for the long, stately driveway on the left that leads to **The Breakers** ❹, built by Flagler in the style of an Italian Renaissance palace. There's limited free parking out front and ample valets under the porte-cochère. Continue south on South County Road about ¼ mi farther to **Bethesda-by-the-Sea** ❺, a Spanish Gothic Episcopal church. Keep driving south on South County Road until you reach Royal Palm Way; turn right, then right again on Cocoanut Row. Within a few blocks you'll see the gardens of the **Society of the Four Arts** ❻. Head south on Cocoanut Row until you reach famed **Worth Avenue** ❼. Park, stroll, and ogle designer goods. Then drive south on South County Road to peek at magnificent estates, including **El Solano** ❽, designed by

Beaches From a tourism marketing standpoint, many towns along this idyllic stretch officially embrace the word *beach,* and why not? Here there are miles of golden strands—some relatively quiet, others buzzing—blessed with shades of blue-green waters you won't encounter farther north. Among the least crowded are those at Hobe Sound National Wildlife Refuge and Fort Pierce Inlet State Recreation Area. To see and be seen, head for Boca Raton's three beaches or Delray Beach's broad stretch of sand.

Fishing Except for ice fishing, you'll find within a 50-mi radius of Palm Beach virtually every form of hook-and-line activity going on any season you please. Charter boats for deep-sea fishing abound from Boca Raton to Sebastian Inlet. West of Vero Beach, there's great marsh fishing for catfish and perch. Lake Okeechobee is the place for bass fishing.

Golf Golfers love this region, starting with the Professional Golfing Association (PGA) headquarters at the PGA National Resort & Spa in Palm Beach Gardens. If you're not ready to go pro, the Academy at PGA National Resort & Spa can help you improve with its golf-school packages. More than 150 public, private, and semiprivate golf courses dot Palm Beach County, and challenging courses also await along the Treasure Coast.

Shopping There's no shortage of baubles to ogle on Palm Beach's Worth Avenue, known locally as the Avenue and often compared to Beverly Hills' Rodeo Drive, even though such California comparisons displease many old-line Palm Beachers. There's plenty of reasonably priced shopping at the Wellington Green, Town Center, and the Gardens malls. For open-air shopping, dining, and entertainment, CityPlace and Mizner Park are great choices. Both have upscale national retailers mixed with unique independent boutiques and art galleries. The art galleries and antiques shops in Vero Beach and Delray Beach are also worth browsing.

Addison Mizner, and the fabled **Mar-a-Lago** ❾, now owned by Donald Trump and operating as a private club. At this point, if you want some sun and fresh air, continue south on South County Road until you reach **Phipps Ocean Park** ❿ and its stretch of beach, or head back toward town along South Ocean Boulevard to the popular **Mid-Town Beach** ⓫.

TIMING   You'll need half a day, minimum, for these sights. A few destinations are closed Sunday, Monday, or in summer. In winter, often-heavy traffic gets worse as the day wears on, so plan exploring for the morning.

What to See

❺ **Bethesda-by-the-Sea.** This Spanish Gothic Episcopal church with stained-glass windows was built in 1925 by the first Protestant congregation in southeast Florida. Guided tours follow some services. Adjacent are the formal, ornamental **Cluett Memorial Gardens.** ✉ *141 S. County Rd.* ☎ *561/655–4554* ⊕ *www.bbts.org* ✆ *Church and gardens daily 8–5.*

Services Sept.–May, Sun. at 8, 9, and 11; Tues. at 8; Wed. and Fri. at 12:05; June–Aug., Sun. at 8 and 10. Call to confirm.

④ The Breakers. Originally built by Henry Flagler in 1895 and rebuilt by his descendants after a 1925 fire, this luxury hotel resembling an Italian Renaissance palace helped launch Florida tourism with its gilded-age opulence, attracting influential, wealthy northerners. Head for the lobby to gaze at painted arched ceilings hung with crystal chandeliers, the ornate Florentine Dining Room with its 15th-century Flemish tapestries, and other museum-quality public spaces. ⊠ *1 S. County Rd.* ☎ *561/655–6611* ⊕ *www.thebreakers.com.*

Fodor'sChoice
★

▶ **① Canyon of Palm Beach.** A road runs through a ridge of reddish-brown sandstone and oolite limestone, providing a brief sense of the desert Southwest. It's the remains of an ancient coral reef, and 15-foot-high canyon walls line both sides of the road. ⊠ *Lake Way Rd.*

⑧ El Solano. No Palm Beach mansion better represents the town's luminous legacy than the Spanish-style home built by Addison Mizner as his residence in 1925. Mizner later sold El Solano to Harold Vanderbilt, and the property was long a favorite among socialites for parties and photo shoots. Vanderbilt, like many of the socially attuned, would open his home to social peers to accommodate worthy causes. Beatle John Lennon and his wife Yoko Ono bought it less than a year before Lennon's death. It's still privately owned and not open to the public. ⊠ *721 S. County Rd.*

② Henry Morrison Flagler Museum. The opulence of Florida's gilded age lives on at Whitehall, the palatial 73-room mansion Henry Flagler commissioned in 1901 for his third wife, Mary Lily Kenan. Architects John Carrère and Thomas Hastings were instructed to create the finest home imaginable, and they outdid themselves. Whitehall rivals the grandeur of European palaces and has an entrance hall with baroque ceiling similar to Louis XIV's Versailles. To create the museum, Flagler's granddaughter, Jean Flagler Matthews, in 1960 purchased the property, which had been operating as the Whitehall Hotel since 1929. You'll see original furnishings, an art collection, a 1,200-pipe organ, and Florida East Coast Railway exhibits, along with Flagler's personal rail car, the *Rambler,* awaiting in an 8,000-square-foot Beaux Arts style pavilion behind the mansion. Tours take about an hour and are offered at frequent intervals. The café offers snacks and afternoon tea. ⊠ *1 Whitehall Way* ☎ *561/655–2833* ⊕ *www.flagler.org* ⊡ *$10* ☉ *Tues.–Sat. 10–5, Sun. noon–5.*

Fodor'sChoice
★

⑨ Mar-a-Lago. Breakfast-food heiress Marjorie Meriweather Post commissioned a Hollywood set designer to create Ocean Boulevard's famed Mar-a-Lago, with Italianate towers silhouetted against the sky. Owner Donald Trump has turned it into a private membership club. ⊠ *1100 S. Ocean Blvd.*

⑪ Mid-Town Beach. Just east of Worth Avenue, this small beach is convenient, but be warned that parking is scarce. The only nearby meters are along Ocean Boulevard between Worth Avenue and Royal Palm Way.

⊠ *400 S. Ocean Blvd.* ☎ *No phone* 🄿 *Parking 25¢ for 15 mins* ⏱ *Daily 8–8.*

③ Palm Beach Post Office. Spanish-style architecture defines the exterior of this 1932 National Historic Site building. Inside, murals depict Seminole Indians in the Everglades and stately royal and coconut palms. ⊠ *95 N. County Rd.* ☎ *800/275–8777.*

⑩ Phipps Ocean Park. In addition to the shoreline, picnic tables, and grills, this park has a Palm Beach County landmark in the **Little Red Schoolhouse.** Dating from 1886, it served as the first schoolhouse in what was then Dade County. No alcoholic beverages are permitted in the park. ⊠ *2185 S. Ocean Blvd.* ☎ *561/832–0731* 🄳 *Free* ⏱ *Daily dawn–dusk.*

⑥ Society of the Four Arts. Feel like unwinding amid Blackberry Lilies and Japanese Sago Palms, Confederate Jasmine, Weeping Juniper, and Fairy Carpet Begonias? Despite widespread misconceptions of members-only exclusivity, this privately endowed institution—founded in 1936 to encourage appreciation of art, music, drama, and literature—is funded for public enjoyment. A gallery building—designed by Addison Mizner, of course—artfully melds an exhibition hall, library, 13 gardens, and the Philip Hulitar Sculpture Garden. As of this writing, Four Arts' gardens were closed due to 2004 hurricane damage; Hulitar Garden is under renovation until late 2006. Open from about Thanksgiving to Easter, programs are extensive and there's ample free parking. ⊠ *2 Four Arts Plaza* ☎ *561/655–7226* ⊕ *www.fourarts.org* 🄳 *$4* ⏱ *Galleries Dec.–mid-Apr., Mon.–Sat. 10–5, Sun. 2–5. Library, children's library, and gardens Nov.–May, weekdays 10–5, Sat. 9–1.*

★ ⑦ Worth Avenue. Called the Avenue by Palm Beachers, this ¼-mi-long street is synonymous with exclusive shopping. Nostalgia lovers recall an era when faces or names served as charge cards, purchases were delivered home before customers returned from lunch, and bills were sent directly to private accountants. Times have changed, but a stroll amid the Moorish architecture of its shops offers a tantalizing taste of the island's ongoing commitment to elegant consumerism. ⊠ *Between Cocoanut Row and S. Ocean Blvd.*

Where to Stay & Eat

$$$$ ✕ **Leopard Supper Club and Lounge.** In the Chesterfield hotel, this enclave feels like an exclusive club. Choose a cozy banquette set off by black-and-red lacquer trim or a table near the open kitchen. Start with sweet corn and crab chowder with Peruvian purple potato or a jumbo crab cake, moving on to an arugula or spinach salad followed by a prime strip steak or a glazed rack of lamb. As the night progresses, the Leopard turns into a popular nightclub for Palm Beach's old guard. ⊠ *363 Cocoanut Row* ☎ *561/659–5800* ▭ *AE, D, DC, MC, V.*

$$$–$$$$ ✕ **Bice Ristorante.** The bougainvillea-laden trellises set the scene at the main entrance on Peruvian Way and weather permitting, many patrons prefer to dine on the outdoor side and back patios. A favorite of Palm Beach society, both the restaurant and the bar become packed during high season. The aroma of basil, chives, and oregano fills the air as wait-

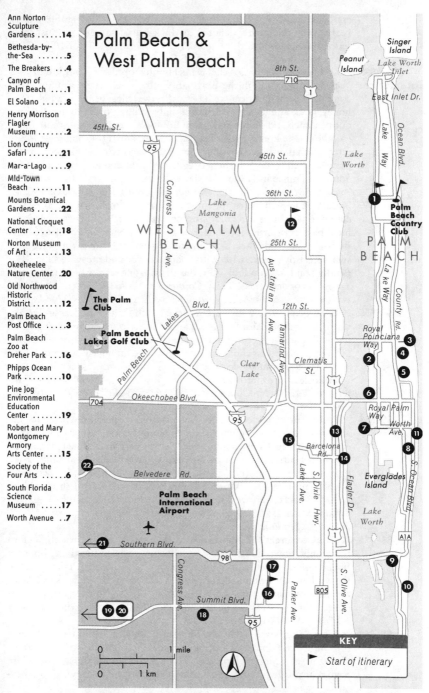

Palm Beach & West Palm Beach

ers bring out home-baked focaccia to accompany delectable pastas, veal chops, and such specialties as duck breast sautéed in mushroom sauce with venison truffle ravioli. ⊠ *313½ Worth Ave.* ☎ *561/835–1600* ⚑ *Reservations essential* ▤ *AE, DC, MC, V.*

$$$–$$$$
Fodor'sChoice
★
✕ **Café Boulud.** Celebrated chef Daniel Boulud opened his outpost of New York's Café Boulud in the Brazilian Court hotel. The warm and welcoming French-American venue is casual yet elegant, with a palette of honey, gold, and citron and natural light spilling through arched glass doors. Lunch and dinner entrées on Boulud's signature four-muse menu include classic French, seasonal, vegetarian, and a rotating selection of international dishes. The lounge, with its backlit amber glass bar, is the perfect perch to take in the jet-set crowd that comes for a hint of the South of France in South Florida. ⊠ *Brazilian Court, 301 Australian Ave.* ☎ *561/655–6060* ⚑ *Reservations essential* ▤ *AE, DC, MC, V.*

$$$–$$$$ ✕ **Café L'Europe.** One of the most enduring Palm Beach enclaves, this classy restaurant is a regular stop on fine diners' itineraries. Management pays close attention to service and consistency of excellence here. Best-sellers include rack of lamb and Dover sole, along with creations such as crispy sweetbreads with poached pear and mustard sauce. Depending on how you look at it, the champagne-caviar bar can provide appetizers or dessert. ⊠ *331 S. County Rd.* ☎ *561/655–4020* ⚑ *Reservations essential* 🏛 *Jacket required* ▤ *AE, DC, MC, V* ☯ *No lunch.*

$$$–$$$$ ✕ **Chez Jean-Pierre.** With walls adorned with Dalí- and Picasso-like art, this is where the Palm Beach old guard likes to let down its guard, all the while partaking of sumptuous French cuisine and an impressive wine list. Forget calorie or cholesterol concerns and indulge in scrambled eggs with caviar or homemade duck foie gras, along with desserts like hazelnut soufflé or profiteroles au chocolat. Waiters are friendly and very attentive. ⊠ *132 N. County Rd.* ☎ *561/833–1171* ⚑ *Reservations essential* ▤ *AE, DC, MC, V* ☯ *Closed Sun. No lunch.*

$$–$$$ ✕ **Amici.** This celebrity-magnet bistro is a crowd-pleaser: when it moved across the street and down the block from its original location, a consistent Palm Beach crowd followed. The northern Italian menu highlights house specialties such as rigatoni with spicy tomato sauce and roasted eggplant, potato gnocchi, grilled veal chops, risottos, and pizzas from a wood-burning oven. There are nightly pasta and fresh-fish specials as well. To avoid the crowds, stop by for a late lunch or early dinner. ⊠ *375 S. County Rd.* ☎ *561/832–0201* ⚑ *Reservations essential* ▤ *AE, DC, MC, V* ☯ *No lunch Sun.*

$$–$$$ ✕ **Chuck & Harold's.** Locals and tourists eager to people-watch flock to this combo power-lunch bar, sidewalk café, and nocturnal jazz hot spot for breakfast, lunch, and dinner. For optimum viewing, take a seat in the outdoor café next to begonia pots mounted on the sidewalk rail. Worthy are local clams from nearby Sebastian, conch chowder, terrific hamburgers, grilled steaks, and key lime pie. ⊠ *207 Royal Poinciana Way* ☎ *561/659–1440* ▤ *AE, DC, MC, V.*

$$–$$$ ✕ **Echo.** Palm Beach's window on Asia has a sleek sushi bar and floor-to-ceiling glass doors separating the interior from the popular terrace dining area. Chinese, Japanese, Thai, and Vietnamese selections are neatly categorized: Wind (small plates starting your journey), Water (beverages, sushi), Fire (from grill, wok, fry pan), Earth (land and sea), and Flavor (desserts, sweets). Pick from dim sum to sashimi, pad Thai to Peking duck, steamed sea bass to lobster lo mein. ⊠ *230-A Sunrise Ave.* ☎ *561/802–4222* ⊟ *AE, D, MC, V* ☉ *Closed Mon. No lunch.*

★ **$$–$$$** ✕ **Ta-boó.** This peach stucco landmark with green shutters has ruled on Worth Avenue for more than 60 years. Pick a good table—the best are by the windows at the front or near the bar or fireplace. Entrées include Black Angus dry-aged beef or roast duck, along with main-course salads, pizzas, and burgers, plus coconut lust, a signature dessert. Drop in late night during the winter season when the nightly music is playing and you'll probably spot a celebrity or two. ⊠ *221 Worth Ave.* ☎ *561/ 835–3500* ⊟ *AE, DC, MC, V*

¢–$ ✕ **Hamburger Heaven.** A favorite with locals since 1945, this spot is loud and casual and has some of the best burgers on the island. Vegetarian meals, fresh salads, sandwiches, homemade pastries, and daily soup and hot-plate specials are also available. During the week, it is a typical lunch stop for working locals. ⊠ *314 S. County Rd.* ☎ *561/655–5277* ⊟ *MC, V* ☉ *Closed Sun.*

¢ ✕ **Pastry Heaven.** Head to the counter of this bakery and sandwich shop to place your breakfast or lunch order. Choose from the daily selection of fresh quiche, pastries, sandwiches (consider turkey on a baked-that-morning croissant) and salads (chicken with grapes and walnuts); eye a chocolate chip cookie; and help yourself to a beverage. If you're lucky to secure one of the few tight tables inside or out on the patio, grab one of the complimentary local papers and magazines and read up on the town's happenings while you eat. ⊠ *375 S. County Rd.* ☎ *561/655– 0610* ⊟ *No credit cards* ☉ *Closed Sun. No dinner.*

¢ ✕ **Pizza Al Fresco.** Off Worth Avenue's beaten path, this European pizzeria (beer and wine only) provides outdoor dining under a canopy of century-old banyans in a charming courtyard. Specialties are 12-inch hand-tossed brick-oven pizzas; calzones, salads, and sandwiches round out the selection. Slices are available with such interesting toppings as prosciutto, arugula, and caviar; there's even a dessert pizza topped with Nutella. Delivery is available, by limo, of course. ⊠ *14 Via Mizner, at Worth Ave.* ☎ *561/832–0032* ⊟ *AE, MC, V* ☉ *No lunch Sun.*

★ **$$$$** ▦ **Brazilian Court.** A short stroll from Worth Avenue shopping, the yellow stucco Spanish-style facade and red-tile roof here underscore this boutique hotel's Roaring '20s origins. All of the studio and one- and two-bedroom suites have rich limestone baths and showers, Sub-Zero wine refrigerators, and personal butler service. Bay windows look out into the impeccably maintained gardens and enchanting flower-filled courtyards. Amenities include video-conference capabilities in a state-of-the-art business center, a Frederic Fekkai hair salon and spa, and Café Boulud, a New York outpost from famed restaurateur Daniel Boulud; hotel guests reportedly have a better shot than outsiders at procuring a table. ⊠ *301 Australian Ave., 33480* ☎ *561/655–7740* ⊜ *561/655–0801* ⊕ *www.braziliancourt. com* ⇌ *80 rooms* ⚭ *Restaurant, room service, refrigerators, some in-room VCRs, in-room data ports, pool, gym, hair salon, spa, bicycles, bar, library, laundry facilities, concierge, meeting rooms, some pets allowed (fee), no-smoking rooms* ⊟ *AE, D, DC, MC, V.*

$$$$
Fodor'sChoice
★

🏨 **The Breakers.** Dating from 1896 and on the National Register of Historic Places, this opulent Italian Renaissance–style resort sprawls over 140 ocean-front acres. Cupids frolic at the main Florentine fountain, while majestic frescoes grace hallways leading to restaurants. More than an opulent hotel, the Breakers is a modern resort packed with amenities, from a 20,000-square-foot luxury spa and beach club to golf and tennis clubhouses that support the 10 tennis courts and two 18-hole golf courses. Jackets and ties are no longer *required* after 7 PM. ⊠ *1 S. County Rd., 33480* ☎ *561/655–6611 or 888/273–2537* 🖷 *561/659–8403* ⊕ *www.thebreakers.com* ⇴ *569 rooms, 57 suites* ⌂ *5 restaurants, room service, room TVs with movies and video games, in-room data ports, 2 18-hole golf courses, putting green, 10 tennis courts, 5 pools, health club, sauna, spa, beach, boating, croquet, shuffleboard, 4 bars, shops, babysitting, children's programs (ages 3–12), concierge, business services* ▤ *AE, D, DC, MC, V.*

★ $$$$

🏨 **Four Seasons Resort Palm Beach.** Relaxed elegance is the watchword at this four-story resort on 6 acres with a delightful beach at the south end of town, approximately 5 mi outside the heart of Palm Beach. Fanlight windows, marble, chintz, and palms are serene and inviting. Rooms are spacious, with separate seating areas and private balconies; many have ocean views. On weekends, piano music accompanies cocktails in the Living Room lounge. Jazz groups perform on some weekends in season. The restaurants are worth sampling, and all three have children's menus. ⊠ *2800 S. Ocean Blvd., 33480* ☎ *561/582–2800 or 800/432–2335* 🖷 *561/547–1557* ⊕ *www.fourseasons.com* ⇴ *200 rooms, 10 suites* ⌂ *3 restaurants, room service, in-room safes, minibars, in-room data ports, golf privileges, 3 tennis courts, pool, health club, hair salon, hot tub, sauna, spa, steam room, beach, boating, fishing, bicycles, 2 bars, shop, babysitting, children's programs (ages 3–12), dry cleaning, concierge, business services, meeting rooms, no-smoking rooms* ▤ *AE, D, DC, MC, V.*

$$$–$$$$

🏨 **The Colony.** What distinguishes this legendary pale-yellow British colonial–style hotel is that it's only steps from Worth Avenue and a beautiful beach on the Atlantic Ocean. An attentive staff, youthful yet experienced, is buzzing with competence and a desire to please. Cool and classical guest rooms, with small baths, have fluted blond cabinetry and matching curtains and bedcovers in floral pastels. In addition to the rooms and suites, there are ample penthouses with refrigerators as well as seven luxurious two-bedroom villas (rentable by the week or month) with laundry facilities and full kitchens with optional private chefs. For convenient in-house fare and fun, check out the nightly dinner cabaret show. ⊠ *155 Hammon Ave., 33480* ☎ *561/655–5430 or 800/521–5525* 🖷 *561/659–8104* ⊕ *www.thecolonypalmbeach.com* ⇴ *68 rooms, 14 suites* ⌂ *Restaurant, 2 pools, spa, bicycles, bar, concierge, meeting rooms* ▤ *AE, DC, MC, V.*

$$–$$$$

🏨 **Heart of Palm Beach Hotel.** Three blocks north of Worth Avenue and a three-minute walk from the beach, this hotel is truly in the center of Palm Beach. Although the two low, pink buildings date from 1960 and 1975, the hotel is constantly being renovated inside and out. Rooms are spacious and sunny, with private balconies and terraces. ⊠ *160 Royal*

Palm Way, 33480 ☎ *561/655–5600 or 800/523–5377* 🖷 *561/832–1201* ⊕ *www.heartofpalmbeach.com* ⇆ *88 rooms, 7 suites* ⚭ *Restaurant, refrigerators, in-room data ports, pool, spa, bicycles, 2 bars, laundry facilities, business services, some pets allowed* ☰ *AE, D, MC, V.*

$–$$$$ 🏨 **The Chesterfield.** Two blocks north of Worth Avenue is this elegant four-story, white stucco, European-style hotel with inviting rooms ranging from small to spacious. All have plush upholstered chairs, antique desks, paintings, and marble baths. Settle on a leather couch near the cozy library's fireplace and peruse an international newspaper or classic book. A quiet courtyard surrounds a large pool where you can relax, and the Leopard Lounge draws a convivial crowd. ✉ *363 Cocoanut Row, 33480* ☎ *561/659–5800 or 800/243–7871* 🖷 *561/659–6707* ⊕ *www.chesterfieldpb.com* ⇆ *44 rooms, 11 suites* ⚭ *Restaurant, room service, some refrigerators, some in-room VCRs, pool, bar, library, concierge, Internet, business services, meeting rooms* ☰ *AE, D, DC, MC, V.*

$–$$$ 🏨 **Palm Beach Historic Inn.** Downtown, tucked between Town Hall and a seaside residential block, this B&B has personal touches that include a deluxe Continental breakfast served in bed or in the courtyard and tea and cookies delivered to your room upon your arrival. Guest rooms tend toward the frilly, with lace, ribbons, and scalloped edges. Most are furnished with Victorian antiques and reproductions and chiffon draped above the bed. ✉ *365 S. County Rd., 33480* ☎ *561/832–4009* 🖷 *561/832–6255* ⊕ *www.palmbeachhistoricinn.com* ⇆ *9 rooms, 4 suites* ⚭ *Refrigerators, some in-room VCRs, library* ☰ *AE, D, DC, MC, V* ⧓ *CP.*

$–$$$ 🏨 **Plaza Inn.** This three-story hotel, deco-designed in the 1930s, operates B&B style. Its Stray Fox Pub Piano Bar, palm- and ficus-lined pool, and courtyard gardens have the intimate charm of a trysting place. Courteous staff and a location in the heart of Palm Beach are pluses. Traditional rooms are individually decorated and have French- and Italian-style furnishings complete with fussy fabrics and finishes. Small pets are welcome. ✉ *215 Brazilian Ave., 33480* ☎ *561/832–8666 or 800/233–2632* 🖷 *561/835–8776* ⊕ *www.plazainnpalmbeach.com* ⇆ *48 rooms, 5 suites* ⚭ *Refrigerators, in-room data ports, pool, hot tub, bar, concierge, some pets allowed* ☰ *AE, MC, V* ⧓ *CP.*

Nightlife & the Arts

The Arts

Society of the Four Arts (✉ 2 Four Arts Plaza ☎ 561/655–7226) has concerts, lectures, and films December–March. Movie tickets can be purchased at time of showing; other tickets may be obtained a week in advance.

Nightlife

Although Palm Beach is teeming with restaurants that turn into late-night scenes and hotel lobby bars perfect for tête-à-têtes, the only true nightclub in town is **251** (✉ 251 Sunrise Ave. ☎ 561/820–9777). Known for its live music and late-night partying, 251 is a locals' hot spot. Popular for lunch and dinner, **Cucina Dell 'Arte** (✉ 257 Royal Poinciana Way ☎ 561/655–0770) later becomes the in place for the younger and trendy

set. The old guard gathers at the **Leopard Lounge** (⊠ 363 Cocoanut Row
☎ 561/659–5800) in the Chesterfield Hotel for piano music during cocktail hour and later to dance until the wee hours. Thursday night happy
hours spiked by Flirtinis and live jazz draw a local crowd to the lobby
lounge and outdoor patios of the **Brazilian Court** (⊠ 301 Australian
Ave. ☎ 561/655–7740).

Sports & the Outdoors

Biking

Bicycling is a great way to get a closer look at Palm Beach. Only 14 mi
long, ½ mi wide, flat as the top of a billiard table, and just as green, it's
a perfect biking place. The palm-fringed **Lake Trail** (⊠ parallel to Lake
Way) skirts the backyards of many palatial mansions and the edge of
Lake Worth. The trail starts at the Society of the Four Arts, heading
north—just follow the signs. A block from the bike trail, the **Palm Beach
Bicycle Trail Shop** (⊠ 223 Sunrise Ave. ☎ 561/659–4583) rents by the
hour or day.

Dog Racing

Since 1932 the hounds have raced year-round at the 4,300-seat **Palm Beach
Kennel Club.** Enjoy simulcasts of jai alai and horse racing, and wager on
live and televised sports; there's also an expanded 30-table card room
with high-stakes wagers, and a restaurant. ⊠ *1111 N. Congress Ave.*
☎ *561/683–2222* ⬚ *50¢, terrace level $1, parking free* ⊙ *Racing
Mon.–Sat. at 12:40, Fri. and Sat. also at 7:30, Sun. at 1. Simulcasts daily
at 11:30 and 7:30.*

Golf

Breakers Hotel Golf Club (⊠ 1 S. County Rd. ☎ 561/659–8407) has the
historic Ocean Course and the Todd Anderson Golf Academy and is open
to members and hotel guests only; green fee: Breakers West $175 in-
cludes range balls, cart, and bag storage; a $175 green fee buys you the
same amenities for the redesigned Ocean Course. The **Town of Palm
Beach Golf Club** (⊠ 2345 S. Ocean Blvd. ☎ 561/547–0598) has 18
holes, including 4 on the Atlantic and 3 on the inland waterway; green
fee: $18/$25.50.

Shopping

★ One of the world's premier showcases for high-quality shopping, **Worth
Avenue** runs ¼ mi east–west across Palm Beach, from the beach to Lake
Worth. The street has more than 250 shops (more than 40 of them sell
jewelry), and many upscale stores (Gucci, Hermès, Pucci, Saks Fifth Avenue, and Tourneau) are represented, their merchandise appealing to the
discerning tastes of the Palm Beach clientele. The six blocks of **South County
Road** north of Worth Avenue have interesting (and somewhat less expensive) stores. For specialty items (out-of-town newspapers, health foods,
and books), try the shops along the north side of **Royal Poinciana Way.**
Most stores are closed on Sunday, and many go on hiatus in summer.

Calypso (⊠ 247-B Worth Ave. ☎ 561/832–5006), tucked into Via Encantada, is where owner Christiane Celle—known for handcrafted fra-

grances—has curated a lively collection of resortwear for the whole family. An institution on the island, the thrift store **Church Mouse** (⊠ 374 S. County Rd. ☎ 561/659–2154) is where many high-end resale boutique owners grab their merchandise. **Déjà Vu** (⊠ Via Testa, 219 Royal Poinciana Way ☎ 561/833–6624) could be the resale house of Chanel, as it has so many gently used, top-quality pieces. There's no digging through piles here; clothes are in impeccable condition and are well organized. **Giorgio's** (⊠ 230 Worth Ave. ☎ 561/655–2446) is over-the-top indulgence, with 50 colors of silk and cashmere sweaters and 22 colors of ostrich and alligator adorning everything from bags to bicycles. Giorgio's also has men's and women's boutiques in the Breakers. Jewelry is very important in Palm Beach and for more than 100 years **Greenleaf & Crosby** (⊠ 236 Worth Ave. ☎ 561/655–5850) has had a diverse selection that includes investment pieces. **Hollywould** (⊠ 36 Via Mizner ☎ 561/366–9016) stocks the Palm Beach It-Girl uniform of bright jersey dresses, shoes from slides to stilettos, and coordinating handbags. Collector and trader Edmund Lo packs the goods into his tiny, closet-size shop **Lo Co** (⊠ Via Encantada, 245 Worth Ave. ☎ 561/832–0565), where he has superb and pricey pre-owned Hermès handbags, antique Louis Vuitton travel bags, and vintage Pucci dresses. **Spring Flowers** (⊠ 337 Worth Ave. ☎ 561/832–0131) has beautiful children's clothing, pajamas, and special occasion outfits from newborn to size 12. Little ones start with a newborn gown set by Kissy Kissy or Petite Bateau and grow into fashions by Cacharel and Lili Gaufrette. The custom-made creations at **Tracey Tooker Hats** (⊠ Via Bice, 313½ Worth Ave. ☎ 561/835–1663) have bone buttons, real and faux fur, double grosgrain silk bows, satin linings, ostrich feathers, and silk flowers. Holding court for more than 60 years, **Van Cleef & Arpels** (⊠ 249 Worth Ave. ☎ 561/655–6767) is where legendary members of Palm Beach society shop for tiaras and formal jewels.

WEST PALM BEACH

2 mi west of Palm Beach.

Long considered Palm Beach's less-privileged relative, sprawling West Palm has evolved into an economically vibrant destination of its own, ranking as the cultural, entertainment, and business center of the entire county and territory to the north. Sparkling buildings like the mammoth Palm Beach County Judicial Center and Courthouse and the State Administrative Building underscore the breadth of the city's governmental and corporate activity. The glittering Kravis Center for the Performing Arts is Palm Beach County's principal entertainment venue. One of the newest additions to the city is the enormous and extravagant Palm Beach County Convention Center, which cost more than $80 million to build; the 350,000-square-foot campus sits on almost 20 acres across from the Kravis Center and CityPlace.

Downtown

The heart of revived West Palm Beach is a small, attractive downtown area, spurred on by active historic preservation. Along beautifully land-

scaped Clematis Street are boutiques and restaurants in restored buildings. An exuberant nightlife has also taken hold of the area. In fact, downtown rocks every Thursday from 5:30 PM on with Clematis by Night,
a celebration of music, dance, art, and food at Centennial Square. Even
on downtown's fringes there are sights of cultural interest.

a good tour From a geographical perspective, the best place to start is at the north
end of the city with a walk through the **Old Northwood Historic District** ⑫ ▶,
which is on the National Register of Historic Places. Drive south on
U.S. 1, take a left onto 12th Street, and then a right onto South Olive
Avenue to view the exceptional art collection at the **Norton Museum of
Art** ⑬. From here, it's just a few blocks south to the peaceful **Ann Norton Sculpture Gardens** ⑭. Finally, drive west across Barcelona Road to
the **Robert and Mary Montgomery Armory Arts Center** ⑮ to check out the
current exhibit.

TIMING Late morning is ideal for starting this tour. Walk through the historic
neighborhood before having lunch on Clematis Street. In the afternoon
you'll need about three hours at the arts-oriented sights. Daytime business hours are the best for this tour.

What to See

⑭ **Ann Norton Sculpture Gardens.** This monument to the late American
sculptor Ann Weaver Norton, second wife of Norton Museum founder
Ralph H. Norton, consists of charming 3-acre grounds displaying seven
granite figures and six brick megaliths. The plantings were designed to
attract native bird life. ✉ *253 Barcelona Rd.* ☎ *561/832–5328* 💲 *$5*
🕐 *Wed.–Sun. 11–4, call ahead as schedule is not always observed, or
by appointment.*

⑬ **Norton Museum of Art.** Constructed in 1941 by steel magnate Ralph H.
Fodor'sChoice Norton, this museum has an extensive permanent collection of 19th-
★ and 20th-century American and European paintings, including works
by Picasso, Monet, Matisse, Pollock, and O'Keeffe, and Chinese, contemporary, and photographic art. There's a sublime outdoor covered
loggia, Chinese bronze and jade sculptures, and a library. Galleries, including the Great Hall, also showcase traveling exhibits. ✉ *1451 S. Olive
Ave.* ☎ *561/832–5196* 🌐 *www.norton.org* 💲 *$8* 🕐 *Tues.–Sat. 10–5,
Sun. 1–5; May–Oct., also Mon. 10–5.*

▶ ⑫ **Old Northwood Historic District.** This 1920s-era neighborhood, on the National Register of Historic Places, hosts special events, Saturday green
markets from November through March, and neighborhood walking
tours. ✉ *West of Flagler Dr. between 26th and 35th Sts.*

⑮ **Robert and Mary Montgomery Armory Arts Center.** Built by the WPA in
1939, the facility is now a visual-arts center hosting rotating exhibitions
and art classes throughout the year. ✉ *1703 Lake Ave.* ☎ *561/832–1776*
💲 *Free* 🕐 *Weekdays 10–5, Sat. 10–2.*

Away from Downtown

West Palm Beach's outskirts, flat stretches lined with fast-food outlets
and car dealerships, may not inspire, but are worth driving through to

reach attractions scattered around the city's southern and western reaches. Several sites are especially rewarding for children and other animal and nature lovers.

a good tour Head south from downtown and turn right on Southern Boulevard, left onto Parker Avenue, and right onto Summit Boulevard to reach the **Palm Beach Zoo at Dreher Park** ⑯ ▶. In the same area (turn right onto Dreher Trail) and also appealing to kids, the **South Florida Science Museum** ⑰, with its Aldrin Planetarium and McGinty Aquarium, is full of hands-on exhibits. If a quick game of croquet intrigues you, head to **National Croquet Center** ⑱, less than 2 mi from the museum, by turning right onto Summit Boulevard from Dreher Trail north and proceeding to Florida Mango Road, where you will again turn right. Backtrack to Summit Boulevard and go west to the 150-acre **Pine Jog Environmental Education Center** ⑲. For more natural adventure, head farther west on Summit until you reach Forest Hill Boulevard, where you turn right to reach the **Okeeheelee Nature Center** ⑳ and its miles of wooded trails. Now retrace your route to Summit Boulevard, drive east until you reach Military Trail, and take a left. Drive north to Southern Boulevard and turn west to reach **Lion Country Safari** ㉑, a 500-acre cageless zoo. For the last stop on this tour, backtrack to Military Trail and travel north to the **Mounts Botanical Gardens** ㉒.

TIMING   Tailor your time based on specific interests, because you could easily spend most of a day at any of these attractions. Prepare yourself for heavy rush-hour traffic, and remember that sightseeing in the morning (not *too* early, to avoid rush hour) will be less congested.

What to See

🖐 ㉑ **Lion Country Safari.** Drive your own vehicle (with windows closed) on 8 mi of paved roads through a 500-acre cageless zoo with 1,000 free-roaming animals. Lions, elephants, white rhinos, giraffes, zebras, antelopes, chimpanzees, and ostriches are among the wild things in residence. Exhibits include the Kalahari, designed after a South African bush plateau and containing water buffalo and Nilgai (the largest type of Asian antelope), and the Gir Forest, modeled after a game forest in India and showcasing a pride of lions. A walk-through park area has bird feeding and a petting zoo, or take a pontoon boat tour. There's also paddleboating, miniature golf, a children's play area with rides and sports fields, a picnic pavilion, restaurant, and snack shop. No convertibles or pets are allowed. ✉ *2003 Lion Country Safari Rd., at Southern Blvd. W, Loxahatchee* 📞 *561/793–1084* ⊕ *www.lioncountrysafari.com* 💲 *$19.95, vehicle rental $9–$17 per 1½ hrs* ⊙ *Daily 9:30–5:30; last vehicle in by 4:30.*

㉒ **Mounts Botanical Gardens.** Take advantage of balmy weather by walking among the tropical and subtropical plants here. Join a free tour or explore the 14 acres of exotic trees, rain-forest area, and butterfly and water gardens on your own. Many plants were significantly damaged during the 2004 hurricanes and new plantings will take years to reach maturity. ✉ *531 N. Military Trail* 📞 *561/233–1749* ⊕ *www.mounts.org* 💲 *Gardens free; tours $2* ⊙ *Mon.–Sat. 8:30–4:30, Sun. 1–5; tours Sat. at 11, Sun. at 2.*

★ ⑱ **National Croquet Center.** The world's largest croquet complex, the 10-acre center is also the headquarters for the U.S. Croquet Association. Vast expanses of manicured lawn are the stage for fierce competitions—in no way resembling the casual backyard games where kids play with wide wire wickets. There's also a clubhouse with a pro shop and Café Croquet, with verandas for dining and viewing, and a museum hall. Half-day and full-day reservations for play on a dozen lawns can be booked. ⊠ *700 Florida Mango Rd., at Summit Blvd.* ☎ *561/478–2300* ⊕ *www.croquetnational.com* ☜ *$20 daily June–Sept., $35 daily Oct.–May* ⊗ *Court times June–Sept., Tues.–Sat. 9–5; Oct.–May, daily 9–5.*

⑳ **Okeeheelee Nature Center.** Explore 5 mi of trails through 90 acres of western Palm Beach County's native pine flatwoods and wetlands. A visitor center–gift shop has hands-on exhibits and offers guided walks by the center's volunteers. ⊠ *7715 Forest Hill Blvd.* ☎ *561/233–1400* ☜ *Free* ⊗ *Visitor center Tues.–Fri. and Sun. 1–4:45, Sat. 8:15–4:45; trails daily dawn–dusk.*

♻ ⚑ ⑯ **Palm Beach Zoo at Dreher Park.** This wild kingdom is a 23-acre complex with 400-plus animals representing more than 125 species, from Florida panthers to the giant Aldabra tortoise and the first outdoor exhibit of Goeldi's monkeys in the nation. The Tropics of America exhibit has 6 acres of rain forest plus Maya ruins, an Amazon river village, and an aviary. Also notable are a nature trail, the otter exhibit, and a children's petting zoo. ⊠ *1301 Summit Blvd.* ☎ *561/533–0887* ⊕ *www.palmbeachzoo.com* ☜ *$9* ⊗ *Daily 9–5.*

♻ ⑲ **Pine Jog Environmental Education Center.** The draw here is 150 acres of mostly undisturbed Florida pine flatwoods with one self-guided ½-mi trail. Formal landscaping around five one-story buildings includes native plants, while dioramas and displays illustrate ecosystems. School groups use the trails during the week; special events include camping and campfires. Call for an event schedule. ⊠ *6301 Summit Blvd.* ☎ *561/686–6600* ⊕ *www.pinejog.org* ☜ *Free* ⊗ *Weekdays 9–5.*

♻ ⑰ **South Florida Science Museum.** Here at the museum, which includes the Aldrin Planetarium and McGinty Aquarium, there are hands-on exhibits with touch tanks, and laser shows with music by the likes of Dave Matthews. Galaxy Golf is a nine-hole science challenge. Weather permitting, you can observe the heavens Friday nights through the most powerful telescope in South Florida. ⊠ *4801 Dreher Trail N* ☎ *561/832–1988* ⊕ *www.sfsm.org* ☜ *$7, planetarium $2 extra, laser show $4 extra, galaxy golf $2 extra* ⊗ *Mon.–Fri. 10–5, Sat. 10–6, Sun. noon–6.*

Where to Stay & Eat

★ **$$–$$$$** ✕ **Tsunami.** Hip crowds hang out here to nibble on Asian fusion fare and wash it down with exotic fruit martinis. Packed into this dramatic multilevel restaurant are an upstairs bar, a late-night lounge, a sushi bar, and an enormous Buddha statue. ⊠ *CityPlace, 651 Okeechobee Blvd.* ☎ *561/835–9696* ☜ *Reservations essential* ▭ *AE, D, DC, MC, V* ⊗ *No lunch.*

$$–$$$ ✕ **Café Protégé.** At this 150-seat restaurant of the Florida Culinary Institute, watch students slicing, dicing, and sautéing in the observation kitchen. Try the rack of lamb served with cabernet mashed potatoes, sautéed mushrooms, and bok choy ragout in a balsamic reduction. Another superb dish is the Floridian bouillabaisse, with shrimp, scallops, clams, mussels, and whitefish. ✉ *2400 Metrocentre Blvd.* ☎ *561/687–2433* 🖹 *AE, MC, V* ⊘ *No lunch weekends, no dinner Sun.–Tues.*

¢–$$ ✕ **Aleyda's Tex-Mex Restaurant.** This casual, family-friendly eatery consistently scores high on local popularity polls. Fajitas, the house specialty, are brought to the table sizzling in the pan, along with such classic Mexican offerings as enchiladas, chili con queso, and quesadillas. The bartenders claim to make the best margaritas in town. ✉ *1890 Okeechobee Blvd.* ☎ *561/688–9033* 🖹 *AE, MC, V* ⊘ *No lunch Sun.*

¢–$$ ✕ **China Cafe.** Located in the Carefree Theatre building, this place isn't fancy and the food is not expensive, yet China Cafe is popular with both the West Palm and Palm Beach crowds. From lunching workers and antique shoppers to theatre goers and barhoppers, they all stop by to fill up on straightforward Chinese food. ✉ *7635 S. Dixie Hwy.* ☎ *561/585–7777* 🖹 *AE, MC, V.*

¢ ✕ **Manzo's Italian Deli.** Slightly off the West Okeechobee Boulevard main drag and tucked inside a shopping center is a fine sandwich shop. Favorite sandwiches include the Number 8 (homemade mozzarella and tomato with basil) and the Number 22 (eggplant parmigiana on warm Italian bread). Sides include tricolor tortellini, macaroni, potato, and mushroom salads. ✉ *400 Village Blvd.* ☎ *561/697–9411* 🖹 *No credit cards* ⊘ *Closed Sun.*

¢ ✕ **Middle East Bakery.** This hole-in-the-wall Middle Eastern bakery, deli, and market fills at lunchtime with regulars who are on a first-name basis with the gang behind the counter. From the nondescript parking lot the place doesn't look like much, but inside, delicious hot and cold Mediterranean treats await. Choose from traditional gyro sandwiches and lamb salads with sides of grape leaves, tabbouleh, and couscous. ✉ *327 5th St., at Olive Ave.* ☎ *561/659–7322* 🖹 *AE, MC, V* ⊘ *Closed Sun.*

$$–$$$ ▥ **Casa de Rosa.** This peach stucco Tuscan-style house, in the Old Northwood area, was restored in 2002 and is now filled with antique furnishings and wood floors; all rooms are decorated with a rose theme. Three rooms are in the main house and a cottage with a full kitchen is next to the pool. There are inviting outdoor spaces, with tropical plants, exotic palms, and rock and rose gardens, and there's a fountain near the pool. Breakfast might include frittatas or Dutch apple pancakes, and the afternoons and evenings bring fresh-baked cookies, snacks, and cocktails. ✉ *520 27th St., 33407* ☎ *561/833–1920 or 888/665–8666* 🖶 *561/835–3566* ⊕ *www.casaderosa.com* ⇆ *4 rooms* ⌕ *Pool* 🖹 *AE, D, MC, V* ▯◯▮ *BP.*

$–$$$ ▥ **Hibiscus House.** The hosts work diligently to promote not only their delightful Cape Cod–style B&B, but also their neighborhood, Old Northwood, which, thanks to their efforts, is listed on the National Register of Historic Places. Rooms are decorated with a mix of antiques and reproductions and all overlook the tropical pool-patio area. There's also a Hibiscus House Downtown near CityPlace. ✉ *501 30th St., 33407*

☎ 561/863–5633 or 800/203–4927 🖷 561/863–5633 ⊕ *www.* *hibiscushouse.com* 🛏 *8 rooms* 👌 *Microwaves, in-room data ports, pool, airport shuttle, some pets allowed* ⊟ *AE, DC, MC, V* ⑩ *BP.*

$–$$$ 🏨 **Hotel Biba.** In the El Cid historic district, this 1940s motel has gotten a fun, stylish revamp from Barbara Hulanicki, designer of the 1960s Biba fashion line. Each room has a vibrant mélange of colors along with handcrafted mirrors, mosaic bathroom floors, and custom mahogany furnishings. Luxury touches include Egyptian-cotton sheets, down pillows and duvets, and lavender-scented closets. The hotel is about a mile from Clematis Street nightlife and the lobby bar attracts a hip happy-hour crowd. ✉ *320 Belvedere Rd., 33405* ☎ *561/832–0094* 🖷 *561/* *833–7848* ⊕ *www.hotelbiba.com* 🛏 *43 rooms* 👌 *Pool, bar, no-smoking rooms* ⊟ *AE, DC, MC, V* ⑩ *CP.*

$–$$ 🏨 **Tropical Gardens Bed & Breakfast.** In the historic Old Northwood area, this cozy, informal cottage house painted in a sunny yellow with white trim has room options, from the twin-bedded Canary Room to the deluxe Carriage House, in a separate building with a kitchenette and French doors leading out to the pool. With its tropical colors and a laid-back approach, this B&B feels very Key West. Included with breakfast are tasty homemade breads and scones. ✉ *419 32nd St., 33407* ☎ *561/848–* *4064 or 800/736–4064* 🖷 *561/848–2422* ⊕ *www.tropicalgardensbandb.* *com* 🛏 *4 rooms* 👌 *Some microwaves, some refrigerators, some in-room VCRs, pool, bicycles; no smoking* ⊟ *AE, D, MC, V* ⑩ *CP.*

Nightlife & the Arts

The Arts

★ Starring amid the treasury of local arts attractions is the **Raymond F. Kravis Center for the Performing Arts** (✉701 Okeechobee Blvd. ☎561/832–7469), a 2,200-seat glass, copper, and marble showcase perched on what passes for high ground near the railroad tracks in West Palm Beach. Its 250-seat Rinker Playhouse has children's programming, family productions, and other events. The outdoor Gosman Amphitheatre is perfect for winter nights and holds 1,400 in seats and on the lawn. A packed year-round schedule unfolds here with drama, dance, and music—from gospel and bluegrass to jazz and classical, including performances of the Palm Beach Pops, New World Symphony, and Miami City Ballet.

Palm Beach Opera (✉ 415 S. Olive Ave. ☎ 561/833–7888) stages four productions each winter at the Kravis Center with English translations projected above the stage. The family opera series includes matinee performances such as "Hansel & Gretel"; tickets are $18 to $225. The **Carefree Theatre** (✉ 2000 S. Dixie Hwy. ☎ 561/833–7305) is Palm Beach County's premier showcase for foreign and art films and live entertainment in an intimate setting. The **Cuillo Center** (✉ 201 Clematis St. ☎ 561/835–9226) has a 377-seat theater on the main floor with off-Broadway shows and a 40-seat theater upstairs with small acting groups.

Nightlife

The **Palm Beach Casino Line** (✉ 1 E. 11th St., Riviera Beach ☎ 561/845–7447 or 800/841–7447) runs a five-hour getaway aboard the *Palm*

Beach Princess, sailing twice daily from the Port of Palm Beach. There's a 15,000-square-foot casino, assorted lounges, a sports booking bar with nine televisions, a gift shop, and entertainment, along with a prime-rib buffet in the evening. Sailings are at 11 AM and 6:30 PM daily, and you'll need to allow time for pre-boarding procedures. Fares are $25–$35 per person. CityPlace comes alive at **Blue Martini** (⊠ 550 S. Rosemary Ave. ☎ 561/835–8601), a bar with eclectic music that attracts a diverse crowd. **ER Bradley's Saloon** (⊠ 104 Clematis St. ☎ 561/833–3520) is an open-air, pavilion-style restaurant and bar where large groups of all ages congregate to hang out and socialize while overlooking the Intracoastal Waterway and the Meyer Amphitheatre. At **Flow** (⊠ 308 Clematis St. ☎ 561/833–9555), DJs spin high-energy dance tunes for an energetic clientele. There are full-size palm trees and trellises bright with bougainvillea blooms, plus a light-and-laser sound system and a 7,500-square-foot dance floor at the Caribbean-theme **Monkeyclub** (⊠ 219 Clematis St. ☎ 561/833–6500) where the music hails from the 1970s, '80s, and '90s.

Sports & the Outdoors

Golf

The plush **Emerald Dunes Golf Course** (⊠ 2100 Emerald Dunes Dr. ☎ 561/687–1700) has 18 holes designed by Tom Fazio; green fee: $120/$175, which includes cart and GPS yardage system. The **Palm Beach National Golf & Country Club** (⊠ 7500 St. Andrews Rd., Lake Worth ☎ 561/965–3381) has an 18-hole classic course with a Joe Lee championship layout; green fee: $40/$60. The Joanne Carner Golf Academy is based here.

Shopping

If you're looking for a mix of food, art, performance, landscaping, and retailing, then head to renewed downtown West Palm around **Clematis Street,** which runs east–west from Dixie Highway to Flagler Drive. Waterview parks with attractive plantings and lighting—and fountains where kids can cool off—add to the pleasure of browsing, window-shopping, and resting at an outdoor café. Hip national retailers such as Design Within Reach, Ann Taylor Loft, and Z Gallerie blend in with stores that specialize in fabrics or tattoos. The 55-acre, $550 million **CityPlace** (⊠ 700 S. Rosemary Ave. ☎ 561/366–1000) attracts people of all ages to enjoy restaurants, cafés, and outdoor bars, a 20-screen Muvico, the Harriet Himmel Gilman Theater, and a 36,000-gallon dance, water, and light show. This family-friendly dining, shopping, and entertainment complex has plenty to see and do. Among CityPlace's stores are popular national retailers Macy's, Armani Exchange, Pottery Barn, and Restoration Hardware and several boutiques unique to Florida. Inside **Artefacto** (☎ 561/822–0004), spaciously organized furniture and creative accessories for the home fill a gallery-like showroom of this Brazilian importer. Behind the punchy, brightly colored clothing in the front window of **C. Orrico** (☎ 561/832–9203) are family fashions and accessories by Lily Pulitzer and girlie casual gear by Three Dots and Trina Turk. **Rhythm Clothiers** (☎ 561/833–7677) attracts fashion-for-

ward types with a stock of men's and women's clothing by Dolce & Gabbana, Catherine Malandrino, Diesel, Miss Sixty, and J. Lindeberg. With shelves displaying sleek and sometimes quirky home goods, **Artifacts & Objects** (☎ 561/653–0001) is an ideal spot for souvenirs. The free downtown trolley runs a continuous loop linking Clematis Street
★ and CityPlace, so you won't miss a shop. West Palm's **Antique Row,** aka South Dixie Highway, is the destination for those who are interested in interesting home decor. From thrift shops to the most exclusive stores, it is all here—furniture, lighting, art, junk, fabric, frames, tile and rugs. So if you're looking for an art deco or French Provincial or Mizner piece de resistance, big or small, schedule a few hours for an Antique Row stroll. You'll find bargains during the off-season (May–November). Antique Row runs north–south from Okeechobee Road to Forest Hill Boulevard, although most stores are bunched between Okeechobee Road and Southern Boulevard.

Lake Okeechobee

40 mi west of West Palm Beach.

Rimming the western edges of Palm Beach and Martin counties, the second largest freshwater lake completely within the United States is girdled by 120 mi of road yet remains shielded from sight for almost its entire circumference. Lake Okeechobee—the Seminole's Big Water and the heart of the great Everglades watershed—measures 730 square mi, roughly 33 mi north–south, and 30 mi east–west, with an average natural depth of only 10 feet (flood control brings the figure up to 12 feet and deeper). Six major lock systems and 32 separate water-control structures manage the water. Encircling the lake is a 30-foot-high grassy levee—locals call it "the wall"—and the Lake Okeechobee Scenic Trail, a segment of the Florida National Scenic Trail, challenging for even the most experienced hikers and mountain bicyclists. This primitive and intriguing 110-mi trail encircles the lake atop the 35-foot Herbert Hoover Dike. Inside the wall, on the lake, you'll spot happy anglers from all over, themselves hooked on some of the best bass fishing in North America.

Small towns dot the lakeshore in this predominantly agricultural area. To the southeast is Belle Glade—motto: HER SOIL IS HER FORTUNE—playing a role as the eastern hub of the 700,000-acre Everglades Agricultural Area, the crescent of farmlands south and east of the lake. Southwest lies Clewiston, billing itself as "the sweetest town in America" thanks to the presence of "Big Sugar," more formally known as the United States Sugar Corporation. At the lake's north end, around Okeechobee, citrus production has outgrown cattle ranching as the principal economic engine, and still-important dairying diminishes as the state acquires more acreage in efforts to reduce water pollution. Set back from the lake, Indiantown is the western hub of Martin County, noteworthy for citrus production, cattle ranching, and timbering. The town reached its apex in 1927, when the Seaboard Airline Railroad briefly established its southern headquarters and a model town here.

Detailing city history, the **Clewiston Museum** tells stories not only of Big Sugar and the Herbert Hoover Dike construction but also of a ramie crop grown here to make rayon, of World War II RAF pilots training at the Clewiston airfield, and of a German POW camp. ⊠ *112 S. Commercio St., Clewiston* ☎ *863/983–2870* 🖾 *Free* ☺ *Mon.–Fri. 1–5.*

In the **Municipal Complex** are the public library and the **Lawrence E. Will Museum,** both with materials on town history. On the front lawn is a Ferenc Verga sculpture of a family fleeing a wall of water rising from the lake during the catastrophic hurricane of 1928. More than 2,000 people perished and 15,000 families were left homeless by torrential flooding. ⊠ *530 Main St., Belle Glade* ☎ *561/996–3453* 🖾 *Free* ☺ *Mon.–Wed. 10–8, Thurs.–Sat. 10–5.*

Where to Stay & Eat

¢–$$ ✕ **Colonial Dining Room.** The Clewiston Inn's restaurant has ladder-back chairs, chandeliers, fanlight windows, and an attitude that's anything but fancy. The regional and Continental dishes—chicken, pork, steak, and the ubiquitous catfish—are mighty tasty. ⊠ *108 Royal Palm Ave., at U.S. 27, Clewiston* ☎ *863/983–8151* 🖃 *MC, V* ☺ *No dinner Sun. and Mon.*

¢–$ ✕ **Lightsey's.** The pick of the lake, this lodgelike restaurant at the Okee-Tantie Recreation Area started closer to town as a fish company with four tables in a corner. Now folks gladly trek out here for lunch and dinner daily. Get most items fried, steamed, broiled, or grilled. The freshest are the catfish, cooter (freshwater turtle), frogs' legs, and gator. ⊠ *10430 Rte. 78 W, Okeechobee* ☎ *863/763–4276* 🖃 *D, MC, V.*

$–$$ 🏨 **Clewiston Inn.** A classic antebellum-style country hotel in the heart of town, this inn was built in 1938. The cypress-paneled lobby, wood-burning fireplace, Colonial Dining Room, and Everglades lounge with a wraparound Everglades mural are standouts. Rooms, with reproduction furniture, are an excellent value, and rates include a full breakfast cooked to order. There's a pool across the street in the park. ⊠ *108 Royal Palm Ave., at U.S. 27, Clewiston 33440* ☎ *863/983–8151 or 800/749–4466* 🖷 *863/983–4602* ⊕ *www.clewistoninn.com* 🛏 *48 rooms, 5 suites* ⚐ *Restaurant, 6 tennis courts, bar* 🖃 *AE, D, DC, MC, V* ⊠◯ *BP.*

¢–$$ 🏨 **Seminole Inn.** Once the Seaboard Airline Railroad's southern headquarters, this two-story, Mediterranean Revival inn, with cypress ceilings and pine hardwood floors, was restored by Holman Wall. It's now run by the late Indiantown patriarch's daughter, Jonnie Wall Williams, a fifth-generation native. Carpeted rooms are done in country ruffles and prints, with comfy beds. Rocking chairs await on the porch, and there's Indiantown memorabilia in the lobby, a sitting area on the 2nd floor, and good local art throughout. ⊠ *15885 S.W. Warfield Blvd., Indiantown 34956* ☎ *772/597–3777* 🖷 *772/597–2883* ⊕ *www.seminoleinn.com* 🛏 *22 rooms* ⚐ *2 restaurants, pool, horseback riding* 🖃 *AE, D, MC, V* ⊠◯ *CP.*

¢–$ 🏨 **Pier II Resort.** This two-story motel on the rim canal has a five-story observation tower for peeking over the lake's levee. Large, motel-plain rooms are nicely maintained. Out back are a 650-foot fishing pier and the Oyster Bar, one of the lake area's best hangouts for shooting pool or watching TV, attracting a mix of locals and out-of-towners. ⊠ *2200*

S.E. U.S. 441, Okeechobee 34974 ☎ *863/763–8003 or 800/874–3744*
🖶 *863/763–2245* ⊕ *www.pier2resort.com* ⇱ *83 rooms, 6 suites*
 ⟋ *Some kitchens, some microwaves, refrigerators, pool, marina, fishing, bar* ⊟ *AE, D, DC, MC, V* ⟋ *CP.*

¢ ⊡ **Okeechobee Inn.** Rooms in this simple, two-story, L-shape motel, 2 mi west of Belle Glade, are done in green floral prints. Large windows let in plenty of light, and balconies overlook the pool. Fishing and boat ramps are a mile away. ⊠ *265 N. U.S. 27, South Bay 33493* ☎ *561/ 996–6517* ⇱ *115 rooms* ⟋ *Pool, playground* ⊟ *AE, D, DC, MC, V.*

¢ ⩕ **Belle Glade Campground.** A few miles north of downtown Belle Glade, just offshore in Lake Okeechobee, is Torry Island. Campsites have horseshoes, shuffleboard, boating, fishing, and docks. ⟋ *Flush toilets, full hookups, partial hookups (electric and water), picnic tables, playground* ⇱ *370 campsites* ⊠ *5000 W. Canal St. N, Torry Island* ☎ *561/ 996–6322* ▨ *$17.60* ⊟ *MC, V.*

¢ ⩕ **Okee-Tantie Recreation Area.** The park has RV sites, tent sites, boating, fishing, and a dock. Lightsey's restaurant overlooks the marina, which has direct access to Lake Okeechobee and the Kissimmee River. ⟋ *Flush toilets, full hookups, partial hookups (electric and water), showers, picnic tables, restaurant, general store, playground* ⇱ *215 RV sites, 38 tent sites* ⊠ *10430 Rte. 78 W, Okeechobee* ☎ *863/763–2622* ▨ *$26.96–$30.75* ⊟ *MC, V.*

Sports & the Outdoors

FISHING **J-Mark Fish Camp** (⊠ Torry Island, Belle Glade ☎ 561/996–5357) has fully equipped bass boats, airboat rides, fishing guides, tackle, bait, and licenses. Since the **Okee-Tantie Recreation Area** (⊠ 10430 Rte. 78 W, Okeechobee ☎ 863/763–2622) has direct lake access, it's a popular fishing outpost. There are two public boat ramps, fish-cleaning stations, a marina, picnic areas and a restaurant, a playground, rest rooms, showers, and a **bait shop** (☎ 863/763–9645) that stocks groceries. In addition to operating the bridge to Torry Island (among Florida's last remaining swing bridges—it's cranked open and closed by hand, swinging at right angles to the road), brothers Charles and Gordon Corbin run **Slim's Fish Camp** (⊠ 215 Marina Dr., Belle Glade ☎ 561/996–3844). Here, on Torry Island, are a complete tackle shop, guides, camping facilities, and bass boats. You can also procure the name of a taxidermist to mount your trophy.

GOLF **Belle Glade Municipal Country Club** (⊠ Torry Island Rd. [W. Lake Rd.], Belle Glade ☎ 561/996–6605) has an 18-hole golf course and restaurant open to the public; green fee: $15/$28.

SOUTH TO BOCA RATON

Strung together by Route A1A, the towns between Palm Beach and Boca Raton are notable for their variety. Although the aura of Palm Beach has rubbed off here and there, there are also pockets of modesty, such as Briny Breezes with its oceanside trailers. In one town is a cluster of art galleries and fancy dining, while the very next town will yield mostly hamburger joints and mom-and-pop stores.

Lake Worth

㉓ *2 mi south of West Palm Beach.*

For years, tourists looked here mainly for inexpensive lodging and easy access to Palm Beach, since a bridge leads from the mainland to a barrier island with Lake Worth's beach. Now Lake Worth has several blocks of restaurants and art galleries, making this a worthy destination on its own. Also known as Casino Park, **Lake Worth Municipal Park** has a beach, Olympic-size swimming pool, fishing pier, picnic areas, shuffleboard, restaurants, and shops. ⊠ *Rte. A1A at end of Lake Worth Bridge* ☎ *561/533–7367* ▣ *Pool $3, parking 25¢ for 15 mins* ⊙ *Daily 9–5.*

Where to Stay & Eat

$–$$ ✕ **Bizaare Avenue Café.** Decorated with a mix of artwork and antiques, this cozy tapas bar/wine bar/bistro fits right into downtown Lake Worth's groovy, eclectic scene. Daily specials are available on both the lunch and dinner menus, where crepes, pizzas, pastas, and salads are the staples. ⊠ *921 Lake Ave.* ☎ *561/588–4488* ▤ *AE, D, DC, MC, V* ⊙ *Closed Sun.*

¢–$ ✕ **John G's.** Count on a line here until closing at 3 PM. The menu is as big as the crowd: grand fruit platters, sandwich-board superstars, grilled burgers, seafood, eggs every which way, and the house specialty, French toast. Breakfast is served until 11. ⊠ *10 S. Ocean Blvd. (Lake Worth Casino)* ☎ *561/585–9860* ⩗ *Reservations not accepted* ▤ *No credit cards* ⊙ *No dinner.*

¢ ✕ **Benny's on the Beach.** Perched on the Lake Worth Pier (and nearly wiped out in Hurricanes France and Jeanne), Benny's has diner-style food that's cheap and nothing fancy, but the spectacular view of the sun (or moon) glistening on the water and the waves crashing directly below is what dining here is all about. Reservations and credit cards are only permitted at dinner. ⊠ *10 Ocean Ave.* ☎ *561/582–9001* ▤ *MC, V* ⊙ *No dinner Mon.–Thurs.*

★ $$–$$$ ▦ **Mango Inn.** It's only a 15-minute walk to the beach from this white frame B&B built as a private house in 1915. The two ground-floor rooms have French doors opening out onto a patio. A poolside cottage has two bedrooms and two bathrooms. Have your complimentary breakfast of homemade raspberry buttermilk pancakes on the veranda overlooking the heated pool, or in the courtyard next to the fountain. ⊠ *128 N. Lakeside Dr., 33460* ☎ *561/533–6900 or 888/626–4619* 🖷 *561/493–3748* ⊕ *www.mangoinn.com* ⇥ *7 rooms, 1 cottage* ♿ *Kitchenettes, some refrigerators, in-room VCRs, in-room data ports, pool; no kids, no smoking* ▤ *AE, D, MC, V* ⏐◉⏐ *BP.*

$$–$$$ ▦ **Sabal Palm House.** Built in 1936, this historic two-story frame enclave is a short walk from the Intracoastal Waterway and a golf course. Three rooms and a suite are in the main house, three others are across a brick courtyard in the carriage house. Each room is inspired by a different artist—including Renoir, Dalí, Norman Rockwell, and Chagall—and all have oak floors, antique furnishings, and private balconies. There's an inviting parlor where afternoon tea and weekend wine and appetizers are served. A full breakfast is offered indoors or in the courtyard, under the palms. ⊠ *109 N. Golfview Rd., 33460* ☎ *561/582–1090 or 888/ 722–2572* 🖶 *561/582–0933* ⊕ *www.sabalpalmhouse.com* ➷ *6 rooms, 1 suite* ♨ *Some in-room hot tubs; no kids under 14* 🖃 *AE, MC, V* ⦿*BP.*

¢–$$$ 🏠 **The Parador.** This Caribbean-style B&B brims with color and light throughout the main house, courtyard, and breezeway, where reggae music plays. All rooms are suites and decorated in yellows, pinks, and blues, with pine or terrazzo floors. A fern garden, deck, and hot tub make the courtyard the perfect place to wind down, especially after the complimentary evening refreshments. Rules are flexible, with well-behaved children and pets allowed and smoking permitted in the two main-house rooms. ⊠ *1000 S. Federal Hwy., 33460* ☎ *561/540–1443 or 561/876– 6000* 🖶 *561/547–1243* ⊕ *www.theparadorinn.com* ➷ *8 rooms* ♨ *Microwaves, refrigerators, hot tub* 🖃 *AE, MC, V* ⦿*BP.*

¢–$ 🏠 **Hummingbird Hotel.** This historic but no-frills B&B offers comfortable rooms and a personable staff. In the heart of downtown Lake Worth, Hummingbird Hotel is very close to art galleries, antiques shops, and eclectic restaurants. Six rooms have private baths. Efficiencies have kitchenettes, but full kitchen and laundry facilities are available to guests. ⊠ *631 Lucerne Ave., 33460* ☎*561/582–3224* 🖶*561/540–8817* ⊕*www.hummingbirdhotel. com* ➷ *25 rooms, 6 with bath* 🖃 *AE, D, MC, V* ⦿*CP.*

Nightlife & the Arts

NIGHTLIFE   Some nights you'll encounter free concerts by local and regional artists, and other nights the headliners are nationally known professionals. But every night, Tuesday through Saturday, there's traditional blues at the **Bamboo Room** (⊠ 25 S. J St. ☎ 561/585–2583).

THE ARTS   **Lake Worth Playhouse** (⊠ 713 Lake Ave. ☎ 561/586–6410) presents drama and popular musicals on its main stage, including works by Andrew Lloyd Webber and Tim Rice. The regular season runs from September through June, with two adjacent venues each showing six shows. Tickets are reasonably priced from $18 to $25.

★   The **Palm Beach Institute of Contemporary Art** (⊠ 601 Lake Ave. ☎ 561/ 582–0006), in a former art deco movie theater, is a 6,400-square-foot exhibition space with a new media lounge, family art workshops, contemporary art lectures, and gallery tours. PBICA is open Tuesday through Sunday from noon to 6 PM; call for extended seasonal hours and guided tours.

Sports & the Outdoors

The **Gulfstream Polo Club,** the oldest such club along the Palm Beaches, began in the 1920s and plays medium-goal polo (for teams with handicaps of 8–16 goals). There are seven polo fields and stabling for more than 60 horses here on the western edge of Lake Worth. ⊠ *4550 Polo Rd.* ☎ *561/965–2057* 🎫 *Free* ☉ *Games Dec.–Apr.*

Lantana

㉔ *2 mi south of Lake Worth.*

Lantana—just a bit farther south from Palm Beach than Lake Worth— has inexpensive lodging and a bridge connecting the town to its own beach on Palm Beach's barrier island. Tucked between Lantana and Boynton Beach is **Manalapan,** a tiny but posh residential community crowned by a luxury Ritz-Carlton beach resort. Ideal for sprawling, beach-combing, or power-walking, **Lantana Public Beach** is also worthy for its proximity to one of the most popular food concessions in town, the **Dune Deck Cafe.** Here the choices are standard, but the food is particularly fresh and the portions are hearty. Try an omelet with a side of potato fries and melon wedges, the homemade yogurt with seasonal fruit topped with honey, or a side of banana nut bread. There are daily breakfast and lunch specials; dining is outdoors under yellow canopies perched over the beach. ⊠ *100 N. Ocean Ave.* ☏ *No phone* 🄿 *Parking 25¢ for 15 mins* ⊙ *Daily 9–4:45.*

Where to Stay & Eat

$$–$$$ ✕ **Station House Restaurant.** The best Maine lobster in South Florida might well reside at this delicious dive, where all the seafood is cooked to perfection. Sticky seats and tablecloths are an accepted part of the scene, so wear jeans and a T-shirt. Although it's casual and family-oriented here, reservations are recommended, since it's a local favorite. Station Grill, across the street, is less seafood-oriented, but every bite as good. ⊠ *233 Lantana Rd.* ☏ *561/547–9487* ▭ *AE, D, DC, MC, V.*

★ **$$–$$$** ✕ **Suite 225.** On a quaint street with other shops and eateries is this stylish restaurant, an inviting older house that's been renovated into a sleek sushi bar. Glass doors and windows open up to outdoor dining areas and a bar nestles under large banyan trees. Start with a sample platter from the extensive list of eclectic "suite rolls," which includes nearly 40 choices. Among the good nonseafood bets are grilled sake skirt steak with ginger barbecue sauce and pork chops with Asian-pear chutney. ⊠ *225 E. Ocean Ave.* ☏ *561/582–2255* ▭ *AE, D, MC, V* ⊙ *No lunch Sun. and Mon.*

$–$$$ ✕ **Old Key Lime House.** Overlooking the Intracoastal Waterway, the 1889 Lyman House has grown in spurts over the years and is now a patchwork of shedlike spaces, housing an informal Old Florida seafood house with local seafood and key lime pie—the house specialty. Although there's air-conditioning, dining is open-air most evenings. ⊠ *300 E. Ocean Ave.* ☏ *561/533–5220* ▭ *AE, MC, V.*

★ **$$$$** 🄷 **Ritz-Carlton, Palm Beach.** Despite its name, this bisque-color, triple-tower landmark is actually in Manalapan, halfway between Palm Beach and Delray Beach. A huge double-sided marble fireplace dominates the elegant lobby and foreshadows the luxury of the guest rooms, which have rich upholstered furnishings and marble tubs. Most rooms have ocean views, and all have balconies. Although much of the beach was eroded by two hurricanes in 2004, there's a large pool and courtyard shaded by coconut palms—all of which are served by attendants who can fulfill whims from iced drinks to cool face towels. ⊠ *100 S. Ocean Blvd., Manalapan 33462* ☏ *561/533–6000 or 800/241–3333* 🖷 *561/588–4555* ⊕ *www.ritz-carlton.com* ⇆ *257 rooms, 13 suites* ♨ *4 restaurants, room service, minibars, in-room data ports, 5 tennis courts, pool, hair salon, massage, sauna, spa, steam room, beach, snorkeling, bicycles, basketball, 2 bars, babysitting, children's programs (ages 5–12),* *laundry service, concierge, business services, no-smoking rooms* ⊟ *AE, D, DC, MC, V.*

$$–$$$ 🏨 **Palm Beach Oceanfront Inn.** Families seeking closer-to-earth prices gravitate to this casual two-story resort on the beach. Don't count on anything fancy, but large, adequately furnished rooms and suites face tropical gardens. Beach frontage is the draw here. A wide wooden sundeck surrounds the free-form pool, and both look to the ocean. The informal restaurant and outdoor bar also overlook the water. ⊠ *3550 S. Ocean Blvd., 33480* ☎ *561/582–5631 or 800/457–5631* 🖶 *561/588–4563* ⊕ *www.palmbeachoceanfrontinn.com* ➪ *50 rooms, 8 suites* ⟡ *Restaurant, room service, some kitchenettes, some microwaves, refrigerators, some in-room VCRs, in-room data ports, pool, beach, bar* ⊟ *AE, D, MC, V.*

THE ARTS **Florida Stage** (⊠ 262 South Ocean Blvd., Manalapan ☎ 561/585–3433), in the Plaza Del Mar shopping center across from the Ritz, is a 258-seat theater that presents five new or developing plays from October through June. Tickets range from $33 for previews to $75 for opening-night receptions.

Sports & the Outdoors

B-Love Fleet (⊠ 314 E. Ocean Ave. ☎ 561/588–7612) offers three deep-sea fishing excursions daily: 8–noon, 1–5, and 7–11. No reservations are needed; just show up 30 minutes before the boat is scheduled to leave. The cost is $30 per person and includes fishing license, bait, and tackle.

Boynton Beach

㉕ *3 mi south of Lantana.*

In 1884, when fewer than 50 settlers lived in the area, Nathan Boynton, a Civil War veteran from Michigan, paid $25 for 500 acres with a mile-long stretch of beachfront thrown in. How things have changed, with today's population at about 118,000 and property values still on an upswing. Far enough from Palm Beach to remain low-key, Boynton Beach has two parts, the mainland and the barrier island—the town of Ocean Ridge—connected by two bridges.

An inviting beach, boardwalk, concessions, grills, a jogging trail, and playground await at **Boynton Beach Oceanfront Park.** Weekend evening concerts are held throughout the year. Parking costs more if you're not a Boynton resident. ⊠ *6415 Ocean Blvd. (Rte. A1A)* ☎ *No phone* 🅿 *Parking $10 per day in winter, $5 per day rest of year* ⊙ *Daily 9 AM–midnight.*

★ ⓒ Boynton Beach's history is highlighted through interactive exhibits that make the **Schoolhouse Children's Museum** a kid and parent pleaser. In this 1913 schoolhouse, children can milk a mock cow or pick and wash plastic vegetables at the Pepper Patch Farm. Kids can buy tickets and dress up for a "time travel" train ride that immerses them in Boynton's history. A great outdoor playground castle is adjacent to the museum. ⊠ *129 E. Ocean Ave.* ☎ *561/742–6780* 🖾 *$5* ⊙ *Tues.–Sat. 10–5.*

Dating from the 1930s, when its trees were planted by the partners of the *Amos & Andy* radio show, **Knollwood Groves** offers a 30-minute, 30-acre tram tour through the orange groves, a processing plant, and an alligator exhibit. Knollwood is a working orange grove where juice is made daily during season. The grocery–gift shop sells assorted juices, jams, breads, and knickknacks with an orange theme. ⊠ *8053 Lawrence Rd.* ☎ *561/734–4800* ⊕ *www.knollwoodgroves.com* ⊡ *Tour $3* ⊙ *Daily 9–5:30* ⊙ *Closed Sun. May–Oct.*

off the
beaten
path

ARTHUR R. MARSHALL–LOXAHATCHEE NATIONAL WILDLIFE REFUGE – The most robust part of the Everglades, this 221-square-mi refuge is one of three huge water-retention areas accounting for much of the Everglades outside the national park. These areas are managed less to protect natural resources, however, than to prevent flooding to the south. Start from the visitor center, where there are two walking trails: a boardwalk through a dense cypress swamp, and a marsh trail to a 20-foot-high observation tower overlooking a pond. There's also a 5½-mi canoe trail, best for experienced canoeists, since it's overgrown. Wildlife viewing is good year-round, and you can fish for bass and panfish. ⊠ *10119 Lee Rd., off U.S. 441 between Boynton Beach Blvd. (Rte. 804) and Atlantic Ave. (Rte. 806), west of Boynton Beach* ☎ *561/734–8303* ⊡ *$5 per vehicle, pedestrians $1* ⊙ *Daily 6 AM–sunset; visitor center weekdays 9–4, weekends 9–4:30.*

Where to Stay & Eat

$$–$$$ ✕ **Nirvana.** Highly stylized dining attracts experimental foodies hungry for Indian food touched with Caribbean, American, and French flavors. Given its strip-mall location, the attentive service is an unexpected treat, as is the intimate interior: sheer fabrics drape from the ceiling, warm woods trim the perimeter, and terra-cotta-color floors and walls contrast the crisp white tablecloths. ⊠ *1701 N. Congress Ave.* ☎ *561/752–1932* ⊟ *AE, MC, V* ⊙ *No lunch.*

¢–$ ✕ **Banana Boat.** A mainstay for local boaters, who cruise up and down the Intracoastal and dock their crafts here, Banana Boat has fish-and-chips, burgers, ribs, and raw seafood. On weekends, casual crowds clad in tank tops, flip-flops, and bikinis dance to live music while downing frozen drinks. ⊠ *739 E. Ocean Ave.* ☎ *561/732–9400* ⊟ *AE, MC, V.*

$–$$ ⌂ **Emerald Shores Resort.** This green-and-white two-story motel has one- and two-bedroom apartments with full kitchens. A large sundeck surrounds the heated pool. The property is well situated—just across Route A1A from the beach—tucked into a quiet residential area with a mix of single and multifamily properties in Ocean Ridge, the barrier island of Boynton Beach. The minimum stay is three nights. ⊠ *6600 N. Ocean Blvd., 33435* ☎ *561/738–2063 or 800/433–0786* ⊷ *16 rooms, 2 suites* ⚴ *Kitchens, pool, laundry facilities* ⊟ *AE, D, DC, MC, V.*

¢–$ ⌂ **Holiday Inn Express.** Conveniently perched right off Interstate 95, this four-story hotel has large rooms with purple-and-green fabrics, blond-wood furniture, and small sitting areas. A large sundeck surrounds the heated pool. Complimentary breakfast is served, and free beverages are on tap at the end of the day. There's a full-service Holiday Inn with restaurant and gym 2 mi away. ⊠ *480 W. Boynton Beach Blvd., 33435* ☎ *561/734–9100* 🖷 *561/738–7193* ⊕ *www.hiexpress.com* ⤵ *105 rooms, 6 suites* ⚲ *In-room data ports, pool, laundry facilities* ☰ *AE, DC, MC, V* ⦿ *BP.*

Sports & the Outdoors

FISHING   Fish the canal at the **Arthur R. Marshall–Loxahatchee National Wildlife Refuge** (☎ 561/734–8303). There's a boat ramp, and the waters are decently productive, but bring your own equipment. On the other side of town, catch fish swimming between the Atlantic and Intracoastal at the **Boynton Beach Inlet Pier** (☎ No phone).

GOLF   **Links at Boynton Beach** (⊠ 8020 Jog Rd. ☎ 561/742–6500) has 18-hole and 9-hole executive courses; green fee: Champion course $13/$30, Family course $39/$49.

Gulf Stream

㉖ *2 mi south of Boynton Beach.*

Quiet money, and quite a lot of it, resides in this small beachfront community, whose architecture reflects Mizner's influence. As you pass the bougainvillea-topped walls of the Gulf Stream Club, don't be surprised if a private security officer stops traffic for a golfer to cross.

Delray Beach

㉗ *2 mi south of Gulf Stream.*

A onetime artists' retreat with a small settlement of Japanese farmers, Delray has grown into a sophisticated beach town. Atlantic Avenue, the once dilapidated main drag, has evolved into an over-a-mile-long stretch of palm-dotted sidewalks, lined with stores, art galleries, and dining establishments. Running east–west and ending at the beach, it's a pleasant place for a stroll, day or night. Another active pedestrian way begins at the eastern edge of Atlantic Avenue and runs along the big, broad swimming beach that extends north to George Bush Boulevard and south to Casuarina Road.

Just off Atlantic Avenue, the **Old School Square Cultural Arts Center** has several museums in restored school buildings dating from 1913 and 1926. The **Cornell Museum of Art & History** offers ever-changing art exhibits. During its season, the **Crest Theatre** showcases performances by local and touring troupes. ⊠ *51 N. Swinton Ave.* ☎ *561/243–7922* ⊕ *www. oldschool.org* 🎟 *$6* ⊙ *Tues.–Sat. 10:30–4:30, Sun. 1–4:30.*

A restored bungalow-style home that dates from about 1915, **Cason Cottage** serves as the Delray Beach Historical Society's offices. It's filled with Victorian-era relics, including a pipe organ donated by descendants of a Delray Beach pioneer family. Periodic displays celebrate the town's architectural evolution. The cottage is a block north of the cultural center. ⊠ *5 N.E. 1st St.* ☎ *561/243–0223* 🎟 *Free* ⊙ *Tues.–Fri. 11–4.*

The chief landmark along Atlantic Avenue since 1926 is the Mediterranean revival–style **Colony Hotel,** which is a member of the National

THE MORIKAMI:
ESSENCE OF JAPAN IN FLORIDA

A MAGICAL 200-ACRE GARDEN where the Far East meets the South lies just beyond Palm Beach's allure of sun and sea and glittering resorts. It's called the Morikami Museum and Japanese Gardens, and it's a testament to one man's perseverance against agricultural angst. The largest Japanese garden outside of Japan, it's also a soothing destination for reflection, with pine forest, trails, and lakes.

In 1904, Jo Sakai, a New York University graduate, returned to his homeland of Miyazu, Japan, to recruit hands for farming what is now northern Boca Raton. With help from Henry Flagler's East Coast Railroad subsidiary they colonized as Yamato, an ancient name for Japan. When crops fell short, everyone left except for George Sukeji Morikami, who carried on cultivating local crops, eventually donating his land to memorialize the Yamato Colony. His dream took on new dimension with the 1977 opening of the Morikami, a living monument bridging cultural understanding between Morikami's two homelands.

The original Yamato-Kan building chronicles the Yamato Colony, and a 32,000-square-foot main museum has rotating exhibits along with 5,000 art objects and artifacts including a 500-piece collection of tea-ceremony items. Enjoy a demonstration of sado, the Japanese tea ceremony, in the Seishin-an tea house, or learn about Japanese history in the 5,000-book library. There are also expansive Japanese gardens with strolling paths, a tropical bonsai collection, small lakes teeming with koi, plus picnic areas, a shop, and a café.

— Lynne Helm

Trust for Historic Preservation. Walk through the lobby to the parking lot of the hotel where original stable "garages" still stand from when hotel guests used to arrive via horse and carriage. ✉ *525 E. Atlantic Ave.* ☎ *561/276–4123.*

The **Museum of Lifestyle & Fashion** hosts rotating exhibits such as the history of the lunchbox or fashion in architecture and holds trolley rides through downtown Delray on the fourth Saturday of the month. ✉ *322 N.E. 2nd Ave.* ☎ *561/243–2662* ⊕ *www.mlfhmuseum.org* ✉ *$5* ☽ *Tues.–Sat. 10–5, Sun. 1–5.*

Traditional and digital photography are on display at the **Palm Beach Photographic Centre,** located in the Pineapple Grove section of town. There's a small museum, gallery, darkroom, and retail shop. ✉ *55 N.E. 2nd Ave.* ☎ *561/276–9797* ⊕ *www.workshop.org* ✉ *$3* ☽ *Mon.–Sat. 9–6.*

Out in the boonies west of Delray Beach seems an odd place to encounter **Fodor's**Choice the inscrutable East, but there awaits **Morikami Museum and Japanese Gardens,** a cultural and recreational facility heralding the Yamato Colony ★ of Japanese farmers. The on-site Cornell Café serves light Asian fare. If you don't get your fill of orchids, the American Orchid Society's 20,000-

square-foot headquarters is across the street. ⊠ *4000 Morikami Park Rd.* ☎ *561/495–0233* ⊕ *www.morikami.org* ⊠ *$9* ⊙ *Tues.–Sun. 10–5.*

★ Enjoy many types of water-sport rentals—sailing, kayaking, windsurfing, boogie boarding, surfing, snorkeling—or scuba diving at a sunken Spanish galleon less than ½ mi offshore at **Seagate Beach.** ⊠ *½ mi south of Atlantic Ave. at Rte. A1A.*

A scenic walking path follows the main stretch of the public **Delray Beach Municipal Beach.** ⊠ *Atlantic Ave. at Rte. A1A.*

Where to Stay & Eat

★ **$$–$$$$** ✕ **32 East.** While restaurants come and go on a trendy street like Atlantic Avenue, 32 East is a consistent staple, if not the best restaurant on any given night in Delray Beach. A daily menu of wood-oven pizzas, salads, soups, seafood, meat, and desserts is all based on what is fresh and plentiful. Dark wood accents and dim lighting make this large restaurant seem cozy. There's a packed bar in front and an open kitchen in back. ⊠ *32 E. Atlantic Ave.* ☎ *561/276–7868* ⊟ *AE, D, MC, V* ⊙ *No lunch.*

$$–$$$ ✕ **Kyoto.** An energetic crew, from the sushi chefs to the waitstaff, keep this bustling restaurant running into the wee hours all week long. Sushi and sake are the main draw here, and the less traditional dishes still have Japanese influences. Indoor dining is in a stylish, contemporary setting with sleek black accents and multicolor lighting. You can dine among a bar crowd and watch your sushi being assembled, or take a table in the front courtyard and watch the crowds meander along happening Pineapple Grove. ⊠ *25 N.E. 2nd Ave.* ☎ *561/330–2404* ⊟ *AE, DC, MC, V* ⊙ *No lunch Sat. and Sun.*

$–$$$ ✕ **Splendid Blendeds Café.** Dine on the sidewalk or in the dining room decorated with original primitive art. The café is popular day and night, and food is a blend of savory Italian, Mexican, Asian, and contemporary. Tasty starters include roasted corn chowder and grilled Thai duck satay. Entrées range from pasta dishes to grilled yellowfin tuna, filet mignon stuffed with roasted garlic, or jerk chicken. ⊠ *432 E. Atlantic Ave.* ☎ *561/265–1035* ⊟ *AE, MC, V* ⊙ *Closed Sun.*

¢–$$$ ✕ **Pineapple Grille.** A magnet for regulars, this informal tropical enclave serves dependable Caribbean fare. An extensive menu includes macadamia nut–crusted crab cakes and mango goat-cheese chicken, along with imaginative pizzas. There's also a good and affordable wine list and live music on weekends. ⊠ *800 Palm Trail, in Palm Trail Plaza* ☎ *561/265–1368* ⊟ *AE, MC, V* ⊙ *No lunch Sat., no dinner Sun.*

¢–$$ ✕ **Blue Anchor.** Yes, this pub was actually shipped from England, where it stood for 150 years as the Blue Anchor Pub in London's historic Chancery Lane. There it was a watering hole for famed Englishmen, including Winston Churchill. The Delray Beach incarnation has stuck to authentic British pub fare. Chow down on a ploughman's lunch (a chunk of Stilton cheese, a hunk of bread, and pickled onions), shepherd's pie, fish-and-chips, and bangers and mash (sausages with mashed potatoes). English beers and ales are on tap and by the bottle. ⊠ *804 E. Atlantic Ave.* ☎ *561/272–7272* ⊟ *AE, MC, V.*

¢–$$ ✕ **Boston's on the Beach.** Restaurants overlooking a beach often rely on location alone to keep tables filled. That's the case at Boston's, where you'll find beer flowing and the ocean breeze blowing. Decent bar fare includes New England clam chowder, several lobster dishes, and fresh fish. The walls are laden with paraphernalia from the Boston Bruins, New England Patriots, and Boston Red Sox, including a shrine to Ted Williams. Kick back on an outdoor deck upstairs. ⊠ *40 S. Ocean Blvd. (Rte. A1A)* ☎ *561/278–3364* ⊟ *AE, MC, V.*

¢–$ ✗ **Señor Torito.** Home-style Mexican favorites abound here. The home-made salsa and chips can fill you up, so save room for the spinach and cheese enchiladas, tacos asada, or mole verde burritos. Someone always orders sizzling fajitas, which fill the rooms with the aroma of onions and peppers. Señor Torito has a brother restaurant, Señor Burrito, in Boca Raton; both are delicious, casual dining. ⊠ *142 S.E. 6th Ave. (Federal Hwy.)* ☎ *561/278–5757* ⊟ *AE, MC, V* ⊗ *No lunch weekends.*

★ ¢ ✗ **Old School Bakery.** Formerly in a much larger shop where they actually baked all the goodies, this purveyor of many restaurants' breads has moved its baking facilities off-site and concentrates on simple sandwich making at its best. Particularly worthy is the cherry chicken salad sandwich with brie on multigrain. Apart from sandwiches and soups served for lunch every day, order from a diverse baked-goods menu with artisan breads, pastries, and several kinds of cookies, even biscotti. The bakery is primarily take-out, but there are a few small tables in an adjacent open-air courtyard. ⊠ *814 E. Atlantic Ave.* ☎ *561/243–8059* ⊟ *AE, MC, V* ⊗ *No dinner.*

★ $$$–$$$$ ✗🏨 **Sundy House.** Just about everything in this bright, bungalow-style inn is executed to perfection. Guest rooms are luxuriously decorated and offer hotel-style amenities, while the cottage has its own Jacuzzi and fireplace and the apartments offer a full kitchen and laundry. Situated a few blocks south of Atlantic Avenue, the only downside is a hearty walk to the beach. Even if you do not stay here, come see the grounds, where rooms are hidden behind extraordinary tropical gardens. Dine at the exceptional restaurant De la Tierra under an expansive indoor canopy, or on the outside patios under trees and among koi ponds. ⊠ *106 Swinton Ave., 33483* ☎ *561/272–5678 or 877/434–9601* ⊕ *www.sundyhouse.com* ➭ *11 rooms* ⚹ *Restaurant, room service, some kitchens, minibars, some refrigerators, in-room data ports, pool, 2 bars, laundry facilities, business services* ⊟ *AE, DC, MC, V.*

$$$–$$$$ 🏨 **Seagate Hotel & Beach Club.** At this lovely garden enclave, all units have at least kitchenettes; less-expensive studios have compact facilities behind foldaway doors, while others have a separate living room and larger kitchen. The one- and two-bedroom suites are chintz and rattan, with many upholstered pieces. Dress up and dine in a smart little mahogany and lattice-trim beachfront salon, or have the same Continental lunch and dinner fare in casual attire in the bar. As a guest, you'll have access to the private beach club, which is on the best stretch of Delray Beach. ⊠ *400 S. Ocean Blvd., 33483* ☎ *561/276–2421 or 800/233–3581* 🖷 *561/243–4714* ⊕ *www.hudsonhotels.com* ➭ *70 suites* ⚹ *Restaurant, kitchenettes, in-room data ports, 2 pools, beach, bar* ⊟ *AE, DC, MC, V* ⊚| *CP.*

$$–$$$$ 🏨 **Delray Beach Marriott.** A bright pink five-story hotel, it's by far the largest property in Delray, with a stellar location at Atlantic Avenue's east end, across the road from the beach and within walking distance

of restaurants, shops, and galleries. Rooms and suites are spacious, and many have stunning ocean views. The giant, free-form pool is surrounded by a comfortable deck. ⊠ *10 N. Ocean Blvd., 33483* ☎ *561/274–3200* 📠 *561/274–3202* ⊕ *www.delraybeachmarriott.com* 🛏 *268 rooms, 88 suites* ⚘ *3 restaurants, room service, in-room safes, minibars, in-room data ports, pool, health club, hot tub, beach, 2 bars, laundry facilities, business services* ☰ *AE, DC, MC, V.*

$–$$$ 🏨 **Colony Hotel & Cabana Club.** In the heart of downtown Delray, this lovely and charming building underwent an exterior renovation that luckily did not do away with stables in the back, which date back to 1926 when the hotel was built. Today it's listed on Delray's local Register of Historic Places and maintains an air of the 1920s with its Mediterranean-revival architecture. The Cabana Club is a separate property on the ocean about a mile away, with a private beach, club, and heated saltwater pool. A convivial bar and live music on weekend nights make the lobby area a great place to wind down. Fine shops selling leather goods, body products, and stationery fill the lower-level storefronts. ⊠ *525 E. Atlantic Ave., 33483* ☎ *561/276–4123 or 800/552–2363* 📠 *561/276–0123* ⊕ *www.thecolonyhotel.com* 🛏 *70 rooms* ⚘ *In-room data ports, pool, beach, bar, shops* ☰ *AE, DC, MC, V* ⧉ *CP.*

Nightlife & the Arts

THE ARTS The **Crest Theater** (⊠ 51 N. Swinton Ave. ☎ 561/243–7922), in the Old School Square Cultural Arts Center, presents productions in dance, music, and theater.

NIGHTLIFE **Bice** (⊠ 110 E. Atlantic Ave. ☎ 561/274–7077) bar is packed with local society, which means a celebrity or two. The drinks flow and so does the food, but there's no dancing, only posing. **Dada** (⊠ 52 N. Swinton Ave. ☎ 561/330–3232) presents live music in the living room of a historic house, while movies play on the wall. It's a place where those who don't drink will also feel comfortable. **Elwood's** (⊠ 301 E. Atlantic Ave. ☎ 561/272–7427) is a fun drinking establishment in a former service station. Harley Davidsons line up on the weekend as locals stop by for the jamming live music and occasional Elvis sighting. **Delux** (⊠ 16 E. Atlantic Ave. ☎ 561/279–4792) is where the young South Beach wannabe crowd goes to dance all night long.

Sports & the Outdoors

BIKING There's a bicycle path in Barwick Park and a special oceanfront lane along Route A1A. **Richwagen's Bike & Sport** (⊠ 32 S.E. 2nd Ave. ☎ 561/276–4234) rents bikes by the hour or day and provides lock, basket, helmet, and maps.

TENNIS Each winter the **Delray Beach Tennis Center** (⊠ 201 W. Atlantic Ave. ☎ 561/243–7360) hosts professional tournaments such as the Chris Evert Tennis Classic and trains top-ranked players—even Andy Roddick. It offers individual lessons and clinics and you can practice or learn on 14 clay courts and 5 hard courts year-round.

WATERSKIING At **Lake Ida Park** (⊠ 2929 Lake Ida Rd. ☎ 561/964–4420), you can waterski whether you're a beginner or a veteran. The park has a boat ramp, a slalom course, and a trick ski course.

Shopping

Street-scaped **Atlantic Avenue** is a showcase for art galleries, shops, and restaurants. This charming area, from Swinton Avenue east to the ocean, has maintained much of its small-town integrity. **Snappy Turtle** (⌧ 1038 Atlantic Ave. ☎ 561/276–8088) is a multiroom extravaganza where Mackenzie Childs and Lily Pulitzer mingle with other fun fashions for the home and family. A store in the historic Colony Hotel, **Escentials Apothecaries** (⌧ 533 Atlantic Ave. ☎ 561/276–7070) is packed with all things good-smelling for your bath, body, and home. **Murder on The Beach** (⌧ 273 N.E. 2nd Ave. ☎ 561/279–7790) specializes in new, used, and antiquarian mystery books, with an impressive selection from local authors. You can also purchase mystery games and puzzles.

Boca Raton

㉘ *6 mi south of Delray Beach.*

Less than an hour south of Palm Beach and anchoring the county's south end, upscale Boca Raton has much in common with its fabled cousin. Both reflect the unmistakable architectural influence of Addison Mizner, their principal developer in the mid-1920s. The meaning of the name Boca Raton (pronounced boca rah-*tone*) often arouses curiosity, with many folks mistakenly assuming it means "rat's mouth." Historians say the probable origin is Boca Ratones, an ancient Spanish geographical term for an inlet filled with jagged rocks or coral. Miami's Biscayne Bay had such an inlet, and in 1823, a mapmaker copying Miami terrain confused the more northern inlet, thus mistakenly labeling this area Boca Ratones. No matter what, you'll know you've arrived in the heart of downtown when you spot the town hall's gold dome on the main drag, Federal Highway.

★ ℭ In a spectacular building in the Mizner Park shopping center (*see* Shopping), the **Boca Raton Museum of Art** has an interactive children's gallery and changing exhibition galleries showcasing internationally known artists. Upstairs galleries house a permanent collection including works by Picasso, Degas, Matisse, Klee, and Modigliani as well as notable pre-Columbian art. ⌧ *501 Plaza Real* ☎ *561/392–2500* ⊕ *www.bocamuseum.org* ⌧ *$8* ☉ *Tues., Thurs., and Fri. 10–5; Wed. 10–9; Sat. and Sun. noon–5.*

ℭ A big draw for kids, **Gumbo Limbo Nature Center** has four huge saltwater tanks brimming with sea life—from coral to stingrays—and a boardwalk through dense forest with a 40-foot tower you can climb to overlook the tree canopy. In spring and early summer, staffers lead nocturnal turtle walks: you can watch nesting females come ashore and lay eggs. ⌧ *1801 N. Ocean Blvd.* ☎ *561/338–1473* ⊕ *www.gumbolimbo. org* ⌧ *Free; turtle tours $5; tickets must be obtained in advance* ☉ *Mon.–Sat. 9–4, Sun. noon–4; turtle tours May–Aug., Mon.–Thurs. 9 PM–midnight.*

Built in 1925 as the headquarters of the Mizner Development Corporation, **2 East El Camino Real** is an example of Mizner's characteristic Spanish revival architectural style, with its wrought-iron grilles and handmade tiles. As for Mizner's grandiose vision of El Camino Real, the architect-promoter once prepared brochures promising a sweeping wide boulevard with Venetian canals and arching bridges. Camino Real is attractive, heading east to the Boca Raton Resort & Club, but don't count on feeling you're in Venice.

Within a shimmering golden dome, **Town Hall Museum** has a vital repository of archival material and special exhibits on the area's development. Tours and the gift shop are hosted by the Boca Raton Historical Society. ✉ *71 N. Federal Hwy.* ☎ *561/395–6766* ⊕ *www.bocahistory.org* ✉ *Free, tours $7* ☉ *Tues.–Fri. 10–4; tour dates and times vary.*

A residential area behind the Boca Raton Art School on Palmetto Park Road, **Old Floresta** was developed by Addison Mizner starting in 1925 and landscaped with varieties of palms and cycads. It includes houses that are mainly in a Mediterranean style, many with upper balconies supported by exposed wood columns. Home tours are held twice a year.

Hands-on interactive exhibits enliven the **Children's Science Explorium**, at Sugar Sands Park. Children can create their own laser-light shows, explore a 3-D kiosk that illustrates wave motion, and try assorted electrifying experiments. There are also wind tunnels, microscopes, and microwave and radiation experiment stations. ✉ *300 S. Military Trail* ☎ *561/347–3913* ✉ *Free* ☉ *Weekdays 9–6, weekends 10–5.*

Where to Stay & Eat

$$$–$$$$ ✗ **La Vieille Maison.** One of the Gold Coast's temples of cuisine, this restaurant in a 1920s-era dwelling is pricey, and worth it. Intimate private dining rooms set the stage for seasonal prix-fixe and à la carte menus showcasing Provençale dishes. Don't miss the *soupe au pistou* (vegetable soup with basil and Parmesan), venison chop with red currant–pepper sauce and roasted chestnuts, and French apple tart, if they're available. ✉ *770 E. Palmetto Park Rd.* ☎ *561/391–6701* ▤ *AE, D, DC, MC, V* ☉ *No lunch.*

$$$–$$$$ ✗ **Mark's at the Park.** Exotic cars pour into valet parking at this Mark Militello property, where a whimsical interpretation of retro and art deco design and a seasonal menu compete for your attention. The eclectic food includes starters of scallops with foie gras–infused mashed potatoes and spicy steamed mussels; main courses range from crab-crusted mahimahi to roast duck with sweet potatoes. Desserts are deliciously old-fashioned. You'll need to make reservations for weekend nights. ✉ *344 Plaza Real, Mizner Park* ☎ *561/395–0770* ▤ *AE, D, MC, V.*

$$–$$$$ ✗ **Tiramisu.** The food is an extravaganza of taste treats; veal chops, tuna, and anything with mushrooms draw raves, but count on hearty fare rather than a light touch. Start with the Portobello mushroom with garlic or the Corsican baby sardines in olive oil. For a main course, try ricotta ravioli; scaloppine of veal stuffed with crabmeat, lobster, and Gorgonzola; or Tuscan fish stew. ✉ *855 S. Federal Hwy.* ☎ *561/338–9692* ▤ *AE, DC, MC, V* ☉ *Closed Sun. No lunch Sat.*

$$–$$$ ✗ **Uncle Tai's.** The draw at Boca's most upscale Chinese restaurant is some of the best Szechuan food on Florida's east coast. Specialties include sliced duck with snow peas and water chestnuts in a tangy plum sauce, and orange beef delight—flank steak stir-fried until crispy and then sautéed with pepper sauce, garlic, and orange peel. They'll go easy on the heat on request. Service is quietly efficient. ✉ *5250 Town Center Circle* ☎ *561/368–8806* ▭ *AE, MC, V* ☺ *No lunch Sun.*

★ **$–$$** ✗ **La Tre.** An adventuresome menu distinguishes this simple Vietnamese eatery. Try the crispy eggplant and the happy pancake, a Vietnamese crepe stuffed with pork, shrimp, and vegetables. Tamarind squid is another winner. The restaurant's decor seems to date from the 1980s, with black lacquer furniture and an odd purple hue cast from fluorescent lighting. Don't anticipate a romantic dinner experience, but rather a very good Vietnamese dining experience. ✉ *249 E. Palmetto Park Rd.* ☎ *561/392–4568* ▭ *AE, DC, MC, V* ☺ *No lunch Sat.–Tues.*

¢–$ ✗ **Draft House.** Sports aficionados love this place. It's decorated with sports equipment, memorabilia, and photos of famed coaches, players, and moments in sports, plus a dozen televisions for can't-miss events. Apart from inexpensive draft beer, regulars favor homemade chili wings, fried chicken tenders, and juicy burgers. For the more ravenous, there are char-grilled New York strips or racks of baby-back ribs. There are additional locations in east Boca Raton and West Palm Beach. ✉ *22191 Powerline Rd.* ☎ *561/394–6699* ▭ *AE, MC, V.*

¢–$ ✗ **TooJay's.** TooJay's has several branches in Florida, and it's definitely the place for huge sandwiches piled high, from corned beef on rye and roast beef and onion on pumpernickel to tuna melts. While here you might also want to give in to your urge for chicken soup, meat loaf, lox and bagels, or killer desserts; they also serve beer and wine. Aside from the Boca locations there are others in Lake Worth, Vero Beach, Palm Beach, and Wellington. All menus are identical, though daily specials and soups of the day may vary. ✉ *5030 Champion Blvd.* ☎ *561/241–5903* ✉ *3013 Yamato Rd.* ☎ *561/997–9911* ✉ *2200 Glades Rd.* ☎ *561/392–4181* ▭ *AE, D, DC, MC, V.*

★ **$$$–$$$$** 🏨 **Boca Raton Resort & Club.** Addison Mizner built the Mediterranean-style Cloister Inn here in 1926, and additions over time have created this sparkling, sprawling resort with a beach accessible by shuttle. There are recreational activities here and many lodging options: traditional Cloister rooms are small but warmly decorated; accommodations in the 27-story Tower are more spacious; Beach Club rooms are light, airy, and contemporary; golf villas are large and attractive. In addition to a re-designed golf course, there's a two-story golf clubhouse, and the deluxe Tennis & Fitness Center. ✉ *501 E. Camino Real, 33432* ☎ *561/447–3000 or 800/327–0101* 📠 *561/447–3183* ⊕ *www.bocaresort.com* 🛏 *840 rooms, 63 suites, 60 golf villas* ♨ *11 restaurants, room service, in-room safes, some kitchens, 36-hole golf course, 40 tennis courts, 5 pools, 3 health clubs, hair salon, beach, snorkeling, windsurfing, boating, marina, fishing, basketball, racquetball, 3 bars, nightclub, shops, children's programs (ages 2–17), laundry service, concierge, business services, convention center, meeting rooms* ▭ *AE, DC, MC, V.*

$$$–$$$$ 🏨 **Radisson Bridge Resort of Boca Raton.** This pink mid-rise resort sits directly on the Intracoastal Waterway yet has views of the ocean that can't be beat, especially from the top-floor restaurant. The beach is a five-minute walk away, as are restaurants, galleries and boutiques. Comfortable accommodations, the kind of attentive service found at smaller resorts, and an amazing location are the draws. Rooms are decorated in typical Boca-style light woods and rattan and a watercolor palette—nothing spectacular, yet quite presentable. ⊠ *999 East Camino Real, 33432* ☎ *561/368–9500 or 800/333–3333* ⊜ *561/362–0492* ⊕ *www.radisson. com* ⟋ *110 rooms, 11 suites* ⟋ *2 restaurants, room service, minibars in suites, in-room data ports, cable TV with movies and games, pool, health club, beach, 2 bars, shop, laundry facilities, business services, meeting rooms* ▤ *AE, DC, MC, V.*

$–$$ ☷ **Ocean Breeze Inn.** If golf is your game, this is an excellent choice. Inn guests can play the outstanding course at the adjoining Ocean Breeze Golf & Country Club, otherwise available only to club members. Rooms are in a three-story building, and most have a patio or balcony. Although the inn is nearly 30 years old, refurbished rooms are comfortable and contemporary. ⊠ *5800 N.W. 2nd Ave., 33487* ☎ *561/994–0400 or 800/ 344–6995* ⊜ *561/998–8279* ⊕ *www.oceanbreezegolf.com* ⟋ *46 rooms* ⟋ *Restaurant, 27-hole golf course, 6 tennis courts, pool, recreation room, laundry facilities* ▤ *AE, DC, MC, V.*

¢–$ ☷ **Ocean Lodge.** The hotel is across the street from rather than on the beach, so the price is nice here. Rooms are in a simple two-story building, and all have refrigerators. Eleven rooms also have small kitchenettes with two-burner stove tops. Restaurants are within walking distance. ⊠ *531 N. Ocean Blvd., 33432* ☎ *561/395–7772 or 800/ 782–9262* ⊜ *561/395–0554* ⟋ *18 rooms* ⟋ *Some kitchenettes, refrigerators, pool, laundry facilities* ▤ *AE, DC, MC, V.*

Nightlife & the Arts

THE ARTS   **Caldwell Theatre Company** (⊠ 7873 N. Federal Hwy. ☎ 561/241–7432) stages four productions each season from November through May in addition to hosting the Play Reading Series for developing playwrights.

NIGHTLIFE   Drop by **Gatsby's Boca** (⊠ 5970 S.W. 18th St., Shoppes at Village Point ☎ 561/393–3900) any night of the week to mingle with a lively crowd. Shoot pool at one of 18 tables or watch sporting events on several giant screens. **Pranzo** (⊠ 402 Plaza Real ☎ 561/750–7442) has a happening weekend bar scene.

Sports & the Outdoors

BEACHES   **Red Reef Park** (⊠ 1400 N. Rte. A1A) has a beach and playground plus picnic tables and grills. Popular **South Beach Park** (⊠ 400 N. Rte. A1A) has a concession stand. In addition to its beach, **Spanish River Park** (⊠ 3001 N. Rte. A1A) has picnic tables, grills, and a large playground.

BOATING   For the thrill of blasting across the water at up to 80 mph, try **Air and Sea Charters** (⊠ 107 E. Palmetto Park Rd., Suite 330 ☎ 561/368–3566). For $175 per person (two-person minimum), spend a wild-eyed hour gripping your life vest aboard a 1,000-horsepower offshore racing boat. More leisurely are the two 55-foot catamarans or 45-foot sailboat; rates start at $35 per person for 2½ hours.

GOLF   Two championship courses and golf programs are at **Boca Raton Resort & Club** (⊠ 501 E. Camino Real ☎ 561/447–3078), green fee: Resort and

Country Club courses $100/$182, which includes cart. The Dave Pelz Golf School is located at the Country Club course.

POLO **Royal Palm Polo Sports Club** (✉ 18000 Jog Rd., at Old Clint Moore Rd. ☎ 561/994–1876), founded in 1959 by Oklahoma oilman John T. Oxley and now home to the $100,000 International Gold Cup Tournament, has seven polo fields within two stadiums. Games take place January through May, Sunday at 1 and 3. Admission is $10 to $15 for seats, $15 per car.

SCUBA & **Force E** (✉ 2181 N. Federal Hwy. ☎ 561/368–0555) has information
SNORKELING on dive trips and also rents scuba and snorkeling equipment. It has PADI affiliation, provides instruction at all levels, and offers charters.

Shopping

Locals know that Boca "strip malls" contain great shops. While stopping by for essentials at Publix, be sure to check out that unassuming consignment, shoe, or fashion boutique next door and you may discover one of Boca's better finds.

★ **Mizner Park** (✉ Federal Hwy., 1 block north of Palmetto Park Rd. ☎ 561/447–8105) is a distinctive 30-acre shopping center with apartments and town houses among its gardenlike retail and restaurant spaces. Some three dozen stores, including national and local retailers, mingle with fine restaurants, sidewalk cafés, galleries, a movie theater, museum, and amphitheater. **Town Center Mall** (✉ 6000 W. Glades Rd. ☎ 561/368–6000) is an upscale shopping mall. Major retailers include Nordstrom, Bloomingdale's, Burdines, Lord & Taylor, Saks Fifth Avenue, and Neiman Marcus. The mall's specialty may be women's fashion, but there are more than 200 stores and restaurants.

THE TREASURE COAST

From south to north, the Treasure Coast encompasses the top of Palm Beach County plus Martin, St. Lucie, and Indian River counties. Although dotted with destinations, this coastal section is one of Florida's quietest. Beyond the Palm Beach County border, most towns are small, with plenty of undeveloped land in between. Vero Beach, the region's most sophisticated beach area, is burgeoning with fine-dining establishments, upscale shops, and new housing construction. Beaches along here are also sought out by nesting sea turtles; join locally organized watches to view the turtles laying their eggs in the sand between late April and August. It's illegal to touch or disturb turtles or their nests.

Palm Beach Shores

㉙ *7 mi north of Palm Beach.*

Rimmed by mom-and-pop motels, this residential town is at the southern tip of Singer Island, across Lake Worth Inlet from Palm Beach. To travel between the two, however, you must cross over to the mainland before returning to the beach. This unpretentious community has affordable beachfront lodging and is near several nature parks.

CloseUp

FLORIDA'S SEA TURTLES: THE NESTING SEASON

FROM MAY TO OCTOBER *it's turtle nesting season all along the Florida coast. Female loggerhead, Kemp's ridley, and other species living in the Atlantic Ocean or Gulf of Mexico swim up to 2,000 mi to the Florida shore. By night, they drag their 100- to 400-pound bodies onto the beach to the dune line. Then each digs a hole with her flippers, drops in 100 or so eggs, covers them up, and returns to sea.*

The babies hatch about 60 days later, typically at night, sometimes taking days to surface. Once they burst out of the sand, the hatchlings must get to sea rapidly or risk becoming dehydrated from the sun or being caught by crabs, birds, or other predators.

Instinctively baby turtles head toward bright light, probably because for millions of years starlight or moonlight reflected on the waves was the brightest light around, serving to guide hatchlings to water. But now light from beach development can lead the babies in the wrong direction, and many hatchlings are crushed by vehicles after running to the street rather than the water. To help, many coastal towns enforce light restrictions during nesting months, and more than one Florida homeowner has been surprised by a police officer at the door requesting that lights be dimmed on behalf of baby sea turtles.

At night, volunteers walk the beaches, searching for signs of turtle nests. Upon finding telltale scratches in the sand, they cordon off the sites, so beachgoers will leave the spots undisturbed. Volunteers also keep watch over nests when babies are about to hatch and assist if the hatchlings get disoriented.

It's a hazardous world for baby turtles. They can die after eating tar balls or plastic debris, or they can be gobbled by sharks or circling birds. Only about 1 in 1,000 survives to adulthood. After reaching the water, the babies make their way to warm currents. East-coast hatchlings drift into the Gulf Stream, spending years floating around the Atlantic.

Males never, ever return to land, but when females attain maturity, in 15–20 years, they return to shore to lay eggs. Remarkably, even after migrating hundreds and even thousands of miles out at sea, most return to the very beach where they were born to deposit their eggs. Sea turtles nest at least twice a season—sometimes as many as 10 times—and then skip a year or two. Each time they nest, they come back to the same stretch of beach. In fact, the more they nest, the more accurate they get, until eventually they return time and again to within a few feet of where they last laid their eggs. These incredible navigation skills remain for the most part a mystery despite intense scientific study. To learn more, check out the Sea Turtle Survival League's and Caribbean Conservation Corporation's Web site at ⊕ www.cccturtle.org.

— Pam Acheson

In the Intracoastal Waterway between Palm Beach Shores and Riviera Beach, the 79-acre **Peanut Island** was opened in 1999 as a recreational park. There's a 20-foot-wide walking path surrounding the island, a 19-slip boat dock, a 170-foot T-shape fishing pier, six picnic pavilions, a visitor center, and 20 overnight campsites. The small **Palm Beach Maritime Museum** (☎ 561/832–7428) is open daily except Friday and showcases the "Kennedy Bunker," a bomb shelter prepared for President John F. Kennedy (call for tour hours). To get to the island, you can use your own boat, take a water taxi (call for schedules and pickup locations), or pick up the ferry at Currie Park. ⊠ *6500 Peanut Island Rd.* ☎ *561/ 540–5147* ⊕ *www.pbmm.org* ✆ *Free, tours $7* ☉ *Daily dawn–dusk for noncampers.*

Where to Stay & Eat

$–$$$ ✕ **Sailfish Marina Restaurant.** Once known as the Galley, this waterfront restaurant looking out to Peanut Island remains a great place to chill out after a hot day of mansion gawking or beach bumming. Sit inside or outdoors to order tropical drinks and mainstays like conch chowder, grouper, or meat loaf. More upscale entrées—this, after all, is still Palm Beach County—include lobster tail or baby sea scallops sautéed in garlic and lemon butter. Breakfast is a winner here, too. ⊠ *98 Lake Dr.* ☎ *561/842–8449* ▤ *AE, MC, V.*

$$–$$$$ ⌂ **Palm Beach Shores Resort.** At the edge of a long stretch of golden beach is this pink, six-story time-share resort with a red tile roof that's a superb family destination. All rooms are suites with a separate bedroom, living room with a sofa bed, plus refrigerator, microwave, and dining area. Suites are tastefully furnished in natural rattan and tropical prints. The oceanfront pool is surrounded by a brick courtyard. The Beach Buddies Kids Club has many programs, including field trips, arts and crafts, seashell hunts, and water sports. ⊠ *181 Ocean Ave., Singer Island 33404* ☎ *561/863–4000* ⊟ *561/863–9502* ⊕ *www.palmbeachshoresfl. com* ➮ *257 suites* ♨ *Restaurant, microwaves, refrigerators, pool, health club, spa, beach, bar, children's programs (ages 3–12)* ▤ *AE, D, DC, MC, V.*

$–$$ ⌂ **Sailfish Marina and Sportfishing Resort.** This one-story motel has a marina with 94 deep-water slips and accommodations that include motel-style rooms, small and large efficiencies, and even a three-bedroom house. All rooms open to landscaped grounds, although none are directly on the water. Units 9–11 have ocean views across the blacktop drive. Rooms have peaked ceilings, carpeting, king-size or twin beds, and stall showers; all have ceiling fans. From the seawall, you'll see fish through the clear inlet water. ⊠ *98 Lake Dr., Singer Island 33404* ☎ *561/844–1724 or 800/446–4577* ⊟ *561/848–9684* ⊕ *www. sailfishmarina.com* ➮ *30 units* ♨ *2 restaurants, grocery, pool, dock, bar* ▤ *AE, MC, V.*

Sports & the Outdoors

BIKING To rent bikes by the hour, half day, or full day, head for the **Sailfish Marina and Resort** (⊠ 98 Lake Dr. ☎ 561/844–1724). Ask for a free map of the bike trails.

FISHING	The **Sailfish Marina and Resort** (⊠ 98 Lake Dr. ☎ 561/844–1724) has a large sportfishing fleet, with 28-foot to 60-foot boats and seasoned captains. Book a full- or half-day of deep-sea fishing for up to six people.

Palm Beach Gardens

㉚ *5 mi north of West Palm Beach.*

About 15 minutes northwest of Palm Beach is this relaxed, upscale residential community known for its high-profile golf complex, the PGA National Resort & Spa. Although not on the beach, the town is less than a 15-minute drive from the ocean.

Where to Stay & Eat

★ $$$	✕ **Café Chardonnay.** At the end of a strip mall, Café Chardonnay is surprisingly elegant inside. Soft indirect lighting, warm woods, and cozy banquettes set the scene for a quiet lunch or romantic dinner. Established by the Eucalitto husband-and-wife team, the restaurant consistently receives praise for its innovative menu and outstanding wine list. Starters include wild mushroom strudel and truffle-stuffed diver sea scallops; entrées might include gorgonzola-crusted filet mignon and pan-seared veal scaloppine with rock shrimp. ⊠ *4533 PGA Blvd.* ☎ *561/627–2662* ▭ *AE, MC, V* ☉ *No lunch Sat. and Sun.*

$–$$$	✕ **Arezzo.** The aroma of fresh garlic will draw you into this Tuscan grill at the PGA National Resort & Spa. Families are attracted by affordable prices (as well as the food), so romantics might be tempted to pass on by, but that would be a mistake. Dishes include chicken, veal, fish, steaks, a dozen pastas, and almost as many pizzas. Thanks to the unusually relaxed attitude of the resort itself, you'll be equally comfortable in khakis or in jacket and tie. ⊠ *400 Ave. of the Champions* ☎ *561/627–2000* ▭ *AE, MC, V* ☉ *Closed Mon. No lunch.*

$–$$	✕ **The Riverhouse.** Patrons keep returning to this waterfront restaurant for large portions of straightforward American fare, the large salad bar, and fresh, slice-it-yourself bread, as well as the competent service. Choices include seafood (with a daily catch), steaks, chops, and seafood-steak combo platters. Booths and freestanding tables are surrounded by light wood, high ceilings, and nautical art. Expect a wait on Saturday night in season; the restaurant does not take reservations. ⊠ *2373 PGA Blvd.* ☎ *561/694–1188* ▭ *AE, D, DC, MC, V* ⌙ *required on weekends* ☉ *No lunch.*

¢–$	✕ **No Anchovies.** Sharing is half the fun here for either lunch or dinner, so don't be shy about it at this casual and generous neighborhood trattoria. Sandwiches come on Italian loaf, semolina, whole wheat, or a spinach tortilla wrap with fillings such as oven-roasted turkey breast with sun-dried tomatoes or chicken salad. Entrées include pastas, chicken, and shrimp. Consider making your own pizza, perhaps with fresh goat cheese from the Turtle Creek dairy. ⊠ *2650 PGA Blvd.* ☎ *561/622–7855* ▭ *AE, MC, V.*

★ $$$–$$$$	▥ **PGA National Resort & Spa.** The entire resort is richly detailed, from the consistently updated and renovated rooms to the lavish landscaping to the extensive sports facilities to the excellent dining. The spa is in a building styled after a Mediterranean fishing village, and six outdoor therapy pools, dubbed Waters of the World, are joined by a collection of imported mineral salt pools. Flowering plants adorn golf courses and croquet courts amid a 240-acre nature preserve. Lodgings include two-bedroom, two-bath cottages with kitchens. Among the restaurants are Shula's Steakhouse and Arezzo. Golf is key here and guests have access to a rotating selection of four of the resort's five private courses. ⊠ *400 Ave. of the Champions, 33418* ☎ *561/627–2000 or 800/633–9150* 🖷 *561/622–0261* ⊕ *www.pga-resorts.com* 🛏 *279 rooms, 60 suites, 80 cottages* ⟨ *5 restaurants, room service, in-room safes, some kitchens, some refrigerators, 90-hole golf course, 19 tennis courts, 9 pools, lake, health club, hot tub, massage, sauna, spa, boating, croquet, 4 bars, babysitting, children's programs (ages 3–12), business services, meeting rooms* ☰ *AE, D, DC, MC, V.*

Nightlife

For DJ'd Top 40, try the **Club Safari** (⊠ Palm Beach Gardens Marriott, 4000 RCA Blvd. ☎ 561/622–7024), except on Thursday, when the focus is on oldies, which now means '50s–'80s.

Sports & the Outdoors

AUTO RACING If you yearn for drag racing action, the **Moroso Motorsports Park** (⊠ 17047 Beeline Hwy. ☎ 561/622–1400) awaits with weekly ¼-mi drag racing; monthly 2¼-mi, 10-turn road racing; and monthly AMA motorcycle road racing. These events and swap meets take place all year long. Spectator admission is $12 on Saturday, $15 on Sunday, and there's a $20 two-day pass.

GOLF **PGA National Resort & Spa** (⊠ 1000 Avenue of the Champions ☎ 561/627–1800) has a reputedly tough 90 holes, which are available to hotel guests and private members. Among them are the Champion Course, designed by Tom Fazio and Jack Nicklaus, green fee: $109/$280; the General Course, designed by Arnold Palmer, green fee: $109/$180; the Haig Course, the first course opened at the resort, green fee: $109/$160; the Estate Course, with a practice range and putting green, green fee: $109/$160; and the Tom Fazio–designed Squire Course, green fee: $109/$180. Lessons are available at the Golf Digest Academy.

Shopping

The **Gardens Mall** (⊠ 3101 PGA Blvd. ☎ 561/775–7750) offers an above-par shopping-mall experience—a calm, spacious, airy, and well-lit environment. Anchors Bloomingdale's, Burdines-Macy's, Nordstrom, Saks Fifth Avenue, and Sears Roebuck support more than 160 specialty retailers including Swarovski, Godiva, Tommy Bahama, J. Jill, Gymboree, and Charles David.

en route **John D. MacArthur Beach State Park.** Almost 2 mi of beach, good fishing and shelling, and one of the finest examples of subtropical coastal habitat remaining in southeast Florida are among treasures here. To learn about what you see, take an interpretive walk to a mangrove estuary along the upper reaches of Lake Worth. Or visit the **William T. Kirby Nature Center** (☎ 561/624–6952), open daily from 9 to 5, which has exhibits on the coastal environment.

✉ *10900 Rte. A1A, North Palm Beach* ☎ *561/624–6950* ⊕ *www. macarthurbeach.org* ▦ *$4 per vehicle, up to 8 people* ☉ *Daily 8–sundown.*

Loggerhead Park Marine Life Center of Juno Beach. Established by Eleanor N. Fletcher, the "turtle lady of Juno Beach," the center focuses on sea turtle history, including loggerheads and leatherbacks, with displays of coastal natural history, sharks, whales, and shells. You can adopt a turtle for a donation and although you can't take it home with you, the center will watch over your pet. ✉ *14200 U.S. Hwy. 1, Juno Beach* ☎ *561/627–8280* ⊕ *www.marinelife.org* ▦ *Free* ☉ *Tues.–Sat. 10–4, Sun. noon–3.*

Jupiter

③① *12 mi north of Palm Beach Shores.*

Jupiter is one of the few little towns in the region not fronted by an island. Beaches here are part of the mainland, and Route A1A runs for almost 4 mi along the beachfront dunes and beautiful estates.

A beach is just one of the draws of **Carlin Park,** which has picnic pavilions, hiking trails, a baseball diamond, playground, six tennis courts, and fishing sites. The Park Galley, serving snacks and burgers, is open daily 9–5. ✉ *400 Rte. A1A* ☎ *No phone* ☉ *Daily dawn–dusk.*

★ Designed by Civil War hero General George Meade, the redbrick Coast Guard **Jupiter Inlet Lighthouse** has operated here since 1860. Tours of the 105-foot-tall landmark unfold every half hour, and there's a small museum. The lighthouse has undergone significant change, courtesy of an $858,000 federal grant, transforming it from bright red to natural brick, the way it looked from 1860 to 1918. ✉ *500 Capt. Armour's Way (U.S. 1 and Beach Rd.)* ☎ *561/747–8380* ⊕ *www.jupiterlighthouse.org* ▦ *Tour $6* ☉ *Sat.–Wed. 10–4; last tour at 3:15.*

Maltz Jupiter Theatre. This renovated 550-seat theater is open all year with comedy and dramatic performances, but the major shows, such as "Anna in the Tropics," run during the season from September to April. Shows have both evening and matinee performances and tickets range from $15 to $50. ✉ *1001 E. Indiantown Rd.* ☎ *561/743-2666* ⊕ *www. jupitertheatre.org.*

Where to Stay & Eat

$–$$$ ✕ **Sinclairs Ocean Grill.** This popular spot in the Jupiter Beach Resort has French doors looking out to the pool, and a menu with a daily selection of fresh fish, such as cashew-encrusted grouper, Cajun-spice tuna, and mahimahi with pistachio sauce. There are also thick juicy steaks—filet mignon is the house specialty—or chicken and veal dishes. Sunday brunch is a big draw. ✉ *5 N. Rte. A1A* ☎ *561/745–7120* ▤ *AE, MC, V.*

$–$$ ✕ **Food Shack.** This bar-like shack filled with locals is a bit tricky to find, but worth the search. Fried-food standards typical to such a casual place are not found at the Food Shack; instead there are fried tuna rolls with basil and fried grouper cheeks with a fruity side slaw. A variety of beers are fun to pair with the creatively prepared seafood dishes that include wahoo, mahimahi, dolphin, and snapper. ⊠ *103 South U.S. 1* ☎ *561/741–3626* ⊟ *DC, MC, V* ⊘ *Closed Sun. No dinner Mon.*

¢–$ ✕ **Lighthouse Restaurant.** Low prices match the plain look in this coffee shop–style building. The same people-pleasing formula has been employed since 1936: round-the-clock service (except 10 PM Sunday–6 AM Monday) and a menu that changes daily to take advantage of in-season market buys. Order chicken breast stuffed with sausage and veggies, burgundy beef stew, crab cakes, and great pastries. ⊠ *1510 U.S. 1* ☎ *561/746–4811* ⊟ *D, DC, MC, V.*

$$–$$$$ ▦ **Jupiter Beach Resort.** While unpretentious, this time-share resort has undergone a multimillion-dollar makeover (again after the 2004 hurricanes), and it shows. Caribbean-style rooms with mahogany sleigh beds and armoires are within a nine-story tower. Most rooms have balconies, and those on higher floors have great ocean views. Plentiful activities and a casual approach draw families here, and the resort offers turtle watches in season, May through October. Snorkeling and scuba equipment, Jet Skis, and bicycles are for rent. ⊠ *5 N. Rte. A1A, 33477* ☎ *561/746–2511 or 800/228–8810* ⊟ *561/747-3304* ⊕ *www.jupiterbeachresort.com* ⇌ *88 rooms, 65 suites* ⚅ *3 restaurants, in-room data ports, tennis court, pool, gym, beach, dive shop, 2 bars, recreation room, shop, babysitting, laundry facilities, business services* ⊟ *AE, D, MC, V.*

Sports & the Outdoors

BASEBALL Both the **St. Louis Cardinals and Florida Marlins** (⊠ *4751 Main St.* ☎ *561/775–1818*) train at the $28 million Roger Dean Stadium, which seats 7,000 and has 12 practice fields.

CANOEING **Canoe Outfitters of Florida** (⊠ 9060 W. Indiantown Rd. ☎ 561/746–7053) runs trips (Thurs.–Mon.) along 8 mi of the Loxahatchee River, Florida's only government-designated Wild and Scenic River, where you can see animals in the wild, from otters to eagles. Canoe rental for two, with drop-off and pickup, costs $40 for the first two hours (two-hour minimum) and then $4 per additional hour plus tax.

GOLF **Abacoa Golf Club** (⊠ 105 Barbados Dr. ☎ 561/622–0036) with 18 holes, is a recommended alternative to nearby private courses; green fee: $50/$105, including cart. The **Golf Club of Jupiter** (⊠ 1800 Central Blvd. ☎ 561/747–6262) has 18 holes of varying difficulty; green fee: $25/$56, including cart. **Jupiter Dunes Golf Club** (⊠ 401 Rte. A1A ☎ 561/746–6654) has 18 holes named Little Monster and a putting green on the water; green fee: $15/$20.

Jupiter Island & Hobe Sound

㉜ *5 mi north of Jupiter.*

Northeast across the Jupiter Inlet from Jupiter is the southern tip of Jupiter Island, including a planned community of the same name. Here expansive and expensive estates often retreat from the road behind screens of vegetation, while at the north end of the island, turtles come to nest in a wildlife refuge. To the west, on the mainland, is the little community of Hobe Sound.

In **Blowing Rocks Preserve,** within the 73-acre Nature Conservancy holding, are plant communities native to beachfront dune, coastal strand (the landward side of the dunes), mangrove, and hammock (tropical hardwood forests). The best time to visit is when high tides and strong offshore winds coincide, causing the sea to blow spectacularly through holes in the eroded outcropping. Park in the lot; police ticket cars parked along the road. ✉ *574 South Beach Rd. (Rte. 707), Jupiter Island* ☎ *561/744–6668* 💲 *$3* 🕙 *Daily 9–4:30.*

Two tracts comprise **Hobe Sound National Wildlife Refuge:** 232 acres of sand-pine and scrub-oak forest in Hobe Sound and 735 acres of coastal sand dune and mangrove swamp on Jupiter Island. Trails are open to the public in both places. Turtles nest and shells wash ashore on the 3½-mi-long beach, which has been severely eroded by hurricanes' high tides and strong winds. ✉ *13640 S.E. Federal Hwy., Hobe Sound* ☎ *772/546–6141* 💲 *$5 per vehicle* 🕙 *Daily dawn–dusk.*

� Although on the Hobe Sound National Wildlife Refuge, **Hobe Sound Nature Center** is an independent organization. Its museum, which has baby alligators and crocodiles, and a scary-looking tarantula, is a child's delight. Interpretive exhibits focus on the environment, and a ½-mi trail winds through a forest of sand pine and scrub oak—one of Florida's most unusual and endangered plant communities. As a result of the 2004 hurricanes, the Nature Center's main building was destroyed and exhibit space is now limited. ✉ *13640 S.E. Federal Hwy., Hobe Sound* ☎ *772/546–2067* 💲 *Donation suggested* 🕙 *Trail daily dawn–dusk; nature center weekdays 9–3, call to verify hours.*

Once you've gotten to **Jonathan Dickinson State Park,** follow signs to **Hobe Mountain.** An ancient dune topped with a tower, it yields a panoramic view across the park's 10,285 acres of varied terrain, as well as the Intracoastal Waterway. The Loxahatchee River, part of the federal government's Wild and Scenic Rivers program, cuts through the park and harbors manatees in winter and alligators year-round. Two-hour boat tours of the river leave daily at 9, 11, 1, and 3. Among amenities here are bicycle and hiking trails, a campground, and a snack bar. ✉ *16450 S.E. Federal Hwy., Hobe Sound* ☎ *772/546–2771* 💲 *$4 per vehicle for up to 8 people, boat tours $12* 🕙 *Daily 8–dusk.*

Sports & the Outdoors
Jonathan Dickinson's River Tours (✉ Jonathan Dickinson State Park ☎ 561/746–1466) offers boat tours of the river and canoe rentals for use around the park from 9–5 daily. The fee is $10 for the first two hours and $4 for each additional hour.

Stuart

33 *7 mi north of Hobe Sound.*

This compact little town on a peninsula that juts out into the St. Lucie River has a remarkable amount of river shoreline for its size as well as a charming historic district. The ocean is about 5 mi east.

★ Strict architectural and zoning standards guide civic renewal projects in **historic downtown Stuart,** which has antiques shops, restaurants, and more than 50 specialty shops within a two-block area. A self-guided walking-tour pamphlet is available at assorted locations downtown to clue you in on this once small fishing village's early days. On the National Register of Historic Places, the **Lyric Theatre** (⊠ 59 S.W. Flagler Ave. ☎ 772/286–7827) has been revived for performing and community events; a gazebo has free music performances. The old courthouse has become the **Court House Cultural Center** (⊠ 80 E. Ocean Blvd. ☎ 772/288–2542) and presents art exhibits. The George W. Parks General Store is now the **Stuart Heritage Museum** (⊠ 161 S.W. Flagler Ave. ☎ 772/220–4600). For information on the historic downtown, contact the **Stuart Main Street** (⊠ 201 S.W. Flagler Ave., 34994 ☎ 772/286–2848).

★ Linking the watery past with a permanent record of maritime and yachting events contributing to Treasure Coast lore, the **Maritime & Yachting Museum** is near a marina with many old ships as well as historic exhibits to explore. Ship modelers are usually on hand, too; call for an events and activities schedule. Among those leading Saturday tours is a retired ship captain who has many interesting stories to share. ⊠ *3250 S. Kanner Hwy.* ☎ *772/692–1234* 🖭 *Free* ☉ *Mon.–Sat. 11–4, Sun. 1–5.*

Where to Stay & Eat

$$-$$$ ✕ **Courtine's.** A husband-and-wife team oversees this quiet and hospitable restaurant located under the new Roosevelt Bridge. The Swiss chef's food represents French Continental and American influences, from his seafood and poultry dishes to the grilled house special of filet mignon stuffed with Roquefort, fresh spinach, and a port wine balsamic reduction. The formal dining room has subtle touches of elegance, such as soft lighting and fresh flowers on each table. A full bar and extensive wine list are available. A more casual and light menu is also available at the bar. ⊠ *514 N. Dixie Hwy. (SR707)* ☎ *772/692–3662* 🖃 *AE, MC, V* ☉ *Closed Sun. and Mon. No lunch.*

¢-$$ ✕ **The Ashley.** Despite the hanging plants and artwork, this restaurant still has elements of the old bank that was robbed three times early in the 20th century by the Ashley Gang (hence the name). Situated at the end of the main drag in downtown Stuart, The Ashley is easy to spot because of its redbrick facade. Spacious tables, comfortable seats, and good service make this restaurant a consistently pleasant place to eat. The Continental menu has lots of salads, fresh fish, and pastas, and all are served in large portions. Crowds head to the lounge for a popular happy hour. Brunch is the only meal served on Sunday. ⊠ *61 S.W. Osceola St.* ☎ *772/221–9476* 🖃 *AE, MC, V.*

$$-$$$ 🏨 **Pirates Cove Resort and Marina.** On the banks of the St. Lucie River and in the heart of Sailfish Alley, this cozy enclave is the perfect place to recoup after a day at sea. This mid-size resort is relaxing and casual but packed with recreational activities for the day. The Pirates Loft Lounge gets lively at night, but the restaurant can be rather dull during the day. The tropically furnished rooms are large, with balconies to enjoy the waterfront views. The few suites include microwaves and refrigerators. ⊠ *4307 S.E. Bayview St., Port Salerno 34997* ☎ *772/287–2500 or 800/*

332–1414 🖨 *772/220–2704* 🌐 *www.piratescoveresortandmarina.com*
🛏 *50 rooms* ⬧ *Restaurant, room service, pool, boating, bar, shop*
🚪 *AE, D, DC, MC, V.*

Sports & the Outdoors
Deep-sea charters are available at the **Sailfish Marina** (✉ 3565 S.E. St. Lucie Blvd. ☎ 772/221–9456).

Shopping
More than 60 restaurants and shops with antiques, art, and fashions have opened along **Osceola Street** in the restored downtown area. Operating for more than two decades, the **B&A Flea Market**, the oldest and largest such enterprise on the Treasure Coast, has a street-bazaar feel with shoppers happily scouting for the practical and unusual. ✉ *2885 S.E. Federal Hwy.* ☎ *772/288–4915* 🎫 *Free* ⊙ *Weekends 8–3.*

Hutchinson Island (Jensen Beach)

34 *5 mi northeast of Stuart.*

Area residents have taken pains to curb the runaway development that has created the commercial crowding found to the north and south, although some high-rises have popped up along the shore. The small town of Jensen Beach, occupying the core of the island, stretches across both sides of the Indian River. Citrus farmers and anglers still play a big community role, anchoring the area's down-to-earth feel. Between late April and August more than 600 turtles come here to nest along the town's Atlantic beach.

★ The **Florida Oceanographic Coastal Center** consists of a coastal hardwood hammock-and-mangrove forest. Expansion has yielded a visitor center, a science center with interpretive exhibits on coastal science and environmental issues, and a ½-mi interpretive boardwalk. Guided nature walks through trails and stingray feedings are offered at various times during the day. Eco-boat tours are 1½ hours long and include a 20-minute stop at a bird sanctuary. Dolphins, manatees and turtles are often seen on the boat tour, for which reservations are required. ✉ *890 N.E. Ocean Blvd.* ☎ *772/225–0505* 🌐 *www.floridaoceanographic.org* 🎫 *$6; $22 boat tour* ⊙ *Mon.–Sat. 10–5, Sun. noon–4; guided nature walks Mon.–Sat. 11 and 3, Sun. 2; boat tours Tues., Thurs.–Sat. 11 and also Thurs. 4.*

The pastel-pink **Elliott Museum** was erected in 1961 in honor of Sterling Elliott, inventor of an early automated addressing machine and a four-wheel cycle. The museum, with its antique cars, dolls, toys, and vintage baseball cards, is a nice stop for anyone fond of nostalgic goods. There are also antique fixtures from an early general store, blacksmith shop, and apothecary shop. ✉ *825 N.E. Ocean Blvd.* ☎ *772/225–1961* 🎫 *$6* ⊙ *Mon.–Sat. 10–4, Sun. 1–4.*

Where to Stay & Eat
★ **$$$** ✕ **11 Maple Street.** With a mere 16 tables, this spot is as good as it gets on the Treasure Coast, with a menu that changes nightly. Soft recorded jazz and friendly staff satisfy, along with food served in ample portions.

Although the food is progressive, the place is filled with antiques and many vintage collectibles. Appetizers run from panfried conch and crispy calamari to spinach salad, and entrées include pan-seared rainbow trout, wood-grilled venison with onion potato hash, and beef tenderloin with white truffle and chive butter. Desserts such as a white-chocolate custard with blackberry sauce are seductive, too. ⊠ *3224 Maple Ave.* ☎ *772/334–7714* ⌂ *Reservations essential* ▭ *MC, V* ⊘ *Closed Mon. and Tues. No lunch.*

$$–$$$ ✕ **Baha Grill.** Replacing the former Scalawags restaurant, but in a slightly different locale (the main dining room is now on the first floor), this spot serves breakfast, lunch, and dinner daily, though from a more limited menu than before. The food is basically the same—assorted soups, salads, and entrées consistent with most Marriott hotels. Standouts include a prime-rib buffet on Friday night and the all-you-can-eat Wednesday-evening seafood extravaganza with jumbo shrimp, Alaskan crab legs, clams on the half shell, marinated salmon, and fresh catch. The decor is also standard for a Marriott dining room—a tasteful assemblage of wood accents, floral patterns and subtle hues. ⊠ *Marriott Beach Resort, 555 N.E. Ocean Blvd.* ☎ *772/225–6818* ▭ *AE, D, DC, MC, V.*

¢–$$ ✕ **Conchy Joe's.** This rustic Florida stilt house full of antique fish mounts, gator hides, and snake skins dates from the 1920s, although Conchy Joe's, like a hermit crab sliding into a new shell, moved up from West Palm Beach in 1983. It's a popular tourist spot, but its waterfront location, supercasual attitude, and seafood continue to attract locals, too. Staples are grouper marsala, broiled sea scallops, and fried cracked conch. There's live music Friday, heady rum drinks on Saturday, and a happy hour daily 3 to 6 and during NFL games. ⊠ *3945 N.E. Indian River Dr.* ☎ *772/334–1130* ▭ *AE, D, MC, V.*

$$–$$$$ ▥ **Hutchinson Island Marriott Beach Resort & Marina.** With golf, tennis, a 77-slip marina, and a full water-sports program, plus many restaurants and bars, this 200-acre self-contained resort is excellent for families. Reception, some restaurants, and many rooms are in a trio of yellow four-story buildings that form an open courtyard with a large pool. Additional rooms and apartments with kitchens are spread over the property, some overlooking the Intracoastal Waterway and marina, others looking onto the ocean or tropical gardens. ⊠ *555 N.E. Ocean Blvd., Hutchinson Island 34996* ☎ *772/225–3700 or 800/775–5936* 🖷 *772/225–0003* ⊕ *www.marriotthotels.com* ⬦ *213 rooms, 70 suites, 70 condominiums* ⌂ *3 restaurants, room service, some kitchens, golf privileges, 13 tennis courts, 3 pools, gym, hot tub, spa, beach, dock, boating, 2 bars, children's programs (2-12), laundry facilities, business services, meeting rooms, pets allowed* ▭ *AE, D, DC, MC, V.*

Sports & the Outdoors

BASEBALL The **New York Mets** (⊠ 525 N.W. Peacock Blvd., Port St. Lucie ☎ 772/871–2115) train at Tradition Field.

BEACHES **Bathtub Reef Park** (⊠ MacArthur Blvd. off Rte. A1A), at the north end of the Indian River Plantation, is ideal for children because the waters are shallow for about 300 feet offshore and usually calm. At low tide bathers can walk to the reef. Facilities include rest rooms and showers.

GOLF **Hutchinson Island Marriott Golf Club** (⊠ 555 N.E. Ocean Blvd. ☎ 772/
225–6819) has 18 holes for private-club members and hotel guests; green
fee: $28/$77. The PGA-operated **PGA Golf Club at the PGA Villages**
(⊠ 1916 Perfect Dr., Port St. Lucie ☎ 772/467–1300 or 800/800–4653)
is a public facility with the PGA Learning Center and three courses designed by Pete Dye and Tom Fazio; green fee for North Course, South
Course, and Dye Course: $25/$89 (fee includes cart).

Fort Pierce

③⑤ *11 mi north of Stuart.*

About an hour north of Palm Beach, this community has a distinctive
rural feel, focusing on ranching and citrus farming. There are several
worthwhile stops, including those easily seen while following Route 707.
As a result of being directly hit by two hurricanes in 2004, the landscape from Fort Pierce to Vero Beach has been greatly altered. While
there are pockets of destruction, there are also pockets of beauty that
have sprung up. It will take years before the trees and plantings are lush
and full again, perhaps hundreds of years for the glorious Banyan and
Australian Pine trees to reach their former statuesque size.

☾ Once a reservoir, the 550-acre **Savannas Recreation Area** has been returned
to its natural state. Today the semi-wilderness area has campsites, boat
ramps, and trails. ⊠ 1400 E. Midway Rd. ☎ 772/464–7855 ☞ $1 per
vehicle ☾ Daily 8–6.

A self-guided tour of the 3½ acre **Heathcote Botanical Gardens** takes in
a palm walk, a Japanese garden, and subtropical foliage. There is also
a pioneer house, orchid house, and gift shop with whimsical and botanical knickknacks. Guided tours are available Tuesday–Saturday by appointment. ⊠ 210 Savannah Rd. ☎ 772/464–4672 ⊕ www.
heathcotebotanicalgardens.org ☞ $4 ☾ Tues.–Sat. 9–5; Nov.–Apr.,
also Sun. 1–5.

As the home of the Treasure Coast Art Association, the **A. E. "Bean" Backus
Gallery** displays works of one of Florida's foremost landscape artists.
The gallery mounts changing exhibits and offers exceptional buys on
work by local artists. ⊠ 500 N. Indian River Dr. ☎ 772/465–0630
⊕ www.backusgallery.com ☞ Free ☾ Tues.–Sat. 10–4, Sun. noon–4;
summer hrs by appointment.

Accessible only by footbridge, the **Jack Island Wildlife Refuge** has 4⅓ mi
of trails. The 1½-mi Marsh Rabbit Trail across the island traverses a
mangrove swamp to a 30-foot-tall observation tower overlooking the
Indian River. ⊠ Rte. A1A ☎ 772/468–3985 ☞ Free ☾ Daily 8–dusk.

★ Commemorating more than 3,000 navy frogmen who trained along Treasure Coast shoreline during World War II, the **Navy SEAL Museum** has
weapons and equipment on view and exhibits depicting the history of
the UDTs (Underwater Demolition Teams). Patrol boats and vehicles are
displayed outdoors. ⊠ 3300 N. Rte. A1A ☎ 772/595–5845 ☞ $5
☾ Mon.–Sat. 10–4, Sun. noon–4.

Highlights of the **St. Lucie County Historical Museum** include early-20th-century memorabilia, photos, vintage farm tools, a restored 1919 American La France fire engine, replicas of a general store and the old Fort Pierce railroad station, and the restored 1905 Gardner House. ⊠ *414 Seaway Dr.* ☎ *772/462–1795* 🖃 *$3* ☉ *Tues.–Sat. 10–4, Sun. noon–4.*

✺ The **St. Lucie Marine Station** is a facility of the Smithsonian Museum in Washington, D.C., and is where Smithsonian scientists come to study ecosystems. Inside are large fish tanks filled with ocean, river, and lagoon ecosystems and one special tank with "Nemo" the fish. The Station's park-like setting, where visitors picnic and children play, make it an ideal stop when you visit the St. Lucie County Historical Museum, which is within walking distance. ⊠ *1420 Seaway Dr.* ☎ *772/462–3474* 🖃 *$2, Tues. free* ☉ *Tues.–Sat. 10–4, Sun. 12–4.*

The 340 acres of the **Fort Pierce Inlet State Recreation Area** contain sand dunes and a coastal hammock. The park has swimming, surfing, picnic facilities, hiking, and a self-guided nature trail. ⊠ *905 Shorewinds Dr.* ☎ *772/468–3985* 🖃 *$3.25 per vehicle, up to 8 people* ☉ *Daily 8–dusk.*

Where to Stay & Eat

★ $$–$$$ ✕ **Ian's Tropical Grill.** Ian's serves fish with many possibilities. Choose from wild salmon, local snapper, pompano, dolphin, and black grouper among others, and then select your method of preparation from grilled, blackened, pan seared, jerked, or broiled. The menu is primarily seafood, but there are a few chicken, pork-chop, and sirloin options such as the macadamia nut–crusted chicken breast. Ian's is a small restaurant where tables are crammed on top of each other, which sometimes means dining elbow to elbow. ⊠ *927 U.S. Hwy. 1* ☎ *772/595–5950* 🖃 *AE, D, DC, MC, V* ☉ *No lunch.*

$$–$$$ ✕ **Mangrove Mattie's.** Since opening in the 1980s, this upscale but rustic spot on Fort Pierce Inlet has provided dazzling waterfront views and delicious seafood. Dine on the terrace or in the dining room, and try the coconut-fried shrimp or the chicken and scampi. Or come by during happy hour (weekdays 5–8) for a free buffet of snacks. ⊠ *1640 Seaway Dr.* ☎ *772/466–1044* 🖃 *AE, D, DC, MC, V.*

$$–$$$ ▦ **Villa Nina Island Inn.** This newly constructed property on 8 acres of North Hutchinson Island is squeaky clean and fresh and has beach access. Housekeeping will cost you $10 per day; but if you don't want to wake for breakfast, you'll save $5. All rooms have private entrances and are decorated with pastels inspired by the ocean, and a mix of wicker and rattan furniture. Creature comforts include TV, coffeemaker, and mini-refrigerator. Suites overlook the Indian River. Children and pets are not allowed, and there is no smoking. Credit card users pay a 10% fee. ⊠ *3851 N. A1A, 34949* ☎ *772/467–8969* ⊕ *www.villanina.com* ➥ *5 rooms* ♨ *Refrigerators, pool; no kids, no smoking* 🖃 *D, MC, V* ❖ *CP.*

Sports & the Outdoors

FISHING For charter boats and fishing guides, try the dockmaster at the **Dockside Harborlight Resort** (⊠ 1152 Seaway Dr. ☎ 772/461–4824).

JAI ALAI **Fort Pierce Jai Alai** (⊠ 1750 S. Kings Hwy., off Okeechobee Rd. ☎ 772/464–7500 or 800/524–2524) sustained significant hurricane damage in

2004. As of this writing, the facility was open for simulcasts only and was expected to be closed for the 2004–2005 season.

SCUBA DIVING   Some 200 yards from shore and ¼ mi north of the Navy SEAL Museum on North Hutchinson Island, the **Urca de Lima Underwater Archaeological Preserve** contains remains of a flat-bottom, round-bellied store ship. Once part of a treasure fleet bound for Spain, it was destroyed by a hurricane. Dive boats can be chartered through the **Dockside Harborlight Resort** (✉ 1152 Seaway Dr. ☎ 772/461–4824).

en route   To reach Vero Beach, you have two options—Route A1A, along the coast, or Route 605 (also called Old Dixie Highway), on the mainland. As you approach Vero on the latter, you'll pass through an ungussied landscape of small farms and residential areas. On the beach route, part of the drive is through an unusually undeveloped section of the Florida coast. Both trips are relaxing.

Vero Beach

③⑥ *12 mi north of Fort Pierce.*

Tranquil and charming, this Indian River County town has a strong commitment to the environment and the arts. There are plenty of outdoor activities here, even though many visitors gravitating to this training ground for the L.A. Dodgers opt to do little at all. In the town's exclusive Riomar Bay area, roads are shaded by massive live oaks, and a popular cluster of restaurants and shops is just off the beach.

★   On the National Register of Historic Places, the 18-acre **McKee Botanical Garden** is both a subtropical garden and a horticulture teaching museum. There's a 1,600-square-foot bamboo pavilion, gift shop, library, and the Hibiscus café, which serves tasty snacks and sandwiches and locally grown tea. ✉ *350 U.S. Hwy. 1* ☎ *772/794–0601* ⊕ *www. mckeegarden.org* ☞ *$6* ☉ *Tues.–Sat. 10–5, Sun. noon–5.*

More grapefruit is shipped from the Indian River area than anywhere else in the world, as you'll learn at the **Heritage Center and Citrus Museum,** where memorabilia harks back to when families washed and wrapped the luscious fruit to sell at roadside stands, and oxen hauled citrus-filled crates with distinctive Indian River labels to the rail station. A video shows current harvesting and shipping methods. ✉ *2140 14th Ave.* ⊕ *www. veroheritage.org* ☎ *772/770–2263* ☞ *Free* ☉ *Tues.–Fri. 10–4.*

In addition to aquariums filled with Indian River Lagoon life, the **Environmental Learning Center,** on 51 acres, has a 600-foot boardwalk through the mangrove shoreline and a 1-mi canoe trail. The center is on the north edge of Vero Beach, on Wabasso Island, and the pretty drive is worth the trip. ✉ *255 Live Oak Dr.* ☎ *772/589–5050* ⊕ *www.elcweb.org* ☞ *Donation suggested* ☉ *Tues.–Fri. 10–4, Sat. 9–4, Sun. 12–3.*

Where to Stay & Eat

$$–$$$$ ✕ **Tangos.** In a yellow three-story building with retail shops on the ground floor, this restaurant offers steak and seafood with a twist. Some

of the more interesting dishes include a lobster quesadilla appetizer with papaya salsa, and roasted duck breast with cabbage and bacon. This casual yet elegant restaurant has great outdoor dining with views of Humiston Park. ⊠ *Park Place, 3001 Ocean Dr.* ☎ *772/231–1550* ⊟ *AE, D, DC, MC, V* ⊙ *Closed Sun. and Mon. No lunch.*

$$–$$$ ✕ **Ocean Grill.** Opened by Waldo Sexton as a hamburger shack in 1938, the Ocean Grill combines its ocean view with Tiffany-style lamps, wrought-iron chandeliers, and paintings of pirates and Seminoles. Count on at least three kinds of seafood any day on the menu, along with pork chops, tasty soups, and salads. The house drink, the Leaping Limey— a curious blend of vodka, blue curaçao, and lemon—commemorates the 1894 wreck of the *Breconshire,* which occurred just offshore and from which 34 British sailors escaped. ⊠ *Sexton Plaza, 1050 Ocean Dr.* ☎ *772/231–5409* ⊟ *AE, D, DC, MC, V* ⊙ *Closed 2 wks following Labor Day. No lunch weekends.*

$$$–$$$$ ▦ **Disney's Vero Beach Resort.** On 71 pristine oceanfront acres, this sprawling family-oriented retreat, operating both as a time-share and a hotel, is Vero's top resort. The main four-story building, three freestanding villas, and six beach cottages, all painted in pastels with gabled roofing in an approximation of turn-of-the-19th-century old-Florida style, are nestled among tropical greenery. Units, some with kitchens and many with balconies, have bright interiors with rattan furniture and tile floors. Shutters, one of two restaurants, has American food. ⊠ *9250 Island Grove Terr., 32963* ☎ *772/234–2000 or 800/359–8000* ☐ *772/234– 2030* ⊕ *www.dvcresorts.com* ⇄ *161 rooms, 14 suites, 6 cottages* ⚫ *3 restaurants, room service, in-room safes, some kitchens, some refrigerators, in-room VCRs, miniature golf, 6 tennis courts, pool, wading pool, gym, hot tub, massage, sauna, beach, boating, bicycles, basketball, bar, video game room, babysitting, children's programs (ages 4–12), laundry facilities, no-smoking rooms* ⊟ *AE, MC, V.*

$$–$$$ ▦ **Vero Beach Inn Resort.** After undergoing a million-dollar renovation and then another renovation after the 2004 hurricanes, this intimate beachfront resort shines. Rooms have either an ocean or pool view and are freshly decorated with tropical furnishings. One- and two-bedroom suites are available with a microwave, refrigerator, and wet bar. ⊠ *4700 N. Rte. A1A, 32963* ☎ *772/231–1600 or 800/227–8615* ☐ *772/231– 9547* ⊕ *www.verobeachinn.com* ⇄ *104 rooms* ⚫ *Some minibars, some microwaves, some refrigerators, in-room data ports, pool, hot tub, beach, lounge, shop, laundry facilities, meeting room* ⊟ *AE, D, DC, MC, V.*

The Arts

The **Civic Arts Center** (⊠ Riverside Park), a cluster of cultural facilities, includes the **Riverside Theatre** (⊠ 3250 Riverside Park Dr. ☎ 772/ 231–6990), which stages six productions each season in its 633-seat performance hall; the **Agnes Wahlstrom Youth Playhouse** (⊠ 3280 Riverside Park Dr. ☎ 772/234–8052), mounting children's productions; and the **Center for the Arts** (⊠ 3001 Riverside Park Dr. ☎ 772/231–0700), which presents exhibitions, art movies, lectures, workshops, and other events, with a focus on Florida artists.

🐾 **Riverside Children's Theatre** (✉ 3280 Riverside Park Dr. ☎ 772/234–8052) offers a series of professional touring and local productions, as well as acting workshops at the Agnes Wahlstrom Youth Playhouse.

Vero Museum of Art (✉ 3001 Riverside Park Dr. ☎ 772/231–0707) is part of the Riverside Park's 26-acre campus dedicated to the arts. The museum is where a full schedule of exhibitions, art movies, lectures, workshops, and classes are hosted. The museum's five galleries and sculpture garden make it the largest art facility in the Treasure Coast.

Sports & the Outdoors

BASEBALL The **Los Angeles Dodgers** (✉ 4101 26th St. ☎ 772/569–4900) train at Holman Stadium in Vero Beach's Dodgertown.

BEACHES **Humiston Park** is one of the beach-access parks along the east edge of town that have boardwalks and steps bridging the foredune. There are picnic tables and a children's play area. ✉ *Ocean Dr. below Beachland Blvd.* ☎ *772/231–5790* 🎫 *Free* ◷ *Daily 7 AM–10 PM.*

Full-service **Round Island Park** (✉ A1A near the Indian River–St. Lucie county line ☎ 772/234–2604) is a good bet for relaxation. There are many services at **Treasure Shores Park** (✉ A1A, 3 mi north of County Rd. 510 at the Wabasso Bridge ☎ 772/581–4997). **Wabasso Beach Park** (✉ County Rd. 510, east of A1A intersection, north of Disney Resort ☎ 772/581–4998) is a good option for a day in the sun.

GOLF **Sandridge Golf Club** (✉ 5300 73rd St. ☎ 772/770–5000) has two public 18-hole courses designed by Ron Garl; green fee: Dunes Course or Lakes Course $16/$42, including cart.

Shopping

Along **Ocean Drive** near Beachland Boulevard, a shopping area includes art galleries, antiques shops, and upscale clothing stores. The eight-block area of Oceanside has an interesting mix of boutiques, specialty shops, and eateries. Just west of Interstate 95, **Outlets at Vero Beach** (✉ 1824 94th Dr. ☎ 772/770–6171) is a discount shopping destination with 85 brand-name stores including Ann Taylor, Ralph Lauren Polo, Mikasa, Bombay, and Jones New York.

Sebastian

37 *14 mi north of Vero Beach.*

One of few sparsely populated areas on Florida's east coast, this fishing village has as remote a feeling as you're likely to find between Jacksonville and Miami Beach. That adds to the appeal of the recreation area around Sebastian Inlet, where you can walk for miles along quiet beaches and catch some of Florida's best waves for surfing.

You'll really come upon hidden loot when entering **Mel Fisher's Treasure Museum.** See some of what was recovered in 1985 from the Spanish treasure ship *Atocha* and its sister ships of the 1715 fleet. The museum certainly piques one's curiosity as to what is still buried at sea: treasures continue to be discovered each year. A similar museum in Key West is also operated by the late Mel Fisher's family. ✉ *1322 U.S. Hwy. 1* ☎ *772/*

589–9875 ⊕ *www.melfisher.com* ✉ *$6.50* ☉ *Mon.–Sat. 10–5, Sun. noon–5.*

Founded in 1903 by President Theodore Roosevelt as the nation's first national wildlife refuge, **Pelican Island National Wildlife Refuge** is in the Indian River Lagoon between Sebastian and Wabasso. The island is only accessible by boat or kayak. Public facilities—a boardwalk and observation tower, built for the refuge's centennial—enable visitors to see birds, endangered species, and habitats.

Because of the highly productive fishing waters of Sebastian Inlet, at the north end of Orchid Island, the 578-acre **Sebastian Inlet State Recreation Area** is one of the Florida park system's biggest draws. Both sides of the high bridge spanning the inlet—views are spectacular—attract plenty of anglers as well as those eager to enjoy the fine sandy shores, known for having some of the best waves in the state. A concession stand on the inlet's north side sells short-order food, rents various craft, and has an apparel and surf shop. There's a boat ramp, and not far away is a dune area that's part of the **Archie Carr National Wildlife Refuge,** a haven for sea turtles and other protected Florida wildlife. ✉ *9700 S. Rte. A1A, Melbourne Beach* ☎ *321/984–4852* ⊕ *www.floridastateparks.org* ✉ *$3 for single occupancy, $5 for more than one in vehicle* ☉ *Daily; bait and tackle shop 7:30–6, concession stand 8–5.*

A National Historical Landmark, the **McLarty Treasure Museum** underscores the credo "Wherever gold glitters or silver beckons, man will move mountains." It has displays of coins, weapons, and tools salvaged from a fleet of Spanish treasure ships which sank in the 1715 storm, leaving some 1,500 survivors struggling to shore between Sebastian and Fort Pierce. The museum's last video showing begins at 3:15. ✉ *13180 N. Rte. A1A* ☎ *772/589–2147* ✉ *$1* ☉ *Daily 10–4:30.*

Where to Stay & Eat

$$–$$$ ✕ **Hurricane Harbor Seafood Company.** Built in 1927 as a garage and used during Prohibition as a smugglers' den, this restaurant draws a year-round crowd for lunch and dinner. Waterfront window seats are especially coveted on stormy nights, when waves break outside in the Indian River Lagoon. Count on seafood, steaks, and grills, along with lighter fare. There's live music most nights. Peek into the Antique Dining Room, with a huge breakfront, used for special occasions. ✉ *1540 Indian River Dr.* ☎ *772/589–1773* ▤ *AE, D, MC, V* ☉ *Closed Mon.*

$–$$ ✕ **Capt. Hiram's Restaurant.** This family-friendly outpost on the Indian River Lagoon is easygoing, fanciful, and fun. Don't miss Capt. Hiram's Sandbar, where kids can play while parents enjoy drinks at stools and booths set in the sand and on wooden decks overlooking the water. Order the fresh catch, crab cakes, stuffed shrimp, raw-bar items, or a juicy steak. There's a weekday happy hour and nightly entertainment in season. ✉ *1606 N. Indian River Dr.* ☎ *772/589–4345* ▤ *AE, D, MC, V.*

$–$$ ▥ **Angler Inn.** Perched on the shores of the Indian River, this 1936 grove house with two floors of wraparound verandas caters to guests who love to fish. Rooms are divided among the main house, guest house, and cottage and all have private entry and bath. Rates at this B&B include expanded Continental breakfast, but early-morning anglers can receive a discounted rate that does not include breakfast. ✉ *805 Indian River Dr., 32958* 🕾 *772/589–1150* ⊕ *www.anglerinn.net* 🗲 *5 suites* ⚲ *Kitchenettes, hot tub, boating, fishing, some pets allowed* ▭ *AE, DC, MC, V* ❮❙❙❯ *CP.*

$–$$ ▤ **Capt. Hiram's Key West Inn.** A Key West–style inn with a lobby embellished with a classic surfboard collection brings the Florida Keys to Sebastian's Riverfront, about 17 mi north of Vero at Marker 66 on the Intracoastal. All rooms have a private balcony and most have oak furnishings. Minisuites include microwave, refrigerator, and wet bar; deluxe suites also include dishwasher and stove. A heated pool has a tropical sun deck, shaded by tables with umbrellas. A complimentary deluxe Continental breakfast is included. ✉ *1580 U.S. 1, 32958* 🕾 *772/388–8588* 🖷 *772/589–4346* ⊕ *www.hirams.com* 🗲 *56 rooms* ⚲ *2 restaurants, some minibars, some microwaves, some refrigerators, in-room data ports, pool, dock, lounge* ▭ *AE, D, MC, V* ❮❙❙❯ *CP.*

Sports & the Outdoors

CANOEING & The boating stand at **Sebastian Inlet State Recreation Area** (✉ 9700 S. Rte.
KAYAKING A1A, Melbourne Beach 🕾 321/724–5424) rents canoes, kayaks, and powerboats daily.

FISHING The region's best inlet fishing is at **Sebastian Inlet State Recreation Area** (✉ 9700 S. Rte. A1A, Melbourne Beach), where the catch includes bluefish, flounder, jack, redfish, sea trout, snapper, snook, and Spanish mackerel. For bottom fishing, try **Incentive Charter Fishing** (✉ Dock at Capt. Hiram's Restaurant 🕾 321/676–1948) and for sport fishing, try **The Big Easy Fishing Charters** (✉ Dock at Capt. Hiram's Restaurant 🕾 772/664–4068).

PALM BEACH & THE TREASURE COAST A TO Z

To research prices, get advice from other travelers, and book travel arrangements, visit www.fodors.com.

AIR TRAVEL

CARRIERS Palm Beach International Airport (PBIA) is served by Air Canada, Air-Tran, American, Bahamasair, CanJet, Comair, Continental, Delta, Jet-Blue, Laker Air, Northwest, Song, Southwest Airlines, Spirit Airlines, United, and US Airways/US Airways Express.

🛪 Airlines & Contacts **Air Canada** 🕾 800/247-2262. **AirTran** 🕾 800/247-8726. **American** 🕾 800/433-7300. **Bahamasair** 🕾 800/222-4262. **CanJet** 🕾 800/809-7777. **Comair** 🕾 800/354-9822. **Continental** 🕾 800/525-0280. **Delta** 🕾 800/221-1212. **Jet-Blue** 🕾 800/538-2583. **Laker Air** 🕾 800/422-7466. **Northwest** 🕾 800/225-2525. **Song** 🕾 800/359-7664. **Southwest Airlines** 🕾 800/435-9792. **Spirit Airlines** 🕾 800/772-7117. **United** 🕾 800/241-6522. **US Airways/US Airways Express** 🕾 800/428-4322.

AIRPORT INFORMATION

PalmTran Routes 44 and 50 run from the airport to Tri-Rail's nearby Palm Beach airport station daily. Palm Beach Transportation provides taxi and limousine service from PBIA. Reserve at least a day in advance for a limo. The lowest fares are $2 per mile, with the meter starting at

$1.25. Depending on your destination, a flat rate (from PBIA only) may save money. Wheelchair-accessible vehicles are available.

🛈 Airport Information **Palm Beach International Airport (PBIA)** ✉ Congress Ave. and Belvedere Rd., West Palm Beach ☎ 561/471-7420. **Palm Beach Transportation** ☎ 561/689-4222. **Tri-Rail Commuter Bus Service** ☎ 800/874-7245.

BUS TRAVEL

Greyhound Lines buses arrive at the station in West Palm Beach. Palm-Tran buses, running between Worth Avenue and Royal Palm Way in Palm Beach and major areas of West Palm Beach, require exact change. Fares are $1.25, or 60¢ for students, senior citizens, and people with disabilities (with reduced-fare I.D.). Service operates seven days a week. Call for schedules, routes, and rates for multiple-ride punch cards.

🛈 Bus Information **Greyhound Lines** ☎ 800/229-9424 ✉ 205 S. Tamarind Ave., West Palm Beach ☎ 561/833-8536. **PalmTran** ☎ 561/841-4200.

CAR TRAVEL

Interstate 95 runs north–south, linking West Palm Beach with Fort Lauderdale and Miami to the south and with Daytona, Jacksonville, and the rest of the Atlantic coast to the north. To access Palm Beach, exit east at Southern Boulevard, Belvedere Road, or Okeechobee Boulevard. Florida's Turnpike runs from Miami north through West Palm Beach before angling northwest to reach Orlando. U.S. 1 threads north–south along the coast, connecting most coastal communities, while the more scenic Route A1A ventures out onto the barrier islands. Interstate 95 runs parallel to U.S. 1 but a few miles inland. A nonstop four-lane route, Okeechobee Boulevard carries traffic from west of downtown West Palm Beach, near the Amtrak station in the airport district, directly to the Flagler Memorial Bridge and into Palm Beach. The best way to access Lake Okeechobee from West Palm is to drive west on Southern Boulevard from Interstate 95 past the cutoff road to Lion Country Safari. From there, the boulevard is designated U.S. 98/441.

EMERGENCIES

Dial 911 for police or ambulance.

🛈 Late-Night Pharmacies **CVS** ✉ 3187 S. Congress Ave., Palm Springs ☎ 561/965-3367. **Walgreens** ✉ 1634 S. Federal Hwy., Boynton Beach ☎ 561/737-1160 ✉ 1208 Royal Palm Beach Blvd., Royal Palm Beach ☎ 561/798-9048 ✉ 1800 W. Indiantown Rd., Jupiter ☎ 561/744-6822 ✉ 2501 Broadway, Riviera Beach ☎ 561/848-6464.

MEDIA

NEWSPAPERS & MAGAZINES
To keep abreast of local issues and find what's new in entertainment options, pick up copies of the *Sun-Sentinel, Palm Beach Post, Palm Beach Daily News, The Press Journal, South Florida Business Journal, New Times,* or *Boca Magazine, Palm Beach Illustrated,* and *Palm Beach Society* magazines.

RADIO
WLRN 91.3 FM is a public radio station. Tune into WLVE 93.9 FM for jazz; WZTA 94.9 for rock; WFLC 97.3 and WRMF 97.9 for adult contemporary; WLDI 95.5 and WHYI 100.7 for top 40; WMXJ 102.7 for oldies; WPBZ 103.1 for alternative; WMGE 103.5 for disco; and WKGR 98.7 and WBGG 105.9 for classic rock.

TAXIS

Palm Beach Transportation has a single number serving several cab companies. Meters start at $1.25, and the charge is $2.00 per mile within West Palm Beach city limits; if the trip at any point leaves the city limits, the fare is still $2 per mile. Some cabs may charge more.

🛈 Taxi Information **Palm Beach Transportation** ☎ 561/689-4222.

TOURS

Capt. Doug's offers three-hour lunch and dinner cruises along the Indian River on a 35-foot sloop. The cost is $100 per couple, including meal, beer, wine, and tips. J-Mark Fish Camp has 45- to 60-minute airboat rides for $30 per person, with a minimum of two people and a maximum of six. Jonathan Dickinson's River Tours runs two-hour guided riverboat cruises daily at 9, 11, 1, and 3. The cost is $12. Loxahatchee Everglades Tours operates airboat tours year-round from west of Boca Raton through the marshes between the built-up coast and Lake Okeechobee. The *Manatee Queen,* a 49-passenger catamaran, offers day and evening cruises November–May on the Intracoastal Waterway and into the park's cypress swamps for $19.99. *Pilgrim Belle* operates two-hour sightseeing cruises along the Intracoastal Waterway. Water Taxi Scenic Cruises has several different daily sightseeing tours in a 16-person launch. All include a close-up look at the mansions of the rich and famous. The southern tour passes Peanut, Singer, and Munyan islands, and Palm Beach mansions. A second tour runs solely along the shore of Jupiter Island. A third tour passes the Craig Norman estate and goes into Lake Worth and Sawgrass Creek.

The Boca Raton Historical Society offers tours of the Boca Raton Resort & Club and trolley tours of city sites during season. Main Street Fort Pierce gives walking tours of the town's historic section, past buildings erected by early settlers, the second Wednesday of each month. The Indian River County Historical Society conducts walking tours of downtown Vero by reservation. Old Northwood Historic District Tours leads two-hour walking tours that include visits to historic home interiors. They leave typically during season Sunday at 2, and a $5 donation is suggested. Tours for groups of six or more can be scheduled almost any day.

🛈 Tours Information **Audubon Society of the Everglades** ⌂ Box 16914, West Palm Beach 33461 ☎ 561/588-6908. **Boca Raton Historical Society** ✉ 71 N. Federal Hwy., Boca Raton ☎ 561/395-6766. **Capt. Doug's** ✉ Sebastian Marina, Sebastian ☎ 772/589-2329. **Indian River County Historical Society** ✉ 2336 14th Ave., Vero Beach ☎ 772/778-3435. **J-Mark Fish Camp** ✉ Torry Island ☎ 561/996-5357. **Jonathan Dickinson's River Tours** ✉ Jonathan Dickinson State Park, 16450 S.E. Federal Hwy., Hobe Sound ☎561/746-1466. **Loxahatchee Everglades Tours** ✉10400 Loxahatchee Rd. ☎561/482-0313. ***Manatee Queen*** ✉ Jonathan Dickinson State Park, 1065 N. Hwy. A1A, Hobe Sound ☎561/744-2191. **Old Northwood Historic District Tours** ✉ 501 30th St., West Palm Beach ☎ 561/863-5633. ***River Rose Riverboat*** ✉ 1 N.E. 1st St., Delray Beach ☎ 561/243-0686. **Water Taxi Scenic Cruises** ✉ Panama Hatties Restaurant, 11511 Ellison Wilson Rd., North Palm Beach ☎ 561/775-2628.

TRAIN TRAVEL

Amtrak connects West Palm Beach with cities along Florida's east coast and the Northeast daily and via the *Sunset Limited* to New Orleans and Los Angeles three times weekly. Included in Amtrak's service is transport from West Palm Beach to Okeechobee; the station is unmanned. Tri-Rail, the commuter rail system, has 13 stops altogether between West Palm Beach and Miami, where tickets can be purchased. The one-way fare is $5.50.

🚆 Train Information **Amtrak** ☎ 800/872-7245 ⊠ 201 S. Tamarind Ave., West Palm Beach ☎ 561/832-6169 ⊠ 801 N. Parrott Ave., Okeechobee. **Tri-Rail** ☎ 800/874-7245.

VISITOR INFORMATION

🚆 Tourist Information **Belle Glade Chamber of Commerce** ⊠ 540 S. Main St., Belle Glade 33430 ☎ 561/996-2745. **Chamber of Commerce of the Palm Beaches** ⊠ 401 N. Flagler Dr., West Palm Beach 33401 ☎ 561/833-3711. **Clewiston Chamber of Commerce** ⊠ 544 W. Sugarland Hwy., Clewiston 33440 ☎ 863/983-7979. **Delray Beach Chamber of Commerce** ⊠ 64-A S.E. 5th Ave., Delray Beach 33483 ☎ 561/278-0424. **Glades County Chamber of Commerce** ⊠ 998 U.S. 27 SE, Moore Haven 33471 ☎ 863/946-0440. **Indian River County Tourist Council** ⊠1216 21st St., Vero Beach 32960 ☎772/567-3491. **Indiantown and Western Martin County Chamber of Commerce** ☎ Box 602, Indiantown 34956 ☎ 772/597-2184. **Okeechobee County Chamber of Commerce** ⊠ 55 S. Parrott Ave., Okeechobee 34974 ☎ 863/763-3959. **Pahokee Chamber of Commerce** ⊠ 115 E. Main St., Pahokee 33476 ☎ 561/924-5579. **Palm Beach County Convention & Visitors Bureau** ⊠1555 Palm Beach Lakes Blvd., Suite 800, West Palm Beach 33401 ☎ 561/233-3000. **St. Lucie County Tourist Development Council** ⊠ 2300 Virginia Ave., Fort Pierce 34982 ☎ 800/344-8443. **Stuart/Martin County Chamber of Commerce** ⊠1650 S. Kanner Hwy., Stuart 34994 ☎ 772/287-1088. **Town of Palm Beach Chamber of Commerce** ⊠ 45 Cocoanut Row, Palm Beach 33480 ☎ 561/655-3282. **U.S. Army Corps of Engineers (Okeechobee area information)** ⊠ South Florida Operations Office, 525 Ridgelawn Rd., Clewiston 33440-5399 ☎ 863/983-8101.

Fort Lauderdale & Broward County

WORD OF MOUTH

"The Fort Lauderdale Taxi was a great way to see the city and get around. The drivers always have a few stories to tell and point out lots of things along the way too and make the trip entertaining. Certainly listening to the driver dishing the dirt on all the rich owners of homes on Millionaire's Row on the Intracoastal Waterway was funny."

—Dave

"At nighttime in Fort Lauderdale, try the Riverwalk area on the New River. Lots of restaurants and bars, right on the river (of course.). If you want something upscale, go east on Las Olas Blvd. $$$! But really nice!"

—birdergirl

Updated by
Lynne Helm

COLLEGE STUDENTS OF THE 1960S returning to Fort Lauderdale for vacations today would be hard pressed to recognize the onetime Sun and Suds Spring Break Capital of the Universe. Back then, Fort Lauderdale's beachfront was lined with T-shirt shops interspersed with quickie food outlets, and downtown consisted of a lone office tower, some dilapidated government buildings, and motley other structures waiting to be razed. Today, the beach has upscale shops and restaurants, and downtown growth of recent years has exploded with new office and luxury residential development.

The 1960 film *Where the Boys Are* changed everything for the city. The movie depicted how college students—upward of 20,000—were swarming to the city for the spring break phenomenon. By 1985 the 20,000 had mushroomed to 350,000. Hotel owners complained of a dozen or more students cramming into a room, with civility hitting new lows. Drug trafficking and petty theft proliferated, along with downscale bars staging wet T-shirt and banana-eating contests. Fed up, city leaders adopted policies and restrictions designed to encourage spring breakers to go elsewhere. They did, and the complaints of lost business are few—given a new era attracting a far more sophisticated, affluent crowd.

A major beneficiary is Las Olas Boulevard, a shopping street once moribund after 5 PM, which has reinvented itself as a hot venue, with a mix of trendy shops. Ever more restaurants have sprung up, and both visitors and locals often make an evening of strolling the boulevard. On-street parking on weekends has slowed traffic, providing more of a village feel. Farther west, along New River, is evidence of Fort Lauderdale's cultural renaissance: the Arts and Entertainment District and its crown jewel, the Broward Center for the Performing Arts. Still farther west, in the community of Sunrise, is the Office Depot Center (formerly the National Car Rental Center), serving as the county's major-league sports and concert venue and as home arena for the National Hockey League's Florida Panthers. Of course, a captivating shoreline with wide ribbons of sand for beachcombing and sunbathing is what continues to make Fort Lauderdale and Broward County a major draw.

Tying this all together is a transportation system that, while becoming more crowded, is relatively hassle free compared to elsewhere in congested South Florida. An expressway connects the city and suburbs and provides a direct route to the Fort Lauderdale–Hollywood International Airport and Port Everglades. For a slower, more scenic way to really see this canal-laced city, simply hop on a water taxi. None of this was envisioned by Napoleon Bonaparte Broward, Florida's governor from 1905 to 1909, for whom the county was named. His drainage schemes opened much of the marshy Everglades region for farming, ranching, and settling (in retrospect, an environmental disaster). But it was for Major William Lauderdale, who built a fort at the river's mouth in 1838 during the Seminole Indian wars, that the city was named.

Incorporated in 1911 with just 175 residents, Fort Lauderdale grew rapidly during the Florida boom of the 1920s. Today its population is 150,000, and suburbs keep growing—1.6 million live in the county's 30 municipalities and unincorporated areas. Once oriented toward retirees,

Broward now attracts younger, working-age families, many living in such newer communities as Weston, southwest of Fort Lauderdale. With a revitalized downtown and a skyline (marked by ever-more high-rises) that now includes multiuse complexes mixing retail and loft housing, the city's teeming with young professionals who are buying and revamping aging beachside condominiums.

Changing the complexion of the area further is gambling. Although South Florida's Indian tribes have long offered bingo, poker, and machines that resemble traditional slots—The Seminole Hard Rock Hotel & Casino in Hollywood is the most prominent example in the region—big change is afoot for gaming in Greater Fort Lauderdale. In March 2005, Broward County residents voted to become the first county in Florida to offer Las Vegas-style gambling with true slot machines at wagering facilities such as Gulfstream Park, the Hollywood Greyhound Track, Dania Jai-Alai, and Pompano Park Harness Track.

Exploring Fort Lauderdale & Broward County

The Fort Lauderdale metro area is laid out in a basic grid system, and only myriad canals and waterways interrupt the mostly straight-line path of streets and roads. Nomenclature is important here. Streets, roads, courts, and drives run east–west. Avenues, terraces, and ways run north–south. Boulevards can (and do) run any which way. For visitors, Las Olas Boulevard is one of the most important east–west thoroughfares from the beach to downtown, whereas Route A1A—referred to as Atlantic Boulevard and Ocean Boulevard along some stretches—runs along the north–south oceanfront. These names can confuse visitors, since there are separate streets called Atlantic and Ocean in Hollywood and Pompano Beach. Boulevards, composed of either pavement or water, give Fort Lauderdale its distinct "Venice of America" character. Honeycombed with more than 260 mi of navigable waterways, the city is home port for about 44,000 privately owned boats. An easy, pleasant way to tour the canals is via the city's water-taxi system, made up of motor launches with names like *Michele,* carrying up to 70 passengers, providing transportation and quick, narrated tours. Larger, multiple-deck touring vessels and motorboat rentals for self-guided tours are other options. The massive Intracoastal Waterway, paralleling Route A1A, is the nautical equivalent of an inter-state highway. It runs north–south between downtown Fort Lauderdale and the beach and provides easy access to neighboring beach communities—Deerfield Beach and Pompano Beach lie to the north while Dania Beach and Hollywood lie to the south.

About the Restaurants

Greater Fort Lauderdale offers some of the finest, most varied dining of any U.S. city its size. From among more than 3,500 wining and dining establishments in Broward, choose from basic Americana or the cuisines of Asia, Europe, or Central and South America and enjoy more than just food in an atmosphere with a subtropical twist.

About the Hotels

Though not as posh as Palm Beach or as trendy as Miami Beach, Fort Lauderdale has respectable lodging choices, from beachfront luxury suites

Since most Broward County sights are close together, it's easy to pack a lot into a day if you have a vehicle. Catch the history, museums, and shops and bistros in Fort Lauderdale's downtown area and along Las Olas Boulevard. Then if you feel like hitting the beach, just take a 10-minute drive east to the intersection of Las Olas and A1A and you're there. Many neighboring communities, with attractions of their own, are just north or south of Fort Lauderdale. As a result, you'll be able to cover most of the high points in 3 days, and with 7 to 10 days, you can experience virtually all of Broward's mainstream charms.

Numbers in the text correspond to numbers in the margin and on the Broward County and Fort Lauderdale maps.

If you have 3 days

With a bigger concentration of hotels, restaurants, and attractions than its suburbs, ▦ **Fort Lauderdale ❶** ☞ –⓭ makes a logical base of operations for any visit. On your first day, see the downtown area, especially Las Olas Boulevard between Southeast 3rd and Southeast 15th avenues. After lunch at a sidewalk café, head for the nearby Arts and Science District and the downtown **Riverwalk ❻**; enjoy it at a leisurely pace in half a day. On your second day, spend some time at the **Fort Lauderdale Beachfront ⓫**, shopping or having a cooling libation at an oceanfront lounge if heat drives you off the sand. Tour the waterways on the third day, either on a rented boat from one of the marinas along Route A1A, or via a sightseeing vessel or water taxi. The latter can be boarded at points along the Intracoastal Waterway. Reachable by water taxi are attractions such as Beach Place, Broward Center for the Performing Arts, Galleria Mall, Las Olas Boulevard shops, Las Olas Riverfront, and the **Museum of Art ❸** and **Museum of Discovery and Science/Blockbuster IMAX Theater ❼**; restaurants such as 15th Street Fisheries, Grill Room at Riverside Hotel, Shula's on the Beach, and dozens of others; and hotels such as the Hyatt Regency Pier Sixty-Six, Radisson Bahia Mar, Riverside Hotel, and Pillars Waterfront.

If you have 5 days

With additional time, see more of the beach and the arts district and still work in some outdoor sports—and you'll be more able to rearrange your plans depending on weather. On the first day, visit the Arts and Science District and the downtown **Riverwalk ❻** ☞. Set aside the next day for an offshore adventure, perhaps a deep-sea fishing charter, a reef diving trip, or some kite surfing or parasailing along the beach. Landlubbers might go for hiking at Markham Park or at Tradewinds Park (home of **Butterfly World ⓮**). On Day 3, shop, dine, and relax along the **Fort Lauderdale Beachfront ⓫**, and at the end of the day, sneak a peak at the Hillsboro Light, at **Lighthouse Point ㉙**. Another good day can be spent at the **Hugh Taylor Birch State Recreation Area ⓬**. Enjoy your fifth day in ▦ **Hollywood ㉒**, perhaps combining time on the Broadwalk with a visit to the Anne Kolb Nature Center, at West Lake Park.

If you have 7 days

With a full week, you have time for more attractions, fitting in beach time around other activities. In fact, enjoy any of the county's public beach areas on your first day. The second day can be spent shopping, either at chic boutiques or at one of the malls. On Day 3, tour the waterways on a sightseeing boat or water taxi. Then shop and dine along Las Olas Boulevard. Your fourth day might be devoted to the many museums in downtown Fort Lauderdale and the African-American Cultural Center on Sistrunk Boulevard west of downtown. Day 5 could be prime for an airboat ride at **Sawgrass Recreation Park** ⑯, at the edge of the Everglades. Since Fort Lauderdale offers plenty of facilities for outdoor recreation, spend the sixth day fishing and picnicking on one of the area's many piers or playing at a top golf course. Set aside your last day for 🎦 **Hollywood** ㉒ to stroll the scenic Broadwalk or head to **Davie** ㉔ to see the aviary at Flamingo Gardens before relaxing in peaceful Hollywood North Beach Park.

to intimate B&Bs to chain hotels along the Intracoastal Waterway. If you want to be on the beach, be sure to ask specifically when booking your room, since many hotels advertise "waterfront" accommodations that are actually on inland waterways, not the beach.

WHAT IT COSTS				
	$$$$	$$$	$$	$	¢
RESTAURANTS	over $30	$20–$30	$15–$20	$10–$15	under $10
HOTELS	over $220	$140–$220	$100–$140	$80–$100	under $80

Restaurant prices are per person for a main course at dinner. Hotel prices are for a standard double room, excluding 6% sales tax (more in some counties) and 1%–4% tourist tax.

Timing

Tourists visit all year long, choosing to arrive in winter or summer depending on budget, interests, hobbies, and the climate where they live. The winter season, roughly Thanksgiving through March, attracts the biggest crowds and "snowbirds"—seasonal residents showing up when snow starts up north. Concert, art, and entertainment seasons are at their height then, and restaurants and roadways are packed. In summer, waits at even the top restaurants are likely to be shorter, although some venues curtail hours. Summer is the rainy season, with showers arriving about mid-afternoon and typically soon gone, but heat and humidity do not quickly subside and summer seems to move at a slow, sticky pace. For golfers, almost any time is great for play, though waits for tee times are longer on weekends year-round. Remember that sun can burn all year long, even in cloudy weather and especially at midday. If you jump in the water to cool off when the sun is strongest, rays reflecting off the water can substantially increase your chance of burning. Try planning beach time for early morning and late afternoon, with sightseeing, shopping, or a siesta in between.

FORT LAUDERDALE

Like many of its southeast Florida neighbors, Fort Lauderdale has been busily revitalizing for several years. In a state where gaudy tourist zones often stand aloof from workaday downtowns, Fort Lauderdale is unusual in that the city exhibits consistency at both ends of the 2-mi Las Olas corridor. The sparkling look results from moves to thoroughly improve both beachfront and downtown. Matching the downtown's innovative arts district, cafés, and boutiques is an equally inventive beach area, with cafés and shops facing an undeveloped shoreline, and new hotels gradually replacing faded icons of yesteryear. Despite wariness of pretentious overdevelopment, city leaders have allowed a striking number of glittering high-rises. Some nostalgia buffs fret over the diminishing vision of sailboats bobbing in waters near downtown, now that high-rise development has erased one of the area's oldest marinas. Sharp demographic changes also are changing the faces of Greater Fort Lauderdale communities, increasingly cosmopolitan with more minorities including Hispanics and people of Caribbean descent, as well as gays and lesbians. In Fort Lauderdale, especially, a younger populace is growing while long-time residents are becoming fewer, to a point where one former city commissioner likens the change to that of the city's historic New River—moving with the tide and sometimes appearing at a standstill. "The river of our population is at still point, old and new in equipoise, one pushing against the other."

Downtown

The jewel of the downtown area along New River is the Arts and Entertainment District, with Broadway shows, the Miami City Ballet and much, much more at the riverfront Broward Center for the Performing Arts. Clustered within a five-minute walk are the Museum of Discovery and Science, the expanding Fort Lauderdale Historical Museum, and the Museum of Art, site of world-class traveling exhibits including "St. Peter and the Vatican: The Legacy of the Popes," and the U.S. debut of "Diana: A Celebration." Restaurants, sidewalk cafés, bars, and blues, folk, jazz, reggae, and rock clubs flourish. Las Olas Riverfront is a multistory entertainment, dining, and retail complex along several waterfront blocks once owned by pioneers William and Mary Brickell. Tying this district together is the Riverwalk, extending 2 mi along the New River's north and south banks. Tropical gardens with benches and interpretive displays fringe the walk on the north, boat landings on the south. East along Riverwalk's north side is the pioneer Stranahan House, and Las Olas shopping and dining begins a block east. Tropical landscaping and trees separate traffic lanes in some blocks, setting off fine shops, restaurants, and popular nightspots. From here, depending on traffic, it's 10 to 15 minutes by car or about a half hour by water taxi back to the beach.

a good tour

Start on Southeast 6th Avenue at Las Olas Boulevard, where you'll find **Stranahan House** ❶ ☞. Between Southeast 6th and 15th avenues, Las Olas has Spanish colonial buildings with fashion boutiques, jewelry shops, and art galleries. Driving east, you'll cross into the Isles, among Fort Lauderdale's most prestigious neighborhoods, where homes line waterways with seawalls embellished by yachts. Return west on Las Olas to Andrews Avenue, turn right, park in one of the municipal garages, and walk around downtown. First stop is the **Museum of Art** ❸. Walk one block north to the **Broward County Main Library** ❹ to see works from Broward County's Public Art and Design Program. Go west on Southeast 2nd Street to Southwest 2nd Avenue, turn left, and stop at the **Old Fort Lauderdale Village & Museum** ❺, surveying the city's beginnings.

Just to the south is the palm-lined **Riverwalk ❻**, a good place for leisurely strolling. Head north toward a cluster of facilities collectively known as the Arts and Science District. The district contains the outdoor Esplanade, whose exhibits include a hands-on display of the science and history of navigation, the **Museum of Discovery and Science/Blockbuster IMAX Theater ❼**; adjacent to the museum is the Broward Center for the Performing Arts. Finally, for a glimpse of one of the city's oldest neighborhoods, go west along Las Olas Boulevard to Southwest 7th Avenue and the entrance to **Sailboat Bend ❽**. Return to the start of the tour by traveling east along Las Olas Boulevard.

TIMING Depending on how long you like to linger in museums and how many hours you want to spend in the shops on Las Olas Boulevard, you can devote anywhere from half a day to an entire day to this tour.

What to See

❾ **African-American Research Library and Cultural Center.** A two-story, $14-million gem, this resource provides locals and researchers from around the world with more than 75,000 books, documents, and artifacts centering on the experiences of people of African descent. There's a gift shop and a small café, and parking is free. ⊠ *2650 Sistrunk Blvd.* ☎ *954/625–2800* ⊛ *http://www.broward.org/library/aarlcc.htm* ⊠ *Free* ⊙ *Mon. noon–8, Tues.–Thurs. 10–8, Sat. 9–5.*

❹ **Broward County Main Library.** One of more than 30 libraries in the Broward County system, this eight-story building of Florida limestone with a terraced glass facade was designed by Marcel Breuer to complement the environment. Works are on display here from Broward County's Public Art and Design Program, including paintings, sculpture, photographs, and weavings by nationally renowned and Florida artists. A community technology center has personal computers for public use and assistant/adaptive devices for patrons with learning and physical disabilities. Productions from theater to poetry readings are presented in a 300-seat auditorium. ⊠ *100 S. Andrews Ave.* ☎ *954/357–7444, 954/357–7457 for self-guided Art in Public Places walking tour brochure* ⊛ *www.broward.org/library* ⊠ *Free* ⊙ *Mon.–Thurs. 9–9, Fri. and Sat. 9–5, Sun. noon–5:30.*

need a
break?

Don't miss **Charcuterie Too** (⊠ 100 S. Andrews Ave. ☎ 954/463–9578), a cozy cafeteria on the 2nd floor of the Broward County Main Library. Breakfast treats include muffins, scones, and coffee cakes, and there's an extensive lunch menu with soups, salads, and entrées. Open weekdays from 8 to 2:30, it caters to library bookworms and downtown worker bees.

❷ **Fort Lauderdale Antique Car Museum.** Retired floral company owner Arthur O. Stone set up a foundation to preserve these eye-poppers. Nostalgia includes nearly two dozen Packards from 1900 to the 1940s, along with a gallery saluting F.D.R. Within a quick commute of both Port Everglades and the airport for visitors with time to while away, this easily accessible museum has everything from spark plugs and gear shift knobs to signage from the Texaco Oil Co. ⊠ *1527 S.W. 1st Ave.* ☎ *954/779–7300* ⊛ *www.antiquecarmuseum.org* ⊠ *$8* ⊙ *Weekdays 10–4.*

Beaches
Broward County's beachfront extends for miles without interruption, although the character of communities along the shoreline changes. In Hallandale, the beach is backed by towering condominiums, whereas in Hollywood you'll find motels and the Broadwalk. Just north of there—blessedly—there's virtually nothing at all.

Fishing
Greater Fort Lauderdale has both freshwater and saltwater fishing. Go bottom or drift-boat fishing from party boats, deep-sea fishing for large sport fish on charters, angling for freshwater game fish, or drop a line off a pier. For bottom fishing, party boats typically charge between $25 and $30 per person for up to four hours, including rod, reel, and bait. For charters, a half day for as many as six people runs about $325, six-hour charters around $495, and full-day charters (eight hours) around $600. Captain and crew, plus bait and tackle, are included. Split parties can be arranged for about $85–$90 per person for a full day. Several Broward municipalities—Dania Beach, Lauderdale-by-the-Sea, Pompano Beach, and Deerfield Beach—have fishing piers that draw anglers for pompano, amberjack, bluefish, snapper, blue runners, snook, mackerel, and Florida lobster.

5

Golf
Nearly 60 courses, including famous championship links, green up Greater Fort Lauderdale. Most area courses are inland, and sometimes offer great bargains. Off-season (May–October) green fees start at $20 or less; peak-season (November–April) charges run from $35 to more than $125. Fees can be trimmed by reserving tee times through a local service, Next Day Golf, and many hotels offer golf packages.

Scuba Diving
There's good diving within 20 minutes of shore. Among the most popular of the county's 80 dive sites is the 2-mi-wide, 23-mi-long Fort Lauderdale Reef, the product of Florida's most successful artificial reef-building program. More than a dozen houseboats, ships, and oil platforms have been sunk at 10- to 150-foot depths to provide a habitat for fish and other marine life, as well as to help stabilize beaches. The most famous sunken ship is the 198-foot German freighter *Mercedes*, blown onto the pool terrace of the late Palm Beach socialite Mollie Wilmot during a violent Thanksgiving storm in 1984; the vessel is now submerged a mile off Fort Lauderdale beach.

★ ❸ **Museum of Art.** In an Edward Larrabee Barnes–designed building that's considered an architectural masterpiece, this museum's impressive permanent collection has 20th-century European and American art, including works by Picasso, Calder, Dalí, Mapplethorpe, Warhol, and Stella, as well as a notable collection of works by celebrated Ashcan School artist William Glackens. When its building opened in 1986, the museum helped launch revitalization of the downtown district and nearby Riverwalk area, and it since has become a magnet for special traveling exhibits (with higher admission fees) including "Tutankhamen and the Golden

Broward
County

Hillsborough Blvd.

Deerfield Beach 21

441 75

Coconut
Creek

Hillsboro Beach

7

811

Sample   Rd.

**Lighthouse
Point** 20

Coral
Springs

834

Margate

**Butterfly
World** 14

Coconut Cr.

W.   Atlantic   Blvd.   Pkwy.

Powerline   Rd.

Dixie Hwy.

Federal Hwy.

Pompano Beach 19

817

North
Lauderdale

Atlantic   Blvd.

95

Tamarac

McNab   Rd.

Florida's Tnpk.

Cypress Creek Rd.

Commercial Blvd.

Commercial Blvd.

18

Lauderhill

**Lauderdale-
by-the-Sea**

Sunrise

Oakland   Park   Blvd.

Sunrise Blvd.

University Dr.

Lauderdale
Lakes

N. Andrews Ave.

A1A

Sunrise   Blvd.

Seminola

Dr.

**Big Cypress
Seminole Reservation** 17

Plantation

Broward   Blvd.

**Fort
Lauderdale**

1 - 13
see detail
map

**Sawgrass
Recreation Park** 16

S.W. 31st   Ave.

Davie Blvd.

Las Olas
Blvd.

595

84

S.E. 17th St.
Causeway

ATLANTIC OCEAN

441

84

Davie 24

817   Dr.

Orange Dr.

595

1

**Fort Lauderdale-Hollywood
International Airport**

Flamingo   Rd.

**Everglades
Holiday Park** 15

Griffin Rd.

Griffin Rd.

Dania Beach
23
Dania Beach
Blvd.

848

Stirling Rd.

A1A

822

Sheridan St.

University   Ave.

95

Snake Creek Rd.

Palm   Ave.

Pines Blvd.

Hollywood Blvd.

Dixie Hwy.

Hollywood 22

820

Pembroke
Pines

Pembroke Rd.

Miramar

Hallandale Blvd.

KEY

Start of itinerary

Ives Dairy Rd.

0   4 miles

0   4 km

Age of the Pharaohs," which as of this writing is slated to run through spring 2006; this will mark the Egyptian king's first appearance in Florida and his first time in the United States in nearly 30 years. ✉ *1 E. Las Olas Blvd.* ☎ *954/763–6464* ⊕ *www.moafl.org* ✆ *$7 and up, depending on exhibit* ⊘ *Daily 11–7, Thurs. open until 9; closed Tues. mid-Dec.–Jan.*

★ ♻ ❼ **Museum of Discovery and Science/Blockbuster IMAX Theater.** The aim here is to show children—*and* adults—the wonders of science in an entertaining fashion. The 52-foot-tall Great Gravity Clock in the courtyard entrance lets arrivals know a cool experience awaits. Inside, exhibits include Choose Health, about healthy lifestyle choices; Kidscience, encouraging youngsters to explore the world around them; and Gizmo City, a look at how gadgets work. Florida Ecoscapes has a living coral reef as well as live bees, bats, frogs, turtles, and alligators. An IMAX theater, part of the complex, shows films (some 3-D) on a five-story-high screen. ✉ *401 S.W. 2nd St.* ☎ *954/467–6637 museum, 954/463–4629 IMAX* ⊕ *www.mods.org* ✆ *Museum $14, includes one IMAX show* ⊘ *Mon.–Sat. 10–5, Sun. noon–6.*

❺ **Old Fort Lauderdale Village & Museum.** Surveying city history from the Seminole era to more recent times, the museum has expanded into several adjacent historic buildings, including the King-Cromartie House, the Historical Society's Hoch Heritage Center archives building, and the New River Inn. The research facility archives original manuscripts, maps, and more than 250,000 photos. ✉ *231 S.W. 2nd Ave.* ☎ *954/463–4431* ⊕ *www.oldfortlauderdale.org* ✆ *$8* ⊘ *Tues.–Fri. 11–5, Sat. and Sun. noon–5.*

★ ▶❻ **Riverwalk.** Fantastic views and entertainment prevail on this lovely, paved promenade on the New River's north bank. On the first Sunday of every month a jazz brunch attracts visitors. The walk has been extended 2 mi on both sides of the beautiful urban stream, connecting the facilities of the Arts and Science District.

❽ **Sailboat Bend.** Between Las Olas and the river lies a neighborhood with much of the character of Old Town in Key West and historic Coconut Grove in Miami. There are no shops or services here. Across the river lies another older tree-lined neighborhood called Tarpon River, alluding to the river that loops off New River from the southeast quadrant and runs to the southwest section, returning to New River near Sailboat Bend.

▶❶ **Stranahan House.** The oldest residence in the city was once home for businessman Frank Stranahan, who arrived in 1892. With his wife, Ivy, the city's first school teacher, he befriended the Seminole Indians, traded with them, and taught them "new ways." In 1901 he built a store and later made it his home. Now it's a museum with many original furnishings. ✉ *335 S.E. 6th Ave., at Las Olas Blvd.* ☎ *954/524–4736* ⊕ *www. stranahanhouse.com* ✆ *$6* ⊘ *Wed.–Sat. 10–3, Sun. 1–3.*

Along the Beach

Fort Lauderdale's beachfront offers the best of all possible worlds, with easy access not only to a wide band of beige sand but also to restaurants and shops. For 2 mi heading north, beginning at the Bahia Mar

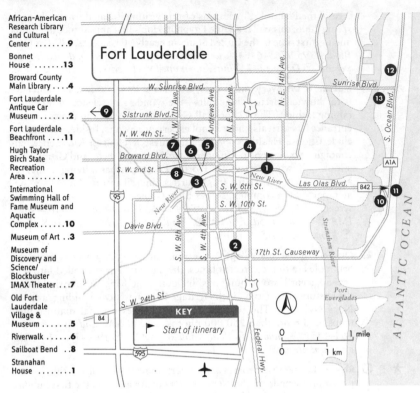

yacht basin along Route A1A, you'll have clear views, typically across rows of colorful beach umbrellas, to the ocean and ships passing in and out of nearby Port Everglades. If you're on the beach, gaze back on an exceptionally graceful promenade. Pedestrians rank ahead of cars in Fort Lauderdale. Broad walkways line both sides of the beach road, and traffic has been trimmed to two gently curving northbound lanes, where in-line skaters skim past slow-moving cars. On the beach side, a low masonry wall doubles as an extended bench, separating sand from the promenade. At night the wall is accented with ribbons of fiber-optic color, occasionally on the blink despite efforts for a permanent fix, but quite pretty when working. The most crowded portion of beach is between Las Olas and Sunrise Boulevards. North of the redesigned beachfront is another 2 mi of open and natural coastal landscape. Much of the way parallels the Hugh Taylor Birch State Recreation Area, preserving a patch of primeval Florida.

a good tour

Go east on Southeast 17th Street across the newly improved (higher and wider) bridge over the Intracoastal Waterway and bear left onto Seabreeze Boulevard (Route A1A). You'll pass through a neighborhood of older homes set in lush vegetation before emerging at the south end of Fort Lauderdale's beachfront strip. On your left is the Radisson Bahia Mar Beach Resort, where novelist John McDonald's fictional hero, Travis

McGee, is honored with a plaque at marina slip F-18; it's here that McGee docked his houseboat, the *Busted Flush*. Three blocks north, visit the **International Swimming Hall of Fame Museum and Aquatic Complex** ⑩ ▶. As you approach Las Olas Boulevard, you'll see the lyrical styling that has given a distinctly European flavor to the **Fort Lauderdale Beachfront** ⑪. Plan to break for lunch and perhaps some shopping at Beach Place, the entertainment, retail, and dining complex just north of Las Olas. Turn left off Route A1A at Sunrise Boulevard, then right into **Hugh Taylor Birch State Recreation Area** ⑫, where outdoor activities can be enjoyed amid vivid flora and fauna. Cross Sunrise Boulevard and visit the **Bonnet House** ⑬ to marvel at both the whimsical home and the surrounding subtropical 35-acre estate.

TIMING   The beach is all about recreation and leisure. To enjoy it as it's meant to be, allow at least a day to loll about. For shade there's a stand of trees at the southern portion near the Yankee Clipper hotel.

What to See

★ ⑬ **Bonnet House.** A 35-acre oasis in the heart of the beach area, this subtropical estate is a tribute to the history of Old South Florida. The charming home was the winter residence of the late Frederic and Evelyn Bartlett, artists whose personal touches and small surprises are evident throughout. Whether you're interested in architecture, artwork, or the natural environment, this is a special place. Be on the lookout for playful monkeys swinging from trees, a source of amusement at even some of the most solemn outdoor weddings on the grounds. Hours can vary, so call first. ⊠ *900 N. Birch Rd.* ☎ *954/563–5393* ⊕ *www. bonnethouse.org* ☞ *$10 for house tours, $6 for grounds only* ⊙ *Wed.–Fri. 10–3, weekends noon–4.*

⑪ **Fort Lauderdale Beachfront.** A wave theme unifies the setting—from the
Fodor'sChoice low, white, wave-shape wall between the beach and beachfront promenade to the widened and bricked inner promenade in front of shops,
★ restaurants, and hotels. Alone among Florida's major beachfront communities, Fort Lauderdale's beach remains gloriously open and uncluttered. More than ever, the boulevard is worth promenading.

⑫ **Hugh Taylor Birch State Recreation Area.** Amid the tropical greenery of this 180-acre park, stroll along a nature trail, visit the Birch House Museum, picnic, play volleyball, pitch horseshoes, and paddle a rented canoe. Since parking is limited on A1A, park here and take a walkway underpass to the beach (between 9 and 5). ⊠ *3109 E. Sunrise Blvd.* ☎ *954/564–4521* ⊕ *www.abfla.com/parks* ☞ *$4 per vehicle with up to 8 people, $1 per pedestrian* ⊙ *Daily 8–sunset; ranger-guided nature walks Fri. at 10:30.*

▶ ⑩ **International Swimming Hall of Fame Museum and Aquatic Complex.** This monument to underwater accomplishments has two 10-lane, 50-meter pools that are open daily to the public, when not hosting international competitions. The exhibition building has photos, medals, and other souvenirs from major swimming events worldwide, as well as a theater that shows vintage Tarzan and Esther Williams films. ⊠ *1 Hall of Fame Dr., 1 block south of Las Olas at A1A* ☎ *954/462–6536 museum, 954/828–4580 pool* ⊕ *www.ishof.org* ☞ *Museum $3 per individual, $5 per fam-*

CloseUp

CRUISING FOR A TAXI

SHOUT "TAXI! TAXI!" IN FORT LAUDERDALE, *and look for your ship to come in.*

Actually, it's a water bus or water taxi depending on your point of view, since the original fleet of water taxis has been replaced by water buses carrying up to 70 passengers, floating "cabs" that you can "hail" from the many docks along the Intracoastal Waterway.

For a day of sightseeing, the taxi will pick you up at any of several hotels along the waterway, and you can stop off at attractions like the Performing Arts Center or Beach Place. For lunch, enjoy a restaurant on Las Olas Boulevard or Las Olas Riverfront. In the evening, water taxis are a great way to go out to dinner or bar-hop.

Water Taxi and Broward County Mass Transit have partnered to create Water

Buses. These environmentally friendly electric ferries can carry up to 70 passengers. Ride all you want from 6:30 AM to 12:30 AM for $5 (one-way adult fare is $4). Passes are available, too, at $10 for a 3-day, $20 for a 7-day, $35 for a 31-day, $85 for a six-month, and $150 for an annual, the latter including value-added savings with discounts at selected restaurants, shops, and attractions, from the Stranahan House to the Mai Kai. Annual pass holders also qualify for discounts on companion tickets and for the shuttle to Miami's South Beach ($17). For family reunions, special group tours such as the Great River Safari and the History Tours are on tap. To catch a water taxi, call 954/467–6677 about 20 minutes ahead of your desired pick-up, or check out the schedule at ⊕ www.watertaxi.com.

— Alan Macher, updated by Lynne Helm

---

ily, pool $3 ⊙ *Museum and pro shop mid-Jan.–late Dec., weekdays 9–7, weekends 9–5; pool mid-Jan.–late Dec., weekdays 8–4, weekends 9–5.*

Where to Eat

American

$$$–$$$$ ✕ **Shula's on the Beach.** It's only fitting that Don Shula, coaching the Miami
Fodor'sChoice Dolphins to that Perfect Season in 1972 and the "winningest" coach in
★ NFL history, should have a winning South Florida steak house. The good news for steak—and sports—fans is that the staff here also turns out winners. Certified Angus beef is cut thick and grilled over a superhot fire for quick charring. Try Steak Mary Anne, named for Shula's wife, consisting of two sliced filets covered in a savory sauce. Seafood is excellent, too, as is the apple cobbler à la mode. Outside tables provide views of sand and ocean; inside seating provides access to sports memorabilia and large-screen TVs. ⊠ *Sheraton Yankee Trader, 321 N. Fort Lauderdale Beach Blvd.* ☎ *954/355–4000* ▭ *AE, D, DC, MC, V.*

$$–$$$ ✕ **Casablanca Cafe.** You'll get a fabulous ocean view and a good meal
Fodor'sChoice to boot at this historic two-story Moroccan-style villa, built in the
★ 1920s by local architect Francis Abreu. The menu is an American potpourri with both tropical and Asian influence (try the mussels in Thai

curry sauce) along with North African specialties like lamb shank and couscous. There's a piano bar downstairs, and a deck for outside dining. Service is friendly and attentive. ⊠ *A1A and Alhambra St.* ☎ *954/ 764–3500* ☰ *AE, D, MC, V.*

$$–$$$ ✕ **Tropical Acres.** Sizzling steaks have been served up from an open-kitchen-style fireplace grill here since 1949—a millennium by South Florida standards. The Studiale family's sprawling icon of a restaurant, with its orange awnings out front, harks back to simpler times on the once-remote, now bustling Griffin Road. There's an inviting lounge for pre-dinner drinks, a main dining room with booths and tables that's quite cozy despite its size, and five private dining rooms. Juicy prime rib is big here, and you'll find some of the best early-bird specials around. Choose from more than 40 other entrées, including sautéed frogs' legs, rack of lamb, boneless New York strip for two, or ask the friendly, knowledgeable waitstaff for recommendations. A wine list of some 50 labels ranges from $17 to $90, with more than a dozen available by the glass. ⊠ *2500 Griffin Rd.* ☎ *954/989–2500* ☰ *AE, DC, MC, V.*

¢–$ ✕ **Floridian.** This Las Olas landmark with photos of Marilyn Monroe, Richard Nixon, and local notables past and present dishes up one of the best breakfasts around, with oversized omelets that come with biscuits, toast, or English muffins, plus a choice of grits or tomatoes. With sausage or bacon on the side, the feast will make you forget about eating again soon. Servers can be brisk, bordering on brusque, but chalk it up as part of the experience. Count on savory sandwiches and hot platters for lunch and dinner. It's open 24 hours every day—even during hurricanes. Feeling flush? Try the Fat Cat Breakfast (New York strip steak, hash browns or grits, toast, and a worthy champagne) or the Not-So-Fat-Cat, with the same grub and a lesser-quality vintage. ⊠ *1410 E. Las Olas Blvd.* ☎ *954/463–4041* ☰ *No credit cards.*

¢–$ ✕ **Joe Picasso's Interactive Art Studio & Cafe.** Hungry artists adult and pint-sized now have a "loft" of their own right on Las Olas where they can throw pottery, bead, bisque-paint, cast plaster face masks, or create "Who Am I" self-portrait projects. All that Picasso-esque creativity can work up appetites. At press time, Joe Picasso's was reworking its menu canvas to focus exclusively on desserts such as orange tangerine white chocolate cake, Chinese confetti cookies, gelatos, and other sweets along with Equator Estate coffees, teas, and espresso. ⊠ *888 E. Las Olas Blvd.* ☎ *954/462–2551* ☰ *AE, MC, V.*

¢–$ ✕ **Lester's Diner.** Home of big cups of coffee, Lester's has stood as a 24-hour haven for the hungry along State Road 84 since 1967. Truckers head here on their way to Port Everglades, as do workers from the area's thriving marine industry, suits from downtown toting briefcases, and tourists packing beach bags. The clientele gets even more eclectic in the wee hours. A stick-to-the-ribs menu includes breakfast anytime, homemade soups, sandwiches, salads, and dinners of generous portions. If your cholesterol count can take the hit, try the country-fried steak ($8.95) or the chicken liver omelet ($5.95). Patio dining under a red awning on the east side of the restaurant accommodates smokers. Two other Lester's are in western Broward's Margate and Sunrise, although they close at midnight on weeknights. ⊠ *250 State Rd. 84* ☎ *954/*

525–5641 ✉ *4701 Coconut Creek Pkwy., Margate* ☎ *954/979–4722* ✉ *1399 N.W. 136th Ave., Sunrise* ☎ *954/838–7473* 🖃 *D, MC, V.*

¢–$ ✕ **Southport Raw Bar.** You can't go wrong at this unpretentious spot where the motto, seen on bumper stickers for miles around, proclaims "Eat fish, live longer, eat oysters, love longer, eat clams, last longer." Raw or steamed clams, raw oysters, and combos, along with peel-and-eat shrimp, are market-priced. Hoagies, subs, and burgers are the ticket for around $5. Side orders range from Bimini bread to key lime pie, with conch fritters, beer-battered onion rings, and corn on the cob in between. Order wine by the bottle or glass and beer by the pitcher, bottle, or can. Eat outside overlooking a canal, or inside at booths, tables, or the bars, in front and back. Limited parking is free, and a shopping-center parking lot is across the street. ✉ *1536 Cordova Rd.* ☎ *954/525–2526* 🖃 *MC, V.*

¢–$ ✕ **Tom Jenkins.** Big portions of drippingly delicious barbecue are dispensed at this handy spot for eat-in or takeout, south of the New River Tunnel and north of the 17th Street Causeway. Furnishings include an old Singer sewing machine and a wringer washer, and diners partake at a half dozen or so picnic-style tables. Side dishes with dinners under $10 include baked beans, collards, and a mighty tasty macaroni and cheese. For lunch, Tom's pork, beef, and catfish sandwiches are a surefire shortcut to appetite satisfaction. Leave room for sweet-potato pie or apple cobbler. ✉ *1236 S. Federal Hwy.* ☎ *954/522–5046* 🖃 *No credit cards* ☺ *Closed Sun. and Mon.*

¢ ✕ **Ernie's Barbecue.** Walls once plastered with philosophical quotes from a former owner have been scrubbed clean at Ernie's, where the menu proclaims "conch is king, barbecue is a way of life, and the bar is open late." Fortunately for patrons, the barbecue platters of pork or beef and conch chowder are as lip-smacking as ever. Bimini bread, thick sliced for sandwiches, is also sold by the loaf to go, along with racks of ribs and conch chowder by the quart. Seafood, salads, and burgers also pass muster here, and there's a children's menu. Eat downstairs, or if you don't mind the buzz of federal-highway traffic, take the stairs to the 2nd-floor open-air patio tables near a couple of pool tables. ✉ *1843 S. Federal Hwy.* ☎ *954/523–8636* 🖃 *AE, D, MC, V.*

¢ ✕ **Georgia Pig.** When you're heading out to the area's western reaches, this postage-stamp-size outpost can add some down-home zing to your day. Breakfast, including sausage gravy and biscuits, is served from 6 to 11 AM. But the big attraction is barbecue, beef, pork, or chicken, on platters or in sandwiches. Alternatives include a spicy Brunswick stew and fried jumbo shrimp. There's apple, peach, cherry, and pecan pie, and also a small-fry menu. Order takeout (25¢ extra) or eat at the counter, at wooden tables, or at a half dozen or so booths. ✉ *1285 S. W. 40 Ave. (State Rd. 7–U.S. 441, just south of Davie Blvd.)* ☎ *954/ 587–4420* 🖃 *No credit cards.*

¢ ✕ **Skyline Chili.** Cincinnati's famed brand has made a name for itself among locals fond of debating the merits of coneys or three-, four-, or five-way chili, each making for a meal well under $10. There's a chili sandwich, made just like the coneys but without the wiener, and also some low-carb variations. Eat inside or at a couple of tables out front. ✉ *2590 N. Federal Hwy.* ☎ *954/566–1541* 🖃 *D, MC, V.*

¢ ✕ **Stork's Café.** In trendy Wilton Manors (a municipality in remarkable renaissance), Stork's Café stands out as a gay-friendly, straight-friendly, and just plain friendly-friendly place to plot sightseeing strategy (or catch up on news from a stack of local papers). Sit indoors or outside under red umbrellas. Custom Barbie cakes (real dolls, edible ball gowns) are popular here. Divine baked goods range from croissants, tortes, cakes, and pies to assorted monster cookies ($1.60 each), including gingersnap and snickerdoodle. The Pilgrim (turkey) or Hello Kitty (tuna) sandwiches go with salads or soups like vegan split pea. An offshoot, Stork's Las Olas, delights with a similar menu, and now there's a third Stork's (with an abbreviated menu and hours) at the Museum of Art, also on Las Olas. ✉ 2505 N.E. 15th Ave. Wilton Manors ☎ 954/567–3220 ✉ 1109 E. Las Olas Blvd., Fort Lauderdale ☎ 954/522–4670 ✉ 1 E. Las Olas Blvd., Fort Lauderdale ☎ 954/761–2344 ☰ AE, D, MC, V.

Asian

$$$ ✕ **Mai-Kai.** You'll think you've tripped off to the South Seas rather than South Florida upon arrival at this landmark, operating with lighted torches along Federal Highway since this particular stretch was a two-laner. It's a trifle touristy yet somehow magnetic. Specialties include lobster Bora Bora and Peking duck, exotic tropical drinks, and a pulsating Polynesian dance review with a flaming finale. Kids' shows are hosted on Sunday evening in summer. Valet parking is available. ✉ 3599 N. Federal Hwy. ☎ 954/563–3272 ☰ AE, D, MC, V.

$–$$ ✕ **Siam Cuisine.** Some locals say this restaurant, tucked away in a small storefront in Wilton Manors, serves the best Thai in the Fort Lauderdale area, and they may be right. The family-run kitchen turns out appealing, flavorful delights from $9.95 up to $21.95 for a whole fish, usually red snapper. Thai curry dishes with chicken or shrimp are favorites, along with steamed dumplings and roast duck. ✉ 2010 Wilton Dr. ☎ 954/564–3411 ☰ AE, MC, V.

Contemporary

★ $$$–$$$$ ✕ **By Word of Mouth.** Unassuming but outstanding, this restaurant never advertises, hence its name. But word has sufficed for nearly a quarter century because locals consistently put this restaurant along the railroad tracks just off Oakland Park Boulevard at the top of "reader's choice" restaurant polls. There's no menu. Patrons are shown the day's specials to make their choice. Count on a solid lineup of fish, fowl, beef, pasta, and vegetarian entrées. A salad is served with each dinner entrée. ✉ 3200 N.E. 12th Ave. ☎ 954/564–3663 ☰ AE, MC, V.

$$–$$$$ ✕ **Mark's Las Olas.** Mark Militello, a star among chefs in South Florida
FodorsChoice and beyond, commands this offshoot of North Miami's long-gone
★ Mark's Place. Militello's loyal following remains enchanted with his Florida-style preparation, blending flavors from Caribbean, Mediterranean and Southwestern traditions. Entrées change daily, but patrons can count on signatures like crab-crusted black grouper. Appearing on occasion is the Italian baby chicken grilled under a brick. And some patrons rave about the wild mushroom polenta with roasted shallots and porcini oil. Dishes are occasionally paired with combos of *callaloo* (West Indian spinach), chayote, ginger, jicama, and plantain. Be aware

that substitutions are frowned upon, although servers are warmly hospitable. To start, the adventurous might try pancetta-wrapped rabbit loin or lobster with truffle mash. To end, Militello recommends his banana bread pudding. The wine list is mostly Californian, with many varieties offered by the glass. ⊠ *1032 E. Las Olas Blvd.* ☎ *954/463–1000* ◬ *Reservations essential* ⊟ *AE, D, DC, MC, V* ☯ *No lunch weekends.*

$–$$$ ✕ **Creolina's.** Since it moved to more upscale environs within the Himmarshee Village area from its modest storefront birthplace not far away, it's not uncommon to see chef-owner Mark Sulzinski cooking up Cajun-Creole delights for city power brokers, including the mayor. Try the Gumbo Ya Ya, crawfish rémoulade, or Alligator Piquant (tender strips fried crisp) for starters. Also consider the catfish with pecans, or plain old red beans and rice. Warm bread pudding with bourbon sauce is a worthy finale. Despite the fancier digs, prices remain down to earth. ⊠*209 S.W. 2nd St.* ☎ *954/524–2003* ⊟ *AE, D, DC, MC, V.*

Continental

$$$–$$$$ ✕ **Grill Room on Las Olas.** After soaking in the area's trendier spots, you may be ready for tried-and-true fare at the historic Riverside Hotel. The room is accented in the grand style of a colonial British officers' club, and the menu has grilled steaks, or chateaubriand and rack of lamb, both prepared for two. Many dishes are prepared tableside, including a grand Caesar salad. Choose from an extensive wine list. The adjacent Golden Lyon Bar has the feeling of a pub somewhere in India. ⊠ *Riverside Hotel, 620 E. Las Olas Blvd.* ☎ *954/467–2555* ⊟ *AE, MC, V.*

French

$$–$$$ ✕ **French Quarter.** This 1920 building, formerly a Red Cross headquarters, sits on a quiet street just off bustling Las Olas Boulevard. French-style architecture has a touch of New Orleans, and the food captures both Creole and traditional French elements. Among favorites are shrimp *maison* (large shrimp sautéed with carrots and mushrooms in beurre blanc), bouillabaisse, crab cakes, and escargot appetizers. French baking, including aromatic bread, is done on site, and a prix-fixe three-course dinner is served until 6:30. ⊠ *215 S.E. 8th Ave.* ☎ *954/463–8000* ⊟ *AE, D, DC, MC, V* ☯ *Closed Sun. No lunch Sat.*

German

$–$$$ ✕ **Old Heidelberg Restaurant & Deli.** Likened to a Bavarian mirage plucked from the Alps and plopped along State Road 84 near airport and seaport, the Old Heidelberg's beer stein–cowbell–cuckoo clock decor accents the veal loaf, sauerkraut, and dessert specialties such as apple strudel and Black Forest cake. Owners Heidi Bruggermann and Dieter Doerrenberg hit South Florida to thaw out in 1984. After opening a wholesale sausage factory, they bought a one-time seafood eatery in 1991 for transformation into a German-style haven for breaded pork cutlets, fried burgers, pan-fried flounder, and stuffed roast pork with bread dumplings. For better or wurst in take-out, the Old Heidelberg Deli next door (open Monday through Saturday 9 AM to 6 PM) stocks kielbasa, liver dumplings, Bitburger beer and nearly a dozen mustards. ⊠ *900 State Road 84* ☎ *954/463–6767* ⊟ *AE, D, MC, V* ☯ *Closed Mon. No lunch Sat.*

Irish

$ ✕ **Biddy Early's.** This dark, somewhat gothic lunch and dinner watering hole with nook-like booths stands out on a somewhat forlorn stretch of Andrews Avenue, beckoning with assorted East Clare Sandwiches, West Clare burgers (harking back to the County Clare home turf of one of the owners), and other Irish fare including beef Guinness stew and bangers and mash. Bread and butter pudding is quite comforting, and there's more comfort in the Monday-through-Friday happy hour, from 4 to 7 PM. ⊠ *3419 N. Andrews Ave. Oakland Park* ☎ *954/567–1990* ▤ *AE, D, MC, V.*

¢–$ ✕ **Maguire's Hill 16.** With the requisite lineup of libations and sandwiches, this comfortable Irish pub has a very tasty potato soup, shepherd's pie, bangers and mash, corned beef and cabbage, and Irish stew. ⊠ *535 N. Andrews Ave.* ☎ *954/764–4453* ▤ *AE, D, DC, MC, V.*

Italian

$$–$$$$ ✕ **Primavera.** Tucked inside an ordinary shopping plaza is this extraordinary find celebrating its 20th anniversary in 2005. Apart from fresh pasta with rich sauces and risotto entrées, choose from creative fish, poultry, veal, and beef dinners. One of chef-owner Giacomo Dresseno's favorites is a double-cut veal chop. If you're in town for a few nights, check out the chef's day or evening cooking classes or wine-appreciation dinners. Ticket holders around town appreciate the pre-theater menu. There's live entertainment on weekends. ⊠ *830 E. Oakland Park Blvd.* ☎ *954/564–6363* ⊕ *www.trueitalian.com* ▤ *AE, D, DC, MC, V* ☾ *Closed Mon. No lunch.*

$–$$$$ ✕ **Casa D'Angelo.** Owner-chef Angelo Elia has re-created his former Café D'Angelo into a gem of a Tuscan-style white tablecloth restaurant, which is tucked inside the Sunrise Square shopping center. Casa D'Angelo's oak oven turns out some marvelous seafood and beef dishes. The pappardelle with porcini mushrooms takes pasta to pleasant heights. Another favorite is the calamari and scungilli salad with garlic and lemon. Be sure to ask about the oven-roasted fish of the day. ⊠ *1201 N. Federal Hwy.* ☎ *954/564–1234* ▤ *AE, D, DC, MC, V* ☾ *No lunch.*

¢–$$$ ✕ **Louie, Louie Bistro.** Some of the best pasta dishes on Las Olas are served at this friendly, tavern-style establishment. Try individual thin-crust pizzas, sandwiches, or complete dinners. Fresh fish specials are offered daily. Grouper, when available, is excellent. Wash it all down with any of eight on-tap beers, or select from the wine list. ⊠ *1404 E. Las Olas Blvd.* ☎ *954/524–5200* ▤ *AE, MC, V.*

Mediterranean

$$$–$$$$ ✕ **Trina.** You might well fill up on eyefuls of Fort Lauderdale beach during breakfast or lunch at this spot on the ground level of The Atlantic hotel, but come dinnertime your focus will shift to the crackling activity in the open kitchen and among the well-heeled crowd. The warm wood tones and minimalist fixtures mirror The Atlantic's restrained elegance, but there's a touch of New York fanfare on the menu, in part because Don Pintabona, former executive chef of Tribeca Grill, is running the kitchen. Seafood dominates, with some interesting results: scallops and sweetbreads mingle in one entrée, while Florida favorites like snapper and sole get Mediterranean touches. One successful leitmotif

is flatbread: a tasty herbed variation with pancetta at breakfast, or with such toppings as rock shrimp or spicy Moroccan lamb at dinner. Another good bet is a Trina Trio, which might include an appetizer of tuna carpaccio, salmon tartare, and snapper ceviche, or a crème brûlée sampler including coffee, chocolate and, most worthy, coconut. Reservations are recommended. ⊠ *601 N. Fort Lauderdale Beach Blvd.* ☎ *954/567–8020* ▤ *AE, D, DC, MC, V.*

Mexican

$$–$$$$ ✕ **Eduardo de San Angel.** Authentic chilies, spices, and herbs enhance classic seafood, meat, and poultry dishes here. Specialties are beef tenderloin tips sautéed with portobello mushrooms and onions in a chipotle chili sauce, and terrific peppercorn-crusted Keys yellowtail. ⊠ *2822 E. Commercial Blvd.* ☎ *954/772–4731* ▤ *AE, D, DC, MC, V* ☉ *Closed Sun.*

¢–$ ✕ **Cafe del Rio.** This Tex-Mex eatery next to an Outback Steakhouse kicks things off with tortilla chips and fresh, zingy salsa. Appetizers, soups, salads, combo plates, and fajitas make it easy for two to dine heartily for around $20. Enchiladas have chunk meat and tamales are stuffed with ground beef. Complimentary serve-yourself soft ice cream provides a cordial finale. Huge, high-ceiling dining rooms are less than cozy, and those in the know often head outside to the landscaped patio where tables are on gliders under canopies. ⊠ *1821 S.E. 10th Ave.* ☎ *954/463–5490* ▤ *AE, MC, V* ☉ *Closed Sun.*

¢ ✕ **Tortilleria Mexicana.** With a machine about the size of an old homestyle Mixmaster cranking out 1,000 pounds of corn-meal tortillas daily (double that on weekends) as you watch, the tiny hole-in-the-wall Tortilleria Mexicana near Oakland Park City Hall has authentic fare that attracts Broward's growing Mexican population and plenty of gringos to boot. Try such staples as tacos, tamales, and chicken with rice and beans; enchiladas, quesadillas and flautas, with chicken, salad, and hot-pepper slices, do the trick for hearty appetites. Don't count on much English being spoken here, but you'll do fine if you can say "taco." With the success of his first store (open 6 AM to 10 PM), owner Eliseo Martinez opened a second tortilla haven, in Pompano Beach, this one with a bakery and butcher shop (open 8 AM to 9 PM). ⊠ *4115 N. Dixie Hwy., Oakland Park* ☎ *954/563-2503* ⊠ *1614 E. Sample Rd., Pompano Beach* ☎ *954/943-0057* ▤ *MC, V.*

Seafood

★ $$$–$$$$ ✕ **Blue Moon Fish Company.** Most tables have stellar views of the Intracoastal Waterway, but Blue Moon's true magic comes from the kitchen, where chefs Baron Skorish and Bryce Statham create moon-and-stars-worthy seafood dishes. Start with the raw bar, a sushi sampler, or the pan-seared fresh shucked oysters. Salads include a hydroponic bibb with hearts of palm, and entrée favorites include shiitake-mushroom-crusted halibut or peppercorn-crusted big eye tuna with sticky rice. Carnivores might opt for prosciutto-stuffed veal tenderloin. To wrap up an evening, indulge in the icky-stick caramel tart or the tartlet of bananas Foster blue moon ($10 each). Sunday champagne brunches ($24.95) are frequently booked in winter high season, making it best to reserve ahead. ⊠ *4405 W. Tradewinds Ave.* ☎ *954/267–9888* ▤ *AE, D, DC, MC, V.*

$$–$$$$ ✕ **15th Street Fisheries.** A view of the Intracoastal Waterway is only the beginning at this two-story seafood landmark. Satisfying dishes include a cold seafood salad and a spicy conch chowder for starters. Homemade breads, a specialty, come with a cheese-and-chive spread. Grilled mahimahi and alligator are among the more than 50 entrées. Try the key lime pie with an Oreo crust. Downstairs seating is more casual. ⊠ *1900 S.E. 15th St.* ☎ *954/763–2777* ⊟ *AE, D, DC, MC, V.*

$$–$$$$ ✕ **Rustic Inn Crabhouse.** Wayne McDonald started with a cozy one-room roadhouse in 1955, when this stretch was a remote service road just west of the little airport. Now, the still-rustic place is huge. The ample menu includes a $24.95 garlic crab dinner, with patrons banging open the crabs with mallets directly on tables covered with newspapers, and peel-and-eat shrimp, served either with garlic and butter or spiced and steamed with Old Bay seasoning. Finish with pie or cheesecake. ⊠ *4331 Ravenswood Rd.* ☎ *954/584–1637* ⊟ *AE, D, DC, MC, V.*

Southwestern

$$–$$$ ✕ **Canyon Southwest Cafe.** Adventurous Southwestern food helps you escape the ordinary at this small but popular spot next to a movie theater. Take, for example, the ostrich skewers, smoked salmon tostada, or Brie and wild-mushroom quesadilla. Brook trout is served with a tempting crabmeat salsa. Start off with Canyon's famous prickly pear margaritas, or choose from a well-rounded wine list or beer selection. The restaurant is at Sunrise Boulevard and Federal Highway. ⊠ *1818 E. Sunrise Blvd.* ☎ *954/765–1950* ⊟ *AE, MC, V* ☉ *No lunch.*

Where to Stay

Downtown & Beach Causeways

$$$–$$$$ ▦ **Hyatt Regency Pier Sixty-Six.** The trademark of this high-rise resort on
Fodor'sChoice the Intracoastal Waterway is the rooftop Pier Top Lounge, making one
★ 360-degree revolution every 66 minutes. The 17-story tower dominates a 22-acre spread that includes Spa 66, a full-service European-style spa. Each room has a balcony with views of the 142-slip marina, pool, ocean, or Intracoastal. Some guests prefer the ground-level lanai rooms. Lush landscaping and convenience to the beach, shopping, and restaurants add to the overall allure. Hail the water bus at the resort's dock for a three-minute trip to the beach. ⊠ *2301 S.E. 17th St. Causeway, 33316* ☎ *954/525–6666 or 800/327–3796* ☐ *954/728–3551* ⊕ *www. pier66.com* ⇆ *380 rooms, 8 suites* ⟁ *6 restaurants, 2 tennis courts, 2 pools, gym, hot tub, spa, snorkeling, boating, marina, parasailing, waterskiing, fishing, 3 bars* ⊟ *AE, D, DC, MC, V.*

$$$–$$$$ ▦ **Schubert Resort.** This restored 1950's art deco property is a gay-friendly luxury boutique resort tucked into tropical landscaping within the Victoria Park neighborhood. Rooms are oversize and have marble and granite baths; most have either a king-size bed or two double-size beds. Continental breakfast is served overlooking the pool and Jacuzzi. The property feels secluded yet is a short walk from shopping and restaurants. ⊠ *855 N.E. 20th Ave., 33304* ☎ *954/763–7434 or 866/338–7666* ☐ *954/763–4132* ⊕ *www.schuberthotel.com* ⇆ *30 rooms* ⟁ *Some kitchenettes, pool, spa, shuffleboard, business services* ⊟ *AE, DC, MC, V.*

$–$$$ ⊞ **Riverside Hotel.** On Las Olas Boulevard, just steps from boutiques, restaurants, and art galleries, this charming hotel was built in 1936 and has taken on unprecedented luster with a $25-million renovation and expansion. Penthouse suites in the newer 12-story executive tower have balconies with sweeping views of Las Olas, New River, and the downtown skyline. Old Fort Lauderdale photos grace the hallways, and rooms are outfitted with antique oak furnishings and framed French prints. Enjoy afternoon tea in the lobby, and dine at Indigo, with Southeast Asian cooking, or the elegant Grill Room. ⊠ *620 E. Las Olas Blvd., 33301* ☎ *954/467–0671 or 800/325–3280* 🖷 *954/462–2148* ⊕ *www.riversidehotel.com* 🖘 *206 rooms, 11 suites* ⚭ *2 restaurants, pool, dock, 2 bars, no-smoking rooms* ⊟ *AE, DC, MC, V.*

¢–$ ⊞ **Banyan Marina Resort.** These outstanding waterfront apartments on
Fodor'sChoice   a residential isle just off Las Olas Boulevard are set amid imaginative
★   landscaping that includes a walkway through the upper branches of a banyan tree. With leather sofas, comfortable carpets, high-quality art, French doors, and jalousies to court sweeping breezes, the luxurious units are competitive with those at any first-class hotel—for half the price. Apartments and efficiencies include a full kitchen and dining area. All units enjoy the property's beautiful gardens, dockage for eight yachts, and exemplary housekeeping. ⊠ *111 Isle of Venice, 33301* ☎ *954/ 524–4430 or 800/524–4431* 🖷 *954/764–4870* ⊕ *www.banyanmarina. com* 🖘 *3 rooms, 1 efficiency, 4 1-bedroom apartments, 2 2-bedroom apartments* ⚭ *Pool, dock* ⊟ *MC, V.*

Along the Beach

$$$$ ⊞ **The Atlantic.** Functional but elegant is the principle behind this luxury condo hotel, a Starwood newcomer steps from Las Olas Boulevard and the Atlantic beyond. In lieu of having you hunch over the front desk, staffers check you in one-on-one while you sip an icy libation in the lobby, a marriage of marble and wood, beiges and browns. This British colonial scheme is picked up in the spacious, unfussy rooms, which have simple, dark-wood furniture, ample marble kitchen areas, and creamy fabrics and plush carpeting that smartly frame rather than compete with the main event—balcony views of the city or ocean (go for the latter). Little in-room touches include Bose Wave CD/radio systems and a host of Internet connection options; among the major on-premises amenities are a European-style spa offering a variety of treatments and massages within the spa or in-room, and the tony Trina lounge and restaurant. ⊠ *601 N. Fort Lauderdale Beach Blvd., 33304* ☎ *954/567–8020* 🖷 *954/567–8040* ⊕ *www.luxurycollection.com/atlantic* 🖘 *61 rooms, 58 suites, 5 penthouses* ⚭ *2 restaurants, kitchens, minibars, cable TV, in-room broadband, in-room data ports, Wi-Fi, pool, health club, spa with, lounge, shop, parking (fee), laundry service, dry cleaning, concierge, meeting rooms, no-smoking rooms* ⊟ *AE, D, DC, MC, V.*

$$$–$$$$ ⊞ **Ireland's Inn.** At the north end of Fort Lauderdale Beach, directly on the shoreline, this long-popular Old Florida–style four-building property has undergone a major revamp while retaining a cordial, intimate feel that delights newcomers and keeps the faithful happily loyal. Lovely rooms with either two queen-size beds or a single king-size bed are among the area's largest, and ocean views are unsurpassed. One-bedroom suites with a separate living area have an extra TV, and there are one-bedroom suites with Jacuzzis for romantic getaways. The main building also has quarters with kitchenettes, and two lavishly decorated penthouses. Ireland's 2220 building has its own courtyard, water fountain, pool, and direct beach access. Windows, the main building's oceanfront dining room, has a cozy fireplace and a diverse menu, including fresh fish and a house specialty, panfried chicken served family style. ⊠ *2220 N. Atlantic Blvd., 33305* ☎ *954/565–6661 or 800/347–7776* ☒ *954/565–8893* ⊕ *www.Irelands.com* ⌁ *120 rooms* ⌂ *Restaurant, 2 pools, bar* ⊟ *AE, D, DC, MC, V.*

$$$–$$$$
Fodor'sChoice
★
🏨 **Marriott's Harbor Beach Resort.** Look down from the upper stories (14 in all) at night, and this 16-acre property, on the secluded south end of Fort Lauderdale Beach, shimmers like a jewel. Spacious guest rooms have rich tropical colors, lively floral art prints, and warm woods. Part of the hotel's big-budget renovation is the addition of a European spa. No other hotel on the beach gives you so many activity options. ⊠ *3030 Holiday Dr., 33316* ☎*954/525–4000 or 800/222–6543* ☒*954/766–6152* ⊕*www. marriottharborbeach.com* ⌁ *602 rooms, 35 suites* ⌂ *3 restaurants, room TVs with movies and video games, in-room data ports, 5 tennis courts, 2 pools, gym, spa, beach, snorkeling, boating, parasailing, volleyball, 2 bars, children's programs (ages 5–12)* ⊟ *AE, D, DC, MC, V.*

★ $$–$$$
🏨 **Best Western Pelican Beach.** On the beach and owned-managed by the hospitable Kruse family, this already lovely property has been transformed into an entirely new non-smoking resort with a restaurant and lounge, an old-fashioned ice cream parlor, and Fort Lauderdale's only Lazy River pool, allowing guests to float around a moat-like "river" via circulating current. For small fry, there's also a Funky Fish program. Rooms include 117 ocean-front suites. With the new building all aglow, the original Sun Tower is getting a makeover. ⊠ *2000 N. Atlantic Blvd., 33305* ☎ *954/568–9431 or 800/525–6232* ☒ *954/565–2622* ⊕ *www. pelicanbeach.com* ⌁ *180 rooms* ⌂ *Restaurant, 2 pools, lounge* ⊟ *AE, DC, MC, V.*

★ $$–$$$
🏨 **Lago Mar Resort & Club.** The sprawling Lago Mar has been owned by the Banks family since the early 1950s and, after renovations, its sparkle remains. Most accommodations are suites, ideal for families. Suite highlights include a king-size bed, pull-out sofa, and full kitchen. Trellises and bougainvillea plantings edge the swimming lagoon, and you have direct access to a large private beach in an exclusive neighborhood. ⊠*1700 S. Ocean La., 33316* ☎ *954/523–6511 or 800/524–6627* ☒ *954/524–6627* ⊕ *www.lagomar.com* ⌁ *52 rooms, 160 suites* ⌂ *4 restaurants, miniature golf, tennis court, 2 pools, shuffleboard, volleyball, playground* ⊟ *AE, DC, MC, V.*

$$–$$$
🏨 **The Pillars Hotel at New River Sound.** Described as Fort Lauderdale's "small secret" by locals in the know, this property is one block in from the beach on the Intracoastal. Its design recalls the colorful architecture of 18th-century British-colonial Caribbean plantations. Most rooms have views of the waterway or pool, with French doors opening to individual patios or balconies. Rooms have rattan and mahogany headboards, antique reproduction desks and nightstands, and lush draperies. Suites include wet bars with refrigerators and microwaves. ⊠*111 N. Birch Rd., 33304* ☎ *954/467–9639* ☒ *954/763–2845* ⊕ *www.pillarshotel.*

com ↩ *19 rooms, 4 suites ♿ Room service, minibars, some microwaves, some refrigerators, in-room VCRs, in-room data ports, pool, concierge, no-smoking rooms; no kids under 12 ☰ AE, D, DC, MC, V.*

$–$$$ ▥ **The Worthington.** This gay-friendly hotel exclusively for men has a 24/7 hot tub for up to 12, great landscaping with rare palms and fountains, and tastefully decorated rooms. It's close to the beach, and Continental breakfast is served poolside with fresh-ground Starbucks coffee. ⊠ *543 N. Birch Rd., 33306* ☎ *954/524-1568 or 800/445-7036* 🖷 *954/563-6819* ↩ *15 units ♿ Pool, hot tub ☰ AE, D, DC, MC, V.*

¢–$$ ▥ **Sea Chateau Resort.** A cozy two-story enclave about a block from the beach, this tropical-motif property has more going for it than affordability. Each room is done differently; many have canopy beds draped with gossamer fabric, and all have puffy comforters of assorted stripes, spacious closets, and tub-showers. Unit 110 boasts a blue nautical motif right down to the napkin holders, while Unit 108's theme centers on palm trees. Efficiencies with kitchenettes anchor the corners. Rooms face the pool next to a quiet, shaded courtyard. Should you fall in love with the area, the owner is a licensed real estate broker. ⊠ *555 N. Birch Rd., 33304* ☎ *954/566–8331* 🖷 *954/564–2411* ↩ *17 rooms ♿ Some kitchenettes, refrigerators, pool ☰ No credit cards.*

Camping

Greater Fort Lauderdale

🛆 **Kozy Kampers RV Park.** This quiet, shaded park with a restaurant next door serves as a central point for exploring Greater Fort Lauderdale or relaxing with such activities as horseshoes and shuffleboard. Leashed dogs up to 35 pounds are allowed, as are big rigs and slide-outs. There are 13 pull-through sites. Stay the night ($38), or pay a weekly ($250) or monthly ($725) rate in winter; rates are lower in summer. Reservations are advised in winter. *♿ Full hookups, dump station, laundry facilities, public telephone* ↩ *104 sites* ⊠ *3631 W. Commercial Blvd.* ☎ *954/731–8570* 🖷 *954/731-3140* ⊕ *www.kozykampers.com* ▨ *$38* ☰ *MC, V* ☉ *Year-round.*

🛆 **Paradise Island RV Resort.** You'll find this long-established park, formerly known as Buglewood, well situated for heading east to the beach or west to attractions. Relax in a large heated pool surrounded by umbrellaed tables or chaise longues. Or, head for the resource room with modem hookup, big-screen TV, and a library. Planned group activities, including cookouts and ice-cream socials, unfold November through April. There's fax service at the front office, and daily trash pickup at no extra cost. Rates for two people November–April range from $38 daily to $228 weekly and $735 monthly, with lower rates available in summer. Reservations are advised, especially in winter. *♿ Full hook-ups, electricity* ↩ *232 paved, level sites* ⊠ *2121 N.W. 29th Ct.* ☎ *800/487–7395* 🖷 *954/485–5701* ⊕ *www.paradiseislandrvresort.com* ☰ *AE, D, MC, V* ☉ *Year-round.*

🛆 **Twin Lakes Travel Park.** Unwind here in the clubhouse or in the adjacent heated pool overlooking the lake. The park offers free daily trash removal. Rates for two people range from $40 daily to $240 weekly to $750 monthly. Reservations are advised, especially in winter. *♿ Full hook-*

AN AFRICAN-AMERICAN GEM

WEST OF DOWNTOWN *Fort Lauderdale's Arts & Sciences District, in the heart of the African-American community along Sistrunk Boulevard, lies a gem once discounted as a grand idea unlikely to get off the ground.*

Yet in late 2002, Fort Lauderdale's African-American Research Library and Cultural Center soared into reality as a sparkling two-story, $14-million repository of history and heritage of African, African-American, and Caribbean cultures, with historic books, papers, and art, much of it pertaining to the African Diaspora. There's a 300-seat auditorium, a storytime area, and 5,000 square feet of gallery space for permanent and traveling exhibits. African symbols, similar to ones on the historic Adinkra cloth, appear as part of the decor. Adinkra, an Akan word that means "to say good-bye," is mostly associated with Asante people of Ghana who developed the art of Adinkra printing around the 19th century.

For Samuel F. Morrison, who retired in 2003 as Broward County Library Director, the center's opening has represented a culmination of his dream, a bold vision to create a worthy showcase reflecting African-American heritage. Broward County government agreed to ante up $5 million for the 60,000-square-foot center, and Morrison raised the rest.

Of the three African-American public research facilities in the country, Fort Lauderdale's is the only one that includes a focus on the Caribbean. (The others are New York's Schomburg Center for Research in Black Culture and Atlanta's Auburn Avenue Research Library.) Among the center's offerings is the Alex Haley Collection, including eight of the late author's unfinished manuscripts. Other

components range from Fisk University research of slave narratives to the Frederic Gomes Cassidy collection of books on Jamaica and the Caribbean.

And there's the collection of Dorothy Porter Wesley—in some observers' eyes the greatest of the black bibliophiles. Her collection includes about 500 inscribed and autographed books— some date to 1836—with personal narratives, biographies, histories, fiction, bibliographies, and reference works. Wesley's daughter, Constance Porter Uzelac, refers to "Mama's stuff," noting that "it's not just books and manuscripts . . .what's interesting is the associations she had with the authors and the people." Wesley was known for going to auctions or the homes of the recently deceased to make sure nothing of value was thrown away. Her daughter recalls "she'd get to the house before the body was cold," heading straight to attics and basements to retrieve bits and scraps of history.

Passionate about his dream, Morrison is also adamant about the library's widespread appeal, noting that "these pieces provide glimpses [into] the hearts and minds of people who have made a difference in the lives of not only people of color and African culture, but people of many colors and cultures."

— Lynne Helm

ups, electricity ↩ 232 paved, level sites ✉ *3055 Burris Rd.* ☎ *954/587–0101* 🖷 *954/587–9512* ☰ *AE, D, MC, V* ☉ *Year-round.*

🐾 **Yacht Haven Park and Marina.** Along the New River, this park is pet-friendly for animals up to 40 pounds. There are scheduled activities in the recreation hall during the winter season. A heated pool and spa and fishing are available on the property. Depending on location, daily rates for two range from $35 to $49 in winter, $28 to $45 in summer, with $5 for each extra person, plus tax. Weekly and monthly rates are also available. Reservations are recommended. ⚒ *Laundry facilities, dump station, showers ↩ 250 paved RV sites, some waterfront* ✉ *2323 State Rd. 84* ☎ *954/583–2322 or 800/581–2322* ⊕ *www.yachthavenpark. com* ☰ *AE, D, MC, V* ☉ *Year-round.*

Nightlife & the Arts

For the most complete weekly listing of events, read the Showtime! entertainment section and events calendar in the Friday *South Florida Sun-Sentinel.* Weekend, in the Friday Broward edition of the *Miami Herald,* also lists area happenings. The weekly *City Link* is principally an entertainment and dining paper with an "underground" look. *New Times* is a free alternative weekly circulating a Broward–Palm Beach County edition. *East Sider* is another free weekly entertainment guide. A 24-hour **Arts & Entertainment Hotline** (☎ 954/357–5700) has updates on attractions and events. Get tickets at individual box offices and through **Ticketmaster** (☎ 954/523–3309); there's a service charge.

The Arts

Broward Center for the Performing Arts (✉ 201 S.W. 5th Ave. ☎ 954/462–0222) is the waterfront centerpiece of Fort Lauderdale's arts district. More than 500 events unfold annually at the 2,700-seat architectural masterpiece, including Broadway-style musicals, plays, dance, symphony and opera, rock, film, lectures, comedy, and children's theater.

Nightlife

BARS & LOUNGES **Café Iguana** (✉ Beach Pl., 17 S. Fort Lauderdale Beach Blvd. ☎ 954/763–7222) has a nightly DJ to keep the dance floor hopping. At the **Interlude Bar & Cabaret** (✉ 4 W. Las Olas Blvd. ☎ 954/779–3339) you can actually hear what companions have to say. **Howl at the Moon Saloon** (✉ Beach Pl., 17 S. Fort Lauderdale Beach Blvd. ☎ 954/522–5054) has dueling piano players and sing-alongs nightly. **Maguire's Hill 16** (✉ 535 N. Andrews Ave. ☎ 954/764–4453) highlights excellent bands in classic Irish-pub surroundings. **O'Hara's Jazz Café** (✉ 722 E. Las Olas Blvd. ☎ 954/524–1764) belts out the live jazz, blues, R&B, and funk nightly. Its packed crowd spills onto this prettiest of downtown streets. **Rush Street** (✉ 220 S.W. 2nd St. ☎ 954/522–6900) is where hipsters line up around the corner to gain access to one of the best martini bar–dance clubs in Broward County. **Side Bar** (✉ 210 S.W. 2nd St. ☎ 954/524–1818) has a contemporary industrial feel and a polished professional crowd. **Tarpon Bend** (✉ 200 S.W. 2nd St. ☎ 954/523–3233) specialties—food, fishing gear and bait, and live bands playing current covers—draw a casual, beer-drinking crowd. **Tavern 213** (✉ 213 S.W. 2nd St. ☎ 954/463–6213) is a small, no-frills club where cover bands do classic rock nightly. **Voodoo Lounge** (⊠ 111 S.W. 2nd Ave. ☎ 954/522–0733) plays the latest in club music inside the nightclub and high hip-hop on the elegant outside deck. The scene here doesn't start until close to midnight.

Sports & the Outdoors
Baseball
From mid-February to the end of March the **Baltimore Orioles** (⊠ Fort Lauderdale Stadium, 1301 N.W. 55th St. ☎ 954/776–1921) are in spring training.

Biking
Among the most popular routes are Route A1A and Bayview Drive, especially in early morning before traffic builds, and a 7-mi bike path that parallels State Road 84 and the New River and leads to Markham Park, which has mountain-bike trails.

Fishing
If you're interested in a saltwater charter, check out the **Radisson Bahia Mar Beach Resort** (⊠ 801 Seabreeze Blvd. ☎ 954/627–6357). Both sportfishing and drift-fishing bookings can be arranged.

Golf
Ten miles from Fort Lauderdale in Dade County, Robert Trent Jones designed the two 18-hole courses at **Turnberry Isle Resort & Club** (⊠ 19999 W. Country Club Dr., Aventura ☎ 305/933–6929 or 800/327–7028 ⊕ www.turnberryisle.com), green fee: $95/$130.

Scuba Diving & Snorkeling
Lauderdale Diver (⊠ 1334 S.E. 17th St. Causeway ☎ 954/467–2822 or 800/654–2073), which is PADI-affiliated, arranges dive charters throughout the county. Dive trips typically last four hours. Nonpackage reef trips are open to divers for $45; scuba gear is extra.

Pro Dive (⊠ 515 Seabreeze Blvd. ☎ 954/761–3413 or 800/776–3483), a PADI five-star facility, is the area's oldest diving operation and offers packages with Radisson Bahia Mar Beach Resort, where its 60-foot boat departs. Snorkelers can go out for $29 on a two-hour snorkeling trip, which includes equipment. Scuba divers pay $45 using their own gear or $84 with all rentals included.

Tennis
With 21 courts, 18 of them lighted clay courts, the **Jimmy Evert Tennis Center at Holiday Park** is Fort Lauderdale's largest public tennis facility. Chris Evert learned the sport here under the watchful eye of her father, Jimmy, who retired after 37 years as the center's tennis professional. ⊠ *701 N.E. 12th Ave.* ☎ *954/828–5378* 🎫 *$5 per person per hr* ⊙ *Weekdays 8 AM–9 PM, weekends 8–6.*

Shopping

Malls
Just north of Las Olas Boulevard on Route A1A is the happening **Beach Place** (⊠ 17 S. Fort Lauderdale Beach Blvd. [A1A]). Browse through shops, have lunch or dinner at restaurants ranging from casual Caribbean

to elegant American, or carouse at a selection of nightspots—all open late. Eateries on the lower level tend toward the upscale, whereas on the upper level, with a superior ocean view, prices are lower. Just west of the Intracoastal Waterway, the split-level **Galleria Mall** (⌧ 2414 E. Sunrise Blvd.) has more than 1 million square feet of retail space, anchored by Neiman Marcus, Dillard's, Macy's, and Saks Fifth Avenue, with 150 specialty shops for anything from cookware to sportswear and fine jewelry. Restaurants include the Capital Grille, Blue Martini, Red Star Tavern, Mama Sbarros, and Seasons 52 (where every item on the menu is under 475 calories and there are some 70 wines by the glass) at this renovated mall, open 10 to 9 Monday through Saturday, and noon to 5:30 Sunday. The **Swap Shop** (⌧ 3291 W. Sunrise Blvd.) is the South's largest flea market, with 2,000 vendors open daily. While exploring this indoor-outdoor entertainment and shopping complex, enjoy the carousel or the free daily circus, or stick around for Swap Shop drive-in movies.

Shopping Districts

When you're downtown, check out the **Las Olas Riverfront** (⌧ 1 block west of Andrews Ave. on the New River), a shopping, dining, and entertainment complex. **Vogue Italia** (⌧ Las Olas Riverfront, 300 S.W. 1st Ave. ☎ 954/527–4568) is packed with trendy fashions by D&G, Ferré, Versus, Moschino, and Iceberg, among others, at wholesale prices.

If only for a stroll and some window-shopping, don't miss **Las Olas Boulevard** (⌧ 1 block off New River east of Andrews Ave.). The city's best boutiques plus top restaurants and art galleries line a beautifully landscaped street. **American Soul** (⌧ 810 E. Las Olas Blvd. ☎ 954/462–4224) carries menswear from suits to socks, along with leather goods and gifts. **Casa Chameleon** (⌧ 619 E. Las Olas Blvd. ☎ 954/763–2543) has antiques, linens, and beautiful things to top your table. The sweet smell of waffle cones lures pedestrians to **Kilwin's of Las Olas** (⌧ 809 E. Las Olas Blvd. ☎ 954/523–8338), an old-fashioned confectionery that also sells hand-paddled fudge and scoops of homemade ice cream. **Lily Pulitzer by Lauderdale Lifestyle** (⌧ 819 E. Las Olas Blvd. ☎ 954/524–5459) specializes in the South Florida dress requisite—clothing and accessories in Lily Pulitzer's signature tropical colors and prints. **Giorgio** (⌧ 825 E. Las Olas Blvd. ☎ 954/522–2479) focuses on sleek shoes, handbags, and belts. **Seldom Seen** (⌧ 817 E. Las Olas Blvd. ☎ 954/764–5590) is a gallery of contemporary and folk art including furniture, jewelry, ceramics, sculpture, and blown glass. **Zola Keller** (⌧ 818 E. Las Olas Blvd. ☎ 954/462–3222) sells special-occasion dresses—cocktail dresses, evening gowns, bridal apparel, and, yes, Miss Florida and Mrs. America pageant dresses.

Side Trips

The Western Suburbs & Beyond

West of Fort Lauderdale is an ever-growing mass of suburbia, with most of the city's golf courses as well as attractions and malls. As you head west, the terrain takes on more characteristics of the Everglades, and you'll occasionally see an alligator sunning on a canal bank. No

SWAP 'TIL YOU DROP

JUST WHEN YOU THOUGHT IT WAS SAFE TO HEAD FOR THE BEACH, the siren's song of bargain-shopping draws you inland to a sprawling, sun-baked patch of land where you can park free, get in free, browse free, and (depending on your negotiation skills) load up with eclectic acquisitions or plain swell stuff for darned-near free.

From Barbie dolls to slightly used miter saws and tubes of off-brand toothpaste, here's a place where you can feel free to squeeze nickels until the buffalos moan. Fort Lauderdale's Swap Shop—among Florida's largest tourist draws long before the arrival of roller-coaster economics—is a 180,000-square-foot shopping-entertainment complex on 88 acres that makes it possible to find a Carly Simon Hotcakes album for a dime, apparel items for 10 cents each (make that a dozen for a dollar), workpants for $5, or 30 sticks of hand-dipped mango incense for $2. Intangible rewards? Psychic readings are $5, and it's $15 for 15 minutes of bliss at the Chinese Backrub Booth, near a stall where you can get tailoring and alterations done while you wait, which is near a place to get palm trees put on your nails. Value-added are a small midway with a Ferris wheel, a giant video arcade, and eateries where aromas are reminiscent of Caribbean food stands. You can also hang around past dusk to catch flicks at the 13-screen Swap Shop Drive-In. Open 365 days, rain or shine, the Swap Shop has elevators and wheelchair-accessible ramps, and plenty of benches.

Established in 1963 by Betty and Preston Henn, the latter a forever-in-faded-blue-jeans Broward power broker, Fort Lauderdale Swap Shop stems from what originally was known as the Thunderbird, one of America's then-ubiquitous drive-in theaters. By 1966, Henn started farming out his land as a weekend flea market, patterned after what he'd spotted in California. As drive-ins went bust across the nation, the Thunderbird held on, propped up by Swap Shop revenues. By 1979, Henn had put up a building as an open-air food court surrounded by vendors hawking Wednesday through Saturday. In 1988 he walled it in, adding air-conditioning and a stage where local bands jammed at no charge. Next came the arrival of the Hanneford Family Circus, still appearing several times daily. In 1990 singer Ronnie Milsap kicked off a free-concert tradition. And the rest, as they say, is bargain-hunter, drive-in-movie-aficionado history.

Tri-Rail runs Swap Shop shuttles on Saturday from points in Broward, Palm Beach, and Dade counties, and some hotels arrange transportation. Fort Lauderdale Swap Shop grounds are between I–95 and Florida's Turnpike at 3291 E. Sunrise Blvd., 954/791–SWAP.

— Lynne Helm

matter how dedicated developers are to building over this area, the Everglades keeps asserting itself. Waterbirds, fish, and other creatures populate canals and lakes throughout the western areas.

As many as 80 butterfly species from South and Central America, the Philippines, Malaysia, Taiwan, and other Asian nations are typically found
⑭ within **Butterfly World**, a 3-acre site inside Tradewinds Park. A screened aviary called North American Butterflies is reserved for native species. The Tropical Rain Forest Aviary is a 30-foot-high construction, with observation decks, waterfalls, ponds, and tunnels where thousands of colorful butterflies flutter about. ⊠ *3600 W. Sample Rd., Coconut Creek* ☎ *954/977–4400* ⊕ *www.butterflyworld.com* ⌧ *$17.95* ☉ *Mon.–Sat. 9–5, Sun. 1–5.*

⑮ The 30-acre **Everglades Holiday Park** provides an excellent glimpse of the Everglades. Take an airboat tour, look at an 18th-century-style Native American village, or watch an alligator-wrestling show. A souvenir shop, TJ's Grill, a convenience store, and a campground with RV hookups ($22 per night) and tent sites ($7 nightly) are also here. ⊠ *21940 Griffin Rd.* ☎ *954/434–8111* ⊕ *www.evergladesholidaypark. com* ⌧ *Free, airboat tour $18* ☉ *Daily 9–5.*

⑯ To understand and enjoy the Everglades, take an airboat ride at **Sawgrass Recreation Park.** You'll see all sorts of plants and wildlife, from birds and alligators to turtles, snakes, and fish. Included in the entrance fee along with the airboat ride is admission to an Everglades nature exhibit, a native Seminole village, and exhibits about alligators, other reptiles, and birds of prey. A souvenir and gift shop, food service, and an RV park with hook-ups are also at the park. ⊠ *U.S. 27 north of I–595* ☎ *954/ 426–2474* ⊕ *www.evergladestours.com* ⌧ *$19.50* ☉ *Weekdays 7–6, weekends 6–6; airboat rides daily 9–5.*

Some distance from Fort Lauderdale's tranquil beaches, but worth the
⑰ one-hour drive, is the **Big Cypress Seminole Reservation** and its two very
☺ different attractions. At the **Billie Swamp Safari,** experience the majesty of the Everglades firsthand. Daily tours of the wetlands and hammocks, where wildlife abounds, yield sightings of deer, water buffalo, bison, wild hogs, hawks, eagles, alligators, and occasionally the rare Florida panther. Animal and reptile shows are also offered. Eco-heritage tours are provided aboard motorized swamp buggies, and airboat rides are available, too. On the property is Swamp Water Café, which serves Seminole foods. ⊠ *19 mi north of I–75 Exit 49* ☎ *863/983–6101 or 800/ 949–6101* ⊕ *www.seminoletribe.com* ⌧ *Free to visit reservation; combined ecotour, show, airboat ride $40* ☉ *Daily 8–5.*

Not far from the Billie Swamp Safari is the **Ah-Tha-Thi-Ki Museum,** whose name means "a place to learn, a place to remember." It is just that. The museum documents and honors the culture and tradition of the Seminole Tribe of Florida through artifacts, exhibits and reenactments of rituals and ceremonies. The site includes a living-history Seminole village, nature trails, and a boardwalk through a cypress swamp. ⊠ *17 mi north of I–75 Exit 49* ☎ *863/902–1113* ⊕ *www.seminoletribe. com* ⌧ *$6* ☉ *Tues.–Sun. 9–5.*

WHERE TO
STAY & EAT
¢–$$$

✕ **Wolfgang Puck Café.** Just in case you lack an excuse, here's another reason to go to the mall. Amid your shopping bags, you'll be treated to excellent service and quality dishes. Wolfgang Puck's crispy pizzas have such tasty toppings as spicy shrimp with peppers, vegetable combinations, and smoked salmon. Also worthy are the roasted pumpkin ravioli, rosemary chicken, and meat loaf with mashed potatoes and mushroom gravy. ⊠ *Sawgrass Mills, 2610 Sawgrass Mills Circle, Sunrise* ☎ *954/846–8668* ⊕ *www.wolfgangpuck.com* ▤ *AE, D, MC, V.*

$–$$$$

🏨 **Bonaventure Resort & Spa.** This resort draws convention crowds with its luxurious amenities, which include a full-service spa and affiliation with two championship golf courses. Spacious guest rooms and suites are done in tropical colors with rattan seating, and most overlook a golf course. Oversize baths have dressing areas. The resort offers separate spa and golf packages. Golf and tennis facilities adjacent to the hotel are independent of the resort. Green fee: east course $95/$99; west course, $85/$99. ⊠ *250 Racquet Club Rd., Westin 33326* ☎ *954/389–3300* 🖷 *954/384–1416* ⊕ *www.wyndham.com* ⬤ *400 rooms, 96 suites* ⬧ *2 restaurants, 2 18-hole golf courses, 16 tennis courts, 5 pools, gym, hair salon, spa, 2 bars, convention center* ▤ *AE, D, DC, MC, V.*

$$–$$$

🏨 **Coral Springs Marriott Hotel, Golf Club and Convention Center.** Formerly a Radisson property, this resort is adjacent to the Tournament Players Club golf course in Heron Bay. Its perch near the Sawgrass Expressway also makes it convenient to area attractions. Spacious, updated rooms are furnished with oak and cherrywood. There's an outdoor terrace and a game room. ⊠ *11775 Heron Bay Blvd., Coral Springs 33076* ☎ *954/753–5598* 🖷 *954/753–2888* ⊕ *www.marriott.com* ⬤ *224 rooms, 7 suites* ⬧ *Restaurant, in-room data ports, golf course, pool, gym, sauna, bar* ▤ *AE, D, MC, V.*

SPORTS & THE
OUTDOORS

Fishing. The marina at **Everglades Holiday Park** (⊠ 21940 Griffin Rd. ☎ 954/434–8111) caters to freshwater fishing. For $72.50 for five hours, rent a 14-foot johnboat (with a 9.9-horsepower Yamaha outboard) that carries up to four people. A rod and reel rent for $10 a day with a refundable $20 deposit; bait is extra. For two people, a fishing guide for a half day (four hours) is $200; for a full day (eight hours), $275. A third person adds $35 for a half day, $70 for a full day. Also buy a freshwater fishing license (mandatory) here; a seven-day nonresident license is $17. At **Sawgrass Recreation Park** (⊠ U.S. 27 and I–75 ☎ 954/426–2474) you can rent boats, get fishing licenses, and buy live bait.

Golf. Functioning like a golf concierge, **Next Day Golf** (☎ 954/772–2582) provides no-fee tee-time booking at both public courses and private ones normally members-only—a big advantage for golfers in summer. Bookings are limited at private courses during the busy winter months. Also offered are last-minute discount tee times (call 12 hours in advance).

Bonaventure Country Club (⊠ 200 Bonaventure Blvd. ☎ 954/389–2100) has 36 holes. Green fee: west course, $29/$49; east course, $34/$54. **Colony West Country Club** (⊠ 6800 N.W. 88th Ave. [Pine Island Rd.], Tamarac ☎ 954/726–8430) offers play on 36 holes, green fee: $15.50/$95. Just west of Florida's Turnpike, the **Inverrary Country Club** (⊠ 3840 Inverrary Blvd., Lauderhill ☎ 954/733–7550) has two 18-hole championship courses and an 18-hole executive course. Green fee: $69/$100. **Jacaranda Golf Club** (⊠ 9200 W. Broward Blvd., Plantation ☎ 954/472–5836) has 36 holes to play. Green fee: $29/$99. **Tournament Players Club at Heron Bay** (⊠ 11801 Heron Bay Blvd., Coral Springs ☎ 954/796–2000 or 800/511–6616) has a public 18-hole course, green fee: $41/$150.

Ice Hockey. Office Depot Center (formerly the National Car Rental Center) is the home of the National Hockey League's **Florida Panthers** (⊠ 2555 N.W. 137th Way [Panther Pkwy.], Sunrise ☎ 954/835–8326).

SHOPPING   Broward's shopping extravaganza, **Fashion Mall at Plantation** (⊠ 321 N. University Dr., north of Broward Blvd., Plantation), is a jewel of a mall. The three-level complex includes Macy's, a Sheraton Suites Hotel, and more than 100 specialty shops. Apart from a diverse food court, there's Brasserie Max for fancier dining. Travel-industry surveys reveal that shopping is vacationers' number one activity. With 26 million visitors annually, **Sawgrass Mills** (⊠ 12801 W. Sunrise Blvd., at Flamingo Rd., Sunrise), 10 mi west of downtown Fort Lauderdale, proves the point, ranking as the second-biggest tourist attraction in Florida, behind Disney. The complex is alligator-shaped, and walking every nook and cranny is about a 2 mi jaunt. There are 11,000 self-parking spaces, valet parking, and two information centers. More than 400 shops—many of them manufacturer's outlets, retail outlets, and name-brand discounters—include Last Call from Neiman Marcus, Nautica, Hugo Boss, Puma, Donna Karan, Liz Claiborne, Off 5th Saks Fifth Avenue, Kenneth Cole, and Ron Jon Surf Shop. At the Oasis, restaurants such as Hard Rock Cafe, Legal Sea Foods, Wolfgang Puck Express, Rainforest Cafe, and others are joined by entertainment venues Regal 23 Cinemas, GameWorks and the socko new Wannado City, a $40-million indoor recreation enterprise that bills itself as the first interactive empowerment environment for kids ages 4 to 11 in the United States. While parents shop, kids can role-play as firefighters, reporters, doctors, chefs, and archeologists, among hundreds of occupations. There's even a special monetary system for "Kidizens" of this Wannado community.

NORTH ON SCENIC A1A

North of Fort Lauderdale's Birch Recreation Area, Route A1A edges away from the beach through a stretch known as the Galt Ocean Mile, and a succession of ocean-side communities lines up against the sea. Traffic can line up, too, as it passes through a changing pattern of beach-blocking high-rises and modest family vacation towns and back again. Here and there a scenic lighthouse or park dots the landscape, and other attractions and recreational activities are found inland.

Lauderdale-by-the-Sea

18 *5 mi north of Fort Lauderdale.*

Just north of Fort Lauderdale's northern boundary, this low-rise family resort town has a tradition of digging in its heels at the thought of multiple-story high-rises. The result is choice shoreline access that's rapidly disappearing in similar communities, and the locals here take delight in making things even better for beachgoers, adding such amenities as showers and bike racks. Dedicated to pioneers Marie White and her late husband Stanley, who settled in when roads were of dirt with little traffic, a beach access portal at the intersection of El Mar Drive and Pal Avenue is one of five (also including Hibiscus, Datura, Washingtonia, and Pine avenues). Enjoy driving along lawn-divided El Mar Drive, lined with garden-style motels. Getting along without a car in Lauderdale-by-the-Sea is easy—it's only 3 mi long, and restaurants and shops are near hotels and the beach. Where Commercial Boulevard meets the ocean, **Anglin's Fishing Pier** (being shored up by new owners after storm damage) stretches 875 feet into the Atlantic. Fish, stop at any of the restaurants clustered around the seafront plaza, or just soak up the scene.

Where to Stay & Eat

$–$$$$ ✕ **Sea Watch.** For more than 25 years this nautical-themed restaurant on the beach has been packed, during lunch and dinner. Among the appetizers are oysters Rockefeller, gulf shrimp, clams casino, and Bahamian conch fritters; daily entrées might include oat-crusted sautéed yellowtail snapper with roasted red bell pepper sauce and basil, or charbroiled swordfish or dolphin fillet marinated with soy sauce, garlic, black pepper, and lemon juice. Try the crème brûlée or the strawberries Romanoff. ✉ *6002 N. Ocean Blvd. (Rte. A1A), Fort Lauderdale* 🕿 *954/ 781–2200* 🖃 *AE, MC, V.*

$–$$$ ✕ **Aruba Beach Café.** This is your best bet at the pier. A big beachside barn of a place—very casual, always crowded, always fun—it serves big portions of Caribbean conch chowder and a Key West soup loaded with shrimp, calamari, and oysters, plus fresh tropical salads, burgers, sandwiches, and seafood. A band performs daily. ✉ *1 E. Commercial Blvd.* 🕿 *954/776–0001* 🖃 *AE, D, DC, MC, V.*

$$–$$$$ ▦ **Tropic Seas Resort Motel.** It's only a block off A1A, but it's a million-dollar location—directly on the beach and two blocks from municipal tennis courts. Built in the 1950s, units are plain but clean and comfortable, with tropical rattan furniture and ceiling fans. Muffins and coffee are served daily. ✉ *4616 El Mar Dr., 33308* 🕿 *954/772–2555 or 800/952–9581* 🖶 *954/771–5711* ⊕ *www.tropicseasresort.com* ⇝ *16 rooms, including 6 efficiencies, 7 apartments* ♨ *Pool, beach* 🖃 *AE, D, DC, MC, V.*

$–$$$$ ▦ **Sea Lord Hotel & Suites.** You won't need to wonder "are we there yet" since Sea Lord is spelled out in huge letters on this attractive oceanside building, which is on a stretch of private beach. Enjoy a complimentary Continental breakfast by the pool overlooking the ocean. Efficiencies and one- and two-bedroom units all have coffeemakers and refrigerators, and some have full kitchens. The staff prides itself on creating a warm, hospitable environment. Depending on the time of year, market conditions, and area events like the Super Bowl, there can be four-night or longer minimum stays on some rooms. ✉ *4140 El Mar Dr., 33308* 🕿 *954/776–1505 or 800/344–4451* 🖶 *954/776–1505* ⊕ *www.sealord. com* ⇝ *48 rooms* ♨ *Some kitchens, pool, beach, laundry facilities* 🖃 *AE, D, MC, V* ⊠ *CP.*

$$–$$$ ▦ **A Little Inn by the Sea.** Innkeeper Uli Brandt and his family maintain tropical charm at this inn, which caters to an international clientele—French, German, and English are spoken here. All rooms have bamboo-and-rat-

tan furniture and nice views from private balconies, many of which face the beach. ☒ *4546 El Mar Dr., 33308* ☎ *954/772–2450 or 800/492–0311* 🖨 *954/938–9354* ⊕ *www.alittleinn.com* ➾ *10 rooms, 7 suites, 12 efficiencies* ♦ *Pool, beach, bicycles* ☰ *AE, D, DC, MC, V* ℃ *BP.*

¢–$$ 🏨 **Blue Seas Courtyard.** Innkeeper Cristie Furth, with her husband, Marc, runs this small one- and two-story motel in a quiet resort area across from the beach. Lattice fencing, fountains, and gardens of cactus and impatiens provide privacy around the brick patio and pool. Guest quarters have a Mexican hacienda look, with hand-painted and stenciled furnishings and terra-cotta tiles. ☒ *4525 El Mar Dr., 33308* ☎ *954/772–3336* 🖨 *954/772–6337* ⊕ *www.blueseascourtyard.com* ➾ *12 rooms* ♦ *Kitchens, pool, laundry facilities* ☰ *MC, V.*

¢–$$ 🏨 **Great Escape Motel.** For comfortable accommodations amid palms and other tropical plants in a poolside courtyard, this could be your great—and economical—escape. Among the units are four hotel rooms, five efficiencies, and two one-bedroom apartments. ☒ *4620 N. Ocean Dr., 33308* ☎ *954/772–1002* 🖨 *954/772–6488* ⊕ *www.greatescapemotel. com* ➾ *11 units* ♦ *Pool, laundry facilities* ☰ *AE, MC, V.*

¢–$$ 🏨 **High Noon Beach Resort.** Flanked by the Nautilus Resort to the north and the Sea Foam Resort to the south, High Noon plays the central role for this resort trio on the beach, where you'll find a comfortable place to relax morning, high noon or night. Accommodations, either poolside or oceanfront, range from rooms to efficiency apartments with kitchens, or apartments with separate bedrooms and one or two baths. Wicker furnishings and a color scheme of sea foam, sage, and beiges prevail at High Noon; Sea Foam rooms have terra-cotta tile, while High Noon and Nautilus rooms have beige tile. ☒ *4424 El Mar Dr., 33308* ☎ *954/776–1121 or 800/382–1265* 🖨 *954/776–1124* ➾ *40 rooms* ♦ *Some kitchens, some microwaves, some refrigerators, pool, beach* ☰ *AE, D, DC, MC, V.*

¢–$$ 🏨 **Villa Orleans.** With just a touch of New Orleans architecture, this beach-area property rests behind an inviting pool and well-groomed grounds. Rooms are spacious. ☒ *4513 N. Ocean Dr., 33308* ☎ *888/301–2363* 🖨🖨 *954/491–2363* ⊕ *www.villaorleans.com* ➾ *12 rooms* ♦ *Pool, laundry facilities* ☰ *AE, MC, V.*

¢ 🏨 **Mardi Gras Motel.** You'll find renovated rooms, a new pool, new kitchens, and new owner-management, but what remains steadfast is a place within the area's affordable small-property lineup. The owner's wife speaks Spanish. ☒ *4312 Ocean Dr., 33308* ☎ *954/776–4566* 🖨 *954/772–8929* ⊕ *www.mardigrasmotel.com* ➾ *16 rooms* ♦ *Cable TV, pool, laundry facilities, Internet* ☰ *AE, D, MC, V.*

¢ 🏨 **Rainbow by the Sea Resort.** There's no smoking at this family-oriented, owner-managed property. A carpeted sundeck equipped with loungers faces the ocean on top of the main building. ☒ *4553 El Mar Dr., 33308* ☎ *954/772–0514* 🖨 *954/772–6569* ➾ *30 rooms* ♦ *2 pools, laundry facilities; no smoking* ☰ *AE, MC, V.*

The Outdoors

★ **Anglin's Fishing Pier** (☎ *954/491–9403*), a long-time favorite for 24-hour fishing, has new ownership and is undergoing major renovation after sustaining storm damage in fall 2004.

Pompano Beach

⑲ *3 mi north of Lauderdale-by-the-Sea.*

As Route A1A enters this town directly north of Lauderdale-by-the-Sea, the high-rise scene resumes. Sportfishing is big in Pompano Beach, as its name implies, but there's more to beachside attractions than the popular Fisherman's Wharf. Behind a low coral-rock wall, Alsdorf Park extends north and south of the wharf along the road and beach.

Where to Stay & Eat

★ **$$$–$$$$** ✕ **Cafe Maxx.** New-wave epicurean dining had its South Florida start here in the early 1980s, and Cafe Maxx remains popular. Chef Oliver Saucy's menu changes nightly, showcasing tropical appeal with jumbo stone-crab claws with honey-lime mustard sauce and black bean and banana pepper chili with Florida avocado. Appetizers include caviar pie and crispy sweetbreads. Desserts such as Hawaiian vintage chocolate soufflé cake stay the tropical course. Select from 300 wines offered by the bottle, another 20 by the glass. ⊠ *2601 E. Atlantic Blvd.* ☎ *954/ 782–0606* ⊟ *AE, D, DC, MC, V* ☉ *No lunch.*

$$–$$$ 🏨 **Beachcomber Resort & Villas.** This property's beach location is central to most Broward County attractions and a mile from the Pompano Pier. Ocean views are everywhere, from the oversize guest-room balconies to dining rooms. Although there are also villas and penthouse suites atop the eight-story structure, standard rooms are spacious. The multilingual staff is attentive to guest requests. ⊠ *1200 S. Ocean Blvd., 33062* ☎ *954/941–7830 or 800/231–2423* 🖷 *954/942–7680* ⊕ *www. beachcomberhotel.com* 🛏 *134 rooms, 9 villas, 4 suites* ♨ *Restaurant, 2 pools, beach, shuffleboard, volleyball, bar* ⊟ *AE, D, DC, MC, V.*

$$–$$$ 🏨 **Fairfield Fairways of Palm-Aire Resort & Spa.** This time-share resort has studios and one-, two-, and four-bedroom apartments that are individually owned but share the same decor. Some units have whirlpool tubs and washers and dryers; kitchens range from partial to full, depending on the unit. Housekeeping is provided on a weekly basis, and more often for a charge. The spa and fitness complex has sauna, steam room, cardiovascular machines, weight equipment, fitness classes, and body treatments. Five championship golf courses at the Palm-Aire Country Club are just a chip shot away. Lunch and drinks are available at the Tiki Hut. ⊠ *2601 Palm-Aire Dr. N, 33069* ☎ *954/972–3300* 🖷 *954/968–2711* ⊕ *www.efairfield.com* 🛏 *298 units* ♨ *37 tennis courts, 3 pools, gym, hot tub, spa* ⊟ *AE, D, DC, MC, V.*

Sports & the Outdoors

FISHING **Pompano Pier** (☎ 954/943–1488) extends 1,080 feet into the Atlantic. Admission is $2.65; rod-and-reel rental is $5.25, plus $5 deposit and a driver's license.

For drift-fishing try **Fish City Pride** (⊠ Fish City Marina, 2621 N. Riverside Dr. ☎ 954/781–1211). Morning, afternoon, and evening trips cost $30 and include fishing gear and bait. Arrange for a saltwater charter boat through the **Hillsboro Inlet Marina** (⊠ 2629 N. Riverside Dr. ☎ 954/ 943–8222). The 10-boat fleet offers half-day charters for $450, including gear for up to six people.

GOLF **Crystal Lake South Course** (✉ 3800 Crystal Lake Dr. ☎ 954/943–2902) has 36 holes. Green fee: $21/$69. **Palm-Aire Country Club** (✉ 3701 Oaks Clubhouse Dr. ☎ 954/978–1737, 954/975–6244 tee line) has five golf courses, including an executive course with four extra practice holes. Green fee: $25/$45.

HORSE RACING **Pompano Park Harness Track,** Florida's only harness track, has world-class trotters and pacers during its October–August meet. The Top o' the Park restaurant overlooks the finish line. The track also has a poker room and afternoon and evening simulcast betting. ✉ 1800 S.W. 3rd St. ☎ 954/972–2000 ✏ Grandstand and clubhouse free ⊘ Racing Mon., Wed., Fri., and Sat. at 7:30 PM.

ICE-SKATING Skate at the **Glacier Ice and Snow Arena** during morning, afternoon, or evening sessions. ✉ 4601 N. Federal Hwy. ☎ 954/943–1437 ✏ Sessions $6, skate rental $2 ($3 for hockey skates) ⊘ Weekdays 9:20 AM–11:50 AM, Fri. also 8:30 PM–11 PM.

Shopping

Bargain hunters head to the **Festival Flea Market Mall** (✉ 2900 W. Sample Rd.), where more than 800 stores, booths, and kiosks sell new brand-name merchandise at a discount. For shopping diversions, there's also an arcade, beauty salon, farmers' market, and food court. The **Pompano Square Mall** (✉ 2001 N. Federal Hwy., at Copans Rd.) has 60 shops, three department stores, and a few places for food.

Lighthouse Point

⑳ 2 mi north of Pompano Beach.

The big attraction here is the view across Hillsboro Inlet to **Hillsboro Light,** the brightest lighthouse in the Southeast. Mariners have used this landmark for decades. When at sea you can see the light almost halfway to the Bahamas. Although the lighthouse is on private property inaccessible to the public, it's well worth a peek.

Where to Eat

★ $-$$$ ✕ **Cap's Place.** On an island that was once a bootlegger's haunt, this seafood spot is reached by launch and has served such luminaries as Winston Churchill, Franklin D. Roosevelt, and John F. Kennedy. Cap was Captain Theodore Knight, born in 1871, who, with partner-in-crime Al Hasis, floated a derelict barge to the area in the 1920s. Today the restaurant, built on the barge, is run by descendants of Hasis. Baked wahoo steaks are lightly glazed, flaky rolls are baked fresh several times a night, and tangy lime pie is a great finale. ✉ Cap's Dock, 2765 N.E. 28th Ct. ☎ 954/941–0418 ═ AE, MC, V ⊘ No lunch.

en route To the north, Route A1A traverses the so-called Hillsboro Mile (actually more than 2 mi), a millionaire's row of some of the most beautiful and expensive homes in Broward County. The road runs along a narrow strip of land between the Intracoastal Waterway and the ocean, with bougainvillea and oleander edging the way and yachts docked along both banks. In winter the traffic often creeps at a snail's pace as vacationers and retirees gawk at the views.

Deerfield Beach

㉑ *3½ mi north of Lighthouse Point.*

☺ The name **Quiet Waters Park** belies what's in store for kids here. Splash Adventure is a high-tech water-play system with slides and tunnels, among other activities. There's also cable waterskiing and boat rental on the park's lake. ⊠ *401 S. Powerline Rd.* ☎ *954/360–1315* 🖃 *Park $1 weekends, free weekdays; Splash Adventure $3* ☉ *Apr.–Sept., daily 8–7; Oct.–May, 8–6:30; Splash Adventure May–Labor Day, daily 9:30–5:30; Labor Day–Apr., Sat. and Sun 9:30–5:30.*

Deerfield Island Park, reached only by boat, is a group of coastal hammock islands. Officially designated an Urban Wilderness Area along the Intracoastal Waterway, it contains a mangrove swamp that provides a critical habitat for gopher tortoises, gray foxes, raccoons, and armadillos. Boat shuttles run on the hour Wednesday 10–noon and Sunday 10–3; space is limited, so call for reservations. Call also for special events. ⊠ *1720 Deerfield Island Park* ☎ *954/360–1320* 🖃 *Free.*

Where to Stay & Eat

★ **$$–$$$$** ✗ **Brooks.** This is one of the area's better restaurants, thanks to a French perfectionist at the helm, Bernard Perron. Meals are served in a series of rooms filled with replicas of old masters, cut glass, antiques, and floral wallpaper. Fresh ingredients go into distinctly Floridian dishes including sea bass. Rack of lamb and rib-eye steak are popular. For dessert, put in your order early in the meal for the chocolate soufflé. ⊠ *500 S. Federal Hwy.* ☎ *954/427–9302* 🖃 *AE, D, MC, V.*

★ **¢–$$$** ✗ **Whale's Rib.** For a casual, almost funky nautical experience near the beach, look no further. For more than 20 years the Williams family has served up fish specials along with whale fries—thinly sliced potatoes that look like hot potato chips. Lesser appetites can choose from a good selection of salads and fish sandwiches. Other favorites are specials from the raw bar, Ipswich clams, and a popular fish dip for starters. ⊠ *2031 N.E. 2nd St.* ☎ *954/421–8880* 🖃 *AE, MC, V.*

$$$–$$$$ 🏨 **Ocean Terrace Suites.** This four-story motel is in one of the quieter sections of North Broward, just south of the Palm Beach County line, across the narrow shore road from the beach. Large units—efficiencies and one- and three-bedroom apartments—all have kitchens worthy of roasting a turkey and big balconies overlooking the sea. The updated furniture is rattan, and colors vary from shore-washed to bright; pink-and-green pastels tint the rooms. ⊠ *2080 E. Hillsboro Blvd., 33441* ☎ *954/427–8400* 🖶 *954/427–0555* ⊕ *www.ocean-terracesuites.com* ⚲ *32 units* ⚙ *Kitchens, pool, laundry facilities* 🖃 *AE, D, DC, MC, V.*

$$–$$$$ 🏨 **Royal Flamingo Villas.** A small community of houselike villas built in the 1970s reaches from the Intracoastal Waterway to the ocean. The roomy and comfortable one- and two-bedroom villas are condominiums. All are so quiet that you hear only the soft click of the ceiling fans. If you don't need lavish public facilities, this is your upscale choice at a reasonable price. ⊠ *1225 Hillsboro Mile (Rte. A1A), Hillsboro Beach 33062* ☎ *954/427–0660 or 800/241–2477* 🖶 *954/427–6110* ⊕ *www.*

royalflamingovillas.com ⌗ *40 villas* ⌂ *Pool, beach, dock, boating, shuffleboard, laundry facilities* ▭ *D, MC, V.*

¢-$$ ▥ **Carriage House Resort Motel.** This tidy motel is one block from the ocean. The white, two-story colonial-style property with black shutters is actually two buildings connected by a second-story sundeck. Steady improvements have been made to the facility, including the addition of Bahama beds that feel and look like sofas. Kitchenettes are equipped with good-quality utensils. Rooms are quiet and have walk-in closets and room safes. ⊠ *250 S. Ocean Blvd., 33441* ☎ *954/427–7670* 🖷 *954/ 428–4790* ⊕ *www.carriagehouseresort.com* ⌗ *6 rooms, 14 efficiencies, 10 1-bedroom apartments* ⌂ *Pool, shuffleboard, laundry facilities* ▭ *AE, D, DC, MC, V.*

Sports & the Outdoors

FISHING The **Cove Marina** (⊠ Hillsboro Blvd. and the Intracoastal Waterway ☎ 954/360–9343) has a deep-sea charter fleet. In winter there are excellent runs of sailfish, kingfish, dolphinfish, and tuna. A half-day charter costs about $425 for six people. Enter the marina through the Cove Shopping Center.

GOLF Off Hillsboro Boulevard west of Interstate 95, **Deer Creek Golf Club** (⊠ 2801 Country Club Blvd. ☎ 954/421–5550) has 18 holes. Green fee: $50/$135; there are six fee structures depending on the season.

SCUBA DIVING One of the area's most popular dive operators, **Dixie Divers** (⊠ Cove Marina, Hillsboro Blvd. and the Intracoastal Waterway ☎ 954/420–0009) has morning and afternoon dives aboard the 48-foot *Lady-Go-Diver,* plus evening dives on weekends. Snorkelers and certified divers can explore the marine life of nearby reefs and shipwrecks. The cost is $45; ride-alongs are welcome for $35.

SOUTH BROWARD

From Hollywood's Broadwalk, a 27-foot-wide thoroughfare paralleling 2 mi of palm-fringed beach, to the western reaches of Old West–flavored Davie, this region has a personality all its own. South Broward's roots are in early Florida settlements. Thus far it has avoided some of the glitz and glamour of its neighbors to the north and south, and folks here like it that way. Still, there's plenty to see and do—excellent restaurants in every price range, world-class pari-mutuels, and a new focus on the arts.

Hollywood

㉒ *7 mi south of Fort Lauderdale.*

Hollywood is in the midst of a revival. The flamboyant Seminole Hard Rock Hotel & Casino, which not-so-quietly came onto the scene in May 2004, has arguably etched the town on the map for good, drawing local weekenders, architecture buffs, and gamblers to the area. But Hollywood's development doesn't end there: new shops, restaurants, and art galleries open at a persistent clip, and the city has spiffed up its Broadwalk, a wide pedestrian walkway along the beach, where rollerbladers are as common as visitors from the North. Trendy sidewalk cafés have opened, vying for space with mom-and-pop T-shirt shops. Downtown, along Harrison Street and Hollywood Boulevard, jazz clubs and still more fashionable restaurants draw young professionals to the scene. Design studios and art galleries are also abundant along these two streets. In 1921 Joseph W. Young, a California real-estate entrepreneur, began developing the community of Hollywood from the woody flatlands. It quickly became a major tourist magnet, with casino gambling and whatever else that made Florida hot. Reminders of the glory days of the Young era remain in places like Young Circle (the junction of U.S. 1 and Hollywood Boulevard) and the stately old homes on east Hollywood streets.

The **Art and Culture Center of Hollywood** is a visual and performing arts center with an art reference library, outdoor sculpture garden, and arts school. It's just east of Young Circle. ⊠ *1650 Harrison St.* ☎ *954/921–3274* ✉ *$5* ⊙ *Tues., Wed., Fri., and Sat. 10–5, Thurs. 10–8, Sun. 1–4.*

Fodor's Choice
★
With the Intracoastal Waterway to its west and the beach and ocean to the east, the 2.2-mi paved promenade known as the **Broadwalk** has been popular with pedestrians and cyclists since 1924. Expect to hear French spoken along this scenic stretch, especially in winter, since Hollywood Beach has been a favorite winter getaway for Québecois ever since Joseph Young hired French-Canadians to work here in the 1920s. Spanish and Portuguese conversations are also frequently heard on this walk.

Hollywood North Beach Park is at the north end of the Broadwalk. No high-rises overpower the scene and there's nothing hip or chic about the park. It's just a laid-back, old-fashioned place for enjoying the sun, sand, and sea. ⊠ *Rte. A1A and Sheridan St.* ☎ *954/926–2444* ✉ *Free; parking $4 until 2, $2 thereafter* ⊙ *Daily 8–6.*

Comprising 1,500 acres at the Intracoastal Waterway, **West Lake Park** is one of Florida's largest urban nature facilities. Rent a canoe, kayak, or boat with an electric motor (no fossil fuels are allowed in the park) or take the 40-minute environmental boat tour. Extensive boardwalks traverse mangroves, where endangered and threatened species abound. A 65-foot observation tower allows views of the entire park. More than $1 million in exhibits are on display at the **Anne Kolb Nature Center,** named after the late county commissioner who was a leading environmental advocate. The center's exhibit hall has 27 interactive displays, an ecology room, and a tri-level aquarium. ⊠ *1200 Sheridan St.* ☎ *954/926–2410* ✉ *Weekends $1, weekdays and holidays free; exhibit hall $1* ⊙ *Daily 9–5.*

At the edge of Hollywood lies **Seminole Native Village,** a reservation where you can pet a cougar, hold a baby alligator, and watch other wildlife demonstrations. The Seminole also sell their arts and crafts here. Across the street from the Seminole Native Village, **Hollywood Seminole Gaming** (⊠ 4150 N. State Rd. 7 ☎ 954/961–3220) is open 24/7 and has high-stakes bingo, high-stakes poker, and more than 1,000 gaming machines. ⊠ *3551 N. State Rd. 7* ☎ *954/961–4519* ✉ *Self-guided tour $5, guided tour including alligator wrestling and snake demonstrations $10* ⊙ *Daily 9–5.*

In addition to displaying a collection of artifacts from the Seminole and other tribes, Joe Dan and Virginia Osceola sell contemporary Native American arts and crafts at the **Anhinga Indian Trading Post.** It's ½ mi south of Seminole Native Village, at the northeast corner of U.S. 441 and Stirling Road, which technically puts it over the Fort Lauderdale border. ⊠ *5980 S. State Rd. 7, Fort Lauderdale* ☎ *954/581–0416* ☉ *Daily 9–5.*

Where to Stay & Eat

$$-$$$$ ✗ **Martha's.** Choose from two dining locations, both with impressive views of the Intracoastal Waterway: Martha's Tropical Grille, on the upper deck, is more informal but often booked for private parties. Martha's Supper Club, on the lower level, is dressier, and piano music accompanies dinner. Both floors offer similar menus, chiefly Florida seafood, including shrimp dipped in a piña colada batter, rolled in coconut, and panfried with orange mustard sauce, and snapper prepared 17 ways. Complimentary dock space is provided for boat arrivals. ⊠ *6024 N. Ocean Dr.* ☎ *954/923–5444* 🖃 *AE, D, DC, MC, V.*

$-$$$$ ✗ **Giorgio's Grill.** Good food and service are hallmarks of this 400-seat restaurant overlooking the Intracoastal Waterway. Seafood is a specialty, but you'll also find pasta and meat dishes. A great water view and friendly staff add to the experience. A surprisingly extensive wine list is reasonably priced. ⊠ *606 N. Ocean Dr.* ☎ *954/929–7030* 🖃 *AE, D, DC, MC, V.*

$$-$$$ ✗ **Las Brisas.** Next to the beach, this cozy bistro offers seating inside or out, and the food is Argentine with Italian flair. A small pot, filled with *chimichurri*—a paste made of oregano, parsley, olive oil, salt, garlic, and crushed pepper—for spreading on steaks, sits on each table. Grilled fish is a favorite, as are pork chops, chicken, and pasta entrées. Desserts include a flan like *mamacita* used to make, and a *dulce con leche* (sweet milk pudding). ⊠ *600 N. Surf Rd.* ☎ *954/923–1500* 🖃 *AE, D, DC, MC, V* ☉ *No lunch.*

$-$$ ✗ **Sushi Blues Café and Blue Monk Lounge.** Raw fish, burgers, and soul food complement the American roots music and vintage lamps at this hip (read: far from stodgy) Hollywood institution, open seven days from 11:30 AM until the wee hours. It's operated by husband-wife team Kenny Millions and Junko Maslak. Japanese chefs prepare conventional and macrobiotic-influenced dishes that range from sushi and rolls (California, tuna, and the Yozo roll, with snapper, flying-fish roe, asparagus, and Japanese mayonnaise) to steamed veggies with tofu and steamed snapper with miso sauce. Poached pears steamed in cabernet sauce and cappuccino custard are popular desserts. The Sushi Blues Band performs on many evenings. ⊠ *2009 Harrison St.* ☎ *954/929–9560* 🖃 *AE, MC, V.*

¢-$$ ✗ **Le Tub.** Formerly a Sunoco gas station, this place is now a quirky waterside saloon with a seeming affection for claw-foot bathtubs. Hand-painted tubs are everywhere—under ficus, sea grape, and palm trees. The eatery is favored by locals for affordable food: mostly shrimp, burgers, and barbecue. ⊠ *1100 N. Ocean Dr.* ☎ *954/921–9425* 🖃 *No credit cards.*

$$-$$$$ 🏨 **Seminole Hard Rock Hotel & Casino.** Springing up from the flatlands of western Hollywood, the Seminole Hard Rock Hotel & Casino is quickly evolving into a destination resort for area weekenders and out-of-towners. The 4½-acre pool complex is nothing short of a wow, where a rock mountain doubles as a backdrop to a 182-foot-long waterslide. A Lazy River circulating pool, waterfalls, hot tubs, and a shallow area with play features are capped by a nearby 22,000-square-foot spa. Partially em-

bracing this subtropical landscaping is a starkly white 12-story tower, whose rooms are equipped with such amenities as Tivoli stereos and ultra-luxe beds dressed in Egyptian cottons and European duvets. Dining options include the memorabilia-packed Hard Rock Cafe Hollywood, the Council Oak, with steak and seafood, and the 24-hour Blue Plate, which borders the casino action.

The facility is designed in a somewhat dizzying fashion so that the eateries, lounges, and elegant outlying lobby area form a peripheral road of sorts for the casino floor, where poker—the genuine, lovably trendy article—pulsates at 40 tables, to the delight of spectators. Also on hand are a couple thousand or so electronic gaming machines. A ballroom theater just off the casino hosts stage extravaganzas like *Singin' in the Rain,* and Hard Rock Live!, a 5,600-seat live performance venue, hosts touring bands, theater, championship boxing, and rodeo. Also on the property is Seminole Paradise, a retail, restaurant, and live-entertainment district. ⊠ *1 Seminole Way, 33314* ☎ *954/364–4171 or 800/937–0010* ⊕ *www.hardrock.com* ➷ *500 rooms, including 100 suites* ♨ *3 restaurants, minibars, in-room data ports, 18-hole golf course, 10 tennis courts, 3 pools, health club, 2 spas, marina, 2 bars, business services, convention center* ▭ *AE, DC, MC, V.*

★ **$$–$$$$** ▦ **The Westin Diplomat Resort & Spa.** Opened in 2002 on the site of the original 1950s hotel of the same name, the Diplomat is a grand 39-story, dual-tower property. The hotel has a lobby-atrium area with ceilings soaring to 60 feet. A signature of the resort is its 120-foot bridged lagoon pool, extending from the lobby to the ocean. A beach replenishment project is in the works to offset erosion. A Mediterranean-inspired spa offers fitness facilities and more than 20 luxury treatments. The Diplomat's country club, across the Intracoastal, has 60 rooms, golf, tennis, and spa. Guests have use of facilities at both properties; shuttle service is provided. ⊠ *1995 E. Hallandale Beach Blvd., 33309* ☎ *954/457–2000 or 800/327–1212* ⊕ *www.starwoodhotels.com* ➷ *900 rooms, 100 suites* ♨ *3 restaurants, minibars, in-room data ports, 18-hole golf course, 10 tennis courts, 3 pools, health club, 2 spas, marina, 2 bars, business services, convention center* ▭ *AE, DC, MC, V.*

$–$$$ ▦ **Greenbriar Beach Club.** In a neighborhood of Hollywood Beach known for its flowered streets, this oceanfront all-suite hotel retains its 1950s style outside, but inside the rooms have been renovated and include full kitchens. The staff is multilingual, and TVs have four Spanish and two French channels. On a 200-foot stretch of beach, the hotel bills itself as Florida's best-kept secret, and it just could be. ⊠ *1900 S. Surf Rd., 33019* ☎ *954/922–2606 or 800/861–4873* ⊟ *954/923–0897* ⊕ *www.greenbriarbc.com* ➷ *47 suites* ♨ *Pool, beach, volleyball, laundry facilities* ▭ *AE, D, MC, V.*

★ **$–$$$** ▦ **Manta Ray Inn.** Canadians Donna and Dwayne Boucher run this immaculate, affordable two-story inn on a beach, perfect for a low-key getaway. Dating from the 1940s, the inn offers casual, comfortable beachfront accommodations with amenities such as cable TV with VCR. Kitchens are equipped with pots, pans, and many appliances that make housekeeping convenient. One-bedroom apartments have marble shower stalls, and two-bedroom units also have tubs. ⊠ *1715 S. Surf*

Rd., 33019 ☎ *954/921–9666 or 800/255–0595* 🖷 *954/929–8220* ⊕ *www.mantarayinn.com* 🖙 *12 units* ⚲ *Beach* ▤ *AE, D, MC, V.*

¢–$$$ ▦ **Sea Downs.** Directly on the Broadwalk, this three-story lodging is a good choice for efficiency or apartment living (one-bedroom units can be joined to make two-bedroom apartments). All but two units have ocean views. Kitchens are fully equipped, and most units have tub-showers and closets. Housekeeping is provided once a week. In between, fresh towels are provided daily and sheets upon request, but you must make your own bed. ⊠ *2900 N. Surf Rd., 33019* ☎ *954/923–4968* 🖷 *954/923–8747* ⊕ *www.seadowns.com* 🖙 *6 efficiencies, 8 1-bedroom apartments* ⚲ *In-room data ports, pool, laundry facilities* ▤ *No credit cards.*

¢–$ ▦ **Driftwood on the Ocean.** Facing the beach at the secluded south end of Surf Road is this attractive late-1950s-era resort motel. The setting is what draws guests, but attention to maintenance and frequent refurbishing are what make it a value. Accommodations range from a studio to a deluxe two-bedroom, two-bath suite. Most units have a kitchen; all have balconies or terraces. ⊠ *2101 S. Surf Rd., 33019* ☎ *954/923–9528 or 800/944–3148* 🖷 *954/922–1062* ⊕ *www.driftwoodontheocean. com* 🖙 *7 rooms, 9 2-bedroom apartments, 13 1-bedroom apartments, 20 efficiencies* ⚲ *Some kitchens, pool, beach, bicycles, shuffleboard, laundry facilities* ▤ *AE, D, MC, V.*

Nightlife & the Arts

THE ARTS **Harrison Street Art and Design District** in downtown Hollywood has galleries that carry original artwork (eclectic paintings, sculpture, photography, and mixed media), Costa Rican collectibles, and African artifacts. Friday night the artists' studios, galleries, and shops stay open late while crowds meander along Hollywood Boulevard and Harrison Street. **Indaba** (⊠ 2029 Harrison St. ☎ 954/920–2029) celebrates African art with an extensive collection of masks, statues, cloth, baskets, and furniture. **Mosaica** (⊠ 2020 Hollywood Blvd. ☎ 954/923–7006) is a design studio with unique mosaic tile tables, mirrors, and art. The colorful home furnishings gallery, **Alliage** (⊠ 2035 Harrison St. ☎ 954/922–7017), has tables, wall consoles, and sculptures handcrafted from brushed aluminum and sand-blasted glass.

NIGHTLIFE Although downtown Hollywood has a small-town feel, it has an assortment of coffee bars, Internet cafés, sports bars, martini lounges, and dance clubs. The downtown area is known for its live jazz and blues venues. **O'Hara's Hollywood** (⊠ 1903 Hollywood Blvd. ☎ 954/925–2555) highlights top local jazz and blues talents six nights a week. Sushi café and wine bar **Sushi Blues** (⊠ 1836 Young Circle ☎ 954/929–9560) serves up live blues Friday and Saturday nights starting at 9. **Warehaus 57** (⊠ 1904 Hollywood Blvd. ☎ 954/926–6633) is where aspiring novelists and poets share their words with the café crowd.

Sports & the Outdoors

DOG RACING **Hollywood Greyhound Track** has live dog-racing action during its December–May season and simulcasting every day. Relax at the Dog House sports bar and grill. ⊠ *831 N. Federal Hwy., Hallandale* ☎ *954/924–3200* 🎫 *Grandstand $1, clubhouse $2, parking free* ⊙ *Racing nightly at 7:30, and Tues., Thurs., and Sat. at 12:30 PM.*

BOATING **Adventure World at the Landing** (✉ 3570 South Ocean Dr. ☎ 954/457–9575) provides Jet Ski, Air Cat and other boat rentals, and runs fishing trips as well as kayak and canoe expeditions through the mangroves and lagoons of local state parks. Motor scooter, Segway, and bicycle rentals are also available, and handy package deals allow you to try out combinations of water and land equipment over a five-hour period.

FISHING **Sea Leg's III** (✉ 5400 N. Ocean Dr. ☎ 954/923–2109) runs drift-fishing trips from 8 AM to 12:30 PM and 1:30 to 6 and bottom-fishing trips from 7 PM to midnight. Trips cost $30 ($35 on longer Friday-night adventures), with a $3 rod and reel rental, if needed.

GOLF The **Diplomat Country Club & Spa** (✉ 501 Diplomat Pkwy., Hallandale ☎ 954/457–2000) has 18 holes and a spa. Green fee: $65/$160. The course at **Emerald Hills** (✉ 4100 N. Hills Dr. ☎ 954/961–4000) has 18 holes. Green fee: $55/$145, depending on the season.

HORSE RACING **Gulfstream Park Race Track** is the winter home of some of the nation's top thoroughbreds, trainers, and jockeys. In addition to races, there are family days with attractions for kids and scheduled concerts with well-known performers. The season is capped by the $1 million Florida Derby, with Kentucky Derby hopefuls. Racing unfolds January through April. ✉ *901 S. Federal Hwy., Hallandale* ☎ *954/454–7000 or 800/771–8873* ⚑ *Grandstand $3, clubhouse $5* ☉ *Racing Wed.–Mon. at 1 and nightly simulcasting.*

Dania Beach

㉓ *3 mi north of Hollywood, 4 mi south of Fort Lauderdale.*

This town at the south edge of Fort Lauderdale is probably best known for its antiques dealers, but there are other attractions as well.

The once pine-dotted **John U. Lloyd Beach State Recreation Area** has lost significant shaded ambiance, thanks to government-driven efforts to pull out all but indigenous plantings. Disappointed park-goers are advised that, eventually, sea grape, gumbo limbo and other native plantings will fill the void. Meanwhile, hurricane damage has closed the jetty pier for fishing, and erosion has done a number on what remains of the beach. Nature trails and a marina remain, along with canoeing on Whiskey Creek. Despite setbacks, this is a prime spot to watch cruise ships enter and depart Port Everglades. ✉ *6503 N. Ocean Dr.* ☎ *954/923–2833* ⚑ *$5 per vehicle with up to 8 people* ☉ *Daily 8–sunset.*

★ **IGFA Fishing Hall of Fame and Museum** is a shrine to the sport. Near the Fort Lauderdale airport at Interstate 95 and Griffin Road, the center is the creation of the International Game Fishing Association. In addition to checking out the World Fishing Hall of Fame, a marina, and an extensive museum and research library, visit seven galleries with virtual-reality fishing and other interactive displays. And in the Catch Gallery, cast off via virtual reality and try to reel in a marlin, sailfish, trout, tarpon, or bass. ✉ *300 Gulfstream Way, Dania Beach* ☎ *954/922–4212* ⊕ *www.igfa.org* ⚑ *$6* ☉ *Daily 10–6.*

Where to Eat

¢–$ ✕ **Jaxson's Ice Cream Parlor Restaurant and Country Store.** Across from the Dania United Methodist Church, Jaxson's, for nearly 50 years, has churned out malts, shakes, and jumbo sundaes, plus sandwiches and salads, amid an antiquated license plate decor. Platters include a mile-long beef hot dog and a chicken parmigiana sandwich. Ice creams and toppings are prepared daily on premises. Owner Monroe Udell has trademarked the Kitchen Sink, reserved for parties of four or more for around $9 per person, with a small sink full of ice cream, topped by sparklers. Less ambitious appetites lean toward Jaxson's sampler (junior or senior), the praline pecan supreme or the banana skyscraper. Chocoholics can ponder the jug-o-fudge or chocolate suicide. ☒ *128 S. Federal Hwy.* ☎ *954/923–4445* ▭ *AE, D, MC, V.*

¢–$ ✕ **Tarks of Dania.** Started in 1966 as a small stand for clams, wings, and beer, Tarks hasn't changed much, with a counter and a few tables for neighbors and drop-ins to eat, drink, and rejuvenate. From Tarks' raw bar come topneck and littleneck clams along with raw oysters. From the fryer are clams (bellies or strips), oysters, scallops, shrimp, wings, and curly fries. For around $10 you can order a gator-tail dinner (gently marinated and deep fried) or a tasty conch salad. Nightly specials include Alaskan snow crab on Friday. Tarks markets its own bottles of "terminator" sauce, and there's a "Frequent Tarks Club" that allows you to accumulate points for special offers. ☒ *1317 S. Federal Hwy.* ☎ *954/925–8275* ▭ *AE, D, MC, V.*

Sports & the Outdoors

FISHING The 920-foot **Dania Pier** (☎ 954/927–0640) is open around the clock. Fishing is $3 (including parking), tackle rental is $6, bait is about $3, and spectators pay $1.

JAI ALAI **Dania Jai-Alai Palace** has one of the fastest ball games on the planet, scheduled year-round. Simulcast wagering from other tracks and a poker room are also available. ☒ *301 E. Dania Beach Blvd.* ☎ *954/920–1511* ▨ *$1.50, reserved seats $2–$7* ☉ *Games Tues. and Sat. at noon, Sun. at 1, nightly Tues.–Sat. at 7:15.*

MINIATURE GOLF **Boomers!** has action games for kids of all ages—go-kart and Naskart racing, miniature golf, batting cages, bumper boats, Lasertron, and a sky-coaster. ☒ *1801 N.W. 1st St.* ☎ *954/921–1411* ☉ *Sun.–Thurs. 10 AM–2 AM, Fri. and Sat. 10 AM–6 AM.*

ROLLER COASTER **Dania Beach Hurricane** roller coaster isn't the highest, fastest, or longest coaster in the world, but it's near the top in all those categories and it's the tallest wooden roller coaster south of Atlanta. This is a retro-feeling ride—a wooden coaster that creaks like an old staircase while you race along its 3,200 feet of track and plummet from a height of 100 feet at speeds of up to 55 mph. ☒ *1760 N.W. 1st St.* ☎ *954/921–7433* ▨ *$6.25* ☉ *Sun.–Thurs. 10 AM–11:30 PM, Fri. and Sat. 10 AM–2 AM.*

Shopping

More than 250 antiques dealers in **Dania Antique Row** buy and sell items from antique furniture to vintage knickknacks. You never know what you'll find here, but Depression-era glassware seems plentiful and shop owners are quite friendly. This two-square-block area is on Federal Highway (U.S. 1), ½ mi south of the Fort Lauderdale airport and ½ mi north of Hollywood. Take the Stirling Road or Griffin Road East exit off Interstate 95.

Davie

㉔ *4 mi west of Dania.*

This town's horse farms and estates are the closest thing to the Old West in South Florida. Folks in Western-wear ride their fine steeds through downtown—where they have the same right of way as motorists—and order up takeout at "ride-through" windows. With 70,000 residents, the town has doubled in size in 15 years, and gated communities are popping up alongside ranches. A monthly rodeo is Davie's most famous activity.

★ ⏱ Gators, crocodiles, river otters, and birds of prey can be seen at **Flamingo Gardens and Wray Botanical Collection,** as can a 25,000-square-foot walk-through aviary, a plant house, and an Everglades museum in the pioneer Wray Home. A half-hour guided tram ride winds through a citrus grove and wetlands area. ⊠ *3750 S. Flamingo Rd.* ☎ *954/473–2955* ⊕ *www.flamingogardens.org* ⊡ *$12, tram ride $3* ☉ *Daily 9:30–5:30; closed Mon. June–Sept.*

⏱ At the **Young at Art Children's Museum,** kids can work with paint, graphics, sculpture, and crafts according to themes that change three times a year. Then they take their masterpieces home with them. ⊠ *11584 W. State Rd. 84, in the Plaza* ☎ *954/424–0085* ⊕ *www.youngatartmuseum. org* ⊡ *$5* ☉ *Mon.–Sat. 10–5, Sun. noon–5.*

Where to Eat

$$–$$$$ ✕ **East City Grill.** Weston's East City Grill, born on Fort Lauderdale beach, quickly grew up to relocate to this fine dining outpost. Amid a casual atmosphere with a lake view, try the lollipop lamb chops or the "Jurassic" shrimp cocktail. Entrées might include seafood jambalaya or barbecue and peanut-crusted pork tenderloin. Among desserts, pear frangipane tartlet is a standout. Martinis—chocolate, butterscotch, mango, or cappuccino—provide liquid dessert refreshment. ⊠ *1800 Bell Tower La.* ☎ *954/659–3339* ⊟ *AE, D, DC, MC, V.*

$–$$$ ✕ **Bangkok Cafe.** Asian influence overrules Western standards at this outpost serving a signature Bangkok duck, pad thai, and shrimp sautéed in sweet-and-sour sauce. For starters, try the sausage salad. Takeout and delivery are convenient at this casual eatery. ⊠ *3400 S. University* ☎ *954/434–4222* ⊟ *AE, D, DC, MC, V.*

Nightlife & the Arts

THE ARTS **Bailey Concert Hall** (⊠ Central Campus of Broward Community College, 3501 S.W. Davie Rd. ☎ 954/201–6884) is a popular place for classical music concerts, dance, drama, and other performing-arts activities, especially from October to April.

NIGHTLIFE **Davie Junction** (⊠ 6311 S.W. 45th St. ☎ 954/581–1132), South Florida's hot venue for country music, is in the heart of Broward's horse country, with dance lessons available. It's open for dinner and dancing until 4 AM Wednesday through Sunday.

The Outdoors

BIKING   Bicycle and in-line-skating enthusiasts can ride at the **Brian Piccolo Skate Park and Velodrome** (✉9501 Sheridan St., Cooper City ☎954/437–2626), south of Davie. Hours are geared to after-school and weekend skating and biking.

RODEO   The local **Davie Rodeo** (✉ 4271 Davie Rd. ☎ 954/384–7075) is held on the Bergeron Rodeo Grounds the fourth weekend of every month. Saturday-night bull riding starts at 8. Special national rodeos come to town some weekends.

FORT LAUDERDALE & BROWARD A TO Z

To research prices, get advice from other travelers, and book travel arrangements, visit www.fodors.com.

AIR TRAVEL

CARRIERS   More than 40 scheduled airlines, commuters, and charters serve Fort Lauderdale–Hollywood International Airport.

🚹 **Major Airline Contacts Air Canada** ☎800/689–2247. **Air Jamaica** ☎800/523–5585. **Air Tran** ☎ 800/247–8726. **America West** ☎ 800/235–9292. **American** ☎ 800/433–7300. **Continental** ☎ 800/525–0280. **Delta** ☎ 800/221–1212. **JetBlue** ☎ 800/538–2583. **MetroJet** ☎ 888/638–7653. **Midway** ☎ 800/446–4392. **Northwest** ☎ 800/225–2525. **Southwest** ☎800/435–9792. **Spirit** ☎800/772–7117. **TWA** ☎800/221–2000. **United** ☎ 800/241–6522. **US Airways** ☎ 800/428–4322.

AIRPORTS

Fort Lauderdale–Hollywood International Airport, 4 mi south of downtown Fort Lauderdale and just off U.S. 1, is one of Florida's busiest, serving nearly 21 million travelers a year. Ongoing expansion has added a terminal, parking, and access roads. Broward County Mass Transit operates bus route No. 1 between the airport and its main terminal at Broward Boulevard and Northwest 1st Avenue, in the center of Fort Lauderdale. Service from the airport is every 20 minutes and begins daily at 5:40 AM; the last bus leaves the airport at 11:15 PM. The fare is $1 (50¢ for senior citizens). Airport Express provides limousine service to all parts of Broward County. Fares to most Fort Lauderdale beach hotels are in the $16 range.

🚹 **Airport Information Fort Lauderdale–Hollywood International Airport** ☎ 954/359–6100. **Airport Express** ☎ 954/561–8888. **Broward County Mass Transit** ☎ 954/357–8400.

BOAT & FERRY TRAVEL

Water Taxi provides service along the Intracoastal Waterway in Fort Lauderdale between the 17th Street Causeway and Oakland Park Boulevard daily from 6 AM until midnight.

🚹 **Boat & Ferry Information Water Bus, Water Taxi** ☎ 954/467–6677.

BUS TRAVEL

Greyhound Lines buses stop in Fort Lauderdale. Broward County Mass Transit bus service covers the county on 275 fixed routes and ventures into Dade and Palm Beach counties. The fare is $1 with reduced rates for seniors; unlimited daily ($2.50), weekly ($9), and monthly ($32) passes are available. Route service starts at 5 AM and continues to 11:30 PM, except on Sunday. Call for route information. City Cruiser is free and covers both the downtown loop and the beach area. The Courthouse Route runs every 10 minutes weekdays from 7:30 until 6. The Las Olas & Beach Route runs on the half hour 5:45 PM–1:45 AM.

CUTTING COSTS   Broward County Mass Transit offers seven-day passes that cost $9 and are good for unlimited use on all county buses. Get passes at some hotels, Broward County libraries, and the main bus terminal.

🚌 Bus Information **Broward County Mass Transit** Main Bus Terminal, ✉ Broward Blvd. at N.W. 1st Ave., Fort Lauderdale ☎ 954/357-8400. **Greyhound Lines** ✉ 515 N. E. 3rd St., Fort Lauderdale ☎ 800/231-2222 or 954/764-6551. **TMAX** ☎ 954/761-3543.

CAR RENTAL

Agencies in the airport include Avis, Budget, Dollar, and National. Other rental companies have shuttle services to nearby rental centers.

🚗 Local Agencies **Alamo** ☎ 954/525-4713. **Avis** ☎ 954/359-3255. **Budget** ☎ 954/359-4700. **Dollar** ☎ 954/359-7800. **Enterprise** ☎ 954/760-9888. **Hertz** ☎ 954/764-1199. **National** ☎ 954/359-8303.

CAR TRAVEL

Access to Broward County from north or south is via Florida's Turnpike, Interstate 95, U.S. 1, or U.S. 441. Interstate 75 (Alligator Alley) connects Broward with Florida's west coast and runs parallel to State Road 84 within the county. Except during rush hour, Broward County is a fairly easy place in which to drive. East–west Interstate 595 runs from westernmost Broward County and links Interstate 75 with Interstate 95 and U.S. 1, providing handy access to the airport. The scenic but slow Route A1A generally parallels the beach. The Sawgrass Expressway (also known as State Road 869 north of I–595 and I–75 south) is a toll road that links to Sawgrass Mills shopping and the ice-hockey arena, both in Sunrise.

EMERGENCIES

Dial 911 for police or ambulance.

🏥 24-Hour Pharmacies **Eckerd Drug** ✉ 1701 E. Commercial Blvd., Fort Lauderdale ☎ 954/771-0660. **Walgreens** ✉ 2855 Stirling Rd., Fort Lauderdale ☎ 954/981-1104 ✉ 601 E. Commercial Blvd., Oakland Park ☎ 954/772-4206 ✉ 289 S. Federal Hwy., Deerfield Beach ☎ 954/481-2993 ✉ 4003 S. University Dr., Davie ☎ 954/475-9375 ✉ 9005 Pines Blvd., Hollywood ☎ 954/392-4749.

MEDIA

NEWSPAPERS &   The *South Florida Sun-Sentinel* and affiliated magazine *City & Shore*
MAGAZINES   cover South Florida news and events.

RADIO   On the FM band: 97.3 WFLC and 101.5 WLIF play adult contemporary; 98.7 WKGR plays rock, 105.9 WBGG, classic rock; try 100.7 WHYI for Top 40; 102.7 WMXJ for oldies; 93.9 WLVE for jazz; 99.9 WKIS for country; and 91.3 WLRN for public radio. AM stations include 560 WQAM for sports; 610 WIOD for news; 1360 WKAT for classical; and 1580 WSRF for reggae-Caribbean.

TAXIS

It's difficult to hail a cab on the street. Sometimes you can pick one up at a major hotel. Otherwise, phone ahead. Meters run at a rate of $3.25 for the first mile and $2 for each additional mile; waiting time is 30¢ per minute. The major company serving the area is Yellow Cab.

🚩 Taxi Information **Yellow Cab** ☎ 954/565-5400.

TOURS

Carrie B., a 300-passenger day cruiser, gives 90-minute tours up the New River and Intracoastal Waterway. Cruises depart at 11, 1, and 3 each day and cost $13.50. *Jungle Queen III* and *Jungle Queen IV* are 175-passenger and 527-passenger tour boats taking day and night cruises up the New River through the heart of Fort Lauderdale. Sightseeing cruises at 10 and 2 cost $13.50, and the evening dinner cruise costs $30.95. You can also take a daylong trip to Miami's Bayside Marketplace ($16.95), on Biscayne Bay, for shopping and sightseeing on Wednesday and Saturday, departing at 9:15. Call in advance for availability. Professional Diving Charters operates the 60-foot glass-bottom boat *Pro Diver II*. On Tuesday through Saturday mornings and Sunday afternoon, two-hour sightseeing trips costing $22 take in offshore reefs; snorkeling can be arranged at $29 per person.

🚩 Tours Information *Carrie B.* ✉ Riverwalk at S.E. 5th Ave., Fort Lauderdale ☎ 954/768-9920. *Jungle Queen III* and *Jungle Queen IV* ✉ Radisson Bahia Mar Beach Resort, 801 Seabreeze Blvd., Fort Lauderdale ☎ 954/462-5596. **Professional Diving Charters** ✉ 515 Seabreeze Blvd., Fort Lauderdale ☎ 954/761-3413.

TRAIN TRAVEL

Amtrak provides daily service to the Fort Lauderdale station as well as other Broward County stops at Hollywood and Deerfield Beach. Tri-Rail operates train service daily 4 AM–11 PM (limited service on weekends) through Broward, Miami-Dade, and Palm Beach counties. There are six Broward stations west of Interstate 95: Hillsboro Boulevard in Deerfield Beach, Pompano Beach, Cypress Creek, Fort Lauderdale, Fort Lauderdale Airport, Sheridan Street in Hollywood, and Hollywood Boulevard.

🚩 Train Information **Amtrak** ✉ 200 S.W. 21st Terr., Fort Lauderdale ☎ 800/872-7245. **Tri-Rail** ☎ 800/874-7245.

VISITOR INFORMATION

🚩 Tourist Information **Chamber of Commerce of Greater Fort Lauderdale** ✉ 512 N. E. 3rd Ave., Fort Lauderdale 33301 ☎ 954/462-6000 ⊕ www.ftlchamber.com. **Davie/ Cooper City Chamber of Commerce** ✉ 4185 S.W. 64th Ave., Davie 33314 ☎ 954/581-0790 ⊕ www.davie-coopercity.org. **Greater Deerfield Beach Chamber of Commerce** ✉ 1601 E. Hillsboro Blvd., Deerfield Beach 33441 ☎ 954/427-1050 ⊕ www. deerfieldchamber.com. **Greater Fort Lauderdale Convention & Visitors Bureau** ✉ 1850 Eller Dr., Suite 303, Fort Lauderdale 33316 ☎ 954/765-4466 ⊕ www.broward.org. **Hollywood Chamber of Commerce** ✉ 330 N. Federal Hwy., Hollywood 33020 ☎ 954/923-4000 ⊕ www.hollywoodchamber.org. **Lauderdale-by-the-Sea Chamber of Commerce** ✉ 4201 N. Ocean Dr., Lauderdale-by-the-Sea 33308 ☎ 954/776-1000 ⊕ www.lbts.com. **Pompano Beach Chamber of Commerce** ✉ 2200 E. Atlantic Blvd., Pompano Beach 33062 ☎ 954/941-2940 ⊕ www.pompanobeachchamber.com.

Miami & Miami Beach

WORD OF MOUTH

"Head to the Little Havana area. Walk around a little and wander into a market in hopes of securing some Cuban or Hispanic soda and a mango."

—ajcolorado

"You must stop by the pool bar at the Delano (a walk through the lobby is a South Beach must) for the very best mojitos in Miami."

—GoTravel

"The club scene in South Beach is ever-changing, and getting a little past its 'That's so hot' stage, so don't be too intimidated. You DO want to dress a bit flashily for the better places, certainly, but don't go too over the top."

—rjw_lgb_ca

Updated by
Jim and
Cynthia Tunstall

MIAMI IS DIFFERENT from any other city in America—or any city in Latin America for that matter, even though it has a distinctly Latin flavor. Both logically and geologically, Miami shouldn't even be here. Resting on a paved swamp between the Everglades and the Atlantic Ocean, the city is subject to periodic flooding, hurricanes, and the onslaught of swallow-size mosquitoes. Despite the downsides, however, Miami is a vibrant city. The Tequesta Indians called this area home long before Spain's gold-laden treasure ships sailed along the Gulf Stream a few miles offshore. Foreshadowing 20th-century corporations, the Tequesta traded with mainland neighbors to the north and island brethren to the south. Today their descendants are the 150-plus U.S. and multinational companies whose Latin American headquarters are based in Greater Miami. For fans of international business and random statistics, Greater Miami has more than 40 foreign bank agencies, 11 Edge Act banks, 23 foreign trade offices, 31 binational chambers of commerce, and 53 foreign consulates.

The city has seen more than a decade of big changes. In the late 1980s Miami Beach was an oceanside geriatric ward. Today's South Beach residents have the kind of hip that doesn't break. The average age dropped from the mid-sixties in 1980 to a youthful early forties today. Toned young men outnumber svelte young women two to one. At night the revitalized Lincoln Road Mall is in full swing with cafés, galleries, and theaters, but it's also suffering vacancies due to rapidly rising rents, and has attracted retail chains including The Gap, Pottery Barn and Williams-Sonoma. The bloom may not be off the rose, but cash-crazy entrepreneurs hoping to strike it rich on Miami's popularity are finding the pie isn't large enough to feed their financial fantasies. Those who have seen how high rents can crush a dream are heading to North Beach and the southern neighborhoods of South Beach, whose few remaining derelict buildings are a flashback to the pre-renaissance days of the 1980s. If the many high-rises under construction are any indication, this is where the next revival is taking place.

As you plan your trip, know that winter *is* the best time to visit, but if money is an issue, come in the off-season—after Easter and before October. You'll find plenty to do, and room rates are considerably lower. Summer brings many European and Latin American vacationers, who find Miami congenial despite the heat, humidity, and intense afternoon thunderstorms. Regardless of when you arrive, once you're here, you'll suspect that you've entered Cuban air space. No matter where you spin your radio dial, virtually every announcer punctuates each sentence with an emphatic "COO-BAH!" Look around, and you'll see Spanish on billboards, hear it on elevators, and pick it up on the streets. But Miami sways to more than just a Latin beat. In addition to populations from Brazil, Colombia, Argentina, El Salvador, Haiti, Jamaica, Nicaragua, Panama, Puerto Rico, Venezuela, and, of course, Cuba, there are also representatives from China, Germany, Greece, Iran, Israel, Italy, Lebanon, Malaysia, Russia, and Sweden. Miami has accepted its montage of nationalities, and it now celebrates this cultural diversity through languages, festivals, world-beat music, and a wealth of exotic restaurants.

6

Numbers in the text correspond to numbers in the margin and on the Miami Beach; Downtown Miami; Miami, Coral Gables, Coconut Grove, and Key Biscayne; and South Dade maps.

If you have 3 days

Grab your lotion and head to the ocean, more specifically **Ocean Drive** on **South Beach,** and catch some rays while relaxing on the white sands. Afterward, take a guided or self-guided tour of the **Art Deco District** to see what all the fuss is about. Keep the evening free to socialize at Ocean Drive cafés. The following day drive through **Little Havana** to witness the heartbeat of Miami's Cuban culture on your way south to Coconut Grove's Vizcaya. Wrap up the evening a few blocks away in downtown **Coconut Grove,** enjoying its party-like mood and many nightspots. On the last day head over to **Coral Gables** to take in the eye-popping display of 1920s Mediterranean revival architecture in the neighborhoods surrounding the city center and the majestic **Biltmore Hotel** ㉕; then take a dip in the fantastic thematic **Venetian Pool** ㉓. That night have a fine meal in Coral Gables.

If you have 5 days

Follow the suggested three-day itinerary, and on Day 4 add a visit to the beaches of **Virginia Key** and **Key Biscayne.** Take a diving trip or fishing excursion, learn to wind surf, or do absolutely nothing but watch the water. On Day 5 step back to the 1950s with a cruise up **Collins Avenue** to some of the monolithic hotels, such as the **Fontainebleau Hilton** and **Eden Roc**; continue north to the elegant shops of **Bal Harbour**; and return to **South Beach** for an evening of shopping, drinking, and outdoor dining at **Lincoln Road Mall.**

If you have 7 days

A week gives you just enough time to experience fully the multicultural, cosmopolitan, tropical mélange that is Greater Miami and its beaches. On Day 6 see where it all began. Use the Miami Metromover to ride above downtown Miami before touring the streets (if possible, on a tour with historian Dr. Paul George). Take time to visit the **Miami-Dade Cultural Center** ⑭, home of art and history museums. Or go check out the **Miami Design District's** art galleries, which showcase up-and-coming local and international artists amidst a hip, urban setting of decorator showrooms, antique stores and hideaway nightclubs. The nearby **Wynwood Art District** is also worth exploring. In the evening check out the shops and clubs at **Bayside Marketplace.** The final day can be used to visit **South Miami,** site of **Fairchild Tropical Garden** ㉙ and the **Shops at Sunset Place.** Keep the evening free to revisit your favorite nightspots.

If you're concerned about Miami crime, you'll be glad to know that criminals are off the street—and seem to be running for public office. Forget about D.C. If you want weird politics, spread out a blanket and enjoy the show. Miamians still talk about Mayor Xavier Suarez's being removed from office after a judge threw out absentee ballots that included votes from dead people. That pales in comparison to the Miami foul-ups in the 2002 gubernatorial primary: in the wake of complaints about hanging chads in the 2000 presidential election, the state had switched to computerized voting. However, bugs in the computer system caused even candidate Janet Reno, a Miami native, to be turned away on her first attempt to vote. Three hours after the election began, 1 out of 10 polling places was still closed. While most of the state was using the new touch-screen machines, only the counties of Miami-Dade and Broward, just to the north, had problems. As for human error, the Miami City Commission chairman was removed following a voter fraud conviction, a county commissioner was arrested and removed from office for using campaign money for her personal use, and a state senator was reelected despite being under indictment for pocketing profits from sham home-health-care companies.

Corrupt politicians aside, Miami has its share of the same crimes that plague any other major city. However, the widely publicized crimes against tourists a decade ago led to the creation of effective visitor-safety programs and neighborhood police stations in high-crime areas. Patrol cars driven by TOP (Tourist Oriented Police) Cops cruise heavily visited areas. Identification that made rental cars conspicuous to would-be criminals has been removed, and multilingual pamphlets on avoiding crime are widely distributed. The precautions have had a positive impact. In the last decade the number of tourist robberies has decreased by more than 80%. While it's still prudent to avoid crime-ridden areas, the incidents of lost tourists being robbed are so rare now that special direction signs—with red-sunburst logos placed at ¼-mi intervals on major roads to guide tourists from the airport to major destinations such as Key Biscayne and Miami Beach—have been taken down.

What *is* on the rise is Miami's film profile. Arnold Schwarzenegger and Jamie Lee Curtis filmed *True Lies* here, Al Pacino and Johnny Depp shot scenes for *Donnie Brasco,* Jim Carrey rose to stardom through the Miami-based *Ace Ventura: Pet Detective,* Robin Williams and Nathan Lane used two deco buildings on Ocean Drive as their nightclub in *The Birdcage,* and traffic on MacArthur Causeway ceased for several days to film an incredible car-carrier wreck scene for *Bad Boys II.* It's a far cry from when Esther Williams used to perform water ballet in Coral Gables' Venetian Pool. Daily fashion-magazine and TV shoots add to the frenetic mix.

Fun here can easily drain your wallet, but look for less flashy ways to explore Miami, too. Skip the chichi restaurant and go for an ethnic eatery. Tour Lincoln Road Mall, downtown Coral Gables, or Coconut Grove on foot. Or take South Beach's colorful Electrowave shuttle, Florida's first electric transportation system, which really works for getting around traffic-clogged SoBe. Nearly 10 million tourists flock annually to Miami-Dade County and discover a multicultural metropolis that invites the world to celebrate its diversity.

EXPLORING MIAMI & MIAMI BEACH

If you had arrived here 40 years ago with Fodor's guide in hand, chances are you'd be thumbing through listings looking for alligator wrestlers

6

Savories

Miami cuisine is what mouths were made for. The city serves up a veritable United Nations of dining experiences, including dishes native to Spain, Cuba, and Nicaragua as well as China, India, Thailand, Vietnam, and other Asian cultures. Chefs from the tropics combine fresh, natural foods—especially seafood—with classic island-style dishes, creating a new American cuisine that is sometimes called Floribbean. Another style finding its way around U.S. restaurants is the Miami-born New World cuisine. The title comes from chefs who realized their latest creations were based on ingredients found along the trade routes discovered by early explorers of the "New World."

Sizzle

Fast, hot, and as transient as the crowds who pass through their doors, Miami's nightspots sizzle, keeping pace with their New York and L.A. counterparts. The densest concentration of clubs is on South Beach along Washington Avenue, Lincoln Road Mall, and Ocean Drive. Other nightlife centers on Little Havana and Coconut Grove, and on the fringes of downtown Miami. Miami's nightspots offer jazz, reggae, salsa, various forms of rock, disco, and Top 40 sounds, most played at a body-thumping, ear-throbbing volume. Some clubs refuse entrance to anyone under 21, others to those under 25. If you prefer to hear what people are saying, try the many lobby bars at South Beach's art deco hotels. Throughout Greater Miami, bars and cocktail lounges in larger, newer hotels operate nightly discos with live weekend entertainment.

Spectator Sports

Greater Miami has franchises in basketball, football, and baseball. Fans still turn out en masse for the Dolphins, and—in the best fair-weather-fan tradition—show up for basketball's Heat and baseball's Marlins, who suddenly regained fans with a surprising victory over the Yankees in the 2003 World Series. Miami also hosts top-rated events in golf, tennis, boat racing, auto racing, and jai alai. Each winter, the FedEx Orange Bowl Football Classic highlights two of the top teams in college football.

Surf

Greater Miami has numerous free beaches to fit every style. A sandy, 300-foot-wide beach with several distinct sections extends for 10 mi from the foot of Miami Beach north to Haulover Beach Park. Between 23rd and 44th streets, Miami Beach built a boardwalk and protective walkways atop a dune landscaped with sea oats, sea grapes, and other native plants whose roots keep the sand from blowing away. Farther north there's even a nude beach, and Key Biscayne adds more great strands to Miami's collection. If you can sail in Miami, do. Blue skies, calm seas, and a view of the city skyline make for a pleasurable outing—especially at twilight, when the fabled "moon over Miami" casts a soft glow on the water. Key Biscayne's calm waves and strong breezes are perfect for sailing and windsurfing, and although Dinner Key and the Coconut Grove waterfront remain the center of sailing in Greater Miami, sailboat moorings and rentals sit along other parts of the bay and up the Miami River. Greater Miami has numerous marinas, and dockmasters can provide information on any marine services you may need.

and you-pick strawberry fields or citrus groves. Well, things have changed. While Disney sidetracked families in Orlando, Miami was developing a grown-up attitude courtesy of *Miami Vice,* European fashion photographers, and historic preservationists. Nowadays the wildest ride is the city itself. Climb aboard and check out the different sides of Greater Miami. Miami on the mainland is South Florida's commercial hub, while its sultry sister, Miami Beach (America's Riviera), encompasses 17 islands in Biscayne Bay. Seducing winter refugees with its sunshine, beaches, palms, and nightlife, this is what most people envision when planning a trip to what they think of as Miami. These same visitors fail to realize that there's more to Miami Beach than the bustle of South Beach and its Deco District. Indeed, there are quieter areas to the north like Sunny Isles Beach, Surfside, and Bal Harbour.

During the day downtown Miami has become the lively hub of the mainland city, now more accessible thanks to the Metromover extension, a supplementary rail system linking many downtown sights that conveniently connects Metrorail's Government Center and Brickell stations. Other major attractions include Coconut Grove, Coral Gables, Little Havana, and, of course, the South Beach–Art Deco District; but since these areas are spread out beyond the reach of public transportation, you'll have to drive. Rent a convertible if you can. There's nothing quite like wearing cool shades and feeling the wind in your hair as you drive across one of the causeways en route to Miami Beach.

To find your way around Greater Miami, learn how the numbering system works. Miami is laid out on a grid with four quadrants—northeast, northwest, southeast, and southwest—which meet at Miami Avenue and Flagler Street. Miami Avenue separates east from west, and Flagler Street separates north from south. Avenues and courts run north–south; streets, terraces, and ways run east–west. Roads run diagonally, northwest–southeast. But other districts—Miami Beach, Coral Gables, and Hialeah—may or may not follow this system, and along the curve of Biscayne Bay, the symmetrical grid may shift diagonally. It's best to buy a detailed map, stick to the major roads, and ask directions early and often. However, make sure you're in a safe neighborhood or public place when you seek guidance; cabbies and cops are good resources.

South Beach–Miami Beach

The hub of Miami Beach is South Beach (SoBe, to anyone but locals), and the hub of South Beach is the 1-square-mi Art Deco District, fronted on the east by Ocean Drive and on the west by Alton Road. The story of South Beach has become the story of Miami. In the early 1980s South Beach's vintage hotels were badly run down, catering mostly to infirm retirees. But a group of visionaries led by the late Barbara Baer Capitman, a spirited New York transplant, saw this collection of buildings as an architectural treasure to be salvaged from a sea of mindless urban renewal. It was, and is, a peerless grouping of art deco architecture from the 1920s to 1950s, whose forms and decorative details are drawn from nature, the streamlined shapes of modern transportation and industrial machinery, and human extravagance.

Investors started fixing up the interiors of these hotels and repainting their exteriors with a vibrant pastel palette—a look that *Miami Vice* made famous and that TV shows such as MTV's *Real World* and *CSI: Miami* continue to keep on the pop-culture radar screen. Fashion photographers and the media took note, and celebrities like singer Gloria Estefan; the late designer Gianni Versace, whose fashions captured the feel of the awakening city; and record executive Chris Blackwell bought a piece of the action. As a result, South Beach now holds the distinction of being the nation's first 20th-century district on the National Register of Historic Places, with more than 800 significant buildings making the roll. New high-rises and hotels spring up, areas like SoFi ("south of fifth" street) blossom, and clubs open (and close) with dizzying speed.

Yet Miami Beach is more than just SoBe. (The northern edge of South Beach is generally considered to be around 24th–28th streets, while Miami Beach extends well north.) It also consists of a collection of quiet neighborhoods where Little Leaguers play ball, senior citizens stand at bus stops, and locals do their shopping away from the prying eyes of visitors. Surprisingly, Miami Beach is a great walking town in the middle of a great city. Two things are particularly plentiful in SoBe: cell phones and meter maids. Tickets are given freely when meters expire, and towing charges are high. Check the meter to see when parking fees are required; times vary by district. From mid-morning on, parking is scarce along Ocean Drive. You'll do better on Collins or Washington Avenue, the next two streets to the west. Fortunately, there are several surface parking lots south and west of the Jackie Gleason Theater, on 17th Street, and parking garages on Collins Avenue at 7th and 13th streets, on Washington Avenue at 12th Street, and west of Washington at 17th Street. Keep these sites in mind, especially at night, when cruising traffic makes it best to park your car and see SoBe on foot. Better yet, catch the colorful Electrowave shuttle buses that cover South Beach well into the wee hours—for 25¢, they're the best deal in town.

a good walk

Ocean Drive—primarily the 10-block stretch from 5th to 15th Street—has become the most talked-about beachfront in America. A bevy of art deco jewels hugs the drive, while across the street lies palm-fringed **Lummus Park** ❶ ⌐, the south end of which is a good starting point for a walk. Beginning early (at 8) gives you the pleasure of watching the awakening city without distraction. Sanitation men hose down dirty streets, merchants prepare window displays, bakers bake, and construction workers change the skyline one brick at a time. Cross to the west side of Ocean Drive, where sidewalk cafés abound, and walk north, taking note of the Park Central Hotel, built in 1937 by deco architect Henry Hohauser. At 10th Street recross Ocean Drive to the beach side and visit the **Art Deco District Welcome Center** ❷ in the 1950s-era Oceanfront Auditorium. Rent tapes or hire a guide for a Deco District tour.

Glance back across Ocean Drive and take a look at the wonderful flying-saucer architecture of the Clevelander, at No. 1020. On the next block you'll see the late Gianni Versace's Spanish Mediterranean **Casa Casuarina** ❸, once known as Amsterdam Palace. You may recognize the Leslie (No. 1244) and **The Carlyle** ❹, from the Robin Williams movie

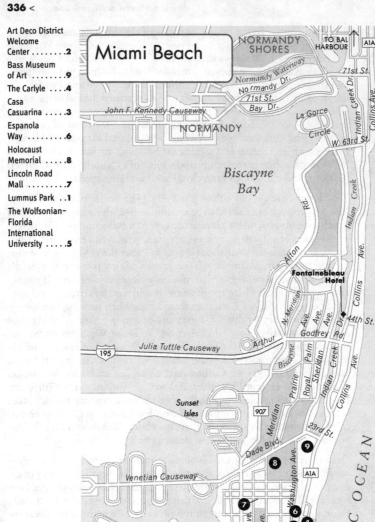

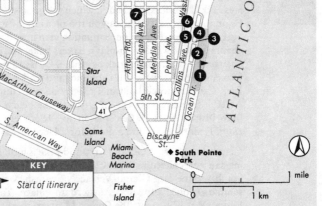

The Birdcage. Walk two blocks west (away from the ocean) on 13th Street to Washington Avenue, where a mix of chic restaurants, avant-garde shops, delicatessens, produce markets, and nightclubs has spiced up a once-derelict neighborhood. Turn left on Washington and walk 2½ blocks south to **Wolfsonian–Florida International University** ❺, which showcases artistic movements from 1885 to 1945. Provided you haven't spent too long in the museum, return north on Washington Avenue past 14th Street, and turn left on **Espanola Way** ❻, a narrow street of Mediterranean revival buildings, eclectic shops, and a weekend market. Continue west to Meridian Avenue and turn right. Three blocks north of Espanola Way is the redesigned **Lincoln Road Mall** ❼, which is often paired with Ocean Drive as part of must-see South Beach. The next main street north of Lincoln Road is 17th Street, and to the east is the Miami Beach Convention Center. Walk behind the massive building to the corner of Meridian Avenue and 19th Street to see the chilling **Holocaust Memorial** ❽, a monumental record honoring the 6 million Jewish victims of the Holocaust. Head east to the **Bass Museum of Art** ❾, a Maya-inspired temple filled with European splendors. Return to Ocean Drive in time to pull up a chair at an outdoor café, order an espresso, and settle down for an evening of people-watching, SoBe's most popular pastime. If you've seen enough people, grab some late rays at one of the area's beaches, with different sands for different tans. Go back to Lummus Park (*the* beach) or head north, where there's a boardwalk for walking but no allowance for skates and bicycles.

TIMING   To see only the art deco buildings on Ocean Drive, allow one hour minimum. Depending on your interests, schedule at least five hours and include a drink or meal at a café and browsing time in the shops on Ocean Drive, along Espanola Way, and at Lincoln Road Mall. Start your walking tour as early in the day as possible. In winter the street becomes crowded as the day wears on, and in summer, afternoon heat and humidity can be unbearable. Finishing by mid-afternoon also enables you to hit the beach and cool your heels in the warm sand.

What to See

❷ **Art Deco District Welcome Center.** Run by the Miami Design Preservation League, the center provides information about the buildings in the District. A gift shop sells 1930s–1950s art deco memorabilia, posters, and books on Miami's history. Several tours—covering Lincoln Road, Espanola Way, North Beach, the entire Art Deco District—start here. Rent audiotapes for $15 per person for a self-guided tour, join the regular Wednesday-, Friday-, Saturday- and Sunday-morning or Thursday-evening walking tours, or take a bicycle tour. Don't miss the special boat tours during Art Deco Weekend in early January. ⊠ *1001 Ocean Dr., at Barbara Capitman Way (10th St.), South Beach* ☎ *305/531–3484 or 305/672–2014* 🖃 *Tours $20* ⊙ *Daily 10–7:30.*

Bal Harbour. Known for its upscale shops, this affluent community has a stretch of prime beach real estate where wealthy condominium owners cluster in winter. Look close and you may spy Bob Dole sunning himself outside his condo. ⊠ *Collins Ave. between 96th and 103rd Sts., Bal Harbour.*

⑨ Bass Museum of Art. European art is the focus of this impressive museum in historic Collins Park, a short drive north of SoBe's key sights. Works on display include *The Holy Family,* a painting by Peter Paul Rubens; *The Tournament,* one of several 16th-century Flemish tapestries; and works by Albrecht Dürer and Henri de Toulouse-Lautrec. An $8 million, three-phase expansion by architect Arata Isozaki added another wing, cafeteria, and theater, doubling the museum's size to nearly 40,000 square feet. ✉ *2121 Park Ave., South Beach* ☎ *305/673–7530* ⊕ *www. bassmuseum.org* ✍ *$12* ۞ *Tues.–Sat. 10–5, Thurs. 10–9, Sun. 11–5.*

④ The Carlyle. Built in 1941, this deco gem was one of the first hotels to be restored and is now shuttered for a second redo. Fans will recognize it and its neighbor, the Leslie, as the nightclub from *The Birdcage.* ✉ *1250 Ocean Dr., South Beach.*

③ Casa Casuarina. In the early 1980s before South Beach became a hotbed of chicness the late Italian designer Gianni Versace purchased this run-down Spanish Mediterranean residence, built before the arrival of deco. Today the home is an ornate three-story palazzo with a guest house and a copper-dome rooftop observatory and pool that were added at the expense of a 1950s hotel, the Revere. Its loss and the razing of the fabled deco Senator became a rallying point for preservationists. Although the Casuarina is now owned by a private investor, picture-taking tourists still flock to see the villa and its broad front stairs where Versace was tragically gunned down by a stalker in 1997 as he returned home from breakfast at the nearby News Café. ✉ *1114 Ocean Dr., South Beach.*

★ **⑥ Espanola Way.** The Mediterranean revival buildings along this road were constructed in 1925 and frequented through the years by artists and writers. In the 1930s future bandleader Desi Arnaz strapped on a conga drum and started beating out a rumba rhythm at a nightclub that is now the Clay Hotel, a youth hostel that covers most of a block. The best time to visit is on a Sunday afternoon, when itinerant dealers and craftspeople set up shop to sell everything from garage-sale items to handcrafted bongo drums. Between Washington and Drexel avenues, the road has been narrowed to a single lane, and Miami Beach's trademark pink sidewalks have been widened to accommodate sidewalk cafés and shops selling imaginative clothing, jewelry, and art. ✉ *Espanola Way between 14th and 15th Sts. from Washington to Jefferson Ave., South Beach.*

★ **Fontainebleau Hilton Resort and Towers.** For a sense of what Miami was like during the Fabulous '50s, take a drive north to see the finest example of Miami Beach's grandiose architecture. By the 1950s smaller deco-era hotels were passé, and architects like Morris Lapidus got busy designing free-flowing hotels that affirmed the American attitude of "bigger is better." Even if you're not a guest, wander through the lobby just to feel the energy generated by an army of bellhops, clerks, concierges, and travelers. ✉ *4441 Collins Ave., between 44th and 45th Sts., South Beach* ☎ *305/538–2000* ⊕ *www.fontainebleau.hilton.com.*

۞ **Haulover Beach Park.** At this county park, far from the action of SoBe, see the Miami of 30 years ago. Pack a picnic, use the barbecue grills, or grab a snack at the concession stand. There are tennis and volleyball courts and paths designed for walking and bicycling. The beach is nice if you want water without long marches across hot sand, and a popular clothing-optional section at the north end of the beach lures people who want to tan every nook and cranny. Other offerings are kite rentals, kayak rentals, charter-fishing excursions, and a par-3, 9-hole golf course. ✉ *10800 Collins Ave., Sunny Isles* ☎ *305/947–3525* ⊕ *www.miamidade. gov/parks/Parks/haulover_park.asp* ✎ *$5 per vehicle* ⊘ *Daily dawn–dusk.*

❽ Holocaust Memorial. The focus of the memorial is a 42-foot-high bronze arm rising from the ground, with sculptured people climbing the arm seeking escape. Don't stare from the street; enter the courtyard to see the chilling memorial wall and hear the eerie songs that seem to give voice to the victims. ✉ *1933–1945 Meridian Ave., South Beach* ☎ *305/ 538–1663* ⊕ *www.holocaustmmb.org* ✎ *Free, donations welcome* ⊘ *Daily 10–9.*

---

need a break? If your feet are still holding up, head to the **Delano Hotel** (✉ 1685 Collins Ave., South Beach ☎ 305/674–6400) for a drink. This surrealistic hotel, like a Calvin Klein ad come to life, delivers fabulousness every step of the way. It's popular among SoBe's fashion models and hepcats.

---

❼ Lincoln Road Mall. The Morris Lapidus–renovated Lincoln Road, just a few blocks from the beach and convention center, is fun, lively, and friendly for people old, young, gay, and straight—and their dogs. Folks skate, scoot, bike, or jog here past the electronics stores at the Collins Avenue end toward the chichi boutiques and outdoor cafés heading west. An 18-screen movie theater anchors the west end of the street. The best times to hit the road are during Sunday-morning farmers' markets and on weekend evenings when cafés are bustling; art galleries, like Romero Britto's Britto Central, schedule openings; street performers take the stage; and bookstores, import shops, and clothing stores are open late. ✉ *Lincoln Rd. between Collins Ave. and Alton Rd., South Beach.*

Fodor'sChoice ★

❶ Lummus Park. Once part of a turn-of-the-last-century plantation owned by brothers John and James Lummus, this palm-shaded park on the beach side of Ocean Drive attracts beach-going families with its children's play area. Senior citizens and health-conscious locals predominate early in the day. Volleyball playing, in-line skating along the wide and winding sidewalk, and a lot of posing go on here. Gays like the beach between 11th and 13th streets. The lush foliage is a pleasing, natural counterpoint to the ultrachic activity across the street, where endless sidewalk cafés make it easy to come ashore for everything from burgers to quiche. Like New York's Central Park, this is a natural venue for big-name public concerts by such performers as Luciano Pavarotti and past Art Deco Weekend stars Cab Calloway and Lionel Hampton. ✉ *East of Ocean Dr. between 5th and 15th Sts., South Beach.*

North Beach. Families and those who like things quiet prefer this section of beach. Metered parking is ample right behind the dune and a block behind Collins Avenue along a pleasant, old shopping street. With high prices discouraging developers from SoBe, this area will no doubt see some redevelopment in years to come. However, without the cafés or 300-foot-wide beach to lure tourists, it may never match SoBe's appeal. ✉ *Ocean Terr. between 73rd and 75th Sts., North Beach.*

off the
beaten
path

OLETA RIVER STATE PARK – At nearly 1,000 acres, this is the largest urban park in Florida. It's backed by lush tropical growth rather than hotels and offers group and youth camping, 14 log cabins, kayak and canoe rentals, mountain-bike trails, and a fishing pier. Popular with outdoors enthusiasts, it also attracts dolphins, ospreys, and manatees, who arrive for the winter. ✉ *3400 N.E. 163rd St., North Miami Beach* ☎ *305/919–1846* ⊕ *www.floridastateparks.org/oletariver* 🎟 *$3 per vehicle with one person, $5 per vehicle for 2 to 8 people, pedestrians $1* ⊙ *Daily 8–dusk.*

Sanford L. Ziff Jewish Museum of Florida. A permanent exhibit, *MO-SAIC: Jewish Life in Florida* depicts more than 235 years of the Florida Jewish experience through lectures, films, storytelling, walking tours, and special events. If you've never seen a crate of kosher citrus or ark ornaments from a Florida synagogue, drop in. And for a flashback to what Miss Florida looked like in the '80s—the 1880s, that is—look for the snapshot of Mena Williams. The building is the former Congregation Beth Jacob Synagogue. ✉ *301 Washington Ave., South Beach* ☎ *305/672–5044* ⊕ *www.jewishmuseum.com* 🎟 *$6, free on Sat.* ⊙ *Tues.–Sun. 10–5.*

South Pointe Park. From the 50-yard Sunshine Pier, which adjoins the 1-mi-long jetty at the mouth of Government Cut, fish while watching huge ships pass. No bait or tackle is available in the park. Facilities include two observation towers, rest rooms, and volleyball courts. ✉ *1 Washington Ave., South Beach.*

Surfside. *Parlez-vous français?* If you do, you'll feel quite comfortable in and around this French Canadian enclave. It's one of the few spots on the beach yet to be reinvented, making it (and down the island to 72nd Street) an affordable place for many folks to spend the winter. ✉ *Collins Ave. between 88th and 96th Sts., Surfside.*

★ ❺ **Wolfsonian–Florida International University.** A converted 1927 storage facility is now both a research center and the site of the 80,000-plus-item collection of modern design and "propaganda arts" amassed by Miami native Mitchell Wolfson Jr., a world traveler and connoisseur. Included in the museum's eclectic holdings, representing art moderne, art nouveau, arts and crafts, and other artistic movements, is a 1930s braille edition of Hitler's *Mein Kampf*. Exhibitions such as World's Fair designs and the architectural heritage of S. H. Kress add to the appeal. ✉ *1001 Washington Ave., South Beach* ☎ *305/531–1001* ⊕ *www.wolfsonian. fiu.edu* 🎟 *$5* ⊙ *Mon., Tues., Fri., and Sat. 11–6, Thurs. 11–9, Sun. noon–5.*

Downtown Miami

Although steel-and-glass buildings have sprung up around downtown, the heart of the city hasn't changed much since the 1960s—except that it's a little seedier. By day there's plenty of activity downtown, as office workers and motorists crowd the area. Staid, suited lawyers and bankers share the sidewalks with Latino merchants wearing open-neck, intricately embroidered shirts called guayaberas. Fruit merchants sell their wares from pushcarts, young European travelers with backpacks stroll the streets, and foreign businesspeople haggle over prices in import-export shops, including more electronics and camera shops than you'd see in Tokyo. You'll hear Arabic, Chinese, Creole, French, German, Hebrew, Hindi, Japanese, Portuguese, Spanish, Yiddish, and even some English. But what's best in the heart of downtown Miami is its Latinization and the sheer energy of Latino shoppers. At night, however, downtown is sorely neglected. Except for Bayside Marketplace, the AmericanAirlines Arena, and a few ever-changing clubs in warehouses, the area is deserted, and arena patrons rarely linger. Travelers spend little time here, since most tourist attractions are in other neighborhoods, but there's a movement afoot to bring a renaissance to downtown. A huge new performing-arts center is scheduled to open in early 2006 and, with it, new cafés and nightspots. Thanks to the Metromover, which has inner and outer loops through downtown plus north and south extensions, this is an excellent tour to take by rail, and it's free. Attractions are within about two blocks of the nearest station. Parking downtown is no less convenient or more expensive than in any other city, but the best idea is to park near Bayside Marketplace or leave your car at an outlying Metrorail station and take the train downtown.

a good tour

Start at the Bayfront Park Metromover stop. There's plenty of parking in lots in the median of Biscayne Boulevard and slightly more expensive covered parking at the Bayfront Marketplace. If you want, wait until you return to walk through the **Mildred and Claude Pepper Bayfront Park** ⑩ ▶, but look south of the park and you'll see the Hotel Inter-Continental Miami, which displays *The Spindle,* a huge sculpture by Henry Moore, in its lobby. A trip to **Brickell Village** ⑪ on the south side of the Brickell Avenue Bridge makes a good detour. Next, board the Metromover northbound and take in the fine view of Bayfront Park's greenery, the bay beyond, the stunning AmericanAirlines Arena, the Port of Miami in the bay, and Miami Beach across the water. The next stop, College–Bayside, serves the downtown campus of **Honors College at Miami Dade College** ⑫, which has two fine (and free) galleries. As the Metromover rounds the curve after the College–Bayside station, look northeast for a view of the vacant **Freedom Tower** ⑬, an important milepost in the history of Cuban immigration now being renovated as a Cuban museum. You'll also see the *Miami Herald* building and the rapidly rising performing-arts center. Survey the city as the train works its way toward Government Center station. Look off to your right (north) as you round the northwest corner of the loop to see the round, windowless, pink Miami Arena.

It's time to hoof it, so get off the train at Government Center, a large station with small shops, restaurants, and a hair salon, in case you're looking shaggy. It's also where the 21-mi elevated Metrorail commuter system connects with the Metromover, so this is a good place to start

Downtown Miami

your tour if you're coming downtown by train. Walk out the east doors to Northwest 1st Street and head a block south to the **Miami-Dade Cultural Center** ⑭, which contains the city's main art museum, historical museum, and library and made an appearance in the movie *There's Something About Mary*. After sopping up some culture, walk east down Flagler Street. On the corner is the **Dade County Courthouse** ⑮, whose pinnacle is accented by circling vultures. Now you're in the heart of downtown, where the smells range from pleasant (hot-dog carts) to rancid (hot-dog carts). If you cleaned up the streets and put a shine on the city, you'd see Miami circa 1950. Still thriving today, the downtown area is a far cry from what it was in 1896, when it was being carved out of pine woods and palmetto scrub to make room for Flagler's railroad. If you're in the market for jewelry, avoid the street peddlers and duck into the Seybold Building, at 36 Northeast 1st Street; it comprises 10 stories with 250 jewelers hawking watches, rings, bracelets, etc. Just a few blocks from your starting point at the Bayfront Park Metromover station, stop in at the **Gusman Center for the Performing Arts** ⑯, a beautiful movie palace that now serves as downtown Miami's concert hall. If there's a show on—even a bad one—get tickets. It's worth it just to sit in here. When you get back to your car and the entrance to the Bayfront Marketplace, opt to hit the road, go shopping, or grab a brew at a bay-front bar.

TIMING   To walk and ride to the various points of interest, allow two hours. If you want to spend additional time eating and shopping at Bayside, allow at least four hours. To include museum visits, allow six hours.

What to See

AmericanAirlines Arena. The stylish bay-front home of the NBA's Miami Heat includes Gloria Estefan's Bongos restaurant and shops. ⊠ *Biscayne Blvd. between N.E. 8th and 9th Sts., Downtown* ☎ *786/777–1000* ⊕ *www.aaarena.com.*

⓫ **Brickell Village.** Brickell (rhymes with fickle) is an up-and-coming downtown area with new low- and high-rise condos, a shopping area, Brickell Park, and plenty of popular restaurants. **Perricone's Marketplace and Café** (⊠ 15 S.E. 10th St., Brickell Village) is the biggest and most popular of the area's many Italian restaurants, in a 120-year-old Vermont barn. The cooking is simple and good. Buy your wine from the on-premises deli and bring it to your table for a small corking fee. ⊠ *Between Miami River and S.W. 15 St., Brickell Village.*

⓯ **Dade County Courthouse.** Built in 1928, this was once the tallest building south of Washington, D.C. Unlike at Capistrano, turkey vultures—not swallows—return to roost here in winter. ⊠ *73 W. Flagler St., Downtown* ☎ *305/349–7000.*

⓭ **Freedom Tower.** In the 1960s this imposing Spanish baroque structure was the Cuban Refugee Center, processing more than 500,000 Cubans who entered the United States after fleeing Fidel Castro's regime. Built in 1925 for the *Miami Daily News,* it was inspired by the Giralda, an 800-year-old bell tower in Seville, Spain. The tower's exterior was restored in 1988 and restoration of the interior is ongoing. ⊠ *600 Biscayne Blvd., at N.E. 7th St., Downtown.*

★ **⑯** **Gusman Center for the Performing Arts.** Carry an extra pair of socks when you come here; the beauty of this former movie palace will knock yours clean off. Reopened in the '70s as a concert hall and given an additional $2.1 million restoration in 2002, it resembles an ornate Moorish court-yard on the inside, with twinkling stars in the sky. You can catch per-formances by the Florida Philharmonic and movies of the Miami Film Festival. If the hall is closed, call the office and they may let you in. ✉ *174 E. Flagler St., Downtown* ☎ *305/372–0925* ⊕ *gusmancenter.org.*

⑫ **Honors College at Miami Dade College.** The campus has two fine galleries: the larger, third-floor **Centre Gallery** hosts photography, painting, and sculpture exhibitions, and the fifth-floor **Frances Wolfson Art Gallery** has smaller photo exhibits. ✉ *300 N.E. 2nd Ave., Downtown* ☎ *305/ 237–3278* 🎟 *Free* ☉ *Mon.–Wed. and Fri. 10–4, Thurs. noon–6.*

★ ♻ **⑭** **Miami-Dade Cultural Center.** Containing three important cultural re-sources, this 3-acre complex is one of the focal points of downtown. The **Miami Art Museum** (☎ 305/375–3000 ⊕ www.miamiartmuseum. org) has a permanent collection and major touring exhibitions of work by international artists, focusing on work completed since 1945. Open Tuesday–Friday 10–5 (and until 9 PM the third Thursday of the month) and weekends noon–5, the museum charges $5 admission ($6 includ-ing the Historical Museum). At the **Historical Museum of Southern Florida** (☎ 305/375–1492 ⊕ www.historical-museum.org) you'll be treated to pure Floridiana, including an old Miami streetcar, cigar labels, and a railroad exhibit as well as a display on prehistoric Miami. Admission is $5 ($6 including the Miami Art Museum), and hours are Mon-day–Saturday 10–5 (until 9 on Thursdays) and Sunday noon–5. The **Main Public Library** (☎ 305/375–2665), which is open Monday–Wednes-day, Friday, and Saturday 9–6, Thursday 9–9, and Sunday 1–5, has nearly 4 million holdings and offers art exhibits in the auditorium and second-floor lobby. ✉ *101 W. Flagler St., Downtown.*

► **⑩** **Mildred and Claude Pepper Bayfront Park.** This respite among the skyscrap-ers borders Bayside Marketplace, making it a natural place for a pre- or post-shopping walk. An urban landfill in the 1920s, it became the site of a World War II memorial in 1943, which was revised in 1980 to include the names of victims of later wars. Japanese sculptor Isamu Noguchi redesigned the park before his death in 1989 to include two amphitheaters, a memorial to the *Challenger* astronauts, and a foun-tain honoring the late Florida congressman Claude Pepper and his wife. At the park's north end the Friendship Torch was created to honor JFK during his presidency and was dedicated in 1964. ✉ *Biscayne Blvd. be-tween 2nd and 3rd Sts., Downtown.*

Little Havana

More than 40 years ago, Cubans fleeing the Castro regime flooded into an older neighborhood west of downtown Miami. Don't expect a sparkling and lively reflection of 1950s Havana, however. What you will find are ramshackle motels and cluttered storefronts. With a million Cubans and other Latinos—who make up more than half the metropolitan population—dispersed throughout Greater Miami, Little Havana and neighboring East Little Havana remain magnets for Hispanics and Anglos alike. That culture, of course, functions in Spanish. Many Little Havana residents and shopkeepers speak little or no English.

a good tour

From downtown go west on Flagler Street across the Miami River to Teddy Roosevelt Avenue (Southwest 17th Avenue) and pause at **Plaza de la Cubanidad** ⓱ ▶, on the southwest corner. The plaza's monument is indicative of the prominent role of Cuban history and culture here. Turn left at Douglas Road (Southwest 37th Avenue), drive south to **Calle Ocho** ⓲ (Southwest 8th Street), and turn left again. You are now on the main commercial thoroughfare of Little Havana. After you cross Unity Boulevard (Southwest 27th Avenue), Calle Ocho becomes a one way street eastbound through the heart of Little Havana. At Avenida Luis Muñoz Marín (Southwest 15th Avenue), stop at **Domino Park** ⓳, where elderly Cuban men, among others, pass the day with their black-and-white tiles. The **Brigade 2506 Memorial** ⓴, commemorating the victims of the unsuccessful 1961 Bay of Pigs invasion, stands at Memorial Boulevard (Southwest 13th Avenue). A block south are several other monuments relevant to Cuban history, including a bas-relief of and quotations by José Martí.

TIMING If the history hidden in the monuments is your only interest, set aside one hour. Allow more time to stop along Calle Ocho for a strong cup of Cuban coffee or to shop for a cigar made of Honduran tobacco hand-rolled in the United States by Cubans.

What to See

⓴ **Brigade 2506 Memorial.** To honor those who died in the Bay of Pigs invasion, an eternal flame burns atop a simple stone monument with the inscription CUBA—A LOS MÁRTIRES DE LA BRIGADA DE ASALTO ABRIL 17 DE 1961. The monument also bears a shield with the Brigade 2506 emblem, a Cuban flag superimposed on a cross. ⊠ *S.W. 8th St. and S.W. 13th Ave., Little Havana.*

⓲ **Calle Ocho.** In Little Havana's commercial heart, experience such Cuban customs as hand-rolled cigars or sandwiches piled with meats and cheeses. Although it all deserves exploring, if time is limited try the stretch from Southwest 14th to 11th Avenue. ⊠ *S.W. 8th St., Little Havana.*

⓳ **Domino Park.** Officially known as Maximo Gomez Park, this is a major gathering place for elderly, guayabera-clad Cuban men, who after 40 years still pass the day playing dominoes while arguing anti-Castro politics. ⊠ *S.W. 8th St. and S.W. 15th Ave., Little Havana* ☽ *Daily 9–6.*

off the beaten path

ELIÁN GONZÁLEZ'S HOUSE – This humble two-bedroom home was where six-year-old González stayed for nearly six months after surviving a raft journey from Cuba that killed his mother. From this same house, he was removed by federal agents in a predawn raid that ultimately united him with his father, who took him home to Cuba. The Miami relatives have since moved but bought the property to turn it into a shrine and museum. ⊠ *2319 N.W. 2nd St., at N.W. 23rd Ave., Little Havana* ⊠ *Free* ☽ *Sun. 10–6.*

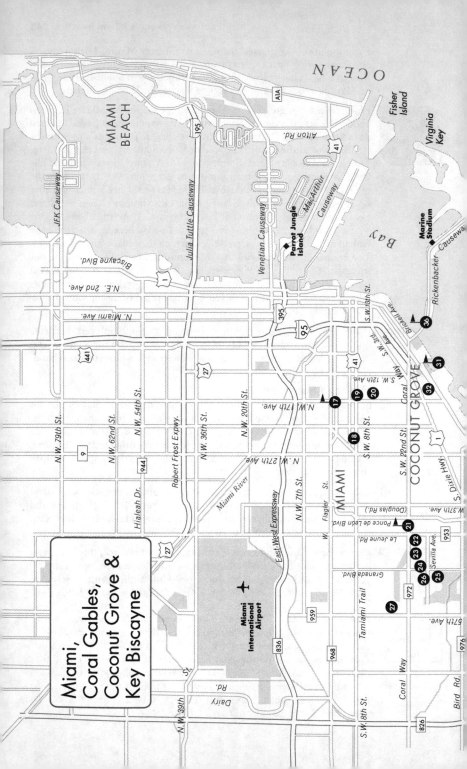

Miami, Coral Gables, Coconut Grove & Key Biscayne

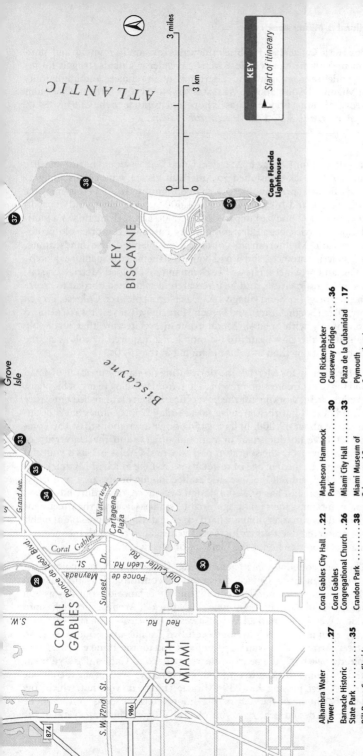

ATLANTIC

KEY
BISCAYNE

Cape Florida
Lighthouse

KEY

▲ Start of itinerary

0 ————— 3 miles

0 ————— 3 km

Biscayne

Grove
Isle

CORAL
GABLES

SOUTH
MIAMI

17 Plaza de la Cubanidad. Redbrick sidewalks surround a fountain and monument with the words of José Martí, a leader in Cuba's struggle for independence from Spain and a hero to Cuban refugees and immigrants in Miami. The quotation, LAS PALMAS SON NOVIAS QUE ESPERAN (The palm trees are waiting brides), counsels hope and fortitude to the Cubans. ⊠ W. Flagler St. and S.W. 17th Ave., Little Havana.

Coral Gables

If it weren't for George E. Merrick, Coral Gables would be just another suburb. Merrick envisioned an American Venice, with canals and gracious homes spreading across the community. In 1911 his minister father died, and Merrick inherited 1,600 acres of citrus and avocado groves; by 1921 he had upped that to 3,000 acres. Using this as a foundation, Merrick began designing a city based on centuries-old prototypes from Mediterranean countries. He planned lush landscaping, magnificent entrances, and broad boulevards named for Spanish explorers, cities, and provinces. His uncle, Denman Fink, helped Merrick crystallize his artistic vision, and he hired architects trained abroad to create themed neighborhood villages, such as Florida pioneer, Chinese, French city, Dutch South African, and French Normandy. The result was a planned community with Spanish Mediterranean architecture that justifiably calls itself the City Beautiful—a moniker it acquired by following the Garden City method of urban planning in the 1920s.

Unfortunately for Merrick the devastating no-name hurricane of 1926 and the Great Depression prevented him from fulfilling many of his plans. He died at 54, working for the post office. His city languished until after World War II but then grew rapidly. Today Coral Gables has a population of about 43,000. In its bustling downtown more than 150 companies have headquarters or regional offices, and the University of Miami campus in the southern part of Coral Gables brings a youthful vibrancy: the median age of residents is 38. Like much of Miami, Coral Gables has realized the aesthetic and economic importance of historic preservation and has passed a design ordinance, rewarding businesses for maintaining their buildings' architectural style. Even the street signs (ground-level markers that are hard to see in daylight, impossible at night) are preserved due to their historical value. They're worth the inconvenience, if only to honor the memory of Merrick.

a good tour

This tour contains some backtracking. Unfortunately, no matter how you navigate Coral Gables, directions get confusing. This plan takes in the highlights first and lets you fill out the balance of your day as you see fit. Heading south on downtown's Brickell Avenue, turn right onto Coral Way—also marked as Southwest 13th Street—and stay on Coral Way even as it turns into Southwest 3rd Avenue and Southwest 22nd Street. An arch of banyan trees prepares you for the grand entrance onto **Miracle Mile 21 ►**, the heart of downtown Coral Gables. Park your car and take time to explore on foot. When you've seen enough, continue driving west, passing the 1930s Miracle Theatre on your left, which now serves as home of the Actors' Playhouse. Keep heading west, cross Le Jeune Road, and bear right onto Coral Way, catching an eyeful of the

MIAMI'S ART DECO HOTELS

WITH APOLOGIES TO THE **FLAMINGO,** Miami's most recognizable icons are the art deco hotels of South Beach. But why here? What did this city do to deserve some of the world's most beautiful and stylish buildings?

The story begins in the 1920s, when Miami Beach established itself as America's Winter Playground. Long before Las Vegas got the idea, Miami Beach sprouted hostelries resembling Venetian palaces, Spanish villages, and French châteaux. To complement the social activities of the hotels, the city provided gambling, prostitution, and bootleg whiskey. Miami became a haven for out-of-town high rollers.

In the early 1930s, drawn south by the prospect of warm beaches and luxurious tropical surroundings, middle-class tourists fueled a second boom. More hotels had to be built, but it wouldn't do for Miami to open the same type of boring, staid hotels found across America. En masse, architects decided the motif of choice would be . . . art deco.

In truth, the design was Art Moderne. For purists, the term Moderne was a bow to the Exposition Internationale des Arts Décoratifs et Industriels Modernes, held in Paris in 1925. Moderne offered a distinctive yet affordable design solution for the hotels, stores, clubs, and apartment buildings that would be built to accommodate the needs of a new breed of tourist.

An antidote to the gloom of the Great Depression, this look was cheerful and tidy. Along South Beach, Miami received an architectural makeover. Elaborating on the styles introduced in Paris, architects borrowed elements of American industrial design. The features of trains, ocean liners, and automobiles were stripped down to their streamlined essentials, inspiring new looks for the art deco hotels.

With a steel-and-concrete box as a foundation, architects dipped into this grab bag of styles to accessorize their hotels. Pylons, spheres, cylinders, and cubes thrust from facades and roofs. "Eyebrows," small ledges over windows, popped out to provide shade. Softening the boxy buildings' edges, designers added curved corners and wraparound windows. Sunlight, an abundant commodity in Miami Beach, was brought indoors by glass-block construction. Landscapers learned to create an illusion of coolness by planting palms and laying terrazzo floors.

A uniform style soon marked Miami's new hotels. A vertical central element raced past the roofline and into the sky to create a sense of motion. To add to the illusion that these immobile buildings were rapidly speeding objects, colorful bands known as racing stripes were painted around the corners. In keeping with the beachside setting, designers adorned hotels with nautical elements. Portholes appeared in sets of three on facades or within buildings. Images of seaweed, starfish, and rolling ocean waves were plastered, painted, or etched on walls. Some of the buildings looked as if they were ready to go to sea.

Art deco design translated the synchronized choreography of Busby Berkeley movie musicals into architecture. Ordinary travelers could now take a low-cost vacation in an oceanfront fantasy world of geometric shapes and amusing colors. All this was created not for millionaires but for regular folks, those who collected a weekly paycheck . . . who, for one brief, shining moment, could live a life of luxury.

— Gary McKechnie

ornate Spanish Renaissance **Coral Gables City Hall** ㉒. Continue a few blocks until you see Toledo Street and make a left. A few blocks up on your left, are the gates surrounding the exotic and unusual Merrick-designed **Venetian Pool** ㉓, created from an old coral quarry. There's parking on your right. Immediately ahead of you is the Merrick-designed **De Soto Plaza and Fountain** ㉔.

As in many areas of Coral Gables, there's a traffic circle surrounding the fountain. Head to 12 o'clock (the opposite side of the fountain) and stay on De Soto for a magnificent vista and entrance to the, yes, Merrick-designed and reborn **Biltmore Hotel** ㉕. On your right, before you reach the hotel, is the **Coral Gables Congregational Church** ㉖, one of the first churches in this planned community. After visiting the hotel, double back to the fountain, this time circling to 9 o'clock and Granada Boulevard. Several blocks away you'll arrive at the Granada Golf Course, where you turn left onto North Greenway. As you cruise up the street, notice the stand of banyan trees that separates the fairways. At the end of the course the road makes a horseshoe bend, but instead cross Alhambra to loop around the restored **Alhambra Water Tower** ㉗, a city landmark dating from 1924. By the way, it's Merrick-designed.

Return to Alhambra and follow it straight to the next light (Coral Way); turn left and ogle beautifully maintained Spanish homes from the 1920s. Afterward, take a right on Coral Way, followed by a left on Granada, which winds south past Bird Road and eventually to Ponce de León Boulevard. Turn right and follow it to the entrance of the main campus of the **University of Miami** ㉘. Turn right at the first stoplight (Stanford Drive) to enter the campus; park in the lot on your right designated for visitors to the Lowe Art Museum.

TIMING   Strolling Miracle Mile should take slightly more than an hour—unless you plan to shop. In that case, allow four hours. Save time for a dip at the Venetian Pool, and plan to spend at least an hour getting acquainted with the Biltmore—longer if you'd like to order a drink and linger poolside. If you can pull yourself away from the lap of luxury, allow an hour to visit the University of Miami campus (if you're into college campuses).

What to See

㉗ **Alhambra Water Tower.** A water tower? Hardly a sight in most places, but this 1924 city landmark was clad in a decorative Moresque lighthouselike exterior. It delights viewers with its copper-rib dome and multicolor frescoes—pretty impressive when you consider its peers are merely steel containers. ⊠ *Alhambra Circle, Greenway Ct., and Ferdinand St., Coral Gables.*

㉕ **Biltmore Hotel.** Bouncing back from dark days as an army hospital, this 1926 hotel is now the jewel of Coral Gables. Reopened a decade ago after extensive renovations, the opulent landmark played host to President Clinton and regularly books visiting heads of state in its presidential suite. Tucked away on the easternmost side of the ground floor is performance space for one of Miami's top theater companies, GablesStage. The coral-color hotel was recently designated a National Historic Landmark. Its 16-story tower, like the Freedom Tower in downtown Miami, is a replica of Seville's Giralda tower. To the west is the Biltmore Country Club, a beaux arts–style structure with a superb colonnade and courtyard; it was reincorporated into the hotel in 1989. Free tours are offered. ⊠ *1200 Anastasia Ave., Coral Gables* ☎ *305/445–1926* ⊕ *www. biltmorehotel.com* ⊗ *Tours Sun. at 12:30, 1:30, and 2:30.*

㉒ Coral Gables City Hall. Far more attractive than today's modular city halls, this 1928 building has a three-tier tower topped with a clock and a 500-pound bell. A mural by Denman Fink (George Merrick's uncle and artistic adviser), inside the dome ceiling on the second floor, depicts the four seasons. (Although not as well known as Maxfield Parrish, Fink demonstrated a similar utopian vision.) Also on display are paintings, photos, and ads touting 1920s Coral Gables. ⊠ *405 Biltmore Way, Coral Gables* ☎ *305/446–5208* ⊗ *Weekdays 8–5.*

need a break? Whether you want to relax or try Miami's "in" snack, you can't miss with **Sushi Maki** (⊠ 2334 Ponce de León Blvd., Coral Gables ☎ 305/443–1884). In the center of the action in the Gables, this corner hangout is a remarkably inexpensive spot to rest your soles while sinking into dark red cushions and chowing down on a few California rolls or savoring a slice of key lime pie.

㉖ Coral Gables Congregational Church. The parish was organized in 1923, and with George Merrick as a charter member (and donor of the land), this small church became the first in the city. Rumor has it Merrick built it in honor of his father, a Congregational minister. The original interiors are still intact. ⊠ *3010 De Soto Blvd., Coral Gables* ☎ *305/448–7421* ⊕ *www.coralgablescongregational.org* ⊗ *Weekdays 8:30–7, Sun. services at 9:15 and 11 AM.*

㉔ De Soto Plaza and Fountain. Water flows from the mouths of four sculpted faces on a classical column on a pedestal in this Denman Fink–designed fountain from the early 1920s. The closed eyes of the face looking west symbolize the day's end. ⊠ *Granada Blvd. and Sevilla Ave., Coral Gables.*

▶ **㉑ Miracle Mile.** This upscale yet neighborly stretch of retail stores is actually only ½ mi long. After years of neglect, it's been updated and upgraded and now offers a delightful mix of owner-operated shops and chain stores, bridal shops, art galleries and bistros, and enough late-night hot spots to keep things hopping. ⊠ *Coral Way between S.W. 37th Ave. (Douglas Rd.) and S.W. 42nd Ave. (Le Jeune Rd.), Coral Gables.*

㉘ University of Miami. With almost 15,000 full-time, part-time, and non-credit students, UM is the largest private research university in the Southeast. Visit the **Lowe Art Museum,** which has a permanent collection of 8,000 works that include Renaissance and baroque art, American paintings, Latin American art, and Navajo and Pueblo Indian textiles and baskets. The museum also hosts traveling exhibitions and the popular Beaux Arts Festival in January. ⊠ *1301 Stanford Dr., Coral Gables* ☎ *305/284–3535 or 305/284–3536* ⊕ *www.lowemuseum.org* ⊠ *$5* ⊗ *Tues., Wed., Fri., and Sat. 10–5, Thurs. noon–7, Sun. noon–5.*

★ ♻ ㉓ **Venetian Pool.** Sculpted from a rock quarry in 1923 and fed by artesian wells, this 825,000-gallon municipal pool remains popular due to its themed architecture—a fantasized version of a waterfront Italian village—created by Denman Fink. The pool has earned a place on the National Register of Historic Places and displays vintage photos depicting 1920s beauty pageants and swank soirees held long ago. Paul Whiteman played here, Johnny Weissmuller and Esther Williams swam here, and you should, too (but no kids under three). A snack bar, lockers, and showers make this must-see user-friendly as well. ⊠ *2701 De Soto Blvd., Coral Gables* ☎ *305/460–5356* ⊕ *www.venetianpool.com* ✉ *Apr.–Oct., $9; Nov.–Mar. $6, free parking across De Soto Blvd.* ⊙ *June–Aug., weekdays 11–7:30, weekends 10–4:30; Sept. and Oct., Apr. and May, Tues.–Fri. 11–5:30, weekends 10–4:30; Nov.–Mar., Tues.–Fri. 10–4:30, weekends 10–4:30.*

South Miami

South of Miami and Coral Gables is a city called South Miami, which is not to be confused with the region known as South Dade. A pioneer farm community, South Miami grew into a suburb but retains its small-town charm. Fine old homes and stately trees line Sunset Drive, a city-designated Historic and Scenic Road to and through the town. The pace in this friendly community has picked up since the arrival of the Shops at Sunset Place, a retail complex larger than Coconut Grove's CocoWalk.

a good tour

Drive south from Sunset Drive on Red Road (watching for the plentiful orchid merchants) and turn left on Old Cutler Road, which curves north along the uplands of southern Florida's coastal ridge toward the 83-acre **Fairchild Tropical Garden** ㉙ ⌐. Just north of the gardens Old Cutler Road traverses Miami-Dade County's **Matheson Hammock Park** ㉚. From here follow the road back to U.S. 1, heading north to Miami.

TIMING Allow half a day for these three natural attractions, a full day if ornithology and botany are your thing. Driving from SoBe should take only 25 minutes—longer during afternoon rush hour.

What to See

★ ♻ ⌐ ㉙ **Fairchild Tropical Garden.** Comprising 83 acres, this is the largest tropical botanical garden in the continental United States. Eleven lakes, a rain forest, and lots of palm trees, cycads, and flowers, including orchids, mountain roses, bellflowers, coral trees, and bougainvillea make it a garden for the senses—and there's special assistance for the hearing impaired. Take the free guided tram tour, which leaves on the hour. Spicing up the social calendar are garden sales (don't miss the Ramble in November or the International Mango Festival in July), moonlight strolls, and symphony concerts. A gift shop in the visitor center is a popular source for books on gardening and horticulture, ordered by botanists the world over. ⊠ *10901 Old Cutler Rd., Coral Gables* ☎ *305/667–1651* ⊕ *www. fairchildgarden.org* ✉ *$10* ⊙ *Daily 9:30–4:30.*

♻ ㉚ **Matheson Hammock Park.** In the 1930s the Civilian Conservation Corps developed this 100-acre tract of upland and mangrove swamp on land donated by a local pioneer, Commodore J. W. Matheson. The park,

Miami-Dade County's oldest and most scenic, has a bathing beach and changing facilities and a popular restaurant housed in a historic coral-rock building that overlooks the swimming lagoon, Redfish Grill. The marina has slips for 243 boats, 71 dry-storage spaces, and a bait-and-tackle shop. Noticeably absent are fishing and diving charters, although there is a sailing school. ⊠ *9610 Old Cutler Rd., Coral Gables* ☎ *305/ 665-5475* ⊕ *www.miamidade.gov/parks/Parks/matheson_beach.asp* ☞ *Parking for beach and marina $5 per car, $12 per RV; limited free upland parking* ⊙ *Daily 6-dusk. Pool lifeguards winter, daily 8:30-5; summer, weekends 8:30-6.*

off the beaten path

PARROT JUNGLE ISLAND – One of South Florida's original tourist attractions, Parrot Jungle opened in 1936 and has now relocated to Watson Island, linked by the MacArthur Causeway (Interstate 395) to Miami and Miami Beach. In addition to a thousand exotic birds, the attraction includes a 17-foot Asian crocodile, a 9-foot albino alligator, a serpentarium filled with venomous snakes, a petting zoo, and a two-story-high aviary with more than 100 free-flying macaws. A restaurant with indoor and outdoor seating overlooks a lake where 60 postcard-perfect Caribbean flamingos hang out. Orchids and ferns and even trees from the original site were transplanted along a Disneyesque jungle river that meanders through the park. The Japanese garden that once stood on the new Parrot Jungle site is being reconstructed adjacent to the attraction. The original site on Southwest 57th Avenue at 111th Street has reopened as a park. The popular trails originally cut through coral rock and shaded by massive oaks and bald cypress remain a draw and showcase the region's natural flora. ⊠ *980 MacArthur Causeway, Watson Island* ☎ *305/258-6453* ⊕ *www.parrotjungle.com* ☞ *$24.95 plus $6 parking* ⊙ *Daily 10-6; last admission 4:30.*

Coconut Grove

South Florida's oldest settlement, "The Grove" was inhabited as early as 1834 and established by 1873, two decades before Miami. Its early settlers included Bahamian blacks, "Conchs" (white Key Westers, many originally from the Bahamas), and New England intellectuals, who built a community that attracted artists, writers, and scientists to establish winter homes. To this day Coconut Grove reflects its pioneers' eclectic origins. Posh estates mingle with rustic cottages, modest frame homes, and stark modern dwellings, often on the same block. To keep Coconut Grove a village in a jungle, residents lavish affection on exotic plantings while battling to protect remaining native vegetation. The historic center of the village of Coconut Grove went through a hippie period in the 1960s, a laid-back funkiness in the 1970s, and a teenybopper invasion in the early 1980s. Today the tone is upscale and urban. On weekends the Grove is jam-packed with locals and tourists—especially teenagers—shopping at the Streets of Mayfair, CocoWalk, and small boutiques. Parking can be a problem, especially on weekend evenings, when police direct traffic and prohibit turns at some intersections to prevent gridlock. Be prepared to walk several blocks from the periphery into the heart of the Grove.

a good
tour

From downtown Miami take Brickell Avenue south and follow the signs pointing to Vizcaya and Coconut Grove. If you're interested in seeing celeb estates, turn left at Southeast 32nd Road and follow the loop— Sylvester Stallone's former estate is the one with the huge gates on the right at the turn, and Madonna's one-time abode is at 3029 Brickell. Turn left back on South Miami Avenue. Immediately on your left is the entrance to the **Vizcaya Museum and Gardens** ㉛ ▶. Less than 100 yards down the road on your right is the **Miami Museum of Science and Space Transit Planetarium** ㉜. The road switches from four lanes to two and back again as you approach downtown Coconut Grove. With 28 waterfront acres of Australian pine, lush lawns, and walking and jogging paths, the bayside David T. Kennedy Park makes a pleasant stop. If you're interested in the history of air travel, take a quick detour down Pan American Drive to see the 1930s art deco Pan Am terminal, which has been horribly renovated inside to become **Miami City Hall** ㉝. You'll also see the Coconut Grove Convention Center, where antiques, boat, and home shows are held, and Dinner Key Marina, where seabirds soar and sailboats ride at anchor. South Miami Avenue, now known as South Bayshore Drive, heads directly into McFarlane Road, which takes a sharp right into the center of the action. If you can forsake instant gratification, turn left on Main Highway and drive less than ½ mi to Devon Road and the interesting **Plymouth Congregational Church** ㉞ and its gardens. Return to Main Highway and travel northeast toward the historic village of Coconut Grove. As you reenter the village center, note on your left the Coconut Grove Playhouse. On your right, beyond the benches and shelter, is the entrance to the **Barnacle Historic State Park** ㉟. After getting your fill of history, relax and spend the evening mingling with Coconut Grove's eccentrics.

TIMING   Plan on devoting from six to eight hours to enjoy Vizcaya, other bayfront sights, and the village's shops, restaurants, and nightlife.

What to See

㉟ **Barnacle Historic State Park.** The oldest Miami home still on its original foundation rests in the middle of 5 acres of native hardwood and landscaped lawns surrounded by flashy Coconut Grove. Built by Florida's first snowbird—New Yorker Commodore Ralph Munroe—the home has many original furnishings, a broad sloping roof, and deeply recessed verandas that channel sea breezes into the house. If your timing is right, you may catch one of the monthly Moonlight Concerts. ✉ 3485 Main Hwy., Coconut Grove 🕾 305/442–6866 ⊕ www.floridastateparks.org/ thebarnacle ✏ $1, concerts $5 ☉ Fri.–Mon. 9–4; tours at 10, 11:30, 1, and 2:30; group tours for 10 or more Tues.–Thurs. by reservation; concerts on evenings near the full moon 6–9, call for dates.

㉝ **Miami City Hall.** Built in 1934 as the terminal for the Pan American Airways seaplane base at Dinner Key, the building retains its nautical-style art deco trim. Sadly, the interior is generic government, but a 1938 Pan Am menu on display (with filet mignon, *petit pois au beurre,* [buttered baby peas] and Jenny Lind pudding) lets you know Miami officials appreciate from whence they came. ⊠ *3500 Pan American Dr., Coconut Grove* ☎ *305/250–5400* ☉ *Weekdays 8–5.*

☝ ㉜ **Miami Museum of Science and Space Transit Planetarium.** This museum is chock-full of hands-on sound, gravity, and electricity displays for children and adults. A wildlife center has native Florida snakes, turtles, tortoises, and birds of prey. Traveling exhibits appear throughout the year, and virtual-reality and life-science demonstrations are on hand every day. If you're here the first Friday of the month, stick around after dark for the laser-light rock-and-roll shows presented in the planetarium. ⊠ *3280 S. Miami Ave., Coconut Grove* ☎ *305/646–4200 museum* ⊕ *www. miamisci.org* ▨ *Museum exhibits, planetarium shows, and wildlife center $10, laser show $7* ☉ *Daily 10–6.*

㉞ **Plymouth Congregational Church.** Opened in 1917, this handsome coral-rock structure resembles a Mexican mission church. The front door, made of hand-carved walnut and oak with original wrought-iron fittings, came from an early 17th-century monastery in the Pyrenees. Also on the 11-acre grounds are the first schoolhouse in Miami-Dade County (one room), moved to this property, and the site of the original Coconut Grove water and electric works. ⊠ *3400 Devon Rd., Coconut Grove* ☎ *305/444–6521* ☉ *Weekdays 9–4:30, Sun. service at 10 AM.*

★ ▶ ㉛ **Vizcaya Museum & Gardens.** Of the 10,000 people living in Miami between 1912 and 1916, about 1,000 of them were gainfully employed by Chicago industrialist James Deering to build this $20 million Italian Renaissance–style winter residence. Once comprising 180 acres, the grounds now cover a still-substantial 30-acre tract, including a native hammock and more than 10 acres of formal gardens and fountains overlooking Biscayne Bay. The house, open to the public, has 70 rooms, 34 of which are filled with paintings, sculpture, and antique furniture dating from the 15th through the 19th centuries and representing the Renaissance, baroque, rococo, and neoclassical styles. Vizcaya's guest list has included Ronald Reagan, Pope John Paul II, Queen Elizabeth II, Bill Clinton, and Boris Yeltsin. It's a shame the guided tour can be far less impressive than the home's guest list and surroundings. ⊠ *3251 S. Miami Ave., Coconut Grove* ☎ *305/250–9133* ⊕ *www.vizcayamuseum. com* ▨ *$12* ☉ *Daily 9:30–4:30, garden 9:30–5:30.*

Virginia Key & Key Biscayne

Government Cut and the Port of Miami separate the city's dense urban fabric from two of its playground islands, Virginia Key and Key Biscayne. Parks occupy much of both keys, providing facilities for golf, tennis, softball, picnicking, and sunbathing, plus uninviting but ecologically valuable stretches of dense mangrove swamp. Key Biscayne's long and winding roads are great for rollerblading and bicycling, and its lush laziness provides a respite from the buzz-saw tempo of SoBe.

a good tour

To reach Virginia Key and Key Biscayne take the Rickenbacker Causeway ($1 per car) across Biscayne Bay from the mainland at Brickell Avenue and Southwest 26th Road, about 2 mi south of downtown Miami. The causeway links several islands in the bay. The William M. Powell Bridge rises 75 feet above the water to eliminate the need for a draw span. The view from the top includes the bay, keys, port, and downtown skyscrapers, with Miami Beach and the Atlantic Ocean in the distance. Just south of the Powell Bridge a stub of the **Old Rickenbacker Causeway Bridge** 🗲 ☞, built in 1947, is now a fishing pier. Immediately after crossing the Rickenbacker Causeway onto Virginia Key, you'll see a long strip of bayfront popular with windsurfers and jet skiers. Nearby rest rooms and a great view of the curving shoreline make this an ideal place to park and have your own tailgate party. Look for the gold dome of the **Miami Seaquarium** 🗲, one of the country's first marine attractions. Opposite the causeway from the Seaquarium, a road leads north to Virginia Key Beach and the adjacent Virginia Key Critical Wildlife Area, which is often closed to the public to protect nesting birds. From Virginia Key the causeway crosses Bear Cut to the north end of Key Biscayne and becomes Crandon Boulevard. The boulevard bisects 1,211-acre **Crandon Park** 🗲, with a popular Atlantic Ocean beach and nature center. On your right are entrances to the Crandon Park Golf Course and the Tennis Center at Crandon Park, home of the Nasdaq 100 Open. Keep your eyes open for pure Miami icons: coconut palms and iguana-crossing signs. From the traffic circle at the south end of Crandon Park, Crandon Boulevard continues to **Bill Baggs Cape Florida State Park** 🗲, a 460-acre park with the brick Cape Florida Lighthouse and light keeper's cottage. Follow Crandon Boulevard back to Crandon Park through Key Biscayne's downtown village, where shops and a 10-acre village green cater mainly to local residents. On your way back to the mainland, pause as you approach the Powell Bridge to admire the Miami skyline. At night the brightly lighted Bank of America building looks like a clipper ship running under full sail before the breeze.

TIMING   Set aside the better part of a day for this tour, and double that if you're into beaches, fishing, and water sports.

What to See

👏 ㊵   **Bill Baggs Cape Florida State Park.** Thanks to its beaches, blue-green waters, amenities, sunsets, and a lighthouse, this park at Key Biscayne's southern tip is well worth the drive. Since Hurricane Andrew, it has returned better than ever, with native trees replacing the once-ubiquitous Australian pines, an additional 54 acres of wetlands, new boardwalks over sea grass–studded dunes, 18 picnic shelters, and two rustic waterfront cafés. A stroll or bike ride along paths and boardwalks provides wonderful views of Miami's skyline. Also on-site are bicycle and skate rentals, a playground, fishing piers, and kayak rental. Guided tours of the cultural complex and the **Cape Florida Lighthouse,** South Florida's oldest structure, are offered, but call for availability. The lighthouse was built in 1845 to replace an earlier one destroyed in an 1836 Seminole attack, in which the keeper's helper was killed. ✉ *1200 S. Crandon Blvd., Key Biscayne* ☎ *305/361–5811 or 305/361–8779* ⊕ *www.*

Fodor'sChoice
★

floridastateparks.org/capeflorida ▨ *$3 per single-occupant vehicle, $5 per vehicle with 2 to 8 people; $1 per person on bicycle, bus, motorcycle, or foot* ☉ *Daily 8–dusk, tours Thurs.–Mon. at 10 and 1; sign up ½ hr beforehand.*

㊳ Crandon Park. This laid-back park in northern Key Biscayne is popular with families, and many educated beach enthusiasts rate the 3½-mi county beach here among the top 10 beaches in North America. The sand is soft, and parking is both inexpensive and plentiful. So large is this park that it includes a marina, a golf course, a tennis center, and ball fields. There is also a kids' section with a playground, splash pool and restored carousel (3 rides for $1). At the north end of the beach is the free **Marjory Stoneman Douglas Biscayne Nature Center** (☎ 305/ 361–6767). Explore natural habitats by taking a tour that includes dragging nets through sea-grass beds to catch, study, and release such marine creatures as sea cucumbers, sea horses, crabs, and shrimp. Nature center hours vary, so call ahead. ⊠ *4000 Crandon Blvd., Key Biscayne* ☎ *305/361-6767* ⊕ *www.miamidade.gov/parks/parks/crandon beach.asp* ▨ *Free, parking $5 per vehicle* ☉ *Daily 8–sunset.*

☝ ㊲ Miami Seaquarium. This old-fashioned attraction has six daily shows with sea lions, dolphins, and Lolita, a killer whale. (Lolita's tank is small for seaquariums—just three times her length—and so some wildlife advocates are trying to get her back to sea.) Exhibits include a shark pool, a 235,000-gallon tropical-reef aquarium, and manatees. Glass-bottom boats take tours of Biscayne Bay. Want to get your feet (and everything else) wet? The Water and Dolphin Exploration (WADE) program enables you to swim with dolphins during a two-hour session. Reservations are required. ⊠ *4400 Rickenbacker Causeway, Virginia Key* ☎ *305/361-5705* ⊕ *www.miamiseaquarium.com* ▨ *$24.95, WADE $149, parking $5* ☉ *Daily 9:30–6, last admission at 5; WADE daily at noon and 3:30.*

▶ ㊱ Old Rickenbacker Causeway Bridge. Watch boat traffic pass through the channel, pelicans and other seabirds soar and dive, and dolphins cavort in the bay. Park at its entrance, about a mile from the tollgate, and walk past anglers tending their lines to the gap where the center draw span across Biscayne Bay was removed. ⊠ *Rickenbacker Causeway south of Powell Bridge, east of Coconut Grove.*

WHERE TO EAT

Restaurants listed here have passed the test of time, but you might double-check by phone before you set out for the evening. At many of the hottest spots, you'll need a reservation to avoid a long wait for a table. And when you get your check, note whether a gratuity is already included; most restaurants add 15% (ostensibly for the convenience of, and protection from, the many Latin-American and European tourists who are used to this practice in their homelands), but reduce or supplement it depending on your opinion of the service.

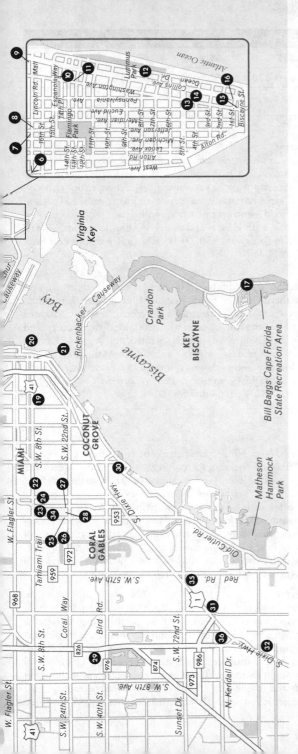

	WHAT IT COSTS				
	$$$$	$$$	$$	$	¢
AT DINNER	over $30	$20–$30	$15–$20	$10–$15	under $10

Restaurant prices are per person for a main course at dinner.

Coconut Grove

Contemporary

$$$ ✕ **Aria.** As pretty as an operatic melody, this dining room in the Ritz-Carlton resort provides a high-end, global experience. Choose your view: the 126-seat restaurant has an exhibition kitchen, although an alfresco area offers views of landscaped gardens or breeze-brushed beaches. Then select your food—entrées range from grilled tuna with chorizo and peppers to veal loin with lobster and morel mushroom ragout. ⊠ *455 Grand Bay Dr., Key Biscayne* ☎ *305/365–4500* ⌔ *Reservations essential* ⊟ *AE, D, DC, MC, V.*

Indian

$–$$$ ✕ **Anokha.** "There is no doubt that all Indians love food," the menu says at Anokha, and there's also no doubt that all Miamians love *this* Indian food. Standouts are mahimahi steamed with green chilies and cilantro and wrapped in a banana leaf, chicken with an almond-cream curry, and chicken marinaded in a puree of spinach, cilantro, and yogurt. The wait between courses can seem as long as a cab ride in Manhattan during rush hour, but don't fret—there's only one cook in the kitchen, and she's worth the wait. ⊠ *3195 Commodore Plaza, Coconut Grove* ☎ *786/552–1030* ⊟ *AE, MC, V* ⊗ *Closed Mon.*

Coral Gables

Caribbean

$$–$$$$ ✕ **Ortanique on the Mile.** Named after an exotic citrus fruit, this restaurant screams "island"—or, more accurately, island resort—from the breezy interior decorated like a Jamaican terraced garden to the exquisite pan-Caribbean cuisine. Proprietor Delius Shirley and chef-proprietor Cindy Hutson offer such favorites as pumpkin soup, spicy fried calamari salad, pan sautéed black grouper, and jerk pork chop. Dessert doesn't get better than drunken banana fritters, unless you accompany them with a press pot of Blue Mountain coffee, direct from Jamaica and practically vibrating with caffeine. ⊠ *278 Miracle Mile, Miracle Mile* ☎ *305/446–7710* ⊟ *AE, DC, MC, V* ⊗ *No lunch weekends.*

Contemporary

$$$–$$$$ ✕ **Norman's.** This destination restaurant, which has won as many awards as it has customers, turns out some of Miami's most imaginative cui-
Fodor'sChoice sine. Chef Norman Van Aken created an international buzz by perfect-
★ ing New World cuisine—a combination rooted in Latin, North American, Caribbean, and Asian influences. Bold tastes pervade the changing selections, which might include grilled wahoo with potato *brandade,* red pepper *pipérade* and thyme scented garlic broth. The ultragracious staff never seems harried, even when all seats are filled (usually every minute

between opening and closing). ✉ *21 Almeria Ave., Coral Gables* ☎ *305/446–6767* ⊟ *AE, DC, MC, V* ☉ *Closed Sun. No lunch.*

$–$$$$ ✗ **Restaurant St. Michel.** While this spot is utterly French, the hotel it's in evokes the Mediterranean, and the food is new American. Stuart Bornstein's window on Coral Gables is a lace-curtained café with sidewalk tables that would be at home across from a railroad station in Avignon or Bordeaux. Lighter dishes include penne pasta with garlic, basil, and tomatoes. Among the heartier entrées are salmon and shrimp with steamed asparagus, sesame-seared loin of tuna, and yellowtail snapper with a fruit salsa. ✉ *162 Alcazar Ave., Coral Gables* ☎ *305/444–1666* ⊟ *AE, DC, MC, V.*

French

$$–$$$ ✗ **Pascal's on Ponce.** Chef-proprietor Pascal Oudin's stream-lined French cuisine disdains trends and discounts flash. Instead, you're supplied with substantive delicacies such as sautéed Australian sea bass with Mediterranean vegetables en croute or tenderloin of beef sautéed with snails and wild mushrooms. Service is proper, textures perfect, and wines ideally complementary. The only dilemma is deciding between Oudin's own tart Tatin or a cheese course for dessert. ✉ *2611 Ponce de León Blvd., Coral Gables* ☎ *305/444–2024* ⊟ *AE, D, DC, MC, V* ☉ *Closed Sun. No lunch Sat.*

Italian

$$–$$$ ✗ **Caffè Abbracci.** Much-beloved, this Italian restaurant is more like a club than an eatery. Start with some cold and hot antipasti, various carpaccios, porcini mushrooms, calamari, grilled goat cheese, shrimp, and mussels. Most pasta is made fresh, so consider sampling two or three, maybe with pesto sauce, Gorgonzola sauce, or fresh tomatoes. Patrons tend to fare better when they're recognized, so go with a local if you can. ✉ *318 Aragon Ave., Coral Gables* ☎ *305/441–0700* ⌔ *Reservations essential* ⊟ *AE, DC, MC, V* ☉ *No lunch weekends.*

Japanese

¢–$ ✗ **Sushi Maki.** At night, the twentysomething set seems to gravitate to this Gables restaurant for the current "in" nibble—sushi, washed down with Japanese beer, sake, or green tea. But if sushi and sashimi make you squeamish, there are cooked rolls and hot dishes such as teriyaki, tempura, and noodle bowls. Diehards dig the Volcano, a roll of smoked salmon, crab, cream cheese, and rice topped with a spicy burnt orange "lava" of conch-spiked mayonnaise. Entrées come with miso soup or a simple salad. ✉ *2334 Ponce de León Blvd., Coral Gables* ☎ *305/443–1884* ⊟ *AE, MC, V* ☉ *No lunch Sun.*

Downtown Miami

Chinese

$–$$$$ ✗ **Tony Chan's Water Club.** Off the lobby of the Doubletree Grand Hotel, this spot overlooks a bayside marina. On the menu of more than 200 appetizers and entrées are minced quail tossed with bamboo shoots and mushrooms wrapped in lettuce leaves. Indulge in a seafood spectacular of shrimp, conch, scallops, fish cakes, and crabmeat tossed with broccoli in a bird's nest, or go for pork chops sprinkled with green pepper in a black bean–garlic sauce. A lighter favorite is steamed sea bass with ginger and garlic. ✉ *1717 N. Bayshore Dr., Downtown* ☎ *305/374–8888* ⊟ *AE, D, DC, MC, V* ☉ *No lunch weekends.*

Contemporary

★ **$$–$$$$** ✕ **Azul.** This sumptuous eatery has truly conquered the devil in the details. In addition to chef Michelle Bernstein's exquisite French–Caribbean cuisine, the thoughtful touches in service graciously anticipate your needs. Does your sleeveless top mean your shoulders are too cold to properly appreciate the Swiss chard–stuffed pompano with caramelized pears? Ask for one of the house pashminas. Forgot your reading glasses and can't decipher the hanger steak with foie gras sauce? Request a pair from the host. Want to see how the other half lives? Descend the staircase to Cafe Sambal, the all-day casual restaurant. ⊠ *Mandarin Oriental Hotel, 500 Brickell Key Dr., Brickell Key* ☎ *305/913–8288* ⚊ *Reservations essential* ⊟ *AE, MC, V* ⊘ *Closed Sun. No lunch Sat.*

Italian

$–$$$ ✕ **Perricone's Marketplace and Café.** Brickell Avenue south of the Miami River is burgeoning with Italian restaurants. This is the biggest and most popular among them, in a 120-year-old barn from Vermont. The recipes were handed down from grandmother to mother to daughter, and the cooking is simple and good. Buy your wine from the on-premises deli and bring it to your table for a small corkage fee. Enjoy a glass with homemade minestrone; a generous antipasto; linguine with a sauté of jumbo shrimp, fresh asparagus, and chopped tomatoes; or gnocchi with four cheeses. The homemade tiramisu and fruit tart are top-notch. ⊠ *15 S.E. 10th St., Brickell Village* ☎ *305/374–9449* ⊟ *AE, MC, V.*

Mexican

¢–$ ✕ **Taquerias el Mexicano.** This modest storefront on the edge of Little Havana is a find for authentic Mexican fare such as enchiladas, chicken *mole* (chocolate sauce), and fajitas. Dinner begins with a basket of chips to dip in a salsa brimming with fresh cilantro. Not a lot of English is spoken here, but the waitstaff is eager to help. ⊠ *521 S.W. 8th St., Downtown* ☎ *305/858–1160* ⊟ *AE, MC, V.*

Little Havana

Cuban

¢–$$$ ✕ **Versailles.** Cubans meet to dine on Calle Ocho in what is quite possibly the most ornate budget restaurant you'll ever see, all mirrors and candelabras. And the royal treatment is not limited to the furnishings. The food is terrific, especially such classics as *ropa vieja* (saucy shredded beef served over rice), *arroz con pollo* (chicken and rice), *palomilla* (thin, boneless) steak, *sopa de platanos* (plantain soup), ham shank, and roast pork. To complete the experience, have ultrastrong Cuban coffee and terrific flan or sweet *tres leches* (literally, "three milks," a creamy Latin dessert) to finish. ⊠ *3555 S.W. 8th St., Little Havana* ☎ *305/444–0240* ⊟ *AE, D, DC, MC, V.*

Vietnamese

★ **¢–$$** ✕ **Hy-Vong Vietnamese Cuisine.** This plain little restaurant is an anomaly on Calle Ocho, and also a novelty—come before 7 PM to avoid a wait. Spring springs forth in spring rolls of ground pork, cellophane noodles, and black mushrooms wrapped in homemade rice paper. Folks will mill about on the sidewalk for hours to sample the whole fish panfried with *nuoc man* (a garlic-lime fish sauce), not to mention the thinly sliced pork barbecued with sesame seeds, almonds, and peanuts. Beer-savvy proprietor Kathy Manning serves a half-dozen top brews (Singha, Sapporo, and Spaten, among them) to further inoculate the experience from the ordinary. ⊠ *3458 S. W. 8th St., Little Havana* ☎ *305/446–3674* ▭ *AE, D, MC, V* ☺ *Closed Mon. No lunch.*

Miami Beach North of South Beach
Contemporary
$–$$$ ✕ **Crystal Café.** Classic dishes like Beef Stroganoff and chicken *paprikash* are updated and lightened up here; osso buco falls off the bone (there's also a seafood version with salmon). More contemporary items include chicken Kiev, stuffed with goat cheese and topped with a tricolor salad, and pan-seared duck breast with raspberry sauce. Multiple Golden Spoon award–winning Macedonian chef-proprietor Klime Kovaceski takes pride in serving more food than you can possibly manage, including home-baked rhubarb pie. ⊠ *726 41st St., Miami Beach* ☎ *305/673–8266* ▭ *AE, D, DC, MC, V* ☺ *Closed Mon. No lunch.*

Continental
$$$–$$$$ ✕ **The Forge.** This landmark bills itself as the Versailles of steak. Each intimate dining salon has historical artifacts, including a chandelier that hung in James Madison's White House. The wine cellar contains 380,000 bottles—including more than 500 dating from 1822. In addition to steak, specialties include Norwegian salmon with spinach vinaigrette and free-range duck roasted with black currants. For dessert try the blacksmith pie. ⊠ *432 Arthur Godfrey Rd., Miami Beach* ☎ *305/ 538–8533* ⌕ *Reservations essential* ▭ *AE, DC, MC, V* ☺ *No lunch.*

Delicatessens
¢–$ ✕ **Arnie and Richie's.** Take a deep whiff when you walk in and you'll know what you're in for: onion rolls, smoked whitefish salad, half-sour pickles, herring in sour cream sauce, chopped liver, corned beef, and pastrami. At this casual-to-the-extreme, family-run operation, most customers are regulars and seat themselves at tables that have baskets of plastic knives and forks; if you request a menu, it's a clear sign you're a newcomer. Service can be brusque, but it sure is quick. ⊠ *525 41st St., Miami Beach* ☎ *305/531–7691* ▭ *AE, MC, V.*

Italian
★ **¢–$$** ✕ **Café Prima Pasta.** One of Miami's many signatures is this exemplary Argentine-Italian spot, which rules the emerging North Beach neighborhood. Service can be erratic, but you forget it all on delivery of fresh-made bread with a bowl of spiced olive oil. Tender carpaccio and plentiful antipasti are a delight to share, but the real treat here is the hand-rolled pasta, which can range from crab-stuffed ravioli to simple fettuccine with seafood. ⊠ *414 71st St., North Beach, Miami Beach* ☎ *305/867–0106* ▭ *MC, V.*

North Miami Beach & North Dade
Contemporary
★ **$$$–$$$$** ✕ **Chef Allen's.** Chef Allen Susser presents his global fare in this art gallery of a dining room. At the 25-foot-wide picture window, watch him create

masterpieces from a menu that changes nightly. After a salad of baby greens and warm wild mushrooms or crisp veal sweetbreads with capers, consider cumin-and-tangerine seared yellowfin tuna with green papaya slaw or Dijon-crusted lamb chops with portobello–goat cheese strudel. It's hard to resist finishing off your meal with a soufflé; order it early to eliminate a wait at the end of your meal. ☒ *19088 N.E. 29th Ave. North Miami Beach* ☎ *305/935–2900* ☝ *Reservations essential* ▤ *AE, DC, MC, V.*

Steak

$$$–$$$$ ✗ **Shula's Steak House.** Prime rib, fish, steaks, and 3-pound lobsters are almost an afterthought to the *objets de sport* in this NFL shrine in the Don Shula's Hotel. Dine in a muscular wood-lined room with a fireplace, surrounded by memorabilia of retired coach Don Shula's perfect 1972 season with the Miami Dolphins. Finish the 48-ounce porterhouse steak and achieve immortality—your name posted on Shula's Web site and an autographed picture of Shula to take home. Also at the hotel is sports-celebrity hangout Shula's Steak 2; there's a Shula's at the Alexander Hotel in Miami Beach as well. ☒ *7601 N.W. 154th St., Miami Lakes* ☎ *305/820–8102* ▤ *AE, DC, MC, V.*

South Beach

American

$$–$$$ ✗ **Joe Allen.** In a neighborhood of condos, town houses, and stores, this casual upscale eatery is a hangout for locals who crave a good martini along with a terrific burger. The eclectic crowd includes kids and grandparents, and the menu, printed daily, has everything from pizzas to calves' liver to steaks. Start with a salad, such as arugula with pear, prosciutto, and Parmesan with a lemon-shallot dressing. Desserts include banana cream pie and ice cream and cookie sandwiches. ☒ *1787 Purdy Ave., South Beach* ☎ *305/531–7007* ▤ *MC, V.*

Cafés

★ ¢–$$ ✗ **News Café.** An Ocean Drive landmark, this 24-hour café attracts a crowd with snacks, light meals, and drinks. Most prefer sitting out along the sidewalk, where they can feel the salt breeze and gawk at the human scenery. Offering a little of this and a little of that—bagels, eggs, stuffed grape leaves, chocolate fondue, sandwiches, and a terrific wine list—this joint has something for all appetites. Although service can be indifferent to the point of laissez-faire, the café remains a scene. ☒ *800 Ocean Dr., South Beach* ☎ *305/538–6397* ☝ *Reservations not accepted* ▤ *AE, DC, MC, V.*

¢–$$ ✗ **Van Dyke Café.** Just as its parent, News Café, draws the fashion crowd, this offshoot attracts the artsy crowd. Indeed, this place seems even livelier than its Ocean Drive counterpart, with pedestrians passing by on the Lincoln Road Mall and live jazz playing upstairs every evening—or, technically, every early morning. The kitchen serves dishes from mammoth omelets with home fries to soups and grilled dolphin sandwiches to chilled poached salmon and shrimp kabobs, though it's best to stick to basics. ☒ *846 Lincoln Rd., South Beach* ☎ *305/534–3600* ▤ *AE, DC, MC, V.*

Contemporary

★ **$$$–$$$$** ✕ **Blue Door at the Delano.** In a hotel where style reigns supreme, this restaurant provides both glamour and tantalizing food. Acclaimed consulting chef Claude Troisgros combines the flavors of classic French fare with South American influences to create dishes such as Maine lobster with caramelized bananas and "crabavocat"—blue crab and guacamole salad in spiced tomato coulis. Equally pleasing is dining with the crème de la crème of Miami (and New York, and Paris) society. ✉ *1685 Collins Ave., South Beach* ☎ *305/674–6400* ✍ *Reservations essential* ▭ *AE, D, DC, MC, V.*

★ **$$$–$$$$** ✕ **Nemo.** The bright colors, copper fixtures, and tree-shaded courtyard lend Nemo casual comfort, but it's the menu that earns raves. Caribbean, Asian, Mediterranean, and Middle Eastern influences blend boldly, and succeed. Appetizers include garlic-cured salmon rolls with Tobiko caviar and wasabi mayo, and crispy prawns with spicy salsa *cruda*. Main courses might include wok-charred salmon or Indian-spice pork chop. Hedy Goldsmith's funky pastries are exquisite. ✉ *100 Collins Ave., South Beach* ☎ *305/532–4550* ▭ *AE, DC, MC, V.*

Italian

$$$–$$$$ ✕ **Escopazzo.** A romantic storefront takes you away, like Calgon, from the din of bustling Washington Avenue. The Roman menu offers some of the area's best—and most expensive—Italian food. Indulge in sea bream with roasted vegetables and toasted almond sauce, risottos with such combinations as goat cheese and arugula, and various soufflés with the freshest produce and seafood. Service can be slow as a speedboat in a manatee zone; pass the time by taking a tour of the 1,000-bottle wine cellar. ✉ *1311 Washington Ave., South Beach* ☎ *305/674–9450* ▭ *AE, DC, MC, V* ☾ *Closed Sun.–Tues. No lunch.*

★ **$$–$$$$** ✕ **Tuscan Steak.** Dark wood and mirrors define this masculine, chic, expensive place, where food is served family style. Tuscan can be busy as a subway stop, and still the staff will be gracious and giving. The chefs take their cues from the Tuscan countryside, where pasta is rich with truffles and main plates are simply but deliciously grilled. Sip a deep red Barolo with any of the house specialties: three-mushroom risotto with white truffle oil, gnocchi with Gorgonzola cream, Florentine T-bone with roasted garlic puree, whole yellowtail snapper with baby artichoke and shrimp risotto, or filet mignon with Gorgonzola crust. ✉ *431 Washington Ave., South Beach* ☎ *305/534–2233* ▭ *AE, DC, MC, V.*

$–$$ ✕ **Spiga.** When you need a break from Miami's abundant exotic fare, savor the modestly priced Italian standards at this neighborhood favorite. Homemade pastas and breads are fresh daily. Carpaccio *di tonno* (thinly sliced tuna with avocado and onion) is a typical appetizer, and the *zuppa di pesce* (fish stew) is unparalleled. Entrées include ravioli *di ricotto* (homemade ravioli stuffed with cheese and spinach). Customers sometimes bring CDs for personalized enjoyment. ✉ *1228 Collins Ave., South Beach* ☎ *305/534–0079* ▭ *AE, D, DC, MC, V* ☾ *No lunch.*

Pan-Asian

★ **$$$–$$$$** ✕ **Pacific Time.** Packed nearly every night, chef-proprietor Jonathan Eismann's superb eatery has a high blue ceiling, banquettes, plank floors, and an open kitchen. The brilliant American-Asian food includes such masterpieces as Sizzling Local Yellowtail Hot & Sour Tempura, a crisp, ginger-stuffed whole fish served filleted over ribbon vegetables with herbs and a dipping sauce, or dry-aged Colorado beef grilled with shiitake mushrooms and bok choy. Diners can start with a spicy coconut curry of local pink shrimp and end with a soothing tropical sorbet. ✉ *915 Lincoln Rd., South Beach* ☎ *305/534–5979* ⌀ *Reservations essential* ▤ *AE, DC, MC, V.*

$$–$$$$ ✕ **China Grill.** This crowded, noisy celebrity haunt turns out not Chinese food but rather "world cuisine" in large portions meant for sharing. Shanghai lobster with ginger, curry, and crispy spinach is one headliner, as is the pan-seared spicy tuna with avocado sashimi. Unless you're a celebrity, don't expect your drinks to arrive before your food. ✉ *404 Washington Ave., South Beach* ☎ *305/534–2211* ⌀ *Reservations essential* ▤ *AE, DC, MC, V* ☉ *No lunch Sat.*

Seafood

$–$$$$ ✕ **Joe's Stone Crab Restaurant.** Joe's stubbornly operates by its own rules: be prepared to wait up to an hour just to register your name for a table, and resign yourself to waiting up to another *two* hours before you finally sit down (consider arriving at 5 or 5:30 to reduce your wait). The centerpiece of the ample à la carte menu is, of course, stone crab, with a piquant mustard sauce. Side orders include creamed garlic spinach, fried sweet potatoes, fried green tomatoes, and hash browns. Desserts include a justifiably famous key lime pie. If you can't stand loitering hungrily, come for lunch; or, go next door for Joe's takeout and consider bringing a blanket to picnic on the beach. ✉ *11 Washington Ave., South Beach* ☎ *305/673–0365, 305/673–4611 takeout, 800/780–2722 overnight shipping* ⌀ *Reservations not accepted* ▤ *AE, D, DC, MC, V* ☉ *Closed May–mid-Oct. No lunch Sun. and Mon.*

South Miami

Barbecue

¢–$$ ✕ **Shorty's.** When "Shorty" opened his barbecue spot in 1951, some folks would ride in on horseback. Now the rustic outpost sits in the shadow of "Downtown Dadeland," and plate glass and air-conditioning have replaced screens, but it still serves the best barbecue in these parts. Sit at long picnic tables and chow down on pork barbecue sandwiches, baby backs, or a combo plate of chicken and ribs; order a side of corn on the cob drenched in butter; and slake your thirst with a glass of iced tea (sweetened or not) while recalling the simpler days before high-rises and Metrorail. Clean off the addictive barbecue sauce with rolls of paper towels and throw the bones into individual brown paper bags. If there's room, key lime pie or a soft-serve ice cream cone makes a great ending. ✉ *9200 S. Dixie Hwy., Miami* ☎ *305/670–7732* ▤ *AE, MC, V.*

Contemporary

$$–$$$ ✕ **Two Chefs.** This restaurant, decorated like a Williams-Sonoma catalog, has an ever-changing menu, but scan for oak-baked Portobello with Gruyère cheese and sourdough toast or New York strip with lobster potato galette and escargots. The chefs pride themselves on the unexpected and think nothing of pairing grilled salmon with a Jerusalem artichoke hash or creating a calzone with lobster, mozzarella, and asparagus. ⊠ *8287 S. Dixie Hwy., South Miami* ☎ *305/663–2100* ▭ *AE, D, DC, MC, V* ⊘ *Closed Sun.*

¢–$$ ✕ **Sunset Tavern.** Innovative food, such as a seafood enchilada topped with fried flat noodles, comes with a relatively low price tag in this preppie tavern near Sunset Place. The open-faced steak sandwich is loaded with sautéed mushrooms and onions, and the burger is a half pound of sirloin. Among many tasty bangs for the buck are handmade Hawaiian pizza, roasted duck and lentil salad, and maple-glazed meat loaf served with potato cake and spring vegetables. ⊠ *7230 S.W. 59th Ave., South Miami* ☎ *305/665–9996* ▭ *AE, MC, V.*

Seafood

$–$$$ ✕ **Captain's Tavern.** This beloved family fish house has an unusually interesting menu fortified with Caribbean and South American influences. The paneled walls and padded captain's chairs may be dated, but the fabulous food and impressive wine list make up for it. Next to good versions of the typical fare—seafood platters and conch fritters—you'll find Portuguese fish stew (*Cataplana*), a hearty conch chowder served with a shot of sherry, fish with various tropical fruits, and oysters in cream sauce with fresh rosemary, not to mention decadent desserts. ⊠ *7495 S.E. 98th St., South Miami* ☎ *305/661–4237* ▭ *AE, MC, V.*

West Miami

Chinese

¢–$$$$ ✕ **Tropical Chinese Restaurant.** This big, lacquer-free room feels and sounds as open and busy as a railway station. The extensive menu is filled with tofu combinations, poultry, beef, and pork, as well as tender seafood. An exuberant dim sum lunch—brunch on the weekends—allows you to choose an assortment of small dishes from wheeled carts. In the open kitchen 10 chefs prepare everything as if for dignitaries. ⊠ *7991 S.W. 40th St. (Bird Rd.), Westchester, West Miami* ☎ *305/262–7576 or 305/262–1552* ▭ *AE, DC, MC, V.*

WHERE TO STAY

Although some hotels (especially on the mainland) have adopted steady year-round rates, many adjust their rates to reflect seasonal demand. The peak occurs in winter, with a dip in summer (prices are often more negotiable than rate cards let on). You'll find the best values between Easter and Memorial Day (which is actually a delightful time in Miami but a difficult time for many people to travel) and in September and October (the height of hurricane season). Keep in mind that Miami hoteliers collect roughly 12.5%—ouch—for city and resort taxes; parking fees can

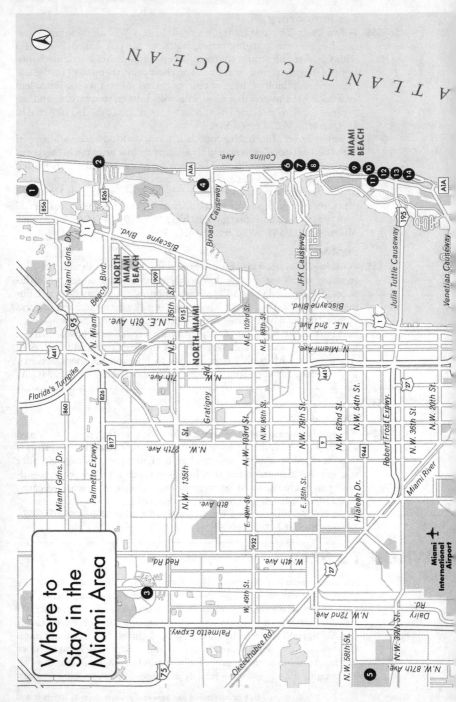

Where to Stay in the Miami Area

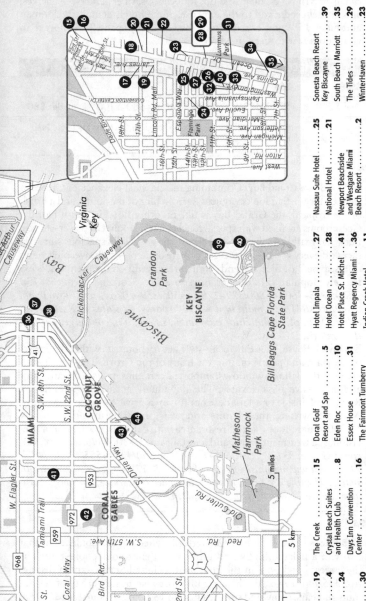

The Albion **19**
Bay Harbor Inn **4**
Bayliss Guest House **24**
Best Western
South Beach **30**
Biltmore Hotel **42**
Cadet Hotel **17**
Casa Grande
Suite Hotel **34**
Claridge Hotel **14**

The Creek **15**
Crystal Beach Suites
and Health Club **8**
Days Inn Convention
Center **16**
Day's Inn North Beach . . . **6**
Days Inn Oceanside
Beach Front **13**
Delano Hotel **20**
Don Shula's Hotel
& Golf Club **3**

Doral Golf
Resort and Spa **5**
Eden Roc **10**
Essex House **31**
The Fairmont Turnberry
Isle Resort & Club **1**
Fontainebleau
Hilton Resort **12**
Four Seasons Miami **38**
Hotel Astor **3**

Hotel Impala **27**
Hotel Ocean **28**
Hotel Place St. Michel . . **41**
Hyatt Regency Miami . . **36**
Indian Creek Hotel **11**
Kent **26**
Loews Miami
Beach Hotel **22**
Mayfair House **43**
Mandarin Oriental Miami . .**37**

Nassau Suite Hotel **25**
National Hotel **21**
Newport Beachside
and Westgate Miami
Beach Resort **2**
Ocean Surf **7**
Raleigh Hotel **18**
Ritz-Carlton
Key Biscayne **40**
Royal South Beach **33**

Sonesta Beach Resort
Key Biscayne **39**
South Beach Marriott . . **35**
The Tides **29**
WinterHaven **23**
Wyndham Grand Bay . . **44**
Wyndham Miami
Beach Resort **9**

run up to $16 per evening; and tips for bellhops, valet parkers, concierges, and housekeepers add to the expense. Some hotels actually tack on an automatic 15% gratuity. All told, you can easily spend 25% more than your room rate to sleep in Miami.

	WHAT IT COSTS				
	$$$$	**$$$**	**$$**	**$**	**¢**
FOR 2 PEOPLE	over $220	$140–$220	$100–$140	$80–$100	under $80

Hotel prices are for a standard double room, excluding 6% sales tax (more in some counties) and 1%–4% tourist tax.

Coconut Grove

★ **$$$–$$$$**   🏨 **Wyndham Grand Bay.** Combining the classical elegance of Greece, a stepped facade that looks vaguely Aztec, a hint of the South, and a brush of the tropical, the Grand Bay is like no other hotel in South Florida. Guest rooms are filled with special touches like in-room CD player–stereos. But what really sets the hotel apart are the atypically spacious suite terraces off every room—perfect for private dinners—with sweeping views of Biscayne Bay. Bice, a trendy Italian restaurant on the premises, is extremely popular. ⊠ *2669 S. Bayshore Dr., Coconut Grove 33133* ☎ *305/858–9600 or 800/327–2788* 🖷 *305/859–2026* ⊕ *www.wyndham. com/hotels/MIAGB/main.wnt* ➲ *130 rooms, 47 suites* ♨ *Restaurant, cable TV, pool, health club, hair salon, sauna, bar, concierge, parking (fee)* ▤ *AE, DC, MC, V.*

$$–$$$$ 🏨 **Mayfair House.** This European-style luxury hotel sits within the Streets of Mayfair, an upscale mall in the heart of the Grove. That feel is mirrored in the Tiffany windows, imported ceramics, polished mahogany, and impressive glass elevator. The individually furnished suites have a Roman tub inside or a Japanese hot tub on a private terrace or balcony. As of this writing, the all-suite hotel was preparing to christen a new 13,000-square-foot rooftop resort area with cabanas, pool, plasma television, spa treatment areas, and a restaurant. ⊠ *3000 Florida Ave., Coconut Grove, 33133* ☎ *305/441–0000 or 800/433–4555* 🖷 *305/447–9173* ⊕ *www.mayfairhousehotel.com* ➲ *179 suites* ♨ *Restaurant, snack bar, cable TV, pool, hot tub, bar, laundry service, concierge, business services, parking (fee)* ▤ *AE, D, DC, MC, V.*

Coral Gables

★ **$$$–$$$$**   🏨 **Biltmore Hotel.** Built in 1926 and still reflecting the opulence of that era with a palatial lobby and grounds, an enormous pool—touted as the largest hotel pool in the continental United States—and a distinctive 315-foot tower, the historic Biltmore also has a variety of restaurants and bars, tennis and spa facilities, an 18-hole golf course, and 76,000 square feet of convention space, including the Conference Center of the Americas (formerly the hotel's country club). ⊠ *1200 Anastasia Ave., Coral Gables 33134* ☎ *305/445–1926 or 800/727–1926* 🖷 *305/913–3159* ⊕ *www.biltmorehotel.com* ➲ *241 rooms, 39 suites* ♨ *4 restau-*

*rants, cable TV, 18-hole golf course, 10 tennis courts, pool, health club,
spa, 4 bars, convention center, meeting rooms* ⊟ *AE, D, DC, MC, V.*

★ **$$$** ▦ **Hotel Place St. Michel.** Art nouveau chandeliers suspended from vaulted
ceilings light the public areas of this intimate hotel within walking dis-
tance of Miracle Mile. Built in 1926, the historic inn is kept filled with
the scent of fresh flowers, circulated by paddle fans. Each room has its
own dimensions, personality, and antiques imported from England,
Scotland, and France, although plusher beds would be welcome. Din-
ner at the superb Restaurant St. Michel is a must, but there's also a more
casual bar-dining area behind the lobby, best suited for quiet breakfasts
or late-night aperitifs. ⊠ *162 Alcazar Ave., Coral Gables 33134* ☎ *305/
444–1666 or 800/848–4683* 🖷 *305/529–0074* ⊕ *www.
hotelplacestmichel.com* 🛏 *24 rooms, 3 suites* ⌂ *Restaurant, cable TV,
bar, laundry service, parking (fee)* ⊟ *AE, DC, MC, V* ⦿ *CP.*

Downtown Miami

$$$$ ▦ **Four Seasons Miami.** Pleasure before business? Maybe, at this down-
town spot, which greets visitors with the soothing sound of a water wall
trickling down from above. Inside, a cavernous lobby is barely big
enough to hold enormous pieces of sculpture—the hotel has a $3.5-mil-
lion collection showcasing the work of local artists. A 2-acre pool ter-
race on the 7th floor overlooks downtown Miami while making you
forget you're in downtown Miami. Four pools include a foot-high wad-
ing pool with 24 "islands" from which cocktails are served. A shoe valet
stands by with slippers and towels. Rooms are elegantly subdued, with
nice touches like glass-enclosed showers, DVD–CD players and window
seats. ⊠ *1435 Brickell Ave., Downtown, 33131* ☎ *305/358–3535 or
800/819–5053* 🖷 *305/358–7758* ⊕ *www.fourseasons.com/miami* 🛏 *182
rooms, 39 suites* ⌂ *Restaurant, in-room safes, cable TV, 4 pools, health
club, spa, 2 bars, children's programs (ages 4–12), Internet, business ser-
vices, meeting rooms* ⊟ *AE, D, DC, MC.*

$$$$ ▦ **Hyatt Regency Miami.** If your trip is based on boats, basketball, busi-
ness, or bargains, you can't do much better than the Hyatt Regency, with
its adjacent convention facilities and location near the Brickell Avenue
business district, Bayside Marketplace, the AmericanAirlines Arena,
the Port of Miami, and downtown shopping. Distinctive public spaces
are more colorful than businesslike, and guest rooms are a blend of av-
ocado, beige, and blond. The James L. Knight International Center is
accessible without stepping outside, as is the downtown Metromover
and its Metrorail connection. ⊠ *400 S.E. 2nd Ave., Downtown, 33131*
☎ *305/358–1234 or 800/233–1234* 🖷 *305/358–0529* ⊕ *www.miami.
hyatt.com* 🛏 *561 rooms, 51 suites* ⌂ *2 restaurants, cable TV, pool, health
club, lounge, laundry service, concierge, business services, parking (fee)*
⊟ *AE, D, DC, MC, V.*

$$$$ ▦ **Mandarin Oriental Miami.** Though it's a favorite of Wall Street tycoons
Fodor's Choice and Latin American CEOs doing business with the Brickell Avenue
★ banks, anyone who can afford to stay here, should. The location is ex-
cellent, at the tip of Brickell Key in Biscayne Bay; rooms facing west have
a dazzling view of the downtown skyline, while those facing east over-

look Miami Beach and the blue Atlantic. Everything is sheer perfection down to the smallest detail, from hand-painted room numbers on rice paper at check-in to the incredibly luxurious spa. ⊠ *500 Brickell Key Dr., Brickell Key, 33131* ☎ *305/913–8288 or 866/888–6780* 🖷 *305/ 913–8300* ⊕ *www.mandarinoriental.com* 🛏 *327 rooms, 31 suites* ⚒ *2 restaurants, in-room safes, cable TV, in-room data ports, pool, spa, 2 bars, dry cleaning, laundry service, concierge, business services, meeting rooms, parking (fee)* 🖃 *AE, D, DC, MC, V.*

Key Biscayne

$$$$ ⬚ **Ritz-Carlton, Key Biscayne.** One of three Ritz-Carltons in Miami, this 14-story oceanfront tower includes rooms and one- and two-bedroom suites. As with most Ritz-Carltons, first-class amenities are plentiful: an oceanfront spa with 21 treatment rooms; an 11-court tennis "garden" with tennis butler; wellness center with such activities as yoga and tai chi; private beach, and beachside watersports. In-room amenities include robes, slippers, toiletries, and scales. They don't call the resort's signature restaurant Aria for nothing: a tenor is on hand to belt out birthday greetings and other requests. ⊠ *455 Grand Bay Dr., Key Biscayne, 33149* ☎ *305/365–4500 or 800/241–3333* 🖷 *305/365–4505* ⊕ *www. ritzcarlton.com* 🛏 *365 rooms, 37 suites* ⚒ *3 restaurants, minibars, cable TV, in-room data ports, 11 tennis courts, 2 pools, spa, beach, 2 lounges, concierge, business services, meeting rooms, parking (fee)* 🖃 *AE, D, DC, MC, V.*

$$$–$$$$ ⬚ **Sonesta Beach Resort Key Biscayne.** Like Miami Beach, Key Biscayne has a strip of oceanfront resorts—though on a much smaller scale. This full-service resort rises like a Mayan pyramid from the sand and offers acres of recreation, including ocean watersports, a European spa, kids' programs, tennis and other court sports. If you want to explore the secluded island of Key Biscayne, rent a Segway Human Transporter on site. ⊠ *350 Ocean Dr., Key Biscayne, 33149* ☎ *305/361–2021 or 800/ 766–3782* 🖷 *305/365–2096* ⊕ *www.sonesta.com/keybiscayne* 🛏 *284 rooms, 15 suites* ⚒ *3 restaurants, snack bar, cable TV, 9 tennis courts, pool, exercise equipment, spa, beach, windsurfing, bicycles, basketball, volleyball, 2 bars, children's programs (ages 5–17), meeting rooms* 🖃 *AE, D, DC, MC, V.*

Miami Beach North of 23rd Street

$$$$ ⬚ **Eden Roc Renaissance Resort & Spa.** This grand 1950s hotel designed by Morris Lapidus, with its free-flowing lines of deco architecture, has a hip lobby bar with low-slung meandering couches, an indoor rock-climbing wall at its 55,000-square-foot spa, and a beachside sports bar. Rooms blend a touch of the '50s with informal elegance. ⊠ *4525 Collins Ave., Mid-Beach, 33140* ☎ *305/531–0000 or 800/327–8337* 🖷 *305/674–5555* ⊕ *www.edenrocresort.com or www.renaissancehotels.com* 🛏 *349 rooms* ⚒ *2 restaurants, cable TV, 2 pools, gym, spa, basketball, racquetball, squash, sports bar, meeting rooms* 🖃 *AE, MC, V.*

$$$–$$$$ ⬚ **Claridge Hotel.** This cool Mediterranean haven is one of the city's most impressive hotel renovations. The exterior has been restored to the canary-yellow glory of the 1928 original; inside, rich Venetian frescoed walls are hung with Peruvian oil paintings, while gleaming floors and majestic columns are crafted from volcanic stone. A Moroccan terrace overlooks the soaring inner atrium, which has a splash Jacuzzi at the far end. Rooms are a mix of Asian and European influences, with straw mats laid over wood floors, and ornate wood furniture. ⊠ *3500 Collins Ave., Mid-Beach, 33140* ☎ *305/604–8485 or 888/422–9111* 🖶 *305/ 674–0881* ⊕ *www.claridgefl.com* ⇱ *42 rooms, 8 suites* ♨ *Restaurant, in-room safes, cable TV, in-room data ports, hot tub, concierge, business services, parking (fee)* ☰ *AE, D, DC, MC, V.*

★ $$$–$$$$ 🖭 **Fontainebleau Hilton Resort.** This big, busy, and ornate grande dame is still going strong after a major renovation. Redesigned rooms are decked out in natural woods and rich tones, while the lobby has been restored to its Rat Pack-era glory, with grand deco flourishes everywhere. Guests enjoy free admission to Club Tropigala, one of the few hotel showrooms left on the beach. And for kids, Cookie's World is a water playground with a water slide and lazy river raft ride. ⊠ *4441 Collins Ave., between 44th and 45th Sts., South Beach* ☎ *305/538–2000 or 800/548–8886* 🖶 *305/673–5351* ⊕ *www.fontainebleau.hilton.com.* ⇱ *920 rooms, 50 suites* ♨ *10 restaurants, cable TV, 2 pools, gym, massage, beach, windsurfing, boating, jet skiing, parasailing, volleyball, lounges, children's programs (ages 5–12), convention center* ☰ *AE, D, DC, MC, V.*

★ $$$–$$$$ 🖭 **Wyndham Miami Beach Resort.** Among the great Miami Beach hotels, this 18-story modern glass tower is a standout, as is its polished staff offering exceptional service, from helping you find the best shopping to bringing you an icy drink on the beach. The bright rooms have a tropical blue color scheme and wonderful details including mini-refrigerators, three layers of drapes (including blackout curtains), big closets, and bathrooms with high-end toiletries and a magnifying mirror. Two presidential suites were designed in consultation with the Secret Service, and a rooftop meeting room offers views of bay and ocean. ⊠ *4833 Collins Ave., Mid-Beach, 33140* ☎ *305/532–3600 or 800/203–8368* 🖶 *305/ 534–7409* ⊕ *www.wyndham.com* ⇱ *378 rooms, 46 suites* ♨ *3 restaurants, cable TV, tennis court, pool, gym, massage, beach, bar, meeting rooms* ☰ *AE, D, DC, MC, V.*

$$–$$$$ 🖭 **Bay Harbor Inn.** The inn's not on the ocean, but the tranquil Indian Creek flowing outside is sure to soothe. One of the most pleasing touches is your own private front porch; sit with a book or a drink and enjoy a view of Bal Harbour, a five-minute walk away. Rooms have queen- and king-size beds, and baths are large. The hotel staff is composed largely of hotel students from Johnson & Wales University, so the service is enthusiastic but not flawlessly professional. ⊠ *9660 E. Bay Harbor Dr., Bal Harbour, 33154* ☎ *305/868–4141* 🖶 *305/867–9094* ⊕ *www. bayharborinn.com* ⇱ *22 rooms, 23 suites* ♨ *Restaurant, cable TV, pool, bar, meeting rooms* ☰ *AE, MC, V* ⦿ *CP.*

★ $–$$$$ 🖭 **Indian Creek Hotel.** This 1936 Pueblo Deco original may just be Miami's most charming and sincere lodge. Owner Marc Levin rescued the inn and filled its rooms with art deco furniture, much of it from the hotel basement. The garden rooms are minimalist in design, in contrast to the creamy tones and plush furniture of the deco rooms. Suites have

VCR–CD players and modem capabilities. The dining room has an eclectic and appetizing menu, which can also be enjoyed by the lush pool and garden. ⊠ *2727 Indian Creek Dr., Mid-Beach, 33140* ☎ *305/531–2727 or 800/491–2772* 🖷 *305/531–5651* ⊕ *www.indiancreekhotelmb.com* ⇌ *55 rooms, 6 suites* ⚐ *Restaurant, refrigerators, cable TV, some in-room VCRs, some in-room data ports, pool, meeting room* ⊟ *AE, D, DC, MC, V.*

$–$$$ 🎦 **Crystal Beach Suites & Health Club.** This updated beachfront hotel is easy to miss, as the entrance and sign are on 71st Street, not Collins Avenue. But for those who prefer modern comforts, it's worth seeking. A large marble-floor lobby leads to a huge fitness center and a beautiful outdoor pool and hot tub surrounded by palm trees. Even the hallways are attractive, with new carpeting, chair railings, and colorful framed paintings. Suites are done in rich jewel tones with floral drapes and upholstery. The bathroom and living areas are spacious, with a sleeper couch and a compact, fully outfitted kitchenette cleverly placed in a corner off by a bar. ⊠ *6985 Collins Ave., North Beach, 33140* ☎ *305/865–9555 or 800/435–0766* 🖷 *305/866–5314* ⊕ *www.crystalbeachsuites.com* ⇌ *84 suites* ⚐ *Microwaves, refrigerators, cable TV, pool, gym, hot tub, massage, steam room, beach, parking (fee)* ⊟ *AE, MC, V.*

$$ 🎦 **Days Inn Oceanside–Beach Front.** Just up the road from South Beach and in the same neighborhood as the more expensive Eden Roc and Fontainebleau resorts, this eight-story budget hotel might surprise you with its ornate lobby, but the value is true to the brand. Expect to pay more for an ocean view, but all rooms are basically a bargain, offering crisp, clean comfort with cable TV, data ports, and other standard amenities. ⊠ *4299 Collins Ave., Mid-Beach, 33141* ☎ *305/673–1513 or 800/329–7466* 🖷 *305/538–0727* ⊕ *www.daysinnmiamibeach.com* ⇌ *145 rooms* ⚐ *3 restaurants, in-room data ports, in-room safes, cable TV, pool, bar, dry cleaning, laundry facilities, parking (fee)* ⊟ *AE, DC, MC, V.*

$–$$ 🎦 **Days Inn North Beach.** Although the rooms and baths are small, the hotel is clean, and it's in a quiet, resurgent strip of Miami Beach. The natural attributes of South Beach—sun and sea—are here as well, with the big advantage of not having to fight for a parking spot or deal with creeping traffic. A good bet for families, this hotel has a game room, plus a bright breakfast room. ⊠ *7450 Ocean Terr., North Beach, 33141* ☎ *305/866–1631 or 888/825–6800* 🖷 *305/868–4617* ⊕ *www.daysinn.com* ⇌ *92 rooms* ⚐ *Restaurant, cable TV, pool, beach, bar, video game room, laundry facilities* ⊟ *AE, DC, MC, V.*

¢–$ 🎦 **Ocean Surf.** For those who dig deco, this is a gem. Built in 1940 at **Fodor's Choice** the height of the art deco era, this three-story hotel looks like it's straight **★** out of South Beach, with large porthole windows, ship-style railings, and wide ribbons of pink-and-white terrazzo swirling through the lobby. If one of the four oceanfront rooms is available, grab it—the view through the large porthole over the bed is remarkable. Rooms are smallish but impeccably clean. The tables on the front porch, with a great view of the beach across a quiet street, are a perfect spot for enjoying breakfast. ⊠ *7436 Ocean Terr., 1 block east of Collins Ave., North Beach, 33141* ☎ *305/866–1648 or 800/555–0411* 🖷 *305/866–1649* ⇌ *49 rooms* ⚐ *Cable TV, beach* ⊟ *AE, MC, V* ⧠ *CP.*

North Miami-Dade County & Sunny Isles

★ **$$$$** 🏨 **The Fairmont Turnberry Isle Resort & Club.** Finest of the grand resorts, even more so with the addition of the Golf Learning Center, Turnberry is a tapestry of islands and waterways on 300 superbly landscaped acres by the bay. You'll stay at the 1920s Addison Mizner–designed Country Club Hotel on the Intracoastal Waterway, where rooms have large terraces and hot tubs. The marina has moorings for 117 boats; there are two Robert Trent Jones golf courses, and a free shuttle to the Aventura Mall. Perks include a private Ocean Club on the Atlantic and a Kids Club at Turnberry. ✉ *19999 W. Country Club Dr., North Miami Beach 33180* 📞 *305/932–6200 or 800/327–7028* 🖶 *305/933–6560* ⊕ *www. fairmont.com* 🛏 *350 rooms, 42 suites* ♿ *4 restaurants, in-room safes, minibars, cable TV, 2 18-hole golf courses, 19 tennis courts, 2 pools, health club, spa, steam room, beach, dock, windsurfing, boating, racquetball, 5 lounges* ☰ *AE, D, DC, MC, V.*

★ **$$–$$$$** 🏨 **Newport Beachside & Westgate Miami Beach Resort.** Built before the present crop of luxury towers sprang up, Newport is still one of the nicest hotels in Sunny Isles Beach. The combination timeshare and hotel is a good place to enjoy the beach and outdoor activities. There's a wading pool and a standard pool, not to mention the ocean and fishing pier—the only remaining hotel fishing pier in Miami ($7 to fish, $1 to watch). Back inside, the lobby is large and bright, and so are the rooms—all one- and two-bedroom suites. ✉ *16701 Collins Ave., Sunny Isles, Miami Beach 33160* 📞 *305/949–1300 or 800/327–5476* 🖶 *305/947–5873* ⊕ *www. newportbeachsideresort.com* 🛏 *290 suites* ♿ *4 restaurants, microwaves, refrigerators, cable TV, pool, wading pool, gym, beach, bar, nightclub, shops, concierge, meeting rooms, some free parking* ☰ *AE, D, DC, MC, V.*

$$–$$$ 🏨 **Don Shula's Hotel & Golf Club.** About 14 mi northwest of downtown Miami, the Don Shula Hotel is part of the Main Street shopping and entertainment complex in Miami Lakes. The Golf Club—less than a mile down the road—sits on a par-72 championship golf course and par-3 executive course. A complimentary shuttle runs between the two properties. When they're not teeing off, guests can work out in the hotel's huge athletic club, which includes racquetball courts and a weight training center. Like steak? Don Shula's Steak House at the club serves hefty cuts of prime beef in an atmosphere that can best be described as "football elegant." ✉ *6842 Main St., Miami Lakes 33014* 📞 *305/821–1150 or 800/ 247–4852* 🖶 *305/820–8071* ⊕ *www.donshulahotel.com* 🛏 *188 rooms, 17 suites in hotel, 84 rooms in club* ♿ *2 restaurants, cable TV, 2 golf courses, 9 tennis courts, 2 pools, health club, sauna, steam room, basketball, racquetball, volleyball, 2 bars, meeting rooms* ☰ *AE, DC, MC, V.*

South Beach

★ **$$$$** 🏨 **Casa Grande Suite Hotel.** A luxe and spicy Eastern-tinged flavor sets this hotel apart from the typical icy-cool minimalism found on Ocean Drive. Luxurious Balinese-inspired suites are done in teak and mahogany, with dhurrie rugs, Indonesian fabrics and artifacts, two-poster beds with ziggurat turns, full kitchens with utensils, and large baths—practically unheard of in the Art Deco District. Insulated windows keep the noise of Ocean Drive revelers at bay. ⊠ *834 Ocean Dr., South Beach, 33139* ☎ *305/672–7003 or 866/420–2272* 🖷 *305/ 673–3669* ⊕ *www.casagrandehotel.com* ➴ *35 suites* ⚬ *Café, in-room safes, kitchenettes, refrigerators, cable TV, in-room VCRs, beach, shops, laundry service, concierge, business services, travel services* ⊟ *AE, D, DC, MC, V.*

$$$$
Fodor'sChoice
★
🏨 **Delano Hotel.** Marvel at the lobby, hung with massive white billowing drapes, and appear aloof while trying to glimpse celeb guests, which have included Jennifer Lopez, Beyonce Knowles, Will Smith, and Ashton Kutcher. Fashion models and moguls gather beneath cabanas and pose by the pool, as heady aromas from the Blue Door restaurant and Robert DeNiro's Ago waft by. Executive services are offered for business travelers, and all guests have the run of a rooftop bathhouse and solarium. Standard rooms average a roomy 400 square feet in size. ⊠ *1685 Collins Ave., South Beach, 33139* ☎ *305/672–2000 or 800/ 555–5001* 🖷 *305/532–0099* ⊕ *www.delano-hotel.net411.com* ➴ *184 rooms, 24 suites* ⚬ *Restaurant, cable TV, pool, health club, spa, beach, bar, lobby lounge, laundry service, concierge, business services* ⊟ *AE, D, DC, MC, V.*

★ **$$$$**
🏨 **Loews Miami Beach Hotel.** Unlike other neighborhood properties, this 18-story, near 800-room gem was built from the blueprints up. Not only did Loews manage to snag 99 feet of beach, it also took over the vacant St. Moritz next door and restored it to its original 1939 art deco splendor, so that the entire complex combines boutique charm with updated opulence. The resort has kids' programs, a health spa, 85,000 square feet of meeting space, and an enormous ocean-view grand ballroom. Dining, too, is a pleasure, courtesy of Emeril Lagasse, who opened here with a "bam" in November 2003. ⊠ *1601 Collins Ave., South Beach, 33139* ☎ *305/604–1601 or 800/235–6397* 🖷 *305/604–3999* ⊕ *www. loewshotels.com* ➴ *733 rooms, 57 suites* ⚬ *6 restaurants, cable TV, pool, gym, beach, lounges, children's programs (ages 4–12), meeting rooms* ⊟ *AE, D, DC, MC, V.*

$$$$
🏨 **Raleigh Hotel.** Hidden behind a thick veil of greenery, this hotel was among the first Art Deco District hotels to be renovated, and it has retained Victorian accents (hallway chandeliers and in-room oil paintings) to soften the 20th-century edges. Standard rooms are spacious, and the suites more so. The fleur-de-lis pool is the focal point year-round, especially on December 31, when synchronized swimmers dive in at the stroke of midnight. Other pluses: the lobby coffee bar, a romantic restaurant (Tiger Oak Room), and the old-fashioned Martini Bar. ⊠ *1775 Collins Ave., South Beach, 33139* ☎ *305/534–6300 or 800/848–1775* 🖷 *305/538–8140* ⊕ *www.raleighhotel.com* ➴ *86 rooms, 18 suites* ⚬ *Restaurant, in-room safes, refrigerators, cable TV, in-room VCRs, in-room data ports, pool, gym, massage, beach, bar, laundry service, concierge, business services, meeting room, parking (fee)* ⊟ *AE, D, DC, MC, V.*

$$$$
🏨 **South Beach Marriott.** Continuing the trend started by Loews, Marriott's move into South Beach was late and big, with nouveau art deco flourishes meant to conceal a pragmatic beach resort. The rooms are

larger than most on the beach, with a liberal helping of very un-Marriott-like tropical color that proves the mega-brand really is trying to fit in. A mini-spa, quiet beach, and reliable service make this a safe bet for business types or families who want to experience South Beach while keeping the wildest partying at a distance. ✉ *161 Ocean Dr., South Beach, 33139* ☎ *305/536–7700 or 800/228–9290* 🖷 *305/536–9900* ⊕ *www.miamibeachmarriott.com* ✒ *236 rooms, 8 suites* ⚘ *Restaurant, cable TV, in-room data ports, pool, health club, beach, 2 bars, laundry service, concierge, business services, meeting rooms, parking (fee)* ▭ *AE, D, DC, MC, V.*

★ **$$$$** ▦ **The Tides.** Miami hotels like white, and this one is no exception. However, hotelier and music magnate Chris Blackwell has put a creative twist on what can often be a sterile design motif by introducing hospitality-inspiring elements, from the small (telescopes in each room, since they all have big windows and face the ocean; a blackboard for housekeeping messages; newspapers on request) to the large (a king-size bed in every room, capacious closets, and generous baths, the result of turning 115 rooms into 45 suites). At the 50-foot-long mezzanine pool, women can go topless. ✉ *1220 Ocean Dr., South Beach, 33139* ☎ *305/604–5070 or 866/438–4337* 🖷 *305/604–5180* ⊕ *www.thetideshotel.com* ✒ *45 suites* ⚘ *Restaurant, in-room safes, minibars, cable TV, in-room data ports, pool, gym, beach, babysitting, dry cleaning, concierge, business services, meeting room, travel services* ▭ *AE, D, DC, MC, V.*

$$$–$$$$ ▦ **Essex House.** A favorite with Europeans, Essex House moved into the upscale category over the past few years with a major renovation and amenities like in-room spa services and a pool with Jacuzzi jets. The large suites are well worth the price: each has a wet bar, king-size bed, pull-out sofa, 100-square-foot bathroom, refrigerator, and hot tub. Rooms weigh in with club chairs, custom carpet and lighting, mahogany entertainment units and matching desks, and marble tubs. ✉ *1001 Collins Ave., South Beach, 33139* ☎ *305/534–2700 or 800/553–7739* 🖷 *305/532–3827* ⊕ *www.essexhotel.com* ✒ *61 rooms, 19 suites* ⚘ *Cable TV, in-room data ports, pool, bar, dry cleaning, laundry service, meeting rooms, parking (fee)* ▭ *AE, D, DC, MC, V.*

★ **$$$–$$$$** ▦ **Hotel Impala.** It's all very European here at the Impala, from the mineral water and orchids to the Mediterranean-style armoires, Italian fixtures, and Eastlake sleigh beds. Everything from wastebaskets to towels to toilet paper is of extraordinary quality. The building, a stunning tropical Mediterranean Revival, is a block from the beach. Iron, mahogany, and stone on the inside are in sync with the sporty white-trim ocher exterior and quiet courtyard. Rooms come with a TV/VCR/stereo and a stock of CDs and videos. ✉ *1228 Collins Ave., South Beach, 33139* ☎ *305/673–2021 or 800/646–7252* 🖷 *305/673–5984* ⊕ *www.hotelimpalamiamibeach.com* ✒ *14 rooms, 3 suites* ⚘ *Restaurant, cable TV, in-room VCRs, in-room data ports, bar, laundry service, concierge* ▭ *AE, D, DC, MC, V* ⦿ *CP.*

$$$–$$$$ ▦ **Hotel Ocean.** If the street signs didn't read Ocean Drive, you might suspect you were whiling away the day on the French Riviera. The tropical European feel is evident when you enter the shaded, bougainvillea-draped courtyard and see diners enjoying a complimentary breakfast in the hotel's brasserie. The two buildings connected by the courtyard contain a few surprises: soft beds, authentic 1930s art deco pieces, large foldout couches, spacious baths, and soundproof windows, which ensure that rooms are comfortable and quiet. ⊠ *1230–38 Ocean Dr., South Beach, 33139* ☎ *305/672–2579 or 800/783–1725* 🖷 *305/672–7665* ⊕ *www.hotelocean.com* 🛏 *14 rooms, 13 suites* 🖒 *Restaurant, in-room safes, minibars, cable TV, in-room VCRs, in-room data ports, bar, concierge* ⊟ *AE, D, DC, MC, V* ⦿ *CP.*

$$$–$$$$ 🏨 **Kent.** There are toys in the Day-Glo–color lobby, beanbag chairs in the rooms, and chrome ceiling fans throughout at this fanciful SoBe hotel. But the highlight here is the third-floor Lucite Suite, where practically everything, from bed to desk to phones to tables, is made from translucent plastic, making it a great place to party (but a bad place to play hide-and-seek). Sure, the rooms are on the small side, and there isn't much of a view, but the vibe, the pumped-up staff, and those great prices make the Kent hard to beat if you're in the mood for a good time. ⊠ *1131 Collins Ave., South Beach, 33139* ☎ *305/604–5068 or 866/826–5368* 🖷 *305/531–0720* ⊕ *www.thekenthotel.com* 🛏 *53 rooms, 1 suite* 🖒 *In-room safes, refrigerators, cable TV, in-room VCRs, business services, meeting room, travel services* ⊟ *AE, D, DC, MC, V.*

$$$–$$$$ 🏨 **Nassau Suite Hotel.** For a boutique hotel one block from the beach, this airy retreat almost qualifies as a steal (by South Beach standards). The original 1937 floor plan of 50 rooms gave way to 22 spacious and smart-looking suites with king beds, hardwood floors, white-wood blinds, and free high-speed Internet access. The Nassau is in the heart of the action yet quiet enough to give you the rest you need. Note: there's no bellhop and very limited parking. ⊠ *1414 Collins Ave., South Beach, 33139* ☎ *305/532–0043 or 866/859–4177* 🖷 *305/534–3133* ⊕ *www.nassausuite.com* 🛏 *22 suites* 🖒 *Kitchenettes, cable TV, in-room data ports, concierge, business services* ⊟ *AE, D, DC, MC, V.*

$$$–$$$$ 🏨 **National Hotel.** The most spectacular feature of this resurrected 1939 hotel is its palm-lined "infinity" pool—Miami Beach's longest, at 205 feet. It's a dramatic backdrop for the film crews that often work here. A major 2003 renovation gave rooms a new design scheme, combining the geometry of art deco with a soothing palette of colors and fabrics. Check out the 1930s-style Martini Room bar. ⊠ *1677 Collins Ave., South Beach, 33139* ☎ *305/532–2311 or 800/327–8370* 🖷 *305/534–1426* ⊕ *www.nationalhotel.com* 🛏 *143 rooms, 9 suites* 🖒 *Restaurant, in-room safes, minibars, in-room data ports, pool, gym, beach, bar, laundry service, concierge, meeting rooms, parking (fee), no-smoking floor* ⊟ *AE, DC, MC, V.*

★ $$–$$$$ 🏨 **Hotel Astor.** The Astor stands apart from the crowd by double-insulating walls against noise and offering such quiet luxuries as thick towels, down pillows, paddle fans, and a seductive pool. Rooms are built to recall deco ocean-liner staterooms, with faux-portholes, custom-milled French furniture, Roman shades, and sleek sound and video systems. A tasteful, muted color scheme and the most comfortable king beds imaginable make for eminently restful nights, and service is excellent. Metro Kitchen & Bar has exceptional fare and service. ⊠ *956 Washington Ave., South Beach, 33139* ☎ *305/531–8081 or 800/270–4981*

🖶 *305/531–3193* ⊕ *www.hotelastor.com* ⟿ *24 rooms, 16 suites* ᕕ *Restaurant, room service, in-room safes, minibars, in-room data ports, massage, bar, laundry service, concierge, Internet, business services, meeting room, parking (fee)* ⊟ *AE, DC, MC, V.*

★ **$$–$$$$** 🏨 **WinterHaven.** "Bright" and "airy" are not words usually associated with South Beach hotels, but this artfully restored classic is both—in spades. WinterHaven is a riot of color, from the garnet-and-aquamarine lobby to the ginger-and-cream upholstery in guest rooms. The two-story lobby and split-level mezzanine regularly play host to parties and fashion shoots, but if you take your complimentary breakfast up to the rooftop sundeck, you'll have a bird's-eye view of South Beach at dawn. ✉ *1400 Ocean Dr., South Beach, 33139* 🕾 *305/531–5571 or 800/ 395–2322* 🖶 *305/538–6387* ⊕ *www.winterhavenhotelsobe.com* ⟿ *71 rooms* ᕕ *In-room safes, cable TV, in-room data ports, bar, concierge, parking (fee)* ⊟ *AE, D, DC, MC, V* ⦿ *CP.*

$–$$$$ 🏨 **The Albion.** Avant-garde Boston architect Carlos Zapata updated this stylish 1939 nautical-deco building by Igor Polevitzky. The two-story lobby sweeps into a secluded courtyard and is framed by an indoor waterfall. A crowd of hip but friendly types makes up the clientele; they like to gather at the mezzanine-level pool, which has portholes that allow courtyard strollers an underwater view of the swimmers. As with other Rubell properties (the Beach House and the Greenview), guest rooms are minimalist in design, though filled with upscale touches. ✉ *1650 James Ave., South Beach, 33139* 🕾 *305/913–1000 or 888/665–0008* 🖶 *305/674–0507* ⊕ *www.rubellhotels.com* ⟿ *87 rooms, 9 suites* ᕕ *Restaurant, minibars, cable TV, in-room data ports, pool, gym, bar, laundry service, concierge, meeting room* ⊟ *AE, D, DC, MC, V.*

$–$$$$ 🏨 **Cadet Hotel.** Clark Gable stayed in Room 225 when he came to Miami for Army Air Corps training in the 1940s. Although this Lincoln Road district hotel doesn't quite have the glamour to attract stars today, it's still a clean, friendly, and perfectly placed little hotel: a few minutes' walk from the Jackie Gleason Theater of the Performing Arts and the convention center and two blocks from the ocean. Room renovations have brought bamboo floors, custom armoires, Egyptian linens, and upgraded bath amenities. Breakfast is on the house. ✉ *1701 James Ave., South Beach, 33139* 🕾 *305/672–6688 or 800/432–2338* 🖶 *305/532–1676* ⊕ *www. cadethotel.com* ⟿ *33 rooms, 3 suites* ᕕ *In-room safes, minibars, cable TV, Internet, meeting rooms* ⊟ *AE, D, DC, MC, V* ⦿ *CP.*

$$–$$$ 🏨 **Days Inn Convention Center.** Nothing flashy and nothing trashy, this link in a well-known chain is a fairly decent one. The lobby is bright and floral, with a fountain and gift shop. Rooms include in-room safes and cable TV; deluxe rooms throw in impressive views of the ocean. If you're more concerned about your wallet than your image, this is a good bet. Keep in mind that if you want something with character, you can find that elsewhere at these rates. Here you'll find the basic franchise dependables seconds from the beach and the Miami Beach Convention Center. ✉ *100 21st St., South Beach, 33139* 🕾 *305/538–6631 or 800/ 451–3345* 🖶 *305/674–0954* ⊕ *www.daysinnsouthbeach.com* ⟿ *172 rooms* ᕕ *Restaurant, in-room safes, some refrigerators, cable TV, pool, beach, bar, laundry service, parking (fee)* ⊟ *AE, D, DC, MC, V.*

★ **$$$-$$$** ▦ **Royal South Beach.** *Austin Powers* meets *2001: A Space Odyssey* in this avant-garde hotel, which doesn't take itself too seriously. Each room really only has two pieces of furniture: a "digital chaise lounge" and a bed, both molded white plastic contortions from designer Jordan Mozer. The bed's projecting wings hold a phone and alarm clock. The headboard arcs back like a car spoiler and doubles as a minibar. The chaise lounge holds a TV–Web TV with keyboard. A wild shag carpet and rainbow-paisley bathrobes remind you you're here to have fun. A cigar shop and onsite bike rentals are among the more unusual amenities. ✉ *758 Washington Ave., South Beach, 33139* ☎ *305/673–9009 or 888/394–6835* ☎ *305/673–9244* ⊕ *www.royalhotelsouthbeach.com* ◄ *38 studios, 4 suites* ⚻ *In-room safes, kitchenettes, microwaves, cable TV, in-room data ports, lounge* ▤ *AE, D, DC, MC, V.*

$-$$$ ▦ **Best Western South Beach.** It's all for one at this complex of five art deco hotels—the Kenmore, Taft, Bel-Aire, Coral House and Davis—offering a total of 135 guest rooms, along with budget-friendly rates that include a Continental breakfast. Each hotel is like a separate "wing" of the whole, yet each retains its unique character. The Kenmore, for example, projects a no-nonsense 1930s utilitarian simplicity, while the Bel-Aire invites relaxation within a walled courtyard sheltering a winding sidewalk. The complex is within walking distance of the Miami Beach Convention Center and Lincoln Road Mall. The main lobby is inside the Kenmore. ✉ *1050 Washington Ave., South Beach, 33139* ☎ *305/ 674–1930 or 888/343–1930* ☎ *305/534–6591* ⊕ *www.bestwestern. com* ◄ *135 rooms* ⚻ *Cable TV, pool, Internet, business services* ▤ *AE, MC, V* ◯ *CP.*

¢-$$$ ▦ **The Creek.** Once a cheap youth hostel called Banana Bungalow, the Creek emerged in late 2002 as a still-inexpensive but spruced-up and arty abode for mostly young travelers looking for a friendly place to crash. They'll find it here, in 18 "signature rooms" each designed by a different artist; basic standard or pool deck rooms; and the mega-budget shared rooms that go for $16–$29 a night, depending on the time of year. The Creek's social center is the large pool area, which has outdoor grills, and is surrounded by a patio bar and game room. Note to the noise-intolerant—the music's loud 'til midnight. ✉ *2360 Collins Ave., South Beach, 33139* ☎ *305/538–1951* ☎ *305/531–3217* ⊕ *www. thecreeksouthbeach.com* ◄ *60 private rooms, 25 dorm-style rooms* ⚻ *Cable TV with video games, pool, billiards, bar, lobby lounge, recreation room, Internet* ▤ *MC, V* ◯ *CP.*

¢-$$ ▦ **Bayliss Guest House.** At the Bayliss, rooms are unexpectedly large and surprisingly inexpensive. Not only are the bedrooms large, so are the kitchens, sitting rooms, and baths. Standard rooms minus kitchens also are available. An easy three blocks west of the ocean, the Bayliss is in a residential neighborhood that's comfortably close to—but far enough away from—the din of the Art Deco District. You can't do much better than this on a budget, if you don't mind carrying your own bags. There's very limited parking. Note: don't be thrown off if the switchboard answers, "The Riviera." Operators handle jointly owned properties. Just ask for the Bayliss. ✉ *500–504 14th St., South Beach, 33139*

☎ *305/531–3488* 🖨 *305/531–4440* ⊕ *www.thebayliss.com* ➟ *12 rooms, 7 efficiencies* ⎕ *Refrigerators, cable TV, laundry facilities* ⊟ *AE, D, DC, MC, V.*

West Dade

$$$$ ⌧ **Doral Golf Resort and Spa.** With its five championship golf courses, including the Blue Monster—home of the annual PGA Ford Championship—this 650-acre resort is definitely golf central in Greater Miami. But wait, there's more: the Arthur Ashe Tennis Center with 11 courts, the lavish Spa at Doral with its own luxury suites, two fitness centers, on-site shops and boutiques, a kids' camp and water park, five restaurants, and extensive meeting space. Add bright, airy rooms that showcase Florida inside and out, and you have a self-contained repository of fun and relaxation just west of the airport. ⊠ *4400 N.W. 87th Ave., West Miami, 33178* ☎ *305/592–2000 or 800/713–6725* 🖨 *305/591–4682* ⊕ *www.doralresort.com* ➟ *696 rooms, 48 suites* ⎕ *5 restaurants, cable TV, 5 18-hole golf courses, golf school, 11 tennis courts, pro shop, pool, exercise equipment, spa, fishing, basketball, volleyball, 3 bars, concierge, business services, meeting rooms* ⊟ *AE, D, DC, MC, V.*

NIGHTLIFE & THE ARTS

Greater Miami's English-language daily newspaper, the *Miami Herald,* publishes reliable reviews and comprehensive listings in its "Weekend" section on Friday and in the "IN South Florida" section on Sunday. It also publishes a free tabloid, *Street,* with entertainment listings. Call ahead to confirm details. *El Nuevo Herald* is the paper's Spanish version. If you read Spanish, check *Diario Las Américas,* the area's largest independent Spanish-language paper, for information on the Spanish theater and a smattering of general performing-arts news. The best, most complete source is the *New Times,* a free weekly distributed throughout Miami-Dade County each Thursday. A good source of information on the performing arts and nightspots is the calendar in *Miami Today,* a free weekly newspaper available each Thursday in downtown Miami, Coconut Grove, and Coral Gables. Various tabloids reporting on Deco District entertainment and the Miami social scene come and go. *Wire* reports on the gay community. The free *Greater Miami & The Beaches Calendar of Events* is published twice a year by the **Miami-Dade County Department of Cultural Affairs** (⊠ 111 N.W. 1st St., Suite 625, Downtown, 33128 ☎ 305/375–4634) and by the **Greater Miami Convention & Visitors Bureau** (☎ 305/539–3000 or 800/283–2707 ⊕ www.gmcvb.com). The GMCVB also publishes a comprehensive list of dance venues, theaters, and museums.

The Arts

Greater Miami's cultural renaissance is a work in progress. The basics are in place: solid cultural institutions such as the Florida Grand Opera, the New World Symphony, the Miami City Ballet, the Concert Association of South Florida; a plethora of multicultural arts groups and festivals year-round; and burgeoning arts districts in South Beach, Coral Gables, and the Design District north of downtown, to name a few. The massive performing-arts center downtown, which spans both sides of Biscayne Boulevard, is sparking a neighborhood revival even before it opens its doors in 2006. Several churches and synagogues run classical-music series with international performers. In theater, Miami offers English-speaking audiences an assortment of professional, collegiate, and amateur productions of musicals, comedy, and drama. Spanish theater also is active.

The not-for-profit **Concert Association of Florida** (⊠ 1470 Biscayne Blvd., Downtown ☎ 877/433–3200 ⊕ www.concertfla.org) led by Judith Drucker, presents classical arts, music, and dance in venues throughout Miami-Dade and Broward counties. On its roster have been some of the greatest names in the worlds of music and dance—Itzhak Perlman, Isaac Stern, Baryshnikov, Pavarotti, and the Russian National Ballet.

To order tickets for performing-arts events by telephone, call **TicketMaster** (☎ 305/358–5885).

Arts Venues

What was once a 1920s movie theater has become the 465-seat **Colony Theater** (⊠ 1040 Lincoln Rd., South Beach, Miami Beach ☎ 305/674–1040). Undergoing a second renovation, the city-owned performing-arts center, which spotlights dance, drama, music, and experimental cinema, is expected to reopen by summer 2004.

If you have the opportunity to attend a concert, ballet, or touring stage production at the **Gusman Center for the Performing Arts** (⊠ 174 E. Flagler St., Downtown, Miami 33131 ☎ 305/374–2444 administration, 305/372–0925 box office ⊕ http://gusmancenter.org), do so. Originally a movie palace, this 1,700-plus-seat theater is as far from a mall multiplex as you can get. The stunningly beautiful hall resembles a Moorish courtyard, with twinkling stars and rolling clouds skirting across the ceiling and freshly restored Roman statues guarding the wings.

Not to be confused with the ornate Gusman theater, **Gusman Concert Hall** (⊠ 1314 Miller Dr., Coral Gables ☎ 305/284–2438) is a 600-seat facility on the University of Miami campus. Presenting primarily recitals and concerts by students, it has good acoustics and plenty of room, but parking is a problem when school is in session.

Acoustics and visibility are perfect for all 2,700 seats in the **Jackie Gleason Theater of the Performing Arts** (TOPA; ⊠ 1700 Washington Ave., South Beach, Miami Beach ☎ 305/673–7300 ⊕ www.gleasontheater.com). A pleasant walk from the heart of SoBe, TOPA hosts the Broadway Series, with five or six major productions annually; guest artists, such as BB King, Stomp, and Shirley MacLaine; and classical-music concerts.

Midway between Coral Gables and downtown Miami, the **Miami-Dade County Auditorium** (⊠ 2901 W. Flagler St., Little Havana, Miami 33135 ☎ 305/545–3395) satisfies patrons with nearly 2,500 comfortable seats, good sight lines, and acceptable acoustics. Opera, concerts, and touring musicals are usually on the schedule, and past performers have included David Helfgott and the late Celia Cruz.

Dance

★ The **Miami City Ballet** (✉ 2200 Liberty Ave., South Beach, Miami Beach ☎ 305/929–7000 ⊕ www.miamicityballet.org/mcbdev/index.shtml) has risen rapidly to international prominence since its arrival in 1985. Under the direction of Edward Villella (a principal dancer with the New York City Ballet under George Balanchine), Florida's first major, fully professional resident ballet company has become a world-class ensemble. The company re-creates the Balanchine repertoire and introduces works of its own during its September–March season. Villella also hosts children's works-in-progress programs. Performances are held at the Jackie Gleason Theater of the Performing Arts; the Broward Center for the Performing Arts; Bailey Concert Hall, also in Broward County; the Raymond F. Kravis Center for the Performing Arts; and the Naples Philharmonic Center for the Arts.

Film

Several theaters and events cater specifically to fans of fine film. In December, Florida International University sponsors the **Jewish Film Festival** (☎305/576–4030), which presents screenings of new work as well as workshops and panel discussions with filmmakers in several Miami Beach locations. Screenings of new films from all over the world—including some made here—are part of the **Miami International Film Festival** (✉ 444 Brickell Ave., Suite 229, Miami ☎305/372–0925). Each year more than 45,000 people descend on the eye-popping Gusman Center for the Performing Arts to watch about 25 movies over 10 days in February. Two more venues—South Beach's Colony Theater and Regal Cinema—have been added, and the number of movies is expected to double.

In April the **Miami Gay & Lesbian Film Festival** (☎ 305/534–9924) presents screenings at various Miami Beach venues. In March the **Miami Latin Film Festival** (☎ 305/279–1809) actually presents French, Italian, and Portuguese movies along with Spanish and Latin American movies. Each May, South Beach hosts the **Brazilian Film Festival** (☎305/899–8998), which unveils on a huge outdoor movie screen built on the beach especially for the occasion.

Music

From October to May, **Friends of Chamber Music** (✉ 169 E. Flagler St., Suite 1619, Downtown, Miami ☎ 305/372–2975) presents a series of chamber concerts by internationally known guest ensembles, such as the Emerson and Guarneri quartets. Concerts are held at the Gusman Concert Hall at the University of Miami, with tickets averaging about $20.

Although Greater Miami has no resident symphony orchestra, the **New World Symphony** (✉ 555 Lincoln Rd., South Beach, Miami Beach ☎ 305/673–3331 or 305/673–3330 ⊕ www.nws.org), known as "America's training orchestra" because its musicians are recent graduates of the best music schools, helps fill the void. Under the direction of conductor Michael Tilson Thomas, the New World has become an artistically dazzling group that tours extensively. In a season that runs October–May, performances take place in its home venue, the Lincoln Theater on Lincoln Road Mall. The symphony's concerts are broadcast live via speaker (and sometimes video) over the Lincoln Road Mall. Guest conductors have included Leonard Bernstein and Georg Solti.

Opera

South Florida's leading company, the **Florida Grand Opera** (✉ 1200 Coral Way, Downtown, Miami ☎ 305/854–1643 ⊕ www.fgo.org), presents five operas each year in the Miami-Dade County Auditorium. The series brings such luminaries as Placido Domingo and Luciano Pavarotti (Pavarotti made his American debut with the company in 1965 in *Lucia di Lammermoor*). Operas are sung in the original language, with English subtitles projected above the stage.

Theater

Actors' Playhouse at the Miracle Theater (✉ 280 Miracle Mile, Coral Gables ☎ 305/444–9293 ⊕ www.actorsplayhouse.org), a professional Equity company, presents musicals, comedies, and dramas year-round in Coral Gables' 600-seat Miracle Theater. Performances of musical theater for younger audiences take place in the 300-seat Children's Balcony Theatre.

Built in 1926 as a movie theater, the **Coconut Grove Playhouse** (✉ 3500 Main Hwy., Coconut Grove ☎ 305/442–4000 or 305/442–2662 ⊕ www.cgplayhouse.org) is now a serious regional theater owned by the state of Florida. The Spanish rococo Grove stages tried-and-true Broadway plays and musicals, many with Broadway actors, as well as experimental productions in its main theater and cabaret-style–black box Encore Room.

The critically acclaimed **GableStage** (✉ 1200 Anastasia Ave., Coral Gables ☎ 305/446–1116 ⊕ www.gablestage.org) presents classic and contemporary theater in an intimate space on the first floor of the Biltmore Hotel.

Productions at the University of Miami's **Jerry Herman Ring Theater** (✉ 1380 Miller Dr., Coral Gables ☎ 305/284–3355 ⊕ www.miami.edu/tha/ring) are often as ambitious as those by its professional counterparts (Broadway legend Jerry Herman is the drama school's most successful alumnus).

Once one of the major centers of entertainment for the African-American community, the **Lyric Theater** (✉ 819 N.W. 2 Ave., Overtown ☎ 305/358–1146 ⊕ www.theblackarchives.org) showcased more than 150 performers, including Aretha Franklin, Count Basie, Sam Cooke, B. B. King, Ella Fitzgerald, and the Ink Spots.

In an intimate 104-seat theater, the **New Theatre** (✉ 4120 Laguna St., Coral Gables ☎ 305/443–5909 ⊕ www.new-theatre.org) company mounts contemporary and classical plays, with an emphasis on new works and imaginative staging.

SPANISH
THEATER   Spanish theater prospers, although many companies have short lives. About 20 Spanish companies perform light comedy, puppetry, vaudeville, and political satire. To find them, read the Spanish newspapers. When

you call, be prepared for a conversation in Spanish—few box office personnel speak English. The city's most successful crossover theater is **Teatro Avante** (✉ 235 Alcazar Ave., Coral Gables ☎ 305/445–8877), programming works that cater to the tastes of its middle-aged Cuban-American audiences and providing subtitles on an overhead screen for the benefit of non-Spanish speakers. Each summer Teatro Avante sponsors the Hispanic Theatre Festival, during which international theater artists converge on Miami, often presenting the most provocative stagings around, all in Spanish, English, and Portuguese and attracting a multicultural audience to various venues in the Greater Miami area.

The 255-seat **Teatro de Bellas Artes** (✉ 2173 S.W. 8th St., Little Havana ☎ 305/325–0515), on Calle Ocho, presents plays, musicals, and other acts.

Nightlife

Bars & Lounges

COCONUT GROVE
Drinking cold beer and gorilla-size margaritas in the middle of the Grove at CocoWalk is part of the fun at touristy **Fat Tuesday** (✉ 3015 Grand Ave., Coconut Grove ☎ 305/441–2992). The bar offers up drinks called 190 Octane (190-proof alcohol), Swampwater (also 190 proof), and Grapeshot (a meager 151-proof rum and bourbon concoction). At the Streets of Mayfair, **Oxygen Lounge** (✉ 2911 Grand Ave., Coconut Grove ☎ 305/476–0202) is a sleek, below-ground nightclub offering Latin and other dance music.

The waterfront **Monty's in the Grove** (✉ 2550 S. Bayshore Dr., at Aviation Ave., Coconut Grove ☎ 305/858–1431) has lots of Caribbean flair, thanks to live calypso and island music. It's very kid-friendly on weekends days, when Mom and Dad can kick back and enjoy a beer and the raw bar while the youngsters dance to live music. Evenings bring a DJ and reggae and Top 40 music. Don't be alarmed if someone answers the phone, "South Beach." Just ask for Monty's.

CORAL GABLES
What fueled the Gables' nightlife renaissance? Some think it was the **Globe** (✉ 377 Alhambra Circle ☎ 305/445–3555). Crowds of twentysomethings spill out onto the street for live jazz on Saturday. Two Irishmen missed the Emerald Isle, so they opened **John Martin's Restaurant and Irish Pub** (✉ 253 Miracle Mile ☎ 305/445–3777). It serves up fish-and-chips, bangers and mash, and shepherd's pie—plus the requisite pints of Guinness, Harp, Bass, and other ales. **Stuart's Bar-Lounge** (✉ 162 Alcazar Ave. ☎ 305/444–1666), inside the charming Hotel Place St. Michel, is favored by locals. The style is created by beveled mirrors, mahogany paneling, French posters, pictures of old Coral Gables, and art nouveau lighting.

MIAMI
Tobacco Road (✉ 626 S. Miami Ave., Downtown ☎ 305/374–1198), opened in 1912, holds Miami's oldest liquor license: Number 0001! Upstairs, in space occupied by a speakeasy during Prohibition, blues bands perform nightly, accompanied by single-malt Scotch and bourbon.

MIAMI BEACH At the **Clevelander** (✉ 1020 Ocean Dr. ☎ 305/531–3485), a giant pool-bar area attracts a young crowd of revelers for happy-hour drink specials and live music. The Rose Bar at the **Delano** (✉ 1685 Collins Ave., South Beach ☎ 305/672–2000) is dramatic and chic, with long gauzy curtains and huge pillars creating private conversation nooks around the outdoor infinity pool. Inside, the cool, chic lounge area creates a glamorous space for the modelesque crowd. Offering more character than chic, the **Marlin** (✉ 1200 Collins Ave. ☎ 305/604–3595) gleams with the high-tech look of stainless steel. DJs spin different music every night for the 25-to-40 crowd. At the upscale **Mynt Ultra Lounge** (✉ 1921 Collins Ave., South Beach ☎ 786/276–6132), the name is meant to be taken literally—not only are the walls bathed in shades of green, but an aromatherapy system pumps out different fresh scents, including mint. The glass-top bar at the **Tides** (✉ 1220 Ocean Dr. ☎ 305/604–5000) is the place to go for martinis and piano jazz. At the chic Shore Club, the **SkyBar** (✉ 1901 Collins Ave., South Beach ☎ 786/276–6772), is a hip garden–poolside spot.

Dance Clubs

MIAMI Want 24-hour partying? **Space** (✉ 34 N.E. 11th St., Downtown ☎ 305/375–0001), created from four warehouses downtown, has three dance rooms, an outdoor patio, a New York industrial look, and a 24-hour liquor license. It's open on Saturdays only, and you'll need to look good to be allowed past the velvet ropes.

MIAMI BEACH South Beach is headquarters for nightclubs that start late and stay open until the early morning. The clientele includes freak-show rejects, sullen male models, and sultry women.

The **Bermuda Bar & Grille** (✉ 3509 N.E. 163rd St., North Miami Beach ☎ 305/945–0196) is way north of SoBe but worth the drive if you want to hang with the locals. Rock radio stations do remote broadcasts, and hard liquor and bottled beer are favored over silly drinks with umbrellas. The music is as loud as the space is large—two floors and seven bars—and it's open from 10 PM to 6 AM. Male bartenders wear knee-length kilts, while female bartenders are in matching minis. The vibe and crowd, though, are stylish, and there's a big tropical-forest scene, booths to hide in, and pool tables. The joint is closed Monday and Tuesday.

Honey (✉ 645 Washington Ave. ☎ 305/604–8222) has soft lighting, cozy couches, and chaise longues, and vibey music every bit as smooth as their trademark honey-dipped apples. **Mansion** (✉ 1235 Washington Ave. ☎ 305/532–1525) is the hip-hop rebirth of a defunct club called Level. Mansion has lots of places to search out fun.

Nikki Beach Club (✉ 1 Ocean Dr., South Beach ☎ 305/538–1231) has seven bars in a beautiful beachfront location—complete with tepee cabanas—and includes Pearl Restaurant and Champagne Bar, a steadfast celeb hangout. Popular with casually chic twenty- and thirtysomethings, **Opium Garden** (✉ 136 Collins Ave., at 1st St., South Beach ☎ 305/674–8360) has a lush waterfall, an Asian temple motif with lots of candles, dragons and tapestries, and a restaurant next door. It's open 11 PM–6 AM Thursday through Sunday.

Gay Nightlife

Aside from a few bars and lounges on the mainland, Greater Miami's gay action centers on the dance clubs in South Beach. That tiny strip of sand rivals New York and San Francisco as a hub of gay nightlife, if not in the number of clubs then in the intensity of the partying. The neighborhood's large gay population, plus the generally tolerant attitudes of the hip straights who live and visit here, encourages gay-friendliness at most South Beach venues that are not specifically gay, so you'll have many options from which to choose. In fact many mixed clubs, like crobar, have one or two gay nights. Laundry Bar has a mixed scene, and also hosts a gay night, including one for the ladies. Generally, gay life in Miami is overwhelmingly male-oriented, and lesbians, although welcome everywhere, will find themselves in the minority. To find out what's going on, pick up the South Beach club rag *Hotspots*, widely available as the weekend approaches, or the alternative weeklies *Wire* and *TWN (The Weekly News)*. The Miami-Dade Gay & Lesbian Chamber of Commerce (⊕ www.gogaymiami.com) is another helpful resource.

SOUTH BEACH Locals continue to flock to **crobar** (⊠ 1445 Washington Ave., at 14th St., South Beach ☎ 305/531–5027), whose exterior is the historic Cameo Theater, while the interior is a *Blade Runner*–esque blend of high-tech marvels with some performance art thrown in. Dazzling and lots of fun, it's open Thursday through Monday.

The popular Lincoln Road hangout **Score** (⊠ 727 Lincoln Rd., at Euclid Ave., South Beach ☎ 305/535–1111) draws a good-looking, largely younger crowd. There's loud dance music and an outdoor patio perfect for people-watching. Sunday is karaoke day.

Twist (⊠ 1057 Washington Ave., at 10th St., South Beach ☎ 305/538–9478) is a longtime hot spot and local favorite with two levels, an outdoor patio, and a game room. It's crowded from 8 PM on, especially on Monday, Thursday (2-for-1), and Friday nights.

SOUTH MIAMI One of the most popular men's dance clubs on the mainland, South Miami multilevel dance complex **O'Zone** (⊠ 6620 Red Rd., 1 block off U.S. 1, South Miami ☎ 305/667–2888) attracts Latin and Anglo patrons in their twenties and thirties. Pool tables and other games offer an alternative to elbow bending.

Jazz

MIAMI BEACH **Jazid** (⊠ 1342 Washington Ave., at 13th St., South Beach ☎ 305/673–9372), a stylishly redecorated standout on the strip, is sultry and candlelighted; the music is jazz, with blues and R&B. More restaurant than jazz club, **Van Dyke Café** (⊠ 846 Lincoln Rd. ☎ 305/534–3600) serves music on the second floor seven nights a week. Its location on the Lincoln Road Mall makes it a great spot to take a break during an evening shopping excursion.

Nightclub

MIAMI BEACH Dine as you watch the show at the Fontainebleau Hilton's **Club Tropigala** (⊠ 4441 Collins Ave., Miami Beach ☎ 305/672–7469 ⊕ www.clubtropigala.com), which tries to blend modern Vegas with 1950s Havana. The four-tier round room is decorated with orchids, banana leaves, and philodendrons. Some of the performances are stellar, with a Latin flavor—Ricky Martin, Julio Iglesias, and Jose Feliciano have made appearances here. Hotel guests are comped, but others pay a $20 cover. Reservations are suggested.

SPORTS & THE OUTDOORS

In addition to contacting the addresses below directly, get tickets to major events from **TicketMaster** (☎ 305/358–5885).

Auto Racing

Hialeah Speedway holds stock-car races on a ⅓-mi asphalt oval in a 5,000-seat stadium. Don't be fooled: the enthusiasm of the local drivers makes this as exciting as Winston Cup races. Five divisions of cars run weekly. The speedway is on U.S. 27, ¼ mi east of the Palmetto Expressway (Route 826). ⊠ *3300 W. Okeechobee Rd., Hialeah* ☎ *305/821–6644* ⊕ *www. hialeahspeedway.com* ☞ *$10, special events $15* ◷ *Sat., gates open at 5:30 PM, races 7–11; closed mid-Dec.–late Jan.*

For Winston Cup events, head south to the **Homestead-Miami Speedway,** which brings the NASCAR Winston Cup Series to South Florida with the Ford 400 NASCAR Winston Cup Series season finale. Held on the third Sunday in November in conjunction with the NASCAR Craftsman Truck Series Season Finale, it's the highlight of the speedway's yearly schedule. The track, built in 1995, was re-engineered with steeper banking in 2003 to increase the challenge to the drivers. The speedway also hosts the Toyota Indy 300 IRL season opener, Indy car racing, and the Grand Am Sports Car Event in spring. From Miami take Florida's Turnpike (Route 821) south to Exit 6, at Southwest 137th Avenue. ⊠ *1 Speedway Blvd., South Dade, Homestead* ☎ *305/230–7223* ⊕ *www. homesteadmiamispeedway.com* ☞ *Varies according to event* ◷ *Weekdays 9–5.*

Baseball

⌘ The **Florida Marlins** (☎ 305/626–7400 or 877/627–5467 ⊕ www. flamarlins.com) did what few thought possible: they came out of nowhere and beat the New York Yankees to win the 2003 World Series. Despite a respectable season in 2004, however, they didn't make the playoffs. The only thing lacking is a baseball-only stadium with a retractable roof to use on rainy days. For now, home games are played at **Pro Player Stadium** (⊠ 2267 N.W. 199th St., Lake Lucerne ☎ 305/626–7400 or 305/ 626–7426 ⊕ www.proplayerstadium.com ☞ $3–$75, parking $10), which is 16 mi northwest of downtown.

Basketball

The **Miami Heat** play their home games at the 19,600-seat waterfront AmericanAirlines Arena, which has restaurants. The regular season runs from November to April. ⊠ *AmericanAirlines Arena, 601 Biscayne Blvd., Downtown, Miami* ☎ *786/777–4328, 800/462–2849 ticket hotline* ⊕ *www.heat.com* ☞ *$10–$180.*

Biking

Perfect weather and flat terrain make Miami-Dade County a popular place for cyclists. A free map that points out streets best suited for bicycles, as well as information about bike rack–equipped buses, is available from bike shops and also from the **Miami-Dade County Bicycle Coordinator** (⊠ Metropolitan Planning Organization, 111 N.W. 1st St., Suite 910, Miami 33128 ☎ 305/375–1647), whose purpose is to share with you the glories of bicycling in South Florida. Information on dozens of monthly group rides is available from the **Everglades Bicycle Club** (☎ 305/598–3998). On Key Biscayne, **Mangrove Cycles** (⊠ 260 Crandon Blvd., Key Biscayne ☎ 305/361–5555) rents bikes for $10 for two hours or $15 per day. On Miami Beach, the proximity of the **Miami Beach Bicycle Center** (MBBC; ⊠ 601 5th St., South Beach, Miami Beach ☎ 305/674–0150) to Ocean Drive and the ocean itself makes it worth the $25 per day (or $10 per hour).

Boating

The popular full-service **Crandon Park Marina** (⊠ 4000 Crandon Blvd., Key Biscayne ☎ 305/361–1281) is a one-stop shop for all things oceany. The office is open daily 8–6. Embark on deep-sea-fishing or scuba-diving excursions, dine at a marina restaurant, or rent power boats through **Key Biscayne Rentals** (⊠ 5420 Crandon Blvd., Key Biscayne ☎ 305/361–9217), a national power boat rental company. Get half- to full-day rentals from $299 to $699 or buy a membership, which costs a bundle at first but cuts the cost of future rentals by 50%.

Named for an island where early settlers had picnics, **Dinner Key Marina** (⊠ 3400 Pan American Dr., Coconut Grove ☎ 305/579–6980 ☼ Daily 7 AM–11 PM) is Greater Miami's largest, with nearly 600 moorings at nine piers. There's space for transients and a boat ramp. Whether you're looking to be on the water for a few hours or a few days, **Cruzan Yacht Charters** (⊠ 3375 Pan American Dr., Coconut Grove ☎ 305/858–2822 or 800/628–0785) is a good choice for renting manned or unmanned sailboats and motor yachts. If you plan to captain the boat yourself, expect a two- to three-hour checkout cruise and at least a $500 daily rate (three-day minimum). If you want to charter a boat with a captain, **Key Biscayne Rentals** (⊠ 2560 Bayshore Dr., Coconut Grove ☎ 305/858–6258) offers half- to full-day rentals from $299 to $699.

Haulover Marine Center is low on glamour but high on service. It has a bait-and-tackle shop, marine gas station, and boat launch. ⊠ *15000 Collins Ave., Sunny Isles, Miami Beach* ☎ *305/945–3934* ☼ *Bait shop and gas station 24 hrs.*

Although **Matheson Hammock Park** has no charter services, it does have 252 slips and boat ramps. It also has **Castle Harbor** (☎ 305/665–4994), which rents sailboats for those with U.S. Sailing certification and holds classes for those without. When you're ready to rent, take your pick of boats, ranging from 20 feet to 41 feet. ⊠ *9610 Old Cutler Rd., Coral Gables* ☎ *305/665–4994* ⊕ *www.castleharbor.com* ☼ *Weekdays 9–4, weekends 9–5.*

Near the Art Deco District, **Miami Beach Marina** has about every marine facility imaginable—restaurants, charters, boat and vehicle rentals, a complete marine-hardware store, a dive shop, excursion vendors, a large grocery store, a fuel dock, concierge services, and 400 slips accommodating vessels of up to 250 feet. There's also a U.S. Customs clearing station. One charter outfit here is the family-owned **Florida Yacht Charters** (☎ 305/532–8600 or 800/537–0050). After completing the requisite checkout cruise and paperwork, take off for the Keys or the Bahamas on a catamaran, sailboat, or motor yacht. Charts, lessons, and captains are available if needed. ⊠ *300 Alton Rd., South Beach, Miami Beach* ☎ *305/673–6000 marina* ⊙ *Daily 7–6.*

Dog Racing

Flagler Greyhound Track has dog races during its June–November season and a poker room that's open when the track is running. Closed-circuit TV brings harness-racing action here as well. The track is five minutes east of Miami International Airport, off Dolphin Expressway (Route 836) and Douglas Road (N.W. 37th Avenue). ⊠ *401 N.W. 38th Ct., Little Havana, Miami* ☎ *305/649–3000* ⊕ *www.flaglerdogs.com* ⊠ *Grandstand and clubhouse free, parking free–$3* ⊙ *Daily at 8:05* PM *and also on Tues., Thurs., and Sat. at 1:05* PM.

Fishing

Before there was fashion, there was fishing. Deep-sea fishing is still a major draw in Miami, and anglers drop a line for sailfish, kingfish, dolphin, snapper, wahoo, grouper, and tuna. Small charter boats cost $450–$500 for a half day and provide everything but food and drinks. If you're on a budget, you might be better off paying around $30 for passage on a larger fishing boat—rarely are they filled to capacity. Most charters have a 50–50 plan, which allows you to take (or sell) half your catch while they do the same. Just don't let anyone sell you an individual fishing license; a blanket license for the boat should cover all passengers.

Crandon Park Marina has earned an international reputation for its knowledgeable charter-boat captains and good catches. Heading out to the edge of the Gulf Stream (about 3 to 4 mi), you're sure to wind up with something on your line (sailfish are catch-and-release). ⊠ *4000 Crandon Blvd., Key Biscayne* ☎ *305/361–1281* ⊠ *6-passenger boats $699 full day, $499 half day (5 hrs).*

Haulover Beach Park. This marina lays claim to the largest charter–drift fishing fleet in South Florida. Among the many charters docked here are the **Kelley Fleet** (☎ 305/945–3801), with 65- or 85-foot party boats charging $33 per person, and *Therapy IV* (☎ 305/945–1578), a six-passenger boat, charging $125 per person for a half day. ⊠ *Haulover Beach Park, 10800 Collins Ave., Sunny Isles, Miami Beach* ☎ *305/947–3525* ⊠ *$4 per vehicle* ⊙ *Daily sunrise–sunset.*

Among the charter services at **Miami Beach Marina** is the two-boat **Reward Fleet** (☎ 305/372–9470). Rates run $35 per person including bait, rod, reel, and tackle. ⊠ *MacArthur Causeway, 300 Alton Rd., South Beach, Miami Beach* ☎ *305/673–6000.*

Football

Consistently ranked as one of the top teams in the NFL, the **Miami Dolphins** (☎ 305/620–2578) have one of the largest average attendance figures in the league. Fans may be hoping to see a repeat of the 1972 perfect season, when the team, led by legendary coach Don Shula, compiled a 17–0 record (a record that has yet to be broken). From September through January, on home-game days, the Metro Miami-Dade Transit Agency runs buses to **Pro Player Stadium**, 16 mi northwest of downtown. ✉ *2267 N.W. 199th St., Lake Lucerne* ☎ *305/573-8326 or 305/626-7426* ⊕ *www.proplayerstadium.com* ✉ *Tickets $25–$175, parking $20.*

Worth checking out is the **University of Miami Hurricanes** (☎ 305/284–2263 or 800/462–2637) football team. Now competing in the powerful Atlantic Coast Conference, the Hurricanes are regularly a top-10 contender, with five national football championships since 1983. During the September–November season, the home-team advantage is measured in decibels, as some 70,000 fans literally rock the stadium when the team is on a roll. They play their home games at downtown's aging but beloved **Orange Bowl Stadium**. ✉ *1145 N.W. 11th St., Downtown* ☎ *305/643-7100* ✉ *Tickets $20–$50, parking $20–$30.*

Golf

Greater Miami has more than 30 private and public courses. Fees at most courses are higher on weekends and in season, but save money by playing weekdays and after 1 PM or 3 PM (call to find out when afternoon or twilight rates go into effect). That said, costs are reasonable. The **"Golfer's Guide for South Florida"** (☎ 800/864–6101 to order) includes information on most courses in Miami and surrounding areas. The cost is $3.

The 18-hole, par-71 championship **Biltmore Golf Course**, known for its scenic layout, has been restored to its original Donald Ross design, circa 1925. The green fee ranges from $48 to $120 in season, and the gorgeous hotel makes a great backdrop. ✉ *1210 Anastasia Ave., Coral Gables* ☎ *305/460–5364* ✉ *Optional cart $22.*

The **California Golf Club** has an 18-hole, par-72 course, with a tight front nine and three of the area's toughest finishing holes. A round of 18 holes will set you back $30 to $45, cart included. ✉ *20898 San Simeon Way, North Miami Beach* ☎ *305/651–3590.*

Overlooking the bay, the **Crandon Golf Course**, formerly the Links at Key Biscayne, is a top-rated 18-hole, par-72 public course in a beautiful tropical locale. Expect to pay around $149 for a round in winter, $65 in summer, cart included. After 3, the winter rate drops to $57. The Royal Caribbean Classic and the Senior PGA are held here. ✉ *6700 Crandon Blvd., Key Biscayne* ☎ *305/361–9129.*

Don Shula's Hotel & Golf Club has one of the longest championship courses in Miami (7,055 yards, par 72), a lighted par-3 course, and a golf school, and it hosts more than 75 tournaments a year. Weekdays you can play the championship course for $105, $145 on weekends ($40 for both after 3); golf carts are included. The lighted par-3 course is $12 weekdays, $15 weekends, and $15 for an optional cart. ⊠ *7601 Miami Lakes Dr., take the 154th Street exit east (Miami Lakes Drive) off Rte. 826, Miami Lakes* ☎ *305/820–8106.*

Among its six courses and many annual tournaments, the **Doral Golf Resort and Spa** is best known for the par-72 Blue Monster course and the annual Ford Championship, with $1 million in prize money. Fees range from $195 to $295. Carts are not required, but there's no discount for walking. ⊠ *4400 N.W. 87th Ave., 36th St. exit off Rte. 826, Doral* ☎ *305/ 592–2000 or 800/713–6725.*

For a casual family outing or for beginners, the 9-hole, par-3 **Haulover Golf Course** is right on the Intracoastal Waterway at the north end of Miami Beach. The longest hole on this walking course is 120 yards; the green fee is only $6. ⊠ *10800 Collins Ave., Sunny Isles, Miami Beach* ☎ *305/940–6719.*

Normandy Shores Golf Course is good for senior citizens, with some modest slopes and average distances; green fee is $55 in season, including cart. ⊠ *2401 Biarritz Dr., Miami Beach* ☎ *305/868–6502.*

The **Turnberry Isle Resort & Club** has 36 holes designed by Robert Trent Jones. The South Course's 18th hole is a killer. Green fee is $134, but since it's private, you won't be able to play unless you're a hotel guest. ⊠ *19999 W. Country Club Dr., North Miami Beach* ☎ *305/933–6929.*

Horse Racing

The **Calder Race Course,** opened in 1971, is Florida's largest glass-enclosed, air-conditioned sports facility. Its season runs from late April to early January. The high point of the season, the Tropical Park Derby for three-year-olds, comes in the final week. The track is on the Miami-Dade–Broward county line near Interstate 95 and the Hallandale Beach Boulevard exit, ¾ mi from Pro Player Stadium. ⊠ *21001 N.W. 27th Ave., Lake Lucerne* ☎ *305/625–1311* 🎟 *Grandstand $2, clubhouse $4, parking $1–$5* ⊘ *Gates open at 11, racing 12:25–5.*

Gulfstream Park, north of the Miami-Dade county line, is open from mid-January through late March. The track's premier race is the Florida Derby. ⊠ *21301 Biscayne Blvd. (U.S. 1), between Ives Dairy Rd. and Hallandale Beach Blvd., Hallandale* ☎ *954/454–7000* 🎟 *Grandstand $3, clubhouse $5, parking free* ⊘ *Wed.–Mon. post time 1 PM.*

Jai Alai

Built in 1926, the **Miami Jai Alai Fronton,** a mile east of the airport, is America's oldest fronton. It presents 13 games (14 on Friday and Saturday) daily except Tuesday—some singles, some doubles. This game, invented in the Basque region of northern Spain, is the world's fastest. Jai alai balls, called pelotas, have been clocked at speeds exceeding 170 mph. The game is played in a 176-foot-long court, and players literally climb the walls to catch the ball in a *cesta* (a woven basket), which has an attached glove. Either place your wager on the team you think will win or on the order in which you think the teams will finish. ⊠ *3500 N.W. 37th Ave., Downtown, Miami* ☎ *305/633–6400* 🎟 *General ad-*

mission $1, reserved seats $2, Courtview Club $5 ◷ *Mon., Wed.–Sat., noon–5, Mon, Fri., and Sat. 7–midnight, Sun. 1–6.*

Jogging

There are numerous places to run in Miami, but these recommended jogging routes are considered among the most scenic and the safest: in Coconut Grove, along the pedestrian-bicycle path on South Bayshore Drive, cutting over the causeway to Key Biscayne for a longer run; from the south shore of the Miami River, downtown, south along the sidewalks of Brickell Avenue to Bayshore Drive, where you can run alongside the bay; in Miami Beach, along Bay Road (parallel to Alton Road) or on the sidewalk skirting the Atlantic Ocean, opposite the cafés of Ocean Drive; and in Coral Gables, around the Riviera Country Club golf course, south of the Biltmore Country Club. **Foot Works** (✉ 5724 Sunset Dr., South Miami ☎ 305/667–9322), a running-shoe store that sponsors races and organizes marathon training, is a great source of information. The **Miami Runners Club** (✉ 8720 N. Kendall Dr., Suite 206, Miami ☎ 305/227–1500) has information on routes and races.

Scuba Diving & Snorkeling

Diving and snorkeling on the offshore coral wrecks and reefs can be comparable to the Caribbean, especially on a calm day. Chances are excellent you'll come face to face with a flood of tropical fish. One option is to find Fowey, Triumph, Long, and Emerald reefs in 10- to 15-foot dives that are perfect for snorkelers and beginning divers. On the edge of the continental shelf a little more than 3 mi out, these reefs are just ¼ mi away from depths greater than 100 feet. Another option is to paddle around the tangled prop roots of the mangrove trees that line the coast, peering at the fish, crabs, and other creatures hiding there. Perhaps the most unusual diving options in Greater Miami are the artificial reefs. Since 1981 **Miami-Dade County's Department of Environmental Resources Management (DERM)** (✉ 1920 Meridian Ave., South Beach, Miami Beach ☎ 305/672–1270) has sunk tons of limestone boulders and a water tower, army tanks, a 727 jet, and almost 200 boats of all descriptions to create a "wreckreational" habitat where you can swim with yellow tang, barracudas, nurse sharks, snapper, eels, and grouper. Most dive shops sell a book listing the locations of these wrecks.

H20 Scuba (✉ 160 Sunny Isles Blvd., Sunny Isles, Miami Beach ☎ 305/956–3483 or 888/389–3483), is the place many local divers recommend for buying or renting your scuba or snorkel equipment. It's an all-purpose dive shop with PADI affiliation and runs night and wreck dives from its Coast Guard–certified charter boat docked right behind the store. **Divers Paradise of Key Biscayne** (✉ 4000 Crandon Blvd., Key Biscayne ☎ 305/361–3483), next to the full-service Crandon Park Marina, has a complete dive shop and diving-charter service. On offer are equipment rental and scuba instruction with PADI affiliation.

Tennis

Greater Miami has more than a dozen tennis centers open to the public, and county-wide nearly 500 public courts are open to visitors. Nonresidents are charged an hourly fee. If you're on a tight schedule, try calling in advance, as some courts take reservations on weekdays. **Biltmore Tennis Center** has 10 lighted hard courts and a view of the beautiful Biltmore Hotel. ⊠ *1150 Anastasia Ave., Coral Gables* ☎ *305/460–5360* ⌨ *Day rate $5.50 per person per hr, night rate $7.50* ☉ *Weekdays 7 AM–10 PM, weekends 7 AM–8 PM.*

Very popular with locals, **Flamingo Tennis Center** has 19 lighted clay courts smack dab in the middle of Miami Beach. You can't get much closer to the action. ⊠ *1000 12th St., South Beach, Miami Beach* ☎ *305/673–7761* ⌨ *Day rate $8 per person per hr, night rate $9.50* ☉ *Weekdays 8 AM–9 PM, weekends 8–8.*

The 30-acre **Tennis Center at Crandon Park** is one of America's best. Included are 2 grass, 8 clay, and 17 hard courts. Reservations are required for night play. The clay and grass courts are closed at night. The courts are open to the public except during the **Nasdaq-100 Open** (☎ 305/442–3367), held for 12 days each spring. Top players such as Andre Agassi, Gustavo Kuerten, Venus and Sabrina Williams, and Jennifer Capriati compete in a 14,000-seat stadium for more than $6 million in prize money. ⊠ *7300 Crandon Blvd., Key Biscayne* ☎ *305/365–2300* ⌨ *Laykold courts: day rate $3, night rate $5, per person per hr. Clay courts: $6 per person per hr. Grass courts: $8 per person per hr* ☉ *Daily 8 AM–9 PM.*

Windsurfing

Windsurfing is more popular than ever in Miami. The safest and most popular windsurfing area is at **Hobie Beach,** sometimes called Windsurfer Beach, just off the Rickenbacker Causeway on your way to Key Biscayne. In Miami Beach the best spots are at **1st Street** (north of the Government Cut jetty) and at **21st Street;** also windsurf on the beach at 3rd, 10th, and 14th streets. **Sailboards Miami** (⊠ 1 Rickenbacker Causeway, Key Biscayne ☎ 305/361–7245), ⅓ mi past the causeway tollbooth, rents equipment and claims to teach more windsurfers each year than anyone else in the United States. Rentals average $25–$30 for one hour and $100 for 4 hours. The outfit promises to teach anyone to windsurf within two hours—for $69.

SHOPPING

In Greater Miami you're never more than 15 minutes from a major shopping area that serves as both a shopping and entertainment venue for tourists and locals. Miami-Dade County has more than a dozen major malls and hundreds of miles of commercial streets lined with stores and small shopping centers. Latin neighborhoods contain a wealth of Latin merchants and merchandise, including children's *vestidos de fiesta* (party dresses) and men's guayaberas (a pleated, embroidered tropical shirt), conveying the feel of a South American *mercado* (market).

Malls

FodorśChoice **Aventura Mall** (⊠ 19501 Biscayne Blvd., North Miami Beach) has more ★ than 250 upscale shops anchored by Macy's, Lord & Taylor, JCPenney, Sears Roebuck, Burdines, and Bloomingdale's, along with a 24-screen theater with stadium seating and a Cheesecake Factory. In a tropical garden, **Bal Harbour Shops** (⊠ 9700 Collins Ave., Bal Harbour, Miami Beach) is a swank collection of 100 shops, boutiques, and department stores, such as Chanel, Gucci, Cartier, Gianfranco Ferré, Hermès, Neiman Marcus, and Saks Fifth Avenue. **Bayside Marketplace** (⊠ 401 Biscayne Blvd., Downtown, Miami), the 16-acre shopping complex on Biscayne Bay, has more than 100 specialty shops, live entertainment, tour-boat docks, and a food court. It's open late (until 10 during the week, 11 on Friday and Saturday), but its restaurants stay open even later. Browse, buy, or simply relax by the bay with a tropical drink.

The heartbeat of Coconut Grove, **CocoWalk** (⊠ 3015 Grand Ave., Co-conut Grove, Miami) has three floors of nearly 40 specialty shops (Vic-toria's Secret, Gap, among others) that stay open almost as late as the popular restaurants and clubs. Kiosks with cigars, beads, incense, herbs, and other small items are scattered around the ground level, while the restaurants and nightlife (e.g., Hooters, Fat Tuesday, an AMC theater) are upstairs. If you're ready for an evening of people-watching, this is the place.

The oldest retail mall in the county, **Dadeland Mall** (⊠ 7535 N. Kendall Dr., Kendall, Miami Beach) also feels like the biggest and busiest. Re-tailers include Saks Fifth Avenue, JCPenney, Lord & Taylor, Florida's largest Burdines department store, Burdines Home Gallery, and more than 185 specialty stores. There are 12 places to eat, that vary from ordering at the counter to ordering from the waiter. It's on the south side of town, and close to the Metrorail station. The **Dolphin Mall** (⊠ 11401 N.W. 12th St., at State Rd. 836 and Florida's Tpke., West Dade, Miami) has more than 200 outlet, dining, and entertainment venues. Major anchors in-clude Linens 'N Things, Marshalls Megastore, Off 5th Saks Fifth Avenue Outlet, and Old Navy. A 400,000-square-foot entertainment center in-cludes Dave & Busters, a 19-screen cinema, and 850-seat food court. **The Falls** (⊠ 8888 S.W. 136th St., at U.S. 1, South Miami), which derives its name from the waterfalls and lagoons inside, is the most upscale mall on the south side of the city. It has a Macy's and Bloomingdale's as well as another 100 specialty stores, restaurants, and a 12-theater multiplex.

As its name suggests, **Loehmann's Fashion Island** (⊠ 18701 Biscayne Blvd., North Miami Beach) is dominated by Loehmann's, the nation-wide retailer of off-price designer fashions for women and men. Fash-ion-conscious shoppers can also visit other specialty boutiques and browse in a Barnes & Noble bookstore.

With a huge banyan tree to welcome visitors, **Shops at Sunset Place** (⊠ 5701 Sunset Dr., at U.S. 1 and Red Rd., South Miami) is even larger than CocoWalk. The three-story, family-oriented center has upped the ante for shopping-entertainment complexes with a 24-screen cinemaplex, IMAX theater, Virgin Megastore, NikeTown, A/X Armani Exchange, Dan Marino's Town Tavern, and GameWorks. **Streets of Mayfair** (⊠ 2911 Grand Ave., Coconut Grove, Miami) is an open-air promenade of shops that bustles both day and night thanks to its Coconut Grove locale. The News Café, Borders Books Music Cafe, a dozen other shops, an improv comedy club and nightclubs provide entertainment.

★ At the Mediterranean-style shopping and dining venue **Village of Merrick Park** (✉ 358 San Lorenzo Ave., Coral Gables), anchors Neiman Marcus and Nordstrom and 115 specialty shops (Burberry, Jimmy Choo, and Boucheron) fulfill most high-fashion and haute-decor shopping fantasies, while 10 international food venues and a day spa round out the indulgent options.

Outdoor Markets

★ **Coconut Grove Farmers Market** (✉ Grand Ave. and Margaret St., Coconut Grove, Miami), open Saturday 10–5:30, originated in 1977 and still specializes in organically grown local produce and ready-to-eat goodies. Each Saturday morning from 8 to 1, mid-January to late March, some 25 produce and plant vendors sell herbs, fruits, fresh-squeezed juices, chutneys, cakes, and muffins at the **Coral Gables Farmers Market** (✉ 405 Biltmore Way, Coral Gables) in Merrick Park. The **Española Way Market** (✉ Española Way, between Drexel and Washington Aves., South Beach, Miami Beach) happens Saturday 10 AM–midnight and Sunday 10–9 along a two-block stretch of storefronts and cafés. Scattered among the handcrafted items and food merchants, musicians beat out Latin rhythms on bongos and steel drums. From 9 to 6 on the second and fourth Sunday of each month, locals set up the **Lincoln Road Antique and Collectibles Market** (✉ Lincoln and Alton Rds., South Beach, Miami Beach). The eclectic goods should satisfy postimpressionists, deco-holics, Edwardians, Bauhausers, and Gothic, atomic, and '50s junkies. The **Lincoln Road Farmers Market** (✉ Lincoln Rd. between Meridian and Euclid Aves., South Beach, Miami Beach), open Sunday 9–7, brings about 20 local produce and bakery vendors. The market is good for people-watching and picking up local plants, especially orchids. **Normandy Village Marketplace** (✉ 900 71st St., Mid-Beach, Miami Beach) convenes every Saturday from 9 to 6 at the Normandy Village Fountain where local vendors present a diverse show of fruits and vegetables, plants and breads, and jewelry and incense.

Shopping Districts

The shopping is great on a two-block stretch of **Collins Avenue** (✉ Between 6th and 8th Aves., South Beach, Miami Beach). Club Monaco, Polo Sport, Intermix, Kenneth Cole, Sephora, Armani Exchange, and Banana Republic are among the high-profile tenants, and a parking garage is just a block away on 7th Avenue. **Lincoln Road Mall** (✉ Between Alton Rd. and Washington Ave., South Beach, Miami Beach) (*see* What to See *in* South Beach/Miami Beach) brims with energy, especially when it swells with locals on weekends.

★ The **Miami Design District** (✉ Between N.E. 36th and N.E. 41st Sts. and between N.E. 2nd Ave. and N. Miami Ave., Design District, Miami) has some 200 designer showrooms and galleries specializing in interior furnishings, decorative arts, antiques, and a rich mix of exclusive and unusual merchandise. The surrounding area is still rough around the edges, but the Design District is an important and visitor-friendly place to view high-quality and cutting-edge interior design. **Miracle Mile** (✉ Coral Way between 37th and 42nd Aves., Coral Gables) consists of some 120 shops, galleries, and restaurants along a wide, tree-lined boulevard.

Shops range from posh bridal boutiques to bargain basements, from beauty salons to chain restaurants. As you go west, the quality improves.

Specialty Stores

ANTIQUES **Alhambra Antiques** (✉ 2850 Salzedo, Coral Gables ☎ 305/446–1688) is a collection of high-quality decorative pieces acquired from annual shopping trips to Europe. **Architectural Antiques** (✉ 2520 S.W. 28th La., Coconut Grove, Miami ☎ 305/285–1330) carries large and eclectic items—railroad crossing signs, statues, English roadsters—in a store so cluttered that shopping here becomes an adventure promising hidden treasures for the determined. **Senzatempo** (✉ 1655 Meridian Ave., South Beach, Miami Beach ☎ 305/534–5588) has a unique collection of watches and vintage home accessories by European and American designers of the 1930s through the 1970s, including electric fans, klieg lights, and chrome furniture. **Valerio Antiques** (✉ 250 Valencia Ave., Coral Gables ☎ 305/448–6779) is a fine collection of French art deco furniture, bronze sculptures, and original art glass by Gallé and Loetz, among others.

BOOKS   Like others in the superstore chain, **Barnes & Noble** (✉ 152 Miracle Mile, Coral Gables ☎ 305/446–4152) manages to preserve the essence of a neighborhood bookstore by encouraging customers to pick a book off the shelf and lounge on a couch without being hassled. A well-stocked national–international magazine rack and coffee bar–café complete the experience here or at its Kendall, North Miami Beach, and South Miami locations. Greater Miami's best English-language bookstore, **Books & Books, Inc.** (✉ 265 Aragon Ave., Coral Gables ☎ 305/442–4408 ✉ 933 Lincoln Rd., South Beach, Miami Beach ☎ 305/532–3222) specializes in books on the arts, architecture, Florida, and contemporary and classical literature. At either store you can lounge at the café, browse through the photography gallery, or sit outside and flip through magazines. Both locations host poetry readings, book signings, and author readings. **Kafka's** (✉ 1464 Washington Ave., South Beach, Miami Beach ☎ 305/673–9669), a bookstore and Argentinian café, sells previously owned books and has a good selection of art books and literature. In addition, the shop carries obscure and familiar periodicals and has computers and Internet access for a fee. **Super Heroes Unlimited** (✉ 1788 N. E. 163rd St., North Miami ☎ 305/940–9539) beckons comic-book readers looking for monthly refills of *Spawn* and *X-Men* and tempts with an enviable selection of Japanese *animé*.

CHILDREN'S   **Sweetdreams Candies** (✉ 708 Lincoln Rd., South Beach, Miami Beach
BOOKS & TOYS   ☎ 305/538–8155) is a candy store with a wild assortment of jelly beans, lollipops, bubblegum, and gummi bears along with toys and homemade chocolates. **Peekaboo** (✉ 6807 Main St., North Miami ☎ 305/556–6910) carries educational toys and exceptional European clothing for kids.

CIGARS   Smoking anything even remotely affiliated with a legendary Cuban has boosted the popularity of Miami cigar stores and the small shops where you can buy cigars straight from the press. **Bill's Pipe & Tobacco** (✉ 2309 Ponce de León Blvd., Coral Gables ☎ 305/444–1764) has everything for the pipe and cigar smoker, including a wide selection of pipes and pipe tobacco, cigars, accessories, and gifts. **Tropical Cigars** (✉ 741 Lincoln Rd., South Beach, Miami Beach ☎ 305/673–3194) is a cigar, coffee, and cocktail bar where you can hang out and buy boxes of cigars with personalized labels. **El Credito Cigars** (✉ 1100 S.W. 8th St., Little Havana, Miami ☎ 305/858–4162) is where workers at wooden benches rip through giant tobacco leaves, cut them with rounded blades, wrap them tightly, and press them in vises. Dedicated smokers find their way here to pick up a $90 bundle or peruse the *gigantes, supremos,* panatelas, and Churchills available in natural or maduro wrappers. **Macabi Cigars** (✉ 3475 S.W. 8th St., Little Havana, Miami ☎ 305/446–2606) carries cigars, cigars, and more cigars, including premium and house brands. Humidors and other accessories make great gifts.

CLOTHING FOR **Base** (✉ 939 Lincoln Rd., South Beach, Miami Beach ☎ 305/531–
MEN & WOMEN 4982) has good karma and great eclectic island wear for men and women. For women's fashions by Barbara Bui, Catherine Malandrino, and Mint mixed in with up-and-coming designer clothing and accessories, **Chroma** (✉ 920 Lincoln Rd., South Beach, Miami Beach ☎ 305/695–8808) is where local fashionistas go. **Koko & Palenki** (✉ CocoWalk, 3015 Grand Ave., Coconut Grove, Miami ☎ 305/444–1772) has a well-edited selection of men's and women's shoes and accessories by Casadei, Charles David, Stuart Weitzman and Donald Pliner in its Coconut Grove, South Miami, and Aventura locations.

Miami Twice (✉ 6562 S.W. 40th St., South Miami ☎ 305/666–0127) has fabulous vintage clothes, costumes, and accessories from the last three decades. Check out the vintage home collectibles and furniture, too. Just ★ off Lincoln Road is **Sasparilla Vintage** (✉ 1630 Pennsylvania Ave., South Beach, Miami Beach ☎ 305/532–6611), a well-edited boutique teeming with gotta-have-it vintage. Find excellent condition resale accessories from Gucci, Dolce, Dries, and Pucci neatly organized among the colorful party dresses.

In the Shore Club Hotel, **Scoop** (✉ 1901 Collins Ave., South Beach, Miami Beach ☎ 305/695–3297) is a small but spaciously arranged store carrying all the latest fashion requirements for men and women by Helmut Lang, Marc Jacobs, Earl, and Seven.

Silvia Tcherassi (✉ 358 San Lorenzo Ave., Coral Gables ☎ 305/461–0009), the Colombian designer's signature boutique in the Village of Merrick Park, has feminine and frilly dresses and separates accented with chiffon, tulle and sequins.

ESSENTIALS Wall-to-wall merchandise is found at the **Compass Market** (✉ 9 Ocean Dr., South Beach, Miami Beach ☎ 305/673–2906), a cute basement shop in the Waldorf Towers hotel. The market stocks sandals, souvenirs, cigars, deli items, umbrellas, newspapers—all the staples you'll need for a day at the beach. If the heat of Miami gets you hot and bothered, try **Condom USA** (✉ 3066 Grand Ave., Coconut Grove, Miami ☎ 305/445–7729). Sexually oriented games and condoms are sold by the gross. ★ **Epicure Market** (✉ 1656 Alton Rd., South Beach, Miami Beach ☎ 305/672–1861) is one of Miami's most cherished establishments. Pick up jars of homemade chicken noodle soup and some of the pricey produce or wander down aisles full of imported chocolate, cheese, and local celebrities.

JEWELRY **Beverlee Kagan** (⊠ 5831 Sunset Dr., South Miami ☎ 305/663–1937) specializes in vintage and antique jewelry, including art deco–era bangles, bracelets, and cuff links. **By Design** (⊠ 297 Miracle Mile, Coral Gables ☎ 305/441–9696) custom designs fine jewelry from precious metals and stones. The 10-story **Seybold Building** (⊠ 36 N.E. 1st St., Downtown, Miami ☎ 305/374–7922) is filled from bottom to top with more than 250 independent jewelry companies. Diamonds, bracelets, necklaces, and rings are sold in this crowded, competitively priced spot; it's closed Sunday.

SOUVENIRS & **Art Deco District Welcome Center** (⊠ 1001 Ocean Dr., South Beach, Miami
GIFT ITEMS Beach ☎ 305/531–3484) hawks the finest in Miami-inspired kitsch, from flamingo salt-and-pepper shakers to alligator-shape ashtrays, along with
★ books and posters celebrating the Art Deco District. **Dog Bar** (⊠ 723 N. Lincoln La., South Beach, Miami Beach ☎ 305/532–5654), just north of Lincoln Road's main drag, caters to enthusiastic animal owners who simply must have that perfect leopard-skin pet bed, gourmet treats, and organic food. The **Indies Company** (⊠ 101 W. Flagler St., Downtown, Miami ☎ 305/375–1492), the Historical Museum of Southern Florida's gift shop, offers interesting artifacts reflecting Miami's history, including some inexpensive reproductions. The collection of books on Miami and South Florida is impressive.

SIDE TRIP, SOUTH DADE

Hurricane Andrew forever changed the face of these scattered suburbs southwest of Miami-Dade County's urban core, with many residents moving out and millions of dollars of aid pouring in, evident today in the charmingly rebuilt Deering Estate, Metrozoo, and Fruit and Spice Park. The Redland, the southernmost area also known as America's winter vegetable basket, offers a welcome change from urbane Miami. A complete exploration of all the attractions would probably take two days. Keep an eye open for hand-painted signs announcing orchid farms, fruit stands, you-pick farms, and horseback riding.

♻ ➍➏ **Coral Castle of Florida.** The castle was born when 26-year-old Edward Leedskalnin, a Latvian immigrant, was left at the altar by his 16-year-old fiancée. She went on with her life, while he went off the deep end and began carving a castle out of coral rock. It's hard to believe that Eddie, only 5-foot tall and 100 pounds, could maneuver tons of coral rock single-handedly. Built between 1920 and 1940, the 3-acre castle is one of South Florida's original tourist attractions. There's a 9-ton gate a child could open, an accurate working sundial, and a telescope of coral rock aimed at the North Star. ⊠ 28655 S. Dixie Hwy. ☎ 305/248–6345 ⊕ www.coralcastle.com ☜ $9.75 ☉ Daily 7 AM–9 PM.

➍➊ **Deering Estate at Cutler.** In 1913 Charles Deering, brother of James Deering, who built Vizcaya in Coconut Grove, bought this property for a winter residence. Nine years later he built the Mediterranean revival stone house that stands here today. Far more austere than its ornate cousin

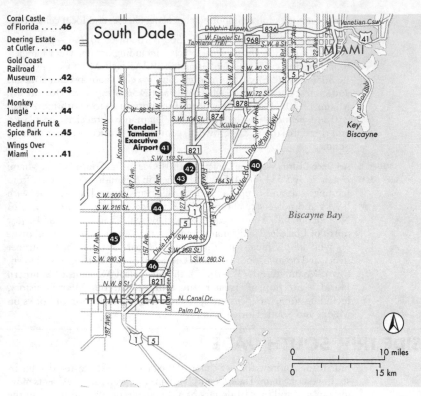

Vizcaya, the stone house, with a magnificent view of Biscayne Bay, has wrought-iron gates, copper doors, and a unique stone ceiling. Next door, the fully restored Richmond Cottage, the first inn to be built between Coconut Grove and Key West (1900), is a fine example of South Florida frame vernacular architecture. Take a naturalist-guided tour to learn more about the area's archaeology: scientists discovered human remains here and carbon-dated them to 10,000 years ago; they may belong to Paleo-Indians. A fossil pit contains the bones of dog-size horses, tapirs, jaguars, peccaries, sloths, and bison. Coastal tropical hardwood hammocks, rare orchids and trees, and wildlife, such as gray foxes, bobcats, limp-kins, peregrine falcons, and cormorants, populate the property. A huge environmental education and visitor center, with wide viewing porches, presents programs for children and adults. Nature tours and canoe trips to nearby Chicken Key are available. Admission includes parking and three guided tours. ⊠ *16701 S.W. 72nd Ave.* ☎ *305/235–1668* ⊕ *www. deeringestate.org* 🎫 *$7* ☉ *Daily 10–5; last admission at 4.*

🐾 **42** **Gold Coast Railroad Museum.** Historic railroad cars on display here in-clude a 1949 *Silver Crescent* dome car and the *Ferdinand Magellan,* the only Pullman car constructed specifically for U.S. presidents. It was used by Franklin Delano Roosevelt, Harry Truman, Dwight Eisenhower, and Ronald Reagan. Every weekend the museum offers $2 train rides; every other weekend you can ride the presidential Pullman for $5 ($10 for the engine car). ⊠ *12450 S.W. 152nd St.* ☎ *305/253–0063* ⊕ *www. goldcoast-railroad.org* ⌲ *$5* ⊗ *Weekdays 10–4, weekends 11–4.*

★ ☾ ㊸ **Metrozoo.** One of the few zoos in the United States in a subtropical environment, the first-class, 290-acre Metrozoo is state of the art. Inside the cageless zoo, some 800 animals roam on islands surrounded by moats. Take the monorail to see major attractions including the Tiger Temple, where white tigers roam, and the African Plains exhibit, where giraffes, ostriches, and zebras graze in a simulated habitat. There are also koalas and Komodo dragons. The free flight aviary, demolished by Hurricane Andrew, reopened in 2003 with 300 birds, waterfalls, and lush tropical foliage. The children's petting zoo has a meerkat exhibit, and Dr. Wilde's World is an interactive facility with changing exhibits. Kids can touch Florida animals such as alligators and possum at the Ecology Theater. ⊠ *12400 S.W. 152nd St.* ☎ *305/251–0400* ⊕ *www.miamimetrozoo. com* ⌲ *$11.50, 45-min tram tour $2.50* ⊗ *Daily 9:30–5:30; last admission at 4.*

☾ ㊹ **Monkey Jungle.** Still a kitschy attraction for adults, more than 300 monkeys representing 25 species—including orangutans from Borneo and Sumatra and golden lion tamarins from Brazil—roam free here. Exhibits include Lemurs of Madagascar, Parrots of the Amazon, and the Cameroon Jungle. Perhaps the most fun is feeding monkeys who scurry across the fences overhead, hauling up peanuts you place in a metal cup. ⊠ *14805 S.W. 216th St.* ☎ *305/235–1611* ⊕ *www.monkeyjungle.com* ⌲ *$17.95* ⊗ *Daily 9:30–5; last admission at 4.*

㊺ **Redland Fruit & Spice Park.** The 35 acres here have been a Dade County treasure since 1944, when it was opened as a 20-acre showcase of tropical fruits and vegetables. Plants are grouped by country of origin and include more than 500 varieties of exotic fruits, herbs, spices, nuts, and poisonous plants from around the world. A sampling reveals 90 types of bananas, 40 varieties of grapes, and dozens of citrus fruits. The park store offers many varieties of tropical-fruit products, jellies, seeds, aromatic teas, and reference books. ⊠ *24801 S.W. 187th Ave.* ☎ *305/247– 5727* ⊕ *www.co.miami-dade.fl.us* ⌲ *$5* ⊗ *Daily 10–5, tours at 11, 1:30, and 3.*

☾ ㊶ Aviation enthusiasts touch down at **Wings Over Miami** to see planes from World War II and the Korean War and earlier vintage bi-planes in a still-evolving museum filling the space that once housed Weeks Air Museum, which moved to the Sun and Fun complex in Lakeland. The museum is inside Tamiami Airport. ⊠ *14710 S.W. 128th St.* ☎ *305/233–5197* ⊕ *www.wingsovermiami.com* ⌲ *$9.95* ⊗ *Thurs.–Sun. 10–5:30.*

MIAMI & MIAMI BEACH A TO Z

To research prices, get advice from other travelers, and book travel arrangements, visit www.fodors.com.

ADDRESSES

Greater Miami is made up of more than 30 municipalities, and tourist favorites Miami and Miami Beach are only two of the cities that make up what is actually Miami-Dade County. Within Greater Miami, addresses fall into four quadrants: NW, NE, SW, and SE. The north–south dividing line is Flagler Street, and the east–west dividing line is Miami Avenue. Numbering starts from these axes and gets higher the farther away an address is from them. Avenues run north–south and streets east–west. Some municipalities have their own street naming and numbering systems, including Miami Beach, Coral Gables, Coconut Grove, and Key Biscayne, so a map is a good idea. In South Beach, all north–south roads are named, and the main drags are Ocean Drive, Collins, and Washington avenues, and Alton Road. Streets are numbered and run east–west; 1st Street is at the beach's southernmost point, and numbers get higher as you head north.

AIR TRAVEL TO & FROM MIAMI

CARRIERS In addition to the multitude of airlines that fly into Miami International Airport (MIA; *see* Air Travel *in* Smart Travel Tips A to Z), there's also Chalk's Ocean Airways—starting over where the original Pan Am began—with seaplane flights. Departing from Watson Island, the 30- to 60-minute rides to Bimini and Paradise Island in the Bahamas are exciting, anachronistic, and somewhat cramped. Still, if you've got an extra $200–$300, a round-trip could be quite fun.

🛪 Chalk's Ocean Airways ☎ 800/424-2557 ⊕ www.flychalks.com.

AIRPORTS & TRANSFERS

Miami International Airport, 6 mi west of downtown Miami, is the only airport in Greater Miami that provides scheduled service. More than 1,400 daily flights make MIA the ninth-busiest passenger airport in the world. Approximately 34 million people pass through annually, more than half of them international travelers. Altogether, more than 100 airlines serve nearly 150 cities and five continents with nonstop or one-stop service from here, making it the nation's top international gateway. Anticipating continued growth, the airport has begun a more than $5 billion expansion program that is expected to be completed by 2015. Passengers will mainly notice rebuilt and expanded gate and public areas, which should reduce congestion. A link to Metrorail is also planned. A greatly underused convenience for passengers who have to get from one concourse to another in this long, horseshoe-shape terminal is the amazingly convenient moving walkway on the skywalk level (third floor), with access points at every concourse. MIA, the first to offer duty-free shops, now has 12, carrying liquors, perfumes, electronics, and various designer goods. Heightened security at MIA has meant that it's suggested you check in two hours before departure for a domestic flight, three hours for an international flight. Services for international travelers include 24-hour multilingual information and paging phones as well as currency conversion booths throughout the terminal. There is an information booth with a multilingual staff across from the 24-hour currency exchange at the entrance of Concourse E on the upper level.

The county's Metrobus still costs $1.25, although equipment has improved. From Concourse E on the ground level, take Bus 7 to downtown (weekdays 5:30 AM–9 PM every 40 minutes, weekends 6:30 AM–7:30 PM every 40 minutes); Bus 37 south to Coral Gables and South Miami (6 AM–10 PM every 30 minutes) or north to Hialeah (5:30 AM–11:30 PM every 30 minutes); Bus J south to Coral Gables (6 AM–12:30 AM every 30 minutes) or east to Miami Beach (4:30 AM–11:30 PM every 30 minutes); and Bus 42 to Coconut Grove (5:30 AM–7:20 PM hourly). Some routes change to 60 minute schedules after 7 PM and on weekends, so be prepared to wait or call the information line for exact times. Miami has more than 100 limousine services, although they're frequently in and out of business. If you rely on the Yellow Pages, look for a company with a street address, not just a phone number. Offering 24-hour service, Club Limousine Service has shuttle vans and minibuses as well as limos. One of the oldest companies in town is Vintage Rolls Royce Limousines of Coral Gables, which operates a 24-hour reservation service and provides chauffeurs for privately owned, collectible Rolls-Royces from the 1940s.

Except for the flat-fare trips described below, cabs cost $1.70 for the first 1/11 of a mile, 20¢ for each additional 1/11 of a mile after that, plus a $1 toll for trips originating at MIA or the Port of Miami. Approximate fares from MIA include $19 to Coral Gables or downtown Miami, $35 to Key Biscayne. In addition, Miami's regulatory commission has established flat rates for five zones of the city, four of which are listed here: $24 to between 63rd Street and the foot of Miami Beach (including South Beach); $45 to Golden Beach and Sunny Isles, north of Haulover Beach Park; $37 to between Surfside and Haulover Beach Park; and $32 to between 63rd and 87th streets. These fares are per trip, not per passenger, and include tolls and $1 airport surcharge but not tip. The fare between MIA and the Port of Miami is a flat fare of $18. For taxi service to destinations in the immediate vicinity, ask a uniformed county taxi dispatcher to call an ARTS (Airport Region Taxi Service) cab for you. These special blue cabs offer a short-haul flat fare in two zones. An inner-zone ride is $8; the outer-zone fare is $11. The area of service is north to 36th Street, west to the Palmetto Expressway (77th Avenue), south to Northwest 7th Street, and east to Douglas Road (37th Avenue). Maps are posted in cab windows.

SuperShuttle vans transport passengers between MIA and local hotels, the Port of Miami, and even individual residences on a 24-hour basis. At MIA the vans pick up at the ground level of each concourse (look for clerks with yellow shirts, who will flag one down). The company's service area extends from Palm Beach to Monroe County (including the Lower Keys). You can also ride from airport to airport—between Miami International Airport and Fort Lauderdale International Airport—for a flat rate of $23. Service from MIA is available around the clock on demand; for the return it's best to make reservations 24 hours in advance, although the firm will try to arrange pickups within Miami-Dade County on as little as four hours' notice. The cost from MIA to downtown hotels runs $9–$13; to the beaches it can be $15–$19 per passenger, depending on how far north you go. Additional members of a party pay a lower rate for many destinations, and children under three ride free with their parents. There's a pet transport fee of $5 for a cat, $8 for a dog under 50 pounds in kennels.

7 Airport Information Miami International Airport (MIA) ☎ 305/876-7000 ⊕ www. miami-airport.com. **Miami International Airport Hotel** ✉ Concourse E, upper level ☎ 305/871-4100.

7 Taxis & Shuttles Carey South Florida limousines ✉ 12050 N.E. 14th Ave., Miami 33161 ☎ 305/892-5800, 800/325-9834 in Florida, 800/824-4820. **Metrobus** ☎ 305/ 770-3131. **SuperShuttle** ☎ 305/871-2000 from MIA, 954/764-1700 from Broward [Fort Lauderdale], 800/874-8885 from elsewhere. **Vintage Rolls Royce Limousines** ✉ 7242 S.W. 42nd Terr., South Miami 33155 ☎ 305/444-7657 or 800/888-7657.

BIKE TRAVEL

Cruise America offers Hondas and Suzukis with daily rentals starting at $109, weekly at $545. You must be 21 with a credit card, valid driver's license, and motorcycle endorsement. Great weather and flat terrain make Miami perfect for cycling enthusiasts, but as a general method of transportation, it shouldn't be your first choice given traffic and limited bike paths. Consider Miami-Dade Transit's "Bike and Ride" program, which lets permitted cyclists take single-seat two-wheelers on Metrorail and select bus routes. **Miami-Dade Bicycle/Pedestrian Coordinator** has details on permits, bike maps, and lockers and is open weekdays 8–5.

7 Bike Rentals Cruise America ✉ 5021 N.W. 79th Ave., Miami Lakes ☎ 800/327-7799 or 305/436-8068. **Miami-Dade Bicycle/Pedestrian Coordinator** ☎ 305/375-4507.

BOAT & FERRY TRAVEL

If you enter the United States in a private vessel along the Atlantic Coast south of Sebastian Inlet, you must call the **U.S. Customs Service.** Customs clears most boats of less than 5 tons by phone, but you may be directed to a marina for inspection. The Port of Miami, in downtown Miami near Bayside Marketplace and the MacArthur Causeway, justifiably bills itself as the Cruise Capital of the World. With 18 ships and the largest year-round cruise fleet in the world, the port accommodates more than 3 million passengers a year. It has 12 air-conditioned terminals, duty-free shopping, and limousine service. Taxicabs are available at all terminals, and Avis is at the port, although other rental companies offer shuttle service to off-site locations. Parking is $12 per day, and short-term parking is a flat rate of $5. From here, short cruises depart for the Bahamas and Eastern and Western Caribbean, with longer sailings to the Far East, Europe, and South America.

7 Cruise Lines Port of Miami ✉ 1015 North American Way, Miami ☎ 305/371-7678 or 305/347-4860 ⊕ www.co.miami-dade.fl.us/portofmiami. **U.S. Customs Service** ☎ 800/432-1216 small-vessel arrival near Miami, 305/536-5263 Port of Miami office.

Carnival Cruise Lines ☎ 800/227-6482 ⊕ www.carnival.com. **Celebrity Cruises** ☎ 800/722-5941 ⊕ www.celebrity.com. **Norwegian Cruise Lines** ☎ 800/327-7030 ⊕ www.ncl.com. **Royal Caribbean International** ☎ 800/722-5045 ⊕ www. royalcaribbean.com.

BUS TRAVEL TO & FROM MIAMI & MIAMI BEACH

Regularly scheduled, interstate **Greyhound** buses stop at five terminals in Greater Miami; the airport terminal is 24-hour.

🚌**Bus Information Greyhound** ☎800/231-2222 ✉Homestead ✉5 N.E. 3rd Rd. ☎305/247-2040 ✉ Miami Bayside/Downtown ✉ 100 N.W. 6th St., Overtown ☎ 305/374-6160 ✉ Miami South ✉ 20505 S. Dixie Hwy., Cutler Ridge ☎ 305/296-9072 ✉ Miami West/Airport ✉ 4111 N.W. 27th St. ☎ 305/871-1810 ✉ North Miami ✉ 16560 N.E. 6th Ave. ☎ 305/688-7267.

BUS TRAVEL WITHIN MIAMI & MIAMI BEACH

Metrobus stops are marked by blue-and-green signs with a bus logo and route information. The frequency of service varies widely, so call in advance to obtain specific schedules. The fare is $1.25 (exact change), transfers 25¢; 60¢ with 10¢ transfers for people with disabilities, senior citizens (65 and older), and students. Some express routes carry surcharges of $1.50. Reduced-fare tokens, sold 10 for $10, are available from Metropass outlets. All trains and stations are accessible to persons with disabilities; lift-equipped buses for people with disabilities are available on more than 50 routes, including one from the airport that links up with many routes in Miami Beach as well as Coconut Grove, Coral Gables, Hialeah, and Kendall. Miami Beach has a tourism hot line with information on accessibility, sign language interpreters, rental cars, and area recreational activities for the disabled. The best thing to arrive in Miami Beach since sand, the Electrowave is a fleet of electric trolleys running every few minutes up and down Washington Avenue between 5th and 17th streets. Fare is 25¢. New service continues south of 5th Street, west to Alton Road, and over by the Miami Beach Marina. Considering the great distances between South Beach attractions, it'll save a lot of shoe leather. Trolleys operate Monday–Saturday 8 AM–1 AM, Sunday and holidays 10 AM–1 AM.

FARES & 🚌 **Bus Information Electrowave** ☎ 305/843–9283. **Special Transportation Ser-**
SCHEDULES **vices** ☎ 305/263–5400.

CAR RENTAL

The following agencies have booths near the baggage-claim area on MIA's lower level: Avis, Budget, Dollar, Hertz, National, and Royal. Avis and Budget also have offices at the Port of Miami. If money is no object, check out Excellence Luxury Car Rental. As the name implies, rent some wheels (a Ferrari, perhaps?) to cruise SoBe. If you can't find the excellent car you want, rent a Dodge Viper, BMW, Hummer, Jag, Porsche, or Rolls from Exotic Toys. Airport pickup is provided.

🚗 **Local Agencies Alamo** ☎ 800/468-2583. **Avis** ☎ 800/331-1212. **Budget** ☎ 800/527-0700. **Dollar** ☎ 800/800-4000. **Excellence Luxury Car Rental** ☎ 305/526-0000. **Exotic Toys Car Rental** ☎ 305/888-8448. **Hertz** ☎ 800/654-3131. **National** ☎ 800/227-7368. **Royal** ☎ 800/314-8616.

CAR TRAVEL

The main highways into Greater Miami from the north are Florida's Turnpike (a toll road) and Interstate 95. From the northwest take Interstate 75 or U.S. 27 into town. From the Everglades, to the west, use the Tamiami Trail (U.S. 41), and from the south use U.S. 1 and the Homestead Extension of Florida's Turnpike. In general, Miami traffic is the same as in any other big city, with the same rush hours and the same likelihood that parking garages will be full at peak times. Many drivers who aren't locals and don't know their way around might turn and stop suddenly, or drop off passengers where they shouldn't. Some drivers are short-tempered and will assault those who cut them off or honk their horn. Motorists need to be careful, even when their driving behavior is beyond censure, however, especially in rental cars. Despite the removal of identifying marks, cars piled with luggage or otherwise showing signs that a tourist is at the wheel remain prime targets for thieves. The city has also initiated a TOP (Tourist Oriented Police) Cops program to assist tourists with directions and safety. For more safety advice on driving in Miami, *see* Car Travel *in* Smart Travel Tips A to Z.

EMERGENCIES

Dial 911 for police or ambulance. Dial free from pay phones. Randle Eastern Ambulance Service Inc. operates at all hours, although in an emergency it'll direct you to call 911. Dade County Medical Association is open weekdays 9–5 for medical referral. East Coast District Dental Society is open weekdays 9–4:30 for dental referral. After hours stay on the line and a recording will direct you to a dentist. Services include general dentistry, endodontics, periodontics, and oral surgery.

🔢 **Doctors & Dentists Dade County Medical Association** ✉ 1501 N.W. North River Dr., Miami ☎ 305/324-8717. **South Florida District Dental Association** ✉ 420 S. Dixie Hwy., Suite 2E, Coral Gables ☎ 305/667-3647.

🔢 **Hot Lines Randle Eastern Ambulance Service Inc.** ✉ 7255 N.W. 19th St., Suite C, Miami ☎ 305/718-6400.

🔢 **Late-Night Pharmacies Walgreens** ✉ 4895 E. Palm Ave., Hialeah ☎ 305/231-7454 ✉ 2750 W. 68th St., Hialeah ☎ 305/828-0268 ✉ 12295 Biscayne Blvd., North Miami ☎ 305/893-6860 ✉ 5731 Bird Rd., Miami ☎ 305/666-0757 ✉ 1845 Alton Rd., South Beach, Miami Beach ☎ 305/531-8868 ✉ 791 N.E. 167th St., North Miami Beach ☎ 305/652-7332.

MEDIA

Greater Miami is a media hub, offering access to information from around the world in many languages. For international and foreign language papers, check one of the larger hotels or bookstore chains, or try the popular News Café in Coconut Grove or South Beach. The main Coral Gables branch of **Books & Books, Inc.** (✉ 265 Aragon Ave. ☎ 305/442–4408 ⊕ www.booksandbooks.com) is a terrific independent bookstore that's worth a trip for magazines and books.

NEWSPAPERS & MAGAZINES Greater Miami's major newspaper is the *Miami Herald*. Your best bet for weekend happenings is the free alternative weekly, *New Times,* or *Street,* a free weekly with entertainment news, local art and film reviews, events, and nightlife. For Spanish-language news, turn to *El Nuevo Herald*. Regional editions of the *Wall Street Journal* and the *New York Times* can be found just about everywhere—including vending machines—and many of Europe's and Latin America's major dailies and fashion glossies are available at newsstands.

RADIO Greater Miami is served by all the major cable networks. Major broadcast television stations include WAMI (Telefutur, Spanish-international),

WBFS (UPN), WBZL (WB), WFOR (CBS), WLTV (Univision, Spanish-international), WPBT (PBS), WPLG (ABC), WSCV (Telemundo, Spanish-international), WSVN (Fox), and WTVJ (NBC).

Radio stations in Greater Miami include WDNA 88.9 (jazz), WEDR 99.1 (urban), WHYI 100.7 (Top 40), WIOD 610 AM (news), WKIS 99.9 (country), WLRN 91.3 (National Public Radio), WQAM 560 AM (sports), WZTA 94.9 (hard rock), and WBGG 105.9 (classic rock). Near the airport, find basic tourist information, broadcast successively in English, French, German, Portuguese, and Spanish, on the low-wattage WAEM 102.3.

TAXIS

One cab "company" stands out above the rest. It's actually a consortium of drivers who have banded together to provide good service, in marked contrast to some Miami cabbies, who are rude, unhelpful, unfamiliar with the city, or dishonest, taking advantage of those who don't know the area. To plug into this consortium—they don't have a name, simply a number—call the dispatch service, although they can be hard to understand over the phone. If you have to use another company, try to be familiar with your route and destination. For information call the Metro-Dade Passenger Transportation Regulatory Service, also known as the Hack Bureau. It takes complaints and monitors all for-hire vehicles. Fares are set at $1.70 for the first $\frac{1}{11}$ of a mile, and 20¢ for each additional $\frac{1}{11}$ of a mile thereafter, with no additional charge for up to five passengers, luggage, and tolls. Taxis can be hailed on the street if you can find them—it's better to call for a dispatch taxi or have a hotel doorman hail one for you. Some companies with dispatch service are Central Taxicab Service, Diamond Cab Company, Metro Taxicab Company, Miami-Dade Yellow Cab, Society Cab Company, Super Yellow Cab Company, Tropical Taxicab Company, and Yellow Cab Company. Many now accept credit cards; inquire when you call.

📱 Taxi Companies **Dispatch service** ☎ 305/888-4444. **Central Taxicab Service** ☎ 305/532-5555. **Diamond Cab Company** ☎ 305/545-5555. **Metro-Dade Passenger Transportation Regulatory Service** ☎ 305/375-2460. **Metro Taxicab Company** ☎ 305/888-8888. **Miami-Dade Yellow Cab** ☎ 305/633-0503. **Society Cab Company** ☎ 305/757-5523. **Super Yellow Cab Company** ☎ 305/888-7777. **Tropical Taxicab Company** ☎ 305/945-1025. **Yellow Cab Company** ☎ 305/444-4444.

TOURS

Coconut Grove Rickshaw centers its operations at CocoWalk. Two-person rickshaws scurry along Main Highway in Coconut Grove's Village Center, nightly 7 PM–midnight. Take a 10-minute ride through Coconut Grove or a 20-minute lovers' moonlight ride to Biscayne Bay; prices start at $5 per person, and you can pick them up curbside.

BOAT TOURS *Island Queen, Island Lady,* and *Pink Lady* are 150-passenger double-decker tour boats docked at Bayside Marketplace. They go on daily 90-minute narrated tours of the Port of Miami and Millionaires' Row, costing $15. Refreshments are available. For something a little more private and luxe, *RA Charters* sails out of the Dinner Key Marina in Coconut Grove. Full- and half-day charters include snorkeling and even sailing lessons on the 40-foot ketch, with extended trips to the Florida Keys and Bahamas. For a romantic night, have Captain Masoud pack some delicious fare and sail sunset to moonlight while you enjoy Biscayne Bay's spectacular skyline view of Miami. Prices range from $400 for a half day to $700 for a full day, depending on the number of people aboard and refreshments provided.

🛈 **Fees & Schedules** Island Queen, Island Lady, and Pink Lady ✉ 401 Biscayne Blvd., Bayside Marketplace ☎ 305/379-5119. RA Charters ☎ 305/854-7341 or 305/666-7979.

PRIVATE GUIDES Professor Paul George, a history professor at Miami-Dade College and past president of the Florida Historical Society, leads walking tours as well as boat tours and tours that make use of the Metrorail and Metromover. Choose from tours covering downtown, historic neighborhoods, cemeteries, Coconut Grove, and the Miami River. They generally last about 2½ hours. Call for each weekend's schedule and for additional tours by appointment. The fee is $12–$20.

🛈 **Professor Paul George** ✉ 1345 S.W. 14th St., Little Havana ☎ 305/858-6021 ⊕ www. historical-museum.org.

WALKING TOURS The Art Deco District Tour, operated by the Miami Design Preservation League, is a 90-minute guided walking tour that departs from the league's welcome center at the Oceanfront Auditorium. It costs $15 (tax-deductible) and starts at 10:30 AM Saturday and 6:30 PM Thursday. Private group tours can be arranged with advance notice. The league's self-guided $10 audio tour takes roughly an hour and a half and is available in English, Spanish, French, and German.

🛈 **Fees & Schedules** Art Deco District Tour ✉ Art Deco Welcome Center, 1001 Ocean Dr., South Beach, Miami Beach 33139 ☎ 305/672-2014 ⊕ www.mdpl.org.

TRAIN TRAVEL

Amtrak provides service from 500 destinations to the Greater Miami area, including three trains daily from New York City. North–south service stops in the major Florida cities of Jacksonville, Orlando, Tampa, West Palm Beach, and Fort Lauderdale. For extended trips, or if you're visiting other areas in Florida, come via Auto Train from Lorton, Virginia, just outside of Washington, D.C., to Sanford, Florida, just outside of Orlando. Tri-Rail, South Florida's commuter train system, offers daily service connecting Miami-Dade with Broward and Palm Beach counties via Metrorail (transfer at the TriRail/Metrorail Station at the Hialeah station, at 79th Street and East 11th Avenue). It also offers shuttle service to and from MIA from its airport station at 3797 Northwest 21st Street. Tri-Rail stops at 18 stations along a 71-mi route. Fares are established by zones, with prices ranging from $3.50 to $9.25 for a round-trip ticket.

Elevated Metrorail trains run from downtown Miami north to Hialeah and south along U.S. 1 to Dadeland, daily 5:30 AM–midnight. Trains run every six minutes during peak hours, every 15 minutes during weekday mid-hours, every 20 minutes on weekends, every 30 minutes after 8 PM. The fare is $1.25. Transfers, which cost 25¢, must be bought at the first station entered. Parking at train stations costs $2. Metromover has two loops that circle downtown Miami, linking major hotels, office buildings, and shopping areas. The system spans 4½ mi, including the 1½-mi Omni Extension, with six stations to the north, and the 1-mi Brickell Extension, with six stations to the south. Quite convenient, and free, thanks to a half-penny sales tax, it beats walking all around downtown. Service runs daily, every 90 seconds during rush hour and every three minutes off-peak, 6 AM–midnight along the inner loop and 6 AM–10:30 PM on the Omni and Brickell extensions. Transfers to Metrorail are $1.25

🚆 **Train Information Amtrak** ⊠ 8303 N.W. 37th Ave., Hialeah ☎ 800/872-7245 ⊕ www.amtrak.com. **Metromover** ☎ 305/770-3131. **Metrorail** ☎ 305/770-3131. **Tri-Rail** ⊠ 1 River Plaza, 305 S. Andrews Ave., Suite 200, Fort Lauderdale ☎ 800/874-7245.

TRANSPORTATION AROUND MIAMI & MIAMI BEACH

Greater Miami resembles Los Angeles in its urban sprawl and traffic. You'll need a car to visit many attractions and points of interest. Some are accessible via the public transportation system, run by a department of the county government—the Metro-Dade Transit Agency, which consists of 650 Metrobuses on 70 routes, the 21-mi Metrorail elevated rapid-transit system, and the Metromover, an elevated light-rail system. Free maps and schedules are available.

🚆 **Miami-Dade Transit** ⊠ Government Center Station, 111 N.W. 1st St., Downtown, 33128 ☎ 305/654-6586 for Maps by Mail, 305/770-3131 for route information weekdays 6 AM–10 PM and weekends 9–5.

VISITOR INFORMATION

Florida Gold Coast Chamber of Commerce serves the beach communities of Bal Harbour, Bay Harbor Islands, Golden Beach, North Bay Village, Sunny Isles Beach, and Surfside.

🚆 **Tourist Information Greater Miami Convention & Visitors Bureau** ⊠ 701 Brickell Ave., Suite 2700, Downtown, 33131 ☎ 305/539-3000 or 800/933-8448 ⊕ www.gmcvb.com ⊠ Bayside Marketplace tourist information center, 401 Biscayne Blvd., Bayside Marketplace, Miami 33132 ☎ 305/539-2980 ⊠ Tropical Everglades Visitor Information Center, 160 U.S. 1, Florida City 33034 ☎ 305/245-9180 or 800/388-9669 🖶 305/247-4335. **Coconut Grove Chamber of Commerce** ⊠ 2820 McFarlane Rd., Coconut Grove, 33133 ☎ 305/444-7270 🖶 305/444-2498 ⊕ www.coconutgrove.com. **Coral Gables Chamber of Commerce** ⊠ 50 Aragon Ave., Coral Gables 33134 ☎ 305/446-1657 🖶 305/446-9900 ⊕ www.gableschamber.org. **Florida Gold Coast Chamber of Commerce** ⊠ 1100 Kane Concourse, Suite 210, Bay Harbor Islands 33154 ☎ 305/866-6020 ⊕ www.flgoldcc.org. **Greater Miami Chamber of Commerce** ⊠ 1601 Biscayne Blvd., Miami 33132 ☎ 305/350-7700 🖶 305/374-6902 ⊕ www.greatermiami.com. **Greater North Miami Chamber of Commerce** ⊠ 13100 W. Dixie Hwy., North Miami 33181 ☎ 305/891-7811 🖶 305/893-8522 ⊕ www.northmiamichamber.com. **Greater South Dade/South Miami Chamber of Commerce** ⊠ 6410 S.W. 80th St., South Miami 33143-4602 ☎ 305/661-1621 🖶 305/666-0508 ⊕ www.chambersouth.com. **Key Biscayne Chamber of Commerce** ⊠ Key Biscayne Village Hall, 88 W. McIntyre St., Key Biscayne, Miami 33149 ☎ 305/361-5207 ⊕ www.keybiscaynechamber.org. **Miami Beach Chamber of Commerce** ⊠ 1920 Meridian Ave., South Beach, Miami Beach 33139 ☎ 305/672-1270 🖶 305/538-4336 ⊕ www.miamibeachchamber.com. **Surfside Tourist Board** ⊠ 9301 Collins Ave., Surfside, Miami Beach 33154 ☎ 305/864-0722 or 800/327-4557 🖶 305/861-1302.

The Florida Keys

7

Updated by
Diane P.
Marshall

A WILDERNESS OF FLOWERING JUNGLES and shimmering seas, a jade necklace of mangrove-fringed islands dangling toward the tropics, the Florida Keys are also, simultaneously and conversely, overburdened. Booming tourism and a growing population have created sewage contamination at beaches and a 110-mi traffic jam lined with garish billboards, hamburger stands, shopping centers, motels, and trailer courts. Unfortunately, in the Keys you can't have one without the other. The river of visitor traffic gushes along U.S. 1 (also called the Overseas Highway), the main artery linking the inhabited islands. Residents of Monroe County live by diverting the river's flow of dollars to their own pockets. In the process, the fragile beauty of the Keys—or at least the 45 that are inhabited and linked to the mainland by 43 bridges—is paying an environmental price. At the top, nearest the mainland, is Key Largo, becoming more congested as it evolves into a bedroom community and weekend hideaway for residents of Miami and Fort Lauderdale. At the bottom, 106 mi southwest, is Key West, where hundreds of passengers from multiple cruise ships swarm the narrow streets in search of the best deal on T-shirts.

Despite designation as "an area of critical state concern" in 1975 and a subsequent state-mandated development slowdown, growth has continued, and the Keys' natural resources remain imperiled. Congress established the Florida Keys National Marine Sanctuary, covering 2,800 square nautical mi of coastal waters. Adjacent to the Keys landmass are spectacular, unique, and nationally significant marine environments, including sea-grass meadows, mangrove islands, and extensive living coral reefs. These fragile environments support rich and diverse biological communities possessing extensive conservation, recreational, commercial, ecological, historical, research, educational, and aesthetic values. The sanctuary protects the coral reefs and water quality, but problems continue. Increased salinity in Florida Bay causes large areas of sea grass to die and drift in mats out of the bay. These mats then block sunlight from reaching the reefs, stifling their growth and threatening both the Keys' recreational diving economy and tourism in general.

Other threats to the Keys' charm also loom. Debate continues on the expansion of U.S. 1 to the mainland to four lanes, opening the floodgates to increased traffic, population, and tourism. Observers wonder if the four-laning of the rest of U.S. 1 throughout the Keys can be far away. For now, however, take pleasure as you drive down U.S. 1 along the islands. Gaze over the silvery blue-and-green Atlantic and its still-living reef, with Florida Bay, the Gulf of Mexico, and the backcountry on your right (the Keys extend east–west from the mainland). At a few points the ocean and gulf are as much as 10 mi apart. In most places, however, they are from 1 to 4 mi apart, and on the narrowest landfill islands, they are separated only by the road. Try to get off the highway. Once you do, rent a boat, anchor, and then fish, swim, or marvel at the sun, sea, and sky. In the Atlantic, dive spectacular coral reefs or pursue grouper, blue marlin, and other deep-water game fish. Along Florida Bay's coastline, kayak and canoe to secluded islands and bays or seek out the bonefish, snapper, snook, and tarpon that lurk in the grass flats and in the shallow, winding channels of the backcountry.

More than 600 kinds of fish populate the reefs and islands. Diminutive deer and pale raccoons, related to but distinct from their mainland cousins, inhabit the Lower Keys. And throughout the islands you'll find such exotic West Indian plants as Jamaican dogwood, pigeon plum, poisonwood, satin leaf, and silver-and-thatch palms, as well as tropical birds, including the great white heron, mangrove cuckoo, roseate spoonbill, and white-crowned pigeon. Mangroves, with their gracefully bowed prop roots, appear to march out to sea. Day by day they busily add more keys to the archipelago. With virtually no distracting air pollution or obstructive high-rises, sunsets are a pure, unadulterated spectacle that each evening attracts thousands to waterfront parks, piers, restaurants, bars, and resorts throughout the Keys. Weather is another attraction: winter is typically 10°F warmer than on the mainland; summer is usually 10°F cooler. The Keys also get substantially less rain, around 30 inches annually, compared to an average 55–60 inches in Miami and the Everglades. Most rain falls in quick downpours on summer afternoons, except in June, September, and October, when tropical storms can dump rain for two to four days. Winter cold fronts occasionally stall over the Keys, dragging overnight temperatures down to the high 40s.

The Keys were only sparsely populated until the early 20th century. In 1905, however, railroad magnate Henry Flagler began building the extension of his Florida railroad south from Homestead to Key West. His goal was to establish a Miami to Key West rail link to his steamships that sailed between Key West and Havana, just 90 mi across the Straits of Florida. The railroad arrived at Key West in 1912 and remained a lifeline of commerce until the Labor Day hurricane of 1935 washed out much of its roadbed. The Overseas Highway, built over the railroad's old roadbeds and bridges, was completed in 1938.

Exploring the Florida Keys

Finding your way around the Keys isn't hard once you understand the unique address system. Many addresses are simply given as a mile marker (MM) number. The markers are small, green rectangular signs along the side of the Overseas Highway (U.S. 1). They begin with MM 126, a mile south of Florida City, and end with MM 0, in Key West. Keys residents use the abbreviation BS for the bay side of U.S. 1 and OS for the ocean side. From Marathon to Key West, residents may refer to the bay side as the gulf side. The Keys are divided into four areas: the Upper Keys, from Key Largo to the Long Key Channel (MM 106–65) and Ocean Reef and North Key Largo, off Card Sound Road and Route 905, respectively; the Middle Keys, from Conch (pronounced *konk*) Key through Marathon to the south side of the Seven Mile Bridge, including Pigeon Key (MM 65–40); the Lower Keys, from Little Duck Key south through Big Coppitt Key (MM 40–9); and Key West, from Stock Island through Key West (MM 9–0). The Keys don't end with the highway, however; they stretch another 70 mi west of Key West to the Dry Tortugas.

Numbers in the text correspond to numbers in the margin and on the Florida Keys and Key West maps.

If you have 3 days

You can fly and then dive; but if you dive, you can't fly for 24 hours, so spend your first morning diving or snorkeling at John Pennekamp Coral Reef State Park in ⊞ **Key Largo** ❷ ▶. If you aren't certified, take a resort course, and you'll be exploring the reefs by afternoon. Afterward, breeze through the park's visitor center. The rest of the afternoon can be whiled away either lounging around a pool or beach. Dinner or cocktails at a bayside restaurant or bar will give you your first look at a fabulous Keys sunset. On Day 2 get an early start to savor the breathtaking views on the two-hour drive to Key West. Along the way make stops at the natural-history museum that's part of the Museums and Nature Center of Crane Point Hammock, in **Marathon** ❽, and Bahia Honda State Park, on **Bahia Honda Key** ❾; stretch your legs on a forest trail or snorkel on an offshore reef. Once in ⊞ **Key West** ❷–❸❹, watch the sunset before dining at one of the island's first-class restaurants. Spend the next morning exploring beaches, visiting any of the myriad museums, or taking a walking or trolley tour of Old Town before driving back to the mainland.

If you have 4 days

Spend the first day as you would above, overnighting in ⊞ **Key Largo** ❷ ▶. Start the second day by renting a kayak and exploring the mangroves and small islands of Florida Bay or take an ecotour of the islands in Everglades National Park. In the afternoon stop by the Florida Keys Wild Bird Rehabilitation Center before driving down to ⊞ **Islamorada** ❹. Pause to read the inscription on the Hurricane Monument, and before day's end, make plans for the next day's fishing. After a late lunch on Day 3—perhaps at one of the many restaurants that will prepare your catch for you—set off for ⊞ **Key West** ❷–❸❹. Enjoy the sunset celebration at Mallory Square, and spend the last day as you would above.

If you have 7 days

Spend your first three days as you would in the four-day itinerary, but stay the third night in ⊞ **Islamorada** ❹. In the morning catch a boat, or rent a kayak to paddle to Lignumvitae Key Botanical State Park, before making the one-hour drive to ⊞ **Marathon** ❽. Visit the natural-history museum that's part of the Museums and Nature Center of Crane Point Hammock and walk or take a train across the Old Seven Mile Bridge to Pigeon Key. The next stop is just 10 mi away at Bahia Honda State Park, on ⊞ **Bahia Honda Key** ❾. Take a walk on a wilderness trail, go snorkeling on an offshore reef, wriggle your toes in the beach's soft sand, and spend the night in a waterfront cabin, letting the waves lull you to sleep. Your sixth day starts with either a half day of fabulous snorkeling or diving at Looe Key Reef or a visit to the National Key Deer Refuge, on **Big Pine Key** ❿. Then continue on to ⊞ **Key West** ❷–❸❹, and get in a little sightseeing before watching the sunset. The next morning take a walking, bicycling, or trolley tour of town or catch a ferry or seaplane to Dry Tortugas National Park before heading home.

About the Restaurants

A number of talented young chefs have settled in the Keys—especially Key West—contributing to the area's image as one of the nation's points of culinary interest. Restaurants' menus, rum-based fruit beverages, and music reflect the Keys' tropical climate and their proximity to Cuba and other Caribbean islands. Better restaurants serve tantalizing fusion cuisine that draws on traditions worldwide. Florida citrus, seafood, and tropical fruits figure prominently, and Florida lobster should be local and fresh from August to March and stone crabs from mid-October to mid-May. Also keep an eye out for authentic key lime pie. The real McCoy has a yellow custard in a graham-cracker crust and tastes like nothing else. Restaurants may close for a two- to four-week vacation during the slow season—between mid-September and mid-November.

About the Hotels

Resorts and water sports marry throughout the Keys, giving couples and families, novices and veterans, chances to snorkel and dive. Some properties do charge a required $15 daily resort fee for equipment rental, which can cover spa use and other services. Key West's lodging portfolio includes historic cottages, restored Conch houses, and large resorts. A few rooms cost as little as $65 a night, but most range from $100 to $300. Some guest houses and inns do not welcome children under 16, and some do not permit smoking.

WHAT IT COSTS				
$$$$	$$$	$$	$	¢
RESTAURANTS over $30	$20–$30	$15–$20	$10–$15	under $10
HOTELS over $220	$140–$220	$100–$140	$80–$100	under $80

Restaurant prices are per person for a main course at dinner. Hotel prices are for a standard double room, excluding 6% sales tax (more in some counties) and 1%–4% tourist tax.

Timing

High season in the Keys is mid-December through March, and traffic on the Overseas Highway is inevitably heavy. From November to the middle of December, crowds are thinner, the weather is superlative, and hotels and shops drastically reduce their prices. Summer, which is hot and humid, is becoming a second high season, especially among families and Europeans. Key West's annual Fantasy Fest is the last week in October; if you plan to attend this popular event, reserve at least six months in advance. Rooms are also scarce the first few weekends of lobster season, which starts in August.

THE UPPER KEYS

The tropical coral-reef tract that runs a few miles off the seaward coast accounts for most of the Upper Keys' reputation. Divers benefit from accessible islands and dive sites and an established tourism infra-

Boating If it floats, local marinas rent it. For up-close exploration of the mangroves and near-shore islands in Florida Bay, nothing beats a kayak or canoe. Paddle within a few feet of a flock of birds without disturbing them. Visiting the backcountry islands and inlets of Everglades National Park requires a shallow-draft boat: a 14- to 17-foot skiff with a 40- to 50-horsepower outboard is sufficient. Rental companies prohibit smaller boats from going on the ocean side. For diving the reef or fishing on the open ocean, you'll need a larger boat with greater horsepower. Houseboats are ideal for cruising the Keys. Only experienced sailors should attempt to navigate the shallow waters surrounding the Keys with deep-keeled sailboats. On the other hand, small shallow-draft, single-hull sailboats and catamarans are ideal. Personal water vehicles, such as Wave Runners and Jet Skis, can be rented by the half hour or hour but are banned in many areas. Flat, stable pontoon boats are a good choice for anyone with seasickness. Those interested in experiencing the reef without getting wet can take a glass-bottom-boat trip.

Fishing These sun-bathed waters have many species of game fish as well as lobster, shrimp, and crabs. Flats fishing and backcountry fishing are Keys specialties. In flats fishing, a guide poles a shallow-draft outboard boat through the shallow, sandy-bottom waters while sighting for bonefish and snook to be caught on light tackle, spin, and fly. Backcountry fishing may include flats fishing or fishing in the channels and basins around islands in Florida Bay. Charter boats fish the reef and Gulf Stream for deep-sea fish. Party boats, which can be crowded, carry up to 50 people to fish the reefs for grouper, kingfish, and snapper. Some operators have a guarantee, or "no fish, no pay" policy. It's customary to tip the crew 15%–20% of the trip price if they were helpful.

Scuba Diving & Snorkeling Diving in the Keys is spectacular. In shallow and deep water with visibility up to 120 feet, explore sea canyons and mountains covered with waving sea plumes, brain and star coral, historic shipwrecks, and sunken submarines. There's no best season for diving, but occasional storms in June, September, and October cloud the waters and make seas rough. Dive the reefs with scuba, snuba (a cross between scuba and snorkeling), or snorkeling gear, using your own boat or a rented boat or by booking a tour with a dive shop. Tours depart two or three times a day, stopping at two sites on each trip. The first trip of the day is usually the best. It's less crowded— vacationers like to sleep in—and visibility is better before the wind picks up in the afternoon. There's also night diving. If you want to scuba dive but are not certified, take an introductory resort course. Although it doesn't result in certification, it allows you to dive with an instructor in the afternoon following morning classroom and pool instruction. Nearly all the waters surrounding the Keys are part of the Florida Keys National Marine Sanctuary and thus are protected; the reef is fragile and shouldn't be touched.

structure. Yet although diving is king here, fishing, kayaking, and nature touring draw an enviable number of people. Within 1½ mi of the bay coast lie the islands of Everglades National Park; here naturalists lead ecotours to see one of the world's few saltwater forests, endangered manatees, dolphins, roseate spoonbills, and tropical-bird rookeries. Although the number of birds has dwindled since John James Audubon captured their beauty on a visit to the Keys, bird-watchers won't be disappointed. At sunset flocks take to the skies, and in spring and autumn migrating birds add their numbers. Tarpon and bonefish teem in the shallow waters surrounding the islands, providing food for birds and a challenge to light-tackle anglers. These same crystal-clear waters attract windsurfers, sailors, and powerboaters. Wherever you go, you'll find a pleasant mix of locals, visitors, snowbirds (in season), and South Floridian weekenders.

With few exceptions, dining in the Upper Keys tends toward the casual in food, service, and dress. Accommodations are as varied as they are plentiful. The majority are in small waterfront resorts, with efficiency and one- or two-bedroom units. They offer dockage and either provide or will arrange boating, diving, and fishing excursions. Depending on which way the wind blows and how close the property is to the highway, noise from U.S. 1 can be bothersome. In high season, expect to pay $85–$165 for an efficiency (in low season, $65–$145). Campground and RV park rates with electricity and water run $25–$55. Some properties require two- or three-day minimum stays during holidays and on weekends in high season. Conversely, discounts are given for midweek, weekly, and monthly stays, and rates can drop 20%–40% April–June and October–mid-December. Keep in mind that salty winds and soil play havoc with anything man-made, and constant maintenance is a must; inspect your accommodations before checking in.

Key Largo

56 mi south of Miami International Airport.

The first Key reachable by car, 30-mi-long Key Largo—named Cayo Largo ("long key") by the Spanish—is also the largest island in the chain. Comprising three areas—North Key Largo, Key Largo, and Tavernier—it runs northeast–southwest between Lake Surprise and Tavernier Creek, at MM 95. Most businesses are on the four-lane divided highway (U.S. 1) that runs down the middle, but away from the overdevelopment and generally suburban landscape are many areas of wilderness. One such area ❶ is **North Key Largo,** which still has a wide tract of virgin hardwood hammock and mangroves as well as a crocodile sanctuary (not open to the public). To reach North Key Largo, take Card Sound Road just south of Florida City, or from within the Keys, take Route 905 north.

Rest rooms, information kiosks, and picnic tables make 2,400-acre **Dagny Johnson Key Largo Hammocks Botanical State Park** a user-friendly place to explore the largest remaining stand of the vast West Indian tropical hardwood hammock and mangrove wetland that once covered most of the Keys' upland areas. Nearly 100 species of protected plants and animals coexist here, including the endangered American crocodile, Key Largo wood rat, Key Largo cotton mouse, and Schaus swallowtail butterfly. Interpretive signs describe many of the tropical tree species along a 1¼-mi paved road (2½ mi round-trip) that invites walking, rollerblading, and biking. Rangers give guided tours and encourage you to taste the fruits of native plants. Pets are welcome if on a 6-foot leash. ✉ *1 mi north of U.S. 1 on Rte. 905, OS, North Key Largo* ☎ *305/451–1202* 🖃 *$1.50* ☉ *Daily 8–5. Tours Thurs. and Sun. at 10.*

▶ **②** Taking the Overseas Highway from the mainland lands you closer to **Key Largo** proper, abounding with shopping centers, chain restaurants, and, of course, dive shops.

Fodor'sChoice ★ Whenever people talk about the best diving sites in the world, **John Pennekamp Coral Reef State Park** is on the short list. The park encompasses 78 square mi of coral reefs, sea-grass beds, and mangrove swamps. Its reefs contain 40 of the 52 species of coral in the Atlantic Reef System and more than 650 varieties of fish. Its visitor center–aquarium has a large floor-to-ceiling aquarium surrounded by smaller tanks, a video room, and exhibits. A concessionaire rents canoes and powerboats and offers snorkel, dive, and glass-bottom-boat trips to the reef. The park also has short nature trails, two man-made beaches, picnic shelters, a snack bar, and a campground. No pets are allowed for visitors who are camping or going on a boat trip. ✉ *MM 102.5, OS, Box 487, 33037* ☎ *305/451–1202* ⊕ *www.dep.state.fl.us/parks* 🖃 *$3.50 for 1 person, $5 per vehicle for 2 people, plus 50¢ each additional person; $1.50 per pedestrian or bicyclist* ☉ *Daily 8–sunset.*

③ The southernmost part of Key Largo is **Tavernier.** Here at the **Florida Keys Wild Bird Rehabilitation Center,** injured and recovering ospreys, hawks, pelicans, cormorants, terns, and herons of various types rest in large, screened enclosures lining a winding boardwalk on some of the best waterfront real estate in the Keys. The center is especially popular among photographers, who arrive at 3:30 PM, when hundreds of wild waterbirds fly in and feed within arm's distance. Rehabilitated birds are set free, while others become permanent residents. A short nature trail runs into the mangrove forest (bring bug spray May–October), and a video explains the center's mission. ✉ *MM 93.6, BS, Tavernier* ☎ *305/852–4486* 🖃 *Free* ☉ *Daily sunrise–sunset.*

Weekends are crowded at **Harry Harris County Park,** which has play equipment, a small swimming lagoon, a boat ramp, ball fields, barbecue grills, and rest rooms. Although the turnoff is clearly marked on the Overseas Highway, the road to the ocean is circuitous. ✉ *MM 93, OS, at Burton Dr., Tavernier* ☎ *305/852–7161 or 888/227–8136* 🖃 *Weekdays free, weekends $5 per person* ☉ *Daily 7:30 AM–sunset.*

☺ **Jacobs Aquatic Center.** Take the plunge at one of three swimming pools: an 8-lane, 25-meter lap pool with a diving well; a 3–4-foot ramp-accessible pool; and an interactive play pool with a water slide, pirate ship, waterfall, and beachfront entry. ✉ *320 Laguna Ave., MM 99.6, OS* ☎ *305/453–7946* ⊕ *www.jacobsaquaticcenter.org* 🖃 *$7, discounted multiday passes available* ☉ *Weekdays 11–6, weekends 10–7.*

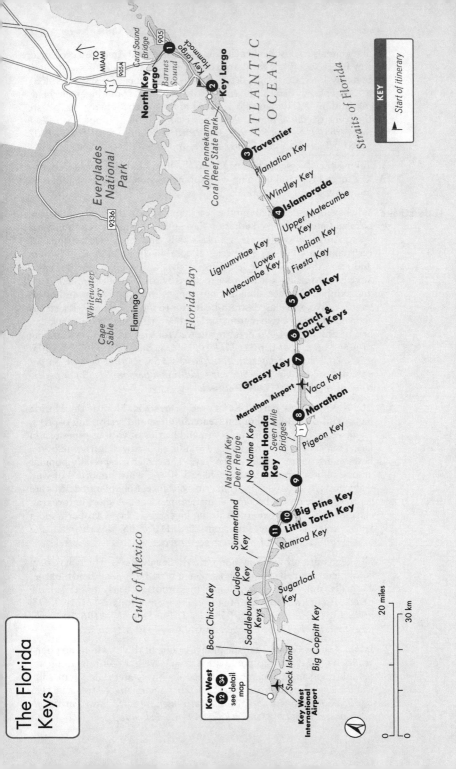

The Florida Keys

KEY
▲ Start of itinerary

TO MIAMI

Card Sound Bridge

905

905A

1

Barnes Sound

Key Largo Hammock

North Key Largo

Everglades National Park

9336

Whitewater Bay

Cape Sable

Flamingo

Florida Bay

Gulf of Mexico

① Key Largo

② Key Largo

ATLANTIC OCEAN

John Pennekamp Coral Reef State Park

③ Tavernier

Plantation Key

Windley Key

④ Islamorada

Upper Matecumbe Key

Lignumvitae Key

Lower Matecumbe Key

Indian Key

Fiesta Key

⑤ Long Key

⑥ Conch & Duck Keys

⑦

Grassy Key

Marathon Airport

Vaca Key

⑧ Marathon

1

Seven Mile Bridges

Pigeon Key

National Key Deer Refuge

No Name Key

Bahia Honda Key

⑨

Big Pine Key

⑩

⑪ Little Torch Key

Ramrod Key

Summerland Key

Cudjoe Key

Sugarloaf Key

Boca Chica Key

Saddlebunch Keys

Big Coppitt Key

Stock Island

Key West ⑫ - ㉞ see detail map

Key West International Airport

Straits of Florida

0   20 miles
0   30 km

Where to Stay & Eat

★ **$–$$$** ✕ **The Fish House.** A nautical, Keys-y casualness and diligent servers create the feeling of dining in the home of a friend, albeit a friend who knows how to prepare seafood like a superchef. Fish is prepared any way you like—from charbroiled or fried to Jamaican-jerked or pansautéed. Nightly specials like shrimp and lobster creole in a spicy tomato sauce keep happy diners coming back. The key lime pie is homemade. To ease the long lines, they added outdoor seating and opened Encore next door; it has many of the same dishes, but with slightly higher prices, a more formal dining room, and a piano-bar dining area, where weekend karaoke performances can be loud. ✉ *MM 102.4, OS* ☎ *305/451–4665 or 305/451–0650* ▭ *AE, D, MC, V* ✆ *Closed early Sept.–early Oct.*

$–$$$ ✕ **Mrs. Mac's Kitchen.** Fortunately, some things never change. The architecture and feel of this rustic, wood-paneled, screened, open-air restaurant hark back to the 1950s, when the Keys had more fishermen than well-heeled visitors. The cooks still serve traditional American sandwiches, burgers, barbecue, and seafood, like the popular TJ Dolphin, a mahimahi fillet with a spicy tomato salsa served with black beans and rice. At breakfast and lunch, the counter and booths fill up early with locals. The chili is always good, and regular nightly specials are also worth the stop. The best seats are around the busy counter or the booths in front. ✉ *MM 99.4, BS* ☎ *305/451–3722* ▭ *No credit cards* ✆ *Closed Sun.*

$–$$$ ✕ **Rib Daddy's Steak & Seafood.** When Bob Marshall's smoking experiments resulted in finger-licking ribs that almost fell off the bone, he whispered to his wife, "who's your rib daddy?" The phrase became the restaurant's name, servers' T-shirts ask the question, and Bob's reads, "I'm your rib daddy." Many people concur after tasting the mesquitesmoked prime rib, beef ribs, and pork baby back and spare ribs flavored with Bob's own rubs and sauces. Smoked turkey drumsticks are a recent addition, and salmon on a plank is in the works. Try the grilled corn on the cob or a fluffy, very sweet, sweet potato casserole. Fish tacos are a local favorite. Key lime pie comes standard or with a chocolate cookie crust and a drizzle of chocolate. ✉ *MM 102.5, BS* ☎ *305/451–0900* ⌚ *Reservations not accepted.* ▭ *MC, V.*

★ **¢–$$$** ✕ **Café Largo.** You're on vacation and someone in your group wants Italian while someone else craves seafood. This bistro-style eatery prepares both quite well. The Tuscan flank steak is grilled, then topped with sweet sautéed onions and fresh basil. There's lobster and shrimp scampi, too. A more-than-ample wine list, international beers, Italian bottled waters, and espresso and cappuccino are offered, and the dessert list is short but sweet. For lunch with a water view, try the sister restaurant, the Bayside Grille, behind the café. ✉ *MM 99.5, BS* ☎ *305/451–4885* ▭ *AE, MC, V* ✆ *No lunch.*

¢–$$ ✕ **Alabama Jack's.** Floating on two roadside barges in an old fishing community 13 mi southeast of Homestead is this weathered open-air seafood restaurant. Regular customers include Keys characters, Sunday cyclists, local retirees, and boaters, who come to admire tropical birds in the nearby mangroves, the occasional crocodile in the canal, or the bands that play on weekends. The menu has traditional Keys dishes like cracked and fried conch, fish sandwiches, burgers, fries, salads, and lots of beer. The crab cakes, made from local blue crabs, are the best thing on the menu. Jack's closes by 7 or 7:30, when the skeeters come out. ⊠ *58000 Card Sound Rd., Card Sound* ☎ *305/248–8741* ▭ *MC, V.*

¢–$$ ✕ **Chad's Deli & Bakery.** After years of requests for dinner service, Chad expanded into the space next door, where he still serves his legendary sandwiches in pita wraps or on one of eight fresh-baked breads. He also turns out white-chocolate macadamia nut and chocolate chip cookies that are a whopping 8 inches around. For dinner he's added pastas with freshly made sauces, pizzas on wheat and whole wheat crusts, and large salads. Chicken parmesan pasta is the most popular dinner item. The chicken breast is tender and the marinara sauce tastes like fresh tomatoes. ⊠ *MM 92.3, BS* ☎ *305/853–5566* ▭ *MC, V.*

¢–$ ✕ **Harriette's Restaurant.** If you're looking for comfort food, try this refreshing throwback. Little has changed over the years in this bright yellow-and-turquoise roadside eatery. Owner Harriette Mattson still personally welcomes her guests, and the regulars—many of whom have been coming here since it opened—still come for breakfast: steak and eggs with hash browns or grits and toast and jelly for $7.95, or old-fashioned hotcakes with butter and syrup and sausage or bacon for $4.75. ⊠ *MM 95.7, BS* ☎ *305/852–8689* ▭ *No credit cards* ☽ *No dinner.*

$$$$ ▥ **Jules' Undersea Lodge.** Had he been a time traveler to this century, 19th-century namesake French writer Jules Verne might have enjoyed this hotel, a former underwater research lab, at 5 fathoms (30 feet) below the surface with a 42-inch round window for viewing sea life. The only way to gain access to the lodge is by diving, and guests must either be certified divers or take the hotel's three-hour introductory course (an additional $80). Two guest rooms share a kitchen and bathroom. Rates include breakfast, dinner, snacks, beverages, unlimited dives, and diving gear. Because of the length of stay underwater, once back on terra firma, you can't fly for 24 hours. The office is only open from 8 AM to 4 PM. ⊠ *MM 103.2, OS, 51 Shoreland Dr., 33037* ☎ *305/451–2353* 🖷 *305/451–4789* ⊕ *www.jul.com* ⇨ *2 rooms* ♻ *Kitchen, cable TV, in-room VCRs, saltwater pool, dive shop; no kids under 10, no smoking* ▭ *AE, D, MC, V* ⧖ *MAP.*

★ $$$$ ▥ **Kona Kai Resort.** One of the prettiest places to stay in the Keys, these beautifully landscaped cottages have tropical furnishings, CD players, and fruit-scented toiletries. Spacious studios and one- and two-bedroom suites—with full kitchens and original art—are light-filled. Beachfront hammocks and a heated pool beckon you to relax, though if you're active, try a paddleboat or kayak, or visit the art gallery or orchid house. Maid service is every third day to prolong your privacy; however, fresh linens and towels are available at any time. The resort closes during the month of September. ⊠ *MM 97.8, BS, 97802 Overseas Hwy., 33037* ☎ *305/852–7200 or 800/365–7829* ⊕ *www.konakairesort. com* ⇨ *8 suites, 5 rooms* ♻ *Fans, some kitchens, refrigerators, cable TV, some in-room VCRs, tennis court, pool, outdoor hot tub, massage, beach, dock, boating, basketball, Ping-Pong, shuffleboard, volleyball,* concierge, Internet; no room phones, no kids under 16, no smoking ⊟ AE, D, MC, V.

$$$$ 🏨 **Marriott's Key Largo Bay Beach Resort.** The Upper Keys are best known for small mom-and-pop-style accommodations. One of the exceptions is this 17-acre bayside resort, whose lemon-yellow, grill-balconied, and spire-topped stories slice between highway and bay and exude an air of warm, indolent days. There are diversions galore. While away the days on the sandy beach or poolside or take an adventurous parasail or personal-watercraft ride. Rooms and suites have rattan tropical-style furnishings and balconies; from some, watch the sunset sweep across the bay. If you plan to spend little time in your room, select one sans view or balcony for significantly lower rates. ⊠ *MM 103.8, BS, 103800 Overseas Hwy., 33037* ☎ *305/453–0000 or 866/ 849–3753* 🖷 *305/453–0093* ⊕ *www.marriottkeylargo.com* ⮐ *132 rooms, 20 2-bedroom suites, 1 penthouse suite* ⟁ *Restaurant, room service, in-room safes, some kitchens, minibars, cable TV with movies, in-room data ports, tennis court, pool, gym, hot tub, spa, beach, dive shop, dock, snorkeling, jet skiing, parasailing, fishing, bicycles, volleyball, 3 bars, shop, children's programs (ages 5–13), dry cleaning, laundry facilities, business services, meeting rooms, no-smoking rooms* ⊟ *AE, D, DC, MC, V.*

$$$–$$$$ 🏨 **Key Largo Resorts &Marina.** You get three for the price of one at this resort trio—Marina del Mar, Holiday Inn, and Ramada—that surrounds a picturesque marina. Guests share all hotel and marina facilities. Recent renovations included the addition of lush vegetation and new furnishings, as well as larger TVs. Some rooms have porches or balconies that overlook the marina or gardens. Stroll the marina past fishing and dive boats, private yachts, the *African Queen* (used in the eponymous Bogey/Bacall movie) and glass-bottom and casino boats. There's live entertainment indoors and poolside. After check-out, guests who dive or spend the day at the beach can return to use shower facilities. The rate includes free casino-cruise tickets. Each hotel has a different personality; for a quieter stay, choose either the Ramada or Marina del Mar. ⊠ *MM 99.7, OS, 99701 Overseas Hwy., 33037* ☎ *305/451–2121 or 800/843–5397* 🖷 *305/451–1891* ⊕ *www. keylargoresorts.net* ⮐ *296 units, 48 rooms, 28 suites* ⟁ *Restaurant, picnic area, fans, in-room data ports, some kitchens, some kitchenettes, refrigerators, cable TV with movies, boating, marina, parasailing, fishing, bicycles, 2 bars, casino (boat), 2 tennis courts, 4 pools, gym, outdoor hot tub, massage, dock, snorkeling, shop, dry cleaning, laundry facilities, Internet, business services, convention center, meeting rooms, some pets allowed (fee), no-smoking rooms* ⊟ *AE, D, DC, MC, V* ⟁ *CP.*

★ $$$–$$$$ 🏨 **Sheraton Beach Resort, Key Largo.** Rather than destroy the vegetation and clutter the roadside landscape with yet another building, the original owners ensconced this compact resort off the road in a bayfront hardwood hammock. Most rooms overlook the water or woods; others face the lushly landscaped parking lot. The spacious, comfortable rooms have tropical furnishings. Lighted nature trails and boardwalks wind through the woods to a small beach. Two small pools are separated by a coral rock wall and waterfall. Both restaurants, one very casual, overlook the water. The beach is small, but the vistas are tremendous. ⊠ *MM 97, BS, 97000 Overseas Hwy., 33037* ☎ *305/ 852–5553 or 800/850–5099* 🖷 *305/852–8669* ⊕ *www.keylargoresort. com* ⤴ *190 rooms, 10 suites* ♧ *2 restaurants, room service, in-room safes, minibars, cable TV with movies and video games, in-room data ports, 2 tennis courts, 2 pools, health club, hair salon, hot tub, sauna, beach, dock, snorkeling, boating, jet skiing, marina, parasailing, fishing, bicycles, 3 bars, lounge, shop, babysitting, business services, meeting rooms, car rental, some pets allowed (fee), no-smoking rooms* ▱ *AE, D, DC, MC, V.*

$$$–$$$$ 🏨 **Tarpon Flats Inn & Marina.** This intimate oceanfront getaway in a quiet residential neighborhood was converted in 2002 from a six-unit apartment complex. Spacious rooms, many with a pullout sofa bed, are done in a mix of vibrant and subdued colors against dark West Indies–style mahogany and wicker furniture, and Oriental carpets on wood and tile floors. Sliding glass doors and sliding louvered wood shutters let you take in the breezes and water views while still enjoying privacy. You can cook in your room or outside on the grill. Breakfast includes made-to-order fruits, cereal, and pastries from a local bakery delivered to your door. The property is eco-friendly; there's a research conch nursery on-site. Room service is only available during breakfast. ⊠ *29 Shoreland Dr., off MM 103.5, OS, 33037* ☎ *305/453–1313 or 866/546–0000* 🖷 *305/453–1305* ⊕ *www.tarponflats.com* ⤴ *6 units* ♧ *Picnic area, room service, fans, some kitchens, some kitchenettes, cable TV with movies, in-room VCRs, in-room data ports, outdoor hot tub, beach, dock, snorkeling, boating, marina, fishing, bicycles, shop, concierge; no smoking* ▱ *AE, D, DC, MC, V* ⑩ *CP.*

$$$ 🏨 **Azul Del Mar.** Advertising director Karol Marsden and husband Dominic Marsden, a commercial travel photographer, transformed a run-down waterfront mom-and-pop resort into the Keys' newest boutique resort in early 2004. As you'd expect of two image makers, the place is lovely to look at, from the marble floors, dark wood furniture, and Provençal yellow leather sofas to the ice-blue bath tiles, Tom Seghi paintings, and dark granite countertops. Beauty here isn't just good looks. With their warm hospitality and desire to create the kind of place they've been promoting throughout their careers, they've also made it a great place to stay for adults. They're avid sailors, so water toys are plentiful. For the ultimate in mixing business with pleasure, take your laptop to the beach; the resort is a Wi-Fi hotspot. ⊠ *MM 104.3, BS, 104300 Overseas Hwy., Key Largo 33037* ☎ *305/451–0337* 🖷 *305/ 451–0339* ⊕ *www.azulkeylargo.com* ⤴ *5 suites* ♧ *Some fans, kitchens, microwaves, refrigerators, cable TV, in-room DVDs/VCRs, beach, dock, snorkeling, boating, fishing, bicycles, Internet, business services; no room phones, no smoking* ▱ *AE, MC, V.*

$$$ 🏨 **Coconut Palm Inn.** This small, casual waterfront lodge in a quiet residential neighborhood of towering gumbo-limbo and buttonwood trees was built in the 1930s to withstand hurricanes. It's still noted for its tranquility, privacy, and fine service. It has more than 400 feet of sandy beach with the requisite hammocks, swaying palm trees, and extensive decks

for relaxing and watching sunsets. Screened porches let you enjoy the outdoors without mosquitoes in summer. Rooms, which are decorated in a sophisticated West Indies–plantation style, vary from one-room efficiencies to one- and two-bedroom suites. It's popular for weddings. ⊠ *MM 92, BS, 198 Harborview Dr., Tavernier 33070* ☎ *305/852–3017 or 800/765–5397* 🖷 *305/852–3880* ⊕ *www.coconutpalminn.com* ⊰ *8 suites, 12 rooms* ⟁ *Picnic area, BBQ, fans, some kitchens, microwaves, refrigerators, cable TV, some in-room VCRs, pool, beach, dock, boating, fishing, laundry facilities; no smoking* ▭ *AE, MC, V.*

★ **$$** 🏨 **Largo Lodge.** A palpable calm hangs over the 1950s-vintage adults-only one-bedroom guest cottages hidden in a tropical garden of palms, sea grapes, and orchids. Accommodations are cozy and equipped with small kitchens, rattan furniture, and screened porches. There's 200 feet of bay frontage for swimming, sitting, or contemplating. Late in the day, wild ducks, pelicans, herons, and other birds come looking for a handout from longtime owner Harriet "Hat" Stokes, who sets the tone at this laid-back, top-value tropical hideaway not too far down the Keys. ⊠ *MM 101.7, BS, 101740 Overseas Hwy., 33037* ☎ *305/451–0424 or 800/468–4378* ⊕ *www.largolodge.com* ⊰ *6 apartments, 1 efficiency* ⟁ *Fans, kitchenettes, cable TV, beach, dock; no room phones, no kids under 16* ▭ *MC, V.*

$–$$ 🏨 **Coconut Bay Resort & Bay Harbor Lodge.** The value at this combined resort with 200 feet of waterfront is as refreshing as the pastel-color buildings with simply furnished and pretty rooms, efficiencies, and cottages. Almost all the rooms were renovated with new tile floors and appliances in 2004. Large gumbo-limbo trees shade the 2½-acre grounds, except at the beach, where palm trees whisper in the breeze. There are lounge chairs for gazing out over the water, and kayaks and paddleboats for when you want to get a little closer. A covered sundeck and new 30-foot dock are perfect for watching watery sunsets. Restaurants are within walking distance. Unit 25 is the best if you want extra space and a water view. ⊠ *MM 97.7, BS, 97770 Overseas Hwy., 33037* ☎ *305/852–1625 or 800/385–0986* ⊕ *www.thefloridakeys. com/coconutbay* ⊰ *21 units, 9 rooms, 5 efficiencies, 7 1-bedroom cottages* ⟁ *Picnic area, some fans, some kitchens, microwaves, refrigerators, cable TV, pool, beach, dock, boating, some pets allowed (fee)* ▭ *AE, D, MC, V.*

$ 🏨 **Hungry Pelican Motel & Sunset Cove.** Decades ago, visitors packed up the kids and station wagon and came to the Keys to stay in basic fishing camps and no-frills, mom-and-pop motels by the beach. These side-by-side resorts form a small village that harks back to that simple lifestyle, albeit with a few modern conveniences such as air-conditioning and TV. Picnic tables, palm trees, hammocks, Adirondack chairs, and lots of kitschy animal statuary abound between the clean, ground-level duplex bungalows, painted white with pastel trim. It's a friendly place, with clientele ranging from seniors and baby-boomer bikers to families and students. Rooms closest to the highway are noisiest. ⊠ *MM 99.3, BS, 33037* ☎ *305/451–3576* 🖷 *305/451–4407* ⊕ *www. hungrypelican.com* ⊰ *16 rooms, 3 efficiencies, 2 trailers* ⟁ *Picnic area, BBQ, fans, some kitchens, microwaves, refrigerators, cable TV, in-*

room VCRs, beach, dock, snorkeling, boating, fishing, bicycles; no room phones ☐ *AE, D, DC, MC, V* ⫶◯⫶ *CP.*

$ ⌨ **Popp's Motel.** A high wall with stylized metal white herons marks the entrance to this 50-year-old family-run motel. It's roomy, homey, breezy, and ideal for families, whose kids can safely play on swings and a sandy beach just yards from their rooms. Clean, well-maintained bedroom units and efficiencies have a kitchen, dark wood paneling, and terrazzo floors. It's simple but a gem of a resort. A weekly stay is required during busy periods. ⊠ *MM 95.5, BS, 95500 Overseas Hwy., 33037* ☎ *305/852–5201* 🖷 *305/852–5200* ⊕ *www.popps.com* ⋧ *10 units* ⚲ *Picnic area, fans, kitchens, cable TV, beach, dock, snorkeling, boating, waterskiing, fishing, shuffleboard, playground* ☐ *AE, MC, V.*

$ ⌨ **Seafarer Resort & Dive Center.** New owners, 20-year residents of the Keys, upgraded the interiors of this budget-priced resort with new air conditioners, tiled floors, appliances, and linens. Outdoors, a new pond, hammocks, and extensive landscaping have opened up water views to more rooms. Rooms 3 and 4 are spacious and best for families. Unit 6, a 1-bedroom cottage called the "beach house," has a large picture window with an awesome view of the bay. Duplexes closest to the highway are cheapest and will get quieter when the louvered windows are replaced. Some units have private patios. Guests like to gather at the beachfront picnic table for al fresco dining and on the dock and lounge chairs for sunset watching. The dive business offers scuba certification and uses state-of-the-art equipment. ⊠ *MM 97.6, BS, 97684 Overseas Hwy., 33037* ☎ *305/852–5349* 🖷 *305/852–0474* ⊕ *www.seafarerresort.com* ⋧ *15 units, 7 rooms, 2 studios, 3 1-bedroom cottages, 1 2-bedroom cottage, 2 apartments* ⚲ *Picnic area, BBQs, fans, some kitchenettes, refrigerators, some microwaves, cable TV, beach, dive shop, dock, hot tub, fishing, bicycles, snorkeling, boating, Internet, no-smoking rooms; no room phones* ☐ *MC, V.*

¢ ⌨ **Ed & Ellen's Lodgings.** Dense foliage separates U.S. Highway 1 from this two-story wooden house with three balconied efficiencies overlooking a garden with picnic tables and chairs. Two queen beds, a dining table for four, and full-size kitchen appliances fit comfortably in about 300 square feet. The carpets are industrial, the decor no-frills, the bathrooms clean. It's within walking distance of John Pennekamp State Park, dive shops, restaurants, and the owners, who reside next door. ⊠ *MM 103.3, OS, 33037* ☎ *305/451–9949 or 888/333–5536* ⊕ *www.ed-ellens-lodgings.com* ⋧ *3 efficiencies* ⚲ *Picnic area, BBQ, fans, kitchens, cable TV; no room phones, no smoking* ☐ *MC, V.*

⚠ **John Pennekamp Coral Reef State Park.** Campsites are carved out of hardwood hammock, providing shade and privacy away from the heavy day-use areas. Nearby water laps the shore, lulling you to sleep. Groups have numerous facilities for spreading out. There's a campground host, campfire programs, and vending machines for late-night snack attacks. Day-use activities and facilities include boating, fishing, hiking, boat-slip rentals, dock, boat tours, nature center, marina, scuba and snorkel, and volleyball. ⚲ *Grills, snack bar, playground, flush toilets, partial hook-ups (electric and water), dump station, drinking water, showers, fire pits, picnic tables, electricity, public telephone, general store, ranger station,* *swimming (ocean)* ⇒ *47 partial hook-ups for RVs and tents* ⊠ *MM 102.5, OS* ☎ *305/451–1202 park, 800/326–3521 reservations* ⊕ *www. reserveamerica.com* 🗺 *$26* ⊟ *AE, D, MC, V.*

Nightlife

The semiweekly *Keynoter* (Wednesday and Saturday), weekly *Reporter* (Thursday), and Friday through Sunday editions of the *Miami Herald* are the best sources of information on entertainment and nightlife.

Local movers and shakers mingle with visitors over cocktails and sunsets at **Breezers Tiki Bar** (⊠ MM 103.8, BS ☎ 305/453–0000), in Marriott's Key Largo Bay Beach Resort. Walls plastered with Bogart memorabilia remind customers that the classic 1948 Bogart-Bacall flick *Key Largo* was shot in the **Caribbean Club** (⊠ MM 104, BS ☎ 305/451–4466). An archetype of a laid-back Keys bar, it draws a hairy-faced, down-home group to shoot the breeze while shooting pool but is friendlier than you might imagine. It also has postcard-perfect sunsets and live entertainment that's good enough to draw late-night crowds on Friday and Saturday and at 5 on Sunday evening, plus karaoke on Wednesday nights. **Coconuts** (⊠ MM 100, OS, 528 Caribbean Dr. ☎ 305/453–9794), next to Marina Del Mar Resort, has nightly entertainment year-round, except Monday during football season. The crowd is primarily thirty- and fortysomething, sprinkled with a few grizzled locals.

The Outdoors

BIKING **Tavernier Bicycle & Hobbies** (⊠ MM 91.9, BS, 91958 Overseas Hwy., Tavernier ☎ 305/852–2859) rents single-speed adult and children's bikes. Cruisers go for $10 a day, $50 a week. Helmets and locks are free with rental. It's closed on Sunday.

FISHING **Sailors Choice** (⊠ MM 99.7, OS ☎ 305/451–1802 or 305/451–0041) runs a party boat twice daily plus a night trip ($40) on Friday and Saturday. The ultramodern 65-foot, 49-passenger boat with air-conditioned cabin costs $35 per half day, and leaves from the Holiday Inn docks. Rods, bait, and license are included.

SCUBA & SNORKELING Much of what makes the Upper Keys a singular dive destination is diversity. Places like Molasses Reef, which rises as high as 3 feet below the surface and descends to 55 feet, have something for snorkelers, novice divers, and experienced divers. The latest addition to the Keys diving wrecks is the Spiegel Grove, a 510-foot vessel that was sunk 6 mi off Key Largo in June 2002. It lies on its starboard side in 130 feet of water, but reaches up as high as 45 feet below the surface. Expect to pay about $70 for a two-tank, two-site dive trip with tanks and weights; $30–$40 for a two-site snorkel outing and for nonswimming accompanying guests. Get big discounts with multiple trips.

Ocean Divers (⊠ MM 105.5, BS and 522 Caribbean Dr., MM 100, OS ☎ 305/451–0037, 877/451–0037, 305/451–1113, or 800/451–1113 ⊕ oceandivers.com) operates two shops in Key Largo. Both are PADI five-star CDC facilities and offer day and night dives, fully stocked stores, instruction, and dive-lodging packages. The cost is $70 for a two-tank reef dive with tank and weight rental, $105 if you need everything; $111–$117 includes a wet suit, suggested in winter. Snorkel trips cost $39 with snorkel, mask, and fins.

Amy Slate's Amoray Dive Resort (⊠ MM 104.2, BS ☎ 305/451–3595 or 800/426–6729) makes diving easy. Get out of bed, walk out of your room and into a full-service dive shop (NAUI, PADI, TDI, and BSAC-certified), then onto a 45-foot catamaran. Ask about multidive discounts, accommodations packages, and underwater weddings.

Coral Reef Park Co. (⊠ John Pennekamp Coral Reef State Park, MM 102.5, OS ☎ 305/451–6322) gives scuba and snorkeling tours of the park aboard sailing and motorized boats.

Divers City, USA (⊠ MM 90.5, OS ☎ 305/852–0430 or 800/649–4659) is eco- and diver-friendly. They repair scuba gear and also have the best prices for "Bubble Watchers"—passengers accompanying a diver ($20).

Quiescence Diving Service, Inc. (⊠ MM 103.5, BS ☎ 305/451–2440) sets itself apart in two ways: it limits groups to six to ensure personal attention and offers day, night, and twilight (in summer) dives an hour before sundown, the time when sea creatures are most active.

WATER SPORTS Kayaking is the fastest growing water sport in the Keys thanks in part to the many new outfitters offering tours, but also because of advances in equipment, such as foot pedals, rudders, and sails, that make kayaking easier. You can kayak for a few hours or the whole day, paddle on your own, or take a guided tour. Some outfitters also offer overnight trips. The new Florida Keys Overseas Paddling Trail, part of a statewide system, runs from Key Largo to Key West. You can paddle the entire trip, which takes seven days, or just cover a section. Contact outfitters for information on campgrounds and participating hotels along the route. **Coral Reef Park Co.** (⊠ John Pennekamp Coral Reef State Park, MM 102.5, OS ☎ 305/451–1621) frequently renews its fleet of canoes and kayaks for scooting around the mangrove trails or the sea. Rent a canoe, a one- or two-person sea kayak, or even camping equipment from **Florida Bay Outfitters** (⊠ MM 104, BS ☎ 305/451–3018). They help with trip planning and match the equipment to the skill level. Rentals are by the half day or full day. They also run myriad tours and sell camping and outdoor accessories, kayaks, and canoes. The shop stages the well-attended annual Florida Keys Paddling Festival the first weekend in February. It features kayak and canoe races, instruction, and demonstrations, as well as food and live entertainment. Owners Monica and Frank Woll are the segment coordinators for the Florida Keys Overseas Paddling Trail.

Shopping

Learn about Keys history, flora and fauna, and fishing through the books, cards, and maps at **Cover to Cover Books** (⊠ Tavernier Towne Shopping Center, MM 91.2, BS, 91272 Overseas Hwy. ☎ 305/853–2464). New owners added a coffee bar, open-mike nights, and author readings. Original works by major international artists—including American photographer Clyde Butcher, French painter Jalinepol W, and French sculptor Polles—are shown at the **Gallery at Kona Kai** (⊠ MM 97.8, BS, 97802 Overseas Hwy. ☏ 305/852–7200), in the Kona Kai Resort. There are lots of shops in the Keys that carry fun souvenirs. **Shellworld** (⊠ MM 97.5, center median ☏ 305/852–8245) is one of the largest. Inside the long Keys-style building are two floors crowded with high-quality home furnishings, CDs of local music, shells, cards, resort clothing, jewelry, and, yes, tacky souvenirs. There's a supersale the weekend after Thanksgiving.

Islamorada

❹ *MM 90.5–70.*

Early settlers named Islamorada after their schooner, the *Island Home,* but to make the name more romantic, they translated it into Spanish— *isla morada* (although the translation endured, the local pronunciation is now the non-Spanish EYE-la-mor-AH-da). The local chamber of commerce prefers to say it means "the purple isles." Early maps show Islamorada as only Upper Matecumbe Key, but the incorporated "Village of Islands" comprises the islands between Tavernier Creek at MM 90 and Fiesta Key at MM 70, including Plantation Key, Windley Key, Upper Matecumbe Key, Lower Matecumbe Key, Craig Key, and Fiesta Key. In addition, two islands—Indian Key, in the Atlantic Ocean, and Lignumvitae Key, in Florida Bay—belong to the group. Islamorada is one of the world's most renowned sportfishing areas. For nearly 100 years, seasoned anglers have fished these clear, warm waters, with game fish as well as lobster, shrimp, and crabs. The rich, famous, and powerful have fished here, including Lou Gehrig, Ted Williams, Zane Grey, and presidents Hoover, Truman, Carter, and Bush Sr. More than 150 backcountry guides and 400 offshore captains operate out of this 20-mi stretch. Activities include fishing tournaments and historic reenactments. During September and October, Heritage Days highlights include free lectures on Islamorada history, a golf tournament, and the Indian Key Festival. Holiday Isle Resort sponsors boating, fishing, car, and golf tournaments as well as bikini and body-building contests.

Between 1885 and 1915, settlers earned good livings growing pineapples at **Plantation Key,** using black Bahamian workers to plant and harvest their crops. The plantations are gone, replaced by a dense concentration of homes, businesses, and a public park. ⊠ *MM 90.5–86.*

At 16 feet above sea level, **Windley Key** is the highest point in the Keys. Originally two islets, the area was first inhabited by Native Americans, who left middens and other remains, and then by settlers, who farmed and fished in the mid-1800s and called the islets the Umbrella Keys. The Florida East Coast Railway bought the land from homesteaders in 1908, filled in the inlet between the two islands, and changed the name. They quarried rock for the rail bed and bridge approaches in the Keys— the same rock used in many historic South Florida structures, including Miami's Vizcaya and the Hurricane Monument on Upper Matecumbe. Although the Quarry Station stop was destroyed by the 1935 hurricane, quarrying continued until the 1960s. Today a few resorts and attractions occupy the island. ⊠ *MM 86–84.*

Islamorada Founder's Park. Formerly part of a commercial resort, this is now a public village park with a beach, marina, dog park, skate park, water-sports equipment rentals, an Olympic-size pool, and clean restroom and shower facilities. If you're staying in Islamorada hotels, enter the park free and pay the village rate of $2 weekdays or $3 weekends for use of the pool. Guests of other Keys hotels pay $4–$6 to enter the park and $4–$6 to use the pool. ⊠ *MM 87, BS* ☎ *305/853–1685.*

The fossilized coral reef at **Windley Key Fossil Reef Geological State Park,** laid down about 125,000 years ago, shows that the Florida Keys were at some time underwater. Excavation of Windley Key's limestone bed by the Florida East Coast Railway exposed the petrified reef. The park contains the **Alison Fahrer Environmental Education Center,** with historic, biological, and geological displays about the area. There also are guided and self-guided tours along trails that lead to the railway's old quarrying equipment and cutting pits, where you can take rubbings of beautifully fossilized brain coral and sea ferns from the quarry walls. There's an annual festival in February. ⊠ *MM 85.5, BS* ☎ *305/664–2540* ⊕ *www.dep.state.fl.us/parks* ⊠ *Education center free, quarry trails $1.50, ranger-guided tours $2.50* ⊙ *Education center Thurs.–Mon. 8–5; tours at 10 and 2.*

ↄ The lush, tropical 17-acre **Theater of the Sea** is the second-oldest marine mammal center in the world. Entertaining and educational shows provide insight into conservation issues, natural history, and mammal anatomy, physiology, and husbandry. Shows run continuously. Ride a glass-bottom boat and take a four-hour Dolphin Adventure Snorkel Cruise or guided tours to view marine life, raptors, and reptiles. Visit dolphins and sea lions and participate in animal interaction programs such as Swim with the Dolphins ($150), Swim with Sea Lions ($100), Stingray Swim ($50), Dolphin Wade ($150) and Meet the Sea Lion ($50). Reservations are recommended for interaction programs. Program fees include general admission, a marine-life tour, and bottomless-boat ride. Try lunch at the grill, shop, and sunbathe at a lagoonside beach. ⊠ *MM 84.5, OS, 84721 Overseas Hwy., 33036* ☎ *305/664–2431* ⊕ *www.theaterofthesea. com* ⊠ *$23.95* ⊙ *Daily 9:30–4.*

Early homesteaders were so successful at growing pineapples in the rocky soil of **Upper Matecumbe Key** that at one time the island had the largest U.S. pineapple crop. However, Cuban pineapples and the hurricane of 1935 killed the industry. Today life centers on fishing and tourism, and the island is lively with homes, charter-fishing boats, bait shops, restaurants, stores, nightclubs, marinas, nurseries, and offices. It's one of the earliest of the Upper Keys to be permanently settled. ⊠ *MM 84–79.*

Although the possibility of a hurricane is something Keys residents live with, few hurricanes actually make landfall here. One major exception was the 1935 Labor Day hurricane, in which 423 people died. Beside the highway, the 65-foot-by-20-foot art deco–style **Hurricane Monument** commemorates their deaths. Many of those who perished were World

War I veterans who had been working on the Overseas Highway. The monument, built of Keys coral limestone with a ceramic map of the Keys, depicts wind-driven waves and palms bowing before the storm's fury. ⊠ *MM 81.6, OS.*

Tucked away behind the Islamorada library is **Islamorada County Park,** with a small beach on a creek. The water isn't very deep, but it is crystal clear. Currents are swift, making swimming unsuitable for young children, but kids can enjoy the playground as well as picnic tables, grassy areas, and rest rooms. ⊠ *MM 81.5, BS.*

off the beaten path

INDIAN KEY HISTORIC STATE PARK – Murder, mystery, and misfortune surround 10½-acre Indian Key, on the ocean side of the Matecumbe islands. Before it became one of the first European settlements outside of Key West, it was inhabited by Native Americans for several thousand years. The islet served as a county seat and base for 19th-century shipwreck salvagers until an Indian attack wiped out the settlement in 1840. Dr. Henry Perrine, a noted botanist, was killed in the raid. Today his plants overgrow the town's ruins. In October the Indian Key Festival celebrates the key's heritage. Take a guided tour, Thursday–Monday at 9 and 1, or roam among the marked trails and sites. The island is reachable by boat—your own, a rental, or a ferry. Robbie's Marina, the official concessionaire, rents kayaks and boats and operates twice-daily ferry service Thursday–Monday. For information, contact Long Key State Park. Locals kayak out from **Indian Key Fill** (⊠ *MM 78.5, BS*). Rentals are available from Florida Keys Kayak and Sail. ⊠ *MM 78.5, OS* ☎ *305/664–9814 ferry service, 305/664–2540 Windley Key State Park* 🎫 *Ferry and tour $15, $25 with Lignumvitae Key* ☉ *Thurs.–Mon. at 9 and 1, last ticket sold 30 minutes before tour.*

LIGNUMVITAE KEY BOTANICAL STATE PARK – On the National Register of Historic Places, this 280-acre bayside island is the site of a virgin hardwood forest and home and gardens that chemical magnate William Matheson built as a private retreat in 1919. Access is by boat—your own, a rental, or a ferry operated by the official concessionaire, Robbie's Marina, which also rents kayaks and boats. (Kayaking out from Indian Key Fill, at MM 78.5, is a popular pastime.) On the key, take a tour with the resident ranger and request a list of native and well-naturalized plants. As a courtesy, you should arrange for a tour in advance with Long Key State Park if you're using your own or a rental boat. On the first weekend in December, the park service holds an annual Lignumvitae Christmas Celebration. ⊠ *MM 78.5, BS* ☎ *305/664–9814 ferry service, 305/664–2540 Windley Key State Park* 🎫 *Free; tour $1.50; ferry and tour $15, $25 with Indian Key* ☉ *Tours Thurs.–Mon. at 10 and 2; last ticket sold 30 minutes before tour.*

Tarpon, large prehistoric-looking denizens of the not-so-deep, congregate around the docks at **Robbie's Marina** on Lower Matecumbe Key, where children—and lots of adults—buy a $2 bucket of bait fish to feed them. ⊠ *MM 77.5, BS* ☎ *305/664–9814 or 877/664–8498* 🖴 *Dock access $1* ☉ *Daily 8–5.*

On Lower Matecumbe Key, **Anne's Beach** is a popular village park whose beach is best enjoyed at low tide. It also has a ½-mi elevated wooden boardwalk that meanders through a natural wetland hammock. Covered picnic areas along the boardwalk provide a place to rest and enjoy the view. Restrooms are at the north end. Weekends are packed with Miami day-trippers. ⊠ *MM 73.5, OS* ☎ *305/853–1685.*

Where to Stay & Eat

$$–$$$$ **✕ Pierre's.** A two-story sister to the Morada Bay restaurant, this spot
Fodor'sChoice marries British colonial decadence with South Florida trendiness. It
★ oozes style with dark wood, rattan, French doors, Indian and Asian architectural artifacts, and a wicker chair–strewn veranda that overlooks the bay. The food, inspired by those same Asian, Indian, and Floridian accents, is complex: layered, colorful, and beautifully presented. Weather permitting, dine outside. The sophisticated downstairs bar provides a perfect vantage point for sunset watching. Reservations are recommended. ⊠ *MM 81.5, BS* ☎ *305/664–3225* 🖃 *AE, MC, V.*

$–$$$$ **✕ Island Grill.** If you sat any closer to the water, you would get wet at this oceanfront restaurant with indoor and outdoor seating. Boats pull up within a few feet of your table discharging diners—and exhaust—so opt for a table a little farther away; you'll still get the sea view, but without the fumes. The radio plays pop music as waiters take orders from an eclectic menu with such dishes as Reuben mahimahi, guava barbecue shrimp with pineapple salsa, and tuna nachos. Southern-inspired fare includes low-country shrimp or shrimp and andouille, both with grits. There's a bar indoors and another outdoors, with live entertainment Wednesday through Sunday. ⊠ *MM 85.5, OS* ☎ *305/664–8400* 🖃 *AE, MC, V.*

$$–$$$ **✕ Uncle's Restaurant.** You'll be well past the center of Islamorada when you finally arrive here, but it's worth the drive. Most Keys restaurants give you a choice of grilled, broiled, or blackened fish. Here you get those choices plus française, milanaise, parmigiana or LePree—the owner's last name—with artichokes, mushrooms, white wine, and lemon butter. Specials sometimes combine wild game with seafood, like the elk and lobster combo. Portions are huge, so plan to split dishes or take home a doggie bag. Weather permitting, sit outdoors in the garden; poor acoustics make dining indoors unusually noisy. ⊠ *MM 81, OS* ☎ *305/664–4402* 🖃 *AE, D, DC, MC, V* ☉ *Closed Sun.*

★ $–$$$ **✕ Morada Bay.** The best part of this wildly popular, bay-front restaurant is the striking scenery and traditional wooden Conch architecture decorated with Clyde Butcher's black-and-white Everglades photos. Popularity has made the kitchen's performance inconsistent in the preparation of a contemporary menu, which includes tapas, mostly from the sea. Dine indoors (noisy) or outdoors overlooking a beach dotted with Adirondack chairs and kids playing in the sand, who, as always, have eaten faster than their parents. There's frequently live entertainment, especially on weekends, and a monthly full-moon party. ⊠ *MM 81, BS* ☎ *305/664–0604* 🖃 *AE, MC, V.*

¢–$$$ ✕ **Kaiyo.** Chef-owner Dawn Sieber designed Kaiyo with as much artistry as she gives to the food. The setting includes a colorful abstract mosaic, polished wood floors and bars, earth tones, and upholstered banquettes. The menu, a fusion of East meets West, has sushi and sashimi, classic rolls, and her signature rolls that combine local ingredients with traditional Japanese tastes. Key lime lobster roll is a blend of Florida lobster with hearts of palm and essence of key lime ($13.75). Kaiyo roll includes local stone crab, wahoo, edamame, sunflower seeds, and stone-ground mustard mayonnaise. ⊠ *MM 82, OS* ☎ *305/664–5556* ⊟ *AE, MC, V* ⊘ *Closed Sun.*

★ ¢–$$$ ✕ **Squid Row.** The food is so good at this seafood eatery that no gimmicks are needed to lure customers. That doesn't prevent the affable staff from offering a playful challenge: if you eat the nightly special seafood bouillabaisse ($28.95)—thick with stone crab claws and other savories— all by yourself, you'll get a free slice of key lime pie. Other fish choices are grilled to divinely flaky perfection or breaded and sautéed. Meals begin with a slice of warm banana bread, also nice with your coffee. ⊠ *MM 81.9, OS* ☎ *305/664–9865* ⊟ *AE, D, DC, MC, V.*

¢–$ ✕ **Caribbean Café & Catering.** Chef David Mansen left one of the Keys' most popular restaurants to open this café with half a dozen tables and bar seating. Word spread fast, even though he only serves until 4 PM and closes at 5 PM (4 PM on Saturdays). Dishes such as his grilled veggie panini and happy-hour chicken—sautéed chicken with apricots, mangoes, ginger, and herbs over jasmine rice with toasted coconut—are worth having as an early dinner. Think of it as a hip early bird special. ⊠ *MM 80.9, OS* ☎ *305/664–0004* ⊟ *AE, D, MC, V* ⊘ *Closed Sun.*

$$$$ 🏨 **Casa Morada.** Three female hoteliers brought their cumulative 50 years
Fodor's Choice of New York and Miami Beach experience to the Keys. Using their trans-
★ formative magic, they've turned this waterfront resort into an all-suites showcase befitting the French Riviera, with a Caribbean accent, of course. Lush landscaping, a pool surrounded by a sandy "beach," artwork, blooming orchids, CD players, and outdoor lounges at the water's edge are just the start. Clean, cool tile and terrazzo floors invite you to kick off your shoes and step out to your private patio overlooking the gardens and bay. Breakfast and lunch are served on the waterside terrace. ⊠ *MM 82, BS, 136 Madeira Rd., 33036* ☎ *305/664–0044 or 888/ 881–3030* 🖷 *305/664–0674* ⊕ *www.casamorada.com* ⇥ *16 suites* ⚲ *Restaurant, room service, fans, in-room safes, some in-room hot tubs, minibars, cable TV, in-room DVDs, in-room data ports, pool, massage, dock, boating, marina, bicycles, boccie, lounge, dry cleaning, laundry service, concierge; no smoking* ⊟ *AE, MC, V* ⱺ⊙ *CP.*

$$$$ 🏨 **Cheeca Lodge & Spa.** Stretching across 27 oceanfront acres, this classy, classic resort has luxury beachfront bungalows, suites, and rooms, as well as fish-filled lagoons. Accommodations include West Indies–style furniture and 42-inch plasma TVs. Beckoning are the beach and water sports, as well as massages, facials, and body treatments at the Avanyu Spa. Rooms have either an ocean, garden, or golf-course view. The resort is the local leader in green activism, with everything from recycling programs to ecotours. Camp Cheeca for kids, $30 per child (ages 5–12) per day, $25 per night, is fun and educational. The room rate does not

include a $39 resort fee. ⊠ *MM 82, OS, Box 527, 33036* ☎ *305/664–4651 or 800/327–2888* 🖷 *305/664–2893* ⊕ *www.cheeca.com* 🔊 *139 rooms, 64 suites* ⚬ *2 restaurants, room service, fans, some minibars, some refrigerators, cable TV with movies, in-room VCRs, in-room data ports, 9-hole golf course, 6 tennis courts, 2 pools, saltwater pool, health club, 4 outdoor hot tubs, spa, beach, dive shop, dock, snorkeling, windsurfing, boating, parasailing, fishing, bicycles, bar, lobby lounge, shops, babysitting, children's programs (ages 4–12), playground, laundry service, concierge, Internet, business services, meeting rooms, no-smoking rooms* ▭ *AE, D, DC, MC, V.*

★ **$$$$** 🏨 **The Moorings.** When you think of a tropical retreat, visions of palm trees, beaches, and wooden houses with porches and wicker furniture may spring to mind. That's what you'll find here at one of the Keys' finest hostelries. Tucked in a beachfront tropical forest are one-, two-, and three-bedroom cottages and two-story houses, outfitted with wicker and artistic African fabrics and pristine kitchens. There are exquisite touches, from thick towels to cushy bedcovers. The beach has Adirondack chairs, hammocks, and a swimming dock. A new spa provides guests with manicures, massages, and beauty treatments. There's a two-night minimum on one-bedrooms and a one-week minimum on other lodgings. ⊠ *MM 81.6, OS, 123 Beach Rd., 33036* ☎ *305/664–4708* 🖷 *305/664–4242* ⊕ *www.themooringsvillage.com* 🔊 *5 cottages, 13 houses* ⚬ *Fans, some kitchens, some kitchenettes, cable TV, in-room data ports, tennis court, pool, beach, windsurfing, boating, laundry facilities* ▭ *AE, MC, V.*

★ **$$–$$$$** 🏨 **The Caribbean Resort and Marina.** On 8½ acres, this resort has a beautiful sandy beach, two docks, and two types of accommodations. Old concrete duplex "villas" were modernized with very tasteful island furnishings, tile floors, and a private deck or patio. You'll smell the sea from all of them. Next door are the gilded lilies: Caribbean-style one- and two-bedroom houses with open-beam ceilings, wraparound porches, and light, breezy, oh-so-tropical furnishings. Public areas are equally appealing. The large walk-in, beach-entry-style pool is surrounded by palm trees and lounge chairs. ⊠ *MM 82, OS, 109 E. Carroll St., Box 1298, 33036* ☎ *305/664–2235 or 800/799–9175* 🖷 *305/664–2093* ⊕ *www. thecaribbeanresort.com* 🔊 *21 units, 9 villas, 12 houses* ⚬ *BBQ, fans, some kitchens, cable TV, some in-room VCRs, pool, outdoor hot tub, beach, dock, snorkeling, marina, fishing* ▭ *AE, MC, V.*

$$$ 🏨 **The Islander Resort.** This is the quintessential island resort: 1,300 feet of sandy beach, tall, curved palm trees bending in the breeze, and blue ocean views as far as you can see. Built in 1951, the hotel made an ugly-duckling-to-swan transformation in 2004. All units have private, screened porches; they lead to sunny living rooms (in suites) and bedrooms painted sunny yellow, trimmed in white, with white furniture and lapis-colored bedding and curtains. The suites in the new oceanfront Beach House are ideal for families, and units farther from the pool area and beach are more tranquil. Stroll or fish from the 200-foot-long lighted dock day or night. ⊠ *MM 81.2, OS , 33026* ☎ *305/664–2031 or 800/ 753–6002* 🖷 *305/664–5503* ⊕ *www.islanderfloridakeys.com* 🔊 *114* ⚬ *Restaurant, picnic area, BBQs, fans, in-room data ports, in-room safes,* *kitchens, cable TV with movies, boating, fishing, bicycles, shuffleboard, volleyball, bar, 2 pools, gym, outdoor hot tub, beach, dock, snorkeling, dry cleaning, laundry facilities, Internet, business services, meeting rooms* ⊟ *AE, D, DC, MC, V* ⦿| *CP.*

$$$ ▦ **White Gate Court.** On the edge of Florida Bay, this well-run inn includes five restored 1940s buildings laid out on three landscaped acres along 220 feet of white-sand beach. Susanne Orias de Cargnelli created this intimate escape, where everyone in the family, including pets, is welcome. All the units, which sleep either two or five, are well equipped, and the backyard has a barbecue and umbrella-shaded table under big old palm trees that sway with the sea breeze. Rates include use of a paddleboat and snorkeling gear. ⊠ *MM 76, BS, 76010 Overseas Hwy., 33036* ☎ *305/664–4136 or 800/645–4283* ⊕ *www.whitegatecourt.com* ⥼ *7 units* ⚲ *Picnic area, BBQ, fans, kitchens, cable TV, in-room data ports, beach, dock, snorkeling, boating, bicycle, laundry facilities, some pets allowed (fee)* ⊟ *MC, V.*

$$–$$$ ▦ **Drop Anchor Resort & Marina.** This newly renovated resort presents a dilemma; time spent indoors means time away from the whispering palm fronds and lolling ocean waves, but the soothing West Indies–style furnishings of the rooms and suites is equally enticing. New owners gutted the place, added lots of tropical hues, coordinating fabrics, art objects, and pillows. The only old thing that remains is the colorful 1950s-style tile in the bathrooms, which is back in vogue. The tiles are accented with matching or contrasting towels for a bit of whimsy. Catch the ocean breezes on your balcony or on one of the chaises that are lined up along the 300 feet of sandy beach. ⊠ *84959 Overseas Hwy., MM 85, OS* ⑇ *Box 222, 33036* ☎ *305/664–4863 or 888/664–4863* ⊜ *305/664–4801* ⊕ *www.dropanchorresort.com* ⥼ *18 rooms* ⚲ *Fans, some kitchens, some kitchenettes, refrigerators, boccie, pool, massage, dock, laundry facilities* ⊟ *AE, D, DC, MC, V.*

¢ ▦ **Bed & Breakfast of Islamorada.** After celebrating the 20th anniversary of her bed-and-breakfast in 2004, veteran traveler Dotty Saunders sold it to Eileen O'Brien and Mike Flynn. They've redecorated the rooms in lively tropical colors, added a tiki bar and patio in the back, and spruced up the landscaping. Rooms in the one-story house are large and clean and have private baths. Breakfast includes fresh fruits from the yard. A two-day minimum stay is required. ⊠ *81175 Old Hwy., MM 81, OS, 33036* ☎ *305/664–9321* ⥼ *2 rooms* ⚲ *Fans, cable TV, bicycles, laundry facilities, some pets allowed (fee); no room phones* ⊟ *MC, V* ⦿| *BP.*

¢ ▦ **Key Lantern Motel and Blue Fin Inn.** These side-by-side no-frills motels are on the highway, in the heart of Islamorada, within walking distance of restaurants and shops. Terrazzo floors and brick walls reveal their age, but rooms are spacious and have well-maintained tile bathrooms with some new fixtures. The staff is helpful and friendly. It's a bargain if you just need a place to rest your body after a long day on the water. ⊠ *MM 82.1, BS, 33036* ☎ *305/664–4572* ⊕ *www.keylantern.com* ⥼ *24 units* ⚲ *BBQ, fans, some kitchenettes, refrigerators, cable TV, laundry facilities* ⊟ *MC, V.*

¢ ▦ **Ragged Edge Resort.** Smack on the water's edge, this laid-back getaway has simple rooms with pine paneling. Many downstairs units have screened porches; upper units have large decks, more windows, and beam ceilings. Congregate under the thatch-roof observation tower by day and at the barbecue pits by night to grill up your catch. Minimal staffing and no in-room phones are among the measures that make this place affordable. There's not much of a beach, but you can swim off the dock. ⊠ *MM 86.5, OS, 243 Treasure Harbor Rd., 33036* ☎ *305/ 852–5389 or 800/436–2023* ⊕ *www.ragged-edge.com* ⇆ *10 units* ⚴ *Picnic area, fans, some kitchens, some kitchenettes, some refrigerators, pool, dock, marina, fishing, bicycles, shuffleboard; no room phones, no TV in some rooms* ⊟ *MC, V.*

Nightlife

Holiday Isle Beach Resorts & Marina (⊠ MM 84, OS ☎ 305/664–2321) is the liveliest spot in the Upper Keys. On weekends, especially during spring break and holidays, the resort's three entertainment areas are mobbed, primarily with the under-30 set. Bands play everything from reggae to heavy metal nightly, and there's a Hawaiian dance show on Saturday and Sunday. Behind the larger-than-life mermaid is the Keys-easy, over-the-water cabana bar, the **Lorelei** (⊠ MM 82, BS ☎ 305/ 664–4656). Live nightly sounds are mostly reggae and light rock. **Zane Grey Long Key Lounge** (⊠ MM 81.5, BS ☎ 305/664–4244), above the World Wide Sportsman, was created to honor Zane Grey, one of South Florida's greatest legends in fishing and writing and one of the most famous members of the Long Key Fishing Club. The lounge displays the author's photographs, books, and memorabilia and has live blues, jazz, and Motown Thursday–Saturday and a wide veranda that invites sunset watching.

Sports & the Outdoors

BOATING **Bump & Jump** (⊠ MM 81.2, OS ☎ 305/664–9404 or 877/453–9463) is a one-stop shop for windsurfing, sailboat, and powerboat rental, sales and lessons. This company understands what you need to make your vacation a blast. They deliver to your hotel, house or beach. They also rent bicycles. Their motto: "we rent nice clean recent equipment, just like what we would like to use while on vacation."

Wildlife in the Keys is most active at sunrise and sunset. Be there comfortably at both times with **Houseboat Vacations of the Florida Keys** (⊠ MM 85.9, BS, 85944 Overseas Hwy. ☎ 305/664–4009 ⊕ www. thefloridakeys.com/houseboats), which rents a fleet of 42- to 44-foot boats that accommodate from six to eight people and come outfitted with safety equipment and necessities—except food. The three-day minimum starts at $1,012; a week costs $1,754. Kayaks, canoes, and 17- to 27-foot skiffs suitable for the ocean are also for hire.

Robbie's Boat Rentals & Charters (⊠ MM 77.5, BS, 77520 Overseas Hwy. ☎ 305/664–9814 ⊕ www.robbies.com) prides itself on service. It delivers boats to hotels, provides orientation and instruction to new users, and rents fishing gear as well as boats, starting from a 16-foot skiff with a 25-horsepower outboard for $70 for four hours and $90 for the day. Boats up to 27 feet are available, but there's a two-hour minimum; pontoon boats have a half-day minimum.

When you're in the Keys, do as the locals do; get out on the water, preferably for a few days. Captains Pam and Pete Anderson of **Treasure Harbor Marine** (⊠ MM 86.5, OS, 200 Treasure Harbor Dr., 33036 ☎ 305/852–2458 or 800/352–2628 ⊕ www.treasureharbor.com) provide everything you'll need for a vacation at sea: linens, safety gear, and, best of all, advice on where to find the best beaches, marinas, and lobster sites. Rent a vessel bareboat or crewed, with sail or with power. Boats range from a 19-foot Cape Dory to a 41-foot Morgan Out Island. Rates start at $110 a day, $450 a week. Captains start at $150 a day. Marina facilities are basic—water, electric, ice machine, laundry, picnic tables, and shower-restrooms—and dockage is only $1.50 a foot. A ship's store sells snacks and beverages.

FISHING   Long before fly-fishing became a trendy sport, Sandy Moret was fishing the Keys for bonefish, tarpon, and redfish. Now he operates **Florida Keys Outfitters** (⊠ MM 82, BS ☎ 305/664–5423 ⊕ www.floridakeysoutfitters.com), with a store and the Florida Keys Fly Fishing School, which attracts anglers from around the world. Two-day weekend fly-fishing classes, which include classroom instruction, equipment, arrival cocktails, and daily breakfast and lunch, cost $895. Add another $970 for two days of fishing. Guided fishing trips cost $345 for a half day, $485 for a full day. Fishing and accommodations packages (at Cheeca Lodge) are available.

The 65-foot party boat **Miss Islamorada** (⊠ Bud n' Mary's Marina, MM 79.8, OS ☎ 305/664–2461) has full-day trips ($55 includes everything). Bring your lunch or buy one from the dockside deli.

★   Captain Ken Knudsen of the **Hubba Hubba** (⊠ MM 79.8, OS ☎ 305/664–9281) quietly poles his flat boat through the shallow water, barely making a ripple. Then he points and his clients cast. Five seconds later there's a zing, and the excitement of bringing in a snook, redfish, trout, or tarpon begins. Knudsen has fished Keys waters since he was 12. That's more than 40 years. Now a licensed backcountry guide, he's ranked among the top 10 guides in Florida by national fishing magazines. He offers four-hour sunset trips for tarpon ($350) and two-hour sunset trips for bonefish ($200), as well as half- ($300) and full-day ($450) outings. Prices are for one or two anglers, and tackle and bait are included.

Like other top fly-fishing and light-tackle guides, Captain Geoff Colmes of **Fishabout Charters** (⊠ 105 Palm La. ☎ 305/853–0741 or 800/741–5955 ⊕ www.floridakeysflyfish.com) helps his clients land double-figure fish in the waters around the Keys ($300–$425). But unlike the others, he also heads across Florida Bay to fish the coastal Everglades on three- and four-day trips (from $3,900 for two anglers) off his 65-foot mother ship, the *Fishabout*. It has four staterooms, private baths, living room, kitchen, satellite TV, phone, and separate crew quarters. It's especially ideal when cold, windy weather shuts out fishing around the Keys. Rates include captain, crew, guide fees, lodging, all meals, tackle, and use of canoes for getting deep into shallow Everglades inlets.

SCUBA &
SNORKELING
Florida Keys Dive Center (✉ MM 90.5, OS ☎ 305/852–4599 or 800/433–8946 ⊕ www.floridakeysdivectr.com) organizes dives from John Pennekamp Coral Reef State Park to Alligator Light. The center has two Coast Guard–approved dive boats, offers scuba training, and is one of the few Keys dive centers to offer Nitrox (mixed gas) diving. With a resort, pool, restaurant, entertainment, store, lessons, and twice-daily dive and snorkel trips, **Holiday Isle Dive Shop** (✉ MM 84, OS, 84001 Overseas Hwy. ☎ 305/664–3483 or 800/327–7070 ⊕ www.diveholidayisle.com) is a one-stop dive shop.

TENNIS
Not all Keys recreation is on the water. Play tennis year-round at the **Islamorada Tennis Club** (✉ MM 76.8, BS ☎ 305/664–5340). It's a well-run facility with four clay and two hard courts (five lighted), same-day racket stringing, ball machines, private lessons, a full-service pro shop, night games, and partner pairing. Rates are from $16 a day.

WATER SPORTS
Florida Keys Kayak and Sail (✉ MM 77.5, BS, 77522 Overseas Hwy. ☎ 305/664–4878) rents kayaks within a 20- to 30-minute paddle of Indian and Lignumvitae keys, two favorite destinations for kayakers. Rates are $15 per hour, $30 per half day. They've added glass-bottom kayaks and a 26-mi, 2½-hour jet-boat tour for $99. It includes a snorkel stop on the reef and trips to the sand bar and several small islands.

Shopping

At **Banyan Tree** (✉ MM 81.2, OS, 81197 Overseas Hwy. ☎ 305/664–3433), a sharp-eyed husband-and-wife team successfully combines antiques and contemporary gifts for the home and garden with plants and pots in a stylishly sophisticated indoor–outdoor setting. At **Down to Earth** (✉ MM 82.2, OS, 82205 Overseas Hwy. ☎ 305/664–9828), indulge your passion for *objets* that are at once practical and fanciful, such as salad tongs carved from polished coconut shells or Indonesian furniture. Prices are reasonable, too. When locals need a one-of-a-kind gift, they head for **Gallery Morada** (✉ MM 81.6, OS, 81611 Old Hwy. ☎ 305/664–3650). Its new home across the street on the ocean side better displays blown glass and glassware, as well as home furnishings, original paintings and lithographs, sculptures, and hand-painted scarves and earrings by top South Florida artists. Among the best buys in town are the used best-sellers and hardbacks that sell for less than $5 after locals trade them in for store credit at **Hooked on Books** (✉ MM 82.6, OS, 82681 Overseas Hwy. ☎ 305/517–2602). There are also new titles, audio books, cards, and CDs. **Island Silver & Spice** (✉ MM 82, OS ☎ 305/664–2714) has women's and men's resort wear, a large jewelry selection with high-end Swiss watches and marine-theme pieces, tropical housewares, cards, toys and games, bedding, and bath goods.

Former U.S. presidents, celebrities, and record holders beam alongside their catches in black-and-white photos on the walls at **World Wide Sportsman** (✉ MM 81.5, BS ☎ 305/664–4615), a two-level attraction and retail center that sells upscale fishing equipment, art, resort clothing, and gifts. You can shop until 9. There's also a marina and the Zane Grey Long Key Lounge.

ART GALLERIES **Art Lovers Gallery** (✉ MM 82.2, OS ☎ 305/664–3675) showcases the work of almost 100 primarily South Florida artists, including Keys water colorist Millard Wells and Jim Lewk (copper creations). The **Rain Barrel** (✉ MM 86.7, BS ☎ 305/852–3084) is a natural and unhurried shopping showplace. Set in a tropical garden of shady trees, native shrubs, and orchids, the 1977 crafts village has shops with works by local and national artists and eight resident artists in studios, including John Hawver, noted for Florida landscapes and seascapes. The **Garden Café** (☎ 305/852–6499) is a beautiful outdoor respite, and serves a primarily vegetarian menu of sandwiches and salads until 5 PM. The **Redbone Gallery** (✉ MM 81.5, OS, 200 Industrial Dr. ☎ 305/664–2002), the largest sporting-art gallery in Florida, has hand-stitched clothing and giftware in addition to work by wood and bronze sculptors such as Kendall Van Sant; watercolorists Chet Reneson, Jeanne Dobie, and Kathleen Denis, and painters C. D. Clarke and Tim Borski. One of the most-photographed subjects in the Upper Keys is the enormous fabricated lobster by artist Richard Blaes that stands in front of **Treasure Village** (✉ MM 86.7, OS, 86729 Old Hwy. ☎ 305/852–0511), a former 1950s treasure museum that has a dozen crafts and specialty shops and a small restaurant.

Long Key

❺ *MM 70–65.5.*

Long Key is steeped in cultural and ecological history. Offering both is **Long Key State Park.** On the ocean side, the Golden Orb Trail leads onto a boardwalk through a mangrove swamp alongside a lagoon, where waterbirds congregate. The park has a campground, picnic area, restrooms and showers, a canoe trail through a tidal lagoon, and a not-very-sandy beach fronting a broad expanse of shallow grass flats. Bring a mask and snorkel to observe the marine life in this rich nursery area. Repairs and replantings following hurricanes have left the park with improved facilities, but with a lot less shade. Replanting efforts continue. Across the road, near a marker partially obscured by foliage, is the **Layton Nature Trail** (✉ MM 67.7, BS), which takes 20–30 minutes to walk and leads through tropical hardwood forest to a rocky Florida Bay shoreline overlooking shallow grass flats. A marker relates the history of the Long Key Viaduct, the first major bridge on the rail line, and the exclusive Long Key Fishing Camp, which Henry Flagler established nearby in 1906 and which attracted sportsman Zane Grey, the noted Western novelist and conservationist, who served as its first president. The camp was washed away in the 1935 hurricane and never rebuilt. For Grey's efforts, the creek running near the recreation area was named for him. ✉ *MM 67.5, OS, Box 776, 33001* ☎ *305/664–4815* ⊕ *www.dep.state.fl.us/parks* 🎟 *$3.50, $6 for 2 or more persons; canoe rental $5 per hr, $10 per day; Layton Nature Trail free* ☉ *Daily 8–sunset.*

Where to Stay & Eat

¢–$$ ✕ **Little Italy.** Good food, good value. It doesn't say it on the menu, but ask locals about this traditional family-style Italian and seafood restaurant and that is often the answer. Lunch favorites include Caesar salad, chicken marsala, stone crabs, and stuffed snapper for $4.95–$8.95. Dinners are equally tasty and well priced—pasta, chicken, seafood, veal, and steak. Try the rich, dreamy hot chocolate–pecan pie. Breakfast, too, is served, and a light-bites menu has smaller portions for kids and calorie-watchers. ⊠ *MM 68.5, BS* ☎ *305/664–4472* ☰ *AE, MC, V.*

$$ ▥ **Lime Tree Bay Resort.** This popular 2½-acre resort is on Florida Bay and far from the hubbub of other hotels and businesses. It offers excellent value. You can participate in water sports or do nothing more energetic than turn the pages of a book, head for the beach, or settle into a hammock in the pleasantly landscaped garden. Colorful bedding and coordinating valances, tropical art, and walls painted in complementary faux finishes create a sophisticated, upscale look. Five new mini and family suites have become the best places to stay, followed by the cottages out back (no bay views) and four deluxe rooms upstairs that have cathedral ceilings and skylights. The best bet for two couples traveling together is the upstairs Tree House. Most units have a balcony or porch. ⊠ *MM 68.5, BS* ⌂ *Box 839, Layton 33001* ☎ *305/664–4740 or 800/723–4519* ⎙ *305/664–0750* ⊕ *www.limetreebayresort.com* ➥ *34 rooms* ⅄ *Picnic area, BBQ, fans, some kitchens, some kitchenettes, some microwaves, refrigerators, cable TV with movies, in-room data ports, tennis court, pool, outdoor hot tub, beach, snorkeling, fishing, bicycles, no-smoking rooms* ☰ *AE, D, DC, MC, V.*

⚠ **Long Key State Park.** Trees and shrubs border all of these oceanfront tent and RV sites. By day there is biking, hiking 10 mi of trail, boating, and fishing for bonefish, permit (bigger than bonefish), and tarpon in the near-shore flats. By night there are seasonal campfire programs. All sites have water and electricity, and campground hostesses are available to help out. Reserve up to 11 months in advance by phone or in person. Sites cost $26 for electricity. ⅄ *BBQs, flush toilets, partial hook-ups (electric and water), dump station, drinking water, showers, picnic tables, electricity, public telephone, ranger station, swimming (ocean)* ➥ *60 partial hook-ups, 50 RV sites, 10 tent sites* ⊠ *MM 67.5, OS, Box 776, 33001* ☎ *305/664–4815* ⊕ *www.reserveamerica.com* ➲ *$26* ☰ *AE, D, MC, V.*

---

en route | As you cross Long Key Channel, look beside you at the old **Long Key Viaduct.** The second-longest bridge on the former rail line, this 2-mi-long structure has 222 reinforced-concrete arches. The old bridge is popular with anglers, who fish off the sides day and night.

THE MIDDLE KEYS

Stretching from Conch Key to the far side of the Seven Mile Bridge, the Middle Keys contain U.S. 1's most impressive stretch, MM 65–40, bracketed by the Keys' two longest bridges—Long Key Viaduct and Seven Mile Bridge, both historic landmarks. Activity centers on the town of Marathon, the Keys' third-largest metropolitan area. Fishing and diving are the main attractions. The deep-water fishing is superb in both bay and ocean, at places like Marathon West Hump, whose depth ranges from 500 to more than 1,000 feet. Anglers successfully fish from a half-dozen bridges, including Long Key Bridge, the Old Seven Mile Bridge, and both ends of Toms Harbor. There are also many beaches and natural areas to enjoy in the Middle Keys.

Conch & Duck Keys

6 *MM 63–61.*

This stretch of islands is rustic. Fishing dominates the economy, and many residents are descendants of immigrants from the mainland South. Across a causeway from the tiny fishing and retirement village of Conch Key is Duck Key, an upscale community and resort.

Where to Stay & Eat

$$–$$$$ ✕ **Waters Edge.** At the Hawk's Cay Resort, this plush yet relaxed restaurant gathers flavors and techniques from the Caribbean, Florida, and Europe. Favorites include St. Thomas, a land-and-sea combo of jumbo shrimp and tournedos of beef; chicken Key West, stuffed with crab, shrimp, and scallops; and Florida stone crab claws (in season); for dessert there is mud pie and coconut ice cream. Soup and a 40-item salad bar are included with dinners. Dine indoors or out. Photos on the walls recall regional history and notable visitors. ☒ *MM 61, OS, Duck Key* ☎ *305/ 743–7000* ⊟ *AE, D, DC, MC, V* ☉ *No lunch mid-Dec.–mid-Apr.*

★ $$$$ ▦ **Hawk's Cay Resort.** Popular with vacationing families is this rambling Caribbean-style retreat, which opened in 1959. Two-bedroom villas and upgrades have improved the tony resort, which has spacious rooms with wicker and earthy colors. Recreational facilities are extensive, as are supervised programs for kids and teens. The Dolphin Connection provides three educational experiences with dolphins, including the in-the-water Dolphin Discovery program, which lets you get up-close and personal with the intelligent mammals. The room rate does not include a $10–$20 daily resort fee. ☒ *MM 61, OS, Duck Key* ☎ *305/743–7000 or 888/ 443–6393* ▤ *305/743–5215* ⊕ *www.hawkscay.com* ➩ *177 rooms, 16 suites, 295 2-bedroom villas* ♿ *4 restaurants, room service, fans, some kitchens, refrigerators, cable TV with movies, in-room data ports, golf privileges, 8 tennis courts, 5 pools, health club, outdoor hot tub, massage, spa, dive shop, snorkeling, boating, jet skiing, parasailing, waterskiing, fishing, basketball, volleyball, 2 bars, shop, children's programs (ages 5–12), laundry facilities, laundry service, concierge, business services, meeting rooms, airport shuttle, car rental, no-smoking rooms* ⊟ *AE, D, DC, MC, V.*

$$ ▦ **Conch Key Cottages.** Flowering shrubs, palm trees, hammocks, a beach, and ocean breezes evoke the spirit of the tropics at this small, secluded resort composed of a fourplex motel efficiency and lattice-trimmed, pastel-color cottages furnished in reed, rattan, and wicker. One- and two-bedroom cottages have kitchens. Three cottages face the beach. Although not on the water, the small honeymoon cottage is very charming. On rare days when the wind shifts, highway noise can be distracting. Complimentary use of a double kayak is included. There's a three-night minimum and check-in or check-out on Wednesday and Saturday only from mid-December through April. ☒ *MM 62.3, OS* ⌖ *R.*

R. 1, Box 424, Marathon 33050 ☎ *305/289–1377 or 800/330–1577*
🖷 *305/743–8207* ⊕ *www.conchkeycottages.com* ⇱ *12 units* ⚒ *Picnic area, BBQ, fans, some kitchens, some kitchenettes, cable TV, some in-room VCRs, pool, hot tub, beach, dock, snorkeling, laundry facilities; no room phones, no smoking* ▤ *D, MC, V.*

Grassy Key

❼ *MM 60–57.*

Local lore has it that this sleepy little key was named not for its vegetation—mostly native trees and shrubs—but for an early settler with the name Grassy. It's primarily inhabited by a few families who operate small fishing camps and motels.

The original *Flipper* movie popularized the notion of dolphins interacting with humans. The film's creator, Milton Santini, also created this facility, the **Dolphin Research Center,** now home to a colony of dolphins and sea lions. The not-for-profit organization has tours, narrated programs every 30 minutes, and several programs that allow interaction with dolphins in the water (Dolphin Encounter) or from a submerged platform (Dolphin Splash). Some programs have age or height restrictions, and some require 30-day advance reservations. ⊠ *MM 59, BS* ⬡ *Box 522875, Marathon Shores 33052* ☎ *305/289–1121 general information, 305/289–0002 interactive program information* ⊕ *www.dolphins.org* ✉ *Tours $17.50, Dolphin Splash $100, Dolphin Encounter $165* ◷ *Daily 9–5; walking tours daily at 10, 11, 12:30, 2, 3:30, 4:30.*

off the beaten path

CURRY HAMMOCK STATE PARK – On the ocean and bay sides of U.S. 1, this littoral park covers 260 acres of upland hammock, wetlands, and mangroves. On the bay side, there's a trail through thick hardwoods to a rocky shoreline. The ocean side is more developed, with a sandy beach, a clean bathhouse, picnic tables, playground, grills, and a parking lot. Brown park signs mark the entrance. Plans for a campground and entrance fees are still undecided. Locals consider the trails that meander under canopies of arching mangroves one of the best areas for kayaking in the Keys. Manatees frequent the area, and it's a rich repository for birders. Information is provided by Long Key State Park. ⊠ *MM 57, OS, Crawl Key* ☎ *305/664–4815* ◷ *Daily 8–sunset.*

Where to Stay

$ 🏨 **Bonefish Resort.** Tucked among palms, banana leaves, and hibiscus flowers, this hideaway sits along a row of small, unfussy beachfront resorts on Grassy Key. Rooms, efficiencies, and suites are decorated with floral linens, wicker, tile floors, and tropical motifs painted by a local artist on entrance doors and some interior walls. The resort has a small beach and a waterfront pool. Hammocks, chaises, and a covered waterfront deck invite relaxation, and kayaks and paddleboats encourage exploration. Check in/out is at next-door sister property Yellowtail Inn, which has cottages and efficiencies starting at $109 in winter. ⊠ *MM 58, OS, 58070 Overseas Hwy., 33050* ☎ *305/743–7107 or 800/274–*

CLOSE ENCOUNTERS OF THE FLIPPER KIND

HERE IN THE FLORIDA KEYS, *where Milton Santini created the original 1963 Flipper movie, close encounters of the Flipper kind are an everyday occurrence at a handful of facilities that allow you to commune with trained dolphins. There are in-water and waterside programs. The former are the most sought-after and require advance reservations. All of the programs emphasize education and consist of three parts: first, you learn about dolphin physiology and behavior from a marine biologist or researcher; then you go waterside for an orientation on dos and don'ts (for example, don't talk with your hands—you might, literally, send the wrong signal); finally, you interact with the dolphins—into the water you go.*

For the in-water programs, the dolphins swim around you and cuddle up next to you. If you lie on your back with your feet out, they use their snouts to push you around; or grab onto a dorsal fin and hang on for an exciting ride. The in-water encounter lasts about 10 to 25 minutes, depending on the program. On waterside-interaction programs, participants feed, shake hands, kiss, and do tricks with the dolphins from a submerged platform. The programs vary from facility to facility but share a few rules, and the entire program, from registration to departure, takes about two hours. The best time to go is when it's warm, from March through December. You spend a lot of time near or in and out of the water, and even with a wetsuit on you can get cold on a chilly day. Call ahead to get information on restrictions (there are often age or height requirements) and other relevant details.

Dolphin Connection at Hawk's Cay Resort. *Marine biologists at the Dolphin Connection inspire awareness and promote conservation through programs at this stylish mid-Keys resort. Dolphin Discovery is an in-water, nonswim program that lasts about 45 minutes and lets you kiss, touch, and feed the dolphins.* ⊠ MM 61, OS, 61 Hawks Cay Blvd., Duck Key ☎ 888/814–9174 ⌨ $100 resort guests, $110 nonguests.

Dolphin Cove. *The educational part of the Dolphin Encounter program takes place on a 30-minute boat ride on adjoining Florida Bay. Then it's back to the facilities lagoon for a get-acquainted session from a platform. Then you slip into the water for the program's highlight: swimming and playing with your new dolphin pals.* ⊠ MM 101.9, BS, 101900 Overseas Hwy., Key Largo ☎ 305/451–4060 ⌨ $160.

Dolphin Research Center. *This not-for-profit organization has a colony of Atlantic bottlenose dolphins and California sea lions. Dolphin Encounter is a swim-interaction program, and in Dolphin Splash you stand on a submerged platform rather than swim.* ⊠ MM 59, Marathon Shores ☎ 305/289–1121 or 305/289–0002 ⌨ Dolphin Encounter $155, Dolphin Splash $80.

Dolphins Plus, Inc. *Programs here emphasize education and therapy. Natural Swim begins with a one-hour briefing; then you don snorkel gear and enter the water to become totally immersed in the dolphins' world.* ⊠ MM 99, 31 Corrine Pl., Key Largo ☎ 305/451–1993 or 866/860–7946 ⌨ $125.

Theater of the Sea. *The Dolphin Swim program at this marine park starts with a 30-minute classroom session and orientation. Then, through trained behaviors, including kisses, dorsal tows, and jumps, dolphins interact with swimmers in a 15-foot-deep saltwater lagoon.* ⊠ MM 84.7, 84721 Overseas Hwy., Islamorada ☎ 305/664–2431 ⌨ $140.

— Diane P. Marshall

9949 🖶 *305/743–9014* ⊕ *www.bonefishresort.com* 🗭 *5 suites, 6 efficiencies, 2 rooms ♨ BBQ, fans, some kitchens, microwaves, refrigerators, cable TV, in-room VCRs, beach, boating, fishing, bicycles, some pets allowed (fee)* ▤ *D, MC, V.*

$ 🏨 **Gulf View Waterfront Resort.** With just 11 guest rooms and one- and two-bedroom apartments, this cozy resort feels more like a large private home than a hotel. Other than the talking, squawking, and singing of exotic birds in large cages, about the only sounds you'll hear while putting on the small green, dozing in a hammock, or floating in the pool are the rustling of palm leaves, the lapping of waves, and the splashing of canoe and kayak paddles. ⊠ *MM 58.5, BS, 58743 Overseas Hwy., 33050* ☎ *305/289–1414* 🖶 *305/743–8629* ⊕ *www.gulfviewwaterfrontresort.com* 🗭 *2 rooms, 6 suites, 3 efficiencies ♨ Picnic area, BBQ, fans, some kitchens, microwaves, refrigerators, cable TV, in-room data ports, putting green, pool, dock, boating, fishing, laundry facilities, some pets allowed (fee)* ▤ *AE, D, MC, V.*

$ 🏨 **Valhalla Beach Motel.** Just steps from the water, this simple motel has rooms, efficiencies, and a suite. Lounge on the beach or read in the Adirondack chairs, grill dinner on a barbecue, or paddle a canoe through mangrove trails in the neighboring state park. It's quiet here, and the views of the undisturbed outdoors are awesome. ⊠ *MM 56.3, OS, 56243 Ocean Dr., Crawl Key 33050* ☎ *305/289–0616* 🗭 *4 rooms, 1 suite, 5 efficiencies ♨ Fans, some kitchens, some refrigerators, cable TV, beach, dock, boating; no room phones* ▤ *No credit cards.*

¢ 🏨 **Valhalla Point.** This unpretentious Crawl Key motel with a to-die-for waterfront location has the feel of a friend's simple beach house. There are hammocks and chaises on a very good beach, a dock from which manatees are frequently sighted, picnic tables, barbecue grills, and kayaks and canoes, a nice touch, since the property borders Curry Hammock State Park. ⊠ *MM 56.2, OS, 56223 Ocean Dr., Crawl Key 33050* ☎ *305/360–2726* ⊕ *www.keysresort.com* 🗭 *1 room, 3 efficiencies, 1 suite ♨ Picnic area, some kitchens, cable TV, beach, dock, boating; no room phones* ▤ *MC, V.*

Marathon

8 *MM 53–47.5.*

Marathon, an independent municipality in the Middle Keys, began as a commercial fishing village in the early 1800s. Pirates, salvagers, fishermen, spongers, and, later, farmers eked out a living, traveling by boat between islands. About half the population were blacks who stoked charcoal furnaces for a living. According to local lore, Marathon was renamed when a worker commented that it was a marathon task to rebuild the railway across the 6-mi island after a 1906 hurricane. The railroad brought businesses and a hotel, and today Marathon is a bustling town by Keys standards. Fishing, diving, and boating are the primary attractions.

Tucked away from the highway behind a stand of trees, Crane Point—part of a 63-acre tract that includes the last-known undisturbed thatch-palm hammock—is delightfully undeveloped greenery. It's the site of the

🐾 **Museums and Nature Center of Crane Point Hammock,** which includes the

Museum of Natural History of the Florida Keys, with a few dioramas, a shell exhibit, and displays on Keys geology, wildlife, and cultural history. Also here is the **Florida Keys Children's Museum,** with iguanas, fish, and a replica of a 17th-century Spanish galleon and pirate dress-up room where children can play as swashbucklers. Two other exhibits explore the rain forest and butterfly meadows. Outside, on the 1-mi indigenous loop trail, visit the remnants of a Bahamian village, site of the restored **George Adderly House,** the oldest surviving example of Bahamian tabby (a cement-type material created from sand and seashells) construction outside of Key West. A newly constructed Cracker house demonstrates the vernacular housing of the early 1900s. A boardwalk crosses wetlands, a river, and mangroves before ending at Adderly Village. From November to Easter, docent-led tours, included in the price, are available; bring good walking shoes and bug repellent during warm weather. Full-moon kayak tours ($30) to an offshore island last two hours. ⊠ *MM 50.5, BS, 5550 Overseas Hwy., Box 536, 33050* ☎ *305/743–9100* 💲 *$7.50* ◷ *Mon.–Sat. 9–5, Sun. noon–5; call to arrange trail tours.*

If you don't get a contact buzz from breathing in the robust aroma at **Leigh Ann's Coffee House** (⊠ 7537 Overseas Hwy. ☎ 305/743–2001), order an espresso shot, Cuban or Italian, for a satisfying jolt. Pastries are baked fresh daily, but the biscuits with sausage gravy and the Italian frittata cooked with no fat are among the big movers. Soups, salads, and sandwiches, as well as beer and wine, make up the rest of the menu, served until 6 PM in season, until 4 PM at other times. They accept major credit cards and are closed on Sunday.

Pleasant, shaded picnic kiosks overlook a grassy stretch and the Atlantic Ocean at **Sombrero Beach.** Separate areas allow swimmers, jet boaters, and windsurfers to share the beach. There are lots of facilities, as well as a grassy park with barbecue grills, picnic kiosks, showers, rest rooms, plus a baseball diamond, a large playground, and a volleyball court. The park is accessible for travelers with disabilities and allows leashed pets. Turn left at the traffic light in Marathon and follow signs to the end. ⊠ *MM 50, OS, Sombrero Rd.* ☎ *305/743–0033* 💲 *Free* ◷ *Daily 8–sunset.*

off the beaten path

PIGEON KEY – There's much to like about this 5-acre island under the Old Seven Mile Bridge. It's reached by walking or riding a tram across a 2¼-mi section of the old bridge. Once there, tour the island on your own with a brochure or join a guided tour. The tour explores the buildings that formed the early-20th-century work camp for the Overseas Railroad, which linked the mainland to Key West. Later, their uses changed as the island became a fish camp, then a park, and then government administration headquarters. Today, the focus is on Florida Keys culture, environmental education, and marine research. Exhibits in a museum and a video recall the history of the railroad, the Keys, and railroad baron Henry M. Flagler. Pick up the shuttle at the depot on Knight's Key (MM 47, OS). ⊠ *MM 45, OS, Box 500130, Pigeon Key 33050* ☎ *305/289–0025 general information, 305/743–5999 tickets* ⊕ *www.pigeonkey.org* 💲 *$8.50* ◷ *Daily 10–5, tours hourly 10–3.*

Where to Stay & Eat

$$–$$$$
Fodor'sChoice
★
✕ **Barracuda Grill.** If you pigeonhole Keys food as grilled fish, Barracuda Grill will be a revelation. The sophisticated, eclectic menu capitalizes on local seafood but is equally represented by tender, aged Angus beef, rack of lamb, and even braised pork shank. Innovation is in everything but not at the expense of good, solid cooking. Local favorites include Francesca's voodoo stew, with scallops, shrimp, and veggies in a spicy tomato-saffron stock, and sashimi of yellowfin tuna with wasabi and tamari. Decadent desserts include a rich key lime cheesecake. The well-thought-out wine list is heavily Californian. ⊠ *MM 49.5, BS, 4290 Overseas Hwy.* ☎ *305/743–3314* ⌂ *Reservations not accepted* ▤ *AE, MC, V* ☻ *Closed Sun. No lunch.*

¢–$$$
✕ **Key Colony Inn.** The inviting aroma of an Italian kitchen pervades this popular family-owned restaurant. The menu has well-prepared chicken, steak, pasta, and veal dishes, and the service is friendly and attentive. For lunch there are fish and steak entrées served with fries, salad, and bread. At dinner you can't miss with traditional Continental dishes like veal Oscar and New York strip, or such Italian specialties as seafood Italiano, a light dish of scallops and shrimp sautéed in garlic butter, served over a bed of linguine with a hint of marinara sauce. ⊠ *MM 54, OS, 700 W. Ocean Dr., Key Colony Beach* ☎ *305/743–0100* ▤ *AE, MC, V.*

¢–$$
✕ **Keys Fisheries Market and Marina.** From the parking lot the commercial warehouse with fishing boats docked alongside barely hints at the restaurant inside. Order at the window outside, pick up your food in the market, then dine at waterfront picnic tables, some under a plastic canopy. Fresh seafood and a token hamburger are the only things on the menu. A lobster Reuben ($13.95) served on thick slices of toasted bread is the signature dish. There's also a 16-flavor ice cream bar and a beer-wine bar. ⊠ *MM 49, BS, end of 35th St.* ☎ *305/743–4353* ▤ *MC, V.*

★ ¢–$$
✕ **7 Mile Grill.** This nearly-50-year-old, weatherworn, open-air restaurant easily could serve as a movie set for a 1950s-era black-and-white movie based in the tropics. At the Marathon end of the Seven Mile Bridge, it serves up friendly service that rivals the casual food at breakfast, lunch, and dinner. Favorites on the mostly seafood menu include creamy shrimp bisque, grouper, and dolphinfish grilled, broiled, or fried. Don't pass up the authentic key lime pie, which won the local paper's "Best in the Keys" award three years in a row. ⊠ *MM 47, BS* ☎ *305/743–4481* ▤ *MC, V* ☻ *Closed Wed.; closed Thurs. mid-Apr.–mid-Nov. and at owner's discretion Aug. and Sept.*

¢–$
✕ **Fish Tales Market and Eatery.** Fans of the Island City Fishmarket won't be too disappointed about its sale once they learn that the new owners are George, Jackie, Johnny, and Gary Eigner of the former Grassy Key DB Seafood Grille (which has closed). They serve some of the DB's favorite dishes, such as grilled fish with homemade wasabi ($9.95) and German snapper sandwich, fried snapper on grilled rye with slaw and melted cheese. The market section ships seafood throughout the country. Plan to dine early, as it's only open until 6:30 Monday–Thursday

and 8:30 Friday and Saturday. ⊠ *MM 53, OS, 11711 Overseas Hwy.* ☎ *305/743–9196 or 888/662–4822* ▤ *AE, MC, V* ⊘ *Closed Sun.*

¢–$ ✕ **Takara.** This is that casual and perhaps unlikely little Japanese restaurant you were hoping to find for fresh sushi, flavorful soba noodles, and light, crispy tempura. While two chefs work at an open dining-room bar making sushi, sashimi, and rolls, another is in the kitchen preparing cooked dishes. Order from a menu of nearly 30 "tapas" appetizers to sample the full range of flavors. Save room for a slice of icy-hot tempura cheesecake. The interior is plain, and the clientele is heavily local. ⊠ *MM 49.5, BS, 3740 Overseas Hwy.* ☎ *305/743–0505* ▤ *D, DC, MC, V* ⊘ *Closed Sun.*

★ $$$ ▦ **Seascape Ocean Resort.** The charming lobby filled with soothing sea colors and original artwork gives way to nine pastel-color guest rooms decorated with more original artwork, hand-painted headboards, and fresh flowers and fruit. Transforming the 5-acre oceanfront property with a large, two-story bay-front house into an exclusive yet unsnobbish retreat was the inspiration of painter Sara Stites and her husband Bill, a magazine photographer. Swim, kayak, or relax around the pool, at the beach, or under a shade tree. Continental breakfast is complimentary as is wine and hors d'oeuvres at 6. Guests can kayak out to a nearby bird rookery. Guests with computers can access the Internet through Wi-Fi. ⊠ *MM 50.5, OS, 1075 75th St., 33050* ☎ *305/743–6455 or 800/332–7327* 🖷 *305/743–8469* ⊕ *www.seascaperesort.us* ➥ *9 rooms* ⌂ *Some BBQs, fans, some kitchens, refrigerators, cable TV, pool, beach, dock, boating; no room phones, no kids under 12* ▤ *AE, MC, V* ⊚ *CP.*

$$ ▦ **Coral Lagoon.** Private sundecks with hammocks have calming views of a deep-water canal and pretty landscaping. Cheerfully painted duplex cottages have king or twin beds, sofa beds, and lots of extras not usually available at this price, including hair dryers, morning coffee, dockage, barbecues, video library ($1 rental), and lots of sports equipment. For a fee, use a private beach club and go on scuba and snorkel trips arranged through the Diving Site, a dive shop that also offers certification. ⊠ *MM 53.5, OS, 12399 Overseas Hwy., 33050* ☎ *305/289–0121* 🖷 *305/289–0195* ⊕ *www.corallagoonresort.com* ➥ *18 efficiencies* ⌂ *BBQ, fans, kitchens, cable TV, in-room VCRs, tennis court, pool, dive shop, dock, snorkeling, fishing, bicycles, laundry facilities, no-smoking rooms* ▤ *AE, D, MC, V.*

$–$$ ▦ **Coconut Cay Resort & Marina.** The whimsically painted one-story buildings along U.S. 1, on a peninsula in Florida Bay, comprise a sprawling village of reasonably priced guest rooms, efficiencies, suites, and cottages. Accommodations have tile floors and wicker and rattan furniture. The sunning beach (not accessible for swimming) and pool are far from the highway. There's free dockage (up to 21 feet) along a canal and in the marina. Adderley's Pavilion, at the end of the sandy peninsula, has BBQs and picnic tables, well-suited for large family gatherings. It's also where guests—an eclectic mix of couples, families, and business travelers—seem to gather harmoniously to watch the sun set. There is an airport nearby, though it does not have commercial airline service. ⊠ *MM*

51, BS, 7196 Overseas Hwy., 33050 ☎ *305/289–7672 or 877/354–7356*
☏ *305/289–0186* ⊕ *www.coconutcay.com* ♿ *Picnic areas, BBQs, some*
kitchens, some kitchenettes, some microwaves, refrigerators, cable TV,
pool, dock, boating, marina, playground, some pets allowed; no smok-
ing ▱ *D, MC, V.*

Sports & the Outdoors

BIKING   Tooling around on two wheels is a good way to see Marathon. There
are paved paths along Aviation Boulevard on the bay side of Marathon
Airport, the four-lane section of the Overseas Highway through Marathon,
Sadowski Causeway to Key Colony Beach, Sombrero Beach Road to
the beach, and the roads on Boot Key (across a bridge on 20th Street,
OS). There's easy cycling on a 1-mi off-road path that connects to the
2 mi of the Old Seven Mile Bridge that leads to Pigeon Key.

"Have bikes, will deliver" could be the motto of **Bike Marathon Bike Rentals**
(☎ 305/743–3204), which gets beach cruisers to your hotel door for $45
per week, including a helmet. It's open Monday through Saturday 9–4
and Sunday 9–2.

Equipment Locker Sport & Cycle (✉ MM 53, BS ☎ 305/289–1670) rents
cruisers for $10 per day, $50 per week, and mountain bikes for $15 per
day and $75 per week for adults and children. It also rents in-line skates
for $25 per day, including pads and helmet. It's open weekdays 9–6, Sat-
urday 9–5, and Sunday 10–3.

BOATING   **Fish 'n' Fun** (✉ MM 53.5, OS ☎ 305/743–2275), next to the Boat
House Marina, lets you get out on the water on 18- to 25-foot powerboats starting at $115 for a half day, $160–$250 for a full day. You also
can pick up bait, tackle, licenses, and snorkel gear. For those who want
a live-aboard vacation, **Florida Keys Bareboat Charters** (☎ 305/743–
0090 ⊕ www.floridakeysbareboatchartercompany.com) rents 27-foot
Catalina and Balboa sailboats for $200 a day, $950 a week, with a two-
day minimum. The fee includes home-port dockage.

FISHING   Morning and afternoon, fish for mahimahi, grouper, and other deep-
sea creatures aboard the 75-foot *Marathon Lady* (✉ MM 53, OS, at 117th
St., 33050 ☎ 305/743–5580) that departs on half-day ($33, plus $3 equipment) excursions from the Vaca Cut Bridge, north of Marathon. Join
them for night fishing ($40, plus $3) from 6:30 to midnight from Memorial Day to Labor Day; it's especially beautiful on a full-moon night.
Captain Jim Purcell, a deep-sea specialist for ESPN's *The American Out-*
doorsman, provides one of the best values in fishing in the Keys. His
★   **Sea Dog Charters** (✉ MM 47.5, BS ☎ 305/743–8255), next to the 7 Mile
Grill, has half- and full-day offshore, reef and wreck, tarpon, and backcountry fishing trips as well as combination fishing and snorkeling trips
on the 32-foot *Bad Dog* for up to six people. The cost is $59.99 per
person for a half day, regardless of whether your group fills the boat,
and includes bait, light tackle, licensing, ice, and coolers. If you prefer
an all-day private charter on a 37-foot boat, he offers those, too, for
$550–$600.

GOLF **Key Colony Golf & Tennis** (✉ MM 53.5, OS, 8th St., Key Colony Beach ☎ 305/289–1533), a 9-hole par-3 course near Marathon, charges $9 for the course, $2 per person for club rental, and $1 for a pull cart. There are no tee times and there's no rush. Play from 7:30 to dusk. A little golf shop meets basic golf needs. There are two lighted tennis courts open from 7:30 to 10. Hourly rates are $4 for singles, $6 for doubles.

SCUBA & **Hall's Diving Center and Career Institute** (✉ MM 48.5, BS, 1994 Over-
SNORKELING seas Hwy., 33050 ☎ 305/743–5929 or 800/331–4255), next to Faro Blanco Resort, has been diving and training divers for more than 40 years. Along with conventional twice-a-day snorkel and two-tank dive trips to the reefs at Sombrero Lighthouse and wrecks, including *Thunderbolt*, the company also offers wet submarine dives, diver propulsion vehicles, rebreathers, and digital and video photography.

en route The **Seven Mile Bridge** is one of the most-photographed images in the Keys. Actually measuring 6.79 mi long, it connects the Middle and Lower Keys and is believed to be the world's longest segmental bridge. It has 39 expansion joints separating its cement sections. Each April, runners gather in Marathon for the annual Seven Mile Bridge Run. The expanse running parallel to it is what remains of the **Old Seven Mile Bridge,** an engineering marvel in its day that's now on the National Register of Historic Places. It rested on a record 546 concrete piers. No cars are allowed on the old bridge today, but a 2.2-mi segment is open for biking, walking, and rollerblading, with a terminus at historic Pigeon Key.

THE LOWER KEYS

In truth, the Lower Keys include Key West, but since it's covered in its own section and is as different from the rest of the Lower Keys as peanut butter is from jelly, this section covers just the limestone keys between MM 37 and MM 9. From Bahia Honda Key south, islands are clustered, smaller, and more numerous, a result of ancient tidal waters' flowing between the Florida Straits and the gulf. Here you're likely to see more birds and mangroves than other tourists, and more refuges, beaches, and campgrounds than museums, restaurants, and hotels. The islands are made up of two types of limestone, both more dense than the highly permeable Key Largo limestone of the Upper Keys. As a result, fresh water forms pools rather than percolating, creating watering holes that support Key deer, alligators, fish, snakes, Lower Keys rabbits, raccoons, migratory ducks, Key cotton and silver rice rats, pines, saw palmettos, silver palms, grasses, and ferns. (Many of these animals and plants can be seen in the National Key Deer Refuge on Big Pine Key.) Nature was generous with her beauty in the Lower Keys, which have both Looe Key Reef, arguably the Keys' most beautiful coral reef tract, and Bahia Honda State Park, considered one of the best beaches in the world for its fine sand dunes, clear warm waters, and panoramic vista of bridges, hammocks, and azure sky and sea.

Bahia Honda Key

❾ *MM 38–36.*

Fodor'sChoice
★ Sun-soaked, 524-acre **Bahia Honda State Park** sprawls across both sides of the highway, giving it 2½ mi of beautiful sandy beaches—the best in the Keys—on both the Atlantic Ocean and the Gulf of Mexico. Although swimming, kayaking, fishing, and boating are the main reasons to come, there are many other activities, including walks on the Silver Palm Trail, with rare West Indian plants and several species found nowhere else in the Keys. Seasonal ranger-led nature programs might include illustrated talks on the history of the Overseas Railroad. There are 3½ mi of flat park roads for biking, rental cabins, a campground, a snack bar, gift shop, 19-slip marina, and a concessionaire for snorkeling. Get a panoramic view of the island from what's left of the railroad—the Bahia Honda Bridge. ⊠ *MM 37, OS, 36850 Overseas Hwy., 33043* ☎ *305/872–2353* ⊕ *www.dep.state.fl.us/parks* 🖀 *$3.50 for 1 person, $6 per vehicle for 2 people, 50¢ each additional person; $1.50 per pedestrian or bicyclist* ☉ *Daily 8–sunset.*

Where to Stay

$$ 🏠 **Bahia Honda State Park.** You usually have to pay big bucks for the caliber of water views available at the cabins here. Each cabin is completely furnished, with air-conditioning (although there's no television, radio, or phone); each has two bedrooms, full kitchen, and bath; and sleeps six. The park also has popular campsites ($26 per night), suitable for motor homes and tents. Cabins and campsites usually book up early, so reserve up to 11 months before your planned visit. ⊠ *MM 37, OS, 36850 Overseas Hwy., 33043* ☎ *305/872–2353 or 800/326–3521* ⊕ *www.reserveamerica.com* 🛏 *80 campsites, 48 RV sites, 32 tent sites; 3 duplex cabins* ♿ *Picnic area, snack bar, BBQ, kitchens, beach, dive shop, dock, snorkeling, boating, marina, fishing, bicycles, shop; no room phones, no room TVs* 🖃 *AE, D, MC, V.*

The Outdoors

Bahia Honda Dive Shop (⊠ MM 37, OS ☎ 305/872–3210 ⊕ www. bahiahondapark.com), the concessionaire at Bahia Honda State Park, manages a 19-slip marina; rents wet suits, snorkel equipment, and corrective masks; and operates twice-a-day offshore-reef snorkel trips ($28 plus $6 for equipment) off-season and thrice-a-day in-season that run almost three hours (with 90 minutes on the reef). Park visitors looking for other fun can rent kayaks ($10 per hour single, $18 double), bicycles, and beach chairs.

Big Pine Key

❿ *MM 32–30.*

In the Florida Keys, more than 20 animals and plants are endangered or threatened. Among them is the Key deer, which stands about 30 inches at the shoulders and is a subspecies of the Virginia white-tailed deer. The 8,542-acre **National Key Deer Refuge** was established in 1957 to protect the dwindling population of Key deer. These deer once ranged throughout the Lower and Middle Keys, but hunting, habitat destruction, and a growing human population had caused their numbers to decline to fewer than 50. However, under the refuge's aegis the deer have made a comeback, increasing their numbers to around 800. The best place to see Key deer in the refuge is at the end of Key Deer Boulevard (Route 940), off U.S. 1, and on No Name Key, a sparsely populated island just east of Big Pine Key. Deer may turn up along the road at any time of day, so drive slowly. Feeding them is against the law and puts them in danger. The refuge also has 22 listed endangered and threatened species of plants and animals, including 5 that are found nowhere else in the world. The **Blue Hole**, a quarry left over from railroad days, is the largest body of fresh water in the Keys. From the observation platform and nearby walking trail, you might see alligators, birds, turtles, Key deer, and other wildlife. There are two well-marked trails: the Jack Watson Nature Trail (⅔ mi), named after an environmentalist and the refuge's first warden; and the Fred Mannillo Nature Trail, one of the most wheelchair-accessible places to see an unspoiled pine rockland forest. The visitor center has exhibits on Keys biology and ecology. The refuge also provides information on the Key West National Wildlife Refuge and the Great White Heron National Wildlife Refuge. Both, accessible only by water, are popular with kayak outfitters. ⊠ *Visitor Center–Headquarters, Big Pine Shopping Center, 28950 Watson Blvd., MM 30.5, BS* ☎ *305/872–0774* ⊕ *nationalkeydeer.fws. gov* ☒ *Free* ☉ *Daily sunrise–sunset; headquarters weekdays 8–5.*

Where to Stay & Eat

¢–$ ✕ **No Name Pub.** If you don't like change you'll be delighted by this ramshackle establishment, in existence since 1936. Locals come for the cold beer, excellent pizza, and sometimes questionable companionship. The owners have conceded to the times by introducing a full menu, adding "city food" like pasta, seafood baskets ($10.95), and chicken wings. The lighting is poor, the furnishings are rough, and the jukebox doesn't play Ricky Martin. It's hard to find but worth the search if you want a singular Keys experience. ⊠ *MM 30, BS, N. Watson Blvd., Turn north at Big Pine Key traffic light, right at the fork, left at the 4-way stop, and then over a humpback bridge; pub is on left, before the No Name Bridge* ☎ *305/872–9115* ☐ *D, MC, V.*

¢ ✕ **Good Food Conspiracy.** Like good wine, this natural-food eatery and market surrenders its pleasures a little at a time. Step inside to the aroma of brewing coffee, then pick up the scent of fresh strawberries or carrots blending into a smoothie, followed by an earthy hummus redolence. Order raw or cooked vegetarian and vegan dishes, organic soups, salads, sandwiches, and desserts, along with organic and vegan coffees, smoothies, juices, and teas. Bountiful sandwiches like the popular organic turkey on whole wheat pita or chapatti bread are served with vegetables, sprouts, and mixed greens. Sit indoors at the bar and chat with local customers, or outdoors in the herb garden. Dine early: it closes at 7, and at 5 on Sunday. ⊠ *MM 30.2, OS* ☎ *305/872–3945.*

$$–$$$ ▦ **The Barnacle.** With very little air pollution in the area, the star-flecked moonlit nights seen from this B&B's atrium are as romantic as the sunny days spent lazing on the beach or on the waterfront balcony. Own-

ers Tim and Jane Marquis offer two second-floor rooms in the main house; one in a cottage with a kitchen; another, below the house, that opens to the beach. Guest rooms are large. Paddle your kayak out to the ocean from the beach, or to a preserve in the bay, where the owners have a boat dock. Olfactory alert at low tide: you'll get a healthy whiff of sulfur. ⊠ *MM 33, OS, 1557 Long Beach Dr., 33043* ☎ *305/872–3298 or 800/465–9100* 🖷 *305/872–3863* ⊕ *www.thebarnacle.net* 🛏 *4 rooms* ♿ *Fans, some kitchens, refrigerators, cable TV, outdoor hot tub, beach, bicycles; no kids under 16, no smoking* ▤ *D, MC, V* ⫶◯⫶ *BP.*

★ **$$** 🏨 **Casa Grande.** On a beautiful white-sand beach abutting a rocky shoreline, this adults-only B&B offers a gracious island stay under the proprietorship of Kathleen Threlkeld. Her warm island personality pervades the Mediterranean-style house, which has a massive Spanish door, mainly contemporary furnishings, and high open-beam ceilings. There are a screened porch and rich Berber carpeting in the spacious guest rooms. A screened, second-story waterfront atrium gives you the opportunity to gaze out across the soothing sea. On cool nights, cozy up to the sitting-room fireplace or watch TV. ⊠ *MM 33, OS, 1619 Long Beach Dr., Box 430378, 33043* ☎*305/872–2878* ⊕*www.floridakeys.net/casagrande* 🛏*3 rooms* ♿ *Picnic area, BBQ, fans, refrigerators, hot tub, beach, dock, snorkeling, windsurfing, boating, fishing, bicycles; no room TVs, no kids, no smoking* ▤ *No credit cards* ⫶◯⫶ *BP.*

$$ 🏨 **Deer Run.** Enjoy Florida wildlife up-close at this 2-acre beachfront B&B. A herd of Key deer regularly forages along the beach a few feet from the back door. Innkeeper Sue Abbott also keeps cats and caged tropical birds. She is caring and informed, well settled and hospitable. Two large oceanfront rooms are furnished with whitewashed wicker, king-size beds, and coffeemakers. An upstairs unit looks out on the sea through trees. Guests share a living room, 52-foot veranda cooled by paddle fans, hammocks, a barbecue grill, and water toys. Breakfast is no longer served. ⊠ *MM 33, OS, 1997 Long Beach Dr., Box 430431, 33043* ☎ *305/872–2015* 🖷 *305/872–2842* ⊕ *floridakeys.net/deer* 🛏*3 rooms* ♿ *Picnic area, BBQ, fans, microwaves, refrigerators, cable TV, outdoor hot tub, beach, snorkeling, windsurfing, boating, fishing, bicycles; no kids under 13, no smoking* ▤ *No credit cards.*

★ **¢–$$** 🏨 **Big Pine Key Fishing Lodge.** It's a family affair at this 30-year-old combination lodge and campground. Rooms and RV and tent sites ($30–$37 per site) are attractively priced. Rooms have tile floors, wicker furniture, doors that allow sea breezes to blow through, queen-size beds, a second-bedroom loft, and vaulted ceilings. A skywalk joins them with a pool and deck. Camping sites range from rustic to full hook-ups. Immaculately clean tile lines the spacious bathhouse for campers. Separate game and recreation rooms have TVs, organized family-oriented activities, and other amusements, and there's dockage along a 735-foot canal. A three-day minimum stay is required. Discounts are available for week- and month-long stays. ⊠ *MM 33, OS, Box 430513, 33043* ☎ *305/872–2351* 🖷 *305/872–3868* 🛏 *16 rooms; 158 campsites, 101 with full hook-ups, 57 without hook-ups* ♿ *Picnic area, BBQ, some kitchens, some microwaves, some refrigerators, cable TV, pool, dock,* *boating, marina, Ping-Pong, shuffleboard, recreation room, playground, Internet* ⊟ *D, MC, V.*

The Outdoors

BIKING A good 10 mi of paved and unpaved roads run from MM 30.3, BS, along Wilder Road, across the bridge to No Name Key, and along Key Deer Boulevard into the National Key Deer Refuge. You might see some Key deer. Stay off the trails that lead into wetlands, where fat tires can do damage to the environment.

Marty Baird, owner of **Big Pine Bicycle Center** (⊠ MM 30.9, BS ☎ 305/ 872–0130), is an avid rider and enjoys sharing his knowledge of great places to ride. He's also skilled at selecting the right bike for customers to rent or purchase, and he knows his repairs, too. His old-fashioned single-speed, fat-tire cruisers for adults rent for $7 per half day, $9 for a full day, and $36 a week, second week $18; children for $6, $7, $28, and $11. Helmets, baskets, and locks are included. Although the shop is closed on Sunday, join Marty there most Sunday mornings at 8 in winter for a free off-road fun ride.

FISHING Fish with pros year-round in air-conditioned comfort with **Strike Zone Charters** (⊠ MM 29.6, BS, 29675 Overseas Hwy. ☎ 305/872–9863 or 800/654–9560 ⊕ www.strikezonecharter.com). Deep-sea charter rates are $500 for a half day, $650 for a full day. It also offers flats fishing in the Gulf of Mexico.

SCUBA & **Strike Zone Charters** (⊠ MM 29.6, BS, 29675 Overseas Hwy. ☎ 305/
SNORKELING 872–9863 or 800/654–9560 ⊕ www.strikezonecharter.com) leads dive excursions to the wreck of the 210-foot *Adolphus Busch* ($50), and scuba ($40) and snorkel ($30) trips to Looe Key Reef.

WATER SPORTS **Big Pine Kayak Adventures** (⊠ Old Wooden Bridge Fishing Camp, MM 30, BS, turn right at traffic light, continue on Wilder Rd. toward No Name Key ☎ 305/872–7474 ⊕ www.keyskayaktours.com) has a complete rental fleet and makes it very convenient to rent kayaks. Along with bringing kayaks to your lodging or put-in point anywhere between Seven Mile Bridge and Stock Island, the group, headed by Captain Bill Keogh, author of *The Florida Keys Paddling Guide*, will rent you a kayak and then ferry you—called taxi-yaking—to remote islands with explicit instructions on how to paddle back on your own. Rentals are by the half day or full day. There are also myriad dolphin excursions, and tours, starting at $125. Kayak fishing charters are his most popular outings.

Little Torch Key

⓫ *MM 29–10.*

With a few exceptions, Little Torch Key and its neighbor islands, Cudjoe Key and Geiger Key, are more jumping-off points for divers headed for Looe Key Reef, a few miles offshore, than destinations themselves. They also serve as a refuge for those who want to make forays into Key West, but not stay there.

The aroma of rich, roasting coffee beans at **Baby's Coffee** (✉ MM 15, OS, Saddlebunch Keys ☎ 305/744–9866 or 800/523–2326) arrests you at the door of "the Southernmost Coffee Roaster." Buy it by the pound or by the cup along with fresh-baked goods.

The undeveloped backcountry is at your door, making this an ideal location for fishing and kayaking, too. Nearby **Ramrod Key**, which also caters to divers bound for Looe Key, derives its name from a ship that wrecked on nearby reefs in the early 1800s.

Where to Stay & Eat

$$$$ ✕ **Little Palm Island Resort & Spa Restaurant.** The waterfront dining room with nightly live music at the exclusive Little Palm Island resort is one of the most romantic spots in the Keys. The menu reflects a mix of Caribbean, French, and Asian tastes, though new chef Anthony Keene had not developed any signature dishes as of this writing. The dining room is open to nonguests on a reservations-only basis. The tropical Sunday brunch buffet and the full-moon jazz dinners are the most popular meals. ✉ *MM 28.5, OS, 28500 Overseas Hwy., 33042* ☎ *305/872–2551* ⚞ *Reservations essential* ▤ *AE, D, DC, MC, V.*

$$–$$$ ✕ **Square Grouper.** Although this restaurant's food draws raves, its name draws snickers—a grouper is a fine eating fish, but a square grouper is the moniker for bales of marijuana dropped into the ocean off the coast during the drug-running 1970s. The setting is suave, with white-clothed tables and West Indies–style sofas separating a wood-topped stainless steel bar from the dining rooms. Owners Lynn and Doug Bell give the dishes whimsical and artistic presentations, making them look as good as they taste. Seared sesame-encrusted tuna looks like a fish and is lightly crunchy outside, like butter inside. The square grouper sandwich is a steaming pan-sautéed grouper fillet with key lime tartar sauce topped with onion rings, lettuce, and tomato on ciabatta. ✉ *MM 22.5, OS, Cudjoe Key* ☎ *305/745–8880* ▤ *MC, V* ⊘ *Closed Sun. and Mon. and several weeks in summer.*

¢–$ ✕ **Geiger Key Marina Smokehouse.** There's a lot of the old Keys at this oceanfront marina restaurant where locals usually outnumber tourists even in high season. They come for the daily dinner specials of meat loaf on Monday, corned beef and cabbage Tuesday, and so on. Weekends are the most popular; the place is packed Saturday for $10 pig roasts, and Sunday for the $11 "Famous Chicken & Ribs BBQ" accompanied by live music. Along with lunch and dinner, this spot serves breakfast, catering to local fishermen and RVers who park their "land cruisers" within shouting distance of their boats for early fishing getaways. ✉ *MM 10, Geiger Key* ☎ *305/296–3553* ▤ *MC, V.*

$$$$ 🛏 **Little Palm Island Resort & Spa.** *Haute tropicale* best describes this luxury retreat on a 5-acre palm-fringed island 3 mi offshore. The 28 ocean-front one-bedroom, thatch-roof bungalow suites have slate-tile baths, mosquito netting–draped king beds, and British colonial–style furnishings. Other comforts include an indoor and outdoor shower, private veranda, a separate living room, and robes and slippers. Two Island Grand Suites are twice the size of the others and offer his-and-her bathrooms, an outdoor hot tub, and uncompromising ocean views. Cellular phones

Fodor'sChoice
★

are verboten in public areas. ✉ *MM 28.5, OS, 28500 Overseas Hwy., 33042* ☎ *305/872–2524 or 800/343–8567* 🖷 *305/872–4843* ⊕ *www. littlepalmisland.com* ➾ *30 suites* 🖔 *Restaurant, dining room, room service, fans, in-room data ports, in-room safes, in-room hot tubs, minibars, refrigerators, pool, gym, hair salon, hot tub, Japanese baths, massage, sauna, spa, steam room, beach, dive shop, dock, snorkeling, windsurfing, boating, marina, fishing, 2 bars, lounge, piano bar, library, piano, recreation room, 2 shops, concierge, airport shuttle, free parking; no room phones, no room TVs, no kids under 16, no smoking* ▤ *AE, D, DC, MC, V* ¶◎¶ *MAP.*

★ **$–$$** 🏨 **Parmer's Place.** This is the perfect spot for a family getaway in the Lower Keys. You'll stay in family-style waterfront cottages with a deck or balcony. It's spread out on 5 landscaped acres, so the kids have room to play. And the price is right. Lots of families agree; many are repeat guests and recommend it, and the proprietors treat them all like family. The motel rooms are comfortable for two people and are the best buy. There are water activities galore, 19 aviaries with more than 70 birds, and a sunny breakfast room. ✉ *MM 29, BS, 565 Barry Ave., 33042* ☎ *305/872–2157* 🖷 *305/872–2014* ⊕ *www.parmersplace.com* ➾ *45 units, 18 rooms, 12 efficiencies, 15 apartments* 🖔 *Dining room, fans, some kitchens, cable TV, pool, dock, boating, bicycles, laundry facilities, Internet, no-smoking rooms; no room phones* ▤ *AE, D, MC, V* ¶◎¶ *CP.*

¢–$ 🏨 **Ed & Ellen's Lodgings.** Homey, in a quiet residential neighborhood, these well-maintained 800-square-foot duplexes scream, "bring the family, the big family." Units (of which there are three) sleep up to seven, with double beds in two bedrooms and three daybeds in the living room. There's a breakfast bar and good appliances in the fully outfitted kitchen, one bathroom, and a small canal-front balcony, where a plastic table and four chairs barely fit. You can tie up a boat at the wooden dock along the canal lined with mangroves and other homes, but bring bug spray. Wildlife abounds, including Key deer, raccoons, squirrels, and iguanas. Rental includes a free pass to Bahia Honda State Park. ✉ *1547 Narcissus Ave., MM 30, BS, 33043* ☎ *305/872–0703 or 888/333–5536* ⊕ *www.ed-ellens-lodgings.com* ➾ *3 duplexes* 🖔 *BBQ, fans, kitchens, cable TV, in-room VCRs, dock, fishing, bicycles; no room phones, no smoking* ▤ *MC, V.*

Sports & the Outdoors

SCUBA & SNORKELING
In 1744 the HMS *Looe*, a British warship, ran aground and sank on one of the most beautiful and diverse coral reefs in the Keys. Today, **Looe Key Reef** (✉ MM 27.5, OS, 216 Ann St., Key West 33040 ☎ 305/292–0311) owes its name to the ill-fated ship. The 5.3-square-nautical-mi reef, part of the **Florida Keys National Marine Sanctuary,** has stands of elkhorn coral on its eastern margin, purple sea fans, and abundant sponges and sea urchins. On its seaward side, it drops almost vertically 50–90 feet. Snorkelers and divers will find the sanctuary a quiet place to observe reef life, except in July, when the annual Underwater Music Festival pays homage to Looe Key's beauty and promotes reef awareness with six hours of music broadcast via underwater speakers. Dive shops and private charters transport hundreds of divers to hear the spec-

tacle, which includes Caribbean, classical, jazz, New Age, and, of course, Jimmy Buffett.

Rather than the customary morning and afternoon two-tank, two-location trips offered by most dive shops, **Looe Key Reef Resort & Dive Center** (✉ MM 27.5, OS, Box 509, Ramrod Key 33042 ☎ 305/872–2215 Ext. 2 or 800/942–5397 ⊕ www.diveflakeys.com), the closest dive shop to Looe Key Reef, runs a single three-tank, three-location dive from 10 to 3. The maximum depth is 30 feet, so snorkelers and divers go on the same boat. On Saturday and Wednesday, they run a 3/3 dive on wrecks (for qualified divers) and reefs in the area. It's part of the full-service Looe Key Reef Resort, which, not surprisingly, caters to divers. The dive boat, a 45-foot Corinthian catamaran, is docked outside the hotel, whose guests get a 10% discount on trips. Bring lunch or buy food and sodas on board.

en route

The huge object that looks like a white whale floating over Cudjoe Key (MM 23–21) is not a figment of your imagination. It's Fat Albert, a radar balloon that monitors local air and water traffic.

KEY WEST

MM 4–0.

Situated 150 mi from Miami and 90 mi from Havana, this tropical island city has always maintained a strong sense of detachment, even after it was connected to the rest of the United States—by the railroad in 1912 and by the Overseas Highway in 1938. The U.S. government acquired Key West from Spain in 1821 along with the rest of Florida. The Spanish had named the island Cayo Hueso (Bone Key) after the Native American skeletons they found on its shores. In 1823 Uncle Sam sent Commodore David S. Porter to chase pirates away. For three decades, the primary industry in Key West was wrecking—rescuing people and salvaging cargo from ships that foundered on the nearby reefs. According to some reports, when pickings were lean, the wreckers hung out lights to lure ships aground. Their business declined after 1849, when the federal government began building lighthouses.

In 1845 the army started construction of Fort Taylor, which held Key West for the Union during the Civil War. After the war, an influx of Cuban dissidents unhappy with Spain's rule brought the cigar industry here. Fishing, shrimping, and sponge-gathering became important industries, and a pineapple-canning factory opened. Major military installations were established during the Spanish-American War and World War I. Through much of the 19th century and into the second decade of the 20th, Key West was Florida's wealthiest city in per-capita terms. But in 1929 the local economy began to unravel. Modern ships no longer needed to provision in Key West, cigar making moved to Tampa, Hawaii dominated the pineapple industry, and the sponges succumbed to a blight. Then the Depression hit, and the military moved out. By 1934 half the population was on relief. The city defaulted on its bond payments, and the Federal Emergency Relief Administration took over the city and county governments.

By promoting Key West as a tourist destination, federal officials attracted 40,000 visitors during the 1934–35 winter season, but when the 1935 Labor Day hurricane struck the Middle Keys, it wiped out the railroad and the tourist trade. An important naval center during World War II and the Korean conflict, the island remains a strategic listening post on the doorstep of Fidel Castro's Cuba. It was during the 1960s that the fringes of society began moving here and the mid-'70s that gay guest houses opened in rapid succession. In April 1982 the U.S. Border Patrol threw a roadblock across the Overseas Highway just south of Florida City to catch drug runners and illegal aliens. Traffic backed up for miles as Border Patrol agents searched vehicles and demanded that the occupants prove U.S. citizenship. City officials in Key West, outraged at being treated like foreigners by the federal government, staged a mock secession and formed their own "nation," the so-called Conch Republic. They hoisted a flag and distributed mock border passes, visas, and Conch currency. The embarrassed Border Patrol dismantled its roadblock, and now an annual festival recalls the secessionists' victory.

Key West reflects a diverse population: native "Conchs" (white Key Westers, many of whom trace their ancestry to the Bahamas), fresh-water Conchs (longtime residents who migrated from somewhere else years ago), black Bahamians (descendants of those who worked the railroads and burned charcoal), Hispanics (primarily Cuban immigrants), recent refugees from the urban sprawl of mainland Florida, navy and air force personnel, and an assortment of vagabonds, drifters, and dropouts in search of refuge. The island is decidedly gay-friendly—gays make up at least 20% of Key West's citizenry. It's not unusual to see gay couples holding hands or to see advertisements aimed at gay customers. Although gay men and lesbians will feel welcome in almost all establishments, there are numerous accommodations, restaurants, clubs, businesses, and visitor information services that cater exclusively to a gay clientele.

Although the rest of the Keys are highly outdoor-oriented, Key West has more of a city feel. Few open spaces remain, as promoters continue to churn out restaurants, galleries, shops, and museums to interpret the city's intriguing past. As a tourist destination, Key West has a lot to sell—an average temperature of 79°F, 19th-century architecture, and a laid-back lifestyle. There's also a growing calendar of festivals and artistic and cultural events—including the Conch Republic Celebration in April and a Halloween Fantasy Fest. Few cities of its size—a mere 2 mi by 4 mi— offer the joie de vivre of this one. Yet, as elsewhere, when preservation has successfully revived once-tired towns, next have come those unmindful of style and eager for a buck. Duval Street can look like a strip mall of T-shirt shops and tour shills. Mass marketers directing the town's tourism have attracted cruise ships, which dwarf the town's skyline, and Duval Street floods with day-trippers who gawk at the earringed hippies with dogs in their bike baskets, gay couples walking down the street holding hands, and the oddball lot of locals.

Old Town

The heart of Key West, this historic area runs from White Street west to the waterfront. Beginning in 1822, wharves, warehouses, chandleries, ship-repair facilities, and eventually in 1891 the U.S. Custom House sprang up around the deep harbor to accommodate the navy's large ships and other sailing vessels. Wealthy wreckers, merchants, and sea captains built lavish houses near the bustling waterfront. A remarkable number of these fine Victorian and pre-Victorian structures have been restored to their original grandeur and now serve as homes, guest houses, and museums. These, along with the dwellings of famous writers, artists, and politicians who've come to Key West over the past 175 years, are among the area's approximately 3,000 historic structures. Old Town also has the city's finest restaurants and hotels, lively street life, and popular nightspots.

a good tour

To cover many sights, take the Old Town Trolley, which lets you get off and reboard a later trolley, or the Conch Tour Train. Old Town is also very manageable on foot, bicycle, or moped, but be warned that this tour is expansive; you'll want either to pick and choose from it or break it into two days. Start on Whitehead Street at the **Ernest Hemingway Home & Museum** ⑫ ▸, and then cross the street and climb to the top of the **Lighthouse Museum** ⑬ for a spectacular view. Exit through the museum's parking lot and cross Truman Avenue to the **Lofton B. Sands African-Bahamian Museum** ⑭ to learn about nearly two centuries of black history in Key West. Return to Whitehead Street and follow it north to Angela Street; then turn right. At Margaret Street, the **City Cemetery** ⑮ has above-ground vaults and unusual headstone inscriptions. Head north on Margaret to Southard Street, turn left, then right onto Simonton Street. Halfway up the block, Free School Lane is occupied by **Nancy Forrester's Secret Garden** ⑯. After touring it, return west on Southard to Duval Street, turn right, and look at the lovely tiles and woodwork in the **San Carlos Institute** ⑰. Return again to Southard Street, turn right, and follow it through Truman Annex to **Fort Zachary Taylor State Park** ⑱; after viewing the fort, take a dip at the beach.

Go back to Simonton Street, walk north, and then turn left on Caroline Street; climb to the widow's walk on top of **Curry Mansion** ⑲. A left on Duval Street puts you in front of the **Duval Street Wreckers Museum** ⑳, Key West's oldest house. Continue west into Truman Annex to see the **Harry S Truman Little White House Museum** ㉑, President Truman's vacation residence. Return east on Caroline and turn left on Whitehead to visit the **Audubon House and Gardens** ㉒, honoring the artist-naturalist. Follow Whitehead north to Greene Street and turn left to see the salvaged sea treasures of the **Mel Fisher Maritime Heritage Society Museum** ㉓. At Whitehead's north end are the **Key West Aquarium** ㉔ and the **Key West Museum of Art and History** ㉕, the former historic U.S. Custom House. By late afternoon you should be ready to cool off with a dip or catch a few rays at the beach. (Heed signs about the water's condition.) From the aquarium, head east two blocks to the end of Simonton Street, where you'll find the appropriately named **Simonton Street Beach** ㉖. On the Atlantic side of Old Town is **South Beach ㉗**, named for its location at the southern end of Duval Street. If you've brought your pet, stroll a few blocks east to **Dog Beach ㉘**, at the corner of Vernon and Waddell streets. A little farther east is **Higgs Beach–Astro Park ㉙**, on Atlantic Boulevard between White and Reynolds streets. As the sun starts to sink, return to the north end of Old Town and follow the crowds to Mallory Square, behind the aquarium, to watch Key West's nightly sunset spectacle. For dinner, head east on Caroline Street to **Historic Seaport at Key West Bight ㉚** (formerly known simply as Key West Bight), a renovated area where there are numerous restaurants and bars.

TIMING   Allow two full days to see all the Old Town museums and homes, especially with a little shopping thrown in. For a narrated trip on the tour train or trolley, budget 1½ hours to ride the loop without getting off, an entire day if you plan to get off and on at some of the sights and restaurants.

What to See

㉒ **Audubon House and Gardens.** If you've ever seen an engraving by ornithologist John James Audubon, you'll understand why his name is synonymous with birds. See his work in this three-story house, which was built in the 1840s for Captain John Geiger but now commemorates Audubon's 1832 stop in Key West while he was traveling through Florida to study birds. Several rooms of period antiques and a children's room are also of interest. Admission includes an audiotape (in English, French, German, or Spanish) for a self-guided tour of the house and tropical gardens, complemented by an informational booklet and signs that identify the rare indigenous plants and trees. ⊠ *205 Whitehead St.* ☎ *305/294–2116* ⊕ *www.audubonhouse.com* ✏ *$10* ☉ *Daily 9:30–4:30, last tour starts at 4.*

★ ⑮ **City Cemetery.** You can learn almost as much about a town's history through its cemetery as through its historic houses. Key West's celebrated 20-acre burial place is no exception. Among the interesting plots are a memorial to the sailors killed in the sinking of the battleship U.S.S. *Maine,* carved angels and lambs marking graves of children, and grand aboveground crypts. There are separate plots for Catholics, Jews, and martyrs of Cuba. You're free to walk around the cemetery on your own, but the best way to see it is on a 60-minute tour given by the staff and volunteers of the Historic Florida Keys Foundation. Tours leave from the main gate, and reservations are required. ⊠ *Margaret and Angela Sts.* ☎ *305/292–6718* ✏ *$10* ☉ *Daily sunrise–6 PM, tours Tues. and Thurs. at 9:30; call for additional times.*

⑲ **Curry Mansion.** See the opulence enjoyed by Key West's 19th-century millionaires in this well-preserved 22-room house. Construction was begun by William Curry, a ship salvager and Key West's first millionaire, and completed in 1899 by his son, Milton Curry. The owners have restored most of the house and turned it into a B&B. Take an unhurried self-guided tour; a brochure describes the home's history and contents. ⊠ *511 Caroline St.* ☎ *305/294–5349* ⊕ *currymansion.com* ✏ *$5* ☉ *Daily 8:30–5.*

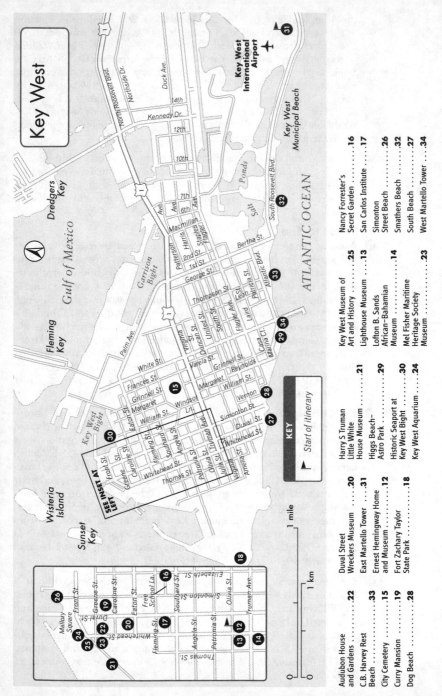

Key West

KEY

▲ *Start of itinerary*

Audubon House
and Gardens **22**

C.B. Harvey Rest
Beach **33**

City Cemetery **15**

Curry Mansion **19**

Dog Beach **28**

Duval Street
Wreckers Museum **20**

East Martello Tower ...**31**

Ernest Hemingway Home
and Museum **12**

Fort Zachary Taylor
State Park **18**

Harry S Truman
Little White
House Museum **21**

Higgs Beach–
Astro Park **29**

Historic Seaport at
Key West Bight **30**

Key West Aquarium ...**24**

Key West Museum of
Art and History **25**

Lighthouse Museum ...**13**

Lofton B. Sands
African-Bahamian
Museum **14**

Mel Fisher Maritime
Heritage Society
Museum **23**

Nancy Forrester's
Secret Garden **16**

San Carlos Institute ...**17**

Simonton
Street Beach **26**

Smathers Beach **32**

South Beach **27**

West Martello Tower ..**34**

28 **Dog Beach.** Next to Louie's Backyard, this small beach—the only one in Key West where dogs are allowed—has a shore that's a mix of sand and rocks. ⊠ *Vernon and Waddell Sts.* ☎ *No phone* 🖾 *Free* ☉ *Daily sunrise–sunset.*

20 **Duval Street Wreckers Museum.** Most of Key West's early wealthy residents made their fortunes from the sea. Among them was Francis Watlington, a sea captain and wrecker, who in 1829 built this house, alleged to be the oldest house in South Florida. Six rooms are open, furnished with 18th- and 19th-century antiques and providing exhibits on the island's wrecking industry of the 1800s, which made Key West one of the most affluent towns in the country. ⊠ *322 Duval St.* ☎ *305/294–9502* 🖾 *$5* ☉ *Daily 10–4.*

★ ▶ **12** **Ernest Hemingway Home & Museum.** Guided tours of Ernest Hemingway's home are full of anecdotes about the author's life in the community and his household quarrels with wife Pauline. While living here between 1931 and 1942, Hemingway wrote about 70% of his life's work, including *For Whom the Bell Tolls*. Few of the family's belongings remain, but photographs help illustrate his life, and scores of descendants of Hemingway's cats have free reign of the property. Literary buffs should be aware that there are no curated exhibits from which to gain much insight into Hemingway's writing career. Tours begin every 10 minutes and take 25–30 minutes; then you're free to explore on your own. ⊠ *907 Whitehead St.* ☎ *305/294–1136* ⊕ *www.hemingwayhome.com* 🖾 *$10* ☉ *Daily 9–5.*

★ **18** **Fort Zachary Taylor State Park.** Construction of the fort began in 1845, and in 1861, even though Florida seceded from the Union during the Civil War, Yankee forces used the fort as a base to block Confederate shipping (more than 1,500 Confederate vessels were detained in Key West's harbor). The fort, finally completed in 1866, was also used in the Spanish-American War. Take a 30-minute guided tour of this National Historic Landmark at noon and 2. On the first weekend in March, a celebration called Civil War Days includes costumed reenactments and demonstrations. The park's uncrowded beach is the best in Key West. There's an adjoining picnic area with barbecue grills and shade trees. ⊠ *End of Southard St., through Truman Annex* ☎ *305/292–6713* ⊕ *www.floridastateparks.org/forttaylor* 🖾 *$3.50 for 1 person, $6 per vehicle for 2 people, plus 50¢ per additional person; $1.50 per pedestrian or bicyclist* ☉ *Daily 8–sunset, tours noon and 2.*

need a break?

For a partying kind of town, Key West restaurants are oddly unaccommodating for those looking for breakfast at noon, or dinner at midnight. If your appetite is out of sync with most serving schedules, **Iguana Cafe** (⊠ 425C Greene St. ☎ 305/296–6420) will come to the rescue 24 hours a day. Just off Duval Street, the simple shacklike dive puts out tasty recipes from around the globe.

Artist Ray Rolston created a lifelike underwater experience with a coral reef diorama of dolphins, turtles, and sharks at the new **Reef World** (⊠ 201 William St., on the boardwalk of the Historic

Seaport, foot of William St. ☏ 305/294–3100) educational center. Watch the sea come alive in the video viewing area, then check out the depths on an interactive computer station. The children's area has a microscope with slides of sea creatures, as well as reef games and activities.

㉑ Harry S Truman Little White House Museum. In a letter to his wife during one of his visits, President Harry S Truman wrote, "Dear Bess, you should see the house. The place is all redecorated, new furniture and everything." If he visited today, he'd write something similar. There's a photographic review of visiting dignitaries and permanent audiovisual and artifact exhibits on the Florida Keys as a presidential retreat; Ulysses S. Grant, John F. Kennedy, and Jimmy Carter are among the chief executives who passed through here. Tours lasting 45 minutes begin every 15 minutes. On the grounds of **Truman Annex,** a 103-acre former military parade grounds and barracks, the home served as a winter White House for presidents Truman, Eisenhower, and Kennedy. The two-bedroom Presidential Suite, with a veranda and sundeck, is available for a novelty overnight stay. ⊠ *111 Front St.* ☏ *305/294–9911* ⊕ *www. trumanlittlewhitehouse.com* ⊒ *$11* ⊘ *Daily 9–5, grounds 8–sunset; last tour at 4:30.*

㉙ Higgs Beach–Astro Park. This Monroe County park is a popular sunbathing spot. A nearby grove of Australian pines provides shade, and the West Martello Tower provides shelter should a storm suddenly sweep in. Across the street, **Astro Park** is a popular children's playground. The beach also has a marker commemorating the gravesite of 295 enslaved Africans who died after being rescued from three South America–bound slave ships in 1860. Archaeologists uncovered several of the forgotten graves and the site was consecrated in 2002. ⊠ *Atlantic Blvd. between White and Reynolds Sts.* ☏ *No phone* ⊒ *Free* ⊘ *Daily 6 AM–11 PM.*

㉚ Historic Seaport at Key West Bight. What used to be a funky—in some places even seedy—part of town is now an 8½-acre historic restoration project of 100 businesses, including waterfront restaurants, open-air people- and dog-friendly bars, museums, clothing stores, bait shops, docks, a marina, a wedding chapel, the Waterfront Market, the Key West Rowing Club, and dive shops. It's all linked by the 2-mi waterfront **Harborwalk,** which runs between Front and Grinnell streets, passing big ships, schooners, sunset cruises, fishing charters, and glass-bottom boats. Additional construction continues on outlying projects.

㉔ Key West Aquarium. Explore the fascinating underwater realm of the Keys without getting wet at this kid-friendly aquarium. Hundreds of tropical fish and sea creatures live here. A touch tank enables you to handle starfish, sea cucumbers, horseshoe and hermit crabs, even horse and queen conchs—living totems of the Conch Republic. Built in 1934 by the Works Progress Administration as the world's first open-air aquarium, most of the building has been enclosed for all-weather viewing. Guided tours include shark petting and feedings. Tickets are good for the entire day. ⊠ *1 Whitehead St.* ☏ *305/296–2051* ⊕ *www.keywestaquarium. com* ⊒ *$10* ⊘ *Daily 10–6; tours at 11, 1, 3, and 4:30.*

HEMINGWAY WAS HERE

N A TOWN WHERE *Pulitzer prize–winning writers are almost as common as coconuts, Ernest Hemingway stands out. Bars and restaurants around the island claim that he ate or drank there, and though he may not have been at all of them, his larger-than-life image continues to grow.*

Hemingway came to Key West in 1928 at the urging of writer John dos Passos and rented a house with wife number two, Pauline Pfeiffer. They spent winters in the Keys and summers in Europe and Wyoming, occasionally taking African safaris. Along the way they had two sons, Patrick and Gregory. In 1931 Pauline's wealthy uncle Gus gave the couple the house at 907 Whitehead Street, now known as Ernest Hemingway Home & Museum and Key West's number one tourist attraction. They renovated it, added a pool, and put in a tropical garden with peacocks.

In 1935, when the visitor bureau included the house in a tourist brochure, Hemingway promptly built the high brick wall that surrounds it today. He wrote of the visitor bureau's offense in a 1935 essay for Esquire, stating, "The house at present occupied by your correspondent is listed as number eighteen in a compilation of the forty-eight things for a tourist to see in Key West. So there will be no difficulty in a tourist finding it or any other of the sights of the city, a map has been prepared by the local F.E.R.A. authorities to be presented to each arriving visitor . . . This is all very flattering to the easily bloated ego of your correspondent but very hard on production."

During his time in Key West, Hemingway penned some of his most important works, including A Farewell to Arms, To Have and Have Not, Green Hills of Africa, and Death in the Afternoon. His rigorous

schedule consisted of writing almost every morning in his second-story studio above the pool, then promptly descending the stairs at midday. By afternoon and evening he was ready for drinking, fishing, swimming, boxing, and hanging around with the boys.

One close friend was Joe Russell, a craggy fisherman and owner of the rugged bar Sloppy Joe's, originally at 428 Greene Street but now at 201 Duval Street. Russell was the only one in town who would cash Hemingway's $1,000 royalty check. Russell and Charles Thompson introduced him to deep-sea fishing, which became fodder for his writing. Another of Hemingway's loves was boxing. He set up a ring in his yard and paid local fighters to box with him, and he refereed matches at Blue Heaven, then a saloon but now a restaurant, at 729 Thomas Street.

Hemingway honed his macho image dressed in cutoffs and old shirts and took on the name Papa. In turn, he gave his friends new names and used them as characters in his stories. Joe Russell became Freddy, captain of the Queen Conch charter boat in To Have and Have Not.

Hemingway stayed in Key West for 11 years before leaving Pauline for wife number three. A foreign correspondent, Martha Gellhorn, arrived in town and headed for Sloppy Joe's, intent on meeting him. When the always restless Hemingway packed up to cover the Spanish Civil War, so did she. Though he returned to Pauline occasionally, he finally left her and Key West to be with Martha in 1939. They married a year later and moved to Cuba, and he seldom returned to Key West after that. Pauline and the boys stayed on in the house, which sold in 1951 for $80,000, 10 times its original cost.

— Diane P. Marshall

㉕ **Key West Museum of Art and History.** When Key West was designated a
Fodor'sChoice U.S. port of entry in the early 1820s, a custom house was established.
★ Salvaged cargoes from ships wrecked on the reefs could legally enter here,
thus setting the stage for Key West to become the richest city in Florida.
Following a $9-million restoration, the imposing redbrick-and-terra-cotta
Richardsonian Romanesque–style U.S. Custom House reopened as a museum. Its main gallery displays major rotating exhibits. Smaller galleries
have long-term and changing exhibits about the history of Key West,
such as *Remember the Maine.* ⊠ *281 Front St.* ☎ *305/295–6616*
⊕ *www.kwahs.com* ⌨ *$7* ⊗ *Daily 9–5.*

⑬ **Lighthouse Museum.** For the best view in town and a history lesson at
the same time, climb the 88 steps to the top of this 92-foot lighthouse.
It was built in 1847. About 15 years later, a Fresnel lens was installed
at a cost of $1 million. The keeper lived in the adjacent 1887 clapboard
house, which now exhibits vintage photographs, ship models, nautical charts, and lighthouse artifacts from all along the Key reefs. ⊠ *938
Whitehead St.* ☎ *305/294–0012* ⌨ *$8* ⊗ *Daily 9:30–4:30; last ad-
mission at 4:15.*

⑭ **Lofton B. Sands African-Bahamian Museum.** Vintage photographs and
memorabilia chronicle the nearly 200-year history of Key West's black
community in this modest 1928 house on the edge of Bahama Village.
The house was built by the namesake owner, a master electrician, in the
mid-1920s in what was then called Black Town or Africa Town. There
are photographs of graduations and dances at the segregated high
school, photos of funeral parades, candids of people at social clubs and
balls, and posed wedding pictures. Crafts and demonstrations of traditional Afro-Caribbean arts are scheduled periodically. ⊠ *324 Truman
Ave.* ☎ *305/295–7337* ⌨ *Free* ⊗ *Daily 10–6; tours by appointment.*

㉓ **Mel Fisher Maritime Heritage Society Museum.** In 1622 two Spanish galleons
loaded with riches from South America foundered in a hurricane 40 mi
west of the Keys. In 1985 Mel Fisher recovered the treasures from the
lost ships, the *Nuestra Señora de Atocha* and the *Santa Margarita.* In
this museum, see, touch, and learn about some of the artifacts, including a gold bar weighing 6.3 troy pounds and a 77.76-carat natural emerald crystal worth almost $250,000. Exhibits on the second floor rotate
and might cover slave ships, including the excavated 17th-century *Hen-
rietta Marie,* or the evolution of Florida maritime history. ⊠ *200 Greene
St.* ☎ *305/294–2633* ⊕ *www.melfisher.org* ⌨ *$10* ⊗ *Daily 9:30–5.*

⑯ **Nancy Forrester's Secret Garden.** It's hard to believe that this green escape exists in the middle of Old Town Key West. Despite damage by
hurricanes and pressures from developers, Nancy Forrester has maintained her naturalized garden for more than 35 years. Growing in harmony are rare palms and cycads, ferns, bromeliads, bright gingers and
heliconias, gumbo-limbos strewn with orchids and vines, and a few surprises. The gardens are popular for weddings. An art gallery has botanical prints and environmental art. One-hour private tours cost $15 per
person, four-person minimum. ⊠ *1 Free School La.* ☎ *305/294–0015*
⊕ *www.keywestsecretgarden.com* ⌨ *$6* ⊗ *Daily 10–5.*

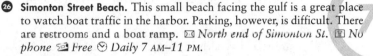

⓱ San Carlos Institute. South Florida's Cuban connection began long before Fidel Castro was born. The institute was founded in 1871 by Cuban immigrants. Now it contains a research library and museum rich with the history of Key West and 19th- and 20th-century Cuban exiles. Cuban patriot Jose Martí delivered speeches from the balcony of the auditorium, and opera star Enrico Caruso sang in the Opera House, which reportedly has exceptional acoustics. It's frequently used for concerts, lectures, films, and exhibits. ✉ 516 Duval St. ☎ 305/294–3887 ☞ $3 ☉ Tues.–Fri. 11–5, Sat. 11–9, Sun. 11–4.

㉖ Simonton Street Beach. This small beach facing the gulf is a great place to watch boat traffic in the harbor. Parking, however, is difficult. There are restrooms and a boat ramp. ✉ North end of Simonton St. ☎ No phone ☞ Free ☉ Daily 7 AM–11 PM.

㉗ South Beach. On the Atlantic, this stretch of sand, also known as City Beach, is popular with travelers staying at nearby motels. It has limited parking and a nearby buffet-type restaurant, the South Beach Seafood and Raw Bar. ✉ Foot of Duval St. ☎ No phone ☞ Free ☉ Daily 7 AM–11 PM.

New Town

The Overseas Highway splits as it enters Key West, the two forks rejoining to encircle New Town, the area east of White Street to Cow Key Channel. The southern fork runs along the shore as South Roosevelt Boulevard (Route A1A), past municipal beaches, salt ponds, and Key West International Airport. Along the north shore, North Roosevelt Boulevard (U.S. 1) passes the Key West Welcome Center, shopping centers, chain hotels, and fast-food eateries. Part of New Town was created with dredged fill. The island would have continued growing this way had the Army Corps of Engineers not determined in the early 1970s that it was detrimental to the nearby reef.

Attractions are few in New Town. The best way to take in the sights is by car or moped. Take South Roosevelt Boulevard from the island's entrance to the historical museum exhibits at **East Martello Tower ㉛** ▶, near the airport. Continue past the Riggs Wildlife Refuge salt ponds and stop at **Smathers Beach ㉜** for a dip, or continue west onto Atlantic Boulevard to **C. B. Harvey Rest Beach ㉝**. A little farther along, at the end of White Street, is the **West Martello Tower ㉞**, with its lovely tropical gardens.

TIMING Allow one to two hours for brief stops at each attraction. If your interests lie in art, gardens, or Civil War history, you'll need three or four hours. Throw in time at the beach and make it a half-day affair.

What to See

㉝ C. B. Harvey Rest Beach. This beach and park were named after former Key West mayor and commissioner Cornelius Bradford Harvey. It has half a dozen picnic areas, dunes, and a wheelchair and bike path. ✉ Atlantic Blvd., east side of White St. Pier ☎ No phone ☞ Free ☉ Daily 7 AM–11 PM.

★ ▶ **③** **East Martello Tower.** As a Civil War citadel this spot never saw any action. Today, however, it serves as a museum, with historical exhibits of the 19th and 20th centuries. Among the latter are relics of the U.S.S. *Maine,* a Cuban refugee raft, and books by famous writers—including seven Pulitzer prize winners—who have lived in Key West. The tower, operated by the Key West Art and Historical Society, also has a collection of Stanley Papio's "junk art" sculptures and Cuban folk artist Mario Sanchez's chiseled and painted wooden carvings of historic Key West street scenes. Hours fluctuate; call in advance. ✉ *3501 S. Roosevelt Blvd.* ☎ *305/296–3913* 🎫 *$6* ☉ *Daily 9:30–4:30; last admission at 4:15.*

③ **Smathers Beach.** This beach has nearly 2 mi of sand, restrooms, picnic areas, and volleyball courts, all of which make it popular with the spring-break crowd. Trucks along the road rent rafts, Windsurfers, and other beach "toys." ✉ *S. Roosevelt Blvd.* ☎ *No phone* 🎫 *Free* ☉ *Daily 7 AM–11 PM.*

③ **West Martello Tower.** Within the ruins of this Civil War–era fort is the Key West Garden Club, which maintains lovely gardens of native and tropical plants. It also holds art, orchid, and flower shows in March and November and leads private garden tours in March. ✉ *Atlantic Blvd. and White St.* ☎ *305/294–3210* 🎫 *Donation welcome* ☉ *Tues.–Sat. 9:30–3.*

Where to Eat

American

$$–$$$ ✕ **Michael's Restaurant.** White tablecloths, subdued lighting, oil paintings, and light music give Michael's the feel of a favorite restaurant in a comfortable urban neighborhood. Garden seating gives it that Key West touch. Try *filet al forno* (tenderloin of beef rubbed with roasted garlic and Roquefort) or grouper Oscar, a fillet stuffed with jumbo lump crab. Chef-owner Michael is especially proud of the prime rib, flown in from Allen Brothers in Chicago, which has supplied top-ranked steakhouses for more than 100 years. Chocolate lovers shouldn't miss the Volcano, a hot Ghirardelli chocolate cake with a molten center that erupts when the cake is broken open. Fondue is served at the garden bar. ✉ *532 Margaret St.* ☎ *305/295–1300* 🖃 *AE, DC, MC, V* ☉ *No lunch.*

$–$$$ ✕ **Pepe's Café and Steak House.** Pepe's is a Key West institution. It was established downtown in 1909 (making it the oldest eating house in the Keys) and moved here in 1962. With few exceptions, it's been serving three squares a day with the same nightly specials for years, such as meat loaf on Monday, seafood on Tuesday, and traditional Thanksgiving every Thursday. Dine indoors or on the garden patio under the trees. The walls are plastered with local color. Service is fast and friendly. ✉ *806 Caroline St.* ☎ *305/294–7192* 🖃 *D, MC, V.*

¢–$$ ✕ **The Deli Restaurant.** Nostalgia is part of the appeal in this fourth-generation family-run 1950s-style eatery with huge desserts in glass display cases, a deli counter, friendly service, and a smoky kitchen. Roast pork and roast beef dinners, papa's fish cakes (stuffed with fish and potatoes), and baked chicken with stuffing and cranberries are among the comfort foods. Most dishes cost $7–$11 and include a choice of two veggies and a biscuit or corn-bread muffin. Although the key lime pie is a bit sweet, it's a favorite among locals. The popular "bumbleberry" pie, a mix of berries, has been replaced by a blueberry pie that's quickly winning converts. You can order breakfast, lunch, and dinner all day. ⊠ *531 Truman Ave.* ☎ *305/294–1464* ▤ *D, MC, V.*

¢–$ ✕ **PT's Late Night Bar and Grill.** Locals like the dimly lighted homeyness (booths, TVs, pool tables), low prices (most entrées are around $9.95), and late hours (open until 4 AM). There's lots of turkey in the potpie and lots of onions on the smothered pork chops. Fajitas are a specialty, with a choice of steak, chicken, shrimp, veggies, or a combo. ⊠ *920 Caroline St.* ☎ *305/296–4245* ▤ *AE, D, MC, V.*

¢ ✕ **Lobo's Mixed Grill.** If White Castle has attained national cult status with its burgers, then the equivalent among Key West denizens might very well be Lobo's burger. The 7-ounce, chargrilled chunk of ground chuck is thick and juicy and served with lettuce, tomato, and pickle on a toasted bun. The menu includes wraps, salads, and quesadillas, as well as a fried shrimp and oyster combo. Beer and wine are also served. It's an outdoor eatery that closes at 6 PM, so eat early. Lobo's offers free delivery within Old Town. ⊠ *5 Key Lime Sq., between Southard and Angela Sts.* ☎ *305/296–5303* ▤ *No credit cards* ☉ *Closed Sun. Apr.–early Dec.*

Contemporary

$$$–$$$$ ✕ **Café Marquesa.** The hospitality machine is well oiled at this refined
Fodor's Choice 50-seat restaurant adjoining the intimate Marquesa Hotel. Chef Susan
★ Ferry, who trained with Norman Van Aken (of Norman's restaurant in Coral Gables), presents 10 or so entrées each night. Although every dish she makes is memorable, frequent guests favor the peppercorn-dusted seared yellowfin tuna. Low-fat options such as grilled meats are often highlighted, but fresh-baked breads and desserts are quite the dietary contrary. There's also a fine selection of wines and a choice of microbrewery beers. Dinner is served until 11. ⊠ *600 Fleming St.* ☎ *305/292–1244* ▤ *AE, DC, MC, V* ☉ *No lunch.*

$$$–$$$$ ✕ **Louie's Backyard.** Feast your eyes on a steal-your-breath-away view and beautifully presented dishes prepared by executive chef Doug Shook. The winter menu might include grilled catch of the day with ginger butter, tomato chutney, and five-spice fried onions. Louie's key lime pie has a pistachio crust and is served with a raspberry coulis. Come for lunch if you're on a budget; the menu is less expensive and the view is just as fantastic. For night owls, the Afterdeck Bar serves cocktails on the water until the wee hours. ⊠ *700 Waddell Ave.* ☎ *305/294–1061* ⌲ *Reservations essential* ▤ *AE, DC, MC, V.*

$$–$$$$ ✕ **Rick's Blue Heaven.** There's much to like about this historic restaurant where Hemingway refereed boxing matches and customers watched cockfights. Fresh eats are served in the house and the big leafy yard. Nightly specials include blackened grouper or lobster with citrus beurre blanc, vegetarian options, and Caribbean foods. Desserts and breads are baked on-site. There's a shop and bar, the latter named after the water tower hauled here in the 1920s. Expect a line—everybody knows how good

this is. ⊠ *305 Petronia St.* ☎ *305/296–8666* ⌕ *Reservations not accepted* ▤ *D, MC, V.*

★ **$$–$$$** ✕ **Alice's Key West Restaurant.** There's a current of excitement in the air here, generated by the enthusiasm that chef-owner Alice Weingarten exudes. Nothing is plain. Everything has to have color, zing, or spice. Take the tuna tartar tower: it's spiced with a garlic-chili paste, topped with tomato ginger jam, and served between crisp wonton wafers. Many restaurants in the Keys serve coconut shrimp; few come close to giving it the spicy tang and aroma that Alice has perfected. The secret is the honey wasabi and papaya ginger chutney. She still serves Aunt Alice's magic meat loaf with a mushroom sauce. You may never eat strawberry shortcake again after trying Alice's tropical fruit shortcake dessert. The feel is calm and cool, the service exemplary. You can end your Duval Crawl here for a breakfast of eggs, fries, and toast for as little as $4. ⊠ *1114 Duval St.* ☎ *305/292–5733* ▤ *AE, D, MC, V* ⊙ *No lunch.*

$$–$$$ ✕ **915 Duval.** Technically this is not a budget restaurant if you judge by the price of the half-dozen entrées, but most of the menu is comprised of amply portioned tapas priced from $8. Two people will easily feel well-fed by ordering two tapas, splitting a salad, such as the wilted spinach with pine nuts, golden raisins and Serrano ham, and ordering dessert; say, "life by chocolate." Dine outdoors and people-watch along upper Duval, or sit inside at a table or the sleek bar while listening to light jazz. ⊠ *915 Duval St.* ☎ *305/296–0669* ▤ *AE, MC, V* ⊙ *No lunch.*

¢–$ ✕ **The Cafe, A Mostly Vegetarian Place.** Travelers who are vegetarians or vegans now have a place of their own in Key West. This New Age-ish café turns out stir fries, grilled tofus, and polentas, pastas, and even pan-seared tuna for your non-vegetarian partner. Local favorites include home-made veggie burgers, as well as portobello mushroom salad, a perfect accompaniment to green and yellow split pea soup. There are fewer than a dozen tables and an eat-at bar with backless stools that fill the dining space, but there's a couch and chairs for waiting, and the food is worth the wait. Service is relaxed. Save room for apple pie with ginger ice cream. ⊠ *509 Southard St.* ☎ *305/296–5515* ▤ *MC, V* ⊙ *Closed Sun.*

Caribbean

$–$$ ✕ **Bahama Mama's Kitchen.** At this colorful indoor-outdoor restaurant in the heart of Bahama Village, Cory Sweeting, a fourth-generation Conch from the Bahamas, prepares traditional island foods, from simple, flavorful conch fritters to complex curries. Choose from chicken—curried, gingered, or spiced and jerked—and seafood, including shrimp, red snapper, and grouper, any way you like them. Traditional sides include salads, hush puppies, collard greens, pigeon peas with rice, plantains, cheese grits, and crab with rice. Try the shrimp hash cakes if you go for breakfast. ⊠ *324 Petronia St.* ☎ *305/294–3355* ▤ *MC, V.*

Cuban

¢–$ ✕ **El Siboney.** Dining at this sprawling three-room, family-style restaurant is like going to Mom's for Sunday dinner—that is, if your mother is Cuban. It's noisy—everyone talks as though they're at home—and the food is traditional Cubano. There's a well-seasoned black-bean soup; local fish grilled, stuffed, and breaded; and a memorable special paella Valencia for two ($38.60). Dishes come with plantains, bread, and two sides. ✉ *900 Catherine St.* ☎ *305/296–4184* ☰ *No credit cards* ☯ *Closed Sun. and 2 wks in June.*

French

★ **$$$** ✗ **Café Solé.** This little piece of France is concealed behind a high wall and a gate in a residential neighborhood. Inside, chef John Correa shows his considerable culinary talents. Marrying his French training with local foods and produce, he creates some delicious takes on classics like half rack of lamb rubbed with *herbes de Provence* and some of the best bouillabaisse that you'll find outside of Marseilles. From the land, there is filet mignon casa nova with a wild mushroom demi-glace with foie gras. His salads are lightly kissed with balsamic vinegar. ✉ *1029 Southard St.* ☎ *305/294–0230* ☰ *D, MC, V.*

Irish

¢–**$$$** ✗ **Finnegan's Wake Irish Pub and Eatery.** From friendly, heavily accented waitresses to pictures of Beckett, Shaw, Yeats, and Wilde to creaky wood floors, this restaurant exudes Irish country warmth. The certified Angus beef is pricey, except for the thick burgers ($7), and most other dishes are bargains. Traditional fare includes Dublin chicken potpie with chunks of chicken and vegetables in a creamy broth, and *colcannon*—rich mashed potatoes with scallions, sauerkraut, and melted aged white cheddar cheese. The strawberry rhubarb tart and Irish cream chocolate mousse are phenomenal. There's live music on weekends, two happy hours, and a boast of the "world's largest selection on tap." ✉ *320 Grinnell St.* ☎ *305/293–0222* ☰ *AE, D, MC, V.*

Italian

★ **$$–$$$** ✗ **Salute Ristorante Sul Mare.** This funky wooden indoor and open-air restaurant is on Higgs Beach, giving it one of the island's best lunch views (and a bit of sand and salt spray on a windy day). The dinner menu includes Italian pastas, antipasto, soups, and dishes such as lobster ravioli with sweet sage butter and baby greens, and grilled black grouper with curry butter and basmati rice. At lunch there are bruschetta, panini, and mussels and calamari marinara, as well as a fresh-fish sandwich. The wine list shows a knowledgeable palate. ✉ *1000 Atlantic Blvd., Higgs Beach* ☎ *305/292–1117* ☰ *AE, MC, V* ☯ *No lunch Sun.*

★ **$–$$** ✗ **Mangia Mangia.** Elliot and Naomi Baron, ex-Chicago restaurateurs, serve large portions of homemade pastas that can be matched with one of the homemade sauces. Tables are arranged in a twinkly brick garden with specimen palms and in a nicely dressed-up old-house dining room. Everything that comes out of the open kitchen is outstanding, including the *bollito misto di mare* (fresh seafood sautéed with garlic, shallots, and white wine, and finished with herb-infused clam broth), as well as the Mississippi mud pie and key lime pie. The wine list—with more than 350 offerings it's the largest in Monroe County—has a good under-$20 selection. ✉ *900 Southard St.* ☎ *305/294–2469* ☰ *AE, MC, V* ☯ *No lunch.*

Japanese

¢–$$ ✕ **Origami.** A wooden bar, artsy ceramic fish on white walls, original art, and black-and-white tile floors decorate this restaurant's dining room that's the size of an average bedroom. Fortunately, there's outdoor seating on a large courtyard that joins several other restaurants. Along with sushi and sashimi there are traditional Japanese entrées like teriyaki, tempura, and katsu. It's kid friendly, too, with dishes such as the Space Shuttle Special, a combo of teriyaki chicken, fried shrimp, rice, salad, and fruit on a themed platter. ⊠ *1075 Duval St.* ☎ *305/294–0092* ▤ *AE, D, MC, V* ⊘ *No lunch July–Dec.*

Steak/Seafood

★ $$$–$$$$ ✕ **Pisces.** Don't be dismayed when you see the sign for Pisces on the Café des Artistes building: Chef Andrew Berman and staff are still there. They've changed the name, updated the menu, and gone contemporary with a granite bar and sparkling mirrors. Some old favorites remain on the menu, such as Lobster Tango Mango, flambéed in cognac and served with a saffron basil butter sauce and sliced mangoes. Other dishes include broiled Hawaiian blue prawns and pan-roasted halibut. Menu names sounded better when they were in French, but the taste lost nothing in the translation. ⊠ *1007 Simonton St.* ☎ *305/294–7100* ▤ *AE, MC, V* ⊘ *No lunch.*

★ $–$$$ ✕ **Seven Fish.** A local favorite, this small, intimate spot is good for an eclectic mix of seafood dishes such as yellowtail snapper in Thai curry sauce, penne with crawfish and scallops, and sashimi and smoked scallop California roll. Filling out the menu are chicken, vegetable dishes, and even a meat loaf with real mashed potatoes. ⊠ *632 Olivia St.* ☎ *305/296–2777* ▤ *AE, MC, V* ⊘ *Closed Tues. No lunch.*

¢–$$ ✕ **Crabby Bill's.** The scene is a warehouse-size room with beer flags, a concrete floor, old surfboards, and a large bar, but what Bill lacks in decorating skills he makes up for in cooking seafood, lots of it—there are nine popular Crabby Bill's in Florida. Oysters and soft-shell crabs are best sellers. Bring the kids: there's lots of space, a pinball machine, free soda refills, and a few dishes just for the 12-and-under set. ⊠ *511 Greene St.* ☎ *305/292–0802* ▤ *AE, D, DC, MC, V.*

Where to Stay

Historic cottages, restored turn-of-the-last-century Conch houses, and large resorts are among the offerings in Key West, with a few properties as low as $75 but the majority charging $100 to $300 a night. Most places raise prices during October's Fantasy Fest week and other events. Many guest houses and inns do not welcome children under 16, and some do not permit smoking indoors but provide ashtrays outside. Most tariffs include an expanded Continental breakfast and, often, afternoon wine or snack.

Guest Houses

★ $$$–$$$$ ▦ **Fleur de Key Guesthouse.** You could easily fill a little notebook with design ideas to take home from this charming guest house, which caters exclusively to a gay clientele. Conch-style architecture harks back to the property's origins as a boarding house and cigar makers' cottages. Standard rooms in the main house are smallish, so opt for a superior room, which is slightly more expensive but much larger. Rooms have antiques and reproductions and are tastefully decorated in whites and tropical colors. Enjoy robes, CDs, and CD players (in suites), and complimentary breakfast and evening cocktails. ⊠ *412 Frances St., 33040* ☎ *305/296–4719 or 800/932–9119* ⊕ *www.fleurdekey.com* ⇋ *2 suites, 14 rooms* ⚬ *Fans, refrigerators, cable TV, in-room VCRs, in-room data ports, pool, outdoor hot tub, concierge, no-smoking rooms; no kids under 16* ⊟ *AE, D, MC, V* ⏐◯⏐ *CP.*

★ **$$$–$$$$** 🏨 **Heron House.** A high coral fence, brilliantly splashed with spotlights at night, surrounds the compound of four Key West–style buildings with wood siding, railed porches, peaked roofs, and columns centered on a pool and orchid house, which supplies the orchids found throughout the guest house. Most units have a complete wall of exquisitely laid wood, entries with French doors, and bathrooms of polished granite. Some have floor-to-ceiling panels of mirrored glass and/or an oversize whirlpool. Complementing the superb interior detailing are daily newspapers, bathrobes, and free breakfast and wine and cheese. ⊠ *512 Simonton St., 33040* ☎ *305/294–9227* 🖷 *305/294–5692 or 888/861–9066* ⊕ *www.heronhouse.com* ⇋ *23 rooms* ⚬ *Fans, in-room safes, some in-room hot tubs, some minibars, some refrigerators, cable TV, in-room data ports, pool, dry cleaning, laundry service, concierge, parking (fee); no kids under 16, no smoking* ⊟ *AE, DC, MC, V* ⏐◯⏐ *CP.*

$$$–$$$$ 🏨 **Island City House Hotel.** There's a real sense of conviviality at this guest house with three buildings, each with a unique style (and price). The vintage-1880s Island City House has a widow's walk, antiques, and pine floors. Arch House, a former carriage house, has a dramatic entry that opens into a lush courtyard. Although all suites front on busy Eaton Street, only Nos. 5 and 6 face it. A reconstructed cigar factory has become the Cigar House, with porches, decks, and plantation-style teak and wicker furnishings. Guests share a private tropical garden. Children are welcome—a rarity in Old Town guest houses. ⊠ *411 William St., 33040* ☎ *305/294–5702 or 800/634–8230* 🖷 *305/294–1289* ⊕ *www. islandcityhouse.com* ⇋ *24 suites* ⚬ *Picnic area, BBQ, fans, some kitchens, some kitchenettes, some microwaves, cable TV, in-room VCRs, Wi-Fi, pool, outdoor hot tub, bicycles, laundry facilities, concierge; no smoking* ⊟ *AE, D, DC, MC, V* ⏐◯⏐ *CP.*

★ **$$$–$$$$** 🏨 **Mermaid & the Alligator.** Rooms in this 1904 Victorian house have a colonial Caribbean style, and wall colors are so luscious that guests frequently request paint chips. Wooden floors, furniture, and trim as well as French doors complement the colors. Some downstairs rooms open onto the deck, pool, and gardens designed by one of the resident owners, a landscape designer. Upstairs room balconies overlook the gardens. The Caribbean Queen suite has a large soaking tub, tiny shower, four-poster queen bed, and wraparound veranda, but its street-side location makes it noisy. A full breakfast is served poolside. The owners and their two retrievers make this a delightful place. ⊠ *729 Truman Ave., 33040* ☎ *305/294–1894 or 800/773–1894* 🖷 *305/295–9925* ⊕ *www. kwmermaid.com* ⇋ *6 rooms* ⚬ *Fans, pool; no room phones, no room TVs, no kids under 16, no smoking* ⊟ *AE, MC, V* ⏐◯⏐ *BP.*

★ **$$$–$$$$** ▣ **Popular House/Key West Bed & Breakfast.** Local art—large splashy canvases, a mural in the style of Gauguin—hangs on the walls, and tropical gardens and music set the mood here. Owner Jody Carlson offers both inexpensive rooms with shared bath and luxury rooms, reasoning that budget travelers deserve the same good style (and lavish Continental breakfast) as the rich. Less-expensive rooms burst with colors; the hand-painted dressers will make you laugh. Balconies added to second-floor rooms overlook the gardens, making these quarters the best in the house after the spacious (and most expensive) third-floor rooms, decorated with a paler palette and original furniture. Two friendly dogs live here, too. ⊠ *415 William St., 33040* ☎ *305/296–7274 or 800/438–6155* 🖷 *305/293–0306* ⊕ *www.keywestbandb.com* ➷ *8 rooms, 4 with bath* ⚤ *Fans, outdoor hot tub, sauna, bicycle, Internet; no room phones, no room TVs, no smoking* ▭ *AE, D, DC, MC, V* ¶⊙¶ *CP.*

★ **$$$** ▣ **Ambrosia House.** If you desire personal attention and a casual mood with a dollop of style, stay at these twin inns with pool-view rooms, suites, town houses, and cottages spread out on nearly 2 acres. Ambrosia is more intimate. Ambrosia Too is a delightful art-filled hideaway. Rooms have original work by Keys artists, wicker or wood furniture, and spacious bathrooms. Each has a private entrance and deck, patio, or porch. Poolside Continental breakfast is included, and children are welcome. ⊠ *615, 618, 622 Fleming St., 33040* ☎ *305/296–9838 or 800/535–9838* 🖷 *305/296–2425* ⊕ *www.ambrosiakeywest.com* ➷ *22 rooms, 3 town houses, 1 cottage, 6 suites* ⚤ *Fans, some in-room hot tubs, some kitchens, some minibars, some microwaves, refrigerators, cable TV, some in-room VCRs, in-room data ports, 5 pools, outdoor hot tub, bicycles, concierge, some free parking, some pets allowed (fee), no-smoking rooms* ▭ *AE, D, MC, V* ¶⊙¶ *BP.*

$$$ ▣ **Center Court Historic Inn & Cottages.** Noisy Duval Street is half a block away, but when you're here, you're enveloped in quiet and calm. Units range from spacious rooms with a queen bed to efficiency cottages (sleeping two to eight) with a deck and spa to studios and fully equipped three-bedroom, two-bath, house-size cottages (they sleep six). There's even a two-bedroom, two-bath house with its own pool. All units are decorated in relaxed tropical style, and both a full breakfast and happy-hour beverages are included. The heated pools are surrounded by lush foliage, whirlpools, and sundeck. ⊠ *915 Center St., 33040* ☎ *305/296–9292 or 800/797–8787* 🖷 *305/294–4104* ⊕ *www.centercourtkw.com* ➷ *4 rooms, 9 suites, 4 efficiencies, 10 cottages, 8 houses* ⚤ *Fans, in-room safes, some in-room hot tubs, some kitchens, some microwaves, some refrigerators, cable TV, some in-room VCRs, in-room data ports, 2 pools, exercise equipment, outdoor hot tub, business services, some pets allowed (fee); no smoking* ▭ *AE, D, MC, V* ¶⊙¶ *BP.*

★ **$$$** ▣ **Key Lime Inn.** This inn, an 1854 Grand Bahama–style house on the National Register of Historic Places with adjacent cottages and cabanas, succeeds by offering amiable service, good value, and pretty, light-filled rooms with natural wood and white furniture. The tropical ambience comes from gardens shaded by fruit and palm trees, tin-roof buildings with clapboard siding, classic white picket fences, and breezy porches. The least expensive Cabana rooms, some with patios, surround the pool. The Garden Cottages have one room; some include a porch or balcony. Some rooms in the historic Maloney House have a porch or patio. ✉ *725 Truman Ave., 33040* ☎ *305/294–5229 or 800/549–4430* 🖨 *305/294–9623* ⊕ *www.keylimeinn.com* 🛏 *30 rooms, 7 cottages* ⚬ *Fans, in-room safes, some microwaves, some refrigerators, cable TV, some in-room VCRs, in-room data ports, pool, free parking; no smoking* ☰ *AE, D, MC, V.*

★ **$$$** 🏨 **Merlin Guesthouse.** Key West guest houses don't usually welcome families, but this one is an exception. Brick walkways connect colorful rooms, suites, and cottages. A courtyard and tropical plantings further accent the grounds. Rooms in the 1930s Simonton House are most suitable for couples. They have four-poster beds and porches. Suites have wooden floors, French doors, rugs, four-poster beds, sundecks or porches, and sofa beds. Bright, roomy cottages have similar furnishings. There's no parking lot—a drawback, since it's a block off Duval Street. ✉ *811 Simonton St., 33040* ☎ *305/296–3336 or 800/642–4753* 🖨 *305/296–3524* ⊕ *www.merlinguesthouse.com* 🛏 *10 rooms, 6 suites, 4 cottages* ⚬ *Some fans, in-room safes, some kitchens, some microwaves, some refrigerators, cable TV, pool, Internet; no room phones, no smoking* ☰ *AE, D, MC, V* ⏐◯⏐ *CP.*

$$$ 🏨 **Pearl's Rainbow.** Originally a cigar factory and cigar makers' cottages, Pearl's is now a guest house for lesbian and lesbian-friendly straight women. It's designed to promote camaraderie; guests sun themselves on lounge chairs around the pools, relax on private and shared balconies, and hang out at Pearl's Patio, a poolside bar and grill that serves breakfast as well as burgers, sandwiches, salads, and drinks for lunch and dinner. Service, from the housekeepers to the reception staff, is friendly and enthusiastic. Flowery furnishings, French doors, and lush gardens give it a tropical feel. ✉ *525 United St., 33040* ☎ *305/292–1450 or 800/749–6696* 🖨 *305/292–8511* ⊕ *www.pearlsrainbow.com* 🛏 *33 rooms, 5 suites* ⚬ *Snack bar, fans, some kitchens, some kitchenettes, cable TV, 2 pools, 2 hot tubs, laundry service, concierge; no kids* ☰ *AE, D, MC, V* ⏐◯⏐ *CP.*

$$–$$$ 🏨 **Eden House.** This 1920s art deco guest house offers something for most budgets. Two levels of accommodations surround a garden courtyard with a pool bordered by lounges and umbrella-shaded tables. Rooms range from small, simple spaces with a double or two twin beds and a squeaky-clean bathroom shared by two rooms to large spaces with a queen bed, kitchenette, and private porch. They all have pleasant furnishings and tropical colors. Spacious suites come in two sizes and have paler decors. The helpful, friendly staff sets up a daily complimentary happy hour. ✉ *1015 Fleming St., 33040* ☎ *305/296–6868 or 800/533–5397* 🖨 *305/294–1221* ⊕ *www.edenhouse.com* 🛏 *35 rooms, 6 with shared bath, 8 suites* ⚬ *Restaurant, fans, some kitchens, some microwaves, some refrigerators, pool, outdoor hot tub, bicycles, library, shop, laundry facilities, concierge, free parking; no TV in some rooms, no smoking* ☰ *AE, MC, V.*

¢–$$$ 🏨 **Olivia By Duval.** This compound of clapboard buildings and mural art contains eccentrically shaped and sized efficiencies and one- and two-bedroom apartments with wood and carpeted floors, immaculate bathrooms, and some private outside sitting areas. A high white picket fence gives privacy to a pool surrounded by a wooden deck outfitted with lounge chairs. The friendly staff, as well as three apartments that convert into a two-story, three-bedroom, three-bath house, make this property especially accommodating to families and spring breakers (throughout March). ⊠ *511 Olivia St., 33040* ☎ *305/296–5169 or 800/413–1978* 🖷 *305/296–5590* ⊕ *www.oliviabyduval.com* 🛏 *8 rooms, 1 suite* ↻ *BBQ, fans, some kitchens, some kitchenettes, microwaves, refrigerators, cable TV, pool, laundry service, some pets allowed (fee); no room phones* ⊟ *MC, V.*

¢–$$$ 🏨 **Speakeasy Inn.** During Prohibition, Raul Vasquez smuggled liquor from Cuba and taxi drivers stopped here to fill suitcases with the bootleg. Today, the Speakeasy survives as an attractively priced inn. Spacious studios, suites, and two-bedroom units have bright white walls offset by bursts of color in rugs, pillows, and seat cushions; queen-size beds and tables made from salvaged pine; Saltillo tiles in the bathrooms; oak floors; and some claw-foot bathtubs. Maid and concierge service are available. Casa 325 Suites, an upscale all-suites property at the opposite end of Duval, is under the same ownership. ⊠ *1117 Duval St., 33040* ☎ *305/296–2680 or 800/217–4884* 🖷 *305/296–2680* ⊕ *www.speakeasyinn.com* 🛏 *4 suites, 4 studios, 2 2-bedroom units* ↻ *Fans, some kitchenettes, cable TV, lobby lounge, concierge; no room phones, no smoking* ⊟ *AE, D, MC, V.*

$$ 🏨 **Courtney's Place.** This "village" of gardens and cottages in a quiet residential neighborhood is a microcosm of Key West architecture, with building styles ranging from Bahamian and cigar-maker cottages to Caribbean and shotgun houses. The interior is equally varied in coloring and furnishings, but all the rooms have at least a refrigerator, microwave, and coffee pot, if not a full kitchen. It's a family-owned and family-friendly inn. ⊠ *720 Whitmarsh La., 33040* ☎ *305/294–3480 or 800/869–4639* ⊕ *www.courtneysplacekeywest.com* 🛏 *6 rooms, 3 suites, 8 cottages* ↻ *Picnic area, BBQ, fans, some kitchens, some kitchenettes, microwaves, refrigerators, cable TV, in-room data ports, pool, bicycles, laundry facilities, concierge, free parking, some pets allowed (fee); no smoking* ⊟ *AE, MC, V* ⦿⦿ *CP.*

$ 🏨 **Angelina Guest House.** Two blocks off Duval Street, in the heart of Old Town Key West, this gambling hall and bordello turned guest house could command top dollar for its rooms. Instead, it offers simple, clean, attractively priced accommodations, from rooms that share a hallway bath and community refrigerator and microwave to spacious rooms with a king bed and sleeper sofa. Built in the 1920s, this charming, rambling, yellow-and-white wooden building has second-floor porches, gabled roofs, and a white picket fence. New owners prettied the rooms with flower-print curtains and linens and added homemade cinnamon rolls, which receive rave reviews in the guest book, to the inclusive breakfast bar. A pool, fountain, and old bricks accent a lovely garden. ⊠ *302 Angela St., 33040* ☎ *305/294–4480 or 888/303–4480* ⊕ *www.angelinaguesthouse.com* 🛏 *13 rooms* ↻ *BBQ, fans, some microwaves, some refrigerators, pool, bicycles; no room phones, no room TVs, no smoking* ⊟ *D, MC, V* ⦿⦿ *CP.*

Hotels

$$$$ ⊞ **Marquesa Hotel.** In a town that prides itself on its laid-back luxe, this
Fodor'sChoice   complex of four restored 1884 houses stands out. Guests—typically shoe-
★   less in Marquesa robes—relax among richly landscaped pools and gardens against a backdrop of steps rising to the villalike suites. Elegant
rooms have antique and reproduction furnishings, botanical-print fabrics, and marble baths. The lobby resembles a Victorian parlor, with antiques, Audubon prints, flowers, and photos of early Key West. The
clientele is mostly straight, but the hotel is very gay-friendly. ⊠ *600 Fleming St., 33040* ☎ *305/292–1919 or 800/869–4631* 🖷 *305/294–2121*
⊕ *www.marquesa.com* ↩ *27 rooms* ⚭ *Restaurant, room service, fans,
in-room safes, minibars, cable TV with movies, in-room data ports, 2
pools, spa, bicycles, laundry service, concierge, business services* ⊟ *AE,
DC, MC, V.*

★ **$$$$**   ⊞ **Ocean Key Resort.** A pool and open-air bar and grill make their homes
on the Sunset Pier here, which provides the perfect view come sundown.
Toast the day's end from private balconies that extend from brightly colored rooms that are both stylish and homey. High ceilings, hand-painted
furnishings, a sleigh bed, plaid couch, and a wooden chest for a coffee
table create a personally designed look; bring some discs for the CD-
alarm clock. Jet skis can be rented at the marina, and the early evening
hubbub of Mallory Square is right behind the hotel. ⊠ *Zero Duval St.,
33040* ☎ *305/296–7701 or 800/328–9815* 🖷 *305/292–7685* ⊕ *www.
oceankey.com* ↩ *75 rooms, 25 suites* ⚭ *2 restaurants, dining room, room
service, fans, some in-room hot tubs, some kitchens, minibars, some microwaves, refrigerators, cable TV, in-room data ports, pool, massage,
spa, dive shop, snorkeling, windsurfing, boating, jet skiing, parasailing,
fishing, bicycles, 2 bars, beer garden, lounge, shop, dry cleaning, laundry service, concierge, Internet, business services, meeting rooms, parking (fee), no-smoking rooms* ⊟ *AE, D, DC, MC, V.*

★ **$$$$**   ⊞ **Pier House Resort & Caribbean Spa.** This convivial, sprawling pleasure
complex of weathered gray buildings, including an original Conch
house, has a courtyard of tall coconut palms and hibiscus blossoms. Rooms
are light-filled, cozy, and colorful and have a water, pool, or garden view.
Most rooms are smaller than those at newer hotels, except in the more
expensive Caribbean Spa section, which has hardwood floors, two-
poster plantation beds, and CD players. The best lodgings are in the Harbor Front, each with a private balcony. Sunset on the Havana Docks is
a special event. Rooms nearest the public areas can be noisy. ⊠ *1 Duval
St., 33040* ☎ *305/296–4600 or 800/327–8340* 🖷 *305/296–7569*
⊕ *www.pierhouse.com* ↩ *126 rooms, 16 suites* ⚭ *3 restaurants, room
service, fans, some in-room hot tubs, minibars, cable TV, some in-room
VCRs, in-room data ports, pool, health club, hair salon, outdoor hot
tub, massage, sauna, spa, beach, dock, fishing, bicycles, 4 bars, shop,
laundry service, concierge, Internet, business services, meeting rooms,
no-smoking rooms* ⊟ *AE, D, DC, MC, V.*

★ **$$$$**   ⊞ **Sunset Key Guest Cottages at Hilton Key West Resort.** Check in, then
board a 10-minute launch to the one-, two-, and three-bedroom cottages on 27-acre Sunset Key. Sandy beaches, swaying palms, flowering
gardens, a delicious sense of privacy—it's all here. The comforts are first-

class and appeal to adults and children. Baked goods, juice, and a newspaper are delivered each morning, grocery shopping service is provided (fee), a private chef is available (fee), and you can use all the facilities at the Key West Hilton. Avail yourself of a VHS/DVD collection, books, board games, and CDs. Shuttle between the island and Key West around the clock at no extra charge, or remain at Sunset Key to dine, play, and relax at the very civilized beach, complete with attendants and cabanas. ⊠ *245 Front St., 33040* ☎ *305/292–5300 or 888/477–7786* ☐ *305/ 292–5395* ⊕ *www.sunsetkeyisland.com* ⇖ *37 cottages* ⚭ *Restaurant, snack bar, room service, fans, in-room safes, kitchens, minibars, cable TV with movies, in-room DVDs/VCRs, in-room data ports, 2 tennis courts, pool, outdoor hot tub, massage, beach, basketball, library, shop, babysitting, laundry facilities, laundry service, concierge, Internet, business services, meeting rooms; no smoking* ☰ *AE, D, DC, MC, V.*

$$$$ 🏨 **Wyndham's Casa Marina Resort.** At any moment, you expect the landed gentry to walk across the oceanfront lawn, just as they did in the 1920s, when this 13-acre resort was built. It has the same rich lobby with a beamed ceiling, polished pine floor, and art. Guest rooms are stylishly decorated. Armoires and wicker chairs with thick cushions add warmth. Fluffy bathrobes and luxurious designer toiletries make it feel like home. Two-bedroom loft suites with balconies face the ocean. The main building's ground-floor lanai rooms open onto the lawn. ⊠ *1500 Reynolds St., 33040* ☎ *305/296–3535 or 800/626–0777* ☐ *305/296– 9960* ⊕ *www.casamarinakeywest.com* ⇖ *311 units, 239 rooms, 72 suites* ⚭ *2 restaurants, room service, fans, in-room safes, minibars, cable TV with movies and video games, in-room data ports, 3 tennis courts, 2 pools, gym, hair salon, outdoor hot tub, massage, sauna, beach, dive shop, snorkeling, windsurfing, boating, jet skiing, fishing, bicycles, volleyball, 2 bars, shop, babysitting, children's programs (ages 4–12), dry cleaning, laundry service, concierge, Internet, business services, meeting rooms, airport shuttle, no-smoking rooms* ☰ *AE, D, DC, MC, V.*

★ $$$–$$$$ 🏨 **Best Western Key Ambassador Inn.** Every room in this well-maintained 7-acre property has a screened balcony, most with a view of the ocean or pool. Accommodations are roomy and cheerful, with Caribbean-style light-color furniture and linens in coordinated tropical colors. There's high-speed Internet access in the lobby, and a wireless network in the lobby, around the pool, and in most rooms. The palm-shaded pool looks over the Atlantic, and a covered picnic area with a large barbecue grill encourages socializing. The outdoor bar serves lunch, drinks, and light dishes. A complimentary Continental breakfast and free weekday newspaper are included. ⊠ *3755 S. Roosevelt Blvd., New Town 33040* ☎ *305/296–3500 or 800/432–4315* ☐ *305/296–9961* ⊕ *www. keyambassador.com* ⇖ *100 rooms* ⚭ *Café, coffee shop, picnic area, BBQs, refrigerators, cable TV with movies, in-room data ports, pool, shuffleboard, bar, laundry facilities, business services, airport shuttle, free parking, no-smoking rooms* ☰ *AE, D, DC, MC, V* ⊙∣ *CP.*

Motels

$$ 🏨 **Harborside Motel & Marina.** This simple little motel neatly packages three appealing characteristics—affordability, safety, and a pleasant location between a quiet street and Garrison Bight (the charter-boat harbor), at the border of Old Town and New Town. Units are boxy, clean, and basic, with little patios, ceramic-tile floors, phones, and lots of peace and quiet. Four stationary houseboats each sleep four. Barbecue grills are available for cookouts. Spring breakers need not apply: the motel likes to maintain a relative calm. ⊠ *903 Eisenhower Dr., 33040* ☎ *305/294–2780 or 800/501–7823* ⊕ *www.keywestharborside.com* ➳ *14 efficiencies, 4 houseboats* ⚘ *BBQ, kitchens, cable TV, pool, dock, marina, laundry facilities* ▤ *AE, D, DC, MC, V.*

$$ 🏠 **Southwind Motel.** If you're looking for a practical, affordable place to stay that's just a short walk from Duval Street, consider this friendly lodging run by the same folks who operate Harborside Motel & Marina. The pastel 1940s-style motel has mature tropical plantings, all nicely set back from the street a block from the beach. Rooms are superclean and have tile floors and basic furnishings. It's as good as you'll find at the price, and although rates have gone up, they drop if demand gets slack. ⊠ *1321 Simonton St., 33040* ☎ *305/296–2215 or 800/501–7826* ⊕ *www.keywestsouthwind.com* ➳ *12 rooms, 3 efficiencies* ⚘ *Fans, some kitchens, refrigerators, cable TV, pool, laundry facilities* ▤ *AE, D, DC, MC, V.*

Nightlife & the Arts

The Arts

Catch the classics and the latest art, independent, and foreign films ($5) shown by the **Key West Film Society** (⊠ 416 Eaton St. ☎ 305/294–5857) now daily in its new two-screen theater, Tropic Cinema. In a wickedly indulgent style that is so Key West, **Cinema Shores** (⊠ 510 South St. ☎ 305/296–2491), at Atlantic Shores Resort, an adult alternative resort, shows classic, foreign, and new films ($5) on a large outdoor screen on Thursday evenings. Viewers enjoy free popcorn and chocolate bars and cocktail service as they stretch out on lounge chairs on the lawn. Sebrina Alfonso directs the **Key West Symphony** (⊠ Florida Keys Community College, 5901 College Rd. ☎ 305/292–1774) during the winter season. Watch for free preconcert lectures at libraries and other venues. With more than 20 years' experience, the **Red Barn Theatre** (⊠ 319 Duval St., rear ☎ 305/296–9911), a small professional theater, performs dramas, comedies, and musicals, including works by new playwrights. The **Tennessee Williams Fine Arts Center** (⊠ Florida Keys Community College, 5901 College Rd. ☎ 305/296–1520), on Stock Island, presents chamber music, dance, jazz concerts, and dramatic and musical plays with major stars, as well as other performing arts events. The **Waterfront Playhouse** (⊠ Mallory Sq. ☎ 305/294–5015) is a mid-1850s wrecker's warehouse that was converted into a 180-seat, non-Equity regional theater presenting comedy and drama from December to June. It begins its 65th season making improvements to the building, from new air-conditioning and handrails to updated lighting.

Nightlife

BARS & LOUNGES Pick your entertainment at the **Bourbon Street Complex** (⊠ 722–801 Duval St. ☎ 305/296–1992), a gay-oriented club with five bars and two restaurants. There are two nightly drag shows in the 801 Bourbon Bar and 10 video screens along with male dancers grooving to the latest music spun by DJs at the Bourbon Street Pub. In its earliest incarnation, back in 1851, **Capt. Tony's Saloon** (✉ 428 Greene St. ☎ 305/294–1838) was a morgue and icehouse, then Key West's first telegraph station. It became the original Sloppy Joe's in the mid-1930s, when Hemingway was a regular. Later, a young Jimmy Buffett sang here. Bands play nightly. Pause for a libation at the open-air **Green Parrot Bar** (✉ 601 Whitehead St., at Southard St. ☎ 305/294–6133). Built in 1890, the bar is said to be Key West's oldest, a sometimes-rowdy saloon where locals outnumber out-of-towners, especially on weekends when bands play. It opened a smokehouse, Meteor, behind it that serves smoked shrimp, pork, chicken, and beef. **LaTeDa Hotel and Bar** (✉ 1125 Duval St. ☎ 305/296–6706) hosts a riotously funny cabaret show nightly in the Crystal Room Cabaret Lounge. There's also live entertainment nightly, including the popular local singer Lenore Troia, in the Terrace Garden Bar. A youngish crowd sprinkled with aging Parrot Heads frequents **Margaritaville Café** (✉ 500 Duval St. ☎ 305/292–1435), owned by former Key West resident and recording star Jimmy Buffett, who has been known to perform here. The drink of choice is, of course, a margarita. There's live music nightly, as well as lunch and dinner.

Nightlife at the **Pier House** (✉ 1 Duval St. ☎ 305/296–4600) begins with a steel drum band (weekends) to celebrate the sunset on the beach, then moves indoors to the piano bar for live jazz (Thursday to Sunday). The **Schooner Wharf Bar** (✉ 202 William St. ☎ 305/292–9520), an open-air waterfront bar and grill in the historic seaport district, retains its funky Key West charm. There's live island music all day, plus happy hour, and special events. There's more history and good times at **Sloppy Joe's** (✉ 201 Duval St. ☎ 305/294–5717), the successor to a famous 1937 speakeasy named for its founder, Captain Joe Russell. Ernest Hemingway came here to gamble and tell stories. Decorated with Hemingway memorabilia and marine flags, the bar is popular with travelers and is full and noisy all the time. Live entertainment plays daily 10 AM–2 AM. The **Top Lounge** (✉ 430 Duval St. ☎ 305/296–2991) is on the 7th floor of the La Concha Holiday Inn and is one of the best places in town to view the sunset and enjoy live entertainment Wednesday to Saturday. In the best traditions of a 1950s cocktail lounge, **Virgilio's** (✉ Applerouth La. ☎ 305/296–8118) serves chilled martinis to the soothing tempo of live jazz and blues nightly. It's part of the La Trattoria restaurant complex.

Sports & the Outdoors

Biking

Key West is a cycling town, but ride carefully: narrow and one-way streets along with car traffic result in several bike accidents a year. Some hotels rent or loan bikes to guests; others will refer you to a nearby shop and reserve a bike for you.

Keys Moped & Scooter (✉ 523 Truman Ave. ☎ 305/294–0399) rents beach cruisers with large baskets as well as scooters. Rates for scooters start at $15 for three hours. Look for the huge American flag on the roof. **Moped Hospital** (✉ 601 Truman Ave. ☎ 305/296–3344) supplies balloon-tire bikes with yellow safety baskets for adults and kids, as well as mopeds and double-seater scooters for adults.

Fishing

Captain Steven Impallomeni works as a flats-fishing guide, specializing in ultralight and fly-fishing for tarpon, permit, and bonefish, as well as near-shore and light-tackle fishing. Charters on the *Gallopin' Ghost* leave from **Murray's Marina** (✉ MM 5, Stock Island ☎ 305/292–9837). **Key West Bait and Tackle** (✉ 241 Margaret St. ☎ 305/292–1961) carries live bait, frozen rigged and unrigged bait, and fishing and rigging equipment. It also has the Live Bait Lounge; unwind and sip ice-cold beer while telling tall tales after fishing.

Golf

Key West Resort Golf Course (✉ 6450 E. College Rd. ☎ 305/294–5232) is an 18 hole course on the bay side of Stock Island. Nonresident fees are $150 for 18 holes (cart included) in season, $85 off-season.

Scuba & Snorkeling

Adventure Charters & Tours (✉ 6810 Front St., 33040 ☎ 305/296–0362 or 888/817–0841) has sail-and-snorkel coral reef adventure tours ($35) aboard the 42-foot trimaran sailboat *Fantasea,* with a maximum of 16 people. There are two daily departures. **Captain's Corner** (✉ Corner of Greene and Elizabeth ☎ 305/296–8865), a PADI five-star shop, has dive classes in several languages and twice-daily snorkel and dive trips to reefs and wrecks aboard the 60-foot dive boat *Sea Eagle.* Safely dive the coral reefs without getting a scuba certification with **Snuba of Key West.** Ride out to the reef on a catamaran, listen to a 20-minute orientation, then follow your guide underwater for a one-hour tour of the coral reefs. You wear a regulator with a breathing hose that is attached to a floating air tank on the surface of the water. No prior diving or snorkeling experience is necessary, but you must know how to swim. The $95 cost includes beverages (✉ Garrison Bight Marina, Palm Ave. between Eaton St. and N. Roosevelt Blvd. ☎ 305/292-4616.).

Shopping

Key West has dozens of characterless T-shirt shops, as well as art galleries and curiosity shops with lots worth toting home.

Bahama Village is an enclave of new and spruced-up shops, restaurants, and vendors leading the way in the restoration of the historic district where black Bahamians settled in the 19th century. The village lies roughly between Whitehead and Fort streets and Angela and Catherine streets. Hemingway frequented the bars, restaurants, and boxing rings in the village.

Arts & Crafts

The **Gallery on Greene** (✉ 606 Greene St. ☎ 305/294–1669) showcases politically incorrect art by Jeff McNally and three-dimensional paintings by local artist Mario Sanchez, among others, in the largest gallery exhibition space in Key West. The oldest private art gallery in Key West, **Gingerbread Square Gallery** (✉ 1207 Duval St. ☎ 305/296–8900), represents mainly Keys artists who have attained national and international prominence, including Sal Salinero and John Kiraly, in media ranging from graphics to art glass. New management at **Haitian Art Co.** (✉ 600

Frances St. ☎ 305/296–8932) instituted monthly exhibits in the front gallery to highlight the more than 4,000 art objects, ranging from paintings to spirit flags. The gallery has one of the largest collections of Haitian art outside Haiti, representing artists working in wood, stone, metal, and papier-mâché. Reen Stanhouse, one of the three female artists who own **Helio Gallery** (✉ 814 Fleming St. ☎ 305/294–7901), is as exuberant and eccentric as you'd expect of someone who makes whimsical, colorful, island-inspired iron work. Her partners create functional and decorative ceramics, art to wear, textiles, beautifully framed botanical prints, photography, pottery, and woven baskets. Historian, photographer, and painter Sharon Wells opened a contemporary photographic art gallery, **KW Light Gallery** (✉ 534 Fleming St. ☎ 305/294–0566) in 2002, with fine art photography and paintings of her own and national artists as well as giclée prints of historic Key West photographs. **Lucky Street Gallery** (✉ 1120 White St. ☎ 305/294–3973) sells high-end contemporary paintings, watercolors, and a few pieces of jewelry by internationally recognized Key West–based artists. **Pelican Poop** (✉ 314 Simonton St. ☎ 305/296–3887) sells Caribbean art around a lush tropical courtyard garden with a fountain and pool. The owners buy direct from Caribbean artisans every year, so prices are very attractive. (Hemingway wrote *A Farewell to Arms* while living in the complex's apartment.) Potters Charles Pearson and Timothy Roeder *are* **Whitehead St. Pottery** (✉ 322 Julia St. ☎ 305/294–5067), where they display their porcelain stoneware and raku-fired vessels. They also have a photo gallery where they exhibit Polaroid image transfers and black-and-white photos. The setting, around two koi ponds with a burbling fountain, is as sublime as the art.

Books

Flaming Maggie's (✉ 830 Fleming St. ☎ 305/294–3931) specializes in books, cards, and magazines for and about gays and lesbians and also carries books—and artwork—by or about local authors. It has a popular coffee bar, too. The **Key West Island Bookstore** (✉ 513 Fleming St. ☎ 305/294–2904) is the literary bookstore of the large Key West writers' community. It carries new, used, and rare titles and specializes in Hemingway, Tennessee Williams, and South Florida mystery writers.

Clothes & Fabrics

Take home a shopping bag full of scarlet hibiscus, fuchsia heliconias, blue parrot fish, and even pink flamingos from the **Seam Shoppe** (✉ 1114 Truman Ave. ☎ 305/296–9830), which specializes in the city's widest selection of tropical fabrics for indoor and outdoor upholstery, as well as quilts and fashions. Since 1964, **Key West Hand Print Fashions and Fabrics** (✉ 201 Simonton St. ☎ 305/294–9535 or 800/866–0333) has been noted for its vibrant tropical prints, yard goods, and resort wear for men and women. It's in the Curry Warehouse, a brick building erected in 1878 to store tobacco. **Tikal Trading Co.** (✉ 129 Duval St. ✉ 910 Duval St. ☎ 305/296–4463) sells its own line of women's and little girl's clothing of handwoven Guatemalan cotton and knit tropical prints.

Food & Drink

The **Blond Giraffe** (⊠ 629 Duval St. ⊠ 1209 Truman Ave. ☎ 305/293–
6998) turned an old family recipe for key lime pie into a commercial
success story. Its two stores often have a line for the pie, with delicate
pastry, sweet-tart custard filling, and thick meringue topping. The key
lime rum cake is the best-selling product for shipping home. On a hot
summer day, nothing quenches the heat like a Pie-Pop, a slice of frozen
key lime pie dipped in dark chocolate and sold on a stick. You'll be pleasantly surprised by what they make wine from at the **Key West Winery**
(⊠ 103 Simonton St. ☎ 305/292–2254 or 866/880–1717). Display
crates hold bottles of wines made from blueberries, blackberries, pineapples, cherries, carrots, citrus, mangoes, watermelons, tomatoes, and, of
course, key limes. Many of the wines, including Pineapple Sunset, won
gold, silver or Best of Show medals at the Florida State Fair and Indiana International Wine Competition. **Fausto's Food Palace** (⊠ 522 Fleming St. ☎ 305/296–5663 ⊠ 1105 White St. ☎ 305/294–5221) may be
under a roof, but it's a market in the traditional town-square sense. Since
1926, Fausto's has been the spot to catch up on the week's gossip and
to chill out in summer—it has groceries, organic foods, marvelous
wines, a sushi chef on duty from 8 to 6, and box lunches to go. You'll
spend your first five minutes at the **Waterfront Market** (⊠ 201 William
St. ☎ 305/296–0778) wondering how to franchise one of these great
markets in your hometown. It sells savory deli items from around the
world, health food, produce, salads, espresso, cold beer, and wine.
Don't miss the fish market, bakery, deli, or juice bar; sushi from the
Origami Restaurant; and vegan dishes from Linda's Vegan Delights. The
market closes at 6 every day but Friday, when it's open until 8.

Gifts & Souvenirs

Like a parody of Duval Street T-shirt shops, the hole-in-the-wall **Art Attack** (⊠ 606 Duval St. ☎ 305/294–7131) throws in every icon and trin-
ket anyone nostalgic for the days of peace and love might fancy: beads,
necklaces, harmony bells, and psychedelic T-shirts. Best-sellers are photographic postcards of Key West by Tony Gregory. It's open until 11 PM
daily. **Fast Buck Freddie's** (⊠ 500 Duval St. ☎ 305/294–2007) sells a classy,
hip selection of crystal, furniture, tropical clothing, and every flamingo
item imaginable. It also carries such imaginative items as a noise-acti-
vated rat in a trap and a raccoon tail in a bag. **Half Buck Freddie's** (⊠ 306
William St. ☎ 305/294–2007) is the discount-outlet store for Fast
Buck's. It's closed Tuesday and Wednesday.

The feel of **Kindred Spirit** (⊠ 1204 Simonton St. ☎ 305/296–1515) is
very New Age, but in addition to aromatherapy candles, inspirational
music, and scented soaps there are delicate picture frames and artwork
and jewelry made by Keys artists. Tea is a specialty. Buy tea leaves, tea
bags, and tea cups and enjoy formal tea—complete with freshly baked
scones, fruit bread, and cake and confections—on comfy overstuffed chairs
inside or outside in a tropical garden. In a town with a gazillion T-shirt
★ shops, **Last Flight Out** (⊠ 503 Greene St. ☎ 305/294–8008) stands out
for its selection of classic namesake Ts, specialty clothing, and gifts that
appeal to aviation types and others who reach for the stars.

Take home a souvenir that maintains the health of the beautiful coral reefs that surround the Keys from the **Reef Relief Environmental Store** (⊠201 William St. ☎ 305/294–3100). Along with *The Reef Relief Book of Coral Reef Fish* for kids, a whimsical coloring book that identifies sea creatures, the shop sells books for adults, caps, mugs, beach towels, posters, and educational materials.

Health & Beauty

Key West Aloe (⊠ 540 Greene St., at Simonton St. ☎ 305/294–5592 or 800/445–2563) was founded in a garage in 1971; today it produces some 300 perfume, sunscreen, and skin-care products for men and women. After years downtown on Front Street, in April 2004 it moved back to a new showroom at the original factory location.

Side Trip

Dry Tortugas National Park

This sanctuary for thousands of birds, 70 mi off the shores of Key West, consists of seven small islands. Its main facility is the long-deactivated Fort Jefferson, where Dr. Samuel Mudd was imprisoned for his alleged role in Lincoln's assassination. Tour the fort; then lay out your blanket on the sunny beach for a picnic before you head out to snorkel on the protected reef. Many people like to camp here, but note that there's no fresh-water supply and you must carry off whatever you bring onto the island. For information and a list of authorized charter boats and water taxis, contact **Everglades National Park** (⊠ 40001 Rte. 9336, Homestead 33034-6733 ☎ 305/242–7700).

The fast, sleek, 100-foot catamaran *Yankee Freedom II*, of the **Yankee Fleet Dry Tortugas National Park Ferry,** cuts the travel time to the Dry Tortugas to 2¼ hours. The time passes quickly on the roomy vessel equipped with three restrooms, two freshwater showers, and two bars. Stretch out on two decks; one an air-conditioned salon with cushioned seating, the other an open sundeck with sunny and shaded seating. Breakfast and lunch are included. On arrival, a naturalist leads a 45-minute guided tour, which is followed by lunch and a free afternoon for swimming, snorkeling (gear included), and exploring. The vessel is ADA-certified for visitors using wheelchairs. ⊠ *Lands End Marina, 240 Margaret St., Key West 33040* ☎ *305/294–7009 or 800/634–0939* ⊕ *www.yankeefreedom.com* ⊠ *$129, plus $5 park fee* ☉ *Trips daily at 8 AM.*

THE FLORIDA KEYS A TO Z

To research prices, get advice from other travelers, and book travel arrangements, visit www.fodors.com.

AIR TRAVEL

Service between Key West International Airport and Miami, Fort Lauderdale/Hollywood, Atlanta, Naples, Orlando, St. Petersburg, and Tampa is provided by American Eagle, Cape Air, Comair/Delta Connection, Gulfstream/Continental Connection, and US Airways/US Airways Express.

The Airporter operates scheduled van and bus pickup service from all Miami International Airport (MIA) baggage areas to wherever you want to go in Key Largo ($35) and Islamorada ($38). A group discount is given for three or more passengers. Reservations are required. Keys Shuttle runs scheduled service six times a day in 15-passenger vans (9 passengers maximum) between Miami Airport and Key West with stops throughout the Keys for $50–$70. Add $10 to Fort Lauderdale Airport. The Super Shuttle charges $151 per passenger for trips to the Upper Keys. To go farther into the Keys, you must book an entire van (up to 11 passengers), which costs $251 to Marathon, $351 to Key West. Super Shuttle requests 24-hours notice for transportation back to the airport.

CARRIERS   🚐 Airlines & Contacts **American Eagle** ☎ 800/433–7300. **Cape Air** ☎ 800/352–0714. **Comair/Delta Connection** ☎ 800/354–9822. **Gulfstream/Continental Connection** ☎ 800/525–0280. **US Airways/US Airways Express** ☎ 800/428–4322.

🚐 Airport Information **Key West International Airport** ✉ S. Roosevelt Blvd., Key West ☎ 305/296–5439. **Miami International Airport** ☎ 305/876–7000. **Airporter** ☎ 305/852–3413 or 800/830–3413. **Keys Shuttle** ☎ 305/289–9997 or 888/765–9997. **Super Shuttle** ☎ 305/871–2000.

BOAT & FERRY TRAVEL

Boaters can travel to and along the Keys either along the Intracoastal Waterway (5-foot draft limitation) through Card, Barnes, and Blackwater sounds and into Florida Bay or along the deeper Atlantic Ocean route through Hawk Channel, a buoyed passage. Refer to NOAA Nautical Charts Numbers 11451, 11445, and 11441. The Keys are full of marinas that welcome transient visitors, but they don't have enough slips for everyone. Make reservations in advance and ask about channel and dockage depth—many marinas are quite shallow.

For nonemergency information contact Coast Guard Group Key West; VHF-FM Channel 16. Safety and weather information is broadcast at 7 AM and 5 PM Eastern Standard Time on VHF-FM Channels 16 and 22A. There are stations in Islamorada and Marathon.

Key West Express operates air-conditioned ferries between the Key West Terminal (Caroline and Grinnell Streets) and Marco Island and Fort Myers Beach, on the mainland's southwest coast. The trip takes 3 to 3½ hours each way, respectively. Ferries depart in the morning between 8 and 9, and return in the afternoon between 5 and 6. Tickets start at $73 one-way, $135 round-trip. The round trip includes Continental breakfast. A current, legal photo ID is required for each passenger. All bags are subject to search. Advance reservations are recommended.

Chambers of commerce, marinas, and dive shops offer free Teall's Guides, land and nautical charts that pinpoint popular fishing and diving areas throughout the Keys.

🚤 Boat & Ferry Information **Coast Guard Group for the Florida Keys** ✉ Key West ☎ 305/292-8779 ✉ Islamorada ☎ 306/664-8077 information, 305/664-4404 emergencies ✉ Marathon ☎ 305/743-6778 information, 305/743-6388 emergencies. **Key West Express Ferry** ☎ 888/539-2628 or 239/394-9700 ⊕ www.keywestferry.com. **Teall's Guides** ✉ Box 522409, Marathon Shores 33052-2409 ☎ 305/872-3123.

BUS TRAVEL

Greyhound Lines runs a special Keys shuttle three or four times a day (depending on the day of the week) between Miami International Airport (departing from Concourse E, lower level) and stops throughout the Keys. Fares run from $15–$30 one-way–round-trip for Key Largo (Howard Johnson, MM 102) to around $35–$68 for Key West (3535 S. Roosevelt, Key West Airport).

City of Key West Department of Transportation has four color-coded bus routes traversing the island from 6:30 AM to 11:30 PM. Stops have signs with the international symbol for bus. Schedules are available on buses and at hotels, visitor centers, and shops. The fare is $1 (exact change) or $3 for an all-day pass that you purchase onboard.

Bone Island Shuttle circles the island from 9 AM to 11 PM, stopping at attractions, hotels, and restaurants. Passengers pay $8 per day or $18 per three days for unlimited riding. Purchase at hotels and the Key West Welcome. Park at the city's Park 'n' Ride 24-hour garage at the corner of Caroline and Grinnell streets and catch a city bus to Old Town at no extra cost. Parking costs $1.50 an hour or $10 a day.

The Dade–Monroe Express provides daily bus service from MM 50 in Marathon to the Florida City Wal-Mart Supercenter on the Mainland. The bus stops at major shopping centers as well as on-demand anywhere along the route during daily round-trips on the hour from 6 AM to 9:55 PM. The cost is $1.50 each way.

🚍 **Bus Information Bone Island Shuttle** ☎ 305/293-8710. **City of Key West Department of Transportation** ☎ 305/292-8160. **Dade-Monroe Express** ☎ 305/770-3131. **Greyhound Lines** ☎ 800/410-5397 or 800/231-2222. **Park 'n' Ride** ✉ 300 Grinnell St. ☎ 305/293-6426.

CAR RENTAL

Two- and four-passenger open-air electric cars that travel about 25 mph are an environmentally friendly way to get around the island. Rent them from Key West Cruisers for $90–$130 a half day for the two- or four-seater, or $140–$190 a day.

Avis, Budget, and Enterprise serve Marathon Airport. Key West's airport has booths for Alamo, Avis, Budget, Dollar, and Hertz. Tropical Rent-A-Car is based in the city center. Enterprise Rent-A-Car has offices in Key Largo, Marathon, and Key West. Thrifty Car Rental has an office in Tavernier.

CUTTING COSTS Avoid flying into Key West and driving back to Miami; there are substantial drop-off charges for leaving a Key West car there.

🚗 **Local Agencies Alamo** ☎ 305/294-6675 or 800/327-9633. **Avis** ✉ Key West Airport ☎ 305/294-4846 ✉ Marathon Airport ☎ 305/743-5428 or 800/331-1212. **Budget** ✉ Key West Airport ☎ 305/294-8868 ✉ Marathon Airport ☎ 305/743-3998 or 800/527-0700. **Dollar** ☎ 305/296-9921 or 800/800-4000. **Enterprise Rent-A-Car** ☎ 800/325-8007. **Hertz** ☎ 305/294-1039 or 800/654-3131. **Key West Cruisers** ✉ 500 Truman Ave., at Duval St. ☎ 305/294-4724. **Thrifty Car Rental** ✉ MM 91.8, OS, Tavernier ☎ 305/852-6088 or 800/847-4389. **Tropical Rent-A-Car** ✉ 1300 Duval St., Key West ☎ 305/294-8136.

CAR TRAVEL

From MIA follow signs to Coral Gables and Key West, which put you on Lejeune Road, then Route 836 west. Take the Homestead Extension of Florida's Turnpike south (toll road), which ends at Florida City and connects to U.S. 1. Tolls from the airport run approximately $2.25. The alternative from Florida City is Card Sound Road (Route 905A), which has a bridge toll of $1. Continue to the only stop sign and turn right on Route 905, which rejoins U.S. 1 31 mi south of Florida City. Avoid flying into Key West and driving back to Miami; there are substantial drop-off charges for leaving a Key West car in Miami.

In Key West's Old Town, parking is scarce and costly ($2 per hour at Mallory Square). It's better to take a taxi, rent a bicycle or moped, walk, or take a shuttle to get around. Elsewhere in the Keys, a car is crucial. Gas costs more than on the mainland, so fill your tank in Miami and top it off in Florida City. Most of the Overseas Highway is narrow and crowded (especially weekends and in high season). Expect delays behind RVs, trucks, cars towing boats, and rubbernecking tourists. The best Keys road map, published by the Homestead–Florida City Chamber of Commerce, can be obtained for $5.50 from the Tropical Everglades Visitor Center.

🚩 **Tropical Everglades Visitor Center** ✉ 160 U.S. 1, Florida City 33034 ☎ 305/245-9180 or 800/388-9669 ⊕ www.tropicaleverglades.com.

EMERGENCIES

Dial 911 for police, fire, or ambulance. Keys Hotline provides information and emergency assistance in six languages. Florida Marine Patrol maintains a 24-hour telephone service to handle reports of boating emergencies and natural-resource violations. Coast Guard Group Key West responds to local marine emergencies and reports of navigation hazards. The Keys have no 24-hour pharmacies. Hospital pharmacists will help with emergencies after regular retail business hours. Fishermen's Hospital, Lower Florida Keys Health System, and Mariners Hospital have 24-hour emergency rooms.

🚩 **Coast Guard Group Key West** ☎ 305/292-8727. **Fishermen's Hospital** ✉ MM 48.7, OS, Marathon ☎ 305/743-5533. **Florida Marine Patrol** ✉ MM 48, BS, 2796 Overseas Hwy., Suite 100, State Regional Service Center, Marathon 33050 ☎ 305/289-2320, 800/342-5367 after 5 PM. **Lower Florida Keys Health System** ✉ MM 5, BS, 5900 College Rd., Stock Island ☎ 305/294-5531. **Mariners Hospital** ✉ MM 91.5, BS, Tavernier ☎ 305/852-4418.

ENGLISH-LANGUAGE MEDIA

NEWSPAPERS & MAGAZINES The best of the publications covering Key West are the weekly *Solares Hill* and the daily *Key West Citizen*. For the Upper and Middle Keys, turn to the semiweekly *Keynoter*. The *Free Press, Reporter,* and *Upper Keys Independent* cover the same area once a week. The *Miami Herald* publishes a Keys edition with good daily listings of local events. The weekly *Celebrate Key West* and the monthly *Southern Exposure* are good sources of entertainment and information for gay and lesbian travelers.

TELEVISION & RADIO WLRN (National Public Radio) is 91.3, 92.1, and 93.5, depending on where you are in the Keys. Try WKLG 102.1 bilingual (English and Spanish) for adult contemporary; WCTH 100.3 for country; WFKZ 103.1 for classic rock; WKEZ 96.9 for easy listening; WFFG AM 1300 Keys for talk radio, sports, and news; and WKYZ 101.3 classic rock.

LODGING

Brenda Donnelly's friendly, efficient, family-run company represents more than 60 guest houses, B&Bs, inns, and small hotels priced from $70 to $545 a night through Inn Touch in Key West. Key West Vacation Rentals lists historic cottages, homes, and condominiums for rent. Although it prefers to handle reservations for all types of accommodations in advance, the Key West Welcome Center gets a lot of walk-in business because of its location on U.S. 1 at the entrance to Key West. Property Management of Key West, Inc. has lease and rental service for condominiums, town houses, and private homes. Rent Key West Vacations specializes in renting vacation homes and condos for a week or longer. Vacation Key West lists all kinds of properties throughout Key West.

VACATION   ☑ **Local Agents Inn Touch in Key West** ⊠ Key West 33040 ☎ 305/296–
RENTALS   2953, 800/492–1911, or 877/526–7775 🖷 305/292–1621 ⊕ www. inntouchinkeywest.com. **Vacation Rentals Key West** ⊠ 525 Simonton St., Key West 33040 ☎ 305/292–7997 or 800/621–9405 🖷 305/ 294–7501 ⊕ www.keywestvacations.com. **Key West Welcome Center** ⊠ 3840 N. Roosevelt Blvd., Key West 33040 ☎ 305/296–4444 or 800/284–4482 ⊕ www.keywestwelcomecenter.com. **Rent Key West Vacations** ⊠ 1107 Truman Ave., Key West 33040 ☎ 305/294–0990 or 800/833–7368 ⊕ www.rentkeywest.com. **Vacation Key West** ⊠ 100 Grinnell St., Key West 33040 ☎ 305/295–9500 or 800/595–5397 ⊕ www.vacationkw.com.

TAXIS

Serving the Keys from Ocean Reef to Key West, Luxury Limousine has luxury sedans and limos that seat up to eight passengers, as well as vans and buses. It'll pick up from any airport in South Florida. In the Upper Keys (MM 94–74), Village Taxi has been operating since 1982 and charges $2 per mi for vans that hold six. It also makes airport runs. Florida Keys Taxi Dispatch operates around the clock in Key West. The fare for two or more from the Key West airport to Old Town or New Town is $7.50 per person. Otherwise meters register $2.25 to start, 50¢ for each ⅕ mi, and 50¢ for every 50 seconds of waiting time.

☑ **Taxi Information Florida Keys Taxi Dispatch** ☎ 305/296–6666 or 305/294–2222. **Luxury Limousine** ☎ 305/367–2329 or 800/664–0124. **Village Taxi** ☎ 305/664–8181.

TOURS

Island Aeroplane Tours flies up to two passengers in a 1941 Waco, an open-cockpit biplane. Tours range from a quick 6- to 8-minute overview of Key West ($80 for two) to a 50-minute look at the offshore reefs ($325 for two). Seaplanes of Key West has half- and full-day trips to the Dry Tortugas; explore Fort Jefferson, built in 1846, and snorkel on the beautiful protected reef. Soft drinks and snorkel equipment are included in the $179 half-day, $305 full-day per-person fee, plus a $5 park fee.

Lloyd's Original Tropical Bike Tour, led by a 30-year Key West veteran, explores the natural, noncommercial side of Key West at a leisurely pace, stopping on back streets and in backyards of private homes to sample native fruits and view indigenous plants and trees; at City Cemetery; and at the Medicine Garden, a private meditation garden. The tours run 90–120 minutes and cost $20, plus $3 for bike rental. Coral Reef Park Co. runs sailing trips on a 38-foot catamaran as well as glass-bottom-boat tours. Captain Sterling's Everglades Eco-Tours operates Everglades and Florida Bay ecology tours ($39 per person), sunset cruises ($29 per person), a seasonal private-charter evening crocodile tour ($369 for up to six passengers), and a new tour, Flamingo Express, a five-hour boat tour from Key Largo to Flamingo, in mainland Everglades National Park.

Key Largo Princess offers two-hour glass-bottom-boat trips ($20) and sunset cruises on a luxury 70-foot motor yacht with a 280-square-foot glass viewing area, departing from the Holiday Inn docks three times a day. M/V *Discovery*'s glass-bottom boats have submerged viewing rooms for 360-degree marine watching ($30). Strike Zone Charters has glass-bottom-boat excursions into the backcountry and Atlantic Ocean. The five-hour Island Excursion ($49) emphasizes nature and Keys history. Besides close encounters with birds, sea life, and vegetation, there's a fish cookout on an island. Snorkel and fishing equipment, food, and drinks are included. This is one of the few nature outings in the Keys with wheelchair access.

Victoria Impallomeni, noted wilderness guide and authority on the ecology of Florida Bay, invites nature lovers—and especially children— aboard the *Imp II*, a 25-foot Aquasport, for four-hour ($400) and seven-hour ($600) ecotours that frequently include encounters with wild dolphins. While island-hopping, you visit underwater gardens, natural shoreline, and mangrove habitats. Play Like a Dolphin lets you get pulled through the water on a dolphin board. Tours also include Dancing Water Spirits retreats, a self-transformational retreat with healing therapies. All equipment is supplied. Tours leave from Murray's Marina.

The Conch Tour Train is a 90-minute narrated tour of Key West, traveling 14 mi through Old Town and around the island. Board at Mallory Square and Flagler Station (901 Caroline St.) every half hour (9–4:30 from Mallory Square, later at other stops). The cost is $22. Old Town Trolley operates trackless trolley-style buses, departing from the Mallory Square and Roosevelt Boulevard depots every 30 minutes (9:15–4:30 from Mallory Square, later at other stops), for 90-minute narrated tours of Key West. The smaller trolleys go places the train won't fit. You may disembark at any of 10 stops and reboard a later trolley. The cost is $22. Key West Business Guild's 75-minute Gay and Lesbian Historic Trolley Tours highlight the contributions gay and lesbian writers, artists, politicians, designers, and celebrities have made to Key West's past. Tours, which cost $22, depart Saturday at 11 AM from 512 South Street. Look for the rainbow flags on the trolley.

Adventure Charters & Tours loads kayaks onto the 42-foot catamaran *Island Fantasea* in Key West and heads out to the Great White Heron National Wildlife Refuge for guided kayak nature tours with a maximum of 14 passengers. Full-day trips ($109) depart at 9:30 and include snorkeling, fishing, a grilled lunch, and drinks. They also offer half-day trips ($35) at 10 and 2 that paddle out from Key West and last 2½ hours. Mosquito Coast Island Outfitters and Kayak Guides runs full-day guided sea-kayak natural-history tours around the mangrove islands just east of Key West. The $55 charge covers transportation, bottled water, a snack, and supplies, including snorkeling gear.

Captain Bill Keogh (naturalist, educator, photographer, and author of *The Florida Keys Paddling Guide*) operates Big Pine Kayak Adventures, which takes visitors into remote areas of two national wildlife refuges in the Lower Keys to explore mangrove hammocks, islands, creeks, and sponge and grass flats on kayak nature tours, shallow-water skiff eco-tours, backcountry catamaran sailing cruises, and shallow-water fishing expeditions. Prices start at $50 per person for a half day.

The folks at Florida Bay Outfitters know Upper Keys and Everglades waters well. Take a full-moon paddle, or a one- to seven-day canoe or kayak tour to the Everglades, Lignumvitae or Indian Key. Trips run $50–$750. In addition to publishing several good guides on Key West, the Historic Florida Keys Foundation conducts tours of the City Cemetery Tuesday and Thursday at 9:30. As the former state historian in Key West and the current owner of a historic-preservation consulting firm, Sharon Wells of Island City Strolls knows plenty about Key West. She's authored many works, including the annually revised, 120,000-copy "Walking and Biking Guide to Historic Key West," which has 10 self-guided tours of the historic district. It's available free at guest houses, hotels, and Key West bookstores. If that whets your appetite, sign on for one of her walking tours, including Architectural Strolls and Literary Landmarks, which cost $25, with a four-person minimum. "Pelican Path" is a free walking guide to Key West published by the Old Island Restoration Foundation. The guide discusses the history and architecture of 43 structures along 25 blocks of 12 Old Town streets. Pick up a copy at the chamber of commerce.

🚩 **Tours Information** **Adventure Charters & Tours** ✉ 6810 Front St., Stock Island 33040 ☎ 305/296-0362 ⊕ www.keywestadventures.com. **Big Pine Kayak Adventures** ✆ Box 431311, Big Pine Key 33043 ☎ 305/872-7474 ⊕ www.keyskayaktours.com. **Conch Tour Train** ☎ 305/294-5161. **Coral Reef Park Co.** ✉ John Pennekamp Coral Reef State Park, MM 102.5, OS, Key Largo 33037 ☎ 305/451-1621. **Everglades Eco-Tours** ✉ Dolphin's Cove, MM 102, BS, Key Largo 33037 ☎ 305/853-5161 or 888/224-6044 ⊕ www. captainsterling.com. **Florida Bay Outfitters** ✉ MM 104, BS, 104050 Overseas Hwy., Key Largo 33037 ☎ 305/451-3018 ⊕ www.kayakfloridakeys.com. **Historic Florida Keys Foundation** ✉ 510 Greene St., Old City Hall, Key West 33040 ☎ 305/292-6718. **Island Aeroplane Tours** ✉ Key West Airport, 3469 S. Roosevelt Blvd. ☎ 305/294-8687 ⊕ www.islandaeroplanetours.com. **Island City Strolls** ☎ 305/294-8380 ⊕ www. seekeywest.com. *Key Largo Princess* ✉ MM 99.7, OS, 99701 Overseas Hwy., Key Largo 33037 ☎ 305/451-4655. **Key West Business Guild (gay)** ✉ 513 Truman Ave. ✆ Box 1208, Key West 33041 ☎ 305/294-4603 or 800/535-7797 ⊕ www.gaykeywestfl.com. **Lloyd's**

Original Tropical Bike Tour ⊠ Truman Ave. and Simonton St., Key West ☎ 305/294–1882. **Mosquito Coast Island Outfitters and Kayak Guides** ⊠ 310 Duval St., Key West 33040 ☎ 305/294–7178 ⊕ www.mosquitocoast.net. **Murray's Marina** ⊠ MM 5, Stock Island. **M/V** *Discovery* ⊠ Land's End Marina, 251 Margaret St., Key West 33040 ☎ 305/293–0099. **Old Town Trolley** ⊠ 6631 Maloney Ave., Key West ☎ 305/296–6688. **Seaplanes of Key West** ⊠ Key West Airport, 3471 S Roosevelt Blvd. ☎305/294–0709 ⊕www.seaplanesofkeywest.com. **Strike Zone Charters** ⊠ MM 29.6, BS, 29675 Overseas Hwy., Big Pine Key 33043 ☎ 305/872–9863 or 800/654–9560 ⊕ www.strikezonecharter.com. **Victoria Impallomeni** ⊠ 5710 U.S. 1, Key West 33040 ☎ 305/304–7562 or 888/822–7366 ⊕ www.captainvictoria.com.

VISITOR INFORMATION

🛈 Tourist Information **Big Pine and the Lower Keys Chamber of Commerce** ⊠ MM 31, OS ✆ Box 430511, Big Pine Key 33043 ☎ 305/872–2411 or 800/872–3722 🖷 305/872–0752 ⊕ www.lowerkeyschamber.com. **Florida Keys & Key West Visitors Bureau** ⊠ 402 Wall St., Box 1146, Key West 33041 ☎ 800/352–5397 ⊕ www.fla-keys.com. **Florida Keys Council of the Arts** ⊠ 1100 Simonton St., Key West 33040 ☎ 305/295–4369 ⊕ www.keysarts.org. **Gay and Lesbian Community Center of Key West** ⊠ 513 Truman Ave. Key West 33040 ☎ 305/292–3223 🖷 305/292–3237 ⊕ www.glcckeywest. org. **Greater Key West Chamber of Commerce (mainstream)** ⊠ 402 Wall St., Key West 33040 ☎ 305/294–2587 or 800/527–8539 🖷 305/294–7806. **Greater Marathon Chamber of Commerce & Visitor Center** ⊠ MM 53.5, BS, 12222 Overseas Hwy., Marathon 33050 ☎305/743–5417 or 800/262–7284 🖷305/289–0183 ⊕www.floridakeysmarathon. com. **Islamorada Chamber of Commerce** ⊠ MM 83.2, BS, Islamorada 33036 ✆ Box 915 ☎ 305/664–4503 or 800/322–5397 🖷 305/664–4289 ⊕ www.islamoradachamber. com. **Key Largo Chamber of Commerce** ⊠ MM 106, BS, 106000 Overseas Hwy., Key Largo 33037 ☎305/451–1414 or 800/822–1088 🖷305/451–4726 ⊕www.keylargochamber. org. **Key West Business Guild (gay)** ⊠ 513 Truman Ave. ✆ Box 1208, Key West 33041 ☎ 305/294–4603 or 800/535–7797 ⊕ www.gaykeywestfl.com. **Reef World Environmental Center & Gift Store** ⊠ 201 William St., Key West 33041 ☎ 305/294–3100 ⊕ www.reefrelief.org.

The Everglades

WORD OF MOUTH

"Check the tides, and plan a bike trip down Snake Bite trail. You want to arrive at the end of the trail at low tide, because the trail ends at Florida Bay, and the birds will be ALL over feeding. When we went last time, we didn't go at low tide, but it was still wonderful, with lots of wildlife. See what ranger programs are going to be held. We went on a 'swamp tromp' in which a ranger led us into swamp—we mucked around and learned so much in addition to having great fun!

Anhinga Trail does give you the most up-close and reliable wildlife sightings."

—birder

Updated by
Chelle Koster
Walton

MIAMI IS THE ONLY CITY IN THE COUNTRY that has two national parks and a national preserve in its backyard. Everglades National Park, created in 1947, was meant to preserve the slow-moving River of Grass—a freshwater river 50 mi wide but only 6 inches deep, flowing from Lake Okeechobee through marshy grassland into Florida Bay. Along the Tamiami Trail (U.S. 41), marshes of saw grass extend as far as the eye can see, interspersed only with hammocks or tree islands of bald cypress and mahogany, while overhead southern bald eagles make circles in the sky. An assembly of plants and flowers, including ferns, orchids, and bromeliads, shares the brackish waters with otters, turtles, alligators, and occasionally that gentle giant, the West Indian manatee. Not so gentle, though, is the saw grass. Deceptively graceful, these tall, willowy sedges have small sharp teeth on the edges of their leaves.

Biscayne National Park, established as a national monument in 1968 and 12 years later expanded and designated a national park, is the nation's largest marine park and the largest national park within the continental United States with living coral reefs. A small portion of the park's almost 274 square mi consists of mainland coast and outlying islands, but 96% is under water, much of it in Biscayne Bay. The islands contain lush, heavily wooded forests with an abundance of ferns and native palm trees. Of particular interest are the mangroves and their tangled masses of stiltlike roots and stems that thicken the shorelines. These "walking trees," as locals sometimes call them, have striking curved prop roots, which arch down from the trunk, while aerial roots drop from branches. The trees draw fresh water from saltwater and create a coastal nursery capable of sustaining myriad types of marine life. Congress established Big Cypress National Preserve in 1974 after buying up one of the least-developed watershed areas in South Florida to protect Everglades National Park. The preserve, on the northern edge of Everglades National Park, entails extensive tracts of prairie, marsh, pinelands, forested swamps, and sloughs. While preservation and recreation are the preserve's mainstay, hunting and off-road vehicle use are allowed.

Unfortunately, Miami's backyard is threatened by suburban sprawl, agriculture, and business development. What results is competition among environmental, agricultural, and developmental interests. The biggest issue is water. Originally, alternating floods and dry periods maintained a wildlife habitat and regulated the water flowing into Florida Bay. The brackish seasonal flux sustained a remarkably vigorous bay, with thriving mangrove thickets and coral reefs at its Atlantic edge, and Ten Thousand Islands National Wildlife Refuge, accessible only by boat, on its gulf side. The system nurtured sea life and attracted anglers and divers. Starting in the 1930s, however, a giant flood-control system began diverting water to canals running to the gulf and the ocean. As you travel Florida's north–south routes, you cross this network of canals built by the South Florida Water Management District, ironically known as "Protector of the Everglades" (ironic because most people feel it's done more for the developers than the environment). The unfortunate side effect of flood control has been devastation of the wilderness. Park visitors decry diminished bird counts (a 90% reduction over 50 years); the black bear population has been nearly eliminated; and the Florida panther is nearing extinction. Meanwhile, the loss of fresh water has made Florida Bay saltier, devastating breeding grounds and creating dead zones where pea-green algae have replaced sea grasses and sponges.

The nearly $8-billion, 10-year Comprehensive Plan worked out between government agencies and a host of conservation groups and industries to restore, protect, and preserve the ecosystem is underway. More than 200 projects will tear down levees, fill canals, construct new water storage areas on land formerly preserved for agriculture or new development, channel water to estuaries and Everglades National Park, and provide flood protection and a reliable water supply. The expectation is that new policies and projects implemented over the next decade will go a long way toward reviving the natural system.

Exploring the Everglades

Biscayne National Park lies almost completely offshore. As a result, most sports and activities in both national parks are based on water, on the study of nature, or both. So even when you're on land, be prepared to get a bit damp on the region's marshy trails. Although relatively compact compared to the national parks of the West, these parks still require time to see. The narrow, two-lane roads through the Everglades make for slow travel, whereas sightseeing by boat, a necessity at Biscayne, takes time. The southern tip of the Florida peninsula is largely taken up by Everglades National Park, and land access to it is primarily by two roads. The main park road traverses the southern Everglades from the gateway towns of Homestead and Florida City to the outpost of Flamingo, on Florida Bay. In the northern Everglades, take the Tamiami Trail (U.S. 41) east from the Greater Miami area to the western park entrance in Everglades City.

About the Restaurants

With a few exceptions, dining centers on low-key mom-and-pop places that serve hearty home-style food, and small eateries that specialize in local fare: alligator, fish, stone crab, frogs' legs, and fresh Florida lobster from the Keys. Native American restaurants add another dimension, serving local favorites as well as catfish, Indian fry bread (a flour-and-water dough), pumpkin bread, Indian burgers (ground beef browned, rolled in fry-bread dough, and deep-fried), and tacos (fry bread with chili, lettuce, tomato, and shredded cheddar cheese on top). Due to its large Hispanic farm-worker population, Homestead is home to restaurants specializing in authentic and inexpensive Mexican cuisine. Restaurants in Everglades City, especially those along the river, have the freshest seafood, particularly stone crab. These places can be casual to the point of rustic, and often close for a month or two in the fall. The nearest fine restaurants are in Naples, 35 mi northwest. Although both Everglades and Biscayne national parks and Big Cypress National Preserve are wilderness areas, there are restaurants within a short drive. Most are between Miami and Shark Valley along the Tamiami Trail (U.S. 41), in the Homestead–Florida City area, in Everglades City, and in the

If you have 1 day

You have three choices. If you're interested in boating or seeing underwater flora and fauna, Biscayne is your best bet. For interpretive trails and exhibits, go with the Everglades. For quiet, wilderness canoeing, and nature, don't miss Big Cypress.

Numbers in the text correspond to numbers in the margin and on the Everglades and Biscayne National Parks map.

For a day in Everglades National Park, begin in **Florida City** ❽ ⌐, the southeastern gateway to the park. Head to the **Ernest F. Coe Visitor Center** ❺ and continue to the **Royal Palm Visitor Center** ❻. Then go to **Flamingo** ❾ and rent a boat or take a tour of Florida Bay. If Biscayne is your preference, begin at **Convoy Point** ❶ for an orientation before forsaking dry land. Sign up for a snorkel or dive trip or an outing on a glass-bottom boat, kayak, or canoe. To spend a day in Big Cypress National Preserve, begin at the **Oasis Visitor Center** ❶❺. Then head to **Everglades City** ❶❾ and rent a canoe for a tour of the Turner River.

If you have 3 days

With three days, explore all three accesses to the Everglades as well as Biscayne National Park. Start at **Homestead** ❼ ⌐ as your base for exploring Biscayne. If you plan to scuba dive or take a glass-bottom-boat trip, get an early start. Explore the visitor center at **Convoy Point** ❶ when you return and finish your day checking out sights in Homestead and ▦ **Florida City** ❽. There's an afternoon snorkel trip also, which would give you time to see Florida City and Homestead, have lunch, and learn about the park's ecosystem at the visitor center first. Head to the Everglades on Day 2, following the one-day itinerary above. Spend the night in **Flamingo** ❾. On Day 3, start by driving west along the Tamiami Trail, stopping at **Everglades Safari Park** ❶❶ for an airboat ride; at **Shark Valley** ❶❷ for a tram tour, walk, or bicycle trip; at the **Miccosukee Indian Village** ❶❸ for lunch; at the **Big Cypress Gallery** ❶❹; and then at the **Ochopee Post Office** ❶❻, before ending in ▦ **Everglades City** ❶❾. From here, visit historic Smallwood Store on Chokoloskee Island and watch the sunset.

If you have 5 days

Follow Day 1 and 2 above. On Day 3, hike a trail or two along the road from Flamingo and stop at ▦ **Robert Is Here** for a snack. Take in ▦ **Fruit & Spice Park** and lunch in **Homestead** ❼, then head across Tamiami Trail, stopping for a tram tour at **Shark Valley** ❶❷ and spending the night in ▦ **Everglades City** ❶❾. On Day 4, see the sights of Everglades City and do a canoe, kayak, or boat tour of the Ten Thousand Islands. The next morning, bike around **Fakahatchee Strand Preserve State Park** ❶❼ and, in the afternoon, visit **Collier-Seminole State Park** ❶❽; then reserve a canoe for the next day's trip to Big Cypress National Preserve's Turner River. On Day 5, drive to the Big Cypress **Oasis Visitor Center** ❶❺ to put in for the canoe tour. If it's December through April, join a ranger-led canoe tour. Visit **Big Cypress Gallery** ❶❹ and the **Ochopee Post Office** ❶❻ before heading back to Everglades City or Homestead for the night.

8

Florida Keys along the Overseas Highway (U.S. 1). The only food service in the preserve or in either of the parks is at Flamingo, in the Everglades, but many restaurants will pack picnics. There are also fast-food establishments on the Tamiami Trail east of Krome Avenue and west of Everglades City in Naples, and along U.S. 1 in Homestead–Florida City.

About the Hotels

If you're spending several days exploring the East Coast Everglades, stay either in the park itself (at the Flamingo Resort or one of the campgrounds), 11 mi away in Homestead–Florida City, where there are reasonably priced motels and RV parks, or in the Florida Keys or the Greater Miami–Fort Lauderdale area. Lodgings and campgrounds are also available on the Gulf Coast in Everglades City, Naples, and Marco Island. Florida City's selection is mostly of the chain variety and geared toward business travelers, with Internet service and Continental breakfast. Accommodations near the parks range from inexpensive to moderate and offer off-season rates in summer months, when rampant mosquito populations essentially preclude going outdoors for any length of time. If you crave luxury and lots of extras, head for Miami or Naples—where you'll pay more.

WHAT IT COSTS				
$$$$	**$$$**	**$$**	**$**	**¢**
RESTAURANTS over $30	$20–$30	$15–$20	$10–$15	under $10
HOTELS over $220	$140–$220	$100–$140	$80–$100	under $80

Restaurant prices are per person for a main course at dinner. Hotel prices are for a standard double room, excluding 6% sales tax (more in some counties) and 1%–4% tourist tax.

Timing

Winter is the best time to visit Biscayne National Park, Everglades National Park, and Big Cypress National Preserve. Temperatures and mosquito activity are low to moderate, low water levels concentrate the resident wildlife around sloughs that retain water all year, and migratory birds swell the avian population. Winter is also the busiest time in the park. Make reservations and expect crowds at Flamingo, the main visitor center (known officially as the Ernest F. Coe Visitor Center), and Royal Palm Visitor Center. Be careful with campfires and matches; this is when the wildfire-prone saw-grass prairies and pinelands are most vulnerable. In late spring the weather turns hot and rainy, and tours and facilities are less crowded. Migratory birds depart, and you must look harder to see wildlife. Even if you're not staying in Everglades National Park, try to stick around until dusk, when dozens of bird species feed around the ponds and trails. While shining a flashlight over the water in marshy areas, look for two yellowish-red reflections above the surface—telltale signs of alligators.

Summer brings intense sun and billowing clouds unleashing torrents of rain almost every afternoon. Start your outdoor activities early to avoid the rain and the sun's strongest rays, and use sunscreen: water levels rise

8

Biking & Hiking In the Everglades there are several scenic places to ride and hike. The Shark Valley Loop Road (15 mi round-trip) makes a good bike trip as does the 12-mi (one-way) W. J. Janes Memorial Scenic Drive off Route 29 through Fakahatchee Strand Preserve State Park. Several tours depart from Flamingo Marina. Inquire about insect and weather conditions before you go and plan accordingly, stocking up on insect repellent, sunscreen, and water, as necessary.

Boating & Canoeing One of the best ways to experience the Everglades is by boat, and almost all of Biscayne National Park is accessible only by water. Boat rentals are available in both parks. Rentals are generally for half day (four hours) and full day (eight hours). In the Everglades, the 99-mi inland Wilderness Trail between Flamingo and Everglades City is open to motorboats as well as canoes, although power-boats may have trouble navigating the route above Whitewater Bay. Flat-water canoeing and kayaking are best in winter, when temperatures are moderate, rainfall is minimal, and mosquitoes are tolerable. You don't need a permit for day trips, but tell someone where you're going and when you expect to return. Getting lost is easy, and spending the night without proper gear can be unpleasant, if not dangerous. On the Gulf Coast explore the nooks, crannies, and mangrove islands of Chokoloskee Bay and Ten Thousand Islands National Wildlife Refuge, as well as the many rivers near Everglades City. The Turner River Canoe Trail, a pleasant day trip with a guarantee of bird and alligator sightings, passes through mangrove, dwarf cypress, coastal prairie, and fresh-water slough ecosystems of Everglades National Park and Big Cypress National Preserve.

Fishing Largemouth bass are plentiful in fresh-water ponds, while snapper, redfish, and sea trout are caught in Florida Bay. The mangrove shallows of the Ten Thousand Islands, along the gulf, yield tarpon and snook. Whitewater Bay is also a favorite spot. **Note:** the state has issued health advisories for sea bass, largemouth bass, and other fresh-water fish, especially those caught in the canals along the Tamiami Trail, due to their high mercury content. Signs are posted throughout the park, and consumption should be limited.

---

and wildlife disperses as the day goes on, and mosquitoes hatch, swarm, and descend on you in voracious clouds, making outdoor activity virtually unbearable, unless you swath yourself in netting. Mosquito repellent is a necessity any time of year.

BISCAYNE NATIONAL PARK

Occupying 180,000 acres along the southern portion of Biscayne Bay, south of Miami and north of the Florida Keys, this national park is 96% under water, and its altitude ranges from 4 feet above sea level to 10 fathoms, or 60 feet, below. Contained within it are four distinct zones, which from shore to sea are mangrove forest along the coast, Biscayne Bay, the undeveloped upper Florida Keys, and coral reefs. Mangroves line the mainland shore much as they do elsewhere in South Florida. Biscayne Bay functions as a lobster sanctuary and a nursery for fish, sponges, and crabs. Manatees and sea turtles frequent its warm, shallow waters. Lamentably, the bay is under assault from forces similar to those in Florida Bay. To the east, about 8 mi off the coast, lie 44 tiny keys, stretching 18 nautical mi north–south and accessible only by boat. There's no commercial transportation between the mainland and the islands, and only a handful can be visited: Elliott, Boca Chita, Adams, and Sands keys. The rest are either wildlife refuges or too small, or have rocky shores or waters too shallow for boats. It's best to explore the Keys between December and April, when the mosquito population is relatively quiescent. Bring repellent just in case. Diving is best in summer, when calmer winds and smaller seas result in clearer waters. Another 3 mi east of the Keys, in the ocean, lies the park's main attraction—the northernmost section of Florida's living tropical coral reefs. Some are the size of a student's desk, others as large as a football field. You can take a glass-bottom boat ride to see this underwater wonderland, but you really have to snorkel or scuba dive to appreciate it fully. A diverse population of colorful fish—angelfish, gobies, grunts, parrot fish, pork fish, wrasses, and many more—flits through the reefs. Shipwrecks from the 18th century are evidence of the area's international maritime heritage. A Native American midden (shell mound) dating from AD 1000, and Boca Chita Key, listed on the National Register of Historic Places for its 10 historic structures, illustrate the park's rich cultural heritage. More than 170 species of birds have been seen around the park. Although all the Keys are excellent for birding, Jones Lagoon, south of Adams Key, between Old Rhodes Key and Totten Key, is one of the best. It's approachable only by nonmotorized craft.

Convoy Point

❶ *9 mi east of Florida City, 30 mi south of downtown Miami.*

★ Reminiscent of area pioneer homes, with wooden walks and a metal roof, the **Dante Fascell Visitor Center** has a wide veranda with views across mangroves and Biscayne Bay. Inside is a museum, where hands-on and historical exhibits and videos explore the park's four ecosystems. Among the facilities are a 50-seat auditorium, the park's canoe and tour concessionaire, rest rooms with showers, a ranger information area, a gift shop, and vending machines. Ranger programs take place daily along with monthly family festivals and bimonthly narrated paddling trips. Outside are picnic tables and grills. A short trail and boardwalk lead to a jetty and launch ramp. This is the only area of the park accessible without a boat. ⊠ *9700 S.W. 328th St., Homestead* ☎ *305/230–7275* ⊕ *www.nps.gov/bisc* 🎫 *Free* ☉ *Daily 9–5.*

The Outdoors

CANOEING **Biscayne National Underwater Park, Inc.** (⊠ Convoy Point Visitor Center, Box 1270, 9710 S.W. 328th St., Homestead 33090 ☎305/230–1100), the park's official concessionaire, has canoes and kayaks for rent on a first-come, first-served basis. Canoe prices are $9 an hour, kayaks $16 an hour. December through April, rangers lead guided paddling trips the second and fourth Saturdays of the month. Visitor areas are open daily 9–3.

DIVING & **Biscayne National Underwater Park, Inc.** (⊠ Convoy Point Visitor Cen-
SNORKELING ter, Box 1270, 9710 S.W. 328th St., Homestead 33090 ☎ 305/230–1100)
★ rents equipment and conducts snorkel and dive trips aboard the 45-foot *Boca Chita*. Three-hour snorkel trips ($35) leave daily at 1:30 PM and include mask, fins, snorkel, buoyancy vest, and instruction. About half the time is spent on the reef and wrecks. Two-tank scuba trips to shallow reef or wall dives depart weekends at 8:30 AM, costing $54, tanks and weights included. Additional trips, including night dives, may be offered according to demand. Complete gear rental ($42 extra) is available. Even with a reservation (recommended), you should arrive one hour before departure to sign up for gear.

Boca Chita Key

★ ❷ *10 mi northeast of Convoy Point.*

This island was once owned by the late Mark C. Honeywell, former president of Minneapolis's Honeywell Company. A ½-mi hiking trail curves around the south side of the island. Climb the 65-foot-high ornamental lighthouse (by ranger tour only) for a panoramic view of Miami and surrounding waters. There's no fresh water, access is by private boat only, and no pets are allowed.

Where to Stay

⚠ **Boca Chita Campground.** This small, flat island has a grassy, waterside campground shaded by palm trees that whisper in the breeze. The views are awesome and a nature trail circles the island. Check with the park concessionaire for drop-off and pickup service ($25.95 round-trip). Reservations are required. There's no running fresh water. Campers must carry out all trash. ♿ *Flush toilets, grills, picnic tables* ⛺ *39 sites* ⊠ *9700 S.W. 328th St., Homestead 33033* ☎ *305/230–7275, 305/230–1100 transportation* ⊕ *www.nps.gov/bisc* ⚑ *$10* ⊟ *No credit cards.*

Elliott Key

❸ *9 mi east of Convoy Point.*

This key, accessible only by boat (on your own or from the concessionaire for $25.95 round-trip or $46.90 if you take a snorkel trip), has a rebuilt boardwalk made from recycled plastic and two nature trails with tropical plant life. Take an informal, ranger-led nature walk or hike the 7-mi trail on your own along so-called Spite Highway, a 225-foot-wide swath of green that developers mowed down in hopes of linking this key to the mainland. Luckily the federal government stepped in and now it's a hiking trail through tropical hardwood hammock. Facilities include rest rooms, picnic tables, fresh drinking water, showers (cold), grills, and a campground. Pets are allowed on the island but not on trails. A 30-

foot-wide sandy beach about a mile north of the harbor on the west (bay) side of the key is the only one in the national park. Boaters like to anchor off it to swim. For day use only, it has picnic areas and a short trail that follows the shore and cuts through the hammock.

Where to Stay

⚠ **Elliott Key Campground.** The grassy, beachfront tent sites are populated with plenty of native hardwood trees, and there's no light pollution here, so the night sky is brilliant with stars. Spend the day swimming, snorkeling, hiking trails, and fishing. Parties of up to 25 people and six tents can share the group campsite, and leashed pets are welcome. Regular ferry service and boat rental are nonexistent, but the park concessionaire's snorkel boat provides drop-off and pickup service to campers ($25.95 round-trip). Reservations are required. If you bring a boat, dock in the marina overnight for an additional $5. Bring plenty of insect repellent and try to pick a breezy spot to plant your tent. Keep in mind you must carry out all garbage, and bring some drinking water: the pumps are known to go out on occasion. ♨ *BBQ, flush toilets, drinking water, showers (cold), picnic tables, swimming (bay)* �⋑ *40 sites* ✉ *9700 S.W. 328th St., Homestead 33033* ☎ *305/230–7275, 305/230–1100 transportation* ⊕ *www.nps.gov/bisc* ⌦ *$10* ▤ *No credit cards.*

Adams Key

❹ *9 mi southeast of Convoy Point.*

This small key, a stone's throw from the western tip of Elliott Key, is open for day use and has picnic areas, rest rooms, dockage, and a short trail that runs along the shore and through a hardwood hammock. Access is by private boat.

EVERGLADES NATIONAL PARK

11 mi southwest of Homestead, 45 mi southwest of Miami International Airport.

The best way to experience the real Everglades is to get your feet wet either by taking a walk in the muck, affectionately called a "slough slog," or by paddling a canoe into the maze of mangrove islands to stay in a backcountry campsite. Most day-trippers don't want to do that, however. Luckily, there are several ways to see the wonders of the park with dry feet. Take a boat tour in Everglades City or Flamingo, ride the tram at Shark Valley, or walk the boardwalks that extend out from the main park road. And there's more to see than natural beauty. Miccosukee Indians operate a number of attractions and restaurants meriting a stop. Admission to Everglades National Park's two pay gates (main entrance and Shark Valley) is valid at both of those entrances for seven days. Coverage in the following section begins in the southeastern Everglades, followed by the northern Everglades, starting in the east and ending in Everglades City.

The Main Park Road

The main park road (Route 9336) travels from the main visitor center to Flamingo, across a section of the park's eight distinct ecosystems: hardwood hammock, fresh-water prairie, pinelands, freshwater slough, cypress, coastal prairie, mangrove, and marine-estuarine. Highlights of the trip include a dwarf cypress forest, the ecotone (transition zone) between saw grass and mangrove forest, the largest living mahogany tree, and a wealth of wading birds at Mrazek and Coot Bay ponds. Boardwalks, looped trails, several short spurs, and observation platforms allow you to stay dry.

⟲ ➎ Numerous interactive exhibits and films make the **Ernest F. Coe Visitor**
Fodor's Choice **Center** a worthy and important stop during your tour of the region. Stand
★ in a simulated blind and peer through a spyglass to watch birds in the wild; although it's actually a film, the quality is so good you'll think you're outside. Move on to a bank of telephones to hear differing viewpoints on the Great Water Debate. Another exhibit recreates sights and sounds of the Everglades. A 15-minute film on the park, a movie on hurricanes, and a 35-minute wildlife film for children are rotated in the theater. Computer monitors present a schedule of daily ranger-led activities park-wide as well as information on canoe rentals and boat tours. In the Everglades Discovery Shop, browse through neat nature, science, and kids' stuff and pick up extra insect repellent. The center provides information on the entire park. Park admission fees permit entry for a seven-day period, including at the Shark Valley access. The Coe Visitor Center, however, has free admission, as it's outside the park gates. ⊠ *11 mi southwest of Homestead on Rte. 9336* ☎ *305/242–7700* ⊕ *www.nps.gov/ever* ◎ *Park $10 per vehicle, $5 per pedestrian, bicycle, or motorcycle* ◷ *Daily 8–5; hours sometimes shortened in off-season.*

★ ➏ A must for anyone who wants to experience the real Everglades, the **Royal**
Palm Visitor Center permits access to the Anhinga Trail boardwalk, where in winter spying alligators congregating in watering holes is almost guaranteed. Or follow the neighboring Gumbo Limbo Trail through a hardwood hammock. Do both strolls, as they're short (½ mi) and expose you to two of the Everglades' ecosystems. Rangers conduct a daily Anhinga Amble in season (mid-December through mid-April) starting at 10:30 AM. Ask also about slough slogs and bike tours. The visitor center has an interpretive display, a bookstore, and vending machines. ⊠ *4 mi west of Ernest F. Coe Visitor Center on Rte. 9336* ☎ *305/242–7700* ◷ *Daily 8–4.*

Homestead

➐ *30 mi southwest of Miami.*

In recent years, the Homestead area has redefined itself as a destination for tropical agro- and eco-tourism. The emphasis is on "tropical," because as you cross Quail Roost Trail along north Krome Avenue, you actually cross latitudes into the tropical zone. Seated at the juncture between Miami and the Keys as well as Everglades National Park and Bis-

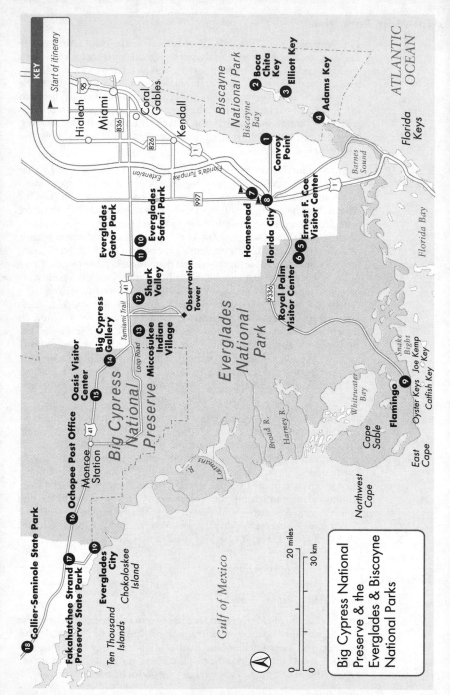

Big Cypress National Preserve & the Everglades & Biscayne National Parks

cayne National Park, it has the added dimension of a shopping center, residential development, hotel chains, and the Miami-Dade Homestead Motorsports Complex—when car races are scheduled there, hotel rates increase and have minimum stays. The historic downtown area has become a preservation-driven Main Street. Krome Avenue (Route 997), which cuts through the city's heart, is lined with restaurants, an arts complex, antiques shops, and low-budget, but often undesirable, accommodations. West of north–south Krome Avenue, miles of fields grow fresh fruits and vegetables. Some are harvested commercially, while others have U-PICK signs, inviting you to harvest your own. Stands selling farm-fresh produce and nurseries that grow and sell orchids and tropical plants abound. In addition to its agricultural legacy, the town has an eclectic flavor, attributable to its population mix: descendants of pioneer Crackers, Hispanic growers and farm workers, professionals escaping Miami's hustle and bustle, and latter-day northern retirees.

With a saltwater atoll pool that's flushed by tidal action, **Homestead Bayfront Park,** adjacent to Biscayne National Park, is popular among local families as well as anglers and boaters. Facilities include a playground, ramps for people with disabilities (including a ramp that leads into the swimming area), and a picnic pavilion with grills, showers, and rest rooms. ⊠ *9698 S.W. 328th St.* ☎ *305/230–3034* ☞ *$4 per passenger vehicle, $10 per vehicle with boat, $12 per RV* ☉ *Daily sunrise–sunset.*

Because it officially qualifies for tropical status, **Fruit & Spice Park,** in Homestead's Redland historic agricultural district, is the only public garden of its type in the United States. More than 500 varieties of herbs, spices, vegetables, citrus, and nuts grow in the 35-acre park, but it is most famous for its exotic fruits, such as pummelo, carambola, custard apple, and monstera. There are 80 varieties of bananas alone. Tours and tastings are available three times daily. ⊠ *24801 S.W. 187th Ave.* ☎ *305/ 247–5727* ⊕ *www.co.miami-dade.fl.us* ☞ *$3.50* ☉ *Daily 10–5.*

I. Stanley Levine and Ellie Schneiderman, founders of the South Florida Art Center in South Beach, are at the forefront of a cultural revival in Homestead. Their fledgling project centers on a 3½-acre complex, **Art-South,** which includes the historic First Baptist Church, 45 artist studios, galleries, workshops, sculpture garden, and stage. Watch artists at work, take classes, and enjoy concert performances. Check Second Saturdays opening exhibits, which include live entertainment, hands-on art demonstrations, self-guided tours, and refreshments from 3 to 8 PM. ⊠ *240 N. Krome Ave.* ☎ *305/247–9406* ⊕ *www.artsouthhomestead.org* ☞ *Free* ☉ *Tues.–Fri. 9–6, weekends noon–6.*

Where to Stay & Eat

★ ¢–$ ✕ **El Toro Taco.** This rustic, family-run favorite gets high marks for its generous portions, homemade tortilla chips (sometimes a little greasy), and friendly service. Selections include tasty fajitas, enchiladas, and burritos, and other traditional Mexican dishes such as *mole de pollo,* which combines unsweetened chocolate and Mexican spices with chicken. Order spicing from mild to tongue-challenging. And if you're tired of the same-old morning fare, consider stopping in here for breakfast, available after 11 AM. ⊠ *1 S. Krome Ave.* ☎ *305/245–8182* ⊟ *AE, D, MC, V* ☖ *BYOB* ☽ *Closed Mon.*

¢–$ ✗ **Hiatari Sushi Bar.** Visit this downtown Japanese-Thai restaurant, in a simple storefront café setting, for a change of pace from Homestead's seafood and Mexican staples. Off the Japanese side of the menu, choose from a dazzling selection of rolls and sushi, including the hometown Homestead Roll, with fried snapper, avocado, and cream cheese. Entrées include pan-seared tuna, teriyakis, and tempura shrimp. Thai takes over with entrées in the curry, noodle, vegetarian, and fried-rice departments. Ask for tatami Japanese-style seating in private booths or American style tables, and stay for karaoke. ⊠ *109 N. Krome Ave.* ☎ *305/ 248–7426* ⊟ *MC, V.*

¢–$ ✗ **Sam's Restaurant.** For good old Southern-style home cooking, Sam's is the choice of the local population. Burgers, sandwiches, and dinners—including chicken livers, hamburger steaks, and fried clams—come with fresh-baked cornbread and a daily selection of sides such as okra with tomatoes, turnip greens, pickled beets, or onion rings. Don't miss out on the changing selection of homemade soups and desserts. All this goodness comes cheaply, but at the expense of an anything-but-glamorous dining area and often slow service. ⊠ *1320 N. Krome Ave.* ☎ *305/246– 2990* ⊟ *MC, V* ☽ *Closed Sun.*

¢ ✗ **Main St. Café.** This place bills itself as "The Music Café" for its Thursday- through Saturday-night dinners with local and touring folk, country, and acoustic rock entertainment. The multipage menu of generously sized sandwiches (including vegetarian choices), wraps, soups, salads, and burgers stays the same for lunch and dinner. A particularly good deal is the "bottomless" (all you can eat) soup-and-sandwich special. Beverages include coffee, espresso, juice, smoothies, and sodas. The cobbler is divine, as is the brownie, a thick double-fudge-walnut confection. ⊠ *128 N. Krome Ave.* ☎ *305/245–7575* ⊕ *www. mainstreetcafe.net* ⊟ *AE, D, MC, V* ☽ *Closed Sun. and Mon. No dinner Tues. and Wed.*

¢ ✗ **NicaMex.** More and more gringos are discovering this spotless "plain-Juanita" restaurant frequented primarily by Latin American immigrant farm workers and their families. Although they term it *comidas rapidas* (fast food), the cuisine is not Americanized. You can get authentic huevos rancheros or *chilaquiles* (corn tortillas cooked in red pepper sauce) for breakfast, and specialties such as *chicharron en salsa verde* (fried pork skin in hot green tomato sauce) and shrimp in garlic all day. Seafood and beef soups are best-sellers and have generous amounts of vegetables and seafood or meat. Choose a domestic or imported beer, pop a coin into the Wurlitzer jukebox, and escape to a foreign land. ⊠ *32 N.W. 1st St., across from the Krome Ave. bandstand* ☎ *305/246–8300* ⊟ *AE, D, MC, V.*

¢ ✗ **Tiffany's Cottage Dining.** A large banyan tree shades this casual restaurant done in a country Victorian style complete with gingerbread on the outside and ruffles and lace inside. Breakfast keeps to the country motif with biscuits, waffles, and cinnamon walnut oatmeal. The lunch menu includes crabmeat au gratin, asparagus rolled in ham with hollandaise sauce, seafood- and egg-salad sandwiches on fresh-baked croissants, and the most popular dish, the daily quiche. Among the homemade desserts, choose from a very tall carrot cake and a harvest pie that has layers of fruits, walnuts, and a caramel topping. Sunday brunch buffet is served, too. ⊠ *22 N.E. 15th St.* ☎ *305/246–0022* ▤ *MC, V* ⊘ *Closed Mon. No dinner.*

★ $ ▦ **Redland Hotel.** When it opened in 1904, the inn was the town's first hotel. It later became the first mercantile store, the first U.S. Post Office, the first library, and the first boarding house. Today, each room has a different layout and furnishings, and some have access to a shared balcony, perfect for gatherings. The style is Victorian, with lots of pastels and reproduction antique furniture. The pub is popular with locals, and there are good restaurants and antiques shops nearby. ⊠ *5 S. Flagler Ave., 33030* ☎ *305/246–1904 or 800/595–1904* ⊕ *www. redlandhotel.com* ⇆ *13 rooms* ⚿ *Restaurant, room service, fans, cable TV, in-room VCRs, in-room data ports, pub, meeting rooms, no-smoking rooms* ▤ *AE, D, DC, MC, V.*

★ ¢ ▦ **Grove Inn Country Guesthouse.** The garden is lush with organic, tropical fruit trees and native plants (instead of a guest book there's a live autograph tree in the courtyard, where people sign the leaves) and the rooms are decorated with antique furnishings and table settings. Paul and Craig, the owners, go out of their way to pamper guests, starting with a country breakfast using local produce, served family-style in a dining room done in Victorian-print pastels. They offer behind-the-scenes tours of orchid nurseries and farms not otherwise open to the public. A vending machine dispenses complimentary cold drinks. ⊠ *22540 S.W. Krome Ave., 6 mi north of downtown, 33170* ☎ *305/247–6572 or 877/247–6572* ⊕ *www.groveinn.com* ⇆ *13 rooms, 1 2-bedroom suite, 1 cottage* ⚿ *Dining room, picnic area, fans, some kitchens, microwaves, refrigerators, in-room data ports, hot tub, piano, laundry facilities, some pets allowed, no-smoking rooms* ▤ *AE, D, MC, V* ◎| *BP.*

Sports & the Outdoors

AUTO RACING The **Miami-Dade Homestead Motorsports Complex** (⊠ 1 Speedway Blvd., 33035 ☎ 305/230–7223 ⊕ www.racemiami.com) is a state-of-the-art facility with two tracks: a 2.21-mi continuous road course and a 1.5-mi oval. There's a schedule of year-round manufacturer and race-team testing, club racing, and other national events.

BOATING Boaters give high ratings to the facilities at **Homestead Bayfront Park.** The 174-slip marina has a ramp, dock, bait-and-tackle shop, fuel station, ice, dry storage, and boat hoist, which can handle vessels up to 25 feet long if they have lifting rings. The park also has a tidal swimming area. ⊠ *9698 S.W. 328th St.* ☎ *305/230–3033* ⤳ *$4 per passenger vehicle, $8 per vehicle with boat, $12 per RV, $10 hoist* ⊘ *Daily sunrise–sunset.*

Shopping

In addition to Homestead Boulevard (U.S. 1) and Campbell Drive (Southwest 312th Street and Northeast 8th Street), **Krome Avenue** is popular for shopping. In the heart of old Homestead, it has a brick sidewalk, art galleries, and antiques stores.

Florida City

► **❽**   *2 mi southwest of Homestead.*

The Florida Turnpike ends in this southernmost town on the peninsula, spilling thousands onto U.S. 1 and eventually west to Everglades National Park, east to Biscayne National Park, or south to the Florida Keys. As the last outpost before 18 mi of mangroves and water, this stretch of U.S. 1 is lined with fast-food eateries, service stations, hotels, bars, dive shops, and restaurants. Hotel rates increase significantly during such special events as the NASCAR races at the nearby Miami-Dade Homestead Motorsports Complex. Like Homestead, Florida City is rooted in agriculture, with hundreds of acres of farmland west of Krome Avenue and a huge farmers market that processes produce shipped nationwide.

Where to Stay & Eat

★ **$-$$$**   ✕ **Capri Restaurant.** Locals have been dining here—one of the oldest family-run restaurants in Miami-Dade County—since 1958. Outside it's a rock-walled building with a big parking lot. The interior has dark-wood paneling and heavy wooden furniture. The tasty fare ranges from pizza with a light, crunchy crust and ample toppings to aged and broiled steaks and seafood-pasta masterpieces. Littleneck clams come in garlic or marinara sauce, and the kitchen prepares veal in six different ways. Bargain hunters have two choices: the daily early-bird entrées, 4:30–6:30 for $12–$14, which include soup or salad and potato or spaghetti, and the Tuesday family night (after 4 PM), which has all-you-can-eat pasta with salad or soup for $6.95. Exotic martinis and tropical libations supplement the small wine list. ⊠ *935 N. Krome Ave.* ☎ *305/247–1544* ⊕ *www.the-capri.com* ⊟ *AE, D, MC, V* ⊘ *Closed Sun.*

$-$$$ ✕ **Mutineer Restaurant.** This roadside steak-and-seafood restaurant with an indoor-outdoor fish-and-duck pond was built in 1980, back when Florida City was barely on the map. Etched glass divides the bilevel dining rooms, with velvet upholstered chairs, an aquarium, and nautical antiques. The big menu has 15 seafood entrées including Florida lobster tails and snapper Oscar, plus another half dozen daily seafood specials, as well as poultry, ribs, and steaks. There's a $9.95 hot buffet and salad bar Monday–Saturday 11 AM to 3 PM and live music and dancing Friday and Saturday evenings. ⊠ *11 S.E. 1st Ave. (U.S. 1), at Palm Dr.* ☎ *305/245–3377* ⊕ *www.mutineer.biz* ⊟ *AE, D, DC, MC, V.*

¢-$$ ✕ **Gusto's Grill & Bar.** This place is mostly about drinking and watching sports on TV, yet it's also good for catching a reasonably priced meal, especially during the happy-hour buffet (4–7 PM). Sit indoors or out (televisions are situated throughout) to order your honey garlic wings, shrimp corn chowder, pasta, burgers, pizza, steak, and seafood. Shoot pool while you wait. ⊠ *326 S.E. 1st Ave.* ☎ *786/243–9800* ⊟ *AE, D, MC, V.*

★ **¢-$**   ✕ **Farmers' Market Restaurant.** Although it's in the farmers' market and serves fresh vegetables, seafood figures prominently on the menu of home-cooked specialties. A family of fishermen runs the place, so fish and shellfish are only hours from the sea. Catering to the fishing and farming crowd, it opens at 5:30 AM, serving pancakes, jumbo eggs, and fluffy omelets with home fries or grits. The lunch and dinner menus have fried shrimp, seafood pasta, country-fried steak, roast turkey, and fried conch, as well as burgers, salads, and sandwiches. ⊠ *300 N. Krome Ave.* ☎ *305/242–0008* ▤ *MC, V.*

¢ ✕ **Rosita's Restaurante.** With its population of immigrant farm workers, this area can boast the real thing in Mexican, a flavor you just don't get in the Tex-Mex chains. Order à la carte specialties or dinners and combos with beans and rice, and salad. Forty-three breakfast, lunch, and dinner entrées are served all day and range from Mexican eggs, enchiladas, and taco salad to stewed beef, shrimp rancheros style, and fried pork chop. Clean and pleasant, with an open kitchen, take-out counter, and booths, it's a favorite with locals and budget-minded guests at the hostel across the street. ⊠ *199 W. Palm Dr.* ☎ *305/245– 8652* ▤ *AE, MC, V.*

$–$$$$ ▥ **Best Western Gateway to the Keys.** If you want easy access to Everglades and Biscayne national parks as well as the Florida Keys, you'll be well placed at this pretty, modern, two-story motel two blocks off the Florida Turnpike. Standard rooms, done in tropical colors, have two queen-size beds or one king-size bed. Rooms around the lushly landscaped pool cost the most. There's high-speed Internet access available in the rooms, plus wireless access in the lobby. ⊠ *411 S. Krome Ave., 33034* ☎ *305/246–5100* ☎ *305/242–0056* ⊕ *www.bestwestern.com* ⤷ *114 rooms* ⚘ *Microwaves, refrigerators, cable TV with movies, in-room data ports, pool, hot tub, laundry facilities, Internet, meeting rooms; no smoking* ▤ *AE, D, DC, MC, V* ⧖ *CP.*

¢–$$$ ▥ **Fairway Inn.** Two stories high with a waterfall pool, this motel has some of the area's lowest chain rates, and it's next to the chamber of commerce. Rooms, with either one king-size bed or two doubles, have tiled bathroom and closet areas. ⊠ *100 S.E. 1st Ave., 33034* ☎ *305/ 248–4202 or 888/340–8578* ☎ *305/245–8578* ⊕ *www. southfloridamotels.com* ⤷ *160 rooms* ⚘ *Dining room, in-room data ports, pool, laundry facilities, business services, no-smoking rooms* ▤ *AE, D, MC, V* ⧖ *CP.*

$$ ▥ **Hampton Inn.** Racing fans can hear the engines roar from this two-story motel next to an outlet mall and within 15 minutes of the raceway and Everglades and Biscayne national parks. Carpeted rooms are bright and clean and have upholstered chairs, coffeemaker, and an iron and ironing board. Included are a Continental breakfast and local calls. ⊠ *124 E. Palm Dr., 33034* ☎ *305/247–8833 or 800/426–7866* ☎ *305/ 247–6456* ⊕ *www.hamptoninnfloridacity.com* ⤷ *123 rooms* ⚘ *Some microwaves, some refrigerators, cable TV with movies, in-room data ports, pool, laundry service, Internet, meeting rooms, no-smoking rooms* ▤ *AE, D, DC, MC, V* ⧖ *CP.*

¢–$$ ▥ **Comfort Inn.** Rooms are large, have contemporary tropical furnishings, and are on one of two floors (there's no elevator). They're outfitted with irons, hair dryers, and coffeemakers. Continental breakfast and newspapers are free. In-room Internet connections are high speed. It's in an asphalt complex of hotels, gas stations, and restaurants just off U.S. 1. ⊠ *333 S.E. 1st Ave., 33034* ☎ *305/248–4009 or 888/352– 2489* ☎ *305/248–7935* ⊕ *www.ciflcity.com* ⤷ *124 rooms* ⚘ *Dining* *room, picnic area, in-room safes, microwaves, refrigerators, cable TV with movies, in-room data ports, pool, laundry facilities, business services, meeting rooms; no smoking* ☰ *AE, D, DC, MC, V* ⧄Ⓞ⧄ *CP.*

¢–$$ ⌘ **Travelodge.** This bargain motor lodge is close to the Florida Turnpike, Everglades and Biscayne national parks, the Florida Keys, and the Miami-Dade Homestead Motorsports Complex. Clean and colorful rooms are smallish, but they have more amenities than usually found in this price range, including complimentary breakfast and newspaper, coffeemaker, hair dryer, iron with ironing board, and voice mail. Fast-food and chain eateries, gas stations, and a visitor's bureau are within walking distance. ✉ *409 S.E. 1st Ave., 33034* ☎ *305/248–9777 or 800/758–0618* 🖷 *305/248–9750* ⊕ *www.travelodgefloridacity.com* ⧂ *88 rooms* ⧄ *Dining room, in-room safes, microwaves, refrigerators, cable TV with movies, pool, dry cleaning, laundry facilities* ☰ *AE, D, DC, MC, V* ⧄Ⓞ⧄ *CP.*

¢–$ ⌘ **Econo Lodge.** Close to the Florida Turnpike and with access to the Keys, this is a good pullover spot for an overnight. The rooms are uncramped, with attractive bedspreads, and have microwaves, coffeemakers, and data ports. The pool sits in the middle of the parking lot. ✉ *553 N.E. 1st Ave., 33034* ☎ *305/248–9300 or 800/553–2666* 🖷 *305/245–2753* ⊕ *www.econolodge.com* ⧂ *42 rooms* ⧄ *Dining room, some refrigerators, in-room data ports, pool, laundry facilities, Internet, business services, no-smoking rooms* ☰ *AE, D, DC, MC, V* ⧄Ⓞ⧄ *CP.*

¢ ⌘ **Everglades Hostel.** This HI-AYH facility is in a minimally restored art-deco building on a lush, private acre between Everglades and Biscayne national parks, 20 mi north of Key Largo. Stay in clean, spacious private and dorm-style rooms ($2 charge for linen); relax in indoor and outdoor quiet areas; watch videos or TV on a big screen; and take airboat, hiking, biking, and sightseeing tours. At mealtime, cook in the communal kitchen, pitch in for a communal dinner (according to demand, $3 each), or walk to a nearby restaurant. Pets are welcome. There's local transportation, and the staff will pick you up from the nearby Greyhound station. Guests can make free domestic long-distance calls from the phone in the lobby. ✉ *20 S.W. 2nd Ave., 33034* ☎ *305/248–1122 or 800/372–3874* 🖷 *305/245–7622* ⊕ *www.evergladeshostel.com* ⧂ *46 beds in dorm-style rooms with shared bath, 2 private rooms with shared bath* ⧄ *Dining room, picnic area, fans, boating, bicycles, hiking, recreation room, laundry facilities, Internet, some pets allowed; no a/c in some rooms, no room phones, no room TVs, no smoking* ☰ *MC, V.*

Shopping

Prime Outlets at Florida City (✉ 250 E. Palm Dr. ☎ 877/466–8853) has
★ nearly 50 discount stores plus a small food court. **Robert Is Here** (✉ 19200 Palm Dr. [S.W. 344th St.] ☎ 305/246–1592), a remarkable fruit stand, sells vegetables, fresh-fruit milk shakes, 10 flavors of honey, more than 100 flavors of jams and jellies, fresh juices, salad dressings, and some 40 kinds of tropical fruits, including carambola, lychee, egg fruit, monstera, sapodilla, soursop, sugar apple, and tamarind. The stand started in 1960, when six-year-old Robert sat at this spot selling his father's bumper crop of cucumbers. Now Robert ships around the world, and everything is first quality. Seconds are given to needy area families. The stand opens at 8 and never closes earlier than 7.

Flamingo

9 *38 mi southwest of Ernest F. Coe Visitor Center.*

Here at the far end of the main road is a cluster of buildings where a former town of the same name was established in 1893. Today it contains a visitor center, lodge, restaurant and lounge, gift shop, marina, and bicycle rentals, plus an adjacent campground. Tour boats narrated by interpretive guides, fishing expeditions of Florida Bay, and canoe and kayak trips all leave from here. Nearby is Eco Pond, one of the most popular wildlife observation areas. Some facilities, such as the restaurant, have abbreviated seasonal hours.

The **Flamingo Visitor Center** provides an interactive display and has natural-history exhibits in the small Florida Bay Flamingo Museum. Check the schedule for ranger-led activities, such as naturalist discussions, evening programs in the campground amphitheater, and hikes along area trails. Some of the park's best birding is at nearby Eco Pond. ☎ *239/ 695–2945* ⊙ *Hrs vary.*

Where to Stay & Eat

For an intense stay in the "real" Florida, consider one of the 48 backcountry campsites deep in the park, many inland, with some on the beach. You'll have to carry your food, water, and supplies in; take care to carry out all your trash. You'll also need a site-specific permit, available on a first-come, first-served basis from the Flamingo or Gulf Coast Visitor Center. These sites cost $10 or more depending on group size.

¢–$$ ✕ **Flamingo Restaurant.** The grand view, convivial lounge, and casual style are great reasons to visit here. Big picture windows on the visitor center's second floor overlook Florida Bay, and its eagles, gulls, pelicans, and vultures. Dine at low tide to see birds flock to the sandbar just offshore. The restaurant menu has seafood and local dishes such as its signature appetizer, coconut fried shrimp with orange-marmalade horseradish sauce, and Jamaican pork loin. Downstairs, the Buttonwood Patio Cafe has pizza, sandwiches, and salads. It sometimes remains open into the off-season according to demand. ⊠ *Flamingo Lodge, 1 Flamingo Lodge Hwy.* ☎ *239/695–3101* ⊕ *www.flamingolodge.com* ⊟ *AE, D, DC, MC, V* ⊙ *Closed May–Oct.*

$ 🏨 **Flamingo Lodge, Marina & Outpost Resort.** This simple low-rise motel is the only lodging inside the park. Accommodations are basic but well kept, and an amiable staff helps you adjust to bellowing alligators, roaming raccoons, and ibis grazing on the lawn. Rooms have worn-in furniture, floral bedspreads, and art prints of birds. They face Florida Bay, but don't necessarily look out over it. Bathrooms are small. Cottages, in a wooded area on the margin of a coastal prairie, can accommodate up to six people; none have televisions. Reservations are essential in winter. ⊠ *1 Flamingo Lodge Hwy., Flamingo 33034* ☎ *239/695–3101 or 800/600–3813* 🖷 *239/695–3921* ⊕ *www.flamingolodge.com* ⇆ *102 rooms, 24 cottages, 1 suite* ⌂ *Restaurant, snack bar, some kitchens, some cable TV, picnic area, beach, boating, fishing, bicycles, hiking, bar, shops, laundry facilities, business services, meeting rooms, some pets allowed, no-smoking rooms* ⊟ *AE, D, MC, V.*

⚠️ **Everglades National Park.** About 12 mi southwest of Florida City, the park has two developed campsites available through a reservation system from mid-November through mid-April; the rest of the year they're first-come, first-served. Six miles west of the park's main entrance, **Long Pine Key** has no-permit hiking, though you will need separate permits for fresh-water and saltwater fishing. ♿ *BBQ, flush toilets, dump station, drinking water, picnic tables, public telephone* 🚐 *108 drive-up sites* ☎ *800/365–2267 campsite reservations, 305/242–7700 or 239/695–2945 park information* 🌐 *reservations.nps.gov* 🖂 *$14* ▭ *D, MC, V.*

★ Thirty-eight miles southwest of the park's main entrance, **Flamingo** has hiking and nature trails. Of its 234 drive-in sites, 55 have a view of the bay; 20 of its walk-in sites are on the water. ♿ *BBQ, flush toilets, dump station, drinking water, showers (cold), general store* 🚐 *234 drive-up sites, 44 walk-in sites, 20 on the water* ☎ *800/365–2267 campsite reservations, 305/242–7700 or 239/695–2945 park information* 🌐 *reservations.nps.gov* 🖂 *$14* ▭ *D, MC, V.*

The Outdoors

BIKING **Flamingo Lodge, Marina & Outpost Resort** (☎ 239/695–3101) rents old but sturdy bikes for $14 a day, $8 per half day. Snake Bight Trail and the park's main road are good places to ride to see wildlife.

BOATING The marina at **Flamingo Lodge, Marina & Outpost Resort** (☎ 239/695–3101)
★ rents 16-foot power skiffs for $90 per day, $65 per half day, and $22 per hour; 19-foot Carolina skiffs for $155 per day and $100 per half day; as well as fully furnished and outfitted houseboats that sleep up to eight. From November to April, houseboat rates (two-day minimum) run $475 without air-conditioning for two days. Off-season (summer) rates are lower. Several private boats are also available for charter. There are two ramps, one for Florida Bay, the other for Whitewater Bay and the backcountry. The hoist across the plug dam separating Florida Bay from the Buttonwood Canal can take boats from 16 feet to 26 feet long. A small store sells food, camping supplies, bait and tackle, propane, and fuel. A concessionaire rents rods, reels, binoculars, and coolers by the half and full day.

CANOEING & Everglades has well-marked canoe trails in the Flamingo area, plus the
KAYAKING southern end of the 99-mi Wilderness Trail from Everglades City to
★ Flamingo. **Flamingo Lodge, Marina & Outpost Resort** (☎ 239/695–3101) rents canoes in two sizes: small (up to two paddlers) and family size (up to four). Small canoes rent for $32 per day, $22 per half day, and $8 per hour; family-size run $40, $30, and $12, respectively. Single-person kayaks cost $43 per day, $27 per half day, and $11 per hour; doubles rent for $54, $38, and $16, respectively. Overnight rentals are also available as are daily morning canoe trips with park rangers. Saltwater crocodiles like to hang out around the marina on Buttonwood Canal, so you're practically guaranteed a sighting.

FISHING **Flamingo Lodge, Marina & Outpost Resort** (☎ 239/695–3101) helps arrange
★ two-person charter fishing trips. The cost is $375 a day for one or two people, $275 for a half day.

Tamiami Trail

141 mi from Miami to Fort Myers.

In 1915, when officials decided to build an east–west highway linking Miami to Fort Myers and continuing north to Tampa, someone suggested calling it the Tamiami Trail. In 1928 the road became a reality, cutting through the Everglades and altering the natural flow of water and the lives of the Miccosukee Indians who eked out a living fishing, hunting, farming, and frogging here.

Today the highway's traffic streams through Everglades National Park, Big Cypress National Preserve, and Fakahatchee Strand Preserve State Park. The landscape is surprisingly varied, changing from hardwood hammocks to pinelands, then abruptly to tall cypress trees dripping with Spanish moss and back to saw grass marsh. Those who slow down to take in the scenery are rewarded with glimpses of alligators sunning themselves along the banks of roadside canals and in the shallow waters, and hundreds of waterbirds, especially in the dry winter season. The manmade landscape has chickee huts, Native American villages, and airboats parked at roadside enterprises.

Businesses along the trail give their addresses either based on their distance from Krome Avenue, Florida Turnpike, and Miami on the east coast or Naples on the west coast or by mile marker. Between Miami and Naples, the road goes by several names, including Tamiami Trail, U.S. 41, Ninth Street in Naples, and, at the Miami end, Southwest 8th Street.

10 A perennial favorite with tour-bus operators, **Everglades Safari Park** has an arena that seats up to 300 people to watch an educational alligator show and wrestling demonstration. Before and after the show, get a closer look at the alligators on Gator Island, walk through a small wildlife museum, or climb aboard an airboat for a 30-minute ride through the River of Grass (included in admission). There's also a restaurant, a gift shop, and an observation platform that looks out over the Glades. Small, private airboat tours are available for an extra charge and last 20 minutes to 2½ hours. ✉ *26700 Tamiami Trail, 15 mi west of Florida Tpke.* ☎ *305/226–6923 or 305/223–3804* ⊕ *www.evsafaripark.com* ✉ *$20* ⊙ *Daily 9–5.*

 11 After visiting **Everglades Gator Park** you can tell your friends you came face-to-face with—and even touched—an alligator, albeit a baby one. You can also squirm in a "reptilium" of venomous and nonpoisonous native snakes or learn about Native Americans of the Everglades through a reproduction of a Miccosukee village. The park also has wildlife shows with native and exotic animals, 45-minute airboat tours, and RV campsites, as well as a gift shop and restaurant. The last airboat ride departs 45 minutes before sunset. ✉ *24050 Tamiami Trail, 12 mi west of Florida Tpke.* ☎ *305/559–2255 or 800/559–2205* ⊕ *www.gatorpark. com* ✉ *Park $10; tours, wildlife show, and park $18* ⊙ *Daily 9–6.*

★ **12** It takes a bit of nerve to walk the paved 15-mi loop in **Shark Valley** because in the winter months alligators lie on and alongside the road, basking in the sun—most, however, do move quickly out of the way. You can also ride a bicycle or take a tram tour (reservations recommended in winter). Stop at the halfway point to climb the concrete observation tower's ramp, which spirals skyward 50 feet. From there the vast River of Grass spreads as far as the eye can see. Observe waterbirds as well as alligators and, if you're lucky, river otters at water holes and follow a short trail into the habitat. Just behind the bike-rental area another short boardwalk trail meanders through the saw grass and one passes through a tropical hardwood hammock. A small visitor center has rotating exhibits, a bookstore, and park rangers ready to answer questions. Shark Valley is the national park's north entrance; however, no roads here lead directly to other parts of the park. ⊠ *23½ mi west of Florida Tpke.* ☎ *305/ 221–8455, 305/221–8776 tram tours* 🚳 *Park $10 per vehicle, $4 per pedestrian, bicyclist, or motorcyclist* ☉ *Visitor center daily 9–5.*

★ ☺ ⑬ For more than 25 years, the cultural center at **Miccosukee Indian Village** has showcased Miccosukee foods, crafts, skills, and lifestyle. It also presents cultural alligator shows and crafts demonstrations. Narrated 30-minute airboat rides take you into the heart of the wilderness to which these Native Americans escaped after the Seminole Wars and Indian Removal Act of the mid-1800s. In modern times, the Miccosukee clans have relocated to this village along Tamiami Trail, but most still maintain their hammock farming and hunting camps. The village's museum shows a film and displays chickee structures and artifacts that explain this ancient culture. Guided tours are available throughout the day. The Everglades Music & Craft Festival falls on a July weekend, and the weeklong Indian Arts Festival is in late December. There's a restaurant and gift shop on site. ⊠ *Just west of Shark Valley entrance, 25 mi west of Florida Tpke.* ☎ *305/223–8380* ⊕ *www.miccosukeetribe.com* 🚳 *Village $5, rides $10* ☉ *Daily 9–5.*

Clyde Butcher does for the River of Grass and Big Cypress Swamp what Ansel Adams did for the West; check out his stunning photographs at his **Big Cypress Gallery.** Working with large-format black-and-white film, Butcher captures every blade of grass, barb of feather, and flicker of light. If you're lucky, Butcher will be on hand to sign your prints. He's always there on Thanksgiving and Labor Day weekends. Special exhibits, lectures, tours, photo expeditions, and slide presentations are given throughout the year, especially Labor Day weekend. ⊠ *52388 Tamiami Trail, 45 mi west of Florida Tpke., Ochopee* ☎ *239/695–2428 or 888/999–9113* ⊕ *www.clydebutcher.com* 🚳 *Free* ☉ *Daily 10–5* ☉ *Closed Tues. and Wed. in summer.*

⑭
★

⑮ Slow down—the **Oasis Visitor Center** is a welcome respite along the Tamiami Trail. If you blow by here as you speed between Miami and Naples you'll miss out on an opportunity to learn about the surrounding preserve. Inside the center, renovated in 2004–2005, are a small exhibit area, an information center, a bookshop, a theater that shows a 15-minute film on the preserve and Big Cypress Swamp, and rest rooms. A new hanging boardwalk allows safe alligator viewing. The center also has myriad seasonal ranger-led and self-guided activities, such as campfire and wildlife talks, bike hikes, slough slogs, and canoe excursions.

The 8-mi Turner River Canoe Trail begins nearby and crosses through Everglades National Park before ending in Chokoloskee Bay, near Everglades City. Rangers lead four-hour canoe trips on Saturday in season beginning at 9:30 AM. Hikers can join the Florida National Scenic Trail, which runs north–south through the preserve for 31 mi. Two 5-mi trails, Concho Billy and Fire Prairie, can be accessed a few miles east off Turner River Road. Turner River Road and Birdon Road form a 17-mi gravel loop drive that's excellent for birding. Bear Island has about 32 mi of scenic, flat, looped trails that are ideal for bicycling. Most trails are hard-packed lime rock, but a few miles are gravel. Cyclists share the road with off-road vehicles, which are most plentiful during General Gun Hunting season, from mid-November through December. The best biking time is January–March, when rangers lead four-hour, bimonthly **bike tours** (☎ 239/695–1201). Access is from State Road 29 north of I–75. All of the trails can be very wet and sometimes impassable during the summer rainy season. Rangers at the visitor center provide road-condition information. Four primitive campsites are available on a first-come, first-served basis. ⊠ *24 mi east of Everglades City, 50 mi west of Miami, 20 mi west of Shark Valley* ☎ *239/695–1201* ⊕ *www.nps.gov/bisc:* ☜ *Free* ☉ *Daily 8:30–4:30.*

⑯ The tiny **Ochopee Post Office** is the smallest in North America. Buy a picture postcard of the little one-room shack and mail it to a friend, thereby helping to keep this picturesque spot in business. ⊠ *75 mi west of Miami, Ochopee* ☎ *800/275–8777* ☉ *Weekdays 9:30–noon and 1–4:30, Sat. 9:30–11:30.*

★ ⑰ The ½-mi boardwalk at **Fakahatchee Strand Preserve State Park** gives you an opportunity to see rare plants, bald cypress, and North America's largest stand of native royal palms and largest concentration and variety of epiphytic orchids, including 31 varieties of threatened and endangered species that bloom most extravagantly in the hot months. From November to April the park's rookery, accessed down a short road 2 mi east of the boardwalk, is a birder's paradise beginning an hour before sunset. The sight of 5,000 to 7,000 wading birds returning to roost for the night is spectacular. Launch a kayak or watch from the shore. You can also drive through the 12-mi-long W. J. Janes Memorial Scenic Drive and hike the spur trails that lead off it. Ranger-led swamp walks are given November–February. ⊠ *Boardwalk on north side of Tamiami Trail 7 mi west of Rte. 29; rookery on south side of Tamiami Trail 5 mi west of Rte. 29; W. J. Janes Scenic Dr. ¼ mi north of Tamiami Trail on Rte. 29; ranger station on W. J. Janes Scenic Dr., Box 548, Copeland 34137* ☎ *239/695–4593* ⊕ *www.dep.state.fl.us/parks* ☜ *Free* ☉ *Daily 8–sunset.*

★ ⑱ Nature trails, biking, camping, and boat tours into Everglades territory make **Collier-Seminole State Park** an easy introduction into this often forbidding land. Of historical interest, a Seminole War blockhouse has been recreated to hold the interpretive center and one of the "walking dredges"—invented to build Tamiami Trail out of the muck—adorns the grounds. ⊠ *20200 E. Tamiami Trail, Naples 34114* ☎ *239/394–3397* ⊕ *www.floridastateparks.org/collier-seminole* ☜ *$4 per car* ☉ *Daily 8–sunset.*

Where to Stay & Eat

¢–$$ ✕ **Coopertown Restaurant.** For more than a half century this small, casual eatery inside an airboat concession storefront has been full of Old Florida style—not to mention alligator skulls, stuffed alligator heads, and gator accessories. House specialties are frogs' legs and alligator tail prepared cornmeal-breaded and deep-fried, served simply on paper ware with a lemon wedge and Tabasco. Also choose from more conventional selections, such as catfish, shrimp, or sandwiches. ✉ 22700 S.W. 8th St., 11 mi west of Florida Tpke., Miami ☎305/226–6048 ☰AE, D, MC, V.

$ ✕ **Empeek Aaweeke.** Whether you're staying at the Miccosukee Resort or just spending the day at the slot machines, the all-day buffet will bolster you with salads, cold cuts, chicken, fish, steak, and desserts. There's a Friday night seafood buffet. The restaurant's bright art deco furnishings and tribal art murals are in keeping with the rest of the resort. Kids under age 6 eat free; ages 6 to 12 eat half-price. ✉ 500 S.W. 177th Ave., 6 mi west of Florida Tpke., Miami ☎ 305/925–2555 or 877/242–6464 ⊕ www.miccosukee.com ☰ AE, D, MC, V.

¢–$ ✕ **Joanie's Blue Crab Café.** Movie-set designers could not have created a more quintessential 1950s-style swamp café than this landmark, with its wood-plank floors, open rafters, postcards from around the globe, and local art. Joanie, the chief cook and bottle washer, and her daughter Terry set up shop here in 1987. A local fisherman supplies the blue crab and whatever fish du jour he catches. There's also gator nuggets, shrimp, grouper sandwiches, and black beans and rice. Chill out on the screened deck with a beer, glass of wine, or frosty strawberry shake. It's open daily 9 AM to 5 PM (or, in season, whenever the live music dies down). ✉ 39395 Tamiami Trail, 50 mi west of Florida Tpke., Ochopee ☎ 239/695–2682 ☰ AE, D, MC, V.

★ ¢–$ ✕ **Miccosukee Restaurant.** A mural depicts Native American women cooking and men engaged in a powwow in this restaurant at the Miccosukee Indian Village, overlooking the River of Grass. Favorites are catfish and frogs' legs breaded and deep-fried, Indian fry bread, pumpkin bread, and Indian burgers and tacos, but you'll also find more common fare, such as burgers and fish. Try the Miccosukee Platter ($22.95) for a sampling of native dishes, including gator bites. Breakfast and lunch are served daily. ✉ 25 mi west of Florida Tpke. ☎ 305/223–8380 Ext. 2374 ☰ AE, D, MC, V.

★ ¢–$ ✕ **Pit Bar-B-Q.** On a day with a breeze, you'll smell this old-fashioned roadside eatery's barbecue and smoke long before you can see it. Order at the counter, pick up your food, and eat at one of the indoor or outdoor picnic tables. Specialties include barbecued chicken and ribs with a tangy sauce, french fries, coleslaw, and a fried biscuit, plus burgers and fish sandwiches. Popular with families on weekends (when pony rides are available), it's reminiscent of a summer backyard barbecue. ✉ 16400 Tamiami Trail, 5 mi west of Florida Tpke., Miami ☎ 305/226–2272 ☰ AE, D, MC, V.

★ $$ ⊞ **Miccosukee Resort & Convention Center.** Big-name entertainers, major sporting events, and gaming draw crowds to this nine-story resort at the crossroads of Tamiami Trail and Krome Avenue. Like an oasis on the horizon, it's the only facility for miles and it's situated to attract the attention of travelers going to the Everglades, driving across the state, or looking for casino action. Most units have a view of Everglades saw grass and wildlife. In addition to an enormous indoor play area for children and a game arcade for older kids, there are tours to Everglades National Park and the Miccosukee Indian Village, shuttles to area malls, and a golf course about 9 mi away. ⊠ *500 S.W. 177th Ave., 6 mi west of Florida Tpke., Miami 33194* ☎ *305/925–2555 or 877/242–6464* ⊕ *www.miccosukee.com* ⤳ *256 rooms, 46 suites* ⚭ *3 restaurants, snack bar, in-room safes, some in-room hot tubs, minibars, some microwaves, cable TV with movies and video games, in-room data ports, 18-hole golf course, indoor pool, health club, hair salon, hot tub, sauna, spa, lounge, showroom, video game room, shops, children's programs (ages 0–12), playground, laundry service, Internet, business services, convention center, meeting rooms, airport shuttle, travel services, no-smoking rooms* ⊟ *AE, D, DC, MC, V.*

⚠ **Everglades Gator Park.** At an airboat tour facility in the heart of the Everglades, this RV park is especially popular with snowbirds, as it's close to the Port of Miami and Miami airport, and it offers short-term RV storage. You can store your RV, then take a cruise or fly to another destination. Campers are surrounded by the sounds of alligators, birds, and frogs by night, departing and arriving air boats by day. There's a restaurant inside the park. ⚭ *Flush toilets, full hookups, drinking water, electricity, public telephone, restaurant, general store, lake* ⤳ *10 full hookups, 20 partial hookups* ⊠ *24050 S.W. 8th St., Miami* ✆ *Box 787, Miami 33194* ☎ *305/559–2255 or 800/559–2205* 🖷 *305/559–2844* ⊕ *www.gatorpark.com* ✉ *$30 full or partial hookup per night, $125 per week, $350 per month* ⊟ *AE, D, DC, MC, V.*

The Outdoors

★ **Shark Valley Tram Tours** (⊠ Shark Valley ☎ 305/221–8455) rents bikes daily 8:30–4 (last rental at 3; bikes must be returned by 4) for $5.50 per hour.

Shopping

The shopping alone should lure you to the **Miccosukee Indian Village** (⊠ 25 mi west of Florida Tpke., just west of Shark Valley entrance ☎ 305/223–8380). Wares include Native American crafts such as beadwork, moccasins, dolls, pottery, baskets, and patchwork fabric and clothes.

Everglades City

⑲ *35 mi southeast of Naples, 83 mi west of Miami.*

Ignore the Circle K and BNP gas stations on the main road into town, and this is perfect Old Florida. No high-rises mar the landscape at this western gateway to Everglades National Park, just off the Tamiami Trail. It was developed in the late 19th century by Barron Collier, a wealthy advertising man. Collier built it as a company town to house workers for his numerous projects, including construction of the Tamiami Trail. It grew and prospered until the Depression and World War II, and in 1953 took the name of Everglades City. Today it draws people to the park for canoeing, fishing, and bird-watching excursions. Airboat tours, though popular with visitors, are banned within the preserve and park because of the environmental damage they cause to the mangroves. The annual Seafood Festival, held the first weekend of February, draws 60,000–75,000 visitors to eat seafood, hear nonstop music, and buy crafts. At other times, dining choices are limited to a few basic eateries. Several dockside fish markets have opened small restaurants inside and outside along the river. The town is small, fishing oriented, and unhurried, making it excellent for boating and bicycling. Pedal along the waterfront or take the 2-mi ride along the strand out to Chokoloskee Island.

There's no better place to find information about the park's watery western side than at the **Gulf Coast Visitor Center.** During the winter season, it's filled with canoeists checking in for trips to the Ten Thousand Islands and 99-mi Wilderness Waterway Trail, visitors viewing interpretive exhibits about local flora and fauna while they wait for the departure of a naturalist-led boat trip, rangers answering questions, and backcountry campers purchasing permits. There are no direct roads from here to other sections of the park. ⊠ *Rte. 29* ☎ *239/695–3311* ☜ *Park free* ☾ *Mid-Nov.–mid-Apr., daily 7:30–5; mid-Apr.–mid-Nov., daily 9–4:30.*

Through artifacts and photographs at the **Museum of the Everglades,** meet the Native Americans, pioneers, businesspeople, and fishermen who played a role in the development of southwest Florida. The museum chronicles the 2,000-year history of human habitation in the southwestern Everglades. The only remaining unaltered structure original to the town of Everglades, where it opened in 1927 as the town's laundry, the building is on the National Register of Historic Places. In addition to the permanent displays, there are traveling exhibits, lectures, and works by local artists. Pick up a free walking guide of the town's historic sites. ⊠ *105 W. Broadway* ☎ *239/695–0008* ⊕ *www.colliermuseum.com* ☜ *Free* ☾ *Tues.–Sat. 10–4.*

off the beaten path

SMALLWOOD STORE – Ted Smallwood pioneered this last American frontier in 1906 and built a 3,000-square-foot pine trading post raised on pilings in Chokoloskee Bay. Smallwood's granddaughter Lynn McMillin reopened it in 1989, after it had been closed for several years, and installed a small gift shop and a museum chock-full of goods from the store: historic photographs; Native American clothing, furs, and hides; and area memorabilia. An annual festival in March celebrates the century-long relationship the store has had with local Native Americans. ⊠ *360 Mamie St., Chokoloskee Island* ☎ *239/695–2989* ☜ *$2.50* ☾ *Dec.–Apr., daily 10–5; May–Nov., daily 11–5.*

Where to Stay & Eat

★ **$–$$$** ✕ **Rod and Gun Club.** The striking, polished pecky cypress woodwork in this historic building dates from the 1920s, when wealthy hunters, anglers, and yachting parties from around the world came for the winter season. The main dining room holds the overflow from the popular enormous screened porch that overlooks the river. Like life in general here, servers move slowly. Fresh seafood dominates a menu that includes stone crab claws in season, a turf-and-surf combo of steak and shrimp, a swamp-and-turf combo of frogs' legs and steak, seafood and pasta pairings, and yummy peanut butter or key lime pie. Come by boat or land. ⊠ *200 Riverside Dr.* ☎ *239/695–2101* ▤ *No credit cards.*

¢–$$ ✕ **Everglades Oar House Restaurant.** Locals line up outside on Saturday nights for $13.95 all-you-can-eat fried grouper at this wood-paneled eatery whose picnic table–style booths and mishmash of kitschy fishing implements give it the look of a diner. The menu has a blend of simple steaks and seafood, including such local specialties as frogs' legs and gator. The service is friendly, prices are reasonable, food is fried in canola and corn oils, and most dishes can be grilled or broiled, if you prefer. It's popular for its country-style breakfasts. ⊠ *305 N. Collier Ave.* ☎ *239/695–3535* ▤ *AE, D, MC, V.*

¢–$$ ✕ **Everglades Seafood Depot.** This 1928 Spanish-style stucco structure on Lake Placid has had many lives. It began as the old Everglades depot, was part of the University of Miami, appeared in the film *Winds across the Everglades,* and has housed several restaurants. Today's menu has a wide selection of well-prepared seafood—from shrimp and grouper to frogs' legs and alligator—and combinations thereof. For big appetites, there are generously portioned entrées of steak and fish specials that include soup or salad, potato or rice, and warm, fresh-baked biscuits. Weekly specials include a taco bar one night and all-you-can-eat fried shrimp another. ⊠ *102 Collier Ave.* ☎ *239/695–0075* ▤ *AE, D, MC, V.*

¢–$$ ✕ **Oyster House Restaurant.** Look for the wooden tower near the Everglades National Park entrance. It marks one of the town's oldest and most old-fashioned fish houses, serving all the local staples—shrimp, gator tail, frogs' legs, oysters, stone crab, and grouper. Shrimp scampi and grouper smothered in tomatoes are among the few exceptions to fried preparation. But deep-frying is an art in these parts, so if you're going to indulge, do it here. Try to dine at sunset. ⊠ *Hwy. 29 S.* ☎ *239/695–2073* ▤ *AE, D, MC, V.*

¢–$ ✕ **JT's Island Grill & Gallery.** In the manner of C. G. McKinney's General Store, which was established here in 1890, the restaurant offers a **Fodor's**Choice little of this and a little of that. The emphasis is on local, from the short ★ seafood-dominated menu with seasonal stone-crab claws, the excellent fresh catch marinaded in key lime and topped with fresh salsa, papaya basil shrimp, and three-crab cakes with pineapple tartar, to the walls with artwork depicting Everglades wildlife and landscapes. But there's also swamp cabbage (hearts of palm) chicken pasta, sandwiches, wraps, burgers, soups, and salads. ⊠ *238 Mamie St., Chokoloskee Island* ☎ *239/695–3633* ⊕ *www.chokoloskee-island.com* ▤ *MC, V* ☉ *Closed mid-May–mid-Oct. No dinner.*

¢–$ ✕ **Triad Seafood.** Along the Barron River, seafood houses, fishing boats, and crab traps populate one shoreline; mangroves the other. Some of the seafood houses, selling fresh off the boat, added picnic tables and eventually grew into restaurants. Triad is the latest, with a deck overhanging the river and holding about nine outdoor tables. Nothing fancy, but you won't find a better grouper sandwich anywhere. From 11 AM to 5 PM the house also serves fresh stone crab in season, plus fried shrimp, conch, crab cake, and soft-shell blue crab baskets, reubens, hamburgers, Philly cheese steak sandwiches, and, on Fridays, smoked ribs. ⊠ *401 School Dr.* ☎ *239/695–2662* ☐ *AE, MC, V* ⊗ *Closed approximately May–Aug.*

¢–$$ ⊞ **Ivey House.** A remodeled 1928 boarding house originally for work-
Fodor'sChoice ers building the Tamiami Trail, the Ivey House today fits many budgets.
★ One part is a friendly B&B bargain with shared baths and a cottage that are open only November–April. The year-round inn, connected to the B&B by a ramp, has rooms with private baths—some of Everglades City's plushest accommodations. Most inn rooms surround the screen-enclosed pool and courtyard. Display cases of local flora and fauna decorate the inn, as do photographs of the Everglades and Ten Thousand Islands taken by photographers who present weekend photo-shoot workshops. The layout is designed to promote camaraderie, but there are secluded patios with chairs and tables for private moments. Rates include a full breakfast. The Ivey House is run by the owners of NACT-Everglades Rentals & Eco Adventures, so stay here before or after the ecotours and save 20% on canoe and kayak rentals and tours. ⊠ *107 Camellia St., 34139* ☎ *239/695–3299* ☐ *239/695–4155* ⊕ *www. iveyhouse.com* ⇨ *31 rooms, 18 with bath; 1 2-bedroom cottage* ⚘ *Restaurant, room service, some fans, some refrigerators, some cable TV, in-room data ports, wading pool, boating, bicycles, library, shop, laundry facilities; no smoking* ☐ *MC, V* ⧖ *BP.*

$ ⊞ **Everglades Spa-Fari & Lodge.** Formerly a bank dating from 1923, this inn focuses on offering spa and tour services. On the 2nd floor are spacious rooms, suites, and efficiencies, all homey, no-frills, and comfortable with private baths. A licensed massage therapist operates the 1st-floor, five-room day spa, offering such services as massages and facials, colon hydrotherapy, and clay baths. State-certified ecotourism guides lead outings to local attractions, packaged with spa services. Continental breakfast is delivered to your door. ⊠ *201 W. Broadway, Box 570, 34139* ☎ *239/695–3151* ☐ *239/695–3335* ⊕ *www.spa-fari.com* ⇨ *7 rooms* ⚘ *Some kitchens, some kitchenettes, cable TV, spa, bicycles, shop; no room phones, no smoking* ☐ *AE, D, DC MC, V* ⧖ *CP.*

¢   ⊞ **Glades Haven Cozy Cabins.** Bob Miller wanted to build a Holiday Inn next to his Oyster House Restaurant on marina-channel shores. When that didn't go through, he sent for cabin kits and set up mobile home–size units around a pool on his property. Guests who rent these cabins get free boat docking. A full cabin, done up in wood, tin roof, and polished floor, has a full kitchen and separate bedroom with screened porch. Duplex cabins—one of the best deals in town—come with a small fridge and microwave, with or without a screened porch. ⊠ *Copeland Ave., 34139* ☎ *239/695–2746 or 888/956–6251* ⊕ *www.gladeshaven.com* ⇨ *24 cabins, 5 3-bedroom houses* ⚘ *2 restaurants, grocery, snack bar, some kitchens, some kitchenettes, cable TV, pool, boating, marina, fishing, shops, laundry facilities; no room phones* ☐ *AE, D, MC, V.*

★   ⚠ **Outdoor Resorts.** This clean, amenity-rich RV resort, set at the water's edge on secluded Chokoloskee Island, has sunny sites with concrete pads. Tropical vegetation adds shade and color. All sites have a view. The property has boat rentals, tennis and shuffleboard, a marina, and a bait shop. A TV hookup and use of a recreation hall and health club are included in the rates and help while the hours away on rainy days. There are rental trailers and a motel for those who come without an RV. ♿ *Flush toilets, full hookups, drinking water, guest laundry, showers, electricity, general store, playground, 3 pools* ⊷ *283 sites, 8 efficiencies with kitchens, 2 rental trailers* ⊠ *Rte. 29, 6 mi south of Tamiami Trail* ☐ *Box 39, Chokoloskee Island, 34138* ☎ *239/695–3788* 🖷 *239/695–3338* ⊕ *www. outdoor-resorts.com* ⊠ *$49–$69 full hookups, $85 efficiencies and RV rental trailers* ☐ *MC, V.*

The Outdoors

BIKING   **NACT-Everglades Rentals & Eco Adventures** (⊠ Ivey House, 107 Camellia St. ☎ 239/695–4666), the Florida arm of North American Canoe Tours (NACT), rents bikes for $5 per hour, $20 per day (free for Ivey House guests).

BOATING   **Glades Haven Marina** (⊠ 801 S. Copeland Ave. ☎ 239/695–2628 ⊕ www. gladeshaven.com) can put you on the water to explore the Ten Thousand Islands in 16-foot Carolina skiffs and 24-foot pontoon boats. Rates start at $110 a day, with multiday discounts, a half-day option, and special rates for families. This is one of the few companies that allow overnight boat rentals. It also rents kayaks, canoes, and fishing tackle, and has a 24-hour boat ramp and dockage for vessels up to 24 feet long.

CANOEING &   **Everglades National Park Boat Tours** (⊠ Gulf Coast Visitor Center ☎ 239/
KAYAKING   695–4731, 800/445–7724 in Florida) rents 17-foot Grumman canoes for day and overnight use. Rates are $25 per day. Car-shuttle service is available, for an additional fee, for canoeists paddling the Wilderness Trail in season, and travelers with disabilities can be accommodated.

Fodor'sChoice   **NACT-Everglades Rentals & Eco Adventures** (⊠ Ivey House, 107 Camellia
★   St. ☎ 239/695–3299 ⊕ www.evergladesadventures.com) is an established source for canoes, sea kayaks, and guided Everglades trips (November–April). Canoes cost from $35 the first day, $25 for each day thereafter, and kayaks are from $65 for the first day. Half-day rentals from 1 to 5 PM are available.

BIG CYPRESS NATIONAL PRESERVE

Through the 1950s and early 1960s, the world's largest cypress-logging industry prospered in the Big Cypress Swamp. The industry died out in the 1960s, and the government began buying parcels. Today, 729,000 acres, or nearly half of the swamp, have become this national preserve. The word "big" in its name refers not to the size of the trees but to the swamp, which juts down into the north side of Everglades National Park like a piece in a jigsaw puzzle. Its size and strategic location make it an important link in the region's hydrological system, in which rainwater first flows through the preserve, then south into the park, and eventually into Florida Bay. Its variegated pattern of wet prairies, ponds, marshes, sloughs, and strands provides a wildlife sanctuary, and thanks to a policy of balanced land use—"use without abuse"—the watery wilderness is devoted to research and recreation as well as preservation. The preserve allows—in limited areas—hunting, off-road vehicle (airboat, swamp buggy) use by permit, and cattle grazing. Compared to Everglades National Park, the preserve is less developed and has fewer visitors. That makes it ideal for naturalists, birders, and hikers who prefer to see more wildlife than humans. Several scenic drives link off Tamiami Trail; some require four-wheel drive vehicles, especially in wet summer months. A few lead to camping areas. Roadside picnic areas are off the Tamiami Trail. There are three types of trails—walking (including part of the extensive Florida National Scenic Trail), canoeing, and bicycling. All three trail types are easily accessed from the Tamiami Trail near the preserve's visitor center. In 2004, the refuge opened several new boardwalk trails, one of them departing from the center. Canoe and bike equipment can be rented from outfitters in Everglades City, 24 mi west, and Naples, 40 mi west.

Camping

⚠ There are four no-fee primitive campgrounds within Big Cypress National Preserve along the Tamiami Trail and Loop Road. A fifth site, Monument Lake Campground, has rest rooms, an amphitheater, and activities and seasonal programs (December–mid-April). Campers can use the dump station on Dona Drive in Ochopee. ♿ *Flush toilets, dump station, running water (non-potable), showers (cold)* 🏕 *10 tent, 26 RV or tent sites* ⊠ *Tamiami Trail (Hwy. 41), between Miami and Naples* 🖃 *HCR 61, Box 110, Ochopee 34141* 🖀 *239/695–1201* ⊕ *www.nps. gov/bicy* 🖭 *$16 Dec.–mid-Apr.; free rest of year* 🖃 *No credit cards.*

THE EVERGLADES A TO Z

To research prices, get advice from other travelers, and book travel arrangements, visit www.fodors.com.

AIRPORTS

Miami International Airport (MIA) is 34 mi from Homestead and 83 mi from Flamingo in Everglades National Park. Airporter runs shuttle buses three times daily that stop at the Hampton Inn in Florida City on their way between MIA and the Florida Keys. Shuttle service, which takes about an hour, runs 6:10–5:20 from Florida City, 7:30–6 from the airport. Reserve at least 24 hours in advance. Pickups can be arranged for all baggage-claim areas. The cost is $25 one-way. Greyhound Lines buses from MIA to the Keys make a stop in Homestead four times a day. Buses leave from Concourse E, lower level, and cost from $10 one-way, from $18.25 round-trip. SuperShuttle operates 11-passenger air-conditioned vans to Homestead. Service from MIA is available around the clock; booths are outside most luggage areas on the lower level. For the return to MIA, reserve 24 hours in advance. The one-way cost can be up to $180, depending on how many people are booked for the trip.

🛪 Airport Information Miami International Airport (MIA) 🖀 305/876-7000 ⊕ www. miami-airport.com. Airporter 🖀 800/830-3413. Greyhound Lines ⊠ 5 N.E. 3rd Rd., Homestead 🖀 305/247-2040 or 800/231-2222. SuperShuttle 🖀 305/871-2000.

BOAT TRAVEL

If you're entering the United States by pleasure boat, you must phone U.S. Customs either from a marine phone or upon first arriving ashore. Bring aboard the proper *NOAA Nautical Charts* before you cast off to explore park waters. The charts run $17 at many marine stores in South Florida, at the Convoy Point Visitor Center in Biscayne National Park, and at Flamingo Marina in the Everglades. The annual *Waterway Guide* (Southern Edition) is widely used by boaters. Bookstores all over South Florida sell it, or order it directly from the publisher for $40 plus shipping and handling.

🛈 **Boat Information U.S. Customs** ☎ 800/432-1216. *Waterway Guide* ✉ 326 1st St., Suite 400, Annapolis, MD 21403 ☎ 800/233-3359 ⊕ www.waterwayguide.com.

BUS TRAVEL

Metrobus travels daily through the Miami-Homestead-Florida City area. Regular fare is $1.25. The Dade-Monroe Express provides daily bus service from the Florida City Wal-Mart Supercenter to Mile Marker 50 in Marathon. The bus makes several stops in Florida City and the Keys, during daily round-trips on the hour from 6 AM to 10 PM. The cost is $1.50 each way.

🛈 **Bus Information Dade-Monroe Express** ☎ 305/770-3131. **Metrobus** ☎ 305/770-3131.

CAR RENTAL

Agencies in the Homestead area include A&A Car Rental, Budget, and Enterprise Rent-a-Car.

🛈 **Local Agencies A&A Car Rental** ✉ 30005 S. Dixie Hwy., Homestead 33030 ☎ 305/246-0974. **Budget** ✉ 29949 S. Dixie Hwy., Homestead 33030 ☎ 305/248-4524 or 800/527-0700. **Enterprise Rent-a-Car** ✉ 29130 S. Dixie Hwy., Homestead 33030 ☎ 305/246-2056 or 800/736-8222.

CAR TRAVEL

From Miami the main highways to the area are U.S. 1, the Homestead Extension of Florida Turnpike, and Krome Avenue (Route 997 [old U.S. 27]). To reach Everglades National Park's Ernest F. Coe Visitor Center and Flamingo, head west on Route 9336 (Palm Drive) in Florida City and follow signs. From Florida City the Ernest F. Coe Visitor Center is 11 mi; Flamingo is 49 mi. The north entrance of Everglades National Park at Shark Valley is reached by taking the Tamiami Trail about 20 mi west of Krome Avenue. To reach the west entrance of Everglades National Park at the Gulf Coast Visitor Center in Everglades City, take Route 29 south from the Tamiami Trail. To reach Biscayne National Park from Homestead, take U.S. 1 or Krome Avenue to Palm Drive and turn east. Follow Palm Drive for about 8 mi until it becomes Southwest 344th Street and follow signs to the park headquarters.

EMERGENCIES

Dial 911 for police, fire, or ambulance. In national parks, rangers answer police, fire, and medical emergencies. The Florida Fish and Wildlife Conservation Commission, a division of the Florida Department of Natural Resources, maintains a 24-hour telephone service for reporting boating emergencies and natural-resource violations. The Miami Beach

Coast Guard Base responds to local marine emergencies and reports of navigation hazards. The base broadcasts on VHF-FM Channel 16. The National Weather Service supplies local forecasts.

⛑ Hospital emergency line ☎ 305/596-6556. **Homestead Hospital** ✉ 160 N.W. 13th St., Homestead ☎ 305/248-3232, 305/596-6557 physician referral. **Florida Fish and Wildlife Conservation Commission** ☎ 305/956-2500. **Miami Beach Coast Guard Base** ✉ 100 MacArthur Causeway, Miami Beach ☎ 305/535-4300 or 305/535-4314. **National Parks** ☎ 305/247-7272. **National Weather Service** ☎ 305/229-4522.

MEDIA

NEWSPAPERS & MAGAZINES The *South Dade News Leader* is published thrice weekly and covers Homestead, Florida City, and the Redland areas. *Everglades Echo* comes out on Wednesday in Everglades City.

TELEVISION & RADIO WLRN is National Public Radio at FM 91.3. Two new FM stations broadcast information on Everglades flora, fauna, and attractions along I–75: tune into FM 98.7 or 107.9. Out of Miami, WLVE 93.9 plays easy listening; WZTA 94.9, rock.

TOURS

Many Everglades-area tours operate only in season, roughly November through April. The National Park Service has free programs, typically focusing on native wildlife, plants, and park history. At Biscayne National Park, for example, rangers give informal tours of Elliott and Boca Chita keys, which you can arrange in advance, depending on ranger availability. Contact the respective visitor center for details. Wings Ten Thousand Islands Aero-Tours operates scenic, low-level flight tours of the Ten Thousand Islands National Wildlife Refuge, Big Cypress National Preserve, Everglades National Park, and the Gulf of Mexico in an Alaskan floatplane. On the 20- to 90-minute flights, see saw-grass prairies, Native American shell mounds, alligators, and wading birds. Prices start at $30 per person. For an all- or multiday outing, opt for flights across the gulf to the Florida Keys or Dry Tortugas in a floatplane. The outfit sells postcards and prints of local scenery shot from the air. Wooten's Everglades Airboat Tours runs airboat and swamp-buggy tours ($17) through the Everglades. (Swamp buggies are giant tractorlike vehicles with oversize rubber wheels.) Tours last approximately 30 minutes. Combination tours, including a visit to the animal sanctuary, cost $42. Southwest of Florida City near the entrance to Everglades National Park, Everglades Alligator Farm runs a 4-mi, 30-minute tour of the River of Grass with departures 20 minutes after the hour. The tour ($17) includes a free hourly alligator, snake, or wildlife show, or take in the show only ($11.50).

From the Shark Valley area, Buffalo Tiger's Florida Everglades Airboat Ride is operated by a former chairman of the Miccosukee tribe. Miccosukee Indian guides narrate the 40-minute trip from the perspective of the Native Americans, who have lived there since the 1800s. Trips run on the north side of Tamiami Trail, where there's more water and wildlife, and include a stop at an old Native American camp. Tours cost $20 each for two people and operate 10–5 daily. Reservations are not required. Coopertown Airboat Ride operates the oldest airboat rides in the Everglades (since 1945). The 30- to 40-minute tour ($14) takes you 9 mi to hammocks and alligator holes. Everglades Gator Park offers 45-minute narrated airboat tours ($18, including park tour and wildlife show). Everglades Safari Park runs 40-minute airboat rides for $20 and small, private airboat tours for an extra charge; they last 20 minutes to 2½ hours. The price includes a show and gator tour. The Miccosukee Indian Village 30-minute narrated airboat ride stops at a 100-year-old family camp in the Everglades to hear tales and allow passengers to walk around and explore ($10).

Everglades Airboat Tours' two-hour personalized excursions, on airboats accommodating 6 to 12 passengers, venture 40 mi into the River of Grass. Daytime trips are exciting, but the tour that departs an hour before sundown lets you see birds and fish in daylight and alligators, raccoons, and other nocturnal animals when night falls. The tour costs $60 per person. Half-day trips for two to four people cost $355 for the group. Tours at Biscayne National Park are run by people-friendly Biscayne National Underwater Park, Inc. Daily trips (at 10, with a second trip at 1 during high season, depending on demand) explore the park's living coral reefs 10 mi offshore on *Reef Rover IV*, a 53-foot glass-bottom boat that can carry 48 passengers. On days when the weather is unsuitable for reef viewing, an alternative three-hour, ranger-led interpretive tour visits Boca Chita Key. Reservations are recommended. The cost is $24.45, and you should arrive at least one hour before departure.

Flamingo Lodge, Marina & Outpost Resort Boat Tours is the official concession operating sightseeing excursions through Everglades National Park. The two-hour backcountry *Pelican* cruise ($18) is the most popular. The boat winds under a heavy canopy of mangroves, revealing abundant wildlife—from alligators, crocodiles, and turtles to herons, hawks, and egrets. A quieter option is the Sailboat Cruise ($18) into Florida Bay that runs mid-December to spring. Sunset cruises cost $20. The 90-minute Florida Bay cruise ($12) ventures into the bay to explore shallow nursery areas and encounter plentiful bird life and often dolphins, sea turtles, and sharks.

Starting at the Shark Valley visitor center, Shark Valley Tram Tours follows a 15-mi loop road into the interior, stopping at a 50-foot observation tower especially good for viewing gators. Two-hour narrated tours cost $12.75 and depart hourly 9–4 December–April; the rest of the year tours run every two hours from 9:30 to 3. Reservations are recommended December–April. On the west side, Everglades National Park Boat Tours operates 1½-hour trips ($16) through the Ten Thousand Islands National Wildlife Refuge and mangrove wilderness, where passengers often see dolphins, manatees, bald eagles, and roseate spoonbills. In the height of season, three tour boats run four times daily for two-hour trips. Boats can accommodate large parties and wheelchairs (not electric), and one large boat has drink concessions. Everglades Rentals & Eco Adventures leads one-day to seven-night Everglades paddling tours November–April. Highlights include bird and gator sightings, mangrove forests, no-man's-land beaches, relics of the hideouts of infamous and just-plain-reclusive characters, and spectacular sunsets. Included in the cost of extended tours ($550–$1,650) are canoes or kayaks, all necessary equipment, a guide, meals, and lodging for the first night at the Ivey House. There's a four-person minimum.

⁊ Tour Information Biscayne National Underwater Park, Inc. ✉ Convoy Point, east end of North Canal Dr., 9710 S.W. 328th St. ⌂ Box 1270, Homestead 33090 ☎ 305/230–1100 ⊕ www.nps.gov/bisc. **Buffalo Tiger's Florida Everglades Airboat Ride** ✉ 30 mi west of Florida Tpke. on Tamiami Trail ☎ 305/559–5250 or 305/382–0719. **Coopertown Airboat Ride** ✉ 11 mi west of Florida Tpke. on Tamiami Trail ☎ 305/226–6048 ⊕ www.coopertownairboats.com. **Everglades Alligator Farm** ✉ 40351 S.W. 192nd Ave. ☎ 305/247–2628 ⊕ www.everglades.com. **Everglades Gator Park** ✉ 12 mi west of Florida Tpke. on Tamiami Trail ☎ 305/559–2255 or 800/559–2205 ⊕ www.gatorpark.com. **Everglades National Park Boat Tours** ✉ Gulf Coast Visitor Center, Everglades City ☎ 239/695–2591, 800/445–7724 in Florida ⊕ www.nps.gov/ever. **Everglades Rentals & Eco Adventures** ✉ Ivey House, 107 Camellia St. ⌂ Box 5038, Everglades City 34139 ☎ 239/695–3299 ⊕ www.evergladesadventures.com. **Everglades Safari Park** ✉ 26700 Tamiami Trail, 15 mi. west of Florida Tpke. ☎ 305/226–6923 or 305/223–3804 ⊕ www.evsafaripark.com. **Flamingo Lodge, Marina & Outpost Resort Boat Tours** ✉ 1 Flamingo Lodge Hwy., Flamingo ☎ 239/695–3101 Ext. 355 ⊕ www.flamingolodge.com. **Miccosukee Indian Village** ✉ 25 mi west of Florida Tpke. on Tamiami Trail ☎ 305/223–8380 ⊕ www.miccosukeetours.com. **Everglades Airboat Tours, Inc.** ✉ Coopertown ⌂ Box 940082, Miami 33194 ☎ 305/852–5339 or 305/221–9888. **Shark Valley Tram Tours** ⌂ Box 1739, Tamiami Station, Miami 33144 ☎ 305/221–8455 ⊕ www.nps.gov/ever/visit/tours.htm. **Wings Ten Thousand Islands Aero-Tours** ✉ Everglades Airport, 650 Everglades City Airpark Rd. ⌂ Box 482, Everglades City 34139 ☎ 239/695–3296. **Wooten's Everglades Airboat Tours** ✉ Wooten's Alligator Farm, 1½ mi east of Rte. 29 on Tamiami Trail ☎ 239/695–2781 or 800/282–2781 ⊕ www.wootensairboats.com.

VISITOR INFORMATION

⁊ Tourist Information Big Cypress National Preserve ⌂ HCR 61, Box 11, Ochopee 34141 ☎ 239/695–1201 ⊕ www.nps.gov/bisc. **Biscayne National Park** Dante Fascell Visitor Center, ✉ 9700 S.W. 328th St., Homestead 33033–5634 ☎ 305/230–7275 ⊕ www.nps.gov/bisc. **Everglades City Chamber of Commerce** ✉ Rte. 29 and Tamiami Trail ⌂ Box 130, Everglades City 34139 ☎ 239/695–3941 ⊕ www.florida-everglades.com/chamber/home.htm. **Everglades National Park** Ernest F. Coe Visitor Center ✉ 40001 Rte. 9336, Homestead 33034–6733 ☎ 305/242–7700 ⊕ www.nps.gov/ever. **Flamingo Visitor Center** ✉ 1 Flamingo Lodge Hwy., Flamingo 33034–6798 ☎ 239/695–2945. **Gulf Coast Visitor Center** ✉ Rte. 29, Everglades City 34139 ☎ 239/695–3311 ⊕ www.nps.gov/ever. **Tropical Everglades Visitor Association** ✉ 160 U.S. 1, Florida City 33034 ☎ 305/245–9180 or 800/388–9669 ⊕ www.tropicaleverglades.com.

The Lower
Gulf Coast

9

WORD OF MOUTH

"Within [Naples] there are only a couple of beachfront hotels as the beach is lined with all private homes at the southern end, and condominiums as you go further north, but that doesn't mean that the beach is private or belongs to any of those people. In fact it means that if you go to the more southern end, particularly south of the pier, you have the beach much more to yourself."

—Patrick

"Spent a day on Sanibel island, enjoyed the beach and wonderful shelling . . . We shopped at Miromar, which was nice, but not much different from our nearby Lancaster outlets, just a more tropical feel!"

—luugis

Updated by
Chelle Koster
Walton

WITH ITS SUBTROPICAL CLIMATE AND BECKONING FAMILY-FRIENDLY BEACHES, the Lower Gulf Coast, also referred to as the state's southwestern region, is a favorite vacation spot of Florida residents as well as visitors. Compact though it is, there's lots to do in addition to the sun and surf scene throughout its several distinct travel destinations. Small and pretty Fort Myers rises inland along the Caloosahatchee River. It got its nickname, the City of Palms, from the hundreds of towering royal palms that inventor Thomas Edison planted between 1900 and 1917 along McGregor Boulevard, the main residential street and site of his winter estate. Edison's idea caught on, and more than 2,000 royal palms now line McGregor Boulevard alone. Museums and educational attractions are the draw here. Off the coast west of Fort Myers are more than 100 coastal islands in all shapes and sizes—among them Sanibel and Captiva, two thoughtfully developed resort islands. Connected to the mainland by a 3-mi causeway, Sanibel is known for its superb shelling, fine fishing, beachfront resorts, and wildlife refuge. Here and on Captiva, to which it is connected by a bridge, most houses hide behind thick vegetation, but the gulf beaches are readily accessible. Just southwest of Fort Myers is Estero Island, home of busy Fort Myers Beach, and farther south, Lovers Key State Park and the growing area north of Naples, Bonita Springs. North of Fort Myers, Punta Gorda is the center of a fishing-frenzied vacationland that remains a well-kept secret. However, the summer of 2004 brought the wrath of Hurricane Charley to Southwest Florida, with Punta Gorda receiving the heaviest damage, followed by Captiva and Sanibel Islands. Most properties had reopened by late 2004, but as of this writing, a few remain closed into 2006. The destruction of vegetation was the most visible damage, particularly on the islands, and plans are underway to replace tree canopies sheared off by the storm.

Farther down the coast lies Naples, once a small fishing village and now a thriving and sophisticated town, a smaller, more understated version of Palm Beach with fine restaurants, chichi shopping areas, and—locals will tell you—more golf courses per capita than anywhere else in the world. There's a lovely small art museum in the 1,473-seat Naples Philharmonic Center, which is the west-coast home of the Miami City Ballet. The beaches are soft and white, and access is relatively easy. East of Naples stretches the Big Cypress National Preserve, and a half hour south basks Marco Island; see tight clusters of pristine miniature mangrove islands when you take a boat tour departing from the island's marinas. Although high-rises line much of Marco's waterfront, natural areas have been preserved, including the tiny fishing village of Goodland, an outpost of Old Florida that is starting to sprout condos at its fringes.

Exploring the Lower Gulf Coast

In this region vacationers tend to spend most of their time outdoors—swimming, sunning, shelling, fishing, boating, and playing tennis or golf. Fort Myers is the only major inland destination; it has several interesting museums and parks. The barrier islands vary from tiny and undeveloped to sprawling and chockablock with hotels and restaurants.

Numbers in the text correspond to numbers in the margin and on the Lower Gulf Coast map.

If you have 2 days

🖼 **Fort Myers ❶** ► is a good base for a short visit. It's not directly on the beach, but its central location makes day trips easy. On the morning of your first day, visit Edison & Ford Winter Estates, in downtown Fort Myers, and then take McGregor Boulevard and Summerlin Road to 🖼 **Sanibel Island ❽**. There, stop by the Bailey-Matthews Shell Museum and the J. N. "Ding" Darling National Wildlife Refuge before heading to Bowman's Beach for shelling, swimming, and its famous sunset. The next day drive down Interstate 75 to 🖼 **Naples ⓬–⓴**. Check out the subtropical plants and exotic animals at **Caribbean Gardens: The Zoo in Naples ⓰**. If you have a soft spot for stuffed toys, stop by the **Teddy Bear Museum of Naples ⓯** before hitting Old Naples for some shopping and relaxing on the nearby beach.

If you have 4 days

Stay near the water on 🖼 **Sanibel Island ❽** ►. Spend your first day shelling and swimming, taking a break from the beach for a stop at the Bailey-Matthews Shell Museum. On Day 2, head into **Fort Myers ❶** to Edison & Ford Winter Estates and, if you have kids, the hands-on Imaginarium nearby. Spend your third day back on Sanibel, dividing your time between the beach and the J. N. "Ding" Darling National Wildlife Refuge; go kayaking or try bird-watching in the early morning or evening. On Day 4, drive south to 🖼 **Naples ⓬–⓴** and the sights mentioned in the two-day itinerary, or for even more wildlife, head to the Corkscrew Swamp Sanctuary, a nature preserve east of **Bonita Springs ⓫**.

If you have 10 days

An extended stay enables you to move your base and explore several areas in more depth. With two days in the area around **Fort Myers ❶** ►, add Babcock Wilderness Adventures and the Calusa Nature Center and Planetarium to the sights on the four-day itinerary. An extra day on 🖼 **Sanibel Island ❽** allows you to visit by boat an isolated island such as **Cabbage Key ❻** or the little town of Boca Grande, on **Gasparilla Island ❹**. For the second half of your trip, relocate to 🖼 **Naples ⓬–⓴**, stopping en route at Lovers Key State Park for some sensational shelling along its 2½ mi of white-sand beach. Once in Naples, divide your time between the beach and the galleries and shops. **Caribbean Gardens: The Zoo in Naples ⓰** and the Corkscrew Swamp Sanctuary are good bets for kids; to try your hand at paddling, rent a canoe or kayak at the **Naples Nature Center ⓱**. Or get your dose of culture at the impressive **Naples Museum of Art ⓭**. As a diversion, head to **Marco Island ㉑** for a day of fishing or a wildlife-viewing boat trip in the Everglades.

9

About the Restaurants

In this part of Florida fresh seafood reigns supreme. Succulent native stone crab claws, a particular treat, in season from mid-October through mid-May, are usually served with drawn butter or tangy mustard sauce. Supplies should remain plentiful, since these crabs are not killed to harvest their claws and their limbs regenerate in time for the next season. In Naples's excellent restaurants, mingle with locals, winter visitors, and other travelers and catch up on the latest culinary trends. Throughout the region, early-bird discounts go to diners who sit down before 6 PM.

About the Hotels

Lodging in Fort Myers and Naples can be pricey, but there are affordable properties even during the busy winter season. If these destinations are too rich for your budget, consider visiting in the off-season, when rates drop drastically. Beachfront properties tend to be more expensive; to spend less, look for properties away from the water. Punta Gorda and Charlotte Harbor have more in the budget range. In high season—Christmas through Easter—always reserve ahead for the top properties. Fall is the slowest season: rates are low and availability is high, but this is also the prime time for hurricanes.

WHAT IT COSTS					
	$$$$	**$$$**	**$$**	**$**	**¢**
RESTAURANTS	over $30	$20–$30	$15–$20	$10–$15	under $10
HOTELS	over $220	$140–$220	$100–$140	$80–$100	under $80

Restaurant prices are per person for a main course at dinner. Hotel prices are for a standard double room, excluding 6% sales tax (more in some counties) and 1%–4% tourist tax.

Timing

In winter this is one of the warmest areas of the United States, although occasionally temperatures drop below freezing in December or January. From January through April you may find it next to impossible to find a hotel room. Fewer people visit off season, but there really is no bad time to come. Discounted room rates make summer attractive, and there's plenty of water for keeping cool.

FORT MYERS AREA

In Fort Myers, old Southern mansions peek out from behind rows of stately palms, and views over the broad Caloosahatchee River, which borders the city's small but businesslike cluster of office buildings downtown, soften the look of the area. These days, it's showing the effects of age and urban sprawl, but renowned planner Andres Duany, father of "new urbanism," has been engaged to help revive it. North of Fort Myers are small fishing communities and new retirement towns, including Boca Grande on Gasparilla Island; Englewood Beach on Manasota Key; Port Charlotte, north of the Peace River; and Punta Gorda, at the convergence of the Peace River and Charlotte Harbor.

Beaches Gorgeous, long, white-sand beaches fringe the Lower Gulf Coast and barrier islands. Many strands, most notably those on Sanibel and Captiva, are well known for their shelling. Find tiny coquina shells, bright conch shells, whelks, augurs, scallops, cockles, and much more. Waters are usually calm and friendly to both swimmers and saltwater anglers.

Canoeing Opened in 2003, the Great Calusa Blueway paddling trail runs through Intracoastal waters between Bonita Springs and the islands north of Captiva for a total of 90-some miles. A network of narrow waterways makes Sanibel Island's J. N. "Ding" Darling National Wildlife Refuge a favorite destination for canoeing. Consider canoeing inland in less-developed areas of the region; several outfits offer half- and full-day as well as overnight trips.

Golf Often referred to as the Golf Capital of the World, Naples is a golfer's delight, with nearly perfect weather most of the year and many beautifully situated courses. There are more than 50 courses in the area, with new ones opening all the time.

Shopping As one of the world's premier shelling grounds, Sanibel Island has numerous shops seriously selling shells (try to say that three times fast). Shells come plain, in all shapes and sizes. But a coterie of crustacean crafters also turns them into everything from picture frames and lamps to jewelry and dozens of supremely kitschy creations (a cowrie turtle, anyone?). Elsewhere on Sanibel, appealing boutiques showcase sea-life jewelry along with fashionable resort wear. Naples shops, unique but often pricey, stock lovely antiques, clothing, shoes, linens, and home-decor accessories. Especially noteworthy are the art galleries and the secondhand shops, where, for a fraction of the original price, you can pick up high-end designer clothing discarded—barely worn—by wintering millionaires from all over the United States.

Fort Myers

▶ ❶ *90 mi southeast of Sarasota, 140 mi west of Palm Beach.*

This small, inviting city lies inland along the banks of the Caloosahatchee River, a half hour from the nearest beach. The town is best known as the winter home of inventors Thomas A. Edison and Henry Ford.

Majestic palms, some planted by Thomas Edison, line **McGregor Boulevard,** one of the city's most scenic streets. It runs from downtown to Summerlin Road, which takes you to the barrier islands.

Fodor'sChoice **Edison & Ford Winter Estates,** Fort Myers's premier attraction, pays
★ homage to two of America's most ingenious inventors: Thomas A. Edison, who gave the world the stock ticker, the incandescent lamp, and the phonograph, among other inventions; and his friend and neigh-

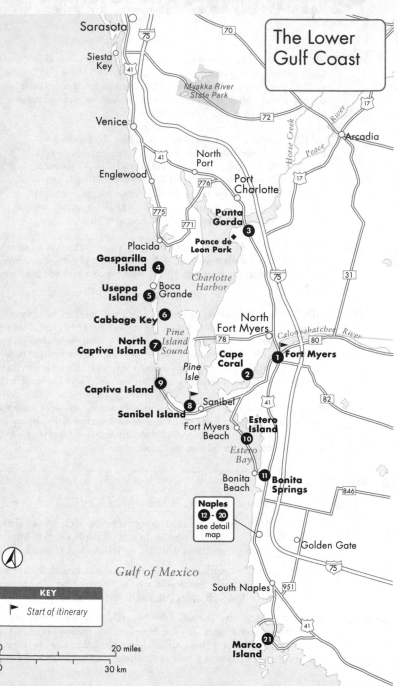

The Lower
Gulf Coast

Sarasota

Siesta
Key

Myakka River
State Park

Venice

North
Port

Englewood

Port
Charlotte

Punta
Gorda ③

Ponce de
Leon Park

Placida

Gasparilla
Island ④

Charlotte
Harbor

Useppa
Island ⑤
Boca
Grande

Cabbage Key ⑥

North ⑦
Captiva Island

Pine
Island
Sound

North
Fort Myers

Cape
Coral ②
① ▶ Fort Myers

Caloosahatchee River

Pine
Isle

Captiva Island ⑨

Sanibel Island ⑧ ▶ Sanibel

Fort Myers
Beach

Estero
Island

⑩

Estero
Bay

Bonita
Beach ⑪ Bonita
Springs

Naples
⑫ - ⑳
see detail
map

Golden Gate

Gulf of Mexico

South Naples

Marco
Island ㉑

0   20 miles
0   30 km

bor, automaker Henry Ford. Donated to the city by Edison's widow, his 14-acre estate, newly renovated in 2004-2005, is a remarkable place with a laboratory, botanical gardens, and a museum. The laboratory is just as Edison left it when he died in 1931. Edison traveled south from New Jersey and devoted much of his time here to inventing things (there are 1,093 patents to his name), experimenting with rubber for friend and frequent visitor Harvey Firestone, and planting some 600 species of plants collected around the world. Next door is Ford's "Mangoes," the more modest seasonal home of Edison's fellow inventor. It's said that the V-8 engine in essence was designed on the back porch. One admission covers both homes. Tours of the river in an electric launch like one Edison kept cost $5.50 extra. ⊠ *2350 McGregor Blvd.* ☎ *239/334–3614* ⊕ *www.edison-ford-estate.com* 🎫 *$16* ⊘ *Tours Mon.–Sat. 9–4, Sun. noon–4.*

In a restored railroad depot, the **Southwest Florida Museum of History** showcases the area's history dating to 800 BC. Displays include prehistoric Calusa artifacts, a reconstructed *chickee* hut, canoes, clothing and photos from Seminole settlements, historical vignettes, and a replicated Florida Crackerhouse. A favorite attraction is the *Esperanza,* a private rail car from the 1930s. ⊠ *2300 Peck St.* ☎ *239/332–5955* 🎫 *$9.50* ⊘ *Tues.–Sat. 10–5.*

★ ℃ Kids can't wait to get their hands on the wonderful interactive exhibits at the **Imaginarium Hands-On Museum,** a lively museum-aquarium combo that explores the environment, physics, anatomy, weather, and other science topics. Check out the marine life in the aquariums, the touch pool, the living-reef tank, and the outdoor lagoon; visit tarantulas, guinea pigs, and other live critters in the Animal Lab; dig for dinosaur bones; then prepare to get blown away in the Hurricane Experience. ⊠ *2000 Cranford Ave.* ☎ *239/337–3332* 🎫 *$8* ⊘ *Mon.–Sat. 10–5, Sun. noon–5.*

℃ For a look at exhibits on wildlife, fossils, and Florida's native animals and habitats, head to the **Calusa Nature Center and Planetarium.** Boardwalks lead through subtropical wetlands, a birds-of-prey aviary, a butterfly house, and a Seminole Indian village. There are snake, alligator, and other live animal demonstrations several times daily. The 90-seat planetarium has astronomy shows daily and special laser shows. ⊠ *3450 Ortiz Ave.* ☎ *239/275–3435* ⊕ *www.calusanature.com* 🎫 *Nature center and planetarium $7* ⊘ *Mon.–Sat. 9–5, Sun. 11–5; call for astronomy and laser show schedule.*

★ ℃ At **Manatee Park** you may glimpse Florida's most famous marine mammal. When gulf waters are cold—usually from November to March—the gentle sea cows congregate in these waters, which are warmed by the outflow of a nearby power plant. Pause at any of the three observation decks and watch for bubbles. Hydrophones allow you to eavesdrop on their songs. Periodically one of the mammoth creatures will surface. They are huge—mature adults weigh hundreds of pounds. The park rents kayaks in winter and on summer weekends, and kayaking clinics and free guided walks are available. ⊠ *1½ mi east of I–75 at 10901 Rte. 80* ☎ *239/694–3537 viewing update, 239/432–2038 office* ⊕ *www.*

leeparks.org/manatee.htm 🅿 *Parking 75¢ per hr to maximum of $3 per day* ⊙ *Apr.–Sept., daily 8–8; Oct.–Mar., daily 8–5. Gates lock automatically and promptly at closing time.*

Where to Stay & Eat

$$–$$$$ ✕ **The Veranda.** A favorite of business and government bigwigs, this spot serves imaginative Continental fare with a trace of a Southern accent. Notable are tournedos with smoky sour-mash whiskey sauce, rack of lamb with rosemary merlot sauce, parmesan-crusted snapper with beurre blanc, and a grilled seafood sampler. The restaurant is a combination of two turn-of-the-20th-century homes, with sconces and antique oil paintings on its pale yellow walls. Meals are also served in the courtyard. ✉ *2122 2nd St.* ☎ *239/332–2065* 🖃 *AE, MC, V* ⊙ *Closed Sun. No lunch Sat.*

$$–$$$ ✕ **Biddle's.** Refined surroundings and a mellow piano bar set the mood for seafood, pasta, and chops infused with flavor and accompanied with creative sides and sauces. Lobster ravioli comes with citrus-wilted spinach; grilled rosemary veal chops with red wine demi-glace; salmon Florentine with porcini risotto; and seafood Wellington is topped with lobster cream sauce. The glamorous chocolate piano dessert brings the meal to a fitting end. Stay for late-night dancing on weekends. ✉ *20351 Summerlin Rd.* ☎ *239/443–4449* 🖃 *AE, MC, V.*

$$–$$$ ✕ **French Roast Café.** Irish omelets, Belgian waffles, tournedos of beef, Vietnamese sea bass, American burgers: French Roast clearly travels farther abroad than its name implies. And it does it with utmost taste and flavor. The best deals are the lunchtime Vietnamese and early-bird (4:30 to 6) meals. At dinner, leave room for crêpes à la Grand Marnier tableside or something from the bakery, and a cup of fresh-roasted coffee (hence the second part of its name). ✉ *15660 San Carlos Blvd.* ☎ *239/ 415–4375* 🖃 *AE, D, MC, V* ⊙ *Closed Sun. and Mon. in off-season.*

★ $–$$ ✕ **Bistro 41.** In this brightly painted bistro the menu roams from chicken potpie and Yucatan pork to seafood paella, rotisserie chicken, and meat loaf. To experience the kitchen at its imaginative best, check the night's specials, which often include daringly done seafood and usually cost more than regular menu items. ✉ *13499 S. Cleveland Ave.* ☎ *239/466–4141* 🖃 *AE, D, MC, V* ⊙ *No lunch Sun.*

$ ✕ **La Casita.** The colorful purple houselike structure in the Kmart parking lot means authentic Mexican done imaginatively. The menu is inspired by Mexico's Guanajuato region and includes traditional breakfast items such as *huevos rancheros*. Try the potato tamales, basil chicken, or grouper topped with spicy roasted tomatoes, and the banana cheesecake chimichanga. Inside is a bright and cheery version of a Mexican cantina. ✉ *15185 McGregor Blvd.* ☎ *239/415–1050* 🖃 *AE, D, MC, V.*

$ ✕ **Shrimp Shack.** Seafood lovers and bargain hunters flock to these two locations with their vivacious staff, bustle, and tropical color. There's often a wait for lunch and a brisk take-out business at both addresses. Southern-style deep frying prevails—whole belly clams, grouper, shrimp, onion rings, hush puppies, and pork loin planks—though you can get some selections broiled or blackened. The Pirate's Pleasure combines broiled grouper, shrimp, and scallops on a bed of crabmeat. ✉ *13361 Metro Pkwy.* ☎ *239/561–6817* ✉ *Royal Palm Sq., 1400 Colonial Blvd. #57* ☎ *239/277–5100* 🖃 *AE, D, DC, MC, V.*

¢–$ ✗ **Mel's Diner.** Comfort food and lots of it: that's what you get at this 1950s-style diner appropriately strewn with memorabilia. The booths are comfortable, and the daily blue-plate specials—pot roast, chicken potpie, country-fried steak, for example—come with real mashed potatoes. Or try the Windy City chili, a burger, ribs, or an omelet. For dessert, the popular mile-high pies hit the spot. ✉ *4820 S. Cleveland Ave.* ☎ *239/275–7850* ⊕ *www.melsdiner.com* ▤ *AE, DC, MC, V.*

¢ ✗ **Philly Junction.** From the bread to the beer, it comes from Philadel-
Fodor'sChoice phia at these two locations. Not only are the Philly cheese steaks deli-
★ cious and authentic, but the burgers and other sandwiches are excellent—and the prices are among the lowest around. Stay for an old-fashioned sundae from the fountain (at the Summerlin location only), or join the Philly natives for pork roll and scrapple at breakfast. ✉ *4600 Summerlin Rd.* ☎ *239/936–6622* ✉ *12901 McGregor Blvd.* ☎ *239/482–8885* ▤ *MC, V* ⊙ *No dinner Sun.*

$$$ 🏨 **Hilton Garden Inn.** This compact, prettily landscaped low-rise lies near Fort Myers's cultural and commercial areas. Rooms, done in florals and light wood, are spacious, with marble vanities in the bath, and have high-speed Internet access and free HBO. A huge aquarium in the lobby adds a nice Florida touch. ✉ *12600 University Dr., 33907* ☎ *239/790–3500* 🖷*239/790–3501* ⊕*www.hilton.com* ⤳*109 rooms, 17 suites* ᗉ *Restaurant, microwaves, refrigerators, cable TV, in-room data ports, pool, exercise equipment, outdoor hot tub, bar, laundry facilities, laundry service, Internet, business services, meeting rooms* ▤ *AE, DC, MC, V.*

$$$ 🏨 **Holiday Inn Riverwalk.** Riverside and close to downtown, this find is known for its lively tiki bar. The dramatic coral rock lobby with sweeping staircase and lush pool courtyard let you know you're in Florida. Rooms and suites have a typical motel-room layout with open closet, but furnishings go a notch above, and some rooms have whirlpools. ✉ *2220 W. 1st St., 33901* ☎ *239/334–3434 or 800/644–7775* 🖷*239/334–3844* ⤳ *133 rooms, 13 suites* ᗉ *2 restaurants, in-room safes, refrigerators, cable TV, pool, exercise equipment, bar, playground, meeting rooms* ▤ *AE, D, DC, MC, V.*

$$–$$$ 🏨 **Country Inn & Suites.** A top option for its value and facilities, this spot is close to the airport and interstate, with complete business services. Restaurants are nearby. ✉ *9401 Marketplace Rd., 33912* ☎ *239/454–0040 or 800/456–4000* 🖷 *239/454–6006* ⊕ *www.countryinns.com* ⤳ *65 rooms, 20 suites* ᗉ *Cable TV with movies and video games, pool, gym, outdoor hot tub, library, laundry service, business services, meeting rooms, airport shuttle, no-smoking rooms* ▤ *AE, D, DC, MC, V* ⦿ *CP.*

Nightlife & the Arts

THE ARTS The **Barbara B. Mann Performing Arts Hall** (✉ Edison Community College, 8099 College Pkwy. SW ☎ 239/481–4849 ⊕ www.bbmannpah.
★ com) presents plays, concerts, musicals, and dance programs. The **Broadway Palm Dinner Theater** (✉ 1380 Colonial Blvd. ☎ 239/278–4422 ⊕ www.broadwaypalm.com) serves buffet dinners along with some of Broadway's best comedies and musicals. There's also a cabaret in a smaller 90-seat theater. In the restored circa-1920 Arcade Theatre downtown,

★ **Florida Repertory Theatre** (✉ 12267 1st St. ☎ 239/332–4488 or 877/787–8053 ⊕ www.floridarep.org) stages professional entertainment, from Neil Simon shows to musical revues.

NIGHTLIFE Lively every night, **Bahama Breeze** (✉ 14701 Tamiami Trail ☎ 239/454–9234) sways tropical with calypso, soca, and other island sounds. **Dwyer's Pub** (✉ 13851 S. Cleveland Ave. ☎ 239/425–0782) hops and jigs on weekends with live Irish bands. **Laugh In Comedy Café** (✉ College Plaza, 8595 College Pkwy. ☎ 239/479–5233), south of downtown, has comedians Thursday, Friday, and Saturday. **Stevie Tomato's Sports Page** (✉ 11491 S. Cleveland Ave. ☎ 239/939–7211) has big-screen TVs and good munchies.

Sports & the Outdoors

BASEBALL The **Boston Red Sox** (✉ 2201 Edison Ave. ☎ 239/334–4700 ⊕ www.redsox.com) train in Fort Myers every spring. The **Minnesota Twins** (✉ Lee County Sports Complex, 14100 Six Mile Cypress Pkwy. ☎ 239/768–4210) play exhibition games in town during March and early April. From April through August, the Miracle, a Twins single-A affiliate, plays home games at the Complex.

BIKING The longest bike path in Fort Myers is along Summerlin Road. It passes through commercial areas, and close to Sanibel's dwindling wide open spaces. Linear Park, which runs parallel to Metro Parkway, offers more natural, less congested views. For a good selection of rentals try the **Bike Route** (✉ 14530 Hwy. 41 S ☎ 239/481–3376).

FISHING Anglers typically head for the gulf, its bays, and estuaries for saltwater fishing—snapper, sheepshead, mackerel, and other species. The Caloosahatchee River, Orange River, canals, and small lakes offer freshwater alternatives.

GOLF The driving range and 18-hole course at the **Eastwood Golf Club** (✉ 4600 ★ Bruce Herd La. ☎ 239/275–4848) are affordable, especially if you don't mind playing at unfavorable times (midday in summer, for example). Many golfers enjoy the lack of development around the course, which poses challenges with its water hazards and doglegs. Fees include cart and tax; fees without cart included are available at certain times. Green fee: $25/$60. The **Fort Myers Country Club** (✉ 3591 McGregor Blvd. ☎ 239/936–2457), with 18 holes, challenges golfers with its small greens. It's the town's oldest course. Lessons are available. Green fee: $25/$52. Head to the **Shell Point Golf Club** (✉ 16401 On Par Blvd. ☎ 239/433–9790) for an 18-hole course and a driving range. Green fee: $34/$79.

ICE-SKATING Recreational ice-skating, in-line skating, ice-hockey programs, and figure-skating plus skate rentals are offered at downtown's **Fort Myers Skatium** (✉ 2250 Broadway Ave. ☎ 239/461–3145 ⊕ www.fmskatium.com).

SAILING **Southwest Florida Yachts** (✉ 3444 Marinatown La. NW ☎ 239/656–1339 ★ or 800/262–7939 ⊕ www.swfyachts.com) charters sailboats and offers lessons.

Shopping

★ **Bell Tower Shops** (✉ U.S. 41 and Daniels Pkwy., South Fort Myers ☎ 239/489–1221), an open-air shopping center, has about 40 stylish boutiques and specialty shops, a Saks Fifth Avenue, and 20 movie screens. **Edison Mall** (✉ Colonial Blvd. at U.S. 41) is the largest mall on the Lower Gulf Coast, with several major department stores and more than 150 specialty shops. **Sanibel Tanger Factory Outlets** (✉ McGregor Blvd. and Summerlin Rd. ☎ 888/471–3939 ⊕ www.tangeroutlet.com) has outlets for Dexter, Van Heusen, Maidenform, Coach, Jones New York, and Samsonite, among others. Just east of Fort Myers, more than 900 vendors sell new and used goods at **Fleamasters Fleamarket** (✉ 1 mi west of I–75 Exit 138 on Rte. 82), Friday through Sunday between 8 and 4.

Cape Coral & North Fort Myers

❷ *13 mi from downtown Fort Myers via North Fort Myers, just across the river (1 mi) from south Fort Myers.*

Four bridges cross from Fort Myers to Cape Coral and its eastern neighbor, North Fort Myers. Families especially find fun in these residential communities and their rural backyards, including undiscovered Pine Island.

Nature walks, bubble bins, Xeriscape displays, an iguana garden, whisper dishes, mazes, telescopes, optical tricks, mind-benders, and brain twisters keep things lively at the **Children's Science Center.** ✉ *2915 N.E. Pine Island Rd.* ☎ *239/997–0012* ⊕ *www.childrenssciencecenter.org* 🎟 *$5* ☉ *Tues.–Fri. 10–4, Sat. 10–4:30.*

Fodor'sChoice
★ **Sun Splash Family Waterpark** has more than two dozen wet and dry attractions, including three large water slides; the Lilypad Walk, where you step from one floating "lily pad" to another; an arcade; a family pool and Tot Spot; and Electric Slide, a lightning-fast tube slide. ✉ *400 Santa Barbara Blvd.* ☎ *239/574–0557* ⊕ *www.sunsplashwaterpark.com* 🎟 *$10.95* ☉ *Mar.–Sept., hrs vary; call ahead.*

> off the beaten path

ECHO – Educational Concerns for Hunger Organization is a small Christian ministry group striving to end world hunger via creative farming. The gardens have one of Florida's largest collections of tropical food plants. On the tour, you watch a video about ECHO's mission and take a 45-minute walk through a simulated rain forest and up a two-story, man-made mountain, and look at farm animals and crops such as sesame and rice grown without soil. ✉ *17391 Durrance Rd., North Fort Myers* ☎ *239/543–3246* ⊕ *www.echonet. org* 🎟 *Free* ☉ *Tours Jan.–Mar., Tues.–Sat. at 10; Apr.–Dec., Tues., Fri., and Sat. at 10; or by appointment.*

Where to Stay & Eat

★ ¢–$ ✕ **Bert's Bar & Grill.** Looking to hang out with the locals on Pine Island? You get that, cheap eats, live entertainment, and a water view to boot at Bert's. Speaking of boots, you're likely to see much of the clientele wearing white rubber fishing boots, known here as Pine Island Reeboks. Order pizza, a burger, fried oysters, or crab cakes from the no-nonsense menu. ⊠ *4271 Pine Island Rd., Matlacha* ⊕ *www.bertsbar.com* ☎ *239/ 282–3232* ▭ *MC, V.*

¢–$ ✕ **Cape Crab & Steak House.** A long-timer in these parts, it's known for its in-shell king, snow, blue, and stone crabs, but sells all sorts of seafood and meat dishes and combinations on its all-day menu. Budgeters can choose from a selection of inexpensive plates and sandwiches. Splurgers can consider crab, crab cakes, stuffed flounder, and daily seafood specials. ⊠ *Coralwood Shopping Center, 2301 Del Prado Blvd. #809* ☎ *239/574–2722* ▭ *AE, D, MC, V.*

¢–$ ✕ **Siam Hut.** Two traditional Thai tables allow you to sit on floor pillows (conveniently with backs) or you can opt for a more conventional table or booth. Lunch and dinner menus at this Cape Coral fixture let you design your own stir-fry, noodle, or fried-rice dish. Dinner specialties include fried crispy frogs' legs with garlic and black pepper, a sizzling shrimp platter, fried whole fish with curry sauce, salads, and *pad thai* (rice noodles, shrimp, chicken, egg, ground peanuts, and vegetables). Get your food fiery hot or extra mild. ⊠ *4521 Del Prado Blvd.* ☎ *239/945–4247* ▭ *MC, V* ⊗ *Closed Sun. No lunch Sat.*

¢–$$$ ▦ **Tarpon Lodge Sportsman Inn.** If you're looking for no-frills escape and fishing, this aptly named lodge, built in 1926 on a sweep of green lawn with magnificent views out to sea, may do the trick. Rooms are small and simple, and the sunny restaurant dishes up creative surprises. It's in the fishing village of Pineland, on the edge of Pine Island Sound, settled in the 16th century by Calusa Indians and stocked with charming Cracker fishing shacks in the 1920s. ⊠ *13771 Waterfront Dr., Pineland 33945* ☎ *239/283–3999* ℻ *239/283–7658* ⊕ *www. tarponlodge.com* ⇆ *20 rooms, 1 cottage* ⌂ *Restaurant, pool, dock, fishing, bar,* ▭ *AE, MC, V.*

$–$$ ▦ **Casa Loma Motel.** At this pretty little motel, 15 minutes from Fort Myers at the end of the Croton Canal, all units are efficiencies with a porch or balcony, some overlooking the canal. ⊠ *3608 Del Prado Blvd., 33904* ☎ *239/549–6000 or 877/227–2566* ℻ *239/549–4877* ⊕ *www. casalomamotel.com* ⇆ *49 efficiencies, 1 suite* ⌂ *Kitchenettes, cable TV, pool, dock, fishing, recreation room, laundry facilities; no smoking* ▭ *AE, D, MC, V.*

Sports & the Outdoors

GOLF **The Golf Club** (⊠ 4003 Palm Tree Blvd. ☎ 239/542–7879) has an 18-hole course (green fee: $20/$80), a driving range, and a putting green. It encompasses 108 bunkers and is considered player-friendly. **Coral Oaks Golf Course** (⊠ 1800 N.W. 28th Ave. ☎ 239/573–3100) has an 18-hole layout and a practice range. Arthur Hill designed the championship par-70 course, which has lots of lakes, ponds, wildlife, and mammoth live oaks. Green fee: $22/$56.25.

TENNIS **Cape Coral Yacht Club Community Park** (⊠ 5819 Driftwood Pkwy. ☎ 239/ 574–0808) has five lighted Har-Tru courts.

Shopping

A survivor from Florida's roadside-attraction era, the vast **Shell Factory & Nature Park** (⊠ 2787 N. Tamiami Trail, North Fort Myers ☏ 239/ 995–2141 or 800/282–5805 ⊕ www.shellfactory.com) claims to have the world's largest display of seashells, coral, sponges, and fossils. But this is as much entertainment complex as store, so you'll find bumper boats, miniature golf, and a musical lighted fountain show (admission $4 each). The nature park contains a petting zoo with camels, llamas, and goats; an EcoLab with reptiles, a hedgehog, and bunnies; a primate pavilion; a prairie dog habitat; and hands-on exhibits (admission $8, open daily 10–7 in season).

Punta Gorda

❸ *23 mi north of Cape Coral and Fort Myers.*

In this small, old town on the mouth of the Peace River, where it empties into Charlotte Harbor, street art, water views, and murals enliven the compact, downtown historic district. It was heavily impacted by Hurricane Charley in 2004, but the vintage buildings stood and the district came back to life with a new influx of creative restaurants and art. Although there's plenty of waterfront in the area, between this town and sprawling adjacent Port Charlotte there's only a single beach—and it's man-made and on the river rather than on the gulf. This is a place to come for fishing, canoeing, walking in the woods, and, most of all, escaping the crowds. The hurricane closed many of the town's waterside lodging options temporarily but indefinitely.

The **Ponce de León Historical Park and Peace River Wildlife Center** is named for the famous *conquistador* who, according to local lore, took a fatal arrow here. A humble shrine and historic marker pay homage, but the park's best features are the fishing, wildlife, and view at the mouth of the Peace River. The rehabilitation facility that shares the point of land conducts tours. ⊠ *3400 W. Marion Ave.* ☏ *941/637–3830* ☑ *Donations accepted* ☉ *Wildlife center daily 11–3; park daily sunrise–sunset.*

Hands-on and glass-encased permanent and changing exhibits explore the region's pirate lore, Native Americans, fishing heritage, and other facets of the past at **Charlotte Harbor Historical Center.** It resides in a lovely new waterfront facility next to a fishing pier park and hosts special kids' programs. ⊠ *22959 Bayshore Rd., Charlotte Harbor* ☏ *941/629–7278* ☑ *$2* ☉ *Weekdays 10–5, Sat. 10–3.*

★ ℭ **BABCOCK WILDERNESS ADVENTURES** – To see what Florida looked like centuries ago, visit 90,000-acre Babcock Crescent B Ranch, southeast of Punta Gorda and northeast of Fort Myers. During the 90-minute swamp-buggy excursion you ride in a converted school bus through several ecosystems, including the unusual and fascinating Telegraph Cypress Swamp. Along the way an informative and amusing guide describes the area's social and natural history while you keep an eye peeled for alligators, wild pigs, all sorts of birds, and other denizens of the wild. The tour also takes in the ranch's bison herd, resident cattle, and Florida panthers in captivity. Reservations are needed for tours. ⊠ *8000 Rte. 31* ☎ *941/637–0551 or 800/500–5583* ⊕ *www.babcockwilderness.com* 🎫 *Bus tour $17.95* ☉ *Tours daily, with varying schedules, weather permitting and by reservation only.*

Where to Stay & Eat

★ **$$–$$$** ✕ **Amimoto Japanese Restaurant.** Sit at the sushi bar or a table in the small dining room decorated simply with Japanese art prints and artifacts. Most popular for lunch, it offers a nice selection of *obentos,* Japanese box lunches, which might include pork loin or shrimp dumplings. The extensive sushi and appetizer menus give you many grazing options. Entrées involve grilled or breaded chicken, pork, beef, and seafood with wasabi or teriyaki sauce. ⊠ *Towles Plaza, 2705 S. Tamiami Trail* ☎ *941/505–1515* ▤ *AE, D, DC, MC, V* ☉ *No lunch weekends.*

$–$$ ✕ **River City Grill.** Sparking a dining renaissance on West Marion Avenue, this eatery remodeled a vintage brick building with artistic panache. Its capacious seating spills out onto the sidewalk and imaginative dishes such as salmon in phyllo and mint and lingonberry roasted lamb shank share the menu with grilled prime cuts of beef and seafood. ⊠ *115 Tamiami Trail* ☎ *941/639–1800* ▤ *AE, D, MC, V.*

¢–$ ▦ **Budget Inn.** Five minutes from downtown's shop-and-dine scene and close to the chain restaurants along the highway, this was one of the first properties to reopen after 2004's hurricane devastation. Rooms look newly painted and furnished and the pool has been restored. ⊠ *1520 Tamiami Trail, Punta Gorda 33950* ☎ *941/639–8000* ⤴ *45 rooms* ⚬ *Refrigerators, cable TV, pool, basketball, laundry facilities* ▤ *AE, D, DC, MC, V.*

Sports & the Outdoors

BIKING   For information on bike trails, which range from bike lanes through local neighborhoods to recreational trails such as the Cape Haze Pioneer Trail and the rails-to-trails Boca Grande Trail, request a copy of the Charlotte County Bikeways brochure from the Charlotte County Chamber of Commerce.

CANOEING   Kayaking and canoeing in Charlotte Harbor and along the Peace River are a good reason to visit this area. Up the Peace River, about 25 mi
★   from Punta Gorda, **Canoe Outpost** (⊠ 2816 Rte. 661, Arcadia ☎ 863/494–1215 or 800/268–0083) conducts all-day and overnight canoe trips, camping equipment included. On this part of the river, the tannin-tinted water runs narrow, and tall cypress trees and birds are plentiful—as are alligators, which pose no threat to canoeists in their vessels.

FISHING   For half- and full-day fishing trips in the bay or the gulf, call **King Fisher Charter** (⊠ Fishermen's Village ☎ 941/639–0969).

GOLF   There are 18 holes to play at the **Deep Creek Golf Club** (⊠ 1260 San Cristobal Ave., Port Charlotte ☎ 941/625–6911), green fee: $17/$45.

TENNIS   **Port Charlotte Tennis Club** (⊠ 22400 Gleneagles Terr., Port Charlotte ☎ 941/625–7222) has four lighted hard courts.

THE COASTAL ISLANDS

A maze of islands in various stages of habitation fronts the mainland from Charlotte County to Fort Myers, separated by the Intracoastal Waterway. Some are accessible via a causeway; to reach others, you may need a boat. If you cut through Pine Island Sound, you have a good chance of being escorted by bottle-nosed dolphins. Mostly birds and other wild creatures inhabit some islands, which are given over to state parks. Traveler-pampering hotels on Sanibel, Captiva, and Fort Myers Beach give way to rustic cottages, old inns, and cabins on quiet Cabbage Key and Pine Island, which have no beaches because they lie between the barrier islands and mainland. Still more are devoted to resorts for the Robinson Crusoe in you. When exploring island beaches, keep one eye on the sand: shelling is a major pursuit in these parts.

Gasparilla Island (Boca Grande)

4 *43 mi northwest of Fort Myers, 23 mi southwest of Punta Gorda.*

Before roads to the Lower Gulf Coast were even talked about, wealthy northerners came by train to spend the winter at the **Gasparilla Inn,** built in 1912 in Boca Grande on Gasparilla Island. Although condominiums and modern sprawl creep up on the rest of Gasparilla, much of the town of Boca Grande looks like another era. The mood is set by the Old Florida homes and tree-framed roadways. The island's calm is disrupted in the spring when anglers descend with a vengeance on Boca Grande Pass, considered among the best tarpon-fishing spots in the world. North of it stretches a long island, home to Don Pedro Island State Park, accessible only by boat, then the off-the-beaten-path island of Manasota Key and its fishing resort community of Englewood Beach.

Where to Stay

★ **$$$$** ⊞ **Gasparilla Inn.** Social-register members such as the Vanderbilts and DuPonts still winter at the gracious, pale-yellow wooden hotel built by shipping industrialists in the early 1900s. Lodge rooms are not lavishly decorated by today's standards. The cottage rooms are more modern and less spartan. The inn takes up most of the town of Boca Grande with its rich-blooded amenities—sprawling lawns, golf course, and beach club. In summer the main lodge closes and cottage rates include breakfast and dinner only. ⊠ *500 Palm Ave., Boca Grande 33921* ☎ *941/964–2201* 🖷 *941/283–1384* 🛏 *140 rooms* ⚬ *Restaurant, dining room, 18-hole golf course, 7 tennis courts, 2 pools, gym, hair salon, beach, croquet* ⊟ *No credit cards* ⑩ *FAP.*

Useppa Island

5 *2 mi south of Boca Grande Pass.*

Unless you're spending the night, the only way to visit this historic island, at Mile Marker 63 on the Intracoastal Waterway and occupied by an exclusive club, is on a tour with the *Lady Chadwick* cruise through Captiva Cruises on Captiva Island. Go for lunch and a tour of the fascinating little Useppa Museum, which tells about the island's ancient Calusa mounds and its role in training fighters for the Cuban Bay of Pigs confrontation.

Where to Stay

★ $$$–$$$$ ⊞ **Collier Inn & Cottages.** Should you decide to spend some time away from civilization, you can lodge at the inn here, built in 1908 as the Izaak Walton Club, a fishing getaway for the rich and tarpon-seeking. Rooms and suites in the inn and a couple of other historic buildings reflect the island's sporting past, but in the finest taste. The Useppa Island Club also has some two-bedroom cottages on a rental program. The club can make transportation arrangements from Pine Island or Boca Grande. Continental breakfast is complimentary for guests without kitchens. *🖉 Box 640, Useppa Island 33922 ☎ 239/283–1061 🖨 239/283–0290 ⊕ www.useppa.com 🛏 8 rooms, 5 suites, 10 2-bedroom cottages ⏶ 2 restaurants, picnic area, some kitchens, refrigerators, cable TV, 3 tennis courts, pro shop, pool, gym, outdoor hot tub, beach, dock, boating, marina, fishing, bicycles, croquet, 2 bars, shop, laundry facilities, Internet ⊟ AE, MC, V ⋈ CP.*

Cabbage Key

❻ *5 mi south of Boca Grande.*

You'll have to take a boat—from Bokeelia, on Pine Island, or from Captiva Island—to get to this island, which sits at Mile Marker 60 on the Intracoastal Waterway. Gone for the foreseeable future is much of the island's lush vegetation, a casualty of the hurricanes that passed through the region in 2004.

Where to Stay

$ ⊞ **Cabbage Key Inn.** Atop an ancient Calusa Indian shell mound and accessible only by boat is the friendly inn built by novelist and playwright Mary Roberts Rinehart in 1938. It's surrounded by 100 acres of tropical vegetation, through which a natural trail runs. In addition to the inn rooms, there are guest cottages scattered throughout the property, some of which have kitchens. Rooms range from barebones to more modern and family friendly. There's a full-service marina and a restaurant whose dining room is papered with thousands of dollar bills. One of the many perks of staying here is access to the remote and pristine beach of Cayo Casto, a short boat trip from Cabbage Key. *🖉 Box 200, Pineland 33945 ☎ 239/283–2278 🖨 239/283–1384 ⊕ www.cabbagekey.com 🛏 6 rooms, 6 cottages ⏶ Restaurant, some kitchens, dock, boating, marina, fishing, bar, shop; no room phones, no room TVs ⊟ MC, V.*

North Captiva Island

❼ *3 mi south of Cabbage Key.*

No bridges lead to this 750-acre island, and most visitors arrive by prearranged water taxi from Pine Island. They come for the isolation and complete absence of "civilization." Some of the private houses can be rented through **North Captiva Island Club Resort** (☎ 239/395–1001 or 800/

576–7343 ⊕ www.northcaptiva.com). The complex has two pools and a sauna, which you're free to use, plus bike and kayak rentals and a restaurant and pool bar that serves food. It's a good idea to bring your own groceries; there's only one small store, and it's quite pricey.

Sanibel & Captiva Islands

23 mi southwest of downtown Fort Myers.

▶ ❽ **Sanibel Island,** accessible from the mainland via the Sanibel Causeway (toll $6 round-trip), is famous as one of the world's best shelling grounds, a function of the unusual east–west orientation of the island's south end. Just as the tide is going out and after storms, the pickings can be superb, and shell seekers with the telltale "Sanibel stoop" patrol every beach laden with bags of conchs, whelks, cockles, and other bivalves and gastropods. (Remember, it's unlawful to pick up live shells.) Away from the beach, flowery vegetation decorates small shopping complexes, pleasant resorts and condo complexes, mom-and-pop motels, and casual restaurants. But much of the narrow road down the spine of the island is bordered by nature reserves that have made Sanibel as well known among bird-watchers as it is among seashell collectors.

❾ **Captiva Island,** connected to the northern end of Sanibel by a bridge, is quirky and engaging. At the end of a twisty road lined with million-dollar mansions lies a delightful village of shops and eateries. South Seas Resort, which takes up one-third of the island, closed in 2004 due to extensive hurricane damage, and as of this writing was scheduled to reopen in 2006.

At Sanibel's southern tip, the frequently photographed **Sanibel Lighthouse,** built in 1884, before the island was settled, guards **Lighthouse Beach.** Although the lighthouse is not open to the public, the area around it has been a wildlife refuge since 1950. A fishing pier, nature trail, and restrooms are available. ⊠ *Periwinkle Way, Sanibel* ☎ *239/472–6477* ⌖ *Parking $2 per hr.*

★ The charming **Sanibel Historical Village and Museum** shows off buildings from the island's past—a 1927 post office, a garage housing a Model T Ford, the Old Bailey general store, a tea house, a 1925 winter vacation cottage, and the 1913 Rutland House Museum, with old documents and photographs and a Calusa Indian exhibit. The newest addition is a 19th-century one-room schoolhouse, which was moved in 2004 from its original location on Periwinkle Way, where it served as a theater for more than 20 years. ⊠ *950 Dunlop Rd., Sanibel* ☎ *239/472–4648* ⌖ *$5* ⊙ *Nov.–May, Wed.–Sat. 10–4; June–mid-Aug., Wed.–Sat. 10–1. Closed mid-Aug.–Oct.*

The beach in **Gulfside Park** is quiet, good for solitude and shells. There are restrooms and picnic tables. ⊠ *Algiers La. off Casa Ybel Rd., Sanibel* ☎ *239/472–6477* ⌖ *Parking $2 per hr.*

Tarpon Bay Beach is centrally located and safer for swimming than beaches at the passes, where waters move swiftly. Sometimes in season there's a mobile concession stand. ⊠ *Tarpon Bay Rd. off Sanibel–Captiva Rd., Sanibel* ☎ *239/472–6477* 🅿 *Parking $2 per hr.*

🆑 To help you identify your Sanibel Island beach finds, stop at the **Bailey-Matthews Shell Museum,** which displays more than a million shells from around the world. A shell-finder display identifies specimens from local waters in sizes ranging from tiny to huge; handle these and sea creatures in the kids' area. A 6-foot revolving globe at the center of the museum rotunda highlights shells from around the world. ⊠ *3075 Sanibel–Captiva Rd., Sanibel* ☎ *239/395–2233 or 888/679–6450* ⊕ *www.shellmuseum.org* 🎫 *$6* 🕙 *Daily 10–4.*

Fodor'sChoice
★

🆑 More than half of Sanibel is occupied by the subtly beautiful **J. N. "Ding" Darling National Wildlife Refuge,** 6,300 acres of wetlands and lush, jungly mangrove forests named after a conservation-minded Pulitzer prize–winning political cartoonist, who became the first director of the government body that later became the U.S. Fish & Wildlife Service. The masses of roseate spoonbills and ibis and the winter flock of white pelicans here make for a good show even if you're not a diehard bird-watcher. Birders have counted some 230 species, including herons, ospreys, and the timid mangrove cuckoo. Raccoons, otters, alligators, and one lone American crocodile also can be spotted. The 4½-mi Wildlife Drive is the main way to explore the preserve; drive, walk, or bicycle along it, or ride a specially designed open-air tram with a naturalist on board. There are also a couple of short walking trails, including one to a Calusa shell mound. Or explore from the water via canoe or kayak (guided tours are available). The best time for bird-watching is in the early morning about an hour before or after low tide, and the observation tower along the road offers prime viewing and is outfitted with a remote camera that broadcasts inside the Education Center for the ultimate in comfortable birding. Interactive exhibits in the Education Center, at the entrance to the refuge, demonstrate the refuge's various ecosystems and explain its status as a rest stop along a major bird migration route. Because Wildlife Drive is closed to vehicular traffic on Friday, try to time your visit for another day. Alternatively, rent a bike for the trip or allow enough time to walk. ⊠ *1 Wildlife Dr., Sanibel* ☎ *239/472–1100, 239/395–0900 tram* 🎫 *$5 per car, $1 for pedestrians and bicyclists, tram $10, Education Center free* 🕙 *Education Center Jan.–Apr., daily 9–4; May–Dec., daily 8–4.*

Fodor'sChoice
★

For a good look at snowy egrets, great blue herons, alligators, and other inhabitants of Florida's wetlands, follow one of the 10 short 🆑 walking trails at the 1,800-acre wetlands managed by the **Sanibel/Captiva Conservation Foundation.** See island research projects and nature displays, visit a butterfly house, and touch sea creatures. Guided walks are available. ⊠ *3333 Sanibel–Captiva Rd., Sanibel* ☎ *239/472–2329* ⊕ *www.sccf.org* 🎫 *$3* 🕙 *Mon.–Fri. 8:30–4, Sat. 10–3.*

★ Long, wide **Bowman's Beach,** on Sanibel's northwest end, is the island's most secluded strand. Walk the length of it and leave humanity behind, finding some of the greatest concentrations of shells along the way. And the sunsets at the north end are spectacular—try to spot the green flash said to occur just as the sun sinks below the horizon.

✉ *Bowman Beach Rd., Sanibel* ☏ *239/472–6477* 🅿 *Parking 75¢ per hr, maximum $3 a day.*

Turner Beach is the sunset-watching spot on the southern tip of Captiva. Strong currents through the pass make swimming tricky, and parking is limited. Surfers head here when winds whip up the waves. ✉ *Captiva Dr., Captiva* 🅿 *Parking $2 per hr.*

Captiva Beach fronts many private homes. The parking lot is small, so arrive early. There are no facilities, but stores and restaurants are nearby. ✉ *Captiva Dr., Captiva* 🅿 *Parking $2 per hr.*

Where to Stay & Eat

$$$–$$$$ ✕ **The Sanibel Steakhouse.** So successful is it at feeding the current craving for top-shelf beef, it has spun off into a local chain with branches in Fort Myers, Bonita Springs, and Naples. Here you can sample the very finest prime meat, including Japan's famous melt-in-your-mouth Kobe beef, plus aged domestic cuts. A more-than-sufficient selection of seafood complements the red meat, including crab cakes, broiled sea bass, and blackened yellowtail snapper. Walls handsomely lined with cushy banquettes and blond wood provide the appropriate setting for unrestrained indulgence. ✉ *1473 Periwinkle Way, Sanibel* ☏ *239/472–5700* 🍴 *Reservations essential* ▤ *AE, D, DC, MC, V* ☉ *No lunch.*

★ $$$ ✕ **Traders Store & Cafe.** In the midst of a warehouse-size import store, this bistro, accented with artifacts from Africa and other exotic places, is a favorite of locals. The marvelous seared tuna appetizer with Asian slaw and wasabi vinaigrette exemplifies the creative fare. Or, go for the barbecued baby back ribs or any of the day's finely crafted specials. ✉ *1551 Periwinkle Way, Sanibel* ☏ *239/472–7242* ▤ *AE, D, MC, V.*

$$–$$$ ✕ **Bubble Room.** At this lively, kitschy favorite, servers wear scout uniforms and funny headgear. Electric trains circle overhead, glossies of 1940s Hollywood stars line the walls, and tabletops showcase old-time toys. After grazing your basket of cheesy bubble bread and sweet, yeasty sticky buns, go for aged prime rib or the grouper steamed in a paper bag. Have a hefty slice of one of the homemade triple-layer cakes; consider the red velvet cake. Be prepared to wait for a table. ✉ *15001 Captiva Dr., Captiva* ☏ *239/472–5558* 🍴 *Reservations not accepted* ▤ *AE, D, DC, MC, V.*

★ $$–$$$ ✕ **Twilight Cafe.** Crawfish mashed potatoes are a tasty specialty at this tiny, artistic nook in Gallery Place. The menu changes daily but often includes such artistic daredevils as grilled scallops over homemade tangerine linguine or pan-seared blackened filet on a bed of braised fennel with black bean salsa. ✉ *751 Tarpon Bay Rd., Sanibel* ☏ *239/472–8818* 🍴 *Reservations essential* ▤ *AE, MC, V* ☉ *No lunch off-season; no lunch weekends in season.*

$–$$$ ✕ **Green Flash.** Good food and second-story, sweeping views of quiet waters and a mangrove island keep boaters and others coming back to this casual indoor-outdoor restaurant. Seafood dominates, but there's a bit of everything on the menu, from shrimp in beer batter and grilled swordfish to pork tenderloin Wellington. For lunch, try the Green Flash sandwich (smoked turkey and prosciutto or vegetables, both with cheese on grilled focaccia). ✉ *15183 Captiva Dr., Captiva* ☏ *239/472–3337* ▤ *AE, D, DC, MC, V.*

$$ ✗ **McT's Shrimphouse and Tavern.** In this informal Sanibel landmark, the menu predictably spotlights fresh seafood. Look for oyster and clam appetizers and the all-you-can-eat shrimp and crab among more than a dozen shrimp entrées, although ribs, prime rib, and blackened chicken are also available. There's always a dessert du jour, but few can resist the Sanibel mud pie, a delicious concoction heavy on the Oreos. ✉ *1523 Periwinkle Way, Sanibel* ☎ *239/472–3161* ⚓ *Reservations not accepted* ▭ *AE, D, MC, V.*

¢–$$ ✗ **Lazy Flamingo.** At two Sanibel locations, this is the friendly neighborhood hang-out enjoyed by locals and visitors alike. The original in Santiva (between Sanibel and Captiva) is small with counter service only; the other provides table service. Both have a nautical look à la Key West and a popular following for their "Dead Parrot Wings" (Buffalo wings coated with tongue-scorching hot sauce), grouper sandwiches, burgers, and steamer pots. ✉ *6520C Pine Ave., Sanibel* ☎ *239/472–5353* ✉ *1036 Periwinkle Way, Sanibel* ☎ *239/472–6939* ⊕ *www.lazyflamingo. com* ⚓ *Reservations not accepted* ▭ *AE, D, MC, V.*

¢–$ ✗ **Amy's Over Easy Café.** Locals head to this bright eatery for breakfast. It caters to Atkins diets, and also serves lunch. Try the egg Reuben sandwich for breakfast or a custom omelet made with whole eggs, whites only, or egg substitute. The lunch menu includes salads, build-your-own burgers, a shrimp roll, a grouper sandwich, and a foot-long hot dog. ✉ *630-1 Tarpon Bay Rd., Sanibel* ☎ *239/472–2625* ⚓ *Reservations not accepted* ▭ *D, MC, V* ☉ *No dinner Apr.–Dec.*

¢–$ ✗ **Redfish Blufish.** Despite the whimsical name and brightly painted, roundly molded furnishings, there's nothing frivolous about the food in this setting à la Seuss. Not a green egg to be found on the "dinner menu petite," which lists well-crafted dishes shrunk to taster size and concentrated with multilevel flavor, such as of scallop ceviche with lemon vinaigrette and tomato water, snapper with sage butter and green-olive sauce, and tournedos of beef with shallot confit. Lunch is more traditional: wraps, fish sandwich, salads, and black beans and rice. ✉ *Captiva Village Square, 14970 Captiva Dr., Captiva* ☎ *239/472–1956* ▭ *AE, D, MC, V.*

$$$$ ⊞ **Casa Ybel Resort.** This time-share dates from the early 20th century. Palms, ponds, a footbridge, and gazebos set the mood on the 23 acres of gulf-facing grounds. Inside, the one- and two-bedroom apartments are contemporary, with full kitchens, tasteful patterns, and big screened-in porches that look out to the beach. The respected Thistle Lodge restaurant is in a re-created historic home with a beach view. In season (February and March), there's a minimum Saturday–Saturday stay requirement. ✉ *2255 W. Gulf Dr., Sanibel 33957* ☎ *239/472–3145 or 800/276–4753* ⊠ *239/472–2109* ⊕ *www.casaybelresort.com* ⊲ *40 1-bedroom units, 74 2-bedroom units* ⚏ *2 restaurants, picnic area, in-room data ports, in-room safes, kitchens, cable TV, in-room VCRs, 6 tennis courts, pool, wading pool, massage, beach, 2 bars, babysitting, children's programs (ages 4–11), playground, business services, meeting rooms* ▭ *AE, D, DC, MC, V.*

$$$$ ☒ **Sanibel Harbour Resort & Spa.** This high-rise resort complex is not on
FodorśChoice   Sanibel proper but instead towers over the bay at the last mainland exit
★   before the causeway. Completely renovated after 2004's hurricane, it
now offers three lodging options—a concierge club-style inn, the hotel,
and condos—all with sweeping views of island-studded San Carlos Bay.
There's also tennis, the exceptional spa and restaurants (one of which
is a dining yacht), a gorgeous circular windowed bar, and the large free-
form pool, among other facilities and activities. Rent a kayak, take a
wildlife-viewing cruise, or go fishing. The beach is small and bayside,
but transportation to Sanibel's beaches is free. ☒ *17260 Harbour Pointe
Dr., Fort Myers 33908* ☎ *239/466–4000 or 800/767–7777* 🖷 *239/
466–6050* ⊕ *www.sanibel-resort.com* ⇆ *278 rooms, 69 suites, 54 condominiums* ⚅ *5 restaurants, coffee shop, snack bar, room service, in-
room safes, cable TV, in-room data ports, golf privileges, 8 tennis courts,
6 pools (1 indoor), health club, hair salon, 2 hot tubs, 4 outdoor hot
tubs, spa, beach, dock, boating, fishing, basketball, 3 bars, children's
programs (ages 5–12), Internet, concierge floor, business services, meeting rooms, no-smoking rooms* ▤ *AE, D, DC, MC, V.*

$$$–$$$$ ☒ **Sanibel's Seaside Inn.** Tucked among the subtropical greenery, right
on the beach, this quiet inn, a part of South Seas Resorts properties, is
a pleasant alternative to the area's larger resorts. Light tropical prints
and rattan furniture fill the guest quarters, which are studios, one- to
three-bedroom units, and individual cottages. Continental breakfast is
complimentary, and videos are on hand to borrow. Transportation is
free to Sundial Beach Resort and other South Seas facilities. ☒ *541 E.
Gulf Dr., Sanibel 33957* ☎ *239/472–1400 or 800/831–7384* 🖷 *239/
481–4947* ⊕ *www.seasideinn.com* ⇆ *12 rooms, 20 suites* ⚅ *Picnic
area, some kitchens, microwaves, refrigerators, cable TV, in-room VCRs,
pool, beach, bicycles, shuffleboard, library, laundry facilities; no smok-
ing* ▤ *AE, D, DC, MC, V* ⛌ *CP.*

$$$–$$$$ ☒ **Shalimar.** Well-maintained grounds and an inviting beach are the ap-
peal of this small property. Units occupy tin-roof two-story cottages and
a two-story motel set back from the beach amid palm trees and other
subtropical greenery. The small pool is in the courtyard, and there are
barbecue grills. ☒ *2823 W. Gulf Dr., Sanibel 33957* ☎ *239/472–1353
or 800/472–1353* 🖷 *239/472–6430* ⊕ *www.shalimar.com* ⇆ *20 effi-
ciencies, 11 1-bedroom units, 2 2-bedroom units* ⚅ *Picnic area, BBQs,
in-room data ports, kitchens, cable TV, in-room VCRs, pool, beach, bi-
cycles, basketball, shuffleboard, laundry facilities* ▤ *AE, D, MC, V.*

$$$–$$$$ ☒ **Waterside Inn.** Palm trees and white sand set the scene at this quiet
beachside vacation spot made up of white one- and two-story buildings.
Rooms and efficiencies are modestly furnished, with bright cobalt-blue-
and-white interiors, and have balconies or patios and at least a partial
view of the gulf. Single-story cottages are named and painted for apri-
cot, kiwi, raspberry, and other fruit. ☒ *3033 W. Gulf Dr., Sanibel
33957* ☎ *239/472–1345 or 800/741–6166* 🖷 *239/472–2148* ⊕ *www.
watersideinn.net* ⇆ *4 rooms, 10 efficiencies, 13 cottages* ⚅ *Picnic area,
BBQs, fans, some kitchens, microwaves, refrigerators, cable TV, in-room
data ports, pool, beach, bicycles, shuffleboard, laundry facilities, some
pets allowed* ▤ *AE, D, MC, V.*

Sports & the Outdoors

BIKING Everyone bikes around flatter-than-a-pancake Sanibel and Captiva—on bikeways that edge the main highway in places, on the road through the wildlife refuge, and along side streets. Free maps are available at bicycle liveries. On Sanibel, rent by the hour or the day at **Billy's Bikes** (⊠ 1470 Periwinkle Way, Sanibel ☎ 239/472–5248). On Captiva, bikes are available at **Jim's Rentals** (⊠ 11534 Andy Rosse La., Captiva ☎ 239/472–1296).

★

BOATING **Boat House of Sanibel** (⊠ Sanibel Marina, 634 N. Yachtsman Dr., Sanibel ☎ 239/472–2531) rents powerboats. **Sweet Water Boat Rental** ('Tween Waters Marina ⊠ 15951 Captiva Dr., Captiva ☎ 239/472–6336) can set you up with a 19-foot center-console boat.

CANOEING & Scout out the wildlife refuge in a canoe or kayak from **Tarpon Bay Ex-**
KAYAKING **plorers** (⊠ 900 Tarpon Bay Rd., Sanibel ☎ 239/472–8900 ⊕ www.tarponbayexplorers.com). Guided tours are also available.

★

FISHING Local anglers head out to catch mackerel, pompano, grouper, reds, snook, bluefish, and shark. To find a charter captain on Sanibel, ask around at its main public marina, **Sanibel Marina** (⊠ 634 N. Yachtsman Dr., Sanibel ☎ 239/472–2723). On Captiva, the place to look for guides is **'Tween Waters Marina** (⊠ 15951 Captiva Dr., Captiva ☎ 239/472–5161).

GOLF Rent clubs and take lessons as well as test your skills against the water hazards on the 18-hole course at the **Dunes Golf & Tennis Club** (⊠ 949 Sandcastle Rd., Sanibel ☎ 239/472–2535), green fee: $50/$118.

TENNIS At the **Dunes Golf & Tennis Club** (⊠ 949 Sandcastle Rd., Sanibel ☎ 239/472–3522), there are seven clay courts and two pros who give lessons.

Shopping

Sanibel is known for its art galleries, shell shops, and one-of-a-kind boutiques; the several small open-air shopping complexes are inviting, with their tropical flowers and shady ficus trees. The largest cluster of shops is **Periwinkle Place** (⊠ 2075 Periwinkle Way, Sanibel), with 55 shops. **Aboriginals** (⊠ 2340 Periwinkle Way, Sanibel ☎ 239/395–2200), at Sanibel Village shops, sells museum-quality textiles, baskets, pottery, sculptures, and jewelry made by Native Americans, Australians, and

Fodor'sChoice Africans. At **She Sells Sea Shells** (⊠ 1157 Periwinkle Way, Sanibel ☎ 239/
★ 395–2266), everything imaginable is made from shells, from decorative mirrors and lamps to Christmas ornaments. Expect the unexpected in wildlife art at **Jungle Drums** (⊠ 11532 Andy Rosse La., Captiva ☎ 239/395–2266), where fish, sea turtles, and other wildlife are depicted with utmost creativity and touches of whimsy.

Estero Island (Fort Myers Beach)

10 *18 mi southwest of Fort Myers.*

Crammed with motels, hotels, and restaurants, this island is one of Fort Myers's more frenetic gulf playgrounds. Dolphins are frequently spotted in Estero Bay, a protected arm of the gulf, and marinas provide a

WEST INDIAN MANATEE

SO THEY WON'T WIN *any beauty contests. Florida's West Indian manatees, also known as sea cows, are enormous aquatic mammals. The average adult male is about 10 feet long and weighs in at around 1,000 pounds, so it should come as no surprise that the manatee's closest relative is the elephant. (What may surprise you, however, is the speculation that early sailor sightings of "mermaids" were actually manatees.) Yet despite their mass, these creatures somehow manage a sweet appeal. Their big lump of a body has wrinkly gray-brown skin, a tiny paddle-shape tail, two little flippers, and a stubby, pug-nose face that is at once whiskery and winsome.*

In spite of their giant size, sea cows are entirely harmless. In fact, they are extremely docile. Moving very slowly, they sometimes submerge and rest, coming up for a breath of fresh air every three to five minutes. These completely herbivorous animals spend the day grazing along the floor and surface of a body of water in search of aquatic greenery. Consummate munchers, the gentle giants can eat close to 15% of their body weight in plants each day.

Male manatees take about nine years to reach adulthood, while females take only five. Baby manatees stay with their mothers for as long as two years.

Although sea cows have no natural enemies and can live to be 60 years old, only about 3,000 are left in all of the United States. They are protected by the Marine Mammal Protection Act of 1972, the federal Endangered Species Act of 1973, and the Florida Manatee Sanctuary Act of 1978. Florida waterways have manatee zones with restricted, no-wake speed limits, yet each year too many manatees are wounded and killed by watercraft and their propellers. Others die from eating fishing line, plastic, or fishhooks and from natural causes.

Manatees live in shallow, slow-moving waters, such as quiet rivers, peaceful saltwater bays, and calm coastal canals. To see them, look in both coasts' Intracoastal Waterways from spring to fall. In winter, the creatures search for warmer waters, heading to inland springs or even to the heated outflow of a power plant. Spotting them can be tricky. Since manatees usually travel together in a long line with their bodies mostly submerged, look for something resembling drifting coconuts. Also look for concentric circles in the water, a signal that manatees are about to surface.

Several organizations are intent on helping manatees. The Save the Manatee Club, which operates under the auspices of the U.S. Fish and Wildlife Service, welcomes new members. If you choose to "adopt" a sea cow, you'll receive a picture of "your" manatee, a little history about him or her, a handbook about manatees, and a certificate of adoption. A newsletter includes periodic updates about your adoptee. For more information contact the **Save the Manatee Club and Adopt a Manatee** (✉ 500 N. Maitland Ave., Maitland 32751 ☎ 800/432–5646 ⊕ www.savethemanatee.org).

—Pam Acheson

starting point for boating adventures, including sunset cruises, sightseeing cruises, and deep-sea fishing. At the southern tip, a bridge leads to Lovers Key State Park.

At the 17-acre **Lynn Hall Memorial Park,** in the commercial northern part of Estero Island, the shore slopes gradually into the usually tranquil and warm gulf waters, providing safe swimming for children. And since houses, condominiums, and hotels line most of the beach, you're never far from civilization. There are picnic tables, barbecue grills, playground equipment, and a free fishing pier. A bathhouse with restrooms, a pedestrian mall, and a number of restaurants are nearby. Parking is metered; 25¢ only buys 8 minutes and meters are closely surveyed. ⊠ *Estero Blvd.* ☎ *239/463–1116* ⊙ *Daily 7 AM–11 PM.*

---

off the
beaten
path

Fodor'sChoice
★

LOVERS KEY STATE PARK – This out-of-the-way park encompasses 1,616 acres on four barrier islands and several uninhabited islets. Bike, hike, or walk the park's trails; go shelling on its 2½ mi of white-sand beach; take a boat tour; or rent a canoe, kayak, or bike. Trams run regularly 9–5 to deliver you and your gear to the beach. Watch for osprey, bald eagles, herons, ibis, pelicans, and roseate spoonbills, or sign up for an excursion to learn fishing or cast-netting, or go birding or biking. Weddings often take place at the romantic gazebo on the beach. There are also restrooms, picnic tables, a snack bar, and showers. ⊠ *8700 Estero Blvd.* ☎ *239/463–4588* ⌂ *$4 2–8 people in one vehicle, $2 one person in one vehicle, $1 per person pedestrians and bicyclists* ⊙ *Daily 8–sunset.*

Where to Stay & Eat

$–$$$ ✕ **Warfields.** The newest sensation in Fort Myers Beach, this spot in a refined, off-the-beach location does steaks with a Latin flair that has locals raving. The lively bar scene adds to its popularity, and the flavorful, exotically prepared meats—oregano sirloin, coffee rib eye with onion-mango soubise sauce, and filet stuffed with roasted shallots and cheese—set it apart from the area's sudden steakhouse proliferation. Intriguing appetizers, entrées, salads, and seafood dishes round out the menu. The interior is warmed by mood lighting and, in the bar, Italian leather couches. ⊠ *19220 San Carlos Blvd.* ☎ *239/463–3510* ⊕ *www.warfieldssteakhouse.com* ⊟ *AE, D, MC, V* ⊙ *No lunch.*

$–$$ ✕ **Matanzas Inn.** Watch boats coming and going whether you sit inside or out at this rustic Old Florida–style restaurant on the Intracoastal Waterway. You can't miss with shrimp from the local fleets—delicately cornmeal-breaded, stuffed, or done Alfredo with scallops. This is true Fort Myers Beach style, meaning service can be a bit gruff—and slow. ⊠ *416 Crescent St.* ⌂ *Reservations not accepted* ☎ *239/463–3838* ⊟ *AE, D, MC, V* ⊕ *www.matanzasrestaurant.com.*

¢–$ ✕ **Plaka.** A casual long-timer and a favorite for a quick breakfast, lunch breaks, and sunset dinners, Plaka—Greek for "beach"—has such typical Greek fare as moussaka, pastitso, gyros, and roast lamb, as well as burgers, hot dogs, sandwiches, fried seafood, and strip steak. There's indoor dining, but grab a seat on the porch. ⊠ *1001 Estero Blvd.* ☎ *239/463–4707* ⌂ *Reservations not accepted* ⊟ *AE, D, MC, V.*

$$$$ 🏨 **DiamondHead.** This 12-story, all-suite resort sits on the beach, and many rooms, especially those on higher floors, have stunning views. Units are done in modern muted earth tones, and each has a living room with queen-size sleeper sofa, a separate bedroom, and a kitchenette. The well-organized children's programs include everything from crafts to scavenger hunts to sand golf. ⊠ *2000 Estero Blvd., 33931* ☎ *239/765–7654 or 888/765–5002* 🖨 *239/765–1694* ⊕ *www.diamondheadfl.com* 🔄 *124 suites ⚲ 2 restaurants, in-room data ports, kitchenettes, cable TV, pool, gym, hot tub, beach, boating, bar, children's programs (ages 4–14), laundry facilities* ⊟ *AE, D, MC, V.*

$$$–$$$$ 🏨 **Lovers Key Beach Club & Resort.** Views can be stupendous from upper floors in this 14-story waterfront resort just north of Lovers Key State Park. The gulf seems to stretch forever, and dolphins and manatees in the estuary put on quite a show. Most of the plantation-style condominiums have spa bathtubs with a window view. All of the one- and two-bedroom units have full kitchens and handsome decor that continues the lobby theme of bamboo, palms, and pineapples. The lagoon-style waterfall pool sits bayside, where a narrow strip of protected sand constitutes the beach. ⊠ *8771 Estero Blvd., 33931* ☎ *239/765–1040 or 877/798–4879* 🖨 *239/765–1055* ⊕ *www.loverskey.com* 🔄 *99 condominiums ⚲ Grill, Restaurant, some in-room hot tubs, kitchens, in-room data ports, pool, gym, hot tub, beach, boating, laundry facilities, Internet, meeting rooms* ⊟ *AE, D, DC, MC, V.*

$$–$$$$ 🏨 **Ramada Inn Beachfront.** In the thick of things at Fort Myers Beach's so-called Times Square, this property is among the prettier in the chain, with gingerbread trim. Inside, cheery florals and wallpaper borders along the ceiling make the rooms homey. It's one of the most affordable options on the beach and its beach bar is a hot spot. ⊠ *1160 Estero Blvd., 33931* ☎ *239/463–6158 or 800/544–4592* 🖨 *239/765–4240* ⊕ *www.ramadainnftmyers.com* 🔄 *56 rooms, 14 suites ⚲ In-room safes, some kitchens, cable TV, in-room data ports, pool, beach, jet skiing, parasailing, bar, Internet, laundry facilities, some pets allowed (fee), no-smoking rooms* ⊟ *AE, D, MC, V.*

$$ 🏨 **Outrigger Beach Resort.** On a wide gulf beach, this casual resort has rooms and efficiencies with configurations to suit different families and budgets. You'll also find a broad sundeck, tiki cabanas, sailboats, and a beachfront pool with a popular tiki bar. ⊠ *6200 Estero Blvd., 33931* ☎ *239/463–3131 or 800/657–5659* 🖨 *239/463–6577* ⊕ *www.outriggerfmb.com* 🔄 *74 rooms, 68 efficiencies ⚲ 2 restaurants, some kitchens, refrigerators, cable TV, in-room data ports, putting green, pool, beach, jet skiing, bicycles, shuffleboard, volleyball, bar; no smoking* ⊟ *AE, MC, V.*

Sports & the Outdoors

BIKING Fort Myers Beach has no designated trails, so most people pedal along the road. **Fun Rentals** (⊠ 1901 Estero Blvd. ☎ 239/463–8844) rents bicycles by the half or full day or for the week. Rent bikes in Lovers Key State Park through **Nature Recreation Management** (⊠ 8700 Estero Blvd., Fort Myers Beach ☎ 239/314–0110 ⊕ www.floridastateparks.org/loverskey). Fees are $10 for a half day, $15 for a full day. No children's bikes are available.

CANOEING   Lovers Key State Park offers both kayak rentals and guided kayaking tours of its bird-rich estuary. The concessionaire, **Nature Recreation Management** (✉ 8700 Estero Blvd., Fort Myers Beach ☎ 239/314–0110), charges $35 for its guided tour, offered Monday, Wednesday, and Saturday. Rentals begin at $20 for a half day, $30 for a full day.

FISHING   **Getaway Deep Sea Fishing** (✉ 18400 San Carlos Blvd. ☎ 239/466–3600 ⊕ www.getawaymarina.com) rents fishing equipment, sells bait, and can arrange half- and full-day charters. Rates start at $40 for a half day and include bait, license, and equipment. Private fishing charters can be arranged at **Deebold's Marina** (✉ 18500 San Carlos Blvd. ☎239/466–3525).

GOLF   The **Bay Beach Golf Club** (✉ Off Estero Blvd., 4200 Bay Beach La. ☎ 239/463–2064) has 18 holes and a practice range. Green fee: $18/$28.

NAPLES AREA

As you head south from Fort Myers on U.S. 41, you soon come to Estero and Bonita Springs, followed by the Naples and Marco Island areas, which are sandwiched between Big Cypress Swamp and the Gulf of Mexico. East of Naples the land is largely undeveloped and mostly wetlands, all the way to Fort Lauderdale. Here, along the northern border of the Florida Everglades, there are stunning nature preserves and parks. Tours and charters out of Everglades City explore the mazelike Ten Thousand Islands. These waters are full of fish and wildlife. Between Naples and Everglades City, acres of breeze-swept sawgrass stretch off to the horizon. Keep your eye peeled, and you may even spot alligators in the waterways alongside the road. Naples itself is a major vacation destination that has sprouted pricey high-rise condominiums and golfing developments, plus a spate of restaurants and shops to match. A similar but not as thorough evolution has occurred on Marco Island, once a quiet fishing community.

Estero/Bonita Springs

⑪ *10 mi south of Fort Myers.*

Towns below Fort Myers have started to flow seamlessly into one another since the opening of Florida Gulf Coast University in San Carlos Park and as a result of the growth of Estero and Bonita Springs, agricultural communities until not long ago. Bonita Beach, the closest beach to Interstate 75, has evolved from a fishing community into a repository of upscale golfing developments. Beach homes and a few resorts line its laid-back strip of white sand.

★   Tour one of Florida's quirkier chapters from the past at **Koreshan State Historic Site.** Named for a religious cult that was active at the turn of the 20th century, Koreshan preserves a dozen structures where the group practiced arts, worshiped a male-female divinity, and created its own branch of science called cosmogony. The cult floundered when leader Cyrus Reed Teed died in 1908, and in 1961, the four remaining members deeded the property to the state. Rangers lead tours, and the grounds, planted with exotic gardens, are lovely for picnicking. Canoeists paddle the woods-fringed Estero River, and there's camping. ✉ *Tamiami Trail, Estero* ☎ *239/992–0311* 💲 *$4 per vehicle with up to 8 passengers; $3 for a single driver; $1 per cyclist, pedestrian, or extra passenger* ◷ *Daily 8 AM–sunset.*

Opened in 1936 and one of the first attractions of its kind in the state, the **Everglades Wonder Gardens** capture the beauty of untamed Florida. The old-fashioned zoological gardens have Florida panthers, black bears, crocodiles and alligators, tame Florida deer, flamingos, and trained otters and birds. There's also a funky natural-history museum. Tours, which include an otter show and alligator feedings, run continuously. The swinging bridge over the alligator pit is a real thrill. ✉ *27180 Old U.S. 41* ☎ *239/992–2591* 💲 *$12* ◷ *Daily 9–5.*

Bonita Springs Public Beach, at the south end of Bonita Beach, has picnic tables, beach concessions, and a restaurant next door. ✉ *Hickory Blvd. at Bonita Beach Rd.* ☎ *239/461–7400* 💲 *Parking 75¢ per hr.*

★ The 342-acre **Barefoot Beach Preserve** is a quiet place, accessible via a road around the corner from the buzzing public beach. It has picnic tables, a nature trail and learning center, a butterfly garden, and refreshment stands. ✉ *Lely Beach Rd.* ☎ *239/498–4364* 💲 *$4.*

off the beaten path

CORKSCREW SWAMP SANCTUARY – To get a feel for what this part of Florida was like before civil engineers began draining the swamps, drive 13 mi east of Bonita Springs (30 mi northeast of Naples) to these 11,000 acres of pine flatwood and cypress, grass-and-sedge "wet prairie," saw-grass marshland, and lakes and sloughs filled with water lettuce. Managed by the National Audubon Society, the sanctuary protects North America's largest remaining stand of ancient bald cypress, 600-year-old trees as tall as 130 feet, as well as endangered birds, such as wood storks, which often nest here. This is a favorite destination for serious birders. If you spend a couple of hours to take the 2¼-mi self-guided tour along the boardwalk, you'll spot ferns, orchids, and air plants, as well as wading birds and possibly alligators and otters. A nature center educates you about this precious, unusual habitat with a dramatic re-creation of the preserve and its creatures in the Swamp Theater. ✉ *16 mi east of I–75 on Rte. 846* ☎ *239/348–9151* ⊕ *www.audubon.org* 💲 *$10* ◷ *In season daily 7–5:30, off-season daily 7–7:30.*

Fodor'sChoice
★

Where to Stay & Eat

$–$$$ ✗ **Toucan Grille.** Spinning lazily from high ceilings, rattan paddle fans swirl cool air and hot reggae around this sandy-hued place, which is done in rattan, wicker, and bamboo and splashed with bright Caribbean colors. With its offerings of coconut shrimp, jerk chicken, and chili rum-glazed salmon, the menu, too, makes an island statement. ✉ *4480 Bonita Beach Rd., Bonita Springs* ☎ *239/495–9464* ⊕ *www.toucangrille. com* ▤ *MC, V* ◷ *Closed Mon. Nov.–mid-May, and Sun. mid-May–Dec.*

$–$$ ✗ **Bonita Bistro.** Hidden behind a Comfort Inn off Bonita Springs' main drag, the bistro draws a devoted clientele by dint of chef-owner Danny Mellman's reputation for fresh ingredients and culinary concepts. In a casual, poolside setting enjoy creations such as peppercorn pork with red cabbage slaw and chili-apple chutney or blackened salmon with barbecue corn butter. You'll want to budget your appetite for the grand finale: pan-blackened bread pudding. ⊠ *9800 Bonita Beach Rd, Bonita Springs* ☎ *239/948–9150* ☰ *AE, D, MC, V.*

¢–$ ✕ **Doc's Beach House.** Right next door to the public access, Doc's has fed hungry beachers for decades. Come barefoot and grab a quick libation or meal downstairs, or try the air-conditioned 2nd floor, with its great view of beach action. Simple fare on the breakfast and all-day menu includes a popular Angus burger, pizza, and seafood plates. ⊠ *27908 Hickory Blvd., Bonita Springs* ☎ *239/992–6444* ⚏ *Reservations not accepted* ⊕ *www.docsbeachhouse.com* ☰ *No credit cards.*

$$$–$$$$ ▦ **Hyatt Coconut Point Resort & Spa.** This secluded luxury Hyatt, with
Fodor'sChoice its marble-and-mahogany lobby and 18 floors, stands in stark contrast
★ to the pristine estuary environment that surrounds it. Man-made water features include a slide pool, lap pool, and fountain-waterfall pool. For nature-made water features, catch a ferry to the hotel's private island beach. Handsomely appointed rooms overlook the gulf or the golf course. The kids' program educates about Calusa Indian heritage and the environment, and an interpretive center showcases natural and prehistoric history. ⊠ *5001 Coconut Rd., Bonita Springs 34134* ☎ *239/444–1234 or 800/554–9288* ⚏ *239/390–4277* ⊕ *www. coconutpoint.hyatt.com* ⚲ *426 rooms, 30 suites* ⚲ *3 restaurants, coffee shop, ice cream parlor, room service, refrigerators, in-room data ports, fans, cable TV with video games, in-room VCRs, 18-hole golf course, 4 tennis courts, 7 pools, health club, outdoor hot tubs, spa, beach, boating, 2 bars, shops, children's programs (ages 3–12), concierge, concierge floor, business services, meeting room, car rental, no-smoking rooms* ☰ *AE, D, DC, MC, V.*

$$$ ▦ **Trianon Bonita.** Convenient to Bonita Springs' best shopping and dining, this branch of a downtown Naples favorite feels European in its peaceful, sophisticated way. Rooms are oversize and the lobby has a vaulted ceiling and marble columns. Cocktails and complimentary breakfast are served in the library, where a fireplace dominates. ⊠ *3401 Bay Commons Dr., Bonita Springs 34134* ☎ *239/948–4400 or 800/859–3939* ⚏ *239/948–4401* ⊕ *www.trianon.com* ⚲ *100 rooms* ⚲ *In-room data ports, in-room safes, cable TV with movies, pool, Internet, meeting rooms, no-smoking rooms* ☰ *AE, D, DC, MC, V* ❢ *CP.*

Sports & the Outdoors

BIKING Rent bicycles by the day or by the week at **Bonita Bike & Baby** (⊠ Bay Landing Shopping Center ☎ 239/947–6377).

BOATING **Bonita Beach Resort Motel** (⊠ 26395 Hickory Blvd. ☎ 239/992–2137) rents pontoon boats for a minimum of two hours or by the half-day and day.

CANOEING The meandering Estero River is pleasant for canoeing as it passes through Koreshan State Historic Site to the bay. **Estero River Tackle and Canoe Outfitters** (⊠ 20991 Tamiami Trail S, Estero ☎ 239/992–4050) provides rental canoes, kayaks, and equipment.

DOG RACING Greyhounds race year-round at the **Naples/Fort Myers Greyhound Track** (⊠ 10601 Bonita Beach Rd. SE ☎ 239/992–2411).

FISHING **Estero Bay Boat Tours** (⊠ 5231 Mamie St., Estero ☎ 239/992–2200) can set you up with a fishing guide or take you out on shelling, nature, and archaeological tours.

GOLF Swamp and thick vegetation border the 36-hole **Pelican's Nest Golf Course** (⊠4450 Pelican's Nest Dr. ☎239/947–4600), green fee: $14/$175. Of the two challenging courses, Gator is considered a bit more difficult than Hurricane. It's the palmetto thickets, not water, that pose problems for the less-than-accurate golfer.

ICE HOCKEY Fort Myers's minor-league hockey team, the **Florida Everblades** (⊠ Germain Arena, 11000 Everblades Pkwy., Estero ☎ 239/948–7825 ⊕ www.floridaeverblades.com), battle their opponents from October to March.

ICE-SKATING ★ Skaters can head to the **Germain Arena** (⊠ 11000 Everblades Pkwy., Estero ☎ 239/948–7825 ⊕ www.germainarena.com) for ice-, in-line, and figure-skating.

Shopping

★ The **Miromar Outlets complex** (⊠ Corkscrew Rd. at I–75 Exit 123 in Estero, near Germain Arena ☎239/948–3766) includes Adidas, Nike, Nautica, and Off-5th Saks Fifth Avenue.

The **Promenade at Bonita Bay** (⊠ South Bay Dr.) in the Bonita Bay subdivision is Bonita Springs' chic shopping venue, with an upscale collection of shops and restaurants.

Naples

⑫–⑳ *21 mi south of Bonita Springs.*

Thirty years ago, Naples was a sleepy relic of Old Florida, a cluster of bungalows, a beach, and a brace of tile-roof stucco buildings painted in pastel hues. Nowadays, Naples is west-coast Florida's Palm Beach, though it's far less brazen about showing off its money. Much of the north shore is lined with 20-story condominiums; their residents crowd the town's many pricey, sophisticated restaurants and run their errands in chichi shopping areas such as tree-lined 5th Avenue South, 3rd Street South, the Waterside Shops, and the Village on Venetian Bay. The beach is stunning, the tennis abundant, and the golf stellar. No wonder it's tough to snag a table—or a room—at the last minute in winter.

⑫ Fodor'sChoice ★ The well-maintained 166-acre **Delnor-Wiggins Pass State Park** has guarded beaches, barbecue grills, picnic tables, a boat ramp, an observation tower, restrooms with wheelchair access, bathhouses, showers, boat ramps, and lots of parking. Fishing is best in Wiggins Pass, at the north end of the park. Rangers conduct sea-turtle walks in summer and kayak tours year-round. ⊠ *11100 Gulf Shore Dr. N, at Rte. 846 ☎ 239/597–6196 ⊕ www.floridastateparks.org/delnor-wiggins ☜ $5 per vehicle with up to 8 people, $3 for single driver, $1 for pedestrians and bicyclists ☉ Daily 8–sunset.*

550 <

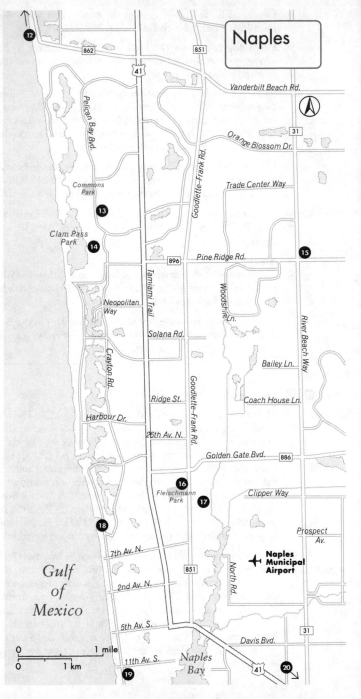

⑬ The cool, contemporary **Naples Museum of Art,** around the corner from
Fodor'sChoice the Waterside Shops in the Naples Philharmonic Center for the Arts, dis-
★ plays provocative, innovative pieces, including American miniatures, antique walking sticks, ancient Asian art, and traveling exhibits. Dazzling
installations by glass artist Dale Chihuly include a fiery cascade of a chandelier and an illuminated ceiling layered with many-hued glass bubbles,
glass corkscrews, and other shapes that suggest the sea; alone, this warrants a visit. ⊠ *5833 Pelican Bay Blvd.* ☎ *239/597–1900 or 800/597–
1900* ⊕ *www.naplesphilcenter.org* ⊠ *$8* ⊙ *Nov.–Apr., Tues.–Sat. 10–5,
Sun. noon–5; May–Oct., Tues.–Sat. 10–4, Sun. noon–4.*

⑭ Kayak through the mangroves or into the surf at **Clam Pass Recreation
Area.** A 3,000-foot boardwalk winds through the mangrove area to the
beach. Tram service is available. ⊠ *Next to the Registry Resort on Seagate Dr.* ☎ *239/353–0404* ⊠ *Parking $4* ⊙ *Daily 8–sunset.*

A life-size Three Bears House and a "libeary" stocked solely with books
about bears keep company with the more than 5,000 bears from around
 ⑮ the world on display at the **Teddy Bear Museum of Naples.** Oil heiress
Frances Pew Hayes, an area resident, had the log structure built when
she ran out of room to keep the bears in her home. Some are just an
inch high, while others are as tall as a basketball player; some are handmade, while others come from well-known manufacturers such as Gund.
The stuffed bruins by Stieff are superb, and the collection of Herrmann
Teddy Originals is the largest anywhere. ⊠ *2511 Pine Ridge Rd.* ☎ *239/
598–2711 or 866/365–2327* ⊕ *www.teddymuseum.com* ⊠ *$8*
⊙ *Tues.–Sat. 10–5.*

 ⑯ The lush and entertaining 52-acre **Caribbean Gardens: The Zoo in Naples,**
established in 1919 as a botanical garden, today draws visitors curious
to see lions, African wild dogs, Indochinese tigers, lemurs, antelope, and
monkeys. Central exhibits include Tiger Forest and Panther Glade, but
it's the shows that distinguish this nationally accredited zoo. The presentations in Planet Predator and Serpents: Fangs & Fiction star the extreme in wild animals. The Primate Expedition Cruise takes you through
islands of monkeys and apes. Youngsters can amuse themselves in three
separate play areas, and there are meet-the-keeper times and alligator
feedings. ⊠ *1590 Goodlette Rd.* ☎ *239/262–5409* ⊕ *www.napleszoo.
com* ⊠ *$15.95* ⊙ *Daily 9:30–5:30; gates close at 4:30.*

⑰ On 14 acres bordering a tidal lagoon teeming with wildlife, the **Naples
Nature Center** includes an aviary, a wildlife rehabilitation clinic, a natural-history museum with a serpentarium, and a 3,000-gallon sea-turtle aquarium. Short trails are dotted with interpretive signs, and there
are free guided walks and boat tours on the mangrove-bordered Gordon River several times daily. Canoes and kayaks are available for rent.
⊠ *1450 Merrihue Dr.* ☎ *239/262–0304* ⊕ *www.conservancy.org*
⊠ *$7.50* ⊙ *Mon.–Sat. 9–4:30; Nov.–Apr. also Sun. noon–4.*

⑱ Stretching along Gulf Shore Boulevard, **Lowdermilk Park** has more than
1,000 feet of beach as well as volleyball courts, a playground, restrooms,
showers, vending machines, and picnic tables. ⊠ *Gulf Shore Blvd. at*

Banyan Blvd. ☎ *239/213–3029* 🅿 *Parking 25¢ per 15 min* ⊙ *Daily 7–sunset.*

⑲ Houses in 19th-century South Florida were often built of a cementlike material made of sand and seashells. For a fine example of such tabby construction, stop by **Palm Cottage**, built in 1895 and one of the Lower Gulf Coast's few surviving tabby homes. The historically accurate interior contains simple furnishings typical of the period. ⊠ *137 12th Ave. S* ☎ *239/261–8164* ⊕ *www.napleshistoricalsociety.org* 🄳 *$6* ⊙ *Guided tours Nov.–Apr., Tues.–Sat. 1–4; May–Oct., Wed.–Sat. 1–4.*

★ ⑳ To get a feel for local history, stop by the **Collier County Museum**, where a Seminole chickee hut, native plant garden, swamp buggy, reconstructed 19th-century trading post, steam logging locomotive, and other historical exhibits capture important developments from prehistoric times to the World War II era. ⊠ *3301 Tamiami Trail E* ☎ *239/774–8476* ⊕ *www.colliermuseum.com* 🄳 *Free* ⊙ *Weekdays 9–5.*

Where to Stay & Eat

$$$$ ✕ **The Dining Room.** The crème de la crème of Naples dining, the Ritz's main restaurant is equally rich in food and decor. Exquisite molding, solid European furnishings, and ever-changing themed exhibits from local galleries set an elegant mood, and the imaginative cuisine reflects what's fresh that day: warm lobster salad, roasted turbot with chanterelle and sauterne sauce, and aged strip steak with rutabaga purée, for instance. Dinners are arranged and priced as three-, four-, and seven-course meals. ⊠ *280 Vanderbilt Beach Rd.* ☎ *239/598–3300* 🍴 *Reservations essential* 🚭 *AE, D, DC, MC, V* ⊙ *No lunch.*

$$$–$$$$ ✕ **Chardonnay.** A bastion of the Naples culinary scene for decades, this classic serves French cuisine with a Florida twist. Look for lobster bisque à l'orange, red snapper in cream of basil sauce, veal sweetbreads, rabbit with champagne sauce, blackened mahimahi, and lobster and scallops St. Jacques. The elegant dining room, with its heavy brocaded drapery and chair cushions and grand brass chandelier, looks out onto a lush garden with pools. ⊠ *2331 N. Tamiami Trail* ☎ *239/261–1744* 🍴 *Reservations essential* 🚭 *AE, DC, MC, V* ⊙ *No lunch. No dinner Sun. Easter through Christmas.*

$$–$$$$ ✕ **Aqua Grill.** This new-wave bistro in the chic Waterside Shops mall is decorated with sea motifs. Traditional bistro dishes such as meat loaf, seafood paella, and rotisserie lemon chicken anchor the menu, while creations such as pancetta-wrapped grouper and nightly specials such as pan-seared skate wing over roasted fennel salad showcase the kitchen's prowess. ⊠ *5555 Tamiami Trail* ☎ *239/254–1234* 🚭 *AE, MC, V.*

★ **$$–$$$**   ✕ **Bha! Bha!** Ocher walls and the stuffed ottomans and exotic tapestries around the room explain the "Persian bistro" on this restaurant's sign. Classic and fusion Middle Eastern cooking—some of Naples's finest ethnic food—fill the menu with wonderful, adventurous taste treats. Specialties include dried plum lamb, garlic eggplant chicken, mango-ginger shrimp, and spicy beef in saffron sauce with cucumber yogurt. Sunday brings a massive brunch buffet. The service lags at times. ⊠ *847 Vanderbilt Rd.* ☎ *239/594–5557* 🚭 *AE, MC, V* ⊙ *Closed Mon. in summer.*

$$–$$$ ✕ **Bice Ristorante.** One of 40 in the world, this exclusive chain restaurant does authentic regional Italian cuisine with a blend of Old World home cooking and artistry in a sleek and modern setting of mahogany, white linens, and mirrors. Starter courses on the seasonally changing menu offer a nice variety of pasta, risotto, and soup. *Secondi piatti* (second plates) consist of classics such as osso buco and contemporary interpretations such as sautéed sea bass with caper vinaigrette. ⊠ *300 5th Ave. S* ☎ *239/262–4044* ⊕ *www.bicenaples.com* ⊟ *AE, DC, MC, V.*

$$–$$$
Fodor'sChoice
★
✕ **Chops City Grill.** This 5th Avenue darling, ultrasophisticated while letting-your-hair-down casual, has become so popular it spawned a spin-off in Bonita Springs. Its name reflects a personality split between chopstick cuisine and fine cuts of meat. Sushi and Pacific Rim inspirations such as beef satay and honey-teriyaki-glazed chicken breast represent the former; lamb chops, dry-aged beef, pork porterhouse, and peppercorn-crusted strip steak with blackberry-cabernet sauce, the latter. ⊠ *837 5th Ave. S* ☎ *239/262–4677* ⊠ *Hwy. 41 at Brooks Grand Plaza, Bonita Springs* ☎ *239/992–4677* ⊕ *www.chopscitygrill.com* ⊟ *AE, DC, MC, V* ☺ *No lunch.*

¢–$$$ ✕ **Tommy Bahama's Tropical Café.** When you're in the mood to be ultra-casual in Naples, this faux-Caribbean spot, the first of five nationwide, is the place to be. On the deck outside, in the spacious dining room inside, and in the bar, everybody's munching sandwiches, salads, ribs, and grilled seafood with a tropical flair and sampling Tommy's Bungalow Brew beer. ⊠ *1220 3rd St. S* ☎ *239/643–6889* ⊟ *AE, MC, V.*

¢–$$ ✕ **Old Naples Pub.** Tucked away from shopping traffic at 3rd Street Plaza, this comfortable pub stays open until late at night. Taste some 20 kinds of beer and order fish-and-chips, burgers, bratwurst, crispy chicken salad, and nachos, as well as such not-so-traditional pub snacks as grilled ahi tuna and fried gator tail. There's musical entertainment nightly between Thanksgiving and Easter. ⊠ *255 13th Ave. S* ☎ *239/649–8200* ⊟ *AE, D, MC, V.*

¢–$ ✕ **Aurelio's Is Pizza.** Transplanted from Chicago, the pizza here is steeped in tradition and flavor. The selections are typical, with a few show-offs such as taco, barbecue, and spinach Calabrese. There's also pasta with homemade sauces and chicken Parmesan or Alfredo. Red-and-white tablecloths and old license plates accent this strip-mall café. ⊠ *590 N. Tamiami Trail* ☎ *239/403–8882* ⊟ *AE, MC, V* ☺ *Closed Mon. No lunch.*

¢–$ ✕ **Cilantro Tamales.** The salsa and chips alone are worth a visit to this bright and lively little spot, with slabs of clay tile for placemats. The signature dish, smoked Gouda-stuffed tamales, sets an example for freshness and authenticity. Imaginative touches are also added to enchiladas, fajitas, rellenos, and a Mexican rice bowl. ⊠ *10823 N. Tamiami Trail* ☎ *239/597–5855* ⊟ *MC, V* ☺ *Closed Mon.*

$$$$ ⊞ **Edgewater Beach Hotel.** This compact waterfront high-rise anchors the north end of fashionable Gulf Shore Boulevard. The one- and two-bedroom suites are brightly decorated and have patios or balconies, many with exquisite gulf views. Have meals by the pool or in the elegant penthouse restaurant, or stop by the lounge for piano music during happy hour. Guests have certain dining and recreational privileges (including golfing) at the Registry Resort, its sister property. ⊠ *1901 Gulf Shore*

Blvd. N, 34102 ☎ *239/403–2000, 800/821–0196, 800/282–3766 in Florida* ▤ *239/403–2100* ⊕ *www.edgewaternaples.com* ⬧ *77 1-bedroom suites, 48 2-bedroom suites* ⚲ *Restaurant, café, grocery, in-room data ports, in-room safes, microwaves, refrigerators, cable TV with movies, 18-hole golf course, pool, gym, beach, boating, bicycles, 2 bars, Internet, meeting rooms* ▭ *AE, DC, MC, V.*

$$$$ ▦ **Inn on Fifth.** To plant yourself in the heart of Naples nightlife and shopping, you can't beat this swank property whose rooms are well-soundproofed to shut out the activity when you're ready to seclude yourself in the comfort of roominess and plush. When you're not, slide open the French doors and tune in to 5th Avenue from the balcony. A spa completes a list of urban amenities that also include a lively Irish pub, a rooftop pool, and an arched, columned marble lobby hung with crystal chandeliers. A theater is next door and the beach is six blocks away. ✉ *699 5th Ave. S, 34102* ☎ *239/403–8777 or 888/403–8778* ▤ *239/403–8778* ⊕ *www.naplesinn.com* ⬧ *76 rooms, 11 suites* ⚲ *Restaurant, cable TV, in-room data ports, in-room safes, pool, gym, spa, bar, laundry service, concierge, business services, meeting rooms* ▭ *AE, D, DC, MC, V* ⭐️⒪ *CP.*

$$$$ ▦ **LaPlaya Beach & Golf Resort.** LaPlaya bespeaks posh and panache down
Fodor'sChoice to the smallest detail—custom-designed duvet covers, for instance. The
★ boutique resort features a Thai-style spa, rock-waterfalls pools, a tony Miami-style beachfront restaurant, and a casual tiki bar that serves food. Of its 189 units, 141 are beachfront with private balconies. Some have jetted soak tubs with a view of the gulf. ✉ *9891 Gulf Shore Dr., 34108* ☎ *239/597–3123 or 800/237–6883* ▤ *239/567–6278* ⊕ *www. laplayaresort.com* ⬧ *180 rooms, 9 suites* ⚲ *Restaurant, snack bar, fans, in-room data ports, cable TV with movies and video games, 18-hole golf course, 3 pools, gym, spa, boating, jet skiing, parasailing, bicycles, volleyball, 2 bars, concierge, Internet, meeting rooms; no smoking* ▭ *AE, D, MC, V.*

$$$$ ▦ **Naples Beach Hotel and Golf Club.** Family-owned and -managed for more than 50 years, this beach resort is a piece of Naples history. On a prime stretch of powdery sand, the resort stands out for its par-72, 18-hole championship golf course, the first resort course in the state. Totally refurbished in 2005, the hotel's new lobby has skylighting, a fireplace, an aquarium, and a bar with outdoor seating. Rooms, decorated in light colors, are in six high- and mid-rise pink buildings, and good packages make an extended stay affordable. ✉ *851 Gulf Shore Blvd. N, 34102* ☎ *239/261–2222 or 800/237–7600* ▤ *239/261–7380* ⊕ *www.naplesbeachhotel.com* ⬧ *255 rooms, 41 suites, 22 efficiencies* ⚲ *3 restaurants, snack bar, in-room data ports, some kitchenettes, cable TV, 18-hole golf course, putting green, 6 tennis courts, pro shop, pool, health club, spa, beach, boating, 3 bars, shop, children's programs (ages 5–12), laundry service, Internet, meeting rooms, no-smoking rooms* ▭ *AE, D, DC, MC, V.*

★ **$$$$** ▦ **Registry Resort.** Rooms are spacious and comfortable at this high-rise hotel with a polished lobby full of marble and crystal. One of the glories of the property—at least for families—is the immense freeform family swimming pool, with zero entry (water begins at a depth of zero feet), and a 100-foot waterslide. The hotel sits behind dusky, twisted mangrove forests; to get to the 3 mi of powdery white sand, it's a short walk or tram ride. Indigenous cypress and pines frame the Naples Grande Golf Club, the hotel's 18-hole Rees Jones layout. ⊠ *475 Seagate Dr., 34103* ☎ *239/597–3232* ⊟ *239/566–7919* ⊕ *www. registryresort.com* ↩ *395 rooms, 79 suites* ⚫ *5 restaurants, coffee shop, room service, in-room data ports, cable TV with movies, 18-hole golf course, 15 tennis courts, 5 pools, health club, hair salon, spa, beach, windsurfing, boating, bicycles, 2 bars, lobby lounge, dance club, video game room, shops, children's programs (ages 4–12), Internet, business services, meeting rooms* ⊟ *AE, DC, MC, V.*

★ **$$$$** ▦ **Ritz-Carlton Golf Resort.** Ardent golfers with a yen for luxury will find their dream vacation at Naples's most elegant golf resort. Ritz style prevails all the way but in a more contemporary verve than at its sister resort, the Ritz-Carlton, Naples. Rooms are regal, and all have balconies with links views. The golf academy can help you polish your skills, and you have access to the spa, kids' program, and other amenities of the beachside Ritz-Carlton, which is nearby. Dining at Tuscan-style Lemonia is divine. ⊠ *2600 Tiburón Dr., 34109* ☎ *239/593–2000 or 800/241–3333* ⊟ *239/593–2010* ⊕ *www.ritzcarlton.com* ↩ *257 rooms, 38 suites* ⚫ *2 restaurants, coffee shop, room service, in-room safes, cable TV with movies and video games, in-room data ports, 36-hole golf course, 4 tennis courts, pro shop, pool, billiards, 3 bars, laundry service, concierge, concierge floors, Internet, no-smoking rooms* ⊟ *AE, D, DC, MC, V.*

$$$$ ▦ **Ritz-Carlton, Naples.** This is a classic Ritz-Carlton, awash in marble,
Fodor'sChoice antiques, and 19th-century European oil paintings. In the rooms, the
★ comforts of home prevail—assuming your home is a palace. Outside, steps away, the beach is soft, white, and dense with seashells. Given the graciousness of the staff, you quickly get over the incongruity of traipsing through the regal lobby in flip-flops, clutching a plastic bag of beach finds. It doesn't hurt that the kitchen is a wonder as well, making meals in the tropical Dining Room and the oh-so-clubby Grill, and even dessert in the lobby, just a little bit special. Then there's the elegant spa, the largest under the Ritz-Carlton brand, themed around the rose garden in its front yard. ⊠ *280 Vanderbilt Beach Rd., 34108* ☎ *239/598–3300 or 800/ 241–3333* ⊟ *239/598–6691* ⊕ *www.ritzcarlton.com* ↩ *435 rooms, 28 suites* ⚫ *7 restaurants, room service, in-room safes, cable TV with movies and video games, golf privileges, 4 tennis courts, pool, health club, spa, beach, boating, 2 bars, babysitting, children's programs (ages 5–12), laundry service, concierge, concierge floors, Internet, no-smoking rooms* ⊟ *AE, D, DC, MC, V.*

$$$ ▦ **Cove Inn.** For the best deal in lodging on the water, check in to this boaters' favorite on the edge of Naples Bay, around the corner from restaurants and shops. Rooms and efficiencies are individually owned and decorated and have private balconies with views of the boats at the city dock. Older and more casual than most other guest quarters in town, this place revolves around fishing and nautical pastimes. ⊠ *900 Broad Ave. S, 34102* ☎ *239/262–7161 or 800/255–4365* ⊟ *239/261–6905* ⊕ *www. coveinnnaples.com* ↩ *50 rooms, 33 efficiencies, 2 apartments* ⚫ *2* *restaurants, coffee shop, some kitchens, microwaves, refrigerators, cable TV, pool, bar, Internet* ▤ *AE, D, DC, MC, V.*

$$$ 🏨 **Trianon Old Naples.** A residential area in the heart of Old Naples is the site of this three-story pink stucco European-style boutique hotel. It's within walking distance of shops and restaurants. Wrought-iron balconies and shade trees set the stage outside; inside, the elegant lobby has high ceilings, a working granite fireplace, plush furnishings, and a library that doubles as a wine-and-beer bar and breakfast room. Rooms are large and lavishly furnished, with heavy draperies. The hotel's historic cottage was restored by Bob Vila and contains two bedrooms and a full kitchen. ⊠ *955 7th Ave. S, 34102* ☎ *239/435–9600 or 877/482–5228* 🖷 *239/261–0025* ⊕ *www.trianon.com* ⌖ *55 rooms, 3 suites, 1 cottage* ⚲ *Cable TV, in-room data ports, in-room safes, pool, wine bar, Internet, meeting room* ▤ *AE, D, DC, MC, V* ⍾*CP.*

$$–$$$ 🏨 **Holiday Inn.** Although this two-story motel is on a major highway, it's set back from the road and the rooms are quiet because most of them are behind the restaurant and pool. Decorated with dark wood and carpeting and pastel bedspreads, they're also clean and comfortable. Landscaping is well maintained and the location convenient if you plan to sightsee. The bar is popular at happy hour. ⊠ *1100 9th St. N, 34102* ☎ *239/263–3434 or 800/325–1135* 🖷 *239/261–3809* ⊕ *www.hinaples. com* ⌖ *137 rooms* ⚲ *Restaurant, in-room data ports, cable TV with movies, pool, bar, Internet* ▤ *AE, D, DC, MC, V.*

$ 🏨 **Tamiami Motel.** South of Naples, this strip of motel rooms is less than 10 minutes from downtown's shopping and beaches. The rooms are small but tidy and equipped with all the basics, including small refrigerators. ⊠ *2164 E. Tamiami Trail, 34112* ☎ *239/774–4626* ⌖ *14 rooms* ⚲ *Refrigerators, cable TV* ▤ *AE, MC, V.*

Nightlife & the Arts

THE ARTS Naples is the cultural capital of this stretch of coast. The **Naples Philharmonic Center for the Arts** (⊠ 5833 Pelican Bay Blvd. ☎ 239/597–1900 or 800/597–1900 ⊕ www.thephil.org) has a 1,473-seat performance center with plays, concerts, and exhibits year-round. It's home to the 85-piece Naples Philharmonic, which presents both classical and pop concerts. The Miami Ballet Company performs here during its winter season. The **Naples Players** (⊠ Sugden Community Theatre, 701 5th Ave. S ☎ 239/263–7990 ⊕ www.naplesplayers.org), on 5th Avenue, performs musicals and dramas year-round; winter shows often sell out well in advance.

NIGHTLIFE **Luna Ultralounge** (⊠ 475 Seagate Dr. ☎ 239/597–3232), at the Registry Resort, is a popular indoor-outdoor multilevel nightclub where DJs pump out Top 40 hits from 9 to 2 Wednesday to Saturday. It's packed on weekends. Downtown's 5th Avenue South is the scene of lively nightclubs and sidewalk cafés. **McCabe's Irish Pub** (⊠ 699 5th Ave. S ☎ 239/403–7170) hosts Irish bands most weekends and some weeknights. Audiences often join in on the lusty lyrics. The **Club at the Ritz-Carlton** (⊠ 280 Vanderbilt Beach Rd. ☎ 239/598–3300) gets lively with contemporary bands on stage Thursday, Friday, and Saturday.

Sports & the Outdoors

BIKING Try **Clem's Bicycle Shoppe of Naples** (✉ 8789 Tamiami Trail N ☎ 239/ 566–3646) for rentals by the day, week, or month.

BOATING **Naples Watersports at Port-O-Call Marina** (✉ 550 Port-O-Call Way ☎ 239/ 774–0479) rents 21-foot deck boats.

FISHING The *Lady Brett* (✉ Tin City ☎ 239/263–4949) makes half-day fishing trips twice daily at $55 each. Take a guided boat and learn to cast and tie flies at **Mangrove Outfitters** (✉ 4111 E. Tamiami Trail ☎ 239/ 793–3370).

GOLF **Tiburón Golf Club** (✉ Ritz-Carlton Golf Resort, 2600 Tiburón Dr. ☎ 239/
★ 593–2000) is one of Naples's newest and brightest, with two 18-hole Greg Norman–designed courses, the Black and the Gold, and a golf academy. Challenging and environmentally pristine, the links include narrow fairways, stacked sod wall bunkers, coquina sand, and no roughs. Green fee: $65/$225. At **Lely Flamingo Island Club** (✉ 8004 Lely Resort Blvd. ☎ 239/793–2600), there are two 18-hole courses—Flamingo and Mustang—plus a golf school. Mustang is easier and more wide-open than the challenging Flamingo, a placement course. Green fee: $35/$149. **Naples Beach Hotel & Golf Club** (✉ 851 Gulf Shore Blvd. N ☎ 239/434– 7007) has 18 holes, a golf school, and a putting green. The region's oldest course, it was built in 1929 and renovated in 1998. Green fee: $55/$120 (cart included). **Naples Golf Center** (✉ 7700 E. Davis Blvd. ☎ 239/775–3337) has a 300-yard driving range and offers private and group lessons by a PGA teaching staff; it even has computerized swing analysis. At affordable **Riviera Golf Club** (✉ 48 Marseille Dr. ☎ 239/774– 1081), there are 18 holes. Green fee: $18/$45 (includes cart).

TENNIS **Cambier Park Tennis Center** (✉ 735 8th St. S ☎ 239/213–3060) offers clinics and play on 12 Hydro-Grid lighted clay courts for members and visitors.

Shopping

Old Naples encompasses two distinct shopping areas marked by historic buildings and flowery landscaping: 5th Avenue South and 3rd Street South. Both are known for their abundance of fine art galleries. Near
★ 5th Avenue South, **Old Marine Market Place at Tin City** (✉ 1200 5th Ave. S), in a collection of tin-roof former boat docks along Naples Bay, has more than 50 boutiques, eateries, and souvenir shops, with everything from jewelry to T-shirts and seafood. At the classy **Village on Venetian Bay** (✉ 4200 Gulf Shore Blvd. ⊕ www.venetianvillage.com), more than 60 shops and restaurants have been built at water's edge. Only in South Florida can you find something like **Waterside Shops** (✉ Seagate Dr. and U.S. 41), with four dozen stores plus eateries wrapped around a series of waterfalls, waterways, and shaded open-air promenades. Saks Fifth Avenue is one of the anchors.

Gattle's (✉ 1250 3rd St. S ☎ 239/262–4791 or 800/344–4552) stocks pricey, beautifully made linens. **Marissa Collections** (✉ 1167 3rd St. S ☎ 239/263–4333) showcases designer women's wear. At the **Mole Hole** (✉ 1201 3rd St. S ☎ 239/262–5115), gift items large and small, from glassware to paperweights to knickknacks, cover every surface. **Kirsten's Boutique** (⊠ Waterside Shops, 5535 Tamiami Trail N ☎ 239/598–3233) is filled with African-inspired clothing, jewelry, and decorative art. Among 5th Avenue South's upscale selection, **Regatta** (⊠ 750 5th Ave. S ☎ 239/262–3929) sells personal and home accessories with a sense of humor and style. Naples's ladies-who-lunch often donate their year-old Armani castoffs and fine collectibles to a spate of terrific thrift shops such as **Options** (⊠ 968 2nd Ave. N ☎ 239/434–7115). The most upscale clothes sometimes go to consignment shops such as **New to You** (⊠ 933 Creech Rd. ☎ 239/262–6869). Pawing through wealthy folks' high-end designer castoffs is a favorite Naples activity for penny-pinching vacationers and residents alike at **Lynne's Consignment** (⊠ 13560 Tamiami Trail N ☎ 239/514–1410). **Encore Shop** (⊠ 3105 Davis Blvd. ☎ 239/775–0032) carries designer furniture, paintings, decorative items, and collectibles. For more bargains, hit **Prime Outlets Naples** (⊠ Rte. 951 west of Marco Island ☎ 239/545–7196 or 877/466–8853), home to more than 40 factory outlets.

Marco Island

㉑ *20 mi south of Naples.*

High-rises line part of the shore of Marco Island, which is connected to the mainland by two bridges. Yet it retains an isolated feeling much appreciated by those who love this corner of the world. Some natural areas have been preserved, and the down-home fishing village of Goodland is resisting change. Fishing, boating, sunning, swimming, and tennis are the primary activities.

In the midst of 110,000-acre Rookery Bay Estuarine Reserve, **Rookery Bay Environmental Learning Center** interprets the Everglades environment with interactive models, aquariums, original art, and classes. It's on the edge of the estuary, about five minutes east of Marco's north bridge on Route 951. ⊠ *300 Tower Rd.* ☎ *239/417–6310* ⊕ *www.rookerybay. org* ⊠ *$5* ⊙ *Tues.–Sun. 9–4.*

Tigertail Beach is on the southwest side of the island, with a view of both developed and undeveloped areas. Facilities include a concession stand, restrooms, and showers. Sailboat and kayak rentals are available. ⊠ *490 Hernando Ct.* ☎ *239/642–0818* ⊠ *Parking $4* ⊙ *Daily 8–sunset.*

Marco Island was once part of the ancient Calusa kingdom. The Marco Cat, a statue found in 1896 excavations, has become symbolic of the island's prehistoric significance. A replica of the original, which is kept by the Smithsonian Institution, is among displays illuminating ancient past to modern present at the **Marco Island Historical Society Museum.** Both it and its branch location interpret local history through vignettes, video, and artifacts. ⊠ *140 Waterway Dr. at Bald Eagle Dr.* ☎ *239/642–7468* ⊠ *Free* ⊙ *Weekdays 9–4* ⊠ *Shops of Olde Marco, 168 Royal Palm Dr., 2nd floor* ☎ *239/389–6447* ⊕ *www.themihs.org* ⊠ *Free* ⊙ *Daily 7-7.*

Where to Stay & Eat

$$$–$$$$ ✕ **Sale e Pepe.** The name means "salt and pepper," an indication that
Fodor'sChoice this palatial restaurant with patio seating overlooking the beach adheres
★ to the basics of home-style Italian cuisine. Pasta, sausage, and sinful pastries are made right here in the kitchen. Simple dishes, such as veal ravioli, risotto, Tuscan bean soup, sautéed salmon with red pepper purée, grilled lamb chops, and veal chops explode with home-cooked, long-cooked flavors. ⊠ *Marco Beach Ocean Resort, 480 S. Collier Blvd.* ☎ *239/393–1600* ⊕ *www.sale-e-pepe.com* ☰ *AE, D, DC, MC, V.*

★ **$$$** ✕ **Olde Marco Island Inn.** Dating from the turn of the 20th century, this inn lends grace to intimate meals. Continental style heavily influences the menu, which includes orange rotisserie duck, broiled Florida lobster tail (market price), sesame tuna, and prime rib. The inn serves lunch and dinner, plus a Sunday brunch. A piano player entertains Wednesday, Friday, and Saturday nights. ⊠ *100 Palm St.* ☎ *239/394–3131 or 977/475–3466* ☰ *AE, D, MC, V* ⊗ *No lunch May–Dec., no brunch May–Nov.*

$$–$$$ ✕ **Café de Marco.** This cozy little bistro serves some of the best food on the island. The kitchen matches up fresh local fish with original preparations, and there are always good daily specials. Try stuffed Florida lobster, sautéed frogs' legs, or the broiled seafood platter. Steaks, chicken, and pasta are also available. ⊠ *244 Palm St.* ☎ *239/394–6262* ☰ *AE, MC, V* ⊗ *Closed Sun. May–Oct. No lunch.*

$$–$$$ ✕ **Verdi's.** Prints and plants add warmth to this spare American bistro, whose reputation is built on friendly, professional service and creative American and fusion cuisine. You might start with steamed littleneck clams or shrimp egg roll, then move on to entrées such as grilled swordfish, seared Chilean sea bass, or tilapia Mediterranean-style (sautéed with fresh tomatoes, olives, and feta). Cuban coffee crème brûlée and bananas Foster are among the tempting desserts. ⊠ *Sand Dollar Plaza, 241 N. Collier Blvd.* ☎ *239/394–5533* ☰ *AE, D, DC, MC, V* ⊗ *Closed Sun. and Mon. No lunch.*

$–$$$ ✕ **Old Marco Lodge Crab House.** Built in 1869, this waterfront restaurant is Marco's oldest landmark, and boaters often cruise in and tie up dockside to sit on the veranda and dine on local-seafood and pasta entrées. Start with a wholesome bowl of vegetable crab soup. The blue crabs in garlic butter are a specialty (market price), but the menu includes all manner of shellfish, pasta, grouper, and steak. Save room for the authentic key lime pie. ⊠ *1 Papaya St., Goodland* ☎ *239/642–7227* ☰ *AE, D, MC, V* ⊗ *Closed Sept.; Mon. and Tues. May–Aug.; and Mon. Oct.–mid-Dec.*

¢–$$ ✕ **The Crazy Flamingo.** Burgers, seafood, and finger foods such as conch fritters and chicken wings are the draw at this neighborhood bar, where there's counter service only and seating indoors and outdoors on the sidewalk. Try the seafood steamer pot, mussels marinara, or grouper sandwich. ⊠ *Marco Island Town Center, 1035 N. Collier Blvd.* ☎ *239/642–9600* ⚐ *Reservations not accepted* ☰ *No credit cards.*

¢–$$ ✕ **Tide Beachfront Bar & Grill.** Head to this local favorite for the best casual dining with a view of the beach and a menu of ribs, thick sandwiches, burgers, chicken-finger and shrimp baskets, pizza, wings, ribs, and pastas. The lively sports bar scene adds to the fun indoors; a porch accommodates al fresco diners with the most inexpensive dining view in Marco. ⊠ *Apollo Condominiums, 900 S. Collier Blvd.* ☎ *239/393–8433* ⊟ *AE, D, MC, V.*

★ **$$$$** 🏨 **Marco Beach Ocean Resort.** One of the area's first condo hotels, this 12-story class act has one- and two-bedroom suites, done in royal blues and golds. All rooms face the gulf and the property's crescent-shape rooftop pool (on the 5th floor). The bathrooms are full of marble. Golf and tennis are nearby. ⊠ *480 S. Collier Blvd., 34145* ☎ *239/393–1400 or 800/260–5089* 🖷 *239/393–1401* ⊕ *www.marcoresort.com* ☞ *87 1- and 16 2-bedroom suites* ♨ *Restaurant, kitchens, cable TV, in-room data ports, golf privileges, 4 tennis courts, pool, health club, outdoor hot tub, spa, beach, boating, 2 bars, shops, concierge, business services, meeting rooms* ⊟ *AE, D, DC, MC, V.*

★ **$$$$** 🏨 **Marco Island Marriott Resort, Golf Club & Spa.** A circular drive and manicured grounds front this beachfront resort made up of two 11-story towers. It's delightfully beachy outside, yet the interior is elegant, with many shops and restaurants and large, plush rooms with good to exceptional water views. A recent makeover yielded a new spa and restaurant plus a rock waterfalls pool with slides. The hotel's golf course is 10 minutes away by tram. ⊠ *400 S. Collier Blvd., 34145* ☎ *239/394–2511 or 800/438–4373* 🖷 *239/642–2672* ⊕ *www.marcoislandmarriott. com* ☞ *727 rooms, 54 suites* ♨ *5 restaurants, coffee shop, snack bar, refrigerators, 18-hole golf course, 4 tennis courts, 2 pools, wading pool, health club, outdoor hot tubs, spa, beach, windsurfing, boating, jet skiing, parasailing, bicycles, 3 bars, shops, babysitting, children's programs (ages 5–12), playground* ⊟ *AE, DC, MC, V.*

$$$$ 🏨 **Olde Marco Island Inn & Suites.** This Victorian with tin roofs and royal blue shutters and awnings used to be the only place to stay on the island. Lodging back then was in the circa-1883 historic building that now holds the restaurant; today guests stay in a much newer, more modern section. Although it's away from the beach, there's a complimentary boat shuttle to a beach on an unbridged island. It's in the heart of Old Marco, and the large one- and two-bedroom tiled suites with screened lanais are ideal for families. ⊠ *100 Palm St., 34145* ☎ *239/394–3131 or 877/475–3466* 🖷 *239/389–5176* ⊕ *www.oldmarco.com* ☞ *52 suites* ♨ *2 restaurants, coffee shop, some kitchens, some kitchenettes, in-room data ports, pool, gym, spa, bar, shops, meeting rooms* ⊟ *AE, D, DC, MC, V.*

$$$ 🏨 **Marco Island Hilton Beach Resort.** This 11-story beachfront hotel is smaller and more conservative than other big-name local resorts, and it seems less crowded. All rooms are spacious and have private balconies with unobstructed gulf views, a sitting area, a dry bar, bathrobes, and a mini-refrigerator. ⊠ *560 S. Collier Blvd., 34145* ☎ *239/394–5000 or 800/394–5000* 🖷 *239/394–8410* ⊕ *www.marcoisland.hilton.com* ☞ *271 rooms, 26 suites* ♨ *2 restaurants, snack bar, in-room safes, refrigerators, cable TV, in-room data ports, 3 tennis courts, pool, health club, outdoor hot tub, massage, beach, windsurfing, boating, parasailing, waterskiing, volleyball, bar, lounge, video game room, children's programs (5–12)* ⊟ *AE, D, DC, MC, V.*

$$$ 🏨 **Radisson Suite Beach Resort.** At this 12-story beachfront property designed for families, all units are tastefully decorated. Rooms are cheerful and amenity-rich; one- and two-bedroom suites are generously proportioned. ⊠ *600 S. Collier Blvd., 34145* ☎ *239/394–4100 or 800/333–3333* 🖷 *239/394–0419* ⊕ *www.radisson.com/marcoislandfl* 🛏 *55 rooms, 214 suites* ⚴ *3 restaurants, 1 pizzeria, some kitchens, microwaves, refrigerators, cable TV, pool, gym, hot tub (outdoor), beach, parasailing, bicycles, 2 bars, video game room, children's programs (ages 4–12)* ⊟ *AE, D, DC, MC, V.*

$$–$$$ 🏨 **Boat House Motel.** For a great location at a good price, check into this two-story motel. Modest but appealing with its white facade and turquoise trim, it's at the north end of Marco Island, on a canal close to the gulf. Units are light and bright and furnished with light woods, rattan, and tropical print fabrics. All have a balcony or walled-in terrace, and some have great water views. You can fish from the motel's dock. ⊠ *1180 Edington Pl., 34145* ☎ *239/642–2400 or 800/528–6345* 🖷 *239/642–2435* ⊕ *www.theboathousemotel.com* 🛏 *20 rooms, 3 condominiums, 1 2-bedroom house* ⚴ *Fans, some kitchens, some microwaves, refrigerators, pool, dock, fishing* ⊟ *MC, V.*

$ 🏨 **Village Inn Motel.** If you're looking for budget accommodations with kitchen facilities (cooktops, but no ovens) on Marco Island, head to Goodland. This unassuming little strip motel bases its nightly rates on the length of your stay; the longer you stay, the cheaper it is. It's within walking distance of the town's funky restaurants and is a popular base for hardcore anglers. ⊠ *212 Harbor Pl., Goodland, 34140* ☎ *239/642–3338* 🖷 *239/642–9793* 🛏 *10 rooms* ⚴ *Kitchenettes* ⊟ *AE, D, MC, V.*

Sports & the Outdoors

BIKING Rentals are available at **Scootertown** (⊠ 845 Bald Eagle Dr. ☎ 239/394–8400) for use on the island's bike path along beachfront condos and resorts.

FISHING **Sunshine Tours** (⊠ Marco River Marina, 951 Bald Eagle Dr. ☎ 239/642–5415 ⊕ www.sunshinetoursmarcoisland.com) operates deep-sea ($75 each for half-day) and backcountry ($47 each for three hours) fishing charters.

SAILING **Kahuna Sea Excursions** (⊠ Marco River Marina, 951 Bald Eagle Dr. ☎ 239/642–7704 ⊕ www.sail-kahuna.com) can help you sail into the sunset or take you out in search of dolphins and shells for $35 to $45.

THE LOWER GULF COAST A TO Z

To research prices, get advice from other travelers, and book travel arrangements, visit www.fodors.com.

AIR TRAVEL

CARRIERS Southwest Florida International Airport (RSW) is served by Air Canada, AirTran Airways, American, ATA, Cape Air, Comair, Condor, Continental, Delta/Song, Frontier Airlines, Hooters Air, JetBlue, LTU International Airways, Midwest, Northwest, Spirit, Sun Country, United, USA 3000 Airlines, and US Airways.

🛈 Airlines & Contacts **Air Canada** ☎ 888/247-2262. **AirTran Airways** ☎ 800/247-8726. **American** ☎ 800/433-7300. **ATA** ☎ 800/435-9282. **Cape Air** ☎ 800/352-0714. **Comair** ☎ 800/221-1212. **Condor** ☎ 800/524-6975. **Continental** ☎ 800/523-3273. **Delta** ☎ 800/221-1212. **Frontier Airlines** ☎ 800/432-1359. **Hooters Air** ☎ 888/359-4668. **LTU International Airways** ☎ 866/266-5588. **Midwest Airlines** ☎ 800/452-2022. **Northwest** ☎ 800/225-2525. **Song** ☎ 800/359-7664. **Spirit** ☎ 800/772-7117. **Sun Country** ☎ 800/359-6786. **United** ☎ 800/241-6522. **USA 3000 Airlines** ☎ 877/872-3000. **US Airways** ☎ 800/428-4322.

AIRPORTS

Southwest Florida International Airport is about 12 mi southwest of Fort Myers and 25 mi north of Naples. A taxi to Fort Myers, Sanibel, or Captiva costs about $8–$65; it's about $45–$65 to Naples. Transportation companies include AAA Airport Transportation, Aaron Airport Transportation, Boca Grande Limo, Charlotte Limousine Service, and Sanibel Island Taxi. The Naples Municipal Airport is a small facility east of downtown principally serving private planes, commuter flights, and charters. Shuttle service to Naples is $15–$25 per person. Once you have arrived, call Naples Taxi.

🛈 Airport Information **Naples Municipal Airport** ☎ 239/643-0733. **Southwest Florida International Airport** ☎ 239/768-1000. **AAA Airport Transportation** ☎ 800/872-2711. **Aaron Airport Transportation** ☎ 239/768-1898 or 800/998-1898. **Boca Grande Limo** ☎ 941/964-0455 or 800/771-7433. **Charlotte Limousine Service** ☎ 941/627-4494. **Naples Taxi** ☎ 239/643-2148. **Sanibel Island Taxi** ☎ 239/472-4160.

BOAT & FERRY TRAVEL

Key West Shuttle operates a ferry from Marco Island (from Thanksgiving through May) and Fort Myers Beach (year-round) to Key West. The cost for the round-trip (four hours each way) from Marco Island and the almost five-hour trip from Fort Myers Beach costs $120 round-trip.

🛈 Boat & Ferry Information **Key West Shuttle** ☎ 239/394-9700 or 888/539-2628 ⊕ www.keywestshuttle.com.

BUS TRAVEL

Greyhound Lines has service to Fort Myers and Naples. LeeTran serves most of the Fort Myers area.

🛈 Bus Information **Greyhound Lines** ☎ 800/231-2222 ✉ 2250 Peck St., Fort Myers ☎ 239/334-1011 ✉ 2669 Davis Blvd., Naples ☎ 239/774-5660 ✉ 26505 N. Jones Loop Rd., Punta Gorda ☎ 941/575-2781. **LeeTran** ☎ 239/275-8726 ⊕ www.rideleetran.com.

CAR TRAVEL

I–75 spans the region from north to south. Once you cross the Georgia border into Florida, it's about six hours to Fort Myers and another half hour to Naples. Alligator Alley, a section of Interstate 75, is a two-lane toll road ($1.50 to enter) that runs from Fort Lauderdale through the Everglades to Naples. The trip takes about two hours. U.S. 41 also runs the length of the region. Also known as the Tamiami Trail, U.S. 41 goes through downtown Fort Myers and Naples and is also called Cleveland Avenue in the former and 9th Street in the latter. McGregor Boulevard

(Route 867) and Summerlin Road (Route 869), Fort Myers's main north–south city streets, head toward Sanibel and Captiva Islands. San Carlos Boulevard runs southwest from Summerlin Road to Fort Myers Beach, and Pine Island–Bayshore Road (Route 78) leads from North Fort Myers through northern Cape Coral onto Pine Island.

EMERGENCIES

Dial 911 for police or ambulance.

🗷 Late-Night Pharmacies **Walgreens Drug Store** ✉ 15601 San Carlos Blvd., Fort Myers ☎ 239/489–3400 ✉ 2710 Del Prado Blvd. S, Cape Coral ☎ 239/574–1928.

MEDIA

NEWSPAPERS & MAGAZINES The local papers are the *Naples Daily News* and Fort Myers's *The News-Press*.

RADIO Tune in WARO 94.5 FM for classic rock, WRXK 96 FM for rock, WAVV 101.1 FM for easy listening, and WCKT 107 FM for country.

TOURS

Boca Grande Seaplane Service operates sightseeing tours in the Charlotte Harbor area. One way to see the cluster of small, undeveloped, protected islands known as the Ten Thousand Islands is on a tour run by Airboat Experience of the Everglades. You'll probably see many birds, including pelicans, egrets, ibises, and hawks, as well as alligators swimming alongside the boat. Nature Recreation Management operates boat tours ($20–$45) out of Lovers Key State Park, including sunset cruises, dolphin and shelling excursions, and backwater fishing. Dolphins play in the boat's wake and a naturalist drags the estuary bottom for marine creatures to study on the Planet Ocean eco-tour into Estero Bay Aquatic Preserve. The two-hour tour includes beach and shelling time at Lovers Key State Park and costs $15. It also runs sunset and fishing excursions. Estero Bay Boat Tours takes you on guided tours of waterways once inhabited by the Calusa Indians. You'll see birds and other wildlife and may even spot some manatees or dolphins. Captiva Cruises runs shelling, nature, luncheon, beach, and sunset cruises to and around the out islands of Cabbage Key, Useppa Island, Cayo Costa, and Gasparilla Island.

J. C.'s Cruises explores the Caloosahatchee and Orange rivers of Lee County. For manatee-sighting tours, hook up with Fort Myers Manatee World or Manatee Sightseeing Adventure at Marco Island. In Punta Gorda, King Fisher Cruise Lines has 90-minute, half-day sightseeing, full-day island, and sunset cruises in Charlotte Harbor, the Peace River, and the Intracoastal Waterway, starting at $9.50. One of the best ways to see the J. N. "Ding" Darling National Wildlife Refuge is by taking a canoe or kayak tour with Tarpon Bay Explorers. The knowledgeable naturalist guides can help you see so much more of what's there among the mangroves and under the water's surface. The national refuge concession also offers pontoon tours of adjacent Tarpon Bay, narrated tram tours, and other educational programs. Take a narrated sightseeing, dinner, or murder-mystery excursion aboard the old-fashioned Seminole Gulf Railway. Daytime trips, which run Wednesday, Saturday, and Sunday and cost $14, travel north for a scenic Caloosahatchee bridge crossing in season. Naples Trolley Tours offers five narrated tours daily, covering more than 100 points of interest. Pick it up at 25 places around town, including the Coastland Mall. The tour ($18) lasts about two hours, but you can get off and reboard at no extra cost. For nature exploration, do a paddling or boat cruise along the wild, preserved Cocohatchee River with Cocohatchee Nature Center.

🚩 **Tours Information Airboat Experience of the Everglades** ✉ 3200 San Marco Rd., Marco Island ☎ 239/642-3141. **Boca Grande Seaplane Service** ✉ 375 Park Ave., Boca Grande ☎ 941/964-0234 or 800/940-0234. **Captiva Cruises** ✉ McCarthy's Marina, Captiva ☎ 239/472-5300 ⊕ www.captivacruises.com. **Cocohatchee Nature Center** ✉ 12345 N. Tamiami Trail, Naples ☎ 239/592-1200 ⊕ www.cocohatchee.org. **Estero Bay Boat Tours** ✉ 5231 Mamie St., Bonita Springs ☎ 239/992-2200. **J. C.'s Cruises** ✉ Fort Myers Yacht Basin, 2313 Edwards Dr., Fort Myers ☎ 239/334-7474. **Fort Myers Manatee World** ✉ Coastal Marine Mart, Rte. 80, Fort Myers ☎ 239/693-1434. **King Fisher Cruise Lines** ✉ Fishermen's Village, 1200 W. Retta Esplanade, Punta Gorda ☎ 239/639-0969 ⊕ www.kingfisherfleet.com. **Manatee Sightseeing Adventure** ☎ 239/642-8818 or 800/379-7440 ⊕ www.see-manatees.com. **Naples Trolley Tours** ☎ 239/262-7300. **Nature Recreation Management** ✉ Lovers Key State Park, Fort Myers Beach ☎ 239/314-0110. **Planet Ocean** ✉ Salty Sam's Marina, Fort Myers Beach ☎ 239/765-1636. **Seminole Gulf Railway** ✉ Colonial Station, Fort Myers ☎ 239/275-8487 or 800/736-4853 ⊕ www.semgulf.com. **Tarpon Bay Explorers** ✉ 900 Tarpon Bay Rd., Sanibel ☎ 239/472-8900.

VISITOR INFORMATION

The following are open weekdays 9–5: Charlotte County Chamber of Commerce, Lee County Visitor & Convention Bureau, and Marco Island Chamber of Commerce. Naples Area Chamber of Commerce also opens Saturday 9–5. The Sanibel & Captiva Chamber of Commerce stays open Monday to Saturday 9–7 and Sunday 10–5.

🚩 **Tourist Information Charlotte County Chamber of Commerce** ✉ 2702 Tamiami Trail, Port Charlotte 33952 ☎ 941/627-2222 ✉ 326 Marion Ave., Suite 112, Punta Gorda 33950 ☎ 941/639-2222 ⊕ www.pureflorida.org. **Lee County Visitor & Convention Bureau** ✉ 12800 University Dr., Suite 550, Fort Myers 33907 ☎ 239/338-3500 or 800/237-6444 ⊕ www.fortmyers-sanibel.com. **Greater Naples Chamber of Commerce** ✉ 2390 N. Tamiami Trail, Naples 34102 ☎ 239/262-6376 ⊕ www.napleschamber.org. **Marco Island Area Chamber of Commerce** ✉ 1102 N. Collier Blvd., Marco Island 34145 ☎ 239/394-7549 or 800/788-6272 ⊕ www.marcoislandchamber.org. **Sanibel-Captiva Chamber of Commerce** ✉ 1159 Causeway Rd., Sanibel 33957 ☎ 239/472-1080 ⊕ www.sanibel-captiva.org.

The Tampa Bay Area

WORD OF MOUTH

"Tampa's International Plaza, with its popular restaurant area, and Westshore Mall are both great, and in Ellenton (across the Skyway Bridge from St. Petersburg) is a designer name-brand outlet mall. Downtown St. Pete has lots of funky shops along Central with retro antiques (the greatest 60's store is there, shag and platform go-go boots, can you dig it?!?)"

—Tandoori_Girl

"Depending on when you are here, baseball spring training may be in full swing. St. Pete, Clearwater, Tampa, and Dunedin all have teams. If it's not on the weekend, you may be able to just walk up and get tickets."

—champ21e

Updated by
Kristin Milavec

THE TAMPA BAY AREA HAS THAT ELUSIVE QUALITY that many attribute to the "real Florida." The state's largest metro area is less fast-lane than Miami, but its strengths are just as varied. Florida's third-busiest airport, a vibrant business community, exceptional beaches, and superior hotels and resorts make this an excellent place to spend a week or a lifetime. Native Americans were the sole inhabitants of the region for many years. (Tampa is a Native American word meaning "sticks of fire.") Spanish explorers Juan Ponce de León, Pánfilo de Narváez, and Hernando de soto passed through in the mid-1500s, and the U.S. Army and civilian settlers arrived in 1824. The Spanish-American War was very good to Tampa, enabling industrialist Henry Plant to create an economic momentum that was sustained through the entire 20th century. A military presence remains in Tampa at MacDill Air Force Base, the U.S. Operations Command.

Today the region offers astounding diversity. Terrain ranges from the pine-dotted northern reaches to the coast's white-sand beaches and barrier islands. Tampa is a full-fledged city, with a high-rise skyline and highways jammed with traffic. Across the bay lies the peninsula that contains Clearwater and St. Petersburg. The compact St. Petersburg downtown, which has interesting restaurants, shops, and museums, is on the southeast side of the peninsula, facing Tampa. Inland is largely classic American suburbia. The peninsula's western periphery is rimmed by barrier islands with beaches, quiet parks, and little, laid-back beach towns. To the north are communities that celebrate their ethnic heritage—such as Tarpon Springs, settled by Greek sponge-divers—and, farther north, mostly undeveloped land dotted with crystal-clear rivers, springs, and nature preserves. To the south lie resort towns, including Sarasota, which fill up in winter with snowbirds escaping the cold.

Exploring the Tampa Bay Area

Whether you feel like walking on white-sand beaches, watching sponge divers, or wandering through upscale shopping districts, there's something to your liking in the diverse Tampa Bay Area. Bright, modern Tampa is the area's commercial center. Peninsular St. Petersburg lies across the bay. Tarpon Springs, to the northwest, is still Greek in flavor. The Manatee Coast, to the north, is quite rural, with extensive nature preserves. To the south are Bradenton, which has several museums and beaches; Sarasota, a sophisticated resort town; and small, canal-crossed Venice.

About the Restaurants

Fresh seafood is plentiful, and raw bars serving oysters, clams, and mussels are everywhere. Tampa's many Cuban and Spanish restaurants serve fresh seafood, perhaps in a spicy paella, along with black beans and rice. Tarpon Springs adds hearty helpings of classic Greek specialties. In Sarasota the emphasis is on ritzier dining, but many restaurants offer extra-cheap early-bird menus for seatings before 6 PM.

About the Hotels

Many convention hotels in the Tampa Bay area double as family-friendly resorts—taking advantage of nearby beaches, marinas, spas, tennis courts, and golf links. However, unlike Orlando and some other parts

Numbers in the text correspond to numbers in the margin and on the Tampa/ St. Petersburg and Bradenton/Sarasota maps.

If you have 3 days

Florida Aquarium ❶ ⊩ and **Busch Gardens ❻**, 8 mi northeast of 🔲 **Tampa ❶–❾**, are probably the two most popular attractions in the area. You need a half day for the aquarium and a full day for Busch Gardens. Then it's on to 🔲 **Sarasota ㊹–㊾**, with the **Ringling Center for the Cultural Arts ㊹** and **Mote Marine Aquarium ㊾**.

10

If you have 4 days

Start in 🔲 **Tampa ❶** ⊩ **– ❾** with a half day at the **Florida Aquarium ❶**. Then it's just a short drive to **Ybor City ❷**. Rest your feet over lunch before an hour or two of strolling through the shops. **Busch Gardens ❻** takes your whole second day. Start your third day in downtown St. Petersburg at the **Florida International Museum ⑮**. Catch lunch in the **BayWalk ⑭** dining and entertainment complex just across the street. A few blocks east is the **Florida Holocaust Museum ⑫**. On Day 4, choose between the beach or the streets of Sarasota. One of the best spots for a day at the beach is pristine **Fort De Soto Park ⑳**, a perfect place to picnic or watch the sun set over the Gulf of Mexico. Spend your last day in **Sarasota ㊹–㊾**, seeing the museums at the **Ringling Center for the Cultural Arts ㊹** and at **Mote Marine Aquarium ㊾**.

If you have 10 days

With this much time, linger three days in 🔲 **St. Petersburg ⑩** ⊩ **– ㉓**. Catch a meal or two and do some shopping at **BayWalk ⑭**, which is across the street from the **Florida International Museum ⑮**, in turn a short walk from the **Florida Holocaust Museum ⑫** and a five-minute drive from the **Salvador Dalí Museum ⑰**. You could easily spend a full day in downtown **Tampa ❶– ❾**. Start the morning with the spectacular **Florida Aquarium ❶**. Then head to **Ybor City ❷** for a bit of touring, shopping, and lunch. End the day with the **Tampa Museum of Art ❸** and the Channelside dining and entertainment district for dinner. The next three attractions, clustered northeast of Tampa, are 45–60 minutes by car from St. Petersburg. Spend a day at **Busch Gardens ❻**. If you are into water slides, set aside another day for **Adventure Island ❼**, Busch Gardens' waterpark cousin. If you opt to skip Adventure Island, try the **Museum of Science and Industry (MOSI) ❽** or one of downtown Tampa's museums. Spend a day around **Tarpon Springs ㉚– ㉞**, the self-described Sponge Capital of the World. Consider Caladesi Island State Park or nearby Honeymoon Island State Park, outside **Dunedin ㉙**, for a day at the beach.

🔲 **Sarasota ㊹– ㊾** is a convenient base for the second part of your stay. Drive up to **Bradenton ㊵– ㊸** to take in its sights and beaches for a day. In Sarasota, allow about four hours to cover the museums at the **Ringling Center for the Cultural Arts ㊹** and **Sarasota Jungle Gardens ㊺**. In the afternoon you might drive to St. Armands Circle on Lido Key to see shops and **Mote Marine Aquarium ㊾**. On another day explore the **Marie Selby Botanical Gardens ㊽** and take a couple of hours to explore downtown Sarasota. **Venice ㊽** makes an enjoyable half- or full-day trip.

of Florida, the area has been bustling for more than a century, and its accommodations often reflect a sense of its history. You'll find a turn-of-the-20th-century beachfront resort where Zelda and F. Scott Fitzgerald stayed, a massive all-wood building from the 1920s, plenty of art deco, and throwbacks to the Spanish-style villas of yore. But one thing they all have in common is a certain Gulf Coast charm.

WHAT IT COSTS					
	$$$$	**$$$**	**$$**	**$**	**¢**
RESTAURANTS	over $30	$20–$30	$15–$20	$10–$15	under $10
HOTELS	over $220	$140–$220	$100–$140	$80–$100	under $80

Restaurant prices are per person for a main course at dinner. Hotel prices are for a standard double room, excluding 6% sales tax (more in some counties) and 1%–4% tourist tax.

Timing

Winter and spring are high season, and the level of activity is double what it is in the off-season. In summer there are huge afternoon thunderstorms, and temperatures hover around 90°F during the day. Luckily the mercury drops to the mid-70s at night, and beach towns have a consistent on-shore breeze that starts just before sundown, which enabled civilization to survive here before air-conditioning was invented.

NORTH & WEST AROUND TAMPA BAY

The core of the northern bay comprises the cities of Tampa, St. Petersburg, and Clearwater. A semitropical climate and access to the gulf make Tampa an ideal port for the cruise industry. The waters around Clearwater and St. Petersburg are often filled with pleasure and commercial craft, including dozens of boats with day trips and night trips featuring what purveyors euphemistically call "Las Vegas action": gambling in international waters. It's fitting that an area with a thriving international port should also be populated by a wealth of nationalities. The center of the Cuban community is the east Tampa enclave of Ybor City, while north of Clearwater, in Dunedin, the heritage is Scottish. North of Dunedin, Tarpon Springs has supported a large Greek population for decades and is the largest producer of natural sponges in the world. Inland, to the east of Tampa, it's all suburban sprawl, freeways, shopping malls, and—the main draw—Busch Gardens.

Tampa

84 mi southwest of Orlando.

The west coast's crown jewel as well as its business and commercial hub, Tampa has numerous high-rises and heavy traffic. Amid the bustle is a concentration of restaurants, nightlife, stores, and cultural events.

★ ▶ ☾ ❶ **Florida Aquarium** is a dazzling architectural landmark with an 83-foot-high multitier glass dome and 152,000 square feet of air-conditioned exhibit space. It has more than 10,000 aquatic plants and animals rep-

Beaches

Every barrier island from Clearwater to Venice has excellent swimming beaches facing out on the Gulf of Mexico. Waters are calmer here than on the Atlantic Coast, a boon to families but a disappointment to surfers. Don't swim in Tampa Bay, Sarasota Bay, or the inland waterway, all of which have been polluted by boaters, marinas, and industry.

Biking

The 35-mi-long Pinellas Trail, a paved route that follows the path of a former railroad, makes it possible to bike all the way from Tarpon Springs, at the north end of Pinellas County, to a spot not far north of the Sunshine Skyway Bridge, at the south end of the county. When completed sometime around 2006, it will cover 47 mi. Opened in 2001, Suncoast Trail runs north from Tampa's outskirts—beginning in north Hillsborough County and ending in north Hernando County—for nearly 42 mi. The paved surface will eventually connect to the Upper Bay Trail and extend another 58 mi.

10

Canoeing

Several inland rivers offer superb canoeing, and outfits at different points along their shores rent equipment and lead guided tours. Sculling teams from the University of Tampa and colleges nationwide train in downtown's Hillsborough River.

Fishing

Anglers flock to southwest Florida's coastal waters to catch tarpon, kingfish, speckled trout, snapper, grouper, sea trout, snook, sheepshead, and shark. Charter a fishing boat or join a group on a party boat for full- or half-day outings. Avoid fishing in polluted Tampa Bay.

---

resenting species native to Florida and the rest of the world. The major exhibit areas reflect the diversity of Florida's natural habitats—Wetlands, Bays and Beaches, and Coral Reef. Creature-specific exhibits are the No Bone Zone (lovable invertebrates) and Sea Hunt, with predators ranging from sharks to exotic lion fish. The aquarium's most impressive single exhibit is the Coral Reef, in a 500,000-gallon tank ringed with viewing windows, including an awesome 43-foot-wide panoramic opening. Part of the tank is a walkable tunnel, almost giving the illusion of venturing into underwater depths. There you see a thicket of elkhorn coral teeming with tropical fish. A dark cave reveals sea life you would normally see only on night dives. For an additional cost, kids six and up can swim with fish, and certified divers 15 and up can dive with sharks. If you have two hours, try Bay Spirit, Wild Dolphin Adventure, an ecotour that takes up to 50 passengers onto Tampa's bays in a 64-foot catamaran for an up-close look at bottlenose dolphins and other native wildlife. The outdoor Explore-a-Shore exhibit, which packs appeal for younger kids, is an aquatic playground with a water slide, water jet spays, and a climbable replica pirate ship. ✉ *701 Channelside Dr., Downtown* ☎ *813/273–4000* ⊕ *www.flaquarium.org* ✍ *Aquarium $17.95, Bay Spirit, Wild Dolphin Adventure $18.95* ☉ *Daily 9:30–5.*

570 <

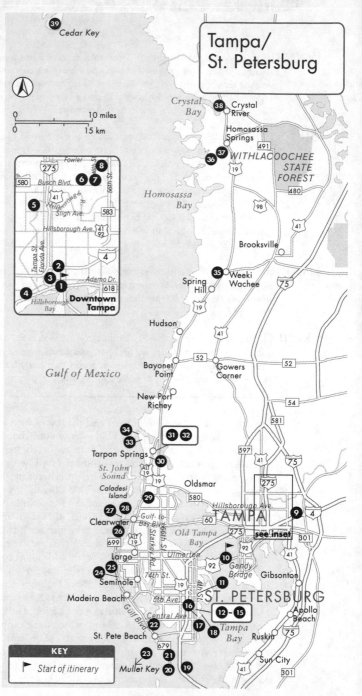

Tampa/
St. Petersburg

Downtown Tampa

KEY

Start of itinerary

Downtown Tampa's **Riverwalk** connects some developed-area waterside entities such as the Marriott Waterside, the Channelside shopping and entertainment complex, and the Florida Aquarium. **Cotanchobee Fort Brooke Park,** which opened in spring 2003, includes a wall of bronze plaques telling the story of Tampa's Seminole War fort from the Seminole perspective. The landscaped park is 6 acres and extends along the Garrison cruise-ship channel and along the Hillsborough River in the downtown area. The walkway is being expanded as waterside development continues.

One of only three National Historic Landmark districts in Florida, lively **Ybor City,** Tampa's Latin quarter, has antique-brick streets and wrought iron balconies. Cubans brought their cigar making industry to Ybor (pronounced *ee*-bore) City in 1886, and the smell of cigars—hand-rolled by Cuban immigrants—still wafts through the heart of this east Tampa area, along with the strong aroma of roasting coffee. These days the neighborhood is emerging as Tampa's hot spot, as empty cigar factories and historic social clubs are transformed into trendy boutiques, art galleries, restaurants, and nightclubs that rival those on Miami's sizzling South Beach. Take a stroll past the ornately tiled **Columbia** restaurant and the stores lining 7th Avenue. Guided walking tours of the area ($6) enable you to see artisans hand-roll cigars following time-honored methods. Step back into the past at **Centennial Park** (⊠ 8th Ave. and 18th St.), which re-creates a period streetscape and hosts the Fresh Market every Saturday. Ybor City's destination within a destination is the dining and entertainment palace **Centro Ybor** (⊠ 1600 E. 7th Ave.). It has shops, trendy bars and restaurants, a 20-screen movie theater, and GameWorks, an interactive playground developed by Steven Spielberg. The **Ybor City Museum State Park** provides a look at the history of the cigar industry. Admission includes a tour of La Casita, one of the shotgun houses occupied by cigar workers and their families in the late 1890s. ⊠ *1818 E. 9th Ave., between Nuccio Pkwy. and 22nd St., from 7th to 9th Ave.* ☎ *813/247–6323* ⊕ *www.ybormuseum. org* ⊠ *$3* ☉ *Daily 9–5; tours Sat. 10:30.*

The 35,000-square-foot **Tampa Museum of Art** has an impressive permanent collection of Greek and Roman antiquities, along with five galleries that host traveling exhibits. A 124,000-square-foot space, designed by internationally renowned architect Rafael Viñoly, was under construction as of this writing; until the new building is ready, the museum will remain open at its current location, closing for a short time when exhibits are moved. ⊠ *600 N. Ashley Dr., Downtown* ☎ *813/274–8130* ⊕ *www. tampamuseum.com* ⊠ *$7* ☉ *Tues.–Sat. 10–5, Sun. 11–5; 3rd Thurs. of month open until 9 PM.*

The **Henry B. Plant Museum** is one part architectural time capsule and one part magic carpet ride to gilded-era America. Originally a luxury hotel built by railroad magnate Henry B. Plant in 1891, the building has classic furnishings that date to when Colonel Theodore Roosevelt made it his U.S. headquarters during the Spanish-American War. The museum displays the finer things of life from the 1890s, including 19th-century artwork and furniture brought from Europe when the hotel opened. On Sunday afternoons (September to May) get a glimpse into the period through "Upstairs/Downstairs," in which actors play the parts of hotel staff and guests. During December, experience a Victorian Christmas stroll through the museum and enjoy hot cider and cookies on the veranda. ⊠ *401 W. Kennedy Blvd., off I–275 Exit 44, Downtown* ☎ *813/254–1891* ⊕ *www.plantmuseum.com* ⊠ *$5* ⊘ *Tues.–Sat. 10–4, Sun. noon–4.*

🕓 ⑤ In the 56-acre **Lowry Park Zoo,** exotic creatures from all seven continents live in their natural habitats. Check out the Asian Domain, with tigers and rhinos, and Primate World, including chimpanzees and colobus monkeys. Spot some fancy flying in the free-flight bird aviary, and come face to face with alligators, panthers, bears, and red wolves at the Florida Wildlife Center. Gentle goats and kangaroos populate the Wallaroo Station family exhibit, and gentle creatures of another kind headline at the Manatee Amphitheater. This zoo is particularly attuned to night events: parties range from food and beer tastings for adults to chaperoned sleepovers for children ages 6–14. New exhibits include Safari Africa, which houses elephants, giraffes, and zebras. ⊠ *1101 W. Sligh Ave., Central Tampa* ☎ *813/935–8552* ⊕ *www.lowryparkzoo.com* ⊠ *$14.95* ⊘ *Daily 9:30–5.*

With a unique blend of thrilling rides, a world-class zoo with more than 2,000 animals, and dazzling live entertainment, the 335-acre **Busch Gardens** provides excitement for the whole family. The park's habitats offer views of some of the world's most endangered and exotic animals. You can experience up-close animal encounters on the **Serengeti Plain,** a 65-acre free-roaming habitat that is home to reticulated giraffe, Grevy's zebra, white rhinos, bongo, eland, impala and more. **Myombe Reserve: The Great Ape Domain** allows you to view gorillas and chimpanzees in a lush, tropical-rainforest environment. **Edge of Africa** is an intense walking tour of lions, hippos, and hyenas. The Broadway-style theater extravaganza **KaTonga: Tales from the Jungle** is a 35-minute celebration of animal folklore. The lush, rhythmic musical reveals life in the jungle through a series of mystical fables and colorful vignettes.

🕓 ⑥ **Fodor's**Choice ★

SheiKra, North America's first dive coaster, opened in mid-2005. On the wings of an African hawk, riders fly through a three-minute journey 200 feet up, then 90 degrees straight down at 70 mi per hour. The park's coaster lineup also includes steel giants **Kumba** and **Montu,** a double wooden roller coaster called **Gwazi,** and **Cheetah Chase**—a five-story family coaster full of hairpin turns and breathtaking dips. The off-road safari **Rhino Rally** brings you face to face with elephants, white rhinos, and Nile crocodiles. **Land of the Dragons** is a 4-acre playland for children that has rides, play areas, and a three-story tree house with towers and stairways. For those 21 years or older, the **Hospitality House** in the Bird Gardens offers complimentary Anheuser-Busch products and the **Budweiser Beer School** hosts a 30-minute lesson in the art, science, and tradition of beer brewing. Allow six to eight hours to experience Busch Gardens. ⊠ *3000 E. Busch Blvd., 8 mi northeast of downtown Tampa and 2 mi east of I–275 Exit 50, Central Tampa* ☎ *813/987–5082 or 888/800–5447* ⊕ *www.buschgardens.com* ⊠ *$56* ⊘ *Daily 9–6; later in summer.*

Water slides, pools, and artificial-wave pools create a 30-acre water wonderland at **Adventure Island,** a corporate cousin of Busch Gardens. Rides such as the Key West Rapids and Tampa Typhoon are creative, if geographically incorrect. (There are no rapids in Key West and *typhoon* is a term used only in Pacific regions—Tampa Hurricane just wouldn't have had the same alliterative allure.) Planners of this water park took the younger kids into account, with offerings such as Fabian's Funport, which has a scaled-down wave pool and interactive water gym. Along with a volleyball complex and a surf pool, there are cafés, snack bars, changing rooms, and video games. ⊠ *1001 Malcolm McKinley Dr., less than 1 mi north of Busch Gardens, Central Tampa* 🕾 *813/987–5660 or 888/800–5447* ⊕ *www.adventureisland.com* 🖅 *$33* ⊙ *Mid-Mar.–late Oct., daily 10–5.*

★ ❽ The **Museum of Science and Industry (MOSI)** is a fun and stimulating scientific playground where you learn about Florida weather, anatomy, flight, and space by seeing *and* by doing. At the Gulf Coast Hurricane Exhibit, experience what a hurricane and its 74-mph winds feel like. The Bank of America BioWorks Butterfly Garden is a 6,400-square-foot engineered ecosystem project that demonstrates how wetlands can clean water plus serve as a home for free-flying butterflies. The 100-seat Saunders Planetarium—Tampa's only planetarium—has afternoon and evening shows, one of them a trek through the universe. For adventurous spirits, there's a high-wire bicycle ride 30 feet above the floor. There's also an impressive IMAX theater, where films are projected on a hemispherical 82-feet dome. As of this writing, two exhibits were slated to open: Kids in Charge, a 41,000-square-foot science center with interactive exhibits aimed at the 12-and-under set; and Disasterville, an exhibit about—you guessed it—natural disasters. ⊠ *4801 E. Fowler Ave., 1 mi north of Busch Gardens, Northeast Tampa* 🕾 *813/987–6300 or 800/995–6674* ⊕ *www.mosi.org* 🖅 *$15.95* ⊙ *Weekdays 9–5, weekends 9–7.*

If you've brought your body to Tampa but your heart's in Vegas, satisfy that urge to hang around a poker table at 4 AM at the **Seminole Hard Rock Hotel & Casino.** The casino has poker tables, high-stakes bingo, and gaming machines. The casino lounge serves drinks 24 hours a day. Floyd's restaurant has lunch, dinner, and nightlife. ⊠ *5223 N. Orient Rd., off I–4 at N. Orient Rd. Exit* 🕾 *813/627–7625 or 866/762–5463* ⊕ *www.seminolehardrock.com* 🖅 *Free* ⊙ *Daily 24 hrs.*

Where to Stay & Eat

$$$–$$$$
Fodor'sChoice
★
✕ **Bern's Steak House.** Fine mahogany paneling and ornate chandeliers define the elegance at legendary Bern's, which many feel is Tampa's best restaurant. Owner David Laxer ages his own beef, grows his own organic vegetables, roasts his own coffee, and maintains his own saltwater fish tanks. Cuts of topmost beef are sold by weight and thickness. The wine list includes some 6,500 selections (with 1,800 dessert wines). After dinner, tour the kitchen and wine cellar before having dessert upstairs in a cozy booth. ⊠ *1208 S. Howard Ave., Hyde Park* 🕾 *813/251–2421, 800/282–1547 in Florida* ⌂ *Reservations essential* ⊟ *AE, D, DC, MC, V* ⊙ *No lunch.*

★ $$–$$$$ ✗ **Armani's.** This northern-Italian–style rooftop restaurant has good service, a great view of the bay and city, and one of the best sunset views along the gulf. Excellent pastas include black-pepper pappardelle with scallops, shrimp, and creamy lemon-pepper sauce. Another front-runner is the signature veal scaloppine Armani (with wild mushrooms, cognac, and truffle sauce). Roast rack of lamb is a house specialty. ⊠ *Grand Hyatt Tampa Bay, 6200 Courtney Campbell Causeway, Airport Area* ☎ *813/207–6800* ▭ *AE, D, DC, MC, V* ☽ *Closed Sun. No lunch.*

$$–$$$$ ✗ **Castaway.** The specialty of this mid-price casual restaurant with bay views is local seafood—grilled, broiled, or blackened—but the menu also includes grilled steaks, such as New York strip, and several pasta dishes. The menu changes frequently, but favorites have included shrimp in gar-lic-chardonnay sauce and coconut shrimp with orange-horseradish sauce. Dine inside or on the expansive deck, popular for lunch and at sunset. The jets dipping down over the bay on their final approach are just far enough away to avoid a noise problem. ⊠ *7720 Courtney Campbell Causeway, east side, 1 mi west of Tampa International Airport, Airport Area* ☎ *813/281–0770* ▭ *AE, D, DC, MC, V.*

$$–$$$$ ✗ **Roy's.** Tampa Bay has a taste for trendy national restaurant names, so it's no surprise that Roy's, the Hawaiian fusion-style restaurant chain that has swept the United States in the past decade, has an outpost here. Chef Roy Yamaguchi flies in fresh ingredients daily from around the Pacific. The menu changes daily, but typical dishes include roasted macadamia-nut-crusted mahimahi with lobster-essence sauce, blackened island ahi tuna with spicy soy-mustard sauce, and tender braised short-rib beef with natural or butter sauce. Dessert choices include a melting chocolate soufflé and a fresh-fruit cobbler. ⊠ *4342 Boy Scout Blvd., Airport Area* ☎ *813/873–7697* ▭ *AE, D, DC, MC, V.*

$$–$$$ ✗ **Bernini.** Named for the 17th-century Italian baroque sculptor Giovanni Bernini, this trendy restaurant is something of a gallery for copies of his works. In the former Bank of Ybor City building, it has a classy look and daring fare like crispy duck with raspberry-pepper glaze and goat cheese potato cake, grilled oregano swordfish, and veal lasagna. The Caesar pizza (basically topped with Caesar salad) is among the best of the wood-fired pizzas. ⊠ *1702 E. 7th Ave., Ybor City* ☎ *813/248–0099* ▭ *AE, D, DC, MC, V* ☽ *No lunch weekends.*

★ $$–$$$ ✗ **Mise en Place.** The menu at one of Tampa's most celebrated restaurants is replete with Floribbean dishes, including creative takes on grouper. The chef combines seemingly incompatible ingredients to make a masterpiece, such as veal scaloppine with goat cheese spaetzle, carrot parsnip sauté, and apple-cider Riesling sauce. ⊠ *442 W. Kennedy Blvd., entrance off Grand Central Pl., Central Tampa* ☎ *813/254–5373* ▭ *AE, D, DC, MC, V* ☽ *Closed Sun. and Mon. No lunch Sat.*

$–$$$ ✗ **Big City Tavern.** The name makes the place sound like it's merely a bar, but it's far more than that. In the ballroom of the historic Cuban social club with an ornate tin ceiling and dark wood furniture, this classy dining room serves many well-prepared dishes, from veal scaloppine with potato lasagna to a tasty shrimp pad thai. A great starter is the coconut shrimp. There's a good selection of wines by the glass and imported beers from Ireland to Australia and in between. The tavern is relatively quiet and removed from the frenzied crowds at street level. ⊠ *Centro Ybor, 1600 E. 8th Ave., 2nd fl., Ybor City* ☎ *813/247–3000* ☷ *AE, D, DC, MC, V* ⊘ *No lunch.*

★ **$–$$$** ✕ **Columbia.** A fixture since 1905, this magnificent structure with spacious dining rooms and a sunny courtyard takes up an entire city block. The paella is possibly the best in Florida, and the Columbia 1905 salad—with ham, olives, cheese, and garlic—is legendary. The menu has Cuban classics such as *ropa vieja* (shredded beef with onions, peppers, and tomatoes) and *arroz con pollo* (chicken with yellow rice). There's flamenco dancing most nights. Buy hand-rolled cigars in the bar. ⊠ *2117 E. 7th Ave., Ybor City* ☎ *813/248–4961* ☷ *AE, D, DC, MC, V.*

$$ ✕ **dish.** At its two hot locations—Centro Ybor in Tampa and St. Petersburg's BayWalk—this restaurant with a bright red-and-yellow color scheme instantly became popular. Plan on standing in line most any evening. Once inside, you get an empty dish, which you fill at different stations before ending up at a big teppanyaki station. Here a chef stir-fries your chicken, pork, beef, fish, and veggies while you watch. The prix-fixe price is $15.95 at dinner, $7.50 at lunch. At dinner, you can make as many trips to the grill station as you'd like. There are more than 40 sauces representing every possible ethnic cuisine. ⊠ *1600 E. 8th Ave., Ybor City* ☎ *813/241–8300* ⊠ *197 2nd Ave. N, St. Petersburg* ☎ *727/894–5700* ☷ *AE, D, DC, MC, V.*

¢–$$ ✕ **GameWorks.** The restaurant (Jax Grill) and bar (Hop Scotch) at this fun factory are secondary attractions to the massive, 128-game arcade designed by Steven Spielberg. Jax Grill has solid offerings like grilled swordfish, baby-back ribs, and a tasty meat loaf, along with quesadillas, fish-and-chips, pizza, and burgers. The Hop Scotch lounge is a full martini bar. ⊠ *1600 E. 8th Ave., Unit A147, Ybor City* ☎ *813/241–9675* ⌔ *Reservations not accepted* ☷ *AE, MC, V.*

¢–$$ ✕ **Kojak's House of Ribs.** Family-run since its doors opened in 1978, this casual eatery has been voted a Tampa favorite year after year in local polls. Day and night the three indoor dining rooms and outdoor dining terrace are crowded with hungry patrons digging into tender barbecued ribs. There's chicken on the menu, too, and heaping sides of coleslaw, potato salad, parsley potatoes, and corn on the cob. ⊠ *2808 Gandy Blvd., South Tampa* ☎ *813/837–3774* ☷ *AE, D, MC, V* ⊘ *Closed Mon.*

¢–$$ ✕ **Stumps Supper Club.** In downtown Tampa's Channelside entertainment center, Stumps promises "Southern cooking and deep-fried dancing." Decorated in flea-market chic, it pokes fun at Southern food while taking it quite seriously. From Brunswick stew to pulled pork barbecue and country-fried steak, it has all the traditions covered. If a bottle of Boone's Farm wine doesn't appeal, look at the martini menu. The key lime version is especially tasty. ⊠ *615 Channelside Dr., Downtown* ☎ *813/226–2261* ☷ *AE, D, DC, MC, V* ⊘ *No lunch weekdays.*

¢–$ ✕ **Estela's Mexican Restaurant.** In the tiny business district of Davis Island, a sidewalk café gives this otherwise nondescript storefront a spark of vibrancy. It's the perfect place to munch on nachos and drink imported Mexican beer on a spring afternoon. The standard Tex-Mex cuisine is nothing special, so go for roasted poblano peppers stuffed with cheese, chicken soup (with a touch of cilantro), or chile Colorado steak (strip steak roasted in a ranchero sauce). ⊠ *209 E. Davis Blvd., 1½ mi across bridge from downtown Tampa, Davis Island* ☎ *813/251– 0558* ⊟ *AE, MC, V.*

¢–$ ✕ **Newk's Lighthouse Cafe.** A popular choice with the downtown work crowd, Newk's has the feel of a neighborhood bar, though a sea-and-sky mural gives the illusion of waterfront dining. Staples are burgers and fish-house fare. Grouper sandwiches come five different ways; notable are the crunchy version, with a corn-flake-and-almond coating, and a spicy buffalo–style. The café has indoor and outdoor seating. ⊠ *514 Channelside Dr., Downtown* ☎ *813/307–6395* ⊟ *AE, D, MC, V* ⊗ *No dinner Mon.*

$$$$ ▥ **Grand Hyatt Tampa Bay.** This large 14-story luxury hotel sits on the west shore of Tampa Bay. It's convenient to Tampa International Airport and downtown Tampa. It has a marble-accented lobby and a scattering of Spanish-style villas with private terraces. In addition to its bay views, the hotel also has a spectacular gazebo and a boardwalk system that wends through a protected salt marsh and bird sanctuary. One of Tampa's best business hotels, the Hyatt has the amenities to attract vacationers as well. ⊠ *2900 Bayport Dr., Airport Area, 33607* ☎ *813/ 874–1234* 🖷 *813/207–6790* ⊕ *www.grandtampabay.hyatt.com* ⊅ *422 rooms, 23 suites* ♿ *3 restaurants, some fans, some kitchenettes, minibars, some refrigerators, cable TV, in-room data ports, 2 tennis courts, 2 pools, gym, 2 hot tubs (1 indoor), massage, boating, fishing, 3 bars, shop, babysitting, dry cleaning, laundry service, concierge, concierge floor, Internet, business services, meeting rooms, airport shuttle, free parking, no-smoking floors* ⊟ *AE, D, DC, MC, V.*

★ $$$$ ▥ **Saddlebrook Resort Tampa.** This is arguably one of Florida's premier resorts of its type, largely because it has so many things in one spot— lots of golf, tennis, and conference space. The Arnold Palmer Golf Academy and the sophisticated spa are especially popular. The heavily wooded grounds sprawl over 480 acres just 12 mi north of Tampa. Varied accommodations include one- and two-bedroom suites; breakfast and dinner are included in the rates and wireless high-speed Internet access is available throughout the hotel. There's also a 5-acre executive challenge course. ⊠ *5700 Saddlebrook Way, Wesley Chapel 33543* ☎ *813/973–1111 or 800/729–8383* 🖷 *813/973–4504* ⊕ *www. saddlebrookresort.com* ⊅ *800 rooms, 420 suites* ♿ *4 restaurants, room service, some kitchens, minibars, cable TV, in-room data ports, driving range, 2 18-hole golf courses, 45 tennis courts, pro shop, 3 pools, health club, spa, fishing, bicycles, 3 bars, babysitting, children's programs (ages 4–12), laundry service, concierge, business services, convention center, meeting rooms* ⊟ *AE, D, DC, MC, V* ❣❣ *MAP.*

$$$$ ▥ **Seminole Hard Rock Hotel & Casino.** If gambling is your game, this property is the place to stay. Rooms are decorated with sophisticated clean lines and neutral tones. Beds have cotton duvets and many of the bathrooms have natural light via a skylight. With the casino open 24 hours, you may not see much of your room. ⊠ *5223 Orient Rd., off I–4 at Orient Rd. Exit, 33610* ☎ *813/627–7625 or 800/937–0010* 🖷 *813/627– 7655* ⊕ *www.seminolehardrock.com* ⊅ *248 rooms, 2 suites* ♿ *2 restau-*

rants, room service, in-room safes, minibars, cable TV, in-room data ports, pool, wading pool, gym, spa, massage, volleyball, hot tubs, steam rooms, 2 bars, lobby lounge, shops, casino, Internet, business services, meeting rooms, free parking ☰ *AE, D, DC, MC, V.*

$$$–$$$$ ▦ **Tampa Marriott Waterside.** Across from the Tampa Convention Center, this downtown hotel was built for conventioneers but is also convenient to popular tourist spots such as the Florida Aquarium, the St. Pete Times Forum hockey arena, and shopping and entertainment districts Channelside, Hyde Park, and Ybor City. At least half of the rooms and most of the suites overlook the channel to Tampa Bay; the bay itself is visible from the higher floors of the 27-story hotel. The lobby coffee bar overlooks the water. Il Terrazzo is the hotel's formal, Italian dining room. ✉ *700 S. Florida Ave., Downtown, 33602* ☎ *813/221–4900* ᗊ *813/221–0923* ⊕ *www.tampawaterside.com* ⇋ *681 rooms, 36 suites* ⚲ *3 restaurants, room service, in-room safes, some kitchens, cable TV, in-room data ports, pool, gym, hair salon, spa, boating, marina, 2 bars, lobby lounge, shop, dry cleaning, laundry facilities, laundry service, concierge, concierge floor, Internet, business services, meeting rooms, car rental, parking (fee), no-smoking floors* ☰ *AE, D, DC, MC, V.*

$$$–$$$$ ▦ **Wyndham Harbour Island Hotel.** Even though this 12-story hotel is on a 177-acre island in Tampa Bay, it's just an eight-minute walk and short drive from downtown Tampa. Many units have terrific views of the water or the downtown skyline. Service is attentive. There's a marina, and you may use the extensive health and fitness center and 20 tennis courts at the Harbour Island Athletic Club, next door, for a fee. Every room has high-speed Internet access. This is a good choice if you want to be downtown without actually being in the midst of the action, yet there's a trolley that takes you from the hotel to the convention center or to the electric street car (TECO) station where you can travel to Channelside, the Florida Aquarium, or Ybor City. ✉ *725 S. Harbour Island Blvd., Harbour Island, 33602* ☎ *813/229–5000* ᗊ *813/229–5322* ⊕ *www. wyndhamharbourisland.com* ⇋ *279 rooms, 20 suites* ⚲ *Restaurant, coffee shop, room service, minibars, some refrigerators, cable TV, in-room data ports, golf privileges, pool, dock, boating, fishing, bar, shop, laundry service, Internet, business services, airport shuttle, parking (fee), no-smoking floors* ☰ *AE, DC, MC, V.*

★ $$–$$$ ▦ **Don Vicente de Ybor Historic Inn.** This boutique hotel is in a restored building constructed in 1895 by Vicente Martinez Ybor, the founder of Ybor City. From the beige stucco exterior to the white marble staircase in the main lobby, the hotel is an architectural tour de force. Rooms have antique furnishings, Persian rugs, and four-poster canopied beds. Most rooms have wrought-iron balconies. The clubs and shops of Ybor City are within a short walk. ✉ *1915 Republica de Cuba, Ybor City, 33605* ☎ *813/241–4545* ᗊ *813/241–6104* ⊕ *www.donvicenteinn.com* ⇋ *13 rooms, 3 suites* ⚲ *Restaurant, cable TV, in-room data ports, bar, dry cleaning, laundry service* ☰ *AE, D, DC, MC, V* ⊠ *BP.*

$$–$$$ ▦ **Hilton Garden Inn Tampa Ybor Historic District.** Architecturally, this property pales when compared to the century-old classic structures around it in Ybor City. But it is convenient: it's across the street from the Centro Ybor complex, 3 mi from downtown Tampa, and 7 mi from Tampa International Airport. The hotel restaurant has a full breakfast buffet and doesn't try to compete with the culinary heavyweights in a six-block radius. Rooms are business traveler–friendly, with high-speed Internet access, dual phone lines, large desks, and ergonomic chairs. ✉ *1700 E. 9th Ave., Ybor City, 33605* ☎ *813/769–9267* 🖷 *813/769–3299* ⊕ *www.tampayborhistoricdistrict.gardeninn.com* ⤳ *84 rooms, 11 suites* ⅛ *Restaurant, microwaves, refrigerators, cable TV, in-room data ports, pool, exercise equipment, laundry facilities, laundry service, business services* ▤ *AE, D, DC, MC, V* ⑩ *EP.*

$$–$$$ ⌸ **Tahitian Inn.** Comfortable rooms and moderate prices are the draws at this three-story family-run boutique hotel, which underwent total reconstruction for a new classic look in 2003. It's 5 minutes from Tampa Stadium and 20 minutes from Busch Gardens. The motel bills itself as the last independently owned and operated lodging option in Tampa. ✉ *601 S. Dale Mabry Hwy., Central Tampa, 33609* ☎ *813/877–6721 or 800/876–1397* 🖷 *813/877–6218* ⊕ *www.tahitianinn.com* ⤳ *62 rooms, 17 suites* ⅛ *Café, minibars, microwaves, refrigerators, in-room data ports, pool, gym, massage, spa, steam room, bar, laundry facilities, Internet, business services, meeting rooms, free parking, some pets allowed (fee), no-smoking rooms* ▤ *AE, D, DC, MC, V.*

$$ ⌸ **Holiday Inn Busch Gardens.** Well maintained and family-oriented, this motor inn is a mile west of Busch Gardens (shuttle provided) and across the street from University Square Mall, one of Tampa's largest. Rooms are functional, but not spectacular, with contemporary furniture and two double beds. The 25 KidSuites have separate bunk-bed cubby rooms decorated and equipped for the preteen set. The kids will also like the pirate-theme children's pool, complete with a ship of slides, water cannons, and fountains. ✉ *2701 E. Fowler Ave., Central Tampa, 33612* ☎ *813/971–4710 or 800/206–2747* 🖷 *813/977–0155* ⊕ *hitampa-buschgardens.felcor.com* ⤳ *375 rooms, 25 suites* ⅛ *Restaurant, some refrigerators, some microwaves, room TVs with video games, in-room data ports, 2 pools, exercise equipment, bar, dry cleaning, laundry service, business services, meeting room, car rental, no-smoking rooms, some pets allowed* ▤ *AE, D, DC, MC, V.*

Nightlife & the Arts

THE ARTS   Occupying 9 acres along the Hillsborough River, the 345,000-square-foot **Tampa Bay Performing Arts Center** (✉ 1010 W. C. MacInnes Pl., Downtown ☎ 813/229–7827 or 800/955–1045) is the largest such complex south of the Kennedy Center in Washington, D.C. Among the facilities are the new 200-seat Teco Theater, the 2,500-seat Carol Morsani Hall, a 1,047-seat playhouse, a 300-seat cabaret theater, and a 120-seat black box theater. Opera, concerts, drama, and ballet performances are presented here. In a restored 1926 movie palace, the **Tampa Theatre** (✉ 711 N. Franklin St., Downtown ☎ 813/274–8981 ⊕ www.tampatheatre.org) has films, concerts, and special events.

NIGHTLIFE   The biggest concentration of nightclubs, as well as the widest variety, is found along 7th Avenue in Ybor City. It becomes a little like Bourbon Street in New Orleans after the sun goes down. Popular **Adobe Gilas** (✉ 1600

E. 8th Ave., Ybor City ☎ 813/241–8588) has live music every day but Monday, karaoke on Wednesday, and a balcony overlooking the crowds on 7th Avenue. There's a large selection of margaritas and more than 50 brands of tequila, and food is served until 2 AM. Considered something of a dive—but a lovable dive—by a loyal local following that ranges from esteemed jurists to nose ring–wearing night owls, the **Hub** (✉ 719 N. Franklin St., Downtown ☎ 813/229–1553) is known for one of Tampa's best martinis and one of its most eclectic jukeboxes. **Improv Comedy Theater & Restaurant** (✉ Centro Ybor, 1600 E. 8th Ave., Ybor City ☎ 813/864–4000 ⊕ www.improvtampa.com) stars top comedians in performances Wednesday through Sunday. **Metropolis** (✉ 3447 W. Kennedy Blvd., Central Tampa ☎ 813/871–2410), a gay club near the University of Tampa, has DJs and male strippers. Catch live comedy Wednesday through Sunday nights at **Side Splitters** (✉ 12938 N. Dale Mabry Hwy., Central Tampa ☎ 813/960–1197 ⊕ www.sidesplitterscomedy.com). **Skippers Smokehouse** (✉ 910 Skipper Rd., Northeast Tampa ☎ 813/971–0666), a junkyard-style restaurant and oyster bar, has live reggae Wednesday, Grateful Dead night on Thursday, blues Friday through Sunday, and great smoked fish every night. **Stumps Supper Club** (✉ 615 Channelside Dr., Downtown ☎ 813/226–2261) serves Southern food, and has live dance music daily and a DJ on Friday and Saturday. The bar **Legends** at the Wyndham Harbour Island Hotel (✉ 725 S. Harbour Island Blvd., Harbour Island ☎ 813/229–5000) has a great bay view, and two TVs behind the bar for viewing sports.

International Plaza's **Bay Street** (✉ 2223 N. West Shore Blvd., Airport Area) has become one of Tampa's dining and imbibing hot spots.

Sports & the Outdoors

BASEBALL Locals and tourists flock each March to see the **New York Yankees** (✉ Legends Field, 1 Steinbrenner Dr., near corner of Dale Mabry Hwy. and Martin Luther King Jr. Blvd., off I–275 Exit 41B, Central Tampa ☎ 813/879–2244 or 813/875–7753) play about 17 spring-training games at their 10,382-seat stadium. Call for tickets. From April through September, the stadium belongs to a Yankee farm team, the **Tampa Yankees,** who play 70 games against the likes of the Daytona Cubs and the Sarasota Red Sox.

CANOEING In northeast Tampa, **Canoe Escape** (✉ 9335 E. Fowler Ave., ½ mi east of I–75, Tampa ☎ 813/986–2067) arranges guided or self-guided trips from two hours' to all-day duration on the upper Hillsborough River, abounding with alligators, ibises, hawks, and other wildlife.

DOG RACING **Tampa Greyhound Track** (✉ 8300 N. Nebraska Ave. ☎ 813/932–4313) holds dog races from early June to December.

FISHING Captain Jim Lemke of **Light Tackle Adventures** (✉ 8613 Beth Ct., Odessa ☎ 813/917–4989 or 813/920–5460) is an outfitter who arranges bay, backwater, offshore, and flats fishing trips for everything from snook to tarpon.

FOOTBALL Seeing the National Football League's **Tampa Bay Buccaneers** (✉ Raymond James Stadium, 4201 N. Dale Mabry Hwy., Central Tampa

☎ 813/870–2700 or 800/282–0683) play isn't easy without connections, since the entire stadium is booked by season-ticket holders years in advance. The Arena Football League team **Tampa Bay Storm** (✉ St. Pete Times Forum, 401 Channelside Dr., Downtown ☎ 813/301–6900) plays about 16 games in its January-to-May season. The Storm is a perennial contender in the Arena League and has a hot rivalry with the Orlando Predators.

GOLF **Babe Zaharias Golf Course** (✉ 11412 Forest Hills Dr., Northeast Tampa ☎ 813/631–4374) is a challenging 18-hole public course with water hazards on 8 holes, green fee: $28/$39. A pro is on hand to give lessons. **Bloomingdale Golfers Club** (✉ 4113 Great Golfers Pl., Southeast Tampa ☎ 813/685–4105) has 18 holes, a two-tiered driving range, a 1-acre putting green, and a restaurant, green fee: $19/$49. **The Claw at USF** (✉ 13801 N. 46th St., North Tampa ☎ 813/632–6893) is named for its many dog-legged fairways. The 18-hole par-71 course is on a preserve with moss-draped oaks and towering pines, and is free of any on-course housing developments; green fee: $27/$52. **The Club at Eaglebrooke** (✉ 1300 Eaglebrooke Blvd., Lakeland, Polk County, 30 mi from Tampa ☎ 863/701–0101) is an 18-hole course, green fee: $45–$69. Twenty miles north of Tampa, **Lake Jovita Golf & Country Club** (✉ 12900 Lake Jovita Blvd., Dade City ☎ 352/588–9200 or 877/481–2652) has a semiprivate 36-hole course, green fee: $119. Golfers rotate from the back nine holes to the front nine. The **Saddlebrook Resort** (✉ 5700 Saddlebrook Way, Wesley Chapel ☎ 813/973–1111) has 36 holes, green fee: $180. There's also a driving range, golf shop, on-site pro, and resort spa. The public, 18-hole course at **Tournament Players Club of Tampa Bay** (✉ 5300 W. Lutz Lake Fern Rd., Lutz ☎ 813/949–0090), 15 mi north of Tampa, was designed by Bobby Weed and Chi Chi Rodriguez, green fee: $79/$153.

HORSE RACING **Tampa Bay Downs** (✉ Race Track Rd., off Rte. 580, Oldsmar ☎ 813/855–4401) holds thoroughbred races from December to May, plus simulcast TV broadcasts of other thoroughbred races at tracks around the nation.

ICE HOCKEY The National Hockey League's **Tampa Bay Lightning** (✉ St. Pete Times Forum, 401 Channelside Dr., Downtown ☎ 813/301–6600) play at the 21,500-seat St. Pete Times Forum (formerly the Ice Palace), a classy, $153-million downtown waterfront arena. It's near the Florida Aquarium and Channelside and close enough to both Ybor City and Hyde Park to venture to either spot to eat before the game. There's a trolley from the forum to Ybor City, and those with a ticket stub can get discounts at several restaurants.

TENNIS & The **City of Tampa Tennis Complex at HCC** (✉ 3901 W. Tampa Bay Blvd.,
RACQUETBALL Central Tampa ☎ 813/223–8602), across from Raymond James Stadium and immediately north of Tampa International Airport, has 12 clay courts and 16 hard courts ($5 an hour for clay courts; $2.50 an hour for hard courts). All courts are lighted. The complex also has four racquetball courts.

Shopping

For bargains, stop at the **Big Top** (✉ 9250 E. Fowler Ave., Northeast Tampa ☎ 813/986–4004), open weekends 9 to 4:30, where vendors hawk new and used items at 1,000-plus booths. The **Channelside shopping and entertainment complex** (✉ 615 Channelside Dr., Downtown) offers movie theaters, shops, restaurants, and clubs; the official Tampa Bay visitors center is also here. If you want to grab something at Neiman-Marcus on your way to the airport, the upscale **International Plaza** (✉ 2223 N. Westshore Blvd., Airport Area) mall, which includes Betsey Johnson, J. Crew, L'Occitane, Louis Vuitton, Tiffany & Co., and many other shops, is immediately south of the airport. Bay Street, the mall's dining "district," is one of Tampa's hot spots. **Old Hyde Park Village** (✉ Swan Ave. near Bayshore Blvd., Hyde Park) is a gentrified shopping district like the ones you find in every major American city. Williams-Sonoma and Brooks Brothers are mixed in with bistros and sidewalk cafés. There are more than 120 shops, department stores, and eateries in one of the area's biggest market complexes, **Westfield Shopping Town at Brandon** (✉ Grand Regency and Rte. 60, Brandon), an attractively landscaped complex near Interstate 75, about 20 minutes east of downtown by car. If you are shopping for hand-rolled cigars, head for 7th Avenue in **Ybor City**, where a few hand-rollers practice their craft in small shops.

St. Petersburg

21 mi west of Tampa.

St. Petersburg and the Pinellas Coast form the thumb of the hand that juts out of Florida's west coast and grasps Tampa Bay. There are two distinct parts of St. Petersburg—the downtown and cultural area, centered on the bay, and the beach area, a string of barrier islands that faces the gulf and includes St. Pete Beach, Treasure Island, and Madeira Beach. Causeways link beach communities to the mainland peninsula.

▶ ⑩ If you can't decide whether to go in-line skating or saltwater fishing, do both at once (depending on your level of athleticism) on Tampa Bay's car-free **Friendship TrailBridge**, formerly the Gandy Bay Bridge (U.S. Highway 92), which connects Tampa and St. Petersburg. The trail runs parallel to the newer Gandy Bridge and can be accessed from either Tampa or St. Petersburg. The 2½-mi bridge will eventually connect to another 21 mi of trails, and when complete, will make it the world's second longest over-the-water recreational trail. It has no facilities except for portable potties that have been placed at either end of the two-lane concrete span. The recreational-trail experience is like going to sea on foot. Long wooden decks on each side of the bridge (open 24 hours) are reserved for anglers, and the former traffic lanes of the bridge are open sunrise to sunset to runners, walkers, bicyclists, and in-line skaters. ☎ 727/549–6099 ⊕ *www.friendshiptrail.org.*

☼ ⑪ **Sunken Gardens** is one of Florida's most beautiful natural attractions. This 100-year-old botanical paradise—check out photos of its colorful past in the gift shop—has cascading waterfalls, koi ponds, a walk-through butterfly house, and exotic gardens where more than 50,000 tropical plants and flowers thrive amid groves of some of the area's most spectacular palm trees. You can arrange a guided tour, and there are special events and workshops year-round. The on-site restaurant, open for dinner, and Great Explorations, a hands-on kids' museum (ask for the dual-admission ticket and save a few bucks), make this place a family favorite. ⊠ *1825 4th St. N* ☎ *727/551–3100* ⊕ *www.sunkengardens. org* ☞ *$8* ☉ *Mon.–Sat. 10–4:30, Sun. noon–4:30.*

Ⓒ ⑱ At **Great Explorations** you'll never hear "Don't touch." The museum is hands-on through and through, with a Robot Lab, Climb Wall, Lie Detector, and other interactive play areas. Smart exhibits like the Tennis Ball Launcher, which uses compressed air to propel a ball through a series of tubes, and Sounds Waves, where Styrofoam pellets in a clear tube show the differences in sound frequencies, employ low-tech to teach kids (and parents) hi-tech principles. ⊠ *1925 4th St. N* ☎ *727/821–8992* ⊕ *www.greatexplorations.org* ☞ *$8* ☉ *Mon.–Sat. 10–4:30, Sun. noon–4:30.*

⑮ In a wonderful conversion of a downtown department store, the **Florida International Museum** has become a major focal point of the central business district. With historic, cultural, and educational exhibitions, the museum displays new treasures each season. The much anticipated exhibition "Diana: A Celebration" opened in winter 2005, direct from the Althorp Estate in England. On display are authentic memorabilia and film footage from the Princess of Wales' childhood, a collection of 28 dresses including her resplendent royal wedding gown, jewels, and other items. ⊠ *100 2nd St. N, off I–275 Exit 23A* ☎ *727/ 822–3693 or 800/777–9882* ⊕ *www.floridamuseum.org* ☞ *$15* ☉ *Mon.–Sat. 10–5, Sun. 12–5.*

Downtown St. Petersburg got a massive infusion of vibrancy with the ⑭ opening of **BayWalk,** a shopping, dining, and entertainment mall in a square-block complex incorporating California mission–style design and courtyard areas lined with trendy eateries, bars, shops, and a 20-screen movie theater. Among the restaurants at 2nd Avenue North and 2nd Street (off I–275 Exit 23A) are Dan Marino's Fine Food & Spirits; dish; Johnny Rockets, of national hamburger-chain fame; and Wet Willies, a see-and-be-seen bar. ⊠ *Bordered by 2nd St. N, 2nd Ave. N, 1st St. N., and 3rd Ave. N.*

⑫ The downtown **Florida Holocaust Museum** is the fourth-largest museum of its kind in the United States. It has the permanent *History, Heritage, and Hope* exhibit, an original boxcar, and an extensive collection of photographs, art, and artifacts. A popular display includes portraits and biographies of Holocaust survivors. The museum was conceived as a learning center for children, so many of the exhibits avoid overly graphic content; parents are warned prior to entering a gallery if any of the subject matter is potentially too intense for kids. ⊠ *55 5th St. S* ☎ *727/ 820–0100 or 800/960–7448* ⊕ *www.flholocaustmuseum.org* ☞ *$8* ☉ *Weekdays 10–5, weekends noon–5.*

Outstanding examples of European, American, pre-Columbian, and ⑬ Asian art are at the **Museum of Fine Arts,** a gorgeous Mediterranean revival structure on the waterfront one block from the Pier. You'll find major works by American artists ranging from Whistler to O'Keeffe to Rauschenberg and Lichtenstein, but the museum is known for its collection of French artists, including Fragonard, Cézanne, Monet, Rodin, Gauguin, and Renoir. There are also photography exhibits that draw from a permanent collection of more than 1,200 works. Docents give narrated gallery tours. Admission prices and museum hours are sometimes increased for special exhibits. ⊠ *255 Beach Dr. NE* ☎ *727/896–2667* ⊕ *www.fine-arts.org* 🖃 *$8* ☉ *Tues.–Sat. 10–5, Sun. 1–5.*

⑯ Learn about the history of the Tampa Bay region, from the Tocobaga Indians to America's first commercial airline, at the **St. Petersburg Museum of History.** Exhibits include those on Native American primitive shell tools, a 400-year-old dugout canoe, an early-European settlement, the railroad era, the growth of tourism, St. Petersburg's own Webb's City (once hailed as the world's largest drug store), and a full-size replica of the Benoist Airboat flown by pioneer aviator Tony Jannus. Admission to the museum is free Monday starting at 5 PM. ⊠ *335 2nd Ave. NE* ☎ *727/894–1052* ⊕ *www.stpetemuseumofhistory.org* 🖃 *$7* ☉ *Mon. 10–7, Tues.–Sat. 10–5, Sun. 1–5.*

⑰
Fodor'sChoice
★ The world's most comprehensive collection of originals by Spanish surrealist Salvador Dalí is at the **Salvador Dalí Museum.** The collection includes 95 oils, more than 100 watercolors and drawings, and 1,300 graphics, sculptures, photographs, and objets d'art, including floor-to-ceiling paintings. Frequent tours are led by well-informed docents. How did the collection end up here? A rich industrialist and friend of Dalí, Ohio magnate A. Reynolds Morse, was looking for a museum site after his huge Dalí collection began to overflow his mansion. The people of St. Petersburg vied admirably for the collection, and the museum was established here as a result. ⊠ *1000 3rd St. S* ☎ *727/823–3767 or 800/442–3254* ⊕ *www.salvadordalimuseum.org* 🖃 *$14* ☉ *Mon.–Wed., Fri., and Sat. 9:30–5:30, Thurs. 9:30–8, Sun. noon–5:30.*

★ ⑲ **Sunshine Skyway,** a 4-mi-long bridge on a section of Interstate 275, connects Pinellas and Manatee counties. The roadway is 183 feet above Tampa Bay at its highest point, and the view out over the bay is spectacular. See the several small islands that dot the bay if you're heading southeast, St. Pete Beach if you're going northwest. Exits off the bridge lead to the old bridge, now known as "the world's longest fishing pier."

⑳ Spread over five small islands, or keys, 1,136-acre **Fort De Soto Park** lies at the mouth of Tampa Bay. It has 7 mi of beaches, two fishing piers, picnic and camping grounds, and a historic fort. The fort for which it's named was built on the southern end of Mullet Key to protect sea lanes in the gulf during the Spanish-American War. Roam the fort or wander the beaches of any of the islands within the park. ⊠ *3500 Pinellas Bayway S, Tierra Verde* ☎ *727/582–2267* 🖃 *Free* ☉ *Beaches, daily 7–sunset; fishing and boat ramp, 24 hrs.*

㉑ **Pass-A-Grille Beach,** at the southern end of St. Pete Beach, has parking meters, a snack bar, restrooms, and showers. ⊠ *Off Gulf Blvd. (Rte. 699), St. Pete Beach.*

㉒ St. Pete Beach (✉ 11260 Gulf Blvd.) is a free beach on Treasure Island. There are dressing rooms, metered parking, and a snack bar.

㉓ In the middle of the mouth of Tampa Bay lies a small (350 acres) and largely unspoiled island, **Egmont Key,** now a state park. On the island are the ruins of Fort De Soto's sister fortification, **Fort Dade,** built during the Spanish-American War to protect Tampa Bay. The primary inhabitant of the 2-mi-long island is the threatened gopher tortoise. Shelling and nature-viewing are rewarding. The only way to get here, however, is by boat. **Dolphin Landings Tours** (☎ 727/360–7411 ⊕ www.dolphinlandings.com) does a four-hour shelling trip, a two-hour dolphin-sighting excursion, back-bay fishing or party-boat fishing, and other outings.

Where to Stay & Eat

$$$–$$$$ ✕ **Chateau France.** Downtown St. Petersburg has grown up around this 1901 Victorian house, which today provides a most legitimate Gallic dining experience. Have traditional French dishes such as coq au vin and Dover sole meunière. Filet mignon is a specialty; it comes in seven variations nightly. Chocolate soufflé and flaming crepes suzette prepared tableside are mainstays. ✉ *136 4th Ave. NE* ☎ *727/894–7163* ⚲ *Reservations essential* ▭ *AE, D, DC, MC, V* ⊘ *No lunch.*

★ **$$–$$$$** ✕ **Marchand's Grill.** Once the Pompeii Room in the former Vinoy Hotel, opened in 1925, this wonderful eatery has frescoed ceilings and a spectacular view of Tampa Bay and the nearby boat docks. The food is impressive as well. The imaginative, changing menu lists temptations such as asparagus ravioli, roasted eggplant soup, browned gnocchi with wild mushrooms and pinot grigio broth, and seafood bouillabaisse. The wine list is extensive, including a number of by-the-glass selections. There's live music Tuesday through Saturday nights. ✉ *Renaissance Vinoy Resort, 501 5th Ave. NE* ☎ *727/894–1000* ▭ *AE, D, DC, MC, V.*

$–$$$$ ✕ **Hurricane Seafood Restaurant.** On Pass-A-Grille Beach, this seafood establishment has been serving the Tampa Bay area since 1977. A steady crowd of tourists now joins regulars for the catch-of-the-day prepared however you like, which could include fried, grilled, blackened, or jerk. Grilled grouper with tomato tapenade, basil olive oil, mango coulis, and seasonal lobster selections are other top menu items. Crowds head to the rooftop sundeck to view the gorgeous sunsets. ✉ *807 Gulf Way* ☎ *727/360–9558* ▭ *AE, D, MC, V.*

$–$$$ ✕ **Bonefish Grill.** A great sampling of local seafood is the trademark of this urbane eatery near downtown. Rock shrimp fettuccine diablo and wood-grilled grouper are local offerings. Mussels sautéed with tomatoes, garlic, basil, and lemon-wine sauce is a must-try appetizer. If you don't care for fish, pork tenderloin portobello piccata is stellar. You won't find the namesake fish on the menu, incidentally; bonefish is popular for sportfishing in the keys, but it's far too bony to eat. ✉ *5901 4th St. N* ☎ *727/521–3434* ▭ *AE, D, DC, MC, V* ⊘ *No lunch.*

$–$$$ ✕ **Captain Al's Waterfront Bar and Grill.** At the end of the St. Petersburg Pier, this cheerful and casual restaurant looks out at the bay. The indecisive will enjoy Captain Al's platter, with shrimp, oysters, crab cake, and conch fritters—all fried. The signature crab-dip appetizer is sure to please while you sip a cocktail at the waterside tiki bar. ✉ *800 2nd Ave. NE* ☎ *727/898–5800* ☐ *AE, D, MC, V.*

$–$$$ ✗ **Gratzzi.** This warm northern-Italian eatery hits local critics' short lists of best restaurants, with tasty classics such as veal saltimbocca and osso buco with pan-seared polenta. Although the *zuppa di pesce* (fish soup) is a pricey dish at $18.99 a bowl, it's also one of the best, with expertly prepared mussels, clams, shrimp, scallops, and whitefish in a red sauce on pasta. Other dishes on the extensive menu are more affordable and include rotisserie-cooked meat and seafood. ✉ *199 2nd Ave. N, BayWalk* ☎ *727/822–7769* ☐ *AE, D, DC, MC, V* ⊘ *No lunch Sun.*

$–$$$ ✗ **Spoto's Steak Joint.** The formula is quite simple here: aged Angus beef, expertly prepared. The restaurant serves about every cut one can imagine, from a huge porterhouse to a petit filet. And if steak is not your thing, smoked baby-back ribs is another specialty. You'll find chicken, duck, and seafood. Dishes are served with hot bread, fresh vegetables, and soup or salad. ✉ *4871 Park St.* ☎ *727/545–9481* ✉ *1280 Main St., Dunedin* ☎ *727/734–0008* ☐ *AE, D, MC, V* ⊘ *No lunch.*

¢–$$$ ✗ **Dan Marino's Fine Food & Spirits.** Upscale yet casual, this restaurant serves American dishes such as steaks, pastas, and burgers; a highlight is the sesame seared tuna. If the weather's right, there's plenty of patio seating. While here you might also enjoy a key lime pie or Snickers martini from the Martini Bar, which is connected to the restaurant. ✉ *BayWalk, 121 2nd Ave. N* ☎ *727/822–4413* ☐ *AE, D, MC, V.*

¢–$$ ✗ **Ted Peters Famous Smoked Fish.** A Pinellas County beach-culture in-
Fodor'sChoice stitution, this place is a favorite with flip-flop–wearing anglers who sit
★ on the picnic benches, soak up a beer or three, and devour the wonderful smoked fish. The menu includes mackerel, mullet, mahimahi, and salmon, but all are smoked and seasoned to perfection and served with heaping helpings of German potato salad and coleslaw. They also serve what many consider to be the best burger in the Tampa Bay region. The popular smoked fish spread is available to go. There's also indoor seating. Closing time is 7:30 PM. ✉ *1350 Pasadena Ave. S, South Pasadena* ☎ *727/381–7931* ⌛ *Reservations not accepted* ☐ *No credit cards* ⊘ *Closed Tues.*

¢–$ ✗ **TooJay's.** Knishes and roast brisket with potato pancakes are the mainstays at this kosher-style deli with a busy dining room at lunch and dinner. Other selections include salmon cakes, shepherd's pie, and shrimp salad. Don't miss the éclair, a house specialty. The restaurant is nothing fancy, but it's bright and friendly, and management ensures you're waited on promptly. Everything on the menu is available for takeout. ✉ *141 2nd Ave. N, BayWalk, St. Petersburg* ☎ *727/823–3354* ⌛ *Reservations not accepted* ☐ *AE, D, DC, MC, V.*

¢ ✗ **Adobo Grill.** The made-to-order Mexican fast food here is light years beyond that of any nationwide chain. House specialties include roast pork burritos and grilled mahi tacos. Service is over-the-counter, and there's seating indoors and under umbrellas on the patio. ✉ *164 2nd Ave. N, BayWalk* ☎ *727/823–8226* ⌛ *Reservations not accepted* ☐ *AE, D, MC, V.*

$$$$ ☷ **Don CeSar Beach Resort, a Loews Hotel.** Once a favorite of Scott and
Fodor'sChoice Zelda Fitzgerald, this sprawling, sybaritic beachfront "Pink Palace,"
★ now part of the Loews hotel chain, has long been a Gulf Coast landmark
because of its remarkable architecture. Steeped in turn-of-the-last-century elegance, the hotel claims a rich history, complete with a resident
ghost. The restaurant, Maritana Grille, specializes in Florida seafood and
is lined with huge fish tanks. The more casual Beach House Suites by the
Don CeSar, less than ½ mi from the main building, has one-bedroom condos and a great little beach bar. The hotel now has Wi-Fi. ⊠ *3400 Gulf
Blvd., St. Pete Beach 33706* ☎ *727/360–1881 or 800/282–1116* 📠 *727/
363–5034* ⊕ *www.doncesar.com or www.loewshotels.com* ⤴ *Resort:
234 rooms, 43 suites; Beach House: 70 condos* ♻ *3 restaurants, ice-cream
parlor, room service, some in-room safes, some kitchens, cable TV, in-
room data ports, 2 pools, health club, hair salon, massage, spa, beach,
boating, jet skiing, parasailing, volleyball, 3 bars, lobby lounge, shops,
babysitting, children's programs (ages 5–12), dry cleaning, laundry service, concierge, Internet, business services, meeting rooms, parking (fee),
some pets allowed, no-smoking rooms* ⊟ *AE, D, DC, MC, V.*

$$$$ ☷ **Renaissance Vinoy Resort and Golf Club.** Rooms in the original 1925
Fodor'sChoice hotel building, listed on the National Register of Historic Places, have
★ more character than others at the property, but all of the spacious units
are comfortable and stylish. They come with three phones and bathrobes.
The resort overlooks Tampa Bay, and a tiny bayside beach several
blocks away is good for strolling (though unswimmable). Transportation is provided to gulf beaches 20 minutes away. Other offerings include a Ron Garl–designed golf course with a stunning clubhouse, a big
marina, and pool attendants who deliver drinks. The hotel is convenient
to downtown museums, the Pier, or BayWalk. ⊠ *501 5th Ave. NE, 33701*
☎ *727/894–1000* 📠 *727/822–2785* ⊕ *www.vinoyrenaissanceresort.
com* ⤴ *345 rooms, 15 suites* ♻ *5 restaurants, room service, minibars,
cable TV, in-room data ports, 18-hole golf course, 12 tennis courts, 2
pools, health club, hair salon, outdoor hot tub, massage, spa, boating,
marina, 4 bars, lobby lounge, shop, babysitting, dry cleaning, laundry
facilities, laundry service, concierge, business services, car rental, no-smoking rooms* ⊟ *AE, D, DC, MC, V.*

$$$$ ☷ **TradeWinds Islands Resort.** Most rooms have a view of the beach at
this sprawling gulf-front property, which is actually two resorts in one.
The resort has some of the showmanship of an Orlando hotel, with a
huge man-made waterway inside the complex, complete with paddleboats. The resort's own kids character, Beaker the Toucan, makes appearances at kids' programs and can even tuck your child into bed at
night for a fee. There are on-site swimming lessons for children and adults.
⊠ *5500 Gulf Blvd., St. Pete Beach 33706* ☎ *727/363–2212* 📠 *727/
363–2222* ⊕ *www.tradewindsresort.com* ⤴ *434 rooms, 310 suites (Island Grand: 378 rooms, 207 suites; Sandpiper: 56 rooms, 103 suites)*
♻ *11 restaurants, ice-cream parlor, pizzeria, in-room safes, kitchenettes,
refrigerators, cable TV, in-room data ports, miniature golf, 4 tennis courts,
7 pools (1 indoor), 2 health clubs, 3 outdoor hot tubs, massage, spa,
beach, boating, jet skiing, volleyball, 3 bars, sports bar, shops, babysitting, children's programs (ages 4–15), dry cleaning, laundry facilities,*

laundry service, concierge, Internet, business services, meeting rooms,
parking (fee), no-smoking floors ⊟ *AE, D, DC, MC, V.*

$$–$$$$ ⊞ **Island's End Resort.** These simply decorated one- and three-bedroom
cottages have water views. Outdoors, attractive wooden walkways lead
to latticework sitting areas and peaceful gazebos. The grounds are nicely
landscaped; walk to the beach, restaurants, and shops. Grills are avail-
able if you want to barbecue. The small resort makes a great place for
families who want to enjoy the beach life. Continental breakfast is
served on Tuesday, Thursday, and Saturday. ⊠ *1 Pass-A-Grille Way, St.*
Pete Beach 33706 ☎ *727/360–5023* 🖨 *727/367–7890* ⊕ *www.*
islandsend.com ⇌ *6 cottages* ⚭ *Kitchens, microwaves, cable TV, in-*
room VCRs, fishing, laundry facilities, some pets allowed ⊟ *MC, V.*

$$$ ⊞ **Inn at the Bay.** In a three-story 1910 Victorian home, this charmer
has four-poster beds and antique furniture in the guest rooms and suites.
The Sailboat Suite has a fireplace and whirlpool bath. A full hot breakfast is served at your leisure. The bed-and-breakfast is near downtown,
a short distance from the museums and the Pier. ⊠ *126 4th Ave. NE,*
33701 ☎ *727/822–1700 or 888/873–2122* 🖨 *727/896–7411* ⊕ *www.*
innatthebay.com ⇌ *7 rooms, 5 suites* ⚭ *Dining room, fans, some in-*
room hot tubs, some minibars, cable TV, in-room data ports, meeting
room, free parking; no kids under 9, no smoking ⊟ *AE, D, DC, MC,*
V ⦿ *BP.*

$$$ ⊞ **Mansion House and the Courtyard on Fifth.** Mansion House I and Man-
sion House II are charming wood-frame homes that are done in the Arts
and Crafts style. The former is rumored to have been the home of the
first mayor of St. Petersburg. The homes are next door to each other
and were built at the beginning of the 20th century. The first and sec-
ond floors of each house have inviting, individually decorated rooms;
the most appealing might be the Carriage Room, which has a cathedral
ceiling and an old-fashioned, custom-made, built-in, four-poster bed. Wi-
Fi is accessible throughout the property, including poolside. A pleasant
15-minute walk from the Pier, this B&B is also within walking distance
of restaurants, shops, and art galleries. ⊠ *105 5th Ave. NE, 33701* ☎ *727/*
821–9391 or 800/274–7520 🖨 *727/821–6906* ⊕ *www.mansionbandb.*
com ⇌ *13 rooms, 1 carriage house* ⚭ *Dining room, fans, cable TV, in-*
room data ports, pool, hot tub, library, Internet, business services, meet-
ing rooms, free parking, some pets allowed (fee); no smoking ⊟ *AE,*
D, DC, MC, V ⦿ *BP.*

Nightlife & the Arts

THE ARTS **American Stage** (⊠ 211 3rd St. S ☎ 727/823–7529) performs in an in-
timate 130-seat theater. In April and May, the company takes Shake-
speare's plays outdoors.

NIGHTLIFE **Carlie's** (⊠ 7020 49th St. N ☎ 727/527–5214) is hopping practically
every night, with plenty of dancing to local bands. At **Cha Cha Coconuts**
(⊠ the Pier ☎ 727/822–6655), crowds catch live contemporary music
Friday through Sunday year-round. **Coliseum Ballroom** (⊠ 535 4th Ave.
N ☎ 727/892–5202) has ballroom dancing and group lessons on most
Wednesday afternoons and Saturday nights. Call ahead. At **Marchand's**
(⊠ 501 5th Ave. NE ☎ 727/894–1000), a fine-dining spot inside the

posh Vinoy Hotel, sophisticated locals and well-informed out-of-town-ers gather at the bar for after-dinner cocktails and dancing to top-notch jazz bands. It's the most genteel place in town for a nightcap. The **Rare Olive** (⊠ 300 Central Ave., corner of 3rd St. ☎ 727/822–7273) adds a touch of class to an otherwise jeans-and-T-shirt nightlife scene with mar-tinis, banquettes, and an assortment of bands and deejays.

Sports & the Outdoors

BASEBALL Hometown favorites, the **Tampa Bay Devil Rays** (⊠ Tropicana Field, 1 Tropicana Dr., off I–275 ☎ 727/825–3250 or 888/326–7297) play in an air-conditioned domed stadium. Spring training is at **Progress En-ergy Park** (⊠ 230 First St. S ☎ 727/898–7297).

DOG RACING Greyhound races are held from early December through mid-June at **Derby Lane** (⊠ 10490 Gandy Blvd. N ☎ 727/812–3339).

GOLF **Mangrove Bay Golf Course** (⊠ 875 62nd Ave. NE ☎ 727/893–7800) has 18 holes and a driving range, green fee: $30/$42.

Shopping

One of the state's more notable bookstores is **Haslam's** (⊠ 2025 Cen-tral Ave. ☎ 727/822–8616), a family-owned emporium that's been doing business just west of downtown St. Petersburg for more than 70 years. The store carries some 300,000 volumes, from cutting-edge best-sellers to ancient tomes. If you value a good book or simply like to browse, you could easily spend an afternoon here. Designer boutiques, movie theaters, and trendy restaurants can be found at the downtown shop-ping plaza **BayWalk** (⊠ 153 2nd Ave. N). **John's Pass Village and Board-walk** (⊠ 12901 Gulf Blvd., Madeira Beach) is a collection of shops and restaurants in an old-style fishing village, where you can pass the time watching pelicans cavorting and dive-bombing for food. A five-story struc-ture on the bay front, the **Pier** (⊠ 800 2nd Ave. NE), near the Museum of Fine Arts, looks like an inverted pyramid. Inside are numerous shops and eating spots. On weekends between 8 and 4, some 1,500 vendors set up a flea market on 125 acres at the **Wagonwheel** (⊠ 7801 Park Blvd., Pinellas Park).

Clearwater

12 mi north of St. Petersburg.

This sprawling town has many residential areas and small shopping plazas. There's a semi-quaint downtown area on the mainland, but the draw is the beaches along the barrier islands offshore.

 When pelicans become entangled in fishing lines, locals sometimes carry them to the nonprofit **Suncoast Seabird Sanctuary,** which is dedicated to the rescue, repair, recuperation, and release of sick and injured birds. At times there are between 500 and 600 land and sea birds in residence, including pelicans, egrets, herons, gulls, terns, sandhill cranes, hawks, owls, and cormorants. Many are kept in open-air pens while they re-cover. The sanctuary backs up to the Indian Rocks Beach. ⊠ *18328 Gulf Blvd., Indian Shores* ☎ 727/391–6211 🖾 *Donation welcome* ☺ *Daily 9–sunset; tours Wed. and Sun. at 2.*

㉕ **Indian Rocks Beach** (✉ Off Rte. 8, south of Clearwater Beach) tends to be a bit quieter and less crowded than Clearwater Beach.

㉖ South of Clearwater Beach, on Sand Key at Clearwater Pass, **Sand Key Park** (✉ 1060 Gulf Blvd. ☏ 727/588–4852) has a lovely beach, plenty of green space, a playground, and a picnic area.

㉗ The **Clearwater Marine Aquarium** is more than just a place to see exotic fish in a big glass tank—it's an opportunity to participate in the work of saving and caring for endangered marine species. Many of the sea turtles, dolphins, and other animals living at the aquarium were brought there to be rehabilitated from an injury or saved from danger. The aquarium conducts tours of the bays and islands around Clearwater, including a daily ecocruise on a pontoon boat (you might just see a dolphin or two), and kayak tours of Clearwater Harbor and St. Joseph Sound. ✉ 249 Windward Passage ☏ 727/441–1790 ⊕ www.cmaquarium.org ☑ $9 ☉ Weekdays 9–5, Sat. 9–4, Sun. 11–4.

㉘ Connected to downtown Clearwater by Memorial Causeway, **Clearwater Beach** (✉ Western end of State Rd. 60, 2 mi west of downtown Clearwater) is on a narrow island between Clearwater Harbor and the gulf. It has a widespread reputation for beach volleyball. There are lifeguards here as well as a marina, concessions, showers, and restrooms. Around Pier 60 there's a big, modern playground. This is the site for a nightly sunset celebration complete with musicians and artisans. It's one of the area's nicest and busiest beaches, but it's also one of the costliest in terms of parking fees.

Fodor'sChoice
★

off the beaten path

PINEWOOD CULTURAL PARK – Three out-of-the-way but worthwhile attractions grace this space. **Florida Botanical Gardens** (✉ 12175 125th St. N, Largo ☏ 727/582–2200 ⊕ www.flbg.org ☑ Free ☉ Daily 7–sunset) welcomes you to 150 acres of native and exotic ornamental plants. Demonstrations teach environmentally friendly gardening techniques. The University of Florida Pinellas County Extension maintains the gardens. More than 24 historic local structures are gathered at **Heritage Village** (✉ 11909 125th St. N, Largo ☏ 727/582–2123 ☑ Donations accepted ☉ Tues.–Sat. 10–4, Sun. 1–4), including a log cabin and Victorian-era home, and they trace local history back to the 1850s. **Gulf Coast Museum of Art** (✉ 12211 Walsingham Rd., Largo ☏ 727/518–6833 ☑ $5 ☉ Tues.–Sat. 10–4, Sun. noon–4) completes the complex with permanent showings of Florida artists and visiting exhibits.

Where to Stay & Eat

¢–$$$ ✕ **PJ's Oyster Bar & Seafood Restaurant.** Follow the crowds to this back-alley long-timer where rolls of paper towels spin overhead on wire hangers and beer flows freely. Seafood selections range from fried catfish to more elegant choices such as orange-glazed sushi-grade tuna. The all-day menu balances seafood with sandwiches and pastas. ✉ 500 1st St., Indian Rocks Beach ☏ 727/596–5898 ▭ AE, MC, V.

$–$$ ✕ **Kaiko Japanese Restaurant.** Step up to the counter or grab a table and settle down for sushi and other dishes. The large appetizer menu gives you a chance to try lots of items, including fried tofu, vegetable sushi, and sashimi. Entrées include grilled seafood and beef, and teriyaki chicken. Try the fried ice cream for dessert. ⊠ *2475 McMullen Booth Rd.* ☎ *727/791–6640* ☰ *AE, D, MC, V* ⊘ *No lunch weekends.*

$$$–$$$$ 🏨 **Safety Harbor Resort & Spa.** The focus here is the 50,000-square-foot spa, with all the latest in therapies and treatments. The pleasant hamlet of Safety Harbor is also a point of interest, with charming shops along the nearby main street. The resort was built over hot springs on Tampa Bay in 1926, but little of the original architecture remains. The springs still function, however, feeding into pools, the spa, and water coolers. The property has on-site golf and tennis instruction, and golf courses are 5 mi away. ⊠ *105 N. Bayshore Dr., Safety Harbor 34695* ☎ *727/ 726–1161 or 888/237–8772* 🖷 *727/724–8772* ⊕ *www.safetyharborspa. com* ⇩ *189 rooms, 4 suites* ⚐ *Restaurant, cable TV, in-room data ports, driving range, golf privileges, 9 tennis courts, 3 pools (1 indoor), fitness classes, gym, spa, laundry facilities, laundry service, Internet, business services, meeting room, some pets allowed, no-smoking rooms* ☰ *AE, D, DC, MC, V.*

$$$–$$$$ 🏨 **Sheraton Sand Key Resort.** This is a supreme spot for those searching for sun, sand, and surf. On 10 well-manicured acres, the nine-story, T-shape resort has many rooms with excellent gulf views, and others that look out over an adjacent park. All rooms have balconies or patios. Considered one of the top corporate meeting and convention hotels in the Clearwater area, the resort has amenities—such as a beautiful private beach—that make it ideal for leisure travelers, too. ⊠ *1160 Gulf Blvd., Clearwater Beach 33767* ☎ *727/595–1611* 🖷 *727/596–8488* ⊕ *www.sheratonsandkey. com* ⇩ *375 rooms, 15 suites* ⚐ *4 restaurants, room service, cable TV with video games, in-room data ports, 3 tennis courts, pool, wading pool, hot tub, health club, massage, sauna, beach, windsurfing, boating, jet skiing, 2 bars, babysitting, children's programs (ages 3–15), playground, some pets allowed, no-smoking floors* ☰ *AE, D, DC, MC, V.*

$$$ 🏨 **Best Western Sea Wake Beach Resort.** This light-terra-cotta-color, concrete, six-story hotel won't win any architectural awards, but it's right on the beach, and major renovations were completed in 2004. Rooms are nicely decorated, and many have balconies with excellent views of the gulf. ⊠ *691 S. Gulfview Blvd., 33967* ☎ *727/443–7652 or 888/329–8910* 🖷 *727/461–2836* ⊕ *www.seawake.com* ⇩ *110 rooms* ⚐ *Restaurant, room service, in-room safes, microwaves, refrigerators, cable TV, in-room data ports, pool, beach, fishing, bar, lounge, playground, dry cleaning, laundry service, business services, meeting room, airport shuttle, no-smoking rooms* ☰ *AE, D, DC, MC, V.*

★ $$–$$$ 🏨 **Belleview Biltmore Resort & Spa.** Built by railroad magnate Henry Plant, this huge 1896 Victorian resort looks like a *Great Gatsby* movie set. It is one of the world's largest wooden structures and is on the National Register of Historic Places. Units range from cozy little rooms to spacious suites that lie off long creaky corridors. The 21 acres overlook a narrow part of Clearwater Bay. The spa matches the Victorian opulence of the rest of the hotel, with the convenience of modern facilities. The hotel staff conducts daily historical tours. ⊠ *25 Belleview Blvd., 33756* ☎ *727/373–3000 or 800/237–8947* 🖷 *727/441–4173* ⊕ *www.*

belleviewbiltmore.com ⟡ 246 rooms, 38 suites ☼ 3 restaurants, in-room data ports, 18-hole golf course, 4 tennis courts, 3 pools (1 indoor), health club, massage, spa, boating, bicycles, 3 bars, playground, business services, meeting rooms, some pets allowed, no-smoking rooms ⊟ AE, D, DC, MC, V.

The Arts

Ruth Eckerd Hall (✉ 1111 N. McMullen Booth Rd. ☎ 727/791–7400 ⊕ www.rutheckerdhall.com) hosts many national performers of ballet, opera, and pop, classical, or jazz music.

Sports & the Outdoors

BASEBALL The **Philadelphia Phillies** (✉ Brighthouse Networks Field, 601 N. Old Coachman Rd. ☎ 727/441–8638, 727/442–8496 tickets) get ready for the season with spring training here. The stadium also hosts the Phillies' farm team.

BIKING **Lou's Bicycle Center** (✉ 8990 Seminole Blvd., Largo ☎ 727/398–2453) rents bikes, does quick repairs, and sells new bikes. There's an access point to the Pinellas Trail a couple of blocks west of Lou's on 86th Avenue Southwest.

The **Pinellas Trail** is a 35-mi paved route that spans Pinellas County. Once a railway, the trail runs adjacent to major thoroughfares, no more than 10 feet from the roadway, so you can access it from almost any point. When completed around 2006, it will run 47 mi. You get the flavor of neighborhoods and an amalgam of suburbs along the way. The trail, also popular with in-line skaters, has spawned trailside businesses such as repair shops and health-food cafés. There are also many lovely rural areas to bike through and plenty of places to rent bikes. Be wary of traffic in downtown Clearwater and on the congested areas of the Pinellas Trail, which still needs more bridges for crossing over busy streets. To start riding from the south end of the trail, park at Trailhead Park (37th Street South at 8th Avenue South) in St. Petersburg. To ride south from the north end, park your car in downtown Tarpon Springs (East Tarpon Avenue at North Stafford Avenue). The 2½-mi car-free **Friendship Trail** is part of the Pinellas Trail system. It's accessible from either Tampa or St. Petersburg, immediately adjacent to the Gandy Bridge.

GOLF **Clearwater Executive Golf Course** (✉ 1875 Airport Dr. ☎ 727/447–5272) has 18 holes and a driving range, green fee: $13/$28. **Largo Municipal Golf Course** (✉ 12500 131st St. N, Largo ☎ 727/518–3024) is an 18-hole par-62 executive course, green fee: $16/$26.

MINIATURE GOLF The live alligators advertised on the roadside sign for **Congo River Golf & Exploration Co.** (✉ 20060 U.S. 19 N, Clearwater ☎ 727/797–4222) are not in the water traps, just in a small, fenced-off lagoon adjacent to the course. The reptiles do, however, add a Florida touch to this highly landscaped course tucked into a small parcel of land adjacent to Clearwater's busiest north–south thoroughfare.

TENNIS **Shipwatch Yacht & Tennis Club** (✉ 11800 Shipwatch Dr., Largo ☎ 727/596–6862) has 11 clay courts, 3 of which are lighted for night play, and 2 hard courts.

Dunedin

㉙ *3 mi north of Clearwater.*

If the sound of bagpipes and the sight of men in kilts appeals to you, head to this town, named by two Scots in the 1880s. In March and April the Highland Games and in November the Celtic Festival pay tribute to the town's heritage. Dunedin also has a nicely restored historic downtown area—only about five blocks long—that has become a one-stop shopping area for antiques hunters and is also lined with gift shops and good, nonchain eateries.

Where to Eat

$$-$$$ ✕ **Bon Appetit.** Known for its creative fare, this restaurant has views of the Intracoastal Waterway and the gulf. European-trained chef-owners Peter Kreuziger and Karl Heinz Riedl change specials twice a month and offer salads and light entrées as well as such selections as broiled rack of lamb in herbed pecan crust and seafood mixed grill with vegetable rémoulade sauce. This is an excellent place to catch a sunset. ☒ *148 Marina Plaza* ☎ *727/733–2151* ▭ *AE, D, DC, MC, V.*

$-$$ ✕ **Sea Sea Riders.** In a pleasant old bungalow with a breezy patio that's enclosed and heated in winter, this seafood eatery has an eclectic menu that includes pasta dishes and homemade chili. Cornmeal-fried catfish and grouper cheek paella are among the best entrées. The cheesecake is worthy as well. Sunday brunch includes great omelets and fresh seafood. ☒ *221 Main St.* ☎ *727/734–1445* ▭ *AE, MC, V.*

★ ¢-$$ ✕ **Casa Tina.** The focus here is on Mexican dishes, including several vegetarian entrées. Try the enchiladas (with veggies or chicken) or chiles rellenos, roasted cheese-stuffed peppers. Cactus salad won't prick your tongue, but the tantalizing flavor created by tender pieces of cactus, cilantro, tomatoes, onions, lime, and *queso fresco* (a mild white cheese) might prick your taste buds. The place is often crowded, and service can be slow, but it's worth it. ☒ *369 Main St.* ☎ *727/734–9226* ▭ *AE, D, DC, MC, V* ☼ *Closed Mon.*

> **off the beaten path**

CALADESI ISLAND AND HONEYMOON ISLAND STATE PARKS – Sharing an entrance and a parking lot, these parks are just a few hundred yards from one another. However, whereas Honeymoon Island is right where you park, Caladesi Island is off the coast across Hurricane Pass and is accessible only by boat or ferry. One of Florida's few undeveloped barrier islands, 600-acre Caladesi Island has a beach on the gulf side, mangroves on the bay side, and a self-guided nature trail winding through the island's interior. Because it's so popular with locals, most of whom have their own boats, don't expect it to feel secluded on weekends. Park rangers are available to answer questions. A good spot for swimming, fishing, shelling, boating, and studying nature, the park has boardwalks, picnic shelters, bathhouses, and a concession stand. If you want to skip the ferry ride to Caladesi Island stay at Honeymoon Island, also an excellent state park, but with a less spectacular beach. It has the same elements as Caladesi, but a bridge connects it to the mainland. The park has the only section of beach north of Venice where it's okay to bring your pets—on a leash. ✉ *Dunedin Causeway to Honeymoon Island, then board ferry* ☎ *727/734–5263 ferry information, 727/469–5918 parks information* ✍ *Honeymoon $5 per car, ferry $8* ⊙ *Daily 8–sunset; ferry hourly 10–4:30 in fair weather.*

Sports & the Outdoors

BASEBALL   The **Toronto Blue Jays** (✉ Knology Park, 373 Douglas Ave., north of State Rd. 580 ☎ 727/733–9302) play about 18 spring training games here in March.

GOLF   **Dunedin Country Club** (✉ 1050 Palm Blvd. ☎ 727/733–7836), a semiprivate course, has 18 holes, a driving range, and a pro shop, green fee: $34/$55.

Tarpon Springs

10 mi north of Dunedin.

Tucked into a little harbor at the mouth of the Anclote River, this growing town was settled by Greek immigrants at the end of the 19th century. They came to practice their generations-old craft of sponge diving. Although bacterial and market forces seriously hurt the industry in the 1940s, sponging has returned, mostly as a focal point for tourism. The docks along Dodecanese Boulevard, the main waterfront street, are filled with sweet old buildings with shops and eateries. Tarpon Springs' other key street is Tarpon Avenue, about a mile south of Dodecanese. This old central business district has become a hub for antiques hunters. The influence of Greek culture is omnipresent; the community's biggest celebration is the annual Greek Orthodox Epiphany Celebration in January, in which teenage boys dive for a golden cross in Spring Bayou, a few blocks from Tarpon Avenue, during a ceremony followed by a street festival in the town's central business district.

㉛ Don't miss **St. Nicholas Greek Orthodox Church**, which is a replica of St. Sophia's in Istanbul and an excellent example of New Byzantine architecture. ✉ *36 N. Pinellas Ave.* ☎ *727/937–3540* ✍ *Donation suggested* ⊙ *Daily 9–4.*

㉜ **The Sponge Factory** is a museum and cultural center that reveals more than you ever imagined about how a lowly sea creature, the sponge, created the industry that built this village. See a film about these much-sought-after creatures from the phylum *porifera* and how they helped the town to prosper in the early 1900s. You'll come away converted to (and loaded up with) natural sponges and loofahs. ✉ *510 Dodecanese Blvd., off Rte. 19* ☎ *727/943–9498* ✍ *Free* ⊙ *Mon.–Sat. 10:30–6, Sun. 11:30–6.*

㉚ The **Konger Tarpon Springs Aquarium** is a privately owned attraction not nearly as extensive as the big aquariums in Tampa or Clearwater, but it's got some good exhibits, including a 120,000-gallon shark tank with a living coral reef inside. Divers feed the sharks in a show performed several times a day. There's also a baby-shark-and-stingray feeding tank, where you can feed the animals yourself—without going in the

CloseUp

BOBBING FOR SPONGES

ANIMALS THAT SWIM *or slither their way through Florida's semitropical waters have a vaunted place in state folklore. Several have been chosen as team mascots—the Miami Dolphins, Florida Marlins, and the University of Florida Gators, to name a few—a sign of the impact these animals have had on the state. But no aquatic creature has had a greater impact on the Tampa Bay area than the sponge.*

Unlike the reputedly intelligent dolphin, the sponge is no genius. It's hard to be smart when you consist of only one cell. The sponge that divers retrieve from the seabed, or perhaps the one you reach for in the shower, is actually a colony of millions of the one-cell organisms bound together in an organic matrix that makes up a soft, flexible lump.

As you learn if you check out Tarpon Springs' aging and modest Spongeorama, sponge diving predates the birth of Christ, and the first Greek sponge seekers actually worshiped the god Poseidon. For the past millennium or so, most spongers have been devoutly Greek Orthodox, and today many sponge boats carry a small shrine to St. Nicholas, the patron saint of mariners. The divers' deep devotion to their religion—and to Greek culture— resulted in the development of Tampa Bay's own little Greek village.

Sponge gathering actually began in the Florida Keys circa 1850, but it gained momentum around Tampa Bay after 1905, when George Cocoris brought to Florida the first mechanical diving apparatus, complete with a brass-helmeted diving suit and pump system, that enabled divers to stay in 75–100 feet of water for two hours at a time. Cocoris and those who worked with him soon discovered a particularly marketable type of sponge: the Rock Island wool sponge, so named because it

resembles fine wool and is found in abundance around Rock Island, off Florida's west coast. When word of Cocoris's success got back to Greece, more sponge-diving families headed west, and within a decade or so, several thousand of his fellow Greeks had settled around Tarpon Springs to share in its prosperity.

By the 1930s, Tarpon Springs was the largest U.S. sponging port, but in the late '40s and early '50s a sponge blight and the growing popularity of synthetic sponges nearly wiped out the local industry. Still, the hardy Greeks held on. They discovered that tourists were drawn more by the town's Hellenic culture than by the sponges sold in the dockside markets. In the ensuing 40 years Tarpon Springs' waterfront area has been turned into a delightful tourist district filled with Greek restaurants, Greek pastry shops, and Greek art galleries. And should you choose to see divers pull sponges from the seabed, you can book passage on one of the glass-bottom boats that leave hourly from the town docks.

And so the town owes its success to the humble sponge. Yet although you'll find bronze statues of sponge divers, with the exception of Spongeorama there is no tribute to the mono-cellular creature itself. Perhaps a future Florida sports team will choose the "Fightin' Sponges" as its mascot.

— Rowland Stiteler

water, of course. The freshwater tank has three 7-foot-long alligators. ⊠ *850 Dodecanese Blvd.* ☏ *727/938–5378* ☏ *$5.25* ⊙ *Mon.–Sat. 10–5, Sun. noon–5.*

③③ Sunset Beach (⊠ Gulf Rd.) is a small public beach with restrooms, picnic tables, grills, and a boat ramp.

③④ Howard Park Beach (⊠ Sunset Dr.) comes in two parts: a shady mainland picnic area and a white-sand beach island. The causeway is a popular hangout for windsurfers. The park has restrooms, picnic tables, and grills.

Where to Stay & Eat

$–$$$ ✕ **Pappas' Riverside Restaurant.** Though a bit institutional, this waterside restaurant allows a great view of the Anclote River and docks. Well-prepared dishes include moussaka and *dolmades* (grape leaves stuffed with rice and ground lamb). Grilled octopus is a more esoteric Greek specialty. Florida classics include grouper. ⊠ *10 W. Dodecanese Blvd.* ☏ *727/937–5101* ☰ *AE, MC, V.*

$–$$ ✕ **Bridie Gannon's Pub & Eatery.** In a town known for its Greek food, you might think it's a mistake to go to an Irish pub, but once you taste the classic Irish dishes, you'll know you've made a good choice. The menu includes bangers and mash, corned beef and cabbage, and shepherd's pie, but also satisfies seafood cravings, with such dishes as grouper piccata and grilled mahi with jalapeño pineapple sauce. There's Guinness on tap, and live Irish music on weekend nights. ⊠ *200 E. Tarpon Ave., Tarpon Springs* ☏ *727/942–3011* ☰ *AE, D, MC, V* ⊙ *Closed Mon. No lunch Tues.–Thurs.*

★ $$$–$$$$ ⊞ **Westin Innisbrook Golf Resort.** A massive pool complex with a 15-foot water slide and sand beach are highlights of this sprawling, 1,100-acre resort. Grounds are beautifully maintained, and guest suites are in 24 two- and three-story lodges tucked among the trees between golf courses. The rooms were all remodeled in 2004, the resort is Wi-Fi equipped, and some of the roomy junior, one- and two-bedroom suites have balconies or patios. The Innisbrook has enough restaurants and lounges to make it self-contained, though today the area around it offers plenty of competition. ⊠ *36750 U.S. 19 N, Palm Harbor 34684* ☏ *727/942–2000 or 800/456–2000* ☏ *727/942–5576* ⊕ *www.golfinnisbrookresort.com* ⇨ *600 suites* ♻ *4 restaurants, in-room safes, some kitchens, some kitchenettes, minibars, cable TV, in-room data ports, 3 driving ranges, 4 18-hole golf courses, miniature golf, 3 putting greens, 11 tennis courts, 3 pro shops, 6 pools, health club, outdoor hot tub, massage, bicycles, racquetball, 4 bars, playground, dry cleaning, laundry facilities, laundry service, concierge, business services, meeting rooms, airport shuttle, car rental, no-smoking rooms* ☰ *AE, D, DC, MC, V.*

¢–$$ ⊞ **Best Value Inn/Tarpon Inn.** On the grounds of a historic inn by the same name, this newer incarnation has only that in common with its namesake. Its location within steps of Spring Bayou and the downtown historic district and its affordability are its greatest assets. ⊠ *110 W. Tarpon Ave., Tarpon Springs 34689* ☏ *727/937–6121* ☏ *727/942–2569* ⇨ *23 rooms, 2 suites, 20 efficiencies* ♻ *Some kitchenettes, cable TV, pool, gym, laundry facilities, no-smoking rooms* ☰ *D, MC, V* ⊙ℐ *CP.*

THE MANATEE COAST

The coastal area north of Tampa is sometimes called the Manatee Coast, and aptly so. Of these gentle vegetarian water mammals, distantly related to elephants, only 2,600 are alive today, and they are threatened by development and speeding motorboats. In fact, many manatees have massive scars on their backs from run-ins with boat propellers. Extensive nature preserves and parks have been created to protect them and other wildlife indigenous to the area, and these are among the best spots to view manatees in the wild. Although they are far from mythical beauties, it is believed that manatees inspired ancient mariners' tales of mermaids. U.S. 19 is the prime route through rural manatee country, and traffic flows freely once you've left the congestion of St. Petersburg, Clearwater, and Port Richey. If you're planning a day trip from the bay area, pack a picnic lunch before leaving, since most of the sights are outdoors.

Weeki Wachee

27 mi north of Tarpon Springs.

35 At **Weeki Wachee Springs,** the spring flows at the remarkable rate of 170 million gallons a day with a constant temperature of 74°F. The spring has long been famous for its live "mermaids," clearly not the work of Mother Nature, as they wear bright costumes and put on an Esther Williams–like underwater choreography show that's been virtually unchanged in the more than 50 years the park has been open. Snorkel tours and canoe trips are available in the river, and a wilderness boat ride gives an up-close look at raccoons, otters, egrets, and the other semitropical Florida wetlands wildlife. There are live shows, and a tour down the river on the Wilderness Riverboat cruise provides views of animals in their natural setting. In summer, Buccaneer Bay water park opens for swimming, beaching, and riding its thrilling slides and flumes. There's a tiki bar on the grounds, and during high season there's live music on Friday and Saturday. ✉ *6131 Commercial Way, at U.S. 19 and Rte. 50* ☎ *352/596–2062* ∰ *www. weekiwachee.com* ✆ *$21.95 mid-Mar.–Sept., $13.95 Oct.–mid-Mar.* ◷ *Hrs vary; call ahead.*

Sports & the Outdoors

The 48 holes at **World Woods Golf Club** (✉ 17590 Ponce de León Blvd., Brooksville ☎ 352/796–5500 ∰ www.worldwoods.com) are some of the best in Florida (green fee: $130). The club also has a 22-acre practice area with a circular driving range and a 2-acre putting course.

Homosassa Springs

20 mi north of Weeki Wachee.

36 At the **Homosassa Springs Wildlife State Park,** see many manatees and species of fish through a floating glass observatory known as the Fish Bowl—

except in this case the fish are outside the bowl and the people inside it. The park's wildlife-walk trails lead you to excellent manatee, alligator, and other animal programs. Among the species are bobcats, western cougars, white-tailed deer, black bears, pelicans, herons, snowy egrets, river otters, and even a hippopotamus, a keepsake from the park's days as an exotic-animal park. Boat cruises on Pepper Creek lead you to the Homosassa wildlife park (which takes its name from a Creek Indian word meaning "place where wild peppers grow"). ⊠ *4150 S. Suncoast Blvd. (U.S. 19)* ☎ *352/628-2311* ⊕ *www.homosassasprings. org* ⊠ *$9* ⊙ *Daily 9-5:30.*

㊲ At the **Yulee Sugar Mill Ruins Historic State Park** are the remains of a circa-1851 sugar mill and other remnants of a 5,100-acre sugar plantation owned by Florida's first U.S. senator, David Levy Yulee. It makes for pleasant picnicking. ⊠ *3 mi off Hwy19/98 on State Rd. 490/Yulee Dr., Old Homosassa* ☎ *352/795-3817* ⊕ *www.floridastateparks.org* ⊠ *Free* ⊙ *Daily 8 AM-sunset.*

Where to Stay & Eat

¢-$$ ✕ **Riverside Crab House.** There's no secret what the specialty is here; buy blue crabs by the bucketful at this Old Florida eatery on the river. Cajun crawfish, mussels, catfish, shrimp, pasta, and prime rib fill the bill. From the windows, watch the monkeys—escapees from the wildlife park—swinging around their own private island. ⊠ *Homosassa Riverside Resort, 5297 S. Cherokee Way* ☎ *352/628-2474* ⊕ *www.riversideresorts. com* ⊟ *D, MC, V* ⊙ *Closed Mon.*

$$$ 🏨 **Homosassa Riverside Resort.** Five villas with multiple guest rooms fill this big (by Homosassa standards) complex. There's a marina with boat and scuba-equipment rentals, a restaurant and bar that overlook the river, and an island where monkeys cavort in the trees. Resort grounds cover 9 acres of semitropical forest along the riverfront. ⊠ *5297 Cherokee Way, 34448* ☎ *352/628-2474 or 800/442-2040* ☎ *352/628-5208* ⊕ *www.riversideresorts.com* ⊅ *43 suites* ⅃ *Restaurant, some kitchens, some microwaves, some refrigerators, cable TV, boating, marina, bar, laundry facilities, no-smoking rooms* ⊟ *D, MC, V.*

¢-$ 🏨 **Park Inn.** Immediately adjacent to the Homosassa Springs Wildlife State Park, this simple motor inn has king-size beds in most rooms. There's a full-service spa next door with water therapy treatments, among other services. The on-site restaurant is popular for its variety of chicken wings. ⊠ *4076 Hwy. 19, 34446* ☎ *352/628-4311* ☎ *352/628-0650* ⊅ *104 rooms* ⅃ *Restaurant, cable TV, pool, hair salon, spa, bar, comedy club, playground, some pets allowed (fee), no-smoking rooms* ⊟ *AE, D, DC, MC, V* 🍽 *CP.*

¢ 🏨 **MacRae's.** Fishing aficionados pick this fixture in the Homosassa lodge scene. Simple rooms occupy one-story structures built to look like log cabins. Efficiencies contain full kitchens. The focus is the riverside marina, complete with boat rentals, bait shop, and fishing charters. ⊠ *5300 Cherokee Way, 34487* ☎ *352/628-2602* ⊅ *12 rooms, 10 efficiencies* ⅃ *Some kitchens, some microwaves, cable TV, boating, marina, bar, laundry facilities; no room phones* ⊟ *AE, D, MC, V.*

Crystal River

7 mi north of Homosassa Springs.

③⑧ The **Crystal River National Wildlife Refuge** is a U.S. Fish and Wildlife Service sanctuary for the endangered manatee. The main spring, around which manatees congregate in winter (generally from November to March), feeds crystal-clear water into the river at 72°F year-round. This is one of the best sure-bet places to see manatees in winter, since more than 700 typically congregate at this 40-acre refuge, which includes the spring that forms the headwaters of the Crystal River. The small visitor center has displays that inform about the manatee and other refuge inhabitants. In warmer months, when most manatees scatter (about 80 stay here year-round), the main spring is fun for a swim or scuba diving. Though accessible only by boat, the refuge provides neither tours nor boat rentals. For these, contact marinas in the town of Crystal River, such as the **American Pro Diving Center** (✉ 821 S.E. Hwy. 19 ☎ 352/563–0041 or 800/291–3483 ⊕ www.americanprodiving.com) or the **Crystal Lodge Dive Center** (✉ Behind Best Western, 614 N.W. U.S. 19 N ☎ 352/795–6798 ⊕ www.manatee-central.com). ✉ *1502 S. Kings Bay Dr.* ☎ *352/563–2088* 🎫 *Free* ☉ *Mid-Nov.–mid-Mar., daily 8–4; mid-Mar.–mid-Nov., weekdays 8–4.*

Where to Stay & Eat

¢–$ ✕ **Charlie's Fish House Restaurant.** This popular, bright, and modern seafood place on the water serves fish caught locally, plus oysters, stone crab claws (in season), and shrimp. It's accessible by boat. ✉ *224 N. W. U.S. 19 N* ☎ *352/795–3949* 🍽 *AE, D, MC, V.*

$$–$$$ 🏨 **Plantation Inn & Golf Resort.** On the shore of Kings Bay, this two-story plantation-style resort is on 232 acres near several nature preserves and rivers. Although the exterior of the resort looks like a huge southern mansion, the rooms are more comfortable than palatial, with blond-wood furniture and wall-to-wall carpeting. Some rooms have patios. Condos and villas have views of the golf course. ✉ *9301 W. Fort Island Trail, 34429* ☎ *352/795–4211 or 800/632–6262* 🖷 *352/795–1368* ⊕ *www. plantationinn.com* ⇆ *126 rooms, 2 suites, 5 condos, 12 villas* ॳ *2 restaurants, some kitchens, some refrigerators, cable TV, in-room data ports, driving range, 27-hole golf course, putting green, 2 tennis courts, pool, hot tub, dive shop, boating, marina, fishing, croquet, horseshoes, shuffleboard, volleyball, 3 bars, shop, business services, meeting rooms, no-smoking rooms* 🍽 *AE, DC, MC, V.*

$ 🏨 **Best Western Crystal River Resort.** Divers favor this cinder-block roadside motel close to Kings Bay and its manatee population. Dive boats depart for scuba and snorkeling excursions from the marina. The property was renovated in 2004 and the rooms are nestled under large oak trees that make the place feel like the Old South. ✉ *614 N.W. U.S. 19, 34428* ☎ *352/795–3171 or 800/435–4409* 🖷 *352/795–3179* ⊕ *www. seawake.com* ⇆ *114 rooms, 18 efficiencies* ॳ *Restaurant, some in-room data ports, some kitchenettes, cable TV, pool, outdoor hot tub, dive shop, dock, snorkeling, boating, bar, shops, laundry facilities, meeting room, airport shuttle, no-smoking rooms* 🍽 *AE, D, DC, MC, V.*

Sports & the Outdoors

GOLF The **Plantation Inn & Golf Resort** (✉ 9301 W. Fort Island Trail ☎ 352/ 795–7211 or 800/632–6262), open to the public, has 27 holes, a lighted driving range, and a putting green, green fee: $27/$48.

Cedar Key

57 mi northwest of Crystal River; from U.S. 19, follow Rte. 24 southwest to the end.

Up in the area known as the Big Bend, Florida's long, curving coastline north of Tampa, you won't find many beaches. You will find an idyllic collection of small cays and a little island village tucked in among the marshes and scenic streams feeding the Gulf of Mexico. Once a strategic port for the Confederate States of America, remote Cedar Key is today a commercial fishing and clamming center. Change is in the air, however. Though the town used to be a well-kept secret with sparse tourism, it's becoming increasingly popular as a getaway, thanks in part to the spring arts festival and fall seafood festival, which take over the streets of the rustic downtown area. There are at least a dozen commercial galleries, a sign that Cedar Key is now attracting travelers who carry platinum credit cards. It's also become a favorite of the college crowd, as it's only an hour from the main campus of the University of Florida in Gainesville. The upside of this popularity is that creative bars and restaurants keep popping up; several are on a Cannery Row–style pier a block from downtown.

㊴ The **Cedar Key Historical Society Museum,** in an 1871 home, displays photographs dating to 1850, Native American artifacts, and exhibits about the area's development. ✉ *Rte. 24 and 2nd St.* ☎ *352/543–5549* 🗔 *$1* 🕑 *Sun.–Fri. 1–4, Sat. 11–5.*

Where to Stay & Eat

$–$$$ ✕ **Island Room.** Like virtually every other downtown restaurant, this place in a waterfront condo complex has a good gulf view and focuses on seafood. Excellent upscale cuisine includes such treats as grouper *piccata* (cooked in white wine and lemon juice), linguine *alle vongole* (with fresh herbs, garlic, and local clams sautéed in oil), and a very worthy crab bisque. Sunday mornings, you can order brunch. ✉ *Cedar Cove Beach and Yacht Club, 10 E. 2nd St.* ☎ *352/543–6520* ▤ *AE, D, MC, V* 🕑 *No lunch Mon.–Sat.*

$–$$ ✕ **Captain's Table.** If you're looking for a good old-fashioned fish house, head to this salty spot with a view of the gulf waters that produced its menu. Have your mullet, grouper, shrimp, and oysters fried or broiled, or try one of the house seafood specialties such as the shrimp feast, a platter of stuffed, char-grilled, and broiled shrimp; or scallop bake in a rich cream sauce with mushrooms. ✉ *On the dock, 590 Dock St.* ☎ *352/543–5441* ▤ *AE, D, MC, V* 🕑 *Closed Mon. and Tues.*

$–$$$ ▦ **Island Place.** Gulf views are the big attraction at this waterfront condo-style hotel, and all the guest rooms have them from their private balconies. Suites, which have either one bedroom and one bath or two bedrooms and two baths, are set up for those who might want to stay in this lovely town a while, and enjoy the historic Old Florida flavor. They come with dining-room areas; the kitchens have dishwashers. ☒ *550 1st St., 32625* ☎ *352/543–5307 or 800/780–6522* ⊕ *www. islandplace-ck.com* ⊷ *30 suites* ♿ *Kitchens, microwaves, refrigerators, cable TV, pool, outdoor hot tub, laundry facilities, no-smoking rooms* ⊟ *AE, D, MC, V.*

$ 🏨 **Island Hotel.** Having enjoyed its heyday during the Confederacy, this property built in 1859 is now on the National Register of Historic Places and has been carefully restored to reflect what it was like a century ago. Rooms have antique furnishings and claw-foot bathtubs. The cooked-to-order breakfast includes a hot specialty item and toasted coconut bread. The small restaurant, which fills up quickly at dinner, serves dishes made from local seafood. ☒ *373 2nd St., 32625* ☎ *352/ 543–5111 or 800/432–4640* 🖶 *352/543–6949* ⊕ *www.islandhotel-cedarkey.com* ⊷ *10 rooms* ♿ *Restaurant, bar, piano; no room phones, no smoking* ⊟ *MC, V* ⦿❘ *BP.*

¢–$ 🏨 **Faraway Inn.** Cheery stucco cottages, efficiencies, and motel rooms accommodate at this typical Old Cedar Key establishment on the gulf. It's made for escaping and fishing. Bikes, canoes, and kayaks are available on the property. ☒ *3rd and G Sts., 32625* ☎ *352/543–5330 or 888/ 543–5330* 🖶 *352/543–5523* ⊕ *www.farawayinn.com* ⊷ *5 rooms, 2 efficiencies, 5 cottages* ♿ *Some kitchens, some kitchenettes, microwaves, refrigerators, cable TV, in-room VCRs, beach, boating, bicycles, some pets allowed (fee), no-smoking rooms* ⊟ *MC, V.*

SOUTH OF TAMPA BAY

Bradenton and Sarasota anchor the southern end of Tampa Bay. A string of barrier islands borders the two cities with fine beaches. Sarasota County has 35 mi of gulf beaches, as well as two state parks, 22 municipal parks, and more than 30 golf courses, many open to the public. Sarasota has a thriving cultural scene, thanks mostly to circus magnate John Ringling, who chose this area for the winter home of his circus and his family. Bradenton, to the north, maintains a lower profile, while Venice, a few miles south on the Gulf Coast, claims beaches known for their prehistoric sharks' teeth.

Bradenton

49 mi south of Tampa.

This city on the Manatee River has some 20 mi of beaches and is well situated for access to fishing, both fresh- and saltwater. It also has its share of golf courses and historic sites dating to the mid-1800s.

40 The **Manatee Village Historical Park** is the real thing. You can see an 1860 courthouse, 1887 church, 1903 general store and museum, and 1912 settler's home. The Old Manatee Cemetery, which dates to 1850, has graves of early Manatee County settlers. An appointment is necessary for a cemetery tour. ☒ *1404 Manatee Ave. E/State Rd. 64* ☎ *941/749–7165* 🎫 *Free* ⊗ *Weekdays 9–4:30, Sun. 1:30–4:30.*

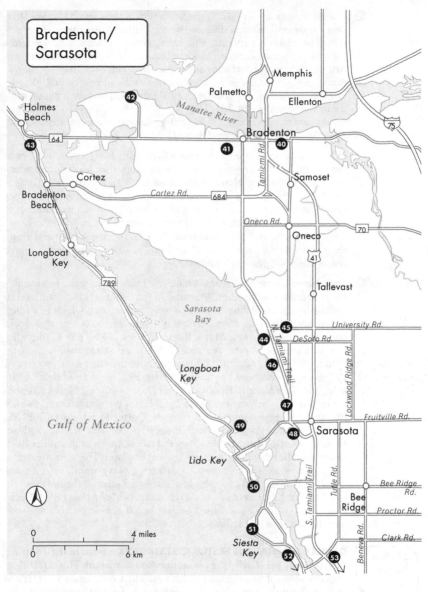

Bradenton/ Sarasota

④ Florida history showcased at the **South Florida Museum and Parker Manatee Aquarium** includes state-of-the-art Native American culture displays, prehistoric artifacts and casts, and a collection of vignettes depicting eras past in South Florida. Snooty, the oldest manatee in captivity, lives here. He performs at feeding time in his 60,000-gallon home. A new planetarium is under construction and will reopen in 2005 (the original was destroyed in a fire in 2001), and will include a digital multipurpose theater. ⊠ *201 10th St. W* ☎ *941/746–4132* ⊕ *www. southfloridamuseum.org* ⊠ *$13.50* ⊗ *Jan.–May and July, Mon.–Sat. 10–5, Sun. noon–5; June and Aug.–Dec., Tues.–Sat. 10–5, Sun. noon–5.*

Hernando de Soto, one of the area's first Spanish explorers, set foot in Florida in 1539 near what is now Bradenton; that feat is commemo-
★ ㊷ rated at the **De Soto National Memorial.** In high season (late December–early April), park employees dressed in 16th-century costumes demonstrate period weapons and show how European explorers prepared and preserved food for their journeys over the untamed land. There's a film, exhibits, and a short nature trail into the mangroves and along the shoreline. ⊠ *75th St. NW* ☎ *941/792–0458* ⊠ *Free* ⊗ *Visitor center daily 9–5, grounds daily dawn–dusk.*

㊸ **Anna Maria Island,** Bradenton's barrier island to the west, has a number of worthwhile beaches. Manatee Avenue connects the mainland to the island via the **Palma Sola Causeway,** adjacent to which is a long, sandy beach fronting Palma Sola Bay. There are boat ramps, a dock, and picnic tables. **Anna Maria Bayfront Park** (⊠ N. Bay Blvd., adjacent to a municipal pier) is a secluded beach fronting the Intracoastal Waterway and the Gulf of Mexico. Facilities include picnic grounds, a playground, restrooms, showers, and lifeguards. In the middle of the island, **Manatee County Beach** (⊠ Gulf Dr. at 44th St., Holmes Beach) is popular with beachgoers of all ages. It has picnic facilities, a snack bar, showers, restrooms, and lifeguards. **Cortez Beach** (⊠ Gulf Blvd., Bradenton Beach) is popular with those who like their beaches without facilities—nothing but sand, water, and trees. Singles and families flock to **Coquina Beach,** at the southern end of the island. There are lifeguards here, as well as a picnic area, boat ramp, playground, refreshment stand, restrooms, and showers. Just across the inlet on the northern tip of Longboat Key, **Greer Island Beach** is accessible by boat or via North Shore Boulevard. The secluded peninsula has a wide beach and excellent shelling, but no facilities.

off the beaten path

GAMBLE PLANTATION HISTORIC STATE PARK – Built in the 1840s, this, the only pre–Civil War plantation house in South Florida, still displays some of its original furnishings. The Confederate secretary of state took refuge here when the Confederacy fell to Union forces. ⊠ *3708 Patten Ave., Ellenton* ☎ *941/723–4536* ⊠ *$5* ⊗ *Thurs.–Mon. 8–4:30; tours at 9:30, 10:30, and hourly 1–4.*

Where to Stay & Eat

★ **$–$$$$** ✕ **Crab Trap and Crab Trap II.** Rustic furnishings, ultrafresh seafood, gator tail, and wild pig are among the trademarks of this casual two-house chain. Crab cakes and three-crab soup are excellent choices. The extensive menu also sways to the exotic with ostrich, octopus, kangaroo, and African rock lobster. ⊠ *5611 U.S. 19 N at Terra Ceia Bridge, Palmetto* ☎ *941/722–6255* ⊠ *4815 17th St. E, Ellenton* ☎ *941/729–7777* ⌣ *Reservations not accepted* ▤ *D, MC, V.*

$–$$$ ✕**Sandbar Seafood & Spirits.** The outside deck here sits right on the beach—the view is spectacular and a great place from which to watch the sunset. Sandbar has a formal indoor menu and a more casual outdoor menu. Options range from hamburgers to sesame-crusted tuna to stuffed snapper. ⊠ *100 Spring Ave., Anna Maria Island* ☎ *941/778–0444* ▤ *AE, D, DC, MC, V.*

¢–$$ ✕ **Gulf Drive Café.** Especially popular for breakfast (served all day), this unassuming landmark squats on the beach and serves cheap sit-down eats: mostly sandwiches, but also a sampling of entrées after 4 PM. ⊠ *900 N. Gulf Dr. N, Bradenton Beach* ☎ *941/778–1919* ▤ *D, MC, V.*

★ $$$–$$$$ ▥ **BridgeWalk, a landmark resort.** An all-in-one beach resort on Bradenton Beach's historic street, the BridgeWalk sits across the road from the beach. It has one- and two-bedroom suites (it calls them "apartos"), with Jacuzzi baths, granite countertops, and terra-cotta tile floors; and town houses with electric fireplaces. The suites range in size from 750 to 1,650 square feet. The handsome tin-roof multicolor resort is within walking distance of a pier that's popular for fishing and strolling, as well as restaurants and shops, including some on-property. Minimum stays may be required during high season (February through April). ⊠ *100 Bridge St., Bradenton Beach 34217* ☎ *941/779–2545 or 866/779–2545* ☐ *941/779–0828* ⊕ *www.silverresorts.com* ⟳ *28 apartments* ⌃ *Restaurant, fans, some kitchens, some kitchenettes, cable TV, in-room data ports, pool, hair salon, massage, spa, bar, shops, laundry facilities, meeting room; no smoking* ▤ *AE, D, DC, MC, V.*

$$–$$$ ▥ **Holiday Inn Riverfront.** Near the Manatee River, this Spanish Mediterranean–style motor inn is easily accessible from Interstate 75 and U.S. 41. Every room has its own balcony, many overlooking the river. ⊠ *100 Riverfront Dr. W, 34205* ☎ *941/747–3727* ☐ *941/746–4289* ⟳ *96 rooms, 57 suites* ⌃ *2 restaurants, room service, some refrigerators, in-room data ports, pool, gym, hot tub, bar, dry cleaning, Internet, meeting rooms* ▤ *AE, D, DC, MC, V.*

$$–$$$ ▥ **Silver Surf Gulf Beach Resort.** It's hard to beat the location of this terra-cotta-color two-story hotel. Its private beach is right out front, there is a heated pool, and many restaurants are nearby. Rooms are comfortable, and all suites were renovated in 2001. There's a free trolley that takes you to and from each tip of Anna Marie Island. ⊠ *1301 Gulf Dr. N, Anna Maria Island, Bradenton Beach 34217* ☎ *941/778–6626* ☐ *941/778–4308* ⊕ *www.silverresorts.com* ⟳ *3 rooms, 46 suites* ⌃ *Some kitchens, some microwaves, some refrigerators, cable TV, pool, beach, bicycles, shuffleboard, volleyball, laundry facilities* ▤ *AE, D, DC, MC, V.*

Sports & the Outdoors

BASEBALL The **Pittsburgh Pirates** (⊠ McKechnie Field, 17th Ave. W and 9th St. ☎ 941/748–4610) have spring training in March.

BIKING **Ringling Bicycles** (✉ 3606 Manatee Ave. W ☎ 941/749–1442) rents racing bicycles and regular bikes for adults and kids starting at $10 a day, $40 a week.

GOLF The excellent county-owned 18-hole **Buffalo Creek Golf Course** (✉ 8100 Erie Rd., Palmetto ☎ 941/776–2611), designed by Ron Garl, resembles a Scottish links course; green fee: $30/$47. Arnold Palmer was among the designers of **The Legacy Golf Course at Lakewood Ranch** (✉ 8255 Legacy Blvd. ☎ 941/907–7067), a public 18-hole course, green fee: $70/$99. **Manatee County Golf Course** (✉ 6415 53rd Ave. W ☎ 941/792–6773) has a driving range and 18 holes of golf, green fee: $42/$47. **Peridia Golf & Country Club** (✉ 4950 Peridia Blvd. ☎ 941/753–9097), an executive course, has 18 holes and a driving range, green fee: $19/$30. **Waterlefe Golf & River Club** (✉ 1022 Fish Hook Cove ☎ 941/744–9771) has a public 18-hole course, green fee: $35/$95.

Shopping

Find discount factory-outlet bargains at **Ellenton Prime Outlets** (✉ 5461 Factory Shops Blvd., off I–75 Exit 224 ☎ 888/260–7608), with more than 135 name-brand and other stores. The **Red Barn** (✉ 1707 1st St. E ☎ 941/747–3794 or 800/274–3532 ⊕ www.redbarnfleamarket.com) is a flea market in the requisite big red barn. A few vendors do business during the week (Tuesday through Sunday 10–4), but on Wednesday (November–April) and year-round Friday through Sunday, the number of vendors skyrockets to more than 650, and many open as early as 8 AM.

Sarasota

16 mi south of Bradenton.

A sophisticated resort town, Sarasota is traditionally the home of some ultra-affluent residents, dating back to John Ringling of circus fame. Cultural events are scheduled year-round, and there is a higher concentration of upscale shops, restaurants, and hotels than in much of the rest of the Tampa Bay area. Across the water from Sarasota lie the barrier islands of **Siesta Key, Longboat Key,** and **Lido Key,** with myriad beaches, shops, hotels, condominiums, and houses.

Decades ago, circus tycoon John Ringling found this area an ideal spot for his clowns and performers to recuperate from their months of travel while preparing for their next journey. Along Sarasota Bay, Ringling built himself a grand home called *Cà d'Zan* ("House of John," in Venetian dialect), patterned after the Palace of the Doges in Venice, Italy. Today

FodorśChoice
★

this winter home is part of the **Ringling Center for the Cultural Arts,** along with the **Museum of the Circus** and the **John and Mable Ringling Museum of Art,** which has a world-renowned collection of Rubens paintings and tapestries. As of this writing, an expansion that will double the exhibit space was slated to open, along with the 30,000-square-foot Tibbals Learning Center, which will focus on the American circus; the historic 18th-century Asolo Theatre Company also will reopen. ✉ *U.S. 41, ½ mi west of Sarasota–Bradenton Airport* ☎ *941/359–5700* ⊕ *www.ringling.org* 💲 *$15* ☉ *Daily 10–5:30.*

45 On display at the **Sarasota Classic Car Museum** are 100 restored antique, classic, and muscle cars—including Rolls-Royces, Pierce Arrows, and Auburns. The collection includes rare cars and vehicles that belonged to famous people, such as John Lennon and John Ringling. ⊠ *5500 N. Tamiami Trail* ☎ *941/355–6228* ⊕ *www.sarasotacarmuseum.org* ☑ *$8.50* ⊙ *Daily 9–6.*

46 It takes about three hours to stroll through the 10-acre spread of tropical plants at the **Sarasota Jungle Gardens.** The lush gardens, created in 1936, are filled with native species and exotic plants from around the world, such as the rare Australian nut tree and the Peruvian apple cactus. Also on-site are a petting zoo and playground, a butterfly garden, and a variety of animal shows and entertainment. ⊠ *3701 Bayshore Rd.* ☎ *941/355–5305* ⊕ *www.sarasotajunglegardens.com* ☑ *$11* ⊙ *Daily 9–5.*

47 Kids and parents alike will be taken with **G.WIZ** (the Hands-on Science Museum). This science center has regularly changing interactive exhibits in the ExploraZone, a butterfly garden, and the ecozone with snakes, a kid's lab, a technology gallery, and other exhibits. ⊠ *1001 Blvd. of the Arts* ☎ *941/309–4949* ⊕ *www.gwiz.org* ☑ *$7* ⊙ *May–Sept., Mon.–Sat. 10–5, Sun. 1–5; Oct.–Apr., Tues.–Sat. 10–5, Sun. 1–5.*

48 At the **Marie Selby Botanical Gardens,** stroll through the Tropical Display House with orchids and colorful bromeliads, wander the garden pathway past plantings of bamboo, under ancient banyans, and through the mangrove along Little Sarasota Bay with spectacular views of downtown. There are rotating exhibits of botanical art and photography in a 1934 restored mansion, a café under the banyans, and the Rainforest Store, with gifts and tropical plants. ⊠ *811 S. Palm Ave.* ☎ *941/366–5731* ⊕ *www.selby.org* ☑ *$12* ⊙ *Daily 10–5.*

49 The 135,000-gallon shark tank at **Mote Marine Aquarium** lets you view its inhabitants from above and below the water's surface. Additional tanks show off sharks, rays, and other marine creatures native to the area. Hugh and Buffett are the resident manatees that have lived at the aquarium since 1995, and there's also a permanent sea turtle exhibit. Handle rays, guitar fish, horseshoe crabs, and sea urchins in the touch tanks. Many visitors take the 105-minute boat trip onto Sarasota Bay, conducted by **Sarasota Bay Explorers** (☎ 941/388–4200 ⊕ www. sarasotabayexplorers.com). The crew brings marine life on board in a net, explains what it is, and throws it back to swim away. You are almost guaranteed to see bottlenose dolphins. Reservations are required for the excursion. ⊠ *1600 Ken Thompson Pkwy., City Island, Sarasota* ☎ *941/388–4441* ⊕ *www.mote.org* ☑ *Aquarium $12, boat excursion $26, combined ticket $31* ⊙ *Aquarium daily 10–5; boat tours daily 11, 1:30, 4.*

50 **South Lido Park,** at the southern tip of the island, has one of the best beaches in the region. The sugar-sand beach offers little for shell collectors, but try your luck at fishing, take a dip in the gulf, roam the 100-acre park, or picnic as the sun sets through the Australian pines into the water. Facilities include nature trails, a canoe trail and kayak launch and trail, volleyball court, playground, horseshoe pits, restrooms, and picnic grounds. ⊠ *2201 Ben Franklin Dr., Lido Key, Sarasota.*

51 **Siesta Beach** and its 40-acre park have nature trails, a concession stand,
Fodor'sChoice fields for soccer and softball, picnic facilities, a playground, restrooms,
★ a fitness trail, and tennis and volleyball courts. In 1987 this beach was recognized internationally as having the whitest and finest sand in the world, a powdery, quartz-based compound that is soft as down. ⊠ *948 Beach Rd., Siesta Key, Sarasota.*

52 Only 14 acres, **Turtle Beach** is a beach-park that's popular with families. It doesn't have the soft, white sand of Siesta Beach, but it does have boat ramps, a canoe and kayak launch, fishing from both the bay and gulf, horseshoe pits, picnic and play facilities, a recreation building, restrooms, and a volleyball court. ⊠ *8918 Midnight Pass Rd., Siesta Key, Sarasota.*

> **off the beaten path**

MYAKKA RIVER STATE PARK – With 28,900 acres, this outstanding wildlife preserve is absolutely lovely and is great for bird-watching and gator-sighting. Tram tours explore hammocks, airboat tours whiz over the lake, and there are hiking trails and bike rentals. A 100-foot-long canopy walkway gives you a bird's-eye view from 25 feet above ground. If you care to stay a while, the park rents cabins that have kitchens, fireplaces, and air-conditioning. There's also a campground. Reservations are essential for the cabins. ⊠ *Rte. 72, 9 mi southeast of Sarasota* ☎ *941/365–0100 tours, 941/361–6511 camping, 800/326–3521 cabin reservations* ⊕ *www.myakkariver.org* ▧ *$3, $5 per vehicle up to 8 people; tours $8; cabins $55 per night* ☉ *Daily 8 AM–dusk; boat tours daily at 10, 11:30, 1, and 2:30.*

Where to Stay & Eat

★ **$$$–$$$$** ✕ **Michael's on East.** Dine in trendy elegance at this downtown Sarasota favorite. The fare ranges from Maine lobster bow-tie pasta to rack of lamb to grilled duck breast to pan-seared Chilean sea bass. Desserts, such as the house specialty chocolate lava, are standouts here. A light menu is served in the intimate bar, where there's often piano music or jazz in the evening. The lunch menu includes unusual sandwiches—grilled portobello mushrooms with smoked Gouda, for example. ⊠ *1212 East Ave. S* ☎ *941/366–0007* ☉ *Closed Sun. No lunch Sat.* ▭ *AE, D, DC, MC, V.*

$$$–$$$$ ✕ **Ophelia's on the Bay.** The menu changes nightly at this intimate waterfront spot. Favorites include grouper with coconut and cashew crust with papaya jam and habañero mashed potatoes; portobello moussaka; grilled bison rib eye with morel mushroom and roasted leek demi-glace; and roast duck. ⊠ *9105 Midnight Pass Rd., Siesta Key* ☎ *941/349–2212* ▭ *AE, D, DC, MC, V* ☉ *No lunch.*

★ **$$–$$$$** ✕ **Bijou Cafe.** Wood, brass, lace, and sumptuous carpeting surround diners in this 1920 gas station turned restaurant. Specialties on the regularly changing menu could include superb crab cakes with rémoulade, a wonderfully spicy shrimp dish inspired by Mozambique, crispy roast duckling with orange-cognac sauce or port-wine cherry sauce, pepper steak, and crème brûlée for dessert. An extensive international wine list includes vintages ranging from an Australian cabernet-shiraz blend to a South African merlot and, of course, numerous selections from France and California. ⊠ *1287 1st St.* ☎ *941/366–8111* ▤ *AE, D, DC, MC, V* ⊘ *Closed Sun. June–Dec. No lunch weekends.*

$$–$$$$ ✕ **Columbia.** On trendy St. Armands Circle, this classic has most of the culinary elements of its mother landmark restaurant in Ybor City, which celebrated its 100th birthday in 2005. The menu reflects Spanish and Cuban cooking, and includes three versions of Spanish paella and a superb black-bean soup. A house specialty is pompano papillote (pompano with shrimp, crabmeat, and artichoke in a white wine sauce, baked in parchment), and the 1905 salad is a classic. ⊠ *411 St. Armands Circle, Lido Key* ☎ *941/388–3987* ▤ *AE, D, DC, MC, V.*

$$–$$$$ ✕ **Marina Jack.** Fresh seafood prevails at this restaurant, whose dining room and outdoor patio seating overlook Sarasota Bay on three sides. Lunch specialties include crab cakes, eggs Benedict, and fried chicken livers with a mushroom demi-glace. Dinner brings lobster tails, red snapper almondine, steaks, and pasta. ⊠ *2 Marina Plaza* ☎ *941/365–4232* ▤ *AE, D, MC, V.*

$–$$$ ✕ **Café Epicure.** This bright and airy café with an Italian flair is downtown and has a unique selection of appetizers, entrées, and drinks. It's a popular place with locals, who sit outside on the terrace enjoying drinks, snacks, and people-watching. Appetizers include roasted peppers with avocado and fresh mozzarella and *insalata tropicale* (arugula, avocado, hearts of palm, and Parmesan), whereas entrées range from standard Italian dishes to New York strip steak. ⊠ *1298 N. Palm Ave., corner of Main St.* ☎ *941/366–5648* ⌂ *Reservations not accepted* ▤ *AE, D, DC, MC, V.*

$–$$$ ✕ **Patricks.** A longtime favorite among locals, this upscale restaurant with a sports bar attracts crowds that belly up to the bar after work and end up staying for steak sandwiches, juicy cheeseburgers, pizza, pasta, and char-grilled steaks. *Sarasota Magazine* continually ranks the burgers here as best in the area. ⊠ *1400 Main St.* ☎ *941/952–1170* ⌂ *Reservations not accepted* ▤ *AE, D, DC, MC, V.*

$–$$ ✕ **Café Baci.** For 13 straight years its northern Italian cuisine has earned Café Baci the best restaurant award from *Sarasota Magazine*. Menu highlights include osso buco; snapper à la Baci, cooked with tomatoes, black olives, rosemary, and white wine; and veal shank. The interior is not as enticing as the entrées, but resembles an English garden, with splashes of green and white and slightly outdated floral accents. ⊠ *4001 S. Tamiami Trail* ☎ *941/921–4848* ▤ *AE, D, DC, MC, V.*

¢–$ ✕ **The Broken Egg.** A local institution in the heart of Siesta Village, the Broken Egg serves breakfast and lunch. Some favorites are crab cakes Benedict, chicken ranch wrap, and banana-nut-bread French toast. The café is decorated with art by local artists and the large patio is surrounded by lush greens. ⊠ *210 Avenida Madera, Siesta Village* ☎ *941/346–2750* ▤ *AE, D, DC, MC, V* ⊘ *No dinner.*

¢–$ ✕ **Old Salty Dog.** A view of New Pass between Longboat and Lido keys and affordable eats make this a popular stop, especially for visitors to Mote Marine Aquarium. It's open-air but comfortable even in summer, thanks to a pleasant breeze. Quarter-pound hot dogs, fish-and-chips, wings, and burgers set the menu's tone. Locals hang out at the beer bar, shaped from the hull of an old boat. ⊠ *1601 Ken Thompson Pkwy., City Island* ☎ *941/388–4311* ⌧ *Reservations not accepted* ⊟ *MC, V.*

¢-$ ✕ **TooJay's.** A sister deli to its St. Pete's location, TooJay's is bright and cheerful and has warm wood tones. The menu has Reubens, matzo ball soup, cheese blintzes, corned beef or pastrami sandwiches, old-fashioned pot roast, and roast chicken. ⊠ *Westfield Shoppingtown-Southgate, 3501 S. Tamiami Trail* ☎ *941/362–3692* ⌧ *Reservations not accepted* ⊟ *AE, D, DC, MC, V.*

¢-$ ✕ **Yoder's.** At this Amish family restaurant in the heart of Sarasota's Amish community, you find great homey cooking. Entrées, served family style—feeding two to three people—typically include liver and onions, turkey and dressing, a wonderful goulash, and other hearty dishes, and breakfasts include big stacks of pancakes. The desserts might be the best part of the meal, particularly the pies. The place gets crowded around noon and early evening. ⊠ *3434 Bahia Vista* ☎ *941/955–7771* ⌧ *Reservations not accepted* ⊟ *No credit cards* ⊙ *Closed Sun.*

¢ ✕ **Panera Bread.** This café in both University Park and mid-Sarasota serves breakfast, lunch, and dinner. The asiago cheese bagels are outstanding and the soup-and-sandwich combo is both reasonably priced and filling. The soups include the popular broccoli cheddar, French onion, and low-fat vegetarian black bean. Hot panini sandwiches include turkey-artichoke and portobello and mozzarella. All breads are freshly baked and there is a wide range of desserts. The café is done in deep earth-tone colors and is both trendy and inviting. ⊠ *University Walk Shopping Center, 2821 University Pkwy., at Tuttle Ave., University Park* ☎ *941/351–9300* ⊠ *Sarasota Pavillion, 6589 S. Tamiami Trail, Sarasota* ☎ *941/924–0800* ⌧ *Reservations not accepted* ⊟ *AE, D, MC, V.*

★ $$$$ ⊞ **Colony Beach & Tennis Resort.** If tennis is your game, this is the place to stay—such tennis greats as Björn Borg have made the Colony their home court, and for good reason. Ten courts are clay hydrosurfaced (the others are hard), and the pros are all USPTA-certified. They run clinics and camps at all levels and with the guaranteed match-making program, you can play with a pro when no one else is available. There are even rackets and lessons for children, plus excellent free kids' programs. The Colony dining room has a local reputation for excellence and fine wine. Suites sleep up to eight. Among the suites are a two-story penthouse as well as three private beach houses that open onto sand and sea. ⊠ *1620 Gulf of Mexico Dr., Longboat Key, 34228* ☎ *941/383–6464 or 800/426–5669* ⊟ *941/383–7549* ⊕ *www.colonybeachresort.com* ⋛ *235 suites* ⌧ *2 restaurants, grocery, in-room safes, kitchens, cable TV, golf privileges, 21 tennis courts, pool, health club, hair salon, massage, sauna, spa, steam room, beach, snorkeling, boating, bicycles, volleyball, 2 bars, babysitting, children's programs (ages 3–17), playground, dry cleaning, laundry facilities, laundry service, concierge, Internet, business services, meeting rooms, car rental, travel services; no smoking* ⊟ *AE, D, DC, MC, V.*

$$$$ ⊞ **Hyatt Sarasota on Sarasota Bay.** The Hyatt is contemporary in design and is in the heart of the city, across from the Van Wezel Performing

Arts Hall. All the spacious rooms overlook Sarasota Bay or the marina and the newly designed lagoon-style pool and hot tub, which have waterfalls flowing into them. ✉ *1000 Blvd. of the Arts, 34236* ☎ *941/953–1234 or 800/233–1234* 🖨 *941/952–1987* ⊕ *www.sarasota.hyatt.com* 🛏 *294 rooms, 12 suites* 🖘 *2 restaurants, room service, some minibars, cable TV, in-room data ports, golf privileges, pool, gym, hot tub, massage, boating, marina, fishing, bicycles, 3 bars, shop, babysitting, dry cleaning, laundry facilities, laundry service, concierge, Internet, meeting room, airport shuttle, no-smoking floors, some pets allowed* ⊟ *AE, D, DC, MC, V.*

$$$$ 🏨 **Lido Beach Resort.** Superb gulf views can be found at this classy beachfront resort. The South Tower was completed in May 2002, and the majority of rooms there have beach and gulf views. There are two free-form pools and three Jacuzzis, all right on the beach. The resort is equipped with Wi-Fi hot spots. ✉ *700 Ben Franklin Dr., Lido Beach, Sarasota 34236* ☎ *941/388–2161 or 800/441–2113* 🖨 *941/388–3175* ⊕ *www.lidobeachresort.com* 🛏 *158 rooms, 64 suites* 🖘 *2 restaurants, some kitchens, microwaves, refrigerators, cable TV with movies and video games, in-room data ports, 2 pools, 3 hot tubs, beach, volleyball, 3 bars, children's programs (ages 8–13), dry cleaning, laundry facilities, concierge, Internet, business services, meeting rooms, no-smoking rooms* ⊟ *AE, D, DC, MC, V.*

$$$$ 🏨 **Resort at Longboat Key Club.** This beautifully landscaped 410-acre property is one of *the* places to golf in the state and one of the top tennis resorts in the country. Water is the test on both golf courses, which have excellent pro shops, lessons, and clinics. Tennis courts are Har-Tru–surfaced. Hobie Cats, kayaks, Sunfish, deep-sea charters, and ecology trips are also available. All rooms have balconies overlooking a golf course, beach, or private lagoon where manatees and bottlenose dolphins are occasionally seen. Golf and dining facilities are for resort guests and club members only. All bathrooms and kitchens were renovated in 2003. ✉ *301 Gulf of Mexico Dr., Longboat Key 34228* ☎ *941/383–8821, 800/237–8821, or 888/237–5545* 🖨 *941/383–0359* ⊕ *www.longboatkeyclub.com* 🛏 *14 rooms, 142 suites* 🖘 *5 restaurants, room service, some kitchens, minibars, microwaves, refrigerators, cable TV, in-room data ports, driving range, 18-hole golf course, 3 9-hole golf courses, putting greens, 38 tennis courts, pro shop, pool, gym, outdoor hot tub, massage, beach, boating, bicycles, 2 bars, library, babysitting, children's programs (ages 5–12), laundry facilities, concierge, Internet, business services, meeting room, no-smoking rooms* ⊟ *AE, DC, MC, V.*

★ **$$$$** 🏨 **Ritz-Carlton, Sarasota.** Developers like to say that this hotel is circus magnate John Ringling's realized dream, and it certainly has a style Ringling would have coveted. Fine artwork and fresh-cut flowers decorate marble-floored hallways. Rooms have marble bathrooms, high-speed Internet access, and private balconies. As of this writing, the Ritz is slated to open a private 18-hole Tom Fazio–designed golf course 12 mi northeast of the property on the Braden River. A European-style spa and guest-and-members-only beach facility on Lido Key, about 3 mi away, make this city resort full-service. Vernona, the contemporary American restaurant, overlooks yachts in the marina. ✉ *1111 Ritz-Carlton Dr., 34236*

☎941/309–2000 or 800/241–3333 🖷941/309–2100 ⊕ *www.ritzcarlton. com/resorts/sarasota* ⇗ *266 rooms, 30 suites ↻ 2 restaurants, room service, in-room safes, minibars, cable TV with movies, in-room data ports, 18-hole golf course, 3 tennis courts, pool, health club, hot tub, massage, sauna, spa, steam room, Turkish bath, 2 bars, lobby lounge, shops, children's programs (ages 5–12), dry cleaning, laundry service, concierge, concierge floor, Internet, business services, meeting rooms, no-smoking floors ☰ AE, D, DC, MC, V.*

★ **$$$–$$$$** ⊡ **Cypress, a Bed & Breakfast Inn.** The only B&B in downtown Sarasota, the inn is across the street from the bay, is convenient to the downtown restaurants, a movie theater, art galleries, and shopping, and is a five-minute drive from the beaches at Lido Key. It's hard to believe this inn is downtown; the grounds are covered with lush tropical plants, and guests can enjoy the view of the bay from the porch in front of the house. The Essie Leigh Key West Room has its own entrance. All four rooms have a Victorian flair, with antique pieces, high-quality linens, oriental rugs, hardwood floors, and wireless Internet access. Breakfast is also a treat: the chef prepares a gourmet entrée, served with fresh-squeezed juice, pastries, and fruit. In the evening the owners serve cocktails on the wraparound porch. ⊠ *621 Gulfstream Ave. S, 34236* ☎ *941/955–4683* 🖷 *941/906–8952* ⊕ *www.cypressbb.com* ⇗ *4 rooms ↻ Dining rooms, fans, some in-room hot tubs, cable TV, concierge, Internet, meeting room, free parking; no room phones, no kids, no smoking* ☰ *AE, D, MC, V* ⏸⏵⏸ *BP.*

$$–$$$ ⊡ **Sea Castle Beachfront Accommodations.** The 10 buildings that make up this property are two-story in the Old Florida style, and all rooms lead out to the beach at Siesta Key. Rooms are bright and decorated in tasteful pastel colors, and have balconies with lounge chairs. During high season, the owners mainly rent out weekly. ⊠ *1001–1019 Seaside Dr., Siesta Key 34242* ☎ *941/349–8858 or 800/720–6885* ⊕ *www.sea-castle.com or www.siestaholiday.com* ⇗ *40 rooms, 11 apartments ↻ Fans, some kitchens, some kitchenettes, microwaves, refrigerators, cable TV, some in-room VCRs, some in-room data ports, pool, beach, laundry facilities, free parking; no smoking ☰ D, MC, V (varies by building).*

$$–$$$ ⊡ **Siesta Key Suites.** This property is made up of five buildings directly across the street from Siesta Key beach. The rooms are fresh, bright, and decorated in the Key West Old Florida style. Some rooms are all-tile, and each suite has sofa beds in the living room. During high season, the owner mainly rents rooms for a week's stay. This is a great place for families, is a couple minutes from Siesta Village, and there are complimentary beach chairs and umbrellas to take with you across the street. ⊠ *523 Beach Rd., Siesta Key 34242* ☎ *941/349–1236* 🖷 *941/349–6277* ⊕ *www.siestakeysuites.com* ⇗ *1 efficiency, 19 suites ↻ Fans, kitchens, microwaves, refrigerators, cable TV, in-room VCRs, some in-room DVDs, 3 pools, laundry facilities, free parking; no smoking ☰ D, MC, V.*

$$ ⊡ **Best Western Midtown.** This three-story motel is comfortable, and very affordable during its off-season, from mid-April through early February. Set back from U.S. 41 and somewhat removed from traffic noise, it's within walking distance of a shopping center and several restaurants—including the popular Michael's on East—and is central to area attractions and downtown. Rooms have sitting areas. ⊠ *1425 S. Tamiami Trail, 34239* ☎ *941/955–9841 or 800/722–8227* 🖶 *941/954–8948* ⊕ *www.bwmidtown.com* 🖘 *100 rooms* ⚘ *In-room data ports, some microwaves, some refrigerators, cable TV, pool, laundry facilities, laundry service, meeting room, no-smoking rooms* 🖿 *AE, D, DC, MC, V* 🅞❘ *CP.*

$–$$ 🏨 **Holiday Inn, Airport–Marina.** Near the airport and just a 10-minute drive from downtown and a 25-minute drive from the beaches, this hotel has its own marina, and the back of the building looks out at Sarasota Bay. Rooms are standard and clean, and the restaurant often has a popular Friday night seafood buffet. ⊠ *7150 N. Tamiami Trail, 34243* ☎ *941/355–2781 or 888/818–2781* 🖶 *941/552–2313* ⊕ *www.hisarasotabradenton.com* 🖘 *178 rooms, 4 suites* ⚘ *Restaurant, room service, some kitchenettes, some microwaves, some refrigerators, cable TV, in-room data ports, pool, gym, dock, marina, 2 bars, shop, dry cleaning, laundry facilities, laundry service, Internet, business services, meeting rooms, airport shuttle, free parking, some pets allowed (fee), no-smoking rooms* 🖿 *AE, D, DC, MC, V.*

¢–$$ 🏨 **Gulf Beach Resort.** This was Lido Key's first motel, and has been named a historic property by the county. The resort is beachfront and is composed of condominium units that are rented out as motel rooms; since each unit is individually owned, renovations at the property are continuous. Rooms are bright and each has a different decor—many return visitors have their favorite rooms and book several years in advance. The hotel staff are friendly, the property is well maintained, and it's just 2 mi from shopping at St. Armands Circle. ⊠ *930 Ben Franklin Dr., Lido Key 34236* ☎ *941/388–2127 or 800/232–2489* 🖶 *941/388-1312* ⊕ *www.gulfbeachsarasota.com* 🖘 *8 rooms, 41 suites* ⚘ *BBQ, picnic area, in-room data ports, cable TV, pool, beach, volleyball, laundry facilities, babysitting, no-smoking rooms* 🖿 *AE, D, DC, MC, V.*

¢ 🏨 **Knights Inn.** Basically a motor inn convenient to the airport and Ringling Center, this property is tidy and appealing, its rooms benefiting from friendly decorative touches. ⊠ *5340 N. Tamiami Trail, 34234* ☎ *941/355–8867 or 800/843–5644* 🖶 *941/351–7718* 🖘 *46 rooms* ⚘ *Some in-room data ports, some microwaves, some refrigerators, cable TV, pool, laundry facilities* 🖿 *AE, D, DC, MC, V* 🅞❘ *CP.*

Nightlife & the Arts

THE ARTS Sarasota has free cultural events most Friday nights. The first Friday of each month, historic Palm Avenue (downtown Sarasota) has **Art Walks** from 6 to 9. Members of the Palm Avenue Arts Alliance open their galleries to the public and entertain with live dancing and singing. The third Friday of each month, from 6 to 10, **Towles Court Artists Colony** (⊠ 1938 Adams La., downtown ⊕ www.towlescourt.com) hosts an evening for folks to wander in and out of its galleries, ask the artists about their work, and enjoy wine and cheese. The fourth Friday night (*October to May, 6–9 PM) brings **Smooth Jazz on St. Armands Circle.** Musicians perform in the center of the circle; bring a blanket, relax, and enjoy refreshments from on-site kiosks.

Among the many theaters in Sarasota, the $10-million **FSU/Asolo Theater Company** (✉ 5555 N. Tamiami Trail ☎ 941/351–8000 or 800/361–8388) mounts productions November through mid-June. The small, professional **Florida Studio Theatre** (✉ 1241 N. Palm Ave. ☎ 941/366–9000) presents contemporary dramas, comedies, and musicals, and has acting classes for both adults and children. Performers at the **Florida West Coast Symphony Center** (✉ 709 N. Tamiami Trail ☎ 941/953–4252 ⊕ www.fwcs.org) include the Florida West Coast Symphony, Florida String Quartet, Florida Brass Quintet, Florida Wind Quintet, and New Artists Piano Quartet. **Golden Apple Dinner Theatre** (✉ 25 N. Pineapple Ave. ☎ 941/366–5454) serves a standard buffet along with musicals. A long-established community theater, **The Players Theatre** (✉ 838 N. Tamiami Trail/U.S. 41 and 9th St. ☎ 941/365–2494) launched such actors as Montgomery Clift and Paul Reubens. The troupe performs comedies, special events, live concerts, and musicals. The **Sarasota Concert Band,** which celebrated its 50th anniversary in 2005, (✉ 1345 Main St. ☎ 941/364–2263) has 50 players, many of them full-time musicians; performance venues change with each event. The **Van Wezel Performing Arts Hall** (✉ 777 N. Tamiami Trail ☎ 941/953–3366 ⊕ www.vanwezel.org) is easy to find—just look for the purple shell rising along the bay front. It hosts some 200 performances each year, including Broadway plays, ballet, jazz, rock concerts, symphonies, children's shows, and ice-skating.

The **Sarasota Film Society** (✉ Burns Court Cinema, 506 Burns La. ☎ 941/364–8662, 941/955–3456 theater ⊕ www.filmsociety.org) shows foreign and art films daily. Call the theater for film titles and show times and see the society's Web site for detailed descriptions of films.

Celebrating its 46th season in 2005, the **Sarasota Opera** (✉ The Edwards Theater, 61 N. Pineapple Ave. ☎ 941/366–8450 or 888/673–7212) performs from February through March in a 1,033-seat, historic theater downtown. Internationally known artists sing the principal roles, supported by a professional chorus of 24 young apprentices.

NIGHTLIFE The **Gator Club** (✉ 1490 Main St. ☎ 941/366–5969), in a classy, historic building downtown, has live music and dancing 365 days a year.

Sports & the Outdoors

BASEBALL The **Cincinnati Reds** (✉ Ed Smith Stadium, 2700 12th St. ☎ 941/954–4101) have spring training here in March.

BIKING **CB's Saltwater Outfitters** (✉ 1249 Stickney Point Rd., Siesta Key ☎ 941/349–4400) rents boats, fishing gear, and bikes hourly or by the day.

DOG RACING The greyhounds run from late November through mid-April at the **Sarasota Kennel Club** (✉ 5400 Bradenton Rd. ☎ 941/355–7744).

FISHING **Flying Fish Fleet** (✉ U.S. 41, on the bay front at Marina Jack ☎ 941/366–3373) has several boats that can be chartered for deep-sea fishing and has daily group trips on its "party" fishing boat.

GOLF **Bobby Jones Golf Course** (✉ 1000 Circus Blvd. ☎ 941/955–8097) has 45 holes and a driving range, green fee: $32/$44. **Bobcat Trail Golf Club**

(⊠ 1350 Bobcat Trail, North Port ☎ 941/429–0500) is a semiprivate 18-hole course 35 mi from Sarasota, green fee: $40/$65. Semiprivate **Forest Lakes Golf Club** (⊠ 2401 Beneva Rd. ☎ 941/922–1312) has a practice range and 18 holes, green fee: $27/$50. Fifteen miles from Sarasota, **Heron Creek Golf & Country Club** (⊠ 5303 Heron Creek Blvd., North Port ☎ 941/423–6955 or 800/877–1433) has a semiprivate 27-hole course, green fee: $60/$80. There are 27 holes at the Ron Garl–designed **University Park Country Club** (⊠ 7671 Park Blvd., University Park ☎ 941/359–9999), green fee: $70/$100. This club is private, but does allow nonmembers limited play after 11 AM.

KAYAKING **Siesta Sports Rentals** (⊠ 6551 Midnight Pass Rd., Siesta Key ☎ 941/346–1797) rents kayaks, bikes, beach chairs, scooters, and beach wheelchairs and strollers. Guided kayaking trips are also available.

Shopping

St. Armands Circle (⊠ John Ringling Blvd. [Rte. 789] at Ave. of the Presidents) is a cluster of oh-so-exclusive shops and restaurants just east of Lido Beach.

Downtown Sarasota has many unique boutiques and eateries. **Sarasota News & Books** (⊠ 1341 Main St., Downtown ☎ 941/365–6332) is an independent bookstore that carries a good selection of books and periodicals, hosts author-signing events, and has a café with outdoor tables. **Lotus** (⊠ 1451 Main St., Downtown ☎ 941/906–7080) is a home-decor and clothing boutique that promotes items made from organic materials, such as bamboo tableware and cotton clothing and bedding. They also display and sell works by local artists. **Rousseau's** (⊠ 1385 Main St., Downtown ☎ 941/365–1072) has fun and unusual women's clothing and jewelry in a SoHo-style boutique. **Whole Foods** (⊠ 1451 1st St. at Lemon Ave., Downtown ☎ 941/955–8500) carries organic produce, has a specialty wine and cheese market, and has a deli with prepared meals that make great picnic lunches for the beach.

Venice

53 *18 mi south of Sarasota.*

This small town is crisscrossed with canals like the city for which it was named. Venice beaches are good for shell collecting, but they're best known for their wealth of sharks' teeth and fossils, washed up from the ancient shark burial grounds just offshore.

Nokomis Beach (⊠ 901 Casey Key Rd., Nokomis) is one of two notable beaches in the area, on the island just north of Venice Beach, across the pass near North Jetty Park. It has restrooms, a concession stand, picnic equipment, play areas, two boat ramps, a volleyball court, and fishing. **North Jetty Park** (⊠ Albee Rd., Casey Key), at the south end of Casey Key, is a favorite for family outings and fishermen. Facilities include restrooms, a concession stand, play and picnic equipment, horseshoes, and a volleyball court. **Caspersen Beach** (⊠ Beach Dr., South Venice) is the county's largest park and is known for its fossil finds. It has a nature trail, fishing, picnicking, restrooms, and lots of beach, but few amenities. **Manasota Beach** (⊠ Manasota Beach Rd., Manasota Key) has a boat ramp, picnic area, and restrooms. Reach it by foot from Caspersen Beach. By road, it's a lot less direct. At **Blind Pass Beach** (⊠ Manasota Beach Rd., Manasota Key), fish, swim, and hike the nature trail. There are restrooms and showers. **Englewood Beach** (⊠ Off Rte. 776, near the Charlotte–Sarasota county line) is popular with teenagers, although beachgoers of all ages frequent it. There are barbecue grills, picnic facilities, boat ramps, a fishing pier, a playground, and showers. There's a charge for parking.

Where to Stay & Eat

$–$$$$　✕ **Crow's Nest Marina Restaurant & Tavern.** This waterfront restaurant on the south jetty is a local favorite, and is always teeming with patrons. The upstairs main dining room, where business-casual dress is enforced, is more formal than the downstairs dark-wood tavern. The menu includes pan-seared grouper Key Largo, which is topped with lobster, shrimp, scallops, and mushrooms, and roasted Bahamian lobster tail. ⊠ *1968 Tarpon Center Dr.* ☎ *941/484–9551* ▭ *AE, D, DC, MC, V.*

$–$$$　✕ **Sharky's on the Pier.** Gaze out on the beach and sparkling waters while dining on grilled seafood at this very casual eatery. You choose whether the catches of the day are broiled, blackened, grilled, or fried. Specialties include macadamia grouper and sea pasta. There's an outdoor veranda and tables indoors, and entertainment five nights a week. ⊠ *1600 S. Harbor Dr.* ☎ *941/488–1456* ▭ *AE, D, MC, V* ☉ *Closed Mon. July–Sept.*

$$$–$$$$　▦ **Inn at the Beach.** Across from the beach, this little one- and two-story resort is popular with families. Some of the one- and two-bedroom suites, which have spacious living rooms, have views of the gulf. Others look out on tropical gardens. A Continental breakfast is served in the lobby each morning. ⊠ *725 W. Venice Ave., 34285* ☎ *941/484–8471 or 800/255–8471* 🖷 *941/484–0593* ⊕ *www. innatthebeach.com* ⊲ *37 rooms, 12 suites* ᗕ *Fans, in-room safes, some kitchens, microwaves, refrigerators, cable TV, in-room data ports, pool, outdoor hot tub, laundry facilities, free parking, no-smoking rooms* ▭ *AE, D, DC, MC, V* ❀❙ *CP.*

$　▦ **Days Inn Venice Resort.** Only 10 minutes from the beach, this simple motel is on the main business route through town. Rooms are comfortable, and there's a Subway sandwich shop on the property. ⊠ *1710 S. Tamiami Trail, 34293* ☎ *941/493–4558* 🖷 *941/493–1593* ⊕ *www.daysinn. com* ⊲ *72 rooms* ᗕ *In-room data ports, cable TV, pool, laundry facilities, laundry service, some pets allowed (fee)* ▭ *AE, D, DC, MC, V.*

The Arts

Venice Little Theatre (⊠ 140 W. Tampa Ave. ☎ 941/488–1115 ⊕ www. venicestage.com) is a community theater showing comedies, musicals, dramas, and contemporary works on two stages during its October–May season.

Sports & the Outdoors

BIKING　**Bicycles International** (⊠ 1744 S. Tamiami Trail ☎ 941/497–1590) rents some of its varied stock weekly and daily.

FISHING   At **Florida Deep Sea Fishing Charters** (✉ 1968 Tarpon Center Dr., Crow's Nest Marina, Venice ☎ 941/473–4603), Captain Dave Pinkham offers half-day and full-day deep-sea-fishing trips for tarpon, shark, amberjack, and other fighting fish.

GOLF   **Bird Bay Executive Golf Course** (✉ 602 Bird Bay Dr. W ☎ 941/485–9333) is a semiprivate course that has 18 holes, green fee: $13/$18.

WATER SPORTS   **Don and Mike's Boat and Jet Ski Rental** (✉ 482 Blackburn Point Rd. ☎ 941/966–4000) rents water skis, jet skis, ski boats, tech boats, and pontoon boats, and has instruction for all activities.

Shopping

If you like flea markets, check out the **Dome** (✉ Rte. 775, west of U.S. 41), where dozens of sheltered stalls sell new and recycled wares. It's open October through August, Friday through Sunday 9–4.

THE TAMPA BAY AREA A TO Z

To research prices, get advice from other travelers, and book travel arrangements, visit www.fodors.com.

AIR TRAVEL

CARRIERS   Many carriers serve Tampa International Airport. Sarasota's airport is served by major carriers (⇨ Smart Travel Tips). Scheduled service to St. Petersburg–Clearwater International is limited, and from many areas of the country, you have to supply your own plane. American TransAir connects to U.S. cities, and Air Transat flies from Toronto.

🗹 Airlines & Contacts **Air Transat** ☎ 877/872-6728 ⊕ www.airtransat.com. **America West Airlines** ☎ 800/235-9292 ⊕ www.americawest.com. **American TransAir** ☎ 800/435-9282 ⊕ www.ata.com. **Cayman Airways** ☎ 800/422-9626 ⊕ www.caymanairways.com. **Gulfstream International** ☎ 800/525-0280 ⊕ www.gulfstreamair.com. **Condor Airlines** ☎ 800/524-6975 ⊕ www.condoramericas.com.

AIRPORTS & TRANSFERS

🗹 Airport Information **Tampa International Airport** ✉ 5503 Spruce St., 6 mi from downtown Tampa ☎ 813/870-8700 ⊕ www.tampaairport.com. **St. Petersburg–Clearwater International** ✉ 14700 Terminal Blvd., off Rte. 686, 9 mi from downtown St. Petersburg ☎ 727/453-7800 ⊕ www.fly2pie.com. **Sarasota–Bradenton International Airport** ✉ 600 Airport Circle, off U.S. 41, just north of Sarasota ☎ 941/359-2777 ⊕ www.srq-airport.com.

AIRPORT   Central Florida Limousine provides Tampa International Airport ser-
TRANSFERS   vice to and from Hillsborough and Polk counties, and Super Shuttle serves Pinellas County. Expect taxi fares to be about $12–$25 for most of Hillsborough County and about twice that for Pinellas County. Transportation to and from Sarasota–Bradenton Airport is provided by West Coast Executive Sedan. The average cab fare between the airport and downtown is $12–$25.

🗹 Taxis & Shuttles **Central Florida Limousine** ☎ 813/396-3730. **Super Shuttle** ☎ 727/572-1111 or 800/282-6817 ⊕ www.supershuttle.com. **West Coast Executive Sedan** ☎ 941/359-8600.

BUS TRAVEL

Service to and throughout the state is provided by Greyhound Lines. Around Tampa, the Hillsborough Area Regional Transit (HART) serves the county, plus the TECO Line Streetcars replicate the city's first electric streetcars, transporting cruise-ship passengers to Ybor City. Around St. Petersburg, Pinellas Suncoast Transit Authority serves Pinellas County. The Looper trolley operates to downtown area attractions. In Sarasota the public transit company is Sarasota County Area Transit (SCAT). Fares for local bus service range from 50¢ to $2.50 (for an all-day pass), and exact change is required.

FARES & SCHEDULES 🚍 Bus Information **Greyhound Lines** ☎ 800/231-2222 ⊕ www.greyhound.com. **Greyhound Sarasota** ✉ 575 N. Washington Blvd., Sarasota ☎ 941/955-5735. **Greyhound Clearwater** ✉ 2811 Gulf-to-Bay Blvd., Clearwater ☎ 727/796-7315. **Greyhound St. Petersburg** ✉ 180 9th St. N, St. Petersburg ☎ 727/822-1497. **Greyhound Tampa** ✉ 610 E. Polk St., Tampa ☎ 813/229-2174. **Hillsborough Area Regional Transit (HART)** ☎ 813/254-4278 ⊕ www.hartline.org. **Pinellas Suncoast Transit Authority (PSTA)** ☎ 727/530-9911 ⊕ www.psta.net. **Sarasota County Area Transit (SCAT)** ☎ 941/316-1234. **TECO Line Street Cars** ☎ 813/254-4278.

CAR TRAVEL

Interstate 75 spans the region from north to south. Once you cross the Florida border from Georgia, it should take about three hours to reach Tampa and another hour to reach Sarasota. Interstate exits are numbered according to mileage from their southern terminus, rather than sequentially. Coming from Orlando, you're likely to drive west into Tampa on Interstate 4. Along with Interstate 75, U.S. 41 (which runs concurrently with the Tamiami Trail for much of the way) stretches the length of the region. U.S. 41 links the business districts of many communities, so it's best to avoid it and all bridges during rush hours (7–9 AM and 4–6 PM). U.S. 19 is St. Petersburg's major north–south artery; traffic can be heavy, and there are many lights, so use a different route when possible. Interstate 275 heads west from Tampa across Tampa Bay to St. Petersburg, swings south, and crosses the bay again on its way to Terra Ceia, near Bradenton. Along this last leg—the Sunshine Skyway and its stunning suspension bridge—you'll get a bird's-eye view of bustling Tampa Bay. The Gandy Bridge (Highway 92) also yields a spectacular view of Tampa Bay, and Route 679 takes you along two of St. Petersburg's most pristine islands, Cabbage and Mullet keys. Route 64 connects Interstate 75 to Bradenton and Anna Maria Island. Route 789 runs over several slender barrier islands, past miles of blue-green gulf waters, beaches, and waterfront homes. The road does not connect all the islands, however; it runs from the village of Anna Maria off the Bradenton coast south to Lido Key, then begins again on Siesta Key and again on Casey Key south of Osprey, and runs south to Nokomis Beach.

EMERGENCIES

Dial 911 for police, ambulance, and fire. There are 24-hour emergency rooms at Bayfront Medical Center, Manatee Memorial Hospital, Sarasota Memorial Hospital, and University Community Hospital.

🏥 Hospitals **Bayfront Medical Center** ✉ 701 6th St. S, St. Petersburg ☎ 727/893-6100. **Manatee Memorial Hospital** ✉ 206 2nd St. E, Bradenton ☎ 941/745-7466. **Sarasota**

Memorial Hospital ✉1700 S. Tamiami Trail, Sarasota ☎ 941/917-9000. **University Community Hospital** ✉ 3100 E. Fletcher Ave., Tampa ☎ 813/971-6000.

ENGLISH-LANGUAGE MEDIA

NEWSPAPERS & MAGAZINES Daily newspapers in the area are the *Bradenton Herald, Sarasota Herald–Tribune, St. Petersburg Times,* and *Tampa Tribune.* The *Cedar Key Beacon, Longboat Observer,* and *Tampa Bay Business Journal* are weekly newspapers. *Tampa Bay Life* is a monthly magazine.

RADIO Local AM stations include WFLA 970 (news and talk radio); WDAE 1250 (ESPN radio, sports talk, and Tampa Bay Lightning broadcasts); WQBN 1300 (all-Spanish); WWMI 1380 (Radio Disney); and WPSO 1500 (Greek-language).

Local FM stations include WJIS 88.1 (Christian music); WMNF 88.5 (alternative and eclectic); WUSF 89.7 (National Public Radio); WYUU 92.5 (oldies); WFLZ 93.3 (Top 40); WQYK 99.5 (country music and Tampa Bay Buccaneers football broadcasts); WHPT 102.5 (classic rock); WBBY 107.3 (soft rock); and WGUL 106.3 (big band).

TOURS

West Florida Helicopters gives bay-area tours. There's a daily hovercraft tour from St. Petersburg, operated by Hover USA. The *American Victory* Mariners Memorial & Museum Ship offers weekend day trips aboard the restored World War II–era merchant marine vessel with historical reenactments of life aboard during its wartime service. Hovercraft tours depart from multiple points around St. Petersburg and to Egmont Key, and private charters are available. Gourmet meals and a stunning view of the Tampa skyline are available aboard StarShip Cruises, which has lunch and dinner cruises aboard its namesake *StarShip,* which seats up to 350 people in the dining room.

On Captain Memo's Pirate Cruise, crew members dressed as pirates take you on sightseeing and sunset cruises in a replica of a 19th-century sailing ship. Dolphin Landing Charter Boat Center has daily, four-hour cruises to unspoiled Egmont Key at the mouth of Tampa Bay. Aboard the glass-bottom boats of St. Nicholas Boat Line, you take a sightseeing cruise of Tarpon Springs' historic sponge docks and see a diver at work. The *Starlite Princess,* an old-fashioned paddle wheeler, and *Starlite Majestic,* a sleek yacht-style vessel, make sightseeing and dinner cruises.

🚩 **Tour Operators** *American Victory* **Mariners Memorial & Museum Ship** ✉705 Channelside Dr., Berth 271, behind Florida Aquarium, Tampa ☎ 813/228-8766 ⊕ www. americanvictory.org. **Captain Memo's Pirate Cruise** ✉ Clearwater Beach Marina, Clearwater Beach ☎727/446-2587. **Dolphin Landings Charter Boat Center** ✉ 4737 Gulf Blvd., St. Pete Beach ☎727/360-7411. **Hover-USA** ☎866/359-4683 ⊕ www.hover-usa.com. **St. Nicholas Boat Line** ✉ 693 Dodecanese Blvd., Tarpon Springs ☎ 727/942-6425. *Starlite Princess* **and** *Starlite Majesty* ✉ Clearwater Beach Marina, at the end of Rte. 60, Clearwater Beach ✉Corey Causeway, 3400 S. Pasadena, St. Pete Beach ☎727/462-2628 ⊕ www.starlitecruises.com. **StarShip Cruises** ✉ 603 Channelside Dr., Tampa ☎ 813/223-7999 or 877/744-7999. **West Florida Helicopters** ✉ Albert Whitted Airport, 107 8th Ave. SE, St. Petersburg ☎ 727/823-5200.

TRAIN TRAVEL

Amtrak trains run from the Northeast, Midwest, and much of the South to the Tampa station.

🚩 Train Information **Amtrak** ✉ Tampa Union Station, 601 N. Nebraska Ave., Tampa ☎ 800/872-7245 or 813/221-7600 ⊕ www.amtrak.com.

VISITOR INFORMATION

🚩 Tourist Information **Bradenton Area Convention & Visitors Bureau Tourist Information Center** ✉ 1 Haven Blvd., Palmetto 34221 ✉ Kiosk in Prime Outlets Ellenton, 5461 Factory Shops Blvd., Ellenton 34222 ☎ 941/729-9177 ⊕ www.flagulfislands.com. **Cedar Key Chamber of Commerce** ✉ 525 2nd St. ⌂ Box 610, Cedar Key 32625 ☎ 352/543-5600 ⊕ www.cedarkey.org. **Clearwater Regional Chamber of Commerce** ✉ 1130 Cleveland St., Clearwater 33755 ☎ 727/461-0011 ⊕ www.clearwaterflorida.org. **Greater Dunedin Chamber of Commerce** ✉ 301 Main St., Dunedin 34698 ☎ 727/733-3197 ⊕ www.dunedin-fl.com. **Greater Tampa Chamber of Commerce** ✉ 615 Channelside Dr. ⌂ Box 420, Tampa 33601 ☎ 813/228-7777, 813/223-1111 Ext. 44 for Visitors Information Department ⊕ www.tampachamber.com. **Sarasota Convention and Visitors Bureau** ✉ 655 N. Tamiami Trail, Sarasota 34236 ☎ 941/957-1877 or 800/522-9799 ⊕ www.sarasotafl.org. **St. Petersburg Area Chamber of Commerce** ✉ 100 2nd Ave. N, St. Petersburg 33701 ☎ 727/821-4069 ⊕ www.stpete.com. **St. Petersburg/Clearwater Area Convention & Visitors Bureau** ✉ 14450 46th St. N, Suite 108, St. Petersburg 33762 ☎ 727/464-7200 or 877/352-3224 ⊕ www.floridasbeach.com. **Tampa Bay Beaches Chamber of Commerce** ✉ 6990 Gulf Blvd., St. Pete Beach 33706 ☎ 727/360-6957 or 800/944-1847 ⊕ www.tampabaybeaches.com. **Tampa Bay Convention and Visitors Bureau** ✉ 400 N. Tampa St., Suite 2800, Tampa 33602 ☎ 800/368-2672 or 813/223-1111 ⊕ www.visittampabay.com. **Tarpon Springs Chamber of Commerce** ✉ 11 E. Orange St., Tarpon Springs 34689 ☎ 727/937-6109 ⊕ www.tarponsprings.com. **Ybor City Chamber Visitor Bureau** ✉ 1600 E. 8th Ave., Suite B104, 33605 ☎ 813/248-3712 ⊕ www.ybor.org.

UNDERSTANDING
FLORIDA

FLORIDA AT A GLANCE

Fast Facts

Nickname: The Sunshine State
Capital: Tallahassee
Motto: "In God we trust"
State Song: *The Swanee River* (Old Folks at Home), written by Stephen C. Foster.
State Bird: Common mockingbird (Mimus polyglottos), which is also the state bird of Arkansas, Mississippi, Tennessee, and Texas
State Flower: Orange blossom
State Tree: Sabal palm
Administrative Divisions: 67 counties
Entered the Union: March 3, 1845, as the 27th state

Population: 16 million
Population density: 316 people per square mi
Median age: 40.1
Life expectancy: Male 75.2, female 90.8
Infant mortality rate: 7.4 deaths per 1,000 births
Literacy: Almost one-quarter of Floridians speak a language other than English at home, usually Spanish.
Ethnic Groups: White 65%; Hispanic 17%; black 15%; Asian 2%; other 1%
Religion: Unaffiliated 59%; Catholic 16%; Southern Baptist 8%; other Christian 8%; other 5%; Jewish 4%

Geography & Environment

Land Area: 53,927 square mi. It's the 22nd largest state
Coastline: 1,197 mi along Atlantic Ocean and Gulf of Mexico
Terrain: Rolling hills in the panhandle; long, low peninsula and islands; swamps
Islands: Florida has 4,500 islands that are 10 acres or larger, including Marco Island, Anna Maria Island, 10,000 Islands, Gasparilla Island/Boca Grande, Isles of Capri, Pine Island, Sanibel Island, Captiva Island, and the Florida Keys
Natural resources: Gravel, phosphate rock, sand, timber

Natural hazards: Flooding from storms; forest fires; hurricanes; tornados, which build annually in the Gulf of Mexico
Environmental issues: Concerns over runoff from industrial farming affecting ground water, as well as Florida Bay and the Gulf of Mexico; growth and its effect on undeveloped lands in Florida Panhandle; new protections for manatees against boats.

In Florida consider the flamingo, Its color passion but its neck a question.
—Robert Penn Warren

Economy

Gross State Product: $550 billion
Per capita income: $30,446
Unemployment: 4.4%
Work force: 8.4 million
Major industries: Construction, farming, fishing, international trade, military, space research and support, tourism
Agricultural products: Cattle and dairy products, corn, crabs, grapefruits, lobsters, oranges, shrimp, sugarcane, tangerines, tomatoes

Exports: $25 billion
Major export products: Chemical products, computers, electronic and electric equipment, fruits and vegetables, industrial machinery, transportation equipment, scientific and measuring instruments
Major import products: Aircraft, automobiles, clothing, oil

A day without orange juice is like a day without sunshine.
—Florida Citrus Commission

Did You Know?

• No U.S. president has ever been born—or died—in Florida.

• In the early 1900s, Jacksonville, known as the Hollywood of the East, had more movie studios than Holly-wood, California.

• Although it seems to dangle out into the Gulf, the state of Florida is actually wider across the top than it is long.

• Florida is one of only seven states where residents pay no state income tax. The others are Washington, Wyoming, Texas, South Dakota, Nevada, and Alaska.

• Lake Okeechobee is the fourth largest lake in the United States, but at its deep-est point, its bottom is only 15 feet from the surface.

• The St. Johns, in northeast Florida, is one of only two rivers in the Western Hemisphere that flows northward.

• Florida has more natural springs than all the other U.S. states combined, and experiences more lightning strikes than any other state.

THE SUNSHINE STATE

IF THE NICKNAME THE OCEAN STATE weren't being used by Rhode Island, Florida could easily adopt it. Jutting into warm waters at the southeastern corner of the United States, this largely flat, finger-shape peninsula is rimmed by more than 1,200 mi of coastline, attracting beachgoers, water-sports enthusiasts, and nature lovers.

Luckily, its real nickname—the Sunshine State—is every bit as accurate. While much of the rest of the country endures Old Man Winter, most of Florida maintains a pleasant, subtropical climate. The net result is that for more than a century, warm weather has drawn—and continues to draw—hordes of vacationers, snowbirds (winter residents), retirees, immigrants, and other new permanent denizens. Among those who have at one time or another been seduced by its charms (and in some cases seduced others to come to the state) are developers Henry Morrison Flagler and Henry Plant, circus tycoon John Ringling, writers Ernest Hemingway and Marjorie Kinnan Rawlings, singers Jimmy Buffett and Gloria Estefan, and inventors Thomas Edison and Henry Ford.

Fly into any Florida airport during the Christmas season or spring break, and you'll have little doubt as to the importance of tourism. Examine the contents of travelers' suitcases—swimsuits, sunscreen, golf clubs, tennis rackets, credit cards—and there's even less doubt about their reasons for visiting: relaxation and recreation.

Of course, the most popular activities center on all that coastline. Florida has a surprising variety of beaches: from the wave-lapped strands along the Atlantic Ocean (east coast) to the sugar-sand, sunset-hung beaches of the Gulf of Mexico (west coast and Panhandle), and from people-watcher beaches to family beaches to secluded beaches. For those with sand aversion, there are the largely sandless, coral-reef-lined shore of Florida's Keys and the mangrove-studded margins in places like the Ten Thousand Islands and Biscayne National Park.

Florida's largest and most cosmopolitan city, Miami, hugs the state's southeastern coast. Whereas Miami Beach has its share of sun and sand, the metropolitan area is equally known for its international trade and international flavor, as well as glitz and celebrity. It seems fitting in this varied state that just a stone's throw from Miami is one of Florida's other distinctive treasures: the Everglades. This national park—comprising a quiet, slow-flowing river of grass—is home to unusual wildlife, including that quintessential Florida creature, the alligator.

In case you think that Florida action is only on the coasts, travel inland; agriculture flourishes here—unfortunately, however, sometimes at the expense of the natural environment. Citrus fruits like oranges and grapefruit are as synonymous with Florida as pineapples are with Hawaii, but Florida farms and ranches also produce sugarcane and cattle. In one formerly sleepy farming town, the soil seems particularly fertile for growing world-famous amusement parks. In just over a quarter century, Orlando has sprouted eight major theme parks, five water parks, and countless other attractions, entertainment options, hotels, restaurants, and shops.

So how did the phenomenon that's Florida come about? Almost from its beginnings as a flat, swampy plateau emerging from the ocean, Florida has been home to all sorts of animals disinclined to the cold (at that time, glaciated) weather up north. It wasn't until 12,000–10,000 BC that humans (probably hunter-gatherers) arrived. These original Floridians began to farm and develop societies, and their descendants would become Florida's Timucuan (central and north), Apalachee (eastern Panhandle), Seminole (south-central to southwest), Calusa (southwest coast), Miccosukee (south), and Tequesta (southeast) tribes.

As in much of the Americas, the sovereignty of Florida's native peoples did not last. By the 16th century, a succession of Spanish explorers, including Pánfilo de Narváez, Hernando de Soto, Tristán de Luna y Arellano, and Pedro Menéndez de Avilés had arrived with visions of wealth. Though they found little gold and often didn't stay long, they still managed to ravage, enslave, and spread disease among the native population. In 1565 the first permanent settlement was founded at St. Augustine, and in the years that followed, the Spanish, French, and British all tried to establish Florida footholds. Pensacola, in fact, got the nickname the City of Five Flags because at one time or another it was under the rule of Spain, France, England, the Confederacy, and the United States.

* * *

EVENTUALLY FLORIDA BECAME a U.S. territory and state, but that didn't end the struggles. An influx of whites from the North, eager to farm and ranch, created friction with Native Americans, and a series of three wars, known as the Seminole Wars, ensued. Led by then General (later president) Andrew Jackson, the Anglos ultimately drove many Native Americans off their lands and out. Conflict returned during the Civil War, though to a lesser degree than in the states to the north. In fact, Tallahassee was the only Confederate capital east of the Mississippi not to fall to Union forces. When the South lost the war, however, Florida rejoined the United States.

By the late 19th century, a group of aggressive developers had begun to see Florida's potential as a tourist destination. Henry Plant built a railroad to the west coast as well as the big Tampa Bay Hotel. Henry Morrison Flagler had even grander plans, extending his Florida East Coast Railway to places like St. Augustine,

Palm Beach, Fort Lauderdale, Miami, and eventually Key West. Flagler also built opulent hotels that attracted Vanderbilts, DuPonts, Rockefellers, and their confreres. Other developers created their own legacies—Addison Mizner in Palm Beach and Boca Raton, Carl Fisher in Miami Beach, George Merrick in Coral Gables. These names live on, in everything from island and street names to museums and shopping malls. Unfortunately, their and others' ideas of progress often meant draining swampland, paving or building over animal habitats, and straightening, damming, dredging, or building new waterways, thereby altering the natural environment forever.

The 20th century saw a succession of land booms and busts as tourists repeatedly rediscovered the appeal of Florida and its climate. The late '20s and early '30s Depression hit tourism hard, as did a 1935 hurricane that cut off Key West from the mainland (except by boat). The '20s and '30s brought art deco to Miami Beach, whereas the '50s brought grand hotels, like Morris Lapidus's Fontainebleau and Eden Roc. But by the '70s and early '80s, Miami Beach and many other Florida towns had become rundown geriatric centers (sometimes pejoratively referred to as "God's waiting room"); Fort Lauderdale was primarily known as a center for spring-break debauchery; and family tourism headed in greater and greater numbers to the new Orlando theme parks.

By the late '80s, however, towns and cities were beginning to renew themselves. By the '90s, Miami Beach, its art deco jewels preserved and restored, became hot again. Miami, with its ever-growing Latin population and flavor, finally began to embrace and even tout its multiculturalism. Fort Lauderdale and West Palm Beach spruced up and added new arts and entertainment attractions. Towns and resorts on both east and west coasts grew, attracting visitors and residents alike. And today, Florida is once again basking in the sunshine.

FLORIDA, MY FLORIDA

HOWDY, KIDS. Looks like you'll be coming to Florida. Personally, I couldn't think of a better place to visit (except that I live here already). And why not? The folks at the tourist board say that Florida is sun-sational! And they're right. Without Florida there would be no space program, no Disney empire, no tropical deco, no pink lawn flamingos. And you know the way Florida sticks down into the Caribbean? If Florida weren't the United States' East Coast counterweight, our nation would just flip right over into the Pacific Ocean—and that's a geological fact.

Florida is *different*. It has almost as many millionaires as migrant workers and an equal number of rednecks and rocket scientists. It houses muck farms and million-dollar condos, and its churches welcome straitlaced Baptists and pious practitioners of Santeria, a mixture of Haitian voodoo, African tribal religions, and Christianity. Florida is where you can spend your vacation clapping happily as a robot bear sings Patsy Cline or screaming in terror as a real live alligator devours a senior citizen's toy poodle. This state may not be schizophrenic, but it does display multiple personalities.

Are you familiar with the saying attributed to Harvey Korman or somebody else that America is the melting pot of the world? Well, Florida is the melting pot of America. In 1990 a U.S. Census Bureau report revealed that fewer than a third of Florida's population are natives and only 13% were born in other states south of the Mason-Dixon line. You'll notice this when you visit, because Florida is the only state in the Deep South where you'll see the Union and Confederacy living side by side. Ironically, down here northerners live in the south and southerners live in the north. No one knows why this is; it just is.

If you're wondering if you'll receive a warm welcome, don't worry. The land of sunshine accommodates just about everybody. In 1950 this was the 20th-most-populous state; now we're number 4. During the Mariel Boatlift of 1980, 125,000 Cuban defectors showed up, and we didn't even call out the National Guard—we only did that when a similar number of New Yorkers arrived for the opening of the new Miami Bloomingdale's.

This influx of outsiders is nothing new. In 1513 Ponce de León decided to land in Florida to avoid the traffic around Newark. That did it. By 1565 Ponce's foothold became the oldest permanent settlement in what would become the United States. Check your history books, and you'll see this was a half century before the English arrived in Jamestown and the Pilgrims knocked on Plymouth Rock. It seemed everybody wanted to be in Florida. While the French, English, and Spanish spent 250 years battling for possession of the territory, Caribbean pirates sailing the Gulf Stream were making withdrawals from the explorers' ships and using Florida's hidden bays and swamps as safe-deposit boxes. Eventually, the pirates and foreign pioneers cleared out, and in 1821 the United States paid Spain $5 million for 59,000 square mi of marshes, mosquitoes, and alligators.

Later, Virginians and Carolinians began moving south to create Panhandle communities like Quincy, Madison, and Monticello. Then in the late 1880s, Henry M. Flagler started building a hotel and railroad empire that started in St. Augustine, arrived in Miami by 1896, and reached the end of the line in Key West in 1912. Thanks to Flagler's promotional and engineering abilities, northern tourists started heading south and have been arriving ever since.

Although it rarely makes the evening news anymore, people are still battling over Florida. Retirees, dropouts, drug runners, natives, multinational companies, and foreign tourists all want to claim Florida for their own. So what's all the fuss about?

The answer, my friend, is blowing in the warm Atlantic winds that comfort us in the middle of January; it's in the primeval pleasures of paddling a canoe down the Wekiva River; in the 3,000-plus varieties of indigenous plants and flowers that color our landscape; and in the fire, smoke, and thunder of the space shuttle as it blazes into the clear blue sky above the Indian River. You'll find it in more than 400 species of birds, ranging from cardinals, ospreys, and bald eagles to wading egrets, herons, and pink flamingos. It is felt in the 220 days of sunshine we savor each year and the approximately 1 inch of snow a century that we don't.

* * *

THESE ARE THE TYPES OF THINGS you may not know about the Shoeshine State. That's why my editors looked at my birth certificate and tan lines to confirm that I was a native and then asked me to share with you the many-splendored things that make up this paradoxical paradise. Even with my more than 35 years of memories and hundreds of thousands of miles spent trekking, biking, motorcycling, and stumbling across my favorite subtropical peninsula, this is a difficult task. Relating all that Florida represents is an impossibility because the typical Floridian could be grunting for worms in Sopchoppy, rounding up cattle in Kissimmee, or posing for the cover of a European fashion magazine in Miami.

And it's not only Americans who come to Florida. Hit Palm Beach during polo season, and you'll find that even Prince Charles is an occasional Floridian. If you stay awhile (and you simply *must*), you'll find yourself eavesdropping on conversations spoken in a Berlitz blitz of mother tongues: Haitian, Chinese, Serbo-Croatian, Portuguese, Yiddish, Italian, Greek, Spanish, Jamaican, Russian, French, Esperanto . . . E Pluribus Unum, y'all. Only California (a relatively insignificant state somewhere out west) challenges Florida in terms of its social, cultural, and environmental diversity. You may have heard its residents claim that in one day they can breakfast on the beach, lunch in the desert, and enjoy dinner in the mountains. So? With a full tank of gas and a fast car (my cousin Chick's got a cherry '74 Pacer), Floridians can leave Pensacola in the western panhandle, drive beside the crystal blue gulf on U.S. 98, head north to Tallahassee to tell the governor not to stay the execution, cruise over to St. Augustine for a carriage ride, and drop down to Daytona Beach to hoist a brew with some bikers.

Then it's lunchtime.

Afterward, they'd head to Disney for a quick twirl in a teacup, race over to Tampa's Ybor City to snag a stogie, fill up the tank, and head south to dine at one of Miami's oceanfront cafés before meeting Jimmy Buffett in Key West to slam a pitcher of margaritas.

There's a whole lotta shakin' goin' on, that's for sure, but there's one thing missing from Florida: Old Florida. October 1, 1971, was the day that Disney drove old Dixie down. Over the last 30 years a new state has emerged, reflecting a not-so-perfect union. It is one of sprawling theme parks that provide a big bang for the buck. It is a place where part-time tourists become full-time residents, and corridors of condos, generic housing developments, strip malls, and highways are built to appease them. The changing nature of Key West is a prime example. A generation ago this was a laid-back island paradise filled with eclectic lodgings and quixotic characters. Then it was popularized in song and literature and through word of mouth until the buzz reached executive boardrooms. Today the island's individuality is endangered by a homogenized mass of Hôtels Banal and rich refugees who are turning the once casual hideaway into the places they left behind.

Keep in mind this is the opinion of someone who knew Florida B. D. (Before Disney). When Disney opened, I was a perceptive nine-year-old who had filed away the singular offerings of this endangered lifestyle. The essence of Florida was in the air as my mom and I drove past thick groves of plump oranges and savored the sweet smell of the delicate blossoms. At night the air was perfumed with Central Florida's omnipresent gardenias, night-blooming jasmine, honeysuckle, and pine. Back then Orlando was so quiet that at night I could hear the lonesome train whistles from 6 mi away.

For entertainment I swam in a creek called Snake Run and took field trips to orange-juice factories. Our family would visit roadside attractions where we could SEE! Walking Catfish! And SEE! Big Sam, the World's Largest Bull! We'd travel to places like Historic Bok Sanctuary, in Lake Wales, and tranquil Tarpon Springs, the Sponge Capital of America. (It's not your fault you were unaware that America had a sponge capital; you didn't own this book yet.)

As a friend, let me give you a tip: when you come to Florida, keep this book with you wherever you go—even in the bath. It will help you find traces of Old Florida in small towns like Micanopy and Mount Dora. You'll find it at Florida's old faithful attractions: Weeki Wachee, Silver Springs, and Monkey Jungle. You'll experience it at Florida's wealth of botanical gardens and at rare winters-only resorts.

* * *

FLORIDIANS LEAP FROM PLANES at 15,000 feet and plunge into blue waters to explore real reefs and artificial ones built upon the hulls of sunken 727s. We motorcycle, ski, sail, paddle, soar, float, climb, cruise, race, run, trek, and, on rare occasions, spelunk. And if you don't like physical activity, what the hell? When you're through sipping margaritas from a coconut shell, sit in the stands and watch pro teams in Miami, Orlando, St. Pete, Tampa, Sunrise, and Jacksonville beat up on visiting players in football, baseball, roller hockey, arena football, ice hockey, and basketball.

Many of our activities are in the great outdoors. We love nature, and we treasure our manatees, sea turtles, and bald eagles. Although it's true that developers and engineers have drained, dredged, and destroyed a million-plus acres of Everglades and other environmentally sensitive land, we're trying to fix things up real nice for your arrival. Stiff fines are handed out to anyone who plucks the sea oats that hold the sandy shoreline in place, and we've set aside hundreds of thousands of acres for wildlife refuges, nature preserves, and state and national parks. Florida, I'll have you know, was the first state to establish a national forest and national bird sanctuary.

Measures such as these have led to fringe benefits. This environmental Valhalla cannot help but foster artistic pursuits. JFK wrote *Profiles in Courage* in Palm Beach, Ernest Hemingway spent 12 years in Key West getting drunk and writing books, and the *National Enquirer* is based in Lantana. Ray Charles attended the Florida School of the Deaf and Blind, in St. Augustine; the Beatles made their second *Ed Sullivan Show* appearance from Miami; and the Rolling Stones wrote "(I Can't Get No) Satisfaction" at (but not as a reflection on) a Clearwater hotel. Artist Robert Rauschenberg lives on Captiva and . . . oh, you get the idea.

If this book doesn't convince you that Florida is the most perfect state in the union, when you get here, ask for me. I'll fill up the DeSoto with some high-test ethyl, put the top down, and we'll take off to see some of Florida's 4,300 square mi of wonderful waterways, where we can swim with manatees or snorkel, scuba, or paddle to our heart's content. I'll take you to a happening diner in Orlando and a great bookstore in St. Pete. If there's time, we'll go tubing down the Ichetucknee and then hook up with some of my hepcat friends down in Coconut Grove.

Now stop reading and get down here.

— Gary McKechnie

BOOKS & MOVIES

What to Read

Suspense novels that are rich in details about Florida include Pulitzer prize–winner Edna Buchanan's *Miami, It's Murder* and *Contents Under Pressure*; Les Standiford's *Done Deal*, about violence in the Miami construction business; former prosecuting attorney Barbara Parker's *Suspicion of Innocence*; Clifford Irving's *Final Argument*; Elmore Leonard's *La Brava*; John D. MacDonald's *The Empty Copper Sea*; Joan Higgins's *A Little Death Music*; and Charles Willeford's *Miami Blues*. James W. Hall features Florida in many of his big sellers, such as *Mean High Tide*, the chilling *Bones of Coral*, and *Hard Aground*.

Marjorie Kinnan Rawlings's classic *The Yearling* poignantly portrays life in the brush country, and her *Cross Creek* re-creates the memorable people she knew there. Peter Matthiessen's *Killing Mister Watson* re-creates turn-of-the-last-century lower southwest Florida. A more recent look at Florida's past is in Bill Belleville's *River of Lakes: A Journey on Florida's St. Johns River*, which shows there are still traces of wilderness here.

Look for *Princess of the Everglades,* a novel about the 1926 hurricane, by Charles Mink, and *Snow White and Rose Red* and *Jack and the Beanstalk,* Ed McBain's novels about a gulf city attorney. Miami's Carl Hiaasen has turned out lots of Florida-based books, including *Double Whammy, Lucky You,* and *Sick Puppy.*

Other recommended titles include Roxanne Pulitzer's *Facade,* set against a backdrop of Palm Beach; Pat Booth's *Miami*; Sam Harrison's *Bones of Blue Coral* and *Birdsong Ascending*; T. D. Allman's *Miami*; Joan Didion's *Miami*; David Rieff's *Going to Miami*; Alice Hoffman's *Turtle Moon*; *Scavenger Reef* and *Florida Straits,* by Laurence Shames; *To Have and Have Not,* by Ernest Hemingway; *The Day of the Dolphin,* by Robert Merle; and *Their Eyes Were Watching God,* by Zora Neale Hurston.

Among recommended nonfiction books are *The Commodore's Story,* by Ralph Munroe and Vincent Gilpin, a luminous reminiscence about the golden years (pre-railroad) of Coconut Grove; *Key West Writers and Their Homes,* by Lynn Kaufelt; *The Everglades: River of Grass,* by Marjory S. Douglas; *The Other Florida,* by Gloria Jahoda; and *Florida's Sandy Beaches,* University Press of Florida. Mark Derr's *Some Kind of Paradise* is an excellent review of the state's environmental follies; John Rothchild's *Up for Grabs: A Trip Through Time and Space in the Sunshine State,* equally good, is about Florida's commercial lunacy. For a great overview on the politics and behind-the-scenes genius that helped build Florida's most popular theme park, look for *Since the World Began: Walt Disney World, the First 25 Years,* by Jeff Kurtti. Good anthologies include *The Florida Reader: Visions of Paradise* (Maurice O'Sullivan and Jack Lane, editors), *The Rivers of Florida* (Del and Marty Marth, editors), and *Subtropical Speculations: An Anthology of Florida Science Fiction* (Richard Mathews and Rick Wilber, editors).

A good companion to this guide, Fodor's *Compass American Guides: Florida* has handsome photos and historical, cultural, and topical essays.

Books that are also available on audiotape include Peter Dexter's *The Paperboy,* as well as several by Carl Hiaasen: *Native Tongue, Skin Tight, Stormy Weather, Strip Tease, Basket Case,* and *Tourist Season,* his immensely funny declaration of war against the state's environment-despoiling hordes. For more on Miami's questionable politics and weird culture, pick up *Kick Ass,* a collection of Hiaasen's newspaper columns.

What to Watch

There's a great misconception that California is the center of the motion picture industry. Never heard of it. Florida is the *true* film capital, and we have the recount to prove it. Well, at least we have more than a century of movie footage that began in 1898 with the spectacular "U.S. Cavalry Supplies Unloading at Tampa." Then consider that Oliver Hardy got his start making movie shorts in Jacksonville, which, between 1910 and 1917, was a film factory town for more than 30 studios and 1,000 actors and extras. That lasted until folks started heading west when a conservative electorate booted the film-friendly mayor from office.

Despite the rocky beginning, the Sunshine State has maintained a high profile on the Silver Screen. Don't think so? Then what about Johnny Weismuller's Tarzan movies that were shot at Wakulla Springs? Or Esther Williams's movies made at the defunct Cypress Gardens? Where do you think Elvis Followed That Dream? Near Ocala! Classics such as *The Creature from the Black Lagoon* (1954) and *Where the Boys Are* (1960)? Shot right here. And Bond fans take note: In *Goldfinger* (1964), remember when 007, nestled in a hotel window, spies the title character cheating at cards? The memorably grand hotel exterior used in that scene is the Fontainebleau Hilton in Miami.

So take a break and run to the video store and check out some more films shot in and around Florida that you may not yet know and love: *Caddyshack* (1980); *Body Heat* (1981); *Cocoon* (1985); *Parenthood* (1989); *Edward Scissorhands* (1990); *My Girl* (1991); *Doc Hollywood* (1991); *Ace Ventura: Pet Detective* (1994); *True Lies* (1994); *The Birdcage* (1996); *Contact* (1997); *Donnie Brasco* (1997); *Rosewood* (1997); *Yulee's Gold* (1997); *There's Something about Mary* (1998); *Instinct* (1999); *Sunshine State* (2002); *Bad Boys 2* (2003); *Monster* (2003); and Tom Hanks's $50-million series, *From the Earth to the Moon* (1998).

Still think that fancy-schmancy Hollywood has anything over Florida? Didn't think you did.

For an in-depth study on Florida's role in the movies, check out *Hollywood East* (1992), by James Ponti.

— Gary McKechnie

INDEX

NOTES

FODOR'S KEY TO THE GUIDES

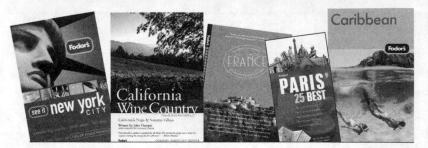

AMERICA'S **GUIDEBOOK LEADER** PUBLISHES GUIDES FOR **EVERY KIND OF TRAVELER**. CHECK OUT OUR MANY SERIES AND FIND YOUR **PERFECT MATCH**.

FODOR'S GOLD GUIDES

America's favorite travel-guide series offers the most detailed insider reviews of hotels, restaurants, and attractions in all price ranges, plus great background information, smart tips, and useful maps.

COMPASS AMERICAN GUIDES

Stunning guides from top local writers and photographers, with gorgeous photos, literary excerpts, and colorful anecdotes. A must-have for culture mavens, history buffs, and new residents.

FODOR'S 25 BEST / CITYPACKS

Concise city coverage in a guide plus a foldout map. The right choice for urban travelers who want everything under one cover.

FODOR'S AROUND THE CITY WITH KIDS

Up to 68 great ideas for family days, recommended by resident parents. Perfect for exploring in your own backyard or on the road.

SEE IT GUIDES

Illustrated guidebooks that include the practical information travelers need, in gorgeous full color. Perfect for travelers who want the best value packed in a fresh, easy-to-use, colorful layout.

FODOR'S FLASHMAPS

Every resident's map guide, with 60 easy-to-follow maps of public transit, parks, museums, zip codes, and more.

FODOR'S LANGUAGES FOR TRAVELERS

Practice the local language before you hit the road. Available in phrase books, cassette sets, and CD sets.

THE COLLECTED TRAVELER

These collections of the best published essays and articles on various European destinations will give you a feel for the culture, cuisine, and way of life.